Transatlantic Anglophone Literatures, 1776–1920

TRANSATLANTIC ANGLOPHONE LITERATURES, 1776–1920

An Anthology

Edited by Linda K. Hughes, Sarah Ruffing
Robbins and Andrew Taylor, with Associate
Editors Heidi Hakimi-Hood and
Adam Nemmers

EDINBURGH
University Press

Edinburgh University Press is one of the leading university presses in the UK. We publish academic books and journals in our selected subject areas across the humanities and social sciences, combining cutting-edge scholarship with high editorial and production values to produce academic works of lasting importance. For more information visit our website: edinburghuniversitypress.com

Edinburgh University Press Ltd
The Tun – Holyrood Road, 12(2f) Jackson's Entry,
Edinburgh EH8 8PJ

Typeset in 10.5/13 Sabon and Gill Sans Nova
by IDSUK (DataConnection) Ltd

A CIP record for this book is available from the
British Library

ISBN 978 1 4744 2982 5 (hardback)
ISBN 978 1 4744 2984 9 (webready PDF)
ISBN 978 1 4744 2983 2 (paperback)
ISBN 978 1 4744 2985 6 (epub)

CONTENTS

2 ART, AESTHETICS AND ENTERTAINMENT

ILLUSTRATIONS

ACKNOWLEDGEMENTS

A project as ambitious as this one requires many supporters. We recognise the invaluable support of our Advisory Board of scholars, listed below, whose expertise guided so many decisions and interpretations. Errors, of course, are our own.

Advisory Board Members

Cari M. Carpenter	West Virginia University
Susan Castillo Street	King's College London
Clare Frances Elliott	Northumbria University
Christopher Gair	University of Glasgow
Barbara McCaskill	University of Georgia
Ifeoma Kiddoe Nwankwo	Vanderbilt University
Clare Pettitt	King's College London
Fiona Robertson	Durham University
Matthew Scott	University of Reading
Marjorie Stone	Dalhousie University
Coll Thrush	University of British Columbia
Tom Wright	University of Sussex

Many students also assisted with the project. We are grateful to our graduate student research associates Abigayle Farrier, Kaylee Henderson, Sofia Prado Huggins, Toya Mary Okonkwo, Dana Shabaan and Alonzo Smith, and to our graduate student editorial assistants Lena Eloy, Abigail Fransen, Saffyre Falkenberg, Kaylee Henderson, Sarah-Marie Horning, Jacquelyn Hoermann-Elliott, Sofia Prado Huggins, Jong-keyong Kim, Larisa Schumann, Susannah Sanford, Micah-Jade Coleman Stanback and Aryn Taylor. Their contributions included checking transcriptions against originals, doing research for headnotes, drafting some headnotes and footnotes, identifying material that would be challenging for other student readers, and tracking down potential illustrations and secondary sources. For feedback on many portions of the draft manuscript, we also thank members of TCU's spring 2021 seminar on transatlantic literatures: Nathan Caballero, Sanjana Chowdhury, Andre Doneskey, Nataly Dickson, Abigayle Farrier, Caylie Jordan, Libby Maack, Shelby Oubre and Mason Patterson. A number of undergraduates also assisted with a range of editorial tasks; thanks to Andreley Bjelland, Blaire Busbee, Sarah Campbell, Will Ehrhardt, Angelica Hernandez, Joel Husleman, Rachel Kimbell, Hattie Lankford, Frank Linton III, Mallory Leitzman, Katie Marler, Susannah Smith, Candace Soto, Ann Tran and Morgan Winspear.

Additional Acknowledgements

In addition to our generous advisory board and numerous graduate and under-graduate student research assistants identified above, we thank the following colleagues:

For support of text selection and interpretation, as well as identifying or providing sources for primary texts and images: Philip Allingham, Jacqueline Banerjee, Frances Smith Foster, Carole Gerson, Colton Johnson, Kevin Kenny, Mark Samuels Lasner, Etta Madden, Laura Mielke, Joseph Rezek, Michael Soto and Derrick Spires.

For assistance with image selection, access and preparation: staff at the American Antiquarian Society, the Archives of Ontario, the British Library, the Free Library of Philadelphia, Guelph Museums (especially Luke Stempien), the Library Company of Philadelphia, the Library of Congress (US), the National Archives of the UK, the National Portrait Gallery (US), the Newberry Library (especially John Powell), the New York Public Library (especially Tom Lisanti), the New York Public Library's Schomburg Center for Research in Black Culture (especially Cheryl Beredo), the Rhode Island Historical Society (especially J. D. Kay), the University of Alberta (CA) Library and the University of Kansas Library.

Special thanks for extensive support to TCU's Mary Couts Burnett Library Staff (especially Kay Edmondson, Ammie Harrison, Kristen Barnes, and Julie Christenson).

We also thank Patricia R. Killian, with support from Kathleen Killian Samaritano, for their French-to-English translation of an excerpt from Jean-Jacques Dessalines's *The Haitian Declaration of Independence* by way of careful reading of the original document, as secured from the British National Archive.

EDITORIAL PRACTICES

Use of Nineteenth-Century Vocabulary

Scholarship on nineteenth-century transatlantic culture necessarily involves working with terminology that has shifted over time. Our guiding principle has been to maintain the diction in original texts as originally published, even when a particular word commonly employed in that earlier era is no longer welcome in today's formal written discourse (or even in culturally sensitive conversations). Thus, for example, if the source text for an entry referred to Native peoples as 'savages' or a Black Caribbean person as a 'n*', we leave the original wording without attaching an explanatory footnote and trust teachers and students to engage such language with appropriate care. In texts we produce ourselves – such as headnotes, footnotes and section introductions – we aim to avoid such terms, even if they were formerly included in scholarly discourse. Hence, we generally choose 'enslaved' or 'enslaved person' rather than 'slave', as well as 'enslaver' or 'slaveholder' rather than 'owner'.[1] We also capitalise 'Black' and 'Native/First Nations' and 'Métis' versus using a lower case for 'white'.[2] And, in our own paratextual writing, we attend to recommendations of the Modern Language Association for adopting gender-neutral language.[3]

We typically use 'First Nations' when referencing Native people in today's Canada; similarly, we might say 'Native American' or 'Indian' in different contexts to refer to Indigenous persons in what is now the United States, typically

---

1 Katy Waldman, '*Slave* or *Enslaved Person*?: It's Not Just an Academic Debate for historians of American slavery', *Slate* (19 May 2015), Web; Nell Irvin Painter, 'How we think about the term "enslaved" matters', *The Guardian* (14 August 2019), Web; National Park Service, 'Language of Slavery' (9 September 2020), Web; Natasha L. Henry, 'Black Enslavement in Canada', *Canadian Encyclopedia* (16 June 2016), Web.
2 David Bauder, 'AP Says It Will Capitalize Black but not white', *AP News* (20 July 2020), Web; Kwame Anthony Appiah, 'The Case for Capitalizing the B in Black', *The Atlantic* (18 June 2020), Web.
3 The online MLA Style Center website is regularly updated, as in recent postings on singular 'they' and on other pronoun usage related to gender identities.

being guided by the choices of Native scholars whose work we are referencing.[4] We include tribal affiliations when possible, and in some contexts use 'Indigenous' when a broader term is more appropriate.

We urge teachers to exercise care when introducing students to material incorporating word choice that might trigger pain or remembered trauma, that is to provide context before assigning a primary text entry using a word like 'squaw' to refer to an Indigenous woman or depicting whole marginalised groups with offensive stereotypes.

Community groups, educational institutions, civic organisations and corporate entities are providing resources to raise awareness about the role language can play in building positive cross-cultural relations.[5] We invite our readers to join in this growing effort by helping those of us teaching about the past to examine how best to introduce troubling terms and concepts from prior eras and cultural networks – including nineteenth-century transatlanticism.[6]

FORMATTING PATTERNS ADOPTED

Our approach to editing primary texts in this volume falls in the 'conservative' editing position outlined by G. Thomas Tanselle in the Modern Language Association's *Scholarly Editing* guide.[7] In presenting the primary text entries to readers, we follow the original's spelling and punctuation choices. Therefore, many entries use long dashes, double quote marks and period placements different from the house style applied in writing of our own. In contrast, an entry first printed in England would duplicate original British spellings and other stylistic patterns as used in the source text.

We silently correct evident typographical errors (such as a repeated word) in all primary texts when such obvious typesetting slips in our source text would impede reader understanding.

Paratextual material such as headnotes, footnotes and section introductions follow Edinburgh University Press's house style, with a few minor variations applied throughout the anthology. US-based readers, therefore, will notice British spelling patterns such as 'labour' versus 'labor' and single quotation marks (') in places where a US style would use double ("). We also follow related

---

4 For examples of the many discussions on preferable naming of Indigenous people in the Americas, see Robert Warrior, 'Indian', in Bruce Burgett and Glenn Hendler (eds), *Keywords for American Cultural Studies* (New York: New York University Press, 2014), 130–2; Marie-Céline Charron, 'No Perfect Answer: Is It First Nations, Aboriginal or Indigenous?', *Indigenous Affairs* (6 March 2019), Web; Don Marks, 'What's in a Name: Indian, Native, Aboriginal or Indigenous?', *CBC News* (22 February 2018), Web; Amanda Blackhorse, 'Blackhorse: Do You Prefer "Native American" or "American Indian"? 6 Prominent Voices Respond', *Indian Country Today* (22 May 2016), Web.

5 See, for example, The World Trust's 'Racial Equity Tools' website, developed in partnership with MP Associates and the Center for Assessment and Policy Development (Web); The Canadian Race Relations Foundation's 'Glossary of Terms' materials (Web); and The Chartered Insurance Institute's 'Inclusive Language Guidelines' (Web).

6 One thoughtful resource is Carolyn Betensky's 'Casual Racism in Victorian Literature', *Victorian Literature and Culture* 47.4 (Winter 2019), 723–51.

7 G. Thomas Tanselle, 'The Varieties of Scholarly Editing', in D. C. Greetham (ed.), *Scholarly Editing: A Guide to Research* (New York: Modern Language Association, 1995), 9–32.

British punctuation practices, such as placing periods and commas outside the end of a quoted phrase or passage.

We have adopted a number of abbreviations to save space in the anthology as we strive to incorporate as many primary texts as possible:

Oxford English Dictionary: OED
Oxford Dictionary of National Biography: ODNB
American National Biography: ANB

When referencing our themes, we use the abbreviations listed below:

Abolition and Aftermath: AA
Art, Aesthetics and Entertainment: AAE
Business, Industry and Labour: BIL
Family and Domesticity: FD
Migration, Settlement and Resistance: MSR
Nationalism and Cosmopolitanism: NC
Religion and Secularism: RS
Science and Technology: ST
Suffrage and Citizenship: SC
Travel and Tourism: TT

We use 'From' in the title of a primary text entry to indicate it is an excerpt. Within primary text presentations, we use [. . .] to designate cuts and omissions made from the original.

A headnote situates each primary text transatlantically and provides additional context for study. For ease of reading, we use only internal citations and not footnotes in those overviews for individual entries; the presentation of primary texts themselves includes explanatory annotations to aid student understanding.

Each entry provides information about its source text and helpful resources for future study in a brief References list. Saving space, citations of Web-based sources omit the URL, since links are sometimes updated or expire.

Each of our thematic sections is introduced by a framing essay that situates its individual entries in dialogue with each other and with scholarship on transatlantic culture. Each section introduction also includes a brief list of references and annotations to guide future study.

CROSS-REFERENCING PRIMARY TEXTS AND TEACHING ACROSS THEMES

We have organised the Contents listing around our ten chosen themes, with texts listed in the order of appearance, following a chronology based on original publication date. A number of authors appear multiple times in the anthology, since their writing engaged with topics crossing our thematic sections. In lieu of a detailed index, we refer readers to our author listing at the close of the volume. Some individual entries complement each other by virtue of their content rather than authorship, and we encourage students and teachers to explore the anthology horizontally, across sections, to discover links and affinities. We include, for instance, two entries in different sections addressing the transatlantic cable, and multiple entries connected with the wide influence of Charles Darwin's work on nineteenth-century culture. Our digital anthology (<https://teachingtransatlanticism.tcu.edu/>) will have the capacity to signal, and link to, a wide range of cross-referencing permutations. Using that digital space to develop additional organising approaches together, we encourage submission of further thematic cluster lists based on such topics as translingualism; the Red, Green or Black Atlantic; and recurring social issues and movements evident in various individual entries, if not directly spotlighted in our current ten themes.

Each of our ten themes could have generated a far more extensive number of entries than this edition accommodates. Furthermore, we recognise that our themes overlap in interesting ways for teaching. To find additional primary texts supplementing the collection here, as well as to see alternative approaches to organising materials for teaching, readers can visit our companion website. Because it includes an ever-growing number of supplementary primary texts, we recommend frequent consultation of the digital anthology there to explore new entries, and we invite our readers to submit proposals for additional texts to join the collection. Formatting of website entries follows the stylesheet developed for the print anthology.

Our 'Teaching Transatlanticism' website also provides resources to support instructional planning and networking in the field. We welcome suggestions for new features, as well as accounts of teaching, syllabi and announcements such as CFPs and new books.

INTRODUCTION

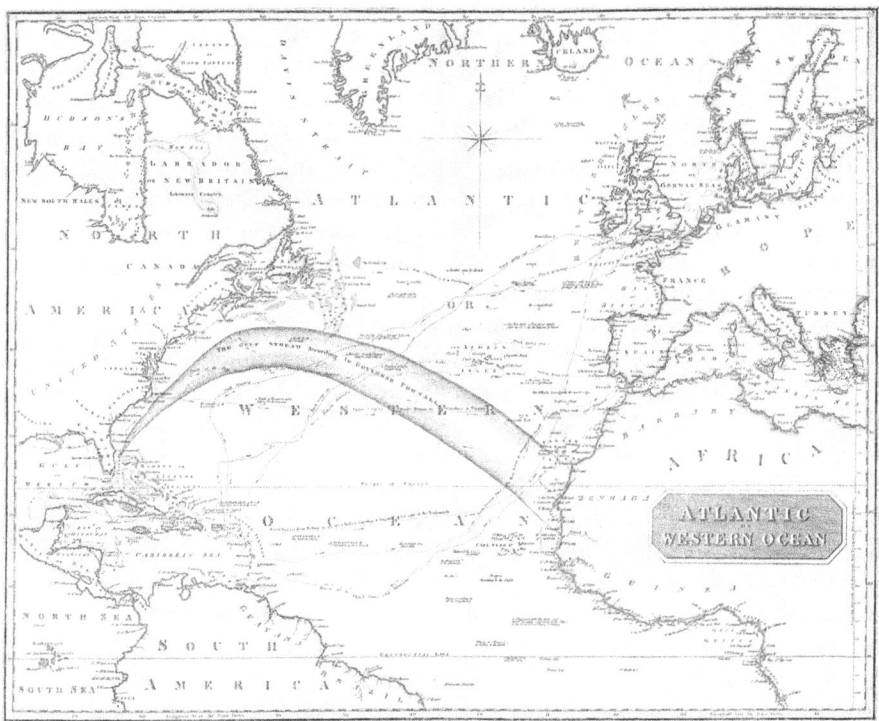

Figure I.1 1814 Map of the Atlantic Ocean drawn by Edinburgh cartographer John Thomson.

This anthology of Anglophone Atlantic writing reflects, and responds to, the consolidation of transatlantic literary studies as a discipline over the last twenty years. While literary history has become far more attuned to transnational frameworks, in which the idea of the 'nation' as an organising category has given way to alternative, often more expansive patterns of interpretation, literary anthologies have tended, with some honourable exceptions, to remain firmly tethered to national traditions as the rubric through which texts are understood. Of course there are no signs that the nation as a concept, and as a space that generates strong affective responses, is going to disappear anytime soon. Yet to acknowledge the ways in which literature travels across vast distances – either as a material object being read in different places, or via those who write about such places as visitors, travellers, workers or enslaved peoples – is to refract expressions and assumptions of national identity in ways that draw attention to their constructed, and therefore contested, nature.

We understand the Anglophone literature of the Atlantic world as being marked by manifold networks of connection and interrelationship, in which hierarchies of centrality and periphery are both enforced and resisted, pro-claimed and undermined, through the circulation of bodies and ideas. The long nineteenth century, the chronology with which we are concerned, is marked by a massive expansion in print culture and literacy, the spread of imperialism in the Atlantic world as a political imperative and rapid advances in transporta-tion technology – all factors that helped facilitate the creation and dissemina-tion of a literature able to look beyond its national borders.

Central to our conceptualisation of this volume has been a desire to expand the kinds of material that students would expect to encounter. While we focus exclusively on Anglophone texts, we present writing from across both hemi-spheres of the Atlantic world to give an indication of the complex and far-reach-ing shapes that transatlantic exchange can take. We have also sought to make visible within our selection the diversity of identities across ethnicity, race and gender that comprise the Atlantic space in this period. While no anthology can hope to be exhaustive – and the transatlantic frame of our volume makes that ambition seem even more illusory – we hope that our careful organisation of material into ten thematic sections allows readers to navigate their way through a wide range of writing from both familiar and less well-known authors, thereby expanding the ways in which the transatlantic frame is understood.

The principal impetus behind the development of this anthology was to provide a volume for classroom instruction. Personally and anecdotally, we found that instructors of transatlantic literature classes were obliged to cobble together a curriculum from various sources, scanning a dozen different books while navigating issues related to public domain and textual authority and fidel-ity. By bringing together a number of these texts within one volume, we hope to offer a resource for teaching Anglophone literature published across the Atlantic world during the long nineteenth century. In addition, the supplementary mate-rial published on our website (more about which below), including additional primary texts, reading guides and lesson plans, offers a number of paratextual elements for instructors and students, as well as digital resources conducive to that environment.

Our ten broad sections, each with its own introduction, are centred on a particular theme or category. Though the sections are themselves expansive (for example, Suffrage and Citizenship encompasses a multitude of movements, issues and identities), they are by no means inclusive or definitive. We encour-age students and scholars to read within a section itself (for instance, assigning several texts on the subject of exploitation within the Business, Industry and Labour section), or to read across sections thematically (focusing, perhaps, on Blacks' experiences in Travel and Tourism, Science and Technology, and more).

Because of the variety of material our anthology offers, it is also possible to curate different collections of texts – for instance Canadian-authored texts, or transatlantic poetry, or texts relating to Darwinism, or texts written during or about the Great War, or even texts across the writing career of a particularly prolific and influential author such as E. Pauline Johnson or Frederick Douglass. We hope that such depth and breadth of textual material allows the instructor or reader to construct a reading cluster or targeted course of study. We recognise, as well, that this anthology will be useful not only in pedagogical settings but also for individual scholarship. To that end we have included a number of valuable scholarly resources in the form of chapter introductions, headnotes, annotations and references following each entry, while also providing citation of the original primary texts for further research.

Languages crossed and recrossed the Atlantic throughout the long nineteenth century, with hybrid mixes emerging from that still continuing process. Thus, although this anthology bears an 'Anglophone' designation in its title, multiple entries are marked by translingualism. The 'Anglophone' label holds for all selected texts within the anthology in that each entered into a nineteenth-century English-speaking community somewhere in the Atlantic world. But many neither started nor remained in Anglophone form. Indeed, a number of our entries ask, implicitly or even explicitly, how language interactions have shaped cultural transmissions and development, and vice versa. Accordingly, for instance, we contextualise our entry excerpted from Benjamin Franklin's autobiography with annotation tracking its passage to French, via a translation of his manuscript that became the first published version and subsequently generated an early example of book history in action when Jared Sparks wrote about the complexity of its later remaking into English. Similarly, we acknowledge the essential role of translations like British writer Mary Howitt's in the social construction of the Danish Hans Christian Anderson's authorial identity for Anglophone readers.

Furthermore, even though all of this anthology's entries are presented in English, a notable number of texts illuminate the many diverse versions of the language circulating within and across nineteenth-century transatlantic communities. John Muir's account of his family's migration from Scotland includes his assertions that their home language was not, in fact, 'English' at all, though he also says he and his siblings could code-switch. Recalling conversations with the British sea captain managing their Atlantic crossing, Muir remembers that he

> seemed surprised to find that Scotch boys could read and pronounce English with perfect accent and knew so much Latin and French. In Scotch schools only pure English was taught, although not a word of English was spoken out of school. All through life, however well educated, the Scotch spoke Scotch among their own folk, except at times when unduly excited on the only two subjects on which Scotchmen get much excited, namely religion and politics. So long as the controversy went on with fairly level temper, only gude braid Scots was used, but if one became angry, as was likely to happen, then he immediately began speaking severely correct English, while his antagonist, drawing himself up, would say: 'Weel, there's na use pursuing this subject only further, for I see ye hae gotten to your English.'

In the same thematic section on Migration, Settlement and Resistance (MSR), Susanna Moodie uses language distinction to signal class as well as ethnic distinctions between her own family and poor Irish immigrants by rendering what those 'Others' say in pronounced dialect. The unnamed presenter of Irish cook Ann McNabb's oral history later in that section makes similar use of dialect indicators, even in a text more affirming of its subject's views and experiences. By including such examples of difference, the anthology underscores how language operates at sites of social power differentials.

Numerous transatlantic translation occasions represented here exemplify how those power differentials often placed English writers in a position of mediating between a marginalised storyteller and an Anglophone audience. With each translation the privilege accorded the English language highlights a language hierarchy, a linguistic imperial prominence. In an attempt to foster voicescapes that illuminate the lives, stories and poetry of original speakers, English translations complicate how messages are received. Translations embody ethical debates across cultures. An Anglophone translation imposes a linguistic message aimed at reaching a specific audience that might well be completely unfamiliar with the author's language and voice. The lyrics of a Barbados work song, for instance, come to us only as transcribed by a British listener: how accurately did his record reflect the sound and sense of the singers he heard? So too, the biting satire of Black Jamaican singers decrying the limits being enslaved had placed on their family life reached nineteenth-century UK readers only via a British official's presentation – along with his efforts at analysis: how trustworthy, we can only guess. Richard Robert Madden plays that intermediary role in two similar entries – one by Abon Becr Sadika in our 'Religion and Secularism' section and another by Juan Francisco Manzano in 'Abolition and Aftermath'. Readers should take that intervening layer of textual production into account, considering that the 'Anglophone' versions of such texts involved translation not only filtering but also reframing the original authorial voice's perspective and intent. One strategy we have used to underscore the interpretive challenges presented by such translations presents accompanying excerpts from alternative translators in annotations – as with Madden's version of Abon Becr Sadika's personal account, which is supplemented by references to George Renouard's longer translation, published by the Royal Geographical Society.

Translation also emerges less directly yet significantly in an entry like our excerpt from Longfellow's *Evangeline*, which chronicles the diasporic experience of Acadians deported from their home in Canada: though the American poet writes in English, his topic reminds us to attend to a dimension of transatlantic linguistic blending that resulted from a British removal resulting in many French language traces in current-day Louisiana in the US. Similarly, while some reports on US Indian removals printed in England drew on the bilingual *Cherokee Phoenix* and thus could be said to offer an 'authentic' Indigenous voice, and some First Nations and Native American speakers and writers generated their own texts (like Joseph Brant early in our chronology or Charles Eastman toward the end of our timeline), their English text-making could also call attention to language as a meaningful site of cultural difference. And, in one complex case of an English speaker translating a Native voice, just how reliable is Henry Rowe Schoolcraft's rendering into English of his wife Jane's poem, originally composed in Ojibwe? Perhaps not as unfiltered as his framing commentary would suggest.

Given that our process of curating such examples has enhanced our own appreciation of translation as both essential to cultural exchange and inherently problematic, we offer with self-aware humility our own occasional translations in annotations and, more substantially, a new translation of the Haitian Declaration of Independence from French. Held in the British Archive, the original now available to the world for easy downloading provides a reminder that the long-standing tendency of European powers to acquire and display artefacts gleaned through empire's determined reach is yet another form of 'Anglophone' dominance which we intend for our anthology to critique as well as acknowledge.

By spotlighting such complex translingual passages and interactions, we complicate our own adoption of an 'Anglophone' focus. We hope our readers will resist, in turn, both by countering any sense of English dominance they find in this collection and by submitting more examples of transatlantic linguistic exchanges for the digital website anthology that complements this print edition.[1]

We deliberately seek inclusiveness across print genres as well as writers' national origins, race, gender and class. Canonical figures and their best-known texts are easily found elsewhere and are thus de-emphasised here; but we suggest that rereading canonical figures from around the Atlantic basin in tandem with our anthology can reframe those familiar voices and resurface the nineteenth-century print conversations taking place across nations, time and oceanic spaces and spark new conversations for scholars, teachers, students and other readers today. Occasionally some writers we hoped to include are absent if their works did not explicitly engage with print or persons active in the Atlantic world beyond the writer's country of origin. For example, to our knowledge Frances Ellen Watkins Harper's immensely important works were not reprinted or reviewed outside North America; thus Harper surfaces here only in a poem looking to Cuba and in an essay that responds in part to *The Spanish Gypsy* by George Eliot. In other respects our selections of texts are purposefully catholic. Ours is a 'literature' anthology in the broad nineteenth-century sense of 'letters' generally. Thanks to their brevity we reprint numerous complete poems as well as several songs, kindred genres with long heritages. Another longstanding written or orally delivered genre, the letter, is likewise represented in several private or published transatlantic exchanges. Other selections emerged from newer modes of connection, whether as transcribed speeches or lectures by transatlantic visitors such as William Wells Brown in London or Emmeline Pankhurst in Connecticut, or as travel writing enabled by modern transport systems. Still other print forms, including visual images, had direct links to new technologies, many in the explosion of mass-produced and circulated long nineteenth-century newspapers and magazines that were churned out using the same steam power that moved print and people across the sea in ships, and that sold far more copies

---

1 See Jessie Reeder, 'Toward a Multilingual Victorian Transatlanticism', *Victorian Literature and Culture* 49.1 (2021), 171–95, for a further compelling argument for the importance of multilingual transatlantic literary studies.

than any books and, as ephemera, were also locally mobile, passing easily from reader to reader. Book reviews and newspaper articles are generously represented too, often in excerpted form. Excerpts not only focus readers on key transatlantic content, but their brevity has also, more crucially, enabled us to include far more writers from Canada, the US, the Caribbean and the British Isles than we otherwise could have. The generous suggestions of our twelve-member advisory board were another crucial factor in moving us closer to the breadth of representation we sought.

As noted already, one sustained element in transatlantic literary studies has been its emphasis on fluidity and motion, and on related patterns of textual exchange. With much of this networking literally occurring by way of the Atlantic ocean (through crossings by people and goods, as well as ideas), one task embraced by the field's scholarship has been to track and analyse such passages: their literal and figurative routes, as well as the material and social forces shaping them. Theorising transatlanticism, therefore, includes marking the material ways that 'culture in motion' – across fluid paths and through social relationships crossing national boundaries – reshapes literature and vice versa.

In our twenty-first-century context, we can benefit from the World Wide Web's echoing the actions of transatlantic cultural passages potent during the long nineteenth century. Following a thread of text and associated concepts through a series of digital paths on a website is admittedly not an equivalent to a ship's captain choosing an oceanic route of exploration based on maps yet open to revision. However, both entail a blend between using charts composed by others and exploring alternative currents. In both cases, the journey makes tangible to the travelling body that experiential knowledge-making draws on structures of prior cultural transmission while inviting new routes of inquiry. At a conceptual level, 'doing' nineteenth-century transatlantic studies should include pushing back against the kind of codifications and boundary-setting implied by a print text like this one.

Hence our companion digital anthology and the Teaching Transatlanticism website where it resides (<www.teachingtransatlanticism.tcu.edu>) are as essential to this project as the volume you are reading now. The digital anthology enacts these principles central to our praxis:

- *Fixed canons, like fixed geographic boundaries, should be constantly undercut by an openness to new/additional texts and new interpretive approaches.* Accordingly, while the digital anthology on our website reiterates the same ten themes of this print collection, it remains open to additional submissions of individual texts. Further, although our echoing there of the print collection's themes hopefully encourages intellectual connections, we resist our own use of seemingly coherent categories by positioning many of the web-presented texts in more than one category, in contrast to this print collection, where entries may seem (despite our cross-referencing of many entries) to be located in relation to a single sequence of reading within a fixed thematic context.
- *Cultural transmission is recursive, sometimes unpredictable in its routing and virtually impossible to retrace exactly.* As our digital anthology demonstrates through any user's travels across particular paths chosen in the

moment, one approach to understanding transatlanticism's culture-making force involves recognising that particular instances of knowledge-making from the past cannot be perfectly recreated, even when they can be contextualised historically and approximated by acts of (re)reading and analysis in a current moment.

- Though individual actors with social power residing in their identities exercise significant influence on how society enacts value systems and understands the world, *social interaction – much of it potentially collaborative – can be vital to knowledge-building.* Consistent with the many social movements of nineteenth-century transatlantic culture, therefore, our website invites ongoing contributions and revision.

We hope you, perhaps now engaging with transatlanticism through reading this text, will soon add your voice to a field-expanding conversation online.

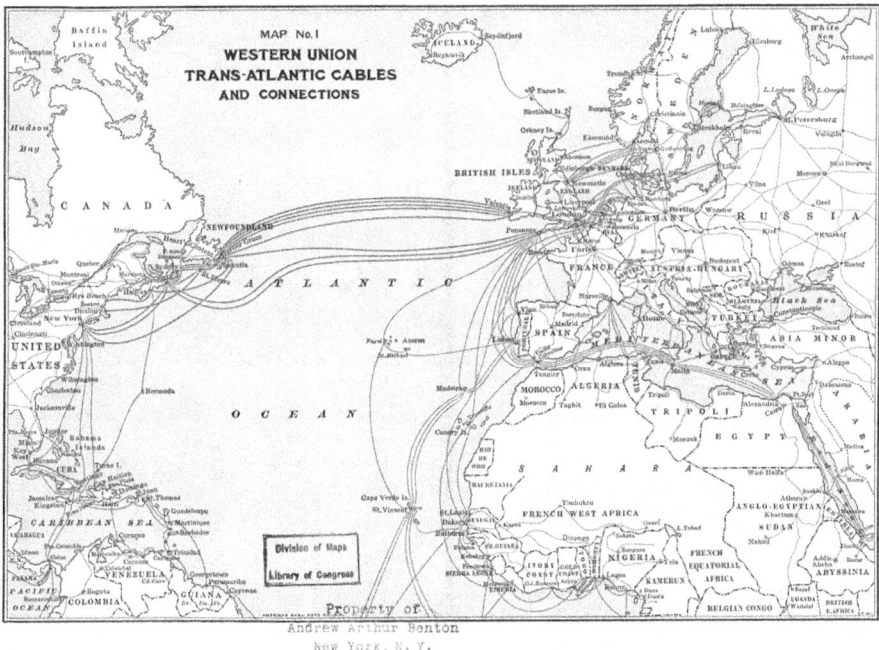

Figure I.2 Western Union Telegraph Company. *Western Union trans-atlantic cables.* [New York?: Publisher not identified, 1900]. Courtesy Geography and Map Division, Library of Congress.

1

ABOLITION AND AFTERMATH

Figure 1.1 Scene in the hold of the 'Blood-Stained Gloria' (Middle Passage)
c.1860. Courtesy Library Company of Philadelphia.

Situated at a conceptual intersection of space and time, this anthology's engagement with nineteenth-century transatlantic 'Abolition and Aftermath' joins an
ongoing intellectual enterprise guided by anti-racist aims and led, most promi-
nently, by Black scholars. Since the 1993 publication of Paul Gilroy's *The Black
Atlantic*, transatlantic studies have foregrounded experiences of enslavement – as

well as resistance against it.[1] On one hand, historicising transatlantic slavery has required noting how evolving ideas about race that emerged beginning in the European Renaissance contributed to a shift in enslavement practices, which in previous eras were not linked to race differences between enslavers and enslaved; once white/Other racial hierarchies crystallised, pro-slavery forces in the so-called 'New World' of the Americas regularly invoked them to justify suppression of peoples of colour – both Indigenous populations and Blacks from West Africa. On the other hand, while pinpointing the history of growing ideologies that enabled slavery's establishment in places like Caribbean sugar plantations was important, so too are more recent moves to demonstrate how the many painful legacies of enslavement have stretched across time, continuing to impact its descendants, large-scale political structures and social relations on both sides of the Atlantic.[2] Our examination of 'Abolition and Aftermath' addresses both these exigencies.

TRANSATLANTIC ANTI-SLAVERY'S INTERPERSONAL CONNECTIONS

One recurring element in studies of abolitionism underscores interpersonal alliances enhancing the social power activists on one side of the Atlantic could exercise over the other. This section documents such transatlantic social connections supporting a shared abolitionist culture. As William Cowper's 'The Negro's Complaint', Mary Prince's 1831 narrative, Elizabeth Barrett Browning's 'Runaway Slave' poem, and William and Ellen Crafts' *Running a Thousand Miles for Freedom* illustrate, North American and Caribbean Blacks' engagement with British supporters – and English authors' eagerness to speak to potential anti-slavery impulses in the Americas – played a major role in sustaining the movement. Relatedly, this section's entry from Phillis Wheatley ('To the Right Honourable WILLIAM, Earl of Dartmouth'), like that for Prince, highlights how print publication, carried out on one side of the Atlantic, could enable voices from the other, while also raising questions about how we should interpret Black agency mediated through white text managers.

If British writers like Barrett Browning sought to influence attitudes toward slavery in America, such efforts to change minds certainly went in the other direction as well. Harriet Beecher Stowe's *Uncle Tom's Cabin* was a bestseller in the US, but even more popular in England, where Stowe's triumphant visit to connect with readers (and lay the groundwork for authorised editions of later writings) presaged today's celebrity book tours, even as it stoked support for the anti-slavery cause. 'Abolition and Aftermath' revisits this *Uncle Tom's Cabin* phenomenon via a review of one London-based performance of the text: Mary Webb's Stafford House reading of *The Christian Slave*, the adaptation

---

1 See Paul Williams, *Paul Gilroy* (Hoboken, NJ: Taylor & Francis, 2013), especially 'The Black Atlantic I' and 'After Gilroy'.

2 Much of this work has been assertively interventionist, as in Alan Rice, *Creating Memorials, Building Identities: The Politics of Memory in the Black Atlantic* (Liverpool: Liverpool University Press, 2010); David Olusoga, *Black and British: A Forgotten History* (London: Macmillan, 2016); and Winfried Siemerling, *The Black Atlantic Reconsidered: Black Canadian Writing, Cultural History, and the Presence of the Past* (Toronto: McGill University Press, 2015). Siemerling, for instance, emphasises connections between 'historical dimensions of black Canada and the work of contemporary writers' (5).

Stowe penned herself with Webb in mind. Later, with the Civil War raging and British failure to unequivocally reject the Confederacy signalling transatlantic abolitionism's limitations, Frances Ann (Fanny) Kemble, an English-turned-American actress who had separated from her Southern plantation-owner spouse, would place her 1863 *Journal of a Residence on a Georgian Plantation* with a London publisher; in doing so, Kemble transformed private writing recorded decades earlier into a public call for her homeland to take a pro-Union, anti-slavery stand.

Print culture fostered imaginative connections as well as interpersonal alliances opposing enslavement. For instance, the 1846 Dublin edition of Frederick Douglass's *Narrative* was an outgrowth of a transatlantic speaking tour whereby he cultivated the network which, Benjamin Fagan explains, supported the subsequent launch of Douglass's *North Star* periodical at home. Similarly, in line with Joseph Rezek's research on Black orators in the northeastern US exhibiting 'a striking self-awareness about the future life of their texts in print' (656), we showcase a British periodical report on an 1849 London speech by William Wells Brown. In-text notations of enthusiastic audience responses to Brown's rousing delivery underscore how print revisitings of oral anti-slavery performances could expand their reach. Earlier, Ryan Butler notes, British publications like the *Christian Observer* crossed the Atlantic to receptive readers like a young Harriet Beecher Stowe, who, though she never met William Wilberforce (represented here in a reprint of one of his speeches), absorbed his anti-slavery ideas. Thus stirring words and associated verbal images could travel transatlantically, whether or not their authors made a related shipboard journey.

INTERTEXTUAL DEBATES ON SLAVERY

Not everyone engaging with anti-slavery goals – as readers, writers or both – became famous. Accordingly, one cluster of texts presented here, listed as 'Transatlantic "Affectionate" Exchanges on Slavery', draws together publications launched through an effort consistent with what Katie Donington and her co-editors designate as an under-studied dimension of abolitionism and its pro-slavery opponents. Recognising that enslavement practices reached into all aspects of 'everyday life' in Britain' (1), *Britain's History and Memory of Transatlantic Slavery* urges deprioritising 'the work of a few "Saints" in . . . abolition campaigns' and incorporating such actions as anti-slavery petitions, which attracted cross-class alliances. Therefore, we begin our 'Exchanges on Slavery' cluster with the 1853 'Affectionate and Christian Address of Many Thousands of Women', one of the most generative petitions of transatlantic culture. Then we balance resistant responses to the petition's call from well-known magazine editor Sarah Josepha Hale and US presidential wife Julia Gardiner Tyler with a letter to the editor penned by a then anonymous escaped slave, Harriet Jacobs. Honouring Jacobs's entrance into anti-slavery discourse, we affirm calls by scholars such as Gwen Bergner and John Oldfield to shine a brighter light on Black agency within the anti-slavery movement. Furthermore, through this multilayered exchange, we can see stirrings of what John Cumbler's *From Abolition to Rights for All* and Julie Holcomb's *Moral Commerce* ask scholars to explore: how one important heritage of the transatlantic anti-slavery movement was casting seeds that would bloom later in a broader 'progressive programme', including campaigns for voting rights and uplift of the working poor, as well as enhanced authorial agency for many women.[3]

ADOPTING A CIRCUM-ATLANTIC MAPPING

Transatlantic studies have often focused on an axis running between the United States and Great Britain. However, Canada and the Caribbean, along with South America and Africa are claiming increased scholarly attention in studies of both nineteenth-century slavery and resistance against it. Donington et al., for instance, analyse longstanding connections between 'British slavery [having] happened, in large part, on the plantations of the Caribbean', geographically distant from the UK itself, and a related 'distancing of the mind' encouraging 'the "forgetting" of Britain's immense role in transatlantic slavery', as well as a focus, when this history is addressed, on 'the more morally comforting narrative of abolition' (10). They advocate for work on the legacy of slavery in Caribbean sites bound to British history and on how, ironically, 'the "anti-slavery mission" drove empire further into the African continent' (10).[4] Similarly, in their study of Africans who, liberated from slave ships, were then turned into 'recaptive captives', DaSilva et al. point to sites 'from Haiti in the west, Britain in the north, Argentina in the south, and colonial Mauritius to the east' as becoming engaged in raids of 'coastal barracoons on both side of the Atlantic, detaining slave vessels at sea, or receiving survivors of wrecked slave ships' (347–8). Exploring the experiences of such recaptive groups includes tracking the diverse Atlantic basin locales where they lived, often enduring long periods of indenture rather than immediate freedom.[5]

Affirming the need to expand geographic mappings, this section offers (besides excerpts from Mary Prince) Caribbean-focused texts such as 'Ode: The Insurrection of the Slave at St. Domingo' and Juan Francisco Manzano's 'Thirty Years' poem. Looking northward, Mary Ann Shadd Cary's 'A Voice of Thanks' should remind readers of the inspiration Canada offered to many US Blacks seeking freedom, while an 1863 essay entitled 'Abolition of Slavery by

---

3 Julie L. Holcomb, in *Moral Commerce: Quakers and the Transatlantic Boycott of the Slave Labor Economy* (Ithaca, NY: Cornell University Press, 2016), argues that efforts like the British boycott-sugar movement appealed to 'politically marginalized' participants (4). She says this approach fostered networking based in shared moral principles, thereby promoting additional, later progressive collaborations throughout the Atlantic world.

4 For more on Caribbean slavery's reach into British culture at home, see Madge Dresser and Andrew Hann (eds), *Slavery and the British Country House* (Swindon: English Heritage, 2013).

5 DaSilva and colleagues also call for increased attention to the 'contract labor that saw a million people leave India and China' for the 'sugar colonies' of the British West Indies, Sierra Leone, St Helena and Brazil once 'slavery was no longer permitted' and 'Europeans and Africans' resisted 'migrat[ing] voluntarily' to those sites (363). Manuel Barcia examines expanded geographies of exchange through complex interactions among healthcare practitioners addressing multiple diseases linked to Middle Passage ships; he suggests shipboard conditions actually worsened after 1807's official end to the slave trade, since 'now-illegal slave vessels had no strong incentives to try to safeguard health among their captives' (3). See Barcia, *The Yellow Demon of Fever: Fighting Disease in the Nineteenth-Century Transatlantic Slave Trade* (New Haven, CT: Yale University Press, 2020).

the Cherokee Indians' underscores the complex entanglements of that Native nation's people with enslavement practices, even as they confronted a diasporic Removal and genocidal policies aimed at their own community.

EXPANDING THE TIME FRAME OF SLAVERY AND ANTI-SLAVERY

Jo Guldi and David Armitage suggest that '*Transnational* history is all the rage', although '*Transtemporal* history has yet to come into vogue' (15, emphasis in original).[6] Scholars of transatlantic slavery might rebuff the latter point. For instance, Donington et al. argue that 'Britain is haunted by the ghost of its slaving past', while former Caribbean colonies retain an even more 'visceral embodiment of a present shaped by [the region's] encounters with slavery and colonialisms' ('Introduction', 5). Proponents of reparations agree, they point out, since 'rather than a horror confined to the past, slavery continues to impact on the lived experiences' of its descendants (4).

For example, the 'Windrush generation', so-called after the ship that brought African-descended Black Jamaicans to Britain in 1948 to redress labour short-ages following the war, arrived as citizens of the 'UK and colonies' but received no confirming documentation of their status, nor did their Caribbean-born children. Besides routine experiences of racism following their arrival, many in the Windrush generation and family members faced denial of citizenship rights and even possible deportation after a 2012 immigration policy was forwarded by then Home Secretary Theresa May – a policy reversed only in 2018 when the annual observance of Windrush Day was founded.[7]

Like pleas to expand the time frame for studying slavery to include its still-current legacies, endeavours like the *New York Times*'s *1619 Project* underscore how public understanding of slavery's impact in the Americas can be enhanced by reaching back into earlier time periods than those (such as the US Civil War era) dominating school textbooks. In a US context, that initiative contends, history-telling needs to address the earliest arrival of enslaved African Blacks in colonies that became the US nation – one flawed from the outset by this lasting moral stain.[8]

Given this anthology's focus on a long nineteenth-century chronology, 'Abolition and Aftermath' affiliates with these calls for a deep and broad time frame in anti-slavery studies by emphasising various legacies from, and responses to, a painful heritage that extends beyond specific events one might cite as marking the 'end' of enslavement in the transatlantic world. Thus, on the one hand, we incorporate such signs of slavery's persistent power as

---

6 Guldi and Armitage call for historians to help build a 'public future' by 'developing a *longue-durée* contextual background against which archival information, events, and sources can be inter-preted' (117).

7 Guy Hewitt, 'The Windrush Scandal: An Insider's Perspective', *Caribbean Quarterly* 66.1 (2020), 108–28.

8 Although Nikole Hannah-Jones won a Pulitzer for her introductory essay in the *1619 Project* anthology of creative writing joined to interpretive essays, the publication drew attacks from both the political right and the left, as outlined by Timothy Messer-Kruse, 'What the 1619 Project Really Means', *Chronicle of Higher Education* (5 March 2020), Web.

lynchings during the Jim Crow era in the US, a recurring horror addressed in Ida B. Wells's anti-lynching campaign. Significantly, Wells's work was bolstered transatlantically by her lecturing in the UK and the endorsement in Celestine Edwards's introduction for a British edition of *United States Atrocities*. Further illustrating how transatlantic enslavements continued into the twentieth century, an entry from Henry W. Nevinson's investigative journalism reveals the contract labour system's pernicious 'new slave trade' along Africa's West Coast. And a 1919 W. E. B. DuBois editorial from *The Crisis* ('Returning Soldiers') bemoans the racist attitudes encountered by Black First World War veterans, whose dedicated service in Europe failed to garner cross-racial acceptance, much less appreciation, at home.

Essential though such acknowledgements of slavery's inheritances must be, honouring the agency of enslaved Black people and their heirs highlights their determined, strategic resistance across time. Accordingly, besides Black leaders of anti-slavery efforts referenced above, 'Aftermath' entries incorporate examples of generative hopefulness in action. Carrie Walls's 'Children's Exchange' column in the *Spelman Messenger*, one installment of which appears here, demonstrates the determination of Black teachers and learners to tap into Anglophone cultural resources aiding education's pathway to communal uplift – a commitment still evident in Black-led classrooms, homes and community literacy practices today. Similarly, song lyrics from the Fisk Jubilee Singers, whose performances crossed both the Atlantic and intercultural boundaries, reassert Black creativity and aspiration for future lives, still marked by inescapable histories, yet looking forward with generative pride.

References

Bergner, Gwen, 'Introduction: The Plantation, the Postplantation, and the Afterlives of Slavery', *American Literature* 91.3 (September 2019), 447–57.

Cumbler, John T., *From Abolition to Rights for All* (Philadelphia: University of Pennsylvania Press, 2008).

Da Silva, Daniel Domingues, David Eltis, Philip Misevich and Ojo Olatunji, 'The Diaspora of Africans Liberated from Slave Ships in the Nineteenth Century', *Journal of African History* 55 (2014), 347–69.

Donington, Katie, Ryan Hanley and Jessica Moody, 'Introduction', in Katie Donington, Ryan Hanley and Jessica Moody (eds), *Britain's History and Memory of Transatlantic Slavery: Local Nuances of a 'National Sin'* (Liverpool: Liverpool University Press, 2016), 1–18.

Fagan, Benjamin, '"The North Star" and the Atlantic 1848', *African American Review* 47.1 (Spring 2014), 51–67.

Gilroy, Paul, *The Black Atlantic: Modernity and Double Consciousness* (Cambridge, MA: Harvard University Press, 1993).

Guldi, Jo and David Armitage, *The History Manifesto* (Cambridge: Cambridge University Press, 2014).

Oldfield, John. 'Afterword', in Katie Donington, Ryan Hanley and Jessica Moody (eds), *Britain's History and Memory of Transatlantic Slavery: Local Nuances of a 'National Sin'* (Liverpool: Liverpool University Press, 2016), 237–46.

Rezek, Joseph, 'The Orations on the Abolition of the Slave Trade and the Uses of Print in the Early Black Republic', *Early American Literature* 45.3 (2010), 655–82.

Phillis Wheatley (1753–84)

'To the Right Honourable WILLIAM, Earl of Dartmouth' (1773)

Wheatley, though enslaved by a Philadelphia family, capitalised on their support of her literacy to cultivate an authorship so at odds with that identity that some doubted her writing's authenticity. Thomas Jefferson, for example, dismissed Wheatley's poetry as 'compositions published under her name', yet 'below the dignity of criticism' (Jefferson, qtd in Coviello, 447). Notably, in that context, Wheatley's poem below anticipates language in the Declaration of Independence he co-authored while extending her claim beyond the literary into transatlantic politics.

Her lyric addresses William, second Earl of Dartmouth (1731–1801), on his arrival in New England as Secretary of State for the colonies. Prior to his 1772 appointment, he had asserted the ultimate governing authority of Parliament but also promoted a generous, conciliatory stance toward the colonies when possible. Thus Wheatley's prediction that the 'iron chain' of prior colonial policy would shift under his leadership seemed possible ('Legge, William', *ODNB*). Wheatley portrays the Earl optimistically, predicting he will end suppressive practices in favour of 'Fair *Freedom*'. Midway through her text, she envisions him reading her poem. She associates her right to address political questions, though 'young in life', as grounded in having lost freedom herself, 'snatch'd from *Afric's* fancy'd happy seat'. If Wheatley elsewhere in her poetry extolled how being enslaved did bring the boon of Christianity, here she asserts the ironic different benefit of enslavement as carrying a type of experience-based knowledge.

'To the Right Honourable WILLIAM, Earl of Dartmouth'

HAIL, happy day, when smiling like the morn,
Fair *Freedom* rose *New-England* to adorn:
The northern clime beneath her genial ray,
Dartmouth, congratulates thy blissful sway:
Elate with hope her race no longer mourns,
Each soul expands, each grateful bosom burns,
While in thine hand with pleasure we behold
The silken reins, and *Freedom's* charms unfold.
Long lost to realms beneath the northern skies
She shines supreme, while hated *faction* dies:
Soon as appear'd the *Goddess* long desir'd,
Sick at the view, she languish'd and expir'd;
Thus from the splendors of the morning light
The owl in sadness seeks the caves of night.
No more, *America*, in mournful strain
Of wrongs, and grievance unredress'd complain,

No longer shall thou dread the iron chain,
Which wanton *Tyranny* with lawless hand
Had made, and with it meant t'enslave the land.

Should you, my lord, while you peruse my song,
Wonder from whence my love of *Freedom* sprung,
Whence flow these wishes for the common good,
By feeling hearts alone best understood,
I, young in life, by seeming cruel fate
Was snatch'd from *Afric's* fancy'd happy seat:
What pangs excruciating must molest,
What sorrows labour in my parent's breast?
Steel'd was that soul and by no misery mov'd
That from a father seiz'd his babe belov'd:
Such, such my case. And can I then but pray
Others may never feel tyrannic sway?[9]

For favours past, great Sir, our thanks are due,
And thee we ask thy favours to renew,
Since in thy pow'r, as in thy will before,
To sooth the griefs, which thou did'st once deplore.
May heav'nly grace the sacred sanction give
To all thy works, and thou for ever live
Not only on the wings of fleeting *Fame*,
Though praise immortal crowns the patriot's name,
But to conduct to heav'ns refulgent fane,
May fiery coursers sweep th' ethereal plain,
And bear thee upwards to that blest abode,
Where, like the prophet, thou shalt find thy God.

Source text

Wheatley, Phillis, *Poems on various subjects, religious and moral* (London: A. Bell, 1773).

References

Coviello, Peter, 'Agonizing Affection: Affect and Nation in Early America', *Early American Literature* 37.3 (2002), 439–68.
Hodgson, Lucia, 'Infant Muse: Phillis Wheatley and the Revolutionary Rhetoric of Childhood', *Early American Literature* 49.3 (2014), 663–82.
'Legge, William, second earl of Dartmouth', *ODNB*.

---

9 Lucia Hodgson argues that in this stanza Wheatley appropriates agency to critique not merely tyrannic rule of the colonies but her own enslaved status and separation from her family, a theme that carried over into much later abolitionist discourse.

Figure 1.2 Wedgwood ceramic anti-slavery piece *c.*1787/88. Catalog number: 68.150 1987.0005.51. Courtesy Division of Cultural and Community Life, National Museum of American History, Smithsonian Institution.

Figure 1.3 The Virginian Slave. John Tenniel, Intended as a Companion to [Hiram] Powers' 'Greek Slave', *Punch* 20 (1851), 236. Courtesy Mary Couts Burnett Library, TCU.

Along with its numerous expressions in print, the transatlantic anti-slavery movement generated a range of material culture texts. Famous examples included pendants representing the cause and art works such as an adaptation of a Greek slave statue from the Classical era.

William Cowper (1731–1800)

'The Negro's Complaint' (1788)

The influence of William Cowper, an English poet and hymn-writer, reached across the Atlantic. Between 1782, the publication of his first major volume, and 1837, when his monumental collected works appeared, more than one hundred editions of his poems were published in Britain and almost fifty in the US.

His humanitarian advocacy found focus in abolitionism in the late 1780s, when the creation in London of the Society for Effecting the Abolition of the Slave Trade coincided with an increase in anti-slavery publications by British writers in multiple genres. Edward Rushton's *West-Indian Eclogues* (1787), Ann Yearsley's *A Poem on the Inhumanity of the Slave-Trade* (1788) and Hannah More's *Slavery: A Poem* (1788) are just three such poetic interventions. Cowper had already addressed slavery's injustices in *The Task* (1785), an epic poem of more than 5,000 lines. In March 1788 Cowper's friend, slave-boat captain turned preacher and abolitionist John Newton, a Society member, forwarded a request that Cowper write a popular abolitionist ballad. Cowper was initially uncertain his verse could capture enslavement's horrors: 'When the condition of our negroes in the islands was first presented to me as a subject for songs, I felt myself not at all allured to the undertaking: it seemed to offer only images of horror, which would by no means be accommodated to the style of that sort of composition' (*Works*, 6: 140). 'The Negro's Complaint' (or lament) was one of two Cowper poems (the other being 'Reflections') published in a Society pamphlet in 1788. 'The Negro's Complaint' gained wider circulation by being reprinted, sometimes in slightly modified form, in numerous periodicals. Martin Luther King would quote lines 13–16 in his Methodist Student Leadership Conference address in Lincoln, Nebraska, in 1964.

'The Negro's Complaint'[10]

> Forced from home and all its pleasures,
>   Afric's coast I left forlorn,
> To increase the stranger's treasures,
>   O'er the raging billows borne.

---

10 Other printings of the poem include these lines after the title: 'To the tune of "Hosier's Ghost" or / As near Porto Bello lying'. 'Hosier's Ghost', a song from 1740 with lyrics by Richard Glover, refers to events in the mid-1720s when Admiral Francis Hosier led a failed attempt to blockade a port in Panama to prevent the Spanish from shipping silver back to Europe. Hosier and thousands of his men died of yellow fever and malaria while circling offshore. Hosier's ghost calls his successor, Admiral Edward Vernon, to retell his story.

Men from England bought and sold me,
    Paid my price in paltry gold;
But, though slave they have enroll'd me,
    Minds are never to be sold.

Still in thought as free as ever,
    What are England's rights, I ask,
Me from my delights to sever,
    Me to torture, me to task?
Fleecy locks and black complexion
    Cannot forfeit Nature's claim;
Skins may differ, but affection[11]
    Dwells in white and black the same.

Why did all-creating Nature
    Make the plant for which we toil?
Sighs must fan it, tears must water,
    Sweat of ours must dress[12] the soil.
Think, ye masters iron-hearted,
    Lolling at your jovial boards,[13]
Think how many backs have smarted
    For the sweets your cane affords.

Is there, as ye sometimes tell us,
    Is there One who reigns on high?
Has He bid you buy and sell us,
    Speaking from his throne, the sky?
Ask Him, if your knotted scourges,
    Matches, blood-extorting screws,
Are the means that duty urges
    Agents of his will to use?

Hark! He answers!—Wild tornadoes
    Strewing yonder sea with wrecks,
Wasting towns, plantations, meadows,
    Are the voice with which he speaks.[14]
He, foreseeing what vexations
    Afric's sons should undergo,
Fix'd their tyrants' habitations
    Where his whirlwinds answer—No.

---

11 Defenders of slavery would routinely argue that enslaved persons were less than fully human.
12 Prepare, treat
13 Table spread for a meal
14 The trope of storms as the expression of divine anger was commonplace. See, for example, Anne Finch's 'Upon the Hurricane' (1713).

By our blood in Afric wasted,
    Ere our necks received the chain;
By the miseries that we tasted,
    Crossing in your barks the main;
By our sufferings, since ye brought us
    To the man-degrading mart,
All sustain'd by patience, taught us
    Only by a broken heart!

Deem our nation brutes no longer
    Till some reason ye shall find
Worthier of regard and stronger
    Than the colour of our kind.
Slaves of Gold, whose sordid dealings
    Tarnish all your boasted powers
Prove that you have human feelings
    Ere ye proudly question ours!

Source text

Cowper, William, 'The Negro's Complaint', in Robert Southey (ed.), *The Works of William Cowper, Esq.*, 15 vols (London: Baldwin & Cradock, 1835–7), 10: 4–6.

References

Carey, Brycchan, *British Abolitionism and the Rhetoric of Sensibility: Writing, Sentiment, and Slavery, 1760–1807* (London: Palgrave, 2005).
Richardson, Alan (ed.), *Slavery, Abolition and Emancipation: Writings in the British Romantic Period, Vol. 4: Verse* (London: Pickering & Chatto, 1999).

'Ode: The Insurrection of the Slaves at St. Domingo' (1792)

This anonymous poem, which first appeared in New York and Long Island's *Courier* in 1792, recounts the 1790–1 revolution of the more than 100,000 enslaved workers who revolted in northern Saint-Domingue, a French sugar colony. Drawing from the political climate prompted by the French Revolution, many initially perceived the enslaved people's actions as barbaric and insupportable. However, with the 1797 republication of the poem in London's *Spirit of the Public Journals*, understandings of the insurrection had altered. Once the British were prepared to invade the French colony in 1791, the uprising's participants could be viewed as the enemies of revolutionary Napoleonic France. As a result, the Blacks might be seen as heroes. Praising the revolt as heroic supported the mythologising of its leader, whom poet William Wordsworth (1770–1850) also addressed in 'To Toussaint L'Ouverture'.

'Ode: The Insurrection of the Slaves at St. Domingo'
(Written in the Year 1792)

> Lowly sinks the ruddy sun,
> Sheathe the blade, the war is done;
> Cried Orrah,[15] to his murderous band,
> Who wearied stood on Cuba's strand.
> But hark! What sound invades the ear?
> Hark!—Sheathe the blade, no danger's near:
> 'Tis the gasp of parting breath,
> 'Tis the hollow voice of death,
> 'Tis the sign, the groan of those,
> Once our tyrants once our foes.
> Loud, loud, ye fiends, shriek loud! your cries
> Pour loud! a grateful sacrifice
> To him, at whose behest ye bleed,
> Who smil'd propitious on the deed!
> And, ye hoar cliffs, that frown around,
> The echos of our shouts resound,
> While around the votive fire!
> —We've soothe'd the spirit of our Sire.
> 'Twas night, when bound in servile chains,
> We sail'd from Afric's golden plains;
> The moon had reach'd its utmost height,
> Its orb disclos'd but half its light;
> Darkling clouds hung o'er the deep,
> And hush'd murmurs seem'd to sleep.
> Sudden floating in the skies
> A shadowy cloud appear'd to rise;
> Sudden gliding o'er the flood
> The dim-seen shade before me stood;
> Thro' its form the moon's pale beam
> Shed a faint, a sickly gleam;
> Thrice its arm I saw it rear,
> Thrice my mighty soul did fear.
> The stillness dread a hollow murmur broke; –
> It was the Genius[16] groan'd; and, lo!—it spoke!
> 'O, my troubled spirit sighs
> When I hear my people's cries!
> Now, the blood which swells their veins
> Flows debas'd by servile chains;
> Desart now my country lies;
> Moss grown now my altars rise:
> O, my troubled spirit sighs
> When I hear my people's cries!
> Hurry, Orrah, o'er the flood,
> Bathe thy sword in Christian blood!

---

15 A participant in the rebellion
16 The 'Genius' or spirit encourages the rebels to rise up against the French.

Whidah[17] will thy side protect;
Whidah will thy arm direct.'
Low'ring frown'd the burthened cloud,
Shrilly roar'd the whirlwind loud,
Livid lightnings gleam'd on high,
And big waves billow'd to the sky.
  Astonished I, in wild affright,
  Knew not 'twas vanished from my sight;
  Whether on the storm it rode,
  Or sunk beneath the troubled flood.
Again! Along the beam-gilt tide,
Ah! see again the spirit glide!
It joins our triumph! on the sight,
It bursts in majesty of light.
Mark! How it bows its wond'rous head,
And hails our deed! Ah! see—'tis fled!
  Now, now ye cliffs, that frown around,
  The echoes of our shouts resound,
  While around the votive fire!
  —We've sooth'd the spirit of our sire.

                                        [Courier.][18]

Source text

'Ode: The Insurrection of the Slaves at St. Domingo. (Written in the year 1792)', *The Spirit of the Public Journals for 1797*, Vol. 1, 2nd edn (London: James Ridgway, 1799), 238–40.

References

Dubois, Laurent, *Avengers of the World: The Story of the Haitian Revolution* (Cambridge, MA: Harvard University Press, 2004).
Horne, Gerald, *Confronting Black Jacobins: The U.S., the Haitian Revolution, and the Origins of the Dominican Republic* (New York: Monthly Review Press, 2015).

William Wilberforce (1759–1833)

From An Appeal to The Religion, Justice, and Humanity of The Inhabitants of The British Empire, in Behalf of The Negro Slaves in The West Indies *(1823)*

Scholarship on the anti-slavery movement emphasises the need to recognise leaders beyond elites with the greatest access to political power.

---

17 A town in the Kingdom of Dahomey, West Africa – now Ouidah in Benin (*OED*); a note in the original offers this explanation: 'The God whom the Africans on the Coast of Guinea worship'.
18 Source from which *The Spirit of the Public Journals* reprinted the poem

Nonetheless, while celebrating middle- and working-class participants (with strategies such as petitions to Parliament) and heeding C. L. R. James's call in *Black Jacobins* to honour Black Caribbean leaders, the historiography of abolition cannot ignore men like Wilberforce.

An 1880 biography exemplifies early moves to sanctify Wilberforce. Within the Heroes of Christian History book series, English minister-author John Stoughton touted Wilberforce's speeches and print interventions beginning as far back as a maiden anti-slavery speech in 1789 – a performance of over three hours. Welcome though partial successes like the abolition of the slave trade in 1807 would be, Stoughton noted, slavery itself continued. Although to 'steal negroes to carry them over to our colonies became illegal and punishable', nonetheless 'negroes still worked as slaves' on West India plantations (77). Such ongoing injustice is the target of the 1823 *Appeal*. Stoughton dubbed this 'manifesto' Wilberforce's 'great work' (78), crucial to the eventual passage of the Emancipation Act in August 1833, a month after the stalwart writer's July death.

From An Appeal

To all the inhabitants of the British Empire, who value the favour of God, or are alive to the interests or honour of their country,—to all who have any respect for justice, or any feelings of humanity, I would solemnly address myself. I call upon them, as they shall hereafter answer, in the great day of account, for the use they shall have made of any power or influence with which Providence may have entrusted them, to employ their best endeavours, by all lawful and constitutional means, to mitigate, and, as soon as it may be safely done, to terminate the Negro Slavery of the British Colonies; a system of the grossest injustice, of the most heathenish irreligion and immorality, of the most unprecedented degradation, and unrelenting cruelty.

At any time, and under any circumstances, from such a heavy load of guilt as this oppression amounts to, it would be our interest no less than our duty to absolve ourselves. But I will not attempt to conceal, that the present embarrassments and distress of our country—a distress, indeed, in which the West Indians themselves have largely participated—powerfully enforce on me the urgency of the obligation under which we lie, to commence, without delay, the preparatory measures for putting an end to a national crime of the deepest moral malignity.

The long continuance of this system, like that of its parent the Slave Trade, can only be accounted for by the generally prevailing ignorance of its real nature, and of its great and numerous evils. Some of the abuses which it involves have, indeed, been drawn into notice: but when the public attention has been attracted to this subject, it has been unadvisedly turned to particular instances of cruelty, rather than to the system in general, and to those essential and incurable vices which will invariably exist wherever the power of man over man is unlimited. Even at this day, few of our countrymen, comparatively speaking, are at all apprised of the Negro population; and, perhaps, many of our non-resident West Indian proprietors are full as ignorant of it as other men. Often, indeed, the most humane of the number, (many of them are men whose humanity is unquestionable,) are least of all aware of it, from estimating, not unnaturally, the actual state of the case, by the benevolence of their own well meant but unavailing, directions to their managers in the western hemisphere.

The persuasion, that it is to the public ignorance of the actual evils of West Indian Slavery that we can alone ascribe its having been suffered so long to remain unreformed and almost unnoticed, is strongly confirmed by referring to what passed when the question for abolishing the Slave Trade was seriously debated in 1792.[19] For then, on the general ground merely of the incurable injustice and acknowledged evils of slavery, aggravated, doubtless, by the consideration that it was a slavery forcibly imposed on unoffending men for our advantage, many of the most strenuous and most formidable opponents of the immediate abolition of the Slave Trade charged us with gross inconsistency, in not fairly following up our own arguments, and proposing the gradual extinction also of slavery itself. "If," they argued, "it is contrary, as you maintain, to the soundest principles of justice, no less than to the clearest dictates of humanity, to permit the seizure, and trans-portation across the Atlantic, of innocent men to labour for our benefit, can it be more just, or less inhuman, to leave the victims of our rapacity to a life of slavery and degradation, as the hopeless lot of themselves and their descendants for ever? If, indeed, it had been true, as was alleged by the African merchants, that the slaves were only the convicts of Africa, condemned after a fair trial, or that they were delivered by the mercy of their British purchasers from becoming the victims of a bloody superstition, or of a relentless despotism, or of cruel intestine wars,—in short, if, as was urged in defence of the traffic, the situation of the slaves in Africa was so bad that it was worth while, even on the plainest principles of humanity, to bring them away, and to place them in a Christian community, though at the price of all the sufferings they must undergo during the process of their deliverance, yet even then our detaining them as slaves longer than should be necessary for civilizing them, and enabling them to maintain themselves by their own industry, would be indefensible. But when, as we maintained, all these pleas had been proved to be not merely gross falsehoods, but a cruel mockery of the wretched sufferers, how much more strongly were we bound not to desert them so soon as they should be landed in the West Indies, but to provide as early as possible for their deliverance from a bondage which we ourselves declared to have been originally unjust and cruel! But whatever shadow of a plea might have existed for reducing the imported Africans to slavery, surely none could be urged for retaining, in the same hopeless state, their progeny to the latest generation."

Such was, I repeat it, the reasoning of many of our greatest and ablest oppo-nents, as well as of some of our warmest friends. Such, more especially, was the argument of our most powerful antagonist in the House of Commons; and, on these grounds, he, thirty years ago, proposed, that in less than eight years, which of course would have expired at the beginning of the present century, not only should the Slave Trade cease, but the extinction of slavery should itself commence. He proposed, that from that hour every new-born Negro infant should be free; subject only, when he should attain to puberty, to a species of apprenticeship for a few years, to repay the owner for the expense of maintaining him during the period

---

19 In 1792, the Society for the Abolition of the Slave Trade and its allies, using print publications and speeches to gather support, presented over 500 petitions with over 300,000 signatures to the House of Commons. The House voted 230 to 85 to abolish the slave trade, but an amendment call-ing for a gradual approach delayed real implementation.

of infancy and boyhood. Can I here forbear remarking, that if the advocates for immediate abolition could have foreseen that the feelings of the House of Commons, then apparently so warmly excited, and so resolutely fixed on the instant extinction of the Slave Trade, would so soon subside into a long and melancholy apathy; and had they in consequence acceded to these proposals, the Slavery of the West Indies would by this time nearly have expired, and we should be now rejoicing in the delightful change which the mass of our Negro population would have experienced, from a state of ignominious bondage to the condition of a free and happy peasantry. [...]

But while we are loudly called on by justice and humanity to take measures without delay for improving the condition of our West-Indian slaves, self-interest also inculcates the same duty, and with full as clear a voice. It is a great though common error, that notwithstanding we must, on religious and moral grounds, condemn the West Indian system, yet, that in a worldly view, it has been eminently gainful both to individuals and to the community at large. On the contrary, I believe it might be proved to any inquiring and unprejudiced mind, that taking in all considerations of political economy, and looking to the lamentable waste of human life among our soldiers and seamen, raised and recruited at a great expense, as well as to the more direct pecuniary charge of protecting the sugar colonies, no system of civil polity was ever maintained at a greater price, or was less truly profitable either to individuals or to the community, than that of our West-Indian settlements. [...]

Before I conclude, may I presume to interpose a word of caution to my fellow-labourers in this great cause,—a caution which I can truly say I have ever wished myself to keep in remembrance, and observe in practice: it is, that while we expose and condemn the evils of the system itself, we should treat with candour and tenderness the characters of the West-Indian proprietors. Let not the friends of the Africans forget that they themselves might have inherited West-Indian property; and that by early example and habit, they might have been subjected to the very prejudices which they now condemn. I have before declared, and I now willingly repeat, that I sincerely believe many of the owners of West-Indian estates to be men of more than common kindness and liberality; but I myself have found many of them, as I have had every reason to believe, utterly unacquainted with the true nature and practical character of the system with which they have the misfortune to be connected.

While, however, we speak and act towards the colonists personally with fair consideration and becoming candour, let our exertions in the cause of the unfortunate slaves be zealous and unremitting. Let us act with an energy suited to the importance of the interests for which we contend. Justice, humanity, and sound policy prescribe our course, and will animate our efforts. Stimulated by a consciousness of what we owe to the laws of God and the rights and happiness of man, our exertions will be ardent, and our perseverance invincible. Our ultimate success is sure; and ere long we shall rejoice in the consciousness of having delivered our country from the greatest of her crimes, and rescued her character from the deepest stain of dishonour.

Source text

Wilberforce, William, *An Appeal to The Religion, Justice, and Humanity of The Inhabitants of The British Empire, in Behalf of The Negro Slaves in The West Indies* (London: J. Hatchard & Son, 1823).

References

James, C. L. R., *Black Jacobins: Toussaint L'Ouverture and the San Domingo Revolution* (New York: Vintage Books, 1989).
Stoughton, John, D. D., *William Wilberforce* (New York: A. C. Armstrong & Son, 1880).

Mary Prince (1788–c.1833)

From The History of Mary Prince: A West Indian Slave. Related by Herself *(1831)*

Mary Prince was born in Bermuda. Prince's movements throughout the Atlantic world would make her life significant to transatlantic studies, even were she not the first enslaved Black woman to publish a narrative in Britain. Appearing shortly before England passed its Slavery Abolition Act of 1833, Prince's text chronicled the physical pain of chattel slavery and the inner life of this remarkable woman.

Like other Black writers' texts mediated through white editing (in this case both by transcriber Susanna Strickland [later Moodie] and abolitionist editor Thomas Pringle), Prince's narrative has been questioned in terms of agency. But Dyanne Martin finds 'critics have not fully examined the ways in which Prince's subtle and sometimes not-so-subtle mutinies against her oppressors exemplify a growing inner freedom' (308).

This excerpt documents Prince's journey from the Caribbean to England. Initially taken along by her enslavers Mr and Mrs Wood, Prince found that, in Britain, she had a different legal standing; a series of cases (including *Somerset* v. *Stewart*, 1772, and *Forbes* v. *Cochrane*, 1824) had established that individuals could not be held enslaved on British soil, even though slavery had not yet been abolished throughout the Empire. Legally free in London, Prince jeopardised that status if she returned to Antigua, where her husband awaited.

From The History of Mary Prince

About this time I asked my master and mistress to let me buy my own freedom. With the help of Mr. Burchell, I could have found the means to pay Mr. Wood; for it was agreed that I should afterwards, serve Mr. Burchell a while, for the cash he was to advance for me. I was earnest in the request to my owners; but their hearts were hard—too hard to consent. Mrs. Wood was very angry—she grew quite outrageous—she called me a black devil, and asked me who had put freedom into my head. "To be free is very sweet," I said: but she took good care to keep me a slave. I saw her change colour, and I left the room.

About this time my master and mistress were going to England to put their son to school, and bring their daughters home; and they took me with them to take care of the child. I was willing to come to England: I thought that by going there I should probably get cured of my rheumatism, and should return with my master and mistress, quite well, to my husband. My husband was willing for me to come away, for he had heard that my master would free me, −and I also hoped this might prove true; but it was all a false report.

The steward of the ship was very kind to me. He and my husband were in the same class in the Moravian Church. I was thankful that he was so friendly, for my mistress was not kind to me on the passage; and she told me, when she was angry, that she did not intend to treat me any better in England than in the West Indies—that I need not expect it. And she was as good as her word.

When we drew near to England, the rheumatism seized all my limbs worse than ever, and my body was dreadfully swelled. When we landed at the Tower, I shewed my flesh to my mistress, but she took no great notice of it. We were obliged to stop at the tavern till my master got a house; and a day or two after, my mistress sent me down into the wash-house to learn to wash in the English way. In the West Indies we wash with cold water—in England with hot. I told my mistress I was afraid that putting my hands first into the hot water and then into the cold, would increase the pain in my limbs. The doctor had told my mistress long before I came from the West Indies, that I was a sickly body and the washing did not agree with me. But Mrs. Wood would not release me from the tub, so I was forced to do as I could. I grew worse, and could not stand to wash. I was then forced to sit down with the tub before me, and often through pain and weakness was reduced to kneel or to sit down on the floor, to finish my task. When I complained to my mistress of this, she only got into a passion as usual, and said washing in hot water could not hurt any one;—that I was lazy and insolent, and wanted to be free of my work; but that she would make me do it. I thought her very hard on me, and my heart rose up within me. However I kept still at that time, and went down again to wash the child's things; but the English washer-women who were at work there, when they saw that I was so ill, had pity upon me and washed them for me. [. . .]

My master quarreled with me another time, about one of our great washings, his wife having stirred him up to do so. He said he would compel me to do the whole of the washing given out to me, or if I again refused, he would take a short course with me: he would either send me down to the brig in the river, to carry me back to Antigua, or he would turn me at once out of doors, and let me provide for myself. I said I would willingly go back, if he would let me purchase my own freedom. But this enraged him more than all the rest: he cursed and swore at me dreadfully, and said he would never sell my freedom—if I wished to be free, I was free in England, and I might go and try what freedom would do for me, and be d——d. My heart was very sore with this treatment, but I had to go on. I continued to do my work, and did all I could to give satisfaction, but all would not do.

Shortly after, the cook left them, and then matters went on ten times worse. I always washed the child's clothes without being commanded to do it, and any thing else that was wanted in the family; though still I was very sick—very sick indeed. When the great washing came round, which was every two months, my mistress got together again a great many heavy things, such as bed-ticks,[20] bed-coverlets, &c. for me to wash. I told her I was too ill to wash such heavy things that day. She said,

---

20 Fabric case stuffed with feathers or other material to form a mattress or pillow (*OED*)

she supposed I thought myself a free woman, but I was not; and if I did not do it directly I should be instantly turned out of doors. I stood a long time before I could answer, for I did not know well what to do. I knew that I was free in England, but I did not know where to go, or how to get my living; and therefore, I did not like to leave the house. But Mr. Wood said he would send for a constable to thrust me out; and at last I took courage and resolved that I would not be longer thus treated, but would go and trust to Providence. This was the fourth time they had threatened turn me out, and, go where I might, I was determined now to take them at their word; though I thought it very hard, after I had lived with them for thirteen years, and worked for them like a horse, to be driven out in this way, like a beggar. My only fault was being sick, and therefore unable to please my mistress, who thought she never could get work enough out of her slaves; and I told them so: but they only abused me and drove me out. This took place from two to three months, I think, after we came to England.

When I came away, I went to the man (one Mash) who used to black the shoes of the family, and asked his wife to get somebody to go with me to Hatton Garden to the Moravian Missionaries:[21] these were the only persons I knew in England. The woman sent a young girl with me to the mission house, and I saw there a gentleman called Mr. Moore. I told him my whole story, and how my owners had treated me, and asked him to take in my trunk with what few clothes I had. The missionaries were very kind to me—they were sorry for my destitute situation, and gave me leave to bring my things to be placed under their care. They were very good people, and they told me to come to the church.

When I went back to Mr. Wood's to get my trunk, I saw a lady, Mrs. Pell, who was on a visit to my mistress. When Mr. and Mrs. Wood heard me come in, they set this lady to stop me, finding that they had gone too far with me. Mrs. Pell came out to me, and said, "Are you really going to leave, Molly?[22] Don't leave, but come into the country with me." I believe she said this because she thought Mrs. Wood would easily get me back again. I replied to her, "Ma'am, this is the fourth time my master and mistress have driven me out, or threatened to drive me—and I will give them no more occasion to bid me go. I was not willing to leave them, for I am a stranger in this country, but now I must go—I can stay no longer to be so used." Mrs. Pell then went up stairs to my mistress, and told that I would go, and that she could not stop me. Mrs. Wood was very much hurt and frightened when she found I was determined to go out that day. She said, "If she goes the people will rob her, and then turn her adrift." She did not say this to me, but she spoke it loud enough for me to hear; that it might induce me not to go, I suppose. Mr. Wood also asked me where I was going to. I told him where I had been, and that I should never have gone away had I not been driven out by my owners. He had given me a written paper some time before, which said that I had come with them to England by my own desire; and that was true. It said also that I left them of my own free will, because I was a free woman in England; and that I was idle and would not do

---

21 While still living in Antigua, Prince had joined the Moravian Church and learned some reading and writing skills from the missionaries there.
22 Diminutive or nickname for Mary

my work—which was not true. I gave this paper afterwards to a gentleman who inquired into my case.[23]

I went into the kitchen and got my clothes out. The nurse and the servant girl were there, and I said to the man who was going to take out my trunk, "Stop, before you take up this trunk, and hear what I have to say before these people. I am going out of this house, as I was ordered; but I have done no wrong at all to my owners, neither here nor in the West Indies. I always worked very hard to please them, both by night and day; but there was no giving satisfaction, for my mistress could never be satisfied with reasonable service. I told my mistress I was sick, and yet she has ordered me out of doors. This is the fourth time; and now I am going out." [...]

About this time, a woman of the name of Hill told me of the Anti-Slavery Society, and went with me to their office, to inquire if they could do any thing to get me my freedom, and send me back to the West Indies. The gentlemen of the Society took me to a lawyer, who examined very strictly into my case; but told me that the laws of England could do nothing to make me free in Antigua.[24] However they did all they could for me: they gave me a little money from time to time to keep me from want; and some of them went to Mr. Wood to try to persuade him to let me return a free woman to my husband; but though they offered him, as I have heard, a large sum for my freedom, he was sulky and obstinate, and would not consent to let me go free.

This was the first winter I spent in England, and I suffered much from the severe cold, and from the rheumatic pains, which still at times torment me. However, Providence was very good to me, and I got many friends—especially some Quaker ladies, who hearing of my case, came and sought me out, and gave me good warm clothing and money. Thus I had great cause to bless God in my affliction.

When I got better I was anxious to get some work to do, as I was unwilling to eat the bread of idleness. Mrs. Mash, who was a laundress, recommended me to a lady for a charwoman.[25] She paid me very handsomely for what work I did, and I divided the money with Mrs. Mash; for though very poor, they gave me food when my own money was done, and never suffered me to want.

In the spring, I got into service with a lady, who saw me at the house where I sometimes worked as a charwoman. This lady's name was Mrs. Forsyth. She had been in the West Indies, and was accustomed to Blacks, and liked them. I was with

---

23 Prince's editor provides this note: 'The paper which Mr. Wood had given her before she left his house, was placed by her in Mr. Stephen's hands. It was expressed in the following terms:—"I have already told Molly, and now give it her in writing, in order that there may be no misunderstanding on her part, that as I brought her from Antigua at her own request and entreaty, and that she is consequently now free, she is of course at liberty to take her baggage and go where she pleases. And, in consequence of her late conduct, she must do one of two things—either quit the house, or return to Antigua by the earliest opportunity, as she does not evince a disposition to make herself useful. As she is a stranger in London, I do not wish to turn her out, or would do so, as two female servants are sufficient for my establishment. If after this she does remain, it will be only during her good behaviour: but on no consideration will I allow her wages or any other remuneration for her services."' John A. Wood. London, 18 August 1828 (24).

24 Original editor's note: She came first to the Anti-Slavery Office in Aldermanbury, about the latter end of November 1828; and her case was referred to Mr. George Stephen to be investigated. More of this hereafter.—ED.

25 Woman employed to do cleaning work

her six months, and went with her to Margate.[26] She treated me well, and gave me a good character when she left London.[27]

After Mrs. Forsyth went away, I was again out of place, and went to lodgings, for which I paid two shillings a week, and found coals and candle. After eleven weeks, the money I had saved in service was all gone, and I was forced to go back to the Anti-Slavery office to ask a supply, till I could get another situation. I did not like to go back—I did not like to be idle. I would rather work for my living than get it for nothing. They were very good to give me a supply, but I felt shame at being obliged to apply for relief whilst I had strength to work.

At last I went into the service of Mr. and Mrs. Pringle, where I have been ever since, and am as comfortable as I can be while separated from my dear husband, and away from my own country and all old friends and connections. My dear mistress teaches me daily to read the word of God, and takes great pains to make me understand it. I enjoy the great privilege of being enabled to attend church three times on the Sunday; and I have met with many kind friends since I have been here, both clergymen and others. The Rev. Mr. Young, who lives in the next house, has shown me much kindness, and taken much pains to instruct me, particularly while my master and mistress were absent in Scotland. Nor must I forget, among my friends, the Rev. Mr. Mortimer, the good clergyman of the parish, under whose ministry I have now sat for upwards of twelve months. I trust in God I have profited by what I have heard from him. He never keeps back the truth, and I think he has been the means of opening my eyes and ears much better to understand the word of God. Mr. Mortimer tells me that he cannot open the eyes of my heart, but that I must pray to God to change my heart, and make me to know the truth, and the truth will make me free.

I still live in the hope that God will find a way to give me my liberty, and give me back to my husband. I endeavour to keep down my fretting, and to leave all to Him, for he knows what is good for me better than I know myself. Yet, I must confess, I find it a hard and heavy task to do so.

I am often much vexed, and I feel great sorrow when I hear some people in this country say, that the slaves do not need better usage, and do not want to be free.[28] They believe the foreign people,[29] who deceive them, and say slaves are happy. I say, Not so. How can slaves be happy when they have the halter round their neck and the whip upon their back? and are disgraced and thought no more of than beasts?—and are separated from their mothers, and husbands, and children, and sisters, just as cattle are sold and separated? Is it happiness for a driver in the field to take down his wife or sister or child, and strip them, and whip them in such a disgraceful manner?—women that have had children exposed in the open field to shame! There is no modesty or decency shown by the owner to his slaves; men, women, and children are exposed alike. Since I have been here I have often wondered how English people can go out into the West Indies and act in such a beastly manner. But when they go to the West Indies, they forget God and all feeling of

---

26 Seaside town to the southeast of London

27 Original editor's note: She refers to a written certificate which will be inserted afterwards.

28 Original editor's note: The whole of this paragraph especially is given as nearly as was possible in Mary's precise words.

29 Original editor's note: She means West Indians.

shame, I think, since they can see and do such things. They tie up slaves like hogs—moor[30] them up like cattle, and they lick them, so as hogs, or cattle, or horses never were flogged;—and yet they come home and say, and make some good people believe, that slaves don't want to get out of slavery. But they put a cloak about the truth. It is not so. All slaves want to be free—to be free is very sweet. I will say the truth to English people who may read this history that my good friend, Miss S——,[31] is now writing down for me. I have been a slave myself—I know what slaves feel—I can tell by myself what other slaves feel, and by what they have told me.[32] The man that says slaves be quite happy in slavery—that they don't want to be free—that man is either ignorant or a lying person. I never heard a slave say so. I never heard a Buckra[33] man say so, till I heard tell of it in England. Such people ought to be ashamed of themselves. They can't do without slaves, they say. What's the reason they can't do without slaves as well as in England? No slaves here—no whips—no stocks—no punishment, except for wicked people. They hire servants in England; and if they don't like them, they send them away: they can't lick them. Let them work ever so hard in England, they are far better off than slaves. If they get a bad master, they give warning and go hire to another. They have their liberty. That's just what we want. We don't mind hard work, if we had proper treatment, and proper wages like English servants, and proper time given in the week to keep us from breaking the Sabbath. But they won't give it: they will have work—work—work, night and day, sick or well, till we are quite done up; and we must not speak up nor look amiss, however much we be abused. And then when we are quite done up, who cares for us, more than for a lame horse? This is slavery. I tell it, to let English people know the truth; and I hope they will never leave off to pray God, and call loud to the great King of England, till all the poor blacks be given free, and slavery done up for evermore.

Source text

Prince, Mary, *The History of Mary Prince, a West Indian Slave. Related by Herself. With a Supplement by the Editor* (London: F. Westley and A. H. Davis, 1831).

References

Martin, Dyanne, 'Island Squalls of Indignation: The Rhetoric of Freedom in *The History of Mary Prince*', CEA Critic 79.3 (2017), 309–15.

Nwankwo, Ifeoma Kiddoe, *Black Cosmopolitanism: Racial Consciousness and Trans-national Identity in the Nineteenth-Century Americas* (Philadelphia: University of Pennsylvania Press, 2005).

---

30 Original editor's note: A West Indian phrase: to fasten or tie up

31 Prince's 'good friend, Miss S' is Susanna Strickland, who wrote down the oral narrative and who would later emigrate to Canada with her husband, afterwards writing as Susanna Moodie.

32 See Chapter 6 in Ifeoma Kiddoe Nwankwo on Mary Prince's 'cosmopolitanism' for an astute analysis of this passage and others.

33 White person, especially a man (*OED*), or in this case likely a boss man

Juan Francisco Manzano (1797–1854)

'Thirty Years', Translated by Richard R. Madden (1840)

Juan Francisco Manzano, born to María del Pilar de Manzano and Toribio de Castro, in Mantanzas, Cuba, wrote his *Autobiografía*, now recognised as the first narrative published by an enslaved writer in Hispanophone America. Self-educated, Manzano frequented *tertulias* (salons promoting discussions of art and literature) hosted by Domingo Del Monte, an abolitionist and liberal intellectual.

Through Del Monte and his associates, Manzano, in his early forties, obtained his manumission and met Richard Madden, who served as a British magistrate and 'superintendent of liberated Africans', as well as 'arbiter in the Court of Mixed Commission established in Havana in 1835' (Malloy, 393; see also 396). With Del Monte's encouragement, Manzano composed his autobiography in Spanish, and the manuscript was initially edited by Anselmo Suárez y Romero. In turn, Madden translated Manzano's work for Anglophone readers and gave him a transatlantic audience via a presentation for the General Anti-Slavery Convention in London in 1840. Although Manzano's work certainly reached a wider audience via Madden's interventions, this translation, reportedly only one-half of the original manuscript, altered and commodified the text for Anglophone readers (Almeida, 140).

Manzano's text focused on growing up enslaved in an urban setting. As illustrated below, he incorporated poetry into his life-writing on slavery's brutality. Manzano's complete work was denied publication in Cuba until 1937. For another example of Madden as translator, see Abon Becr Sadika and Madden, 'Letter XXXI: The Scherife of Timbuctoo', RS.

'THIRTY YEARS'

WHEN I think on the course I have run,
From my childhood itself to this day,
I tremble, and fain would I shun,
The remembrance its terrors array.

I marvel at struggles endured,
With a destiny frightful as mine,
At the strength for such efforts:—assured
Tho' I am, 'tis in vain to repine.

I have known this sad life thirty years,
And to me, thirty years it has been
Of suff'ring, of sorrow and tears,
Ev'ry day of its bondage I've seen.

But 'tis nothing the past—or the pains,
Hitherto I have struggled to bear,
When I think, oh, my God! on the chains,
That I know I'm yet destined to wear.

Source text

Manzano, Juan Francisco, *Poems by a Slave in the Island of Cuba, Recently Liberated; Translated from the Spanish, by R. R. Madden, M.D. With the History of the Early Life of the Negro Poet, Written by Himself; to Which Are Prefixed Two Pieces Descriptive of Cuban Slavery and the Slave-Traffic, by R. R. M.* (London: Thomas Ward, 1840).

References

Almeida, Joselyn, *Reimagining the Transatlantic, 1787–1890* (Farnham: Ashgate, 2011).

Luis, William, *Literary Bondage: Slavery in Cuban Narrative* (Austin, TX: University of Texas Press, 1990).

Molloy, Sylvia, 'From Serf to Self: The Autobiography of Juan Francisco Manzano', *Modern Language Notes* 104. 2 (March 1989), 393–417.

'Slavery in Cuba', *The Friend; A Religious and Literary Journal* (30 January 1841), 138.

Frederick Douglass (1818–95)

'Preface' to the Second Dublin Edition, Narrative of the Life of Frederick Douglass (1846)

Abolitionist leader Frederick Douglass wrote a new Preface to his first autobiography while abroad on a transatlantic lecture tour. Unlike the previous Preface, written by William Lloyd Garrison, here Douglass speaks directly to readers himself. Through global lectures and newspaper reports, Douglass had garnered the authority to introduce his own work and, in a strategically organised Appendix, to reassert the validity of his experience as an American slave.

Offering powerful insights into the horrors of enslavement, Douglass's updated autobiography also marked his social position as a transatlantic figure. This new edition of the *Narrative* extended the transnational reputation its author had already burnished in such oratorical performances as his 'American Prejudice Against Color', delivered in Cork in October of 1845. Douglass would hold fond memories of Ireland, writing to Garrison: 'I can truly say, I have spent some of the happiest moments of my life since landing in this country. I seem to have undergone a transformation. I live a new life' (qtd in Chaffin, 102).

'Preface', Second Dublin Edition, Narrative of the Life of Frederick Douglass

In May last,[34] the present Narrative was published in Boston, Massachusetts,[35] and when I sailed[36] for England in September, about 4,500 copies had been sold. I have lately heard that a fifth edition has been called for. This rapid sale may be accounted for by the fact of my being a fugitive slave, and from the circumstance that for the last four years I have been engaged in travelling as a lecturing agent of the American Anti-slavery Society,[37] by which means I became extensively known in the United States.

My visit to Great Britain had a threefold object. I wished to be out of the way during the excitement consequent on the publication of my book; lest the information I had there given as to my identity and place of abode, should induce my owner[38] to take measures for my restoration to his 'patriarchal care.' For it may not be generally known in Europe, that a slave who escapes from his master is liable, by the Constitution of the United States, to be dragged back into bondage, no matter in what part of the vast extent of the States and their territories he may have taken refuge.

My next inducement was a desire to increase my stock of information, and my opportunities of self-improvement, by a visit to the land of my paternal[39] ancestors.

My third and chief object was, by the public exposition of the contaminating and degrading influences of Slavery upon the slaveholder and his abettors, as well as the slave, to excite such an intelligent interest on the subject of American Slavery, as may react upon my own country, and may tend to shame her out of her adhesion to a system so abhorrent to Christianity and to her republican institutions.

My last object is, I am happy to say, in a fair way of being accomplished. I have held public meetings in Dublin, Wexford, Waterford, Cork, Youghal, Limerick, Belfast, Glasgow, Aberdeen, Perth, and Dundee, within the five months which have elapsed since I landed in England. An edition of 2000 copies of my Narrative has been exhausted, and I am in great hopes that before my visit to Great Britain shall be completed, thousands and tens of thousands of the intelligent and philanthropic will be induced to co-operate with the noble band of American abolitionists, for the overthrow of the meanest, hugest, and most dastardly system of iniquity that ever disgraced any country laying claim to the benefits of religion and civilization.

I beg to refer my reader to the Preface to the First edition, and the Letter which follows it; to some notices of my Narrative from various sources, which will be found

---

34 1845

35 Douglass would later write two additional autobiographies: *My Bondage and My Freedom* (1855) and *Life and Times of Frederick Douglass* (1881/1892).

36 Douglass sailed aboard the RMS *Cambria* from 16 to 28 August from Boston to Liverpool with James N. Buffum (1807–88), an anti-slavery activist who in September 1841 had protested along with Douglass when the Eastern Railroad Company refused to allow the two to ride together in first class.

37 This abolitionist group founded by William Lloyd Garrison published the previous edition of Douglass's autobiography.

38 Thomas Auld, whose son Hugh Auld legally filed manumission papers for Douglass in December 1846 after some of Douglass's allies in England raised the $711 payment to 'purchase' his freedom

39 The identity of Douglass's father is 'shrouded in mystery' to use his own words from *My Bondage and My Freedom* (1855). Based on what little he had been told, Douglass believed his father to be a white man, possibly a slaveholder (Aaron Anthony or Thomas Auld).

at the end of the book; and to the following notice of a public meeting held the evening previous to my departure from home, in the town of Lynn, Massachusetts, where I have resided for the last two years: —

"Last Friday evening a meeting was held in Lyceum Hall, for the purpose of exchanging farewells with Frederick Douglass and James N. Buffum, prior to their departure, on the ensuing day, for the Old World. The spacious hall was crowded to its utmost capacity—hundreds of men and women being obliged to stand all the evening. This was a most gratifying fact, and spoke volumes for the onward progress of the anti-slavery movement—since but six or seven years back, the people, instead of meeting with two such anti-slavery men for the interchange of kindly feelings, would have been more likely to meet them for the purpose of inflicting some summary punishment. Hundreds of persons enjoyed on this occasion the first good opportunity they have had to judge of Frederick Douglass's ability as a speaker and a reasoner; and unless I am much mistaken, their judgment was such as not only to increase their respect for him, but for his race, and the great movement now on foot to release it from thraldom.[40] He spoke twice, and both times with great power. His second effort sparkled with wit from beginning to end.

"The following resolutions were adopted, nem. con.[41]

"Resolved"—As the sense of this great gathering of the inhabitants of Lynn and vicinity, that we extend to our esteemed fellow-citizens Frederick Douglass and James N. Buffum, whose proposed departure for England has brought this multitude together, our heartiest good wishes for a successful issue of their journey.

"Resolved"—That we are especially desirous that Frederick Douglass, who came to this town a fugitive from slavery, should bear with him to the shores of the Old World, our unanimous testimony to the fidelity with which he has sustained the various relations of life, and to the deep respect with which he is now regarded by every friend of liberty throughout our borders."

It gives me great pleasure to be able to add, in an Appendix to the present edition, an attempted Refutation of my Narrative, lately published in the "Delaware Republican" by Mr. A. C. C. Thompson.[42] My reply will be found along with Mr. Thompson's letter. I have thanked[43] him there; but I cannot refrain from repeating my acknowledgments for the testimony he bears to the substantial truth of my story. We differ in our details, to be sure. But this was to be expected. He is the friend of slave-holders; he resides in a slave state, and is probably a slave-holder himself. He dares not speak the whole truth, if he would. I am an American slave, who have given my tyrant the slip. I am in a land of liberty, with no man to make me afraid. He agrees with me at least in the important fact, that I am what I proclaim

---

40 Bondage or being enslaved

41 Abbreviation of Latin *nemine contradicente* (no one contradicting, unanimously)

42 Thompson was neighbour to the slaveholder Thomas Auld. Following publication of Douglass's *Narrative*, Thompson's published letter (12 December 1845) challenged the veracity of the autobiography.

43 Douglass's response, printed in the Appendix, declares: 'I entreat you to accept my thanks for his [Thompson's] full, free and unsolicited testimony in regard to my identity. There now need be no doubt on that point, however much there might have been before. You, Mr. Thompson, have for ever settled them. I give you the fullest credit for the deed, saying nothing of the motive' (cxxvi).

myself to be, an ungrateful fugitive from the 'patriarchal institutions' of the Slave States; and he certifies that many of the heroes of my Narrative are still living and doing well, as 'honoured and worthy members of the Methodist Episcopal Church.'

FREDERICK DOUGLASS.

Glasgow, Feb. 6th, 1846.

Source text

Douglass, Frederick, *Narrative of the Life of Frederick Douglass, an American Slave. Written by Himself*, 2nd Dublin edn (Dublin: Webb & Chapman, 1846).

References

Chaffin, Tom, *Giant's Causeway: Frederick Douglass's Irish Odyssey and the Making of an American Visionary* (Charlottesville, VA: University of Virginia Press, 2014).
Lee, Maurice S. (ed.), *The Cambridge Companion to Frederick Douglass* (Cambridge: Cambridge University Press, 2009).

Elizabeth Barrett Browning (1806–61)

'The Runaway Slave at Pilgrim's Point' (1848)

Elizabeth Barrett Browning, née Elizabeth Barrett Moulton Barrett, had a close connection to Jamaica and slavery all her life. Her maternal grandfather, as Marjorie Stone notes in the *ODNB*, 'owned Jamaican sugar plantations, ships trading between Newcastle and Jamaica, a brewery, flax spinning mills, and glassworks'. Her father, Edward Barrett Moulton Barrett (1785–1857), was born on his maternal grandfather's slave-run estate, Cinnamon Hill in Jamaica, and inherited the property, which purportedly earned £50,000 a year prior to the poet's marriage. Her brother Sam spent part of the 1830s helping to manage the Jamaican family estate, where he died of a tropical fever in 1840.

Like her husband Robert Browning (1812–89) and his father, however, EBB (as she dubbed herself) repudiated slavery, just as she repudiated her father's forbidding any of his children to marry and eloped with poet Browning to Italy in 1846, where she gave birth to their son Robert Wiedemann Barrett Browning (1849–1912) and died in 1861. A radical in politics who at the age of twelve read and endorsed Mary Wollstonecraft's *Vindication of the Rights of Woman* and supported the Italian cause of independence from Austrian rule, she also endorsed the 1833 British abolition of slavery that in part led to the loss of her family's country home in England and removal to London, where she met her future husband in 1844. Even after their marriage, however, the Brownings' income derived in part from the ship *David Lyon*, which she inherited from her slave-owning uncle Samuel.

She was a childhood poet-prodigy but first achieved fame with her two-volume *Poems* of 1844, which Edgar Allan Poe enthusiastically praised in the *Broadway Journal* in January 1845. Her most famous poems remain *Sonnets from the Portuguese* (1850) and *Aurora Leigh* (1857), a novel in verse addressing feminist issues ranging from women's careers to marriage. *Aurora Leigh* so inspired Susan B. Anthony that she carried her personal copy of the poem for years and ultimately donated it to the Library of Congress. When invited to contribute to the *Liberty Bell*, EBB sent 'The Runaway Slave at Pilgrim's Point', which directly confronted the open secret of slave-owners' sexual violence against women in addition to other oppressions. This work is one of the few poems to inspire a postcolonial novel, *Strange Music* (2008), by Black British writer Laura Fish.

'The Runaway Slave at Pilgrim's Point'

I

I stand on the mark,[44] beside the shore,
   Of the first white pilgrim's bended knee;
Where exile changed to ancestor,
   And God was thanked for liberty.
I have run through the night – my skin is as dark –
I bend my knee down on this mark –
   I look on the sky and the sea.

II.

O, pilgrim-souls, I speak to you:
   I see you come out proud and slow
From the land of the spirits, pale as dew,
   And round me and round me ye go.
O, pilgrims, I have gasped and run
All night long from the whips of one
   Who, in your names, works sin and woe!

III.

And thus I thought that I would come
   And kneel here where ye knelt before,
And feel your souls around me hum
   In undertone to the ocean's roar;
And lift my black face, my black hand,
Here in your names, to curse this land
   Ye blessed in Freedom's, heretofore.

---

44 Plymouth Rock in Massachusetts

IV.

I am black, I am black,
    And yet God made me, they say:
But if He did so – smiling, back
    He must have cast his work away
Under the feet of His white creatures,
With a look of scorn, that the dusky features
    Might be trodden again to clay.

V.

And yet He has made dark things
    To be glad and merry as light;
There's a little dark bird sits and sings,
    There's a dark stream ripples out of sight;
And the dark frogs chant in the safe morass,[45]
And the sweetest stars are made to pass
    O'er the face of the darkest night.

VI.

But we who are dark, we are dark!
    O God, we have no stars!
About our souls, in care and cark,[46]
    Our blackness shuts like prison-bars!
And crouch our souls so far behind,
That never a comfort can they find,
    By reaching through their prison-bars.

VII.

Howbeit God's sunshine and His frost
    They make us hot, they make us cold,
As if we were not black and lost;
    And the beasts and birds in wood and wold,[47]
Do fear us and take us for very men; —
Could the whippoorwill or the cat of the glen[48]
    Look into my eyes and be bold?

VIII.

I am black, I am black,
    And once I laughed in girlish glee;
For one of my color stood in the track
    Where the drivers'[49] drove, and looked at me:
And tender and full was the look he gave!
A Slave looked so at another Slave, –
    I look at the sky and the sea.

---

45 Swamp
46 That which burdens the spirit, trouble (*OED*)
47 A piece of open country; a plain (*OED*)
48 A mountain-valley (*OED*)
49 Overseer of a gang of slaves (*OED*)

IX.

And from that hour our spirits grew
    As free as if unsold, unbought;
We were strong enough, since we were two,
    To conquer the world, we thought.
The drivers drove us day by day:
We did not mind; we went one way,
    And no better a liberty sought.

X.

In the open ground, between the canes,[50]
    He said "I love you," as he passed:
When the shingle-roof rang sharp with the rains,
    I heard how he vowed it fast.
While others trembled, he sate[51] in the hut
And carved me a bowl of the cocoa-nut,
    Through the roar of the hurricanes.

XI.

I sang his name instead of a song;
    Over and over I sang his name:
Backward and forward I sang it along,
    With my sweetest notes, it was still the same!
But I sang it low, that the slave-girls near
Might never guess, from what they could hear,
    That all the song was a name.

XII.

I look on the sky and the sea!
    We were two to love, and two to pray, –
Yes, two, O God, who cried on Thee,
    Though nothing didst thou say.
Coldly thou sat'st behind the sun,
And now I cry, who am but one, –
    Thou wilt not speak to-day!

XIII.

We were black, we were black,
    We had no claim to love and bliss –
What marvel, ours was cast to wrack[52]?
    They wrung my cold hands out of his –
They dragged him – why, I crawled to touch
His blood's mark in the dust – not much,
    Ye pilgrim-souls, – though plain as THIS!

---

50 Sugar-cane plants
51 Sat
52 A disastrous change in a state or condition of affairs; wreck, ruin, subversion (*OED*)

XIV.

Wrong, followed by a greater wrong![53]
   Grief seemed too good for such as I;
So the white men brought the shame ere long
   To stifle the sob in my throat thereby.
They would not leave me for my dull
Wet eyes! – it was too merciful
   To let me weep pure tears, and die.

XV.

I am black, I am black!
   I wore a child upon my breast, –
An amulet[54] that hung too slack,
   And, in my unrest, could not rest!
Thus we went moaning, child and mother,
One to another, one to another,
   Until all ended for the best.

XVI.

For hark! I will tell you low – low –
   I am black, you see;
And the babe, that lay on my bosom so,
   Was far too white – too white for me.
As white as the ladies who scorned to pray
Beside me at church but yesterday,
   Though my tears had washed a place for my knee.

XVII.

And my own child – I could not bear
   To look in his face, it was so white:
So I covered him up with a kerchief rare,
   I covered his face in, close and tight!
And he moaned and struggled as well as might be,
For the white child wanted his liberty, –
   Ha, ha! he wanted his master's right.

XVIII.

He moaned and beat with his head and feet –
   His little feet that never grew!
He struck them out as it was meet
   Against my heart to break it through.
I might have sung like a mother mild,
But I dared not sing to the white-faced child
   The only song I knew.

---

53 The 'greater wrong' here is rape.
54 Anything worn about the person as a charm or preventive against evil (*OED*), hence here bitterly ironic

XIX.

And yet I pulled the kerchief close:
    He could not see the sun, I swear,
More then, alive, than now he does
    From between the roots of the mangles[55] – where?
I know where! – close! – a child and mother
Do wrong to look at one another,
    When one is black and one is fair.

XX.

Even in that single glance I had
    Of my child's face, – I tell you all, –
I saw a look that made me mad, –
    The master's look, that used to fall
On my soul like his lash, – or worse, –
Therefore, to save it from my curse,
    I twisted it round in my shawl.

XXI.

And he moaned and trembled from foot to head, –
    He shivered from head to foot, –
Till, after a time, he lay, instead,
    Too suddenly still and mute;
And I felt, beside, a creeping cold, –
I dared to lift up just a fold,
    As in lifting a leaf of the mango fruit.

XXII.

But MY fruit! ha, ha! – there had been
    (I laugh to think on't at this hour!)
Your fine white angels, – who have seen
    God's secret nearest to His power, –
And gathered my fruit to make them wine,
And sucked the soul of that child of mine,
    As the humming-bird sucks the soul of the flower.

XXIII.

Ha, ha! for the trick of the angels white!
    They freed the white child's spirit so;
I said not a word, but day and night
    I carried the body to and fro;
And it lay on my heart like a stone – as chill;
The sun may shine out as much as he will, –
    I am cold, though it happened a month ago.

---

55 A thicket of mangroves (*OED*), or trees and plants that thrive in salty marshes near the ocean

XXIV.

From the white man's house and the black man's hut
   I carried the little body on;
The forest's arms did around us shut,
   And silence through the trees did run!
They asked no questions as I went, –
They stood too high for astonishment, –
   They could see God rise on his throne.

XXV.

My little body, kerchiefed fast,
   I bore it on through the forest – on –
And when I felt it was tired at last,
   I scooped a hole beneath the moon.
Through the forest-tops the angels far,
With a white fine finger in every star
   Did point and mock at what was done.

XXVI.

Yet when it all was done aright,
   Earth twixt me and my baby strewed, –
All changed to black earth, – nothing white, –
   A dark child in the dark, – ensued
Some comfort, and my heart grew young;
I sate down smiling there, and sung
   The song I told you of, for good.

XXVII.

And thus we two were reconciled,
   The white child and black mother, thus;
For, as I sang it, – soft and wild,
   The same song, more melodious,
Rose from the grave whereon I sate!
It was the dead child singing that,
   To join the souls of both of us.

XXVIII.

I look on the sea and the sky!
   Where the Pilgrims' ships first anchored lay,
The great sun rideth gloriously!
   But the Pilgrims' ghosts have slid away
Through the first faint steaks of the morn!
My face is black, but it glares with a scorn
   Which they dare not meet by day.

XXIX.

Ah, in their stead their hunter-sons!
   Ah, ah! they are on me! they form in a ring!
Keep off, – I brave you all at once, –

I throw off your eyes like a noisome[56] thing!
You have killed the black eagle at nest, I think;
Did you never stand still in your triumph, and shrink
    From the stroke of her wounded wing?

XXX.

(Man, drop that stone you dared to lift! –)
I wish you, who stand there, seven abreast,
Each for his own wife's grace and gift,
    A little corpse as safely at rest,
Hid in the mangles! yes, but *she*
May keep live babies on her knee,
    And sing the song she liketh best.

XXXI.

I am not mad, – I am black!
    I see you staring in my face, –
I know you staring, shrinking back, –
    Ye are born of the Washington race!
And this land is the Free America, –
And this mark on my wrist, – (I prove what I say)
    Ropes tied me up here to the flogging-place.

XXXII.

You think I shrieked there? not a sound!
    I hung as a gourd hangs in the sun;
I only cursed them all around
    As softly as I might have done
My own child after. From these sands
Up to the mountains, lift your hands
    O Slaves, and end what I begun.

XXXIII.

Whips, curses! these must answer those!
    For in this UNION, ye have set
Two kinds of men in adverse rows,
    Each loathing each! and all forget
The seven wounds in Christ's body fair;
While He sees gaping everywhere
    Our countless wounds that pay no debt.

XXXIV.

Our wounds are different – your white men
    Are, after all, not gods indeed,
Nor able to make Christs again
    Do good with bleeding. *We* who bleed, –

---

56 Offensive

(Stand off!) – we help not in our loss, –
We are too heavy for our cross,
    And fall and crush you and your seed.

                    XXXV.
I fall, – I swoon, – I look at the sky!
    The clouds are breaking on my brain:
I am floated along, as if I should die
    Of Liberty's exquisite pain!
In the name of the white child waiting for me
In the deep black death where our kisses agree, –
White men, I leave you all curse-free,
    In my broken heart's disdain!

    ENGLAND.

Source text

[Browning, Elizabeth Barrett,] 'The Runaway Slave at Pilgrim's Point', *The Liberty Bell: By Friends of Freedom* (Boston: National Anti-Slavery Bazaar, 1848), 29–44.

References

ODNB
Sampson, Fiona, *Two-Way Mirror: The Life of Elizabeth Barrett Browning* (London: Profile Books, 2021).
Stone, Marjorie and Beverly Taylor (eds), *Elizabeth Barrett Browning: Selected Poems* (Peterborough, Ontario: Broadview Press, 2009).

William Wells Brown (1814?–84)

London Anti-slavery Speech of September 1849

In an introduction to William Wells Brown's 1852 *Three Years in Europe*, British abolitionist William Farmer praised his colleague's transatlantic impact. Revisiting details from Brown's earlier 1847 narrative on his enslavement, Farmer cast Brown as a compelling lecturer who, building on skills cultivated as a speaker for the American Anti-Slavery Society (AASS) in the US, had progressed to international events in France and Britain. Thus, proposed Farmer: 'Perhaps no coloured individual, not excepting that extraordinary man, Frederick Douglass, has done more good in disseminating anti-slavery principles in England, Scotland, and Ireland' (xxv). Strikingly, Farmer admitted that Great Britain still harboured attitudes making 'an intelligent representative of the oppressed coloured Americans' crucial to the cause, 'not only to describe in language of fervid eloquence, the wrongs inflicted upon his race in the United States', but also to keep the transatlantic bonds among movement supporters strong (xxvii).

The 1849 speech below, delivered during a reception for Brown at the Store Street Concert Rooms in London on 27 September 1849, typified his sophisticated oratory in ways that anticipated his subsequent success as a novelist while also illustrating his keen awareness of a live audience. Utilising such features as repetition, parallel structure, humour, vivid imagery and irony, Brown responded to speeches before his – including one recycling tired arguments to justify slavery's continuation within the US – by asserting his personal experience as an authoritative standpoint. Reprinted in the Boston-based *Liberator*, the publications of Brown's rousing speech, his opponent's and others delivered that evening enabled readers of that periodical to capture a sense of the solidarity-building power that such events exercised for the transnational anti-slavery cause.

London Anti-slavery Speech of September 1849

Sir, I wish to make a remark or two in seconding the resolution which is now before the meeting. I am really glad that this meeting has produced this discussion, for I think it will all do good; in fact, I know it will, for the cause of truth. Reference has been made to slavery having been carried to America by the sanction of this country.[57] Now, that is an argument generally used in America by slaveholders themselves. (Hear, hear.)[58] Go to the United States; talk to slaveholders about the disgrace of slavery being found in a professedly Christian republic, and they will immediately reply, 'England imposed it upon us; Great Britain was the cause of it, for she established slavery in America, and we are only reaping the fruits of her act.' Now, gentlemen, I would reply to our friend here, as I have replied to Americans again and again – If you have followed England in the bad example of the institution of slavery, now follow her in the good example of the abolition of slavery. (Cheers.) Some remarks were also made by that gentleman respecting the Americans having abolished the slave trade. It is true that they did pass a law, but not in 1808, that the slave trade should be abolished: they passed a law in 1788 that they would only continue the slave trade for twenty years longer, and at the end of that period there should not be any more slaves imported into the United States. They said, 'We will rob Africa of her sons and daughters for twenty years longer, and then stop.' (Hear and laughter.) But why did they determine that the slave trade should be put an end to? The honorable gentleman has not told you that. Why, it was to give to Virginia,

---

57 Brown here references a previous address by another American, Mr. Jones, who self-identified as having 'held property in Virginia' but 'refus[ing] to hold a slave'. Jones claimed, 'I abhor, from my very soul, every form of slavery'. Yet, he excused its continuation in the US by blaming 'Englishmen, Anglo-Saxons' for its introduction into North America and praising 1808 American legislation setting a date after which no more captured Africans could be brought into the United States (i.e. in Jones's terms, 'making the slave trade piracy'), thereby limiting enslavement afterwards to being 'a domestic institution' ('Public Reception', 1).

58 Here and in other places in its presentation of the address, *The Liberator* used a then-familiar strategy of inserting markers of audience response (such as 'Cheers' or 'Laughter') to alert readers to the speech's original oratorical impact.

Kentucky and Maryland a monopoly in the trade of raising slaves to supply the Southern market. (Cheers.) That was the reason, and the only reason, why they abolished the foreign slave trade in America. They allowed the foreign slave trade to be carried on for twenty years from that time, and during the whole of that period made those who were engaged in the internal slave traffic pay a duty of ten dollars for every slave brought into the country, the whole of the money going into the exchequer of the United States. The Government said, 'We will have a tariff of so much per head upon God's children that are stolen from Africa, and the revenue derived therefrom shall be the support of the republican institutions of the United States.' (Hear, hear.) Do the Americans claim credit for an act like that? Claim credit for abolishing the foreign slave trade, in order that they might make a lucrative domestic slave trade! (Cheers.) Why, ladies and gentlemen, only a few years since, 40,000 slaves were carried out of the single State of Virginia, in one year, and driven off to the far South, to supply the market there. Claim credit for abolishing the slave trade! Claim credit for husbands torn from their wives, and children from their parents! Claim credit for herds of human beings carried off in coffle gangs, and to be worked to death in the rice and cotton fields! That is the character of the domestic slave trade now carried on, even in the capital of America. No, no; the people of the United States can claim no credit on that score. They can find no apology in the fact of slavery being a domestic institution. A pretty 'domestic institution,' truly! (Hear, hear.) Why, in 1847, only two years since, a woman and her daughter were sold in the very capital of America, in the very city of Washington, by the U.S. marshal, on the 3d day of July, the day before the national anniversary of the glorious Declaration of Independence, by which all men were declared free and equal, and the product of the sale of these immortal beings was put into the treasury of the United States. That is one specimen among many of the working of the 'domestic institution' of America. (Cheers.) It dooms me, for example, to be a slave as soon as I shall touch any part of the United States. (Hear, hear.) Yes, Sir, it is indeed domestic enough; it is domesticated all over the country; it extends from one end of America to the other, and is as domesticated as is the Constitution of the United States itself; it is just as domesticated as is the territory over which the United States Government have jurisdiction. Wherever the Constitution proclaims a bit of soil to belong to the United States, there it dooms me to be a slave the moment I set my foot upon it; and all the 20,000 or 30,000 of my brethren who have made their escape from the Southern States, and taken refuge in Canada or the Northern States, are in the same condition. And yet this American slavery is apologized for as a 'domestic institution'! I am glad that our eloquent friend, Mr. Thompson, has impressed the fact upon your minds, that slavery is a *national institution*, and that the guilt of maintaining it is *national guilt*. I am anxious that that circumstance should be understood, and that Englishmen should know, that the slave is just as much a slave in the city of Boston; of which this gentleman is just as much a citizen as he is in Charleston, South Carolina: he is just as much a slave in any of the Eastern States as he is in the Southern States. If I am protected in my person in the city of Boston, and if I have been protected there for the last two or three years, and the slaveholder has not been able to catch me and carry me back again into slavery, I am not at all indebted for that privilege to the Constitution of the United States, but I owe it entirely to that public sentiment which my friend Mr. Thompson, at the peril of his life, so nobly helped to create in America. (Loud cheers.) I am indebted to the anti-slavery sentiment, and that alone, when I am in Boston itself, for the personal protection I enjoy. I cannot look at the Constitution or laws of

America as a protection to me; in fact, I have no Constitution, and no country. I cannot, like the eloquent gentleman who last addressed you, say—'I am bound to stand up in favor of America.' (Hear.) I would to God that I could; but how can I! America has disfranchised me, driven me off, and declared that I am not a citizen, and never shall be, upon the soil of the United States. Can I, then, gentlemen, stand up for such a country as that? Can I have any thing to say in favor of a country that makes me a chattel, that renders me a saleable commodity, that converts me into a piece of property? Can I say any thing in favor of a country, or its institutions, that will give me up to the slaveholder, if he can only find out where I am, in any part of America? Why I am more free here tonight, in monarchical England, than I should be in my own republican country! Whatever our friend from Boston may do, I would that I could say with him, 'I must, in honor, stand up in favor of America.' And yet I love America as much as he does. I admire her enterprising and industrious people quite as ardently as he can; but I hate her hideous institution, which has robbed me of a dear mother, which has plundered me of a beloved sister and three dear brothers, and which institution has doomed them to suffer, as they are now suffering, in chains and slavery. Whatever else there may be to admire in the condition of America, at all events, I hate that portion of her Constitution. I hate, I fervently hate, those laws and institutions of America, which consign three millions of my brethren and sisters to chains for life. Talk about going to the slaveholders with money! Talk about recognizing their right to property in human beings! What! property in man! property in God's children! I will not acknowledge that any man has a right to hold me as property, till he can show his right to supersede the prerogative of that Creator whose alone I am. [Cheers.] Just read the letter which you will find in the preface to my narrative, where my own master has very kindly offered to sell me to myself for half price. [Laughter.] He imagines that the anti-slavery movement has depreciated his property in me, and therefore he offers to take half price for his runaway property. [Renewed laughter.] My answer to him was, that he should never receive a single dollar from me, or any one else in my behalf, with my consent. [Cheers.] I said so, because I am not willing to acknowledge the right of property in man under any circumstances. I believe that the same God who made the slaveholder made the slave—[hear, hear]—and that the one is just as free as the other.

Before resuming my seat, I would say to our friend from Boston, as I said to another gentleman a short time before I left America, who talked in a similar manner about the slave States, and the good treatment the slaves received, and so forth. At the close of a meeting, that gentleman rose, and requested permission to ask me some simple questions, which were as follows: Had I not enough to eat when I was in slavery? Was I not well clothed while in the Southern States? Was I ever whipped? and so forth. I saw that he only wanted a peg on which to hang a pro-slavery speech, but I answered his questions in the affirmative. He immediately rose and made a speech, in which he endeavored to make his audience believe that I had run away from a very good place indeed. [Laughter.] He asked them if they did not know hundreds and thousands of poor people in America and England, who would be willing to go into the State of Missouri and there fill the situation I had run away from. [Cries of Oh, Oh!] A portion of the assembly for a moment really thought his plea for slavery was a good one. I saw that the meeting was anxious to break up, in consequence of the lateness of the hour, and therefore that it would not do for me to reply at any length, and I accordingly rose and made a single remark in answer to this pro-slavery speech. I said, the gentleman has praised up the situation I left, and made it appear quite another thing to what it ever appeared to me when

I was there; but however that may be, I have to inform him that that situation is still vacant, and as far as I[59] have any thing voluntary to do with it, it shall remain so; but, nevertheless, if that gentleman likes to go into Missouri and fill it, I will give him a recommendation to my old master, and I doubt not that he would receive him with open arms, and give him enough to eat, enough to wear, and flog him when ever he thought he required it. (Loud cheers and laughter.) So I say to our friend from Boston, tonight, if he is so charmed with slavery, he shall have the same recommendation to my old master. [Loud cheers.]

Source text

Wells Brown, William, 'Public Reception of Wm. W. Brown in the Metropolis of England', *The Liberator* 9.44 (2 November 1849), 1.

References

Brown, William Wells, *Narrative of William W. Brown, a Fugitive Slave Written by Himself* (Boston: The Anti-slavery office, 1847).

Brown, William Wells, *Three Years in Europe: or, Places I Have Seen and People I Have Met with A Memoir of the Author by William Farmer, Esq.* (London: Charles Gilpin, 1852).

Ruff, Loren K., 'William Wells Brown: Dramatic Apostle for Abolition', *New England Theatre Journal* 2.1 (1991), 73–83.

Salenius, Sirpa, 'Troubling the White Supremacy-Black Inferiority Paradigm: Frederick Douglass and William Wells Brown in Europe', *Journal of Transatlantic Studies* 14.2 (April 2016), 152–63.

Transatlantic Exchanges on Slavery (1853–63)

In the upcoming cluster of entries, we feature an instigating text – an anti-slavery epistle addressed to US women – and a series of responses. After first presenting 'The Affectionate and Christian Address of Many Thousands of Women of Great Britain', we then summarise a widely read response from American magazine editor Sarah Hale. We next spotlight another pro-slavery reaction text, by American First Lady Julia Tyler. Another entry presents in full a letter by Harriet Jacobs, later author of *Incidents in the Life of a Slave Girl*. (Her text replied not to the original British text but to Tyler, whose claims about enslavement Jacobs refutes.) The concluding entry briefly summarises yet another publication related to the original 'Address' – a pamphlet from Harriet Beecher Stowe, which did not appear until after the US Civil War had begun. Source texts and references for all appear at the end of this omnibus selection.

---

59 'I' does not appear in *The Liberator* text but is inserted here for clarity.

Harriet Sutherland-Leveson-Gower, Duchess of Sutherland (1806–68) and Anthony Ashley-Cooper, 7th Earl of Shaftesbury (1801–85) with signatures by thousands of British women

'The Affectionate and Christian Address of Many Thousands of Women of Great Britain and Ireland to Their Sisters the Women of the United States of America' (1853)

After the 1833 abolition of slavery throughout the British Empire, British anti-slavery advocates turned their attention to the United States. Especially after the 1852 publication of *Uncle Tom's Cabin*, British women's groups circulated petitions to bring political pressure to bear on the Southern United States. A particularly ambitious effort, composed by the influential social reform leader the 7th Earl of Shaftesbury, passed hand to hand and door to door for more than a year. The final product contained some 562,848 signatures filling twenty-six leather-bound volumes, all expressing support for the abolitionist cause. Harriet Beecher Stowe (1811–96) was presented with a copy during her first British tour and the text below was widely disseminated through the press on both sides of the Atlantic. Printings in the US and England sometimes also included accounts of how the Duchess of Sutherland, herself an avid abolitionist, helped catalyse this epistolary project by assembling women at Stafford House, London, in November 1852 and reading them a draft of the letter.

Born into a prominent Whig family (the Howards, Earls of Carlisle), Harriet Elizabeth Georgiana Leveson-Gower enhanced her social position and wealth by marrying George Granville Leveson-Gower, who became Duke of Sutherland. Friend to Queen Victoria (and serving several times as mistress of the robes), she became a political ally of W. E. Gladstone. Linking her social role to political causes, including anti-slavery, she famously hosted such events as Harriet Beecher Stowe's visit to Stafford House and a performance by Mary Webb of a one-woman reading based on *Uncle Tom's Cabin*.

Evangelical leader Lord Shaftesbury, who may well have been the primary author of the 'Affectionate and Christian Address', also helped host Stowe during her first British visit. Accompanying the US anti-slavery star on visits to schools for poor children and Model Lodging Houses for London's destitute, for instance, he garnered high praise from her for his activism (Stowe, *Sunny Memories*, vol. II, 'Letter XXVIII', 'Letter XXIX'). Lord Shaftesbury also campaigned to protect women and young children from dangerous coal-mine labour and to re-envision approaches to treating mental illness.

Via commentary in the 'Introductory' chapter for *Sunny Memories*, Stowe would enthusiastically support the 'Affectionate and Christian

Address'. Ever the self-promoter, she framed her own presentation of the letter by printing Lord Shaftesbury's remarks made at the Stafford House reception for her. There he described the letter as aiming 'to cultivate the most friendly and affectionate relations between the two countries', a goal he said was affirmed by the event's welcome to Stowe as 'an American lady' devoting her genius 'to the glory of God and the temporal and eternal interests of the human race' (I, xli). In the US, the letter and its petitioners garnered a wide range of responses, as the entries below demonstrate.

'Affectionate and Christian Address of Many Thousands of Women of Great Britain'

"A common origin, a common faith, and, we sincerely believe, a common cause, urge us, at the present moment, to address you on the subject of that system of negro slavery which still prevails so extensively, and, even under kindly disposed masters, with such frightful results, in many of the vast regions of the western world.

"We will not dwell on the ordinary topics — on the progress of civilization; on the advance of freedom every where, on the rights and requirements of the nineteenth century; but we appeal to you very seriously to reflect, and to ask counsel of God, how far such a state of things is in accordance with his holy word, the inalienable rights of immortal souls, and the pure and merciful spirit of the Christian religion.

"We do not shut our eyes to the difficulties, nay, the dangers, that might beset the immediate abolition of that long-established system; we see and admit the necessity of preparation for so great an event; but in speaking of indispensable preliminaries, we cannot be silent on those laws of your country which, in direct contravention of God's own law, instituted in the time of man's innocency, deny, in effect, to the slave the sanctity of marriage, with all its joys, rights, and obligations; which separate, at the will of the master, the wife from the husband, and the children from the parents. Nor can we be silent on that awful system which, either by statute or by custom, interdicts to any race of man or any portion of the human family education in the truths of the gospel and the ordinances of Christianity.

"A remedy applied to these two evils alone would commence the amelioration of their sad condition. We appeal to you, then, as sisters, as wives, and as mothers, to raise your voices to your fellow-citizens, and your prayers to God, for the removal of this affliction and disgrace from the Christian world. We do not say these things in a spirit of self-complacency, as though our nation were free from the guilt it perceives in others. We acknowledge with grief and shame our heavy share in this great sin. We acknowledge that our forefathers introduced, nay, compelled the adoption of slavery in those mighty colonies. We humbly confess it before Almighty God; and it is because we so deeply feel, and so unfeignedly avow, our own complicity that we now venture to implore your aid to wipe away our common crime and our common dishonor."

Responses to the 'Affectionate Letter'
Sarah Josepha Hale (1788–1879)

Summary and Commentary: 'Editors' Table' (1853)

To some extent American reception of 'The Affectionate and Christian Address' split along the Mason-Dixon Line. While abolitionist groups praised and reprinted the petition, pro-slavery authors countered with parodies, ridicule and direct criticism. Among their targets were the British economic system (for sponsoring wage slavery), the Duchess of Sutherland herself (for the treatment of her tenants) and British women in general (for their meddlesomeness).

Not all of the negative responses to the 'Affectionate and Christian Address' emerged from the US South, however. Sarah Josepha Hale, who served for decades as editor of the popular Boston-based *Godey's Lady's Book*, may be best known today for her promotion of Thanksgiving as a national holiday, her 'Mary Had a Little Lamb' children's poem and her fund-raising for a Bunker Hill Monument. But Hale, like numerous American women writers of her day, also wrote her way into the transnational debate over slavery. First came an 1852 reissuing of her novel (*Northwood*, 1827) with new chapters added to promote the 'repatriation' movement of sending Blacks 'back' to Africa. Also in 1852, she published *Liberia*, an extended pro-'return' narrative from the Southern perspective. And in 1853, invoking her editorial position at *Godey's*, she presented a stinging reply to her British 'Sisters'.

Dubbing her text 'Candid' in its title, Hale penned a rebuke, despite an opening paragraph complimenting the 'kind manner' of the 'Affectionate Letter', acknowledging a shared religious faith and commending the sincere zeal of the British missive. Most of Hale's essay addressed such faults as 'the original sin of . . . this evil system' of slavery having been 'the work of the British government, which upheld the slave trade till our country achieved her independence'. She excoriated the transatlantic letter-writers for hypocrisy, given the suffering of their own underclass: 'Pardon us when we say you seem little aware, Christian Women of England, while shedding tender tears over the fictitious woes of imaginary negroes in America, of the real condition of the poor white people in your own country', particularly 'the London poor' trapped in 'such pestilential dens [as] could not be found or made on the plantations where our colored people are employed'. And she called on her transatlantic women counterparts to redirect their energies toward support for the Liberian colony and 'the negroes under British care at Sierra Leone', as well as for 'the free colored subjects of Britain in the West Indies' (274). Closing with a reminder that 'Charity, to be Christian, must begin at home', Hale sarcastically promised: 'We assure you of our fervent prayers for your success' (275).

Julia Gardiner Tyler (1820–59)

Summary and Commentary: 'To the Duchess of Sutherland and Ladies of England' (1853)

Tyler, the eleventh First Lady of the United States, was born and raised in New York but became a Southerner through her 1844 marriage to President John Tyler. She served as his political helpmate until their retirement to his Virginia plantation. A staunch defender of slavery, Tyler composed her 'To the Duchess of Sutherland and Ladies of England' as a rebuttal. Her letter first appeared on 28 January 1853 in both the *Richmond Enquirer* and *New York Herald*, and later in the February issue of the *Southern Literary Messenger*, where it found much support among proslavery sympathisers. That periodical's editor opined:

> The moral weight of Mrs. Tyler's communication is greatly enhanced by the fact that she is herself a Northern lady, who came to the Southern home which she adorns, as the bride of an eminent Southern Statesman, an ex-president of the United States. Her view of the institution of slavery is not therefore effected by early prejudices, while her social position, it must be admitted, is as high as that of the proud mistress of Stafford House or any other titled lady of Great Britain.

Tyler warned that 'the women of the South, especially, have not received your address in the kindest spirit', accusing English women of unduly meddling in others' affairs. She then invoked a standard litany of Southern defences of the 'peculiar institution', including the charge of English hypocrisy: 'England not only permitted but encouraged the slave trade, for a period of a century and a half, as a means of swelling her coffers' (122). Comparing the plight of working-class wage-slaves in England and Irish peasants to America's slaves, she envisioned: 'There, on the roadside, sinks an attenuated and exhausted mother, still straining her perishing child to her breast, while the unhappy husband and father, himself foodless and raimentless, sheds drops of agony over the heartrending scene' (125). In contrast, she described the comfort and happiness of America's enslaved people: 'The negro of the South lives sumptuously in comparison with the 100,000 of the white population of London. He is clothed warmly in winter, and has his meat twice daily, without stint of bread' (124). She advised: 'We are content to leave England in the enjoyment of her peculiar institutions; and we insist upon the right to regulate ours without her aid' (125–6).

Harriet Ann Jacobs (1813–97)

'Letter from a Fugitive Slave' (1853)

Harriet Ann Jacobs was born enslaved in Edenton, North Carolina, fled her abusive enslaver in 1835 and spent seven years hiding in her grandmother's attic before escaping to the North in 1842. In June of 1853, Jacobs, then a fugitive living in New York, came across Julia Tyler's 'To the Duchess of Sutherland' in an old copy of *The New York Tribune*. Outraged at the former First Lady's defence of slavery, she immediately penned a response of her own and sent it off to the *Tribune*, signing it as 'A Fugitive Slave'. The letter appeared in print only a few days later and was soon reprinted in other periodicals. Encouraged by the audience her text found, Jacobs began writing additional letters and eventually published her full-length memoir, *Incidents in the Life of a Slave Girl*, under the pseudonym 'Linda Brent', in 1861. Much of Jacobs's argument in that volume is forecast in the 1853 *Tribune* letter, which actually offers a more explicit critique of white enslavers' abuse of young enslaved women than Jacobs would feel she could address as directly in portraying her own personal experiences in her longer narrative.

'Letter from a Fugitive Slave'

Slaves Sold Under Peculiar Circumstances

> We publish the subjoined communication exactly as written by the author with the exception of corrections in punctuation and spelling and the omission of one or two passages. –Ed.

> *To the Editor*[60] *of the N. Y. Tribune.*
> Sir: Having carefully read your paper for some months I became very much interested in some of the articles and comments written on Mrs. Tyler's Reply to the Ladies of England. Being a slave myself, I could not have felt otherwise. Would that I could write an article worthy of notice in your columns. As I never enjoyed the advantages of an education, therefore I could not study the arts of reading and writing, yet, poor as it may be, I had rather give it from my own hand, than have it said that I employed others to do it for me.[61] The truth can never be told so well through the second and third person as from yourself. But I am straying from the question. In that Reply to the Ladies of England, Mrs. Tyler said that slaves were never sold only

---

60 Horace Greely (1811–72), editor and founder of the newspaper, was an abolitionist and former Whig Congressman; he transformed *The New York Tribune* into the highest-circulating newspaper in the country.
61 Jacobs's comment here is important in light of later speculation about her *Incidents* text having been written not by her but by her white editor, Lydia Maria Child.

under very peculiar circumstances. As Mrs. Tyler and her friend Bhains[62] were so far used up, that he could not explain what those peculiar circumstances were, let one whose peculiar sufferings justifies her in explaining it for Mrs. Tyler.[63]

I was born a slave, reared in the Southern hot-bed until I was the mother of two children, sold at the early age of two and four years old. I have been hunted through all of the Northern States, but no, I will not tell you of my own suffering—no, it would harrow up my soul, and defeat the object that I wish to pursue. Enough—the dregs of that bitter cup have been my bounty for many years.

And, as this is the first time that I ever took my pen in my hand to make such an attempt, you will not say that it is fiction, for had I the inclination I have neither the brain or talent to write it. But to this very peculiar circumstance under which slaves are sold.

My mother was held as property by a maiden lady; when she married, my younger sister was in her fourteenth year, whom they took into the family. She was as gentle as she was beautiful. Innocent and guileless child, the light of our desolate hearth! But oh, my heart bleeds to tell you of the misery and degradation she was forced to suffer in slavery. The monster[64] who owned her had no humanity in his soul. The most sincere affection that his heart was capable of, could not make him faithful to his beautiful and wealthy bride the short time of three months, but every stratagem was used to seduce my sister. Mortified and tormented beyond endurance, this child came and threw herself on my mother's bosom, the only place where she could seek refuge from her persecutor; and yet she could not protect the child that she bore into the world. On that bosom, with *bitter tears*, she told her troubles, and entreated her mother to save her. And oh, Christian mothers! You that have daughters of your own, can you think of your sable sisters without offering a prayer to that God who created all in their behalf! My poor mother, naturally high-spirited, smarting under what she considered as the wrongs and outrages which her child had to bear, sought her master, entreating him to spare her child. Nothing could exceed his rage at this what he called impertinence. My mother was dragged to jail, there remained twenty-five days, with negro traders to come in as they liked to examine her, as she was offered for sale. My sister was told she must yield, or never expect to see her mother again. There were three younger children; on no other condition could she be restored to them, without the sacrifice of one. That child gave herself up to her master's bidding, to save one that was dearer to her than life itself. And can you, Christian, find it in your heart to despise her? Ah, no! not even Mrs. Tyler; for though we believe that the vanity of a name would lead her to bestow her hand where her heart could never go with it, yet, with all her faults and follies, she is nothing more than a *woman*. For if her domestic hearth is surrounded with slaves, ere long before this she has opened her eyes to the evils of slavery, and that the mistress as well as the slave must submit to the indignities and vices imposed on them by their lords of body and soul. But to one of those peculiar circumstances.

At fifteen, my sister held to her bosom an innocent offspring of her guilt and misery. In this way she dragged a miserable existence of two years, between the

---

62 Bhains remains unidentified in Jacobs's letter.
63 Belying her claim to be limited in her writing abilities, Jacobs repeatedly riffs on the word 'peculiar', a term often used in the nineteenth century to refer to slavery.
64 Dr James Norcom, a physician in Edenton, North Carolina

fires of her mistress's jealousy and her master's brutal passion. At seventeen, she gave birth to another helpless infant, heir to all the evils of slavery. Thus life and its sufferings was meted out to her until her twenty-first year. Sorrow and suffering had made its ravages upon her—she was less the object to be desired by the fiend who had crushed her to the earth; and as her children grew, they bore too strong a resemblance to him who desired to give them no other inheritance save Chains and Handcuffs, and in the dead hour of the night, when this young, deserted mother lay with her little ones clinging around her, little dreaming of the dark and inhuman plot that would be carried into execution before another dawn, and when the sun rose on God's beautiful earth, that broken-hearted mother was far on her way to the capital of Virginia.[65] That day should have refused her light to so disgraceful and inhuman an act in your boasted country of Liberty. Yet, reader, it is true, those two helpless children were the *sons* of one of your sainted Members in Congress;[66] that agonized mother, his victim and slave. And where she now is God only knows, who has kept a record on high of all that she has suffered on earth.

And, you would exclaim, Could not the master have been more merciful to his children? God is merciful to all of his children, but it is seldom that a slaveholder has any mercy for his slave child. And you will believe it when I tell you that mother and her children were sold to make room for another sister, who was now the age of that mother when she entered the family. And this selling appeased the mistress's wrath, and satisfied her desire for *revenge*, and made the path more smooth for her young rival at first. For there is a strong rivalry between a handsome mulatto girl and a jealous and *faded* mistress, and her liege lord sadly neglects those little attentions for a while that once made her happy. For the master will either neglect his wife or double his attentions, to save him from being suspected by his wife. Would you not think that Southern Women had cause to despise that Slavery which forces them to bear so much deception practiced by their *husbands*? Yet all this is true, for a slaveholder seldom takes a white mistress, for she is an expensive commodity, not submissive as he would like to have her but more apt to be tyrannical; and when his passion seeks another object, he must leave her in quiet possession of all the gewgaws that she has sold herself for. But not so with his poor *slave victim*, that he has robbed of everything that makes life desirable; she must be torn from the little that is left to bind her to life, and sold by her *seducer* and *master*, caring not where, so that it puts him in possession of enough to purchase another victim. And such are the peculiar circumstances of American Slavery—of all the evils in God's sight the most to be abhorred.

Perhaps while I am writing this you too, dear Emily,[67] may be on your way to the Mississippi River, for those peculiar circumstances occur every day in the midst of my poor oppressed fellow-creatures in bondage. And oh, ye Christians, while your arms are extended to receive the oppressed of all nations, while you exert every power of your soul to assist them to raise funds, put weapons in their hands, tell them to return to their own country to slay every foe until they break the accursed yoke from off their necks, not buying and selling; this they never do under any circumstances. But while Americans do all this, they forget the millions of slaves they have at home, bought and sold under very peculiar circumstances.

---

65 Richmond, Virginia, some 130 miles from Edenton
66 Samuel Tredwell Sawyer, later elected as North Carolina Representative (1837–9)
67 'Emily' is likely the 'handsome mulatto girl' referenced above.

And because one friend of the slave[68] has dared to tell of their wrongs you would annihilate her. But in Uncle Tom's Cabin she has not told the half. Would that I had one spark from her store house of genius and talent I would tell you of my own sufferings[69]—I would tell you of wrongs that Hungary has never inflicted, nor England ever dreamed of in this free country where all nations fly for liberty, equal rights, and protection under your stripes and stars. It should be stripes and scars, for they go along with Mrs. Tyler's peculiar circumstances, of which I have told you only one.

A Fugitive Slave

Harriet Beecher Stowe (1811–96)

Summary and Commentary: A Reply to 'The Affectionate and Christian Address of Many Thousands of Women of Great Britain and Ireland, to Their Sisters, the Women of the United States of America' (1863)

In early 1863, Harriet Beecher Stowe, who had received bound copies of the original 'Affectionate' text during her first trip to Britain, published a belated reply 'in behalf of many thousands of American women'. (She released this text both in *The Atlantic*, in January, and as a sixty-three-page pamphlet published in London). She begged forgiveness for being slow to respond in print. She justified the delay by referencing the conflict leading up to the Civil War and its ensuing, still-ongoing trauma as having required focused energy from America's anti-slavery women. After recounting several of the War's major events, Stowe proffered observations from 'an eye-witness' Union military leader who described having 'liberated two thousand slaves' (29), turning many of the men into soldiers and establishing the women and children in temporary quarters in South Carolina's Sea Islands. Discussing Lincoln's Emancipation Proclamation, she opined that it had 'been much misunderstood and misrepresented in England' and extolled its call for 'Slaveholding States' to 'emancipate peaceably with compensation' or suffer consequences (45–6).

Purposefully echoing the earlier 'Affectionate' letter, Stowe then begged her 'Sisters' in Britain to support the Northern (i.e. Union) cause in the War. She reproached them for various signs of Britain's hypocritical affiliation with the Confederacy. She bitterly cited the example of 'a war-steamer, built for a man-stealing Confederacy with English gold in an English dockyard,

---

68 Harriet Beecher Stowe
69 Sadly, though Jacobs praises Stowe here, the famous author rebuffed later requests from Lydia Maria Child and Jacobs for assistance toward publication of the autobiography of this 'fugitive slave'. Instead, Stowe sought to appropriate Jacobs's narrative for inclusion in her own *Key to Uncle Tom's Cabin*; fortunately, Jacobs persisted and published her own account.

going out of an English harbor, manned by English sailors, with the full knowledge of English Government-officers, in defiance of the Queen's proc-lamation of neutrality' (53). Urging her Sisters to reject rhetoric presenting the South as 'fighting for *independence*', Stowe insisted they were instead fighting to 'establish the doctrine that the white may enslave the negro' (49). Recycling words and sentiments from the original 'Address' to American women, Stowe called on her anticipated British readers 'as sisters, as wives, and as mothers, to raise [their] voices' (62) against 'the decline of the noble anti-slavery fire in England' (63).

Source texts

[Hale, Sara Josepha], 'Editor's Table: The Candid and Christian Reply of the Women of America to "The Affectionate and Christian Address of Many Thousands of the Women of England"', *Godey's Lady's Book* 8.3 (March 1853), 274–5.

[Jacobs, Harriet A.], 'Letter from a Fugitive Slave', *New York Daily Tribune* (21 June 1853), 6.

Stowe, Harriet Beecher, *A Reply to "The Affectionate and Christian Address of Many Thousands of Women of Great Britain and Ireland, to Their Sisters, the Women of the United States of America"* (London: Sampson Low, Son, and Co., 1863).

Stowe, Mrs. Harriet Beecher, *Sunny Memories of Foreign Lands*, Vols I and II (Boston: Phillips, Sampson, 1854), I, xli–xlii (for the 'Affectionate and Christian Address') and II, *passim*.

Tyler, Julia Gardiner, 'To the Duchess of Sutherland and Ladies of England', *Southern Literary Messenger* 19 (February 1853), 120–6.

References

Foreman, P. Gabrielle, *Activist Sentiments: Reading Black Women in the Nineteenth Century* (Urbana, IL: University of Illinois Press, 2009).

Jacobs, Harriet A., *Incidents in the Life of a Slave Girl*, ed. Lydia Maria Child (Boston: Thayer & Eldridge, 1861).

Taketani, Etsuko, 'Postcolonial Liberia: Sarah Josepha Hale's Africa', *American Literary History* 14.3 (2002), 479–504.

'Dramatic Readings by a Coloured Native of Philadelphia' (1856)

Harriet Beecher Stowe's *Uncle Tom's Cabin* (1852) generated an unprec-edented level of transatlantic reader response dubbed a 'mania' by the British press and embodied in cultural products ranging from pirated edi-tions to 'Uncle Tomitudes' such as decorative plates, dolls and toys. Fur-ther, in this era before copyright restrictions, playwrights quickly adapted the narrative, with elaborately staged scenes like Eliza Harris's crossing of the Ohio River to freedom and the death of little Eva becoming audience favourites. These plays also tapped into minstrelsy traditions depicting negative stereotypes of Black characters, thereby reinforcing racist attitudes.

Stowe herself penned only one dramatic adaptation of her novel, *The Christian Slave*, written for African American Mary Webb to perform. After touring in the northern US, Webb took letters of introduction from Stowe to smooth the way for formal readings in Britain, the most famous of which was held at the Duchess of Sutherland's Stafford House.

Such a one-woman staging eschewed the 'special effects' becoming staples in the elaborate *Uncle-Tom*-based melodramas but gave more attention to Stowe's message and treatment of enslaved women characters than other dramatic adaptations (Clark, 339–40). Additionally, as Eric Gardner suggests, Webb's performance enabled audiences to engage 'the novel voiced through a black body', one seen as both refined and exotic (105). Periodical reviews of Webb's British performances – including the unsigned one from the widely read *Illustrated London News* featured here – can thus illuminate the transatlantic anti-slavery movement's complex responses to Black identities.

MRS. MARY E. WEBB (A COLOURED NATIVE OF PHILADELPHIA) READING " UNCLE TOM'S CABIN," IN THE HALL OF STAFFORD-HOUSE.

Figure 1.4 'Mrs. Mary Webb (A Coloured Native of Philadelphia) Reading "Uncle Tom's Cabin," in the Hall of Strafford House', *Illustrated London News* 29 (2 August 1856), 122. Courtesy Division of Rare and Manuscript Collections, Cornell University Library.

'Dramatic Readings by a Coloured Native of Philadelphia'

The great hall of Stafford House[70] was on Monday last the scene of an event which would have caused considerable astonishment to any gentleman of the Southern States of America who might have happened to be present. A large audience was gathered together in that hall—one of the most magnificent in London—to listen to a lady of colour giving dramatic readings. The Duchess of Sutherland had devoted her mansion, for the time, to the service of a Mrs. F. Webb, and our Southerner would have been confounded and disgusted at the sight of what he would call a "tarnation nigger"[71] being listened to with the most respectful attention by no inconsiderable number of the aristocracy of England.

However, Mrs. Webb is not a "nigger." She is the daughter indeed of a woman of full African blood; but her father was a European. Her colour is a rich olive, and her features are remarkably delicate and expressive. Her mother, after three efforts, succeeded in making her escape from Virginia to Massachusetts, just three weeks before the daughter's birth. The daughter was brought up for some time in luxury, but hard times succeeded, and the indomitable negro-mother had to work incessantly that her daughter might complete the education begun under happier circumstances. After-events showed the wisdom of her determination. Her daughter married Mr. Webb, a tradesman of Philadelphia, in good circumstances. On his failure Mrs. Webb resolved to devote her talents to practical account; and, after taking lessons in elocution, delivered dramatic readings with great success before American audiences. She is accredited to the Duchess of Sutherland by Mrs. Stowe, who has dramatised her own novel of "Uncle Tom's Cabin" for Mrs. Webb's especial benefit.

During the first portion of the readings on Monday there was not much to strike the observer. All that could be said was that Mrs. Webb had a remarkably sweet and flexible voice, apparently without much power; that she displayed considerable feeling in the rendering of particular passages; and that she was careful on the side of restraint rather than exuberance. There was nothing to excite the sympathies of the hearer very violently; and, had the readings terminated here, the reader would have made a pleasant impression and no more. In the second part, however, Mrs. Webb showed that she possessed considerable and rather peculiar dramatic power. With very little gesticulation, and simply by judicious modulations of the voice, combined with earnest and effective delivery, she gave great effect to the last dark, powerful scenes of the drama. The manner in which Cassy's story was told was especially pathetic; and although, from its length, it threatened to be tedious, the attention of the audience seldom flagged. But Mrs. Webb was most successful in the character of Tom himself. The hoarse negro voice, the solemn tones—those of a man living in a world which seems to be a perpetual contradiction to the laws of that God in whom he firmly believes—were very striking. The piety, the resignation, the humility, and, at the same time, the confidence of Tom's character were brought out fully. The singing of the hymns was remarkably effective. The peculiar negro intonation, the struggle after correctness of melody, the solemn meaning which the

---

70 Stafford House was famous during this era as a glittering site of aristocratic liberal politics with distinguished guests drawn to causes the Duchess supported, including anti-slavery.

71 The anonymous reviewer's use of the racist term 'nigger' seems designed to critique an imagined attendee from the US South, not to demean Webb – yet nonetheless enshrines racist sentiment within the text.

singer threw into the words, gave great prominence to this portion of the readings. It was a mixture of solemnity and pathos quite indescribable; and it was evident that Mrs. Webb had, in the latter part of the entertainment, regained a portion of that confidence which she had lost at the commencement. She was heartily applauded. We understand that she has produced a great sensation in America by reading portions of "Hiawatha,"[72] dressed in Indian costume. We can easily imagine that the peculiarity of her delivery would be well adapted to that curious poem. It is unlucky for Mrs. Webb that she has visited London just as "all the world," that is to say, the small fraction of London which is the peculiar patron of entertainments of this kind, is absent, or going to be absent. Nevertheless, we trust that there will be enough friends of the dark races left in London to carry out to a successful termination the attempt which the Duchess of Sutherland has so kindly and powerfully assisted.

Source text

'Dramatic Readings by a Coloured Native of Philadelphia', *Illustrated London News* (2 August 1856), 121–2.

References

Clark, Susan F., 'Solo Black Performance before the Civil War: Mrs. Stowe, Mrs. Webb, and "The Christian Slave"', *New Theatre Quarterly* 13.52 (November 1997), 339–48.

Gardner, Eric, '"A Nobler End": Mary Webb and the Victorian Platform', *Nineteenth-Century Prose* 29.1 (Spring 2002), 103–16.

Meer, Sarah, *Uncle Tom Mania: Slavery, Minstrelsy, and Transatlantic Culture in the 1850s* (Athens, GA: University of Georgia Press, 2005).

Stowe, Harriet Beecher, *The Christian Slave: A Drama Founded on a Portion of Uncle Tom's Cabin. Dramatized by Harriet Beecher Stowe, Expressly for the Readings of Mrs. Mary E. Webb* (Boston: Phillips, Sampson & Co., 1855).

From 'British Abolitionist Movements: Slavery and the American Churches' (1856)

After their abolition of slavery in the West Indies, British anti-slavery leaders made America's continued acceptance of 'the peculiar institution' a focus of their energies. One target for critique was the role of US Christian religious leaders in sustaining the system. For example, the *Anti-Slavery Reporter* printed numerous articles excoriating the American Board of Commissioners of Foreign Missions (ABCFM) for helping enable slavery, including among Native Americans.

This campaign drew from and contributed to British leaders' print-supported networking with US-based abolitionists, as illustrated by the excerpt below from an unsigned *Anti-Slavery Reporter* article and

---

72 *The Song of Hiawatha* (1855) by US poet Henry Wadsworth Longfellow (1807–82)

similar 1850s reports in that publication ('Illustrations' and 'Mrs. H. B. Stowe'). In addressing elite Native Americans' enslavement practices, the piece deflects blame away from those slaveholders themselves, following a strategy sometimes employed by Cherokee author-activists, who understood that enslaving people undermined their efforts to garner white abolitionists' support against the Removal and post-Removal abuses. The article also challenges whites on both sides of the Atlantic to recognise their own complicity in the ongoing enslavement of Blacks within Native American nations. By linking slaveholding among white Southerners and Native American elites with a hypocritical brand of Christianity, this contribution to the transatlantic anti-slavery campaign spotlighted social relationships that were constraining abolitionism's progress.

From 'British Abolitionist Movements: Slavery and the American Churches'

We extract the following from Edinburgh and Leeds Journals: .[...]

"The principal address was delivered by Mr. Parker Pillsbury, of the *American Anti-Slavery Society*,[73] who said that the strong security of American slavery was the Church, and that it was the only barrier to its abolition which they could not remove, and this barrier was almost as insurmountable in the North as in the South. [...]

Pillsbury [...] chiefly directed his remarks to exposing the pro-slavery character of nearly all the American Churches and great Religious Associations. [...] The most powerful Religious Association in the United States is the American *Board of Missions*;[74] next to it stand the *American Bible Society* and the *American Tract Society*;[75] all of which are supported by the leading men of the various religious denominations. At great length he reviewed the operations of these Societies, and shewed that the *Board of Missions*, in its own documents, proved its pro-slavery character; that it had introduced the slave-laws of the Southern States amongst the Indians; thus converting the Cherokees,[76] the Choctaws, and

---

73 Founded in 1833, the American Anti-Slavery Society (AASS) promoted immediate (not gradual) abolition. With over a thousand local auxiliaries and membership above 200,000, under the leadership of William Lloyd Garrison the organisation sponsored events with keynotes supplied by formerly enslaved orators like William Wells Brown and Frederick Douglass. A dedicated Garrisonian, Pillsbury went as an official representative of the AASS to Great Britain, where he drew on his extensive experience as a lecturer in the US to seek transatlantic support.

74 The largest US missionary organisation, the American Board of Commissioners for Foreign Missions (ABCFM), founded in 1810, positioned its work with Native Americans under its 'foreign' rubric, ironically affirming Indigenous tribes' continued assertions of nationhood.

75 The American Bible Society (ABS), launched in 1816, continues its focus on Bible distribution today; the American Tract Society was founded in 1825 to promote widespread circulation of Protestant print materials in inexpensive, accessible formats.

76 For analysis of related texts by Cherokee authors David Brown and Elias Boudinot, see Joy, 'Cherokee Slaveholders'. Joy argues that, rhetoric blaming missionaries for introducing slavery to Native people aside, slaveholding by American Indians 'predated the arrival of Europeans, as Native Americans of the precontact Southeast had captured and enslaved one another for centuries'.

the Sioux to Christianity, but at the same time forcing upon them the horrible and brutalizing doctrines inseparable from slaveholding; and that its chief Secretary had publicly declared, in answer to an appeal from the Southern States, that the Board were astonished that anybody could have supposed them capable of regarding slaveholding or slavetrading as a disciplinary offence. Prior to their conversion, the Cherokees and the Choctaws had regarded all men as free, and would not recognize the right of one man to hold another as chattel; but the *American Board of Missions* 'converted' them, not to the Christianity of the Bible, but to the Christianity of the American pro-slavery Church, which taught that man might brutalize and chattelize his fellow-man; thus compassing sea and land to make proselytes, who, when made such, become more children of darkness than they were before. (Applause.) He then pointed to the operations of the *American Bible and Tract Societies*, and declared that they had ever been found on the side of the slaveholder, and the enemies of the slave. With these revolting principles and doctrines, the *American Board of Missions* had actually come to England, and endeavoured to ally itself with the Churches of this country. [...] Alas! The Board had already succeeded in raising 1000*l.* from the friends of Missions in England, by pretending that the Association was anti-slavery in its character and operations. But now that the truth had come out − now that the imposture was unmasked−would the Christian people of England fling their anti-slavery principles to the winds, and with open arms receive these upholders of Slavery, these defenders of the slaveholder?[77] (Applause) Mr. Pillsbury concluded by an earnest appeal to the religious bodies of England to speak out boldly against American Slavery, and to tell their mind freely to those Churches and Religious Associations of America who countenanced and encouraged the slaveholding system of that country. (Applause.)

Source text

'British Abolitionist Movements: Slavery and the American Churches', *The Anti-Slavery Reporter* 4.1 (1 January 1856), 7–8.

References

'The American Board of Foreign Missions and Slavery', *The Anti-Slavery Reporter* 3.1 (January 1855), 15–20.
'Illustrations of American Slavery', *The Anti-Slavery Reporter* 6.66 (June 1851), 93.
Joy, Natalie, 'Cherokee Slaveholders and Radical Abolitionists', *Commonplace* 10.4 (July 2010), Web.
'Mrs. H. B. Stowe on Pro-Slavery Advocates', *The Anti-Slavery Reporter* 7.1 (January 1859), 17–22.
Whipple, Charles K., *Relation of the American Board of Commissioners for Foreign Missions to Slavery* (Boston: R. F. Wallcut, 1861).

---

77 Pillsbury's address drew strong responses from several attendees, such as Rev. G. W. Condor, who declared he would 'rather resign his pastorate' than admit any 'pro-slavery minister, to enter his pulpit for the purpose of advocating the claims of the *American Board of Missions*' (8).

William and Ellen Craft (1824–1900; 1826–91) and Samuel J. May (1797–1871)

'Preface' and 'Letter to Mr. Estlin' from Running a Thousand Miles for Freedom (1860)

The daring escape of the Crafts from enslavement in Georgia holds a central place in their *Running* narrative. With the mixed-race Ellen disguised as a male slaveholder and William pretending to be 'his' servant, the two made their way North by train – only to find themselves in continued danger from slave-catchers emboldened by the Fugitive Slave Law. As outlined in William's 'Preface' to their London-published book, the Crafts joined other abolitionists on both sides of the Atlantic in invoking the disjunction between the US Revolution's aspirational documents and the nation's persistent enabling of slavery – not only by plantation owners in the South but also by complicit Northerners.

Allied with US anti-slavery activists like Reverend Samuel J. May, the Crafts had extended their escape route to England, where they tapped into transnational networks for financial and emotional support. That community is exemplified by the longstanding correspondence between May and John Estlin of Bristol. May's letter to Estlin, as reprinted in the Crafts' account, underscores the role that Britain played as a haven for African Americans like William and Ellen, particularly in the years between the passage of the Fugitive Slave Law and the post-Civil War era.

'Preface' to Running a Thousand Miles for Freedom

HAVING heard while in Slavery that "God made of one blood all nations of men," and also that the American Declaration of Independence says, that "We hold these truths to be self-evident, that all men are created equal; that they are endowed by their Creator with certain inalienable rights; that among these, are life, liberty, and the pursuit of happiness;" we could not understand by what right we were held as "chattels." Therefore, we felt perfectly justified in undertaking the dangerous and exciting task of "running a thousand miles" in order to obtain those rights which are so vividly set forth in the Declaration.

I beg those who would know the particulars of our journey, to peruse these pages.

This book is not intended as a full history of the life of my wife, nor of myself; but merely as an account of our escape; together with other matter which I hope may be the means of creating in some minds a deeper abhorrence of the sinful and abominable practice of enslaving and brutifying our fellow-creatures.

Without stopping to write a long apology for offering this little volume to the public, I shall commence at once to pursue my simple story.

W. CRAFT
12, Cambridge Road, Hammersmith, London.

'Letter to Mr. Estlin'

"21, Cornhill, Boston,
"November 6th, 1850.

"My dear Mr. Estlin,

"I trust that in God's good providence this letter will be handed to you in safety by our good friends, William and Ellen Craft. They have lived amongst us about two years, and have proved themselves worthy, in all respects, of our confidence and regard. The laws of this republican and Christian land (tell it not in Moscow, nor in Constantinople) regard them only as slaves—chattels—personal property. But they nobly vindicated their title and right to freedom, two years since, by winning their way to it; at least, so they thought. But now, the slave power, with the aid of Daniel Webster and a band of lesser traitors, has enacted a law, which puts their dearly-bought liberties in the most imminent peril; holds out a strong temptation to every mercenary and unprincipled ruffian to become their kidnapper; and has stimulated the slaveholders generally to such desperate acts for the recovery of their fugitive property, as have never before been enacted in the history of this government.

"Within a fortnight, two fellows from Macon, Georgia, have been in Boston for the purpose of arresting our friends William and Ellen. A writ was served against them from the United States District Court; but it was not served by the United States Marshal; why not, is not certainly known: perhaps through fear, for a general feeling of indignation, and a cool determination not to allow this young couple to be taken from Boston into slavery, was aroused, and pervaded the city. It is understood that one of the judges told the Marshal that he would not be authorized in breaking the door of Craft's house. Craft kept himself close within the house, armed himself, and awaited with remarkable composure the event. Ellen, in the meantime, had been taken to a retired place out of the city. The Vigilance Committee (appointed at a late meeting in Fanueil Hall[78]) enlarged their numbers, held an almost permanent session, and appointed various sub-committees to act in different ways. One of these committees called repeatedly on Messrs. Hughes and Knight, the slave-catchers, and requested and advised them to leave the city. At first they peremptorily refused to do so, ''till they got hold of the niggers.' On complaint of different persons, these two fellows were several times arrested, carried before one of our county courts, and held to bail on charges of 'conspiracy to kidnap,' and of 'defamation,' in calling William and Ellen 'slaves.' At length, they became so alarmed, that they left the city by an indirect route, evading the vigilance of many persons who were on the lookout for them. Hughes, at one time, was near losing his life at the hands of an infuriated coloured man. While these men remained in the city, a prominent whig gentleman sent word to William Craft, that if he would submit peaceably to an arrest, he and his wife should be bought from their owners, cost what it might. Craft replied, in effect, that he was in a measure the representative of all the other fugitives in Boston, some 200 or 300 in number; that, if he gave up, they would all be at the mercy of the slave-catchers, and must fly from the city at any sacrifice;

---

78 Near Boston's waterfront, Faneuil Hall opened before the American Revolution and had already, by the time of Estlin's letter, been the site of many famous political speeches and gatherings.

and that, if his freedom could be bought for two cents, he would not consent to compromise the matter in such a way. This event has stirred up the slave spirit of the country, south and north; the United States government is determined to try its hand in enforcing the Fugitive Slave law; and William and Ellen Craft would be prominent objects of the slaveholders' vengeance. Under these circumstances, it is the almost unanimous opinion of their best friends, that they should quit America as speedily as possible, and seek an asylum in England! Oh! shame, shame upon us, that Americans, whose fathers fought against Great Britain in order to be FREE, should have to acknowledge this disgraceful fact! God gave us a fair and goodly heritage in this land, but man has cursed it with his devices and crimes against human souls and human rights. Is America the 'land of the free, and the home of the brave?' God knows it is not; and we know it too. A brave young man and a virtuous young woman must fly the American shores, and seek, under the shadow of the British throne, the enjoyment of 'life, liberty, and the pursuit of happiness.'

"But I must pursue my plain, sad story. All day long, I have been busy planning a safe way for William and Ellen to leave Boston. We dare not allow them to go on board a vessel, even in the port of Boston; for the writ is yet in the Marshal's hands, and he *may* be waiting an opportunity to serve it; so I am expecting to accompany them to-morrow to Portland, Maine, which is beyond the reach of the Marshal's authority; and there I hope to see them on board a British steamer.

"This letter is written to introduce them to you. I know your infirm health; but I am sure, if you were stretched on your bed in your last illness, and could lift your hand at all, you would extend it to welcome these poor hunted fellow-creatures. Henceforth, England is their nation and their home. It is with real regret for our personal loss in their departure, as well as burning shame for the land that is not worthy of them, that we send them away, or rather allow them to go. But, with all the resolute courage they have shown in a most trying hour, they themselves see it is the part of foolhardy rashness to attempt to stay here longer.

"I must close; and with many renewed thanks for all your kind words and deeds towards us,

"I am, very respectfully yours,
"SAMUEL MAY, JUN."

Source texts

Craft, W[illiam], *Running a Thousand Miles for Freedom; or, The Escape of William and Ellen Craft from Slavery* (London: William Tweedie, 1860).

May, Samuel, 'Letter', in Craft, *Running a Thousand Miles*, 88–92.

References

Estlin, J. B., *A Brief Notice of American Slavery, and the Abolition Movement* (London: William Tweedie, 1853).

McCaskill, Barbara, *Love, Liberation, and Escaping Slavery: William and Ellen Craft in Cultural Memory* (Athens, GA: University of Georgia Press, 2015).

May, Samuel J., *Memoir of Samuel Joseph May* (Boston: Roberts, 1873).

Mary Ann Shadd Cary (1823–93)

'A Voice of Thanks': Letter to William Lloyd Garrison, Esq. (1861)

Mary Ann Shadd Cary found compelling role models in her parents, Abraham Shadd and Harriet Burton Parnell, free Blacks who supported the Underground Railroad. After passage of the US Fugitive Slave Act, she joined a growing number of African Americans relocating to Canada, where slavery had been outlawed since 1834.

In Windsor, Ontario, she met her husband Thomas F. Cary, with whom she had two children. In Canada she worked as an educator, journalist and activist fighting for racial integration, challenging the then common practice of social segregation in daily life despite legal freedom for Blacks. In 1853, Shadd Cary launched *The Provincial Freeman*, 'intended to report about the lives of blacks in Canada, to encourage black emigration to Canada, and to promote their status as black Canadians' (Paul, 171). Though the name of Samuel Ringgold Ward (an escaped enslaved person) appeared on the masthead, Shadd Cary's veiled leadership role did not prevent her from producing powerful writing. In1860 Thomas Cary died and Shadd Cary had to close the newspaper for financial reasons. With the outbreak of the American Civil War, she returned to the US and recruited for the Union Army.

In her letter to Garrison, editor of the *Liberator*, Shadd Cary opposes calls for Blacks to be sent to Caribbean islands. Overall, her letter affirms the transnational social justice network to which she contributed, in both the US and Canada.

'A VOICE OF THANKS'

WM. LLOYD GARRISON, ESQ.:

Dear Sir — Could the friends of freedom know the effect that a good word timely spoken in behalf of the fleeing slave has upon the colored residents in this country, and the deep gratitude they feel for your many acts of kindness, and your solicitude, and, above all, for that sterling, out-spoken sentiment–as true in its services to them, and in its results upon their destiny, as the needle is to the tempest-tossed mariner–I think there would be more faith in the colored people as a responsible moral element, necessary component of the anti-slavery forces, destined now and in the future to enter largely into the moral and political makeup of this continent. I say this continent, because, the importance of islands and other continents admitted,[79] as far as it goes, whatever new-fangled theories may be afloat

---

79 Shadd Cary likely refers to the Caribbean islands and Africa, touted by the American Colonization Society (ACS) as desirable emigration destinations for Blacks then in North America.

about our destiny as colored native Americans[80] away from here, and out in an island any where, we, at least, realize the truth, that the masses have a fixed destiny here, and we do not believe, and do not intend, that it must always be as the sub-stratum of the body politic.

There are certain plain land-marks by means of which we have come to this conclusion, and upon which the beams of this new policy of our removal from the continent to Hayti break like Samson's withes.[81]

I am led to this train of thought by a very noticeable, and, to us, very impor-tant paragraph in your re-marks in reply to the letter of friend Hiram Wilson,[82] in the last *Liberator*, wherein you say: "Although it is probable that the number of fugitives, seeking freedom and safety in Canada, will be somewhere diminished for the present; still, there is reason to believe that many of them will go there this winter," &c. &c.

For this gleam of the old light—this stray beam from the old beacon so well-known to our people, we give you sincerest thanks. This says, as plain as English can, that the well-worn friends of the refugee and contraband[83] are not to be turned aside, by every wind of doctrine, from the long-established custom of aiding them to settle upon this free soil, without, in their extremity, either attempting to bias their imperfectly formed judgments against Canada and America generally, or join-ing in the now seeking-to-be popular cry that they must leave the country because of the hatred to pursue them as the cause of the war, which the stupid among them know that the slave-holder, not the poor slave, is the cause, and that once he and his system are crushed out, the cause will have been destroyed, and America must become a desirable country for the masses.

Pointed and easily understood paragraphs as your own say plainly enough, that the Abolitionists of America, who labored and suffered long ago, do not join in the crusade against the colored people, but are right upon this question of residence on this continent for the colored men of the land. There has of late been much silence upon this point—so much, that now the new emigration scheme, about which Mr. Higginson[84] wrote, and for which others work, is thought by many to have absorbed all the Anti-Slavery of the United States worth having.

I have often thought that there was a misapprehension somewhere of the rela-tion in which the refugees here stand to the cause proper.

It is a debatable question with some, whether or not, after being once helped to Canada, they are any longer connected with the Anti-Slavery polity. Some are out-spoken, and say that any consideration of the fugitive in Canada is not Anti-Slavery work; others, less sincere, regard this Canada as a vast poaching-ground for

---

80 '[N]ative Americans' here designates Blacks born in North America, not First Nations people.
81 Flexible branches or bands, used by Delilah to bind Samson, who easily broke them (see Judges 16)
82 After earning a theology degree from Oberlin College, Hiram Wilson (1803–64) emigrated to Canada and supported escaped slaves in Ontario. He opened a night school that reportedly provided refuge for travellers crossing the border with Harriet Tubman through the Underground Railroad.
83 Already in 1861, enslaved people in the South were leaving their former slaveholders and seek-ing protection from the Union Army. Though Union forces initially had no formal policy for dealing with them, Major General Benjamin Butler took the ironic step of classifying those arriving to his command area as property, thus making them a 'contraband of war' that need not be returned to previous 'owners'.
84 Thomas Wentworth Higginson, Unitarian minister and militant abolitionist

negro game,[85] from which they may get the material for experience in the islands without loss to the cause, and certainly without loss to the experiment-makers. A few there are who are honest in believing that they would profit by removal to the British islands.[86]

That you do not share the views of the two first, I infer from your recommendation for "local provision" in behalf of the refugees, should the contingencies of travel make it necessary. This explicit acknowledgment of it, as Anti-Slavery work, is subject of congratulation here.

The institution of slavery has despoiled the colored man of America wofully; the injury done to him intellectually, physically, morally, is not of his seeking; those, therefore, whose sympathies do not care to reach beyond your geographical boundaries, and who choose to forget his perils and the difficulties which he must encounter in his new position by reason of former deprivations in slavery, yet scruple not when here, to arouse prejudice by deprecating further emigration of fugitives and contrabands to the Canadas, clearly forfeit the right to the confidence of the colored Canadian, and must not complain, if they do not command his respect.

The fugitives in Canada, though assuming new and important political relations to this government—relations not to be trifled with by every theorizer, who, upon a flying or discursive visit, may hope to sharpen his axe upon their instability and credulity—have keen sympathies for friends and kindred left behind; their better selves remember *for ever* the friends who helped them on, and aid others with help when needed here: they divide to the last morsel with the wayfarer when he escapes, and they gladly welcome and will welcome the many you may send the coming winter, whether to St. Catherines or this western section. They hail also every organized and responsible society for the necessary relief of the really deserving, as an earnest of the ever kind regards of long-tried friends; and your endorsement of Fugitive Aid Societies, under proper auspices and limitations, must, as I hear that the one at St. Catherines does, receive their grateful acknowledgements and fullest approbation.

MARY A. SHADD CARY.

Source text

Cary, Mary A. Shadd, 'A Voice of Thanks', *Liberator* (29 November 1861), 191.

Reference

Paul, Heike, 'Out of Chatham: Abolitionism on the Canadian Frontier', *Atlantic Studies: Literary, Cultural, and Historical Perspectives* 8.2 (June 2011), 165–88.

---

85 'Negro game' (linked to the 'poaching ground' phrase earlier) ironically invokes racist language casting Blacks as animals to hunt.
86 'A few' references advocates assuming that sending North American Black persons away to the 'British' [i.e. Caribbean] islands (or Africa) would actually be a positive move.

Elizabeth Gaskell (1810–65) and Charles Eliot Norton (1827–1908)

Letters on the Civil War (1861, 1863)

English novelist Elizabeth Gaskell is best known for her industrial novel *Mary Barton* (1848), which moves its heroine from Manchester, England, to Canada, and the *Life of Charlotte Brontë* (1857). After finishing Brontë's biography, she became part of a circle that included American man of letters Charles Eliot Norton, sculptor William Wetmore Story (1819–95), and his wife Emelyn (1820–94). Thereafter transatlantic relations became increasingly important to Gaskell. She and Norton started a correspondence that lasted until her death. Gaskell also began to publish transatlantically. Beginning with 'The Poor Clare', first published in Dickens's *Household Words* (13, 20, 27 December 1856), her stories also appeared serially in *Harper's Weekly Magazine*. The tales thus published include 'Lois the Witch' (*All the Year Round*, 8, 15, 22 October 1859; *Harper's Weekly*, 22, 29 October, 5, 12 November 1859), her fictionalised account of the Salem witch trials.

Norton is best known today as co-editor of the *North American Review* (1863–8), the translator of Dante's *Vita Nuova* (1867), and the inaugural professor of art history at Harvard University (1875–98). His many transatlantic friends included, in addition to Gaskell, Robert (1812–89) and Elizabeth Barrett Browning (1806–61), William Morris (1834–96), Edward (1833–98) and Georgiana Burne-Jones (1840–1920), and John Ruskin (1819–1900). Gaskell's lively style, for which her correspondence is famous, informs her 10 June 1861 letter to Norton, which demonstrates the bafflement the American Civil War could inspire in Britons and is notable as well for its anticolonial sentiment. Norton's 1863 letter captures the warmth of their friendship; more importantly, it reflects his role as editor for the pro-Union New England Loyal Publication Society and offers an account of Black troops in the Massachusetts Infantry.

Elizabeth Gaskell to Charles Eliot Norton

Monday, June 10th, 1861
Dining room in Plymouth Grove, breakfast things not as yet removed, your letter came *at* breakfast.
My dear Mr. Norton:
    Yesterday —a quiet Sunday, with somehow less of bustle about it than Sunday School and Ragged School[87] usually make, Meta[88] and I were having a long *yearning*

---

87 Ragged schools offered free education to poor children.
88 Margaret Emily Gaskell (1837–1913), second oldest daughter of Gaskell, nicknamed 'Meta'

talk about America, and our dear friends there. I am not sure that we did not shake hands upon a resolution that if we lived we *would* go over to America. I know we calculated time and expense, and knocked off Niagara, because we would rather see friends. (That is to say Meta did. I was not so clear in my own mind about giving up Niagara, so I won't pretend I was). Then we talked over your politics and could *not* understand them; and I half determined to do what I am doing now—take myself and Meta for average specimens of English people,—*most* kindly disposed to you, our dear cousins, hating slavery intensely, but yet thoroughly *puzzled by* what is now going on in America. I don't mind your thinking me dense or ignorant, and I think I can be sure you will give me a quiet *unmetaphorical* statement of what is the end proposed in this war. Now don't be indignant at me, (or at the English) when I tell you exactly how much I (average English) know, and how much I don't know. I understood 'the Union' to be an *expansive,* or *contractive* contract. Expansive (as being capable of including more than the original thirteen United States) it has proved itself to be. But it seems to me that the very fact of its power of expansion involved that of its *dissolution* (or contraction as I have called it above) if need were. No over great empire has long preserved itself in vigour. You included (by your annexations) people of different breeds, and consequently different opinions and habits of thought; the time was sure to come when you could not act together as a nation; the only wonder to me is that you have cohered so long. And yet you say in this letter 'I do not feel sure that under *any* circumstances the *right* of secession could or would have been allowed' etc. You will perhaps say that our great unwieldy British Empire coheres—that the Roman did—yes, but we do not come in frequent contact with our colonies,—as you North and South do. People of diametrically opposite opinions on many points may keep good friends on the whole if they are not brought into intimate daily communion. Doubtless a good quantity of grumbling goes on, both with just and unjust cause, at our antipodes, at our government of them; but we do not hear it 'hot and hot'.—(Besides I heartily wish our colonies would take to governing themselves, and sever the connexion with us in a comfortable friendly way). So that altogether I (average English) cannot understand how you (American) did not look forward to 'secession' at some time not very far distant. As to the manner in which it has been done nothing it appears to me *could* have been more treacherous and base on the part of the Southerners,—and I hear no other opinion. Moreover I have heard some letters from Southern Sea Island Cotton[89] planters—apparently kindly good old-fashioned people named Giraudet, or something like it, expressive of deep regret at the behaviour of such men as Jefferson Davis[90] etc. But I should have thought (I feel as if I were dancing among eggs,) that separating yourselves from the South was like getting rid of a diseased member (possibly there are cases where amputation is a more impatient and consequently a more cowardly thing than the slower process of trying to bring the leg back to a healthy state). We have a proverbial expression in Lancashire[91] 'Good riddance of bad rubbish' that I think I should have applied to the Southern secessions. From what we read of the attack on Fort Sumter,[92] 'no one killed', it sounds like a piece

---

89 Sea Island Cotton, considered the finest cotton then available, was grown on islands off South Carolina, Georgia and Florida. Giraudet: unidentified
90 (1808–89), President of the Confederate States
91 Manchester was then part of Lancashire county.
92 The fort was captured by Confederate troops on 14 April 1861, launching the Civil War.

of bravadoing child's play,—insolent enough, but of a piece with the sort of bullying character one always heard attributed to the South. Now comes my great puzzle. What are you going to do when you have conquered the South, as no one doubts that you will. Mr. Channing[93] says 're-assert the right of letting the U. S. flag float over the fortresses of the South, throwing out liberty to the breeze' or something like this, which just tells me nothing of what I really and with deep interest want to know. *Conquering* the South won't turn them into friends, or pre-dispose them to listen to reason or argument, or to yield to influence instead of to force. You must *compel* them then to what you want them to do. (And what *do* you want them to do? —abolish slavery? return to their allegiance to the Union?) *Compelling* them implies the means of compulsion. You will have to hold them in subjection by force, i. e. by military occupation. At present your army is composed of volunteers, —but can they ever leave their business etc. for years and years of military occupation of a country peopled by those adverse to them? Shall you not have henceforward to keep a standing army?—If you were here I could go on multiplying questions of this kind, but I dare say you are already tired and think me very stupid. I sometimes try and compare your position to what ours in England would be if Ireland took it into her head to *secede* but after all that is not a fair comparison —Scotland would do better because Scotland was never *conquered*, but agreed to the Union with England in a kind of a way, —I suppose we should fight and conquer and then we should have to garrison all her forts, and keep her down— But I think I should not feel it to be *right* to do this, (and it is the nearest parallel case I can think of)—and it certainly would involve the standing army which I thought you were all so proud at being able to do without. I have been reading your letter again—I see you speak as if the anarchical minority would have been able to upset the law and order of the *majority*. (They are thieves and rascals, that is clear.) But I feel as if their attack on Fort Sumter was just to get rid of the little nest of Northerners in the heart of their town not to attack formally the 'majority'.—And as for the mob (in Baltimore, was it not?) attacking the Northern regiment,[94] *that* was very bad; but your New York mobs—(nay, even your Boston mobs in abolition-meeting times[95]) have got ahead of law and order without bringing on a national war. Now I have said out the very worst I have ever *heard* said, and you know I live in S. Lancashire where all personal and commercial intimacies are with the South.[96] Every one looks and feels sad (—oh so sad) about this war; it would do Americans good to see how warm the English *heart* is towards them, although we may all be blundering in our *minds* as to the wisdom or otherwise. [...] You owe me a *personal* as well as a *National* letter. Put me right where I am wrong,—(you'll say I'm wrong throughout—) [...]

Your ever affectionate friend

E. C. Gaskell

---

93 William Henry Channing (1810–84), American Unitarian minister
94 A Baltimore mob fired on a Massachusetts regiment, which returned fire, on 19 April 1861. Four soldiers and twelve civilians were killed.
95 Likely a reference to the riot on 21 October 1835, when a Boston mob sought to lynch the prominent abolitionist William Lloyd Garrison (1805–79)
96 Manchester's principal industry was textile manufacturing, to which the supply of Southern cotton was vital.

Charles Eliot Norton to Elizabeth Gaskell

Shady Hill. 23d April 1863

My dearest Mrs. Gaskell

[...] I am occupied a good deal with the selection of articles on public affairs, short newspaper articles for the most part containing what seem to me true views in regard to the great questions of the time, which are printed off on slips & sent to several hundred, (nearly a thousand) newspapers in the free States, to supply them with good matter for the filling up of their columns. In this way a great deal of sound doctrine is spread abroad, and I am glad to give what time is necessary for the work as my contribution to the cause for which we are at war. Of course one has to select from such material as is afforded & to make such selections as are likely to be effective,—so that often in the making up of the 'slips' there is some sacrifice required both of fastidious taste, & of critical judgment of style. But these are minor considerations, and it is not without interest to circulate through a country & among a people like ours the opinions which are the expression of one's own principles & faith. On the whole our cause makes progress, & the war is accomplishing a good work. There is a very rapid growth of the feeling of nationality, & an increasing conviction of the necessity of nationality & an undivided Union. Nor is the growth of antislavery feeling less rapid. Missouri, Maryland and Delaware will soon be added to the list of Free States. And in a letter I have from Mr. Olmsted, written from Louisville, Kentucky last month, he says, 'Kentucky & Tennessee need only to be rightly managed to come out Anti-Slavery States.'[97] Meanwhile in all the loyal States the Emancipation policy is gaining support, and the people generally are becoming confident in it as a means of success in the War,—while thoughtful men see more & more clearly that it is the necessary policy for securing a healthy & permanent peace.

The experiment of enlisting black troops is now being fairly tried. The first South Carolina (negro) Volunteers have distinguished themselves in action. There are two other regiments of freed men in South Carolina, & many similar regiments are now being formed in the West, to take charge of the works on the Mississippi River, as well as to serve actively in the war. The prejudice among the white soldiers against the black is rapidly dying out,—and this military training seems to be as good a school as possible for educating the freed slaves into the independence & self-dependence of free citizens.—In Massachusetts a regiment of black volunteers is being formed, as part of the quota of troops of the State, and the success has been so great that orders have been issued for another. The one now formed & nearly full is under the command of Colonel Robert Shaw, the son of your correspondent Mrs. Shaw.[98] He is a fine young fellow; exceedingly well fitted to fill so responsible a position, & full of the true spirit of a soldier & a believer in the equal rights of man. He expects to have his regiment full in a few days, & to be ordered off in about a fortnight,—but before he goes he is to be married to a very charming person, a Miss Haggerty.[99] Public duties & private interests intermingle very much in these days. [...]

Your grateful & affectionate friend

Charles Eliot Norton

---

97 In 1863 Frederick Law Olmsted (1822–1903) served as general secretary of the US Sanitary Commission, dedicated to maintaining the health of Union Army volunteers.

98 Robert Gould Shaw (1837–63), son of Boston abolitionist Sarah Sturgis Shaw, led the Black 54th Massachusetts Infantry and fell in battle on 18 July while urging forward the regiment that had proven its fighting mettle.

99 Annie Kneeland Haggerty, whom Shaw married in 1863

Source text

Whitehall, Jane (ed.), *Letters of Mrs. Gaskell and Charles Eliot Norton 1855–1865* (London: Oxford University Press, 1932), 82–7, 99–102.

References

Greenwood, John, '"Our Happy Days in Rome": The Gaskell-Norton Correspondence', *Gaskell Journal* 28 (2014), 97–104.
Pettitt, Claire, 'Time Lag and Elizabeth Gaskell's Transatlantic Imagination', *Victorian Studies* 54.4 (2012), 599–623.
Whitehill, Jane, 'Introduction', in Whitehill (ed.), *Letters of Mrs. Gaskell and Charles Eliot Norton 1855–1865*, vii–xxix.

Frances Anne (Fanny) Kemble (1809–93)

From Journal of a Residence on a Georgian Plantation *(1863)*

Frances Anne Kemble was the niece of the celebrated British actors John Philip Kemble (1757–1823) and Sarah Siddons (1755–1831), siblings to her father Charles Kemble (1775–1854), himself a notable presence on the London stage. Fanny Kemble became an acclaimed actress in 1829 through her first appearance as Shakespeare's Juliet in Covent Garden. With her father, she toured the US in 1832–4, performing with great success before retiring from the stage following her marriage to Pierce Butler of Philadelphia. In 1836 Butler inherited vast sugar cane plantations in Georgia, and in 1838 he moved his family south. Kemble, as the extract reprinted below shows, was an opponent of slavery even before moving to her husband's home but was initially prepared to countenance the possibility that conditions under which enslaved persons lived might be better than she anticipated. *Journal of a Residence on a Georgian Plantation* is testament to the realisation of her fears. The book covers the winter and spring of 1838–9, and represents the first eyewitness testimony by a white woman – and a plantation mistress – to condemn the system of enslavement. The *Journal* also charts the unravelling of a marriage.

Shortly after its composition, Kemble declined to publish the book, a position she held until the outbreak of the Civil War and the radically transformed conditions of both the nation and her marriage (she and Butler having divorced in 1849). Appearing first in England and then in the US, the book garnered strong reviews, especially from the Northern US press.

From Journal of a Residence on a Georgian Plantation

Philadelphia, December, 1838.[100]

My Dear E——,[101] — I return you Mr. ——'s letter.[102] I do not think it answers any of the questions debated in our last conversation at all satisfactorily: the *right* one man has to enslave another, he has not the hardihood to assert; but in the reasons he adduces to defend that act of injustice, the contradictory statements he makes appear to me to refute each other. He says, that to the Continental European protesting against the abstract iniquity of slavery, his answer would be, "The slaves are infinitely better off than half the Continental peasantry." To the Englishman, "They are happy compared with the miserable Irish."[103] But supposing that this answered the question of original injustice, which it does not, it is not a true reply. Though the negroes are fed, clothed, and housed, and though the Irish peasant is starved, naked, and roofless, the bare name of freeman—the lordship over his own person, the power to choose and will—are blessings beyond food, raiment, or shelter; possessing which, the want of every comfort of life is yet more tolerable than their fullest enjoyment without them. Ask the thousands of ragged destitutes who yearly land upon these shores to seek the means of existence—ask the friendless, penniless foreign emigrant, if he will give up his present misery, his future uncertainty, his doubtful and difficult struggle for life at once, for the secure, and, as it is called, fortunate dependence of the slave: the indignation with which he would spurn the offer will prove that he possesses one good beyond all others, and that his birthright as a man is more precious to him yet than the mess of pottage[104] for which he is told to exchange it because he is starving. [. . .]

Mr. —— (and many others) speaks as if there were a natural repugnance in all whites to any alliance with the black race; and yet it is notorious, that almost every Southern planter has a family more or less numerous of illegitimate colored children. Most certainly, few people would like to assert that such connections are formed because it is the *interest* of these planters to increase the number of their human property, and that they add to their revenue by the closest intimacy with creatures that they loathe, in order to reckon among their wealth the children of their body. Surely that is a monstrous and unnatural supposition, and utterly unworthy of belief. That such connections exist commonly is a sufficient proof that they are not abhorrent to nature; but it seems, indeed, as if marriage (and not concubinage) was the horrible enormity which can not be tolerated, and against which, moreover, it has been deemed expedient to enact laws.[105] Now it appears very evident that there is no law in the white man's nature which prevents him from making a colored woman

---

100 After her retirement from the stage in 1834, Kemble lived in Philadelphia (other than a trip to England in 1836–7) until moving with her family to the Georgia Sea Islands in December 1838.
101 Elizabeth Dwight Sedgwick (1801–91), an abolitionist and teacher, ran the Young Ladies' School in her home at Lenox, Massachusetts, from 1828 until her death. The *Journal* is dedicated to her.
102 Pierce Butler (1810–67), Kemble's husband
103 Irish immigrants to the US in the nineteenth century often faced prejudice and persecution on religious and economic grounds. Among Southern apologists for Black slavery, the condition of white Northern labourers was held as an example of a more brutal form of exploitation.
104 Stew or porridge; Kemble alludes to Esau's sale of his birthright in Genesis 25: 29–34.
105 Anti-miscegenation laws were first passed in Georgia in 1750, when African slaves were admitted to the colony, and not finally overturned until 1967, with the Supreme Court decision of *Loving v. Virginia*.

the mother of his children, but there *is* a law on his statute-books forbidding him to make her his wife; and if we are to admit the theory that the mixing of the races is a monstrosity, it seems almost as curious that laws should be enacted to prevent men marrying women towards whom they have an invincible natural repugnance, as that education should by law be prohibited to creatures incapable of receiving it. As for the exhortation with which Mr. —— closes his letter, that I will not "go down to my husband's plantation prejudiced against what I am to find there," I know not well how to answer it. Assuredly I *am* going prejudiced against slavery, for I am an Englishwoman, in whom the absence of such a prejudice would be disgraceful. Nevertheless, I go prepared to find many mitigations in the practice to the general injustice and cruelty of the system—much kindness on the part of the masters, much content on that of the slaves; and I feel very sure that you may rely upon the carefulness of my observation, and the accuracy of my report, of every detail of the working of the thing that comes under my notice; and certainly, on the plantation to which I am going, it will be more likely that I should some things extenuate, than set down aught in malice.

Yours ever faithfully.

Source text

Kemble, Frances Anne, *Journal of a Residence on a Georgian Plantation in 1838–1839* (New York: Harper & Brothers, 1863).

References

Barnes, Mollie, '"My Mere Narration": Fanny Kemble's Intercessions in *Journal of a Residence on a Georgian Plantation*', *Nineteenth-Century Gender Studies* 13.3 (Winter 2017), Web.
Deirdre, David, *Fanny Kemble: A Performed Life* (Philadelphia: University of Pennsylvania Press, 2007).

'Abolition of Slavery by the Cherokee Indians' (1863)

This unsigned account, describing the Cherokee National Council's vote to emancipate enslaved persons, appeared in both *The Liberator* (US) and *The Anti-Slavery Reporter* (Britain). Abolitionist writers on both sides of the Atlantic regularly borrowed texts from each other's publication venues, thereby reinforcing their shared commitments. Here, an additional dimension of transnational identity comes into play: Native peoples continuing to assert nationhood status, despite having had to endure Removal from their homelands to the West.

In this case, acknowledging Cherokee sovereignty requires reading beyond the seemingly straightforward celebration of this article to take into account the complex politics of their Nation's shifting Civil War alliances. Early in that conflict, Chief John Ross favoured neutrality. But a rival party, led by Stand Watie, combined calls for allegiance to the Confederacy with efforts to oust Ross from power. When Ross abandoned his original position and supported the Confederacy, his shift did not dissuade Watie from forming a rival government. Meanwhile, many individual Cherokee men went into hiding rather than fight for the South. In contrast, when federal troops invaded the Cherokee Nation in summer 1863, supporters of the South there, many themselves enslavers, fled into the Choctaw and Chickasaw nations, taking enslaved people with them.

By February 1863, the Ross party was ready to disavow the alliance. But the group's associated vote to emancipate all enslaved people in the Nation did not free those who had already been carried away by their owners. Thus, while anti-slavery whites on both sides of the Atlantic touted the votes described below as a watershed in abolitionism, doing so required ignoring the Watie party's continued support of the Confederacy – and their still having enslaved people within their community.

See 'British Abolitionist Movements: Slavery and the American Churches', AA.

'Abolition of Slavery by the Cherokee Indians'

The subjoined is from the *National Anti-Slavery Standard* of 8 March,[106] from the correspondence of the *Missouri Democrat*. We need add no comment upon the remarks of the writer.

> "Camp Blunt, Ark., Feb. 26, 1863.
>
> "The Cherokee National Council has just adjourned. It convened in Delaware District, Cherokee Nation, a few miles from Camp John Ross, where Colonel Phillips camped the 3rd Brigade, to guard its proceedings. The result of this Legislative Assembly is the most significant and instructive. The members of the body were elected nearly two years ago. They are the old Legislature—the Legislature that was coerced into an ordinance of secession by the rebel army. The first act of the Legislature was to repeal the ordinance of secession, which was done unanimously. The next act was to deprive of office in the nation, and disqualify all who should continue to be rebellious or disloyal to the United States' Government. The courts and other legal business of the nation will go on as heretofore the moment the country is peaceable enough to warrant it.
>
> "A law was enacted appointing a delegation to visit Washington about the military and civil affairs of the nation, and this delegation was authorised to abolish Slavery in the nation should the Congress extend the same privilege to the nation

---

106 We have been unable to find a copy of the report in the *National Anti-Slavery Standard* under any winter/spring 1863 date. The same article did appear in *The Liberator* of 27 March 1863, under the title 'The Cherokee Nation Abolishes Slavery and Repents of Secession', 51.

as to the Border States. This was to be a remunerated emancipation, hanging to the clause of a bargain.

"But this could neither meet the wishes or the notions of the Cherokee legislators. Captain Bird Geitz, somewhat noted for fighting the rebels in the mountains before he joined the Federal service, a full-blooded Indian, and good lawyer, framed a Bill for unconditional emancipation. He introduced his Bill with a fine speech, and was eloquently supported by Captain James Vand, Lieut.-Col. Lewis Deming, and others. The argument was this: 'That Slavery had precipitated this peaceful, happy, and glorious nation in war. Slavery was responsible for all the ills that had befallen the Cherokee people and the country. That President Lincoln had struck at the head of the monster in his Emancipation Proclamation, and that it beho[o]ves every patriot and statesman to sustain the President and meet the issue. That without this there was no peace for our distracted country.' A few clung to the hope of emancipation with compensation,[107] and urged the losses of the people already, but the majority urged that the Bill ought not to be so clogged. If the Government chose to pay the loyal, very well; but they would leave such a necessary act as the abolition of Slavery to no contingencies, and no one should do it for them. It was their work. To the question that 'free negroes would crowd in,' &c., Lieut.-Col. Deming made an eloquent reply, in which he said that, awakened by the grandeur of this struggle, the Cherokee nation could surely afford to do right, and look for God's blessing on our cause, if a million refugees should flock to it.

"Nothing could be more instructive to us as a nation than this simple and great action of the Cherokee people. We boast of ourselves, of our intelligence and shrewdness, yet debate and cavil at this late day over selfish interests that have betrayed us, and base prejudices that have led us to ruin. Surely God, in his infinite wisdom, has raised up these people to rebuke those who would still fight against the providences of God. When the history of this great rebellion, and of this nation, is written, the Cherokees shall make no mean figure. Under the leadership of Col. Phillips, they fought desperately at Newtonia, and Cane Hill, and have distinguished themselves in every battle of the South-west this past season. They have fought fearlessly and bravely, second to no other troops, even while their families have suffered untold misery and disaster; and now they come cheerfully up to offer the slavery of their nation to the cause of Liberty and Union. "He that hath ears to hear, let him hear."

KAW.

Source text

'Abolition of Slavery by the Cherokee Indians', *The Anti-Slavery Reporter* 11.5 [New Series] (1 May 1863), 112.

References

Finkelman, Paul, 'Lincoln and Emancipation: Constitutional Theory, Practical Politics, and the Basic Practice of Law', *Journal of Supreme Court History* 35.3 (2010), 243–66.
Yarbrough, Fay A., *Race and the Cherokee Nation: Sovereignty in the Nineteenth Century* (Philadelphia: University of Pennsylvania Press, 2007).

---

107 See Finkelman (especially 258) on President Lincoln's gradual steps toward freeing enslaved people in the Confederate states via the Emancipation Proclamation.

Fisk Jubilee Singers (1871–today)

'Steal Away' and 'Go down, Moses' (1872)

In the midst of segregation and economic oppression after the Civil War, educational institutions serving formerly enslaved people and their children emerged across the US South. These Historically Black Colleges and Universities (HBCUs) shared the goal of providing race uplift. One of these, Fisk University in Nashville, opened its doors in 1866. Like its sister institutions, Fisk faced financial challenges. To raise funds as well as the institution's profile, music professor George L. White organised the Fisk Jubilee Singers.

Every 6 October, Fisk celebrates Jubilee Day in honour of the 1871 date when the first Jubilee Singers launched a national fundraising tour, which prompted an invitation in 1872 to the White House. The singers soon afterwards performed for Queen Victoria in London in May 1873, then went to Scotland, the Netherlands and Germany. The choir presented hymns and songs that W. E. B. DuBois, in *The Souls of Black Folk*, would famously dub 'sorrow songs', such as 'Swing Low Sweet Chariot' and 'Didn't My Lord Deliver Daniel'.

While the choir's preservation of such spirituals is valued today, Director White faced opposition from some African Americans who found the performances called up dark memories of enslavement. Others felt the music's sacred nature should preclude secular performances. Reviews of the group's European tour demonstrated that white audiences' strong sense of racial hierarchies could complicate their evaluations of the singers and their music. One British article described their repertoire as 'rude' yet 'at least genuine, and though it may not perhaps satisfy the artistic standard of educated musicians, it is impossible not to feel a certain amount of charm with the novel and natural effects produced' ('Jubilee', 320). Below, we give opening stanzas of two songs.

'Steal Away' (1872)

> Steal away, steal away, steal away to Jesus!
> Steal away, steal away home, I hain't got long to stay here.
> 1.   My Lord calls me, He calls me by the thunder;
> The trumpet sounds it in my soul, – I hain't got long to stay here.
> 2.   Green trees are bending, poor sinners stand trembling;
> The trumpet sounds it in my soul, – I hain't got long to stay here.

'Go down, Moses' (1872)

> When Israel was in Egypt's land;
>   Let my people go,
> Oppressed so hard they could not stand,
>   Let my people go.

Go down, Moses, way down in Egypt land,
Tell ole Pha-roh,
> Let my people go.

Thus saith the Lord, bold Moses said,
> Let my people go;
If not, I'll smite your first-born dead,
> Let my people go.
Go down, Moses, etc.

No more shall they in bondage toil,
> Let my people go;
Let them come out with Egypt's spoil,
> Let my people go.
Go down, Moses, etc.

Source text

Jubilee Songs: As Sung by the Jubilee Singers, of Fisk University (New York: Biglow & Main, 1872), 28, 22.

References

'The Jubilee Singers', *Musical Standard* 4.459 (17 May 1873), 312.
Milner, Gabriel, 'The Tenor of Belonging: The Fisk Jubilee Singers and the Popular Cultures of Postbellum Citizenship', *Journal of the Gilded Age and Progressive Era* 15.4 (October 2016), 399–417.
Newland, Marti, 'Concert Spirituals and the Fisk Jubilee Singers', *American Music Review* 40.1 (October 2010), 4–15.
Thurman, Kira, 'Singing the Civilizing Mission in the Land of Bach, Beethoven, and Brahms: The Fisk Jubilee Singers in Nineteenth-century Germany', *Journal of World History* 27.3 (September 2016), 443–71.

Carrie Walls (1859–1935)

'Children's Exchange' (1887)

Why would a young African American woman, writing for a monthly school publication in the late 1880s, join her classmates in regularly incorporating material from her studies of English history and literature into her texts? What did her stories for young readers accrue in cultural capital from such moves? The article below, originally printed in the *Spelman Messenger*, exemplifies how Carrie Walls and her classmates drew on their knowledge of transatlantic culture to affirm their liberal arts learning in the face of forces demeaning their racial identity.

During post-Reconstruction, US Black leaders and their white allies turned to education as a source of strength. Basic literacy was necessary for navigating the politics in a 'New South' restricting Black males' newly won voting rights. Acquiring cultural literacy, meanwhile, provided a means for countering depictions of African Americans as inferior. While some race leaders embraced vocational education as the pragmatic avenue for uplift, others sought a liberal-arts-based curriculum (at least for those W. E. B. DuBois called the 'talented tenth' of well-educated leaders); though tensions between these viewpoints are often cast as a dichotomy between Booker T. Washington and DuBois, the range of educational enterprises operating in African American communities complicates this picture. Spelman, founded in Atlanta in 1881, offers one such counter-narrative by blending vocational training like that provided by its print shop with liberal arts study.

Spelman's teacher-administrators launched the *Messenger* to celebrate students' learning in action. One strategy for representing cultural literacy there involved appropriation of British literary-historical resources, an approach comparable to writing by professional African American authors as documented by Daniel Hack. Thus, in her columns, Carrie Walls demonstrated her knowledge of transatlantic culture while modelling for young readers a pathway to claim social capital through education.

'Children's Exchange'

Little folks: Send us your questions and ideas, and in exchange Cousin Carrie (a Spelman Student) will answer the questions and give items of interest from the field. Address—Miss Carrie P. Walls,[108] Spelman Seminary, Atlanta, Ga.[109]

DEAR CHILDREN:—

I wonder if others of you will be interested in the answer to Lillie's question?[110] Long[,] long years ago, a printer, living in "Merrie England,"[111] went to Gloucester to attend to some business. While there he set out one Sunday for a walk. As he passed through the streets his attention was drawn to the large number of neglected children, spending their Sundays so carelessly, and wickedly, never once thinking of God and His holy day. The tender heart of Robert Raikes—for it was he—was moved with pity, and he began to think what he could do for these neglected ones.[112] Within

---

108 Thanks to Carrie Walls Gassaway's great-grandson, Charles Kellogg, for sharing important details of her family history.

109 Walls's young readers did indeed respond via letters back to her, with at least one published text coming from Canada and numerous others from across the US.

110 Walls here references a letter printed in an earlier issue. Her 'Exchange' approach also showed up in this issue, as she presented two recent letters from other child readers, one in Washington DC, and one in Thomasville, Georgia.

111 Walls's quotes around "Merrie England" suggest she was aware of the ways in which that phrase conjured nostalgia for an earlier, better version of the country – one pre-industrial and resisting class divides – then popular in Victorian culture. See 'Merrie England' in the online *Oxford Reference*.

112 Robert Raikes (1736–1811) succeeded his father as manager of the *Gloucester Journal* in 1757. While a myth-like aura has grown up around the story of his founding a local Sunday School, it appears to have some basis in real-life experience, and he certainly used his periodical to promote the movement (*ODNB*).

their dirty, ragged, little bodies he could see souls, sin-stained and defiled, which, if brought into the sunlight of God's truth, would, like slender sickly plants carried from the darkness to the sunlight, grow fresh and strong, making this beautiful, bright world more beautiful and bright. Like all good thoughts, his were not in vain; soon a house was hired and four ladies were engaged to teach, every Sunday afternoon, just as many children as would come. Gladly the little ones flocked to hear the truth, till very soon there were many schools instead of one. God's smile of approval must have rested on this noble man as he quietly set about and carried on this work of love. But does it not seem strange to us, in this land of Sunday schools that those who taught in Gloucester were paid for their service? Nor were those schools much like what we have. Before many years there were Sunday schools all over England; and hundreds of poor little children, who once were sad and neglected now rejoiced and were "Merrie" in the sunshine of Christain [*sic*] love and care.

So the grand work grew and grew till the little island of England could no longer hold it and it came across the water to bless the children and the homes of our own dear land. Our first school was started over ninety-six years ago, in Philadelphia.[113] Do you wonder that good men love to talk of Robert Raikes and that when one hundred years had passed away, a grand celebration was held throughout this and other lands, in honor of the founder of Sabbath schools? Do not my little friends all wish to become earnest Sunday school teachers when they are grown? You can be very helpful little workers now by your presence in the school and by paying close attention to all that is said and done, that you may tell it to others and interest them, then they too will want to be Sunday school scholars.[114]

Lovingly, COUSIN CARRIE[115]

Source text

Walls, Carrie, 'Children's Exchange', *Spelman Messenger* 3.6 (April 1887), 6.

References

Hack, Daniel, *Reaping Something New*: *African American Transformations of Victorian Literature* (Princeton, NJ: Princeton University Press, 2017).

Robbins, Sarah Ruffing, '"That My Work May Speak Well for Spelman": *Messengers* Recording History and Performing Uplift', *Learning Legacies: Archive to Action through Women's Cross-Cultural Teaching* (Ann Arbor, MI: University of Michigan Press, 2017), 37–78.

---

113 Walls may be referring to schools opened in Philadelphia by an inter-denominational organisation, the Sunday School Union, in 1791.

114 One way of appreciating Walls's invocation of Raikes's efforts is to see how, in her final sentences, she shifts from noting that 'good men love to talk of Robert Raikes' to asking her child readers to imagine themselves not just attending a school but, when they are older, teaching one. Thus, to use Hack's term, Walls draws from a transatlantic cultural resource gleaned from her studies to generate an 'African Americanisation' of that resource – in this case, the Sunday School. Accordingly, she shifts from revisiting the movement's history in the UK to reconfiguring Sunday School as an uplift site for her race.

115 Walls herself continued to draw on her studies for teaching after graduation. She worked from 1890 to 1919 at a school in Belton, South Carolina (near Anderson), with her spouse Mark H. Gassaway (1854–?), serving 1,200 students. Sadly, however, a family move to the Midwest came not by choice. The Gassaways had to hurriedly escape Anderson, abandoning their beloved school, due to death threats associated with Mark's NAACP leadership – a devastating personal and communal loss demonstrating that race uplift through education remained a fragile goal. The NAACP's magazine reported in chilling detail on the threats made against the Gassaway family and their narrow escape in 'Modern Migrants', *The Crisis* 19.2 (December 1919), 70–2.

Celestine Edwards (1857?–94)

Introduction, United States Atrocities: Lynch Law, by *Ida B. Wells (1892)*

The son of formerly enslaved West Indians, Samuel Jules Celestine Edwards was born in Dominica, travelled the world as a sailor starting in his teens, and ultimately settled in Britain, first in Edinburgh, then London. In Britain he discovered his talent for oratory in lectures and lay sermons. A committed Christian, Edwards converted during his early education in Antigua to Methodism, influenced by his tutor Rev. Henry Mason Joseph, future head of Britain's African Association, and in London earned a Diploma in Theology from King's College, becoming a popular lecturer among white East End workers. Though Protestant himself, his journalism ultimately attributed the origins of Western slavery and Anglo-Saxon racism to England and the linkage of English Protestantism to commerce (Lorimer, 739–41). Both as an orator and writer, he advocated tirelessly for all African descendants, whether situated transatlantically or in Africa.

Figure 1.5 S. J. Celestine Edwards, Editor of *Lux*, with a copy of his journal displayed (1894). Courtesy National Archives, London, catalogue number COPY1-417-501.

When he founded *Lux*, a weekly Christian paper, in 1892, he became the first Black editor in Britain. The same year his newspaper company published the anti-lynching pamphlet by US journalist and activist Ida B. Wells (1862–1931), *United States Atrocities*. In 1893 Wells toured Britain and, with her English friend Catherine Impey (1847–1923), founder of *Anti-Caste*, a journal dedicated to fighting global racial discrimination, and Isabella Fyvie Mayo (1843–1914), established the Society for the Recognition of the Brotherhood of Man. They recruited Edwards as their organisation's secretary and editor of the journal *Fraternity*.

Edwards's introduction to Wells's pamphlet was prefaced by Frederick Douglass's 25 October 1892 letter to Wells and 'Scene of a Lynching in Clanton, Alabama', a photo later reproduced in *Anti-Caste* (1893) and Wells's own *A Red Record* (1895) (Bressey, 114–15).

Introduction, **United States Atrocities: Lynch Law,** *by Ida B. Wells*

Although this is neither the time nor place to make an exhaustive defence for the unfortunate Negro race—in the United States of America—for the highly-coloured charges brought against him by the "mean whites," and those who are influenced by their prejudices, I will assume that all the charges are true, and that the Negro "difficulty must last till the way has been found out by which the Ethiopian may change his skin, or till either the white man or the black man departs out of the land." In the meantime, the white man's deadly hatred for the Negro is so great that Mr. W. Laird Clowes observed in 1891 that, "If the racial crimes and outrages which are of daily occurrence in the Southern States were taking place in a semi-civilised part of Europe, and were only half as well advertised as the events in Bulgaria were, the public sentiment of Europe would at once insist upon, and would within six months secure reform, even at the cost of war. Such a situation as sullies the South is a disgrace to the fair name of Anglo-Saxon civilisation."[116] As every effect is said to have a cause, it is only proper that the reader should ask, why do white men murder, torture, and lynch the Negro in the South as they do? If the white man was just and straightforward he would not make the answer which Mr. Laird Clowes has put in his mouth, viz., that it is "Because no white woman is safe from hour to hour in the black country district," because he would have sufficient common sense to know that the chastity of white women is perfectly safe in every country where the Negro is in the majority, and that the *real* cause lies, not in the Negro's fondness to outrage white women, but in the fact that slavery was abolished by force—physical force, and without compensation to the slaveholder.[117] Seeing that he cannot reek[118] his vengeance upon those who suddenly sprang upon him and forced the Negro's freedom at the point of the bayonet—seeing that he received no compensation, and, therefore, was left a mere pauper to struggle for existence alongside the ex-slave, whom the United States constitution placed upon the same political level as himself, the white man, who aforetime fared sumptuously upon, and at the moral degradation of the Negro, brings, for pure spite, foul charges against him, in the hope that he will once more enslave or exterminate the Negro. Besides, the white man, who boasts of superior mental power, must know that the immoral tendencies which he attributes to the Negro of to-day is greatly due to himself, because for three hundred years he kept him like a horse and bred him as a pig. Is it likely, therefore, that the vice which he so carefully sowed in his nature should be erased by twenty-six years of freedom? Where is the race or nation that was ever regenerated in the same time, or anyway near it? Is it not expecting too much from a people who are said to be ever so much inferior to the white man? How is it we do not find similar charges brought against the West Indian Negroes, as the trumped-up stories of rape and outrage in the southern states? How is it that missionaries in Africa do not impeach the Negroes who are much more savage than those in the South? Moreover, if it is true that Negroes thus misconduct themselves, what right have white men to withhold a fair trial in a Court of Law, or brutally Lynch men who could be easily convicted, if the charges are true? That their ruthless barbarity will not go on for ever is obvious, for already some Southern whites are crying

---

116 Sir William Laird Clowes (1856–1905), *Black America: A Study of the Ex-Slave and His Late Master* (London: Cassell & Co. 1891), 130.
117 Clowes, 131–2.
118 To inflict or take (vengeance, etc.) *on* or *upon* a person (*OED*)

shame upon the reckless lynchers, and justice for the Negro. Mr. W. Laird Clowes was good enough to publish the following in 1891, which appeared in the Augusta (Georgia) *Chronicle* of January 5th, 1890:—

> "Laws are powerless either to prevent the commission of crimes or to punish criminals, unless public sentiment forbids the one and commands the other. Where there is little regard for human life, and we fear this is the case in many portions of our country, the Courts are often to blame for not hanging those who slay their fellowmen. Is it not a fact that it is almost impossible to convict a man of the crime of murder who has any social position or means to defend himself. Fortunately, crimes of this sort do not often occur, but if they did, public sentiment is so demoralised that the Courts would fail of conviction. This is true as to white men who kill their equals. If a Negro kills a white man, he is pretty sure to be lynched or hung; but if a white man slays a Negro, he is in no danger of being lynched, and as to his being hung for the crime, there is no such probability."[119]

There is not a word said about a Negro outraging white women here; it is a mere statement of the evil effects of racial hatred in the South. If a white man thinks that a Negro has offended him, that is quite enough; he kills the Negro with perfect impunity; and the more it is done without punishment, the more it will be done. I do not ask for cantish[120] sympathy for the Negro, but justice—the common birthright of every man. What a hubbub there would be in Europe if the Africans were to turn upon the whites in any part of Africa, under similar pretence, and kill white people without their having the option of defending themselves. Let a Turkish Pasha[121] issue an edict against American missionaries and see how the United States and other representatives will busy themselves in endeavouring to secure justice for the white man and Christian. The Negro did not go to America by choice, he had very little to say in securing his freedom, his moral character has been formed for him by the slaveholder, which character suffered in consequence of the condition in which he lived; the Negro has adopted his religion and language, his tastes and habits, the same as the English copied somebody else's. In short, the Negro is exactly what the slave system made him; is it likely that in the short period of emancipation he should become a better man than the ex-slave-holder? Is not the life of a Negro as precious to him as the white man's, is to himself and his friends? If the Negro abuses the law under which he lives, he should be tried and punished accordingly to that law, and conversely, because the white man violates the law of the country by murders, lynches, and other outrages, he, too, should be tried and punished accordingly. The Negro asks for nothing more than justice. He does not require another Civil War to settle the vexed racial question, because experience has taught that "Peace hath her own victories, no less renowned than war,"[122] and the object of the present pamphlet is to create a strong public feeling against injustice, and to awaken the right kind of sympathy for a people who under the most provoking circumstances have on the whole, shown much more forbear-ance than many other races would have done under like circumstances. It is believed

---

119 Clowes, 128.
120 Affected or unreal use of religious or pietistic phraseology (*OED*)
121 High-ranking member of the Ottoman Empire's political system, presumably allied with Islam
122 John Milton (1608–74), Sonnet XVI, addressed 'To the Lord General [Oliver] Cromwell', lines 10–11

that by giving this pamphlet to the English people, it will not only direct attention to a condition of things which have been allowed to continue too long, but it will, I hope, awaken the love of fairness in the mind of every Englishman, so that influence—moral and religious influences—will be brought to bear upon the American Government, as it was their good fortune to bring upon the Turks, and thereby ameliorated the condition of the Bulgarians and Egyptians, and conferred untold blessings upon a people who will ever be grateful to England.[123] I know how grateful the Negroes of Canada and the West Indies are to English people, and it is certain that those of the United States will be equally so, if this nation will use her mighty moral and religious influence on their behalf. In collecting her facts, Miss Ida B. Wells has taken the greatest possible care, and, knowing the strong hatred of the race, and their general disabilities in the South, I trust that her pamphlet will have a very wide circulation, and awaken public sympathy, such as will tend to secure justice for the poor down-trodden Negro, on whose behalf it is written.

    S.J. CELESTINE EDWARDS (Editor of *Lux*.)

Source text

Edwards, S. J. Celestine, 'Introduction', in I. B. Wells, *United States Atrocities: Lynch Law* (London: 'Lux' Newspaper and Publishing Company, 1892), v–vii. Copy for this project provided by the Schomburg Center for Research in Black Culture, Manuscripts, Archives and Rare Books Division, New York Public Library.

References

ANB
Bressey, Caroline, *Empire, Race and the Politics of* Anti-Caste (London: Bloomsbury Academic, 2013).
Fryer, Peter, *Staying Power: The History of Black People in Britain* (London: Pluto Press, 2010).
Lorimer, Douglas A., 'Legacies of Slavery for Race, Religion, and Empire: S. J. Celestine Edwards and the *Hard Truth* (1894)', *Slavery and Abolition* 39.4 (2018), 731–5.
ODNB
Zackodnik, Teresa, 'Ida B. Wells and "American Atrocities" in Britain', *Women's Studies International Forum* 28 (July–August 2005), 259–73.

Henry W. Nevinson (1856–1941)

From 'The New Slave-Trade: Introductory—Down the West Coast' (1905)

Henry Woodd Nevinson, an English journalist, landed on the coast of Portuguese West Africa (now Angola) in December 1904. On assignment

---

123 In 1876 the US Consul General in Istanbul, Eugene Schuyler, and US journalist Januarius MacGahan investigated reports of a Turkish massacre of Bulgarian Christians. The coverage of the atrocities helped sway opinion in both the US and Britain, which had earlier supported the Turks against the Russians.

for the American periodical *Harper's Monthly Magazine*, he gathered information for a series of articles describing the inhumane conditions of contract labour. Excerpts from Part I appear below.

Though Portugal had abolished slavery in its colonies in the 1870s, plantation owners enacted a state-enabled replacement whose corrupt goals Nevinson revealed. Local peoples, though often illiterate, could 'sign' papers, supposedly of their own free will, committing to years of low-wage labour for the European colonisers' benefit.

Nevinson witnessed many indicators of how the contract labour system had created a 'new slave-trade'. Human bones littered the sides of trails, marking the death of enslaved workers who had become too weak to walk. Nevinson also found shackles that had bound hands and legs hanging from them. Crossing into Caconda, a largely abandoned town, he encountered a Catholic mission whose priests opposed this 'new' enslavement practice but were afraid to challenge the system overtly. Preparing to sail home, Nevinson suffered from a suspicious fever. Evidence suggested a poisoning aimed at stopping his investigation. Nevinson responded by arranging to have his reports sent to England, should he die. The intrepid reporter left São Tomé on 30 June 1905, arriving back in Britain on 21 July. He then published his series, including graphic photographs, in *Harper's*, followed by his 1906 book, *A Modern Slavery*.

From 'The New Slave-Trade: Introductory—Down the West Coast'

Since the Berlin Conference of 1885[124] *the African slave-trade is said to have ceased. As a matter of fact, it has assumed a more subtle and a more insidious form. In the summer of 1904 the management of* Harper's Magazine *arranged to send an expedition to Africa, under Henry W. Nevinson, to make an investigation of present conditions, and to find out and report the truth concerning the slave-trade of to-day. Mr. Nevinson is one of the most distinguished of English war correspondents, the author of several important books, and a man of standing, who has already given much time to philanthropic work. Mr. Nevinson sailed from England, October, 1904, to make his first investigations in Portuguese West Africa. At this writing he is somewhere in the interior.—EDITOR.*

For miles on miles there is no break in the monotony of the scene. Even when the air is calmest the surf falls heavily upon the long, thin line of yellow beach, throwing its white foam far up the steep bank of sand. And beyond the yellow beach runs the long, thin line of purple forest—the beginning of that dark forest belt which stretches from Sierra Leone through West and Central Africa to the lakes of the Nile. Surf, beach, and forest—for two thousand miles that is all, except where some great estuary makes a gap, or where the line of beach rises to a low cliff, or where a few distant hills, leading up to Ashanti, can be seen above the forest trees.

It is not a cheerful part of the world—"the Coast." Every prospect does not please, nor is it only man that is vile. Man, in fact, is no more vile than elsewhere;

---

124 At the Berlin Conference European nations met to create rules to divide Africa up for colonisation, marking the climax of their competition for territory in the continent.

but if he is white he is very often dead. We pass in succession the white man's settlements, with their ancient names so full of tragic and miserable history—Axim, Sekundi, Cape Coast Castle, and Lagos. We see the old forts, built by Dutch and Portuguese to protect their trade in ivory and gold and the souls of men. They still gleam, white and cool as whitewash can make them, among the modern erections of tin and iron that have a meaner birth. And always, as we pass, some "old Coaster" will point to a drain or an unfinished church, and say, "That was poor Andersson's last bit." And always when we stop and the officials come off the ship, drenched by the surf in spite of the skill of native crews, who drive the boats with rapid paddles, hissing sharply at every stroke to keep the time—always the first news is of sickness and death. Its form is brief: "Poor Smythe down—fever." "Poor Cunliffe gone—blackwater."[125] "Poor Tomkinson scuppered[126]—natives." Everyone says, "Sorry," and there's no more to be said.

It is not cheerful. The touch of fate is felt the more keenly because the white people are so few. For the most part, they know each other, at all events by classes. A soldier knows a soldier. Unless he is very military, indeed, he knows the district commissioner, and other officials as well. An official knows an official, and is quite on speaking terms with the soldiers. A trader knows a trader, and ceases to watch him with a malignant jealousy when he dies. It is hard to realize how few the white men are, scattered among the black swarms of the natives. I believe that in the six-mile radius round Lagos (the largest "white" town on the Coast) the whites could not muster 150 among the 140,000 blacks. And in the great walled city of Abbeokuta, to which the bit of railway from Lagos runs, among a black population of 205,000 the whites could hardly make up twenty, all told. So that when one white man disappears he leaves a more obvious gap than he would in a London street, and any white man may win a three days' fame by dying.

Among white women, a loss is naturally still more obvious and deplorable. Speaking generally, we may say the only white women on the Coast are nurses and missionaries. A benevolent government forbids soldiers and officials to bring their wives out. The reason given is the deadly climate, though there are other reasons, and an exception seems to be made in the case of a governor's wife. She enjoys the liberty of dying at her own discretion. But Accra, almost alone of the Coast towns, boasts the presence of two or three English ladies, and I have known men overjoyed at being ordered to appointments there. Not that they were any more devoted to the society of ladies than we all are, but they hoped for a better chance of surviving in a place where ladies live. Vain hope; in spite of cliffs and clearings, in spite of golf and polo, and ladies too, Death counts his shadows at Accra much the same as anywhere else. [...]

Until the white man develops a new kind of blood and a new kind of inside, the Coast will kill him. Till then we shall know the old Coaster by the yellow and streaky pallor of a blood destroyed by fevers, by a confused and uncertain memory, and by a puffiness that comes from enfeebled muscle quite as often as from insatiable thirst.

It is through swamps like these that those unheard-of "punitive expeditions" of ours, with a white officer or two, a white sergeant or two, and a handful of trusty Hausa men, have to fight their way, carrying their Maxim[127] and three-inch guns

---

125 Probably blackwater fever, a dangerous, often fatal, complication of malaria
126 To force a failure
127 A repeating early machine gun; see Rogers, 'Gun of the Age', in ST.

upon their heads. "I don't mind as long as the men don't sink above the fork," said the commandant of one of them to me. And it is beside these swamps that the traders, for many short-lived generations past, have planted their "factories."

The word "factory" points back to a time when the traders made the palm-oil themselves. The natives make nearly the whole of it now and bring it down the rivers in casks, but the "factories" keep their name, though they are now little more than depots of exchange and retail trade. Formerly they were made of the hulks of ships, anchored out in the rivers, and fitted up as houses and stores. A few of the hulks still remain, but of late years the traders have chosen the firmest piece of "beach" they could find, or else have created a "beach" by driving piles into the slime, and on these shaky and unwholesome platforms have erected dwelling-houses with big verandas, a series of sheds for the stores, and a large barn for the shop. Here the "agent" (or sometimes the owner of the business) spends his life, with one or two white assistants, a body of native "boys" as porters and boatmen, and usually a native woman, who in the end returns to her tribe and hands over her earnings in cash or goods to her chief. [...]

In the midst of all such contradictions, what is to be the real relation of the white races to the black races? That is the ultimate problem of Africa. We need not think it has been settled by a century's noble enthusiasm about the Rights of Man and Equality in the sight of God. Outside a very small and diminishing circle in England and America, phrases of that kind have lost their influence, and for the men who control the destinies of Africa they have no meaning whatever. Neither have they any meaning for the native. He knows perfectly well that the white people do not believe them.

The whole problem is still before us, as urgent and as uncertain as it has ever been. It is not solved. What seemed a solution is already obsolete. The problem will have to be worked through again from the start. Some of the factors have changed a little. Laws and regulations have been altered. New and respectable names have been invented. But the real issue has hardly changed at all. It has become a part of the worldwide issue of capital, but the question of African slavery still abides.

We may, of course, draw distinctions. The old-fashioned export of human beings as a reputable and staple industry on a level with the export of palm-oil, has disappeared from the Coast. Its old headquarters were at Lagos, and scattered about that district and in Nigeria and up the Congo one can still see the remains of the old barracoons[128] where the slaves were herded for sale or shipment. In passing up the rivers you may suddenly come upon a large square clearing. It is overgrown now, but the bush is not so high and thick as the surrounding forest, and palms take the place of the mangrove-trees. Sometimes a little Ju-ju house[129] is built by the water's edge, with fetishes inside; and perhaps the natives have placed it there with some dim sense of expiation. For the clearing is the site of an old barracoon, and misery has consecrated the soil. Such things leave a perpetual curse behind. The English and the Portuguese were the largest slave-traders upon the Coast, and it is their descendants who are still paying the heaviest penalty. But that ancient kind of slave-trade may for the present be set aside. The British gunboats have made it so difficult and so unlucrative that slavery has been driven to take subtler forms, against which gunboats have hitherto been powerless.

---

128 An enclosure in which Black slaves were confined for a limited period
129 Juju is a spiritual belief system incorporating objects, such as amulets, and spells used in religious practice, as part of witchcraft in West Africa.

Figure 1.6 Slaves on Ship, Wearing Tin Disk and Cylinder; from Henry Nevinson, 'The Slave-Trade of To-Day: Part VI—The Slaves at Sea', *Harper's Monthly Magazine* 112 (January 1906), 239. Courtesy Mary Couts Burnett Library, TCU.

We may draw another distinction still.

Quite different from the plantation slavery under European control, for the profit of European capitalists, is the domestic slavery that has always been practised among the natives themselves. Legally, this form of slavery was abolished in Nigeria by a proclamation of 1901, but it still exists in spite of the law, and is likely to exist for many years, even in British possessions. It is commonly spoken of as domestic slavery, but perhaps tribal slavery would be the better word. Or the slave might be compared to the serf of feudal times. He is nominally the property of the chief, and may be compelled to give rather more than half his days to work for the tribe. Even under the Nigerian enactment, he cannot leave his district without the chief's consent, and he must continue to contribute something to the support of the family. But in most cases a slave may purchase his freedom if he wishes, and it frequently happens that a slave becomes a chief himself and holds slaves on his own account. [. . .]

When a woman who has been hired as a white man's concubine is compelled to surrender her earnings to the chief, we may call it a survival of tribal slavery, or of the patriarchal system, if you will. But when, as happens, for instance, in Mozambique, the agents of capitalists bribe the chiefs to force laborers to the Transvaal mines, whether they wish to go or not, we may disguise the truth as we like under talk about "the dignity of labor" and "the value of discipline," but, as a matter of fact, we are on the downward slope to the new slavery. It is easy to see how one system may become merged into the other without any very obvious breach of native custom. But, nevertheless, the distinction is profound. As Mr. Morel has said in his admirable book on *The Affairs of West Africa*, between the domestic servitude of Nigeria and plantation slavery under European supervision there is all the difference in the world. The object of the present series of sketches is to show, by one particular instance, the method under which this plantation slavery is now being carried on, and the lengths to which it is likely to develop.

Source text

Nevinson, Henry W., 'The New Slave-Trade: Introductory. Down the West Coast', *Harper's Monthly Magazine* 111. 663 (August 1905), 341–50.

References:

'African Slavery: Mr. Henry W. Nevinson's Graphic Study of Conditions On The West Coast Of Africa', *New York Times*, Book Review (9 June 1906), 369.
Satre, Lowell J., *Chocolate on Trial: Slavery, Politics, and the Ethics of Business* (Athens, OH: Ohio University Press, 2005).

W. E. B. DuBois (1868–1963)

'Returning Soldiers' (1919)

As a US sociologist, civil rights activist, educator and historian, W. E. B. DuBois laboured tirelessly to promote social justice. Serving from 1910 to 1934 as editor of *The Crisis* magazine of the National Association for the Advancement of Colored People (NAACP), he wrote hundreds of articles championing civil rights, resisting racial terror and promoting African American artistic productivity.

In a July 1918 *Crisis* editorial, shifting focus and thereby surprising many readers, DuBois called for support of the global World War:

> This is the crisis of the world. For all the long years to come men will point to the year 1918 as the great Day of Decision, the day when the world decided whether it would submit to military despotism and an endless armed peace—if peace it could be called—or whether they would put down the menace of German militarism and inaugurate the United States of the World. ('Close Ranks', 111)

He called for temporarily setting aside the campaign for racial justice: 'Let us, while this war lasts, forget our special grievances and close our ranks shoulder to shoulder with our own white fellow citizens and the allied nations that are fighting for democracy.' He linked race pride with long-term hope: 'We make no ordinary sacrifice, but we make it gladly and willingly with our eyes lifted to the hills' ('Close Ranks', 111).

In 1919, as soldiers returned from transatlantic service, DuBois published a related piece, this one marking his disappointment – indeed, his righteous anger – at the continued unjust treatment of his race. He decried the hypocrisy of a nation that had claimed to defend global freedom abroad, yet still purposefully upheld white supremacy at home.

'Returning Soldiers'

We are returning from war! THE CRISIS and tens of thousands of black men were drafted into a great struggle. For bleeding France and what she means and has meant and will mean to us and humanity and against the threat of German race arrogance, we fought gladly and to the last drop of blood; for America and her highest ideals, we fought in far-off hope; for the dominant southern oligarchy entrenched in Washington, we fought in bitter resignation. For the America that represents and gloats in lynching, disfranchisement, caste, brutality and devilish insult—for this, in the hateful upturning and mixing of things, we were forced by vindictive fate to fight, also.

But today we return! We return from the slavery of uniform which the world's madness demanded us to don to the freedom of civil garb. We stand again to look America squarely in the face and call a spade a spade. We sing: This country of ours, despite all its better souls have done and dreamed, is yet a shameful land.

It *lynches*.

And lynching is barbarism of a degree of contemptible nastiness unparalleled in human history. Yet for fifty years we have lynched two Negroes a week, and we have kept this up right through the war.

It *disfranchises* its own citizens.

Disfranchisement is the deliberate theft and robbery of the only protection of poor against rich and black against white. The land that disfranchises its citizens and calls itself a democracy lies and knows it lies.

It encourages *ignorance*.

It has never really tried to educate the Negro.[130] A dominant minority does not want Negroes educated. It wants servants, dogs, whores and monkeys. And when this land allows a reactionary group by its stolen political power to force as many black folk into these categories as it possibly can, it cries in contemptible hypocrisy: "They threaten us with degeneracy; they cannot be educated."

It *steals* from us.

It organizes industry to cheat us. It cheats us out of our land; it cheats us out of our labor. It confiscates our savings. It reduces our wages. It raises our rent. It steals our profit. It taxes us without representation. It keeps us consistently and universally poor, and then feeds us on charity and derides our poverty.[131]

---

130 During this era when access to higher education was elusive for Black Americans, DuBois himself represented an exception. He earned his first bachelor's degree from Fisk University in 1888 and another from Harvard in 1890. He subsequently studied abroad on a doctoral fellowship at the University of Berlin from 1892 to 1894. After returning to the US, DuBois in 1895 became the first African American to earn a PhD from Harvard.

131 See Dialika Sall and Shamus Khan on DuBois's moving beyond his famous 'talented tenth' construction of Black elites as a source of race uplift (514).

It *insults* us.

It has organized a nation-wide and latterly a world-wide propaganda of deliberate and continuous insult and defamation of black blood wherever found. It decrees that it shall not be possible in travel nor residence, work nor play, education nor instruction for a black man to exist without tacit or open acknowledgment of his inferiority to the dirtiest white dog. And it looks upon any attempt to question or even discuss this dogma as arrogance, unwarranted assumption and treason.

This is the country to which we Soldiers of Democracy return. This is the fatherland for which we fought! But it is *our* fatherland. It was right for us to fight. The faults of *our* country are *our* faults. Under similar circumstances, we would fight again. But by the God of Heaven, we are cowards and jackasses if now that that war is over, we do not marshal every ounce of our brain and brawn to fight a sterner, longer, more unbending battle against the forces of hell in our own land.[132]

We *return.*

We *return from fighting.*

We *return fighting.*

Make way for Democracy! We saved it in France, and by the Great Jehovah, we will save it in the United States of America, or know the reason why.

Source text

DuBois, W. E. B., 'Returning Soldiers', *The Crisis*, 18.1 (May 1919), 13–14.

References

DuBois, W. E. B., 'Close Ranks', *The Crisis* 16.3 (July 1918), 111.

Lomotey-Nakon, Leah Lomoki, 'DuBois's Decolonial Pragmatism: Teaching Community Psychology Toward Epistemological Liberation', *Community Psychology* 62.3–4 (December 2018), 364–73.

Sall, Dialika and Shamus Khan, 'What Elite Theory Should Have Learned, and Can Still Learn, from W. E. B. DuBois', *Ethnic and Racial Studies* 40.3 (2017), 512–14.

---

132 See Lomotey-Nakon on DuBois and 'decolonial theory' (366).

2

ART, AESTHETICS AND ENTERTAINMENT

Figure 2.1 Zitkala-Ša, Sioux Indian and Activist, photographed by Gertrude Käsebier, 1898. Courtesy Photographic History Collection, Division of Work and Industry, National Museum of American History, Smithsonian Institution.

As with many ideas, institutions and inventions referenced in this transatlantic anthology, the terms 'art' and 'aesthetics' emerged in the long nineteenth century. As Raymond Williams comments, 'The now normal association [of "art"] with *creative* and *imaginative*, as a matter of classification', essentially dates from the late eighteenth and early nineteenth centuries, while 'aesthetic', a German invention from Greek *aisthesis* designating 'sense perception', became common only in the mid-nineteenth century, its origin connoting 'an emphasis on subjective sense activity, and on the specialized human creativity of art'.[1]

These influential new terms emerged in tandem with increased cultural and symbolic power (or 'capital', in Pierre Bourdieu's phraseology)[2] attributed to creative writing. An oft-used alternative term dating back at least to the early eighteenth century was *belles lettres* (French for 'fine letters' [*OED*]). Both the older and newer designations connoted what was beautiful, set apart from the merely utilitarian – even if no print production ever escaped the literary marketplace that enabled publication in the first place. Still, the goal of those pursuing literature as an art rather than trade was beauty and cultural significance that superseded the (in)famous dictum of utilitarian philosopher Jeremy Bentham (1748–1832): 'Prejudice apart, the game of push-pin is of equal value with the arts and sciences of music and poetry. If the game of push-pin furnish more pleasure, it is more valuable than either.'[3] Here, in a nutshell, was the rationale for small- or large-scale popular entertainments, our third term in this section, a prime example in this section being William Cody's wildly popular Wild West Show that travelled to London in 1887. Entertainments had far wider appeal to audiences and involved a more diverse range of creative performers than the poetry, fiction, drama, and fine arts that demanded greater degrees of literacy, education, leisure and income if audiences were to access and fully appreciate them.

HIGH ART, LOW CULTURE

Given the high prestige of art and the aesthetic in the nineteenth century, two important themes in the poetry, criticism, reviews, lectures and song lyric included here are, first, transatlantic rivalries for cultural prestige in an era that associated great nations with great art, and second, contested standards of aesthetic achievement. In keeping with what counted as art, critics and theorists increasingly distinguished between 'high art' and 'low' (the merely popular), terms that have scant purchase on cultural production today but that registered personal and national prestige in the long nineteenth century.[4]

It is worth pausing to note performance arts both 'high' and 'low' in this and other sections of this anthology. For example, the songs and spirituals sung by enslaved workers in fields (see BIL) were later performed by the touring

---

1 Raymond Williams, *Keywords: A Vocabulary of Culture and Society* (Oxford: Oxford University Press, 1983), 41, 30.
2 Pierre Bourdieu, *Distinction: A Social Critique of the Judgment of Taste*, tr. Richard Nice (Cambridge, MA: Harvard University Press, 1984) and *The Field of Cultural Production* (New York: Columbia University Press, 1993).
3 Jeremy Bentham, *The Rationale of Reward* (London: John and H. L. Hunt, 1825), 206.
4 Because ours is a print anthology (albeit with a digital accompaniment), we necessarily take up the vital role of performing arts only insofar as discussions of them entered print.

African American Jubilee Singers (see AA); and their transatlantic presence today persists through concerts, recordings and special public occasions.[5] Music surfaces in this section in Frederick Douglass's review of Scottish ballads performed by William Dempster in Rochester, New York, at a Robert Burns celebration in 1849, and in Albert Chevalier's turn-of-the-century song 'The Yankee in London', based on popular music-hall traditions but performed at Queen's Hall in London, which opened in 1893 and hosted classical music concerts as well as celebrity performers like Chevalier. His performances, then, occurred at an intersection of low and high culture. Native writer Zitkala-Ša (excerpted in SC), a classically trained violinist, was also invited to merge high and popular culture by performing violin solos with the touring Carlisle Indian School band and reciting selections from Longfellow's *The Song of Hiawatha*; in addition to stops in the northeast US in 1900, the band travelled transatlantically to Paris, where Zitkala-Ša again performed solos.[6] The democratisation of visuality was another key development of the nineteenth century, both in printed illustrations (of which we give many samples throughout this anthology) and in the founding of public art galleries, which enabled popular audiences to view paintings and sculpture formerly sequestered in private collections.[7] The British Museum, which included art, opened in 1759 followed by London's National Gallery in 1824; the US opened its first major art gallery, the Metropolitan Museum of Art ('the Met'), in 1870. This last was itself a transatlantic event, since the idea for it was hatched at a 4 July 1866 dinner in Paris celebrating American Independence and subsequently carried forward by abolitionist and attorney John Jay II (1817–94) when he returned to New York.[8] British and US reviews of art exhibitions were regularly printed in periodicals, sometimes profusely illustrated (as in the *Illustrated London News*) and exhibition catalogues were an important revenue source for printers.[9] In this section art is represented by William Cullen Bryant's 'Sonnet – To an American Painter Departing for Europe' and Oscar Wilde's lecture in the US on decorative art. It should be recalled too that the London-published volume of Phillis Wheatley's poems, three of which appear in this anthology (see AA, RS and NC), featured a frontispiece portrait thought to be by enslaved artist

---

5 For example, when the distinguished judge and civil rights advocate Supreme Court Justice Ruth Bader Ginsburg died late in 2020, the spiritual 'Deep River' was performed by a favourite opera singer of Ginsburg's, Denyce Graves, at the US Capitol memorial service (25 September 2020). A counter use of music associated with the enslaved occurred in racist minstrel shows, in which white and sometimes Black cast members performed in blackface.

6 Ruth Spack, 'Zitkala-Ša, *The Song of Hiawatha*, and the Carlisle Indian School Band: A Captivity Tale', *Legacy* 25.2 (2008), 211–24; 'Observations', *Violin Times* 7 (June 1900), 138.

7 British country houses opened their doors and private collections to visitors, but, as Jocelyn Anderson notes, only to 'genteel travellers' ('"Worth viewing by travellers": Arthur Young and Country House Picture Collections in the Late Eighteenth Century', in Jon Stobart (ed.), *Travel and the British Country House: Cultures, Critiques and Consumption in the Long Eighteenth Century* (Manchester: Manchester University Press, 2017), 127).

8 Winifred E. Howe, *A History of the Metropolitan Museum of Art* (New York: Metropolitan Museum of Art, 1913), 99–101ff.

9 The Yale Center for British Art alone has over 6,000 catalogues dating from the eighteenth and nineteenth centuries.

Scipio Moorhead, to whom Wheatley addresses another poem in her book; a print of this portrait now forms part of the Met's collection in New York.

Theatre likewise crossed from high to low culture, from Shakespearean tragedies to melodramas or plays speedily adapted from popular novels, such as the best-selling *Uncle Tom's Cabin* by Harriet Beecher Stowe, including the solo performance by Black actress Mary Webb (see the review of Webb in AA). Charles Dickens's novels were likewise adapted to the stage in both London and New York, in some cases even before serialisation of a new novel was complete. Celebrity actors led to a convergence of theatre and painting in 'high' art, including the 1826 portrait by James Northcote of American-born Black actor Ira Frederick Aldridge (1807–67), the first Black actor to perform the role of Shakespeare's *Othello* in Britain.[10]

Charismatic preachers provided not only occcasions for worship but sometimes, additionally, forms of public entertainment (see Trollope, RS). We include few sermons in the anthology but do feature another form of oratory, the lecture, an important transatlantic medium (and income generator) for writers. Many of these lectures have been lost because they were not transcribed and printed.[11] An important exception is 'Decorative Art in America', one of three lectures presented across the US by Oscar Wilde in 1882. Theatre, music and literature converged in Wilde's lectures since, garbed in the 'aesthetic dress' memorably photographed by Napoleon Sarony (1821–96), he was promoting the comic operetta *Patience* by W. S. Gilbert (1836–1911) and Arthur Sullivan (1842–1900) prior to its opening in New York. *Patience* mocked aesthetes' pretensions to high art through the popular medium of broadly comic songs and acting.

Decorative art including handicrafts, the focus of Wilde's lecture, was another important source of transatlantic creative invention and production, from Native American beadwork, basket weaving, masks and headdresses to transatlantic silver smithing and crafting of timepieces to Black and white women's quilting.[12] Social protest handicrafts brought visibility to reform movements, with examples ranging from the Josiah Wedgwood abolitionist medallion of 1787, *Am I not a Man and a Brother*, to transatlantic women's suffrage banners, flags and poster art.

In addition to Wilde numerous other lecturers traversed the Atlantic, from Americans Frederick Douglass, William Wells Brown, William and Ellen Craft (see AA), Ralph Waldo Emerson and also Mark Twain in Britain to Dickens,

10 The portrait by Northcote (1746–1831) can be viewed at the Manchester Art Gallery, or in the copy included in London's National Portrait Gallery. For additional treatments of transatlantic celebrity see the special issue entitled 'Transatlantic Celebrity: European Fame in Nineteenth-Century America', ed. Paraic Finnerty and Rod Rosenquist, *Comparative American Studies* 14.1 (2016), 1–89.

11 See Tom Wright (ed.), *Transatlantic Rhetoric: Speeches from the American Revolution to the Suffragettes* (Edinburgh: Edinburgh University Press, 2020).

12 For Native arts, see Dan L. Monroe (ed.), *Gifts of the Spirit: Works by Nineteenth-Century and Contemporary Native American Artists* (Salem, MA: Peabody Essex Museum, 1996) and Steven C. Brown (ed.), *Spirits of the Water: Native Art Collected on Expeditions to Alaska and British Columbia, 1774–1910* (Seattle, WA: University of Washington Press, 2000).

Matthew Arnold and Emmeline Pankhurst in the US (see SC for this last).[13] These figures are a vivid reminder that both artists and art continuously travelled across the Atlantic throughout the long nineteenth century.

TRANSATLANTIC LITERARY CRITICISM

A majority of the following selections on art and aesthetics represent literary criticism. Particularly in the early nineteenth century, when Britain was still smarting from losing its former colony, British critics often scoffed at the upstart country's pretensions to art, as when Francis Jeffrey used the powerful voice of the *Edinburgh Review* in 1809 to dismiss American Joel Barlow's epic poem *The Columbiad* (1807) and charged not only that Barlow was no better than provincial British scribblers but also that the epic was a bygone genre in any case. His judgment was premature, belied by the outpouring of epic poems in the century, including Elizabeth Barrett Browning's *Aurora Leigh* (1856), which Susan B. Anthony identified as one of her best beloved books.[14] Sydney Smith, another *Edinburgh* reviewer, added further insult to Jeffrey's when he asked, 'Who reads an American book?' Though Dickens's reprinted fiction was enormously popular in the US, Charles Dickens further rankled American literary sensibilities when he excoriated American newspapers in *American Notes* (1842).[15] Nor did Matthew Arnold's US lecture tour of 1883–4 win him many sympathisers when he dismissed Ralph Waldo Emerson's poetry to secondary status. Arnold's final and equally unwelcome word on US culture came in 1888, the year of his death, in 'Civilisation in the United States', which censured Americans for their indifference to beauty.

The tables turned inevitably, perhaps most memorably when Walt Whitman called Arnold 'one of the dudes of literature'.[16] Much earlier in the century, one of the chapters in Washington Irving's *Sketches of Geoffrey Crayon* (1819–20), an undisputed influence on British writers including Dickens, was 'English Writers on America', which called out British 'animosity' against the fledgling country and warned that continued hostility might tell against Britain in the long run. Yet Irving also took care to affirm elements of English culture he admired. Decades later E. C. Stedman in 'Victorian Poets' (1873) deflated British literary

---

13 See Amanda Adams, *Performing Authorship in the Nineteenth-Century Transatlantic Lecture Tour* (Farnham: Ashgate, 2014). As Adams notes, transatlantic writers like Harriet Martineau and Harriet Beecher Stowe were widely feted when visiting abroad, but gender norms did not favour public presentation of the respectable female body (though Harriet Beecher Stowe sat on the stage). With the early twentieth century these conventions rapidly faded. In 1901 poet and essayist Alice Meynell gave lectures on seventeenth-century literature and Dickens as she travelled from New York to San Francisco in 1901; see Damian Atkinson (ed.), *The Selected Letters of Alice Meynell: Poet and Essayist* (Newcastle upon Tyne: Cambridge Scholars, 2013), 159. See also Daphne Brooks, *Bodies in Dissent: Spectacular Performances of Race and Freedom, 1850–1910* (Durham, NC: Duke University Press, 2006).

14 See Herbert F. Tucker, *Epic: Britain's Heroic Muse, 1790–1910* (Oxford: Oxford University Press, 2008).

15 Meredith McGill, *American Literature and the Culture of Reprinting, 1834–1853* (Philadelphia, PA: University of Pennsylvania Press, 2003), 109–40.

16 Horace Traubel, *With Walt Whitman in Camden*, volume 1 (Boston: Small, Maynard & Co., 1906), 45.

prestige when he suggested that Tennyson's work already seemed 'over-refined' and contended that British poetry's increasing sense of belatedness required new vigour and innovation. William Sharp, in 'The Sonnet in America' (1889), saw a similar 'lull' in American poetry at the century's end.

Two nineteenth-century literary movements mark the remaining selections: realism and aestheticism. Realism was especially relevant to commentary on the realist novel, and several excerpts we present also impinged on race and difference. George Eliot warmly praised Harriet Beecher Stowe's genius and her novel *Dred* in 1856, claiming (dubiously in retrospect) that Stowe had '*invented* the Negro novel' but closed by bringing a realist aesthetic to bear on the novel as she questioned whether Stowe had not overidealised her Black characters. In 1885 African American author Frances Ellen Watkins Harper turned to Eliot's 1868 poem of racial conflict, *The Spanish Gypsy*, to call for racial solidarity and shared commitment to education in her 'Factor in Human Progress'. In *A Voice from the South* (1892), Anna Julia Cooper partly echoed Eliot's praise of Stowe as she theorised two schools of Anglo-American writers, the didactic versus the truth tellers who wrote to please themselves; above all, she upheld the centrality of race and representations of Black life to American fiction, which set American apart from British literary creativity. Applying a realist aesthetic to critique stereotypical Black characters in white writers' fiction, she called on Black writers to write the truths they alone knew. In 1892 as well, First Nations author E. Pauline Johnson directed a parallel charge against white writers' stereotypical Indian characters. 'A Strong Race Opinion: On the Indian Girl in Modern Fiction' deftly reversed terminology, pointing out the absurdity of clumping all Americans or Europeans into a single homogeneous group just as white novelists too often presented a generic 'Indian' irrespective of crucial tribal differences. In essence, Cooper and Johnson were protesting the reification of people of colour into literary tropes and demanding equivalent complexity of realist characterisation seen in other figures.

Insofar as Cooper attributed lasting art only to those 'who write to please – or rather who write because *they* please' and censured 'writers with a purpose or a lesson', she was also writing from within a framework of aestheticism, which invoked art for art's sake and, especially in England, the pursuit of beauty apart from any morality. Edgar Allan Poe anticipated aestheticism in his review of *Barnaby Rudge* (1842) in critiquing Dickens's 'inartistic' fabrication of mystery by so wording a key passage as to obscure the obvious clues, thus driving his novel forward by inciting mere readerly curiosity. Arnold's praise of beauty above righteousness was likewise allied with aestheticism, as was John Addington Symonds's queer reading of Whitman's 'Calamus' poems. But the prime exemplar in this section is Oscar Wilde, whose lecture endorsed beauty *in* what was useful, from carpets to teacups, a key dimension of aestheticism and decorative arts manufacture that anticipated the transatlantic Arts and Crafts movement to follow.[17]

---

17 See Eileen Boris, *Art and Labor: Ruskin, Morris, and the Craftsman Ideal in America* (Philadelphia: Temple University Press, 1986).

References

Codell, Julie and Linda K. Hughes (eds), *Replication in the Long Nineteenth Century: Re-makings and Reproductions* (Edinburgh: Edinburgh University Press, 2018).

Krotz, Sarah Wylie, *Mapping with Words: Anglo-Canadian Literary Cartographies, 1789–1916* (Toronto: University of Toronto Press, 2018).

Lee, Maurice S., *Overwhelmed: Literature, Aesthetics, and the Nineteenth-Century Information Revolution* (Princeton, NJ: Princeton University Press, 2019).

Nasta, Susheila and Mark U. Stein (eds), *The Cambridge History of Black and Asian British Writing* (Cambridge: Cambridge University Press, 2019).

Siemerling, Winfried, *The Black Atlantic Reconsidered: Black Canadian Writing, Cultural History, and the Presence of the Past* (Montreal: McGill-Queen's University Press, 2015).

Taylor, Melanie Benson (ed.), *The Cambridge History of Native American Literature* (Cambridge: Cambridge University Press, 2020).

Joel Barlow (1754–1812)

From **The Columbiad** *(1807)*

Joel Barlow, born into a prosperous Connecticut farming family, was educated at Yale University and served as a chaplain during the Revolutionary War, before embarking on a successful career as a diplomat, most notably as US Minister to France. For a brief period he was associated with a group of conservative Federalist poets, known as the Connecticut Wits, whose members included Timothy Dwight, John Trumbull and David Humphreys. An early poem, *The Vision of Columbus* (1787), imagines Christopher Columbus granted sight of the future of the America that he has discovered. *The Columbiad* is an expanded version of this earlier work, in every sense. Its ten books present a political perspective that is more radical, embracing republican values against feudal, aristocratic ones, with a wider geographical scope and advocating a system of global trade built on 'navigators from Columbus through to Cook and Magellan who redefined the shape of the earth through their voyages of discovery' (Giles, 145). Columbus in this poem is offered a series of visions by Hesper, the star of the West, that now include those drawn from the Revolutionary Wars and which culminate, in Book 10, in a 'general congress' of nations united through free trade and commerce.

Barlow's epic poem draws on several well-established poetic traditions of the eighteenth century, many of which are now lost to us. As a result, *The Columbiad* has alienated modern readers, and only recently has it received the critical attention it deserves. It is written in heroic couplets, the form most favoured by Alexander Pope, whose translation of *The Iliad* influenced Barlow, while its references to classical mythology also represent a conventional structuring trope of the epic form. The English poet John Milton is the poem's other significant interlocutor, whose *Paradise Lost* is an eschatological vision of origins and, in Milton's case, decline.

The excerpt reprinted here is from the opening lines of the poem.

From **The Columbiad**

I sing the Mariner[18] who first unfurl'd
An eastern banner o'er the western world,
And taught mankind where future empires lay
In these fair confines of descending day;
Who sway'd a moment, with vicarious power,
Iberia's sceptre on the new found shore,
Then saw the paths his virtuous steps had trod
Pursued by avarice and defiled with blood,
The tribes he foster'd with paternal toil
Snatch'd from his hand, and slaughter'd for their spoil.
Slaves, kings, adventurers, envious of his name,
Enjoy'd his labours and purloin'd his fame,
And gave the Viceroy, from his high seat hurl'd,
Chains for a crown, a prison for a world.[19]
　Long overwhelm'd in woes, and sickening there,
He met the slow still march of black despair,
Sought the last refuge from his hopeless doom,
And wish'd from thankless men a peaceful tomb:
Till vision'd ages, opening on his eyes,
Cheer'd his sad soul, and bade new nations rise;
He saw the Atlantic heaven with light o'ercast,
And Freedom crown his glorious work at last.
　Almighty Freedom! give my venturous song
The force, the charm that to thy voice belong;
Tis thine to shape my course, to light my way,
To nerve my country with the patriot lay,
To teach all men where all their interest lies,
How rulers may be just and nations wise:
Strong in thy strength I bend no suppliant knee,
Invoke no miracle, no Muse but thee.
　Night held on old Castile[20] her silent reign,
Her half orb'd moon declining to the main;
O'er Valladolid's[21] regal turrets hazed
The drizzly fogs from dull Pisuerga[22] raised;
Whose hovering sheets, along the welkin[23] driven,
Thinn'd the pale stars, and shut the eye from heaven.
Cold-hearted Ferdinand his pillow prest,
Nor dream'd of those his mandates robb'd of rest,

---

18 Christopher Columbus (1451–1506)
19 After his third voyage to the Americas (1498–1500), Columbus was imprisoned on his return to Spain amid accusations of misrule in his governance of the West Indies. This is not something that Barlow chooses to acknowledge in his poem.
20 The Kingdom of Castile, a state in the Iberian peninsula, ruled over by Ferdinand II (1452–1516) and Isabella I (1451–1504)
21 City in Spain, the capital of Castile and location of Columbus's death in 1506
22 A river passing through the city of Valladolid
23 Sky, firmament (OED)

Of him who gemm'd his crown, who stretch'd his reign
To realms that weigh'd the tenfold poise of Spain;
Who now beneath his tower indungeon'd lies,
Sweats the chill sod and breathes inclement skies.
   His feverish pulse, slow laboring thro his frame,
Feeds with scant force its fast expiring flame;
A far dim watch-lamp's thrice reflected beam
Throws thro his grates a mist-encumber'd gleam,
Paints the dun vapors that the cell invade,
And fills with spectred forms the midnight shade;
When from a visionary short repose,
That nursed new cares and temper'd keener woes,
Columbus woke, and to the walls addrest
The deep felt sorrows bursting from his breast:
   Here lies the purchase, here the wretched spoil
Of painful years and persevering toil.
For these damp caves, this hideous haunt of pain,
I traced new regions o'er the chartless main,
Tamed all the dangers of untraversed waves,
Hung o'er their clefts, and topt their surging graves,
Saw traitorous seas o'er coral mountains sweep,
Red thunders rock the pole and scorch the deep,
Death rear his front in every varying form,
Gape from the shoals and ride the roaring storm,
My struggling bark her seamy planks disjoin,
Rake the rude rock and drink the copious brine.
Till the tired elements are lull'd at last,
And milder suns allay the billowing blast,
Lead on the trade winds with unvarying force,
And long and landless curve our constant course.
   Our homeward heaven recoils; each night forlorn
Calls up new stars, and backward rolls the morn;
The boreal vault descends with Europe's shore,
And bright Calisto[24] shuns the wave no more,
The Dragon[25] dips his fiery-foaming jole,[26]
The affrighted magnet flies the faithless pole;
Nature portends a general change of laws,
My daring deeds are deemed the guilty cause;
The desperate crew, to insurrection driven,
Devote their captain to the wrath of heaven,
Resolve at once to end the audacious strife,
And buy their safety with his forfeit life.
   In that sad hour, this feeble frame to save,
(Unblest reprieve) and rob the gaping wave,

---

24 In Greek mythology, Callisto was a nymph who, after being raped and becoming pregnant by Zeus, was transformed into a bear and placed among the stars as the constellation Ursa Major.
25 Draco (Latin for Dragon), a constellation in the northern sky
26 Jawbone (*OED*)

The morn broke forth, these tearful orbs descried
The golden banks that bound the western tide.
With full success I calm'd the clamorous race,
Bade heaven's blue arch a second earth embrace;
And gave the astonish'd age that bounteous shore,
Their wealth to nations, and to kings their power.
    Land of delights! ah, dear delusive coast,
To these fond aged eyes forever lost!
No more thy flowery vales I travel o'er,
For me thy mountains rear the head no more,
For me thy rocks no sparkling gems unfold,
Nor streams luxuriant wear their paths in gold;
From realms of promised peace forever borne,
I hail mute anguish, and in secret mourn.
    But dangers past, a world explored in vain,
And foes triumphant show but half my pain.
Dissembling friends, each early joy who gave,
And fired my youth the storms of fate to brave,
Swarm'd in the sunshine of my happier days,
Pursued the fortune and partook the praise,
Now pass my cell with smiles of sour disdain,
Insult my woes and triumph in my pain.
    One gentle guardian once could shield the brave;
But now that guardian slumbers in the grave.
Hear from above, thou dear departed shade;
As once my hopes, my present sorrows aid,
Burst my full heart, afford that last relief,
Breathe back my sighs and reinspire my grief;
Still in my sight thy royal form appears,
Reproves my silence and demands my tears.
Even on that hour no more I joy to dwell,
When thy protection bade the canvass swell;
When kings and churchmen found their factions vain,
Blind superstition shrunk beneath her chain,
The sun's glad beam led on the circling way,
And isles rose beauteous in Atlantic day.
For on those silvery shores, that new domain,
What crowds of tyrants fix their murderous reign!
Her infant realm indignant Freedom flies,
Truth leaves the world, and Isabella dies.
    Ah, lend thy friendly shroud to veil my sight,
That these pain'd eyes may dread no more the light;
These welcome shades shall close my instant doom,
And this drear mansion moulder to a tomb.
    Thus mourn'd the hapless man: a thundering sound
Roll'd thro the shuddering walls and shook the ground;
O'er all the dungeon, where black arches bend,
The roofs unfold, and streams of light descend;
The growing splendor fills the astonish'd room,
And gales etherial breathe a glad perfume.

Robed in the radiance, moves a form serene,
Of human structure, but of heavenly mien;
Near to the prisoner's couch he takes his stand,
And waves, in sign of peace, his holy hand.
Tall rose his stature, youth's endearing grace
Adorn'd his limbs and brighten'd in his face;
Loose o'er his locks the star of evening hung,
And sounds melodious moved his cheerful tongue:
　　Rise, trembling chief, to scenes of rapture rise;
This voice awaits thee from the western skies;
Indulge no longer that desponding strain,
Nor count thy toils, nor deem thy virtues vain.
Thou seest in me the guardian Power who keeps
The new found world that skirts Atlantic deeps,
Hesper[27] my name, my seat the brightest throne
In night's whole heaven, my sire the living sun,
My brother Atlas with his name divine
Stampt the wild wave; the solid coast is mine.
This hand, which form'd, and in the tides of time
Laves and improves the meliorating clime,
Which taught thy prow to cleave the trackless way,
And hail'd thee first in occidental day,
To all thy worth shall vindicate thy claim,
And raise up nations to revere thy name.
　　In this dark age tho blinded faction sways,
And wealth and conquest gain the palm of praise;
Awed into slaves while groveling millions groan,
And blood-stain'd steps lead upward to a throne;
Far other wreaths thy virtuous temples twine,
Far nobler triumphs crown a life like thine;
Thine be the joys that minds immortal grace,
As thine the deeds that bless a kindred race.
Now raise thy sorrowed soul to views more bright,
The vision'd ages rushing on thy sight;
Worlds beyond worlds shall bring to light their stores,
Time, nature, science blend their utmost powers,
To show, concentred in one blaze of fame,
The ungather'd glories that await thy name.
　　As that great seer,[28] whose animating rod
Taught Jacob's sons their wonder-working God,
Who led thro dreary wastes the murmuring band,
And reach'd the confines of their promised land,
Opprest with years, from Pisgah's[29] towering height,

---

27 In Greek mythology, Hesperus is the Evening Star, or the planet Venus. In the 'Argument' to
Book 1 of the poem, Barlow makes him 'the guardian of the western continent'.
28 Moses. Barlow summarises the narrative of Moses leading the Israelites to the Promised Land,
found in the Old Testament books of Exodus and Deuteronomy.
29 In the Bible, the name of a mountain (Mount Nebo in Jordan)

On fruitful Canaan feasted long his sight;
The bliss of unborn nations warm'd his breast,
Repaid his toils and sooth'd his soul to rest;
Thus o'er thy subject wave shalt thou behold
Far happier realms their future charms unfold,
In nobler pomp another Pisgah rise,
Beneath whose foot thy new found Canaan lies;
There, rapt in vision, hail my favorite clime,
And taste the blessings of remotest time.
　　So Hesper spoke; Columbus raised his head;
His chains dropt off; the cave, the castle fled.
Forth walked the Pair; when steep before them stood;
Slope from the town, a heaven-illumined road;
That thro disparting shades arose on high,
Reach'd o'er the hills, and lengthen'd up the sky,
Show'd a clear summit, rich with rising flowers,
That breathe their odors thro celestial bowers.
O'er the proud Pyrenees it looks sublime,
Subjects the Alps, and levels Europe's clime;
Spain, lessening to a chart, beneath it swims,
And shrouds her dungeons in the void she dims.
　　Led by the Power, the Hero gain'd the height,
New strength and brilliance flush'd his mortal sight;
When calm before them flow'd the western main,
Far stretch'd, immense, a sky-encircled plain.
No sail, no isle, no cloud invests the bound,
Nor billowy surge disturbs the vast profound;
Till, deep in distant heavens, the sun's blue ray
Topt unknown cliffs and call'd them up to day;
Slow glimmering into sight wide regions drew,
And rose and brighten'd on the expanding view;
Fair sweep the waves, the lessening ocean smiles,
In misty radiance loom a thousand isles;
Near and more near the long drawn coasts arise,
Bays stretch their arms and mountains lift the skies,
The lakes, high mounded, point the streams their way,
Slopes, ridges, plains their spreading skirts display,
The vales branch forth, high walk approaching groves,
And all the majesty of nature moves.
　　O'er the wild hemisphere his glances fly,
Its form unfolding as it still draws nigh,
As all its salient sides force far their sway,
Crowd back the ocean and indent the day.
He saw, thro central zones, the winding shore
Spread the deep Gulph[30] his sail had traced before,
The Darien isthmus[31] check the raging tide,

---

30 The Gulf of Darien, the southernmost region of the Caribbean Sea
31 The Isthmus of Darien, a strip of land dividing the Pacific Ocean and Caribbean Sea

Join distant lands, and neighboring seas divide;
On either hand the shores unbounded bend,
Push wide their waves, to each dim pole ascend;
The two twin continents united rise,
Broad as the main, and lengthen'd with the skies.
    Long gazed the Mariner; when thus the Guide:
Here spreads the world thy daring sail descried,
Hesperia call'd, from my anterior claim;
But now Columbia, from thy patriarch name.
So from Phenicia's peopled strand of yore
Europa[32] sail'd, and sought an unknown shore;
There stampt her sacred name; and thence her race,
Hale, venturous, bold, from Jove's divine embrace,
Ranged o'er the world, predestined to bestride
Earth's elder continents and each far tide.
    Ages unborn shall bless the happier day,
That saw thy streamer shape the guideless way,
Their bravest heroes trace the path you led,
And sires of nations thro the regions spread.
Behold yon isles, where first they flag unfurl'd
In bloodless triumph o'er the younger world;
As, awed to silence, savage bands gave place,
And hail'd with joy the sun-descended race.

Source text

Barlow, Joel, *The Columbiad. A Poem* (Philadelphia: C. and A. Conrad & Co., 1807).

References

Buel, Jr, Richard, *Joel Barlow: American Citizen in a Revolutionary World* (Baltimore, MD: Johns Hopkins University Press, 2011).
Blakemore, Steven, *Joel Barlow's* Columbiad: *A Bicentennial Reading* (Knoxville, TN: University of Tennessee Press, 2007).
Dowling, William C., *Poetry and Ideology in Revolutionary Connecticut* (Athens, GA: University of Georgia Press, 1990).
Giles, Paul, '"To gird this watery globe": Freneau, Barlow, and American Neoclassical Poetry', in Eve Tavor Bannet and Susan Manning (eds), *Transatlantic Literary Studies, 1660–1830* (Cambridge: Cambridge University Press, 2012), 139–53.

---

32 In Greek mythology, Europa was a Phoenecian princess abducted by Zeus and taken to Crete. She would later give her name to the continent of Europe.

Francis Jeffrey (1773–1850)

From Review of Joel Barlow, The Columbiad: A Poem (1809)

Francis Jeffrey was one of the founders in 1802 (along with Francis Horner and Sydney Smith) of the *Edinburgh Review*, a periodical published four times a year. It was intended as a forum for the promotion of liberal political views and of essay-length reviews of recently published books on literature, politics and science. In 1803 Jeffrey became its editor, a post he would hold until 1829. Contributors to its pages included the novelist Walter Scott, the essayists William Hazlitt and Thomas Carlyle, and the scientist John Playfair. The *Review* published frequent reviews of American travel narratives along with accounts of its geography and the state of transatlantic political relations. Jeffrey himself would travel to the United States in 1813, where he met President James Madison. Jeffrey's response to the literary culture of the US was generally unsympathetic: in an 1806 review of the works of Benjamin Franklin (whom he admired), he lamented 'the singular want of literary enterprise or activity' (Jeffrey, 327) in the country. His review of Barlow's *The Columbiad*, excerpts from which we include here, represents an extended engagement with the question of the US's ability to adopt inherited, often classical, modes of poetry for its own national narrative.

From Review of Joel Barlow, The Columbiad: A Poem

As epic poetry has often been the earliest, as well as the most precious production of national genius, we ought not, perhaps, to be surprised at this goodly firstling of the infant Muse of America. The truth however is, that though the American government be new, the people is in all respects as old as the people of England; and their want of literature is to be ascribed, not to the immaturity of their progress in civilization, but to the nature of the occupations in which they are generally engaged. These federal republicans, in short, bear no sort of resemblance to the Greeks of the days of Homer,[33] or the Italians of the age of Dante;[34] but are very much such people, we suppose, as the modern traders of Manchester, Liverpool, or Glasgow. They have all a little Latin whipped into them in their youth; and read Shakespeare, Pope and Milton, as well as bad English novels, in their days of courtship and leisure. They are just as likely to write epic poems, therefore, as the inhabitants of our trading towns at home; and are entitled to no more admiration when they succeed, and to no more indulgence when they fail, than would be due, on a similar occasion, to any of those industrious persons.

---

33 Author of the *Iliad* and the *Odyssey*, epic poems central to classical Greek literature
34 Dante Alighieri (*c*.1265–1321), author of the *Divine Comedy* (*c*.1308–20), an epic narrative poem

Be this, however, as it may, Mr Barlow, we are afraid, will not be the Homer of his country; and will never take his place among the enduring poets either of the old or of the new world. [...] Though not deficient in literature, therefore, nor unread in poetry, he has evidently none of the higher elements of a poet in his composition; and has accordingly made a most injudicious choice and unfortunate application of the models which lay before him. Like other persons of a cold and coarse imagination, he is caught only by what is glaring and exaggerated; and seems to have no perception of the finer and less obtrusive graces which constitute all the lasting and deep-felt charms of poetry. In his cumbrous and inflated style, he is constantly mistaking hyperbole for grandeur, and supplying the place of simplicity with huge patches of mere tameness and vulgarity. [...] Instead of aspiring to emulate the sublime composure of Milton, or the natural eloquence and flowing nervousness of Dryden,[35] Mr Barlow has bethought him of transferring to epic poetry the light, sparkling, and tawdry diction of Darwin,[36] and of narrating great events, and delivering lofty precepts in an unhappy imitation of that picturesque, puerile, and pedantic style, which alternately charms and disgusts us in the pages of our poetical physiologist.

[...] If it will be any comfort to Mr Barlow, we will add, that we doubt very much whether any long poem of the Epic character will ever again be very popular in Europe. All such works have necessarily so much of imitation about them, as nearly to extinguish all interest or curiosity in the reader, and at the same time to lead to dangerous comparisons. The style and title of an Epic poem immediately puts us in mind of Homer, Virgil,[37] and Milton;—and who can stand against such competitors? We even suspect, if we must tell the whole truth, that the works of those great masters themselves were better suited to the times that produced them, than to the present times. Men certainly bore long stories with more patience of old, than they do now. Witness the genealogies and monkish legends and romances which delighted our remoter ancestors, and through which even vanity is now scarcely sufficient to drag a few of their descendants. Epic poetry is the stage beyond these; and though the inimitable merit of the composition, as well as traditionary fame, will insure the immortality of a few great models, we doubt very much whether it would be in the power, even of equal talents, to add another name to that illustrious catalogue. In the present state of society, we require, in poetry, something more natural or more impassioned, and, at all events, something less protracted and monotonous than the sober pomp and deliberate stateliness of the Epic.

Source text

Jeffrey, Francis, Review of Joel Barlow, *The Columbiad: A Poem, Edinburgh Review* 15.29 (October 1809), 24–40.

References

Hook, Andrew, 'Scotland, the USA, and National Literatures in the Nineteenth Century', *Scottish Cultural Review of Language and Literature* 18 (2012), 37–52.

---

35 John Dryden (1631–1700), English poet, translator and critic
36 Erasmus Darwin (1731–1802), English physician and poet, grandfather of Charles Darwin (1809–82)
37 Ancient Roman author of the epic poem the *Aeneid*

Jeffrey, Francis, Review of *The Complete Works, in Philosophy, Politics, and Morals, of the late Dr. Benjamin Franklin, Edinburgh Review* 16 (July 1806), 327–44.

Perkins, Pam, 'Reviewing America: Francis Jeffrey, *Edinburgh Review* and the United States', *Scottish Cultural Review of Language and Literature* 18 (2012), 53–69.

Washington Irving (1783–1859)

From 'English Writers on America' (1819–20)

Washington Irving is transatlantic in origin, fame and literary impact. The son of a Scot and English immigrant who arrived in pre-revolutionary America in 1763, Irving was expected to enter the family's transatlantic import business but was drawn to writing early and began publishing at the encouragement of his older brother. He eventually became a lawyer as well as businessman but above all a popular, highly respected writer who left his mark on literary canons in the US and Britain. His stories 'Rip van Winkle' and 'The Legend of Sleepy Hollow' appear in standard American literature anthologies; Irving's description of traditional Christmas festivities at Bracebridge Hall in England also influenced the Dingley Dell episode in Charles Dickens's *Pickwick Papers* (1836–7) and Mr Fezziwig's Christmas celebration in *A Christmas Carol* (1843). Irving's two stories and British sketch were first published in *The Sketch Book of Geoffrey Crayon, Gent.* serially published in the US and Britain in 1819–20, in which 'English Writers on America' also appeared. Though Irving complained of the treatment of the US by British travel writers, he acknowledged the work of British literary models. He thus managed both to criticise Britain and to find favour with, for example, the conservative British *Quarterly Review*, which, if noting America's 'intoxication of national vanity' and new-found delight in 'military glory' following the Anglo-American war of 1812–15, still praised Irving thus: '"*English Writers on America*," written for the most part in a spirit of good sense and moderation [. . .] [hardly] expected from an American', contained 'much that is praiseworthy and excellent; and we think the perusal of it may be of great service on both sides of the Atlantic' (*The Sketch Book*, 51, 53).

From 'English Writers on America'

It is with feelings of deep regret that I observe the literary animosity daily growing up between England and America. Great curiosity has been awakened of late with respect to the United States, and the London press has teemed with volumes of travels through the Republic; but they seem intended to diffuse error rather than knowledge; and so successful have they been, that, notwithstanding the constant intercourse between the nations, there is no people concerning whom the great mass of the British public have less pure information, or entertain more numerous prejudices.

English travellers are the best and the worst in the world. Where no motives of pride or interest intervene, none can equal them for profound and philosophical views of society, or faithful and graphical descriptions of external objects; but when either the interest or reputation of their own country comes in collision with that of another, they go to the opposite extreme, and forget their usual probity and candor, in the indulgence of splenetic remark, and an illiberal spirit of ridicule.

Hence, their travels are more honest and accurate, the more remote the country described. [...]

It has also been the peculiar lot of our country to be visited by the worst kind of English travellers. While men of philosophical spirit and cultivated minds have been sent from England to ransack the poles, to penetrate the deserts, and to study the manners and customs of barbarous nations, with which she can have no permanent intercourse of profit or pleasure; it has been left to the broken-down tradesman, the scheming adventurer, the wandering mechanic,[38] the Manchester and Birmingham agent,[39] to be her oracles respecting America. From such sources she is content to receive her information respecting a country in a singular state of moral and physical development; a country in which one of the greatest political experiments in the history of the world is now performing; and which presents the most profound and momentous studies to the statesman and the philosopher. [...]

I shall not, however, dwell on this irksome and hackneyed topic; nor should I have adverted to it, but for the undue interest apparently taken in it by my countrymen, and certain injurious effects which I apprehended it might produce upon the national feeling. We attach too much consequence to these attacks. They cannot do us any essential injury. The tissue of misrepresentations attempted to be woven round us are like cobwebs woven round the limbs of an infant giant. Our country continually outgrows them. One falsehood after another falls off of itself.[40] We have but to live on, and every day we live a whole volume of refutation. [...]

But why are we so exquisitely alive to the aspersions[41] of England? Why do we suffer ourselves to be so affected by the contumely[42] she has endeavored to cast upon us? It is not in the opinion of England alone that honor lives, and reputation has its being. The world at large is the arbiter of a nation's fame; with its thousand eyes it witnesses a nation's deeds, and from their collective testimony is national glory or national disgrace established.

For ourselves, therefore, it is comparatively of but little importance whether England does us justice or not; it is, perhaps, of far more importance to herself. She is instilling anger and resentment into the bosom of a youthful nation, to grow with its growth and strengthen with its strength. If in America, as some of her writers are laboring to convince her, she is hereafter to find an invidious[43] rival, and a gigantic foe, she may thank those very writers for having provoked rivalship and irritated hostility. [...]

The present friendship of America may be of but little moment to her; but the future destinies of that country do not admit of a doubt; over those of England there lower[44] some shadows of uncertainty. Should, then, a day of gloom arrive;

---

38 Manual labourer
39 Business representative
40 In the sense of 'by itself'
41 Aspersion: 'charge that tarnishes the reputation' (*OED*)
42 'Insolent reproach or abuse' (*OED*)
43 'Fitted to excite ill feeling or envy' (*OED*)
44 'To descend, sink down' (*OED*)

should these reverses overtake her, from which the proudest empires have not been exempt; she may look back with regret at her infatuation, in repulsing from her side a nation she might have grappled to her bosom, and thus destroying her only chance for real friendship beyond the boundaries of her own dominions. [...]

But above all let us not be influenced by any angry feelings, so far as to shut our eyes to the perception of what is really excellent and amiable in the English character. We are a young people, necessarily an imitative one, and must take our examples and models, in a great degree, from the existing nations of Europe. There is no country more worthy of our study than England. The spirit of her constitution is most analogous to ours. The manners of her people—their intellectual activity—their freedom of opinion—their habits of thinking on those subjects which concern the dearest interests and most sacred charities of private life, are all congenial to the American character; and, in fact, are all intrinsically excellent; for it is in the moral feeling of the people that the deep foundations of British prosperity are laid; and however the superstructure may be time-worn, or overrun by abuses, there must be something solid in the basis, admirable in the materials, and stable in the structure of an edifice, that so long has towered unshaken amidst the tempests of the world.

Source text

[Irving, Washington], *The Sketch-Book of Geoffrey Crayon, Gent.* (London: John Miller, 1820).

References

ANB
Andrews, Malcolm, 'Dickens, Washington Irving, and English National Identity', *Dickens Studies Annual* 29 (2000), 1–16.
Hanssen, Jessica Allen, 'Transnational Narrativity and Pastoralism in *The Sketch Book of Geoffrey Crayon, Gent* by Washington Irving', *Transnational Literature* 9.1 (November 2016), Web.
Sizemore, Michelle R., '"Changing by Enchantment:" Temporal Convergence, Early National Comparisons, and Washington Irving's Sketchbook', *Studies in American Fiction* 40.2 (2013), 157–83.
'*The Sketch Book of Geoffrey Crayon, Gent.*' [review], *Quarterly Review* 25 (April 1821), 50–67.

Sydney Smith (1771–1845)

From Review of Statistical Annals of the United States of America. By Adam Seybert (1820)

The *Edinburgh Review* notice by Scottish writer Sydney Smith of Adam Seybert's *Statistical Annals of the United States of America* (Philadelphia, 1818) posed a question that would by turns haunt and anger American writers: 'Who reads an American book?' Smith, co-founder of the *Edinburgh Review* with Francis Jeffrey (1773–1850), Francis Horner (1778–1817) and Henry Brougham (1778–1868), was a Church of England clergyman but most remembered as an important intellectual, prolific author and wit. The *Edinburgh* was more progressive than the Tory *Quarterly Review*, founded in 1809 to oppose it. In keeping with his journal's policy of open inquiry, Smith took care to survey Dr Seybert's book disinterestedly and to note American achievements before his conclusion (excerpted below). But his conclusion asserts British cultural superiority to the US, counterpointing American pride in achievements with a catalogue of premier British contributions to modern knowledge and a reminder of the hypocrisy and injustice of enslavement in a country founded on the Declaration of Independence – though slavery was also still practised in British Caribbean possessions at the time.

From Review of Statistical Annals of the United States of America. *By Adam Seybert*

Such is the land of Jonathan[45]—and thus has it been governed. In his honest endeavours to better his situation, and in his manly purpose of resisting injury and insult, we most cordially sympathize. We hope he will always continue to watch and suspect his Government as he now does—remembering, that it is the constant tendency of those entrusted with power, to conceive that they enjoy it by their own merits, and for their own use, and not by delegation, and for the benefit of others. Thus far we are the friends and admirers of Jonathan: But he must not grow vain and ambitious; or allow himself to be dazzled by that galaxy of epithets by which his orators and newspaper scribblers endeavor to persuade their supporters that they are the greatest, the most refined, the most enlightened, and the most moral people on earth. The effect of this is unspeakably ludicrous on this side of the Atlantic—and, even on the other, we should imagine, must be rather humiliating to the reasonable part of the population. The Americans are a brave, industrious, and acute people; but they have hitherto given no indications of genius, and made no approaches to the heroic, either in their morality or character. They are but a recent offset indeed from England; and should make it their chief boast, for many generations to come, that they are sprung from the same race with Bacon and Shakespeare and Newton.[46] Considering their numbers, indeed, and the favourable circumstances in which they have been placed, they have yet done marvellously little to assert the honour of such a descent, or to show that their English blood has been exalted or refined by their republican training and institutions. Their Franklins and Washingtons,[47] and all the other sages and heroes of their revolution, were born and bred subjects of the King of England,—and not among the freest or most valued of his subjects: And, since the period of their separation, a far greater proportion of their statesmen and artists and political writers have been foreigners, than ever occurred before in the history of any civilized and educated people. During the thirty or forty years of their independence, they have

---

45 'A generic name for the people of the United States' (*OED*)
46 Francis Bacon (1561–1626), William Shakespeare (1564–1616), Isaac Newton (1642–1727)
47 Benjamin Franklin (1706–90), George Washington (1732–99); Smith's point is borne out in the inclusion of Franklin and Washington in the *ODNB*.

done absolutely nothing for the Sciences, for the Arts, for Literature, or even for the statesman-like studies of Politics or Political Economy. Confining ourselves to our own country, and to the period that has elapsed since *they* had an independent existence, we would ask, Where are their Foxes, their Burkes, their Sheridans, their Wind-hams, their Horners, their Wilberforces?—where their Arkwrights, their Watts, their Davys?—their Robertsons, Blairs, Smiths, Stewarts, Paleys and Malthuses?—their Porsons, Parrs, Burneys, or Blomfields?—their Scotts, Campbells, Byrons, Moores, or Crabbes?—their Siddonses, Kembles, Keans, or O'Neils?—their Wilkies, Laurences, Chantrys?[48]—or their parallels to the hundred other names that have spread them-selves over the world from our little island in the course of the last thirty years, and blest or delighted mankind by their works, inventions, or examples? In so far as we know, there is no such parallel to be produced from the whole annals of this self-adulating[49] race. In the four quarters of the globe, who reads an American book? or goes to an American play? or looks at an American picture or statue? What does the world yet owe to American physicians or surgeons? What new substances have their chemists discovered? or what old ones have they analyzed? What new constellations have been discovered by the telescopes of Americans?—what have they done in the mathematics? Who drinks out of American glasses? or eats from American plates? or wears American coats or gowns? or sleeps in American blankets?—Finally, under which of the old tyrannical governments of Europe is every sixth man a Slave, whom his fellow-creatures may buy and sell and torture?

When these questions are fairly and favourably answered, their laudatory epithets may be allowed: But, till that can be done, we would seriously advise them to keep clear of superlatives.

Source text

[Smith, Sydney], Review of *Statistical Annals of the United States of America*. By Adam Seybert. Philadelphia, 1818, *Edinburgh Review* 33 (January 1820), 69–80.

---

48 Smith's catalogue includes British statesmen, inventors, philosophers, scholars, poets, actors, and artists, to wit: Charles James Fox (1749–1806), politician; Edmund Burke (1730–97), politician and author; Richard Brinsley Sheridan (1751–1816), playwright and politician; William Windham (1750–1810), politician; Francis Horner (1778–1817), politician; William Wilberforce (1759–1833), politician, philanthropist, abolitionist; Sir Richard Arkwright (1732–92), inventor of cotton-spinning machinery; James Watt (1736–1819), engineer and steam engine manufacturer; Sir Humphry Davy (1778–1829), chemist and inventor; possibly Joseph Robertson (1726–1802), Church of England cler-gyman and writer, but more likely William Robertson (1721–93), historian and Church of Scotland minister; Hugh Blair (1718–1800), Church of Scotland minister and rhetorician; Adam Smith (1723–90), political economist, professor, rhetorician and philosopher; Dugald Stewart (1753–1828), phi-losopher, professor, mathematician; William Paley (1743–1805), theologian and moralist; (Thomas) Robert Malthus (1766–1834), political economist and theorist of population growth; Richard Por-son (1759–1808), classical scholar; possibly Bartholomew Parr (1750–1810), physician and medical author, but more likely Samuel Parr (1747–1825), prominent schoolmaster, author and controver-sialist; Dr Charles Burney (1726–1814), music historian and musician; Edward Valentine Blomfield (1788–1816), classical scholar; Walter Scott (1771–1832), poet and novelist; Thomas Campbell (1777–1844), poet; George Gordon Noel Byron (1788–1824), poet; Thomas Moore (1779–1852), poet; George Crabbe (1754–1832), poet and Church of England clergyman; Sarah Siddons, *née* Kem-ble (1755–1831), actress; Stephen George Kemble (1758–1822), actor and theatre manager, and his wife Elizabeth Kemble (1763?–1841), actress; Edmund Kean (1787–1833), actor; most likely Eliza-beth O'Neill (1791–1872), actress, who retired from the stage in 1819; David Wilkie (1785–1841), painter; Thomas Lawrence (1769–1830), painter; Francis Leggatt Chantrey (1781–1841), sculptor.
49 Adulating: given 'to praise or admire uncritically or excessively' (*OED*)

References

ODNB

Seybert, Adam, *Statistical Annals of the United States of America* (Philadelphia, PA: Thomas Dobson & Son, 1818).

Shattock, Joanne, '*Edinburgh Review* (1802–1929)', in Laurel Brake and Marysa Demoor (eds), *Dictionary of Nineteenth-Century Journalism* (Ghent and London: Academia Press and the British Library, 2009), 190–1.

William Cullen Bryant (1794–1878)

'*Sonnet – To an American Painter Departing for Europe*' (1829)

William Cullen Bryant produced only six volumes of poetry, as well as a few pieces of fiction and some translations of Homer, yet his stature within nineteenth-century US culture was monumental. Washington Irving, in recommending Bryant to an English publisher, judged his poetry 'among the highest of their class' (Untermeyer, xi), and James Fenimore Cooper claimed that 'Bryant is the author of America' (Godwin, 1:368). Born into a middle-class Massachusetts family, Bryant first entered the law profession, before moving to New York in 1825 to become editor of the *New-York Review and Atheneum Magazine* and subsequently editor and part-owner of the New York *Evening Post*. The most important poetic influence on his writing was William Wordsworth, whose work he discovered in 1810, reading the Philadelphia edition of Wordsworth and Samuel Taylor Coleridge's *Lyrical Ballads* (1798). The English poet's celebration of nature in the construction of national identity would go on to influence Bryant's own project to write the US landscape. Bryant was also an inveterate traveller, writing accounts of his trips to Canada, Mexico, the Caribbean and Europe. The poem reprinted here, a sonnet addressed to the famous landscape painter Thomas Cole, is a celebration and a reminder of the aesthetic potential of the United States, its availability for Cole's 'glorious canvas', even as the painter is confronted with the visual spectacles of Europe.

'*Sonnet – To an American Painter Departing for Europe*'

>Thine eyes shall see the light of distant skies:
>>Yet, Cole![50] thy heart shall bear to Europe's strand
>>A living image of thy native land,
>Such as on thy own glorious canvass lies.
>Lone lakes – savannahs where the bison roves –
>>Rocks rich with summer garlands – solemn streams –

---

50 Thomas Cole (1801–48), English-born US painter, founder of the Hudson River School, whose trip to Europe in 1829 was the provocation for Bryant's poem

> Skies, where the desert eagle wheels and screams –
> Spring bloom and autumn blaze of boundless groves.
> Fair scenes shall greet thee where thou goest – fair,
>   But different – every where the trace of men,
>   Paths, homes, graves, ruins, from the lowest glen
> To where life shrinks from the fierce Alpine air.
>   Gaze on them, till the tears shall dim thy sight,
>   But keep that earlier, wilder image bright.

Source text

Bryant, William Cullen, *Poems* (New York: E. Bliss, 1832).

References

Godwin, Parke, *A Biography of William Cullen Bryant, With Extracts from His Private Correspondence* (1883) 2 vols (New York: Russell & Russell, 1967).
Muller, Gilbert H. *William Cullen Bryant: Author of America* (Albany, NY: State University of New York Press, 2008).
Schuyler, David, *Sanctified Landscape: Writers, Artists, and the Hudson River Valley, 1820–1909* (Ithaca, NY: Cornell University Press, 2012).
Untermeyer, Louis, Introduction to *The Poems of William Cullen Bryant* (New York: Heritage Press, 1947).

Edgar Allan Poe (1809–49)

From Review of Barnaby Rudge by Charles Dickens (1842)

Charles Dickens (1812–70) was famous transatlantically in his own day and remains so due to fiction from *Oliver Twist* (1837–9) and *A Christmas Carol* (1843) to *Bleak House* (1852–3). Edgar Allan Poe (1809–49) attained less fame and fortune before dying of acute alcohol poisoning in Baltimore. But he, too, is now a major transatlantic author based on groundbreaking detective fiction (e.g. 'The Murders in the Rue Morgue', 1841), horror writing (e.g. 'The Tell-Tale Heart', 1843) and poems like 'The Raven' (1845), all of which drew enthusiastic European readership. Poe's review of Dickens's fifth novel, *Barnaby Rudge: A Tale of the Riots of Eighty* (1841), is also famous because Poe claimed to have solved Dickens's murder mystery while reading Dickens's first chapter (published 13 February 1841 in Dickens's short-lived journal *Master Humphrey's Clock*). Dickens's serial novel is an important depiction of fanaticism and civil strife surrounding the 1780 anti-Catholic Gordon Riots in London, which were sparked by radical Protestants objecting to the 1778 Catholic Relief Act granting modest civil rights to Catholics (who still could not vote or sit in Parliament). The excerpt below omits discussion of the Gordon Riots to focus on Poe's aesthetic critique of Dickens based on an author's obligation to deal fairly with readers and his subordination of higher artistic qualities to the pleasures of suspense and eager curiosity. The excerpt also suggests contested cultural prestige between an American critic and a British novelist.

From Review of Barnaby Rudge by Charles Dickens

Those who know us will not, from what is here premised, suppose it our intention, to enter into any wholesale *laudation* of "Barnaby Rudge." In truth, our design may appear, at a cursory glance, to be very different indeed. [. . .]

On the night of the nineteenth of March, 1733, Rudge murders his master for the sake of a large sum of money which he is known to have in possession. During the struggle, Mr. [Reuben] Haredale grasps the cord of an alarm-bell which hangs within his reach, but succeeds in sounding it only once or twice, when it is severed by the knife of the ruffian, who then, completing his bloody business, and securing the money, proceeds to quit the chamber. While doing this, however, he is disconcerted by meeting the gardener, whose pallid countenance evinces suspicion of the deed committed. The murderer is thus forced to kill his fellow servant. Having done so, the idea strikes him of transferring the burden of the crime from himself. He dresses the corpse of the gardener in his own clothes, puts upon its finger his own ring and in its pocket his own watch—then drags it to a pond in the grounds, and throws it in. He now returns to the house, and, disclosing all to his wife, requests her to become a partner in his flight. Horror-stricken, she falls to the ground. He attempts to raise her. She seizes his wrist, *staining her hand with blood in the attempt.* She renounces him forever; yet promises to conceal the crime. Alone, he flees the country. The next morning, Mr. Haredale being found murdered, and the steward and gardener being both missing, both are suspected. Mrs. Rudge leaves The Warren, and retires to an obscure lodging in London (where she lives upon an annuity allowed her by Haredale) having given birth, *on the very day after the murder,* to a son, Barnaby Rudge, who proves an idiot, who bears upon his wrist a red mark, and who is born possessed with a maniacal horror of blood. [. . .]

In the meanwhile, and immediately subsequent to [his] re-appearance [. . .] Rudge, in a midnight prowl about the scene of his atrocity, is encountered by an individual who had been familiar with him in earlier life, while living at The Warren. This individual, terrified at what he supposes, very naturally, to be the ghost of the murdered Rudge, relates his adventure to his companions at the Maypole, and John Willet conveys the intelligence, forthwith, to Mr. [Geoffrey] Haredale.[51] Connecting the apparition, in his own mind, with the peculiar conduct of Mrs. Rudge, this gentleman imbibes a suspicion, at once, of the true state of affairs. This suspicion (which he mentions to no one) is, moreover, very strongly confirmed by an occurrence happening to Varden, the locksmith, who, visiting the woman late one night, finds her in communion of a nature apparently most confidential, with a ruffian whom the locksmith knows to be such, without knowing the man himself. Upon

---

51 The murdered man's brother, and uncle to Emma Haredale, Reuben's daughter

an attempt, on the part of Varden, to seize this ruffian, he is thwarted by Mrs. R.; and upon Haredale's inquiring minutely into the personal appearance of the man, he is found to accord with Rudge. We have already shown that the ruffian was in fact Rudge himself. Acting upon the suspicion thus aroused, Haredale watches, by night, alone, in the deserted house formerly occupied by Mrs. R. in hope of here coming upon the murderer, and makes other exertions with the view of arresting him; but all in vain. [...]

But the riots have now begun. The idiot is beguiled into joining the mob, and, becoming separated from his mother (who, growing ill through grief, is borne to a hospital) meets with his old playmate Hugh, and becomes with him a ringleader in the rebellion. [...]

We have given, as may well be supposed, but a very meagre outline of the story, and we have given it in the simple or natural sequence. That is to say, we have related the events, as nearly as might be, in the order of their occurrence. But this order would by no means have suited the purpose of the novelist, whose design has been to maintain the secret of the murder, and the consequent mystery which encircles Rudge, and the actions of his wife, until the catastrophe of his discovery by Haredale. The *thesis* of the novel may thus be regarded as based upon curiosity. Every point is so arranged as to perplex the reader, and whet his desire for elucidation:—for example, the first appearance of Rudge at the Maypole; his questions; his persecution of Mrs. R.; the ghost seen by the frequenter of the Maypole; and Haredale's impressive conduct in consequence. What *we* have told, in the very beginning of our digest, in regard to the shifting of the gardener's dress, is sedulously[52] kept from the reader's knowledge until he learns it from Rudge's own confession in jail. We say sedulously; for, *the intention once known*, the *traces* of the design can be found upon every page. [...]

Now there can be no question that, by such means as these, many points which are comparatively insipid in the natural sequence of our digest, and which would have been comparatively insipid even if given in full detail in a natural sequence, are endued with the interest of mystery; but neither can it be denied that a vast many more points are at the same time deprived of all effect, and become null, through the impossibility of comprehending them without the key. The author, who, cognizant of his plot, writes with this cognizance continually operating upon him, and thus *writes to himself* in spite of himself, does not, of course, feel that much of what is effective to his own informed perception, must necessarily be lost upon his uninformed readers; and he himself is never in condition, as regards his own work, to bring the matter to test. But the reader may easily satisfy himself of the validity of our objection. Let him *re-peruse* "Barnaby Rudge," and, with a pre-comprehension of the mystery, these points of which we speak break out in all directions like stars, and throw quadruple brilliance over the narrative—a brilliance which a correct taste will at once declare unprofitably sacrificed at the shrine of the keenest interest of mere mystery.

The design of *mystery*, however, being once determined upon by an author, it becomes imperative, first, that no undue or inartistical means be employed to conceal the secret of the plot; and, secondly, that the secret be well kept. Now, when, at page 16, we read that "the body of *poor Mr. Rudge, the steward, was found* " months after the outrage, &c. we see that Mr. Dickens has been guilty of no misdemeanor

---

52 Constantly

against Art in stating what was not the fact; since the falsehood is put into the mouth of Solomon Daisy, and given merely as the impression of this individual and of the public. The writer has not asserted it in his own person, but ingeniously conveyed an idea (false in itself, yet a belief in which it is necessary for the effect of the tale) by the mouth of one of his characters. The case is different, however, when Mrs. Rudge is repeatedly denominated "the widow." It is the author who, himself, frequently so terms her. This is disingenuous and inartistical: accidentally so, of course. We speak of the matter merely by way of illustrating our point, and as an oversight on the part of Mr. Dickens.

That the secret be well kept is obviously necessary. A failure to preserve it until the proper moment of *dénouement*,[53] throws all into confusion, so far as regards the *effect* intended. If the mystery leak out, against the author's will, his purposes are immediately at odds and ends; for he proceeds upon the supposition that certain impressions *do* exist, which do *not* exist, in the mind of his readers. We are not prepared to say, so positively as we could wish, whether, by the public at large, the whole *mystery* of the murder committed by Rudge, with the identity of the Maypole ruffian with Rudge himself, was fathomed at any period previous to the period intended, or, if so, whether at a period so early as materially to interfere with the interest designed; but we are forced, through sheer modesty, to suppose this the case; since, by ourselves individually, the secret was distinctly understood immediately upon the perusal of the story of Solomon Daisy, which occurs at the seventh page of this volume of three hundred and twenty-three. In the number of the "Philadelphia Saturday Evening Post," for May the 1st, 1841, (the tale having then only begun) will be found a *prospective notice* of some length, in which we made use of the following words—

> That Barnaby is the son of the murderer may not appear evident to our readers—but [. . .] it is not the author himself who asserts that *the steward's body was found*; he has put the words in the mouth of one of his characters. His design is to make it appear, in the *dénouement*, that the steward, Rudge, first murdered the gardener, then went to his master's chamber, murdered *him*, was interrupted by his (Rudge's) wife, whom he seized and held *by the wrist* [. . .].

The differences between our pre-conceived ideas, as here stated, and the actual facts of the story, will be found immaterial. The gardener was murdered not before but after his master; and that Rudge's wife seized *him* by the wrist, instead of his seizing *her*, has so much the air of a mistake on the part of Mr. Dickens, that we can scarcely speak of our own version as erroneous. The grasp of a murderer's bloody hand on the wrist of a woman *enceinte*,[54] would have been more likely to produce the effect described (and this every one will allow) than the grasp of the hand of the woman upon the wrist of the assassin. We may therefore say of our supposition as Talleyrand said of some cockney's bad French—*que s'il ne soit pas Francais, assurément donc il le doit être*[55]—that if we did not rightly prophesy, yet, at least, our prophecy *should have been* right. [. . .]

---

53 'Unravelling of the complications of a plot in a drama' (*OED*)
54 Pregnant
55 If he is not French, then he must assuredly be.

It is, perhaps, but one of a thousand instances of the disadvantages, both to the author and the public, of the present absurd fashion of periodical novel-writing, that our author had not sufficiently considered or determined upon *any* particular plot when he began the story now under review. In fact, we see, or fancy that we see, numerous traces of indecision—traces which a dexterous supervision of the complete work might have enabled him to erase. [...]

The effect of the present narrative might have been materially increased by confining the action within the limits of London. The "Notre Dame" of Hugo[56] affords a fine example of the force which can be gained by concentration, or unity of place. The unity of time is also sadly neglected, to no purpose, in "Barnaby Rudge." [...]

The wood-cut *designs* which accompany the edition before us are occasionally good. The copper engravings are pitiably ill-conceived and ill-drawn; and not only this, but are in broad contradiction of the wood-designs and text. [...]

From what we have here said — and, perhaps, said without due deliberation — (for alas! the hurried duties of the journalist preclude it) there will not be wanting those who will accuse us of a mad design to detract from the pure fame of the novelist. But to such we merely say in the language of heraldry "ye should wear a plain point sanguine in your arms."[57] If this be understood, well; if not, well again. There lives no man feeling a deeper reverence for genius than ourself. If we have not dwelt so especially upon the high merits as upon the trivial defects of "Barnaby Rudge" we have already given our reasons for the omission, and these reasons will be sufficiently understood by all whom we care to understand them. The work before us is not, we think, equal to the tale which immediately preceded it; but there are few—very few others to which we consider it inferior. Our chief objection has not, perhaps, been so distinctly stated as we could wish. That this fiction, or indeed that any fiction written by Mr. Dickens, should be based in the excitement and maintenance of curiosity we look upon as a misconception, on the part of the writer, of his own very great yet very peculiar powers. He has done this thing well, to be sure—he would do anything well in comparison with the herd of his contemporaries—but he has not done it so thoroughly well as his high and just reputation would demand. We think that the whole book has been an effort to him—solely through the nature of its design. He has been smitten with an untimely desire for a novel path. The idiosyncrasy of his intellect would lead him, naturally, into the most fluent and simple style of narration. In tales of ordinary sequence he may and will long reign triumphant. He has a *talent* for all things, but no positive *genius* for *adaptation*, and still less for that metaphysical art in which the souls of all *mysteries* lie. "Caleb Williams"[58] is a far less noble work than "The Old Curiosity-Shop;"[59] but Mr. Dickens could no more have constructed the one than Mr. Godwin could have dreamed of the other.

Source text

Poe, Edgar Allan, Review, *Barnaby Rudge*; By Charles Dickens (Boz) Author of 'The Old Curiosity-Shop,' 'Pickwick,' 'Oliver Twist,' etc. etc. With numerous Illustrations, by

---

56 The 1831 novel *Notre-Dame de Paris* by Victor Hugo (1802–85), known in English as *The Hunchback of Notre-Dame*
57 That is, make clear your intention to draw blood, since sanguine in heraldry is blood-red
58 *Things as They Are; or The Adventures of Caleb Williams* (1794), by William Godwin (1756–1836)
59 *The Old Curiosity Shop* by Dickens, was serialised in 1840–1

Cattermole, Browne & Sibson. Lea & Blanchard: Philadelphia, *Graham's Lady's and Gentleman's Magazine* 20 (February 1842), 124–9.

References

Garrett, Peter K., 'The Force of a Frame: Poe and the Control of Reading Author(s)', *Yearbook of English Studies* 26 (1996), 54–64.

Frederick Douglass (1818–95)

'Dempster' (1849)

Accounts of Frederick Douglass's life rightly emphasise his abolitionist endeavours, situating his literary contributions within that context. Yet, even amid the time-consuming commitments of public work to promote social justice, he took genuine pleasure in the arts. That aesthetic engagement is reflected in his 1849 review of Scottish singer William Dempster, then performing in the US.

While the review clearly illustrates the nineteenth-century transatlantic network linking artists and audiences, another story in the same issue documents Douglass's deep personal investment in poetry and song from Scotland. 'Burns' Anniversary Festival' shows that, besides attending Dempster's concert in Rochester (home city of the anti-slavery *North Star* newspaper Douglass edited), he joined the singer at a local Old Scotia society's soirée commemorating Roberts Burns.

That account notes that the songster and the orator contributed to the gathering's 'social feeling, brotherly love, and innocent amusement' via 'stirring music' and parlour oratory. Dempster offered a rendering of 'Highland Mary' that 'brought the sympathizing tear to the eyes' of attendees and followed up with 'that song of Burns' which is, and will always be, the admiration of all men—"A man's a man for a' that"'. The group subsequently called on Douglass to speak. And, in a moving account of his 'pilgrimage [while abroad] to see the cottage in which [Burns] was born', Douglass reiterated his 'high appreciation of Scotch genius', which, he proposed, resonated with an adopted 'Scotch heart throb[bing] beneath these ribs'. He then asserted: 'though I am not a Scotchman, and have a colored skin, I am proud to be among you', a stance he proposed came from studying Burns, 'who taught me that "a man's a man for a' that"' (J. D., 1).

'Dempster'

This sweet songster gave a delightful entertainment at the new Concert Hall, in this city, on Tuesday evening last; and proposes to offer another in the course of a few days, of which due notice will be published in the daily papers. The merits of Mr.

Dempster, as a vocalist, are well known, and widely appreciated.[60] As a composer, he ranks with the best of the age;[61] and as a performer of the songs, especially those of his native land, we think he has no superior. He has not a deep bass voice, such as Henry Russell or Asa Hutchinson,[62] to awaken terror by its roaring grandeur; but he has just such a voice as is proper to the performance of the songs of his country, and kindred music. The crystal clearness and melting sweetness of his voice, while admirably adapted to express the beautiful tenderness of love, and the warmth of domestic affection, possesses a loftier quality and compass, which soars on high, bearing his audience into the concert of angels. No one could listen to his performance on Tuesday evening, without having the better elements of his nature highly gratified and improved. The song of the "Indian Women," by Whittier, the "Rainy Day," by Longfellow, "'Tis sweet to love in childhood," by Mary Cook, "The May Queen," by Tennyson, and "The Dying Child," by Mary Howitt, and several Scotch songs,[63] were all sung with enchanting beauty and sweetness. To all who love music in which there is nothing to injure the feelings of the helpless, divested of all low vulgarity, creates no fever in the brain, leaves no stain upon the soul, but refines and purifies the heart, elevates the mind, and [fills?] it with loving sentiments[64] – we say, Go and hear Dempster. – F.D.

Source text

Douglass, Frederick, 'Dempster', *The North Star* (2 February 1849), 2.

References

J. D., 'Burns' Anniversary Festival', *The North Star* (2 February 1849), 1.

Tawa, Nicholas E., 'The Performance of Parlor Songs in America, 1790–1860', *Anuario Interamericano de Investigación Musical* 11 (1975), 69–81.

Tawa, Nicholas E., *Sweet Songs for Gentle Americans: The Parlor Song in America, 1790–1860* (Bowling Green, OH: Bowling Green University Popular Press, 1980).

---

60 Tawa emphasises the popularity of 'ballad singers' like Dempster and Henry Russell over more high-art-type operatic performers (*Sweet Songs*, 16). To illustrate Dempster's popularity, in particular, Tawa references an 1847 occasion when the singer drew huge crowds sufficient to finance a new concert hall for the Musical Fund Society of Philadelphia ('Performance', 70).

61 Tawa's history of the 'parlour song' genre emphasises the role that composers (and singer-composers) played in building the audience for these ballads, whose sheet music made them widely available, first in middle-class urban homes and eventually in rural areas (*Sweet Songs*, 3–4).

62 Henry Russell: English composer, pianist, and baritone who brought British music to America in the 1820s and took American Black spirituals back home when he returned to England in the 1840s. American Asa Hutchinson was one member of a popular family quartet that performed throughout New England beginning in 1841 and in the mid-1840s had a highly successful tour in the British Isles. Influenced by Frederick Douglass, Hutchinson began writing abolitionist lyrics for anti-slavery rallies. He also wrote temperance songs.

63 Tawa links the appeal of singers like Dempster to performing pieces from their homelands (*Sweet Songs*, 70). The blending of American (Longfellow, Whittier) and British (Howitt, Tennyson) authors cited as sources for Dempster's lyrics underscores his repertoire's transatlanticism.

64 In an article preceding his book-length study, Tawa characterises the nineteenth-century appeal of such ballads in terms reminiscent of Douglass's assessment of Dempster: 'the singer should experience or at least simulate the affection contained in the song so that his audience is convinced the performer's own feelings are involved. [. . .] [N]o aesthetic distance is to exist between song and performer' ('Performance', 70).

George Eliot (1819–80)

Review of Dred, by Harriet Beecher Stowe (1856)

The author who became famous as George Eliot (1819–80) had not yet assumed that name when she wrote her review of *Dred* (1856), the second novel of Harriet Beecher Stowe (1811–96). Born Mary Anne Evans in Coventry in the West Midlands of England, she had adopted the name Marian Evans Lewes by the time her anonymous review appeared. Markedly intelligent, the young Evans grew up as a devout Evangelical, but when Evans lost her faith in Christianity she moved to London to pursue a career in journalism. By 1851 she had become the de facto editor of the progressive *Westminster Review*, though not publicly recognised as such. Meantime her new London network brought her into contact with writer and journalist George Henry Lewes (1817–78). The married Lewes and Evans were soon romantically involved, but because he had tolerated his wife's infidelity, he could not obtain a divorce. Lewes and Evans eloped to Germany in 1854, a momentous decision that brought ostracisation to Evans by her family and many friends. Anonymity at this point aided her journalism career, and she continued to contribute articles to the *Westminster Review* from the Continent. As Bonnie Shannon McMullen points out, 'only four days after writing the review [of *Dred*, Eliot's] own career in fiction began with "The Sad Fortunes of the Reverend Amos Barton".' Eliot's tribute to Stowe's genius thus testifies to how much she had learned from Stowe's example (McMullen, n.p.). The next year Marian Evans Lewes became George Eliot in her professional correspondence and fiction.

Stowe's *Uncle Tom's Cabin* (1852) had been a runaway best-seller in England. In this brief *Westminster* notice Eliot underscores the importance of anti-slavery themes to Stowe's genius, criticising only her tendency to paint enslaved African Americans in ideal terms.

Review of Dred, by Harriet Beecher Stowe

At length we have Mrs. Stowe's new novel,[65] and for the last three weeks there have been men, women, and children reading it with rapt attention—laughing and sobbing over it—lingering with delight over its exquisite landscapes, its scenes of humour, and tenderness, and rude heroism—and glowing with indignation at its terrible representation of chartered barbarities. Such a book is an uncontrollable power, and critics who follow it with their objections and reservations—who complain that Mrs. Stowe's plot is defective, that she has repeated herself, that her book is too long and too full of hymns and religious dialogue, and that it creates an unfair

---

65 "Dred; a Tale of the Great Dismal Swamp." By Harriet Beecher Stowe. London: Sampson Low & Co. (*Westminster Review* note).

bias—are something like men pursuing a prairie fire with desultory[66] watering-cans. In the meantime, "Dred" will be devoured by the million, who carry no critical talisman against the enchantments of genius. We confess ourselves to be among the million, and quite unfit to rank with the sage minority of Fadladeens.[67] We have been too much moved by "Dred" to determine with precision how far it is inferior to "Uncle Tom;" too much impressed by what Mrs. Stowe *has* done to be quite sure that we can tell her what she ought to have done. Our admiration of the book is quite distinct from any opinions or hesitations we may have as to the terribly difficult problem of Slavery and Abolition—problems which belong to quite other than "polite literature." Even admitting Mrs. Stowe to be mistaken in her views, and partial or exaggerated in her representations, "Dred" remains not the less a novel inspired by a rare genius—rare both in intensity and in range of power.

Looking at the matter simply from an artistic point of view, we see no reason to regret that Mrs. Stowe should keep to her original ground of negro and planter life, any more than that Scott[68] should have introduced Highland life into "Rob Roy" and "The Fair Maid of Perth," when he had already written "Waverley."[69] Mrs. Stowe has *invented* the Negro novel, and it is a novel not only fresh in its scenery and its manners, but possessing that *conflict of races* which Augustin Thierry[70] has pointed out as the great source of romantic interest—witness "Ivanhoe."[71] Inventions in literature are not as plentiful as inventions in the paletôt[72] and waterproof department, and it is rather amusing that we reviewers, who have, for the most part, to read nothing but imitations of imitations, should put on airs of tolerance towards Mrs. Stowe because she has written a second Negro novel, and make excuses for her on the ground that she perhaps would not succeed in any other kind of fiction. Probably she would not; for her genius seems to be of a very special character: her "Sunny Memories"[73] were as feeble as her novels are powerful. But whatever else she may write, or may not write, "Uncle Tom" and "Dred" will assure her a place in that highest rank of novelists who can give us a national life in all its phases—popular and aristocratic, humorous and tragic, political and religious.

But Mrs. Stowe's novels have not only that grand element—conflict of races; they have another element equally grand, which she also shares with Scott, and in which she has, in some respects, surpassed him. This is the exhibition of a people to whom what we may call Hebraic Christianity is still a reality, still an animating belief, and by whom the theocratic conceptions of the Old Testament are literally applied to their daily life. Where has Scott done anything finer than the character

---

66 Marked by a lack of definite plan, regularity or purpose
67 Fadladeen, an emissary in the entourage of the Princess Lalla Rookh as she journeys to her wedding in *Lalla Rookh* (1817) by Irish author Thomas Moore (1779–1852), first authorises Feramorz to entertain the princess with tales, then 'subjects each of these to a splenetic commentary in imitation of Francis Jeffrey, editor of the *Edinburgh Review*', a means by which Moore could also 'revenge' himself upon his own hostile critics (Rudd, 58).
68 Sir Walter Scott (1771–1832), who pioneered the historical novel with his novels set in the Scottish Highlands, was a pre-eminent figure in the nineteenth century and deeply admired by Eliot.
69 Novels published respectively in 1817, 1828, 1814
70 French historian (1795–1856)
71 Sir Walter Scott first published *Ivanhoe*, which turns on conflicting cultures and beliefs of a medieval Anglo-Saxon knight, French Knight Templar and Jewish woman.
72 A coat, here a reference to styles in fashion
73 *Sunny Memories of Foreign Lands*, a travel book by Stowe (1854)

of Balfour of Burley,[74] the battles of Drumclog and Bothwell Brigg,[75] and the trial of Ephraim MacBriar?[76] And the character of Dred, the death scenes in the Swamp, and the Camp Meeting of Presbyterians and Methodists, will bear comparison—if we except the fighting—with the best parts of "Old Mortality." The strength of Mrs. Stowe's own religious feeling is a great artistic advantage to her here; she never makes you feel that she is coldly calculating an effect, but you see that she is all a-glow for the moment with the wild enthusiasm, the unreasoning faith, and the steady martyr-spirit of Dred, of Tiff, or of Father Dickson. But with this, she has the keen sense of humour which preserves her from extravagance and monotony; and though she paints her religious negroes *en beau*,[77] they are always specifically negroes—she never loses hold of her characters, and lets dramatic dialogue merge into vague oratory. Indeed, here is her strongest point: her dramatic instinct is always awake; and whether it is the grotesque Old Tiff or the aërial Nina, the bluff sophist Father Bonim or the gentlemanly sophist Frank Russell, her characters are always like themselves; a quality which is all the more remarkable in novels animated by a vehement polemical[78] purpose.

The objection which is patent to every one who looks at Mrs. Stowe's novels in an argumentative light, is also, we think, one of their artistic defects; namely, the absence of any proportionate exhibition of the negro character in its less amiable phases. Judging from her pictures, one would conclude that the negro race was vastly superior to the mass of whites, even in other than slave countries – a state of the case which would singularly defeat Mrs. Stowe's sarcasms on the cant of those who call Slavery a "Christianizing Institution." If the negroes are really so very good, slavery has answered as moral discipline. But apart from the argumentative suicide involved in this one-sidedness, Mrs. Stowe loses by it the most terribly tragic element in the relation of the two races – the Nemesis lurking in the vices of the oppressed. She alludes to demoralization among the slaves, but she does not depict it; and yet why should she shrink from this, since she does not shrink from giving us a full-length portrait of a Legree or a Tom Gordon?[79]

It would be idle to tell anything about the story of a work which is, or soon will be, in all our readers' hands; we only render our tribute to it as a great novel, leaving to others the task of weighing it in the political balance.

Source text

[Eliot, George], Review of *Dred*, by Harriet Beecher Stowe, *Westminster Review* 66 (October 1856), 571–3.

References

McMullen, Bonnie Shannon, 'Harriet Beecher Stowe', in John Rignall (ed.), *Oxford Reader's Companion to George Eliot* (Oxford: Oxford University Press, 2001).

---

74 Leader of the Covenanters in Sir Walter Scott's *Old Mortality*, a novel (1816)
75 Battles of the Covenanters in Scotland in June 1679
76 An enthusiast and preacher in *Old Mortality*
77 'In a favourable manner' (*OED*)
78 'Contentious, disputatious' (*OED*), especially by way of intervening in public debate
79 Vicious slave owners in, respectively, *Uncle Tom's Cabin* (1852) and *Dred*

ODNB
Rudd, Andrew, '"Oriental" and "Orientalist" Poetry: The Debate in Literary Criticism
    in the Romantic Period', *Romanticism* 13.1 (2007), 53–62.

Edmund Clarence Stedman (1833–1908)

From 'Victorian Poets' (1873)

Edmund Clarence Stedman was an American poet, critic, and stockbroker
who in 1873 invented the label 'Victorian poets' for those writing verse
during Victoria's reign (a term not then current in Britain) (Cohen, 166–7).
Stedman, like many nineteenth-century poetry critics, noted the challenge
of belatedness for the era but more especially emphasised the impact of
writing in a scientific age. According to Robert Scholnick, science was also
germane to Stedman's criticism: 'Influenced by the ideas of French critic
Hippolyte Taine, Stedman brought a scientific rigor to American criticism'
(*ANB*). His book *Victorian Poets* (1875) won praise on both sides of the
Atlantic when it appeared in 1875. His aims were likewise transatlantic.
He had begun by examining American poetry but, he noted in his 1875
preface, seeing that American and British poets shared notable cultural
contexts, he turned to Britain: 'In order to formulate my own ideas of
poetry and criticism, it seemed to me that I could more freely and graciously begin by choosing a foreign paradigm than by entering upon the
home-field' (*Victorian Poets*, xiii–xiv). Not surprisingly, the concluding
paragraph of his book's forerunner, the 1873 article excerpted below also
titled 'Victorian Poets', yoked American and British poetries in a common
Anglophone tradition.

From 'Victorian Poets'

There are passages in modern poems which nearly indicate the approaching harmony of Poetry and Science; [...] In all this we discern the remaining features which,
though less radical in their importance than the scientific revolution, have marked
the Victorian period as one of transition, and as composite in its thought and structure of its poetic art. [...]
    Never was the technique of poetry so well understood as since the time of
Keats and the rise of Tennyson and his school.[80] The *best* models are selected by
the song-writers, the tale-tellers, the preachers in verse; and a neophyte[81] of to-day
would disdain the triteness and crudeness of the master-workmen of fifty years ago.
[...] The rhythm of every dainty lyrical inspiration which heralded the morning of
English minstrelsy has been caught and adapted by the song-writers, all of whom,

---

80 John Keats (1795–1821); Alfred Lord Tennyson (1809–92), appointed poet laureate in 1850
81 Neophyte: beginner

from Barry Cornwall and Hood to Kingsley and Jean Ingelow, have new arrangements and fantasia of their own.[82] [...]

But a period of transition is also one of doubt and turbulence [...]. Conscious
of this, a few, with a spasmodic[83] effort to be original, break away in disdain of all
art, palming off a "saucy roughness"[84] for strength and coarseness for vigor; and
even this return to chaos wins the favor of many who, from very sickness of over-
refinement, pass to the other extreme, and welcome the meaner work for a time
because it is a change. The effect of novelty gives every fashion a temporary hold;
but the calmer vision looks above and along the succession of modes, and seeks
what is in itself ennobling. [...]

[T]hat the years of transition are near an end, and that, in England and America,
a creative poetic literature, adapted to the new order of thought and the new aspirations of humanity, will speedily grow into form, I believe to be evident wherever our
common tongue is the language of imaginative expression. The idyllic philosophy in
which Wordsworth[85] took refuge from the cant and melodrama of his predecessors,
has fulfilled its immediate mission; the art which was born with Keats and found its
perfect work in Tennyson, already seems faultily faultless[86] and over-refined. A crav-
ing for more dramatic, spontaneous utterance is prevalent with the new generation.
There is an instinct that to interpret the hearts and souls of men and women is
the poet's highest function; a disposition to throw aside precedents—to study life,
dialect, and feeling, as our painters study landscape, out of doors and at first hand[87].
[...] The transition-period, doubtless, will be prolonged by the ceaseless progress
of the scientific revolution, occupying men's imaginations and constantly readjusting
the basis of language and illustration. Ere long, some new Lucretius[88] may come to
reinterpret the nature of things, confirming many of the ancient prophecies, and
substituting for the wonder of the remainder the still more wondrous testimony of
the lens, the laboratory, and the millennial rocks. The old men of the Jewish captivity
wept with a loud voice when they saw the foundations of the new temple, because
its glory in their eyes, in comparison of that builded by Solomon, was as nothing;
but the prophet assured them that the Desire of all nations should come, and that
the glory of the latter house should be greater than of the former.[89] But I do not

---

82 Barry Cornwall: pseudonym of poet Bryan Procter (1787–1874); Thomas Hood (1799–1845):
humourist and poet famous for 'The Song of the Shirt' about a starving seamstress; Charles Kingsley (1819–75): Anglican clergyman, novelist and poet; Jean Ingelow (1820–97): poet and novelist;
fantasia: any highly fanciful composition

83 Though 'spasmodic' can merely indicate jerky movement, the term is a likely literary reference included in the OED definition: 'Agitated, excited; emotional, high-strung; given to outbursts
of excitement; characterized by a disjointed or unequal style of expression', as in the 'Spasmodic
School", a name given by W. E. Aytoun [1813–65] to a group of poets chiefly represented by Alexander Smith [1829–67], Philip James Bailey [1816–1902], and Sydney Dobell [1824–74]'.

84 William Shakespeare, King Lear, II.ii.3

85 William Wordsworth (1770–1850), appointed poet laureate in 1843

86 A quote from Tennyson's Maud: A Monodrama (1855), Part I, line 82

87 An allusion to plein-air or outdoor painting associated with emerging impressionist art

88 The Roman poet Lucretius, who flourished in the first century preceding the current era, was
a poet and philosopher who propounded an early version of atomic theory in his Latin poem De
rerum natura ('On the Nature of Things').

89 The temple ordered to be built in Jerusalem by King Solomon, son of King David, was completed in 957 BCE. It was destroyed in 587–6 BCE by the Babylonian king Nebuchadnezzar II, who
deported Jews to Babylonia. In 538 BCE Cyrus II, the Persian conqueror of Babylonia, allowed the
Jews to return to Jerusalem and build a new temple, which was completed in 515 BCE.

endeavor to anticipate the future of English song. It may be lowlier or loftier than now, but certainly it will show a change, and my faith in the reality of progress is broad enough to include the field of poetic art.

Source text

Stedman, Edmund C., 'Victorian Poets', *Scribner's Monthly* 5 (January 1873), 357–64.

References

ANB
Cohen, Michael, 'E. C. Stedman and the Invention of Victorian Poetry', *Victorian Poetry* 43.2 (Summer 2005), 165–88.
Stedman, E. C. *Victorian Poets* (Boston: James R. Osgood & Co., 1875).

Oscar Wilde (1854–1900)

From 'Decorative Art in America' (1882)

Oscar Fingal O'Flahertie Wills Wilde was born in Dublin to a surgeon specialising in ear and eye disorders and to the poet who signed her work as Speranza (1821–96). After training in classics at Trinity College Dublin, Wilde matriculated at Magdalen College, Oxford, where he was awarded a double first in classical moderations and *literae humaniores* or Greats (classics) for his BA. While still at Oxford he showed his gift for wit and penchant for publicity; his quip 'I find it harder and harder every day to live up to my blue china' was circulating publicly as early as 1876 and led to his first caricature in *Punch* in the 30 October 1880 issue. Thus it is unsurprising that, prior to opening their Gilbert and Sullivan comic opera *Patience* (which spoofed aesthetes in the character Bunthorne) in New York, the D'Oyly Carte company hired Wilde to present himself as an aesthete to US audiences and to lecture on art. The success of the plan was evident in the interview published in the 8 July 1882 *Charleston News and Courier*: 'The face, form, figure, attitude and movement of the man brought "Bunthorne" forcibly to mind' (Hofer and Scharnhorst, 162).

Wilde landed in New York on 2 January 1882 and thereafter gave almost 150 lectures throughout the US and in parts of Canada before departing for England on 27 December 1882. For most of his itinerary he was accompanied by Black valet William Traquair, whose own story African-American novelist Louis Edwards fictionalised in 2003 (Ellmann, 185, 201; Edwards). Wilde's lecture topics were 'The English Renaissance', 'The House Beautiful', 'The Decorative Arts' (from May 1882) (Glaenzer, 182 n.1), and 'Irish Poets and Poetry in the Nineteenth Century'. He left a permanent impress on North American literature, aided by photographs of him in velvet knee breeches and silk stockings as well as other accoutrements taken by Napoleon Sarony (1821–96). For example, the clothing worn by Little Lord Fauntleroy in the eponymous novel (1885–6) by Frances Hodgson Burnett (1849–1924) – and by Burnett's own son – derive from Wilde's aesthetic dress. The US in turn left its impress on Wilde's depiction of Americans in Britain in 'The Canterville Ghost' (1887) and the character Hester Worsley in *A Woman of No Importance* (1893).

Figure 2.2 Sarony, Napoleon, photographer. *Oscar Wilde/Sarony. Ca.1882.* Courtesy Library of Congress Prints and Photographs Division.

From 'Decorative Art in America'

I have been through your country to some fifty or sixty cities, I think. I find what your people need is not so much high imaginative art, but that which hallows the vessels of every-day use. [. . .] Your people love art, but do not sufficiently honour the handicraftsmen. [. . .]

And what is the meaning of this beautiful decoration which we call art? In the first place, it means value to the workman, and it means the pleasure which he must necessarily take in making a beautiful thing. The mark of all good art is not that the thing done is done exactly or finely, for machinery may do as much, but that it is worked out with the head and the workman's heart.[90] [. . .] I did not imagine until I went into

---

90 Here Wilde follows his Oxford professor John Ruskin (1819–1900), who in 'The Nature of the Gothic' in *The Stones of Venice* (1851–3) extols work that engages the whole worker and condemns the manufacture of glass beads – perfect, but separate from human hands or thought.

some of your simpler cities that there was so much bad work done. I found where I went bad wall-papers, horribly designed, and coloured carpets, and that old offender, the horse-hair sofa, whose stolid look of indifference is always so depressing. [...]

It must always be remembered that what is well and carefully made by an honest workman after a rational design, increases in beauty and value as the years go on. The old furniture brought over by the Pilgrims two hundred years ago, which I saw in New England, is just as good and beautiful to-day as it was when it first came here. [...]

I regard Mr. Whistler's famous "Peacock room" as the finest thing in colour and art decoration which the world has known since Correggio painted that wonderful room in Italy where the little children are dancing on the walls.[91] Mr. Whistler finished another room just before I came away—a breakfast room in blue and yellow. The ceiling was a light blue, the cabinet-work and furniture were of a yellow wood, the curtains at the windows were white and worked in yellow, and when the table was set for breakfast with dainty blue china, nothing can be conceived at once so simple and so joyous.

The fault which I have observed in most of your rooms is that there is apparent no definite scheme of colour. Everything is not attuned to a keynote as it should be. [...]

We should see more of the workman than we do. We should not be content to have the salesman stand between us—the salesman, who knows nothing of what he is selling save that he is charging a great deal too much for it. And watching the workmen, will teach that most important lesson, the nobility of all rational workmanship. [...]

If children grow up among all fair and lovely things, they will grow to love beauty and detest ugliness before they know the reason why. [...] If everything is dainty and delicate, gentleness and refinement of manner are unconsciously acquired. When I was in San Francisco I used to visit the Chinese Quarter frequently. There I used to watch a great hulking Chinese workman at his task of digging, and used to see him every day drink his tea from a little cup as delicate in texture as the petal of a flower, whereas in all the grand hotels of the land, where thousands of dollars have been lavished on great gilt mirrors and gaudy columns, I have been given my coffee or my chocolate in cups an inch and a quarter thick. I think I have deserved something nicer.

The art systems of the past have been devised by philosophers who looked upon human beings as obstructions. They have tried to educate boys' minds before they had any. How much better it would be in these early years to teach children to use their hands in the rational service of mankind! [...] What we want is something spiritual added to life. Nothing is so ignoble that art cannot sanctify it.

Source text

Glaenzer, Richard Butler (ed.), *Decorative Art in America: A Lecture by Oscar Wilde* (New York: Brentano's, 1906).

References

Carlson, Katherine L., '*Little Lord Fauntleroy* and the Evolution of American Boyhood', *Journal of the History of Childhood and Youth* 3.1 (2010), 39–64.

---

91 'The celebrated dining-room known as the "Peacock Room" was in the residence of Frederick R. Leyland, 49 Prince's Gate, London. Whistler's decorative scheme in blue and gold was carried out by him in 1876–77' (Glaenzer, 183 n.10). The 'Peacock Room' of American James Abbott McNeill Whistler (1834–1903) is today at the Freer Gallery, Washington DC.

Edwards, Louis, *Oscar Wilde Discovers America* (New York: Scribner, 2003).

Ellmann, Richard, *Oscar Wilde* (New York: Alfred A. Knopf, 1988).

Hofer, Matthew and Gary Scharnhorst (eds), *Oscar Wilde in America: The Interviews* (Urbana, IL: University of Illinois Press, 2010).

ODNB

Frances E. W. Harper (1825–1911)

From 'A Factor in Human Progress' (1885)

As Frances Smith Foster's recovery scholarship demonstrated, Frances Harper 'became not only the most popular African-American writer of the nineteenth century but also one of the most important women in United States history' (4). Harper's prominence during her lifetime arose partly through her poetry. Meanwhile, her intellectual leadership in political causes – including abolition, suffrage, temperance and education for Blacks – further strengthened her legacy.

In speeches and essays, as in poetry, Harper touted the power of patient knowledge-building, even in discouraging times such as the post-Reconstruction era ('Democratic Victory', 6–7). When addressing race issues, she spoke extemporaneously from a 'repertoire of speeches' pitched 'to recent or local events' and further adaptable for print (Foster, 37). 'A Factor in Human Progress' fits that pattern.

This essay was also typical of Harper's *oeuvre* in being sponsored by the Black church press. For Harper and her readers, publications like the *Christian Recorder* and the *African Methodist Episcopal Church Review* fostered race community through texts blending literary and socio-political concerns (Gardner).

Harper's 'A Factor' was also consistent with her post-Reconstruction focus on education, an emphasis echoed in the serialised *Trial and Triumph* novel (1888). A major goal of these texts entailed resisting white arbiters like Atticus Haygood and Rutherford B. Hayes, leaders of the Slater Fund, a white-run philanthropic organisation whose vision for teaching former slaves and their children promoted 'industrial education' limited to basic job skills (Robbins, 82). A key tool in Harper's rhetorical arsenal marshalled her own literary knowledge of transatlantic resources for moral learning, like the poetry of George Eliot, as seen below.

From 'A Factor in Human Progress' (1885)

In the last number of the A.M.E Review[92] was a thoughtful paper entitled, "We must educate." The first question asked was: How shall we educate? and a line of action

---

[92] Founded in 1841 and originally *The A.M.E. Church Magazine*, this journal (still publishing) changed its name to *The A.M.E. Church Review* in 1884. Like its sister publication *The Christian Recorder*, in the nineteenth century the magazine promoted race uplift through multiple genres.

was finely mapped. Alongside the suggestions of that paper arises the query, How can we best utilize this education? The culture of the moral and spiritual faculties is destined to play the most important part in our future development. Knowledge is power, the great mental lever which has lifted up man in the scale of social and racial life; but a towering intellect, grand in its achievements, and glorious in its possibilities, may, with the moral and spiritual faculties held in abeyance, be one of the most dangerous and mischievous forces in the world. [. . .] A wicked man, intellectual and gifted, may send his influence for evil across the track of unborn ages, and hurl with mortmain hand a legacy of maledictions to future generations;[93] while, on the other hand, from some bulrush ark and lowly manger or humble habitation, has come the teacher with the chrism[94] of a new era upon his brow, and left upon the centuries the fragrance of his memory.

We are living in the midst of a people who have in their veins the blood of some of the strongest nations on earth – nations who have been pioneers of civilization, macadamizers[95] of paths untrod, masters of achievement, and we have need of the best educational influences of the home, school and church to prepare us to fill our places nobly and grandly in the arena of life; for this we need more than the training of the intellectual faculties. I have heard of a scientist, who, in trying an experiment in hatching chickens, made an unequal distribution of temperature, applying cold where heat should have been more uniform, and the result was deformity and malformation. The education of the intellect and the training of the morals should go hand-in-hand.[96] The devising brain and the feeling heart should never be divorced, and the question worth asking is not simply, What will educations do for us? but, What will it help us to do for others? Do you point me with pride to your son, and tell me the best college in the country is his *alma mater*, that he has passed triumphantly through its curriculum; that he is well versed in ancient lore and modern learning, and that his mind is an arsenal of well-stored facts, fully equipping him for the battle of life? I ask, in reply, Is he noble and upright? Does he prefer integrity to gold, principle to ease, true manhood to self-indulgence? Is he chaste in his conversation, and pure in his life? If not, I answer, his education is unfinished. He may be brilliant and witty; eager, keen and alert for the main chance; but he is not prepared to be a moral athlete, armed for glorious strife, ready to win on hotly-contested fields new battles for humanity. George Eliot in her poem, "The Spanish Gypsy,"[97] has for one of her characters a Gypsy chieftain, a captain of the Spaniards, who discovers in the affianced bride of the Duke of Alva his long-lost daughter, who years before was stolen from him and reared by the duke's mother. Before her the vista of the future is opening with all the light and joy of young wedded love in a ducal palace, when suddenly her father appears upon the scene and discloses her origin, and with words of peculiar power he urges her to join the Zincalas, and clasp with him their fortunes in her hand. In revealing himself to her, he says:

---

93 Property held by a church or other organisation; maledictions: curses (*OED*)
94 Holy oil
95 Road-builder
96 See Robbins (87) for the limitations this philosophy might have for some current readers.
97 On Harper's use of Eliot's poem as an example of the African Americans' transformative repurposing of Victorian literature, see Hack (78–84). As a narrative about 'unwitting passing and voluntary racial affiliation' (83), one appeal of *The Spanish Gypsy* lay in its writing against 'the equation of African ancestry with tragedy' (Hack, 80).

"I lost you as a man may lose a diamond
Wherein he has compressed his total wealth,
On the right hand whose cunning makes him great:
I lost you by a trivial accident.
Marauding Spaniards, sweeping like a storm
Over a spot within the Spanish bounds,
Near where our camp lay, doubtless snatched you up,
When Zind, your nurse, as she confessed, was urged
By burning thirst to wander towards the stream,
And leave you on the sand some paces off,
Playing with pebbles, while she, dog-like, lapped.
It was so I lost you ..."

But now, in finding her, he tells her that she is a Zincala –

                              "Of a blood,
        Unmixed as virgin wine-juice."

Fedalma asks, –

                              "Of a race
        More outcast and despised than Moor or Jew?"

To which Zarca replies –

        "Yes: wanderers whom no God took knowledge of
        To give them laws, or fight for them, or blight
        Another race to make them ample room;
        A people with no home even in memory;
        No dimmest lore of giant ancestors
        To make a common hearth for piety."

Fedalma, his daughter, answers:

        "A race that lives on prey, as foxes do
        With stealthy, petty repine; so despised,
        It is not persecuted, only spurned,
        Crushed under foot, warred on by chance, like rats,
        Or swarming flies, or reptiles of the sea
        Dragged in the net unsought, and flung far off
        To perish as they may?"

Zarca: –

                              "You paint us well.
        So abject are the men whose blood we share;
        Untutored, unbefriended, unendowed;
        No favorites of heaven or of men,
        Therefore I cling to them! Therefore no lure
        Shall draw me to disown them or forsake

The meagre, wandering herd that lows for help
And needs me for its guide, to seek my pasture
Among the well-fed beeves that graze at will.
Because our race have no great memories
I will so live they shall remember me
For deeds of such divine beneficence
As rivers have, that teach men what is good
By blessing them. I have been schooled, – have caught
Lore from the Hebrew, deftness from the Moor, –
Know the rich heritage, the milder life,
Of nations fathered by a mighty Past;
But were our race accursed (as they who make
Good luck a god count all unlucky men)
I would espouse their cause, sooner than take
My gifts from brethren naked of all good,
And lend them to the rich for usury."[98]

Where, in the wide realms of poet[r]y and song, will we find nobler sentiments expressed with more tenderness, strength and beauty? However low down a people may be in the scale of character and condition, absorbed in providing for their physical wants, or steeped in sensuous gratifications, the moment their admiration is awakened and their aspirations kindled by the recital, or the example of deeds of high and holy worth, and the spirit of self-sacrifice and self-surrender for some good cause is awakened and developed, there comes in that race a dividing line between the sensuous and material, and the spiritual and progressive. [...] In the poem to which I have referred, the Gypsy tells his daughter, "No curse has fallen upon us till we have ceased to help each other." Men cannot help each other in the right spirit without helping themselves. The reflex of good deeds is in their own lives. Do you wish to know anything of the moral and spiritual status of a people, find out, not simply how they use their working hours, but how they spend their leisure moments. If these moments are only devoted to amusements and entertainments; if their religion largely consists of emotional fervors, without corresponding practice; if, in the midst of grog-shops and debauchery, they can shout and sing, and be unwilling to make any effort, or practice any self-denial to stay those tides of death whose dreadful breakers dash around the church and home, submerging youth and manhood beneath the waves of intemperance, such a people may produce gifted and brilliant talkers and thinkers, and religious enthusiasts, but it is only as the spirit of self-surrender enters into their lives that its true strength is developed. Self-sacrifice and self-surrender have been the golden cords that have lifted men nearer to God, and brought heaven closer to earth. Had Moses preferred the luxury of an Egyptian palace to the endurance of hardships with his people, would the Jews have been the race to whom we owe the most, not perhaps for science and art, but for the grandest of all sciences, the science of a true life of joy and trust in God, of God-like forgiveness and divine self-surrender?[99] [...] During the days of slavery we read

---

98 Harper's quotations likely came from the author-approved US edition printed with 'Advance Sheets': Eliot, George, *The Spanish Gypsy, A Poem* (Boston, Ticknor & Fields, 1868), Book I, 106–9.
99 As signalled earlier in her reference to 'some bulrush ark', Harper considered Moses a model for African Americans. Her *Moses: A Story of the Nile* narrative poem (1869) retells the Bible story with that emphasis. Relatedly, Hubbard positions Harper as an exemplar of 'Africana womanism' (69), thereby underscoring the poet-activist's position as a transatlantic thinker.

of a man who knew the plan of some of his fellow slaves to obtain their freedom, but rather than betray them, he received seven hundred and fifty lashes, and died. Among the annals of the civil war is the story of a colored man who was in a boat which became stranded, and there was a lack of strength to shove her from the sand, unless some one would expose himself to fire of rebel bullets, and this man, comprehending the situation, exclaimed, "Some one must die to get us out of this. I mought's well be him as any. You are soldiers and can fight. If they kill me it is nothing." And facing danger and death, he shoved the boat from the treacherous sands, received a number of bullets, and died.[100] Who shall say that the race out of which such men could spring from under the dark shadow of slavery has not within it the elements out of which a great people may yet be produced? What a field of usefulness lies before the educated young men and women of our race! What possibilities are in their hands! As "sculptors of life, they stand with their work before them." What shall the carving be? Images of beauty, love and truth? or weakness, vanity and selfishness? I remember once talking with a school teacher in a Southern State, who, speaking of her lack of society, said of those by whom she was surrounded: "They all talk gossip, and wouldn't improve me." Suppose she had viewed the social condition of her neighbors from another standpoint, and said, These women cannot improve me, but I will try to improve them. If they talk nothing but gossip, I will try to raise the tone of conversation, and show them a more excellent way. I will study to teach these mothers how to take care of their little ones; I will learn something of the sophistries of strong drink, of the effect of stimulants and narcotics on the human system, and teach them how intemperance adds to the burdens, waste and miseries of society; because I have had advantages that were denied them; as a friend and sister, I will gladly share with them my richer heritage. Would not such a resolution have given a new significance to her life, and added power which no wealth of intellectual attainments could have given without it? for the best test of a good education is not simply what we know, but what we do, and what we are. When the last lay of the minstrel shall die upon his ashy lips and the sweetest numbers of the poet shall cease to charm the death-dulled ear, when we are ready to lay aside much that we learned as a garment we have outworn and outgrown, then we hope that the science of well-spent hours will go with us through the valley and shadow of death, only to grow brighter and brighter through the eternities.

Philadelphia, Pa.

Source text

Harper, Frances E. W., 'A Factor in Human Progress', *African Methodist Episcopal Church Review* 2 (July 1885), 14–18.

References

Foster, Frances Smith (ed.), *A Brighter Coming Day: A Frances Ellen Watkins Harper Reader* (New York: Feminist Press, 1990).

Gardner, Eric, *Black Print Unbound: The* Christian Recorder, *African American Literature, and Periodical Culture* (Oxford: Oxford University Press, 2015).

---

100 Harper adapted this tale, and the same quote, in Chapter 7 of her 1892 novel *Iola Leroy, Or, Shadows Uplifted* (53).

Hack, Daniel, *Reaping Something New: African American Transformations of Victorian Literature* (Princeton, NJ: Princeton University Press, 2017).

Harper, Frances E. W., *Iola Leroy, or, Shadows Uplifted* (Boston: James H. Earle, Publisher, 1892).

Harper, Mrs. Frances E. W., 'The Democratic Victory and the Negro: Mrs. Frances E. W. Harper of Philadelphia', *The Independent* (15 January 1885), 6–7.

Hubbard, LaRese, 'Frances Ellen Watkins Harper: A Proto-Africana Womanist', *Western Journal of Black Studies* 36.1 (2012), 68–75.

Robbins, Sarah, 'Gendering the Debate over African Americans' Education in the 1880s', *Legacy* 19.1 (January 2002), 81–9.

'Buffalo Bill and the Wild West' (1887)

Today the *Saturday Review* account of 'Buffalo Bill' (William F. Cody, 1846–1917) and his Wild West show is notable for its white supremacist framework and quiescent acceptance of bison's wholesale slaughter. In 1887 the article was part of a mass-media advertising blitz that Cody both orchestrated and benefitted from to promote the six-month London run of 'Buffalo Bill's Wild West: America's National Entertainment', which opened 9 May 1887 and sold some two million tickets (Christianson, xxii). Mark Twain (1835–1910) had encouraged Cody to take his show to England after seeing it in US, arguing that it provided a more realistic glimpse of American culture than most US cultural exports (Christianson, xxi). The show rapidly became the most popular attraction of the larger American Exhibition showcasing American achievements in manufacture, technology and the arts.

The show could claim some authenticity, since Cody had experienced the West as a settler, army scout, buffalo hunter and combatant against Native Americans (Christianson, xxi). On one hand the show and its recurring 'victories' over 'Indians', who were crucial members of the troupe's cast, underlay a performance of Manifest Destiny that anticipated the 'Frontier Thesis' of historian Frederick Jackson Turner (1861–1932); this asserted that the ever-moving western frontier, rather than European settlement (or enslavement) was the lynchpin of America's development (Christianson, xvii–xix, xxvii). On the other hand, the entertainment was in part an ethnographic exhibition, since ticket buyers could visit the recreated Native American village onsite, composed mostly of Sioux Indians.

No contemporaneous Native American accounts are available, but two retrospects came decades later. The account of Black Elk given in 1932 to John G. Neihardt (whose transcription might be compared to Thomas Pringle's role in Mary Prince's history) said of the show he first joined in New York, 'I liked the part of the show we made, but not the part the Wasichus [whites] made'. *Black Elk Speaks* also narrates the exchange between the Native American troupe members and Queen Victoria, who expressed disapproval of Cody's taking Native Americans around for show; as the episode ends, 'we could see that she was a fine woman. [. . .] Maybe if she had been our Grandmother, it would have been better for our people' (Neihardt, 135–9). Standing Bear, who joined the troupe in an early twentieth-century London iteration, noted that on days when the crowd was small he sometimes acted as a cowboy instead of his usual role as 'Chief Interpreter of the Sioux Nation' (Standing Bear, 254).

According to Flint, the show's sequence always included Indian attacks on 'an emigrant wagon [. . .] terrorizing the women and children' or on 'the Deadwood stage coach (with Cody, inevitably, coming to the rescue)' (230). If the Americans projected Manifest Destiny, British audiences were fascinated by exotic Native Americans and Mexicans who peopled the multi-racial spectacle and also gratified by a display of Anglo-Saxon supe-riority centred in the show's daring white hero. As a conservative weekly aimed at the educated classes, the *Saturday Review* was an excellent venue to circulate both the fascination and Anglo-Saxon ideology (Flint, 234–5, 241; Powell, 379–81).

'Buffalo Bill and the Wild West'

Within the memory of not a few who are still young we had to travel for weeks and months in order to reach the "Wild West," and revel in the fresh breezes which blow over that ocean of flowers and grasses – the Prairie. To-day all is changed. Three weeks takes us to the portals of the Golden Gate; and now a reflex wave of American borderland has flowed to our very feet, and the "Wild West" has actually come to London. On a recent visit to the Indian encampment at West Brompton,[101] it needed very little stretch of imagination to believe one's self four thousand miles from England. A long range of Indian tents, bedecked with bright patches of colour, stretched on either side, whilst seated or standing in picturesque groups around were no less than 150 Red Indians, bivouacking within a stone's throw of our great, and, to them, curious civilization, the counterpart of which in their own country is gradually sweeping them off the face of the soil, which has been theirs for count-less generations. In a huge tent hard by a number of Mexicans—tall, lithe, athletic fellows, wearing broad-brimmed sombrero hats, and striped scarves hanging from shoulder to shoulder—sat cheerfully eating their midday meal; a little further on a score or so of Vaqueros and Cowboys were preparing theirs, and at the door of his tent Buffalo Bill himself was chatting to a party of ladies and gentlemen. It was indeed easy to imagine oneself away in the Far West. The very Indian babies, with their faces oddly painted lemon colour, toddling about with their tattooed mothers, in their long crimson blankets, with their hair bedecked with beads and even with scalps, added to the illusion. But it is by night, when the campfires are lighted, and their glow alone illuminates this uncouth extemporized comfort, and the Pawnee and Ogalalla[102] chiefs stride along from tent to tent, wrapped up in their sweeping

---

101 In 1887 a quiet neighbourhood in southwest London
102 The Pawnee People are a Plains tribe, while the Oglala Sioux are a subtribe of the Lakota People.

blankets, looking like the "ghosts of a departed glory," that the scene assumes its weirdest aspect, and quite justifies the intense curiosity which has taken possession of the inhabitants of the neighbourhood, who spend hours at their windows and even on the roofs of their houses watching intently.

A little further to the left of the encampment is a menagerie with buffaloes, Mexican horses, donkeys, ponies, stags, and antelopes, all living happy-family like together, not a very happy family either, as occasionally there is disorder even here; for only last Monday one of the buffaloes grew ugly and "ripped" a horse, but such accidents are fortunately very rare.

It will be worth going to Brompton to see this encampment in all its aspects, and it will always be accessible, let alone the remarkable display of horsemanship and of "wild sports," which have proved such an attraction throughout America during the last two years. The Hon. W. F. Cody, *alias* "Buffalo Bill," and one or two other men of his company played a prominent part in the history of his country during the Civil War. He was a Government scout and guide, and in the terrible conflicts which endured from 1863 to 1867 he participated in many great battles, and was at the close of the war honourably discharged. Then it was that he began his hunting expedition, and in a period of less than eighteen months killed 4,280 buffaloes, hence his popular nickname. In 1872 he was elected a member of the Nebraska Legislature, and thus acquired the title of "Honourable." Some time afterwards he proceeded to Chicago, and began his dramatic career; for he is an actor, and the "Wild Sports of the West" is nothing more nor less than an immense dramatic performance, illustrating life as it is witnessed on the plains—the Indian encampments, the Cowboys and Vaqueros, the herds of buffaloes and elk, the lassoing of animals, the manner of robbing mail-coaches, feats of agility, horsemanship, marksmanship, archery, and the kindred scenes and events characteristic of the American borderland. Mr. Cody's troupe of actors and actresses have lived the hard life of the plains, and some of them have taken a prominent part in the history of that portion of their country.

The American Exhibition itself, of which this entertainment will doubtless be an exceptional attraction, consists of a building 1,282 feet long, by about 250 feet broad, which will be devoted to the ordinary purposes for which exhibitions are created. It is at present not sufficiently advanced for us to be able to judge fairly of its future merits and demerits. The Fine Art Gallery will prove remarkably interesting, as affording us an idea of the vast progress made by the arts of sculpture and painting in America since the days of West and Sully.

Source text

'Buffalo Bill and the Wild West', *Saturday Review* (23 April 1887), 583.

References

Christianson, Frank, 'Editor's Introduction', in *The Wild West in England*, by William F. Cody, ed. Frank Christianson (Lincoln, NE: University of Nebraska Press, 2012), xiii–xxxv.

Flint, Kate, *The Transatlantic Indian, 1776–1930* (Princeton, NJ: Princeton University Press, 2009).

Moses, L. G., 'Performative Traditions in Indian History', in Philip J. Deloria and Neal Salisbury (eds), *A Companion to American Indian History* (Malden: Blackwell, 2002), 193–208.

Neihardt, John G., *The Complete Black Elk Speaks* (1932), introd. by Philip J. Deloria, notes by Raymond J. DeMallie (Lincoln, NE: University of Nebraska Press, 2014).

Powell, Kerry, '*Saturday Review*', in Alvin Sullivan (ed.), *British Literary Magazines: The Victorian and Edwardian Age, 1837–1913* (Westport, CT: Greenwood Press, 1984), 379–83.

Standing Bear, Luther, *My People, The Sioux* (Lincoln, NE: University of Nebraska Press, 1975).

Waegner, Cathy Covell, '"Buffalo Bill Takes a Scalp": Mediated Transculturality on Both Sides of the Atlantic with William F. Cody's Wild West, from Show to Hollywood and You Tube', in Cathy Covell Waegner (ed.), *Mediating Indianness* (East Lansing, MI: Michigan State University Press, 2015), 45–72.

Matthew Arnold (1812–88)

From 'Civilisation in the United States' (1888)

Matthew Arnold, son of the famous Rugby headmaster and Oxford's Regius Professor of Modern History Thomas Arnold (1795–1842), met William Wordsworth (1770–1850) in early childhood when the family visited its holiday home in the Lake District. Arnold also moved in elevated circles as a student at Balliol College, Oxford (1841). His first poems appeared in 1849, succeeded by lyrics such as 'Dover Beach' in 1853. Thereafter Arnold increasingly turned to essays and, with *Culture and Anarchy* (1869), became a leading man of letters on both sides of the Atlantic. He undertook an American lecture tour in 1883–4, apparently for money, his fame attracting standing room only at his inaugural lecture in New York on 30 October 1883, which General and Mrs Grant attended. But Arnold was inaudible beyond the first few rows and the Grants were among the first to leave, joined by a stream of others. Taking elocution lessons, Arnold made himself better heard subsequently, but he alienated American audiences anew by asserting, according to the 15 December 1883 *Literary World*, that Emerson was not '"a great poet, a great writer, a great philosophy maker"' (Lawrence, 69). The lecture tour thus harmed Arnold's US reputation and entrenched American impressions of British cultural snobbery (Lawrence, 63). Arnold's last word on the US, excerpted below, appeared the same month that he died of a sudden heart attack. As Lawrence notes, Arnold's judgement was that 'American civilization was "uninteresting" because of its lack of "distinction" and "beauty," . . . the newspapers were bad, and . . . the national character was inflated and self-important' (78).

Figure 2.3 Caricature of Matthew Arnold, *Punch* 81 (26 November 1881),
250. Courtesy Mary Couts Burnett Library, TCU.

From 'Civilisation in the United States'

I have said how much the word civilisation really means—the humanisation of man
in society; his making progress there towards his true and full humanity. Partial and
material achievement is always being put forward as civilisation. We hear a nation
called highly civilised by reason of its industry, commerce, and wealth, or by reason
of its liberty or equality, or by reason of its numerous churches, schools, libraries,
and newspapers. But there is something in human nature, some instinct of growth,
some law of perfection, which rebels against this narrow account of the matter. And
perhaps what human nature demands in civilisation, over and above all those obvious things which first occur to our thoughts—what human nature, I say, demands in
civilisation, if it is to stand as a high and satisfying civilisation, is best described by the
word *interesting*. Here is the extraordinary charm of the old Greek civilization—that
it is so *interesting*. Do not tell me only, says human nature, of the magnitude of your
industry and commerce; of the beneficence of your institutions, your freedom, your
equality; of the great and growing number of your churches and schools, libraries
and newspapers; tell me also if your civilisation—which is the grand name you give
to all this development—tell me if your civilisation is *interesting*. [. . .]

   Now, the great sources of the *interesting* are distinction and beauty: that which
is elevated, and that which is beautiful. Let us take the beautiful first, and consider
how far it is present in American civilisation. Evidently this is that civilisation's weak
side. There is little to nourish and delight the sense of beauty there. In the long-
settled States east of the Alleghanies the landscape in general is not interesting,

the climate harsh and in extremes. The Americans are restless, eager to better themselves and to make fortunes; the inhabitant does not strike his roots lovingly down into the soil, as in rural England. In the valley of the Connecticut you will find farm after farm which the Yankee settler has abandoned in order to go West, leaving the farm to some new Irish immigrant. The charm and beauty which comes from ancientness and permanence of rural life the country could not yet have in a high degree, but it has it in an even less degree than might be expected. Then the Americans come originally, for the most part, from that great class in English society amongst whom the sense for conduct and business is much more strongly developed than the sense for beauty. If we in England were without the cathedrals, parish churches, and castles of the catholic and feudal age, and without the houses of the Elizabethan age, but had only the towns and buildings which the rise of our middle class has created in the modern age, we should be in much the same case as the Americans. We should be living with much the same absence of training for the sense of beauty through the eye, from the aspect of outward things. The American cities have hardly anything to please a trained or a natural sense for beauty. They have buildings which cost a great deal of money and produce a certain effect—buildings, shall I say, such as our Midland Station at St. Pancras; but nothing such as Somerset House or Whitehall. [. . .] In general, where the Americans succeed best in their architecture—in that art so indicative and educative of a people's sense for beauty—is in the fashion of their villa-cottages in wood. These are often original and at the same time very pleasing, but they are pretty and coquettish, not beautiful. Of the really beautiful in the other arts, and in literature, very little has been produced there as yet. I asked a German portrait-painter, whom I found painting and prospering in America, how he liked the country? 'How *can* an artist like it?' was his answer. The American artists live chiefly in Europe; all Americans of cultivation and wealth visit Europe more and more constantly. The mere nomenclature of the country acts upon a cultivated person like the incessant pricking of pins. What people in whom the sense for beauty and fitness was quick could have invented, or could tolerate, the hideous names ending in *ville*, the Briggsvilles, Higginsvilles, Jacksonvilles, rife from Maine to Florida; the jumble of unnatural and inappropriate names everywhere?[103] On the line from Albany to Buffalo you have, in one part, half the names in the classical dictionary to designate the stations; it is said that the folly is due to a surveyor who, when the country was laid out, happened to possess a classical dictionary; but a people with any artist-sense would have put down that surveyor. The Americans meekly retain his names; and indeed his strange Marcellus or Syracuse is perhaps not much worse than their congenital Briggsville. [. . .]

It is often said that every nation has the government it deserves. What is much more certain is that every nation has the newspapers it deserves. The newspaper is the direct product of the want felt; the supply answers closely and inevitably to the demand. I suppose no one knows what the American newspapers are, who has not been obliged, for some length of time, to read either those newspapers or none at all. Powerful and valuable contributions occur scattered about in them. But on the whole, and taking the total impression and effect made by them, I should say that if one were searching for the best means to efface and kill in a whole nation the discipline of respect, the feeling for what is elevated, one could not do better than take

---

103 Arnold likewise complained in 1865 of ugly British names such as Wragg, Higginbottom, Stiggins and Bugg ('The Function of Criticism at the Present Time' in *Essays*, 23).

the American newspapers. The absence of truth and soberness in them, the poverty in serious interest, the personality and sensation-mongering, are beyond belief. There are a few newspapers which are in whole, or in part, exceptions. The *New York Nation*, a weekly paper, may be paralleled with the *Saturday Review* as it was in its old and good days; but the *New York Nation* is conducted by a foreigner, and has an extremely small sale.[104] In general, the daily papers are such that when one returns home one is moved to admiration and thankfulness not only at the great London papers, like the *Times* or the *Standard*, but quite as much at the great provincial newspapers too—papers like the *Leeds Mercury* and the *Yorkshire Post* in the north of England, like the *Scotsman* and the *Glasgow Herald* in Scotland. [...]

I once declared that in England the born lover of ideas and of light could not but feel that the sky over his head is of brass and iron. And so I say that, in America, he who craves for the *interesting* in civilisation, he who requires from what surrounds him satisfaction for his sense of beauty, his sense of elevation, will feel the sky over his head to be of brass and iron. The human problem, then, is as yet solved in the United States most imperfectly; a great void exists in the civilisation over there: a want of what is elevated and beautiful, of what is interesting. [...]

Common-sense criticism, I repeat, of all this hollow stuff there is in America next to none. There are plenty of cultivated, judicious delightful individuals there. They are our hope and America's hope; it is through their means that improvement must come. They know perfectly well how false and hollow the boastful stuff talked is; but they let the storm of self-laudation rage, and say nothing. For political opponents and their doings there are in America hard words to be heard in abundance; for the real faults in American civilisation, and for the foolish boasting which prolongs them, there is hardly a word of regret or blame, at least in public. Even in private, many of the most cultivated Americans shrink from the subject, are irritable and thin-skinned when it is canvassed. Public treatment of it, in a cool and sane spirit of criticism, there is none. In vain I might plead that I had set a good example of frankness, in confessing over here, that, so far from solving our problems successfully, we in England find ourselves with an upper class materialised, a middle class vulgarised, and a lower class brutalised. But it seems that nothing will embolden an American critic to say firmly and aloud to his countrymen and to his newspapers, that in America they do not solve the human problem successfully, and that with their present methods they never can. Consequently the masses of the American people do really come to believe all they hear about their finer nervous organisation, and the rightness of the American accent, and the importance of American literature; that is to say, they see things not as they are, but as they would like them to be; they deceive themselves totally. And by such self-deception they shut against themselves the door to improvement, and do their best to make the reign of *das Gemeine*[105] eternal. In what concerns the solving of the political and social problem they see clear and think straight; in what concerns the higher civilisation they live in a fool's paradise. This it is which makes a famous French critic speak of 'the hard unintelligence of the people of the United States'—*la dure inintelligence des Américains du Nord*—of the very people who in general pass for being specially intelligent—and so, within certain limits, they are. But they have

---

104 The *Nation*, still publishing, was founded in Manhattan in July 1865; its first editor was Irish immigrant Edwin Lawrence Godkin (1831–1902). The *Saturday Review*, a British weekly sometimes nicknamed the 'Saturday Reviler' for its acerbic reviews, ran from 1855 to 1938.
105 Community, public at large

been so plied with nonsense and boasting that outside those limits, and where it is a question of things in which their civilisation is weak, they seem, very many of them, as if in such things they had no power of perception whatever, no idea of a proper scale, no sense of the difference between good and bad. And at this rate they can never, after solving the political and social problem with success, go on to solve happily the human problem too, and thus at last to make their civilisation full and interesting.

To sum up, then. What really dissatisfies in American civilisation is the want of the *interesting*, a want due chiefly to the want of those two great elements of the interesting, which are elevation and beauty. And the want of these elements is increased and prolonged by the Americans being assured that they have them when they have them not. And it seems to me that what the Americans now most urgently require, is not so much a vast additional development of ortho-dox Protestantism, but rather a steady exhibition of cool and sane criticism by their men of light and leading over there. And perhaps the very first step of such men should be to insist on having for America, and to create if need be, better newspapers.

To us, too, the future of the United States is of incalculable importance. Already we feel their influence much, and we shall feel it more. We have a good deal to learn from them; we shall find in them, also, many things to beware of, many points in which it is to be hoped our democracy may not be like theirs. As our country becomes more democratic, the malady here may no longer be that we have an upper class materialised, a middle class vulgarised, and a lower class brutalised. But the predominance of the common and ignoble, born of the predominance of the average man, is a malady too. That the common and ignoble is human nature's enemy, that, of true human nature, distinction and beauty are needs, that a civili-sation is insufficient where these needs are not satisfied, faulty where they are thwarted, is an instruction of which we, as well as the Americans, may greatly require to take fast hold, and not to let go. We may greatly require to keep, as if it were our life, the doctrine that we are failures after all, if we cannot eschew vain boasting and vain imaginations, eschew what flatters in us the common and ignoble, and approve things that are truly excellent.

Source text

Arnold, Matthew, 'Civilisation in the United States', *Nineteenth Century* 23 (April 1888), 481–96.

References

Adams, Amanda, *Performing Authorship in the Nineteenth-Century Transatlantic Lecture Tour* (Farnham: Ashgate, 2014).
Arnold, Matthew, *Essays in Criticism* (London: Macmillan, 1865).
Butler, Leslie, *Critical Americans: Victorian Intellectuals and Transatlantic Liberal Reform* (Chapel Hill, NC: University of North Carolina Press, 2007).
Jones, Howard Mumford, 'Arnold, Aristocracy, and America', *American Historical Review* 49.3 (April 1944), 393–409.
Lawrence, E. P. 'An Apostle's Progress: Matthew Arnold in America', *Philological Quarterly* 10 (1931), 62–79.
ODNB

William Sharp (1855–1905)

From 'The Sonnet in America' (1889)

William Sharp, Scottish poet, critic, editor, novelist and mystic, is today most famous for writing visionary verse as Fiona MacLeod, a woman Highlander, during the Celtic Twilight (or Revival). Prior to adopting this pseudonym, he was also active as a literature and art critic and poet in London, then editor of *The Pagan Review* (1892), another facet of the Celtic Twilight. 'The Sonnet in America' in the Conservative British journal *National Review* is important for indicating shifting British attitudes toward American literature and the growing confidence of American poets. Nonetheless residual elements of condescension toward American poets among British commentators remain.

From 'The Sonnet in America'

To our benefit, as well as to our credit, it is no longer the vogue with literary critics to speak slightingly of American poetry. The time has gone by when the dilletante reviewer demanded, as Professor Richardson complains, that American poetry, if it was to exist at all, must be limited to pictures of the wharf, the prairie, and the gulch; to city directories and geographical indices, to axe-swinging pioneers and impromptu assassins.[106]

A close study, however, of the last fifty years of Transatlantic poetic literature, certainly does not reveal a body of first-rate work comparable with that produced among ourselves, an assertion which may be set forth without implied disparagement of the great names so dear to thousands in this country as well as to millions in America. But what more nearly concerns us is the work of very recent and contemporary poets. The test of a poetic period is not that of the absolute or relative greatness of its most eminent exemplars, any more than the production of the largest and finest apple would be the test of the best orchard. How do the secondary poets of a period sing? What is the substance of their song? What are their limits? To what does their collective voicing tend? What degree of mental individuality and poetic originality do they possess and maintain? These are the questions which the student of literature has to consider before he can formulate any general opinion.

It is not to be gainsaid—as that acute and able critic, Mr. E. C. Stedman,[107] admits—that there is "a lull in the force and efficacy of American song." Longfellow

---

106 A reference to Charles F. Richardson's *American Literature, 1607–1885*, Volume 2: *American Poetry and Fiction* (1889)
107 Edmund Clarence Stedman (1833–1908), poet, critic and stockbroker

has ceased his clear and beautiful singing, and Bryant's stately measures seem to belong to an altogether bygone period.[108] Poe, the most exaggeratedly praised and the most exaggeratedly condemned of all modern poets, long since threw away the lute of Israfel on which he played so "wildly well."[109] Emerson, potentially the greatest of American poets, rests beside a comrade to whom rhythmic metrical speech was still more emphatically denied, his friend Thoreau, who, like him, now slumbers deep in Sleepy Hollow.[110] [...] Walt Whitman, stricken in years and health, but as serene as of yore, [is] still alert to all the infinite possibilities of his own soul and of mankind in general, still oblivious to the irredeemable commonplace of so much of his barbaric chant [...].[111]

But if we compare the general body of our minor (or, to use a term that seems less weighted with the possibility of covert disparagement, our secondary) poets of the last decade or two with that of the contemporary minor singers of America, I certainly do not think it any foregone conclusion that acknowledgment of our superiority would be our due. It is not flattering, it is not pleasant, to note what a quantity of our relatively popular verse has been the merest trifling of an idle hour – ballads and rondeaux, and triolets,[112] which generally bear the same relation to poetry that flirtation does to passion.[113] [...]

Foremost among American sonneteers stands Longfellow, the only member of the supreme group who uses this form with ease and dignity. Some score of examples—including the beautiful *Divina Commedia* series[114]—might be selected from his works and compared with twenty by any modern English poet save Wordsworth, nor lose thereby for nobility of sentiment and graciousness of diction.[115]

---

108 Henry Wadsworth Longfellow (1807–82), poet and professor; William Cullen Bryant (1794–1878), poet and journalist

109 A reference to the early death of Edgar Allan Poe (1809–49). His poem 'Israfel' was first published in 1831.

110 Ralph Waldo Emerson (1803–82), American transcendentalist writer and lecturer; and Henry David Thoreau (1817–62), writer and naturalist. 'Sleepy Hollow' alludes to 'The Legend of Sleepy Hollow' by Washington Irving (1783–1859) in *The Sketchbook of Geoffrey Crayon, Gent.* (1820), a Gothic story written when Irving lived in Birmingham, England.

111 Walt Whitman (1819–92) celebrates his 'barbaric yawp' (verse 52) in 'Song of Myself', *Leaves of Grass* (1855, thereafter revised in successive editions).

112 A ballade consists of three eight-line stanzas rhyming ababbcbc and an envoy four lines long (bcbc); the rondeau is a fifteen-line poem of three stanzas (five, three and six lines long) with a refrain based on the first half or word of line 1 to form a pattern of aabba, aabR, aabbaR; and a triolet is an eight-line poem with two rhymes (abaaabab), with the first two lines repeated at the end.

113 A reference to the fixed form transatlantic vogue of the 1880s; see Hughes, *passim*.

114 *Divina Commedia*: the *Divine Comedy* of Dante Alighieri (1265–1321), completed in 1320

115 A series of five sonnets published in *Flower-de-Luce* (1867); William Wordsworth (1770–1850): British Romantic poet and Poet Laureate from 1843 to 1850

Source text

[Sharp, William], 'The Sonnet in America', *National Review* 13 (April 1889), 191–201.

References

ANB
Hughes, Linda K., 'Enclosing Forms, Opening Spaces: The 1880s Fixed-Verse Revival', in Penny Fielding and Andrew Taylor (eds), *The Literary 1880s* (Cambridge: Cambridge University Press, 2019), 34–52.
ODNB

Anna Julia Cooper (1858[?]–1964)

From 'The Negro as Presented in American Literature' (1892)

Anna Julia Cooper's groundbreaking translation of *Le Pelerinage de Charlemagne* during her graduate studies at Columbia University, like her advanced work at the Sorbonne, would come decades later than the *Voice from the South* chapter excerpted below. Shirley Moody-Turner and other contributors to a 2009 special section in *African American Review* urge inclusion of such post-*Voice* writings in any evaluation of Cooper's approach to educating African Americans (including Black women's learning) and of her vision for Black transnational intellectualism (in her 1925 dissertation's analysis of the Haitian Revolution). Vivian May offers a related argument for honouring Cooper's early engagement in what would become the négritude movement, whose intellectual history May judges as inaccurately spotlighting only male thinkers. May sees Harper's links to that transatlantic enterprise beginning with her 1900 participation in the first Pan-African Congress in London and continuing via multiple years of summer studies in Paris.

Despite these essential steps toward fully valuing Cooper's transatlanticism, 1892's *Voice* already offers ample evidence of its centrality to her thought, particularly her efforts to situate Black Americans' cultural work in dialogue with Anglophone literary culture (Hack).

Though Cooper is sometimes faulted for elitism, the chapter excerpted below highlights how her argument progresses toward asserting Black culture itself. Outlining 'phases' in the place of the 'Negro' in American literature, she first marks an evolution away from dependence on British models in all of American literature, then identifies a few white writers who have thoughtfully depicted her race (versus authors who stereotype), and finally envisions a time when Black writers themselves will take centre stage in depicting Black American life.

From 'The Negro as Presented in American Literature'[116]

Figure 2.4 Anna Julia Cooper, frontispiece, *A Voice from the South* (Xenia, OH: Aldine Printing, 1892). Courtesy Mary Couts Burnett Library, TCU.

For nations as for individuals, a product, to be worthy the term literature, must contain something characteristic and *sui generis*.[117]

So long as America remained a mere English colony, drawing all her life and inspiration from the mother country, it may well be questioned whether there was such a thing as American literature. "Who ever reads an American book?"[118] it was scornfully asked in the eighteenth century. Imitation is the worst of suicides; it cuts the nerve of originality and condemns to mediocrity: and 'twas not till the pen of our writers was dipped in the life blood of their own nation and pictured out its own peculiar heart throbs and agonies that the world cared to listen. The nightingale and the skylark had to give place to the mocking bird, the bobolink and the whippoorwill, the heather and the blue bells of Britain, to our own golden-rod and daisy; the insular and monarchic customs and habits of thought of old England

---

116 Though this title appears in her table of contents, Cooper's first edition of *Voice* gives another at the head of the chapter: 'One Phase of American Literature'. We follow the influential edition co-edited by Lemert and Bhan in using the table of contents title.

117 Unique as a kind or type

118 See Sydney Smith's essay – to which a number of nineteenth-century Americans defensively responded – earlier in this section.

must develop into the broader, looser, freer swing of democratic America, before her contributions to the world of thought could claim the distinction of individuality and gain an appreciative hearing. [. . .]

For two hundred and fifty years there was in the American commonwealth a great *silent* factor. [. . .] Imported merely to be hewers of wood and drawers of water, no artist for many a generation thought them worthy the sympathetic study of a model. No Shakespeare arose to distil from their unmatched personality and unparalleled situations the exalted poesy and crude grandeur of an immortal Caliban. [. . .] With massive brawn and indefatigable endurance they wrought under burning suns and chilling blasts, in swamps and marshes, – they cleared the forests, tunneled mountains, threaded the land with railroads, planted, picked and ginned the cotton, produced the rice and the sugar for the markets of the world. Without money and without price they poured their hearts' best blood into the enriching and developing of this country. *They wrought but were silent.* [. . .]

In the days of their bitterest persecution, their patient endurance and Christian manliness inspired Uncle Tom's Cabin, which revolutionized the thought of the world on the subject of slavery and at once placed its author in the front rank of the writers of her country and age. Here at last was a work which England could not parallel. Here was a work indigenous to American soil and characteristic of the country – a work which American forces alone could have produced. [. . .]

By a rough classification, authors may be separated into two groups: first, those in whom the artistic or poetic instinct is uppermost – those who write to please – or rather who write because *they* please; who simply paint what they see, as naturally, as instinctively, and as irresistibly as the bird sings – with no thought of an audience – singing because it loves to sing, – singing because God, nature, truth sings through it. For such writers, to be true to themselves and true to Nature is the only canon. They cannot warp a character or distort a fact in order to prove a point. [. . .] [T]he singer sings on with his hat before his face, unmindful, it may be unconscious, of the varied strains reproduced from him in the multitudinous echoes of the crowd. Such was Shakespeare, such was George Eliot, such was Robert Browning. Such, in America, was Poe, was Bryant, was Longfellow; and such, in his own degree perhaps, is Mr. Howells.[119]

In the second group belong the preachers, – whether of righteousness or unrighteousness, – all who have an idea to propagate, no matter in what form their talent enables them to clothe it, whether poem, novel, or sermon, – all those writers with a purpose or a lesson, who catch you by the buttonhole and pommel you over the shoulder till you are forced to give assent in order to escape their vociferations; or they may lure you into listening with the soft music of the siren's tongue – no matter what the expedient to catch and hold your attention, they mean to fetter you with their one idea, whatever it is, and make you, if possible, ride their hobby. In this group I would place Milton in much of his writing, Carlyle in all of his, often our own Whittier, the great reformer-poet, and Lowell; together with such novelists as E. P. Roe, Bellamy, Tourgée and some others.[120]

---

119 Americans Edgar Allan Poe, William Cullen Bryant, Henry Wadsworth Longfellow and William Dean Howells
120 James Russell Lowell is often classified along with Whittier and Longfellow as Fireside or Schoolroom Poets, partly given their popularity, partly given their regular inclusion in school curricula well into the twentieth century. Novelists Cooper names are Edward Payson Roe, Edward Bellamy, and Albion Winegar Tourgée, who (Lemert and Bhan indicate, 137 n.4) wrote an appreciative review of *Voice*.

Now in my judgment writings of the first class will be the ones to withstand the ravages of time. [...]

Now owing to the problematical position at present occupied by descendants of Africans in the American social polity [...] most of the writers who have hitherto attempted a portrayal of life and customs among the darker race have belonged to our class II: they have all, more or less, had a point to prove or a mission to accomplish, and thus their art has been almost uniformly perverted to serve their ends; and, to add to their disadvantage, most, if not all the writers on this line have been but partially acquainted with the life they wished to delineate and through sheer ignorance ofttimes, as well as from design occasionally, have not been able to put themselves in the darker man's place. [...] Not many have had Mrs. Stowe's power because not many have studied with Mrs. Stowe's humility and love. They forget that underneath the black man's form and behavior there is the great bed-rock of humanity, the key to which is the same that unlocks every tribe and kindred of the nations of earth. Some have taken up the subject with a view to establishing evidences of ready formulated theories and preconceptions; and, blinded by their prejudices and antipathies, have altogether abjured all candid and careful study. Others with flippant indifference have performed a few psychological experiments on their cooks and coachmen, and with astounding egotism, and powers of generalization positively bewildering, forthwith aspire to enlighten the world with dissertations on racial traits of the Negro. A few with really kind intentions and a sincere desire for information have approached the subject as a clumsy microscopist, not quite at home with his instrument, might study a new order of beetle or bug. Not having focused closely enough to obtain a clear-cut view, they begin by telling you that all colored people look exactly alike and end by noting down every chance contortion or idiosyncrasy as a race characteristic. [...]

It is in no captious spirit, therefore, that we note a few contributions to this phase of American literature which have been made during the present decade; we shall try to estimate their weight, their tendency, their truthfulness and their lessons, if any, for ourselves.

Foremost among the champions of the black man's cause through the medium of fiction must be mentioned Albion W. Tourgée.[121] No man deserves more the esteem and appreciation of the colored people of this country for his brave words. For ten years he has stood almost alone as the enthusiastic advocate, not of charity and dole to the Negro, but of justice. The volumes he has written upon the subject have probably been read by from five to ten millions of the American people. Look over his list consecrated to one phase or another of the subject: "A Fool's Errand," "A Royal Gentleman," "Bricks without Straw," "An Appeal to Cæsar," "Hot Ploughshares," "Pactolus Prime," – over three thousand pages – enough almost for a life work, besides an almost interminable quantity published in periodicals. [...]

[W]e must say, we do not think of him a novelist primarily; that is, novel making with him seems to be a mere incident, a convenient vehicle through which to convey those burning thoughts which he is constantly trying to impress upon the people of America, whether in lecture, stump speech, newspaper column or magazine article. His power is not that already referred to of thinking himself imaginatively

---

121 Carolyn Karcher dubs Tourgée (1838–1905) 'the man nineteenth-century African Americans widely regarded as their most reliable white ally' (2) and, in accord with Cooper, suggests he 'turned to literature as a medium for mobilizing the public to demand that the nation fulfill its obligation to the emancipated slaves' (6).

into the experiences of others. He does not create many men of many minds. All his offspring are little Tourgées – they preach his sermons and pray his prayers. [...]

The colored people do not object to the adequate and truthful portrayal of types of their race in whatever degree of the scale of civilization, or of social and moral development, is consonant with actual facts or possibilities. As Mr. Howells himself says, "A man can be anything along the vast range from angel to devil, and without living either the good thing or the bad thing in which his fancy dramatizes him, he can perceive it" – and I would add, can appreciate and even enjoy its delineation by the artist. The average Englishman takes no exception to the humorous caricatures of Dickens or to the satires and cynicisms of Thackeray. [...] But were Dickens to introduce an average scion of his countrymen to a whole congregation of *Quilps*,[122] at the same time sagely informing him that these represented *the best there was* of English life and morals, I strongly suspect the charming author would be lifted out on the toe of said average Englishman's boot, in case there shouldn't happen to be a good horsewhip handy.

Our grievance then is not that we are not painted as angels of light or as goody-goody Sunday-school developments; but we do claim that a man whose acquaintanceship is so slight that he cannot even discern diversities of individuality, has no right or authority to hawk "the only true and authentic" pictures of a race of human beings. Mr. Howells' point of view is precisely that of a white man who sees colored people at long range or only in certain capacities. His conclusions about the colored man are identical with the impressions that will be received and carried abroad by foreigners from all parts of the globe, who shall attend our Columbian Exposition[123] for instance, and who, through the impartiality and generosity of our white countrymen, will see colored persons only as boot-blacks and hotel waiters, grinning from ear to ear and bowing and courtesying for the extra tips. [...]

[A]n authentic portrait, at once aesthetic and true to life, presenting the black man as a free American citizen, not the humble slave of *Uncle Tom's Cabin* – but the *man*, divinely struggling and aspiring yet tragically warped and distorted by the adverse winds of circumstance, has not yet been painted. It is my opinion that the canvas awaits the brush of the colored man himself. It is a pathetic—a fearful arraignment of America's conditions of life, that instead of that enrichment from the years and days, the summers and springs under which, as Browning[124] says,

"The flowers turn double and the leaves turn flowers," –

the black man's native and original flowers have in this country been all hardened and sharpened into thorns and spurs. In literature we have no artists for art's sake. Albery A. Whitman[125] in *"Twasinta's Seminoles"* and *"Not a Man and Yet a Man"* is

---

122 Daniel Quilp: a memorably drawn violent villain from *The Old Curiosity Shop* (1840–1)
123 The long-awaited World's Fair would open in Chicago in 1893, envisioned as a celebration of Columbus's 'discovery' of the New World in 1492. Ida B. Wells, Frederick Douglass, Irvine Garland Penn and Ferdinand L. Barnett co-authored a critique of the Fair's marginalising of African Americans, *The Reason Why the Colored American Is Not in the World's Columbian Exposition* (1893).
124 Robert Browning (1812–89), whose 'Cleon' Cooper quotes below
125 Albery Allson Whitman (1851–1901), like Cooper, signalled in his writings a deep knowledge of English literature yet sought to carve out an American authorial identity aligned with race leadership. His *Not a Man, and Yet a Man* (1877) and *Twasinta's Seminoles* (1884) were followed by 1893's 'The Freedman's Triumphant Song' (which he recited at the Columbian Exposition) and his epic, *An Idyl of the South* (1901).

almost the only poet who has attempted a more sustained note than the lyrics of Mrs. Harper,[126] and even that note is almost a wail.

The fact is, a sense of freedom in mind as well as in body is necessary to the appreciative and inspiring pursuit of the beautiful. A bird cannot warble out his fullest and most joyous notes while the wires of his cage are pricking and cramping him at every heart beat. His tones become only the shrill and poignant protest of rage and despair. And so the black man's vexations and chafing environment, even since his physical emancipation has given him speech, has goaded him into the eloquence and fire of oratory rather than the genial warmth and cheery glow of either poetry or romance. And pity 'tis, 'tis true. A race that has produced for America the only folk-lore and folk songs of native growth, a race which has grown the most original and unique assemblage of fable and myth to be found on the continent, a race which has suggested and inspired almost the only distinctive American note which could chain the attention and charm the ear of the outside world—has as yet found no mouthpiece of its own to unify and perpetuate its wondrous whisperings [. . .].

Source text

Cooper, Anna Julia, *A Voice from the South* (Xenia, OH: Aldine Publishing, 1892).

References

Hack, Daniel, *Reaping Something New: African American Transformations of Victorian Literature* (Princeton, NJ: Princeton University Press, 2017).

Karcher, Carolyn, *A Refugee from His Race: Albion W. Tourgée and His Fight against White Supremacy* (Chapel Hill, NC: University of North Carolina Press, 2006).

Lemert, Charles and Esme Bhan (eds), *The Voice of Anna Julia Cooper* (Lanham: Rowman & Littlefield, 1998).

May, Vivian M., '"It Is Never a Question of the Slaves": Anna Julia Cooper's Challenge to History's Silences in Her 1925 Sorbonne Thesis', *Callaloo* 31.3 (2008), 903–18.

Moody-Turner, Shirley, 'Preface: Anna Julia Cooper: A Voice beyond the South', *African American Review* 43.1 (Spring 2009), 7–9.

E. Pauline Johnson (Tekahionwake) (1861–1913)

From 'A Strong Race Opinion: On the Indian Girl in Modern Fiction' (1892)

Emily Pauline Johnson occupied an in-between space in racial identity as the daughter of Mohawk chief George Henry Martin Johnson (Onwanonsyshon)

---

126 Frances E. W. Harper, Black poet, novelist, orator and educator; see, in the SC section, her 'Maceo' poem, which depicts an Afro-Cuban resistance fighter, and 'A Factor of Human Progress' earlier in this section.

and English-born Emily Susanna Howells (related to American author W. D. Howells, discussed in this section by Anna Julia Cooper). Canadian federal law classed Johnson as Indian based on her father, but tribal law dictated that she could inherit no Mohawk rank because of her white mother (Strong-Boag and Gerson, 47–9). Johnson intriguingly foregrounded her hybrid identity as a poet-performer from 1892 until her death in 1913, appearing both in her constructed Native costume and in European evening dress in North America and England (Strong-Boag and Gerson, 102–6, 113). Though she benefitted from her upbringing in a comfortable middle-class home with servants and a piano and her bicultural education in both her heritages, E. Pauline Johnson strongly identified as Mohawk, adding her grandfather's name of Tekahion-wake to her Euro-Canadian name in her signature and performances. Educated at Brantford Collegiate in her teens (Rose, web), she also aligned herself with Canadian New Women (Strong-Boag and Gerson, 59), those who sought enlarged educational and employment opportunities and personal freedoms for women (see also Johnson's 'The Lodge of the Law-Makers' in SC). Johnson's firm commitments to Six Nations peoples and to women's advancement are evident in her essay on the representation of the 'Indian Girl in Modern Fiction'. 'A Strong Race Opinion' appeared in the Toronto *Globe* in 1892 while she was crafting her public authorial persona. As her biographers comment, her bold critique of 'Indian' female stereotypes in contemporary fiction was a 'testament to early daring and confidence' that preceded the more complicated negotiations with authorship she later experienced as a mixed-race woman writer (Strong-Boag and Gerson, 187).

'A Strong Race Opinion: On the Indian Girl in Modern Fiction'

Every race in the world enjoys its own peculiar characteristics, but it scarcely follows that every individual of a nation must possess these prescribed singularities, or otherwise forfeit in the eyes of the world their nationality. Individual personality is one of the most charming things to be met with, either in a flesh and blood existence, or upon the pages of fiction, and it matters little to what race an author's heroine belongs, if he makes her character distinct, unique and natural.

The American book heroine of to-day is vari-colored as to personality and action. The author does not consider it necessary to the development of her character, and the plot of the story to insist upon her having American-colored eyes, an American carriage, an American voice, American motives, and an American mode of dying; he allows her to evolve an individuality ungoverned by nationalisms – but the outcome of impulse and nature and a general womanishness.

Not so the Indian girl in modern fiction, the author permits her character no such spontaneity, she must not be one of womankind at large, neither must she have an originality, a singularity that is not definitely 'Indian.' I quote 'Indian' as there seems to be an impression amongst authors that such a thing as tribal distinction does not exist among the North American aborigines.

Tribal Distinctions.

The term 'Indian' signifies about as much as the term 'European,' but I cannot recall ever having read a story where the heroine was described as 'a European.' The Indian girl we meet in cold type, however, is rarely distressed by having to belong to any tribe, or to reflect any tribal characteristics. She is merely a wholesome sort of mixture of any band existing between the Mic Macs of Gaspé and the Kwaw-Kewiths of British Columbia, yet strange to say, that notwithstanding the numerous tribes, with their aggregate numbers reaching more than 122,000 souls in Canada alone, our Canadian authors can cull from this huge revenue of character, but one Indian girl, and stranger still that this lonely little heroine never had a prototype in breathing flesh-and-blood existence![127]

It is a deplorable fact, but there is only one of her. The story-writer who can create a new kind of Indian girl, or better still portray a 'real live' Indian girl who will do something in Canadian literature that has never been done, but once. The general author gives the reader the impression that he has concocted the plot, created his characters, arranged his action, and at the last moment has been seized with the idea that the regulation Indian maiden will make a very harmonious background whereon to paint his pen picture, that, he, never having met this interesting individual, stretches forth his hand to his library shelves, grasps the first Canadian novelist he sees, reads up his subject, and duplicates it in his own work.

After a half dozen writers have done this, the reader might as well leave the tale unread as far as the interest touches upon the Indian character, for an unvarying experience tells him that this convenient personage will repeat herself with monotonous accuracy. He knows what she did and how she died in other romances by other romancers, and she will do and die likewise in his (she always does die, and one feels relieved that it is so, for she is too unhealthy and too unnatural to live).

The Inevitable "Winona."

The rendition of herself and her doings gains no variety in the pens of manifold authors, and the last thing that they will ever think of will be to study 'The Indian Girl' from life, for the being we read of is the offspring of the writer's imagination and never existed outside the book covers that her name decorates. Yes, there is only one of her, and her name is 'Winona.'[128] Once or twice she has borne another appellation, but it always has a 'Winona' sound about it. Even Charles Mair, in that masterpiece of Canadian-Indian romances, 'Tecumseh,' could not resist 'Winona.'[129] We meet her as a Shawnee, as a Sioux, as a Huron, and then, her tribe unnamed, in the vicinity of Brockville.

She is never dignified by being permitted to own a surname, although, extraordinary to note, her father is always a chief, and had he ever existed, would doubtless have been as conservative as his contemporaries about the usual significance that his people attach to family name and lineage.

---

127 Mic Macs, known today as Mi'kmaq, on the Gaspé Peninsula along the south shore of the Saint Lawrence River, Quebec; Kwaw-Kewiths are today called the Kwakwaka'wakw people associated with the Pacific Northwest Coast, primarily Vancouver Island.

128 A Dakota name meaning first-born daughter; the legendary Winona was a Dakota woman reputed to have leapt to her death rather than enter a forced marriage.

129 Charles Mair (1838–1927), white Canadian poet and journalist, authored the blank verse drama *Tecumseh* (1886), based on Shawnee Chief Tecumseh (*c.*1738–1813), born in south-central Ohio, who led the First Nations Confederacy allied with the British to resist American territorial appropriations in the war of 1812. Tecumseh died at the Battle of the Thames at Moraviantown, Ohio.

In addition to this most glaring error this surnameless creation is possessed with a suicidal mania. Her unhappy, self-sacrificing life becomes such a burden to both herself and the author that this is the only means by which they can extricate themselves from a lamentable tangle, though, as a matter of fact suicide is an evil positively unknown among Indians. To-day there may be rare instances where a man crazed by liquor might destroy his own life, but in the periods from whence 'Winona's' character is sketched self-destruction was unheard of. This seems to be a fallacy which the best American writers have fallen a prey to. Even Helen Hunt Jackson, in her powerful and beautiful romance of 'Ramona,'[130] has weakened her work deplorably by having no less than three Indians suicide while maddened by their national wrongs and personal grief.

To Be Crossed in Love Her Lot.

But the hardest fortune that the Indian girl of fiction meets with is the inevitable doom that shadows her love affairs. She is always desperately in love with the young white hero, who in turn is grateful to her for services rendered the garrison in general and himself in particular during red days of war. In short, she is so much wrapped up in him that she is treacherous to her own people, tells falsehoods to her father and the other chiefs of her tribe, and otherwise makes herself detestable and dishonourable. Of course, this white hero never marries her![131] Will some critic who understands human nature, and particularly the nature of authors, please tell the reading public why marriage with the Indian girl is so despised in books and so general in real life? Will this good far-seeing critic also tell us why the book-made Indian makes all the love advances to the white gentleman, though the real wild Indian girl (by the way, we are never given any stories of educated girls, though there are many such throughout Canada) is the most retiring, reticent, non-committal being in existence! [. . .]

And here follows the thought – do authors who write Indian romances love the nation they endeavour successfully or unsuccessfully to describe? Do they, like Tecumseh, say, 'And I, who love your nation, which is just, when deeds deserve it,' or is the Indian introduced into literature but to lend a dash of vivid colouring to an otherwise tame and sombre picture of colonial life: it looks suspiciously like the latter reason, or why should the Indian always get beaten in the battles of romances, or the Indian girl get inevitably the cold shoulder in the wars of love?

Surely the Redman has lost enough, has suffered enough without additional losses and sorrows being heaped upon him in romance. There are many combats he has won in history from the extinction of the Jesuit Fathers at Lake Simcoe to Cut Knife Creek.[132] There are many girls who have placed dainty red feet figuratively

---

130 The 1884 novel by US author Helen Hunt Jackson (1830–85)

131 Johnson herself reversed this scenario in her story 'A Red Girl's Reasoning', first published in Montreal's *Dominion Illustrated* in February 1893 (Fee and Nason, 163) and republished in *The Moccasin Maker* (1913). In the story Christine, the daughter of an Englishman and Native mother, weds Charlie McDonald, a fair-haired Englishman who falls passionately in love with her, in a Christian ceremony. Christine leaves Charlie when he betrays her own sense of honour by contending that she disgraced *him* in telling their Euro-Canadian acquaintances that Christine's parents married only in a Native ceremony, not in the church.

132 Jesuit Fathers: killed during the Iroquois Wars at Lake Simcoe, Ontario, 1648 (Gerson and Strong-Boag (eds), 324 n.); Cut Knife Creek: 'the scene of an attack on 2 May 1885, by troops under Lieutenant-Colonel Otter Against the Cree and Assiniboine camps of Chief Pitikwahanapi-wiyin (Poundmaker); after several hours' fighting, Otter retreated [. . .] and [. . .] was not pursued; this battle was part of the 1885 conflict between Canadian government forces and the Métis and First Nations peoples over land and treaty issues' (Parks Canada, Web).

upon the white man's neck from the days of Pocahontas to those of little 'Bright Eyes,' who captured all Washington a few seasons ago.[133] Let us not only hear, but read something of the North American Indian 'besting' some one at least once in a decade, and above all things let the Indian girl of fiction develop from the 'dog-like,' 'fawnlike,' 'deer-footed,' 'fire-eyed,' 'crouching ,' 'submissive' book heroine into something of the quiet, sweet womanly woman she is, if wild, or the everyday, natural, laughing girl she is, if cultivated and educated; let her be natural, even if the author is not competent to give her tribal characteristics.

Source text

Johnson, E. Pauline, 'A Strong Race Opinion: On the Indian Girl in Modern Fiction', *Toronto Sunday Globe* (22 May 1892), 1.

References

ANB
Fee, Margery and Dory Nason (eds), *Tekahionwake: E. Pauline Johnson's Writings on Native North America* (Peterloo: Broadview Press, 2016).
Gerson, Carole and Veronica Strong-Boag (eds), E. Pauline Johnson/Tekahionwake, *Collected Poems and Selected Prose* (Toronto: University of Toronto Press, 2002).
Johnson, E. Pauline, 'A Red Girl's Reasoning', *The Moccasin Maker* (Toronto: William Briggs, 1913), 116–43.
Parks Canada, 'Battle of Cut Knife Hill National Historic Site of Canada', Web.
Rose, Marilyn J., 'Johnson, E. Pauline', *Dictionary of Canadian Biography*, vol. 14 (Toronto: University of Toronto, 1998–2020), Web.
Strong-Boag, Veronica, and Carole Gerson, *Paddling Her Own Canoe: The Times and Texts of E. Pauline Johnson* (Tekahionwake) (Toronto: University of Toronto Press, 2000).

John Addington Symonds (1840–93)

From **Walt Whitman** *(1893)*

During his lifetime, English writer and critic John Addington Symonds (1840–93) was best known transatlantically for his multi-volume *Renaissance in Italy* (1875–86) and *Studies of the Greek Poets* (1873; Second Series 1876). He also contributed prolifically to periodicals, translated Michelangelo's sonnets, and authored the Renaissance artist's biography (1893).

---

133 Pocahontas (1596–1617), also known as Matoaka, mediated Anglo-Native American relations between her father, Algonquinian chief Powatan (?–1618), and John Smith (1580–1631) at Jamestown, Virginia. 'Bright Eyes' (1854–1903): Indian Rights Advocate also known as Susette La Flesche (*ANB*)

Today Symonds is best known for his work and life experiences as a queer man, from which his literary analysis was inseparable. Given an elite education at Harrow and Balliol College, Oxford, he fell in love with other men in the process, confessing an affair to his father, who counselled ending it. After suffering health ailments subsequently, he was encouraged by his physician to marry as a form of alleviating sexual repression. This he did in 1864, fathering four children before he reached an amicable agreement with his wife Catherine in 1869 that theirs would be a platonic union and he would be free to have male companions. His health thereafter notably improved, although a tubercular lung forced him to settle in Davos, Switzerland, for much of the year, while he lived with his wife and children in Venice in spring and autumn.

According to Rictor Norton, Symonds was denied an Oxford professorship because the last chapter of his 1876 volume on Greek poets too evidently defended the Greek paiderastia, a cultural practice of close bonds between adult males and young boys, often including sexual relations (*ODNB*). Even earlier, in 1873, he wrote *A Problem in Greek Ethics*, of which he privately published only ten copies in 1883. This was 'the first history of homosexuality in English' (Norton). He followed with *A Problem in Modern Ethics* in 1891, approaching homosexuality in its social, scientific and psychological aspects; of this, fifty copies were printed. He next proposed that he and sexologist Havelock Ellis (1859–1939) collaborate on a study of 'sexual inversion' but died before the work could be completed. The uproar over Oscar Wilde's trial for 'gross indecency with another man' in 1895 prevented any immediate publication of the completed study; hence *Sexual Inversion*, in which 'Case XVIII' is Symonds's own, was first published in Germany in 1896, then in England in 1897.

In both Symonds's life and his studies of literature and sexuality, Walt Whitman's poetry played an important role. After first reading Whitman in 1865, Symonds began corresponding with the poet in 1871. As Andrew Higgins notes, in 1890 Symonds asked Whitman directly about 'homosexual content' in the 'Calamus' section of *Leaves of Grass*, prompting an assertive denial from Whitman and Whitman's claim to have fathered six children (Higgins, 'Symonds, John Addington'). Symonds's own conclusions are evident in the following excerpt from his commentary on Whitman's 'Calamus' poems in his 1893 study, republished in the US in 1906.

From Walt Whitman *(1893)*

The section of Whitman's works which deals with adhesiveness, or the love of comrades, is fully as important, and in some ways more difficult to deal with, than his "Children of Adam." He gave it the title "Calamus," from the root of a water-rush, adopted by him as the symbol of this love.[134] Here the element of spirituality in passion, of romantic feeling, and of deep enduring sentiment, which was almost

---

134 'Its botanical name is Acorus Calamus. We call it "sweet-rush" or "sweet sedge."' [Symonds's note]

conspicuous by its absence from the section on sexual love,[135] emerges into vivid prominence, and lends peculiar warmth of poetry to the artistic treatment. We had to expect so much from the poem quoted by me at the commencement of this disquisition.[136] There Whitman described the love of man for woman as "fast-anchor'd, eternal"; the thought of the bride, the wife, as "more resistless than I can tell." But for the love of man he finds quite a different class of descriptive phrases: "separate, disembodied, another born, ethereal, the last athletic reality, my consolation." He hints that we have left the realm of sex and sense, and have ascended into a different and rarer atmosphere, where passion, though it has not lost its strength, is clarified. "Largior hic æther, et campos lumine vestit purpureo."[137]

This emphatic treatment of an emotion which is usually talked about under the vague and formal term of friendship, gives peculiar importance to "Calamus." No man in the modern world has expressed so strong a conviction that "manly attachment," "athletic love," "the high towering love of comrades," is a main factor in human life, a virtue upon which society will have to lay its firm foundations, and a passion equal in permanence, superior in spirituality, to the sexual affection. Whitman regards this emotion not only as the "consolation" of the individual, but also as a new and hitherto unapprehended force for stimulating national vitality.

There is no softness or sweetness in his treatment of this theme. His tone is sustained throughout at a high pitch of virile enthusiasm, which, at the same time, vibrates with acutest feeling, thrills with an undercurrent of the tenderest sensibility. Not only the sublimest thoughts and aspirations, but also the shyest, most shame-faced, yearnings are reserved for this love. At one time he exclaims:

> O I think it is not for life that I am chanting here my chant
>   of lovers—I think it must be for Death,
> For how calm, how solemn it grows, to ascend to the atmo-
>   sphere of lovers,
> Death or life I am then indifferent—my soul declines to
>   prefer,
> I am not sure but the high soul of lovers welcomes death
>   most;
> Indeed, O Death, I think now these leaves mean precisely the
>   same as you mean;
> Grow up taller, sweet leaves, that I may see! Grow up out
>   of my breast!
> Spring away from the concealed heart there!
> Do not fold yourselves so, in your pink-tinged roots, timid
>   leaves!
> Do not remain down there so ashamed, herbage of my breast!

The leaves are Whitman's emotions and the poems they engender; the root from which they spring is "manly attachment," "athletic love," symbolised for him in the blushing root of the pond-calamus which he plucked one day and chose to be the emblem of the love of lovers.

---

135 Symonds refers to heterosexual love of men for women.
136 'Fast-anchored Eternal O love!'; see Symonds, 55.
137 Virgil (70–19 BCE), *Aeneid*, 6.640–1: 'A freer and purer sky here decks the fields, and clothes them with resplendent light' (Anthon, 650).

Source text

Symonds, John Addington, *Walt Whitman: A Study* (London: John C. Nimmo, 1893).

References

Anthon, Charles, *The Æneïd, with English Notes, Critical and Explanatory* (New York: Harper & Brothers, 1843).
Elzer, Bernd, 'Queer Paths: Walt Whitman's "Calamus" Poems in the Context of His Sexuality/ies', in Christel Baltes-Löhr and Karl Hölz (eds), *Gender-Perspektiven: interdisziplinär-transversal-actuell* (Frankfurt am Main: Peter Lang, 2004), 61–77.
Friedman, Dustin, *Before Queer Theory: Victorian Aestheticism and the Self* (Baltimore, MD: Johns Hopkins University Press, 2019).
Higgins, Andrew C., 'Symonds, John Addington [1840–93]', in J. R. LeMaster and Donald D. Kummings (eds), *Walt Whitman, An Encyclopedia*, 1998; reproduced on *The Walt Whitman Archive*, Web.
Norton, Rictor, 'Symonds, John Addington', *ODNB*.

Albert Chevalier (1861–1923)

'The Yankee in London' (1900)

London-born Albert Chevalier debuted as an actor on the London stage in 1877 and, while performing character roles in the 1880s, began writing his own shows and songs. Chevalier achieved his greatest success when he shifted his performances to popular late-century London music halls. In 1891, in costermonger costume, he began performing his original coster songs. As Simon Featherstone remarks:

> The performance drew upon an older music-hall tradition of the stage cockney established by Alfred Vance [1839?–88] and others, and upon the London characters of Charles Dickens, particularly that of Sam Weller (in *Pickwick Papers*, 1836–7), whom Chevalier had played in an unsuccessful touring show. However, Chevalier modernized the speech of Weller and the mid-century cockney performers, and recast the criminal coster of Vance as a sentimental version of a working-class Londoner. (*ODNB*)

Chevalier also wrote and performed other monologues in character, including a country vicar and unsuccessful actor. After touring in the US and Canada in 1896–7, he began offering the first of one thousand recitals in Queen's Hall, London in 1899. Having first debuted 'The Yankee in London' in Worcester, England, he introduced this song into his Queen's Hall performances (Chevalier, 192). This song reprised the longstanding British charge aired by Sydney Smith (see AAE above) against American boasting of American greatness, even as both sides acknowledged affiliation. Chevalier's 'Yankee' directly resulted from his travels in America, and the photo of himself as the 'Yankee' included in his autobiography (200) suggests British stereotypes of New Yorkers at the time.

Figure 2.5 Albert Chevalier as 'The Yankee in London', *Before I Forget: The Autobiography of a Chevalier d'Industrie* (London: T. Fisher Unwin, 1901), facing 201. Courtesy Mary Couts Burnett Library, TCU.

'The Yankee in London'

I've just arrived from New York and I'm real glad that I came,
This city's out of sight! Yes sir! It's worthy of Its fame.
I've visited Chicago, Paris, Berlin, Cairo, Rome,
But here I somehow kind of, sort of, feel that I'm at home.
America just owns the sun, you get it here in bits,
We loan it, we're not selfish, we have more than we require,
Besides our hearts are warm enough to generate a fire.
We're quicker on the other side, we can't afford to wait,
We always like to get in first, you bet, we're seldom late.
There is, I know, some difference in Transatlantic time,
That may not p'r'aps explain it but it helps me with a rhyme.

Your buses and your cabs strike us Americans as slow,
Your theatres are Okay when New York supplies the show.
You can't say we're remiss, no sir, we send you of the best,
Why, in your aristocracy we've been known to invest.
We've many points in common with our cousins over here,
We come of good old stock, our sires were men who knew no fear.
We may at times run England down, I'm sorry, but I know
That relatives will squabble. It's their priv'lege, that is so.
The only real difference so far as I can see,
Is the language that you speak, which is not pure enough for me.
You have a horrid accent, you should hustle round and git,
A genuine New Yorker just to tone it down a bit.
Great country sir, America, my own, I'm proud to state
And Britain is its momma, so Great Britain's vurry great!

Source text

Music Hall Lyrics, Web.

References

Chevalier, Albert, *Before I Forget: The Autobiography of a Chevalier D'Industrie* (London: T. Fisher Unwin, 1901).
ODNB

3

BUSINESS, INDUSTRY AND LABOUR

Figure 3.1 Scene from the Hotel of Mrs Mary 'Mother' Seacole in Crimea.
Courtesy Victorian Web Foundation.

In the eighteenth century, transatlantic passages took a minimum of six weeks, and often longer, if the vessel were to arrive at all. Transatlantic commerce was therefore slow and unreliable for colonial economies dependent on regular shipments from their mother country to keep them solvent and supplied with goods and technologies. Thus the narrative of nineteenth-century commercial progress involves increasingly expedited and efficient transportation across the Atlantic. By the turn of the twentieth century the passage of goods and people regularly occurred in under a week; transatlantic communication, thanks to the undersea telegraph cable, had become nearly instantaneous. This section's inclusion of Cherokee author John Rollin Ridge's 'The Transatlantic Cable' poem acknowledges how this milestone also fostered an enthusiastic imagined community of innovative labour enterprises, while enabling expansion of transnational commercial potential.

The first European colonies in North America were a venture of private business, and subsequent east-west transatlantic immigration was largely driven by the prospect of material advancement in the New World. This overarching narrative underscores commerce's place at the heart of the Atlantic world: as nineteenth-century nations proclaimed their independence and asserted themselves through commercial as much as military might, systems of economics changed from colonialism to capitalism.

While a major form of transatlantic business shipped goods from one side to the other, plenty of activity took place on and in the ocean itself, including fishing, mineral extraction, recreation, tourism and, notably, the whaling industry portrayed in texts like *Moby-Dick*. The flow of commerce was frequently interrupted by armed conflict: piracy in the late eighteenth century, the impressment of merchant sailors that led to the War of 1812 (as in Elizabeth Gaskell's novel *Sylvia's Lovers*), European powers seeking control of various Caribbean islands, the blockade running of Confederate privateers during the American Civil War, and the onset of the Great War, wherein tons of material were shipped from Canada and the supposedly neutral US in support of the Allied cause. Such an endeavour was dangerous, of course, and the spectre of German submarine warfare lay heavily on the minds of merchant mariners, as represented in this section by British (and, for a time, Canadian) author Cicely Fox Smith's seaman's shanty 'The Ballad of the "Dinkinbar"' (1919). Though the *Dinkinbar* successfully reached its destination, hundreds of shipwrecks littering the ocean floor testify to the peril of crossing the Atlantic in times of both peace and war.

Although most transatlantic commerce involved goods exchanged between legal business partners, the system of trade itself was predicated upon the exploitation of enslaved labour, wherein Africans were treated as a commodity exchanged as part of the notorious 'Triangle Trade' among Africa, Great Britain and the Caribbean and southern US. Before the passage of the US Act Prohibiting Importation of Slaves and the UK's Act for the Abolition of the Slave Trade (both in 1807), millions of kidnapped Africans were transported as human cargo and subsequently auctioned to the highest bidder – a practice continuing illicitly into the mid-century. One major import to the UK that depended on enslaved people's labour was Caribbean sugar, which encouraged some Britons to justify (or at least tolerate) slavery on economic grounds. But sugar (along with rum) also became a symbolic and actual boycott point for English anti-slavery activists. In that context, anti-slavery women's strategic deployment of print culture to promote the sugar boycott and other protest strategies should be seen as one form of social justice labour, shaped by gender and class identities (including varying religious affiliations) that incorporated savvy literary business skill. Examples include Martha Gurney and Anna Laetitia Barbauld.[1]

Despite her abolitionist writing elsewhere, Harriet Martineau's novel *Demerara* (1832) romanticises the plantation economy of a representative British colony in South America through the eyes of travellers inbound from England. The economics of slavery also found support in prominent political settings, as evinced by James Henry Hammond's 1858 'Cotton is King' speech to the US Senate; extolling Great Britain's dependency on cotton from the American South, Hammond claimed this economic tie made a potential southern US 'empire' unassailable.

Though the US Civil War supposedly ended African Americans' enslavement, its vestiges remained in systems of sharecropping, indentured manufacturing and contract labour. Hence, even as late as 1899, the UK's *Anti-Slavery Reporter* affirmed its continuing mission in accounts such as one critiquing US convict-leasing.[2] (See, relatedly, Henry Nevinson's report on a 'Modern Slavery' in São Tomé and Principé in 'Abolition and Aftermath'.)

Earlier in the century, pro-slavery writers had pointed to the exploitative system of 'wage slavery' common to the northern United States and the United Kingdom as evidence of abolitionists' hypocrisy. So too, *Sharpe's London Magazine* detailed the 'deplorable' 'Women's Condition in Great Britain, From an American Point of View' (1860): in the UK, the editorial claimed, women were forced into menial labour as field and house hands and lacked opportunities for education and employment afforded to women in the United States. The Industrial Revolution did generate harsh conditions for workers on both sides of the Atlantic: long hours, low pay and an emphasis on speed and productivity that inevitably caused injuries and death. In response, labourers formed unions, some envisioning global ties – notably the Industrial Workers of the World (IWW), founded in Chicago in 1905. (For an examination of labour organising in Chicago viewed through the transatlantic lens of a Shakespearean analogy between magnate George Pullman and King Lear, see Jane Addams's essay in 'Family and Domesticity'.)

---

1 On Gurney and other women bringing management acumen to anti-slavery religious activism, see Elizabeth J. Clapp and Julie Roy Jeffrey (eds), *Women, Dissent, and Anti-Slavery in Britain and America, 1790–1865* (Oxford: Oxford University Press, 2011). Timothy's Whelan's 'Martha Gurney and the Anti-Slave Trade Movement, 1788–94' (44–65) chronicles the skill Baptist publisher Gurney drew upon to circulate William Fox's *An Address to the People of Great Britain, on the Propriety of Abstaining from West-India Produce* (1791), generating widespread support for boycotting West Indian sugar. Barbauld's personal support of the sugar boycott was consistent with publications like her *Epistle to William Wilberforce* (1791).

2 This unsigned essay follows a common practice of drawing from a publication originally released on the other side of the Atlantic, the pamphlet *Freed, but Not Free*, to spotlight 'the wrongs inflicted on the coloured race in some of the Southern States of America' through convict-leasing, which the British editor dubbed 'practically a revival of Slavery' ('The Convict-Leasing System in the United States', *Anti-Slavery Reporter* 19 (January–February 1899), 42).

INTELLECTUAL AND POLITICAL WORK ON LABOUR AND COMMERCE

The intellectual strand of the labour movement is often now illustrated in historical analysis by referencing the publication of Friedrich Engels's *The Condition of the Working Class in England* (1845) and Engels's and Karl Marx's *The Communist Manifesto* (1848), which detailed the antipathy bred between labour and capital by the capitalist system. The conditions observed by Engels in Manchester were swiftly followed up by the monumental *London Labour and the London Poor* by Henry Mayhew, first serialised weekly beginning in 1849 and published in four volumes in 1851. Before English-language translations of those texts circulated widely,[3] Marx reached an English-speaking transatlantic audience himself by reporting for the *New York Tribune*, as exemplified in his 1853 'Strikes' story, included here. In that entry, Marx notes the prospect of a 'civil war' brewing between mill masters and operatives, with the spirit of general strikes and revolution in the air.

Within Britain, James Bronterre O'Brien's career offers one example of intellectual work aimed at improving individual labourers' lives. O'Brien 'was dubbed the Chartist movement's "schoolmaster", because he gave it an intellectual basis' (Turner, 44). As Turner notes, British Chartists[4] like O'Brien found 'hope and inspiration' through study of 'America's political system and social condition' (43). Similar to networks helping to sustain anti-slavery, temperance and women's suffrage movements, Chartism could turn to the US for ideas (despite such shortcomings as its brutal treatment of immigrant sweatshop and meatpacking workers). Meanwhile, American settlement clubs like Jane Addams's Hull House sponsored study groups whose members read European manifestos and organised strikes informed by examples from across the Atlantic.

CONSTRAINTS AGAINST FREE-FLOWING COMMERCIAL EXCHANGE

Various barriers impeded free transatlantic commerce, most notably the system of customs and tariffs protecting domestic industries from overseas influence. Early in the nineteenth century, colonial economies were prohibited from trade with each other, a system that gave way to international commerce with US independence, and eventually transnational cooperation such as the international copyright agreements reached in Berne (1886) and Buenos Aires (1910). Copyright reforms sought by American and British writers underscored the lucrative business side of literature[5] and associated financial challenges writers faced without

---

3 Both texts, initially published in German, claimed a limited English-language readership at first. Engels's single-author text was not translated until 1885. The *Manifesto*'s first English translation (by Helen McFarlane) appeared in 1850 in a short-lived London socialist periodical, *Red Republican*, with more widely read versions in both the UK and US in the 1870s and 1880s. See Robert J. Usher, 'The Bibliography of the Communist Manifesto', *Papers of the Bibliographical Society of America* 5 (1910), 109–14.

4 Chartism, a working-class movement, emerged in the 1830s, reaching its peak activity late in that decade into the 1840s. Taking its name from a People's Charter advocating political advances for labourers, the movement petitioned Parliament multiple times, failing in each effort but sowing seeds later reflected in Reform Acts in 1867 and 1884.

5 On production innovations making print more profitable, see Fyfe.

effective transatlantic regulations of intellectual property.[6] American advocates of strengthened copyright protection included Washington Irving, Mark Twain, Oliver Wendell Holmes and James Russell Lowell, their cause supported by growing membership in the American Copyright League (Stokes), while in Britain Charles Dickens and Henry James were equally vocal. With the US long withholding signature to the Berne agreement, British writers continued to be victims of pirated editions for which they received no royalties. Meanwhile, even so genteel and purportedly progressive an author as Harriet Beecher Stowe travelled to the UK to secure copyright for her writings there and filed a copyright lawsuit against Philadelphian F. W. Thomas's unauthorised German translation of *Uncle Tom's Cabin* (Homestead).

This section also spotlights connections between publishing and transnational industry with selections from politically active periodicals inaugurated by African Americans (*Freedom's Journal*) and Native Americans (*Cherokee Phoenix*), though the latter's entry comes refracted through Charles Dickens's *Bentley's Miscellany*. Significantly, though individual authors writing professionally fought for more stringent international copyright, publications like these, whose main goal was social justice work, benefited from the free flow of reprintings that transferred their arguments and documentation of wrongs into transatlantic reprintings for potentially sympathetic audiences, making nationally produced texts transnational.

COMPETITIVE CONNECTIONS

Driven by varying agendas, nineteenth-century writers explored the links and disparities between economies on either side of the Atlantic. Examples provided here include Maria Edgeworth in 'Tomorrow' (1804) (relating the tragedy of a young British gentleman who ruins his life in America through inveterate procrastination) and Harriet Beecher Stowe in her memoir *Sunny Memories of Foreign Lands* (1854) (detailing the efforts of British reformers to address public welfare, child labour and education).

Colonies in North America and the Caribbean had earlier sought to boost fledgling domestic industries through the importation of technology from mother countries, as famously shown by Samuel Slater who memorised the design of British mill machines for his own New England factories. Some saw a turning of proverbial tables by century's end; in *The Americanization of the World* (1902), William Thomas (W. T.) Stead argued that by the turn of the century the United States had eclipsed Great Britain as the world's foremost industrial power. Measured in railways, bridges and engines, Stead posited, the flow of technology had reversed, with the US superseding its mother country. (Ridge's celebration of the transatlantic cable, referenced above, made similar arguments, if more poetically.)

---

6 Seville's *Internationalisation* notes that the failure of the 1886 Berne Convention to secure American participation was disastrous for authors, especially in Britain and Canada, since the US, 'a huge consumer of creative works', 'recognised foreign copyrights only in 1891, and even then only under stringent conditions' (3).

Indeed, as the twentieth century dawned, national economies increasingly moved beyond transatlanticism toward globalisation, looking to new markets in the Pacific and Asia, as evinced by the Boxer Rebellion (1899–1901) and the circumnavigation of the US Great White Fleet (1907–9). The infamous scramble for African resources affords another telling – and still reverberating – illustration of connections between a transnational brand of capitalism and colonising impulses. Joseph Conrad's *Heart of Darkness* (1899) memorably depicted the Belgian colonial enterprise through fiction, while Mark Twain's gruesome reporting-cum-images in *King Leopold's Soliloquy* (1905) critiqued the same regime in biting non-fiction.

TELLING STORIES OF WORKERS THEMSELVES

Overall, this section chronicles nineteenth-century business, industry and labour as multidirectional and multidimensional. In tracking such processes, clearly shaped by large-scale social movements and organisational cultures, we should not lose sight of the individual workers' everyday experiences. Some, like creative and determined Jamaican Mary Seacole, could have accepted marginalisation when initially excluded from the wartime nursing work she sought. Instead, as her autobiography's excerpts here and in 'Family and Domesticity' show, Seacole travelled on her own to Crimea, set up a successful boarding house and provided much-needed support for injured soldiers; she then recorded her own story of that work. (See, similarly, accounts by First Nations writer Louis Jackson in 'Science and Technology' and on our website.)

Adopting a different tone, American Fanny Fern playfully depicted a much-stereotyped worker, the Irish domestic, in 'Bridget As She Was, and Bridget As She Is' (1868). With her reminder that such domestic labour was often the only available income source for working-class immigrants, Fern satirised their class-climbing aspirations while also critiquing the systemic social divides in which they were enmeshed.

Hans Christian Andersen's 'The Little Match-Girl: A Christmas Story' (1847), also in this section, illuminated the lives of forgotten child labourers toiling in the street, selling their wares either for self-sufficiency or to support their families. By adapting Andersen's poignant portrait for his own book of children's stories (*The Happy Prince*, 1888), Oscar Wilde reaffirmed the appeal that stories of child labour could exercise in nineteenth-century literature's engagement with work as a social issue.[7]

Some literary legacies relevant to this section's theme, though difficult to retrace clearly, remain crucial to acknowledge. One of these – maintained in the transatlantically generated and ever-evolving labour songs of enslaved people – is represented here by this section's opening entry. Though written versions of these oral texts generally come down through white intermediaries, they convey

---

7 On connections between Andersen's match girl and a figure in Wilde's *Happy Prince*, see Regina Puleo, 'Altruism and Redemption in the Fairy Tales of Hans Christian Andersen and Oscar Wilde', *The Wildean* 32 (January 2008), 78–87.

both the pain imposed on Black bodies through white-controlled labour and, as enshrined by W. E. B. DuBois in *The Souls of Black Folk* (1903), uniquely dignified and moving tributes to their singers' determined resilience.

References

Fyfe, Aileen, *Steam-Powered Knowledge: William Chambers and the Business of Publishing, 1820–1860* (Chicago: University of Chicago Press, 2012).

Homestead, Melissa J., '"When I Can Read My Title Clear": Harriet Beecher Stowe and the Stowe v. Thomas Copyright Infringement Case', *Prospects: An Annual of American Cultural Studies* 27 (2002), 201–45.

Seville, Catherine, *The Internationalisation of Copyright Law: Books, Buccaneers and the Black Flag in the Nineteenth Century* (Cambridge: Cambridge University Press, 2006).

Stokes, Claudia, 'Copyrighting American History: International Copyright and the Periodization of the Nineteenth Century', *American Literature* 77.2 (2005), 291–317.

Turner, Michael J., 'Chartism, Bronterre O'Brien and the "Luminous Political Example of America"', *History: The Journal of the Historical Association* 97.326 (2012), 43–69.

'An African Work Song, Barbados' (c.1770s–1780s)

As Pinky Isha explains: 'The oral tradition of the Caribbean was a synthesis of various literary and linguistic influences' which, despite vibrant diversity, often demonstrate shared themes around 'a struggle for survival' (214), particularly during the era of enslavement. That dynamic hybridity continues today in forms such as Reggae and Calypso, with lyrics of Jamaican Bob Marley claiming a special status for addressing social issues in memorable performances. Similar assertions of this heritage emerge via David Dabydeen, in collections such as *Slave Song* (1984), which (in poems like 'The Canecutters' Song') celebrate Guyanese-infused Caribbean-Creole culture.

To study inscribed examples of this tradition from the pre-abolition period is possible now, however, only through mediated texts such as those recorded by white visitors to the island, enslavers themselves, or their clerks and overseers. Thus Mathew Gregory 'Monk' Lewis kept a journal during his 1815–16 and 1817–18 trips to Jamaica, later publishing *Journal of a West Indian Proprietor* (1834) which included scattered lyrics and commentary on local songs. Decades prior to this, J. B. Moreton's *West India Customs and Manners* (1793) printed several songs that he explicated from the point of view of a white employee on a sugar plantation.

The song lyrics below draw from a handwritten transcription of an even earlier date. They illustrate a Barbados work-song tradition described by several white observers in the long nineteenth century: enslaved islanders 'sing[ing] when they are about any occupation, and when their labor is over' (Handler and Frisbie, 15). A call-and-response chant, this text comes

from notes made by anti-slavery activist Granville Sharp based on reminiscences from Dr William Dickson, who served as secretary to the Governor
while living in Barbados. One singer leads. Others join in a chorus. In its
characterisation of the song, the United Nations' Preservation of Documentary Heritage Project emphasises how the song 'captures thoughts and
emotions of enslaved sugar workers' labouring 'under arduous, depressing conditions', with lyrics 'evok[ing] pathos and suffering at the hands
of a brutal colonial system' but also honouring a 'strength of spirit and
resistance'.

'An African Work Song, Barbados'

An African Song or chant – taken down in notes[8] by G. S.[9] from the information
of Dr.W[m.] Dickson,[10] who lived several years in the West Indies & was Secretary
to a Governor of Barbadoes.[11] A single Negro (while at Work with the rest of
the Gang) leads the Song, and the others join in chorus at the end of every
verse. (Generally in a minor key – suppose E with minor 3[d].)
(Key Note)
Massa buy[12] me he won't killa me
Oh – Massa buy me he won't kill a me
Oh Massa buy me he won't kill a me
Oh 'for he kill me he ship me regulaw
Chorus of laboring Negroes as they – proceed in their work.
NB a̠ is sounded by them like the French a̠i or English a
a̠ a a a a a a a a a a a a a a, a

---

8 As Rickford and Handler observe, how well the transcriber's version of this song matches its
actual performance patterns cannot be determined. 'Aside from the dangers inherent in sound transcription,' they point out, 'especially if sounds are largely alien to the transcriber, the musical training of Dickson is unknown, as are the conditions under which the transcription was made'. In that
context, they caution, 'it is unknown if Dickson recorded the musical notation in situ in Barbados
and later transmitted it in writing to Sharp, or if Sharp made the transcription from information
Dickson recalled' (231). Nonetheless, they suggest, the level of attention accorded to such details
as pronunciation, musical key and musical notes all point to authenticity – a judgement consistent
with the UN's acceptance of the manuscript into its Preservation of Documentary Heritage Project.
Further, based on transcriptions Dickson made of other oral texts, they believe that 'he was a reliable recorder/interpreter of Black speech' (233).
9 G. S. is Granville Sharp, a leading British anti-slavery crusader.
10 Rickford and Handler dub Dickson 'one of the most useful and intelligent observers of Barbadian society in the late 18th century', not only because he served as the governor's secretary for over
a decade but also because he 'was unusually interested in, and sympathetic to, the enslaved, and
advocated an end to the slave trade, albeit not immediate emancipation' (230). Upon his return to
England, Dickson was active in the abolitionist movement.
11 Handler and Frisbie date the manuscript as follows: 'Since Dickson left Barbados in 1785 or
1786 and Sharp died in 1814, we assume the manuscript dates from sometime within this period'
(23). This dating cannot set a time for the song's first use – whether in Barbados or Africa.
12 Rickford and Handler point to Caribbean Creole patterns suggesting the verb would have past
tense meaning here: bought (232).

Figure 3.2 African Song or Chant from Barbados, *c*.1820s. Melody and words to a song chanted by enslaved workers in the sugar fields. Transcribed by Dr William Dickson from Barbadian Creole. Courtesy Mr Henry Lloyd-Baker of the Lloyd-Baker Family Heritage.

'For I live with a bad Man[13] oh la –
'For I live with a <u>bad</u> man <u>Obudda</u> - bo
'For I live with a bad man oh la –
'For I woud go to the River side Regulaw

Chorus a a a a a a a a   O

Source text

'An African Work Song, Barbados, ca. 1770s–1780s', *Slavery Images: A Visual Record of the African Slave Trade and Slave Life in the Early African Diaspora*. Web.

References

'Barbados and United Kingdom – An African Song Chant from Barbados', *Memory of the World*. Web.

---

13 Rickford and Handler read this sequence as meaning 'Before I would live, or rather than live' (232).

Birat, Kathie, '"Taak prappa": Voice, Orality and Absence in David Dabydeen's Slave
    Song', *Sillages critiques* 25 (2018). Web.
Handler, Jerome S. and Charlotte J. Frisbie, 'Aspects of Slave Life in Barbados: Music
    and Its Cultural Context', *Caribbean Studies* 11.4 (January 1972), 5–46.
Isha, Pinky, 'Oral Literature and Its Bearing on Caribbean Slave Songs of the Colonial
    Era', *Rupkatha Journal on Interdisciplinary Studies in Humanities* 4.2 (2012), 211–20.
Rickford, John R. and Jerome S. Handler, 'Textual Evidence on the Nature of Early
    Barbadian Speech, 1676–1835', *Journal of Pidgin and Creole Languages* 9.2 (1994),
    221–55.

Maria Edgeworth (1768–1849)

From 'To-Morrow' (1804)

Maria Edgeworth was one of the great Anglo-Irish writers of the nineteenth century, noted for her children's literature, moral and realist fiction, and tales of Irish life. Under her father's editorship, she began to write as a teenager, producing *The Parent's Assistant*, a volume of loosely autobiographical moral tales for children, in 1796. Her *Castle Rackrent* (1800) was one of the first British regional novels, followed by *Belinda* (1801), *Leonora* (1806) and *The Absentee* (1812). Against the trend of novels focusing on the aristocracy, Edgeworth's writings promoted co-education and women's rights while exploring controversial issues surrounding race, nation and religion. In adulthood Edgeworth became one of the wealthiest and most famous novelists of the period (alongside Jane Austen and Walter Scott), earning a transatlantic reputation for realism and didacticism grounded in what one 1817 Philadelphia feature story dubbed 'pure morals and engaging manners' ('Edgeworth Family', 353).

Edgeworth's *Popular Tales* (1804) embodied this approach. As her father's preface noted, the stories aimed to 'be current beyond circles which are sometimes exclusively considered as polite'. True to his wishes, it was a popular and commercial success, praised as an educational and entertaining text for children.

'To-morrow, or The Dangers of Delay' relates the tragedy of Basil, a British gentleman who is imbued with the flaw of procrastination, squandering every opportunity by putting off today's goals until tomorrow. When Basil and his family cross the Atlantic to try their luck in America, he demonstrates his virtue by redeeming the indentured servitude of immigrant Barnaby O'Grady along with the Irishman's sons. Yet even this second chance goes awry, for Basil delays inoculating his child for smallpox (little Basil then dies), forgets to purchase fire insurance for his country estate (which then burns) and loses all his money (again). Thus, Edgeworth combines moral, didactic and melodramatic elements to warn readers against the vice of procrastination. The following excerpt is from Chapter VII.

From 'To-Morrow'

My situation in Philadelphia was now so disagreeable, and my disgust and indignation were so great, that I determined to quit the country. My real friend, Mr. Croft, was absent all this time from town. I am sure, if he had been at home, he would have done me justice; for, though he never liked me, he was a just slow-judging man, who would not have been run away with by the hurry of popular prejudice. I had other reasons for regretting his absence: I could not conveniently quit America without money, and he was the only person to whom I could or would apply for assistance. We had not many debts, for which I must thank my excellent wife; but, when every thing to the last farthing[14] was paid, I was obliged to sell my watch and some trinkets, to get money for our voyage. I was not accustomed to such things, and I was ashamed to go to the pawnbroker's, lest I should be met and recognized by some of my friends. I wrapped myself up in an old surtout,[15] and slouched my hat over my face.

As I was crossing the quay,[16] I met a party of gentlemen walking arm in arm. I squeezed past them, but one stopped to look after me; and, though I turned down another street to escape him, he dodged me unperceived. Just as I came out of the pawnbroker's shop, I saw him posted opposite to me: I brushed by; I could with pleasure have knocked him down for his impertinence. By the time that I had reached the corner of the street, I heard a child calling after me. I stopped, and a little boy put into my hands my watch, saying, 'Sir, the gentleman says you left your watch and these thing-em-bobs[17] by mistake.'

'What gentleman?'

'I don't know, but he was one that said I looked like an honest chap, and he'd trust me to run and give you the watch. He is dressed in a blue coat. He went toward the quay. That's all I know.'

On opening the paper of trinkets, I found a card with these words:

"*Barny*—with kind thanks."

Barny! Poor Barny! The Irishman whose passage I paid coming to America three years ago. Is it possible?

I ran after him the way which the child directed, and was so fortunate as just to catch a glimpse of the skirt of his coat as he went into a neat good-looking house. I walked up and down some time, expecting him to come out again; for I could not suppose that it belonged to Barny. I asked a grocer, who was leaning over his hatch door, if he knew who lived in the next house?

'An Irish gentleman, of the name of O'Grady.'

'And his christian name?'

'Here it is in my books, Sir—Barnaby O'Grady.'

I knocked at Mr. O'Grady's door, and made my way into the parlour; where I found him, his two sons, and his wife, sitting very sociably at tea. He and the two young men rose immediately, to set me a chair.

---

14 Formerly a unit of money in the UK, worth less than a penny
15 A man's overcoat of a style similar to a frock coat
16 A concrete, stone, or metal platform lying alongside or projecting into water for loading and unloading ships
17 Something whose specific name or designation has been forgotten or is not known

'You are welcome, kindly welcome, Sir,' said he. 'This is an honour I never expected any way. Be pleased to take the seat near the fire. 'Twould be hard indeed if you *would*[18] not have the best seat that's to be had in this house, where we none of us never should have sat, nor had seats to sit upon, but for you.'

The sons pulled off my shabby great coat, and took away my hat, and the wife made up the fire. There was something in their manner, altogether, which touched me so much, that it was with difficulty I could keep myself from bursting into tears. They saw this, and Barny (for I shall never call him any thing else), as he thought that I should like better to hear' of public affairs than to speak of my own, began to ask his sons if they had *seen the day's* papers, and what news there was?

As soon as I could command my voice, I congratulated his family upon the happy situation in which I found them; and asked by what lucky accidents they had succeeded so well?

'The luckiest accident ever *happened me* before or since I came to America,' said Barny, 'was being on board the same vessel with such a man as you. If you had not given me the first lift, I had been down for good and all, and trampled under foot long and long ago. But, after that first lift, all was as easy as life. My two sons here were not taken from me—God bless you! for I never can bless you enough for that. The lads were left to work for me and with me; and we never parted, hand or heart, but just kept working on together, and put all our earnings as fast as we got them, into the hands of that good woman, and lived hard at first, as we were bred and born to do, thanks be to Heaven! Then we swore against drink of all sorts entirely. And, as I had occasionally served the masons, when I lived a labouring man in the county of Dublin, and knew something of that business, why, whatever I knew I made the most of, and a trowel felt no ways strange to me; so I went to work, and had higher wages at first than I deserved. The same with the two boys: one was as much of a black-smith as would shoe a horse; and t'other a bit of a carpenter; and the one got plenty of work in the forges, and t'other in the dock-yards, as a ship-carpenter. So early and late, morning and evening, we were all at the work, and just went this way struggling even on for a twelvemonth, and found, with the high wages and constant employ we had met, that we were getting greatly better in the world. Besides, the wife was not idle. When a girl, she had seen baking, and had always a good notion of it, and just tried her hand upon it now, and found the loaves went down with the customers, and the customers coming faster and faster for them; and this was a great help. Then I grew master mason, and had my men under me, and took a house to build by the job, and that did; and then on to another, and another; and after building many for the neighbours, 'twas fit and my turn, I thought, to build one for myself, which I did out of theirs, without wronging them of a penny. And the boys grew master-men, in their line; and when they got good coats, nobody could say against them, for they had come fairly by them, and became them well perhaps for that *rason*.[19] So, not to be tiring you too much, we went on from good to better, and better to best; and if it pleased God to question me how it was we got on so well in the world, I should answer, Upon my conscience, myself does not know; except it be that we never made saint-monday,[20] nor never put off till the morrow what we could do the day.'

---

18 Should [Edgeworth's note]
19 Reason
20 *Saint Monday*, or Saint Crispin. It is a custom in Ireland, among shoemakers, if they intoxicate themselves on Sunday, to do no work on Monday; and this they call making a saint-monday, or keeping Saint Crispin's day. Many have adopted this good custom from the example of the shoe-makers. [Edgeworth's note]

I believe I sighed deeply at this observation, notwithstanding the comic phrase-ology in which it was expressed.

'But all this is no rule for a gentleman born,' pursued the good-natured Barny, in answer, I suppose, to the sigh which I uttered: 'nor is it any disparagement to him if he has not done as well in a place like America, where he had not the means; not being used to bricklaying, and slaving with his hands, and striving as we did. Would it be too much liberty to ask you to drink a cup of tea, and to taste a slice of my good woman's bread and butter? And happy the day we see you eating it, and only wish we could serve you in any way whatsoever.'

I verily believe the generous fellow forgot, at this instant, that he had redeemed my watch and wife's trinkets. He would not let me thank him as much as I wished, but kept pressing upon me fresh offers of service. When he found I was going to leave America, he asked what vessel we should go in? I was really afraid to tell him, lest he should attempt to pay for my passage. But for this he had, as I afterwards found, too much delicacy of sentiment. He discovered, by questioning the captains, in what ship we were to sail; and, when we went on board, we found him and his sons there to take leave of us, which they did in the most affectionate manner; and, after they were gone, we found in the state cabin, directed to me, every thing that could be useful or agreeable to us, as sea stores for a long voyage.

How I wronged this man, when I thought his expressions of gratitude were not sincere, because they were not made exactly in the mode and with the accent of my own countrymen! I little thought that Barny and his sons would be the only persons who would bid us a friendly adieu when we were to leave America.

We had not exhausted our bountiful provision of sea-stores when we were set ashore in England. We landed at Liverpool; and I cannot describe the melancholy feelings with which I sat down, in the little back parlour of the inn, to count my money, and to calculate whether we had enough to carry us to London. Is this, thought I, as I looked at the few guineas and shillings spread on the table—Is this all I have in this world? I, my wife and child! And is this the end of three years absence from my native country? As the negroes say of a fool who takes a voyage in vain, I am come back, *"with little more than the hair upon my head."* Is this the end of all my hopes, and all my talents? What will become of my wife and child? I ought to insist upon her going home to her friends, that she may at least have the necessaries and comforts of life, till I am able to maintain her.

The tears started from my eyes; they fell upon an old newspaper, which lay upon the table under my elbow. I took it up to hide my face from Lucy and my child, who just then came into the room; and, as I read without well knowing what, I came among the advertisements to my own name.

"If Mr. Basil Lowe, or his heir, will apply to Mr. Gregory, attorney, No. 34, Cecil-street, he will hear of something "to his advantage."

I started up, with an exclamation of joy, wiped my tears from the newspaper, put it into Lucy's hand, pointed to the advertisement, and ran to take places in the London coach for the next morning. Upon this occasion, I certainly did not delay. Nor did I, when we arrived in London, put off one moment going to Mr. Gregory, No. 34, Cecil-street.

Upon application to him, I was informed that a very distant relation of mine, a rich miser, had just died, and had left his accumulated treasures to me, "because I was the only one of his relations who had never cost him a single farthing." Other men have to complain of their ill fortune, perhaps with justice; and this is a great satisfaction, which I have never enjoyed: for I must acknowledge that all my disasters have arisen from my own folly. Fortune has been uncommonly favourable to me.

Without any merit of my own, or rather, as it appeared, in consequence of my neg-
ligent habits, which prevented me from visiting a rich relation, I was suddenly raised
from the lowest state of pecuniary distress to the height of affluent prosperity.

Source text

Edgeworth, Maria, *Popular Tales*, Vol. 3 (London: J. Johnson, 1804).

References

Cohen, Ashley, 'Wage Slavery, Oriental Despotism, and Global Labor Management in
    Maria Edgeworth's "Popular Tales"', *The Eighteenth Century* 5.2/3 (2014), 193–215.
'The Edgeworth Family', *The Analectic Magazine* (November 1817), 353–5.
Fernández-Rodríguez, Carmen María, 'Leaving Utopia Behind: Maria Edgeworth's
    Views of America', *Estudios Irlandeses* 4 (2009), 9–20.
Narain, Mona, 'Not the Angel in the House: Intersections of the Public and Private in
    Maria Edgeworth's *Moral Tales* and *Practical Education*', in Julie Nash (ed.), *New
    Essays on Maria Edgeworth* (New York: Ashgate, 2006), 57–72.

'European Colonies in America' and 'Hayti'

Freedom's Journal *(13 July 1827 and 12 December 1828)*

'European Colonies in America' and 'Hayti' were published in *Freedom's
Journal*, the first African-American newspaper in the United States, having
been launched in New York in 1827, the same year that slavery came to a
legal end there. As Wendell Bourne notes, the newspaper had a transatlantic identity as 'the brainchild of a group of prominent black Northerners
who, coming together at the New York home of M. Boston Crummell, a
self-emancipated oysterman born in West Africa, were looking for a way
to respond to the many articles in white newspapers attacking the black
community' (21). Samuel E. Cornish, a Presbyterian Minister, and John B.
Russwurm, one of the first 'college-educated blacks in America', served as
editors. The 'first newspaper produced solely by, and intended specifically
for, African Americans' (Bourne, 21), *Freedom's Journal* helped establish
the Black press as a venerable African-American institution.

These articles on Spain's transatlantic attempts to cede Haiti by negotiating for a treaty in London highlight the barbarity of Europeans' inclination to colonise, re-colonise and maintain systems of enslavement.
After years of struggle, Haiti had fought for and claimed its independence
in 1804. But Europeans would reoccupy Haiti, and, as Anne Eller suggests, rumours of re-enslavement persisted since 'Dominicans and Haitian
allies who opposed the Spanish reoccupation in 1861 – forced to defend
emancipation and independence at the same time – felt both fear and
determination' (658).

By emphasising the history of African nations and the intellectual heritage of African populations, these two texts extol the cultural and political superiority of Egypt and Ethiopia, in contrast with European influences. Moreover, *Freedom's Journal* recognises Haiti as a self-governing, independent state fully capable of advancing politically without European guidance or control. In particular, 'Hayti' promotes self-governance for the island and argues against the then-commonplace intellectual denigration of people of colour.

'European Colonies in America'

[We recommend to the attentive perusal of our readers, the following extract from an interesting work, entitled 'America, or a General Survey,' &c. &c. By a citizen of the United States.]

The republic of *Hayti*, without belonging precisely to the class of European colonies in America, seems to hold its independence by a somewhat doubtful tenure, (the price that is to be given for it being not yet paid,) and may be considered with propriety in the same section. Notwithstanding the very questionable character of the late transaction with France, (which does, however, quite as little honour to that powerful kingdom as to its colony,) the example of *Hayti* has been upon the whole of a nature to encourage the expectations of the friends of humanity, in regard to the capacity of the black race, for self-government and the arts and habits of a civilized life. It would be difficult indeed to assign any sufficient ground for the supposition of an essential inferiority in this branch of the human family, or in fact of any real inequality among the varieties of the species indicated by their differences of colour, form, or physical structure. If (which may well be doubted) such a prejudice has ever prevailed among enlightened men, it is probably rare at present, and may be expected to become continually more and more so. There are no facts, as far at least as I am acquainted with the subject, which authorize the conclusion that any one of the several varieties of our race is either intellectually or morally superior or inferior to the rest, and there are certainly enough that attest the contrary. – Each great division of the species has had in its turn the advantage in civilization, that is in industry, wealth, and knowledge, and the power they confer; and during this period of conscious triumph, each had doubtless been inclined to regard itself as a favoured race, endowed by nature and Providence with an essential superiority over all the others. – But on reviewing the course of history, we find this accidental difference uniformly disappearing after a while, and the sceptre of civilization passing from the hands of the supposed superior race into those of some other, before inferior, which claims in its turn, for a while, a similar distinction. As respects the immediate question, it would seem from even a slight examination, that the blacks, (whether of African or Asiatic origin) have not only a fair right to be considered as naturally equal to men of any other colour, but are even not without some plausible pretensions to a claim of superiority. At the present day they are doubtless, as far as we have any knowledge of them, much inferior to the whites, and have been so for several centuries; but at more than one preceding period, they have been for a length of time at the head of civilization and political power, and must be regarded as the real authors of most of the arts and sciences which give us at present the advantage over them. While Greece and Rome were yet barbarous, we find the light of learning and improvement emanating from this, by supposition, degraded and accursed continent of Africa, out of the midst of this very woolly haired, flat nosed, thick lipped, coal black race, which some persons are tempted to station at a pretty low intermediate point between men and monkies. It is to Egypt, if to any nation, that we must look as the real *antiqua mater*[21] of the ancient and modern refinement of Europe. – The colonies that civilized Greece, the founders of Argos, Athens, Delphi, and so forth, came from Egypt, and for centuries afterwards their descendants constantly returned to Egypt as the source and centre of civilization. There it was that the generous and stirring spirits of those days, Pythagoras, Homer, Solon, Herodotus, Plato,[22] and the rest, made their noble journies of intellectual and moral discovery, as ours now make them in England, France, Germany, and Italy. – The great lawgiver of the Jews was prepared for his divine mission by a course of instruction in all the wisdom of the Egyptians. But Egypt, as we know from Herodotus who travelled there, was peopled at that time by a black race with woolly hair; and the historian adds in the same passage, that these physical qualities were also proper to so many other nations, that they hardly formed a distinction. It appears in fact, that the whole south of Asia and north of Africa were then possessed by a number of powerful, polished, and civilized communities of kindred origin, differing among themselves in some points of their outward conformation, but all black. – Ethiopia, a country of which the history is almost entirely shrouded in the right of ages and of which we know little or nothing, except that it must have been in its day a seat of high civilization and great power, probably the fountain of the improvement of Egypt and western Asia, was inhabited by blacks. It then comprehended the country on both sides of the Red Sea, whence the Ethiopians are said by Homer to be divided into two parts. The great Assyrian empires of Babylon and Nineveh, hardly less illustrious than Egypt in arts and arms, were founded by Ethiopian colonies, and peopled by blacks. Hence it was a doubtful question, at a time when the historical traditions of these countries had become a little obscure, whether the famous black Prince Memnon who served among the auxiliaries on the side of Troy, at the siege of that city by the Greeks, was a native of Babylon or Ethiopia proper, and he was claimed as a citizen in both these places. Strabo tells us that the whole of Assyria south of Mount Taurus, (including, besides Babylon and Nineveh, Phoenicia, Tyre, and all Arabia,) was inhabited by blacks; but there seems to have been some mixture of whites among them, for the Jews fall within this region, and the Arabs of the present day, although dark, can hardly be called black. These, like the Medes and Persians, who were also white, were probably colonies of the white Syrians, described by the same author as dwelling beyond Mount Taurus, which had emigrated to the south. But Palestine or Canaan, before its conquest by the Jews, is represented in Scripture, as well as other histories, as peopled by blacks, and hence it follows that Tyre and her colony Carthage, the most industrious, wealthy, and polished states of their time, were of this colour. In these swarthy regions were first promulgated the three religions which have exercised the strongest influence on the fortunes of the world, two of which we receive as

---

21 Ancient mother (Latin)
22 Pythagoras (*c.*570–495 BCE), Greek philosopher and mathematician; Homer (*c.*750–*c.*700 BCE), Greek poet, author of *The Odyssey* and *The Iliad*; Solon (*c.*630–*c.*560 BCE), Greek poet and statesman; Herodotus (*c.*484–*c.*425 BCE), Greek historian; Plato (*c.*428–*c.*347 BCE), Greek philosopher

divine revelations; and, as far as human agency was concerned in it, we must look to Egypt, as the original fountain of our faith, which, though developed and completed in the new Testament, reposes on the basis of the old. This consideration alone should suffice with Christians to rescue the black race and the continent they inhabit, from any suspicion of inferiority. It appears, in short, that this race, from the period immediately following the deluge down to the conquest of Assyria and Egypt by the Persians, and the fall of Carthage, enjoyed a decided preponderance throughout the whole ancient western world. (To be Continued.)[23]

'Hayti'

Recent and authentic accounts from this island represent the state of affairs as uncommonly peaceable. Reports concerning the cession of the late Spanish part of the Republic to Spain, had reached there, and been almost officially contradicted. In fact, we have never entertained the least idea that they were true, knowing from the tone which has ever marked the public documents, and the public feeling on this subject, that no other government will ever be suffered to retain any portion of this beautiful island. The Republic is indivisible. The Haytiens, would certainly after having poured out their best blood in defence of their soil, be considered as infatuated beings, were they even to dream of such a scheme: as the occupation of a part of their territory by a foreign government.

As for the treaty which is said to have been lately negociated in London, the report carries its own absurdity on the face of it. The Haytien Government at present have no accredited Agent at the Court of St. James; and if they had, so important a trust would not be vested in one person. What does Spain want with more territory? The bigoted Ferdinand[24] can hardly sway what he now has. With exhausted finances, rotten ships, and degenerate men; Spain, in our humble opinion, should be the last of all the European powers, to attempt new conquests, or even to recover what she has lost, through the mal administration of her officers. *Hayti* is safe, the friends of civil liberty need feel but little concern, that she ever will permit the establishment of a foreign government within her borders. Let schools be established in every city, town, and village, of the Republic. Let all her youth, like those ancient Sparta, be considered the property of the Republic; and in a few years, we shall behold her take her rank among the nations of the earth, respected and honoured for the talents, industry, and bravery of her children.

The Haytiens can look back on the past with great satisfaction; they have fought the good fight of Liberty, and conquered: and all that is won required of them, is, to enjoy this invaluable blessing, as accountable beings, who look forward to what man, even the descendant of Africa, may be, when blessed with Liberty and Equality and their concomitants.

Source texts

'European Colonies in America', *Freedom's Journal* I (13 July 1827), 69.
'Hayti', *Freedom's Journal* II (12 December 1828), 291.

23 First in a multi-part series, 'European Colonies' continues on 20 July and concludes on 27 July 1827 issues of *Freedom's Journal*.
24 Ferdinand VII (1784–1833), King of Spain in 1808 and again between 1813 and 1833

References

Bourne, Wendell, 'Power of the Printed Word: Freedom's Journal – The First Black Newspaper', *Black History Bulletin* 69.2 (2006), 21–6.

Eller, Anne, 'Rumors of Slavery', *American Historical Review* 122.3 (2017), 653–79.

Fraser, Gordon, 'Emancipatory Cosmology: *Freedom's Journal, The Rights of All*, and the Revolutionary Movements of Black Print Culture', *American Quarterly* 68.2 (2016), 263–86.

Harriet Martineau (1802–76)

From **Demerara** (1832)

Harriet Martineau was one of the most prominent women of Victorian England, a prolific writer, theorist and translator who transcended women's domestic sphere. She grew up in a religious household under a mother initially forbidding her daughters any public appearance with the pen; yet Martineau began writing for religious periodicals at age nineteen, eventually earning a steady income after the family textile business collapsed in 1829. Martineau became famous for iconoclast views on feminism, secularism and naturalism, at the same time popularising emerging disciplines of sociology and economics.

Illustrations of Political Economy was Martineau's first series publication, issued in twenty-five parts during a two-year period from 1832 to 1834. Comprised of tales and vignettes, the volumes were wildly popular, reaching an acme of selling 10,000 copies a month and vaulting her into international fame, especially as a woman writing in what was considered the male sphere of economics. The stories illustrated economic concepts and principles, sometimes – as is the case with *Demerara* – through juxtaposition of white and non-white peoples. Combining straightforward domestic plots with subjects as varied as debt, banking, unionism and free trade, Martineau instructed readers in the political philosophy of Adam Smith. Recently, *Illustrations* has garnered increased scholarly scrutiny of Martineau's often clumsy plotting and her racist and sexist caricatures. However, the volume still stands as an early accomplishment of a woman who sought to collapse gendered divides by combining fiction and economics. Our excerpt comes from the *Demerara* volume's Chapter I.

From *Demerara*

The winter of the tropics is the most delicious of all seasons of any climate to inhabitants of the temperate zone. The autumnal deluge is over: there is no further apprehension of hurricanes for many months: the storms of hail are driven far southwards by the steady north winds, which spread coolness and refreshment among the groves and over the plains. The sea, whose rough and heavy swell seemed but lately to threaten to swallow up the island and desolate the coasts, now spreads as blue as the heavens themselves, and kisses the silent shore. Inland, the woods are as leafy as in an English June; for there, buds, blossoms, and fruits abound throughout the year. The groves of cedar and mahogany, of the wild cotton-tree and the fig, form an assemblage of majestic columns, roofed by a canopy of foliage which the sun never penetrates, while the winds pass through, and come and go as they list. In the richest regions of this department of the globe, the cane-fields look flourishing at this season, and coffee-plantations clothe the sides of the hills. All inanimate things look bright; and birds of gay plumage, and animals of strange forms and habits add to the interest and beauty of the scene in the eye of a stranger.

The brightest beauty, the deepest interest, however, is not for strangers, but for those who return to a region like this after years of absence, like two travellers who were hastening, one fine January day, to reach their long-left home,—a plantation in Demerara.[25] Alfred Bruce and his sister Mary had been sent to England for their education when they were, the one seven, the other six years of age. They had spent fourteen years without seeing their parents, except that their father paid one short visit to England about the middle of the time. Of him, they had, of course, a very vivid recollection, as they believed they had of their mother, of their nurse, of the localities of the plantation, and the general appearance of the country. They now, however, found themselves so much mistaken in the last particular, that they began to doubt the accuracy of their memories about the rest.

On landing, they had been full of delight at the contrast between an English and a Guiana winter. When they had gone on board, in the Thames, a thick fog had hung over London, and concealed every object from them but the houses on the banks, which looked all the more dingy for the snow which lay upon their roofs. When they landed, their native shores reposed in the serene beauty of an evening sunshine. By as bright a sunshine they were lighted on the next day; and it still shone upon them as they approached their father's estate; but it no longer seemed to gladden them, for they became more and more silent, only now and then uttering an exclamation.

'How altered every place looks!' said Mary. 'The birds seem the only living things.'

A servant, who had come to meet the travellers with the carriage, reminded her that it was now the time of dinner, and that in an hour or so the slaves would be seen in the fields again.

'It is not only that we see no people,' said Alfred; 'but the country, cultivated as it is, looks uninhabited. No villages, no farm-houses! Only a mansion here and there, seemingly going to decay, with a crowd of hovels[26] near it. I remembered nothing of this. Did you, Mary?'

No. Mary thought the face of the country must have changed very considerably; but the old servant said it was much the same as it had always been in his time.

'Something must have befallen the cattle, surely?' observed Mary. 'I never saw such wretched, starved-looking cows in England.'

The servant, who had never beheld any better, smiled at his young mistress's prejudices, and only answered that these were her father's cattle, and that yonder mansion was his house.

---

25 A historical region in the Guianas on the north coast of South America which is now part of the country of Guyana. It was a Dutch colony until 1815 and a county of British Guiana from 1838 to 1966.

26 Sheds or small and dilapidated houses, usually poorly constructed

In a few minutes more, the long-anticipated meeting had taken place. Alfred, sitting beside his mother's couch, with his beautiful little sister Louisa on his knee; and Mary, with her father's arm about her waist, forgot all their expectations, all their confused recollections, in present happiness. Their only anxiety was for Mrs Bruce, who looked as if recovering from an illness. They would not believe her when she declared, with a languid smile, that she was as well as usual; but her husband added his testimony that she had never been better. Mrs Bruce would have been as much surprised at her daughter's fresh color and robust appearance, if she had not been more in the habit of intercourse with Europeans than her daughter with West Indians.

These young people were far happier this first day—far more exempt from disappointment—than many who return to the home of their childhood after years of absence. Their father was full of joy,—their mother, of tenderness. Louisa was as spirited, and clever, and captivating a little girl as they had ever seen; and her perfect frankness and ease of manner showed them how much liberty of speech and action was allowed her by her parents, and how entirely they might therefore reckon on the freedom which is so precious to young people when they reach what appears to them the age of discretion. Alfred was as much surprised as pleased to observe this spirit of independence in other members of the family. The white servants, as well those whom he had never seen before as the companions of his childhood, met him with an outstretched hand and a hearty welcome; and he observed that they addressed his father more as if they were his equals than his domestics. Alfred immediately concluded that his most sanguine hopes were justified, and that his father was indeed no tyrant, no arbitrary disposer of the fortunes of his inferiors, but a just and kind employer of their industry.

Mary, meanwhile, could not help observing the strangeness of the domestic management she witnessed. The black servants whom she met about the house were only half-clothed, and many of them without shoes and stockings; while her mother was as splendidly dressed as if she had been going to a ball. The rich sideboard of plate, and the whole arrangement of the table, answered to her dim but grand remembrances of the magnificence in which her parents lived; but the house was in as bad repair, and every apartment as unfinished, as if the mansion was going to decay before it was half completed. Having been told, however, before she left England, that she must not look for English comfort in another climate, she presently reconciled herself to whatever displeased her eye or her taste.

Before Louisa went to bed, her brother asked her if she would take a walk with him and Mary in the cool of the morning: they remembered the sound of the conch[27] of old, and they wished to see the people go forth to their work. Louisa laughed heartily, supposing her brother to be in jest; and Mrs Bruce explained that nobody in the house was up for many hours after the conch sounded; but when it appeared that Alfred was serious, Louisa, liking the idea of a frolic, promised to be ready. There was no occasion, as there would have been in England, to make any proviso about the weather being fine.

It was a delicious morning, bright and balmy, when the young people went forth. The sun was just peeping above the horizon, and the families of slaves appearing from their dwellings. They came with a lagging step, as if they did not

---

27 A large shell used to make loud noises. In this instance, it functions as a factory bell announcing the beginning of a work day.

hear the impatient call of the white man who acted as superintendent, or the crack of the driver's whip. Their names were called over, and very few were missing. The driver pointed with his whip to the sun, and observed that there was no excuse for sluggards on so bright a morning.

'Do you find the weather make much difference?' inquired Alfred.

'All the difference, sir. On a chill, foggy morning, such as we sometimes have at this season, it is impossible to collect the half of them before breakfast; and those that come do little or no work. They like the whip better than a fog, for they are made to live in sunshine.'

'Does my father insist on their working in raw weather?' asked Alfred. 'I should not have thought it could answer to either party.'

'They are so lazy,' replied the overseer, 'that it does not do to admit any excuse whatever, except in particular cases. If we once let them off on such a plea, we should soon hear of more just as good.'

'True enough,' thought Alfred, who, earnestly as he had endeavoured to keep his mind free from prejudice respecting the institution of slavery, yet entertained a deep dislike of the system.

More than a third of the slaves assembled were men and women of the ages most fitted for hard labor, and of the greatest strength of frame that negroes attain in slavery. These brought with them their hoes and knives, and each a portion of provision for breakfast. Having delivered their vegetables to the women who were to cook their messes, they were marched off to their labour in the coffee walks. The second gang consisted of young boys and girls, women who were not strong enough for severe toil, and invalids who were sufficiently recovered to do light work: these were dispersed in the plantations, weeding between the rows of young plants. Little children, with an old woman near to take care of them, were set to collect greens for the pigs, or to weed the garden, or to fetch and carry what was wanted. These formed the third gang; and they showed far more alacrity, and were found to do much more in proportion to their strength, than the stoutest man of the first company. They alone showed any interest in the presence of the strangers. They looked back at Mary from time to time as the old woman sent them before her to the garden, and were seen to peep from the gates as long as Alfred and his sisters remained in sight. The other gangs did not appear to observe that any one was by; and such of them as were spoken to scarcely looked at their young master as they made their reply.

The young people took a turn through the walks, where the slaves were setting coffee plants. There could not be better materials to work upon, a finer climate to live in, a richer promise of a due reward for labour, than Alfred saw before him; but never had he beheld employment so listlessly pursued, and such a waste of time. When he observed how the walks were sheltered from the north winds, how thriving the young plants appeared, how fit a soil the warm gravelly mould formed for their growth, he almost longed to be a laborer himself, at least during the cool morning hours. But the people before him did not seem to share his taste. At a little distance he could scarcely perceive that any of them moved; and when they did, it was in a more slow and indolent manner than he could have conceived. He had seen laborers in an English plantation marking out the ground, and digging the holes, and spreading the roots, and covering them with so much despatch,[28] that

---

28 Speed or alacrity

the business of the superintendent was to watch that they did not get over their ground too fast; while here it took eight minutes to measure eight feet from stem to stem; and as for laying the roots, one would have thought each fibre weighed a stone[29] by the difficulty there seemed to be in the work. He reminded Mary how, at this hour of the morning, an English ploughman leads forth his team in the chill of a February mist, and whistles, while eye and hand are busy marking out his furrows; while, in this bright and fragrant season, the black laborers before them seemed to heed neither their employment on the one hand nor the sunshine on the other. Quite out of patience, at last, at seeing a strong man throw down his hoe, when the hole he was preparing was all but cleared, Alfred snatched up the tool, finished the business, and went on to another, and another till he had done more in half-an-hour than any slave near him since sunrise. Louisa looked on in horror; for she had never seen a white man, much less a gentleman, at work in a plantation; but when she perceived that her sister looked more disposed to help than to find fault, she ran away laughing to tell the overseer what Alfred was doing.

'You look well pleased to have your work done for you,' said Alfred to the slave; 'but I hope you will now bestir yourself as briskly for your master as I have done for you.'

When Alfred looked at the man for an answer, he fancied that he knew his face.

'What is your name?'

'Willy.'

'What, old Mark's son, Willy?'

'Yes, old Mark is my father.'

'Why, Willy, have you forgotten me as I had nearly forgotten you? Don't you remember master Alfred?'

'O yes, very well.'

'Is this Willy who used to carry you on his shoulders?' asked Mary, 'and who used to draw my little chaise round the garden? He was a high-spirited, merry boy, at—what age was he then?'

'Twelve when we went away. But, Willy, why did not you come and speak to me as soon as you saw me? You might have been sure that I should remember you when you told me your name.'

Willy made no answer, so Alfred went on—

'I find your father is alive still, and I mean to go and see him today; for I hear he keeps at home now on account of his great age. Can you show me his cottage?'

Willy pointed out a cottage of rather a superior appearance to some about it, and said his father was always within or in the provision ground beside it. His mother was dead, but his two sisters, Becky and Nell, were at hand; one was now in the field yonder, and the other was one of the cooks, whom he would see preparing breakfast under the tree.

There was time to see the slaves at breakfast before the same meal would be ready at home. They assembled in the shade at the sound of the conch, and each had his mess served out to him. The young people did not wish to interfere with this short period of rest, and therefore, after speaking kindly to two or three whom they remembered, they walked away. As they were going, they met a few of the sluggards who had not put up their appearance at the proper hour, and who sauntered along, unwilling (as they well might be) to meet the driver.

---

29 6.35 kilograms, or 14 pounds

'What will be done to them?' asked Mary.

'They will only be whipped a little,' said Louisa. Her sister stared to hear her speak so lightly of being whipped.

'O, I do not mean flogged so that they cannot work; but just a stroke or two, this way.'

And she switched her brother with the cane she snatched from his hand. Seeing that both looked still dissatisfied, she went on—

'What better can they do in England when people are late at their work? for I suppose people sleep too long there sometimes, as they do here.'

Her brother told her, to her great surprise, that lazy people are punished in England by having their work taken from them; there being plenty of industrious laborers who are glad to get it. She said there was nothing her papa's slaves would like so much as not to have to work; but she had never heard of such a thing being allowed, except on Sundays and holidays.

In their way home, they looked in on old Mark, whom they found eating his breakfast, attended upon by his daughter Becky, who had come in from the field for that purpose. Mark had been an industrious man in his day—in his own provision-ground at least; and, in consequence, he was better off than most of his neighbors. His cottage consisted of three rooms, and had a boarded floor. He had a chest for his clothes, and at holiday times he was more gaily dressed than any of his younger neighbors. A few orange-trees and bananas shaded the cottage, and gave the out-side a somewhat picturesque appearance, but the inside looked anything but agree-able, Mary thought. The walls were merely wattled and smeared with plaster; and the roof, thatched with cocoa-nut leaves, had holes in it to let out the smoke of the nightly fire, which is necessary to keep negroes warm enough to sleep. In the day-time they cook out of doors.

Mark had never been very bright in his intellects during his best days; and now the little light he had was clouded with age. He was easily made to understand, however, who his guests were. He told some anecdotes of Alfred's childhood; and when once set talking, went on as if he would never have done. He appeared exces-sively conceited; for the tendency of all he said was to prove his own merits. He related how he had told the truth on one occasion, and been brave on another; and how the overseer had been heard to say that he made the most of his provision-ground,[30] and how the estimate of his value had been raised from time to time. Even when he gave instances of his master's kindness to him, it appeared that he only did so as proving his own merit. What was yet more strange, Becky had exactly the same taste in conversation. She not only listened with much deference to all her father had to say, but took up the strain when he let it fall. The young people soon grew tired of this, and cut short the rambling narratives of the compliments which Becky had received from white people in her time. The conceit only took a new form, however; at every word of kindness which either Alfred or Mary spoke, both the slaves looked prouder and prouder.

'What odd, disagreeable people!' exclaimed Mary, as she turned away from the door; 'I always thought we should find slaves too humble, servile: I hardly know how to treat them when they are proud.'

'Our slaves are particularly proud, because papa has treated them kindly,' observed Louisa. 'Mr Mitchelson laughs at us when we are tired of hearing them

---

30 The small plots of land where, working in their 'free' time, slaves grew food crops for their own use

praise themselves, and says that if we used them properly they would never tease us in that way; and I have heard that Mrs Mitchelson says to her daughter, 'My dear, do not look so conceited, or I shall think you have been talking with Mr Bruce's slaves.'

Louisa could not satisfy her brother as to why slaves were made disagreeable by being kindly treated. All she knew was, that slaves were either silent and obstinate, like Willy, or talkative and conceited, like his father and sisters. Alfred pondered the matter as he went home. 'My loves!' said their mother, in her usual feeble voice, as the young folks entered the breakfast room, 'how weary you must be with all you have done! I would have had breakfast an hour earlier than usual if you had been in; for I am sure you must all be tired to death. Louisa, love, rest yourself on my couch.'

Louisa did so; and her brother and sister were not believed when they declared they were untired.

'When you know our climate a little better,' said Mr. Bruce, 'you will no more dream of such long walks than the English of staying at home all a fine summer's day; which I suppose they seldom do. But if you really are not tired, Alfred, we will ride over to Paradise by and by. I promised to take you to see your old friends, the Mitchelsons, as soon as you arrived; and they are in a hurry to welcome you.'

Source text

Martineau, Harriet, *Illustrations of Political Economy. No. IV. Demerara* (Boston: Leonard C. Bowles, 1832).

References

Dalley, Lana L., 'On Martineau's *Illustrations of Political Economy*, 1832–34', in Dino Franco Felluga (ed.), *BRANCH: Britain, Representation and Nineteenth-Century History*, Extension of *Romanticism and Victorianism on the Net*. Web.

Logan, Deborah A., *Harriet Martineau, Victorian Imperialism, and the Civilizing Mission* (Aldershot: Ashgate, 2010).

Peterson, Linda H., *Becoming a Woman of Letters: Myths of Authorship and Facts of the Victorian Market* (Princeton, NJ: Princeton University Press, 2009).

'Periodical Literature of the North American Indians' (1837)

Bentley's Miscellany, a monthly London publication, ran from 1837 to 1868. Its first editor was Charles Dickens, and it featured work by transatlantic authors such as Wilkie Collins and Catharine Sedgwick. Nodding to such transnational textual exchanges, the writer of the text below recognises the *Cherokee Phoenix*, a path-making Native American-owned business and bilingual (Cherokee and English) periodical published in the US.

The article positions the *Cherokee Phoenix* within comparative transatlantic contexts by noting its similarities to provincial English periodicals as well as emphasising its superiority to certain continental publications.

The writer also establishes that the heroes present in Native American poetry share common bonds with legends and heroic figures in European balladry and folktales.

On 21 February 1828, Elias Boudinot had published the first number of the *Cherokee Phoenix* in New Echota, Cherokee Nation (now in Georgia, US). In a related 1826 Philadelphia speech, 'An Address to the Whites', Boudinot credited the innovative syllabary writing system invented by Sequoya and documented how this new system had impacted the lives of the Cherokee (9).

Boudinot himself was a controversial figure. Of mixed-racial heritage, he married Harriett Gold, a white woman from a prominent Connecticut family. They moved to New Echota at a time when, as Theresa Gaul writes, the 'Cherokees were entering a period of their struggle with the United States government that marks a watershed in the history of Indian-white relations' (48). This era anticipated the brutal Removal of Cherokee from their own Nation to areas west of the Mississippi River after the passage of the Indian Removal Act of 1830.

Though this *Bentley's* assessment of extracts it prints from the *Cherokee Phoenix* is noteworthy today for its patronising tone, the article nonetheless attests to the transatlantic reach of a printing business far removed geographically and culturally from the London periodical's British readers.

'Periodical Literature of the North American Indians'

It is an astounding but gratifying proof of the rapid march of civilization, that periodical literature springs up and flourishes among tribes and nations which, but twenty or thirty years ago, had hardly advanced a few steps beyond barbarism. A Cherokee newspaper has for some time been published, and in the Sandwich Islands a gazette has recently been established; and a file of paper called "the Indian Phoenix," published in the United States, under the superintendence of an Indian editor, and addressed exclusively to his countrymen, has just fallen under our notice. These are pleasing acts for the consideration of every true philanthropist, and stable data on which the philosopher may argue that the day is not far distant when the rays of knowledge shall illumine every nation of the earth. Wherever a newspaper is established, ignorance must diminish; for the newspaper is not only the effect, but the cause of civilization, – not only the work itself, but the means by which the work is performed. The Indian Phoenix is published in the English language at Washington, and is from thence distributed among these roving aborigines, not only in every part of the United States, but throughout the vast territories of Mexico and Texas. The paper is not only edited, but printed by Indians; and, whatever may be said of the intellectual portions of it, the mechanical parts will certainly bear comparison with the provincial journals of England, and are much before the newspapers of several of the nations of Europe, those of Germany and Portugal for instance, which are as wretched specimens of typography as it is now possible to meet with.

For the amusement of our readers we shall proceed to make a few extracts from these very curious journals. The principles which are advocated therein will, no doubt, appear startling at first sight; but a little reflection will show, that, although strange, they are not altogether unfounded. These men have, by the strong arms of European civilization, been driven from the wild forests inherited by their fore fathers, the woods they hunted in have been converted into corn-fields, and the clear waters of the lonely rivers beside which they dwelt have been contaminated by the refuse of smoky manufactories, and rendered busy with the sails and paddle-wheels of enterprising commerce. The civilization which thus came upon the land from afar has now reached its original inhabitants; and the Indians, savages no more, have begun to employ the arts of peace and the powerful weapons of opinion to reconquer a portion of the broad lands of which they have been despoiled. The struggles in Texas, and the unsettled state of Mexico, have caused them to turn their eyes in that direction; and they have been inspired by the hope that Mexico is to be the region in which all the scattered tribes will be collected together to form one great independent nation. It is not intended in this brief notice to specu-late upon the probability or improbability of such a scheme, or to say whether or not these dispersed and dismembered clans, without leader or bond of union, will ever be able to accomplish so gigantic a project. It is sufficient to state that such is their object, in order that the reader may understand the allusions in the extracts which we shall place before him. The following will show the prose these Indians are capable of writing (we shall come to their poetry by and by), and will also give an idea of their political creed. In the leading article of the first number, the editor says,

"Our creed may be met with in these words. We render unto the self-esteemed civilized world the things which are the self-esteemed civilized world's, and unto the long-oppressed, yet noble, elevated, and dignified Indian the things which once belonged and shall again belong to him."

These sentiments, and their open avowal, although they may not cause the settler to tremble for the safety of his homestead, ought nevertheless to make the statesman ponder well on the condition and aspirations of this ill-used race. The editor continues:

"In the deep gloom of the future position of these countries we see no evidence of a single periodical grasping with energetic vision the coming time. Alone, there-fore, do we step on the arena of public opinion. With nerved heart and nerved hand shall we advance: the curiosity of the many, the surprise of others, the encourage-ment of the few, the denunciations of the National Gazette, or New York American, or all who may follow in their fetid and nauseous trail, shall not turn aside one of the barbed arrows which shall now and henceforth be launched unsparingly at all who cross our path." – "We are not mad, most noble Festus, but speak the words of truth and soberness."

The following little bit of Scriptural exposition will, no doubt, cause a smile even on the grave faces of the learned doctors who are versed in Biblical knowledge. The Indians, stigmatized by the civilized nations of the earth for the cruel practice of scalping their fallen enemies, bring forward the authority of our sacred book in their justification. Even David, the man after God's own heart, and one of the fin-est poets the world ever produced, went out on the war-path like a Mohican or a Cherokee, and bore away the scalps of his enemies! The editor hints that this alone would warrant the assertion which has been so often put forth, that America was peopled by the lost ten tribes of Israel. He says,

"We invite the attention—we throw down the gauntlet of defiance to all and every civilized Christian in Europe or America to gainsay or dispute the correctness or validity of the inferences and facts stated below. The Scriptures say,

"'And Michal, Saul's daughter, loved David; and they told Saul, and the thing pleased him.

"'And Saul said, I will give him her that she may be a snare to him, and that the hand of the Philistines may be against him.

"And Saul said, Thus shall ye say to David: the king desireth not any dowry, but a hundred foreskins of the Philistines, to be avenged on the king's enemies, But Saul thought to make David fall by the hand of the Philistines.

"Wherefore David arose, he and his men, and slew of the Philistines two hundred men, and David brought their foreskins, and they gave them in full toll to the king, that he might be the king's son in-law.'

"We see from this," (continues the editor of the Phoenix,) "that David, who was a great Jewish warrior, went out on the war-path not from any motive of war, or to revenge the death of his fallen comrades; but for what? Why, to get a marriage portion to lay before the king of the Jewish nation. And what was this marriage portion? Lo! it was one hundred scalps of the Philistines. * * * * * At the conclusion we are told that Michal, Saul's daughter, loved him. Why? *Because he was a great warrior, who had taken many scalps, and, moreover, David behaved himself wisely, that is, cunning, in taking of scalps from the Philistines, so that his name was much set by.* As the Jews were in the time of Saul and David, so are the Indian tribes of the West and of North America. They go out on the war path, they return with scalps; and the daughters of the tribe sing, as in the days of David, "The warrior Dutch hath slain his tens, but the warrior Smith hath slain his fifties in the villages of the Tarwargans."

The following is a specimen of the poetry, one of the war-songs of these regenerated Indians. We cannot say it is quite equal to the prose, but it is certainly more curious.

> "Indian chiefs, arise!
> The glorious hour's gone forth,
> And in the world's eyes
> Display who gave you birth!
> Indian chiefs, let us go
> In arms to Mexico;
> Till the Spanish blood shall flow
> In a river at our feet.
> Then, manfully despising
> The pale faces' yoke,
> Let your tribes see you rising
> Till your chains is broke!"

Fastidious readers may object both to the vigour and the grammar of the above; but we have still richer specimens in store for them. The song continues:

> "As rose the tribes of *Judah*
> In days long past and gone,
> I'll lead you to as good a
> Land to be your own.
>
> Cherokee! in slumbers
> Why lethargic wilt thou lie?
> Arise, and bring thy numbers
> Us to ally.

> Arouse! Oh, then, awake thee!
> And hasten to my standard;
> For I will ne'er forsake thee,
> But ever lead the vanguard!
>
> Come on, the brave Oneida,
> Seneca, Delaware,
> The promised land divide a-
> -Mong you when you're there."

The rhymes of "Judah" and "good a," and "standard" and "van guard," are tolerably original; but they are beaten hollow by that of the last verse, "Oneida" and "divide a-"! – "-Mong you when you're there," is a sequel which has much more truth than elegance in it. "-Mong you (*when you're there?*)" we would suggest as a new and improved reading of the passage. The following is in a much more elevated style; there is a rough vigour about it which many of our own namby-pamby poetasters would do well to imitate. The rhymes are also more felicitous, and the measure and grammar less objectionable.

> "The mountain sheep are sweeter,
> But the valley sheep are fatter;
> We therefore deemed it meeter
> To carry off the latter.
> We planned an expedition:
> We met a host, and quelled it;
> We took a strong position,
> And killed the men who held it!"

The above stanza is unique. Every line tells; and there is a raciness, a tartness about it, if we may so express it, which is quite delightful.

> *"The valley sheep are fatter;*
> *We therefore deemed it meeter*
> *To carry off the latter."*

Many ballads have been written about Rob Roy, who also had a sneaking inclination for the "fat sheep" of other people: but the daring simplicity of these lines has never been surpassed. The song continues:

> "On Norte's richest valley,
> There herds of kine[31] were browsing;
> We made a nightly sally
> To furnish our carousing.
> Fierce soldiers rushed to meet us,
> We met them, and o'erthrew them;
> They struggled hard to beat us,
> But we conquered them, and slew them!

---

31 Cattle or sheep

As we drove our prize at leisure,
Santa Anna marched to catch us;
His rage surpassed all measure,
Because he could not match us.
He fled to his hall pillars;
But, ere our force we led off,
Some sacked his house and cellars,
While others cut his head off."

Poetry has always been allowed some licence, and we suppose we must pass over the assertion in the last line, by merely observing by the way that Santa Anna is, in vulgar phrase, still "alive and kicking." The song ends thus:

"We then, in strife bewildering,
Spilt blood enough to swim in;
We orphaned many children, (*childering*)
And widowed many women.

The eagles and the ravens
We glutted with the foemen;
Their heroes and their cravens,
Their lancers and their bowmen.

As for Santa Anna, their blood-red chief,
His head was borne before us;
His wine and beasts supplied our feasts,
And his overthrow our chorus."

The foregoing extracts are all in a warlike strain. We will now give a few specimens of the softer lyrics in which these *scalpers* indulge. The Irish melodies of Moore are, it appears, not unknown even amongst them; and that they are admired, the following imitation, or rather parody, of one of the most beautiful of them will sufficiently show.

"There is not in the wide world a valley so sweet
As that Mexican vale in whose bosom "lakes" meet.
Oh! the last ray of feeling and life must depart,
Ere the bloom of that valley shall fade from my heart!

Yet it was not that nature had shed o'er the scene
Her purest of crystal, and brightest of green;
'Twas not the soft magic of streamlet or hill:
Oh, no, it was something more heart-touching still!

Twas remembrance of all,—Montezuma—his throne—
The power and the glory of Aztek all gone!
Like the leaves of the forest in autumn are strewn,
Were the splendour and hope of that race overthrown.

But the day-star is rising unclouded and bright,
That shall clear and illumine long ages of night,

And restore to that valley the Indian race,
And leave of their white lords no longer a trace.

Sweet "Mexican valley," how calm shall we rest
In thy bosom of shade, when thy sons are all blest!
When 'neath the fig-tree and the vine of each man
They shall sing to the praise of the Almighty one!
When the storm of the war, and its bloodshed, shall cease,
And our hearts, like her lakes, be mingled in peace!"

Interspersed through the papers are various imitations of our poets, especially of Scott, Byron, and Mrs. Hemans.[32] As an apology for the plagiarisms, the editor places over the poet's corner the following motto:

"To the living poets we beg to say, that it not being fair for them to monopolize the best words in the language we write in, to say nothing of the ideas, we take free liberty with them when need is. We will make them amends two years hence when they come to see us in the valleys of Mexico. To the illustrious dead we shall fully explain our reasons when we may chance to meet them in the 'great elsewhere.'"

The next specimen is an imitation of Ossian, a bard whose poetry must necessarily possess many charms for them.

"Come, all ye warriors! come with your chief—come! The song rises like the sun in my soul! I feel the joys of other times. Cherokee was on the land of Arkansas. The strange warriors of the prairie were rich in horses. We said in our souls, why not give the Tarwargans of their abundance? Six of our warriors were found on the great prairie, advancing like the moon among clouds, concealed from the view. Days had passed when they approached the wigwams of the Tarwargans. A narrow plain spreads beneath, covered with grass and aged trees. The blue course of a stream is there. The horses were secured. Their feet were slowly advancing towards the wigwams. Not without eyes were the Tarwargans. The warriors had not been invisible. High hopes of prairie horses and the scalps of the enemy fill their souls. A blast came upon them. The sound of rifles was heard in the air. Three of the warriors fell. The tomahawk descended, and they were left in their shame without scalps. Two warriors fled together. SMOKE (a warrior) fled not: he rushed for safety, and laid himself low with his rifle among the briers. Shouts of triumph are heard. The Tarwargans return. The slain are dragged to the dancing-ground— oh, grief! oh, revenge! Did you not know the heart of *Smoke?* Placed in the ground are three stakes; tied are the scalpless dead! Upright they sit. Oh, grief: the derision of the Tarwargans! "Cunning warriors are ye, oh, Cherokees! but your scalps are at our feet.'"

The following, which the editor assures us is a literal translation from an old song highly popular among the aboriginal tribes of Mexico, is interesting. The poetry of the original is so sublime that the translator, in despair of equalling it in rhyme, has given it us in plain prose.

---

32 Sir Walter Scott (1771–1832), George Gordon Byron (1788–1824), typically known as Lord Byron, and Felicia Hemans (1793–1835) – British writers all highly popular in North America

"Mexitli Tetzauhteotl! (the Terrible God) o-ah! o-ah! o-ah! The son of the woman of Tula. The green plume is on his head, the wing of the eagle is on his leg; his forehead is blue, like the firmament. He carries a spear and buckler, and with the fir-tree of Colhuacan he crushes the mountains! O-ah o-ah! o-ahl Mexitli Tetzauhteotl!"

"Mexitli Tetzauhteotl! o-ah! o-ah! o-ah! my father ate the heart of Xochimilco! Where was Painalton, the god of the swift foot, when the Miztecas ran to the mountains? 'Fast, warrior, fast!" said Painalton, the brother of Mexitli. His foot-print is on the snows of Istaccihuatl, and on the tops of the mountains of Orizaba. Toktepec, and Chinantla, and Matlalzinco were strong warriors, but they shook under his feet as the hills shake when the king of hell groans in the caverns. So my father killed the men of the south, the men of the east, and the men of the west, and Mexitli shook the fir-tree with joy, and Painalton danced by night among the stars! O-ah! o-ah! Mexitli Tetzauhteotl!"

"Mexitli Tetzauhteotl! o-ah! lo-ah! Where is the end of Mexico? It begins in Huehuetapallan in the north, and who knows the end of Huehuetapallan? In the south it sees the land of crocodiles and vultures, – the bog and the rock where man cannot live. The sea washes it on the east, the sea washes it on the west, and that is the end; who has looked to the end of the waters? Mexico is the land of blossoms – the land of the tiger-flower, and the cactus-bud that opens at night like a star, – the land of the dahlia, that ghosts come to snuff at. It is a land dear to Mexitli! O-ah! o-ah! Mexitli Tetzauhteotl!

"Mexitli Tetzauhteotl! o-ah o-ah o-ah! Who were the enemies of Mexico? Their heads are in the wall of the house of skulls, and the little child strikes them as he goes by with a twig. Once Mexico was a bog of reeds, and Mexitli slept on a couch of bulrushes. Our god now sits on a world of gold, and the world is Mexico. Will any one fight me? I am a Mexican. Mexitli is the god of the brave. Our city is fair on the island, and Mexitli sleeps with us. When he calls me in the morning, I grasp the quiver, – the quiver and the axe, – and I am not afraid. When he winds his horn from the woods, I know that he is my father, and that he will look at me while I fight. Sound the horn of battle; I see the spear of a foe. Mexitli Tetzauhteotl, we are the men of Mexico! O-ah! o-ah! Mexitli Tetzauhteotl!

With this extract we shall conclude our notice of this very curious subject, promising, however, to return to it at a future period.

Source text

'Periodical Literature of the North American Indians', *Bentley's Miscellany* 1 (January 1837), 534–40.

References

Boudinot, Elias, *An Address to the Whites, Speech Delivered in the First Presbyterian Church, on the 26th of May, 1826* (Philadelphia: W. F. Geddes, 1826).

Gaul, Theresa Strouth, *To Mary an Indian: The Marriage of Harriett Gold & Elias Boudinot in Letters, 1821–39* (Chapel Hill, NC: University of North Carolina Press, 2005).

Hans Christian Andersen (1805–75)

'The Little Match-Girl' (1849), trans. Charles Boner (1815–70)

As Seth Koven remarks of Hans Christian Anderson's 'The Little Match Girl', 'Its Anglo-American life began in [January] 1847 with the *Bentley's Miscellany* publication of "The Little Match Girl" as a "Christmas Story." Mary Howitt's translation of Andersen's *The True Story of My Life: A Sketch* (published . . . that same year) . . . [helped make] him into something of a literary celebrity' (81). In keeping with the 'culture of reprinting' (McGill), American magazines quickly reprinted 'The Little Match Girl' in February 1847. The story appeared in more durable form in transatlantic books published 1848–9. *Hans Andersen's Story Book, with a Memoir by Mary Howitt and Illustrations* (from which our version is drawn) publicised both Andersen and the British poet, children's writer and translator well known to Americans (Karbiener, 49–52; see FD). The 1849 text, in fact, is an exemplar of transatlantic translation and reprinting: the 'Memoir' of the title first appeared in *Howitt's Journal*, 26 June 1847 (the same month Howitt published her authorised book-length translation of Andersen's *True Story of My Life*). Part I also included Howitt's earlier translations of seven Andersen tales. Part III included 'The Red Shoes' translated by Howitt's daughter Anna Mary (*Howitt's Journal*, 11 September 1847) plus 'The Little Match Girl' and other tales translated by the British poet and journalist Charles Boner, whose volumes of Andersen tales appeared transatlantically in 1846 and 1848.

Hans Christian Andersen, considered a Danish national treasure, was born in Odense and enrolled in the Royal Danish Theatre after his early studies. Most famous for his fairy tales, Andersen published 'The Little Match Girl' in *Dansk Folkekalender* in 1845 (when Howitt published the first ever translations of his tales into English). Because Charles Beckwith's translation was the earliest English version of the story, it appears on this anthology's companion website. As Frederike Felcht observes, Andersen's career exemplified a growing 'modern textual culture . . . in which books, newspapers, and letters are widespread' internationally, with growing 'social and geographical mobility' shaping the business of the literary marketplace and its access to mass production (82). 'The Little Match-Girl' is sometimes associated with Dickens's 'A Christmas Carol' (1843). In this story, however, there is no miraculous rescue for the poor little girl, one of the countless millions of urchins forced into child labour during this time period.

'The Little Match-Girl'

Most terribly cold it was; it snowed, and was nearly quite dark, and evening—the last evening of the year. In this cold and darkness there went along the street a poor little girl, bareheaded, and with naked feet. When she left home she had slippers on, it is true; but what was the good of that? They were very large slippers, which her mother had hitherto worn; so large were they; and the poor little thing lost them as she scuffled away across the street, because of two carriages that rolled by dreadfully fast. One slipper was nowhere to be found; the other had been laid hold of by an urchin, and off he ran with it; he thought it would do capitally for a cradle when he some day or other should have children himself. So the little maiden walked on with her tiny naked feet, that were quite red and blue from cold. She carried a quantity of matches in an old apron, and she held a bundle of them in her hand. Nobody had bought anything of her the whole livelong day; no one had given her a single farthing.[33]

She crept along trembling with cold and hunger—a very picture of sorrow, the poor little thing!

The flakes of snow covered her long fair hair, which fell in beautiful curls around her neck; but of that, of course, she never once now thought. From all the windows the candles were gleaming, and it smelt so deliciously of roast goose, for you know it was new year's eve; yes, of that she thought.

In a corner formed by two houses, of which one advanced more than the other, she seated herself down and cowered together. Her little feet she had drawn close up to her, but she grew colder and colder, and to go home she did not venture, for she had not sold any matches and could not bring a farthing of money: from her father she would certainly get blows, and at home it was cold too, for above her she had only the roof, through which the wind whistled, even though the largest cracks were stopped up with straw and rags.

Her little hands were almost numbed with cold. Oh! a match might afford her a world of comfort, if she only dared take a single one out of the bundle, draw it against the wall, and warm her fingers by it. She drew one out. "Rischt!"[34] how it blazed, how it burnt! It was a warm, bright flame, like a candle, as she held her hands over it: it was a wonderful light. It seemed really to the little maiden as though she were sitting before a large iron stove, with burnished brass feet and a brass ornament at top. The fire burned with such blessed influence; it warmed so delightfully. The little girl had already stretched out her feet to warm them too; but—the small flame went out, the stove vanished: she had only the remains of the burnt-out match in her hand.

She rubbed another against the wall: it burned brightly, and where the light fell on the wall, there the wall became transparent like a veil, so that she could see into the room. On the table was spread a snow-white tablecloth; upon it was a splendid porcelain service, and the roast goose was steaming famously with its stuffing of apple and dried plums. And what was still more capital to behold was, the goose hopped down from the dish, reeled about on the floor with knife and fork in its breast, till it came up to the poor little girl; when—the match went out and nothing but the thick, cold, damp wall was left behind. She lighted another match. Now there she was sitting under the most magnificent Christmas tree: it was still larger, and more decorated than the one which she had seen through the glass door in the rich merchant's house. Thousands of lights were burning on the green branches, and gaily-colored pictures, such as she had seen in the shop-windows, looked down upon her. The little maiden stretched out her hands towards them when—the match went out. The lights of the Christmas tree rose higher and higher, she saw them now as stars in heaven; one fell down and formed a long trail of fire.

---

33 English coin now withdrawn from circulation; valued at less than a penny
34 The onomatopoeic sound of the match being struck

"Some one is just dead!" said the little girl; for her old grandmother, the only person who had loved her, and who was now no more, had told her, that when a star falls, a soul ascends to God.

She drew another match against the wall: it was again light, and in the lustre there stood the old grandmother, so bright and radiant, so mild, and with such an expression of love.

"Grandmother!" cried the little one; "oh, take me with you! You go away when the match burns out; you vanish like the warm stove, like the delicious roast goose, and like the magnificent Christmas tree!" And she rubbed the whole bundle of matches quickly against the wall, for she wanted to be quite sure of keeping her grandmother near her. And the matches gave such a brilliant light that it was brighter than at noon-day: never formerly had the grandmother been so beautiful and so tall. She took the little maiden, on her arm, and both flew in brightness and in joy so high, so very high, and then above was neither cold, nor hunger, nor anxiety—they were with God.

But in the corner, at the cold hour of dawn, sat the poor girl, with rosy cheeks and with a smiling mouth, leaning against the wall—frozen to death on the last evening of the old year. Stiff and stark sat the child there with her matches, of which one bundle had been burnt. "She wanted to warm herself," people said: no one had the slightest suspicion of what beautiful things she had seen; no one even dreamed of the splendor in which, with her grandmother she had entered on the joys of a new year.

Source text

Andersen, Hans Christian, *Hans Andersen's Story Book, with a Memoir by Mary Howitt and Illustrations* (New York: C. S. Francis & Co., 1849).

References

Felcht, Frederike, '"Constantly in Motion": Appropriation and Hans Christian Andersen's Texts', *Transfers* 2.3 (Winter 2012), 81–9.

Karbiener, Karen, 'Scribbling Woman into History: Reconsidering a Forgotten British Poetess from an American Perspective', *Wordsworth Circle* 32.1 (2001), 48–52.

Koven, Seth, *The Match Girl and the Heiress* (Princeton, NJ: Princeton University Press, 2015).

McGill, Meredith L., *American Literature and the Culture of Reprinting, 1834–1853* (Philadelphia, PA: University of Pennsylvania Press, 2003).

ODNB

Karl Marx (1818–83)

From 'Great Britain: Strikes' (1853)

German-born Karl Marx, known for *Das Kapital* (1867) and co-authoring the *Communist Manifesto* (1848) with Friedrich Engels, established the central tenets of Marxism and critiqued capitalism's treatment of the labouring classes. In addition to their *Communist Manifesto* collaboration, Marx and Engels also contributed several articles to the *New York Daily Tribune* at the onset of the 1850s.

Heinz Kurz concludes, 'The articles Marx and Engels wrote for the *Tribune* discuss a great many themes, mostly on political, social, economic, and military matters. The focus of attention is Great Britain, the then-most-advanced capitalist economy, its parliamentary system, the role of political parties and of the opposition, the situation of the press, and the formation of public opinion' (642). Marx and Engels would publish over 200 articles in the *Tribune* up until 1862, soon after the start of the Civil War in the US.

A stateless individual, Marx lived in London at the time of his writing for New York's *Tribune*. The piece that follows unpacks labour disputes and anticipated strikes in the United Kingdom. Of note is the Preston Lockout, a conflict involving cotton mill labourers who had demanded wage increases. Mill owners locked the labourers out and brought in Irish and poorhouse workers from other parts of England to take their place. Susanne S. Cammack has identified similarities in Elizabeth Gaskell's *North and South* (serialised in *Household Words* in 1854), which provides a fictional account of Milton, a mill town, reminiscent of Preston (113).

From 'Great Britain: Strikes'

In my letter of August 12, I stated that the master spinners and manufacturers were getting up "An Association for the purpose of aiding the trade in regulating the excitement among the operatives in the Manchester District," that that Association was to consist of local Associations, with a Central Committee, and that it intended "resisting all demands made by *associated bodies* of mill-hands, fortifying the monopoly of capital by the monopoly of combination, and dictating terms as an Associated body."

Now, is it not a very curious fact, that this scheme, of which I informed you about two months ago, has, to this very moment, never been alluded to by the London papers, although silently carried out in the meantime, and already doing its work at Preston, Bolton and Manchester? The London press, it appears, was anxious to withhold the fact from the eyes of the world, that the Factory Lords were systematically arraying their class against the class of Labor, and that the successive steps taken by them, instead of being the spontaneous result of circumstances, are the premeditated effects of a deep-laid conspiracy of an organized Anti-Labor League! This English Capitalist League of the Nineteenth century is yet to find its historian, as the French Catholic League did in the authors of the Satyre Menappée, at the end of the sixteenth century.[35]

The workpeople, in order to succeed in their demands, must naturally try to keep the one party in till the strike of the others has proved victorious. Where this

---

35 A 1594 political satire that criticised the Catholic League's influence in France

plan is acted upon, the mill-owners combine to close *all* their mills, and, thus, to drive their hands to extremities. The Preston manufacturers, as you know, were to begin the game. Thirteen mills are already closed, and, at the expiration of another week, every mill is to be shut up, throwing out of work more than 24,000 men. The weavers have addressed a memorial to the masters, soliciting an interview, or offering to refer the matters in dispute to arbitration, but their request was rejected. As the Preston weavers are assisted by penny collections from the operatives of the surrounding districts, from Stalybridge, Oldham, Stockport, Bury, Withnell, Blackburn, Church-Parish, Acton, Irwell-Vale, Enfield, Burnley, Colne, Bacup, &c.; the men having discovered that the only means of resisting the undue influence of capital, was by union among themselves; the Preston factory-lords, on their part, have sent out secret emissaries to undermine the means of succor for the men on strike, and to induce the mill-owners of Burnley, Colne, Bacup, &c., to close their establishments, and to cause a general cessation of labor. In certain places, as at Enfield, the overlookers have been induced to inform their masters, who had taken a part in forwarding the movement, and accordingly a number of penny collectors have been discharged. While the Preston men are exhorted by the work-people of the surrounding districts to remain firm and united, the Preston masters meet with an immense applause from the other manufacturers, being extolled as the true heroes of the age.

At Bury, matters are taking a similar turn as at Preston. At Bolton, the bedquilt makers having lots cast to decide which of them were to begin striking, the masters of the whole trade at once closed their mills.

Besides the simultaneous closing of mills, other means of combination are resorted to. At Keighly, for instance, the weavers of Mr. Lund struck for an advance of wages, the principal cause of their turn-out being his giving less than was received by the weavers of Mr. Anderton, at Bingley. A deputation of the weavers having asked for an interview with Mr. Lund, and proceeded to his lodgings, they had the door politely shut in their faces. But, a week afterward, Mr. Anderton's work-people were informed by notice that a reduction would be made in the wages of his weavers of 3d. per piece, and of his woolcombers of one farthing per pound, Mr. Lund and Mr. Anderton having, in the meantime, concluded an alliance offensive and defensive, with a view to fight the weavers of the one by pulling down the wages of the other. Thus, it is supposed, Mr. Lund's weavers will be driven to submission or Mr. Anderton's weavers to a turn-out, and the additional weight of another turn-out doing away with all chance of support, both sets will bend to a general reduction.

In other instances the masters try to enlist the shop-keepers against the working men. Thus Mr. Horsfall, the coal king of Darby main pit, when, in consequence of a reduction of wages, his hands struck, went to all the butchers, bakers and provision dealers of the neighborhood the colliers trade with, to prevail on them not to let his men have anything on credit.

In all localities where the Association for "regulating the excitement among the operatives" exists, the associated masters have pledged themselves to heavy fines, in case of any individual member violating the status of their League, or yielding to the demands of the "hands." At Manchester these fines amount to £5,000, at Preston to £3,000, at Bolton to £2,000, etc.

There is one feature which, above all, distinguishes the present conflict from past ones. At former periods—as in 1832, 1839, 1840, 1842—a *general holiday*, as it was called, viz.: a general and simultaneous stopping of labor throughout the whole kingdom, was a favorite idea with the operatives, and the great object they aimed at. This time, it is capital which threatens a general withdrawal. It is the masters who endeavor to bring about a general closing of mills. Do you not think that, if successful, it may prove a very dangerous experiment? Is it their intention to drive the English people to an insurrection of June, in order to break their rising spirit, and to lay them prostrate for a series of years to come?

At all events, we cannot too closely watch the symptoms of the civil war preparing in England, especially as the London press intentionally shuts its eyes to great facts, while it diverts its readers with descriptions of such trifles as the banquet given by Mr. Titus Salt, one of the factory princes of Yorkshire, at the opening of his palace-mill, where not only the local aristocracy were regaled, but his hands, too. "Prosperity, health, and happiness to the working class," was the toast proposed by him, as the public is told by the Metropolitan press, but it is not told, that, some days afterwards, his moreen weavers received notice of *another reduction* in their wages from 2/3 to 2/1. "If this means either health or prosperity to the moreen weavers," writes one of his victims to *The People's Paper*, "I, for one, do not want it."

Source text

Marx, Karl, 'Great Britain: Strikes', *New York Daily Tribune* (21 October 1853), 6.

References

Cammack, Susanne S., "'You Have Made Him What He Is": Irish Laborers and the Preston Strike in Elizabeth Gaskell's *North and South*', *New Hibernia Review* 20.4 (Winter 2016), 113–27.

Kurz, Heinz D., 'Transatlantic Conversations: Observations on Marx and Engels' Journalism and Beyond', *Social Research: An International Quarterly* 81.3 (Fall 2014), 637–55.

Harriet Beecher Stowe (1811–96)

'Letter XXIX', Sunny Memories of Foreign Lands (1854)

Harriet Beecher Stowe was perhaps the most famous American author at mid-century, after the 1852 publication of her abolitionist novel *Uncle Tom's Cabin* sold 300,000 copies within a year. The novel also won her international renown, particularly in England, where she embarked upon an extended promotional tour in March 1853. Although gendered decorum rules of the day repeatedly required her husband to speak in her stead while she demurely sat by, she won popular adoration from the abolitionist masses and was feted by aristocracy, whose attentions encouraged Stowe to craft gushing assessments of their social influence, as seen below.

During her tour Stowe paid keen attention to the condition of British workers, including meeting with reformers and lawmakers. The plight of the British underclass was a favourite counter-argument of pro-slavery southerners, who held that enslaved Blacks were better treated than British labourers under 'wage slavery'. Stowe encountered mixed examples on this front: she found working conditions in many instances abysmal (including the employment of children as young as four, as she says), but also noted legislative reforms then underway.

Drawing on letters sent home, Stowe later composed a volume recounting her experiences abroad, *Sunny Memories of Foreign Lands*, which itself became a best-seller in the United States, stoking increased interest in European travel (Robbins, 84–5). In the preface Stowe writes that the volume was prepared primarily for American readers, though it was also republished in England, France and Germany. In the following excerpt, Stowe addresses her father, a renowned minister and a major influence on her career, Rev. Lyman Beecher.

'Letter XXIX', Sunny Memories

DEAR FATHER:—

I wish in this letter to give you a brief view of the movements in this country for the religious instruction and general education of the masses. If we compare the tone of feeling now prevalent with that existing but a few years back, we notice a striking change. No longer ago than in the time of Lady Huntington[36] we find a lady of quality ingenuously confessing that her chief source of scepticism in regard to Christianity was, that it actually seemed to imply that the educated, the refined, the noble, must needs be saved by the same Savior and the same gospel with the ignorant and debased working classes. Traces of a similar style of feeling are discernible in the letters of the polished correspondents of Hannah More.[37] Robert Walpole[38] gayly intimates himself somewhat shocked at the idea that the nobility and the vulgar should be equally subject to the restraints of the Sabbath and the law of God—equally exposed to the sanctions of endless retribution. And Young[39] makes his high-born dame inquire,

> "Shall pleasures of a short duration chain
>   A *lady's* soul in everlasting pain?"

In broad contrast to this, all the modern popular movements in England are based upon the recognition of the equal value of every human soul. The Times, the most aristocratic paper in England, publishes letters from needlewomen and dressmakers' apprentices, and reads grave lectures to duchesses and countesses on their duties to their poor sisters. One may fancy what a stir this would have made in the courtly circles of the reign of George II.[40] Fashionable literature now arrays itself on the side

---

36 Selina Hastings, the Countess of Huntingdon (1707–91), an English religious leader in early Methodism
37 Hannah More (1745–1833), a writer, poet and playwright on religious, political and political issues
38 Robert Walpole, the 1ˢᵗ Earl of Oxford (1676–1745), and the first and longest-serving Prime Minister of Great Britain
39 Edward Young (1683–1765), an English poet; the allusion is from his 'Satire VI. On Women' in *Love of Fame, the Universal Passion* (1725–27).
40 George II (1683–1760), who reigned over Great Britain and Ireland from 1727 to 1760

of the working classes. The current of novel writing is reversed. Instead of milliners and chambermaids being bewitched with the adventures of countesses and dukes, we now have fine lords and ladies hanging enchanted over the history of John the Carrier, with his little Dot, dropping sympathetic tears into little Charlie's wash tub, and pursuing the fortunes of a dressmaker's apprentice, in company with poor Smike, and honest John Brodie and his little Yorkshire wife.[41] Punch[42] laughs at every body but the work people; and if, occasionally, he laughs at them, it is rather in a kindly way than with any air of contempt. Then, Prince Albert[43] visits model lodging houses, and commands all the ingenuity of the kingdom to expend itself in completing the ideal of a workman's cottage for the great World's Fair. Lords deliver lyceum lectures; ladies patronize ragged schools; committees of duchesses meliorate the condition of needlewomen. In short, the great ship of the world has tacked, and stands on another course.

The beginning of this great humanitarian movement in England was undoubtedly the struggle of Clarkson, Wilberforce, and their associates,[44] for the overthrow of the slave trade. In that struggle the religious democratic element was brought to bear for years upon the mind of Parliament. The negro, most degraded of men, was taken up, and for years made to agitate British society on the simple ground that he had a human soul.

Of course the religious obligations of society to *every* human soul were involved in the discussion. It educated Parliament, it educated the community. Parliament became accustomed to hearing the simple principles of the gospel asserted in its halls as of binding force. The community were trained in habits of efficient benevolent action, which they have never lost. The use of tracts, of committees, of female coöperation, of voluntary association, and all the appliances of organized reform were discovered and successfully developed. The triumphant victory then achieved, moreover, became the pledge of future conquests in every department of reform. Concerning the movements for the elevation of the masses, Lord Shaftesbury[45] has kindly furnished me with a few brief memoranda, set down as nearly as possible in chronological order.

In the first place, there has been reform of the poor laws. So corrupt had this system become, that a distinct caste had well nigh sprung into permanent existence, families having been known to subsist in idleness for five generations solely by means of skilful appropriation of public and private charities.

The law giving to paupers the preference in all cases where any public work was to be done, operated badly. Good workmen might starve for want of work: by declaring themselves paupers they obtained employment. Thus, virtually, a bounty was offered to pauperism. His lordship remarks,—

---

41 Using references to Dickensian characters like Smike in *Nicholas Nickleby* (1838–9), Stowe illustrates her point about readers' fascination with members of a different social class than their own having taken a reverse course from when the lower classes read about experiences of 'countesses and dukes' to what she sees as 'current': readers from upper classes being fascinated with common folks' lives.

42 *Punch*, a weekly satirical magazine which popularised the cartoon

43 Prince Albert (1819–61), the husband of Queen Victoria, who supported a number of public causes

44 Thomas Clarkson (1760–1846) and William Wilberforce (1759–1833), prominent British abolitionists

45 Anthony Ashley-Cooper, 7th Earl of Shaftesbury (1801–85), a prominent British social reformer

"There have been sad defects, no doubt, and some harshness, under the new system; but the general result has been excellent; and, in many instances, the system has been reduced to practice in a truly patriarchal spirit. The great difficulty and the great failure are found in the right and safe occupation of children who are trained in these workhouses, of which so much has been said."

In the second place, the treatment of the insane has received a thorough investigation. This began, in 1828, by a committee of inquiry, moved for by Mr. Gordon.[46]

An almost incredible amount of suffering and horrible barbarity was thus brought to light. For the most part it appeared that the treatment of the insane had been conducted on the old, absurd idea which cuts them off from humanity, and reduces them below the level of the brutes. The regimen in private madhouses was such that Lord Shaftesbury remarked of them, in a speech on the subject, "I have said before, and now say again, that should it please God to visit me with such an affliction, I would greatly prefer the treatment of paupers, in an establishment like that of the Surrey Asylum, to the treatment of the rich in almost any one of these receptacles."

Instances are recorded of individuals who were exhumed from cells where they had existed without clothing or cleansing, as was ascertained, *for years after they had entirely recovered the exercise of sound reason.* Lord Shaftesbury procured the passage of bills securing the thorough supervision of these institutions by competent visiting committees, and the seasonable dismissal of all who were pronounced cured; and the adoption for the pauper insane of a judicious course of remedial treatment.

The third step was the passage of the ten hour factory bill. This took nearly eighteen years of labor and unceasing activity in Parliament and in the provinces. Its operation affects full half a million of actual workers, and, if the families be included, nearly two millions of persons, young and old. Two thirds as many as the southern slaves.

It is needless to enlarge on the horrible disclosures in reference to the factory operatives, made during this investigation. England never shuddered with a deeper thrill at the unveiling of American slavery than did all America at this unveiling of the white-labor slavery of England. In reading the speeches of Lord Shaftesbury, one sees, that, in presenting this subject, he had to encounter the same opposition and obloquy[47] which now beset those in America who seek the abolition of slavery.

In the beginning of one of his speeches, his lordship says, "Nearly eleven years have now elapsed since I first made the proposition to the house which I shall renew this night. Never, at any time, have I felt greater apprehension, or even anxiety. Not through any fear of personal defeat; for disappointment is 'the badge of our tribe;' but because I know well the hostility that I have aroused, and the certain issues of indiscretion on my part affecting the welfare of those who have so long confided their hopes and interests to my charge." One may justly wonder on what conceivable grounds any could possibly oppose the advocate of a measure like this. He was opposed on the same ground that Clarkson was resisted in seeking the abolition of the slave trade. As Boswell[48] said that "to abolish the slave trade would be to shut the gates of mercy on mankind," so the advocates of eighteen hours labor in factories said that the ten hour system would diminish produce, lower wages, and

---

46 The County Asylums Act of 1828 required asylum authorities to send annual records to the Home Office, and for the Secretary of State to send visitors to any asylum.
47 Strong public criticism or verbal abuse
48 James Boswell, 9th Laird of Auchinleck (1740–85), best known for his biography of Samuel Johnson

bring starvation on the workmen. His lordship was denounced as an incendiary, a meddling fanatic, interfering with the rights of masters, and desiring to exalt his own order by destroying the prosperity of the manufacturers.

In the conclusion of one of his speeches he says, "Sir, it may not be given me to pass over this Jordan; other and better men have preceded me, and I entered into their labors; other and better men will follow me, and enter into mine; but this consolation I shall ever continue to enjoy—that, amidst much injustice and somewhat of calumny,[49] we have at last 'lighted such a candle in England as, by God's blessing, shall never be put out.'"

The next effort was to regulate the labor of children in the calico and print works. The great unhealthiness of the work, and the tender age of the children employed,—some even as young as four years—were fully disclosed. An extract from his lordship's remarks on this subject will show that human nature takes the same course in all countries: "Sir, in the various discussions on these kindred subjects, there has been a perpetual endeavor to drive us from the point under debate, and taunt us with a narrow and one-sided humanity. I was told there were far greater evils than those I had assailed—that I had left untouched much worse things. It was in vain to reply that no one could grapple with the whole at once; my opponents on the ten hour bill sent me to the collieries;[50] when I invaded the collieries I was referred to the print works; from the print works I know not to what I shall be sent; for what can be worse? Sir, it has been said to me, more than once, 'Where will you stop?' I reply, Nowhere, so long as any portion of this mighty evil remains to be removed. I confess that my desire and ambition are to bring all the laboring children of this empire within the reach and opportunities of education, within the sphere of useful and happy citizens. I am ready, so far as my services are of any value, to devote what little I have of energy, and all the remainder of my life, to the accomplishment of this end. The labor would be great, and the anxieties very heavy; but I fear neither one nor the other. I fear nothing but defeat."

From the allusion, above, to the colliery effort, it would seem that the act for removing women and children from the coalpits preceded the reform of the printworks. Concerning the result of these various enterprises, he says, "The present state of things may be told in few words. Full fifty thousand children under thirteen years of age attend school every day. None are worked more than seven, generally only six, hours in the day. Those above thirteen and under eighteen, and all women, are limited to ten hours and a half, exclusive of the time for meals. The work begins at six in the morning and ends at six in the evening. Saturday's labor ends at four o'clock, and there is no work on Sunday. The printworks are brought under regulation, and the women and children removed from the coalpits." His lordship adds, "The report of inspectors which I send you will give you a faint picture of the physical, social, and moral good that has resulted. I may safely say of these measures, that God has blessed them far beyond my expectation, and almost equal to my heart's desire."

The next great benevolent movement is the ragged school system. From a miserable hole in Field Lane,[51] they have grown up to a hundred and sixteen in number.

---

49 False and slanderous statement

50 Coal mines

51 The Field Lane Ragged School was founded in 1841 by Andrew Provan, a London City Missioner. Beyond the education of children, the charity sought to ameliorate unemployment, sickness, housing, violence and other societal issues in the area.

Of these Lord Shaftesbury says, "They have produced—I speak seriously—some of the most beautiful fruits that ever grew upon the tree of life. I believe that from the teachers and from the children, though many are now gone to their rest, might have been, and might still be, selected some of the most pure, simple, affectionate specimens of Christianity the world ever saw." Growing out of the ragged school is an institution of most interesting character, called "a place for repentance." It had its origin in the efforts of a young man, a Mr. Nash,[52] to reform two of his pupils. They said they wished to be honest, but had nothing to eat, and *must* steal to live. Though poor himself, he invited them to his humble abode, and shared with them his living. Other pupils, hearing of this, desired to join with them, and become honest too. Soon he had six. Now, the *honest* scholars in the ragged school, seeing what was going on, of their own accord began to share their bread with this little band, and to contribute their pennies. Gradually the number increased. Benevolent individuals noticed it, and supplies flowed in, until at last it has grown to be an establishment in which several hundreds are seeking reformation. To prevent imposition, a rigid probation is prescribed. Fourteen days the applicant feeds on bread and water, in solitary confinement, with the door unfastened, so that he can depart at any moment. If he goes through with that ordeal it is thought he really wants to be honest, and he is admitted a member. After sufficient time spent in the institution to form correct habits, assistance is given him to emigrate to some of the colonies, to commence life, as it were, anew. Lord Shaftesbury has taken a deep interest in this establishment; and among other affecting letters received from its colonists in Australia, is one to him, commencing, "Kind Lord Ashley," in which the boy says, "I wish your lordship would send out more boys, and use your influence to convert all the prisons into ragged schools. As soon as I get a farm I shall call it after your name."

A little anecdote related by Mr. Nash shows the grateful feelings of the inmates of this institution. A number of them were very desirous to have a print of Lord Shaftesbury, to hang up in their sitting room. Mr. Nash told them he knew of no way in which they could earn the money, except by giving up something from their daily allowance of food. This they cheerfully agreed to do. A benevolent gentleman offered to purchase the picture and present it to them; but they unanimously declined. They wanted it to be their own, they said, and they could not feel that it was so unless they did something for it themselves.

Connected with the ragged school, also, is a movement for establishing what are called ragged churches—a system of simple, gratuitous religious instruction, which goes out to seek those who feel too poor and degraded to be willing to enter the churches.

Another of the great movements in England is the institution of the Laborer's Friend Society,[53] under the patronage of the most distinguished personages. Its principal object has been the promotion of allotments of land in the country, to be cultivated by the peasantry after their day's labor, thus adding to their day's wages the produce of their fields and gardens. It has been instrumental, first and last, of establishing nearly four hundred thousand of these allotments. It publishes, also, a monthly paper, called the Laborer's Friend, in which all subjects relative to the elevation of the working classes receive a full discussion.

---

52 The London Colonial Training Institution and Ragged Dormitory, run by Charles Nash
53 A society founded by Lord Shaftesbury in 1830, intended to ameliorate the conditions of the working class

In consequence of all these movements, the dwellings of the laboring classes throughout Great Britain are receiving much attention; so that, if matters progress for a few years as they have done, the cottages of the working people will be excelled by none in the world.

Another great movement is the repeal of the corn laws,[54] the benefit of which is too obvious to need comment.

What has been doing for milliners and dressmakers, for the reform lodging houses, and for the supply of baths and wash houses, I have shown at length in former letters. I will add that the city of London has the services of one hundred and twenty city missionaries.

There is a great multiplication of churches, and of clergymen to labor in the more populous districts. The Pastoral Aid Society and the Scripture Reading Society are both extensive and fruitful laborers for the service of the mass of the people.

There has also been a public health act, by which towns and villages are to be drained and supplied with water. This has gone into operation in about one hundred and sixty populous places with the most beneficial results.

In fine, Lord Shaftesbury says, "The best proof that the people are cared for, and that they know it, appeared in the year 1848. All Europe was convulsed. Kings were falling like rotten pears. We were as quiet and happy in England as the President of the United States in his drawing room."

It is true, that all these efforts united could not radically relieve the distress of the working classes, were it not for the outlet furnished by emigration. But Australia has opened as a new world of hope upon England. And confirmatory of all other movements for the good of the working classes, come the benevolent efforts of Mrs. Chisholm and the colonizing society[55] formed under her auspices.

I will say, finally, that the aspect of the religious mind of England, as I have been called to meet it, is very encouraging in this respect; that it is humble, active, and practical. With all that has been done, they do not count themselves to have attained, or to be already perfect; and they evidently think and speak more of the work that yet remains to be done than of victories already achieved. Could you, my dear father, have been with me through the different religious circles it has been my privilege to enter, from the humble cotter's fireside to the palace of the highest and noblest, your heart would share with mine a sincere joy in the thought that the Lord "has much people" in England. Called by different names, Churchman, Puseyite, Dissenter, Presbyterian, Independent, Quaker, differing widely, sincerely, earnestly, I have still found among them all evidence of that true piety which consists in a humble and childlike spirit of obedience to God, and a sincere desire to do good to man. It is comforting and encouraging to know, that while there are many sects and opinions, there is, after all, but one Christianity. I sometimes think that it has been my peculiar lot to see the exhibition of more piety and loveliness of spirit in the differing sects and ranks in England than they can see in each other. And it lays in my mind a deep foundation of hope for that noble country. My belief is, that a regenerating process is going on in England; a gradual advance in religion, of which contending parties themselves are not aware. Under various forms all are energizing

---

54 British tariffs in place between 1815 and 1846 that favoured domestic grain producers at the expense of the food-buying public

55 Caroline Chisholm (1808–77), an English humanitarian who founded the Family Colonisation Loan Society, which lent half the fare of travel for migrants to Australia

together, I trust, under the guidance of a superior spirit, who is gently moderating acerbities, removing prejudices, inclining to conciliation and harmony, and preparing England to develop, from many outward forms, the one, pure, beautiful, invisible church of Christ.

Source text

Stowe, Mrs. Harriet Beecher, *Sunny Memories of Foreign Lands*, Vol. 2 (Boston: Phillips, Sampson, & Co., 1854).

References

Fields, Annie (ed.), *Life and Letters of Harriet Beecher Stowe* (Boston: Houghton, Mifflin, 1897).
Fisch, Audrey, 'Uncle Tom and Harriet Beecher Stowe in England', in Cindy Weinstein (ed.), *The Cambridge Companion to Harriet Beecher Stowe* (Cambridge: Cambridge University Press, 2004) 96–112.
Kohn, Denise, Sarah Meer and Emily B. Todd (eds), *Transatlantic Stowe: Harriet Beecher Stowe and European Culture* (Iowa City, IA: University of Iowa Press, 2006).
Robbins, Sarah, *The Cambridge Introduction to Harriet Beecher Stowe* (Cambridge: Cambridge University Press, 2007).

Mary Seacole (1805–81)

From 'My Work in the Crimea' and 'My Customers at the British Hotel', Wonderful Adventures of Mrs. Seacole in Many Lands (1857)

Mary Seacole was born in Kingston, Jamaica. Her father was a Scottish soldier and her mother a Jamaican doctor and entrepreneur, the proprietor of a boarding house where British military officers resided with their families.

Sandra Paquet notes that Seacole's narrative eschews 'victimization' themes to stress 'accomplishment and achievement'. She positions herself as a 'subject of the British Empire', but also a 'unique individual who challenges the boundaries of race, gender, and privilege within the parameters of that Empire' (864). While 'explicitly addressing an English reading public' whose recognition and approval she seeks, Seacole nonetheless portrays herself as 'an adventurer, entrepreneur, and professional healer' (865).

Seacole journeyed to London at least two times in the 1820s. She married Edwin Horatio Seacole, Lord Nelson's godson, in 1836, but he died shortly thereafter. Later, she helped her brother run a hotel in Panama and served as a 'nursing superintendent' at a military camp in Jamaica. In 1854, soon after the onset of the Crimean War, Seacole funded her own travel to the front and opened a British hotel with Thomas Day, her late husband's relative. While managing the hotel, she also provided medical care for British forces, as well as Italian, French and Russian soldiers. In the passages that follow, Seacole outlines her experiences labouring in the Crimea and presents accolades from patients she treated there. Her account continues to draw back-and-forth responses from her admirers and from defenders of Florence Nightingale, who some feel has been unfairly denigrated as a means of uplifting Seacole's image (Trubuhovich and Merridew; McDonald); others, meanwhile, urge a robust honouring of both women's contributions to gendering nineteenth-century healthcare work (Gander).

From Chapter XIII 'My Work in the Crimea'

I hope the reader will give me credit for the assertion that I am about to make, viz., that I enter upon the particulars of this chapter with great reluctance; but I cannot omit them, for the simple reason that they strengthen my one and only claim to interest the public, viz., my services to the brave British army in the Crimea. But fortunately, I can follow a course which will not only render it unnecessary for me to sound my own trumpet, but will be more satisfactory to the reader. I can put on record the written opinions of those who had ample means of judging and ascertaining how I fulfilled the great object which I had in view in leaving England for the Crimea; and before I do so, I must solicit my readers' attention to the position I held in the camp as doctress, nurse, and "mother."

I have never been long in any place before I have found my practical experience in the science of medicine useful. Even in London I have found it of service to others. And in the Crimea, where the doctors were so overworked, and sickness was so prevalent, I could not be long idle; for I never forgot that my intention in seeking the army was to help the kind-hearted doctors, to be useful to whom I have ever looked upon and still regard as so high a privilege.

But before very long I found myself surrounded with patients of my own, and this for two simple reasons. In the first place, the men (I am speaking of the "ranks" now) had a very serious objection to going into hospital for any but urgent reasons, and the regimental doctors were rather fond of sending them there; and, in the second place, they could and did get at my store sick-comforts and nourishing food, which the heads of the medical staff would sometimes find it difficult to procure. These reasons, with the additional one that I was very familiar with the diseases which they suffered most from, and successful in their treatment (I say this in no spirit of vanity), were quite sufficient to account for the numbers who came daily to the British Hotel for medical treatment.

That the officers were glad of me as a doctress and nurse may be easily understood. When a poor fellow lay sickening in his cheerless hut and sent down to me, he knew very well that I should not ride up in answer to his message empty-handed. And although I did not hesitate to charge him with the value of the necessaries I took him, still he was thankful enough to be able to *purchase* them. When we lie ill at home surrounded with comfort, we never think of feeling any special gratitude for the sick-room delicacies which we accept as a consequence of our illness; but the poor officer lying ill and weary in his crazy hut, dependent for the merest necessaries of existence upon a clumsy, ignorant soldier-cook, who would almost prefer eating his meat raw to having the trouble of cooking it (our English soldiers are bad campaigners), often finds his greatest troubles in the want of those little delicacies with which a weak stomach must be humoured into retaining nourishment. How often have I felt sad at the sight of poor lads who in England thought attending early parade a hardship, and felt harassed if their neckcloths set awry, or the natty little boots would not retain their polish, bearing, and bearing so nobly and bravely, trials and hardships to which the veteran campaigner frequently succumbed. Don't you think, reader, if you were lying, with parched lips and fading appetite, thousands of miles from mother, wife, or sister, loathing the rough food by your side, and thinking regretfully of that English home where nothing that could minister to your great need would be left untried – don't you think that you would welcome the familiar figure of the stout lady whose bony horse has just pulled up at the door of your hut, and whose panniers[56] contain some cooling drink, a little broth, some homely cake, or a dish of jelly or blanc-mange – don't you think, under such circumstances, that you would heartily agree with my friend *Punch's* remark: –

> "That berry-brown face, with a kind heart's trace
> Impressed on each wrinkle sly,
> Was a sight to behold, through the snow-clouds rolled
> Across that iron sky."

I tell you, reader, I have seen many a bold fellow's eyes moisten at such a season, when a woman's voice and a woman's care have brought to their minds recollections of those happy English homes which some of them never saw again; but many did, who will remember their woman-comrade upon the bleak and barren heights before Sebastopol.

Then their calling me "mother" was not, I think, altogether unmeaning. I used to fancy that there was something homely in the word; and, reader, you cannot think how dear to them was the smallest thing that reminded them of home.

Some of my Crimean patients, who were glad of me as nurse and doctress, bore names familiar to all England, and perhaps, did I ask them, they would allow me to publish those names. I am proud to think that a gallant sailor, on whose brave breast the order of Victoria rests – a more gallant man can never wear it – sent for the doctress whom he had known in Kingston, when his arm, wounded on the fatal 18th of June, refused to heal, and I think that the application I recommended did it good; but I shall let some of my patients' letters, taken from a large bundle, speak for me. Of course I must suppress most of their names. Here are two from one of my best and kindest sons.

> "MY DEAR MAMMA, –Will you kindly give the bearer the bottle you promised me when you were here this morning, for my jaundice. Please let me know how much I am to take of it. Yours truly,
>
>> "F. M., C. E."

You see the medicine does him good, for a few days later comes another from the same writer: –

---

56 In an eighteenth- or nineteenth-century woman's dress, a pocket for holding items, similar to a handbag today

"MY DEAR MRS. SEACOLE, – I have finished the bottle, which has done my jaundice a deal of good. Will you kindly send another by bearer. Truly yours,
"F. M."

It was a capital prescription which had done his jaundice good. There was so great a demand for it, that I kept it mixed in a large pan, ready to ladle it out to the scores of applicants who came for it.

Sometimes they would send for other and no less important medicines. Here is such an application from a sick officer: –

"Mrs. Seacole would confer a favour on the writer, who is very ill, by giving his servant (the bearer) a boiled or roast fowl; if it be impossible to obtain them, some chicken broth would be very acceptable.
"I am yours, truly obliged,
"J. K., 18th R. S."

Doesn't that read like a sick man's letter, glad enough to welcome any woman's face? Here are some gentlemen of the Commissariat anxious to speak for me: –

"Arthur C—, Comm. Staff Officer, having been attacked one evening with a very bad diarrhœa at Mrs. Seacole's, took some of her good medicine. It cured me before the next morning, and I have never been attacked since. – October 17th, 1855."

"Archibald R. L—, Comm. Staff. Crimea, was suffering from diarrhœa for a week or more; after taking Mrs. Seacole's good medicines for two days, he became quite well and remained so to this day. – October 17th, 1855."

Here is Mr. M—, paymaster of the Land Transport Corps, ready with a good account of my services: –

"I certify that Madam Seacole twice cured me effectually of dysentery while in the Crimea, and also my clerk and the men of my corps, to my certain knowledge."

And some of the men shall speak for themselves: –
"Stationary Engine, December 1, 1855.

"I certify that I was severely attacked by diarrhœa after landing in the Crimea. I took a great deal of medicine, but nothing served me until I called on Mrs. Seacole. She gave me her medicine but once, and I was cured effectually.
"WM. KNOLLYS, Sergt., L.T.C."

"This is to certify that Wm. Row, L. T. C., had a severe attack of illness, and was in a short time restored to health by the prompt attention and medical skill of Mrs. Seacole, British Hotel, Spring Hill, Crimea" [. . .]

And now that I have made this a chapter of testimonials, I may as well finish them right off, and have done with them altogether. I shall trouble the patient reader with four more only, which I have not the heart to omit.
"Sebastopol, July 1, 1856."

"Mrs. Seacole was with the British army in the Crimea from February, 1855, to this time. This excellent woman has frequently exerted herself in the most praiseworthy manner in attending wounded men, even in positions of great danger, and in assisting sick soldiers by all means in her power. In addition, she kept a very good store, and supplied us with many comforts at a time we much required them.

"WM. P—,

"Adjutant-General of the British Army in the Crimea."

"July 1, 1856.
"I have much pleasure in stating that I am acquainted with Mrs. Seacole, and from all that I have seen or heard of her, I believe her to be a useful and good person, kind and charitable.

"C. A. W—,
Lt.-Gen. Comm. of Sebastopol."

The third is from the pen of one who at that time was more looked to, and better known, than any other man in the Crimea. In the 2nd vol. of Russell's "Letters from the Seat of War," p. 187, is the following entry: –

"In the hour of their illness these men (Army Works Corps), in common with many others, have found a kind and successful physician. Close to the railway, half-way between the Col de Balaclava and Kadikoi, Mrs. Seacole, formerly of Kingston and of several other parts of the world, such as Panama and Chagres, has pitched her abode – an iron storehouse with wooden sheds and outlying tributaries – and here she doctors and cures all manner of men with extraordinary success. She is always in attendance near the battle-field to aid the wounded, and has earned many a poor fellow's blessings."

Yes! I cannot – referring to that time – conscientiously charge myself with doing less for the men who had only thanks to give me, than for the officers whose gratitude gave me the necessaries of life. I think I was ever ready to turn from the latter to help the former, humble as they might be; and they were grateful in their way, and as far as they could be. They would buy me apples and other fruit at Balaclava, and leave them at my store. One made me promise, when I returned home, to send word to his Irish mother, who was to send me a cow in token of her gratitude for the help I had been to her son. I have a book filled with hundreds of the names of those who came to me for medicines and other aids; and never a train of sick or wounded men from the front passed the British Hotel but its hostess was awaiting them to offer comforts to the poor fellows, for whose suffering her heart bled.

Punch, who allowed my poor name to appear in the pages which had welcomed Miss Nightingale home – *Punch*, that whimsical mouthpiece of some of the noblest hearts that ever beat beneath black coats – shall last of all raise its voice, that never yet pleaded an unworthy cause, for the Mother Seacole that takes shame to herself for speaking thus of the poor part she bore of the trials and hardships endured on that distant shore, where Britain's best and bravest wrung hardly Sebastopol from the grasp of Britain's foe: –

"No store she set by the epaulette,
  Be it worsted or gold lace;
 For K. C. B. or plain private Smith,
  She had still one pleasant face.

"And not alone was her kindness shown
  To the hale and hungry lot
 Who drank her grog and ate her prog,
  And paid their honest shot.

"The sick and sorry can tell the story
  Of her nursing and dosing deeds;
 Regimental M.D. never worked as she,
  In helping sick men's needs.

"Of such work, God knows, was as much as she chose
  That dreary winter-tide,
 When Death hung o'er the damp and pestilent camp,
  And his scythe swung far and wide.

"She gave her aid to all who prayed,
  To hungry and sick and cold;
 Open hand and heart, alike ready to part
  Kind words and acts, and gold.

"And – be the right man in the right place who can –
 The right woman was Dame Seacole."

Reader, now that we have come to the end of this chapter, I can say what I have been all anxiety to tell you from its beginning. Please look back to Chapter VIII., and see how hard the right woman had to struggle to convey herself to the right place.

From Chapter XIV 'My Customers at the British Hotel'

I shall proceed in this chapter to make the reader acquainted with some of the customers of the British Hotel, who came there for its creature comforts as well as its hostess's medicines when need was; and if he or she should be inclined to doubt or should hesitate at accepting my experience of Crimean life as entirely credible, I beg that individual to refer to the accounts which were given in the newspapers of the spring of 1855, and I feel sure they will acquit me of any intention to exaggerate. If I were to speak of all the nameless horrors of that spring as plainly as I could, I should really disgust you; but those I shall bring before your notice have all something of the humorous in them – and so it ever is. Time is a great restorer, and changes surely the greatest sorrow into a pleasing memory. The sun shines this spring-time upon green grass that covers the graves of the poor fellows we left behind sadly a few short months ago: bright flowers grow up upon ruins of batteries and crumbling trenches, and cover the sod that presses on many a mouldering token of the old time of battle and death. I dare say that, if I went to the Crimea now, I should see a smiling landscape, instead of the blood-stained scene which I shall ever associate with distress and death; and as it is with nature so it is with human kind. Whenever

I meet those who have survived that dreary spring of 1855, we seldom talk about its horrors; but remembering its transient gleams of sunshine, smile at the fun and good nature that varied its long and weary monotony. And now that I am anxious to remember all I can that will interest my readers, my memory prefers to dwell upon what was pleasing and amusing, although the time will never come when it will cease to retain most vividly the pathos and woe of those dreadful months.

I have said that the winter had not ended when we began operations at the British Hotel; and very often, after we considered we were fairly under spring's influence, our old enemy would come back with an angry roar of wind and rain, levelling tents, unroofing huts, destroying roads, and handing over May to the command of General Fevrier; But the sun fought bravely for us, and in time always dispersed the leaden clouds and gilded the iron sky, and made us cheerful again. During the end of March, the whole of April, and a considerable portion of May, however, the army was but a little better off for the advent of spring. The military road to the camp was only in progress – the railway only carried ammunition. A few hours' rain rendered the old road all but impassable, and scarcity often existed in the front before Sebastopol, although the frightened and anxious Commissariat toiled hard to avert such a mishap; so that very often to the British Hotel came officers starved out on the heights above us. The dandies of Rotten Row[57] would come down riding on sorry nags, ready to carry back – their servants were on duty in the trenches – anything that would be available for dinner. A single glance at their personal appearance would suffice to show the hardships of the life they were called upon to lead. Before I left London for the seat of war I had been more than once to the United Service Club, seeking to gain the interest of officers whom I had known in Jamaica; and I often thought afterwards of the difference between these I saw there trimly shaven, handsomely dressed, with spotless linen and dandy air, and these their companions, who in England would resemble them. Roughly, warmly dressed, with great fur caps, which met their beards and left nothing exposed but lips and nose, and not much of those; you would easily believe that soap and water were luxuries not readily obtainable, that shirts and socks were often comforts to dream about rather than possess, and that they were familiar with horrors you would shudder to hear named. Tell me, reader, can you fancy what the want of so simple a thing as a pocket-handkerchief is? To put a case – have you ever gone out for the day without one; sat in a draught and caught a sneezing cold in the head? You say the question is an unnecessarily unpleasant one, and yet what I am about to tell you is true, and the sufferer is, I believe, still alive.

An officer had ridden down one day to obtain refreshments (this was very early in the spring); some nice fowls had just been taken from the spit, and I offered one to him. Paper was one of the most hardly obtainable luxuries of the Crimea, and I rarely had any to waste upon my customers; so I called out, "Give me your pocket-handkerchief, my son, that I may wrap it up." You see we could not be very particular out there; but he smiled very bitterly as he answered, "Pocket-handkerchief, mother – by Jove! I wish I had one. I tore my last shirt into shreds a fortnight ago, and there's not a bit of it left now."

Shortly after, a hundred dozen of these useful articles came to my store, and I sold them all to officers and men very speedily.

For some time, and until I found the task beyond my strength, I kept up a capital table at the British Hotel; but at last I gave up doing so professedly, and my hungry

---

57 The bridle path in London's Hyde Park frequented by elegant riders on horseback

customers had to make shift with whatever was on the premises. Fortunately they were not over-dainty, and had few antipathies. My duties increased so rapidly, that sometimes it was with difficulty that I found time to eat and sleep. Could I have obtained good servants, my daily labours would have been lightened greatly; but my staff never consisted of more than a few boys, two black cooks, some Turks – one of whom, Osman, had enough to do to kill and pluck the poultry, while the others looked after the stock and killed our goats and sheep – and as many runaway sailors or good-for-noughts in search of employment as we could from time to time lay our hands upon; but they never found my larder entirely empty. I often used to roast a score or so of fowls daily, besides boiling hams and tongues. Either these or a slice from a joint of beef or mutton you would be pretty sure of finding at your service in the larder of the British Hotel.

Would you like, gentle reader, to know what other things suggestive of home and its comforts your relatives and friends in the Crimea could obtain from the hostess of Spring Hill? I do not tell you that the following articles were all obtainable at the commencement, but many were. The time was indeed when, had you asked me for mock turtle and venison, you should have had them, preserved in tins, but that was when the Crimea was flooded with plenty – too late, alas! to save many whom want had killed; but had you been doing your best to batter Sebastopol about the ears of the Russians in the spring and summer of the year before last, the firm of Seacole and Day would have been happy to have served you with (I omit ordinary things) linen and hosiery, saddlery, caps, boots and shoes, for the outer man; and for the inner man, meat and soups of every variety in tins (you can scarcely conceive how disgusted we all became at last with preserved provisions); salmon, lobsters, and oysters, also in tins, which last beaten up into fritters, with onions, butter, eggs, pepper, and salt, were very good; game, wild fowl, vegetables, also preserved, eggs, sardines, curry powder, cigars, tobacco, snuff, cigarette papers, tea, coffee, tooth powder, and currant jelly. When cargoes came in from Constantinople, we bought great supplies of potatoes, carrots, turnips, and greens. Ah! what a rush there used to be for the greens. You might sometimes get hot rolls; but, generally speaking, I bought the Turkish bread (ekmek), baked at Balaclava.

Or had you felt too ill to partake of your rough camp fare, coarsely cooked by a soldier cook, who, unlike the French, could turn his hand to few things but fighting, and had ridden down that muddy road to the Col, to see what Mother Seacole could give you for dinner, the chances were you would have found a good joint of mutton, not of the fattest, forsooth;[58] for in such miserable condition were the poor beasts landed, that once, when there came an urgent order from headquarters for twenty-five pounds of mutton, we had to cut up one sheep and a half to provide the quantity; or you would have stumbled upon something curried, or upon a good Irish stew, nice and hot, with plenty of onions and potatoes, or upon some capital meat-pies. I found the preserved meats were better relished cooked in this fashion, and well doctored with stimulants. Before long I grew as familiar with the mysteries of seasoning as any London pieman, and could accommodate myself to the requirements of the seasons as readily. Or had there been nothing better, you might have gone further and fared on worse fare than one of my Welch rabbits,[59] for the manufacture of which I became so famous. And had you been

---

58 Indeed, or in truth
59 Seacole refers to the toast and cheese dish more commonly known as Welsh rarebit.

fortunate enough to have visited the British Hotel upon rice-pudding day, I warrant you would have ridden back to your hut with kind thoughts of Mother Seacole's endeavours to give you a taste of home. If I had nothing else to be proud of, I think my rice puddings, made without milk, upon the high road to Sebastopol, would have gained me a reputation. What a shout there used to be when I came out of my little caboose, hot and flurried, and called out, "Rice-pudding day, my sons." Some of them were baked in large shallow pans, for the men and the sick, who always said that it reminded them of home. You would scarcely expect to finish up your dinner with pastry, but very often you would have found a good stock of it in my larder. Whenever I had a few leisure moments, I used to wash my hands, roll up my sleeves and roll out pastry. Very often I was interrupted to dispense medicines; but if the tarts had a flavour of senna, or the puddings tasted of rhubarb, it never interfered with their consumption. I declare I never heard or read of an army so partial to pastry as that British army before Sebastopol; while I had a reputation for my sponge-cakes that any pastry-cook in London, even Gunter, might have been proud of.[60] The officers, full of fun and high spirits, used to crowd into the little kitchen, and, despite all my remonstrances, which were not always confined to words, for they made me frantic sometimes, and an iron spoon is a tempting weapon, would carry off the tarts hot from the oven, while the good-for-nothing black cooks, instead of lending me their aid, would stand by and laugh with all their teeth. And when the hot season commenced, the crowds that came to the British Hotel for my claret and cider cups, and other cooling summer drinks, were very complimentary in their expressions of appreciation of my skill [. . .].

Before I bring this chapter to a close, I should like, with the reader's permission, to describe one day of my life in the Crimea. They were all pretty much alike, except when there was fighting upon a large scale going on, and duty called me to the field. I was generally up and busy by daybreak, sometimes earlier, for in the summer my bed had no attractions strong enough to bind me to it after four. There was plenty to do before the work of the day began. There was the poultry to pluck and prepare for cooking, which had been killed on the previous night; the joints to be cut up and got ready for the same purpose; the medicines to be mixed; the store to be swept and cleaned. Of very great importance, with all these things to see after, were the few hours of quiet before the road became alive with travellers. By seven o'clock the morning coffee would be ready, hot and refreshing, and eagerly sought for by the officers of the Army Works Corps engaged upon making the great high-road to the front, and the Commissariat and Land Transport men carrying stores from Balaclava to the heights. There was always a great demand for coffee by those who knew its refreshing and strengthening qualities, milk I could not give them (I kept it in tins for special use); but they had it hot and strong, with plenty of sugar and a slice of butter, which I recommend as a capital substitute for milk. From that time until nine, officers on duty in the neighbourhood, or passing by, would look in for breakfast, and about half-past nine my sick patients began to show themselves. In the following hour they came thickly, and sometimes it was past twelve before I had got through this duty. They came with every variety of suffering and disease; the cases I most disliked were the frostbitten fingers and feet in the winter. That over, there was the hospital to visit across the way, which was sometimes overcrowded with patients. I was a good deal there, and as often as possible would take over

---

60 Gunter's Tea Shop was well known in London for the quality of its pastries and ice creams.

books and papers, which I used to borrow for that purpose from my friends and the officers I knew. Once, a great packet of tracts was sent to me from Plymouth anonymously, and these I distributed in the same manner. By this time the day's news had come from the front, and perhaps among the casualties over night there would be some one wounded or sick, who would be glad to see me ride up with the comforts he stood most in need of; and during the day, if any accident occurred in the neighbourhood or on the road near the British Hotel, the men generally brought the sufferer there, whence, if the hurt was serious, he would be transferred to the hospital of the Land Transport opposite. I used not always to stand upon too much ceremony when I heard of sick or wounded officers in the front. Sometimes their friends would ask me to go to them, though very often I waited for no hint, but took the chance of meeting with a kind reception. I used to think of their relatives at home, who would have given so much to possess my privilege; and more than one officer have I startled by appearing before him, and telling him abruptly that he must have a mother, wife, or sister at home whom he missed, and that he must therefore be glad of some woman to take their place.

Until evening the store would be filled with customers wanting stores, dinners, and luncheons; loungers and idlers seeking conversation and amusement; and at eight o'clock the curtain descended on that day's labour, and I could sit down and eat at leisure. It was no easy thing to clear the store, canteen, and yards; but we determined upon adhering to the rule that nothing should be sold after that hour, and succeeded. Any one who came after that time, came simply as a friend. There could be no necessity for any one, except on extraordinary occasions, when the rule could be relaxed, to purchase things after eight o'clock. And drunkenness or excess were discouraged at Spring Hill in every way; indeed, my few unpleasant scenes arose chiefly from my refusing to sell liquor where I saw it was wanted to be abused. I could appeal with a clear conscience to all who knew me there, to back my assertion that I neither permitted drunkenness among the men nor gambling among the officers. Whatever happened elsewhere, intoxication, cards, and dice were never to be seen within the precincts of the British Hotel. My regulations were well known, and a kind-hearted officer of the Royals, who was much there, and who permitted me to use a familiarity towards him which I trust I never abused, undertook to be my Provost-marshal, but his duties were very light.

At first we kept our store open on Sunday from sheer necessity, but after a little while, when stores in abundance were established at Kadikoi and elsewhere, and the absolute necessity no longer existed, Sunday became a day of most grateful rest at Spring Hill. This step also met with opposition from the men; but again we were determined, and again we triumphed. I am sure we needed rest. I have often wondered since how it was that I never fell ill or came home "on urgent private affairs." I am afraid that I was not sufficiently thankful to the Providence which gave me strength to carry out the work I loved so well, and felt so happy in being engaged upon; but although I never had a week's illness during my campaign, the labour, anxiety, and perhaps the few trials that followed it, have told upon me. I have never felt since that time the strong and hearty woman that I was when I braved with impunity the pestilence of Navy Bay and Cruces. It would kill me easily now.

Source text

Seacole, Mrs. [Mary], *Wonderful Adventures of Mrs. Seacole in Many Lands, Edited by W. J. S.* (London: James Blackwood, 1857).

References

Gander, Kashmira, 'Mary Seacole Statue: Why Florence Nightingale Fans Are Angry the Crimean War Nurse Is Being Commemorated', *Independent* (24 June 2016), Web.

McDonald, Lynn, 'Florence Nightingale and Mary Seacole on Nursing and Health Care', *Journal of Advanced Nursing* 70.6 (2013), 1436–44.

ODNB

Paquet, Sandra Pouchet, 'The Enigma of Arrival: *The Wonderful Adventures of Mrs. Seacole in Many Lands*', *African American Review* 50.4 (2017), 864–76.

Trubuhovich, R. V. and C. G. Merridew, 'I. K. Brunel's Crimean War Hospital. Re: Crimean Mortality, Florence Nightingale and Mary Seacole; Response', *Anaesthesia and Intensive Care* 43 (July 2015), 47–8.

James Henry Hammond (1807–64)

From 'Speech on the Admission of Kansas' (1858)

James Henry Hammond was the epitome of the Old South gentleman and planter. Born and raised in South Carolina, Hammond secured entry to the planter class through marriage and established himself in Charleston society, serving in a series of political offices: US House of Representatives starting in 1835, Governor of South Carolina in 1842 and US Senate in 1857. One of the South's strongest proponents of slavery, Hammond allied with the Nullification Party (which held that states could disregard federal laws) before converting to the Democrat ticket later in life. He literally wrote the book on plantation slavery, co-authoring *The Pro-Slavery Argument* (1852, Charleston; 1853, Philadelphia) with William Gilmore Simms and others, as well as *Plantation manual 1857–58*, which held up his Redcliffe Plantation as a blueprint for success in the business of enslavement and included such details as how long enslaved mothers should be allowed to nurse their infants.

When Hammond entered the Senate in 1857, the nation was already deep in turmoil over slavery, with tensions exacerbated around the potential admission of Kansas to the Union. Pro-secessionists (such as Hammond) viewed British dependency on southern cotton as a bulwark against northern aggression, so much so that they considered a boycott to highlight the power of 'King Cotton'. Indeed, southern economic power was on full display during the Panic of 1857, when for the first time the interconnected international economy suffered from the widespread failure of investments firms, stock market declines and bank runs. In England the financial crisis caused the Bank of England to violate the Bank Charter Act to remain solvent. Meanwhile the economy of the US South was largely unaffected on account of its exports, leading many southerners to believe they were building an unassailable cotton-based empire.

The following is an excerpt from Hammond's speech delivered in the US Senate on 4 March 1858.

From 'Speech on the Admission of Kansas'

[...] If we never acquire another foot of territory for the South, look at her. Eight hundred and fifty thousand square miles. As large as Great Britain, France, Austria, Prussia and Spain. Is not that territory enough to make an empire that shall rule the world? With the finest soil, the most delightful climate, whose staple productions none of those great countries can grow, we have three thousand miles of continental sea-shore line so indented with bays and crowded with islands, that, when their shore lines are added, we have twelve thousand miles. Through the heart of our country runs the great Mississippi, the father of waters, into whose bosom are poured thirty-six thousand miles of tributary rivers; and beyond we have the desert prairie wastes to protect us in our rear. Can you hem in such a territory as that? You talk of putting up a wall of fire around eight hundred and fifty thousand square miles so situated! How absurd.

But, in this territory lies the great valley of the Mississippi, now the real, and soon to be the acknowledged seat of the empire of the world. The sway of that valley will be as great as ever the Nile knew in the earlier ages of mankind. We own the most of it. The most valuable part of it belongs to us now; and although those who have settled above us are now opposed to us, another generation will tell a different tale. They are ours by all the laws of nature; slave-labor will go over every foot of this great valley where it will be found profitable to use it, and some of those who may not use it are soon to be united with us by such ties as will make us one and inseparable. The iron horse[61] will soon be clattering over the sunny plains of the South to bear the products of its upper tributaries of the valley to our Atlantic ports, as it now does through the ice-bound North. And there is the great Mississippi, a bond of union made by Nature herself. She will maintain it forever. [...]

But if there were no other reason why we should never have war, would any sane nation make war on cotton? Without firing a gun, without drawing a sword, should they make war on us we could bring the whole world to our feet. The South is perfectly competent to go on, one, two, or three years without planting a seed of cotton. I believe that if she was to plant but half her cotton, for three years to come, it would be an immense advantage to her. I am not so sure but that after three years' entire abstinence she would come out stronger than ever she was before, and better prepared to enter afresh upon her great career of enterprise. What would happen if no cotton was furnished for three years? I will not stop to depict what every one can imagine, but this is certain: England would topple headlong and carry the whole civilized world with her, save the South. No, you dare not make war on cotton. No power on earth dares to make war upon it. Cotton *is* king. Until lately the Bank of England was king; but she tried to put her screws as usual, the fall before last, upon the cotton crop, and was utterly vanquished. The last power has been conquered. Who can doubt, that has looked at recent events, that cotton is supreme?[62] When the abuse of credit had destroyed credit and annihilated confidence; when thousands of the strongest commercial houses in the world were coming down, and hundreds of millions of dollars of supposed property evaporating in thin air; when you came to a dead lock, and revolutions were threatened,

---

61 Railroad train

62 Hammond refers to the Financial Crash or Panic of 1857, in which the worldwide banking system collapsed, partly due to a lack of gold reserves (with the US South largely immune due to the stability of its cotton crop).

what brought you up? Fortunately for you it was the commencement of the cotton season, and we have poured in upon you one million six hundred thousand bales of cotton just at the crisis to save you from destruction. That cotton, but for the bursting of your speculative bubbles in the North, which produced the whole of this convulsion, would have brought us $100,000,000. We have sold it for $65,000,000 and saved you. Thirty-five million dollars we, the slaveholders of the South, have put into the charity box for your magnificent financiers, your "cotton lords," your "merchant princes." [. . .]

Source text

Hammond, James H., *Selections from the Letters and Speeches of the Hon. James H. Hammond of South Carolina* (New York: John F. Trow & Co., 1866).

References

Harper, Robert Goodloe et al., *Cotton is King, and Pro-slavery Arguments: Comprising the Writings of Hammond, Harper, Christy, Stringfellow, Hodge, Bledsoe, and Cartwright, on this Important Subject* (Augusta, GA: Pritchard, Abbott & Loomis, 1860).
Woodman, Harold D., *King Cotton and His Retainers: Financing and Marketing the Cotton Crop of the South, 1800–1925* (Lexington, KY: University of Kentucky Press, 1968).

'Women's Condition in Great Britain, From an American Point of View' (1860)

As Charles Dickens observed in his *American Notes*, women factory workers in Lowell, Massachusetts, were noteworthy for having more access to educational opportunities than counterparts in the United Kingdom. Beyond Lowell's well-documented learners, in the US 'middle-class women were increasingly the beneficiaries of a [relatively] privileged education', even as 'wage-earning factory workers were also acquiring the tools of literacy in an expanding public school system as well as through libraries, lyceums, and improvement societies' (Jenkins Cook, 220). Conversely, the following article claims, British young men and boys benefitted from education via private, philanthropic endeavours, whereas young working-class women were denied such privileges.

Transatlantic comparisons like those this writer proposes between American and British working-class factory women are complicated to trace, however. In England, June Purvis argues, 'the struggle by the working class to control their own education and not simply to be recipients of what middle-class patrons wished them to receive opened a debate' about the types of education they desired and could access (100). In that context, Teresa Gerrard and Alexis Weedon examine the curriculum of the

Huddersfield Female Educational Institute (which shared aims with other programmes set up in Leeds, Nottingham and Birmingham). Gerrard and Weedon describe lessons in 'writing, reading and arithmetic, sewing, history, geography, and singing', but explain that 'By the time of the institute's closure in 1883, this narrow curriculum had been further curtailed, and, other than the three Rs, the only lessons on offer were domestic economy and cookery' (239).

'Woman's Condition in Great Britain, From an American Point of View'

In the April number of the "Edinburgh Review" is an able article on woman's work and its reward in Great Britain, from the days of King Alfred, when the surplus women and girls of England were sold into slavery in Ireland, down to the present time, when, under the factory and other systems of labour, they are scarcely *less* slaves now than then.

The reviewer makes some good suggestions, urging an improved system of education for women dependent upon their own labour for support, such as schools for a higher order of instruction in household duties and in the lighter mechanical arts, such as watchmaking, printing, telegraphing, drawing, painting, and also in the liberal professions, especially medicine and surgery.

At present, the only modes of self-subsistence for English women who rise above the lowest kinds of menial or out-door labour are the needle and teaching. As there is no public-school system in England, no free-schools for children—except charity-schools, *which are all for boys*; where female teachers are never employed, except for very small children—the women who teach are chiefly governesses in private families. The situation of women, educated ladies, engaged in this profession is absolutely painful, and their pay is so scanty that the greater wonder is, not that the greater proportion die paupers, but that any ever contrive to lay by provision for sickness and old age.

The jealousy of Englishmen pushes the women from some occupations for which she is in every way better fitted than he. Our author tells us that a manufacturer in Staffordshire, employing women to paint porcelain, in which they were eminently successful, was compelled, by the cruel injustice of his workmen, *to oblige the women to paint without any rest for the hand.*

We are thankful, ay, proud, to record that the reviewer frankly acknowledges that the women of America now enjoy many advantages which the philanthropists of England are but just beginning to seek for their own country-women. He tells of our medical colleges for women, mentions Miss Dr. Blackwell with high approbation, instances our schools of design, and offers the example of the Lowell factory-girls to prove that education and morality are not incompatible with factory-labour. He speaks with great force and reason on the subject of school for girls. In England, as we have already stated, there is no provision for public education. For boys there are private, charitable, and civic foundations; but girls have no place in these, and, with few exceptions of parochial schools, English girls have to rely upon the ability of their families or upon individual beneficence for all educational privileges.

How very different is our condition here in America, let our school-reports and school-examinations testify. Girls have in our country opportunities of education, and women of professions—that of educator and physician—which are not enjoyed by the sex in any other part of the world, which never were before enjoyed by the women of any nation or people; neither are they so hampered by imaginary restrictions, the pride of rank and the prejudices of society, as is the case with the women of Great Britain. The women of America should turn their educational privileges to good account. Let them, when needed, assist their fathers, brothers, or husbands in commercial or professional pursuits, which are not beyond their physical and mental force, and which do not derogate from the propriety and delicacy without which woman is not worthy of her calling as the moral civilizer of our race.

In the little country of Switzerland over *twenty thousand women* are, as we learn from statistics, employed in the delicate fabrication of watches. In England and America this work is done exclusively by men. Is it more suitable to feminine delicacy to scrub, to milk, and to churn butter than to touch the delicate interior of a watch? Should a woman become coarser or more masculine by keeping her husband's books, or copying his law papers, or aiding him in his medical preparations, than she is when washing clothes, sewing on his buttons, and doing the common drudgery? There can be no doubt which would be the more profitable of the two offices. Still, we should never lose sight of this important truth, that the best pursuit of woman is "household good, and good works in her husband [and children] to promote." Nature and revelation alike lay the burden of work on man. He is made strong for his task, and endowed with inventive mechanical genius, excited by the love of gain, which women do not, as a general rule possess, or but in small degree, compared with him. Man should be the worker or provider—woman the preserver and dispenser. It is putting woman nearly on a level with animals when she is sent out of the home which she should keep as the family citadel of hope, safety, virtue, and happiness, and made 'to till the ground'—man's appointed work; yet British women are reduced to this miserable drudgery. We find that over *sixty thousand* of the women of England and Scotland are engaged in agricultural labour, hard, wearing, and ill-paid field-labour; and the British reviewer looks very complacently on their degraded lot, because he thinks "their work is not unfavourable to health, and that women house-servants are worse off than these field-hands."

There are about *forty thousand housemaids* in Great Britain, whose wages average *five or six pounds* a year. Out of this salary nothing can be saved. Their youth is passed in constant drudgery, unpitied and crushing slavery of every faculty they possess, to the one object of keeping soul and body together; in their premature and incapable old age they have no resource save the almshouse. The statistics of London mortality show that, in 1858, of the deaths in that great city, *one out of every five* took place in the hospitals or workhouses. We should like to know how large a proportion of these miserable paupers were women or girls.

Truly, the condition of women-servants—ay, of all working women—in Great Britain, is deplorable, and we rejoice that this important matter is beginning to engage public attention.

Source text

'Woman's Condition in Great Britain, From an American Point of View', *Sharpe's London Magazine of Entertainment and Instruction for General Reading* 17 (January 1860), 44–5.

References

Cook, Sylvia Jenkins, '"Oh Dear! How the Factory Girls Do Rig Up!"': Lowell's Self-Fashioning Workingwomen', *New England Quarterly* 83.2 (June 2010), 219–49.

Gerrard, Teresa and Alexis Weedon, 'Working-Class Women's Education in Huddersfield: A Case Study of the Female Educational Institute Library, 1856–1857', *Information & Culture* 49.2 (2014), 234–64.

Purvis, June, *Hard Lessons: The Lives and Education of Working-Class Women in Nineteenth-Century England* (Cambridge: Polity Press, 1989).

Sara Willis Parton [Fanny Fern] (1811–72)

From 'Bridget As She Was, And Bridget As She Is' (1868)

In this excerpt (companion to another from Part I of the same text in MSR), Fanny Fern satirises, yet attempts to establish sympathy for, both the transatlantic immigrant domestic worker and the middle-class lady-of-the-house who employs her. She takes employers to task for treating servants poorly, including for expecting that they dress a certain way, in line with class differentiation. Fern questions why a housewife chooses to wear finery on public transportation and then expresses concern about working-class women aspiring to wear nice clothing too.

Fern further comments on how working- and middle-class women both contribute to the economy, since domestic workers, like their wealthier counterparts, purchase commodities that, Nan Enstad has argued, exemplify efforts at appropriation for 'display, self-statement, and glamour' (18). Thus Fern here envisions a working-class agency anticipating Vanessa May's analysis of turn-of-the-century domestic labouring women: 'We sometimes imagine domestics as cloistered workers, trapped in middle-class homes and communities far away from the vibrant labor activism of shops and industry. Working class activism could be in the home or neighborhood'(May, 8).

From 'Bridget As She Was, And Bridget As She Is': Part 2

[...] The other day, in running my eye over a daily paper, I read this advertisement: "A *genteel* girl wishes a situation as chambermaid." Now if there is one word in the English language that I hate more than another, it is the word *genteel*. No matter where, or how, or to whom, or by whom it is applied, my very soul sickens at it. It is the universal and never-failing indorser of every sham ever foisted upon disgusted human nature. From the "genteel" cabbage-scented boarding-house, where tobacco emasculated young men "feed," and mindless, be-flounced, cheap jewel-ried married and un-married women smile sweetly on them, to the seventh-rate dry-goods store in some obscure street, whose clerk sells only the most "genteel" goods at a shilling per yard; to the "genteel" school-girl who, owning one greasy silk dress, imagines that she understands her geography better in that attire than in a quiet, clean, modest "delaine;"[63] to the "genteel" shop-girl who, pitiably destitute of comfortable under-clothes, yet always owns a "dress hat," and swings about the last showy fashion in trimming, on some cheap fabric; to the "genteel" cook who goes to market with her hair dressed as near as may be like her mistress, fastening it up with a brassy imitation of her gold comb; to the "genteel" seminary for young ladies, who ride to school in a carriage with liveried servants, their papa having formerly been one himself.

But a "genteel" chambermaid! Now, why should this patrician creature seek such a prosaic, vulgar occupation? Could she be aware that chambermaids must wield brooms, and dust-pans, and scrubbing brushes, and handle pokers, and shovel, and tongs, and ashes. That they may even be asked to stand at the wash-tub, and be seen by the neighbors in the disgraceful occupation of hanging out clothes. That they may occasionally have to answer the door-bell in an apron, and usher finely-dressed ladies into the parlor; or be asked to take a baby out for an airing, and be stamped at once by the public as a person who "works for a living." How can a "genteel" chamber-maid calmly contemplate such degradation, least of all perform such duties faithfully and well? Would not any sensible lady, wishing a chamber maid, see at once that the thing was impossible? Would she not know that she might ring her bell till the wire gave out, before this "genteel" young woman would think it expedient to answer it till she was ready? And when she sent her up stairs to tidy her chamber, would she not be sure that this "genteel" creature would probably spend the time in trying on her mistress' last new opera-hat before the toilet-glass? And if she sent her out on an errand, involving even a moderately sized bundle, would not this "genteel" young woman probably take a circuitous route through back streets to hide her ignominy?

Bridget, sometimes, at the glass,
Tries Miss Julia's bonnet on ;
Making, thus, a face of brass
Edged with lace of Honiton.

Figure 3.3 Cartoon of an Irish domestic; *c*.1840–80. Text reads: Bridget, sometimes, at the glass, / Tries Miss Julia's bonnet on; / Making, thus, a face of brass, / Edged with lace of Honiton. Courtesy Library Company of Philadelphia.

---

63 Lightweight fabric, made of cotton and wool, for dresses

Heavens! What a relief it is to see people self-poised and satisfied with their honest occupations, making no attempt to veneer them over with a thin polish of gentility. Such I am happy to say there still are, in humble circumstances, notwithstanding the bad example constantly set them by the moneyed class in our country, who are servilely and snobbishly bent on aping all the aristocratic absurdities of the old country. *"Genteel!"* Faugh![64] even the detestable expression-word "FUST-rate" is music to my ears after it.

AFTER all, I am not sure that my sympathies are not enlisted much more strongly on the side of servants than of their mistresses, who at any moment can show them the door at their capricious will, without a passport to any other place of shelter. Their lot is often at best a hard one; the best wages being a very inadequate equivalent for the great gulf which, in many cases, separates the servant from her employer as effectually, as if her woman's nature had no need of human love and human sympathy; as if she did not often bear her secret burden of sorrow with a heroism, which should cause a blush on the cheek of her who sits with folded hands in the parlor, all neglectful of woman's mission to her dependent sister. They who have listened vainly for kind words know how much they may lighten toil. They who have shut up in their aching hearts the grief which no friendly look or tone has ever unlocked, know how it will fester and rankle. They who have felt every ounce of their flesh taxed unrelentingly day by day to the utmost, with no approving "well done" to lighten slumber when the heavy yoke is nightly cast down, know what is servitude of *soul*, as well as body.

I could wish that mistresses oftener thought of this; oftener sat down in the gloomy, underground kitchen or basement, and inquired after the absent mother, or brother, or sister, in the old country; oftener placed in the toil-hardened hand the book or paper, or pamphlet, to shorten the tedious evening in the comfortless kitchen, while the merry laugh in which the servant has no share, resounds from the cheerful parlor above.

I do not forget that there are bad servants, as that there are unfeeling, inhuman mistresses who make them. I know that some are wasteful and improvident; and I know, from experience, that there are cases where the sympathy and kindness I speak of are repaid with ingratitude; but these are exceptional cases; and think how much hard usage from the world such an one must have received, ere all her sweet and womanly feelings could be thus blunted. I must think that a humane mistress generally makes a good servant. I know that some of the servants of the present day dress ridiculously above their station, – so does often the mistress; and why is a poor, unenlightened girl more reproachable, for spending the wages of a month on a flimsy, gaudy bonnet, or dress, than is her employer, for trailing a seventy-five or one hundred dollar robe through ferryboats and omnibuses, while her grocer and milliner dun[65] in vain for their bills?

Let the reform in this and other respects begin in the parlor. Our mothers and grandmothers were not always changing servants. *They* did not disdain to lend a helping hand, when a press of work, or company, made the burden of servitude too heavy. A headache in the kitchen, to them, meant the same as a headache in the parlor, and, God be thanked, a heart-ache too. The soul of a servant was of as much account as that of her mistress; her creed was respected, and no elaborate dinner came between her and the church-door. How can you expect such unfaltering,

---

64 A term expressing disgust or contempt
65 To make multiple requests – or even demands – for (late) payments

unswerving devotion to your interests, when you so wholly ignore theirs? —when you spur and goad them on like beasts of burden, and with as little thought for their human wants and needs? No wonder if you have poor service—eye-service. I would like to see you do better in their place. Lift up the cloud, and let the sun shine through into their underground homes, if it is not a mockery to use the word home. We exact too much—we give too little, —too little sympathy—too little kindness—too little encouragement. "Love thy neighbor as thyself" would settle it all. You don't do it—I don't do it, though I try to. Human laws may require only of the mistress that she pay her servant's wages punctually; God's law requires much more—let conscience be its interpreter;—then, and not till then, we shall have good servants.

I SUPPOSE the most jealous fault-finders on this subject will concede that mistresses themselves are not quite perfect; of course, they have often real causes of irritation and vexation apart from the kitchen, which, we are afraid, do not dispose them to look leniently upon any additional trouble there. A "flare up" with Betty or Bridget, is apt to be the last drop in the bucket, the last feather in the balance. But, unfortunately, it is not taken into account that Betty and Bridget, being human, may have their little world of hopes and joys, fears and sorrows, quite disconnected with your gridiron, and dustpan, and ash-barrel. They also have heads and backs to ache, and hearts too, though this may not always be taken into the account, by employers, who, satisfied with punctually paying the stipulated wages when due, and getting as much as possible out of them as an equivalent, consider their duty ended. Some day your dinner is over or under cooked; that day Bridget received a letter from the "old country" with a "black seal."[66] She did not come to you with her trouble; why should she? when she might have been a mere machine for any sympathetic word or look that has ever passed from your woman's heart or eyes to hers. All you know is that your dinner is overcooked, and a sharp rebuke follows, and from the fulness of a tried spirit an "impertinent " answer comes, and you show Bridget the door, preaching a sermon on the neglectfulness and insolence of servants. Had you been the mistress you should have been, Bridget would naturally have come to you with her trouble, and you would willingly have excused at such a time any little oversight in her duty to you, even though on that day you "had company to dinner." Take another case. On some day in the week, when the heaviest family labor falls due, your girl whose province it is to accomplish it, rises with an aching head, or limbs, as you sometimes do yourself, and as you do not, she rises from bed all the same as if she were well. As you have no use for your lips in the kitchen, save to give an order, and no eyes, save to look after defects of economy or carefulness, you do not see her languid eyes, or ask the cause of any apparent dilatoriness; you simply "hurry up" things generally, and go up stairs. Now, suppose you had kindly asked the girl if she felt quite well, and finding she did not, offered to lift from her aching shoulders that day s burden; *suppose* that? why, ten to one, it would have done her more good than could any doctor who ever took a degree, and the poor thing, under its inspiration, might actually have staggered through the day's work, had you been so cruel as to allow her.

I wish mistresses would sometimes ask themselves how long, under the depressing conditions and circumstances of servitude above alluded to, *they* could render faithful conscientious labor? Feeling that doing well, there was no word of praise; and that doing ill, there was no excuse or palliation; that falling sick or disabled, from

---

66 Black sealing wax would connote a need for mourning, so the letter may report a death.

over work or natural causes, there was no sympathy, but only nervous anxiety for a speedy substitute.

Again. Many mistresses utterly object to "a beau" in the kitchen. Now could anything be more unnatural and absurd than this? though, of course, there should be limitations as to late hours. Marriage, with many of these domestics, is the heaven of rest and independence to which they look forward; and even if they are to work quite as hard "for a living," as a poor man s wife, as they have for you, they may possibly have, as wives – heaven help them – a little love to sweeten it; and surely no wife or mother should shut her heart utterly to this view of the case. As to the girl's "bettering herself," let her take the chances, if she chooses, as you have. Possibly, some lady who reads this may say, oh, all this talk about servants is nonsense. I've often petted girls till I have spoiled them, and it is of no use. Very true, madam, "petting" *is* of no use; but it *is* of use to treat them at all times kindly, and humanely, and above all things *justly*, as we – women – in their places, should wish to be treated ourselves. It *is* of use to make a little sunshine in those gloomy kitchens, by a kind good night, or good morning, or some such recognition of their presence, other than a desire to be waited upon. It *is* of use, when they are sick or down-hearted, to turn *to*, not *from* them. All this can be done, and not "spoil" them. And how much better, even as far as yourself is concerned, to feel that their service is that of love and good-will, instead of mere "eye-service." A lady once asked a servant for her references. There was more justice and less "impertinence," than appears at the first blush, in her reply, "and where are *yours*, ma'am?"

Source text

Fern, Fanny, 'Bridget as She Was, and Bridget as She Is', *Folly As It Flies; Hit At* (New York: G. W. Carleton, 1868), 109–17.

References

Enstad, Nan, *Ladies of Labor, Girls of Adventure: Working Women, Popular Culture, and Labor Politics at the Turn of the Twentieth Century* (New York: Columbia University Press, 1999).

May, Vanessa, *Unprotected Labor: Household Workers, Politics, and Middle-Class Reform in New York, 1870–1940* (Chapel Hill, NC: University of North Carolina Press, 2011).

John Rollin Ridge (1827–67)

'The Atlantic Cable' (1868)

John Rollin Ridge is best known today for *The Life and Adventures of Joaquín Murieta* (1854), often touted as the first novel published by a Native American writer (Carr, Hickey). But he was also a journalist and a poet. The enthusiastic lyric below includes features in many of his *Poems* collection, which signalled his self-presentation as a 'Civilized

Indian' (a US Census category by 1860) well-schooled in European-based poetic forms and affiliating with cultural assimilation.

Born in the Cherokee capital of New Echota (in today's US state of Georgia) before the Removal, he was the son and nephew of John and Major Ridge, vocal opponents of Principal Chief John Ross. In 1839, when not yet a teenager, John Rollin Ridge witnessed the assassination of his father, who had advocated accepting monetary compensation and land in the West for Cherokee homelands coveted by the United States rather than fighting a doomed battle against Removal. The remaining Ridges settled in Arkansas. There young John sought to re-establish his family's status and access to leadership, only to find himself a fugitive after killing a longtime rival who had stolen a horse. In a 'Preface' (perhaps prepared by his white wife) for his posthumously published *Poems*, Ridge's own voice takes centre stage in long quotes revisiting his family's rightful place in Cherokee history.

Ridge had moved to California in 1850. There, he became a newspaper writer, praised for public recitations of his poetry and for editorial writing. Ridge's *Joaquín Murieta* presented an anti-racist critique of white abuses against California's indigenous peoples, a stance also informing his journalism. Yet Ridge himself embraced concepts of racial hierarchy, especially in relation to local 'Digger' communities in California (Hickey, 73), which he depicted as inferior to well-educated Natives like himself, who had attended a northeastern boarding school.

Ridge sometimes published his poems under the signature Yellow Bird, an English rendering of his Cherokee name, Cheesquatalawny. But his book-length collection of *Poems* lists its author as 'John R. Ridge', and his frontispiece portrait depicts him as a distinguished businessman.

Like that self-portrait, 'The Atlantic Cable' aligns Ridge with his personal embrace of white Americans' global leadership in industry, particularly as enshrined in the famous laying of the cable. Linking the cable's social power to a history of innovations in sea travel, labour tools and communications, he also salutes individual American inventor figures like Benjamin Franklin and Samuel Morse.

'The Atlantic Cable'

> Let Earth be glad! for that great work is done,
> Which makes, at last, the Old and New World one!
> Let all mankind rejoice! for time nor space
> Shall check the progress of the human race!
> Though Nature heaved the Continents apart,
> She cast in one great mould the human heart;
> She framed on one great plan the human mind,
> And gave man speech to link him to his kind;
> So that, though plains and mountains intervene,
> Or oceans, broad and stormy, roll between,

If there but be a courier for the thought—
Swift-winged or slow—the land and seas are nought,
And man is nearer to his brother brought.

First, ere the dawn of letters was, or burst
The light of science on the world, men, nurs't
In distant solitudes apart, did send
Their skin-clad heralds forth to thread the woods,
Scale mountain-peaks, or swim the sudden floods,
Next, beasts were tamed to drag the rolling car,
Or speed the mounted rider on his track;
And then came, too, the vessels, oar-propelled,
Which fled the ocean, as the clouds grew black,
And safe near shore their prudent courses held.
Next came the wingéd ships, which, brave and free,
Did skim the bosom of the bounding sea,
And dared the storms and darkness in their flight,
Yet drifted far before the winds and night,
Or lay within the dead calm's grasp of might.
Then, sea-divided nations nearer came,
Stood face to face, spake each the other's name,
In friendship grew, and learned the truth sublime,
That Man is Man in every age and clime!
They nearer were by months and years—but space
Must still be shortened in Improvement's race,
And steam came next to wake the world from sleep,
And launch her black-plumed warriors of the deep;
The which, in calm or storm, rode onward still,
And braved the raging elements at will.
Then distance, which from calms' and storms' delays
Grew into months, was shortened into days,
And Science's self declared her wildest dream
Reached not beyond this miracle of steam!
But steam hath not the lightning's wondrous power,
Though, Titan[67]-like, mid Science's sons it tower
And wrestle with the ocean in his wrath,
And sweep the wild waves foaming from its path.
A mightier monarch is that subtler thing,
Which gives to human thought a thought-swift wing;
Which speaks in thunder like a God,
Or humbly stoops to kiss the lifted rod;
Ascends to Night's dim, solitary throne,
And clothes it with a splendor not its own—
A ghastly grandeur and a ghostly sheen,
Through which the pale stars tremble as they're seen;
Descends to fire the far horizon's rim,
And paints Mount Etnas[68] in the cloudland grim;

---

67 According to Greek mythology, twelve pre-Olympian gods of immense power
68 A mountain and active volcano in on the Italian island of Sicily

Or, proud to own fair Science's rightful sway,
Low bends along th' electric wire to play,
And, helping out the ever-wondrous plan,
Becomes, in sooth, an errand-boy for man!

This Power it was, which, not content with aught
As yet achieved by human will or thought,
Disdained the slow account of months or days,
In navigation of the ocean ways,
And days would shorten into hours, and these
To minutes, in the face of sounding seas.
If Thought might not be borne upon the foam
Of furrowing keel, with speed that Thought should roam,
It then should walk, like light, the ocean's bed,
And laugh to scorn the winds and waves o'er head!
Beneath the reach of storm or wreck, down where
The skeletons of men and navies are,
Its silent steps should be; while o'er its path
The monsters of the deep, in sport or wrath,
The waters lashed, till like a pot should boil
The sea, and fierce Arion[69] seize the upcast spoil.

America! to thee belongs the praise
Of this great crowning deed of modern days.
'T was Franklin[70] called the wonder from on high;
'T was Morse[71] who bade it on man's errands fly—
'T was he foretold its pathway 'neath the sea:
A daring Field[72] fulfilled the prophecy!
'T was fitting that a great, free land like this,
Should give the lightning's voice to Liberty;
Should wing the heralds of Earth's happiness,
And sing, beneath the ever-sounding sea,
The fair, the bright millennial days to be.

Now may, ere long, the sword be sheathed to rust,
The helmet laid in undistinguished dust;
The thund'rous chariot pause in mid career,
Its crimsoned wheels no more through blood to steer;
The red-hoofed steed from fields of death be led,
Or turned to pasture where the armies bled;
For Nation unto Nation soon shall be
Together brought in knitted unity,

---

69 An ancient Greek poet renowned for his lyre-playing and invention of the dithyramb
70 Benjamin Franklin (1706–90), a prominent American statesman and inventor who conducted notable experiments in electricity, most famously with a kite and lightning
71 Samuel Morse (1791–1872), American inventor known for his contested innovation of the single-wire telegraph
72 Cyrus West Field (1819–92), American businessman who, through his Atlantic Telegraph Company, enabled the launch of the first transatlantic telegraph cable, on 16 August 1858

And man be bound to man by that strong chain,
Which, linking land to land, and main to main,
Shall vibrate to the voice of Peace, and be
A throbbing heartstring of Humanity!

Source text

Ridge, John R., *Poems* (San Francisco: Henry Payot, 1868).

References

Carr, Ryan, 'Lyric X-Marks: Genre and Self-Determination in the Harp Poems of John Rollin Ridge', *MELUS* 43.3 (Fall 2018), 42–63.
Hickey, Alanna, '"Let Paler Nations Vaunt Themselves": John Rollin Ridge's "Official Verse" and Racial Citizenship in Gold Rush California', *Studies in American Indian Literature* 27.4 (Winter 2015), 66–100.
Whitley, Edward, 'The First White Aboriginal: Walt Whitman and John Rollin Ridge', *ESQ: A Journal of the American Renaissance* 52.1–2 (2006), 105–39.

Figure 3.4 The Old Slater Mill, Pawtucket, RI. The first cotton-spinning mill operated in America. Pawtucket, RI. Graphic Collection, Pawtucket Factories. RHi X3 7735. Copyright and ownership Rhode Island Historical Society, illustration provided Courtesy the Rhode Island Historical Society.

The Old Slater Mill was the first site of textile technology imported (via memorisation of written plans) by English-American engineer Samuel Slater, a transfer exercised against British law. While in the US Slater is considered the 'Father of the American Industrial Revolution', he was branded 'Slater the Traitor' by the British public and press. In time, the United States would come to surpass its 'mother country' in technological prowess and material production, with transatlantic transfers of knowledge like Slater's contributing to that process.

William Thomas (W. T.) Stead (1849–1912)

From **The Americanization of the World** *(1901)*

After a precocious childhood, W. T. Stead in 1870 joined the liberal news-paper *The Northern Echo*, where he served as the youngest newspaper edi-tor in England before moving onto the *Pall Mall Gazette* in 1880. There, Stead revolutionised the journalism industry by adding his personal opin-ions to articles, popularising the interview format and featuring diagrams and subheadings to enhance design. Under Stead the *Pall Mall* often railed against the English criminal codes and other social injustices. He was best known for his 1885 series of articles, 'The Maiden Tribute of Modern Babylon', where he strongly advocated both to end child prostitution and to raise the legal age of child marriage from thirteen to sixteen. Stead died aboard the ill-fated *RMS Titanic* on 15 April 1912, while traveling to America to attend a peace conference at Carnegie Hall.

Stead's *The Americanization of the World* centres on the rising influence of the United States in politics, culture and industry. His pro-American perspective resists a then-prevailing Anglo attitude; as he notes in the vol-ume's first sentence, 'The Americanization of the world is a phrase which excites, quite needlessly, some resentment in Great Britain.' Though writing at perhaps the height of the British Empire, he foresees the coming century as a US-American one, largely due to that nation's massive population, land area and resource base. In Chapter VII, 'Railways, Shipping, and Trusts', excerpted below, Stead characterises the massive presence of US-made rail-ways in England and provides examples of why British railways have fallen behind.

From **The Americanization of the World**

ALTHOUGH there are 200,000 miles of railway in the United States alone, the railway itself is but a thing of yesterday. A curious reminder of this was afforded us this year by the unearthing in Iowa by some enterprising pressmen of the very man who drove Stephenson's "Rocket"[73] on the eventful day when on the opening of the Liverpool and Manchester Railway the train knocked down and killed Mr. Huskis-son. Edward Entwistle was a Lancashire lad of eighteen when George Stephenson took him out of the engine-shop and put him at the throttle of the "Rocket" on the opening day. He is now a man of eighty-six.

After acting as engine-driver on the Liverpool and Manchester for over two years, he emigrated to America in 1837, where he took up the trade of station-ary engineer. He is still in good health and sufficiently alert to be capable of giving

---

73 The world's first modern steam locomotive, invented by father–son duo George and Robert Stephenson

occasional addresses on his reminiscences of Stephenson, in which, judging from the newspaper reports, Mr. Huskisson reappears as Lord Erkinson, so that the span of a single life easily covers the whole of the railway era.

It may be regarded as symbolic that the first engine-driver should so soon have emigrated to the United States, as if divining from some secret unconscious instinct that it was there the genius of Stephenson would bear its richest fruits. By every test, whether quantitative or qualitative, the American stands out *facile princeps*[74] in all things connected with the railway. To begin with, he has built nearly half the railways in the world.

Not only has he spanned his own continent with a perfect gridiron of metalled way, but he is now carrying off contracts for the bridge work, which, with the exception of tunnelling, constitutes the most difficult and delicate of all the operations of railway structure. But it was only yesterday that their pre-eminence as bridge builders dawned upon the British public, which has even yet hardly recovered from the shock of discovering that all the Queen's horses and all the Queen's men were incapable of conquering the Soudan without resorting to the humiliating necessity of accepting an American tender for the building of a bridge across the Atbara.[75]

The British could have built it themselves, no doubt, but they could not do the work up to time. Few incidents caused more chagrin,[76] and the most conclusive explanations were speedily forthcoming to prove how easily the British builders could have done the task if they had only had a reasonable notice and been treated with reasonable fairness.

These explanations, apparently conclusive, temporarily allayed John Bull's[77] ill-humor, but it was only for a time. Last Autumn the American Bridge Company carried off contracts for constructing no fewer than twenty-eight bridges and viaducts required to complete the Uganda Railway.

The work is now in active progress, and the bridges are in process of shipment across the Atlantic for Uganda, one of the territories which was occupied for the express purpose of developing British trade in South Africa. Money is being poured out like water in order to secure this market for British manufactured goods, and lo! the American steps in and carries off the contracts for building these bridges without having incurred a penny of expense or an atom of responsibility in opening up the country.

The same thing is occurring in other parts of the world. The Americans have just built the largest bridge in the world over the Goktein in Upper Burma. And as it is with bridges, so it promises to be with rails. Mr. Rhodes experienced a cruel shock when in opening tenders for the construction of the southern end of his Cape to Cairo Railway, he discovered that Mr. Carnegie was able to deliver steel rails in South Africa at a lower price than any English manufacturer.

The patriotic pride of the South African Colossus prompted him to take advantage of a technical flaw in Mr. Carnegie's contract in order to accept the tender of a British firm; but to this day he feels uneasy at the remembrance of the subterfuge[78] to which he had to resort in order to keep the trade in British hands. "It would have

---

74 An easily acknowledged leader
75 River in northwest Ethiopia, and the site of a decisive 1898 battle in the Second Sudan War
76 Embarrassment; humiliation
77 Imaginary figure often personifying England
78 Deception used to obtain a desire or goal

been too bad," he said, somewhat pathetically, "to think of my Cape to Cairo line being made with American rails!"

In war, as in peace, it is the same thing. While the Imperial Government was importing American mules by the thousand from New Orleans to give mobility to its flying columns[79] at the seat of war, the Cape Government was placing contracts with American engineers for engines which could not be supplied from British workshops, even although, as the Colonial Government plaintively explained, it gave a ten percent[80] preference to British manufacturers. But it is impossible long to carry on business in which contracts, like kissing, go by favor, and not to the best tender; and such devices as ten percent preferences and the like are neither more nor less than a confession of defeat. If British engineers can only hold their own with a ten percent adverse handicap against their American competitors, the question is ended, and the superiority of the Yankee is attested by the very terms of the competition insisted upon by his rival.

As it is with bridges and with rails, so it is even more conspicuously with American locomotives. They are not artistic toys, the giant engines which do the haulage of a continent, neither do they require one month in a paintshop, as is said to be the case in our own Midland Railway. But they are the strongest haulers in the world, and they go at the greatest speed. America holds the world's record both for speed at all distances and the weight of the trains hauled by a single locomotive. Philadelphia railway expresses are constantly timed to run at sixty-six miles an hour, and it is nothing unusual for trains when under pressure to dash along the metal way at the rate of eighty to eighty-four miles an hour. The tendency is ever towards more and more powerful engines, with heavier haulage capacity.

The Americans laugh to scorn what they regard as the toy cars in use in the Old World. At one time their average freight cars weighed ten tons, and only carried their own weight. To-day they weigh fifteen tons and carry thirty. A single engine will grapple a quarter of a mile of these cars, loaded to their utmost capacity, and make no complaint, if half a dozen extra are hitched on behind. The result of this continual development in the direction of greater haulage capacity is that the freight on American railways is about half of what it is in this country.

The United States at one time imported locomotives from this country. They are now exporting locomotives to all parts of the British Empire. Recently the reputation of the American engine has been somewhat prejudiced, first, by the inferior quality of locomotives sent to Australia; secondly, by an adverse report made by the Locomotive Superintendent of the Midland Railway as to the extra working cost of an American engine. He reported that as the result of a six months' trial, the American engine cost 20 to 25 percent more for fuel, 50 percent more for oil, and 60 percent more for repairs. This report was received with a chorus of delight in English papers; but, as was immediately pointed out by an American writer in an interesting paper published in the World's Work for November, under the title "The American Locomotive Abroad," the Midland Report was far from conclusive for several reasons.

First, the so-called American engines were not of the pure American type, but were modified to meet English ideas; secondly, the report gives no information as

---

79 A small, independent military land unit capable of rapid mobility
80 Typesetting of the 'percent' word is somewhat inconsistent and potentially confusing in the source text, often breaking into two words and adding a period; we have standardised to 'percent'.

to the amount of coal burned, oil used, or money spent in repairs. The American locomotives have burned 25 percent more coal, but, on the other hand, they may have been capable of hauling 50 percent more freight; and as for the repairs, 60 percent against the Americans looks very formidable, but if the total repairs on either engine did not amount to more than 10s., a difference even of 100 percent would mean nothing. All attempts to draw information from the Midland superintendent on this point have failed to elicit any facts beyond those contained in the report.

It is a notable fact, says the author of the article already quoted, that the first American locomotive ever imported into England was built sixty years ago for the purpose of enabling the English railway manager to prove that it was possible to haul loaded trains up a steep incline in the Birmingham-Gloucester Railway. Four engines were ordered in 1840, and they triumphantly accomplished their task. Thus, says Mr. Cunnliff, the author of "The American Locomotive Abroad," the Birmingham and Gloucester line, on which the American engines first made their reputation, is now part of the Midland, whose officers have recently tried to ruin that reputation. The engines of 1840 and those of 1900 were both built in the same workshops. [...]

For heavy hauls on steep gradients the American engines appear to leave all their rivals far behind. There is said to be only one English locomotive left in the United States. It is on the Pennsylvania Railroad, and its driver is said to have reported as follows: "It is a good enough engine when it has nothing to do, but when it has a load beyond its drawbar, it sits down and looks at you with tears in its eyes."

Patriotic prejudice, no doubt, impedes for a time the introduction of American locomotives into many countries, and in Russia it would seem the distribution of orders is often governed more by political than by commercial considerations. Another obstacle against which they have to contend, is that their enormous weight requires the rebuilding of bridges and relaying of contracts.

Mr. Cunnliff tells a story that an English firm, having received notice that the engines which they supplied to New Zealand were unsuited to the colonial tracks and bridges, replied: "Then rebuild your tracks and bridges, and we will furnish you with this sort of locomotives or none." Mr. Cunnliff maintains that an American builder would have replied, "Expect new designs by the first of the month." This is no doubt true, but as a matter of fact the American locomotive builder is compelling the reconstruction of tracks and bridges, none the less certainly because he is less domineering in relation to individual contractors. The American practice of standardising all parts of the machine, and of continually increasing the weight in order to get a still increased haulage power, necessitates alteration in the permanent way, for the railway in the long run has always to be built to suit the locomotive, not the locomotive to suit the railway.

Mr. Cunnliff thus lucidly explains the contrast between engine-building in the New World and the Old: "An American builder builds an engine to wear it out. Scrupulous attention is paid to all working parts, as any one can see who visits a great locomotive plant. The mechanism of each machine is made easily accessible. Parts are interchangeable, so that repairs can be made with speed. No unnecessary paint is wasted. As soon as the machine is finished, it is put in commission and driven day and night with the heaviest loads it can stagger under. It goes into the repair shop only when it requires overhauling. Men are hired to run it at good wages, men of ability and intelligence, with a typically American personal interest in their charge. Under such methods the engine is banged through a quarter century of strenuous activity, and then antiquated, worn out, superseded by advanced types, it goes to the scrap heap. The result is profit.

"In England—and in France, for that matter—an engine is built to last. Twenty years after it has been superseded by newer and better types, a locomotive is as tenderly cared for as ever. The result is decreasing dividends."

Of course, if, as Mr. Cunnliff asserts, Americans can deliver engines in Japan at £2,000, which do better work than English engines which cost £3,000, it is out of the question to talk about competition, except such competition as is said to prevail between Lombard Street and a China orange. The moral of it all is in this, as in everything else, that the American success has been obtained by skilled workmanship and businesslike methods.

Mr. Chauncey M. Depew in his address to railway men at the Buffalo Exhibition gave some very interesting figures as to the growth of the American railroad. Railway freight rates in the United States were, he said, almost exactly one-third of what they were when he entered the service in 1866. At the same time the wages of the railway men have nearly doubled, the precise increase being 87½ percent.

As there are more than a million of them, the gain in the weekly wage bill of America from this source alone is enormous. Their annual pay bill for wages is £125,000,000 or 60 percent of the cost of operating the lines. The United States with only 6 percent of the land surface of the world has 40 percent of the railroad track. Its 193,000 mileage is six times that of any other nation, and Mr. Depew declares that they haul more freight every year than is moved by all the railways and all the ships of Great Britain, France, and Germany combined.

An American engine recently hauled a train three fourths of a mile in length at the rate of 20 miles an hour. The gross weight behind the engine was over 3,000 tons. Another engine on a New York railway developed 1,142 horse power. The average load of an American freight train is 2,000 tons, that of the English only 600. The General Superintendent of the London and Western Railway, who has just returned from an inspection of American lines, reported that in passenger traffic we have little to learn, but that we ought to revolutionize our goods traffic.

He said: "Our freight system is wasteful. American goods engines can haul two or three times as much weight by one train as we can. We must have heavier goods locomotives. We must also have air brakes on goods trains. At present the only brakes on our trains are the engine brakes and the brakes at the end of the train. In consequence of improved appliances the American railways not only haul heavier freights, but run much faster than ours. I shall urge the extension of the American system of pneumatic signalling for interlocking, which gives such excellent results on American lines." [. . .]

Source text

Stead, W. T., *The Americanization of the World or The Trend of the Twentieth Century* (New York and London: Horace Markley, 1902).

References

Brown, Stewart J., *W. T. Stead: Nonconformist and Newspaper Prophet* (Oxford: Oxford University Press, 2019).

Snowdon, Trevor K., *Diverging Tracks: American Versus English Rail Travel in the 19th Century* (Jefferson, NC: McFarland, 2018).

Cicely Fox Smith (1882–1954)

'The Ballad of the "Dinkinbar"' (1919)

Transatlantic poet Cicely Fox Smith was born in England. Relocating to Canada in 1911, she lived in Alberta and British Columbia, but returned to England in 1913. When she was sixteen, both England's *The Sketch* and the US's *The Independent* had briefly reviewed her 'Songs of Greater Britain', a collection of poems about the British Empire. *The Sketch* reviewer noted that such poetry was typically 'a man's art' and assessed Smith's work as possessing a 'touch of individuality' along with its 'cheery freshness' with 'a fine swing about most of the verses' ('Small Talk', 281).

By 1923, when London's *The Bookman* revisited her career, Fox Smith's poetry writing was primarily viewed as 'sing[ing] of seamen and shipping', though she had not lived a seafaring life herself. Readers, *The Bookman* asserted, often assumed she was a man and an experienced seagoer at that. Fox Smith signed many poems with initials only; therefore, *The Bookman* reported, 'Seamen wrote many letters to "C. F. S." testifying that here at last was the genuine thing, something worth reading' (273). Her work regularly appeared in such popular periodicals as *Punch*.

For Graeme J. Milne, Fox Smith is one of a number of 'collectors' of sea shanty work songs whose commitment to the form aligns it with a vision of imagined British homogeneity and imperial greatness, ignoring its patterns of global communal composing and revision (381–5), even to the point of her having written comments (in language using racially demeaning stereotypes) that forcefully rejected the reality of Black African and Caribbean influences on its oral transmission (383).

The sea ballad presented here comes from a book-length collection Fox Smith published in the second decade of the twentieth century. Though, by then, as *The Bookman* observed, chantys/shanties and sea ballads themselves had to some extent 'gone out with the going of the sailing ship' (274), Fox Smith underscored a twentieth-century angle for this ballad by depicting a civilian steamship and its crew as caught up in the intense labour of warfare when meeting up with a German U-boat.

THE BALLAD OF THE "DINKINBAR"

It was the steamship "Dinkinbar,"
From the Gulf of Mexico
For Liverpool in time of war
With a thousand mules below,
And a bunch of polyglot[81] muleteers
To tend on them also.

---

81 When applied to people, 'polyglot' would indicate they knew multiple languages; here, the term references linguistic diversity (and thus the global make-up) of the ship's crew.

A swarthy breed from Eagle Butte,
And a greaser from Brazil,
And Daly of the broken nose,
And Ike, and Texas Bill,

In divers tongues that yarned and swore
And wrangled o'er their play,
As they dealt their decks of greasy cards
To pass the hours away,

And talked of how to burn good pay
And play the blooming fool
Among the wenches and the sharks
In the port of Liverpool.[82]

But Texas Bill a bitter laugh
He'd laugh and shake his head:
"It's me for a new style jamboree
When I strike land," he said.

"My brother lies in deep water
Not over far from here,
Where a U-boat sank both ship and men,
A bit beyond Cape Clear.

"They left him to drown with his drownin' mules
In the light of open day,
An' I guess I'll not sleep easy o' nights
While that score's yet to pay.

"So I'm goin' in for a khaki suit[83]
When I get in from sea,
I kin shift my birthplace north o' the line
As handy as kin be,
An' ...I guess there'll sure be a fightin' job
For a big long thing like me!"

It was the steamship "Dinkinbar,"
At the stormy end o' the year
That came in sight of the Bull and Cow
Which are beside Cape Clear.

And soon as rang the lookout's cry
That hailed the sight of land,
Oh, they were aware of a U-boat[84] there
That signalled them to stand.

---

82 See the section introduction to RS on efforts to address sailors' raucous in-port behaviours.
83 Texas Bill's plan to enlist in the ongoing World War is based in a hope for revenge that will be met later in the poem.
84 U-boats (an anglicised version of the German 'U-Boot', itself a condensed version of 'Untersee-boot'), were German submarines.

She fired a shot across their hawse[85]
And they had to heave to them,[86]
For she could make her fifteen knots,
And the "Dinkinbar" but ten,
And she had her machine gun ready to fire
On all but unarmed men.

Her captain he came over the side,
A cold-eyed swaggering Hun
That wore the Iron Cross on his breast
To tell of murders done,—

And his squarehead crew brought up their bombs
To send the ship below
With the poor living things she bore
That knew not friend from foe.

It was a British ship of war
Was swiftly drawing near,
For she had word of a submarine
Was lurking off Cape Clear.

She came from the South with a bone in her mouth,
Her shot sang over the sea,
And straight for the pirate's conning tower
It sped like a hiving bee,
It struck—it smashed it like a shell—
That down like a stone went she.

Then the pirate captain ran to the rail
To signal to his crew,
But all he saw was a smear of oil
On the water's face that grew.

And first he swore and gnawed his lip,
And glanced around in fear,
Till a thought came into his mind again
That brought him better cheer.

"Are not the English easy folk
With pirates ta'en in war?
And my luck is good that safe I stand
On the deck of the 'Dinkinbar.'"

He turned—he saw the muleteers
Come surging from below,
(Like a rustlers' crowd you see on the screen
At a moving picture show).

---

85 Part of a ship's bow
86 The *Dinkinbar* here slows down and essentially stops, with the U-boat's commander soon boarding.

And once he looked on Texas Bill,
And then he turned and ran,
For the look he saw it was not good
To see on the face of man.

Then in and out among the boats,
By hatch and alleyway,
Hunter and hunted, to and fro
In deadly chase sped they.

And through the engine-room where stilled
Was now the engine's clang,
On steel ladder and steel grating
Their footsteps slipped and rang,

Till in the screw shaft's stifling dark,
With spent and gasping breath
The U-boat's captain turned at last
To pay his dues to death . . .

And twice Bill lifted his hand to strike,
And twice he turned aside,
But his brother's blood it called so loud
It would not be denied,
And down in the dark (like those he slew)
The U-boat's captain died.

The cruiser's boat came under the side,
They hailed her with a cheer,
And Texas Bill looked over the rail
And called both loud and clear,
"Come up, come up, now, Lootenant,
But you'll find no prisoner here.

"For Texas law is life for life
Alike in peace and war,
And life for life has paid this day
On board o' the 'Dinkinbar.'"

Source text

Smith, C[icely] Fox, *Small Craft: Sailor Ballads and Chantys* (New York: George H. Doran, 1919).

References

Milne, Graeme, 'Collecting the Sea Shanty: British Maritime Identity and Atlantic Musical Cultures in the Early Twentieth Century', *International Journal of Maritime History* 29.2 (2017), 370–86.
'Small Talk of the Week', *The Sketch* 25.319 (8 March 1899), 275–84.
W. A. F., 'Miss Cicely Fox-Smith', *The Bookman* 64.384 (September 1923), 273–4.

Figure 3.5 Sheet music cover depicting a sailor remembering his loved one.
Courtesy the Lester S. Levy Collection of Sheet Music, Sheridan Libraries,
Johns Hopkins University.

4

FAMILY AND DOMESTICITY

Figure 4.1 Illustration by E. A. Abbey. Harper and Brothers American Household Edition (1876) of Charles Dickens's *Christmas Stories*, image for *A Christmas Carol*, 28. Courtesy Philip Allingham and Victorian Web Foundation.

In 1875, a group of Anglophone transplants living in Italy co-published *A Wreath of Stray Leaves: To the Memory of Emily Bliss Gould*.[1] In his introductory note, T. Adolphus Trollope explained that the volume, originally envisioned as a fund-raiser for a school for poor Italian children being led by Mrs Gould, had been transformed into a memorial in the wake of her untimely death. In a preface, Mary Howitt credited Emily Gould's vision for 'twenty orphans' to join a new home school where, by learning to typeset while developing their own personal literacies, they would blend 'education, intellectual and moral' in Rome's 'Via in Arcione' (xix–xxi). As Howitt explained, the authors hoped that, supported by the book's proceeds, 'the motherless and homeless children, whom she [Gould] gathered into a home of labour and love' might continue prospering there (xxiii). Affirming the public work of Mrs Gould, wife of an American diplomat and social activist in her own right, they drew on intimate family-like knowledge of her endeavour and each other to celebrate and support her goals.

These same co-authors – a team that included familiar literary figures from both sides of the Atlantic – had already co-constructed an alternative family for themselves as expatriates in Italy. In the stories, poems, sketches and aphorisms gathered for the *Wreath of Stray Leaves*, therefore, they saluted not only their friend Emily Gould but also the cultural bonding achieved through family-inflected social practices transported abroad. In their range of contributions – from the playful to the sentimental – readers could see the community they had built with writing, lively conversations, excursions and many an evening's entertainment. Accordingly, Alfred Pearson served up an 'Ode to My Pipe'. Mrs Trollope revisited a haunted rectory she and her pastor spouse had happily vacated for a smaller but less scary home. 'N. Lawless' penned a riff on Poe's 'Raven' – such parodies being a frequent entertainment in nineteenth-century salons. Though writing in an era when treatments of domesticity often cast it as a private bubble, the *Wreath*'s portraits of family-like sociality supported a public-facing project for children (who set the book's type) and thus demonstrated the actual interconnectedness of homes and the larger culture.

Extended continental living (a treasured advantage of nineteenth-century intellectual and cultural elites) had brought these authors together. But their shared appreciation of family-like social practices fostered their social network, which in turn supported their shared writing in connection with a social cause – supporting orphan Italian children.[2] Such bonds – both normative ones glimpsed in this *Wreath* and non-normative variations represented by Emily Gould's semi-domesticated school – make up the contents of our 'Family and Domesticity' section.

---

1 Thanks to Etta Madden for alerting us to this collection, discussed in her *Engaging Italy: American Women's Utopian Visions and Transnational Networks* (Albany, NY: SUNY Press, forthcoming).

2 For a related analysis of expatriates-in-Italy British women writers' poetic constructions of authorial networks in line with Bruno Latour's concept of action strings producing 'poetry [that] could act in the world to influence readers' (277), see Alison Chapman, 'Poetry, Network, Nation: Elizabeth Barrett Browning and Expatriate Women's Poetry', *Victorian Studies* 55.2 (Winter 2013), 275–85.

IDEALISED VISIONS

Nineteenth-century depictions of domesticity often promoted an idealised view of family life that was available only to white, well-to-do readers. One dimension of this ideological construct cast women as home-based mothers, men as providers and children as learning those same roles along with expectations for contributing to capitalist society. Transatlantically exchanged texts depicting such relationships encouraged a shared adoption of this ideal. For instance, in this section's excerpt from Anna Barbauld's groundbreaking primer, *Lessons for Children*, we see both the empowering opportunity that home-based education could provide for (some) mothers and the cultural work involved in passing middle-class values from one generation to the next. Though Barbauld's home literacy programme appeared first in England, a speedy adaptation process generated many Americanised editions and imitations.

We find a similar affirmation of transatlantic family life in Mary Howitt's *Our Cousins in Ohio*, which narrates the experiences of a family relocating to the US yet continuing domestic traditions carried from Britain. Inscribing transatlantic domestic bonds into her text, Howitt developed her book from her sister's writings sent back to England. Meanwhile, Charles Dickens's *A Christmas Carol* joined his curation of numerous seasonal stories for his periodicals, including his special Christmas numbers, in promoting a secular, domesticated version of the holiday. Ranging from descriptions of such occasions in England to an account of a hybrid model in South America (which he featured in his *Household Words* magazine), this section showcases how Dickens's Christmas promotions circulated transatlantically, as did their embodiment in images like the American edition's portrait of the Cratchit family, now an illustration in this introduction.

In replicating visions of idealised domestic life, transatlantic texts like these could also underscore the damage to cultural stability imposed by challenges to such spaces, social practices and familial bonds. In one of his most popular narrative poems, accordingly, Henry Wadsworth Longfellow spun opening passages of *Evangeline* (excerpted here) to limn the French Acadians who were forcibly relocated by a British colonial power as, pre-diaspora, enacting a beloved domestic community.

SAFEGUARDING DOMESTIC NORMS

Evangeline's assertion of French-Canadians' communal family life may be undercut, for today's readers, by its plot focused on a pair of separated lovers. Other writers adopted a more direct approach when portraying the dominant Anglophone culture's white, middle-class domesticity as a model to protect. From *New America*, for example, our excerpt spotlights how William Dixon drew on ideas about proper roles for women back in his British homeland to critique polygamy in the Mormon Utah community.[3] As another example of

---

3 On Victorian writers' insistent attacks on polygamy, see Eileen Cleere, 'Chaste Polygamy: Mormon Marriage and the Fantasy of Sexual Privacy in *East Lynne* and *Verner's Pride*', *Victorian Studies* 57.2 (Winter 2015), especially 201–2. For more on Dickens's and others' (e.g. Doyle's) sustained engagement with Mormonism, see Scott Dransfield, 'Charles Dickens and the Victorian "Mormon Moment"', *Religion and the Arts* 17.5 (2013), 489–506.

literature that countered social practices undermining family life, we include the World's Woman's Christian Temperance Union's 'Pledge', regularly printed in the organisation's far-reaching publications and programmes for events like the conventions rotating transatlantically between Europe and North America. Though editorial cartoons would incessantly caricature temperance leaders, their campaign reflected an understanding of alcohol's close connection with domestic abuse of women and children.

Finding the right stance and tone for texts aimed at safeguarding domesticity could be difficult. One telling example of a would-be defender's transatlantic domestic narrative gone awry emerges in the furious responses to Harriet Beecher Stowe's account of Lord and Lady Byron's marriage. By culling from the British *Public Opinion*'s 1869 collection of critical responses to Stowe's interventionist reporting rather than from her *Lady Byron Vindicated* itself, we document how the widespread condemnation of Stowe's publicising a 'private' family scandal foreshadowed questions still with us around public figures' home life as fair game – or not – for the world to read about.

Sara Willis Parton (who wrote as 'Fanny Fern') adopted a less shrill approach than Stowe. Blending satire with a sentimental touch, Fern proposed that gentle parenting, kind treatment of servants and companionate marriage could foster domestic ideals. A periodical columnist of unsurpassed popularity in the US, Fern marked her appeal to transatlantic readers in the British anthology of her sketches, *Folly as It Flies*. For Fern and her enthusiastic readers, humour set in the home had reliable border-crossing appeal.

Domesticity at Society's Margins

As noted above, the gap between idealised portraits of domesticity and actual family lives within diverse transatlantic communities could be wide indeed. Writers sometimes addressed that gap as a problem to be solved, such as explaining, for middle-class women readers, how to manage one's servants better, including the many Irish immigrants who became American domestic workers.[4] Others invoked domesticity-associated language to link differences with social critique. Sarah Piatt did so poetically in 'Two Sabbath Parties', set in Ireland. Encountering an upper-class family on a Sunday stroll, working-class counterparts assess the contrasting familial responsibilities and access to social resources this encounter makes visible.

Writers also sought readers' acceptance of non-traditional family-oriented models. Such claims might need to remain veiled, however, as in those subtly conveyed within the Lowell Mill women's *Offering* publication, where, Kathryn A. Cady explains, same-sex relations outside heteronormative man-and-wife expectations were affirmed to attentive American and British readers of the popular working-class publication.[5]

---

4 Martha Baldwin, 'Stoicism and the Servants: Philosophy and the Periodical Press', *Victorian Periodicals Review* 51.2 (2018), 307–19, tracks parallel approaches to this issue by the American *Godey's Lady's Book* and British counterpart the *Englishwoman's Domestic Magazine*. See primary texts by and about Irish-American domestics in BIL and MSR sections.

5 Kathryn A. Cady, '"Ann and Myself": Rhetoric, Sexualities, and Silence at Lowell', *Southern Communication Journal* 77.1 (2012), 24–44.

Across the Atlantic, Frances Power Cobbe (1822–1904), who suggested alternative family living arrangements to marriage for women in the November 1862 *Fraser's Magazine* article 'What Shall We Do with Our Old Maids?' – quickly reprinted in New York's *Eclectic Magazine* in February 1863 – was then happily living with her life partner, Welsh sculptor Mary Lloyd (1819–96). At the same time, even hints of non-normative same-sex connections gleaned worried transatlantic commentary in connection with Boston Brahmin Elizabeth Peabody's close friendship with and promotion of fellow educator Sarah Winnemucca, author of *Life Among the Piutes* (1883), their connection doubly worrisome given the latter's being 'an untutored Indian woman'.⁶

On an interpretive flip side, when reading nineteenth-century transatlantic portrayals of family life now, we should avoid imposing straightforward interpretations aligned more with our own era than a text's original time. Our *Little Lord Fauntleroy* excerpt offers an example. Exuding sweetness in his language toward his mother and self-display in his (in)famous suits, Burnett's protagonist may invite (hyper-)masculinity guardians to recoil, dubbing him overly feminised. But being attuned to class-linked domestic culture of Burnett's time, and to biographical dimensions of her characterisation of Fauntleroy as a version of her own son Vivian, would caution against simplified ahistorical readings of a domestic story that spawned affirming nineteenth-century copycat clothing and stage adaptations, as well as caricatures.

Other texts in this section benefit from analysis coupling their original historical context with current relevance. Jamaican author-traveller Mary Seacole's reporting on her domesticated activities in Crimea both addresses restrictions on women's place in her day and anticipates the era-crossing persistence of calls to extend women's social roles outside the nuclear family. Seacole's entry shows her embracing aspects of Anglophone white, middle-class domestic maternalism, including preparing favourite foods for the Christmas holiday and serving as care giver to war-injured patients. Yet, she enacted these tasks in norm-expanding spaces (a hotel business setting, a hospital) beyond the literal familial sphere envisioned for most readers of a Barbauldian primer or a Fanny Fern sketch. Ultimately, in gaining renown for its author, her memoir may have helped shift transatlantic perceptions of gendered work.

Like questions about gender, race-linked identities also shaped transatlantic depictions of family relations. Different community contexts interacting with the dominant culture led individual minority authors to careful rhetorical choices. Charles Eastman (Ohiyesa) faced such a challenge when addressing a 1911 London symposium on race. Eastman faced the daunting assignment of speaking 'for' Indigenous communities whose rich diversity was then generally collapsed into false homogeneity by white cultural arbiters. As our excerpt demonstrates, he cast Native peoples' family life in over-generalised terms that might make it recognisable and appealing to his audience.

---

6 In December 1888, such far-flung periodicals as the *Ross Gazette* (UK) and Ireland's *Lisburn Standard* reprinted critical accounts of Peabody's and Winnemucca's connection. These stories described a 'curious idiosyncrasy [. . .] hav[ing] possessed Miss Elizabeth Peabody of Boston', who, at '86 years old, and though surrounded by intellectual friends of both sexes', was 'devot[ing] herself exclusively to Sarah Winnemucca, an untutored Indian woman, even sharing her room with her' (*The York Herald* [8 December 1888], 5).

Earlier on, in Henry Schoolcraft's mid-century presentation of his wife Jane's poem about leaving her children at a school far from their home, we find details seemingly calibrated to showcase her love of her Native homeland while also situating this Métis woman author within a landscape of white-appropriate maternalism. Given Henry's translation, we should ask: what might his portrait of maternal care omit, add or mis-represent?[7] In any case, his paired printing of that translation with a version in Jane's own language spotlights broader cultural losses sustained through colonising encroachments into Indigenous family life, such as through the assimilationist boarding school movement.

Texts like the Schoolcrafts' transmit particularly complex portrayals of domesticity constrained by a dominant power's control of another group's lived experiences. In reading J. B. Moreton's 1790 renderings of Jamaican songs, for instance, we must question both the accuracy of his transcriptions and the degree to which his interpretive commentary did, or did not, convey singers' feelings about familial ties.[8] Since such accounts can be read only at a remove from the subjects' own experiences, we should attend closely to their critiques of colonialism's impositions on suppressed communities' domestic situations, however indirectly conveyed.

ADDRESSING POLITICAL ISSUES THROUGH DOMESTIC LENSES

Our section on family and domesticity begins with an excerpt from Thomas Paine's *Common Sense* because, like so many documents advocating revolt against colonialism, this one framed a political relationship in domestic terms. Thus, Paine rejects the premise that North American British colonies were children needing a king's paternal management.

Not all domestic analogies in political arguments were progressive. Often, nineteenth-century pro-slavery advocates trotted out 'family' rhetoric to justify enslavement of an 'inferior' race supposedly requiring parent-like care. Anti-slavery rhetors, in turn, countered these arguments, as documented in several entries in our Abolition and Aftermath (AA) section (see Berman). Relatedly, the FD section's episode from the British edition of Harriet Jacobs's memoir (*The Deeper Wrong*) refutes comparisons depicting poor British workers as supposedly abused on a par with enslaved people in the Americas; Jacobs insists that, however 'oppressed' Europe's poor man might be, 'No master could come and take him from his wife, or his daughter.'

Jane Addams adopted another variation on this tactic of explicating political issues through a domestic context. In her critique of industrialist George Pullman's

---

7 See, in the section entry, information on Robert Dale Parker's providing a new translation more closely tied to Jane's original. Christine R. Cavalier argues for valuing Schoolcraft's own rhetorical control (99). Touting the poet's 'engagement with transatlantic gender and literary values' (106), Cavalier sees Jane as taking advantage of teaching from her father and husband without giving up her Ojibwe ties – in daily family life or in writing (106). See Christine R. Cavalier, 'Jane Johnston Schoolcraft's Sentimental Lessons: Native Literary Collaboration and Resistance', *MELUS* 38.1 (Spring 2013), 98–118.

8 On related analysis of white Cuban elites' control of mid-nineteenth-century domestic lives of enslaved women, see Aisha K. Finch, 'Scandalous Scarcities: Black Slave Women, Plantation Domesticity, and Travel Writing in Nineteenth-Century Cuba', *Journal of Historical Sociology* 23.1 (March 2010), 101–43.

paternalistic treatment of the workers who struck against his company in 1894, she compared Pullman to an angry King Lear and argued in the strikers' favour. Significantly, her attempt at presenting a balanced argument by connecting the workers to Shakespearean daughter Cordelia's seeming ingratitude for paternal generosity failed to mollify potential publishers enough to gain publication for her speech-turned-essay until years later – perhaps in part due to the offence of a woman invading so public a debate through a domestic analogy.

As these examples show, however cherished ideals of family life might have been in transatlantic Anglophone culture, many social forces undermined aspirational visions of domesticity. We close our section with an especially forceful example in texts linked to Canadian John McCrae's service during the Great War: his iconic 'Flanders Fields' lyric, which vividly acknowledges that conflict's monumental losses to families, presented here with excerpts from letters he sent to his mother from the Front.

References

Berman, Carolyn Vellenga, *Creole Crossings: Domestic Fiction and the Reform of Colonial Slavery* (Ithaca, NY: Cornell University Press, 2006).

Stewart, David M., 'Working Away, Writing Home', in Celeste-Marie Bernier, Judie Newman and Matthew Pethers (eds), *The Edinburgh Companion to Nineteenth-Century American Letters and Letter-Writing* (Edinburgh: Edinburgh University Press, 2016), 185–97.

Trollope, Thomas Adolphus and others, *A Wreath of Stray Leaves: To the Memory of Emily Bliss Gould* (Rome: Italo-American School Press, 1875).

Thomas Paine (1737–1809)

From **Common Sense** *Part III, 'Thoughts on the Present State of American Affairs' (1776)*

Thomas Paine's *Common Sense* claimed enormous readership on both sides of the Atlantic, stoking calls favouring the American colonies' break with Britain and leaving its imprint on subsequent Revolutionary-era documents such as the Declaration of Independence. Paine masked his authorship for the first edition, signing simply as 'an Englishman'. And, indeed, Paine (originally Pain) had been in North America only since 1774, having been persuaded to emigrate by none other than Benjamin Franklin, whom he had met in London. Franklin and Paine became philosophical adherents, sharing a commitment to Enlightenment thought, with the elder statesman even dubbing Paine an 'adopted political son' (Nelson, 229).

The first run of *Common Sense* became a runaway best-seller. Paine himself claimed over 120,000 copies sold in 1776 alone, but the easy-to-share pamphlet format meant the text may have quickly garnered a readership of five times that figure (Everton, 88). Having collaborated originally with the printer Robert Bell, Paine complained of being cheated out of royalties and contracted with William and Thomas Bradford for a cut-rate reprinting to which he signed his name. The ensuing Bell/Bradford charges and counter-charges reflected the fledgling status of intellectual property in pre-copyright America. Paine soon gave up any claims of copyright himself, asking for proceeds to support the need for mittens within the Continental Army (Nelson, 243). Transatlantic editions (at that time generating no royalties for either American publishers or the author) multiplied rapidly both in Britain and on the continent. Thus, when he re-crossed the Atlantic and, for a time, promoted the French Revolution, Paine was already a famous radical thinker. Central to the argument of this first of Paine's well-known political writings was his refutation of the idea that the North American British colonies were children in a family for which the King served as paternal head.

From **Common Sense** *Part III, 'Thoughts on the Present State of American Affairs'*

In the following pages I offer nothing more than simple facts, plain arguments, and common sense; and have no other preliminaries to settle with the reader, than that he will divest himself of prejudice and prepossession, and suffer his reason and his feelings to determine for themselves: that he will put on or rather that he will not put off the true character of a man, and generally enlarge his views beyond the present day. [...]

It hath lately been asserted in parliament, that the colonies have no relation to each other but through the Parent Country, *i.e.* that Pennsylvania and the Jerseys, and so on for the rest, are sister colonies by the way of England; this is certainly a very round-about way of proving relationship, but it is the nearest and only true way of proving enemy-ship, if I may so call it. France and Spain never were, nor perhaps ever will be our enemies as *Americans*, but as our being the *subjects of Great-Britain*.

But Britain is the parent country say some. Then the more shame upon her conduct. Even brutes do not devour their young, nor savages make war upon their families; wherefore the assertion if true, turns to her reproach; but it happens not to be true, or only partly so, and the phrase, *parent* or *mother country*, hath been jesuitically adopted by the King and his parasites, with a low papistical design of gaining an unfair bias on the credulous weakness of our minds.[9] Europe and not England is the parent country of America. This new World hath been the asylum for the persecuted lovers of civil and religious liberty from *every part* of Europe. Hither have they fled, not from the tender embraces of the mother, but from the cruelty of the monster; and it is so far true of England, that the same tyranny which drove the first emigrants from home, pursues their descendants still.

---

9 Founded in the sixteenth century in Spain, the Jesuit order of Catholic monks was known for its work in education, missionary work (including in the New World among Indigenous peoples) and scholarship. By the late eighteenth century, Jesuits were often critiqued by Protestants, in particular, for over-zealousness in debates and were feared even among Catholics as having too much influence with the Pope – with this anti-Jesuit political pressure within the Church eventually leading to a disbanding of most of the Order until it was allowed to reemerge in the early nineteenth century.

In this extensive quarter of the Globe, we forget the narrow limits of three hundred and sixty miles (the extent of England) and carry our friendship on a larger scale; we claim brotherhood with every European Christian, and triumph in the generosity of the sentiment.

It is pleasant to observe by what regular gradations we surmount the force of local prejudice, as we enlarge our acquaintance with the World. A man born in any town in England divided into parishes, will naturally associate most with his fellow parishioners (because their interests in many cases will be common) and distinguish him by the name of *neighbour*, if he meet him but a few miles from home, he drops the narrow idea of a street, and salutes him by the name of *townsman*: if he travel out of the county, and meet him in any other, he forgets the minor divisions of street and town, and calls him *countryman*, i.e. *county-man*: but if in their foreign excursions they should associate in France, or any other part of *Europe*, their local remembrance would be enlarged into that of *Englishmen*. And by a just parity of reasoning, all Europeans meeting in America, or any other quarter of the Globe, are *countrymen*; for England, Holland, Germany, or Sweden, when compared with the whole, stand in the same places on the larger scale, which the divisions of street, town, and county do on the smaller ones; Distinctions too limited for Continental minds. Not one third of the inhabitants, even of this province, are of English descent. Wherefore I reprobate the phrase of parent or mother country applied to England only, as being false, selfish, narrow and ungenerous.

But admitting, that we were all of English descent, what does it amount to? Nothing. Britain being now an open enemy, extinguishes every other name and title: and to say that reconciliation is our duty, is truly farcical. The first king of England, of the present line (William the Conqueror) was a Frenchman, and half the Peers of England are descendants from the same country; wherefore, by the same method of reasoning, England ought to be governed by France.

Much hath been said of the united strength of Britain and the Colonies, that in conjunction, they might bid defiance to the world: But this is mere presumption, the fate of war is uncertain, neither do the expressions mean any thing; for this Continent would never suffer itself to be drained of inhabitants, to support the British arms in either Asia, Africa, or Europe.

Besides, what have we to do with setting the world at defiance. Our plan is commerce, and that well attended to, will secure us the peace and friendship of all Europe, because it is the interest of all Europe to have America a *free port*. Her trade will always be a protection, and her barrenness of gold and silver secure her from invaders.

I challenge the warmest advocate for reconciliation, to shew, a single advantage that this Continent can reap, by being connected with Great Britain. I repeat the challenge, not a single advantage is derived. Our corn will fetch its price in any market in Europe, and our imported goods must be paid for buy them where we will.

But the injuries and disadvantages we sustain by that connection, are without number, and our duty to mankind at large, as well as to ourselves, instruct us to renounce the alliance: Because, any submission to, or dependance on Great Britain, tends directly to involve this Continent in European wars and quarrels. As Europe is our market for trade, we ought to form no partial connection with any part of it. 'Tis the true interest of America, to steer clear of European contentions, which she never can do, while by her dependance on Britain, she is made the make-weight in the scale of British politics.

Europe is too thickly planted with Kingdoms to be long at peace, and whenever a war breaks out between England and any foreign power, the trade of America goes to ruin, *because, of her connection with Britain*. The next war may not turn out like the last, and should it not, the advocates for reconciliation now, will be wishing for separation then, because neutrality in that case, would be a safer convoy than a man of war. Every thing that is right or natural pleads for separation. The blood of the slain, the weeping voice of nature cries, 'TIS TIME TO PART. Even the distance at which the Almighty hath placed England and America, is a strong and natural proof, that the authority of the one over the other, was never the design of Heaven. The time likewise at which the Continent was discovered, adds weight to the argument, and the manner in which it was peopled encreases the force of it. – The Reformation was preceded by the discovery of America; as if the Almighty graciously meant to open a sanctuary to the persecuted in future years, when home should afford neither friendship nor safety.

The authority of Great Britain over this Continent is a form of government which sooner or later must have an end: And a serious mind can draw no true pleasure by looking forward, under the painful and positive conviction, that what he calls "the present constitution," is merely temporary. As parents, we can have no joy, knowing that *this government* is not sufficiently lasting to ensure any thing which we may bequeath to posterity: And by a plain method of argument, as we are running the next generation into debt, we ought to do the work of it, otherwise we use them meanly and pitifully. In order to discover the line of our duty rightly, we should take our children in our hand, and fix our station a few years farther into life; that eminence will present a prospect, which a few present fears and prejudices conceal from our sight.

Though I would carefully avoid giving unnecessary offence, yet I am inclined to believe, that all those who espouse the doctrine of reconciliation, may be included within the following descriptions. Interested men who are not to be trusted, weak men, who *cannot* see, prejudiced men who *will not* see, and a certain set of moderate men who think better of the European world than it deserves; and this last class, by an ill-judged deliberation, will be the cause of more calamities to this continent, than all the other three. [...]

To talk of friendship with those in whom our reason forbids us to have faith, and our affections wounded thro' a thousand pores instruct us to detest, is madness and folly. Every day wears out the little remains of kindred between us and them, and can there be any reason to hope, that as the relationship expires, the affection will encrease, or that we shall agree better, when we have ten times more and greater concerns to quarrel over than ever?

Ye that tell us of harmony and reconciliation, can ye restore to us the time that is past? Can ye give to prostitution its former innocence? Neither can ye reconcile Britain and America. The last cord now is broken, the people of England are presenting addresses against us. There are injuries which nature cannot forgive; she would cease to be nature if she did. As well can the lover forgive the ravisher of his mistress, as the Continent forgive the murders of Britain. The Almighty hath implanted in us these unextinguishable feelings for good and wise purposes. They are the guardians of his image in our hearts. They distinguish us from the herd of common animals. The social compact would dissolve, and justice be extirpated the earth, or have only a casual existence were we callous to the touches of affection. The robber and the murderer would often escape unpunished, did not the injuries which our tempers sustain, provoke us into justice.

O ye that love mankind! Ye that dare oppose not only the tyranny, but the tyrant, stand forth! Every spot of the old world is overrun with oppression. Freedom hath been hunted round the globe. Asia and Africa have long expelled her.—Europe regards her like a stranger, and England hath given her warning to depart. O! receive the fugitive, and prepare in time an asylum for mankind.

Source text

[Paine, Thomas], *Common Sense: Addressed to the Inhabitants of America* (Philadelphia: R. Bell, 1776).

References

Everton, Michael, '"The Would-be-Author and the Real Bookseller": Thomas Paine and Eighteenth-Century Printing Ethics', *Early American Literature* 40.1 (2005), 79–110.
Nelson, Craig, 'Thomas Paine and the Making of "Common Sense"', *New England Review* 27.3 (2006), 228–50.

Anna Laetitia Aikin Barbauld (1743–1825)

From **Lessons for Children** *(1778)*

Anna Laetitia Aikin benefited from her father's giving her access to the curriculum being taught at the innovative Dissenting Academy in Warrington, England, where he served as a tutor. Cultivating a friendship with Joseph Priestley, also teaching there, she wrote one her earliest poems in honour of his wife. Encouraged by her brother John, Anna began publishing poetry in the early 1770s. Later, with her husband Rochemont Barbauld, she co-founded a boarding school where they co-taught until his deteriorating mental health led to their separation in 1808.

When Barbauld published *Lessons for Children*, her welcoming statement at the start of the book invited readers to 'use' it freely. Publishers in the US quickly obliged. Reprintings of British texts represented a major route to book-making in the young nation. And Barbauld's primers tapped into a nascent vision of US white middle-class Republican motherhood.

Situated primarily in the home and immediate environs, *Lessons* presents dialogues between a mother and her son Charles, a character based on Barbauld's nephew, her adopted son. Besides teaching language skills, the narrative's at-home educator also prepares the novice reader for class-inflected social expectations, sometimes via anecdotes about misbehaving boys. As a growing number of Americanised versions of the primer appeared, changes within these texts, such as adding new characters and American settings, signalled a strengthened sense of US national identity distinct from British ties. Nonetheless, multiple internal features affirmed the continuation of shared, class-linked Anglo-American domestic values, as did the decades-long popularity in the US of *Evenings at Home* (1792), the collection of family stories Barbauld co-authored with her brother.

From **Lessons for Children** *(1778)*

Advertisement

This little publication was made for a particular child, but the public is welcome to the use of it. It was found that, amidst the multitude of books professedly written for children, there is not one adapted to the comprehension of a child from two to three years old. A grave remark, or a connected story, however simple, is above his capacity; and *nonsense* is always below it; for Folly is worse than Ignorance. Another great defect is the want of *good paper, a clear and large type,* and *large spaces.* They only, who have actually taught young children, can be sensible how necessary these assistances are. The eye of a child and of a learner cannot catch, as ours can, a small, obscure, ill-formed word, amidst a number of others all equally unknown to him.—To supply these deficiencies is the object of this book. The task is humble but not mean; for to lay the first stone of a noble building, and to plant the first idea in a human mind, can be no dishonor to any hand.

From *Part I*

COME hither, Charles, come to mamma.
Make haste.
Sit in mamma's lap.
Now read your book.
Where is the pin to point with?
Here is a pin.
Do not tear the book.
Only bad boys tear books.
Charles shall have a pretty new lesson.
Spell that word. Good boy.
Now go and play. [. . .]

Letters make syllables.
Syllables make words.
Words make a sentence.
It is a pleasant thing to read well.
When you are older you shall learn to write; but you must know how to read first.
Once Papa could not read, nor tell his letters.
If you learn a little every day, you will soon know a great deal.
Mamma, shall I ever have learned all there is to be learned?
No, never, if you were to live longer than the oldest man, but you may learn something every day. [. . .]

It is dark.
Bring candles.
Snuff the candles.
Shut the window-shutters.
Do not shut them yet.
Look at the moon.
O bright moon! O pretty moon!

The moon shines at night, when the sun is out of our sight.
Is the sun out of sight[?]
Then it is time for little boys to go to bed. [...]

From *Part II*

Good morning, little boy; how do you do? Bring your little stool and sit by me, for I have a great deal to tell you.

I hope you have been a good boy, and read all the pretty words I wrote for you before. You have, you say; you have read them till you are tired, and you want some more new lessons. Come then, sit down. Now you and I will tell stories. [...]

It is December, and Christmas is coming, and Betty is very busy. What is she doing? She is paring apples, and chopping meat, and beating spices. What for, I wonder? It is to make mince pies. Do you love mince pies? O they are very good! Little boys come from school at Christmas. Pray wrap them up warm, for it is very cold. Well, spring will come again some time.

Figure 4.2 Frontispiece, *Lessons for children. By Mrs. Barbauld* (Newark, NJ: B. Olds, 1842). Courtesy New York Public Library.

From *Part IV*

I will tell you a story.

There was a little boy whose name was Harry; and his papa and mamma sent him to school. Now Harry was a clever fellow, and loved his book; and he got to be first in his class. So his mamma got up one morning very early, and called Betty, the maid, and said, Betty, I think we must make a cake for Harry, for he has learned his book very well. And Betty said, Yes, with all my heart. So they made a nice cake. It was very large, and stuffed full of plums and sweetmeats, orange and citron: and it was iced all over with sugar: it was white and smooth on the top like snow. So this cake was sent to the school. When little Harry saw it he was very glad, and jumped about for joy; and he hardly stayed for a knife to cut a piece, but gnawed it like a little dog. So he ate till the bell rang for school, and after school he ate again, and ate until he went to bed; nay, his bed-fellow told me that he laid his cake under his pillow, and sat up in the night to eat some. So he ate until it was all gone.—But presently after, this little boy was very sick. [. . .] So they sent for Dr. Camomile,[10] and he gave him I do not know how much bitter stuff. Poor Harry did not like it at all, but he was forced to take it, or else he would have died, you know. So at last he got well again, but his mamma said she would send him no more cakes. [. . .]

The Moon says, my name is Moon; I shine to give you light in the night when the sun is set. I am very beautiful and white like silver. You may look at me always, for I am not so bright as to dazzle your eyes, and I never scorch you. I am mild and gentle. I let even the little glowworms shine, which are quite dark by day. The stars shine all round me, but I am larger and brighter than the stars, and I look like a large pearl amongst a great many small sparkling diamonds. When you are asleep I shine through your curtains with my gentle beams, and I say, Sleep on, poor little tired boy, I will not disturb you. The nightingale sings to me, who sings better than all birds of the air. She sits upon a thorn and sings melodiously all night long, while the dew lies upon the grass, and every thing is still and silent all around.

THE END

Source text

Barbauld, Mrs. [Anna Laetitia], *Lessons for Children* (New York: Pendleton and Hill, 1831).

References

Ferguson, Frances, 'The Novel Comes of Age: When Literature Started Talking with Children', *Differences: Journal of Feminist Cultural Studies* 28.1 (May 2017), 37–63.

Robbins, Sarah, 'Re-Making Barbauld's Primers: A Case Study in the Americanization of British Literary Pedagogy', *Children's Literature Association Quarterly* 21.4 (1996), 158–69.

10 Camomile, a plant sometimes used against indigestion and also a type of tea, likely inspired Barbauld's name for the doctor in this episode.

David Humphreys (1752–1818)

From 'A Poem on the Happiness of America. Addressed to the Citizens of the United States' (1786)

Born in Connecticut, David Humphreys first gained fame during the Revolutionary War for his military valour, rewarded with his appointment as aide-de-camp of George Washington's headquarters. Subsequent to the war, he was instrumental in negotiating commerce treaties with several European nations, as well as becoming first minister to Portugal in 1791, in which post he helped to establish peace treaties with a number of Barbary Coast nations (present-day Morocco, Algeria, Tunisia and Libya) then involved in the piracy of American ships. Humphreys was a member of the Hartford Wits, a group of Yale-educated poets, including Joel Barlow and John Trumbull, whose satirical writings owed much, in form and tone, to those of the English writer Alexander Pope. Collectively they wrote 'The Anarchiad' (1786–7), a biting satire of US anti-federalism modelled on Pope's *The Dunciad* (1728–43). 'A Poem on the Happiness of America' eulogises, in Popean rhyming couplets, the new nation's qualities and potential after the trauma of revolution. The passage excerpted here, contrasting the unadorned attributes of American womanhood with the artificial cultivations of those in Europe, is indicative of the poem's political celebration of the 'simple manners' and 'golden mean' of the United States.

From 'A Poem on the Happiness of America'

[...] Nor here the wedded fair in splendor vie,
To shine the idols of the public eye;
Nor place their happiness, like Europe's dames,
In balls and masquerades, in plays and games;
Each home felt bliss exchang'd for foreign sports,
A round of pleasures, or th' intrigues of courts;
Nor seek of government to guide the plan,
And wrest his bold prerogatives from man.
What though not form'd in affectation's school,
Nor taught the wanton eye to roll by rule,
Nor how to prompt the glance, the frown, the smile,
Or practice all the little arts of guile—
What though not taught the use of female arms,
Nor cloth'd in panoply of conqu'ring charms,
Like some fine garnish'd heads—th' exterior fair,
In paints, cosmetics, powder, borrow'd hair:
Yet theirs are pleasures of a diff'rent kind,
Delights at home, more useful, more refin'd;
Theirs are th' attentions, theirs the smiles that please,

With hospitable cares and modest ease:
Their youthful taste, improv'd by finer arts,
Their minds embellish'd, and refin'd their hearts—
'Tis theirs to act, in still sequester'd life,
The glorious parts of parent, friend, and wife:
What nameless grace, what unknown charm is theirs,
To soothe their partners, and divide their cares,
Calm raging pain, delay the parting breath,
And light a smile on the wan cheek of death!

No feudal ties the rising genius mar,
Compel to servile toils or drag to war;
But, free, each youth, his fav'rite course pursues,
The plough paternal, or the sylvan muse;
For here exists, once more, th' Arcadian scene,
Those simple manners, and that golden mean:
Here holds society its middle stage,
Between too rude and too refin'd an age:
Far from that age, when not a gleam of light
The dismal darkness cheer'd of Gothic night,
From brutal rudeness of that savage state—
As from refinements which o'erwhelm the great,
Those dissipations which their bliss annoy,
And blast and poison each domestic joy.

Source text

Humphreys, David, *The Miscellaneous Works of Colonel Humphreys* (New York: Hodge, Allen, and Campbell, 1790).

Reference

Wells, Colin, *Poetry Wars: Verse and Politics in the American Revolution and Early Republic* (Philadelphia, PA: University of Pennsylvania Press, 2018).

Enslaved Jamaican Singers and J. B. Moreton (n.d.)

Two Jamaican Songs From West India Customs and Manners (1790)

Enslaved men and women in the Black Atlantic world struggled determinedly and creatively against systemic undermining of their aspirations for shared family life. One striking record of this pattern resides in Caribbean songs whose written versions may come to us only in print text generated by whites. British author J. B. Moreton's book based on his five years' service as a bookkeeper in Clarendon Parish, Jamaica, exemplifies one such record.

Some English reviews of Moreton's book took him to task for 'coarse' language and 'licentious remarks' on Jamaica as 'profligate' ('Art. 22', 337–8) and for his 'gloomy' and 'displeasing' depiction of 'lust' there ('Manners', 357). Moreton had taken then-unusual steps by suggesting, within some commentaries, that interracial sexual connections were often coerced; still, in other portions of the text, he encouraged stereotypes of Black West Indian women as Jezebel figures. These inconsistencies have led to conflicting assessments of the publication and Moreton himself. One 1790 British reviewer found Moreton's account 'prudent', 'judicious and humane' overall and 'impartial' in its advice 'on the manner of living among the negroes', yet faulted the writing as sometimes 'dashing, superficial, and trite' (130). More recently, Henrice Altink classified Moreton as a pro-slavery writer but credited his depiction of 'the conditions of slavery' as 'responsible for enslaved women's promiscuity' (205).

Carolyn Cooper notes that Moreton's and other white versions of local island lyrics represent an inherently complex record with internal contradictions, since 'English grammar and metre are imposed on the Jamaican text', alongside 'patronising anglo-scribal editorialising'. Nonetheless, she asserts, 'any record at all, however vagrant, is valuable', because these mediated echoes of the original oral songs can provide access (however limited) to their original meaning and intention (22).

The two texts below published by Moreton present one lyric in the voice of a Black man frustrated by his inability to keep the woman he loves at home tending to his needs and another offering a Black woman's poignant revisiting of her white master's sexual abuse and its perverse impact on her and her children.

Two Jamaican Songs from **West India Customs and Manners**

How wretched's my time been of late![11]
    How severe and how bitter my woe!
I've no one to louse my rough pate,[12]
    Nor the chigger to pick from my toe:

For Quashiba's gone to the town,
    To see smarter beaumen than me;
Tho' I often compell'd her to own
    How false and how fickle they be.

---

11 Moreton gives no title for this song lyric. He introduces it with this context: 'Those [enslaved people] who live in pairs together, as man and wife, are mutual helpmates to each other: the men build their huts, and assist to work their grounds; the women prog [i.e. forage (*OED*)] for food, boil their pots at noon and night, louse their heads, extract chiggers from their toes, and wash their frocks and trowsers. I shall here submit the complaint of a negroe man, whose helpmate had deserted him, to your perusal' (150).
12 De-lousing (removing lice from) someone's head

My sungee, alas! is unboil'd,
    My hut is all cover'd with dirt;
I've no one to nurse my dear child,
    Nor to wash the salt sweat from my shirt!

Then join, sable swains, to bemoan
    The hardships of poor Custy's lot;
He sighs the whole night all alone,
    In the day he's deprived of his pot.

He's depriv'd of his pot in the day,
    And of love's softer pleasure at night;
O! ye youths who give ear to my lay,
    Know, Custy's quite lost to delight!

AIR. What care I for Mam or Dad.[13]

Altho' a slave me is born and bred,
    My skin is black, not yellow:
I often sold my maidenhead
    To many a handsome fellow.

My massa keep me once, for true,
    And gave me clothes, wid busses:[14]
Fine muslin coats, wid bitty, too,
    To gain my sweet embraces.

When pickinniny him come black,
    My massa starve and fum[15] me;
He tear the coat from off my back,
    And naked him did strip me.

Him turn me out into the field,
    Wid hoe, the ground to clear-o;
Me take pickinniny on my back,
    And work him te-me weary.

---

13 Recent reprintings of Moreton's presentation of this second song sometimes give as its title a line from later in the lyric, 'Me know no law, me know no sin'. Moreton introduces this text as follows: 'Some masters and overseers, of jealous, pimping dispositions, flog, and otherwise ill treat their black wenches, when they chance to get black children. I have been often diverted, and laughed heartily, when a raw, infatuated gaukey, or a doating, debilitated debauchee has been disappointed, after all his endearing fondness and amorous exertions, with his soft, slobber-chop [i.e. one who drools or slobbers excessively (*OED*)] bundle, to get a black, instead of an olive babe. I shall annex the song of a young woman who was in this predicament: —it is in the negroe dialect, and is no less true than curious' (153–4).
14 Buss/'Busses' carries multiple potentially relevant meanings here: kisses and 'To clothe, dress' or adorn (*OED*) but also, as seen in a Jamaican slang dictionary, a possible punning on 'buss' as both 'a (big) break' [i.e. a supportive move] or a verb meaning to punch, strike, or burst.
15 Flog or beat

Him, Obissha,[16] him de come one night,
       And give me gown and busses;
Him get one pickinniny, white!
       Almost as white as missess.

Then missess fum me wid long switch,
       And say him da for massa;
My massa curse her, "lying bitch!"
       And tell her, "buss my rassa!"

Me fum'd when me no condescend;
       Me fum'd too if me do it;
Me no have no one for 'tand my friend,
       So me am forc'd to do it.

Me know no law, me know no sin,
       Me is just what ebba them make me;[17]
This is the way dem bring me in;
       So God nor devil take me!

Source text

Moreton, J. B., ESQ., *West India Customs and Manners: Containing Strictures on the Soil, Cultivation, Produce, Trade, Officers, and Inhabitants; with the Method of Establishing and Conducting a Sugar Plantation. To Which is Added, The Practices of Training New Slaves*, new edn (London: J. Parsons, 1793).

References

Altink, Henrice, 'Forbidden Fruit: Pro-Slavery Attitudes Towards Enslaved Women's Sexuality and Interracial Sex', *Journal of Caribbean History* 39.2 (2005), 201–35.

'Art. XII: Manners and Customs in the West-India Islands', *English Review, or, an Abstract of English and Foreign Literature* 16 (August 1790), 127–30.

'Art. 22. Manners and Customs of the West India Islands', *Monthly Review* 4 (March 1791), 337–8.

Cooper, Carolyn, *Noises in the Blood: Orality, Gender, and the 'Vulgar' Body of Jamaican Popular Culture* (Durham, NC: Duke University Press, 1995).

'Manners and Customs of the West India Islands', *Critical Review, or, Annals of Literature* 2 (July 1791), 357.

---

16 The overseer, now apparently taking the place of the master

17 Moreton comments immediately after his presentation of the song: 'The virtue and chastity, as well as the lives and properties of the women, are at the command of the masters and overseers; they are perpetually exposed to the prostitution of them and their friends: it is pity that there is not some law to protect them from abuses so tyrannic, cruel and abominable' (155).

Felicia Hemans (1793–1835)

'The Landing of the Pilgrim Fathers in New England' (1828)

Felicia Dorothea Hemans (née Browne) was one of the most widely-read women poets of the nineteenth century in both Britain and North America. Born in Liverpool, England, she was one of six children whose father left for Quebec around 1806 and never returned. In 1812 she married Captain Alfred Hemans (b.1781) and bore five sons. The same year she wed, she also published a new book of poems, *The Domestic Affections*. In 1818 Hemans and her husband separated, and he soon settled in Rome. Of Hemans's many volumes of poetry, the most popular was *Records of Woman* (1828), first published in Edinburgh and quickly reprinted in New York.

'The Landing of the Pilgrim Fathers in New England' initially appeared in *New Monthly Magazine* (London, November 1825) with an epigraph by Robert Treat Paine and the author identified only as 'An American Poet'. Hemans reprinted the poem in 1828 among her volume's 'Miscellaneous Pieces' with a new epigraph by William Cullen Bryant (Feldman, 205). Hemans's heroic depiction of pious British exiles seeking religious freedom through settlement in the New World became a staple of nineteenth-century US celebrations of Thanksgiving. Today it is notable for its erasure of diverse Native Americans whose homes were in the territory later claimed for the English colony Massachusetts (Lootens, 15ff.). Hemans's poem is usefully read in dialogue with Elizabeth Barrett Browning's 'The Runaway Slave at Pilgrim's Point' (see AA).

'The Landing of the Pilgrim Fathers in New England'

> Look now abroad—another race has fill'd
>   Those populous borders—wide the wood recedes,
> And towns shoot up, and fertile realms are till'd;
>   The land is full of harvests and green meads.
>
>   BRYANT.[18]

———

The breaking waves dash'd high
  On a stern and rock-bound coast,
And the woods against a stormy sky
  Their giant branches toss'd;

And the heavy night hung dark,
  The hills and waters o'er,
When a band of exiles moor'd their bark
  On the wild New-England shore.

---

18 Lines 280–3 from 'The Ages' (1822), by US poet William Cullen Bryant (1794–1878).

Not as the conqueror comes,
    They, the true-hearted came;
Not with the roll of the stirring drums,
    And the trumpet that sings of fame:

Not as the flying come,
    In silence and in fear;—
They shook the depths of the desert gloom
    With their hymns of lofty cheer.

Amidst the storm they sang,
    And the stars heard and the sea!
And the sounding aisles of the dim woods rang
    To the anthem of the free.

The ocean-eagle soar'd
    From his nest by the white wave's foam,
And the rocking pines of the forest roar'd—
    This was their welcome home!

There were men with hoary hair,
    Amidst that pilgrim band;—
Why had *they* come to wither there,
    Away from their childhood's land?

There was woman's fearless eye,
    Lit by her deep love's truth;
There was manhood's brow serenely high,
    And the fiery heart of youth.

What sought they thus afar?
    Bright jewels of the mine?
The wealth of seas, the spoils of war?—
    They sought a faith's pure shrine!

Ay, call it holy ground,
    The soil where first they trod!
They have left unstain'd what there they found—
    Freedom to worship God.

Source text

Hemans, Felicia, *Records of Woman: with Other Poems* (New York: William B. Gilley, 1828).

References

Hemans, Felicia, *Records of Woman, with Other Poems* (1828), Paula R. Feldman (ed.) (Lexington, KY: University Press of Kentucky, 1999).

Lootens, Tricia, 'States of Exile', in Meredith L. McGill (ed.), *The Traffic in Poems: Nineteenth-Century Poetry and Transatlantic Exchange* (New Brunswick, NJ: Rutgers University Press, 2008), 15–36.

ODNB

Charles Dickens (1812–70)

From 'A Good-Humoured Christmas Chapter' in Pickwick Papers (1836)

'Preface' to A Christmas Carol (1843)

In scholarship across decades and in popular press stories appearing every December, Charles Dickens is often dubbed the 'Father' of Christmas as celebrated in transatlantic culture. David Parker stresses that Dickens's advocacy for the holiday extended well beyond his most famous depiction in *A Christmas Carol*. Indeed, Dickens's promotion of Christmas can be tracked to earlier starting points in 1835's *Sketches by Boz* and in 1836's *Pickwick Papers*. Additionally, for years after Dickens's most famous Christmas book appeared, he would regularly publish others, as well as shorter holiday pieces in periodicals he edited (such as *All the Year Round*). Accordingly, we present excerpts from both *Pickwick* (here) and his *Household Words* magazine (in our subsequent entry by Samuel Rinder).

Still, *A Christmas Carol*'s ongoing impact on the holiday as a shared social practice of transatlantic (even global) domestic culture is unrivalled. Far-ranging examples include perennial community theatre productions, numerous films (including cartoons, the loveable Muppets and singing versions of Scrooge), as well as twenty-first-century literary riffs like Canadian Margaret Atwood's *Payback: Debt and the Shadow Side of Wealth* (2008). Dickens's vision of Christmas, marked in his brief 1843 *Christmas Carol* 'Preface' as a hopeful, domesticity-focused celebration, continues to exercise a powerful intercultural reach.

From 'A Good-Humoured Christmas Chapter' in Pickwick Papers

As brisk as bees, if not altogether as light as fairies, did the four Pickwickians[19] assemble on the morning of the twenty-second day of December, in the year of grace in which these, their faithfully-recorded adventures, were undertaken and accomplished. Christmas was close at hand, in all his bluff and hearty honesty; it was the season of hospitality, merriment, and open-heartedness; the old year was preparing, like an ancient philosopher, to call his friends around him, and amidst the

---

19 The four: Samuel Pickwick (founder), Tracy Tupman (self-identified adventurer), Augustus Snodgrass (would-be, yet unsuccessful, poet) and Nathaniel Winkel (aspiring sportsman)

sound of feasting and revelry to pass gently and calmly away.[20] Gay and merry was the time; and right gay and merry were at least four of the numerous hearts that were gladdened by its coming.[21]

And numerous indeed are the hearts to which Christmas brings a brief season of happiness and enjoyment. How many families whose members have been dispersed and scattered far and wide, in the restless struggles of life, are then re-united, and meet once again in that happy state of companionship and mutual good-will, which is a source of such pure and unalloyed delight, and one so incompatible with the cares and sorrows of the world, that the religious belief of the most civilized nations, and the rude traditions of the roughest savages, alike number it among the first joys of a future state of existence, provided for the blest and happy! How many old recollections, and how many dormant sympathies, does Christmas time awaken! [. . .]

[. . .] Happy, happy Christmas, that can win us back to the delusions of our childish days, that can recal[l] to the old man the pleasures of his youth, and transport the sailor and the traveller, thousands of miles away, back to his own fire-side and his quiet home!

Preface to A Christmas Carol (1843)

I have endeavoured in this Ghostly little book to raise the Ghost of an Idea which shall not put my readers out of humour with themselves, with each other, with the season, or with me. May it haunt their houses pleasantly, and no one wish to lay it.

Their faithful Friend and Servant, C.D.
December, 1843

Source texts

Dickens, Charles, *The Posthumous Papers of The Pickwick Club* (London: Chapman & Hall, 1837).
Dickens, Charles, 'Preface', *A Christmas Carol* (Philadelphia, PA: J. B. Lippincott, 1843).

References

Allingham, Philip V., 'Dickens "the man who invented Christmas"', *The Victorian Web*, Web.
Barzilai, Shuli, '"Scrooge Nouveau": Margaret Atwood Resites *A Christmas Carol*', *Dickens Quarterly* 31.4 (December 2014), 298–311.

---

20 Intriguingly, Dickens's vision of holiday cheer here and elsewhere may owe a debt to American writer Washington Irving (1783–1859). Irving's account of seasonal festivities in 'Bracebridge Hall' (1822), penned after spending time in an English manor house, were, Richard Kelly suggests, a source for Dickens's later descriptions in *Pickwick Papers*'s Dingley Dell celebration and, subsequently, in *A Christmas Carol*. See Kelly, 'Washington Irving and Dickens's *A Christmas Carol*', *The Victorian Web*, Web.
21 In contrast to this portrait of good cheer, Allingham sees a forerunner of *A Christmas Carol*'s Scrooge in *Pickwick Papers*'s subsequent chapter, where Dickens depicts the 'sexton and grave-digger in the church-yard, one Gabriel Grub' as 'an ill-conditioned, cross-grained, surly fellow—a morose and lonely man, who consorted with nobody but himself' even on Christmas eve (*Pickwick*, 299).

Parker, David, 'Dickens and the American Christmas', *Dickens Quarterly* 19.3 (2002), 160–9.

Taft, Joshua, 'Disenchanted Religion and Secular Enchantment in *A Christmas Carol*', *Victorian Literature and Culture* 43.4 (December 2015), 659–73.

Samuel Rinder (1825[?]–1907)

From 'South American Christmas' in Dickens's Household Words (1852)

Anne Lohrli's attentive scholarship on *Household Words* credits Samuel Rinder as author of 'South American Christmas', one of many holiday-linked stories Charles Dickens published in his periodical each December in line with his self-described role as 'conductor' of the periodical. Lohrli's profile of Rinder for *Dickens Journals Online* focuses on the much-travelled Leeds-born businessman as having journeyed to such far-flung locales as New York in the US and Callao, Peru, before settling in Victoria, Australia. A successful merchant, Rinder also became an active civic leader. Several of his writings critiqued the harsh conditions faced by merchant seamen during oceanic voyages.

The feature story below invites readers to see how cultural practices associated with celebrating Christmas were taking on a hybrid character in increasingly British-influenced global settings such as the South American city whose holiday activities he describes here. At the same time, racist-tinged descriptions of 'negroes' and 'Indian women' illustrate how power dynamics operating in colonised spaces were complicating these ongoing cultural exchanges, even within depictions of a holiday and its related social interactions so often being idealised in Dickensian publication sites.

From 'South American Christmas' in Dickens's Household Words[22]

FOR many years I have been accustomed to eat my Christmas dinner in a white jacket and a loose shirt collar, the doors and windows thrown wide open, admitting with the warm and sluggish breeze the scent of summer flowers and newly made hay. A much prized lump of ice cooling my tepid lemonade, has long been to me

---

22 Looking back on Dickens's leadership of this periodical, Percy Fitzgerald highlighted the notation of 'Conducted by Charles Dickens' appearing 'at the top of every page' as affirming 'how great his supreme position was then' in managing the publication. Though individual stories were intended 'to be quite anonymous', Fitzgerald recalled, 'a wit' of the time joked about how 'Charles Dickens's name [was] on every page' (135). In particular, Fitzgerald linked the 1850s' December holiday issues of the periodical with both his own decades-long 'treasur[ing of] all these Christmas numbers' and his re-reading them 'with each recurring anniversary' in 'a royal feast of retrospection' (146) and Dickens's savvy, yet sincere, dissemination of a 'deep-seated, passionate longing after Christmas feeling' (145).

the only sign of frost—the sole memento of old-country Christmas weather. In Tasmania, a dessert of juicy English cherries, ripe jolly-looking gooseberries, ruddy bunches of newly-gathered currants, and delicious strawberries, formed a repast far more in keeping with the weather, than the dinner of roast beef and hot plum-pudding which, in obedience to the good old custom, we vainly strove to swallow. But still, in Australia, as in every English colony whatever be its latitude, Christmas retains its old associations, and loved usages; and the Yule log, and midnight waits, the rich spice cake and mellow cheese, recall to the long absent settler many a happy Christmas of his boyhood. In the bunch of mistletoe that hangs above his head (for Australia has her mistletoe), the newly landed emigrant sees the bright eyes and sunny smiles of that fair cousin who was his partner all last Christmas eve; and in whose company he was continually losing himself among the dancers, and as often turning up beneath the glistening bough that hung in the ball-room kitchen of the old house at home.

But, although thus inured to hot Decembers and no longer wondering to meet old Christmas dressed in flowers instead of holly, and adding to his English winter cheer the fruits of summer; yet, in some southern countries, I have seen him so disguised as scarcely to admit of recognition: and in none, perhaps, does he wear a stranger garb, than in the half Indian and half Spanish cities of the South American republics. Of these cities not one presents so singular and so interesting an aspect as Lima, the capital of Peru. Its Moorish architecture, its magnificent religious festivals; its many-coloured population; its picturesque costumes; and its strange mixture of the customs of old Spain with those of the ancient empire of the Incas; combine to form a picture that offers to the traveller many rare attractions.

On Christmas Eve—*noche buena*, the good night, as the Spaniards call it—the whole city is alive with preparations for the approaching festivity. Droves of asses crowd the streets, laden with fruit, liquors, and merchandise; ugly calezas,[23] orna-mented with gaudy paper instead of paint, rattle over the rough pavement; and Indians with ice pails on their heads, elbow through the crowd, crying in musical tones *helado! helado!*[24]

Suddenly the great bell of the cathedral, with three slow and heavy strokes, calls to *oraciones* or evening prayers. The effect is magical. The life of the city is instantly suspended. Every foot is arrested; every tongue is silent, and the whole population kneel or bow in whispered prayer. With the last stroke of the bell the silence is bro-ken; each individual turning to his neighbour wishes him "good night," and the busy stream flows on all the more rapidly for the transient interruption.

This scene is enacted in the streets of Lima every evening in the year; but on Christmas Eve it is more especially the signal for the cessation of toil, and the com-mencement of the merry festival.

The Alemadas or public walks outside the walls are, on Christmas Eve, crowded with pleasure seekers; and the great square is filled by a motley throng, whose faces present every shade of human colour, from the aristocratic white and slen-der figure of the pure Spanish creole through fifty crosses and gradations, to the jetty black and robust frame of the equally pure negro; each deepening of the tint marking a new and more degraded race, distinguished by a different name,

---

23 Carriages
24 Ice cream or water ice

and scornfully looked down on by the lighter-hued mulatto or mestizo, in whose veins a drop of pure white blood has mingled with the darker stream. Numerous ice stalls surrounded with chairs and benches, are scattered over the square, and drive a busy trade; for, to the Limeña ice is a necessary of life, and never is it more welcome than during the sultry Christmas tide. As the night darkens the crowd increases, and presently is heard above the hum of voices the wild chanting of the Peruvian waits: bands of negroes dressed in flowing robes of red; with thin, black faces, sometimes disguised by ugly and still blacker masks, and carrying in their hands small painted gourds or calabashes filled with pebbles. To the monotonous music of the guitar and clattering castanets, they sing strange guttural songs, and dance wild and uncouth measures, rattling the pebbles in their gourds to mark the time: and, seen by the flickering lamplight, they bear to us a greater likeness to a mosque of devils than to English waits.

After the negroes, come groups of Indian women, loosely dressed—their long black hair, unbound, falling round them—carrying long slender wands fluttering with ribbons. In the low soft tones peculiar to their race they sing sweet melodies, and move in circles performing the most graceful dances, waving their light wands in time to the music of a flute and harp.

As we wander through the streets we find the doors all open, and hear music in every house, catching sometimes a glimpse of the dark faces of the dancers as they move through the graceful evolutions of the zambacucca— the favourite dance of the coloured races. Lima is, perhaps, the most hospitable city in the world; although many of its old customs are falling into disuse. Even yet, as you traverse its streets after nightfall, you may see shining in many a gateway, the "welcome-lamp," once universal; which tells to the passing friend or stranger than the family is "at home" and ready to receive him. At Christmas every house is open. Strangers enter without fear. To be a foreigner is to have a double claim and to be greeted with a double welcome. The ceremony and restraint which we associate with Spanish manners have no existence here, and no introduction is necessary. With the prettiest girl in the room for a partner (if she be disengaged, and the stranger can muster sufficient courage and Spanish to ask her) he may join the waltzers, who are spinning round the saloon; or, he will find in the adjoining apartment, cigars, ices, liquors, sherbet, and pastry, to which he is expected to help himself without ceremony. A sudden intimacy springs up between him and sundry gorgeous little officers in small moustaches and large silver-hilted swords, or with beautiful women, who introduce themselves by some startling Christian name—the surname being seldom used in conversation. A child born on any festival or Saint's day receiving the name of such Saint or festival, and it is amusing to hear names, which translated into English, would be Donna Nativity, or Donna Ascension; or not unfrequently Donna Holy Ghost (*Espiritu Santo*) or Jesuita. The visitor is at once invested with a title; and by the lips of a fair companion, the plain John, which his godfather gave him, is transformed into the more sonorous Don Juan. [. . .]

In many private houses a sort of theatrical representation of the Nativity is displayed on Christmas Eve; resembling, in some respects, the old English mysteries. It is often got up with considerable skill and at a great expense; the child being sometimes cradled in a silver manger. [. . .]

On one side of the market-place stands a gloomy building which gives its name to the square—the Plazuela de la Inquisicion. But the Inquisition has long been banished from the land, and its deserted palace now looks sullenly over the busy market, once the scene of many a terrible martyrdom; for here were performed the fearful "acts of faith." Now, the only faggots to be seen are those brought from the mountains to serve as fuel for cooking our Christmas dinner.

Upon the ground of the square are heaped great piles of fruit, – plump, juicy melons, yellow plantains, luscious grapes, and fragrant limes. Baskets of crimson chilis and red-hot love-apples shine conspicuously among the green heaps of vegetables. Scattered round are monster yams and feathery corn-cobs, oranges, ripe dates and cocoa-nuts. The butchers' stalls display their stores of beef and mutton; and rows of fowls and turkeys promise plenty of good Christmas cheer. In the great square the flower-market displays a richly scented bouquet, such as Lima only can produce. Upon a large green leaf rests a foundation of small, beautifully-coloured fruits; above them glows a posy of bright flowers tastefully arranged, giving forth a most delicious fragrance, and brightened by a sprinkling of some delicate perfume. The whole is crowned by a single fruit, on which the sun has lavished all those soft, yet brilliant hues unknown beyond the tropics. One of these much esteemed *pucheros de flores*[25] is the most acceptable present to be offered to the Lima ladies; who are all passionately fond of perfumes. Pastiles[26] are constantly burning in their houses, and showers of scented water frequently salute their visitors, who receive such marks of attention as high compliments.

By eight o'clock the markets are almost deserted, and at nine the bell gives notice of the elevation of the host during the celebration of high mass. The scene at evening prayers is reacted, and again the whole city is wrapped in momentary silence; not a whisper nor a footfall sounds in the crowded streets. Every festival in Lima is marked by a religious procession, and the frequent repetition of these shows, does not appear to lessen in the slightest degree the intense gratification which they afford to the inhabitants. The festival of St. Rose, the patron saint of the city, and the twenty-eighth of October, the anniversary of the great earthquake of 1746, are especially noted for the magnificent ceremonies with which they are celebrated, and Christmas Day is always inaugurated by one of these splendid spectacles. In the church of San Domingo, which almost equals the cathedral in grandeur, is a beautiful marble statue of St. Rose, richly decorated with gold and precious stones. [. . .]

So far our Christmas day has been well spent, but now there comes a blot upon it; though to the Limeña that blot is its greatest beauty and its chief attraction. It is a bull-fight, to which barbarous amusement the latter part of the day is always devoted. During the season these exhibitions are of almost weekly occurrence, and Monday being usually set apart for them, that day becomes a general holiday. The excitement that prevails on these occasions is astonishing. The bull-fight is the sole topic of conversation; for the Peruvians are more enthusiastically attached to this sport than even the old Spaniards, and Lima surpasses her ancient mistress, Madrid, in the number and splendor of these national diversions. The Christmas bull-fight is commonly the best of the season, and eight or ten bulls are frequently killed on that day, besides several horses, and not unfrequently one or two of the riders. [. . .]

---

25 Flower pots
26 Small glob of aromatic paste burned as a pleasant deodoriser

Willingly we turn from this bad feature of our Lima festival to see again the merry groups collected round the ice-stalls; to wander through the streets, listening once more to the sweet songs of the Indian women, or to the solemn chanting of the choristers. Or, as we pass the wide court-yards, up which the welcome-lamp is gleaming, we enter again the hospital saloon; and, watching the graceful dancers, think of by-gone days, and far-off friends with whom we have passed so many Christmas Days, and wonder if they think of us amidst their merriment, and if they drink our health as we do theirs, coupling their names with many a hearty wish.

Source text

[Rinder, Samuel], 'South American Christmas', *Household Words* 6 (18 December 1852), 325–8.

References

Fitzgerald, Percy, *Memories of Charles Dickens* (Bristol: J. W. Arrowsmith, 1913).
Lohrli, Anne, 'Samuel Rinder', *Dickens Journals Online* (Toronto: University of Toronto Press, 1971), Web.

Henry Wadsworth Longfellow (1807–82)

From Evangeline *Part I (1847)*

Henry Wadsworth Longfellow, born in Maine and educated at Bowdoin College, was an immensely popular poet and teacher. He studied European languages and cultures for three years (1826–9) and would be instrumental in the reading and teaching of foreign literatures in the United States. His anthology, *The Poets and Poetry of Europe* (1845), was one of the earliest collections of European writing in translation for the American reader. *Evangeline*, one of Longfellow's most famous poems, depicts the 'Great Upheaval' expulsion into exile of the French settlers in Acadie, Nova Scotia, by British troops during the French and Indian War (1754–63), and specifically the enforced separation of its two central characters, the lovers Evangeline and Gabriel. The poem's lines are unrhymed dactylic hexameters, a form traditionally associated with Greek and Latin classical poetry; *Evangeline* is constructed as an American epic in the tradition of Homer's *Iliad* and Ovid's *Metamorphoses*. One early British reviewer celebrated it as 'the first genuine Castalian fount which has burst from the soil of America' (Whewell, 295). The passage excerpted here, from the beginning of the poem, is indicative of its concern with imagining an idyll of domesticity as yet untouched by the forces of historical conflict soon to drive the Acadian community into exile.

Figure 4.3 Celebration of the engagement of the heroine and Gabriel, just before the diaspora begins. *Evangeline: A Tale of Acadie, by Henry Wadsworth Longfellow, with notes* (New York: T. Y. Crowell, 1893), inter-page 40–1. Courtesy HathiTrust.

From Evangeline

In the Acadian land, on the shores of the Basin of Minas,[27]
Distant, secluded, still, the little village of Grand-Pré
Lay in the fruitful valley. Vast meadows stretched to the eastward,
Giving the village its name, and pasture to flocks without number.
Dikes, that the hands of the farmers had raised with labor incessant,
Shut out the turbulent tides; but at stated seasons the flood-gates
Opened, and welcomed the sea to wander at will o'er the meadows.
West and south there were fields of flax, and orchards and cornfields
Spreading afar and unfenced o'er the plain; and away to the northward
Blomidon[28] rose, and the forests old, and aloft on the mountains
Sea-fogs pitched their tents, and mists from the mighty Atlantic
Looked on the happy valley, but ne'er from their station descended.

---

27 The Minas Basin is an inlet in Nova Scotia, Canada. Acadia was a colony of New France in north eastern North America, populated by Indigenous First Nations people and (from 1604) by French settlers.
28 Cape Blomidon is a headland above the Minas Basin.

There, in the midst of its farms, reposed the Acadian village.
Strongly built were the houses, with frames of oak and of chestnut,
Such as the peasants of Normandy built in the reign of the Henries.[29]
Thatched were the roofs, with dormer-windows; and gables projecting
Over the basement below protected and shaded the door-way.
There in the tranquil evenings of summer, when brightly the sunset
Lighted the village street, and gilded the vanes on the chimneys,
Matrons and maidens sat in snow-white caps and in kirtles
Scarlet and blue and green, with distaffs spinning the golden
Flax for the gossiping looms, whose noisy shuttles within doors
Mingled their sound with the whir of the wheels and the songs of the maidens.
Solemnly down the street came the parish priest, and the children
Paused in their play to kiss the hand he extended to bless them.
Reverend walked he among them; and up rose matrons and maidens,
Hailing his slow approach with words of affectionate welcome.
Then came the laborers home from the field, and serenely the sun sank
Down to his rest, and twilight prevailed. Anon from the belfry
Softly the Angelus sounded, and over the roofs of the village
Columns of pale blue smoke, like clouds of incense ascending,
Rose from a hundred hearths, the homes of peace and contentment.
Thus dwelt together in love these simple Acadian farmers, –
Dwelt in the love of God and of man. Alike were they free from
Fear, the reigns with the tyrant, and envy, the vice of republics.
Neither locks had they to their doors, nor bars to their windows;
But their dwellings were open as day and the hearts of the owners;
There the richest was poor, and the poorest lived in abundance.

Source text

Longfellow, Henry Wadsworth, *Evangeline, A Tale of Acadie*, 3rd edn (Boston: William D. Ticknor & Company, 1847–8).

References

Eckel, Leslie Elizabeth, *Atlantic Citizens: Nineteenth-Century American Writers at Work in the World* (Edinburgh: Edinburgh University Press, 2013).

Irmscher, Christoph, *Longfellow Redux* (Urbana, IL: University of Illinois Press, 2006).

Niemeyer, Mark, 'Henry Wadsworth Longfellow's *Evangeline: A Tale of Acadie* and the Ambiguous Afterlife of the History of the Acadeians', *Canadian Review of American Studies* 48.2 (May 2018), 121–45.

[Whewell, William], Review of *Evangeline, a Tale of Acadie*, *Fraser's Magazine for Town and Country* 37 (1848), 295–8.

---

29 French monarchs between 1547 and 1610

Mary Howitt (1799–1888)

From **Our Cousins in Ohio: From a Mother's Diary** (1849)

English writer Mary Howitt's best-known work is 'The Spider and the Fly', but she published in many genres: poems, children's literature, sketches for literary annuals and periodicals, as well as an autobiography documenting her career, family connections and literary friendships. Author of over a hundred books, she also briefly co-edited *Howitt's Journal* with her husband William. Advocate for women's rights and other radical causes, she fostered her daughter Anna Mary's professional work as a translator and visual artist.

Linda Peterson notes: 'Mary Howitt viewed writing as a family business, as a professional endeavor pursued by father, mother, and children gifted with literary ability' (97). *Our Cousins in Ohio* embodies this context. In her autobiography, Howitt explains its grounding in a journal her sister Emma sent back to Britain from the US. Howitt's daughter Anna Mary produced illustrations for multiple editions, as she had for 1848's *The Children's Year*, which depicted the characters Meggy and Herbert (Howitt's own children) as playing at housekeeping. Similarly, the *Cousins* narrative presented a year in the life of Emma's children, acculturating to a new home in the American West while maintaining transatlantic ties.

In its premise of drawing from a mother's diary, Howitt's *Our Cousins* built on the Anglo-American tradition of women's authorship as maternal enterprise, a view traceable back to figures like Anna Barbauld and Hannah More in England, as well as US-based writers like Lydia Sigourney.

From **Our Cousins in Ohio**

Preface

The little book which I promised as a companion volume to the Children's Year, I now present to the public; and in so doing, I would express my grateful sense of the kind and flattering manner in which that little work, an experiment in children's books, has been received.

Here then is another book which is entirely true; and if it interests the child and satisfies the parent, so much the better.

To me its compilation has been a work of pleasure mingled with deep sorrow. It is the twelvemonths' chronicle of the domestic life of a beloved Sister, far removed by distance, and whom it has pleased a good Providence, since then, to remove by death.

The days at The Cedars, made joyous by the presence of that affectionate and wise mother, are now over for ever. This volume contains the brief record of her last Christmas on earth.

M. H.

From Chapter I, 'Our Cousins and Their Home'

I told you last year about Herbert and Meggy. Herbert and Meggy had cousins who lived in America; and it afforded them great pleasure to hear, month by month, what these children did for one whole year. I think that you also may like to hear it, because it is very probable that you may have cousins likewise in America, who may resemble in some particulars Herbert's and Meggy's; and, therefore, you can fancy that it is of *your* cousins and not of *theirs*, that you are reading.

Of these young cousins and their home I must, however, in the first place, tell you something.

Their home was called "The Cedars"; it was in the State of Ohio, on the banks of that noble river which gives its name to the State, and about four miles from the fine city of ――. "The Cedars" lay upon a road which went on and on, through little clusters of houses and log cabins, called "towns" and "villes", and by farms and through woods, and across valleys and creeks, to nobody knows where; at least I cannot tell you where. Well, a little way out of this road lay "The Cedars." It was a large, handsome, and somewhat commanding-looking place, a brick house, white-washed, and one of the oldest thereabout. It stood on the highest land in the neigh-bourhood; and yet it was only after ascending the mile-long hill that lay between it and the river, as well as by observing that the cedar trees which surrounded it and which gave to it its name were landmarks to the whole district, that any one per-ceived how high it really was. This elevation, which made it bleak in winter, caused it to be breezy and particularly pleasant during the fervid heats of summer.

The house, which, as I told you, was white, had green Venetian outside shutters to the windows. In front there was a large two-storied porch, up which grew in wild luxuriance a beautiful prairie rose, which in summer hung about it like garlands of flowers. On the sunny side of the house, which was consequently very hot in summer, there ran along its whole length a broad piazza; which, like the porch, was two-storied; so that both the upper and lower rooms opened into it. This piazza in winter was the favourite play-place of the children; and as it was shaded with vines and trumpet creepers, it was in warm weather like a beautiful summer parlour. Here, in summer, the family frequently took their meals, and often, after supper, sate in the delicious moonlight evenings, till bedtime.

As I told you, the house stood at a little distance from the road. It stood sur-rounded by its own land and in a beautiful smooth field, called "The Lawn." It was approached from the road by an avenue of locust-trees; and the lawn itself was scattered over and grouped with cedar and catalpa trees, which grow there to a large size, and which were, in fact, the remains of the primeval forest. Beautiful flower-beds surrounded the house, and others were cut here and there in the open lawn, which was kept nicely mown to a considerable distance round the house; and, besides these, lovely flowering trees and shrubs grew in clumps and thickets; among which seats were set and pleasant arbours were made. All this, which was properly the pleasure-garden, was uninclosed from the lawn itself by palings or fence of any kind; because, as cattle were never admitted into the field, there was no occasion for it, and thus the lawn itself formed a portion of the whole.

At the back of the house were the outbuildings; on the left stood rather a picturesque building, called the wood-house, where the fuel was kept, and upon the gable of which was perched the little bird-house; where the bluebirds, which came regularly every spring, built their nests, and reared two or three broods in the course of the summer. Further back was the farm-yard, where stood the carriage-house, the waggon-shed, the corn-crib, a hen-house, and a large barn. Beyond, lay the kitchen-garden; and beyond that again, on a fine slope to the south-east, was the vineyard. The orchard adjoined the vineyard, and at one corner of the orchard, hidden by a little grove of willows, stood a log-cabin, in which lived a German farmer, named Eberhard, who managed the land at The Cedars; and with him lived his brother-in-law, Heinrich, likewise employed on the farm, their wives and children, and the old grandmother of the family. To reach Eberhard's it was not necessary to go through kitchen-garden, orchard, and vineyard, because a pleasant little lane led from the farmyard to his cabin; and this lane was remarkable for a beautiful spring of water, which, in the driest seasons, came pouring like liquid crystal into a picturesque water-trough, round which grew six locust-trees and an immense button-wood tree.

A gentle ascent from the vineyard was occupied by pasture land, called the "Far Meadows," which were bounded by a wood belonging to another proprietor. This was Jack's Wood; and as in the course of this history much will be said about it, I may as well introduce you to it here.

Jack's Wood was one of the favourite resorts of our cousins and their mother during spring and summer. It was an unbroken portion of the primeval forest, and had been left uncleared purposely for a supply of fire-wood; and from this cause its beautiful timber was fast vanishing away. From time to time a noble hickory or sugar-maple was felled and cut up; and this our friends never failed to deplore, for they yet retained the Englishman's love of trees; and they were here continually reminded of what is a very common experience in America: "Never," say the lovers of the picturesque there, "set your heart upon a tree; for as sure as you do, somebody will come with an axe and cut it down."

However, notwithstanding all the demands which had been made upon Jack's Wood for fuel, it was wonderful what an innumerable variety of trees and flowers were still collected within its bounds. [...] Here grew hickory, maple, birch, and walnut trees—the splendid American linden—the red-bud or Judas tree, by the budding of which the Indian, in olden time, regulated the sowing of his corn. The wild clematis, sweet-briar, and American hawthorn, were among its abundant undergrowth; and here also were thickets of black-berries, which produced such splendid fruit as English children can form no idea of. [...]

Such was Jack's Wood, the southern boundary of The Cedars. The northern boundary was likewise a wood—a beautiful upland covered with trees— and it was called, also from its proprietor who was a German, Diedrich's Wood. [...]

The house at Diedrich's Hof, was a log-house of a very picturesque appearance, with its log-stables and sheds, all extremely comfortable, as such places always are in winter. In summer, people, like our Cousins, who lived in more commodious dwellings, wondered how any body could live in such pent-up places, with such small windows, and so few of them, and with fire, and beds, and chairs, and tables all in one, or at most two rooms. And yet thousands of families in America are happy and healthy in log-cabins; and magistrates, and judges, and even senators have often lived in them. [...]

Near the gate which opened from the locust-tree avenue to the road stood two log-cabins. In the one lived Lotte, a German joiner, who only twelve-months before left his native land, and came here an emigrant with his old father and mother, his wife and two children, the eldest of whom, named Friedrich, was a pretty, fair-complexioned boy, very well behaved, and a great favourite of our cousins. The grown-up people, even before they could speak one word of English, bowed, and smiled, and said "*guten Tag*" whenever they met any of the family, which everybody understood; and as to little Friedrich, whether it was German or English that he and the Squire's children spoke, it was very intelligible to them.

The inhabitants of the other cabin were Germans also, but very unlike the Lottes. They were old residents, and their name was Brandenburg; and between their children, a boy and a girl, and our cousins there was, and had always been a great feud. Martin Brandenburg, the boy, threw stones at them, and called them ugly names, which greatly incensed them; and besides this, he would go into their fields and shoot their singing and other birds with his pistols, and his bow and arrows, which was very displeasing to our cousins, because it was their father's opinion that birds did a deal of good by devouring insects and worms and grubs in the fields; and for this reason, independently of the pleasure he took in hearing their songs and watching their peculiar habits, he never allowed them to be destroyed; and therefore they pulled up Brandenburg's traps whenever they found them, and this greatly displeased him. [...]

Such is a sketch of the house and friends of the little American Cousins; as to themselves, something more must be said. They were four in number; but three only make much figure in our pages. Will, the eldest, was nine; Florence between seven and eight; and Anna, or as she was called, Nanny, six. The fourth was the baby—the American-born, Cornelia, or Nelly, the pet, the darling of all; but with her, as we have said, we have very little to do. [...]

Figure 4.4 Frontispiece, *Our Cousins in Ohio. With Four Illustrations on Steel, From Original Designs by Anna Mary Howitt*, 2nd edn (London: A. W. Bennett, 1866). The image forecasts an episode when a family friend arrives in a 'Yankee jumper' sledge with jolly sleigh-bells. Courtesy HathiTrust.

From Chapter XIII. 'December'

It was in the commencement of this month, when, amidst all the plenty which surrounded them, the children first heard of the famine and awful suffering which prevailed in Ireland. Every one was speaking of it. [...] [I]t came to the children's ears; but it was hard for them, who only saw the earth bring forth abundantly, and every barn and store-house full to overflowing, at first to realise what was meant. Nanny, for instance, who heard so much of this "horrible famine" in Ireland, which destroyed thousands of men, women, and children, pictured to herself a huge monster, like an ancient dragon, which swallowed up whole provinces at a mouthful; and it was a long time before she could get this idea out of her head. At length, however, she, as well as the rest, were made perfectly to understand what this new and strange misery meant, and then their sympathy for the poor starving people was unspeakable. If they sate down to a remarkably good and plentiful dinner, they wished that the children of poor Ireland could do the same, or partake with them. If any of them were dissatisfied with what was set before them, the others would gravely lecture on the sinfulness of ingratitude when such thousands were wanting bread.

After the great talk of the famine, came the great talk of what America should do to relieve the sufferings of their distant kinspeople in Ireland; and subscription on subscription was set on foot to purchase provisions and other things for their relief. The children's purses at this time were empty enough. Willie now wished that he had not bought his beautiful jointed fishing-rod, and Florence her new fan. However, they were resolved to save anew, and to get all they could, that they too might have something to send. [...]

December 12th. — Ella helped the children to prepare little Christmas presents. As their money was to go to Ireland this year, they would have but very little to give away in presents. Florence, therefore, with Ella's help, made pincushions, needle-books, kettle-holders, spectacle wipers, and even iron-holders; for these cost nothing. [...]

December 24th.—Many a little present had this day to be completed; and even Nanny did wonders with her needle. Louise, the Lottes, Eberhard's people, and Bernard, were all remembered in some little gift or other. [...]

Late in the evening their mother sate with the children, and talked to them of the glorious music which the shepherds heard on the plains of Bethlehem, nearly eighteen centuries and a half ago, and of the beautiful array of angels which sang the divinest song which ever saluted human ears, and of the journey of the wondering men to behold that marvellous child whose birth-place was indicated by a heavenly star. The children listened to the words of their mother, and wished that they too could have heard the angelic anthem; and then they sang—

"When shepherds watched their flocks by night,
All seated on the ground,
The angel of the Lord came down,
And glory shone around."[30]

---

30 This popular hymn by Irish poet Nahum Tate (1652–1715) draws on an account of the Nativity in Luke 2: 8–14.

But their conversation did not end with the Saviour's birth merely: the mother spoke of his life, and how he laid his divine hands on the heads of little children and blessed them. She spoke of his death, and of the part which we all have in redemption through Him; and the children's hearts, like those of the disciples on their way to Emmaus, kindled as she spoke. Little Nelly even, who lay with her sweet head nestled on her mother's bosom, and looking with her dovelike eyes into her face, felt the effect of her holy words; and when, shortly afterwards, the beloved mother laid her in her little bed, she clasped her hands together, and exclaimed with a beaming countenance, "Good Jesus, bless little Nelly!"

The next morning all were up early. The Germans—Bernard, Eberhard, Heinrich, and their wives and children—were going to spend the day in the city. They were to go in the large covered wagon, and the children from The Cedars were to go with them, and to be brought back by them at night.

Willie was up by five o'clock, and Florence and Nanny were not long after him. The shoes on the hearth, the best shoes for the day's visiting, were found filled with presents. Queen Victoria and the Prince, and the wonderful windmill, and the trumpet, were there, and so many other things that the shoes would not hold them. Besides the brimful shoes, the little table near the hearth was covered with presents, of which nobody had any idea—none of the little folks at least. There were new dresses for them all—new silk-aprons for the little girls, even for Nelly—new winter-bonnets—new fur-tippets and muffs, and all sorts of things. Santa Claus must have been busy the night before! [...]

Among the other shoes stood also the best shoes of the beloved mother. That was really a surprise to her; and in one of them sate Willie's snow-white dove! How happy it made him to see that she was greatly pleased. She put it on the chimney piece of her own room; and it was the prettiest ornament there. [...]

At nine o'clock, off they went in the great covered wagon, seated among the German women and children; and each with a little present in their hand, for their friends in the city.

They were the only guests invited to dinner, but scarcely was this meal over, when other company began to arrive, and they kept arriving, and arriving, and arriving, until there were between thirty and forty. The furniture had all been removed from one large room; and here they played at all imaginable games— blind man's buff, turn the trencher, forfeits, and the rest,—and then supper was announced, and each little boy, taking a little girl by the hand, led her to the supper-table. And what a supper there was! There was tea and cakes, and fruit and sweetmeats, and pies of every possible kind, and cheesecakes and candies, and heaped-up plates of sugar-kisses wrapped in bright coloured paper with mottoes; and huge cakes covered with sugar; and there they sate eating and talking, and laughing, and the grown-up people waiting on them, and laughing, and as merry as anybody.

As soon as supper was over, it was announced to our cousins that Eberhard was waiting at the door with the wagon, and afterwards he had to call for the women and the children, so Willie and his sisters took their leave, and having called for the German women, they all drove off amid the most glorious Christmas moonlight, the Germans singing beautiful hymns as they drove along. [...]

December 29th.— The weather was remarkably mild and beautiful; it was like April in England. The children made new little gardens, and spent part of the morning in paving the little walks with pebbles. [...]

December 31st.— A great change now took place in the weather. It was a day of tremendous storms; and Ella read, and read, and read all day long in "Robinson Crusoe."

Willie cut shoe-pegs, and Florence sewed; they were again bent on earning another dollar for the Irish.

In the evening, spite of the storm, which still continued, a large parcel of New Year's gifts came up from the city. Books, and pictures, and toys— books both English and American.

Thanks to good friends! The children were unspeakably happy; and Nanny, as she folded her hands on her breast, and lifted up her large brown eyes, said, with the solemnity of true feeling,

"For these, and all our other good gifts, we ought to be thankful!"

So ended the Old Year at The Cedars.

Source text

Howitt, Mary, *Our Cousins in Ohio with Four Illustrations on Steel, from Original Designs by Anna Mary Howitt* (London: Darton & Co., 1849).

References

Hughes, Linda K., 'Mary Howitt and the Business of Poetry', *Victorian Periodicals Review* 50.2 (Summer 2017), 273–94.
Peterson, Linda H., 'Working Collaboratively: Mary Howitt and Anna Mary Howitt as Women of Letters', in *Becoming a Woman of Letters: Myths of Authorship and Facts of the Victorian Market* (Princeton, NJ: Princeton University Press, 2009), 96–130.

Henry Rowe Schoolcraft (1793–1864) and Jane J. Schoolcraft (1800–42)

From Personal Memoirs of a Residence of Thirty Years with the Indian Tribes on the American Frontiers *(1851)*

Henry Schoolcraft, an American author and ethnologist, was born on a farmstead on Black Creek, New York. In 1822, he commenced a nineteen-year career in the federal Indian service as the first agent at Sault Ste. Marie in today's Michigan. In 1823, he married Jane Johnston. Johnston's father was Irish-born fur trader John Johnston, whose wife, Susan Johnston, née Oshawguscodawayqua, came from a respected Ojibwe family and educated her daughter in Native traditions. With essential support from his wife and her family, Schoolcraft embarked on a formal study of Ojibwe language and oral literature, which he presented as *Algic Researches* (1839), a collection of Native American myths and legends aimed at white readers. That same year, having spent time in several northeastern US cities, the Schoolcrafts sent their children to boarding school before returning home to Michigan. Henry's translation of Jane's poem, presented below as it appeared within his 1851 *Personal Memoirs*, addressed this family event. Like other nineteenth-century printed versions of her poems, this one raises questions about the degree to which her husband – who often edited but also expanded her work when 'translating' – may have taken what today would be viewed as excessive control over her texts.

From **Personal Memoirs**

Mrs. Schoolcraft, having left her children at school, at Philadelphia and Princeton, remained pensive, and wrote the following lines in the Indian tongue, on parting from them, which I thought so just that I made a translation of them.

> Nyau nin de nain dum
> May kow e yaun in
> Ain dah nuk ki yaun
> Waus sa wa kom eg
> Ain dah nuk ki yaun
>
> Ne dau nis ainse e
> Ne gwis is ainse e
> Ishe nau gun ug wau
> Waus sa wa kom eg
>
> She gwau go sha ween
> Ba sho waud e we
> Nin zhe ka we yea
> Ishe ez hau jau yaun
> Ain dah nuk ke yaun
>
> Ain dah nuk ke yaun
> Nin zhe ke we yea
> Ishe ke way aun e
> Nyau ne gush kain dum

[Free Translation.][31]
Ah! when thought reverts to my country so dear,
My heart fills with pleasures, and throbs with a fear:
My country, my country, my own native land,

---

31 In Schoolcraft's *Personal Memoirs*, the original Ojibwe poem and Mr Schoolcraft's free translation are untitled. Robert Dale Parker gave the title 'On leaving my children John and Jane at School, in the Atlantic states, and preparing to return to the interior' to Mrs Schoolcraft's text in his 2005 edition of Jane Schoolcraft's works, where he also offered a new translation of her poem, seeking to align more closely with her original. By comparatively reading Schoolcraft's and Parker's translations, we see how Mr Schoolcraft re-framed Jane's original, which precedes Henry's translation in *Personal Memoirs* (682).

So lovely in aspect, in features so grand,
Far, far in the West. What are cities to me,
Oh! land of my mother, compared unto thee?

Fair land of the lakes! thou are blest to my sight,
With thy beaming bright waters, and landscapes of light;
The breeze and the murmur, the dash and the roar,
That summer and autumn cast over the shore,
They spring to my thoughts, like the lullaby tongue,
That soothed me to slumber when youthful and young.

One feeling more strongly still binds me to thee,
There roved my forefathers, in liberty free—
There shook they the war lance, and sported the plume,
Ere Europe had cast o'er this country a gloom;
Nor thought they that kingdoms more happy could be,
White lords of a land so resplendent and free.

Yet it is not alone that my country is fair,
And my home and my friends are inviting me there;
While they beckon me onward, my heart is still here,
With my sweet lovely daughter, and bonny boy dear:
And oh! what's the joy that a home can impart,
Removed from the dear ones[32] who cling to my heart.

It is learning that calls them; but tell me, can schools
Repay for my love, or give nature new rules?
They may teach them the lore of the wit and the sage,
To be grave in their youth, and be gay in their age;
But ah! my poor heart, what are schools to thy view,
While severed from children thou lovest so true!

I return to my country, I haste on my way,
For duty commands me, and duty must sway;
Yet I leave the bright land where my little ones dwell,
With a sober regret, and a bitter farewell;
For there I must leave the dear jewels I love,
The dearest of gifts from my Master above.
New York, *March 18th*, 1839.

Source text

Schoolcraft, Henry Rowe, *Personal Memoirs of a Residence of Thirty Years with the Indian Tribes on the American Frontiers: with Brief Notices of Passing Events, Facts and Opinions* (Philadelphia: Lippincott, Grambo and Co., 1851).

---

32 The Schoolcraft children, Jane (age eleven) and Johnston (age nine)

References

Cavalier, Christine R., 'Jane Johnston Schoolcraft's Sentimental Lessons: Native Literary Collaboration and Resistance', *MELUS: Multi-Ethnic Literature of the U.S.* 38.1 (2013), 98–118.

Parker, Robert Dale (ed.), *The Sound the Stars Make Rushing Through the Sky: The Writings of Jane Johnston Schoolcraft* (Philadelphia, PA: University of Pennsylvania Press, 2007).

Schneider, Bethany, 'Not for Citation: Jane Johnston Schoolcraft's Synchronic Strategies', *ESQ: A Journal of the American Renaissance* 54 (2008), 111–44.

Mary Seacole (1805–81)

From Wonderful Adventures of Mrs. Seacole in Many Lands *(1857)*

With a multifaceted identity that has led her to be 'a figurehead for a number of different groups including Jamaicans, black British people and nurses' (Salih, 171), Mary Seacole is transatlantic through her early Caribbean-to-England migration; transnational via her travels to 'many lands', including Central America and Crimea; and, increasingly, a site of intersectional identity contested among scholars (Salih, 174). Salih calls for focusing on Seacole's own presentations of self and context, especially when analysing Seacole's time as a Crimean hotel manager and wartime nurse for the empire. Thus, we draw from the memoirist's recollections of Christmas in Crimea to spotlight how she situated herself in a context of British cultural practices as transportable far beyond the UK through individuals linked to a militarised global empire. Aligning with a Dickensian holiday vision, Seacole's mid-century account highlighted preparations of a traditional menu of English Christmas foods for her hotel's clients and visiting with hospitalised soldiers in a season when they longed for ties to home.

After work in Crimea, Seacole returned to Britain destitute and encountered the results of private, yet influential complaints from Florence Nightingale about the Jamaican-British nurse's purportedly 'improper' behaviour abroad. Associating this stereotyping characterisation with prejudice linked to Seacole's mixed-race identity, Tan-Feng Chang identifies an underlying conflict over who qualified for a gendered role supporting Britain's empire (528). If, as Chang suggests, a goal of *Wonderful Adventures* had been to assert a 'Creole' yet British-sanctioned maternal subjectivity, then one anecdote articulating that aspiration is Seacole's revisiting her Christmas cooking and nursing of soldiers as a site of domesticity-invoking maternal agency.

From Wonderful Adventures of Mrs. Seacole in Many Lands

So Christmas came, and with it pleasant memories of home and of home comforts. With it came also news of home—some not of the most pleasant description—and kind wishes from absent friends. "A merry Christmas to you," writes one, "and many of them. Although you will not write to us, we see your name frequently in the newspapers, from which we judge that you are strong and hearty. All your old Jamaica friends are delighted to hear of you, and say that you are an honour to the Isle of Springs."

I wonder if the people of other countries are as fond of carrying with them every-where their home habits as the English. I think not. I think there was something purely and essentially English in the determination of the camp to spend the Christmas-day of 1855 after the good old "home" fashion. It showed itself weeks before the eventful day. In the dinner parties which were got up—in the orders sent to England—in the supplies which came out, and in the many applications made to the hostess of the British Hotel for plum-puddings and mince-pies. The demand for them, and the material necessary to manufacture them, was marvellous. I can fancy that if returns could be got at of the flour, plums, currants, and eggs consumed on Christmas-day in the out-of-the-way Crimean peninsula, they would astonish us. One determination appeared to have taken possession of every mind—to spend the festive day with the mirth and jollity which the changed prospect of affairs warranted; and the recollection of a year ago, when death and misery were the camp's chief guests, only served to heighten this resolve.

For three weeks previous to Christmas-day, my time was fully occupied in mak-ing preparations for it. Pages of my books are filled with orders for plum-puddings and mince-pies, besides which I sold an immense quantity of raw material to those who were too far off to send down for the manufactured article on Christmas-day, and to such purchasers I gave a plain recipe for their guidance. Will the reader take any interest in my Crimean Christmas-pudding? It was plain, but decidedly good. However, you shall judge for yourself:—"One pound of flour, three-quarters of a pound of raisins, three-quarters of a pound of fat pork, chopped fine, two table-spoonfuls of sugar, a little cinnamon or chopped lemon, half-pint of milk or water; mix these well together, and boil four hours."

From an early hour in the morning until long after the night had set in, were I and my cooks busy endeavouring to supply the great demand for Christmas fare. We had considerable difficulty in keeping our engagements, but by substituting mince-pies for plum-puddings, in a few cases, we succeeded. The scene in the crowded store, and even in the little over-heated kitchen, with the officers' servants, who came in for their masters' dinners, cannot well be described. Some were impatient themselves, others dreaded their masters' impatience as the appointed dinner hour passed by— all combined by entreaties, threats, cajolery, and fun to drive me distracted. Angry cries for the major's plum-pudding, which was to have been ready an hour ago, alter-nated with an entreaty that I should cook the captain's mince-pies to a turn—"Sure, he likes them well done, ma'am. Bake 'em as brown as your own purty face, darlint."

I did not get my dinner until eight o'clock, and then I dined in peace off a fine wild turkey or bustard, shot for me on the marshes by the Tchernaya.[33] It weighed twenty-two pounds, and, although somewhat coarse in colour, had a capital flavour.

Upon New Year's-day I had another large cooking of plum-puddings and mince-pies; this time upon my own account. I took them to the hospital of the Land Trans-port Corps, to remind the patients of the home comforts they longed so much for. It was a sad sight to see the once fine fellows, in their blue gowns, lying quiet and still, and reduced to such a level of weakness and helplessness. They all seemed glad for the little home tokens I took them.

---

33 A river in Crimea where a battle was fought in 1855

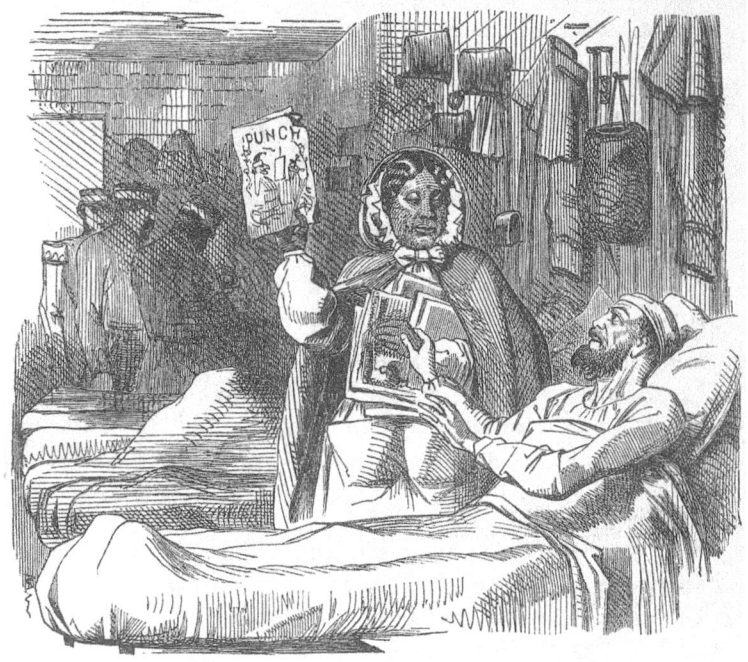

Figure 4.5 'Mother Seacole' carries *Punch* to a hospitalised soldier in
'Our Own Vivandière', *Punch* 32 (30 May 1857), 221.
Courtesy Mary Couts Burnett Library, TCU.

There was one patient who had been a most industrious and honest fellow, and
who did not go into the hospital until long and wearing illness compelled him. I was
particularly anxious to look after him, but I found him very weak and ill. I stayed with
him until evening, and before I left him, kind fancy had brought to his bedside his
wife and children from his village-home in England, and I could hear him talking to
them in a low and joyful tone. Poor, poor fellow! the New Year so full of hope and
happiness had dawned upon him, but he did not live to see the wild flowers spring
up peacefully through the war-trodden sod before Sebastopol.[34]

Source text

Seacole, Mrs, *Wonderful Adventures of Mrs. Seacole in Many Lands, with an Introductory Preface by W. H. Russell, Esq., The "Times" Correspondent in the Crimea* (London: James Blackwood, 1857).

References

Chang, Tan-Feng, 'Creolizing the White Woman's Burden: Mary Seacole Playing "Mother" at the Colonial Crossroads between Panama and Crimea', *College Literature* 44.4 (Fall 2017), 527–57.

34 A large city on the Crimean Peninsula

Salih, Sara, '"A Gallant Heart to the Empire", Autoethnography and Imperial Identity in Mary Seacole's *Wonderful Adventures*', *Philological Quarterly* 83.2 (2004), 171–95.

Harriet Ann Jacobs (c.1813–97)

From The Deeper Wrong; or, Incidents in the Life of a Slave Girl *(1862)*

Harriet Jacobs was born enslaved in North Carolina. After years of hiding from her abusive owners in her grandmother's attic, she escaped in 1842 to the North. Her freedom was tenuous, however. Her former owners tracked down her whereabouts and almost recaptured her in 1852, when her then-employer Cornelia Willis (wife of editor Nathaniel Parker Willis) arranged to have an agent of the Colonization Society pay for Jacobs's freedom (Yellin, 115–16).

Active in abolitionist circles, Jacobs launched her authorship by drawing on her own experiences as an enslaved person to write several anonymous letters for periodical publication (Yellin, 120–4). Encouraged by supporter Amy Post to tell a fuller life story for the anti-slavery cause, she began composing *Incidents* in 1853, while still working at the Hudson River home of the Willis family. Having completed a draft by 1858, Jacobs was unable to secure a publisher for her book until Lydia Maria Child, the celebrated author and abolitionist, agreed to write a preface (Yellin, 140). Child's investment in the project expanded, so that she edited Jacobs's text and ultimately arranged for its publication in Boston in 1861, under the pseudonym Linda Brent. The British edition of Jacobs's narrative, published as *The Deeper Wrong*, appeared in 1862, with the help of the London Emancipation Committee. The passage excerpted here gives an account of Jacobs's visit to England in 1845 with Willis (called Mr Bruce) and his family. One theme contrasts English domesticity and conditions of labour with those for enslaved people in the United States.

From The Deeper Wrong, or, Incidents in the Life of a Slave Girl

XXXVII. A Visit to England

In the spring, sad news came to me. Mrs. Bruce was dead.[35] Never again, in this world, should I see her gentle face, or hear her sympathizing voice. I had lost an excellent friend, and little Mary had lost a tender mother. Mr. Bruce wished the child to visit some of her mother's relatives in England, and he was desirous that I should take charge of her.[36] The little motherless one was accustomed to me, and attached

---

35 Mrs Bruce is the pseudonym for Mary Stace Willis, the first wife of Nathaniel Parker Willis.
36 This first of three trips Jacobs would take to England occurred in 1845–6.

to me, and I thought she would be happier in my care than in that of a stranger. I could also earn more in this way than I could by my needle. So I put Benny to a trade, and left Ellen to remain in the house with my friend and go to school.[37]

We sailed from New York, and arrived in Liverpool after a pleasant voyage of twelve days. We proceeded directly to London, and took lodgings at the Adelaide Hotel. The supper seemed to me less luxurious than those I had seen in American hotels; but my situation was indescribably more pleasant. For the first time in my life I was in a place where I was treated according to my deportment, without reference to my complexion. I felt as if a great millstone had been lifted from my breast. Ensconced in a pleasant room, with my dear little charge, I laid my head on my pillow, for the first time, with the delightful consciousness of pure, unadulterated freedom.

As I had constant care of the child, I had little opportunity to see the wonders of that great city; but I watched the tide of life that flowed through the streets, and found it a strange contrast to the stagnation in our Southern towns. Mr. Bruce took his little daughter to spend some days with friends in Oxford Crescent, and of course it was necessary for me to accompany her. I had heard much of the systematic method of English education, and I was very desirous that my dear Mary should steer straight in the midst of so much propriety. I closely observed her little playmates and their nurses, being ready to take any lessons in the science of good management. The children were more rosy than American children, but I did not see that they differed materially in other respects. They were like all children— sometimes docile and sometimes wayward.

We next went to Steventon, in Berkshire.[38] It was a small town, said to be the poorest in the county. I saw men working in the fields for six shillings, and seven shillings, a week, and women for sixpence, and sevenpence, a day, out of which they boarded themselves. Of course they lived in the most primitive manner; it could not be otherwise, where a woman's wages for an entire day were not sufficient to buy a pound of meat. They paid very low rents, and their clothes were made of the cheapest fabrics, though much better than could have been procured in the United States for the same money. I had heard much about the oppression of the poor in Europe. The people I saw around me were, many of them, among the poorest poor. But when I visited them in their little thatched cottages, I felt that the condition of even the meanest and most ignorant among them was vastly superior to the condition of the most favored slaves in America. They labored hard; but they were not ordered out to toil while the stars were in the sky, and driven and slashed by an overseer, through heat and cold, till the stars shone out again. Their homes were very humble; but they were protected by law. No insolent patrols could come, in the dead of night, and flog them at their pleasure. The father, when he closed his cottage door, felt safe with his family around him. No master or overseer could come and take from him his wife, or his daughter. They must separate to earn their living; but the parents knew where their children were going, and could communicate with them by letters. The relations of husband and wife, parent and child, were too sacred for the richest noble in the land to violate with impunity. Much was being done to enlighten these poor people. Schools were established among them, and

---

37 Benny and Ellen are pseudonyms for Harriet's children, Joseph and Louisa Matilda, whose father was an unmarried white lawyer, Samuel Tredwell Sawyer.
38 A village now in Oxfordshire, England, but part of Berkshire prior to 1974

benevolent societies[39] were active in efforts to ameliorate their condition. There was no law forbidding them to learn to read and write; and if they helped each other in spelling out the Bible, they were in no danger of thirty-nine lashes, as was the case with myself and poor, pious, old uncle Fred. I repeat that the most ignorant and the most destitute of these peasants was a thousand fold better off than the most pampered American slave.

I do not deny that the poor are oppressed in Europe. I am not disposed to paint their condition so rose-colored as the Hon. Miss Murray paints the condition of the slaves in the United States.[40] A small portion of *my* experience would enable her to read her own pages with anointed eyes. If she were to lay aside her title, and, instead of visiting among the fashionable, become domesticated, as a poor govern-ess, on some plantation in Louisiana or Alabama, she would see and hear things that would make her tell quite a different story.

My visit to England is a memorable event in my life, from the fact of my having there received strong religious impressions. The contemptuous manner in which the communion had been administered to colored people, in my native place; the church membership of Dr. Flint,[41] and others like him; and the buying and selling of slaves, by professed ministers of the gospel, had given me a prejudice against the Episcopal church. The whole service seemed to me a mockery and a sham. But my home in Ste-venton was in the family of a clergyman, who was a true disciple of Jesus. The beauty of his daily life inspired me with faith in the genuineness of Christian professions. Grace entered my heart, and I knelt at the communion table, I trust, in true humility of soul.

I remained abroad ten months, which was much longer than I had anticipated. During all that time, I never saw the slightest symptom of prejudice against color. Indeed, I entirely forgot it, till the time came for us to return to America.[42]

Source text

[Jacobs, Harriet Ann], *The Deeper Wrong; or, Incidents in the Life of a Slave Girl. Written by Herself*, ed. L[ydia] Maria Child (London: W. Tweedie, 1862).

References

Jacobs, Harriet, *Incidents in the Life of a Slave Girl: Contexts, Criticisms*, eds Nellie Y. McKay and Frances Smith Foster (New York: W. W. Norton, 2001).

Murray, Amelia M., *Letters from the United States, Cuba and Canada* (New York: G. P. Putnam & Co., 1856).

---

39 Benevolent societies were locally organised charitable institutions for relieving poverty.

40 Amelia Matilda Murray (1795–1884) was a British aristocrat and botanist who had written: 'With all my love of liberty, if I was of the black race, I should much prefer being a slave upon one of the Southern plantations than any free black man or woman I ever met in America' (274).

41 Jacobs's pseudonym for her enslaver in North Carolina

42 Salenius argues Jacobs's second and third journeys to England helped her extend a version of 'sisterhood' she had developed with white women like Amy Post and Lydia Maria Child in the US (184). During her 1858 trip, Jacobs formed a friendship with Amelia Thompson Chesson, daughter of MP George Thompson, a bond Salenius views as both 'blurr[ing] boundaries between sisterhood and friendship' and fostering political solidarity (185). Her final visit in 1867–8 raised money for a school she and her daughter would open in Savannah, Georgia, yet through some social encounters revealed British women's racial prejudices (187).

Salenius, Sirpa, 'Transatlantic Interracial Sisterhoods: Sarah Remond, Ellen Craft, and Harriet Jacobs in England', *Frontiers: A Journal of Women Studies* 38.1 (2017), 166–96.

Yellin, Jean Fagan, *Harriet Jacobs: A Life* (New York: Basic Civitas Books, 2004).

William Hepworth Dixon (1821–79)

From **New America** *(1867)*

Nineteenth-century print texts addressing Mormon polygamy ranged from impassioned attacks by critics to determined defences of plural marriage by members of the Latter-Day Saints (LDS) community. Our excerpt addressing this controversial topic comes from William Dixon, who served for a time as editor of London's *The Athenaeum* and whose multifaceted oeuvre included works on political history as well as travel writing. One travelogue, *New America*, devoted substantial content to his visit to Salt Lake City and presented both praise for LDS industriousness and questions about Mormons' domestic gender politics, particularly around plural marriage.

Dixon was not the first author to situate an assessment of LDS plural marriage in a transatlantic frame, but he sought a relatively balanced view in comparison with other British authors. Perhaps more typical in its angry approach was John Bowes's *Mormonism Exposed* (1850), which, as early as its subtitle, linked leaders like Joseph Smith with 'licentious abominations'. For Bowes, polygamy was just one example of the 'knavery' exercised by Mormons who came to England purportedly as missionaries but actually seeking to defraud naive converts of money and moral domestic life—a situation Bowes cast as further exacerbated for individuals enticed to relocate to the LDS colony in Utah (64).

By the early 1850s, Latter-Day Saints leaders were mounting public defences 'not only scriptural but practical and scientific' (Hardy and Erickson, 40). Jesse Haven's 1854 pamphlet, published in Cape Town during his missionary service there, joined this effort to counter 'slanderous reports, and scandalous misrepresentations in regard to the doctrine of the Plurality of Wives' (1). Rejecting depictions linking LDS polygamy and licentiousness, Haven's eight-page defence highlighted the heaven-sent mandate to be fruitful and multiply. He also stressed that Latter-Day Saints envisioned 'marrying for time and for all eternity', thereby potentially achieving 'a re-union with their companions in the morning of the resurrection and an eternal exaltation in the kingdom of God' (4–5).

Dixon's 1867 inquiry into the practice included positive explanations from LDS Utah leaders on the one hand, alongside his more sceptical portrayals of wives and unmarried girls on the other. Dixon identified some women he interviewed as English converts, and he contrasted their domestic experiences with those of women in his home country.

An unsigned review in *All the Year Round* dubbed Dixon's book 'careful' and 'wise', while underscoring its depiction of polygamy as undermining family life (252). By stoking negative views of Salt Lake as 'the harem of the young Jerusalem of the West' and 'polygamous life' as leaving women 'Saddened, secluded' (254), Charles Dickens's periodical strengthened a critical transatlantic stance that would memorably reappear within Utah-set episodes in Arthur Conan Doyle's 1887 launch of the detective Sherlock Holmes, *A Study in Scarlet*.

From 'Polygamous Society', New America

On the political strength which this fashion of plurality lends to the Saints of Salt Lake City, a few words may be said. Two questions present themselves, – In the first place, has the promise of a plurality of wives proved to be a good bribe, inducing men of a certain class to join the Mormon Church? And, in the second place, has the practice of plurality shown itself to be a means by which, when converts have been won, they can be made to multiply in numbers far beyond the ordinary rate?

To the first query, only one answer can be truly given. Name the motive as you please; call it, with the Saints, desire of the spirit; call it, with the Gentiles, desire of the flesh; the fact will remain—that a license for making love to many women, for sealing them as wives, for gathering them into secluded harems, has acted in the past, and is acting in the present, as a powerful and seductive bribe. [...]

To the second query two answers may be returned. In a fixed society, like that of Turkey, of Syria, of Egypt, the existence of polygamy would have no great influence on the powers of increase. [...]

[...] The question, however, is, not as to the growth of a whole nation; but as to that of a particular family, of a particular community, of a mere sect within the boundaries of that nation. Even in Arabia, it is clear that if a particular sheikh could invent some means of getting from other tribes a great many of their women, until he had enough females in his power to give three wives to every male in his camp, the tribe of that sheikh would increase in numbers faster than their neighbors who had only one wife apiece. This is something like the case in America with the Saints. Their own society could not give them the plurality of wives which they announce as the social law of all coming time. But granted that, by either good or evil means, they could get the women into their church, it is idle to deny that the possession of such a treasure gives them enormous powers of increase. One man may be the father of a hundred children; one woman can hardly be the mother of a score. [...]

It is not an easy thing to count the number of children in the different households at Salt Lake. [...] Every house seems full; wherever we see a woman, she is nursing; and in every house we enter two or three infants in arms are shown to us. This valley is, indeed, a true baby land. For a man to have twenty boys and girls in his house is a common fact. A merchant with whom we were dining yesterday, could not tell us the number of his children until he had consulted a book then lying on his desk. One of his wives, a nice English lady, with the usual baby at her breast, smiled sweet reproof on his ignorance; but the fact was so; and it was only after counting and consulting that he could give us the exact number of his descendants. This patriarch is thirty-three years old.

From 'Woman at Salt Lake', New America

And what, as regards the woman herself, is the visible issue of this strange experiment in social and family life? [...]

In my opinion, Mormonism is not a religion for woman. I will not say it degrades her, for the term degradation is open to abuse; but it certainly lowers her, according to our Gentile ideas, in the social scale. In fact, woman is not in society here at all. The long blank walls, the embowered cottages, the empty windows, doorways, and verandas, all suggest to an English eye something of the jealousy, the seclusion, the subordination of a Moslem harem, rather than the gayety and freedom of a Christian home. Men rarely see each other at home, still more rarely in the company of their wives. Seclusion seems to be a fashion wherever polygamy is the law. Now, by itself, and apart from all doctrines and moralities, the habit of secluding women from society must tend to dim their sight and dull their hearing; for if conversation quickens men, it still more quickens women; and we can roundly say, after experience in many households at Salt Lake, that these Mormon ladies have lost the practice and the power of taking part even in such light talk as animates a dinner-table and a drawing-room. [...]

I am convinced that the practice of marrying a plurality of wives is not popular with the female Saints. Besides what I have seen and heard from Mormon wives, themselves living in polygamous families, I have talked, alone and freely, with eight or nine different girls, all of whom have lived at Salt Lake for two of three years. They are undoubted Mormons, who have made many sacrifices for their religion; but after seeing the family life of their fellow-Saints, they have one and all become firmly hostile to polygamy. [...] All of these girls prefer to remain single,—to live a life of labor and dependence—as servants, chambermaids, milliners, charwomen,—to a life of comparative ease and leisure in the harem of a Mormon bishop. [...]

It is an open question in Utah whether it is better for a plural household to be gathered under one roof or not. Young[43] sets the example of unity, so far at least as his actual wives and children are concerned. A few old ladies, who have been sealed to him for heaven, whether in his own name or in that of Joseph, dwell in cottages apart; but the dozen women, who share his couch, who are mothers of his children, live in one block close to another, dine at one table, and join in the family prayers. Taylor,[44] the apostle, keeps his families in separate cottages and orchards; two of his wives only live in his principal house; the rest have tenements of their own. Every man is free to arrange his household as he likes; so long as he avoids contention, and promotes the public peace. [...]

[...] I cannot wonder that girls who remember their English homes should shrink from marriage in this strange community, even though they have accepted the doctrine of Young, that plurality is the law of heaven and of God. "I believe it's right," said to me a rosy English damsel, who has been three years in Utah, "and I think it is good for those who like it; but it is not good for me, and I will not have it."

"But if Young should command you?"

---

43 Brigham Young (1801–77), second president of the LDS church after founder Joseph Smith (1805–44)

44 John Taylor (1808–87), born in England, immigrated to Canada in 1832, becoming an LDS apostle. After missionary service back in Britain, he settled in Utah, eventually becoming the only president of the church not born in the US.

"He won't!" said the girl with a toss of her golden curls; "and if he were to do so, I would not. A girl can please herself whether she marries or not; and I, for one, will never go into a house where there is another wife."

"Do the wives dislike it?"

"Some don't, most do. They take it for their religion; I can't say any woman likes it. Some women live very comfortably together; not many; most have their tiffs and quarrels, though their husbands may never know of them. No woman likes to see a new wife come into the house."

A Saint would tell you that such a damsel as my rosy friend is only half a Mormon yet; he would probably ask you to reject such evidence as trumpery and temporary; and plead that you can have no fair means of judging such an institution as polygamy, until you are able to study its effects in the fourth and fifth generation.

Meanwhile, the judgment which we have formed about it from what we have seen and heard may be expressed in a few words. It finds a new place for women, which is not the place she occupies in the society of England and the United States. It transfers her from the drawing-room to the kitchen, and when it finds her in the nursery it locks her in it. We may call such a change a degradation; the Mormons call it a reformation. We do not say that any of these Mormon ladies have been worse in their moralities and their spiritualities by the change; probably they have not; but in everything that concerns their grace, order, rank, and representation in society, they are unquestionably lowered, according to our standards. Male Saints declare that in this city women have become more domestic, wifely, motherly, than they are among the Gentiles; and that what they have lost in show, in brilliancy, in accomplishment, that have gained in virtue and in service. To me, the very best women appear to be little more than domestic drudges, never rising into the rank of real friends and companions of their lords. Taylor's daughters waited on us at table; two pretty, elegant, English-looking girls. We should have preferred standing behind their chairs and helping them to dainties of fowl and cake; but the Mormon, like the Moslem, keeps a heavy hand on his female folks. Women at Salt Lake are made to keep their place. A girl must address her father as "Sir," and she would hardly presume to sit down in his presence until she had received his orders.

Source text

Dixon, William Hepworth, *New America* (Philadelphia: J. B. Lippincott, 1867).

References

Bowes, John S., *Mormonism Exposed, in its swindling and licentious abominations, refuted in its principles, and in the claims of its head, the Modern Mohammed, Joseph Smith, Who Is Proved to Have Been a Deceiver, and No Prophet of God* (London: E. Ward, 1850[?]).

Hardy, B. Carmon and Dan Erickson, '"Regeneration—Now and Evermore!": Mormon Polygamy and the Physical Rehabilitation of Humankind', *Journal of the History of Sexuality* 10.1 (January 2001), 40–61.

Haven, Jesse, *Celestical [sic] Marriage and the Plurality of Wives* (Cape Town: W. Foelscher, 1854).

'New America', *All the Year Round* (9 March 1867), 252–6.

Whittaker, David J., 'Early Mormon Polygamy Defenses', *Journal of Mormon History* 11 (1984), 43–63.

Sara Willis Parton [Fanny Fern] (1811–72)

From 'Mistakes About Our Children' from
Folly As It Flies (1868)

In a round-up of noteworthy autumn 1872 deaths, Britain's *St. James's Magazine* included an enthusiastic salute to Sara Parton, 'better known by her *nom de plume* of "Fanny Fern"'. For this appreciative English report, Fern's position as a best-selling transatlantic author was all the more noteworthy in that she had not begun publishing 'until she was 40 years of age' ('Obituary'). Discreetly avoiding direct reference to what, earlier in her life, had been a scandalous divorce from her second husband (her first having died young) and longstanding conflicts with her influential publisher brother, Nathaniel P. Willis, the London magazine profile aligned itself with what was, by then, the dominant view of Fern: 'well-known authoress' of popular domestic sketches, widely read in both England and America.

Although often celebrated for her satire on social norms constraining women, Fern blended those barbed critiques with sentimental pieces honouring the cultural work of mothers and a reverence for childhood. Notably, one English review of an early collection, *Fern Leaves* (1853), predicted she might be appreciated more in Britain in the long run for her 'saucy' and 'funny' sketches than for her more sentimental ones 'devoted to sweet wives, dying infants, the flowers in the field, the clouds in the sky,—and such topics'. But Fern wove both elements into sketches like the one below, from a collection published in New York and London.

From 'Mistakes About Our Children'

[...] I wonder is it foreordained[45] that there shall be one child in every family whom "nobody can do anything with?" Who tears around the paternal pasture with its heels in the air, looking at rules, as a colt does at fences, as good things to jump over. We all know that the poor thing must be "broken in," and all its graceful curvetings[46] sobered down to a monotonous jog-trot; that it must be taught to bear heavy burdens, and to toil up many a steep ascent at the touch of the spur; but who that has climbed the weary height does not pass the halter round the neck of the pretty creature with a half-sigh, that its happy day of careless freedom should be soon ended?[47]

---

45 Appointed or decreed beforehand, by God or Fate
46 Prancings
47 Fern's dedication of the *Folly* collection to her longtime publisher, Robert Bonner, is striking in the context of this sketch's opening metaphor on taming a recalcitrant young girl: 'For fourteen years, the team of Bonner and Fern, has trotted over the road at 2.40 pace, without a snap of the harness, or a hitch of the wheels. –Plenty of oats, and a skilful rein, the secret'. Bonner, *New York Ledger* editor, had made Fern the best-paid US columnist of her day.

How it bounds away from you, making you almost glad that your attempt was a failure; how lovingly your eye follows it, as it makes the swift breathless circle and stops at a safe distance to nod you defiance. Something of all this every loving parent has felt, while trying to reduce to order the child whom "nobody can do anything with."

Geography, grammar and history seem to be put into one ear, only to go out the other. The multiplication table might as well be written in Arabic, for any idea it conveys, or lodges, if conveyed, in the poor thing's head. Temperate, torrid, and frigid zones may all be of a temperature, for all she can remember, and her mother might have been present at the creation of the world, or at the birth of the Author of it, for aught she can chronologically be brought to see.

But look! she is tired of play, and has taken up her pencil to draw; she has had no instruction; but peep over her shoulder and follow her pencil; there is the true artist touch in that little sketch, though she does not know it—a freedom, a boldness which teaching may regulate, never impart. Now she is tired of drawing and takes up a volume of poems, far beyond the comprehension, one would think, of a child of her years, and though she often miscalls a word, and knows little and cares less about commas and semi-colons, yet not the finest touch of humor or pathos escapes her, and the poet would be lucky, were he always sure of so appreciative a reader. She might tell you that France was bounded south by the Gulf of Mexico, but you yourself could not criticise Dickens or Thackeray with more discrimination.[48]

Down goes the book, and she is on the tips of her toes pirouetting. She has never seen a dancing-school, nor need she; perfectly modeled machinery cannot but move harmoniously; she does not know, as she floats about, that she is an animated poem. Now she is tired of dancing, and she throws herself into an old armchair, in an attitude an artist might copy, and commences to sing; she is ignorant of quavers, crotchets and semi-breves, of tenors, baritones and sopranos, and yet you, who have heard them with rapturous encores, stop to listen to her simple melody.

Now she is down in the kitchen playing cook; she turns a beef steak as if she had been brought up in a restaurant, and washes dishes for fun, as if it had been always sober earnest; singing, dancing and drawing the cook's portrait at intervals, and all equally well done.

Now send that child to any school in the land, where "Moral Science"[49] is hammered remorselessly and uselessly into curly heads, and she would be pronounced an incorrigible dunce. Idiotically stupid parrot-girls would ride over her shrinking, sensitive shame-facedness, rough-shod. She would be kept after school, kept in during recess, and have a discouraging list of bad recitation marks as long as Long Island; get a crooked spine, grow ashamed of throwing snow-balls, have a chronic headache, and an incurable disgust of teachers and schools, as well she might.

She is like a wild rose, creeping here, climbing there, blossoming where you least expect it, on some rough stone wall or gnarled trunk, at its own free, graceful will. You may dig it up and transplant it into your formal garden if you like, but you would never know it more for the luxuriant wild-rose, this "child whom nobody can do anything with."

---

48 Fern suggests here that the child can interpret British authors Charles Dickens and William Thackeray with as much skill as her parent. The satirist's invoking these two writers affirms how popular major English authors were in the US in her day.

49 Possibly Fern references US writer Francis Wayland's textbook, based on lectures he gave as President of Brown University, published in 1835 and adopted in many schoolrooms.

Some who read this may ask, and properly, is such a child never to know the restraint of rule? I would be the last to answer the negative, nor (and here it seems to me the great agony of outraged childhood comes in) would I have parents or teachers stretch or dwarf children of all sorts, sizes and capacities, on the same narrow Procrustean[50] bed of scholastic or parental rule. No farmer plants his celery and potatoes in the same spot, and expects it to bear good fruit. Some vegetables he shields from the rude touch, the rough wind, the blazing sun; he knows that each requires different and appropriate nurture, according to its capacities. Should they who have the care of the immortal be less wise?

"You have too much imagination, you should try to crush it out," was said many years ago to the writer in her school-days, by one who should have known that "He who seeth the end from the beginning,"[51] bestows *no* faculty to be "crushed out;" that this very faculty it is which has placed the writer, at this moment, beyond the necessity of singing like so many of her sex, the weary "Song of the Shirt."[52]

Source text

Fern, Fanny. *Folly As It Flies* (London: S. Low; New York: G. W. Carleton, 1868).

References

[Fern, Fanny], *Beauties of Fanny Fern; with a Brief Sketch of Her Genius and Writings* (London: Knight and Son, 1855).
'Obituary of the Month', *The St. James's Magazine* 10 (October 1872), 388.
'Our Library Table: *Fern Leaves from Fanny's Portfolio*', *The Athenaeum* (22 October 1853), 1254.

From 'Home: The Byron Scandal' in *Public Opinion* (1869)

Public Opinion, published weekly in London from 1861 to 1951, sought to provide 'a comprehensive summary of the press throughout the world on all important current topics'. In 1869, the topic of 'The Byron Scandal' undeniably fit that bill. Transatlantic articles that were revisited in the periodical's mid-September issue arose from Harriet Beecher Stowe's recently published story on Lady Byron, appearing in both England (*Macmillan's*) and the US (*Atlantic Monthly*).

Stowe had met Lady Byron when travelling abroad in the 1850s' wake of *Uncle Tom's Cabin*'s creating another kind of sensation as a best-selling anti-slavery narrative. As a youthful reader, Stowe had idolised Byron. So,

---

50 Enforcing uniformity without regard to natural variation or individuality
51 Biblical reference: Isaiah 46: 10
52 A poem by US writer Thomas Hood written in 1843, 'Song of the Shirt' depicts a care-worn seamstress trying to keep her spirits up as she works many hours but generates only limited earnings.

the account his former wife gave of their marriage – particularly her claim of his incest with his sister (Augusta Leigh) – surely horrified the American author. Nonetheless, she counselled dignified silence. But when a biography of Lord Byron appearing after both his and Lady Byron's deaths cast him as a romantic hero and his wife as a shrew, Stowe spoke out, first in her *Atlantic/Macmillan's* article and later in an 1870 book.

T. Austin Graham suggests this defence of Lady Byron actually aimed at a more comprehensive target: women's rights. Indeed, reading Stowe's text today, through a gender studies lens alert to movements like #MeToo, illuminates her argument as a complaint against the limited options for redress then available to married women, however grievous a husband's behaviour. Yet, for Graham, sensation overshadowed any larger liberatory goals, because of 'the inflammatory means by which Stowe made her point' (173). Graham further argues that, though the *Atlantic* lost many subscribers, it was Stowe's career that never recovered.

Indeed, *Public Opinion*'s roundup of response stories demonstrates how much Stowe's writing on the Byrons violated shared transatlantic norms about gendered propriety, including a commitment to home as an inviolably private space and a related unwillingness to trust women's reports of abuse.

From 'Home[53]: The Byron Scandal' in Public Opinion[54]

(*Daily Telegraph*, Sept. 6)

Mrs. Stowe's revelations have been published simultaneously in periodicals which deservedly hold high rank, the one in England [and] the other in America; and all the mechanism of quotations from advance sheets and anticipatory paragraphs has been employed to stimulate a morbid curiosity which unfortunately needed but little provocation. Commercially speaking, the result has doubtless been satisfactory to all concerned. The publishers of this painful story stand too high in reputation to be suspected of anything more than an error of judgment; but, for the credit of literature, we could wish that a disclosure which, whether false or true, is almost equally terrible, had not been made in such a manner as to suggest the idea of a pecuniary speculation. Meanwhile, it is some consolation to see that public opinion, both in England and America, has been singularly unanimous in denouncing alike the disclosure itself, and the manner in which it has been made. The condemnation of course proceeds on the idea that the authoress can produce no other warrant

---

53 *Public Opinion* regularly used 'Home' as reference not to literal domestic space but rather to designate a recurring feature (or section) presenting stories significant to readers in the home nation, versus other segments focused on 'America' and various European countries (such as 'France', 'Greece', 'Austria'). In this case, though, as 'The Byron Scandal' subtitle forecast, the reprints rounded up from multiple periodicals would locate their salacious storytelling as being about 'home' on multiple levels.

54 Besides the articles presented here, *Public Opinion* reprinted texts from London's *Times* and Paris's *La Liberté*.

for telling the secret intrusted to her—no further recital of the reasons which in her judgment rendered its revelation obligatory—no fuller corroboration of its truth—than she has made in her original statement. It is with much reluctance that we incline to regard such an assumption as correct. Mrs. Stowe, her friends, and her publishers in London as well as in Boston, have now been aware for a considerable period of the demand for proof which has been raised by all to whom the cause of literary and historic truth is dear. The telegraph has conveyed the opinion of England to America, and that of America to England; and yet no attempt has been made to relieve Mrs. Stowe from the stigma of having revealed a dead secret without cause, without authority, and without confirmatory proof. Under these circumstances we are almost compelled to abandon the hope that the lady who has taken upon herself the responsibility of telling the true story of Lady Byron's life can furnish us with evidence on which either to accept or reject her ghastly narrative. Nor is it likely, we fear, that an absolute corroboration or refutation of the tale will be furnished at present by the few persons who could throw light upon the mystery. Messrs. Wharton & Fords, the solicitors for the late Lady Byron and her representatives, have addressed a letter to the public journals, in which, while they comment severely upon the breach of confidence committed by Mrs. Stowe, they express no opinion one way or the other upon the truth or falsehood of her statement, and hold out no prospect of their publishing the documents which Lady Byron placed in the hands of her trustees, with the condition that no one, "however nearly connected with her, was upon any pleas whatsoever to be allowed to have access to or to inspect them." In the same way Dr. Lushington, who is known to have been intrusted with the secret of the separation, has as yet made no sign; and it seems probable that, for the present, the true story of the Byron scandal will remain, as it has remained for the last half-century, a matter of controversy. [...]

(Morning Star, Sept. 7)

Mrs. Stowe's story appears to have been met in the United States, as in this country, with a general expression of incredulity. In America the genius of Byron has always been appreciated at its true value; and it was, therefore, not likely that a reading and intelligent nation would be tempted to swallow, without reflection, a scandal which is unsupported by a single particle of evidence. The interest excited by the controversy is so great that a shrewd American journalist suggests that a publisher, desirous of making a hit and levying a tribute on the almighty dollar, could not do better than at once issue a cheap edition of "Don Juan." Byron's fame does not in any measure depend upon the factitious interest of his domestic life. This is a fact which Mrs. Stowe forgot in her tilt with the windmill. But in the endeavour to make it impossible to read him she has greatly multiplied his readers among the present generation. We see proofs of this in the innumerable references to his poems, and in the quotations, apt and inapt, from "Moore's Life,"[55] which meet the eye at every turn. Another sign of the Byronic fever is the appearance of articles descriptive of the places and scenes which are associated with his memory. One of these, which appears in the current number of an American magazine, is interesting in emanating from the pen of Mrs. Nathaniel Hawthorne, the widow of a man who

---

55 *Letters and Journals of Lord Byron. With Notices of his Life,* by Thomas Moore, first published in 1830

was one of the bright intellectual luminaries of our age. Mrs. Hawthorne merely describes a visit which she has recently paid to Newstead Abbey; but she imparts an amount of feeling to her narrative which is wholly inconsistent with the "moral monster" theory of Byron, now in vogue among the least charitable of her sex. She does not tell anything which has not been told before—for, to speak the truth, her own incomparable countryman, Washington Irving, exhausted the subject in a composition which makes it difficult for another to travel over the same ground. From Mrs. Hawthorne, however, we learn that some years ago Barnum[56] made an attempt to lay vulgar hands upon one of the most interesting memorials of the poet which yet remain within the classic precincts of Newstead. The withered tree on which trunk Byron, on the occasion of his last visit, cut his own name and that of his sister Augusta—the lady concerning whom, eighteen years after her death, Mrs. Stowe makes so incredible an accusation—is still preserved in the principal avenue. Mrs. Hawthorne relates that Barnum, with an effrontery which certainly he never surpassed, requested Colonel Wildman, the then proprietor of Newstead, to sell the tree to him for five hundred pounds. The colonel's reply was, that he would not take five thousand pounds for it, and that the showman, for making such a proposition, deserved to be shot. We are afraid that Mrs. Stowe will regard this as another evidence of the weakness and perversity of poor human nature. What she will think of Mrs. Hawthorne's article we fear to speculate upon; but we think that of the two ladies, both English and American readers will prefer the one who deals tenderly with the memory of a great though erring man.

(New York Weekly Review, Aug. 21)[57]

In the *Atlantic Monthly*, for September, appears an article the impudent audacity of which is, we believe, absolutely unparalleled. It proceeds from the pen of Mrs. Harriet Beecher Stowe, the author of the novel of "Uncle Tom's Cabin." It concerns itself with the domestic afflictions of the poet Byron. It states, in a fervid manner, and with an earnestness which expresses on the part of the writer, conviction that what it states is true—that Byron was guilty of a crime which is almost nameless among men, and which we shudder to mention even at second hand—the crime of incest. This, it says, was the cause of Byron's separation from his wife—that deplorable domestic catastrophe which has borne the upas[58] fruit of an evergreen scandal. It makes these statements upon the authority of Lady Byron, who is dead. It does not offer one jot or tittle of evidence that they are true. One woman, who does not even pretend that she has investigated the matter, tells the story which was told to

---

56 P. T. (Phineas Taylor) Barnum (1810–91) was known for both spectacular showmanship and sometimes over-the-top publicity stunts.

57 A longer version of this piece appeared, under the title 'Byron Vampirized' in London's *The Orchestra* No. 312 (17 September 1869), 412–3. That text offered additional rebuke of Stowe and defence of Byron, asserting that, 'If all that she says were true, it would not lessen the grandeur of "Childe Harold" nor dispel the spirt of poetry' from his works since, although, he might be criticised for 'moral delinquencies' he remained 'a poet who, in imagination, sublimity, and beauty, ranks but a little way below Shakespeare' (413). The additional commentary also classifies those who would condemn Byron as 'paltry Pharisees' and 'narrow-minded religious zealots'. Overall, the supplemental text in that version posits, 'the disposition to disparage Byron's genius . . . and to paint him as a moral monster because he was not a model husband, is one that critical patience ought no longer tolerate' (413).

58 A poison

her by another woman, who is beyond the reach of appeal. All the world knew that Byron was married, and that after a little more than one year of married life, his wife left him, never to meet him again on earth. All the world knew that the cause of their separation was a secret, and was kept so—as it ought to have been. But—so great is the influence which that stupendous genius has exerted upon the world—society has never been content to let this trivial subject alone. There was some reason why Lord and Lady Byron parted as man and wife: —what was it? That has been the mental attitude of thousands of curious readers of Byron's poetry. Nearly fifty years have passed since he was laid in the grave. The wife, who long survived him, is also under the sod. And now, after all this time, comes the foulest charge against his nature and his conduct which human ingenuity could devise or human malice could propagate. It is made, too, upon the flimsiest of pretexts. A poor, addle-pated woman, in Italy, who was once Byron's mistress, has put forth a stupid book, which nobody could read, and which was fast drifting to the limbo of all waste paper, in which Byron's domestic affairs were made the subject of some twaddling[59] comment. And this book, it appears, required answer—this pitiful farrago[60] of inconsequential gossip demanded that Byron should be dragged out of his grave and trampled into the mire of public ignominy. The work of the vampire has been done, and, we blush to say it—has been done by an American. Not one jot of evidence, as before remarked, has been adduced, to prove that the terrible assertion is true. Lady Byron thought it was true, and expressed herself to that effect to Mrs. Harriet Stowe. That is the sum and substance of the matter. Lady Byron was an old woman at the time she told this story, was broken in health, was in a morbid condition, and, from all we have heard, was that worst of all moral lunatics, a religious bigot. A cheap edition of Byron's works was to be published. Some cheap editions of mankind got the ear of Lady Byron (having enough ear of their own, meanwhile, the Lord knows!) and tried to persuade her to tell her secret, if she had any, so as to show that he was a monster, and to prevent the sale of his poems! And thereupon she sent for Mrs. Stowe and imparted this horrible tale. We do not doubt that she was telling what she fancied was the truth. A gentleman in a lunatic asylum once informed us that he was Emperor Nero, and he had every appearance of being perfectly convinced that such was the fact. But he offered no evidence in support of his startling proposition, and neither did the unfortunate woman, who—out of her grave—now strikes at the memory of one of the most illustrious men of genius that have ever come upon earth. On the contrary, her story defies all the laws of probability. It says that the wife lived two years with the husband, knowing that, all the time—under their very roof—he was in incestuous intercourse with his own sister: a thing morally impossible, and, in the matter of time, actually false—because the married life of Byron extended only a week or two past one year. It ignores the fact that the wife, after leaving him, wrote to him in the fondest and gentlest strain. It ignores the fact that his life, then as at all times, was subjected to the meridian blaze of observation, and that no such damnable foulness was perceived by anybody.

Source text

'Home: The Byron Scandal', *Public Opinion* 16 (11 September 1869), 313–15.

---

59 Silly, foolish commentary or speech
60 A mixed-up hodgepodge; confused mess

References

Graham, T. Austin, 'The Slaveries of Sex, Race, and Mind: Harriet Beecher Stowe's *Lady Byron Vindicated*', *New Literary History* 41.1 (Winter 2010), 173–90.

Robbins, Sarah, 'Additional late-career writing', in *The Cambridge Introduction to Harriet Beecher Stowe* (Cambridge: Cambridge University Press, 2007), 94–8.

Stowe, Harriet Beecher, *Lady Bryon Vindicated: A History of the Byron Controversy from its Beginning in 1816 to the Present Time* (Boston: Fields, Osgood, & Co., 1870).

World's Woman's Christian Temperance Union, 'Pledge' (1883)

Taking as its motto 'For God and Home and Every Land', the World's Woman's Christian Temperance Union, beginning in 1883, officially envisioned its mission in global terms. The American WCTU had been founded in 1874. Though many local, regional and national temperance groups had been operating on both sides of the Atlantic since the early nineteenth century, the WCTU became especially visible and vocal, building the largest worldwide women-led organisation of its day. Beginning in 1891, a series of biennial conventions contributed to the strength of the network, which, under the leadership of Frances Willard, expanded its advocacy to include causes such as suffrage and fair labour legislation.

Publications like the biennial meeting reports and the international version of the *Union Signal* promoted border-crossing temperance affiliations by reporting on activities from around the world. For example, one 1891 feature story for the newsletter touted how US and English leaders had extended their influence to such far-flung locations as Australia and Japan, Sweden and Russia, and pointed to 'the World's Petition' for abstinence, with 'signatures of hundreds of thousands of women of every tribe and people', as confirming the goal to 'protect the homes of all nations' ('Exodus', 8).

The list of biennial convenings held between 1891 and 1920 points to a transatlantic 'Anglo' tilt (if not outright dominance) of the organisation: London (1895 and 1920), Edinburgh (1900) and Glasgow (1910) hosted conventions on one side of the Atlantic, with Chicago (1893), Toronto (1897), Boston (1906) and Brooklyn (1913) the sites for all others except one in Geneva in 1903 (*Report*, 1920, 2). Overall, the organisation's transnational energies found expression in gendered rhetoric like that of the regularly reprinted 'Pledge' text below, as well as in prayers, temperance hymns and the wearing of the organisation's white ribbon

'Pledge'

"I hereby solemnly promise, God helping me, to abstain from all Alcoholic Liquors as beverages, whether distilled, fermented or malted; from opium in all its forms, and to employ all proper means to discourage the use of and traffic in the same."

To confirm and enforce the *rationale* of the pledge, we declare our purpose to educate the young; to form a better public sentiment; to reform, so far as possible, by religious, ethical and scientific means, the drinking classes; to seek the transforming power of Divine grace for ourselves and all for whom we work, that they and we may wilfully transgress no law of pure and wholesome living; and, finally, we pledge ourselves to labour, and pray that all these principles, founded upon the Gospel of CHRIST, may be worked out into the Customs of Society and the Laws of the Land.

To this end we plead with all good women throughout Christendom to join with us heart and hand in the holy endeavour to protect and sanctify the Home as that Temple of the Holy Spirit which, next to the human body itself, is dearest of all to our Creator; that womanhood and manhood in equal purity, equal personal liberty and peace, may climb to those blest heights where there shall be no more curse.

We ask all women like-minded with us in this sacred cause, to wear the white ribbon as the badge of loyalty; to lift up their hearts with us to GOD at the noon-tide hour of prayer; to take as their motto, "For GOD and Home and Every Land," and to unite with us in allegiance to the foregoing Declaration of Principles and to the summary of our plans and purposes, as embodied in the Preamble of our Constitution adopted in Faneuil Hall, Boston, U.S.A., November 11, 1891.

Source text

World's Woman's Christian Temperance Union, 'Pledge', *Report of the Fourth Biennial Convention of the World's Woman's Christian Temperance Union, Held in The Pavilion, and Massey Music Hall, Toronto, Canada* (London: White Ribbon Company, 1897), 234.

References

'The Exodus of the World's W.C.T.U.', *The Union Signal* 17.20 (14 May 1891), 8.
Woman's Christian Temperance Union, *Report of the Tenth Convention of the World's Woman's Christian Temperance Union* (West Norwood, England: Truslove and Bray, 1920).
'World's Congress and Temperance Convention', *The National Advocate* 35.8 (1900), 118.

Frances Hodgson Burnett (1849–1924)

From Little Lord Fauntleroy (1885–6)

Frances Hodgson Burnett was born in England but emigrated in 1865 to the US, where she began her long writing career. Though many of her early writings were popular romances, in 1877 Burnett began writing children's literature, her most enduring genre. In 1885, Burnett sold *Little Lord Fauntleroy* to Mary Mapes Dodge, editor of *St. Nicholas* children's magazine. The text appeared serially November 1885 – October 1886 and was quickly published as a novel in America and Great Britain, becoming a transatlantic best-seller, with near ubiquitous Fauntleroy suits for young boys just one marker of a popular response which detractors would dub the 'Fauntleroy plague' (Stover, 339).

Little Lord Fauntleroy is transatlantic in both plot and theme. Cedric Errol, an American boy living with his widowed mother, inherits a lordship from the grandparent who had disowned the boy's father. Cedric travels to England, with the young lord gradually reforming his crusty grandfather's stern ways. Our excerpts focus on Cedric's relationships with the two most influential men in his life: his US neighbourhood grocer and friend Mr Hobbs, a proud American who shaped Cedric's interest in democratic politics; and the little lord's grandfather, the cranky, selfish earl whom Cedric naïvely believes to be a benefactor interested in the well-being of tenants on the estate. Taken together, these scenes show how Lord Fauntleroy, though ostensibly acculturating to a new home, introduces idealised American perspectives on class to his British grandfather.

From Chapter I of *Little Lord Fauntleroy*

His name was Mr. Hobbs, and Cedric[61] admired and respected him very much. He thought him a very rich and powerful person, he had so many things in his store,—prunes and figs and oranges and biscuits,—and he had a horse and wagon. Cedric was fond of the milkman and the baker and the apple-woman, but he liked Mr. Hobbs best of all, and was on terms of such intimacy with him that he went to see him every day, and often sat with him quite a long time, discussing the topics of the hour.[62] It was quite surprising how many things they found to talk about—the Fourth of July,[63] for instance. When they began to talk about the Fourth of July there really seemed no end to it. Mr. Hobbs had a very bad opinion of "the British," and he told the whole story of the Revolution, relating very wonderful and patriotic stories about the villainy of the enemy and the bravery of the Revolutionary heroes, and he even generously repeated part of the Declaration of Independence.[64] Cedric was so excited that his eyes shone and his cheeks were red and his curls were all rubbed and tumbled into a yellow mop. He could hardly wait to eat his dinner after he went home, he was so anxious to tell his mamma. It was, perhaps, Mr. Hobbs who gave him his first interest in politics. Mr. Hobbs was fond of reading the newspapers, and so Cedric heard a great deal about what was going on in Washington;

---

61 Cedric is based on Burnett's youngest son, Vivian, who was said to be as outgoing and interested in politics as his namesake character. Illustrations of Lord Fauntleroy are also modelled after Vivian's likeness (Gerzina, 108–10).

62 Burnett used Vivian's relationship with their 'African American cook and manservant, Carrie and Dan', as well as his 'conversations with the real local bootblack and grocer', as the inspiration for various American characters in the novel (Gerzina, 108).

63 Independence Day in the US

64 The 'Declaration' announced the separation of the thirteen North American British colonies from Great Britain in 1776.

and Mr. Hobbs would tell him whether the President[65] was doing his duty or not. And once, when there was an election, he found it all quite grand, and probably but for Mr. Hobbs and Cedric the country might have been wrecked. Mr. Hobbs took him to see a great torchlight procession, and many of the men who carried torches remembered afterward a stout man who stood near a lamp-post and held on his shoulder a handsome little shouting boy, who waved his cap in the air.

It was not long after this election, when Cedric was between seven and eight years old, that the very strange thing happened which made so wonderful a change in his life. It was quite curious, too, that the day it happened he had been talking to Mr. Hobbs about England and the Queen,[66] and Mr. Hobbs had said some very severe things about the aristocracy, being specially indignant against earls and marquises. It had been a hot morning; and after playing soldiers with some friends of his, Cedric had gone into the store to rest, and had found Mr. Hobbs looking very fierce over a piece of the *Illustrated London News*,[67] which contained a picture of some court ceremony.

"Ah," he said, "that's the way they go on now; but they'll get enough of it some day, when those they've trod on rise and blow 'em up sky-high,—earls and marquises and all ! It's coming, and they may look out for it!"

Cedric had perched himself as usual on the high stool and pushed his hat back, and put his hands in his pockets in delicate compliment to Mr. Hobbs.

"Did you ever know many marquises, Mr. Hobbs?" Cedric inquired,— "or earls?"

"No," answered Mr. Hobbs, with indignation; "I guess not. I'd like to catch one of 'em inside here; that's all! I'll have no grasping tyrants sittin' 'round on my cracker-barrels!"

And he was so proud of the sentiment that he looked around proudly and mopped his forehead.

"Perhaps they would n't be earls if they knew any better," said Cedric, feeling some vague sympathy for their unhappy condition.

"Would n't they !" said Mr. Hobbs. "They just glory in it! It's in 'em. They're a bad lot."

They were in the midst of their conversation, when Mary appeared. Cedric thought she had come to buy some sugar, perhaps, but she had not. She looked almost pale and as if she were excited about something.

"Come home, darlint," she said; "the misthress is wantin' yez."

Cedric slipped down from his stool.

"Does she want me to go out with her, Mary?" he asked. "Good-morning, Mr Hobbs. I'll see you again."

He was surprised to see Mary staring at him in a dumfounded fashion, and he wondered why she kept shaking her head.

"What's the matter, Mary ?" he said. "Is it the hot weather?"

"No," said Mary; "but there's strange things happenin' to us."

---

65 In 1884, the year before *The Little Lord Fauntleroy* was serialised, Grover Cleveland was elected the twenty-second US President.
66 Queen Victoria ruled from June 1837 to January 1901, a reign only recently surpassed by Elizabeth II.
67 Lavishly illustrated periodical first published in 1842

"Has the sun given Dearest[68] a headache ?" he inquired anxiously. But it was not that. When he reached his own house there was a coupé[69] standing before the door, and some one was in the little parlor talking to his mamma. Mary hurried him upstairs and put on his best summer suit of cream-colored flannel, with the red scarf around his waist, and combed out his curly locks.

"Lords, is it?" he heard her say. "An' the nobility an' gintry. Och! bad cess to them! Lords, indade — worse luck."

It was really very puzzling, but he felt sure his mamma would tell him what all the excitement meant, so he allowed Mary to bemoan herself without asking many questions. When he was dressed, he ran downstairs and went into the parlor. A tall, thin old gentleman with a sharp face was sitting in an arm-chair. His mother was standing near by with a pale face, and he saw that there were tears in her eyes.

"Oh! Ceddie!" she cried out, and ran to her little boy and caught him in her arms and kissed him in a frightened, troubled way. "Oh! Ceddie, darling!"

The tall old gentleman rose from his chair and looked at Cedric with his sharp eyes. He rubbed his thin chin with his bony hand as he looked.

He seemed not at all displeased.

"And so," he said at last, slowly,— "and so this is little Lord Fauntleroy."

From Chapter VI of Little Lord Fauntleroy

And as the Reverend Mr. Mordaunt walked under the great trees, he remembered that this questionable little boy had arrived at the Castle only the evening before, and that there were nine chances to one that his lordship's worst fears were realized, and twenty-two chances to one that if the poor little fellow had disappointed him, the Earl was even now in a tearing rage, and ready to vent all his rancor on the first person who called — which it appeared probable would be his reverend self.

Judge then of his amazement when, as Thomas opened the library door, his ears were greeted by a delighted ring of childish laughter.

"That's two out!" shouted an excited, clear little voice. "You see it's two out!"

And there was the Earl's chair, and the gout-stool, and his foot on it; and by him a small table and a game on it; and quite close to him, actually leaning against his arm and his ungouty knee, was a little boy with face glowing, and eyes dancing with excitement. "It's two out!" the little stranger cried. "You hadn't any luck that time, had you?"—And then they both recognized at once that some one had come in.

The Earl glanced around, knitting his shaggy eyebrows as he had a trick of doing, and when he saw who it was, Mr. Mordaunt was still more surprised to see that he looked even less disagreeable than usual instead of more so. In fact, he looked almost as if he had forgotten for the moment how disagreeable he was, and how unpleasant he really could make himself when he tried.

"Ah!" he said, in his harsh voice, but giving his hand rather graciously. "Good-morning, Mordaunt. I've found a new employment, you see."

He put his other hand on Cedric's shoulder,— perhaps deep down in his heart there was a stir of gratified pride that it was such an heir he had to present; there was a spark of something like pleasure in his eyes as he moved the boy slightly forward.

---

68 Lionel and Vivian, Burnett's sons, referred to their mother as 'Dearest' (Gerzina, 108).
69 The *OED* defines this term as a carriage seating two passengers inside and a driver outside.

"This is the new Lord Fauntleroy," he said. "Fauntleroy, this is Mr. Mordaunt, the rector of the parish."

Fauntleroy looked up at the gentleman in the clerical garments, and gave him his hand.

"I am very glad to make your acquaintance, sir," he said, remembering the words he had heard Mr. Hobbs use on one or two occasions when he had been greeting a new customer with ceremony. Cedric felt quite sure that one ought to be more than usually polite to a minister.

Mr. Mordaunt held the small hand in his a moment as he looked down at the child's face, smiling involuntarily. He liked the little fellow from that instant — as in fact people always did like him. And it was not the boy's beauty and grace which most appealed to him; it was the simple, natural kindliness in the little lad which made any words he uttered, however quaint and unexpected, sound pleasant and sincere. As the rector looked at Cedric, he forgot to think of the Earl at all. Nothing in the world is so strong as a kind heart, and somehow this kind little heart, though it was only the heart of a child, seemed to clear all the atmosphere of the big gloomy room and make it brighter.

"I am delighted to make your acquaintance, Lord Fauntleroy," said the rector. "You made a long journey to come to us. A great many people will be glad to know you made it safely."

"It *was* a long way," answered Fauntleroy, "but Dearest, my mother, was with me and I was n't lonely. Of course you are never lonely if your mother is with you; and the ship was beautiful."

"Take a chair, Mordaunt," said the Earl. Mr. Mordaunt sat down. He glanced from Fauntleroy to the Earl.

"Your lordship is greatly to be congratulated," he said warmly.

But the Earl plainly had no intention of showing his feelings on the subject.

"He is like his father," he said rather gruffly. "Let us hope he'll conduct himself more creditably." And then he added: "Well, what is it this morning, Mordaunt? Who is in trouble now?"

This was not as bad as Mr. Mordaunt had expected, but he hesitated a second before he began.

"It is Higgins," he said; "Higgins of Edge Farm. He has been very unfortunate. He was ill himself last autumn, and his children had scarlet fever. I can't say that he is a very good manager, but he has had ill-luck, and of course he is behindhand in many ways. He is in trouble about his rent now. Newick tells him if he does n't pay it, he must leave the place; and of course that would be a very serious matter. His wife is ill, and he came to me yesterday to beg me to see about it, and ask you for time. He thinks if you would give him time he could catch up again."

"They all think that," said the Earl, looking rather black.

Fauntleroy made a movement forward. He had been standing between his grandfather and the visitor, listening with all his might. He had begun to be interested in Higgins at once. He wondered how many children there were, and if the scarlet fever had hurt them very much. His eyes were wide open and were fixed upon Mr. Mordaunt with intent interest as that gentleman went on with the conversation.

"Higgins is a well-meaning man," said the rector, making an effort to strengthen his plea.

"He is a bad enough tenant," replied his lordship. "And he is always behindhand, Newick tells me."

"He is in great trouble now," said the rector.

"He is very fond of his wife and children, and if the farm is taken from him they may literally starve. He can not give them the nourishing things they need. Two of the children were left very low after the fever, and the doctor orders for them wine and luxuries that Higgins can not afford."

At this Fauntleroy moved a step nearer.

"That was the way with Michael," he said.

The Earl slightly started.

"I forgot *you!*" he said. "I forgot we had a philanthropist in the room. Who was Michael?" And the gleam of queer amusement came back into the old man's deep-set eyes.

"He was Bridget's husband, who had the fever," answered Fauntleroy; "and he couldn't pay the rent or buy wine and things. And you gave me that money to help him."

The Earl drew his brows together into a curious frown, which somehow was scarcely grim at all. He glanced across at Mr. Mordaunt.

"I don't know what sort of landed proprietor he will make," he said. "I told Havisham the boy was to have what he wanted—anything he wanted—and what he wanted, it seems, was money to give to beggars."

"Oh! but they weren't beggars," said Fauntleroy eagerly. "Michael was a splendid bricklayer! They all worked."

"Oh!" said the Earl, "they were not beggars. They were splendid bricklayers, and bootblacks, and apple-women."

He bent his gaze on the boy for a few seconds in silence. The fact was that a new thought was coming to him, and though, perhaps, it was not prompted by the noblest emotions, it was not a bad thought. "Come here," he said, at last.

Fauntleroy went and stood as near to him as possible without encroaching on the gouty foot.

'What would *you* do in this case?' his lordship asked.

It must be confessed that Mr. Mordaunt experienced for the moment a curious sensation. Being a man of great thoughtfulness, and having spent so many years on the estate of Dorincourt, knowing the tenantry, rich and poor, the people of the village, honest and industrious, dishonest and lazy, he realized very strongly what power for good or evil would be given in the future to this one small boy standing there, his brown eyes wide open, his hands deep in his pockets; and the thought came to him also that a great deal of power might, perhaps, through the caprice of a proud, self-indulgent old man, be given to him now, and that if his young nature were not a simple and generous one, it might be the worst thing that could happen, not only for others, but for himself.

"And what would *you* do in such a case?" demanded the Earl.

Fauntleroy drew a little nearer, and laid one hand on his knee, with the most confiding air of good comradeship.

"If I were very rich," he said, "and not only just a little boy, I should let him stay, and give him the things for his children; but then, I am only a boy." Then, after a second's pause, in which his face brightened visibly, "*You* can do anything, can't you?" he said.

"Humph!" said my lord, staring at him. "That's your opinion, is it?" And he was not displeased either.

"I mean you can give any one anything," said Fauntleroy. "Who's Newick?"

"He is my agent," answered the Earl, "and some of my tenants are not over-fond of him."

"Are you going to write him a letter now?" inquired Fauntleroy. "Shall I bring you the pen and ink? I can take the game off this table."

It plainly had not for an instant occurred to him that Newick would be allowed to do his worst.

The Earl paused a moment, still looking at him. "Can you write?" he asked.

"Yes," answered Cedric, "but not very well."

"Move the things from the table," commanded my lord, "and bring the pen and ink, and a sheet of paper from my desk."

Mr. Mordaunt's interest began to increase. Fauntleroy did as he was told very deftly. In a few moments, the sheet of paper, the big inkstand, and the pen were ready.

"There!" he said gayly, "now you can write it."

"You are to write it," said the Earl.

"I!" exclaimed Fauntleroy, and a flush overspread his forehead. "Will it do if I write it? I don't always spell quite right when I haven't a dictionary, and nobody tells me."

"It will do," answered the Earl. "Higgins will not complain of the spelling. I'm not the philanthropist; you are. Dip your pen in the ink."

Fauntleroy took up the pen and dipped it in the ink-bottle, then he arranged himself in position, leaning on the table.

"Now," he inquired, "what must I say?"

"You may say, 'Higgins is not to be interfered with, for the present,' and sign it, 'Fauntleroy,'" said the Earl.

Fauntleroy dipped his pen in the ink again, and resting his arm, began to write. It was rather a slow and serious process, but he gave his whole soul to it. After a while, however, the manuscript was complete, and he handed it to his grandfather with a smile slightly tinged with anxiety.

"Do you think it will do?" he asked.

The Earl looked at it, and the corners of his mouth twitched a little.

"Yes," he answered; "Higgins will find it entirely satisfactory." And he handed it to Mr. Mordaunt.

What Mr Mordaunt found written was this:

"Dear mr. Newik if you pleas mr. higins is not to be inturfeared with for the present and oblige. Yours rispecferly, "FAUNTLEROY."

"Mr. Hobbs always signed his letters that way," said Fauntleroy; "and I thought I'd better say 'please.' Is that exactly the right way to spell 'interfered'?"

"It's not exactly the way it is spelled in the dictionary," answered the Earl.

"I was afraid of that," said Fauntleroy. "I ought to have asked. You see, that's the way with words of more than one syllable; you have to look in the dictionary. It's always safest. I'll write it over again."

And write it over again he did, making quite an imposing copy, and taking precautions in the matter of spelling by consulting the Earl himself.

"Spelling is a curious thing," he said. "It's so often different from what you expect it to be. I used to think 'please' was spelled p-l-e-e-s, but it is n't, you know; and you'd think 'dear' was spelled d-e-r-e, if you did n't inquire. Sometimes it almost discourages you."

When Mr. Mordaunt went away, he took the letter with him, and he took something else with him also — namely, a pleasanter feeling and a more hopeful one than he had ever carried home with him down that avenue on any previous visit he had made at Dorincourt Castle.

Source text

Burnett, Frances Hodgson, *Little Lord Fauntleroy* (New York: Charles Scribner's Sons, 1886).

References

Gerzina, Gretchen Holbrook, *Frances Hodgson Burnett: The Unexpected Life of the Author of The Secret Garden* (New Brunswick, NJ: Rutgers University Press, 2004).
Stover, Deanna, 'Alternative Family and Textual Citizenship in Frances Hodgson Burnett's *Little Lord Fauntleroy*: A Drama in Three Acts', *Children's Literature Association Quarterly* 40.4 (Winter 2015), 339–54.

Sarah Morgan Bryan Piatt (1836–1919)

'Two Sabbath Parties' (1893)

Sarah Piatt lived and travelled extensively in the US and Europe. Born in Lexington, Kentucky, where she spent her youth on her grandmother's plantation, Piatt moved to the North as a young adult, marrying fellow poet John James Piatt in 1861. In 1882, the couple relocated from Washington, DC, to Cork, Ireland. Sarah spent seven years (1882–93) in Ireland, finding inspiration for several books of verse, including *A Voyage to the Fortunate Isles and Other Poems* (1885), *An Irish Garland* (1884) and *Child's World Ballads: Three Little Emigrants, a Romance of Cork Harbour, 1884* (1887). A prolific writer, Piatt produced in excess of six hundred poems, including in premier publications like *The Independent*, *The Atlantic Monthly* and *Harper's*.

In *An Enchanted Castle and Other Poems*, a collection published simultaneously in London and New York, Piatt portrays what her subtitle identifies as *Pictures, Portraits and People in Ireland*. 'Two Sabbath Parties' critiques social class distinctions evident in the contrast between a peasant's nurturing interactions with his young child and the disruption of that idealised familial scene by a 'gentleman . . . with his pet greyhounds, / And his delicate children following him'. Here, perhaps, Piatt brings her own experiences witnessing post-bellum southern poverty in America to bear on her observations of Irish class differences in Cork.

'Two Sabbath Parties'

> Picturesque, comfortless, lonely and low,
>   In the greenest island of all the earth,
> With room on the roof for ferns to grow
>   In the blackened thatch, and room on the hearth
> For hearts to beat, though the rain dropped through,
> Was the cabin wherein they breathed, these two.

The one was a man, not young nor old,
    Whose tall silk hat, toward the chapel's chime,
(Where few, you'd say, were the sins he told,)
    Had started gravely this many a time—
(A most ridiculous hat, and such
As the Irish peasant prizes much!)

And one was a child, with a sea-shell's blush
    And a bare brown head, that was bright to see;
And I heard in the hedges an old-world thrush
    (Or a robin, at home in an apple-tree!)
That broke one's heart with its song, while they
Walked, hand-in-hand, on their pleasant way.

Suddenly, out of his sacred grounds,
    Walled-in by ages, and shadow-dim,
A gentleman came, with his pet greyhounds,
    And his delicate children following him,
In a violet velvet and long gold hair
Under drooping feathers, a pretty pair.

But the child from the cabin held her head
    As high as theirs, for she seemed to know
That *her* holiday-dress[70] was a radiant red,
    And her Sabbath apron as clean as snow:
I could see no envy nor surprise,
At the little ladies, in her eyes.

She only said: "They are going to walk."
    "And sure they are. It's a lovely day.
Why shouldn't they go?" (I could hear their talk)—
    'If it pleases the gentleman. Any way,
He can afford it." "Do you wish that you
Could afford to be walking too?" "I do."

"But *you* can't afford[71] to walk, do you know,
    On a lovely day?—and you can't that's it.
For you have to work—and *he* hasn't though!"
    She prattled as if she cared no whit,
While the face of the other grew sad and still,—
But he cheerily said: "If I must, I will."

Source text

Piatt, Sarah, *An Enchanted Castle and Other Poems: Pictures, Portraits and People in Ireland* (London and New York: Longmans, Green, and Co., 1893).

---

70 Piatt uses details about dress, such as a 'ridiculous hat' that an 'Irish peasant prizes much' and 'drooping feathers', to mark class distinctions.
71 Piatt underscores the irony that the Sabbath is a day of rest, but only the wealthy can afford to rest.

References

Bennett, Paula (ed.), *Palace-Burner: The Selected Poetry of Sarah Piatt* (Champaign, IL: University of Illinois Press, 2001).

Giordano, Matthew, 'A Lesson from the Magazines: Sarah Piatt and the Postbellum Periodical Poet', *American Periodicals* 16.1 (2006), 23–51.

Wearn, Mary McCartin, 'Subjection and Subversion in Sarah Piatt's Maternal Poetics', *Legacy: A Journal of American Women Writers* 23.2 (2006), 163–77.

Charles Alexander Eastman, MD (Ohiyesa) (1858–1939)

From 'Economic', 'The Social Law' and 'Inter-racial Marriage' in 'The North American Indian' Address (1911)

Native American writer Charles Eastman's prolific publication output included numerous texts for children's home reading, such as stories for America's *St. Nicholas Magazine* and autobiographical books like *Indian Boyhood* (1902) and *Old Indian Days* (1907). Although his white wife Elaine Eastman claimed that his authorial successes were due, in substantial part, to her editing and knowledge of publishing venues, Anglo-American readers' fascination with Native culture made his narratives more appealing to audiences of their time than her own books for young readers (Eastman, *Voice*, 30–1).

Charles Eastman's Indian background also made him a strong draw on the lecture circuit. Elaine's frustration at often being left at home to care for their children is clear in her memoir: 'Saving the joys of motherhood, my pleasures must be vicarious ones. He travelled widely, even to London, and met hosts of interesting people. I was inevitably house-bound' (Eastman, *Voice*, 30).

If his wife resented his celebrity, Eastman himself bore a burden when positioned by white cultural arbiters as spokesman for an entire race. In a text like his 1911 address for the Universal Race Congress in London, as in a children's story like 'Recollections of the Wild Life', he struggled rhetorically to assert distinctive features of various tribal nations while also advocating for whites' appreciation of Indigenous peoples as having a sophisticated culture. Thus, portions of his URC speech dealing with Indian domestic life vacillate between defending some Native social practices as misunderstood and positioning Indigenous peoples as worthy of acceptance into white society via paths such as inter-racial marriages like his own.

From 'Economic', 'The Social Law' and 'Inter-racial Marriage'

Economic– [. . .] The Indian was a tiller of the soil to a very limited extent. He lived almost entirely upon the natural products of the country, and his main dependence was hunting and fishing, together with two native cereals of great value (corn and rice), acorns, berries, wild fruits, and roots of many kinds. The food was always divided until it became abundant; then the women began to gather and store provisions for the colder months of the year. [...] The prairie Indians covered more territory than the forest dwellers, and yet had less variety of food. [...]

All clothing was made and ornamented by the women with much skill, according to the tribal pattern, and they also tanned the skins of which it was made. The tents or lodges were constructed by different tribes from various materials—rush mats, birch-bark, or buffalo skins, entirely prepared by the women. A few lived in dwellings made of poles thatched with brush or sods. Canoes were made by both sexes, but pipes and weapons entirely by the men. Except in cases of emergency, to them fell all hunting and fishing, while the women tilled the small patches of maize or beans, gathered berries, dug roots, and prepared maple sugar. Basket-weaving was done by the women, and blankets and pottery made by both women and men. The men carved the bowls and shaped the spoons of wood, bone, horn, and shell.

The division of labour between the sexes was natural and far from unjust. It must be remembered that in a society like theirs there could be no merely ornamental members. Upon the men devolved those labours involving the severest hardship, peril and exposure—war and the chase; while the women undertook all the care of the home, including the drudgery of providing wood and water. [...]

The Social Law.—The unwritten codes of the wild tribes were not easily changed nor often broken. The punishment of the transgressor was direct and sure. It should never be forgotten that primitive life on this continent was not a life of licence, but in many respects of a strict etiquette and an austere morality.

There was never any promiscuous intermingling of the sexes permitted among us. Girls and boys were not allowed to play together after reaching the age of ten or twelve years. No young man could talk to a girl unless he desired to make her his wife. Even brothers and sisters might not talk and jest freely together, but were expected to preserve the utmost dignity and decorum.

Marriage was not allowed within the clan. It was considered that the reproductive power was the most mysterious and sacred gift of the Divine to man, and it was safeguarded with much anxiety and reverence. The honour and trust given to woman in motherhood won for her a peculiar precedence, as all-important among created beings. The lineage of our chiefs was reckoned in the maternal line, and the purity of our girls was sacredly guarded by each succeeding generation. The annual "Feast of Virgins" was established as evidence and incentive to such purity; and the Sioux had a custom which allowed a young man to reject his bride publicly if upon receiving her she was found to be unchaste.

It is true that in the wild life a plurality of wives was permitted under certain conditions. The reasons for it are thus explained. Our young men, being so ambitious for honour in the "feather count," or record of brave deeds, many of them were killed without leaving successors. Furthermore, it was customary to limit the children of one mother to five, some of whom would probably not live to maturity, therefore the tribe increased very slowly, if at all, in numbers. The conditions imposed were, first, that only a man of superb physique and superior ability should have more than one wife; second, that the wives should be sisters; third, that all concerned should be agreed in the matter, and it was thought better that the proposition should come from the woman's parents. In this manner, the blood of the family was kept distinct, and the relation both honourable and happy. [...]

Inter-racial Marriage.—The intermingling of the blood of the aborigines of America with that of their white conquerors began at an early period, and has continued in growing measure to the present day. In their origin these were usually mere temporary alliances, entered into solely for the pleasure and convenience of the border white man, and opposed by the better class of Indians, who saw in them a menace to their racial integrity.[72] The children of these unions form the numerous and much abused race of "half-breeds," whose fathers are of all nationalities, the French and Scotch predominating, and of all classes from army officers and gentlemen through wealthy Indian traders and rough pioneers to fugitives from justice. The great majority have cast in their lot with their mothers' people and grown up as "Indians," with slight if any advantage over the mass of these. The common slur which attributes to the mixed-blood "the vices of both races and the virtues of neither" is absolutely unjust. Many of them have been men and women of good abilities and fine character; and of the reckless and dissipated class, it should in fairness be said that their weaknesses are due not to a mixture of blood, which has many times proved fortunate, but to a vicious heredity or indifferent bringing up, or both together.

Within the past twenty or thirty years, and occasionally before that time, there have been a great many inter-marriages of a different character, between educated Indians and Caucasians; and whereas in the early days only Indian women contracted these alliances, of late years almost as many Indian men choose Anglo-Saxon wives.[73] Such marriages, based upon mutual sympathy and affection, have been generally happy and have had the best results.

Since it is admittedly impossible for the Indian to continue to exist as a separate race, with his proper racial characteristics and customs, within the limits of the United States, race amalgamation is the only final and full solution of the problem, and only in this sense, implying no lack of vitality, but quite the reverse, is the American Indian a "dying race." In remote parts of Canada, where there is as yet no pressure of white population, the process may take a longer time; but at the present rate, it will not be two hundred years, perhaps not even a hundred, before the full-blooded Indian is extinct.

---

72 On mixed-race alliances and formally recognised marriages between First Nations people and Euro-Canadians, from the initial colonial period to the late nineteenth and early twentieth centuries, see Sylvia Van Kirk, 'From "Marrying-in" to "Marrying-Out": Changing Patterns of Aboriginal/Non-Aboriginal Marriage in Colonial Canada', *Frontiers: A Journal of Women Studies* 23.3 (2002), 1–11.

73 Cathleen D. Cahill has noted that 'During the closing decades of the nineteenth century, the [US] federal government's strategies for changing Indian societies tacitly encouraged interracial marriage', and 'the rhetoric administrators used to describe the government's assimilation policy offered both white women and Native men compelling reasons to believe that their personal relationships had wider social and political implications', potentially 'bring[ing] Indians into citizenry. This rhetoric led some white women to see marriage to Indian men as a logical extension of assimilation policy'. See '"You Think It Strange That I Can Love an Indian": Native Men, White Women, and Marriage in Indian Service', *Frontiers: A Journal of Women Studies* 29.2/3 (2008), 107. Press coverage of Elaine Eastman's marriage to Charles reflected this ideology.

Figure 4.6 Dr Charles H. Eastman, Santee Dakota (1858–1939) and Elaine Goodale Eastman (1863–1953). Edward E. Ayer Digital Collection. Courtesy Newberry Library.

Source text

Eastman, Charles Alexander, MD (Ohiyesa), 'The North American Indian', in Gustav Spiller (ed.), *Papers on Inter-Racial Problems Communicated to the First Universal Race Congress Held at the University of London; July 26–29, 1911* (London: P. S. King; Boston: World's Peace Foundation, 1911), 367–76.

References

Calcaterra, Angela. 'A "Second Look" at Charles Alexander Eastman', *Studies in American Indian Literatures* 27.4 (Winter 2015), 1–36.

Eastman, Dr Charles Alexander, 'Recollections of the Wild Life: II. Early Hardships', *St. Nicholas; an Illustrated Magazine for Young Folks* 21.3 (January 1894), 226–8.

Eastman, Elaine Goodale, *The Voice at Eve* (Chicago: The Bookfellows, 1930).

Robbins, Sarah Ruffing, 'The "Indian Problem" in Elaine Goodale Eastman's Authorship: Gender and Racial Identity Tensions Unsettling a Romantic Pedagogy', in Monika M. Elbert and Lesley Ginsberg (eds), *Romantic Education in Nineteenth-Century Literature: National and Transatlantic Contexts* (New York: Routledge, 2015), 192–208.

Jane Addams (1860–1935)

From 'A Modern Lear' (1915)

Scholarship on Jane Addams situates her within American Progressivism through her work at Chicago's Hull-House. Yet, her own view of the
settlement – and other projects – evinced a transatlantic perspective. Her
best-selling *Twenty Years at Hull-House* (1910) underscored her debt to
London's Toynbee Hall (111–12, 120, 371). Similarly, *Peace and Bread in
Time of War* (1922) honoured the collaboration linking US women with
transatlantic compatriots. Overall, *Peace* invoked Addams's recurring
argument for women's domestically inflected moral leadership by tracing
one gendered transnational enterprise's evolution from seeking to end the
World War, to providing literal bread to hungry Europeans in the conflict's aftermath, to organising a post-war Women's International League
for Peace and Freedom.

Addams's approach for addressing issues by using transatlantic cultural
resources extended back to her time at Rockford College. There, she led
a club of young women who studied European writers to become activist
'breadgivers', extending beyond the 'family claim' of marriage and motherhood often constraining middle-class women's social roles. Personally,
Addams sought to reconcile her ambition with partial reaffirmation of her
era's domestic ideology.

'A Modern Lear' began as a public talk and, after being rejected by
several mainstream publishers as too radical, especially for a woman's
public voice, finally appeared in print in 1915 in a multi-author collection of essays on urban life. The event undergirding Addams's speech
was one of the most bitter labour conflicts in US history: a railroad strike
prompted by George M. Pullman's cutting the already low wages of his
employees by about a quarter. Casting Pullman as a new capitalist version of Shakespeare's King Lear, Addams followed a frequent pattern in
her writing by drawing on canonical English literature for social analysis.
In this case, she critiqued domestic culture's dark side in its hierarchy-
sustaining exercise of patriarchal authority extending well beyond the
actual home into power politics.

From 'A Modern Lear'

> This analysis of paternalism was written in 1894 immediately after the great
> Pullman strike. It was not published at the time because of its personal
> nature, although much of the material, omitting the Lear analogy, was used
> later in "Democracy and Social Ethics." Miss Addams interprets forces which
> were at the height of their power twenty years ago. [...] But the problem
> which she thus dramatizes reasserts itself to-day in the conflict between
> corporation control and community life throughout many of our newer
> industrial districts. [Editor Graham Romeyn Taylor's note.]

Those of us who lived in Chicago in the summer of 1894 were confronted by a drama which epitomized and, at the same time, challenged the code of social ethics under which we live, for a quick series of unusual events had dispelled the good nature which in happier times envelops the ugliness of the industrial situation. It sometimes seems as if the shocking experiences of that summer, the barbaric instinct to kill, roused on both sides, the sharp division into class lines, with the resultant distrust and bitterness, can only be endured if we learn from it all a great ethical lesson. To endure is all we can hope for. It is impossible to justify such a course of rage and riot in a civilized community to whom the methods of conciliation and control were open. Every public-spirited citizen in Chicago during that summer felt the stress and perplexity of the situation and asked himself, "How far am I responsible for this social disorder? What can be done to prevent such outrageous manifestations of ill-will?"[74]

If the responsibility of tolerance lies with those of the widest vision, it behooves us to consider this great social disaster, not alone in its legal aspect nor in its sociological bearings, but from those deep human motives, which, after all, determine events.

During the discussions which followed the Pullman strike, the defenders of the situation were broadly divided between the people pleading for individual benevolence and those insisting upon social righteousness; between those who held that the philanthropy of the president of the Pullman Company had been most ungratefully received and those who maintained that the situation was the inevitable outcome of the social consciousness developing among working people.

In the midst of these discussions the writer found her mind dwelling upon a comparison which modified and softened all her judgments. Her attention was caught by the similarity of ingratitude suffered by an indulgent employer and an indulgent parent. *King Lear* came often to her mind. We have all shared the family relationship and our code of ethics concerning it is somewhat settled. We also bear a part in the industrial relationship, but our ethics concerning that are still uncertain. A comparative study of these two relationships presents an advantage, in that it enables us to consider the situation from the known experience toward the unknown. The minds of all of us reach back to our early struggles, as we emerged from the state of self-willed childhood to a recognition of the family claim.[75]

We have all had glimpses of what it might be to blaspheme against family ties; to ignore the elemental claim they make upon us, but on the whole we have recognized them, and it does not occur to us to throw them over. The industrial claim is so difficult; the ties are so intangible that we are constantly ignoring them and shirking the duties which they impose. It will probably be easier to treat of the tragedy of the Pullman strike as if it were already long past when we compare it to the

---

74 Hudson sees responses to the Pullman strike as exemplifying 1890s' concerns among 'anxious urban elites' that America was being swept up in Marxist class war. In contrast, Hudson reads Addams's 'Lear' as resisting calls to view 'unions as "un-American"' and instead 'cast[ing] industrial capitalist George Pullman' as behaving 'out of step' with 'American values' (904).

75 Addams's reference to 'the family claim' evoked a phrase that, by the 1915 publication of this talk, would have been familiar to readers of her best-selling 1910 *Twenty Years at Hull-House*. Addams there complained that social norms taught women (even those with advanced educations) 'to be self-forgetting and self-sacrificing, to consider the good of the whole before the good of the ego', and to place 'the family claim' ahead of any 'social claim' to activism (119).

family tragedy of *Lear* which has already become historic to our minds and which we discuss without personal feeling.[76]

Historically considered, the relation of *Lear* to his children was archaic and barbaric, holding in it merely the beginnings of a family life, since developed. We may in later years learn to look back upon the industrial relationships in which we are now placed as quite as incomprehensible and selfish, quite as barbaric and undeveloped, as was the family relationship between *Lear* and his daughters. We may then take the relationship of this unusually generous employer at Pullman to his own townful of employees as at least a fair one, because so exceptionally liberal in many of its aspects. *King Lear* doubtless held the same notion of a father's duty that was held by the other fathers of his time; but he alone was a king and had kingdoms to bestow upon his children. He was unique, therefore, in the magnitude of his indulgence, and in the magnitude of the disaster which followed it. The sense of duty held by the president of the Pullman Company doubtless represents the ideal in the minds of the best of the present employers as to their obligations toward their employees, but he projected this ideal more magnificently than the others. He alone gave his men so model a town, such perfect surroundings. The magnitude of his indulgence and failure corresponded and we are forced to challenge the ideal itself: the same ideal which, more or less clearly defined, is floating in the minds of all philanthropic employers. [...]

[...] The relation of the British King to his family is very like the relation of the president of the Pullman Company to his town;[77] the denouement of a daughter's break with her father suggests the break of the employees with their benefactor. If we call one an example of the domestic tragedy, the other of the industrial tragedy, it is possible to make them illuminate each other.

It is easy to discover striking points of similarity in the tragedies of the royal father and the philanthropic president of the Pullman Company. The like quality of ingratitude they both suffered is at once apparent. It may be said that the ingratitude which *Lear* received was poignant and bitter to him in proportion as he recalled the extraordinary benefits he had heaped upon his daughters, and that he found his fate harder to bear because he had so far exceeded the measure of a father's duty, as he himself says. What, then, would be the bitterness of a man who had heaped extraordinary benefits upon those toward whom he had no duty recognized by common consent; who had not only exceeded the righteousness of the employer, but who had worked out original and striking methods for lavishing goodness and generosity? More than that, the president had been almost persecuted for this goodness by the more utilitarian members of his company and had at one time imperiled his business reputation for the sake of the benefactions to his town, and he had thus reached the height of sacrifice for it. This model town embodied not only his hopes and ambitions, but stood for the peculiar effort which a man makes for that which is misunderstood.[78]

---

76 Addams suggests that her audience tap into knowledge of a highly canonical author (Shakespeare) and one of his best-known dramas (*King Lear*) and thus avoid being swayed by 'personal feeling' when evaluating the Pullman strike.

77 Equating George Pullman with a king – a position inimical to American democracy – echoes the Declaration of Independence's depiction of King George as tyrannical toward American colonists.

78 Footnote in original: While the town of Pullman was in process of construction the Pullman stock was sometimes called out on the New York Exchange: "How much for flower-beds and fountains?"—to which the company naturally objected.

It is easy to see that although the heart of *Lear* was cut by ingratitude and by misfortune, it was cut deepest of all by the public pity of his people, in that they should remember him no longer as a king and benefactor, but as a defeated man who had blundered through oversoftness. So the heart of the Chicago man was cut by the unparalleled publicity which brought him to the minds of thousands as a type of oppression and injustice, and to many others as an example of the evil of an irregulated sympathy for the "lower classes." He who had been dined and fêted throughout Europe as the creator of a model town, as the friend and benefactor of workingmen, was now execrated by workingmen throughout the entire country. He had not only been good to those who were now basely ungrateful to him, but he felt himself deserted by the admiration of his people. [. . .]

[. . .] If we may take the dictatorial relation of *Lear* to *Cordelia* as a typical and most dramatic example of the distinctively family tragedy, one will asserting its authority through all the entanglement of wounded affection, and insisting upon its selfish ends at all costs, may we not consider the absolute authority of this employer over his town as a typical and dramatic example of the industrial tragedy? One will directing the energies of many others, without regard to their desires, and having in view in the last analysis only commercial results?

It shocks our ideal of family life that a man should fail to know his daughter's heart because she awkwardly expressed her love, that he should refuse to comfort and advise her through all difference of opinion and clashing of will. That a man should be so absorbed in his own indignation as to fail to apprehend his child's thought; that he should lose his affection in his anger, is really no more unnatural than that the man who spent a million of dollars on a swamp to make it sanitary for his employees, should refuse to speak to them for ten minutes, whether they were in the right or wrong; or that a man who had given them his time and thought for twenty years should withdraw from them his guidance when he believed them misled by ill-advisers and wandering in a mental fog; or that he should grow hard and angry when they needed tenderness and help.

Lear ignored the common ancestry of *Cordelia* and himself. He forgot her royal inheritance of magnanimity, and also the power of obstinacy which he shared with her. So long had he thought of himself as the noble and indulgent father that he had lost the faculty by which he might perceive himself in the wrong. Even when his spirit was broken by the storm he declared himself more sinned against than sinning. He could believe any amount of kindness and goodness of himself, but could imagine no fidelity on the part of *Cordelia* unless she gave him the sign he demanded.

The president of the Pullman Company doubtless began to build his town from an honest desire to give his employees the best surroundings. As it developed it became a source of pride and an exponent of power, that he cared most for when it gave him a glow of benevolence. Gradually, what the outside world thought of it became of importance to him and he ceased to measure its usefulness by the standard of the men's needs. The theater was complete in equipment and beautiful in design, but too costly for a troupe who depended upon the patronage of mechanics, as the church was too expensive to be rented continuously. We can imagine the founder of the town slowly darkening his glints of memory and forgetting the common stock of experience which he held with his men. He cultivated the great and noble impulses of the benefactor, until the power of attaining a simple human relationship with his employees, that of frank equality with them, was gone from him. He, too, lost the faculty of affectionate interpretation, and demanded a sign. He and his employees had no mutual interest in a common cause. [. . .]

Lear had doubtless swung a bauble before *Cordelia's* baby eyes that he might have the pleasure of seeing the little pink and tender hands stretched for it. A few years later, he had given jewels to the young princess, and felt an exquisite pleasure when she stood before him, delighted with her gaud and grateful to her father. He demanded the same kind of response for his gift of the kingdom, but the gratitude must be larger and more carefully expressed, as befitted such a gift. At the opening of the drama he sat upon his throne ready for this enjoyment, but instead of delight and gratitude he found the first dawn of character. His daughter made the awkward attempt of an untrained soul to be honest, to be scrupulous in the expressions of its feelings. It was new to him that his child should be moved by a principle outside of himself, which even his imagination could not follow; that she had caught the notion of an existence so vast that her relationship as a daughter was but part of it.

Perhaps her suitors, the *King of France* or the *Duke of Burgundy*, had first hinted to the young Cordelia that there was a fuller life beyond the seas. Certain it is that someone had shaken her from the quiet measure of her insular existence and that she had at last felt the thrill of the world's life. She was transformed by a dignity which recast her speech and made it self-contained, as is becoming a citizen of the world. She found herself in the sweep of a notion of justice so large that the immediate loss of a kingdom seemed of little consequence to her. Even an act which might be construed as disrespect to her father was justified in her eyes because she was vainly striving to fill out this larger conception of duty.

The test which comes sooner or later to many parents had come to *Lear*, to maintain the tenderness of the relation between father and child, after that relation had become one between adults; to be contented with the responses which this adult made to the family claim, while, at the same time, she felt the tug upon her emotions and faculties of the larger life, the life which surrounds and completes the individual and family life, and which shares and widens her attention. He was not sufficiently wise to see that only that child can fulfill the family claim in its sweetness and strength who also fulfills the larger claim, that the adjustment of the lesser and larger implies no conflict. The mind of *Lear* was not big enough for this test. He failed to see anything but the personal slight involved; the ingratitude alone reached him. It was impossible for him to calmly watch his child developing beyond the strength of his own mind and sympathy.

Without pressing the analogy too hard may we not compare the indulgent relation of this employer to his town to the relation which existed between *Lear* and *Cordelia*? He fostered his employees for many years, gave them sanitary houses and beautiful parks, but in their extreme need, when they were struggling with the most difficult question which the times could present to them, when, if ever, they required the assistance of a trained mind and a comprehensive outlook, he lost his touch and had nothing wherewith to help them. He did not see the situation. He had been ignorant of their gropings toward justice. His conception of goodness for them had been cleanliness, decency of living, and above all, thrift and temperance. He had provided them means for all this; had gone further, and given them oppor-tunities for enjoyment and comradeship. But he suddenly found his town in the sweep of a world-wide moral impulse. A movement had been going on about him and through the souls of his workingmen of which he had been unconscious. He had only heard of this movement by rumor. The men who consorted with him at his club and in his business had spoken but little of it, and when they had discussed it had contemptuously called it the "Labor Movement," headed by deadbeats and agitators. Of the force and power of this movement, of all the vitality within it, of that conception of duty which induces men to go without food and to see their wives and children suffer for the sake of securing better wages for fellow-workmen whom they have never seen, this president had dreamed absolutely nothing. But his town had at last become swept into this larger movement, so that the giving-up of comfortable homes, of beautiful surroundings, seemed as naught to the men within its grasp. [. . .]

That the movement was ill-directed, that it was ill-timed and disastrous in results, that it stirred up and became confused in the minds of the public with the elements of riot and bloodshed, can never touch the fact that it started from an unselfish impulse. [. . .]

The diffused and subtle notion of dignity held by the modern philanthropist bears a curious analogy to the personal barbaric notion of dignity held by *Lear*. The man who persistently paced the seashore, while the interior of his country was racked with a strife which he alone might have arbitrated, lived out within himself the tragedy of "King Lear." The shock of disaster upon egotism is apt to produce self-pity. It is possible that his self-pity and loneliness may have been so great and absorbing as to completely shut out from his mind a compunction of derelict duly. He may have been unconscious that men were charging him with a shirking of the issue. [. . .]

In so far as philanthropists are cut off from the influence of the *Zeit-Geist*, from the code of ethics which rules the body of men, from the great moral life springing from our common experiences, so long as they are "good to people," rather than "with them," they are bound to accomplish a large amount of harm. [. . .]

In reading the tragedy of "King Lear," *Cordelia* does not escape our censure. Her first words are cold, and we are shocked by her lack of tenderness. Why should she ignore her father's need for indulgence, and be so unwilling to give him what he so obviously craved? We see in the old king "the overmastering desire of being beloved, which is selfish, and yet characteristic of the selfishness of a loving and kindly nature alone." His eagerness produces in us a strange pity for him, and we are impatient that his youngest and best-beloved child cannot feel this, even in the midst of her search for truth and her newly acquired sense of a higher duty. It seems to us a narrow conception that would break thus abruptly with the past, and would assume that her father had no part in her new life. We want to remind her that "pity, memory and faithfulness are natural ties," and surely as much to be prized as is the development of her own soul. [. . .]

As the vision of the life of Europe caught the sight and quickened the pulses of *Cordelia*, so a vision of the wider life has caught the sight of workingmen. After the vision has once been seen it is impossible to do aught but to press toward its fulfillment. We have all seen it. We are all practically agreed that the social passion of the age is directed toward the emancipation of the wage-worker; that a great accumulation of moral force is overmastering men and making for this emancipation as in another time it has made for the emancipation of the slave; that nothing will satisfy the aroused conscience of men short of the complete participation of the working classes in the spiritual, intellectual and material inheritance of the human race. But just as *Cordelia* failed to include her father in the scope of her salvation and selfishly took it for herself alone, so workingmen in the dawn of the vision are inclined to claim it for themselves, putting out of their thoughts the old relationships: and just as surely as *Cordelia's* conscience developed in the new life and later drove her back to her father, where she perished, drawn into the cruelty and wrath which had now become objective and tragic, so the emancipation of working people will have to be inclusive of the employer from the first or it will encounter many failures, cruelties and reactions. It will result not in the position of the repentant *Cordelia* but in that of *King Lear's* two older daughters. [...]

The new claim on the part of the toiling multitude, the new sense of responsibility on the part of the well-to-do, arise in reality from the same source. They are in fact the same "social compunction," and, in spite of their widely varying manifestations, logically converge into the same movement. Mazzini[79] once preached, "the consent of men and your own conscience are two wings given you whereby you may rise to God." It is so easy for the good and powerful to think that they can rise by following the dictates of conscience by pursuing their own ideals, leaving those ideals unconnected with the consent of their fellow-men. The president of the Pullman Company thought out within his own mind a beautiful town. He had power with which to build this town, but he did not appeal to nor obtain the consent of the men who were living in it. The most unambitious reform, recognizing the necessity for this consent, makes for slow but sane and strenuous progress, while the most ambitious of social plans and experiments, ignoring this, is prone to the failure of the model town of Pullman. [...]

If only a few families of the English-speaking race had profited by the dramatic failure of *Lear*, much heartbreaking and domestic friction might have been spared. Is it too much to hope that some of us will carefully consider this modern tragedy, if perchance it may contain a warning for the troublous times in which we live? By considering the dramatic failure of the liberal employer's plans for his employees we may possibly be spared useless industrial tragedies in the uncertain future which lies ahead of us.

Source text

Addams, Jane, 'A Modern Lear: A Parenthetical Chapter by Jane Addams', in Graham Romeyn Taylor (ed.), *Satellite Cities: A Study of Industrial Suburbs* (New York and London: Appleton, 1915), 68–90.

References

Addams, Jane, *Twenty Years at Hull-House, with Autobiographical Notes* (New York: Macmillan, 1910).

Hudson, Cheryl, 'The "Un-American" Experiment: Jane Addams's Lessons from Pullman', *Journal of American Studies* 47.4 (November 2013), 903–13.

Robbins, Sarah Ruffing, 'Sustaining Gendered Philanthropy through Transatlantic Friendship: Jane Addams, Henrietta Barnett, and Writing for Reciprocal Mentoring', in Frank Q. Christianson and Leslee Thorne-Murphy (eds), *Philanthropic Discourse in Anglo-American Literature, 1850–1920* (Bloomington, IN: Indiana University Press, 2017), 211–35.

---

79 Italian Joseph (Guiseppe) Mazzini was one of Addams's favourite thinkers. In *Twenty Years*, she credits her father's conviction that Mazzini promoted 'the genuine relationship which may exist between men who share large hopes and like desires, even though they differ in nationality' (21). Addams dubs Mazzini 'that greatest of all democrats', a staunch advocate for education to uplift the poor (427).

John McCrae (1872–1918) and Sir Andrew Macphail (1864–1938)

From In Flanders Fields, and Other Poems *(1919)*

The First World War generated many global firsts, among them initial uses of the term 'home front' to designate the civilian life of people whose country is engaged in foreign warfare (*OED*). One enshrinement of that domestic engagement with faraway conflict appears in Canadian physician John McCrae's 'In Flanders Fields' lyric, penned in 1915 during the Second Battle of Ypres and first published anonymously in the popular English magazine *Punch* that December.

Early reprintings of the poem in the US followed *Punch*'s lead in omitting the author's name, while feeding into calls for Americans to resist President Woodrow Wilson's neutral stance and enter the war. Once the US joined the Allies in 1917, reprintings with the author's name proliferated. Jennifer Ward reports that over fifty different American composers, including John Philip Sousa, set the lyric to music. In Canada, McCrae's text reached iconic status soon after his death of pneumonia in a wartime hospital – its elevation aided by publication of his poems with a biographical narrative by Sir Andrew Macphail.

As Teresa Gilbert and Nancy Holmes have noted in two different interpretive essays ('Challenging the Myths' and '"In Flanders Fields"' respectively), the poem's appropriation by politicians to mythologise war – and questions about the text's aesthetic value – have led some to decry its canonisation. Yet, its power to evoke home-front identification with wartime experiences endures, seen in Canada's placing a quote on the ten dollar bill, recitations on Remembrance Day every November, veneration of its poppy image – and intertextual responses (some critical, some appreciative) by writers ranging from Canadians L. M. Montgomery and Margaret Atwood, to Americans R. W. Lillard and Henry Polk Lowenstein, to British author Martin Bell.

From In Flanders Fields, and Other Poems

In Flanders fields the poppies blow
    Between the crosses, row on row,
  That mark our place; and in the sky
  The larks, still bravely singing, fly
Scarce heard amid the guns below.

We are the Dead. Short days ago
We lived, felt dawn, saw sunset glow,
    Loved and were loved, and now we lie,
      In Flanders fields.

Take up our quarrel with the foe:
To you from failing hands we throw
    The torch; be yours to hold it high.
    If ye break faith with us who die
We shall not sleep, though poppies grow
    In Flanders fields.

Figure 4.7 John McCrae, Bonneau, Bonfire and Herbert Cruickshank, *c.*1917.
Image from a postcard. Courtesy Guelph Museums, McCrae House.

From 'John McCrae': Profile by Sir Andrew Macphail

[...] It is little wonder then that "In Flanders Fields" has become the poem of the army. The soldiers have learned it with their hearts, which is quite a different thing from committing it to memory. It circulates as a song should circulate, by the living word of mouth, not by printed characters. [...]

Nor has any piece of verse in recent years been more widely known in the civilian world. It was used in every platform from which men were being adjured to adventure their lives or their riches in the great trial through which the present generation has passed. Many "replies" have been made. The best I have seen was written in the *New York Evening Post*. None but those who were prepared to die before Vimy Ridge that early April day of 1916[80] will ever feel fully the great truth of Mr. Lillard's opening lines, as they speak for all Americans:

---

80 Macphail gives a 1916 date, but the Vimy Ridge battle occurred in April 1917. Jacqueline Hucker says Vimy holds a place of honour in Canadian history, since the battle 'marked the first time all four Canadian divisions launched a simultaneous attack on one front under Canadian command'. Despite 'high cost in human life [over 3,500 deaths], the successful outcome of the attack boosted the country's military confidence' and 'reinforce[d] Canada's awakening sense of independence and nationhood'. See Jacqueline Hucker, '"Battle and Burial": Recapturing the Cultural Meaning of Canada's National Memorial on Vimy Ridge', *Public Historian* 31.1 (2009), 90.

"Rest ye in peace, ye Flanders dead.
The fight that ye so bravely led
We've taken up."

[...] It was in April, 1915. The enemy was in full cry of victory. All that remained for him was to occupy Paris, as once he did before, and to seize the Channel ports. Then France, England, and the world were doomed. All winter the German had spent in repairing his plans, which had gone somewhat awry on the Marne. He had devised his final stroke, and it fell upon the Canadians at Ypres. This battle, known as the second battle of Ypres, culminated on April 22nd, but it really extended over the whole month.

The inner history of war is written from the recorded impressions of men who have endured it. John McCrae in a series of letters to his mother, cast in the form of a diary, has set down in words the impressions which this event of the war made upon a peculiarly sensitive mind. [...]

Monday, April 26th, 1915

Another day of heavy actions, but last night much French and British artillery has come in, and the place is thick with Germans. There are many prematures (with so much firing) but the pieces are usually spread before they get to us. It is disquieting, however, I must say. And all the time the birds sing in the trees over our heads. Yesterday up to noon we fired 3000 rounds for the twenty-four hours; to-day we have fired much less, but we have registered fresh fronts, and burned some farms behind the German trenches. About six the fire died down, and we had a peaceful evening and night, and Cosgrave and I in the dugout made good use of it.[81] [...]

France, May 12th, 1915

I am glad you had your mind at rest by the rumour that we were in reserve. What newspaper work! The poor old artillery never gets any mention, and the whole show is the infantry. It may interest you to note on your map a spot on the west bank of the canal, a mile and a half north of Ypres, as the scene of our labours. There can be no harm in saying so, now that we are out of it. The unit was the most advanced of all the Allies' guns by a good deal except one French battery which stayed in a position yet more advanced for two days, and then had to be taken out. I think it may be said that we saw the show from the soup to the coffee. [...]

The last letter from the Front is dated June 1st, 1915. Upon that day he [McCrae] was posted to No. 3 General Hospital at Boulogne, and placed in charge of medicine with the rank of Lieutenant-Colonel as of date 17th April, 1915. Here he remained until the day of his death on January 28th, 1918.

Source text

McCrae, John, *In Flanders Fields, and Other Poems, with an Essay in Character by Sir Andrew Macphail* (New York and London: G. P. Putnam's Sons, 1919).

---

81 Situated close to or within a trench wall, First World War dugouts offered added protection for soldiers, creating a space for possible rest or for shelter during meals.

References

Gilbert, Teresa, 'Challenging the Myths of the Great War: John McCrae's "In Flanders Fields" Revisited', *Anglo Saxonica* 3.16 (2018), 95–120.

Holmes, Nancy, '"In Flanders Fields" – Canada's Official Poem: Breaking Faith', *Studies in Canadian Literature* 30.1 (2005), 11–13.

McCrae, John and Henry Polk Lowenstein, 'In Flanders Fields', *Journal of Education* 97.21 (24 May 1923), 581.

McCrae, John and R. W. Lillard, 'In Flanders Fields' and 'America's Answer', *Journal of Education* 94.17 (10 November 1921), 461.

Ward, Jennifer A., 'American Musical Settings of "In Flanders Fields" and the Great War', *Journal of Musicological Research* 33 (2014), 96–129.

5

MIGRATION, SETTLEMENT AND RESISTANCE

Figure 5.1 Frontispiece: First Canadian edition of *Roughing It in the Bush* (1871), illustrators Charles F. Damoreau and Seymour Toro.

In 1855, William Nesbit published a critique of the American Colonization Society's campaign to send US Blacks 'back' to Africa – specifically, to Liberia. Martin Delany's introduction to the publication forcefully seconded Nesbit's depiction of Liberia as an unacceptable settlement site. Interestingly, Delany's own earlier 1852 publication, *The Condition, Elevation, Emigration and Destiny of the Colored People of the United States*, had taken a somewhat different stand, arguing that, in the wake of the dangers imposed by the passage of the 1850 Fugitive Slave Law, the best pathway to Black safety lay in emigration to the Caribbean or Central or South America. And, in yet another text addressing ideas about migration, Delany's serialised novel, *Blake; or, the Huts of America* (1859–62), offered a pro-emigration argument by having his protagonist relocate from the southern US to Canada and then Cuba.

One key to Delany's differing positions lies in the previous transatlantic movement of Black bodies into enslavement. Unlike the majority of white journeys in the long era this anthology explores, Blacks' transatlantic crossings through the heinous Middle Passage were brutally coerced rather than voluntary. Later, when enslaved or free nineteenth-century Blacks in the Caribbean or North America did have opportunities to relocate by choice (whether escaping via an Underground Railroad to the Northern US or Canada, or travelling to Britain after that government had outlawed enslavement), a claim of personal agency guided their migrations. Whether travelling on the anti-slavery lecture circuit like William Wells Brown or Frederick Douglass, or arriving first in Britain as un-manumitted domestic workers like Mary Prince and then claiming freedom, nineteenth-century Blacks choosing transatlantic migrations from West to East asserted a powerful counterpoint to Middle Passage voyages in the other direction. Nesbit's and Delany's rejection of Liberia thus represented not a dismissal of Africa or travel there, per se. Rather, they posed, based on careful research, in Liberia Black–white relations too clearly echoed the 'master–slave' relationship which both sought for their race to escape.

Overall, whatever route a transatlantic journey-by-choice entailed for free Blacks, it was part of a pattern of migratory race history far different from idealised passages to a new life associated with mythic narratives like the 'American Dream', with its images of economic uplift and democratic social relations.[1] Acknowledging such differences lies at the heart of this anthology section, 'Migration, Settlement and Resistance'.

MIGRATION MYTHS

As a time marked (and shaped) by many migrations and diasporas, the long nineteenth century generated persistent narratives of movement, settlement and acculturation whose place in today's Anglophone cultural memory would be difficult to dislodge. However, cultivating a critical transatlantic perspective on this topic can illuminate how some actual individuals' lives helped construct these myths in the first place, but also how such accounts suppress (or even erase) experiences of others. That goal has helped guide our choice of texts here.

Fanny Fern's satirical portrait of an Irish 'Bridget' who longs to pass beyond 'greenhorn' status clearly depended on ethnic immigrant stereotypes to entertain

---

1 For whites, too, as several entries will show, idealised migration myths were far from reliable portraits of transatlantic migration. Thus, as Susanna Moodie emphasised in *Roughing It in the Bush*, the distance between the propaganda of recruitment and the reality of relocating to a place like the Upper Canada of her day was immense. See above image from an 1871 edition.

the popular author's transatlantic readership. Yet many a young Irish woman did actually make the ocean crossing to a successful version of the domestic labour skewered in Fern's sketch.[2] And our 'Irish Female Emigration' report of Vere Foster's funding thousands of such relocations shows this social pattern in action. Meanwhile, if Irish-American cook Ann McNabb's oral history of her family's chain migration to the US invoked already-beloved tropes of shared socio-economic rise, then successful marketing of the multi-ethnic stories where her account originally appeared affirmed the role that nineteenth-century print culture exercised in nurturing associated mythology. So too did later reviews, on both sides of the Atlantic, of Mary Antin's *The Promised Land*, a tale of a Jewish family's escape from religious persecution to North America. Hopeful transatlantic migration myths were both grounded in real-life experiences and nurtured through communal, often unrealistic memory-making.

FLUID SPACES WITH MULTIPLE CURRENTS

Balancing chronicle and critique, and in line with our entire anthology's oceanic emphasis, one organising idea for this section is spatial. Thus the Atlantic itself situates our themes of migration, settlement and resistance geographically in a fluid locale without stable borders. We can think, for example, of settlements that stretched across North America and into Caribbean islands more as an ongoing inflow of cultural activity mixing with the many communities already there, rather than as an inevitable, self-sufficient march across an empty continental space. This approach operates in contrast to studies that emphasise either immigration 'in' to North America or emigration 'out' of Europe. Rather, our work joins scholarship on the Black, Red, and Green Atlantics which traces migrations through frameworks resisting what David Armitage and Jace Weaver have critiqued as imperialistic and/or nationalist perspectives imagining historical currents as white-driven only.

To foreground multiple iterations of diverse Atlantics also complicates histories of whites' transatlantic migrations. So, when we re-envision narratives like Susanna Moodie's account of her family's journey to Upper Canada through a transatlantic lens interrogating race, ethnicity and class, we choose excerpts from her *Roughing It in the Bush* that ask readers to study her portrayals of other immigrants with intersectional identities different from her own. Similarly, in place of straightforward portraits of an expatriate like Henry James renouncing the US for a high-culture European life, a more complex transatlantic version links his anxious revisiting of his youthful New York neighbourhoods in *The American Scene* with his nativist response to Ellis Island as symbolising immigrant hordes' infiltration of America. Further, juxtaposing the Scottish-youth-

---

2 See Lynch-Brennan, *The Irish Bridget*. Though the Bridget figure reflects both substantial real-life numbers and negative stereotyping, recent research reminds us that other labour contexts merit study beyond that gendered, domestic focus. See Harper's 'Obstacles', which uses empirical data to track 'globetrotting British settlers and sojourners who went to Canada, the United States and Australia between 1815 and the 1880s' (43), especially Scottish and Welsh miners, Scottish weavers and granite tradesmen – all of whom Harper sees as remaining self-conscious members of an expanded 'British World' (57–8).

turned-American environmentalist John Muir's memoir of his family's settlement in a land he casts as empty wilderness with poems by First Nations author E. Pauline Johnson prompts critique of his nostalgia about his 'new' home in an 'empty' American West.

MULTI-DIRECTIONALITY

As a group, texts here resist the familiar myth of journeys across the ocean from Europe to the Caribbean and North America as a one-way relocation line toward uplift. See, for instance, the periodical essay by Edith Maude Eaton, which describes how ethnic identity, gender and class could complicate efforts by migrating minorities to achieve economic stability and social acceptance. For Eaton, coming to America became both multi-directional and multicultural.

In another dimension of multi-directionality, we include migrations from the 'New' World to the Old, such as a retrospective account by Benjamin Franklin of his colonial-era move to England, a home country where he considered remaining. Similarly, Caroline Norton's 'The Creole Girl' poem illustrates how British colonisation of the Caribbean brought people from that region to England. Relatedly, while this section excerpts Mary Ann Shadd Cary's pamphlet encouraging Black migration to Canada as a welcoming home in the post-Fugitive Slave Law period, both the headnote for that account (tracking Cary's later return to the US) and her entry's cross-reference to writing by William and Ellen Craft signal how, for many Blacks seeking to flee enslavement, journeys beyond a Canadian borderline became essential to achieving full freedom, given the long reach of transatlantic slavery.

RESISTANCE

Another vital dimension of transatlantic studies' push-back on familiar versions of migration highlights the sustained resistance of Indigenous people against Europeans' encroachment into Native lands. To articulate that opposition from a stance affirming Native nations' political rights, in 1776 Joseph Brant (Thayendenegeh) journeyed from North America to England. The Brant speech we include here proclaimed Indigenous sovereignty and pressed the British government to mitigate the dire impact of white migration on his homeland. In 1911, Charles Eastman (Ohiyesa) retraced Brant's transatlantic route from North America to London to lecture at the First Universal Races Conference. Speaking on the same day when W. E. B. DuBois delivered an address on 'The Negro Race in the United States of America', Eastman characterised the pernicious influence of white settlement on Indigenous lands, people and cultural practices. As an echo and extension of Brant's rhetoric, the segment here from Eastman's speech (additionally excerpted in other sections) demonstrates that attention to time, as well as space, should be part of transatlantic studies. In this case, for instance, while these two Native speakers both underscore how white transatlantic migration created challenges to Indigenous homelands, their different delivery dates lead to content underscoring how nineteenth-century settler colonialism begat more intense social changes across time. Brant's self-identification as a would-be ally from a specific Native nation's sovereign community uses language announcing equal standing (as in addressing his British counterpart political leader as 'brother'). Eastman's nuanced self-presentation characterises his own complex identity as both revelatory of the abuses white migration has imposed on Indigenous people and as embodying successful assimilation, thereby exemplifying how many transatlantic social relationships shifted across time in the long nineteenth century.

In addition, honouring Native resistance to nineteenth-century transatlantic settler colonialism requires underscoring that this vital history was often enacted – and recorded in print – in complicated records. Many accounts documenting this resistance come down to us only in mediated ways. As exemplary of this pattern – one demanding, in response, analysis of both absence and presence, of both bias and insight – see James Boswell's 'Account' of Joseph Brant's time in England and the excerpt from James Seaver's *Narrative in the Life of Mrs. Mary Jemison* (who went from captive to choosing a Native American identity). We urge equally careful readings of Lydia Sigourney's anti-Removal poem ('Indian Names') and of the 1856 post-Removal periodical piece entitled 'The Sorrows of the Cherokees'. In all these texts, even though their authors wrote from a stance seeking to be empathetic advocates, we should ask how such stories of resistance to white incursion are shaped by who is speaking, as well as how these writers envisioned their audiences. In cultivating a critical perspective aware of the particular time of each text's composition and circulation on both sides of the ocean, we should address rhetorical distances between what is said and what could have been said, if the author had been operating from a position of greater epistemic authority, that is from the actual standpoint of the marginalised person or group.

Asking such questions not only enables us to see the restricted viewpoints of white authors writing about nineteenth-century transatlantic migrations. It also invites us to notice the liminal standpoint from which a poem like E. Pauline Johnson's 'Joe: An Etching' arises. A mixed-race speaker with both a First Nations affiliation and a white heritage that led her to self-position as 'Canadian Born' within a British empire's political space, Johnson chooses – in this poem, at least – to depict settler colonialism in the person of a young white child. Then, when we juxtapose that text's view of transatlantic Irish migration with her portrait of an elderly First Nations woman in 'The Corn Husker', we have a far more vexed relationship to take into account.

READING THE GAPS AND ERASURES

Overall, this section on 'Migration, Settlement and Resistance' promotes a transatlantic studies that examines the gaps around, and within, nineteenth-century Anglophone texts, as much as the elements directly inscribed there. One aspect of this approach entails remembering how social practices long valued by a particular group came under pressure when relocated through migration; acculturation involved more than just learning to eat unfamiliar foods, needing to wear different clothes or acquiring new language. It brought both gains and losses. Elizabeth Errington's *Emigrant Worlds and Transatlantic Communities* provides a helpful model by suggesting that any study of migration as an individual experience also needs to track social networks, such as the family circles, but that such efforts will yield only incomplete results.

Errington's study lays out what she dubs as the 'intriguing' yet incomplete stories of transatlantic migration and settlement captured in 'information wanted' stories printed in nineteenth-century Canadian newspapers. These pleas for help finding lost relatives illustrate that aspirations for successful chain migration were not always achievable. Relatives in search of family members to reunify a domestic unit often arrived, post-crossing, to find a father, brother or sister had disappeared.

When seeking to reconstruct social networks linked to migration, settlement and resistance experiences, we must often depend upon conjecture, however well-informed by historical trends. We must be humble and tentative, therefore, in offering any arguments grounded in this attempted recovery process – including that represented in the accounts collected here. On that note, we direct readers to Irish immigrant-to-America Ann McNabb's transcribed oral history. Even as she celebrates the financial and personal victories of family members who followed her to the northeastern US, McNabb poignantly remembers two brothers who instead traversed another ocean: 'John an' Matthew they went to Australia. Mother was layin' by for five year to get their passage money. They went into the bush. We heard twice from them and then no more. Not another word and this is forty year gone now.' McNabb strives to end their unfinished migration story on a positive yet realistic note: 'I suppose they're dead now—John would be ninety now—and in heaven. They were honest men.'

Echoing McNabb, we have gathered diverse, though ever-incomplete, stories of 'Migration, Settlement and Resistance'. We invite our readers to pursue the many gaps in and around these stories, by continuing to recover examples from other networks and to raise questions about the texts and interpretive frameworks offered here.

References

Armitage, David, 'The Red Atlantic', *Reviews in American History* 29.4 (December 2001), 479–86.

Belish, James, *Replenishing the Earth: The Settler Revolution and the Rise of the Anglo-World, 1783–1939* (Oxford: Oxford University Press, 2011).

Errington, Elizabeth, *Emigrant Worlds and Transatlantic Communities: Migration to Upper Canada in the First Half of the Nineteenth Century* (Montreal: McGill-Queen's University Press, 2007).

Gilroy, Paul, *The Black Atlantic: Modernity and Double-Consciousness* (Cambridge, MA: Harvard University Press, 1993).

Gough, Kathleen M., *Kinship and Performance in the Black and Green Atlantic: Haptic Allegories* (New York: Routledge, 2018).

Harper, Marjory, 'Obstacles and Opportunities: Labour Emigration to the "British World" in the Nineteenth Century', *Continuity and Change* 34 (2019), 43–62.

Lynch-Brennan, Margaret, *The Irish Bridget: Irish Immigrant Women in Domestic Service in America, 1840–1930* (Syracuse, NY: Syracuse University Press, 2009).

Weaver, Jace, *The Red Atlantic: American Indigenes and the Making of the Modern World, 1000–1927* (Chapel Hill, NC: University of North Carolina Press, 2014).

Zeleza, Paul Tiyambe, 'Rewriting the African Diaspora: Beyond the Black Atlantic', *African Affairs* 104.414 (January 2005), 35–68.

Joseph Brant (1742–1807)

'Speech of Captain Brant to Lord George Germain' (1776)

Joseph Brant (Thayendenegeh) was a dedicated spokesman (or, in Jace Weaver's term, a 'red diplomat') for First Nations people on pressing issues such as land rights. Early in the US Revolutionary War era, Brant travelled to England to pledge support for King George and to seek, in return, the monarch's promise to honour Native sovereignty in the face of ongoing white settler colonialism. Known for eloquence, Brant was equally noted for his ability to switch performative features such as his dress depending on his listeners, trading the Indian moccasins and blanket English audiences would have expected for broadcloth suits on occasion, while self-presenting in Native dress when such attire was advantageous to his rhetorical situation. Brant's choice to side with the King was similarly strategic. With American colonists already overrunning Native lands up and down the Atlantic seaboard, Brant hoped that supporting the British would garner his homeland's security.

The Six Nations (Haudenosaunee) Confederacy (including Brant's Mohawks and the Oneidas, Onondagas, Cayugas, Senecas and Tuscaroras) held a Constitutional system, making them one of the world's oldest democracies. But the American Revolutionary War ripped their confederation apart, as most Senecas and Cayugas followed the Mohawk 'King' Brant's lead in supporting the British, while many Tuscaroroas and Oneidas sided with the colonists. At the direction of George Washington, in 1779, Major General John Sullivan and Brigadier General James Clinton would lead a brutal campaign against Haudensaunee communities, with thousands of the homeless refugees fleeing to Canada. In response to this punitive strategy, the Iroquois dubbed Washington 'Town Destroyer' or 'Conotocautious'.

When Brant gave this speech, he could not foresee the conflict's eventual results. Thus he repeatedly praises both King George and English government representatives. Asserting a language of familial affiliation yet also affirming national rights for his people, Thayendenegeh/Brant invokes a brand of rhetorical sovereignty anticipating scholarship on Native agency such as Scott Lyons's. Sadly, his call to England's leaders to recognise Native nationhood would be brushed aside in Britain's peace treaty with the former colonists: the king ceded to the new white nation lands that actually belonged to his faithful Six Nations allies.

'Speech of Captain Brant to Lord George Germain'

The Speech of Thayendenegeh a Chief, accompanied by Oteroughyanento a Warrior, both of the Six Nations. 14 March, 1776.

To the Right Honble Lord George Germaine[3] one of His Majestys Principal Secretarys of State.

Brother Gorah.[4]

    We[5] have cross'd the great Lake[6] and come to this kingdom with our Superintendant Col. Johnson,[7] from our Confederacy the Six Nations and their Allies, that we might see our Father, the Great King, and joyn in informing him, his Councillors and wise men, of the good intentions of the Indians our bretheren, and of their attachment to His Majesty and his Government.

    Brother. The Disturbances in America give great trouble to all our Nations, as many strange stories have been told to us by the people in that country. The Six Nations who alwayes loved the King, sent a number of their Chiefs and Warriors with their Superintendant to Canada last summer, where they engaged their allies to joyn with them in the defence of that country, and when it was invaded by the New England people, they alone defeated them.[8]

    Brother. In that engagement we had several of our best Warriors killed and wounded, and the Indians think it very hard they should have been so deceived by the White people in that country, the enemy returning in great numbers, and no White people supporting the Indians, they were obliged to retire to their villages and sit still. We now Brother hope to see these bad children chastised, and that we may be enabled to tell the Indians, who have always been faithfull and ready to assist the King, what His Majesty intends.

    Brother. The Mohocks our particular Nation, have on all occasions shown their zeal and loyalty to the Great King; yet they have been very badly treated by the people in that country, the City of Albany laying an unjust claim to the lands on which our Lower Castle is built, as one Klock, and others do to those of Conijoharrie our Upper Village. We have been often assured by our late great friend, Sr William Johnson[9] who never deceived us, and we know he was told so that the King and wise men here would do us justice; but this notwithstanding all our applications has never been done, and it makes us very uneasie. We also feel for the distress in which our Bretheren on the Susquehanna are likely to be involved by a mistake made in the Boundary we settled in 1768.[10] This also our Superintendant has laid before

---

3 George Germain (1716–85), Secretary of State for the Colonies

4 Gorah might be interpreted as 'Great One', or perhaps 'person of honor'.

5 Consistent with Native practice of sending multiple envoys for important missions, John Hill (Oteroughyanento) accompanied Brant.

6 Atlantic Ocean

7 Guy Johnson (c.1740–88), military officer and Crown diplomat during the Revolutionary War, appointed Superintendent of Northern Indian Affairs in 1774

8 Brant here refers to a battle fought near Montreal in 1775, when the American Ethan Allen was taken prisoner. The captive Allen was sent to Britain in the same ship that brought Brant.

9 William Johnson (c.1715–74), Superintendent of the Iroquois Confederacy and thus responsible for maintaining peace between the Indigenous peoples of the region and the British settlers. He has been credited with helping gain Mohawk support for the British during earlier conflicts with the French in North America. Impressed by Brant's intellect, Johnson supported the younger man's education.

10 The settlement of the boundary was part of a Treaty set at Fort Stanwix.

the King, and we beg it may be remembered.[11] And also concerning Religion and the want of Ministers of the Church of England, he knows the designs of those bad people and informs us he has laid the same before the King. We have only therefore to request that his Majesty will attend to this matter: it troubles our Nation & they cannot sleep easie in their beds. Indeed it is very hard, when we have let the Kings subjects have so much of our lands for so little value, they should want to cheat us in this manner of the small spots we have left for our women and children to live on. We are tired out in making complaints & getting no redress. We therefore hope that the Assurances now given us by the Superintendant may take place, and that he may have it in his power to procure us justice.

Brother. We shall truly report all that we hear from you, to the Six Nations on our return. We are well informed there has been many Indians in this Country who came without any authority, from their own, and gave much trouble. We desire Brother to tell you this is not our case. We are warriors known to all the Nations, and are now here by approbation of many of them, whose sentiments we speak.

Brother. We hope that these things will be considered and that the King or his great men will give us such answer as will make our hearts light and glad before we go, and strengthen our hands, so that we may join our Superintendant Col. Johnson in giving satisfaction to all our Nations, when we report to them, on our return; for which purpose we hope soon to be accomodated with a passage.

Dictated by the Indians and taken down by Jo: Chew. Sec[y]

Source text

Brant, Captain [Joseph (Thayendenegeh)], 'Speech of Captain Brant to Lord George Germain', in E. B. O'Callaghan (ed.), *Documents Relative to the Colonial History of the State of New York; Procured in Holland, England and France, by John Romeyn Brodhead, ESQ.* (Albany, NY: Weed Parsons, 1857), Vol. 8, 670–1.

References

Elbourne, Elizabeth, 'Family Politics and Anglo-Mohawk Diplomacy: The Brant Family in Imperial Context', *Journal of Colonialism and Colonial History* 6.3 (Winter 2006), Web.

Lyons, Scott Richard, 'Rhetorical Sovereignty: What Do American Indians Want from Writing?', *College Composition and Communication* 51.3 (2000), 447–68.

Monture, Rick, *We Share Our Matters: Two Centuries of Writing and Resistance at Six Nations of the Grand River* (Winnepeg: University of Manitoba Press, 2014).

Weaver, Jace, *The Red Atlantic: American Indigenes and the Making of the Modern World, 1000–1927* (Chapel Hill, NC: University of North Carolina Press, 2014).

---

11 Brant may still be referencing the deceased William Johnson, his mentor, or he may here be referring to Guy Johnson, who, along with Daniel Claus, accompanied Brant on the mission to England represented in this speech.

JOSEPH   THAYENDANEKEN
The . Mohawk Chief

Figure 5.2 From an original drawing in the possession of James Boswell,
Esqr.- Illus. in: *The London Magazine*, 1776 (July), p. 339. Joseph
Thayendaneken the Mohawk chief, 1776. [1 July]. Photograph.
Courtesy Library of Congress Prints and Photographs Division.

James Boswell (1740–95)

'An Account of the Chief of the Mohock Indians, who lately visited England (With an exact Likeness)' (1776)

Although best known today for his *Life of Samuel Johnson* (1791), James
Boswell frequently wrote for *The London Magazine* earlier in his career.
One of his articles presented a profile of Joseph Brant (Thayendenegeh),
the Mohawk (or, as Boswell says, 'Mohock') chief who visited London
in 1776.

Boswell's account suggests how England's social leaders viewed their
North American Indian allies – even someone as fluent in the English
language, astute about politics and refined in social skills as Brant. Thus
Boswell's presentation of 'Mohock' people prior to the 'civilising' influence
of white settler colonialism exemplifies how Anglophone print discourse
could ignore such features of their history as a sophisticated system of

government including a confederacy of multiple sovereign Native nations. Further, Boswell's story illustrates how confident a white English writer could then feel about casting himself as an expert on Indigenous North American peoples despite never having crossed the Atlantic.

To underscore the limitations of Boswell's assessment of Brant, one might turn to A. Zuercher Reichardt's appreciation of Thayendenegeh's skilled translation of the Gospel of Mark, published in 1787, but originally completed in 1774 ('Translation'). For Reichardt, Brant's notable translation skills embodied his blending of formal English education via both tutors and boarding school with being 'steeped in Mohawk and Haudenosaunee literary traditions', as also seen in the *Primer* co-published with Daniel Claus in 1786.

As noted in its subtitle, Boswell's *London Magazine* story on Brant also featured a line-drawn, black-and-white portrait. This would end up being just one of a number of portraits of Brant painted by such famous artists as Gilbert Stuart and George Romney. Their visual rhetoric would further extend whites' often romanticised perceptions of Brant, even as, among his people, he remained a dedicated and heroic leader.

'An Account of the Chief of the Mohock Indians, who lately visited England'

IT is well known that the chief of the Mohock[12] Indians visited England in the reign of Queen Anne,[13] and was very well received at the court of that princess. His picture is preserved in the British museum. At that time the Mohocks were a very rude and uncivilized nation. The periodical essays of the Augustan age of England, as Queen Anne's reign has been called, shew us that the very name of Mohock was then terrible in London; and we find many ingenious and entertaining remarks produced from speculating upon the visit of the wild American chief. But somewhat more than half a century has made a very great change upon the Mohock nation. They are now so well trained to civil life, as to live in a fixed place, to have good commodious houses, to cultivate land with assiduity and skill, and to trade with the British colonies. They are also converted to the Christian faith, and have among them a priest[14] of the church of England, who regularly performs the sacred functions as prescribed in the Liturgy, which is translated into their language.

The grandson of the chief who visited England in Queen Anne's reign is their chief at present. He is in the prime of life, and has seen a good deal of service along with the late Sir William Johnson.[15]

---

12 Spelled 'Mohawk' today, the Mohock community within the Iroquois federation was led by Brant.
13 Anne (1665–1714), Queen of England, Scotland and Ireland from 1702 to 1707; Queen of Great Britain and Ireland from 1707 to 1714
14 The priest was likely John Stuart (1740–1811), who served at Fort Hunter, New York, starting in late 1770 and became close friends with Joseph Brant. After the American Revolution, Stuart moved to Upper Canada and provided pastoral support for Mohawk refugees.
15 William Johnson (c.1715–74), Superintendent of the Iroquois Confederacy

The present unhappy civil war in America occasioned his coming over to England. He was solicited by both sides to give his assistance, and found himself perplexed amidst a contrariety of arguments upon a great subject, which he could not well understand. Before coming to a decisive resolution, he resolved to go himself into the presence of THE GREAT KING, as the British sovereign is styled amongst the American Indians. He accordingly came to London in 1776, accompanied by Captain Tice, an officer of English extraction born in America, and who has a settlement just in the neighbourhood of the Mohock nation.

By what mode of reasoning this chief was convinced of the justice of the demands of Great Britain upon her colonies, and the propriety of enforcing them, we have not been informed: but it is said, that he has promised to give his assistance to government, by bringing three thousand men into the field. He and Captain Tice sailed for America early in May.

This chief had not the ferocious dignity of a savage leader; nor does he discover any extraordinary force either of mind or body. We have procured for the satisfaction of our readers, a print of him in the dress of his nation, which gives him a more striking appearance; for when he wore the ordinary European habit, there did not seem to be any thing about him that marked preeminence. Upon his tomahawk is carved the first letter of his Christian name, *Joseph*, and his Mohock appellation thus, *Thayendaneken* (pronounced *Theandenaigen*) the g being founded hard as in *get*. His manners are gentle and quiet; and to those who study human nature, he affords a very convincing proof of the tameness which education can produce upon the wildest race. He speaks English very well; and is so much master of the language, that he is engaged in a translation of the New Testament into the Mohock tongue. Upon his arrival in London, he was conducted to the inn, called *The Swan with Two Necks*, in Lad Lane. Proper lodgings were to be provided for him; but he said the good people of the inn were so civil, that he would not leave them; and accordingly he continued there all the time he was in London. He was struck with the appearance of England in general; but he said he chiefly admired the ladies and the horses.

Source text

[Boswell, James], 'An Account of the Chief of the Mohock Indians, who lately visited England', *The London Magazine* 45 (July 1776), 339.

References

Hutchinson, Elizabeth. '"The Dress of His Nation": Romney's Portrait of Joseph Brant', *Winterthur Portfolio* 45.2/3 (2011), 209–28.
Reichardt, A. Zuercher, 'Translation', *Early American Studies* 16.4 (Fall 2018), 801–11.

Benjamin Franklin (1706–90)

From **Memoirs of the Life and Writings of Benjamin Franklin** *(1818)*

While he is best remembered as a Founding Father of the United States, and as the oldest signatory of the Declaration of Independence, Franklin was also a naturalist, scientist, political theorist, merchant, investor, printer, publisher, author and inventor. Late in his career he became an advocate for women's rights and the abolition of slavery, although he owned at least five enslaved people during his lifetime. His many nation-building activities, including his roles as US Postmaster and President of Pennsylvania (an office now termed governor), could have left him little time to be a transatlantic cosmopolitan. Yet his youthful travels took him to England, and he eventually journeyed to France as US Ambassador after the Revolutionary War.

In his memoir, he vividly recalls his time spent in Britain between 1724 and 1726. Because this portion of the narrative records life experiences before the War for Independence, Franklin positions himself as a colonial subject. Our excerpt begins soon after eighteen-year-old Franklin reaches England with James Ralph, a friend with whom the author lodged upon arrival in London.

From Memoirs of the Life and Writings of Benjamin Franklin[16]

For myself, I immediately got into work at Palmer's, a famous printing-house in Bartholomew Close,[17] where I continued near a year. I was pretty diligent, but I spent with Ralph a good deal of my earnings at plays and public amusements: we had nearly consumed all my pistoles,[18] and now just rubbed on from hand to mouth. [. . .]

At Palmer's I was employed in composing for the second edition of Wollaston's *Religion of Nature.*[19] Some of his reasonings not appearing to me well founded, I wrote a little metaphysical piece in which I made remarks on them. It was intitled *"A Dissertation on Liberty and Necessity, Pleasure and Pain."*[20] I inscribed it to my friend Ralph; I printed a small number. It occasioned my being more considered by Mr. Palmer, as a young man of some ingenuity, though he seriously expostulated with me upon the principles of my pamphlet, which to him appeared abominable. My printing this pamphlet was another *erratum.*[21] While I lodged in *Little Britain*, I made an acquaintance with one Wilcox, a bookseller, whose shop was next door. He had

---

16 The first version of Franklin's memoir, published in France in 1791 and based on a translation of his manuscript, generated numerous re-translations back into English – passing along errors and omissions created in the initial published version. In 1818, Franklin's grandson brought out a new edition based on the original English manuscript. Still later, an 1884 edition, prepared by Jared Sparks and published in London, revisited how the early versions had led to inaccurate later ones, thus offering up a form of book history for the memoir. See 'Preface by Jared Sparks', in Franklin's *The Autobiography of Benjamin Franklin* (London: George Bell & Sons, 1884), 12.
17 Street in the borough of Wandsworth, London
18 Various seventeenth- and eighteenth-century European gold coins
19 Composing: setting the pieces of movable type; William Wollaston (1659–1724) published *The Religion of Nature Delineated* in 1722. It claimed to derive moral laws from mathematics.
20 Published in London in 1725
21 Error in printing

an immense collection of second-hand books. Circulating libraries were not then in use; but we agreed that on certain reasonable terms (which I have now forgotten,) I might take, read, and return any of his books: this I esteemed a great advantage, and I made as much use of it as I could. [. . .]

I now began to think of getting a little before-hand, and expecting better employment, I left Palmer's to work at Watts's, (near Lincoln's Inn Fields)[22] a still greater printing-house. Here I continued all the rest of my stay in London.

At my first admission into the printing-house I took to working at press, imagining I felt a want of the bodily exercise I had been used to in America, where press-work is mixed with the composing. I drank only water; the other workmen, near 50 in number, were great drinkers of beer. On occasion I carried up and down stairs a large form of types in each hand,[23] when others carried but one in both hands; they wondered to see, from this and several instances, that the *Water-American*, as they called me, was *stronger* than themselves, who drank *strong* beer! We had an ale-house boy, who attended always in the house to supply the workmen. My companion at the press drank every day a pint before breakfast, a pint at breakfast with his bread and cheese, a pint between breakfast and dinner; a pint at dinner, a pint in the afternoon about 6 o'clock, and another when he had done his day's work. I thought it a detestable custom; but it was necessary, he supposed, to drink *strong* beer that he might be *strong* to labor. I endeavored to convince him that the bodily strength afforded by beer, could only be in proportion to the grain or flour of the barley dissolved in the water of which it was made; that there was more flour in a pen-nyworth of bread, and therefore if he could eat that with a pint of water, it would give him more strength than a quart of beer. He drank on however, and had four or five shillings to pay out of his wages every Saturday night for that vile liquor; an expence I was free from. And thus these poor devils keep themselves always under.

Watts, after some weeks, desiring to have me in the composing-room, I left the pressmen; a new *bien venu*[24] for drink, (being five s.[25]) was demanded of me by the compositors.[26] I thought it an imposition, as I had paid one to the pressmen; the master thought so too, and forbad my paying it. I stood out two or three weeks, was accordingly considered as an excommunicate, and had so many little pieces of private malice practiced on me, by mixing my sorts, transposing and breaking my matter, &c &c. if ever I stepped out of the room; and all ascribed to the *chapel ghost*,[27] which they said ever haunted those not regularly admitted; that notwith-standing my master's protection, I found myself obliged to comply and pay the money; convinced of the folly of being on ill terms with those one is to live with continually. [. . .]

---

22 A public square in London
23 After individual metal type letters were set on a composing line, those sequenced letters were placed in a full-page holder, sometimes called a single-page 'form'.
24 French term meaning 'welcome'
25 Shillings
26 Compositors assembled and positioned the pieces of metal type, which were arranged by letter, size, and kind, in a wooden box. A compositor set each letter on a metal composing stick to form full lines of words. One challenge was that the type had to be set backwards, since printing reversed the images. Once the type was set into a wooden frame, called a form, ink was spread over it (i.e. acting as a 'beater') and then press workers laboriously pushed and pulled paper through the press, one sheet at a time – a step requiring much strength.
27 Printing companies were called 'chapels', a term growing out of their having evolved from the scriptoria where monks painstakingly created copies of manuscripts.

At Watts's printing-house, I contracted an acquaintance with an ingenious young man, one Wygate, who, having wealthy relations, had been better educated than most printers; was a tolerable Latinist, spoke French, and loved reading. I taught him and a friend of his to swim, at twice going into the river, and they soon became good swimmers. They introduced me to some gentlemen from the country, who went to Chelsea[28] by water, to see the college and Don Saltero's curiosities.[29] In our return, at the request of the company, whose curiosity Wygate had excited, I stripped and leaped into the river, and swam from near Chelsea to Blackfriars; performing in the way many feats of activity, both upon and under the water, that surprised and pleased those to whom they were novelties. I had from a child been delighted with this exercise, had studied and practised Thevenot's motions and positions,[30] added some of my own; aiming at the graceful and easy, as well as the useful. All these I took this occasion of exhibiting to the company, and was much flattered by their admiration; and Wygate, who was desirous of becoming a master, grew more and more attached to me on that account, as well as from the similarity of our studies. He at length proposed to me travelling all over Europe together, supporting ourselves everywhere by working at our business. I was once inclined to it; but mentioning it to my good friend Mr. Denham, with whom I often spent an hour when I had leisure, he dissuaded me from it; advising me to think only of returning to Pennsylvania, which he was now about to do. [. . .]

He now told me he was about to return to Philadelphia, and should carry over a great quantity of goods, in order to open a Store there. He proposed to take me over as his clerk, to keep his books, (in which he would instruct me) copy his letters, and attend the Store. He added that as soon as I should be acquainted with mercantile business, he would promote me by sending me with a cargo of flour and bread, &c. to the West Indies, and procure me commissions from others which would be profitable; and, if I managed well, would establish me handsomely. The thing pleased me; for I was grown tired of London, remembered with pleasure the happy months I had spent in Pennsylvania, and wished again to see it; therefore I immediately agreed on the terms of fifty pounds a year, Pennsylvania money; less indeed than my then present gettings as a compositor, but affording better prospect.

I now took leave of printing, as I thought, for ever, and was daily employed in my new business, going about with Mr. Denham among the tradesmen to purchase various articles, and see them packed up, delivering messages, calling upon workmen to dispatch, &c.; and when all was on board, I had a few days' leisure. On one of these days, I was, to my surprise, sent for by a great man, I knew only by name, (Sir William Wyndham,) and I waited upon him. He had heard by some means or other of my swimming from Chelsea to Blackfriars, and of my teaching Wygate and another young man to swim in a few hours. He had two sons, about to set out on their travels; he wished to have them first taught swimming, and proposed to gratify me handsomely if I would teach them. They were not yet come to town, and my stay was uncertain; so I could not undertake it. But from the incident I thought it likely, that if I were to remain in England and open a swimming school, I might get a good deal of money; and it struck me so strongly that had the overture been made me sooner, probably I should not so soon have returned to America. [. . .]

---

28 An area in southwest London
29 Coffeehouse in Chelsea that boasted cabinets of 'curiosities'
30 French author and cartographer Melchisédec Thévenot (*c.*1620–92) was famous for writing *The Art of Swimming* (1696).

Thus I passed about eighteen months in London; most part of the time I worked hard at my business, and spent but little upon myself except in seeing plays, and in books. [...] I had improved my knowledge, however, though I had by no means improved my fortune: but I had made some very ingenious acquaintance, whose conversation was of great advantage to me; and I had read considerably.

We sailed from Gravesend on the 23rd of July, 1726. For the incidents of the voyage, I refer you to my journal, where you will find them all minutely related. Perhaps the most important part of that journal is the *plan* to be found in it, which I formed at sea, for regulating the future conduct of my life. It is the more remarkable, as being formed when I was so young, and yet being pretty faithfully adhered to quite through to old age.

Source text

Franklin, Benjamin, *Memoirs of the Life and Writings of Benjamin Franklin, LL.D. F.R.S. &c.*, ed. William Temple Franklin, 3rd edn (London: Henry Colburn, 1818).

References

Darnton, Robert, 'Work and culture in an eighteenth-century printing shop', *Quarterly Journal of the Library of Congress* 39.1 (1982), 34–47.

Franklin, Benjamin, *Poor Richard's Almanac for 1851, as Written by Benjamin Franklin for the Years 1736–1737–1738* (New York: John Doggett, 1850).

Goodwin, George, *Benjamin Franklin in London: The British Life of America's Founding Father* (New Haven, CT: Yale University Press, 2016).

Thomas Campbell (1777–1844)

'The Emigrant' (1823)

Though little read today, Thomas Campbell, a Scot whose radical sympathies led him to support abolition and Polish freedom, became a major poet in 1799 when *The Pleasures of Hope* won him immediate renown. Only the year before he had been considering relocating to the US, his four brothers having already emigrated to work in British Guiana in South America. In 1809 his transatlantic romantic epic in Spenserian stanzas, *Gertrude of Wyoming: A Pennsylvanian Tale*, also found popularity, especially in America. Though he never left the public spotlight, his poetic career slowed in the 1810s, but he enjoyed new success when Henry Colburn (1784/5–1855), owner of *New Monthly Magazine*, appointed Campbell editor. 'The Emigrant', which approaches migration to Canada in a dark rather than hopeful mood, appeared in January 1823. Though never included in Campbell's collected poems, it was reprinted in the Cape Colony newspaper *South African Commercial Advertiser* on 7 April 1824. Lara Atkin contextualises the poem's print migration to

South Africa by noting white settler anxiety at the time over colonists' potential for success. The text's reprinting attests to the global reach of circulating periodicals and the local specificity, yet also interactivity, of British global colonies.

'The Emigrant'

When fire sets the forests on blaze,
>   It expires on their desolate track;
But the love which has lighted our days,
>   Still burns when our prospects are black.

I must go to the Huron's[31] wild grounds,
>   Whilst thou bloom'st to thine own native sun;
Oh, the ocean that parts us has bounds,
>   But the grief of our parting has none.

Can the eagle fly home to his mate?
>   Can he build by Niagara's foam?
And are we interdicted by fate
>   From a spot of the world for our home?

Thou art lost to me ev'n as the dead,
>   And our tears unavailingly flow;
Yet to think they could cease to be shed,
>   Would be worse than this burden of woe.

Source text

Campbell, Thomas, 'The Emigrant', *New Monthly Magazine* 8 (January 1823), 552.

References

Atkin, Lara, '(Re)settling Poetry: The Culture of Reprinting and the Poetics of Emigration in the 1820s Southern Settler Colonies', in Matthew Sangster and Jon Mee (eds), *Remediating the 1820s* (Edinburgh: Edinburgh University Press, forthcoming).
ODNB

---

31 The Northern Iroquoian people in Ontario

James E. Seaver (1787–1827) and Mary Jemison (1743–1833)

'Introduction' to A Narrative of the Life of Mrs. Mary Jemison *(1824)*

Literally a transatlantic figure through her birth on shipboard during her family's 1743 crossing from Ireland, Mary Jemison remains a compelling figure for scholars of Native and comparative race studies – and for readers of captivity narratives. As London's *Observer* would note in 1929, her 'little book, which first appeared in 1824', based on a narrative 'taken down from her own lips', was still drawing audiences over one hundred years later, through its mix of vivid accounts of '"Red" Indians' and their 'barbaric' ways, combined with admittedly appealing portraits of the 'ordinary life and fortunes of the tribe', who always treated Mary kindly ('Strange Case', 6). Overall, the 130-plus editions of her as-told-to narrative testify to a lingering transatlantic fascination with Jemison.

Jemison's family squatted on land belonging to the Iroquois Confederacy. In 1755 she was captured by a raiding party. Though Mary's parents and her siblings were killed, she was given to two Seneca, who adopted her, named her Den-he-wa-mis (meaning 'a good thing' or 'pretty girl') and began an acculturation process affirmed by her refusal to return to white life later.

Jemison's life of ninety years brought historical sweep to her narrative. Events of transatlantic significance reflected there ranged from the French and Indian (Seven Years) War (1754–63), through the United States Revolution and the War of 1812, along with longstanding conflicts between white settlers and Native peoples over land. Seaver's introduction nods to such contexts while asserting racial hierarchies. We cannot know how trustworthy he was as transcriber-editor, but we need not wonder about his didactic motives. His text envisions children as his primary audience, for whom he hoped Jemison's life would be 'well calculated to excite their attention, inform their understanding, and improve them in the art of reading'. In Seaver's words, we can trace both verbal flashes of Jemison herself and language reflecting patronising nineteenth-century Anglo-American ideas about Native communities. Therefore, analysing her full narrative (while recognising that even that story is filtered through white transmission) would be a worthwhile next step after studying the excerpt below.

'Introduction' to A Narrative of the Life of Mrs. Mary Jemison[32]

The Peace of 1783,[33] and the consequent cessation of Indian hostilities and barbarities, returned to their friends those prisoners who had escaped the tomahawk, the gauntlet, and the savage fire, after their having spent many years in captivity, and restored harmony to society.

The stories of Indian cruelties which were common in the new settlements, and were calamitous realities previous to that propitious event, slumbered in the minds that had been constantly agitated by them, and were only roused occasionally, to become the fearful topic of the fireside.

It is presumed that at this time there are but few native Americans[34] that have arrived to middle age, who cannot distinctly recollect of sitting in the chimney corner when children, all contracted with fear, and there listening to their parents or visitors, while they related stories of Indian conquests, and murders, that would make their flaxen hair nearly stand erect, and almost destroy the power of motion.

[Editorial Note: The following 5 paragraphs are in the 1842 US edition, but not the 1826 British one, which had only the short overview provided in the note below.[35]]

Time however, has produced a confusion of incidents in those tales, and enveloped the fidelity of their transmission to us, in clouds of doubt: to rescue from oblivion, and preserve in their primitive purity, some of those legends, and to exemplify and record, for the use of posterity, as well as for the present generation, a faithful delineation of the characteristic traits of the Mingoes,[36] is the object of these memoirs.

At the same treaty, the Six Nations or Mingoes, were left in undisturbed possession of the greater portion of the state of New-York, and had the right of possession guaranteed to them by the United States, of all the territory west of a line called the property line, running nearly parallel with, and less than eighty miles west of the Hudson river, two small tracts excepted. At this time Mary Jemison had been with the Indians twenty-nine years; seven had transpired during the French war with

---

32 Reflecting transatlantic interest in Jemison's story, we draw primarily from an 1826 London edition. Illustrating Seaver's continued efforts to benefit from American republications, we include some text tracking differences between the 1826 British version and another of his US versions from 1842.

33 In later editions, such as in 1842, Seaver would open with a more detailed reference to the Peace Treaty process. As noted in the texts by and about Joseph Brant earlier in this section, the Six Nations people incurred a heavy loss of lands in this treaty.

34 Seaver's use of 'native Americans' here refers to whites born in America, not to the Indigenous people certainly far more entitled to be called 'native' than were any colonisers, whatever their birthplace.

35 This paragraph appears in 1826 in place of the longer historical background given in 1842: 'At the close of the revolutionary war, all that part of the State of New-York that lies west of Utica was uninhabited by white people, and few indeed had ever passed beyond Fort Stanwix, except when engaged in war against the Indians, who were numerous, and occupied a number of large towns between the Mohawk river and lake Erie. [. . .]' (vii).

36 Iroquoian-speaking Natives who moved west toward Ohio

the British, in which the Six Nations raised the tomahawk against the British and Americans; and seven during the revolutionary war, in which the Indians arrayed themselves on the side of the British against the Americans; there being an interval of peace of fifteen years between, if peace it could be called, when they were constantly sending war parties against other Indian tribes, south and north from the torrid to the frigid zone, and west to the Rocky Mountains.

During this time Mrs. Jemison had been twice married to Indian chiefs and had a husband and seven children then living. She too, was nearly two hundred miles from any white settlement, and knew not that she had a white relative or friend on earth: she therefore resolved not to accept of her freedom, but to spend the remainder of her days with the Indians, where she knew she had affectionate relatives, and many kind friends; this resolution she carried fully into effect, and became their faithful and correct chronicler for more than three fourths of a century.

At this time, 1784, and for several years afterwards, no settlements of white people were made in the state, west of Cherry Valley, on the head waters of the Susquehannah;[37] and the German Flats, on the Mohawk;[38] as those places were situated nearly as far west as the property line, the boundary of the Indian lands. So fresh were the wounds which the whites had received from their savage neighbors, that the Indians were viewed with a jealous eye, even when unmolested and unprovoked; under these circumstances, peaceable citizens were little inclined to trespass on their lands, or give them the least pretext for a quarrel, by even travelling into their country. No white people therefore, visited their villages, except some half-savage traders, and a few of the refuse of society, who, to escape the meshes of civil or criminal law, bade adieu to civilized life, and took shelter in the recesses of the forest, under the protection of its lords.

The Indian title to the lands surrounding Mrs. Jemison's residence, was not sold to the whites until the great council in 1797, when may be dated the first time of her associating with moral, social, civilized man, from the time of her childhood; after a lapse of forty-two years. Still she had retained her native language with great purity; and had treasured up, and constantly kept in her own breast, all those moral and social virtues, by the precepts of which civilized society profess to be guided, and by their directions always to be governed.

[Editorial Note: Beginning below, we return to the 1826 London edition.]

At length, the richness and fertility of the soil excited emigration, and here and there a family settled down and commenced improvements in the country which had recently been the property of the aborigines. Those who settled near the Genesee river, soon became acquainted with "The White Woman," as Mrs. Jemison is called, whose history they anxiously sought, both as a matter of interest and curiosity. Frankness characterized her conduct, and without reserve she would readily gratify them by relating some of the most important periods of her life.

Although her bosom companion was an ancient Indian warrior, and notwithstanding her children and associates were all Indians, yet it was found that she possessed an uncommon share of hospitality, and that her friendship was well worth courting and preserving. Her house was the stranger's home; from her table the hungry were refreshed; she made the naked as comfortable as her means would admit of; and in all her actions discovered so much natural goodness of heart, that

---

37 A river flowing from New York into Philadelphia all the way into Washington
38 Mohawk River Valley, New York

her admirers increased in proportion to the extension of her acquaintance, and she became celebrated as the friend of the distressed. She was the protectress of the homeless fugitive, and made welcome the weary wanderer. Many still live to commemorate her benevolence towards them when prisoners during the war, and to ascribe their deliverance to the mediation of "The White Woman."

The settlements increased, and the whole country around her was inhabited by a rich and respectable people, principally from New England, as much distinguished for their spirit of inquisitiveness as for their habits of industry and honesty, who had all heard from one source and another a part of her life in detached pieces, and had obtained an idea that the whole taken in connection would afford instruction and amusement.

Many gentlemen of respectability felt anxious that her narrative might be laid before the public, with a view not only to perpetuate the remembrance of the atrocities of the savages in former times, but to preserve some historical facts which they supposed to be intimately connected with her life, and which otherwise must be lost.

Forty years had passed since the close of the revolutionary war, and almost seventy years had seen Mrs. Jemison with the Indians, when Daniel W. Banister, Esq., at the instance of several gentlemen, and prompted by his own ambition to add something to the accumulating fund of useful knowledge, resolved, in the autumn of 1823, to embrace that time, while she was capable of recollecting and reciting the scenes through which she had passed, to collect from herself, and to publish to the world, an accurate account of her life.

I was employed to collect the materials, and prepare the work for the press; and accordingly went to the house of Mrs. Jennet Whaley in the town of Castile, Genesee co. N. Y. in company with the publisher, who procured the interesting subject of the following narrative, to come to that place, (a distance of four miles,) and there repeat the story of her eventful life. She came on foot in company with Mr. Thomas Clute, whom she considers her protector,[39] and tarried almost three days, which time was busily occupied in taking a sketch of her narrative as she recited it.

Her appearance was well calculated to excite a great degree of sympathy in a stranger, who had been partially informed of her origin, when comparing her present situation with what it probably would have been, had she been permitted to have remained with her friends, and to have enjoyed the blessings of civilization.[40]

In stature she is very short, and considerably under the middle size, and stands tolerably erect, with her head bent forward, apparently from her having for a long time been accustomed to carrying heavy burdens in a strap placed across her forehead. Her complexion is very white for a woman of her age, and although the wrinkles of fourscore years are deeply indented in her cheeks, yet the crimson of youth is distinctly visible. Her eyes are light blue, a little faded by age, and naturally brilliant and sparkling. Her sight is quite dim, though she is able to perform her necessary labour without the assistance of glasses. Her cheek bones are high, and rather prominent, and her front teeth, in the lower jaw, are sound and good. When

---

39 Thomas Clute assisted Mary Jemison with such matters as a sale of land (from an allotment she had received in 1797 as part of a treaty between the US and the Seneca) and management of the land she chose to keep. Though Mary apparently viewed Thomas as a protector, much of the land she sold went to his brother, Jellis.

40 This paragraph (from 'Her appearance' to 'civilization') is deleted from the 1842 US edition.

she looks up and is engaged in conversation, her countenance is very expressive; but from her long residence with the Indians, she has acquired the habit of peeping from under her eyebrows, as they do, with the head inclined downwards. Formerly her hair was of a light chesnut brown—it is now quite grey, a little curled, of middling length, and tied in a bunch behind. She informed me that she had never worn a cap nor a comb.

She speaks English plainly and distinctly, with a little of the Irish emphasis,[41] and has the use of words so well as to render herself intelligible on any subject with which she is acquainted. Her recollection and memory exceeded my expectation. It cannot be reasonably supposed, that a person of her age has kept the events of seventy years in so complete a chain as to be able to assign to each its proper time and place; she, however, made her recital with as few obvious mistakes as might be found in that of a person of fifty.[42]

She walks with a quick step without a staff, and I was informed by Mr. Clute, that she could yet cross a stream on a log or pole as steadily as any other person.

Her passions are easily excited. At a number of periods in her narration, tears trickled down her grief-worn cheek, and at the same time a rising sigh would stop her utterance.

Industry is a virtue which she has uniformly practised from the day of her adoption to the present. She pounds her samp,[43] cooks for herself, gathers and chops wood, feeds her cattle and poultry, and performs other laborious services. Last season she planted, tended and gathered corn—in short, she is always busy.

Her dress at the time I saw her, was made and worn after the Indian fashion, and consisted of a shirt, short gown, petticoat, stockings, moccasins, a blanket and a bonnet. The shirt was of cotton, and made at the top, as I was informed, like a man's without collar or sleeves—was open before and extended down about midway of the hips. The petticoat was a piece of broad cloth, with the list at the top and bottom and the ends sewed together. This was tied on by a string that was passed over it and around the waist, in such a manner as to let the bottom of the petticoat down halfway between the knee and ankle, and leave one fourth of a yard at the top to be turned down over the string—the bottom of the shirt coming a little below, and on the outside of the top of the fold so as to leave the list and two or three inches of the cloth uncovered. The stockings were of blue broad cloth, tied, or pinned on, which reached from the knees into the mouth of the moccasins.—Around her toes only she had some rags, and over these her buckskin moccasins. Her gown was of undressed flannel, coloured brown. It was made in old yankee style, with long sleeves, covered the top of the hips, and was tied before in two places with strings of deer skin. Over all this she wore an Indian blanket. On her head she wore a piece of old brown woollen cloth made somewhat like a sun bonnet.

Such was the dress that this woman was contented to wear, and habit had rendered it convenient and comfortable. She wore it not as a matter of necessity, but

---

41 Jemison's retention of this aspect of her Irish identity would have interested both British and American readers.

42 The 1842 US edition adds examples of her accuracy in referencing historical events, while attributing her occasional gaps and slips to the idea that her Native community would not have been invested in interactions between 'English' and 'Yankee traders' or changes in different nations holding a particular fort in the region (19).

43 Porridge or ground corn

from choice, for it will be seen in the sequel, that her property is sufficient to enable her to dress in the best fashion, and to allow her every comfort of life.[44]

Her house in which she lives, is 20 by 28 feet; built of square timber, with a shingled roof, and a framed stoop. In the centre of the house is a chimney of stones and sticks, in which there are two fire-places. She has a good framed barn, 26 by 36, well filled, and owns a fine stock of cattle and horses. Besides the buildings above-mentioned, she owns a number of houses that are occupied by tenants, who work her flats upon shares.

Her dwelling is about one hundred rods north of the Great Slide, a curiosity that will be described in its proper place, on the west side of the Genesee river.

Mrs. Jemison appeared sensible of her ignorance of the manners of the white people, and for that reason was not familiar, except with those with whom she was intimately acquainted. In fact she was (to appearance) so jealous of her rights, or that she should say something that would be injurious to herself or family, that if Mr. Clute had not been present, we should have been unable to have obtained her history. She, however, soon became free and unembarrassed in her conversation, and spoke with a degree of mildness, candor and simplicity, that is calculated to remove all doubts as to the veracity of the speaker. The vices of the Indians she appeared disposed not to aggravate, and seemed to take a pride in extolling their virtues. A kind of family pride inclined her to withhold whatever would blot the character of her descendants, and perhaps induced her to keep back many things that would have been interesting.

For the life of her last husband we are indebted to her cousin, Mr. George Jemison,[45] to whom she referred us for information on that subject generally. The thoughts of his deeds probably chilled her old heart, and made her dread to rehearse them, and at the same time she well knew they were no secret, for she had frequently heard him relate the whole, not only to her cousin, but to others.

Before she left us she was very sociable, and she resumed her naturally pleasant countenance, enlivened with a smile.

Her neighbours speak of her as possessing one of the happiest tempers and dispositions, and give her the name of never having done a censurable act to their knowledge.

Her habits are those of the Indians—she sleeps on skins without a bedstead, sits upon the floor or on a bench, and holds her victuals on her lap, or in her hands.

Her ideas of religion correspond in every respect with those of the great mass of the Senecas. She applauds virtue, and despises vice. She believes in a future state, in which the good will be happy, and the bad miserable; and that the acquisition of that happiness depends primarily upon human volition, and the consequent good deeds of the happy recipient of blessedness. The doctrines taught in the Christian religion she is a stranger to.

Her daughters are said to be active and enterprising women, and her grandsons, who have arrived to manhood, are considered able; decent and respectable men in their tribe.[46]

---

44 Seaver elaborated in the 1842 US edition, stressing the contradiction he perceived between her wealth and her choice of attire (20).

45 George Jemison may or may not have been Mary's white cousin. Some accounts suggest he tried to bilk her of part of her land, and she eventually evicted him.

46 The 1842 edition adds: 'and many of them are greeted with respect in civilized society' (22).

Having in this cursory manner introduced the subject of the following pages, I proceed to the narration of a life that has been viewed with attention, for a great number of years, by a few, and which will be read by the public with the mixed sensations of pleasure and pain, and with interest, anxiety and satisfaction.[47]

Source texts

Jemison, Mary, and James E. Seaver, *Deh-he-wa-mis: or A Narrative of the Life of Mary Jemison: Otherwise Called The White Woman*, 2nd edn (Batavia, NY: William Seaver and Son, 1842).

Jemison, Mary, and James E. Seaver, *A Narrative of the Life of Mrs. Mary Jemison, Who Was Taken by the Indians, in the Year 1755, When only about twelve years of age, and has continued to reside amongst them to the present time* (London: Howden, 1826).

References

'The Strange Case of Mary Jemison', [London] *Observer* (3 November 1929), 6.

Wallace, Arminta, 'Irish Connections: Mary Jemison, the Irishwoman Who Joined a Native American Tribe', *The Irish Times* (6 May 2017), C9.

Wood, Karenne, 'Prisoners of History: Pocahontas, Mary Jemison, and the Poetics of an American Myth', *Studies in American Indian Literatures* 28.1 (2016), 73–82.

Lydia H. Sigourney (1791–1865)

'To the First Slave Ship' (1827)

'Indian Names' (1834)

Many nineteenth-century migrations were enforced rather than chosen, as reflected in two poems by Lydia Sigourney, below. Sigourney devoted much writing to gendered social issues, ranging from promoting mothers' important roles as home-based teachers of their children to calls for their enhanced educational opportunities. An avid student of British writers like Felicia Hemans (1793–1835) and Hannah More (1745–1833), Sigourney was extolled on both sides of the Atlantic, but sometimes cast as derivative, for embracing their didactic goals and emotion-cultivating techniques. Poe, for example, skewered her overly sentimental lapses, yet he also praised her craft. Meanwhile, one appreciative British reviewer dubbed her 'Hemans in mind, and Hannah More in heart' ('Lydia Huntley Sigourney', 444), while joining several others in highlighting her poetry on Native Americans (445; 'Book Review', 146; 'Lays', 255).

---

47 Seaver's prediction that Jemison's life would continue to fascinate has proven true transatlantically. Her story draws regular visitors to her statue in Letchworth Park in New York State, and another in Pennsylvania, near her family's original American homeplace.

Sigourney often turned her sentiment-evoking pen to social causes beyond those advocating rights for white women of her own social class. With Catharine Beecher (1800–78), she co-published a spirited 1829 anti-Indian-Removal argument evoking Christian principles and circulated a petition often cited as an early example of women's political activism (Miles).

Some of Sigourney's poetry on Native Americans can certainly be critiqued today for stereotypes, as in the title poem of her London-published *Pocahontas* collection. Still, in a lyric like 'Indian Names', widely circulated transatlantically, we see a complicated blend of nostalgic erasure themes using tropes of the vanished Indian, but also a call to affirm Indigenous peoples' pre-white-settler presence and enduring influence.

Overall, Sigourney can be applauded for her calls to empathise with others' suffering – whether a 'Cherokee Mother' enduring the Removal with her child in an 1831 poem originally published in that nation's own *Cherokee Phoenix*, or captured Africans in a text like the lyric just below – one of the earliest poems decrying Middle Passage horrors.

'To the First Slave Ship'

> First of that train which cursed the wave,
>   And from the rifled cabin bore,
> Inheritor of wo, — *the slave*
>   To bless his palm-tree's shade no more,
>
> Dire engine!—o'er the troubled main[48]
>   Borne on in unresisted state,—
> Know'st thou within thy dark domain
>   The secrets of thy prison'd freight?—
>
> Hear'st thou *their* moans whom hope hath fled?—
>   Wild cries, in agonizing starts?—
> Know'st thou thy humid sails are spread
>   With ceaseless sighs from broken hearts?—
>
> The fetter'd chieftain's burning tear, —
>   The parted lover's mute despair,—
> The childless mother's pang severe,—
>   The orphan's misery, are there.

---

48 Ocean

Ah!—could'st thou from the scroll of fate
    The annal[49] read of future years,
Stripes,—tortures,—unrelenting hate,
    And death-gasps drown'd in slavery's tears,

Down,— down,—beneath the cleaving main
    Thou fain would'st plunge where monsters lie,
Rather than ope[50] the gates of pain
    For time and for Eternity.—

Oh Afric!—what has been thy crime?—
    That thus like Eden's fratricide,[51]
A mark is set upon thy clime,
    And every brother shuns thy side.—

Yet are thy wrongs, thou long-distrest!—
    Thy burdens, by the world unweigh'd,
Safe in that *Unforgetful Breast*
    Where all the sins of earth are laid.—

Poor outcast slave!—Our guilty land
    Should tremble while she drinks thy tears,
Or sees in vengeful silence stand,
    The beacon of thy shorten'd years; —

Should shrink to hear her sons proclaim
    The sacred truth that heaven is just,—
Shrink even at her Judge's name,—
    "Jehovah,—Saviour of the opprest."

The Sun upon thy forehead frown'd,
    But Man more cruel far than he,
Dark fetters on thy spirit bound:—
    Look to the mansions of the free!

Look to that realm where chains unbind,—
    Where the pale tyrant drops his rod,
And where the patient sufferers find
    A friend,—a father in their God.

---

49 Historical account
50 Open
51 Eden: paradise; fratricide: Cain's killing of his brother Abel; both in Genesis

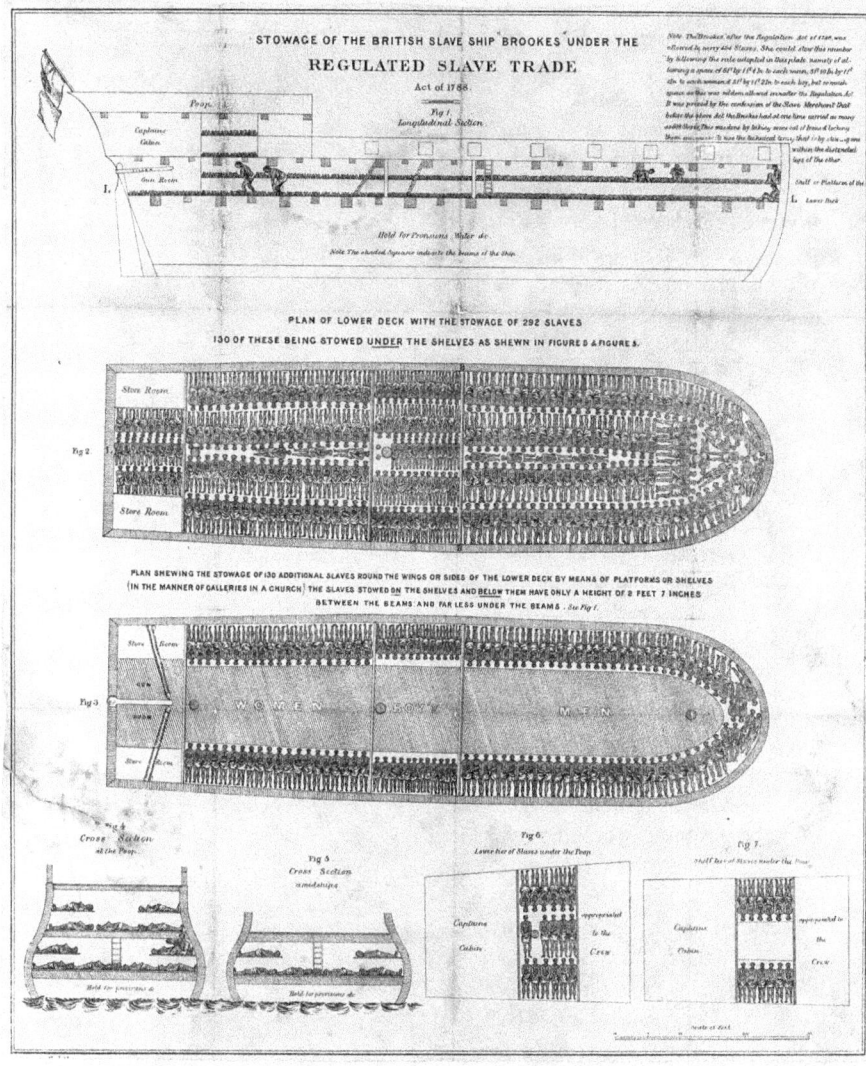

Figure 5.3 Printed Ephemera Collection Dic. *Stowage of the British slave ship 'Brookes' under the Regulated Slave Trade Act.* Liverpool British Great Britain, 1788. [N.P.?] Photograph. Courtesy US Library of Congress Printed Ephemera.

'Indian Names'

"How can the Red Men be forgotten, while so many of our states and territories, bays, lakes, and rivers, are indelibly stamped by names of their giving?"

Ye say, they all have passed away,
    That noble race and brave,
That their light canoes have vanished
    From off the crested wave;
That 'mid the forests where they roamed
    There rings no hunter shout;

But their name is on your waters,
      Ye may not wash it out.

'Tis where Ontario's billow
      Like Ocean's surge is curl'd,
Where strong Niagara's thunders wake
      The echo of the world.
Where red Missouri[52] bringeth
      Rich tribute from the west,
And Rappahannock[53] sweetly sleeps
      On green Virginia's breast.

Ye say, their cone-like cabins,
      That clustered o'er the vale,
Have fled away like withered leaves
      Before the autumn gale:
But their memory liveth on your hills,
      Their baptism on your shore,
Your everlasting rivers speak
      Their dialect of yore.

Old Massachusetts wears it[54]
      Within her lordly crown,
And broad Ohio bears it
      Amid his young renown;
Connecticut hath wreathed it
      Where her quiet foliage waves,
And bold Kentucky breathes its hoarse
      Through all her ancient caves.

Wachuset[55] hides its lingering voice
      Within his rocky heart,
And Alleghany graves its tone
      Throughout his lofty chart;
Monadnock on his forehead hoar
      Doth seal the sacred trust,
Your mountains build their monument,
      Though ye destroy their dust.

Source texts

[Sigourney, Lydia H.], *Poems; by the Author of "Moral Pieces in Prose and Verse."* (Boston: S. G. Goodrich, 1827).
Sigourney, Mrs L. H., *Pocahontas, And Other Poems* (London: Robert Tyas, 1841).

---

52 The longest North American river, running from the Rocky Mountains and flowing east and south for over 2,000 miles before feeding into the Mississippi River
53 A river in eastern Virginia in the US
54 This stanza names a series of states within the US that bear 'Indian names'.
55 A mountain in the US state of Massachusetts; other US mountains and peaks (such as Monadnock) appear later in the stanza.

References

'Book Review', *The Literary Gazette: A Weekly Journal of Literature, Science, and the Fine Arts* 1.676 (3 March 1849), 146–7.

'Lays of the Heart', *Sharpe's London Journal* 9 (March 1849), 254–5.

'Lydia Huntley Sigourney', *Leisure Hour: A Family Journal of Instruction and Recreation* 1.28 (8 July 1852), 444–6.

Miles, Tiya, '"Circular Reasoning": Recentering Cherokee Women in the Antiremoval Campaigns', *American Quarterly* 61.2 (2009), 221–43.

Caroline Norton (1808–77)

'The Creole Girl; or, The Physician's Story', Part I (1840)

Caroline Norton, an aristocratic English writer with strong social justice commitments, published her first volume of verse when only twenty-one. She was thrice married; her abusive first marriage caused her many legal troubles, and the last began only two years before she died.

Norton was known during her lifetime for prose pamphlets advocating women's rights, such as *English Laws for Women* (1854) and *A Letter to the Queen on Lord Chancellor Cranworth's Marriage and Divorce Bill* (1855). She also employed poetry to promote social reform, as in *A Voice from the Factories* (1836).

Having fought for the right to maintain custody of her children in court, Norton was no stranger to tragedy, loss or disappointed love. 'The Creole Girl' addresses each of these themes while also advocating for marginalised voices. Part I, presented below, details the experience of a young girl who comes to England from the West Indies. A white Englishman could travel to the islands, take advantage of a local woman, and father a child never fully welcome anywhere. Part II of the poem offers the point of view of a white man (the 'Physician' of the subtitle) who loved the doomed Creole girl. Although she had wealth and beauty, she was as untouchable as a 'cloister'd nun'. Overall, Norton's poem invites readers to cultivate empathy by highlighting complex transatlantic questions associated with Britain's longstanding rule of Caribbean spaces.

'The Creole Girl;[56] or, The Physician's Story', Part I

> *Elle était de ce monde, où les plus belles choses*
> *Ont le pire destin;*

---

[56] The *OED* today defines 'creole' as 'any person of mixed ancestry born in a country previously colonized by white Europeans'. In the nineteenth century, however, the term could also designate a white Caribbean resident.

Et Rose, elle a vécu ce que vivent les Roses,
		L'espace d'un matin![57]

I.

SHE came to England from the island clime[58]
		Which lies beyond the far Atlantic wave;
She died in early youth—before her time—
		"Peace to her broken heart, and virgin grave!"

II.

She was the child of Passion, and of shame,
		English her father, and of noble birth;
Though too obscure for good or evil fame,
		Her unknown mother faded from the earth.

III.

And what that fair West Indian did betide,[59]
		None knew but he, who least of all might tell,—
But that she lived, and loved, and lonely died,
		And sent this orphan child with him to dwell.

IV.

Oh! that a fair and innocent young face
		Should have a poison in its looks alone,
To raise up thoughts of sorrow and disgrace
		And shame most bitter, although not its own!

V.

Cruel were they who flung that heavy shade
		Across the life whose days did but begin;
Cruel were they who crush'd her heart, and made
		Her youth pay penance for *his* youth's wild sin;

VI.

Yet so it was;—among her father's friends
		A cold compassion made contempt seem light,
But, in "the world," no justice e'er defends
		The victims of their tortuous wrong and right:—

VII.

And "moral England," striking down the weak,
		And smiling at the vices of the strong,
On her, poor child! her parent's guilt would wreak,[60]
		And that which was her grievance, made her wrong.

---

57 Translation: She was of this world, where the most beautiful things/ Have the worst destiny;/ And being a Rose, she lived as Roses live,/ Only the space of a morning!; from François de Malherbe (1555–1628), 'Consolation à M. Du Périer sur la mort de sa fille' (Consolation addressed to Monsieur Du Périer on the death of his daughter), 1598
58 Climate
59 'That fair West Indian': the Creole girl's mother who, lacking the status of the English nobleman, her lover, remained unmarried.
60 Inflict

VIII.

The world she understood not; nor did they
     Who made that world,—her, either, understand;
The very glory of her features' play
     Seem'd like the language of a foreign land;

IX.

The shadowy feelings, rich and wild and warm,
     That glow'd and mantled in her lovely face,—
The slight full beauty of her youthful form,
     Its gentle majesty, its pliant[61] grace,—

X.

The languid lustre of her speaking eye,
     The indolent smile of that bewitching mouth,
(Which more than all betray'd her natal[62] sky,
     And left us dreaming of the sunny South,)—

XI.

The passionate variation of her blood,
     Which rose and sank, as rise and sink the waves,
With every change of her most changeful mood,
     Shock'd sickly Fashion's pale and guarded slaves.[63]

XII.

And so in this fair world she stood alone,
     An alien 'mid the ever-moving crowd,
A wandering stranger, nameless and unknown,
     Her claim to human kindness disallow'd.

XIII.

But oft would passion's bold and burning gaze,
     And curiosity's set frozen stare,
Fix on her beauty in those early days,
     And coarsely thus her loveliness declare;

XIV.

Which she would shrink from, as the gentle plant,
     Fern-leaved Mimosa[64] folds itself away;
Suffering and sad;—for easy 'twas to daunt
     One who on earth had no protecting stay.

---

61 Supple
62 Relating to a person's birthplace
63 Possibly an ironic, oblique reference to Caribbean enslavement prior to 1833; Norton's poem, first published in 1840 in London, was dedicated to the Duchess of Sutherland, the great friend of Queen Victoria and a known abolitionist (see 'Transatlantic Exchanges on Slavery', AA).
64 A plant, native to Central and South America, whose leaves close when touched

XV.

And often to her eye's transparent lid
    The unshed tears would rise with sudden start,
And sink again, as though by reason chid,[65]
    Back to their gentle home, her wounded heart;

XVI.

Even as some gushing fountain idly wells
    Up to the prison of its marble side,
Whose power the mounting wave forever quells,—
    So rose her tears—so stemm'd by virgin pride.

XVII.

And so more lonely each succeeding day,
    As she her lot did better understand,
She lived a life which had in it decay,
    A flower transplanted to too cold a land,—

XVIII.

Which for a while gives out a hope of bloom,
    Then fades and pines, because it may not feel
The freedom and the warmth which gave it room
    The beauty of its nature to reveal.

XIX.

For vainly would the heart accept its lot
    And rouse its strength to bear avow'd contempt;
Scorn *will* be felt as scorn,—deserved or not,—
    And from its bitter spell none stand exempt.

XX.

There is a basilisk[66] power in human eyes
    When they would look a fellow-creature down,
'Neath which the faint soul fascinated lies,
    Struck by the cold sneer, or the with'ring frown.

XXI.

But one there was, among that cruel crowd,
    Whose nature *half* rebell'd against the chain
Which fashion flung around him; though too proud
    To own that slavery's weariness and pain.

XXII.

Too proud; perhaps too weak; for custom still
    Curbs with an iron bit the souls born free;
They start and chafe, yet bend them to the will
    Of this most nameless ruler,[67]—so did he.

---

65 Chided
66 Basilisk: mythical snake that can kill with its gaze
67 'Nameless ruler' references social expectations or the aforementioned 'Custom'.

XXIII.

And even unto *him* the worldly brand
     Which rested on her, half her charm effaced;
Vainly all pure and radiant did she stand,—
     Even unto *him* she was a thing disgraced.

XXIV.

Had she been early doom'd a cloister'd nun,
     To Heaven devoted by a holy vow—
His union with that poor deserted one
     Had seem'd not *more* impossible than now.

XXV.

He *could* have loved her—fervently and well;
     But still the cold world, with its false allure,
Bound his free liking in an icy spell,
     And made its whole foundation insecure.

XXVI.

But not like meaner souls, would he, to prove
     A vulgar admiration, her pursue;
For though his glances after her would rove,
     As something beautiful, and strange, and new,

XXVII.

They were withdrawn if but her eye met his,
     Or, for an instant if their light remain'd,
They soften'd into gentlest tenderness,
     As asking pardon that his look had pain'd.

XXVIII.

And she was nothing unto him,—nor he
     Aught unto her; but each of each did dream
In the still hours of thought, when we are free
     To quit the real world for the things which seem.

XXIX.

When in his heart love's folded wings[68] would stir,
     And bid his youth choose out a fitting mate,
Against his will his thoughts roam'd back to her,
     And all around seem'd blank and desolate.

XXX.

When, in his worldly haunts, a smother'd sigh
     Told he had won some lady of the land,
The dreaming glances of *his* earnest eye
     Beheld far off the Creole orphan stand;

---

68 Reference to the Greek winged god of love Eros (or Cupid)

XXXI.

And to the beauty by his side he froze,
    As though she were not fair, nor he so young,
And turn'd on her such looks of cold repose
    As check'd the trembling accents of her tongue,

XXXII.

And bid her heart's dim passion seek to hide
    Its gathering strength, although the task be pain,
Lest she become that mock to woman's pride—
    A wretch that loves unwoo'd, and loves in vain.

XXXIII.

So in his heart she dwelt,—as one may dwell
    Upon the verge of a forbidden ground;
And oft he struggled hard to break the spell
    And banish her, but vain the effort found;

XXXIV.

For still along the winding way which led
    Into his inmost soul, unbidden came
Her haunting form,—and he was visited
    By echoes soft of her unspoken name,

XXXV.

Through the long night, when those we love *seem* near,
    However cold, however far away,
Borne on the wings of floating dreams, which cheer
    And gives us strength to meet the struggling day.

XXXVI.

And when in twilight hours *she* roved apart,
    Feeding her love-sick soul with visions fair,
The shadow of *his* eyes was on her heart,
    And the smooth masses of his shining hair

XXXVII.

Rose in the glory of the evening light,
    And, where she wander'd, glided evermore,
A star which beam'd upon her world's lone night,
    Where nothing glad had ever shone before.

XXXVIII.

But vague and girlish was that love,—no hope,
    Even of familiar greeting, ever cross'd
Its innocent, but, oh! most boundless scope;
    She loved him,—and she knew her love was lost.

XXXIX.

She gazed on him, as one from out a bark,
    Bound onward to a cold and distant strand,

Some lovely bay, some haven fair may mark,
    Stretching far inward to a sunnier land;

XL.

Who, knowing he must still sail on, turns back
    To watch with dreaming and most mournful eyes
The ruffling foam which follows in his track,
    Or the deep starlight of the shoreless skies.

XLI.

Oh! many a hopeless love like this may be,—
    For love will live that never looks to win;
Gems rashly lost in passion's stormy sea,
    Not to be lifted forth when once cast in!

Source text

Norton, Caroline, 'The Creole Girl, or, The Physician's Story' (Part I), in John Aikin, John Frost and Samuel Carter Hall (eds), *Select Works of the British Poets, in a Chronological Series from Southey to Croly* (Philadelphia, PA: Thomas Wardle, 1845), 668–70.

References

Dolin, Kieran, 'The Transfigurations of Caroline Norton', *Victorian Literature and Culture* 30.2 (2002), 503–27.
ODNB

Mary Ann Shadd [Cary] (1823–93)

From **A Plea For Emigration; Or, Notes Of Canada West** *(1852)*

Born the oldest of thirteen children to a free Black family in the US, Mary Ann Shadd used her elite social position and education to advocate for many causes, including abolition, Black emigration and suffrage.

In 1850, the US passed the Fugitive Slave Act. This law, requiring any citizen (even in 'free' states) to return escaped enslaved individuals to their enslavers, sparked increased emigration by Black Americans to Canada, the West Indies, Britain and Africa. As an advocate for this transnational diaspora, Shadd herself moved in 1851 to Canada. *A Plea For Emigration* appeared in 1852 and, addressing Blacks still in the US, detailed her claims for the advantages African Americans would have as residents of 'Canada West'.

Neither marriage to Thomas Cary nor his death in 1860 slowed her activism. Beyond her work as a writer-editor, she founded a primary school open to all races. She returned to the United States during the Civil War to support the Union cause and eventually studied law at Howard University.

From A Plea For Emigration; Or, Notes Of Canada West

INTRODUCTORY REMARKS.

THE increasing desire on the part of the colored people, to become thoroughly informed respecting the Canadas, and particularly that part of the province called Canada West[69] —to learn of the climate, soil and productions, and of the inducements offered generally to emigrants, and to them particularly, since that the passage of the odious Fugitive Slave Law[70] has made a residence in the United States to many of them dangerous in the extreme,—this consideration, and the absence of condensed information accessible to all, is my excuse for offering this tract to the notice of the public. The people are in a strait,—on the one hand, a pro-slavery administration,[71] with its entire controllable force, is bearing upon them with fatal effect: on the other, the Colonization Society,[72] in the garb of *Christianity* and *Philanthropy,* is seconding the efforts of the first named power, by bringing into the lists a vast social and immoral influence, thus making more effective the agencies employed. Information is needed.—Tropical Africa, the land of promise of the colonizationists, teeming as she is with the breath of pestilence, a burning sun and fearful maladies, bids them welcome; —she feelingly invites to moral and physical death, under a voluntary escort of their most bitter enemies at home. Again, many look with dreadful forebodings to the probability of worse than inquisitorial inhumanity in the Southern States, from the operation of the Fugitive Law. Certain that neither a home in Africa, nor in the Southern States, is desirable under present circumstances, inquiry is made respecting Canada.[73] I have endeavored to furnish information to a certain extent, to that end, and believing that more reliance would be placed upon a statement of facts obtained in the country, from reliable sources and from observation, than upon a repetition of current statements made elsewhere, however honestly made, I determined to visit Canada, and to there collect such information as most persons desire. These pages contain the result of much inquiry— matter obtained both from individuals and from documents and papers of unquestionable character in the Province.

M. A. S.

A PLEA FOR EMIGRATION, &C.
BRITISH AMERICA.

BRITISH AMERICA, it is well known, is a country equal in extent, at least, to the United States, extending on the north to the Arctic Ocean, from the Atlantic on the east, to the Pacific on the west, and the southern boundary of which is subject to the inequalities in latitude of the several Northern States and Territories[74] belonging

---

69 Also Upper Canada, now known as Ontario
70 The Fugitive Slave Acts were actually a pair of laws passed by Congress that allowed the capture and return of runaways within United States territory. The first was enacted in 1793. The second was part of the Compromise of 1850 and created much harsher penalties for runaways and anyone aiding them.
71 After President Zachary Taylor's sudden death, Millard Fillmore became the thirteenth US president. Although he personally opposed slavery, Fillmore believed the 1850 Compromise necessary for preserving the Union and enforced the associated Fugitive Slave Law.
72 The American Colonization Society was founded in 1816 by Reverend Robert Finley, a Presbyterian minister, to encourage and assist free Black people emigrating to Africa.
73 The Abolition Act of 1834 abolished slavery throughout the British Empire, including British North America.
74 The Treaty of Guadalupe-Hidalgo after the Mexican American War in 1848 recognised Texas as a US state and ceded to the US a large area of western land to be categorised as US Territory.

to the United States government. This vast country includes within its limits, some of the most beautiful lakes and rivers on the Western Continent. The climate, in the higher latitudes, is extremely severe, but for a considerable distance north of the settled districts, particularly in the western part, the climate is healthy and temperate: epidemics[75] are not of such frequency as in the United States, owing to a more equable temperature, and local diseases are unknown. The province claiming especial attention, as presenting features most desirable in a residence, is Canada, divided into East and West; and of these Canada West is to be preferred. [...]

LABOR—TRADES.

In Canada, as in other recently settled countries, there is much to do, and comparatively few for the work. The numerous towns and villages springing up, and the great demand for timber and agricultural products, make labor of every kind plenty: all trades that are practiced in the United States, are there patronized by whomsoever carried on—no man's complexion affecting his business. If a colored man understands his business, he receives the public patronage the same as a white man. He is not obliged to work a little better, and at a lower rate—there is no degraded class to identify him with, therefore every man's work stands or falls according to merit, not as is his color. Builders, and other tradesmen, of different complexions, work together on the same building and in the same shop, with perfect harmony, and often the proprietor of an establishment is colored, and the majority or all of the men employed are white. Businesses that in older communities have ceased to remunerate, yield a large percentage to the money invested. [...]

CHURCHES – SCHOOLS.

In the large towns and cities, as in similar communities in other Christian countries, the means for religious instruction are ample. There are costly churches in which all classes and complexions worship, and no "negro pew," or other seat for colored persons, especially. I was forcibly struck, when at Toronto, with the contrast the religious community there presented, to our own large body of American Christians. In the churches, originally built by the white Canadians, the presence of colored persons, promiscuously[76] seated, elicited no comment whatever. They are members, and visitors, and as such have their pews according to their inclination, near the door, or remote, or central, as best suits them. The number of colored persons, attending the churches with whites, constitutes a minority, I think. They have their "own churches." That that is the feature in their policy, which is productive of mischief to the entire body, is evident enough; and the opinion of the best informed and most influential among them, in Toronto and the large towns, is decided and universal. I have heard men of many years residence, and who have, in a measure, been moulded by the better sentiment of society, express deep sorrow at the course of colored persons, in pertinaciously refusing overtures of religious fellowship from the whites; and in the face of all experience to the contrary, erecting Colored Methodist, and Baptist, and other Churches. This opinion obtains amongst many who, when in the United States, were connected with colored churches. Aside from their caste character, their influence on the colored people is fatal. The character of the exclusive church in Canada tends to perpetuate ignorance, both of their true position as

---

75 Cholera, with a very high mortality rate, was a massive public health issue throughout the world in the nineteenth century, including in the Midwestern US.

76 In the nineteenth century, this term often referred to social occasions when men and women mixed together in the same space (a practice generally discouraged unless in private homes or refined, semi-private occasions). Here, Shadd refers to a 'promiscuous' mixing of races – unlikely to occur in the US, even in the North.

British subjects, and of the Christian religion in its purity. It is impossible to observe thoughtfully the workings of that incipient Zion,[77] (the Canadian African Church, of whatever denomination,) in its present imperfect state, without seriously regretting that it should have been thought necessary to call it into existence. In her bosom is nurtured the long-standing and rankling prejudices, and hatred against whites, without exception, that had their origin in American oppression, and that should have been left in the country in which they originated – 'tis that species of animosity that is not bounded by geographical lines, nor suffers discrimination. [. . .]

RECAPITULATION.

The conclusion arrived at in respect to Canada, by an impartial person, is, that no settled country in America offers stronger inducements to colored people. The climate is healthy, and they enjoy as good health as other settlers, or as the natives; the soil is of the first quality; the laws of the country give to them, at first, the same protection and privileges as to other persons not born subjects; and after compliance with Acts of Parliament affecting them, as taking oath, &c., they may enjoy full "privileges of British birth in the Province."[78] The general tone of society is healthy; vice is discountenanced, and infractions of the law promptly punished; and, added to this, there is an increasing anti-slavery sentiment, and a progressive system of religion.

Source text

Shadd, Mary A.[nn], *A Plea for Emigration; or, Notes of Canada West, in its Moral, Social, and Political Aspect; with Suggestions Respecting Mexico, West Indies and Vancouver's Island, for the Information of Colored Emigrants* (Detroit, MI: George W. Pattison, 1852).

References

Calloway-Thomas, Carolyn, 'Mary Ann Shadd Cary: Crafting Black Culture Through Empirical and Moral Arguments', *Howard Journal of Communications* 24 (2013), 239–56.

Steadman, Jennifer Bernhardt, 'Traveling Uplift: Mary Ann Shadd Cary Creates and Connects Black Communities', in Jennifer Bernhardt Steadman (ed.), *Traveling Economies: American Women's Travel Writing* (Columbus, OH: Ohio State University Press, 2007), 85–111.

Susanna Moodie (1803–85)

From Roughing It in the Bush; or, Forest Life in Canada *(1852)*

Susanna Strickland Moodie was born in Bungay, England, in December 1803, to a family of six sisters. She spent much of her adult life in North

---

77 The African Methodist Episcopal Zion Church was established in New York in 1794.
78 A series of Naturalization Acts between 1828 and 1845 allowed alien men who had lived in Canada for five years to take an oath of allegiance and become British subjects.

America, having crossed the Atlantic with her husband and young daughter in 1832. After arriving in the 'bush' of Upper Canada (Ontario), the
Moodies struggled financially. Susanna was already an experienced writer
in genres ranging from children's literature to gift books to anti-slavery
texts, including serving as transcriber for Mary Prince's oral narrative. So,
like her sister Catherine Traill (an immigrant to the same region), Susanna
augmented family income by publishing in Canadian and US magazines.
Her work also appeared in British venues such as the *Lady's Magazine* and
Bentley's Miscellany.

Roughing It in the Bush*, drawing from prior periodical sketches and
poetry, was first published in London in 1852, succeeded by *Life in the
Clearings* (1853) and the novel *Flora Lyndsay* (1854). Moodie tried to con-
trol transnational finances for her authorship, negotiating not only with
Richard Bentley (a purveyor of travel literature) for the British edition of
Roughing It and subsequent writings but also with US publishing houses.

Moodie is honoured now as a founding mother of Canadian literature.
She was not always so well-received in her second homeland. Her depictions of pioneer life present witty but unflattering sketches of local people,
and she complains forcefully about the day-to-day challenges of settler life.
As sample reviews in Michael Peterman's critical edition show, Moodie's
contemporaries needled her back. But twentieth- and twenty-first- century
readers, including major Canadian feminist authors, have been more appreciative. Margaret Atwood, for instance, crafted a poetry collection inspired
by *Roughing It*, and, more recently, Moodie's text was re-conceived as a
graphic novel co-authored by Carol Shields and Patrick Crowe.

In this excerpt, Moodie describes life on shipboard just after arrival
near Montreal.

From Roughing it in the Bush[79]

CHAPTER III
OUR JOURNEY UP THE COUNTRY

Fly this plague-stricken spot! The hot, foul air
Is rank with pestilence—the crowded marts
And public ways, once populous with life,
Are still and noisome as a churchyard vault;
Aghast and shuddering, Nature holds her breath
In abject fear, and feels at her strong heart
The deadly pangs of death.[80]

---

79 'Bush' refers to rural land that is underdeveloped or uninhabited. Our excerpt comes from the
Canadian edition of 1871, which, as indicated in a title page note, presented 'a new and revised
edition, with an introductory chapter, in which Canada of the present is contrasted with Canada of
forty years ago'. See the frontispiece ahead of this section's introductory essay.
80 Moodie includes poems throughout her chapters, both as headnotes and within.

Of Montreal I can say but little. The cholera was at its height, and the fear of infection, which increased the nearer we approached its shores, cast a gloom over the scene, and prevented us from exploring its infected streets. That the feelings of all on board very nearly resembled our own might be read in the anxious faces of both passengers and crew. Our captain, who had never before hinted that he entertained any apprehensions on the subject, now confided to us his conviction that he should never quit the city alive: "This cursed cholera! Left it in Russia——found it on my return to Leith[81]—meets me again in Canada. No escape the third time." If the captain's prediction proved true in his case, it was not so in ours. We left the cholera in England, we met it again in Scotland, and, under the providence of God, we escaped its fatal visitation in Canada.

Yet the fear and the dread of it on that first day caused me to throw many an anxious glance on my husband and my child. I had been very ill during the three weeks that our vessel was becalmed upon the Banks of Newfoundland, and to this circumstance I attribute my deliverance from the pestilence. I was weak and nervous when the vessel arrived at Quebec, but the voyage up the St. Lawrence, the fresh air and beautiful scenery were rapidly restoring me to health.

Montreal from the river wears a pleasing aspect, but it lacks the grandeur, the stern sublimity of Quebec. The fine mountain that forms the back-ground to the city, the Island of St. Helens in front, and the junction of the St. Lawrence and the Ottawa—which run side by side, their respective boundaries only marked by a long ripple of white foam, and the darker blue tint of the former river,—constitute the most remarkable features in the landscape.

The town itself was, at that period, dirty and ill-paved; and the opening of all the sewers, in order to purify the place, and stop the ravages of the pestilence, rendered the public thoroughfares almost impassable, and loaded the air with intolerable effluvia,[82] more likely to produce than stay the course of the plague, the violence of which had, in all probability, been increased by these long-neglected receptacles of uncleanliness.

The dismal stories told us by the excise-officer[83] who came to inspect the unloading of the vessel, of the frightful ravages of the cholera, by no means increased our desire to go on shore.

"It will be a miracle if you escape," he said. "Hundreds of emigrants die daily; and if Stephen Ayres had not providentially come among us, not a soul would have been alive at this moment in Montreal."

"And who is Stephen Ayres?" said I.

"God only knows," was the grave reply. "There was a man sent from heaven, and his name was John."

"But I thought this man was called Stephen?"

"Ay, so he calls himself; but 'tis certain that he is not of the earth. Flesh and blood could never do what he has done, —the hand of God is in it. Besides, no one knows who he is, or whence he comes. When the cholera was at the worst, and the hearts of all men stood still with fear, and our doctors could do nothing to stop its progress, this man, or angel, or saint, suddenly made his appearance in our streets. He came in great humility, seated in an ox-cart, and drawn by two lean oxen

---

81 A shore settlement that became part of Edinburgh in Scotland
82 An offensive, perhaps harmful, odour or discharge
83 A government officer working in customs

and a rope harness. Only think of that! Such a man in an *old ox-cart*, drawn by *rope harness!* The thing itself was a miracle. He made no parade about what he could do, but only fixed up a plain pasteboard notice, informing the public that he possessed an infallible remedy for the cholera, and would engage to cure all who sent for him."

"And was he successful?"

"Successful! It beats all belief; and his remedy so simple! For some days we all took him for a quack, and would have no faith in him at all, although he performed some wonderful cures upon poor folks, who could not afford to send for the doctor. The Indian village was attacked by the disease, and he went out to them, and restored upwards of a hundred of the Indians to perfect health. They took the old lean oxen out of the cart, and drew him back to Montreal in triumph. This 'stablished him at once, and in a few days' time he made a fortune. The very doctors sent for him to cure them; and it is to be hoped that, in a few days, he will banish the cholera from the city."

"Do you know his famous remedy?"

"Do I not? – Did he not cure me when I was at the last gasp? Why, he makes no secret of it.[84] It is all drawn from the maple-tree. First he rubs the patient all over with an ointment, made of hog's lard and maple-sugar and ashes from the maple-tree; and he gives him a hot draught of maple-sugar and ley, which throws him into a violent perspiration. In about an hour the cramps subside; he falls into a quiet sleep, and when he awakes he is perfectly restored to health." Such were our first tidings of Stephen Ayres, the cholera doctor, who is universally believed to have effected some wonderful cures. He obtained a wide celebrity throughout the colony.

The day of our arrival in the port of Montreal was spent in packing and preparing for our long journey up the country. At sunset I went upon deck to enjoy the refreshing breeze that swept from the river. The evening was delightful; the white tents of the soldiers on the Island of St. Helens glittered in the beams of the sun, and the bugle-call, wafted over the waters, sounded so cheery and inspiring, that it banished all fears of the cholera, and the heavy gloom that had clouded my mind since we left Quebec. I could once more hold sweet converse with nature, and enjoy the soft loveliness of the rich and harmonious scene. [...]

Our luggage having been removed to the Custom-house,[85] including our bedding, the captain collected all the ship's flags for our accommodation, of which we formed a tolerably comfortable bed; and if our dreams were of England, could it be otherwise, with her glorious flag wrapped around us, and our heads resting upon the Union Jack?

In the morning we were obliged to visit the city to make the necessary arrangements for our upward journey.

The day was intensely hot. A bank of thunder-clouds lowered heavily above the mountain, and the close, dusty streets were silent, and nearly deserted. Here and there might be seen a group of anxious looking, care-worn, sickly emigrants, seated against a wall among their packages, and sadly ruminating upon their future prospects.

---

84 A friend of mine, in this town, has an original portrait of this notable empiric—this man sent from heaven. The face is rather handsome, but has a keen, designing expression, and is evidently that of an American, from its complexion and features. [Author's note original to the text.]
85 Office at a port or frontier where customs duty is collected

The sullen toll of the death-bell, the exposure of ready-made coffins in the undertakers' windows, and the oft-recurring notice placarded on the walls, of funerals furnished at such and such a place, at cheapest rate and shortest notice, painfully reminded us, at every turning of the street, that death was everywhere – perhaps lurking in our very path; we felt no desire to examine the beauties of the place. With this ominous feeling pervading our minds, public buildings possessed few attractions, and we determined to make our stay as short as possible.

Compared with the infected city, our ship appeared an ark of safety, and we returned to it with joy and confidence, too soon to be destroyed. We had scarcely re-entered our cabin, when tidings were brought to us that the cholera had made its appearance: a brother of the captain had been attacked.

It was advisable that we should leave the vessel immediately, before the intelligence could reach the health officers. A few minutes sufficed to make the necessary preparations; and in less than half-an-hour we found ourselves occupying comfortable apartments in Goodenough's hotel, and our passage taken in the stage for the following morning.

The transition was like a dream. The change from the close, rank ship to large, airy, well-furnished rooms and clean attendants, was a luxury we should have enjoyed had not the dread of the cholera involved all things around us in gloom and apprehension. No one spoke upon the subject; and yet it was evident that it was uppermost in the thoughts of all. Several emigrants had died of the terrible disorder during the week, beneath the very roof that sheltered us, and its ravages, we were told, had extended up the country as far as Kingston; so that it was still to be the phantom of our coming journey, if we were fortunate enough to escape from its headquarters.

At six o'clock the following morning, we took our places in the coach for Lachine, and our fears of the plague greatly diminished as we left the spires of Montreal in the distance. The journey from Montreal west-ward has been so well described by many gifted pens, that I shall say little about it. The banks of the St. Lawrence are picturesque and beautiful, particularly in those spots where there is a good view of the American side. The neat farmhouses looked to me, whose eyes had been so long accustomed to the watery waste, homes of beauty and happiness; and the splendid orchards, the trees at that season of the year being loaded with ripening fruit of all hues, were refreshing and delicious. [. . .]

Our journey during the first day was performed partly by coach, partly by steam. It was nine o'clock in the evening when we landed at Cornwall, and took coach for Prescott. The country through which we passed appeared beautiful in the clear light of the moon; but the air was cold, and slightly sharpened by frost. This seemed strange to me in the early part of September, but it is very common in Canada. Nine passengers were closely packed into our narrow vehicle, but the sides being of canvas, and the open space allowed for windows unglazed, I shivered with cold, which amounted to a state of suffering, when the day broke, and we approached the little village of Matilda. It was unanimously voted by all hands that we should stop and breakfast at a small inn by the road-side, and warm ourselves before proceeding to Prescott. [. . .]

At Prescott we embarked on board a fine new steamboat, *William IV.*, crowded with Irish emigrants, proceeding to Cobourg and Toronto.

While pacing the deck, my husband was greatly struck by the appearance of a middle-aged man and his wife, who sat apart from the rest, and seemed struggling with intense grief, which, in spite of all their efforts at concealment, was strongly impressed upon their features. Some time after, I fell into conversation with the woman, from whom I learned their little history. The husband was factor to a Scotch gentleman, of large landed property, who had employed him to visit Canada, and report the capabilities of the country, prior to his investing a large sum of money in wild lands. The expenses of their voyage had been paid, and everything up to that morning had prospered with them. They had been blessed with a speedy passage, and were greatly pleased with the country and the people; but of what avail was all this? Their only son, a fine lad of fourteen, had died that day of the cholera, and all their hopes for the future were buried in his grave. For his sake they had sought a home in this far land; and here, at the very onset of their new career, the fell disease had taken him from them for ever, – here, where, in such a crowd, the poor heart-broken mother could not even indulge her natural grief!

"Ah, for a place where I might greet!" she said; "it would relieve the burning weight at my heart. But with sae many strange eyes glowering upon me, I tak' shame to mysel' to greet."

"Ah, Jeannie, my puir woman," said the husband, grasping her hand, "ye maun bear up; 'tis God's will; an sinfu' creatures like us mauna repine.[86] But oh, madam," turning to me, "we have sair hearts the day!"

Poor bereaved creatures, how deeply I commiserated their grief, – how I respected the poor father, in the stern efforts he made to conceal from indifferent spectators the anguish that weighed upon his mind! Tears are the best balm that can be applied to the anguish of the heart. Religion teaches man to bear his sorrows with becoming fortitude, but tears contribute largely both to soften and to heal the wounds from whence they flow.

At Brockville we took in a party of ladies, which somewhat relieved the monotony of the cabin, and I was amused by listening to their lively prattle, and the little gossip with which they strove to wile away the tedium of the voyage. The day was too stormy to go upon deck, – thunder and lightning, accompanied with torrents of rain. Amid the confusion of the elements, I tried to get a peep at the Lake of the Thousand Isles; but the driving storm blended all objects into one, and I returned wet and disappointed to my berth. We passed Kingston at midnight, and lost all our lady passengers but two. The gale continued until daybreak, and noise and confusion prevailed all night, which was greatly increased by the uproarious conduct of a wild Irish emigrant, who thought fit to make his bed upon the mat before the cabin door. He sang, he shouted, he harangued his countrymen on the political state of the Emerald Isle, in a style which was loud if not eloquent. Sleep was impossible, whilst his stentorian[87] lungs continued to pour forth torrents of unmeaning sound.

Our Dutch stewardess was highly enraged. His conduct, she said, "was perfectly ondacent."[88] She opened the door, and, bestowing upon him several kicks, bade him get away "out of that," or she would complain to the captain.

In answer to this remonstrance, he caught her by the foot, and pulled her down. Then waving the tattered remains of his straw hat in the air, he shouted with an air of triumph, "Git out wid you, you ould witch! Shure the ladies, the purty darlints, never sent you wid that 'ugly message to Pat,' who loves them so intirely, that he means to kape watch over them through the blessed night." Then making us a

---

86 'Maun': must; 'mauna': must not
87 Loud and powerful
88 Indecent

ludicrous bow, he continued, "Ladies, I'm at yer service; I only wish I could get a dispensation from the Pope, and I'd marry yeas all." The stewardess bolted the door, and the mad fellow kept up such a racket, that we all wished him at the bottom of the Ontario.

The following day was wet and gloomy. The storm had protracted the length of our voyage for several hours, and it was midnight when we landed at Cobourg.

Source text

Moodie, Susanna, *Roughing It in the Bush; or, Forest Life in Canada* (Toronto: Maclear & Co. Publishers, 1871).

References

Atwood, Margaret, *The Journals of Susanna Moodie* (Toronto: Oxford University Press, 1970).
Peterman, Michael A. (ed.), *Roughing It in the Bush by Susanna Moodie: A Norton Critical Edition* (New York: W. W. Norton, 2007).
Shields, Carol and Patrick Crowe, *Susanna Moodie: Roughing It in the Bush* (Toronto: Second Story Press, 2016).
Thomas, Christa Zeller, '"I had never seen such a shed called a house before": The Discourse of Home in Susanna Moodie's "Roughing it in the Bush"', *Canadian Literature* 203 (2009), 105–21.

'The Sorrows of the Cherokees' (1856)

The Trail of Tears – the forced relocation of Cherokee people from their southeastern US homelands to what is now the state of Oklahoma – caused thousands of deaths along the journey. That diaspora has left lasting marks on both the Eastern Band (descended from those who hid in the Appalachian Mountains to avoid Removal) and the Western Band. Meanwhile, the *story* of the Trail of Tears has claimed a notable place among the many Indian Removals in North America, partly because of the eloquence of Cherokee leaders resisting at the time, partly because of writers revisiting this enforced migration in genres ranging from novels and poetry to the *Unto These Hills* outdoor drama in North Carolina.

For scholars, studying this watershed event often involves critique of President Andrew Jackson and the 1830 Removal Act, along with review of related court decisions. John P. Bowes argues, however, that understanding this painful history requires recognition that 'removal was also an act of all-encompassing violence'; that US 'federal removal policy should be viewed as a continuation of, rather than a transition from, the civilization policy begun in the late eighteenth century'; and that geography and chronology for such study should 'be traced back to early English colonization on the Atlantic seaboard' (Bowes, 66–7). For the Cherokee, for instance, a transatlantic understanding of their Removal would include studying visits by Cherokee chiefs to London in 1730 to seek recognition of their national sovereignty from King George II. Cultivating a transatlantic perspective on the Removal also entails tracking the longstanding print-culture-supported engagement of the British public in questions about Native American sovereignty, as illustrated by texts such as 'The Cherokee Indians' (1829) in *The Morning Chronicle*.

Below, we provide one transatlantic narrative illustrating this multi-faceted discourse, a reprinting by a British periodical of a US source. This essay revisits the Removal during a period when the inaccurate stereotype of the 'vanishing Indian' was increasingly deployed by whites eager to shift from tropes of diaspora to full erasure.

'The Sorrows of the Cherokees'[89]

What can be more melancholy than the history of North American Indians? Two centuries ago the smoke of their wigwams, and the light of their council-fires, might have been seen in every valley from the St. Croix to the Sabine, and from the ocean to the lakes. Now the winds of the Atlantic fan not a country they can call their own. We have heard their footsteps rustling in the leaves of autumn – and they are gone. Everywhere fading away at the approach of the white man, they have passed mournfully by us to return no more for ever. Of all the tribes who roamed in their native freedom over the American continent, none were more daring, none more constant, than the Cherokees. Little more than half a century ago, their shouts of victory rang along the river and across the glades in sight of where I now write. Their council-fires were kindled on the spots where stand our flourishing cities; their thick arrows and deadly tomahawks whistled through the forests that lately stood around; and their dark encampments and trace of hunters startled nought save the wild beasts in their lairs.

The warriors then stood forth in their glory. The young listened to the songs of other days, while the aged sat down, but wept not. They believed they would soon be at rest in a happier home, where dwelt the Great Spirit – far beyond the western skies. Braver men never lived; truer men never drew the bow. Their courage, fortitude, and sagacity were astonishing. They shrunk from no dangers; they feared no hardships. They had the vices, but they also had the virtues, of savage life. They were true to their country, their friends, and their homes. If they forgave not injury, neither did they forget kindness. Their vengeance was terrible, but their fidelity was unconquerable. Their love, their hate, stopped not on this side [of] the tomb. But where are they? They have passed away from the graves of their fathers and the homes of their hearts. I saw them as they passed. It was in 1838. The last remnant of that once-powerful tribe were driven from their mountain-homes in North Carolina, to seek a temporary resting-place beyond the Mississippi. There

---

89 Note in the original source: A writer in the 'National Magazine' (U.S. America) furnishes this touching record. – Editors.

was that in their hearts which defied the power of speech. There was something in their looks that spoke not of vengeance, nor of submission, but of hard necessity, which defied both; which choked all utterance; which had no aim nor method. It was courage absorbed in despair. They lingered but for a moment; their look and step were onward, and soon they passed the "father of waters," to return to the homes of their childhood and the graces of their fathers no more for ever!

But there is not yet, between us and them, an impassable gulf. There is one star whose rays gild their sorrowing pathway—whose cheering influence inspires their hearts with hope, and points them out a better state. God's blessed word found its way into their midst: ere they were driven from their early homes, and while the "fire-water"[90] and oppressions of the pale-faced man continued to scatter "fire-brands and death" among the many, a few took heed to this, as unto a "light that shineth in a dark place," and found that peace "the world cannot give." How unspeakably dear was this to their hearts, when driven from their homes to the far west! A majority of the nation removed willingly; but a large minority were forced, by armed troops, hunted up one by one, dragged into camp, and thence far away. Some years before their removal, characters had been invented, their language written,[91] and a portion of the holy Scriptures, with many excellent hymns, and a few other books, translated for their use. How fondly they clung to these when stripped of almost everything else, I had many opportunities to witness. The Indians were collected by the United States' troops, carried to camp, and kept under guard preparatory to their removal in the midst of summer. It was my fate to pass their country again and again during the process of removal; and never can I forget the sight, or the feeling it produced. They took with them what few clothes they had, but scarce anything else; and the sight of their deserted cabins, their flourishing corn and fruitful beans, with the howling of the dogs and piteous lowing of the cattle, produced a melancholy feeling that haunts me to this hour. Rather than leave their country, scores of them fled to the mountains, where, alas! many perished with hunger, and left their unburied bones to bleach the sun.[92] Weeks after the main body had been removed, one after another of those who had fled to the mountains would straggle in the settlements weak and emaciated almost to a skeleton, and piteously ask for bread. "Where is your wife?" "Dead." "Where are your children?" "Dead too—die in the mountains—nothing to eat—all die!" It was enough to melt a heart of stone! Such was the suffering, such the distress, consequent upon the order for their removal, that officers and soldiers, while executing that order, were often seen to weep like children. Yes, hardy soldiers, who perhaps had not wept for years, would go to the cabin, seize the father and mother, and perhaps some of the older children, while the younger and more timid would flee to the fields or thickets to hide themselves; and, on witnessing the deep, unaffected distress of the now ruined family, would sit down and weep as though their hearts would break. I said that many of the smaller children fled and hid themselves on the approach of the soldiers: and so it was. Many of them were found, and dragged from their hiding-places to accompany their parents; but many others *were never found*. Many a hearty, sprightly Indian child,

---

90 Liquor, introduced to Native Americans by white settlers
91 Sequoyah created a Cherokee syllabary early in the nineteenth century, enabling reading and writing in the Cherokee language.
92 Traditionally, a lengthy funeral officiated by a Shaman preceded a seven-day mourning period. Burials were sacred, so having to leave bodies in such a condition was a travesty.

whose father, mother, brothers, sisters, were all gone, never to return, was left to perish and die alone!

Of the many affecting scenes which came to my knowledge during the forcible removal of these hapless people, I select one. I knew the man well. He and most of his family were worthy members of the Methodist church, and for several years under my charge. He lived in a secluded part of the nation, among the mountains of North Carolina, and seemed to have formed his opinions of the white man from his knowledge of the Missionary who had brought him the Gospel of Christ, baptized him into the Christian faith, and often afforded him the consolations of the blessed word. He was slow to believe he would ever be forced from his humble but quiet home; and some months elapsed ere he was molested. His was among the last families in all that region visited by the soldiers. But they came at last. An officer, with guard and interpreter, presented himself at the cabin-door, and the old man was told that he and his family must go into the camp immediately. As if doubting their sincerity, he hesitated, and offered several common-place excuses. But finding these of no avail, with a heavy heart and sad countenance he made one request—just one—which he hoped would be granted. What was it? That he might be allowed *to pray in this cabin once more with his wife and children ere he left it for ever!* It was granted. The old man took from a rude shelf a portion of the Scriptures, and some hymns that had been translated into his native tongue; he read, he sang, and kneeled to pray. He kneeled near the middle of the cabin-floor, while his wife and children, eight in number, closed around him. He stood upright on his knees: they bowed their heads to the floor. With a tremulous voice he began. First, he thanked God for life, health and preservation; for the Gospel; for the privilege of reading His word, and calling on His name. Next, he prayed for the white man, all white men, especially those who persecuted the Indian and took his home; begged that God would pity and forgive them. He particularly mentioned those at the door, excusing them in his prayer, because they had been commanded to do as they did. Then he prayed for the Indian—the poor Indian, as he called him—once strong and powerful, now few and weak: his property was gone; his friends were gone; *all was gone!* "O good Spirit," he cried, "O blessed Jesus, help poor Indian; *he can't help himself any more!*"

The prayer was frequently interrupted by the groans and sobs of his family; and such was its earnestness, unaffected simplicity, and pathos, that the interpreter, though a wicked man, found it impossible to restrain his feelings, and cried aloud. The officer and soldiers, without understanding a word that was said, were overcome by the scene, and mingled their tears and sobs with those of the afflicted family. At the close of the prayer the officer bade the interpreter tell the Indian *he might come into camp whenever he chose;* and turning away, declared he might be punished for disobedience, but he could not and would not lay hands on such a man or such a family as that.

Reader, that Indian and his family were never removed west. He fairly prayed himself out of the hands of the troops; and long did he live, and, for aught I know, still lives, at his quiet home in the mountains of western North Carolina, to witness the truth, excellence, and power of our holy religion. One of his sons became an Exhorter, and another a Leader, in the Methodist church organized among a few hundred Cherokees, who remained on a reservation by the State, some forty or fifty miles from where the family lived at the time mentioned; and often did I share their homely fare, and join with them in prayers and hymns of praise to the "Father of us all."

Source text

'The Sorrows of the Cherokees', *The Wesleyan-Methodist Magazine* 79.9 (London: John Mason, 1856), 802–5.

References

Bowes, John P., 'American Indian Removal beyond the Removal Act', *Native American and Indigenous Studies* 1.1 (2014), 65–87.
'The Cherokee Indians', *Morning Chronicle* (19 October 1829), 1.
Jones, Hunter S., 'Cherokee Chieftains at the British Court', *Historia: Magazine of the Historical Writers Association* (16 September 2016), Web.
Lyons, Scott Richard, *X-Marks: Native Signatures of Assent* (Minneapolis, MN: University of Minnesota Press, 2010).

Sarah Parker Remond (1815–94)

'Colonization. To the Editor of the "Freed-Man"' (1866)

Sarah Parker Remond was born to free people of colour, successful entrepreneurs living in Salem, Massachusetts, who taught her to value education and self-sufficiency. Remond gave her first anti-slavery address when just sixteen years old, leading to multiple speaking tours representing the American Anti-Slavery Society.

In that role, Remond arrived in England in early 1859, following her brother Charles, also an anti-slavery lecturer. British abolitionists enthusiastically welcomed Sarah Remond's speeches, sometimes given along with Frederick Douglass'. Remond's oratory sought to tug the hearts of white mothers by addressing the separation of families. She also boldly addressed sexual exploitation of enslaved Black women. Newspapers on both sides of the Atlantic praised Remond's lectures, with her intense treatment of the Margaret Garner case (which Toni Morrison would later depict in *Beloved* [1987]) described as especially compelling.

Her letter to the editor of *The Freed-Man* illustrated her rhetorical skill and the transatlantic reach of her advocacy. Remond's text appeared in a period when a number of leaders were pushing 'return' to Africa for Blacks living in the US as a viable strategy. No less a supporter of anti-slavery than Harriet Beecher Stowe had depicted 'Back to Africa' positively in *Uncle Tom's Cabin*, though she later changed her position.

Remond's letter appealed to reason and civility, while also critiquing advocates of the colonisation scheme, whether in the US or Britain.

'Colonization: To the Editor of the "Freed-Man"'[93]

Sir, – The negro haters in the United States, and their allies on this side of the Atlantic are now doing all they can to prove the negro unfit for freedom. Among other devices our old enemy "Colonization" seems destined to another revival. It is the custom of this foe to appear at intervals like "the famous Sea Serpent." I have no word of objection to offer against free emigration either for white or black men, if they emigrate of their own *free will*. But I do oppose any coercion or pressure of any kind which in the least forces anyone to live anywhere, but in the locality which their own head and heart dictates. Still more will I oppose colonization, when this pressure grows out of hatred to an oppressed race, or because a dominant race has neither the moral courage, nor the justice to do as they would like to be done by. I well know the other side of the question: that there are honest men, some who wish well to the negro, and who think it would elevate his *hated race* if they could build up a Republic for themselves. But it will be proved in the long run, in fact the only sound policy which will be effective, and the only way to really elevate any oppressed race is to bring them within the influence of the most civilized races. And this is particularly true of races long enslaved. This has long been the opinion of the most eminent friends of the negro on both sides of the Atlantic, and history also gives abundant proof of the result. Never until our friends as well as our enemies understand and act upon the principle which underlies this essential fact and to which they may add another fact of much importance, that coloured men and women desire to be treated according to their intellectual and moral worth, or in other words without any reference to their complexion, exactly the same as any white person would be treated when placed in similar circumstances. Until this is done no real advance to their advantage can be made. The spirit of colonization so lamentably exhibited by President Johnson,[94] and so malignantly imitated by the London *Times*, will I believe be a failure. The propositions similar in character which have been put forth during many *many* years have been complete failures.[95] Colonization for the freed negroes at this period of their history is most wicked in its conception and I hope is destined to an early death. Wendell Phillips, Esq.,[96] delivered a speech at Boston, U.S. on the 17th of October. It is most forcible, and eloquent, every line of it "the truth, the whole truth, and nothing but the truth." He speaks with genuine knowledge of the negro race, and with equal knowledge of his own race. He speaks for us, and of us as he has a right to do; no moment during the history of the negro was ever so critical as the present. Mr. Phillips is more than equal to the hour; that man has more moral courage than almost an army of ordinary men. Negro character is not unfrequently supposed to be delineated by a

93 *The Freed-Man* was a British periodical that ran from 1865 to 1868. Backed by the Freed-Men's Aid Society, it promoted the interests of the newly-freed men and women of colour in the United States. The Society aimed to keep the British informed and encourage their donations to the anti-slavery cause.
94 Andrew Johnson (1808–75), who had been serving as Vice President, assumed the US presidency after the assassination of Abraham Lincoln.
95 The American Colonization Society (ACS) had allies within white American abolitionist ranks, although Black abolitionists resisted the ACS.
96 Abolitionist Wendell Phillips (1811–84) worked closely with William Lloyd Garrison.

class of vulgar men called "Ethiopian Minstrels,"[97] or the negro-hating press on both sides of the Atlantic. To those who wish to know something of the negro character from one who has studied it well for many years, and who has had an opportunity to learn something of the bitterness and agony through which the negro has been forced to pass, I again ask both friend and foe of the negro to read that most opportune speech. At the present moment some portion of the influential press of England and the United States are doing all they can to make the negro the scorn of the civilized world, as if the negro had not received his full cup of bitterness.

"We sue for simple justice at your hands
Nought else we ask nor less will have."[98]

SARAH P. REMOND.

Source text

Remond, Sarah P., 'Colonization', *The Freed-Man: A Monthly Magazine, Devoted to the Interests of the Freed Coloured People* (London: S. W. Partridge, 1866), 162–3.

References

Brown, David, 'William Lloyd Garrison, Transatlantic Abolitionism and Colonisation in the Mid Nineteenth Century: The Revival of the Peculiar Solution?', *Slavery & Abolition* 33.2 (2012), 233–50.
Salenius, Sirpa, 'Transatlantic Interracial Sisterhoods: Sarah Remond, Ellen Craft, and Harriet Jacobs in England', *Frontiers: A Journal of Women Studies* 38.1 (2017), 166–96.

Sara Willis Parton [Fanny Fern] (1811–72)

From 'Bridget As She Was, And Bridget As She Is' (1868)

Fanny Fern (pen name of Sara Parton) achieved unprecedented literary popularity by writing witty newspaper features and publishing book-length sketch collections such as *Fern Leaves* (1853). As noted in a gushing obituary for *The London Reader*, which dubbed her the 'distinguished

---

97 Also known as the 'Ethiopian Serenaders', the group was a popular blackface minstrel troupe.
98 Remond appears here to be adapting (by shifting it from first person singular to plural) an epigraph to a book by North Carolina writer Hinton Rowan Helper, one of a small number of anti-slavery Southerners, in *The Impending Crisis of the South: How to Meet It* (New York: A. B. Burdick, 1857). Helper lists Shakespeare as his source. However, Michèle Vignaux notes that only the final part of Helper's quotation (which Remond does not incorporate) 'appears to be genuinely Shakespeare's', from *Macbeth*. Shakespeare scholar Daniel Gil of TCU indicates Remond's extract is unlikely to be Shakespearean. Still, Remond's adopting the lines could signal her appreciation of Helper's anti-slavery stance, her wish to associate her writing with Shakespearean ethos, or both. Michèle Vignaux, 'A Southern Shakespeare?', *Transatlantica: Revue d'études américaines* 1 (2010), 4; Daniel Gil, E-mail correspondence, 29 March 2021.

transatlantic authoress', Fern was a celebrity in the UK as well as in the US. At a time of fierce competition in the burgeoning world of print, she became the highest paid US periodical columnist. Cultivating a satirical tone, sometimes leavened with sentimental storytelling, Fern made her advocacy for women and children broadly appealing. As *London Reader*'s 'Fanny Fern' report noted, 'She always took aim at something that deserved to be hit, and wrote on subjects in which the great honest masses of people were interested' (100).

'Bridget' (excerpted below) aligns with the *London Reader*'s assessment. Drawn from a jointly published British/American edition of *Folly as It Flies*, it lampoons young Irish women immigrants, but also takes aim at the hierarchical social structures they entered through domestic service in North America. Fern invokes a familiar stereotype of 'Bridget' as fumbling in her duties and insecure in her identity. However, Fern mixes her satire with empathy, in a tone less biting than pieces by her former seminary instructor Harriet Beecher Stowe in *House and Home Papers*, or cartoons in image-heavy periodicals like *Harper's* and *Frank Leslie's Magazine*. Meanwhile, within the same satirical profile, she makes fun of (apparently US-born) chambermaids who (just a social notch above the Irish worker) seek to be 'genteel'. See more of this same sketch in our BIL section.

From 'Bridget As She Was'

A square, solid form, innocent of corsets; a thick, dark "stuff"-dress,[99] raised high above ankles which are shaped for use; stout leather shoes; hands red and gloveless; a bonnet of obsolete shape and trimmings; a face round as the moon, from which the rich red blood, made of potatoes and pure air, seems ready to burst; great, honest eyes, always downcast when addressed by those whom the old country styles "superiors." Such is Bridget when she first steps from the deck of the good ship "Maria," at Castle Garden.[100]

Bridget goes to a "place."[101] The pert house-maid[102] titters when she appears, square and wholesome, like a human cow. Bridget's ears catch the word "greenhorn,"[103] and "she might as well be a grandmother as to be only seventeen." Bridget looks furtively at the smart, though cheap dress of the chambermaid, with its inevitable flimsy ruffled skirt and tinsel buttons, and then at her despised "best dress," which she has been wont to keep so tidy for Sundays and holidays. She looks at the thin, paper-soled gaiters[104] of the critical housemaid, and then at her stout,

---

99 A dress made of fabric other than silk, typically marking the wearer as from a lower class
100 Manhattan port where many immigrants were processed before entering the US
101 Household where a domestic labourer is employed
102 In the multilayered social hierarchy within well-to-do North American homes, a 'house-maid' would have outranked a domestic worker who did the heaviest labour, such as laundry, cooking and cleaning. See 'Managing the "Help"', *Women's Work in the Long 19th Century*, Kennesaw State University, Web.
103 An immigrant recently arrived was 'green' and naive about local customs and expectations.
104 Boots, the paper soles suggesting that the wearer does not do manual labour

dew-defying brogans.[105] She looks at her own thick masses of hair, fastened up with only one idea—to keep it out of the way—and then at the housemaid's elaborate parlor-imitation of puff and braid and curl.[106] The view subdues her. She is for the first time ashamed of her own thick natural tresses. She looks at her peony-red cheeks, and contrasts them with the sickly but "genteel" pallor of the house-maid's, and gradually it dawns upon her why they whispered "greenhorn" when she stepped into the kitchen that first day. But the housemaid, overpowering as she is to Bridget, suffers a total eclipse when the lady of the house sweeps past, in full dress. Bridget looks – marvels, adores, and vows to imitate. *That* hair! *Those* jewels! *That* long, trailing silk skirt and embroidered petticoat! *Did* anybody ever? *Could* Bridget in any way herself reach such perfection? She blushes to think that only last night in her home-sickness she actually longed to milk once more the old red cow in the cherished barn-yard. How ridiculous! She doubts whether that sumptuous lady ever saw a cow. The idea that she – Bridget – had been contented all her life to have only cows look at her! By the way – why should that curly-headed grocer-boy talk so much to the housemaid, when he brings parcels, and never to her? A light dawns on her dormant brain. She will fix her hair the way to catch grocer-boys. She too will have a ruffled skirt to drag through the gutter, though she may never own any underclothes. She will have some brass ear-rings and bracelets and things, and some paper-soled boots, with her very first wages; and as to her bonnet, it is true, she can afford only one for market and for "mass;" for rain and shine; for heat and for cold; but by St. Patrick,[107] it shall be a fourteen-dollar "dress-hat," anyhow, though she may never own a pair of India-rubbers,[108] or a flannel petticoat, or a pocket-handkerchief, or an umbrella. Just as if this wasn't a "free country?" Just as if that spiteful housemaid was going to have all the grocer-boys to herself? Bridget will see about that! Her eyes are a pretty blue; and as to her hair, it is at least her own; yes, ma'am; no "rats"[109] will be necessary for *her*; that will save something.

And so the brogans, and the dark "stuff"-dress, and the thick stockings, and shawl, come to grief; and in two months' time flash is written all over Bridget, from the crown of her showy hat to the tips of her crucified toes, squeezed into narrow, paper-soled, fashionable, high-heeled gaiters. And as to her "superiors," gracious goodness! America is not Ireland, nor England either, I'd have you to know. You had better just mention that word in Bridget's hearing now, and see what will come of it!

Source text

Fern, Fanny, *Folly As It Flies; Hit At* (London: S. Low, Son & Co.; New York: G. W. Carleton & Co., 1868).

References

'Fanny Fern', *The London Reader: Of Literature, Science, Art and General Information* 20.500 (1 December 1872), 100.

---

105 A stout, coarse shoe, typically made of leather, to withstand weather and labour
106 Imitating the hair styles and clothing of well-to-do employees was a strategy for trying to claim a higher-class identity.
107 Patron Saint of Ireland
108 Applying India-rubber to shoes made them sturdier and (semi)water-proof.
109 Swatch of hair (typically brushings) or silk, adding volume and shape to natural hair

Stowe, Harriet Beecher [under pseud. Christopher Crowfield], 'What Is a Home?', *House and Home Papers* (Boston: Ticknor and Fields, 1865), 48–78.

Warren, Joyce W., 'Fanny Fern (1811–1872)', *Legacy* 35.2 (2018), 210–20.

Figure 5.4 'The Departure', *The Illustrated London News* (6 July 1850), 20, within an article on 'The Tide of Emigration to the United States and to the Colonies', 17–22, depicting a ship leaving Liverpool for North America. The same image reappeared as 'The Departure' in *Frank Leslie's Illustrated Newspaper* (12 January 1856), 77, without the original print story. Courtesy University of Michigan.

'Irish Female Emigration' (1884)

Single Irish women represented one of the largest groups of nineteenth-century immigrants to North America. In accounts of this gendered diaspora, a stereotype of the female Irish domestic has emerged, based on actual immigration data, but also on popular representations of 'Bridget'.

Less attention has been paid to how these women got to North America in the first place. The article below exemplifies one way. Vere Foster, philanthropist son of a British politician and foreign minister, gave large sums and his own time to the improvement of Irish school buildings and curriculum. He also supported single Irish women seeking to emigrate. He came to this work during the mid-century Famine and returned to it with renewed energy starting in 1879, during a second wave of Irish economic catastrophes. He continued support of the project until his death in 1900, at eighty-one. Along the way, he pushed for better conditions shipboard, based on investigating through three trips he took to America in steerage, despite his personal wealth.

Not all sponsors of 'assisted emigration' were as caring. Tyler Anbinger reports that some landlords – like Viscount Palmerston – relieved themselves of moral calls to support starving tenants during famine years by sending Irish from their estates across the Atlantic, delivering impoverished migrants ashore seriously ill, unable to work and clad in ragged clothing inadequate for the climate – thus in immediate need of extensive social services.

'Irish Female Emigration'

Mr. Vere Foster, of Belfast, has issued another appeal on behalf of his Irish Female Emigration Fund, which has already been the means of granting assisted passages to twenty thousand two hundred and fifty girls from the west of Ireland to the United States and colonies, at an expenditure of about thirty thousand pounds. This scheme has the support – as it should have – of the clergy of all denominations, and there is little doubt that if carefully gone about, it will prove a benefit both to Ireland and the colonies. Mr Foster, who has exhausted what he can spare of his own means and the funds placed at his disposal, has also given assistance by loan to four hundred girls, who have promised to repay him. We trust they may do so, as the good fortune of four hundred more hangs on this contingency.

The purpose of the fund is the relief of present poverty in the densely peopled district of the west of Ireland, by assisting the emigration of young women of good character of the farm and domestic-servant class. To such it gives a chance of well-doing impossible at home, where, if they marry and rear families, there is but a prospect of poverty for themselves and all concerned. The scheme is a resumption of that adopted with gratifying results immediately after the great famine of 1846–7.

The plan which Mr. Foster has had in operation for helping these young women for the past five years is a very simple one. Blank forms of application are issued to inquirers, when, if returned and approved of, vouchers to a certain value are issued in their favour. These vouchers are available within three months of issue for embarkation from Liverpool or from any port in Ireland where the necessary arrangements have been made. The promoter of this scheme does not approve of shipping young girls in large companies, but leaves them the utmost freedom in their choice of ship and port and time of embarkation. This enables them to take a passage when perhaps they can have the company of friends and neighbours. The young women thus assisted were between eighteen and thirty years of age; and it is satisfactory to know that most of them are going on well, and that many of them have sent home money to their friends more than once.

One of the most satisfactory forms of good doing is to help people to help themselves. This is the object of the Irish Female Emigration Fund.

Source text

'Irish Female Emigration', *Chambers's Journal of Popular Literature, Science and Art*, Series 5, 1.52 (27 December 1884), 830–1

References

Anbinder, Tyler, 'Lord Palmerston and the Irish famine emigration', *Historical Journal* 44.2 (June 2001), 441–69.
'Vere Foster Is Dead', *New York Times* (22 December 1900), 9.
'Vere Foster, the Irish Philanthropist', *Chicago Daily Tribune* (25 January 1880), 4.

E. Pauline Johnson (1861–1913)

'Joe: An Etching' (1888, 1895), 'Inscription' (1903), 'Canadian Born' (1900, 1903), 'The Corn Husker' (1896, 1903)

First Nations people in Canada, like Native communities in the US, saw their lands shrink and sovereign rights undermined through whites' colonisation. By the close of the nineteenth century, when Emily Pauline Johnson (Tekahionwake) began publishing her writing, policies like enforced boarding school education, along with the ever-growing numbers of immigrants, had increased settlers' devastating impact on Indigenous communities. Yet, within *The White Wampum* collection (1895), Johnson offered her British, Canadian, and US readers a sympathetic portrait of a boyish Irish settler in 'Joe: An Etching'.

Perhaps Johnson's casting of settler colonialism in the unthreatening body of a child is understandable. In performances that had already attracted appreciative audiences and reviews, Johnson famously wore a Native costume for the first half and then switched to a formal 'white' gown for a second part. Similarly, for her first book-length poetry collection, she listed a double signature on the title page (both Tekahionwake and E. Pauline Johnson), acknowledging both her father's Indigenous line and her mother's white Canadian one.

Marilyn Rose argues Johnson always emphasised her First Nations identity. Indeed, *White Wampum*'s front-page illustration shows a natural setting of pines, mountains and a circle of tipis. Carole Gerson, meanwhile, posits that Johnson's 'texts enabled White Canadians to feel at home' through 'Aboriginal stories that they could appropriate into their desire to belong to the places to which they or their families had immigrated' (Gerson, 46). 'Wolverine', one poem in *White Wampum*, can be read accordingly, depicting a Canadian past when French fur traders and First Nations people forged complex cross-race relationships. 'Joe', in contrast, limns a youthful Irish immigrant immersed in a natural setting retaining only limited reminders of Indigenous peoples' continued presence.

This theme of white takeover becomes more overt in Johnson's 1903 collection, *Canadian Born*. 'The Corn Husker' paints a poignant portrait of an elderly Native woman counterpart to 'Joe'. Meanwhile, the 'Canadian Born' title poem strives (as in the book's inscription) to envision First Nations and white Canadians as one community, yet also acknowledges British imperial political power.

'Joe: An Etching'[110]

A Meadow brown; across the yonder edge
A zigzag fence is ambling; here a wedge
Of underbush has cleft its course in twain,
Till where beyond it staggers up again;
The long, grey rails stretch in a broken line
Their ragged length of rough, split forest pine,
And in their zigzag tottering have reeled
In drunken efforts to enclose the field,
Which carries on its breast, September born,
A patch of rustling, yellow, Indian corn.
Beyond its shriveled tassels, perched upon
The topmost rail, sits Joe, the settler's son,
A little semi-savage boy of nine.
Now dozing in the warmth of Nature's wine,
His face the sun has tampered with, and wrought,
By heated kisses, mischief, and has brought
Some vagrant freckles, while from here and there
A few wild locks of vagabond brown hair
Escape the old straw hat the sun looks through,
And blinks to meet his Irish eyes of blue.
Barefooted, innocent of coat or vest,
His grey checked shirt unbuttoned at his chest,
Both hardy hands within their usual nest—
His breeches pockets—so, he waits to rest
His little fingers, somewhat tired and worn,
That all day long were husking Indian corn.
His drowsy lids snap at some trivial sound,
With lazy yawns he slips towards the ground,
Then with an idle whistle lifts his load
And shambles home along the country road
That stretches on fringed out with stumps and weeds,
And finally unto the backwoods leads,
Where forests wait with giant trunk and bough
The axe of pioneer, the settler's plough.

Inscription from Canadian Born[111]

Let him who is Canadian born regard these poems as written to himself—whether he be my paleface compatriot who has given to me his right hand of good fellowship, in the years I have appealed to him by pen and platform, or whether he be that

---

110 In *Paddling Her Own Canoe: The Times and Texts of E. Pauline Johnson* (Toronto: University of Toronto Press, 2000), Veronica Strong-Boag and Carole Gerson note that 'Joe: An Etching' first appeared under a slightly different title of 'Joe (A Sketch from Memory)' in *The Week* in May 1888 (221). It was later incorporated into *The White Wampum* (1895) and appeared again in *Flint and Feather* (1912).
111 The poems in this section all reappeared in the 1912 compendium of Johnson's poetry, *Flint and Feather*, but this inscription from 1903's *Canadian Born* was omitted.

dear Red brother of whatsoever tribe or Province, it matters not—White Race or
Red are one if they are but Canadian born.

The Author

'Canadian Born'[112]

We first saw light in Canada, the land beloved of God;
We are the pulse of Canada, its marrow and its blood;
And we, the men of Canada, can face the world and brag
That we were born in Canada beneath the British flag.

Few of us have the blood of kings, few are of courtly birth,
But few are vagabonds or rogues of doubtful name and worth;
And all have one credential that entitles us to brag—
That we were born in Canada beneath the British flag.

We've yet to make our money, we've yet to make our fame,
But we have gold and glory in our clean colonial name;
And every man's a millionaire if only he can brag
That he was born in Canada beneath the British flag.

No title and no coronet is half so proudly worn
As that which we inherited as men Canadian born.
We count no man so noble as the one who makes the brag
That he was born in Canada beneath the British flag.

The Dutch may have their Holland, the Spanish have his Spain,
The Yankee to the south of us must south of us remain;
For not a man dare lift a hand against the men who brag
That they were born in Canada beneath the British flag.

'The Corn Husker'[113]

Hard by the Indian lodges, where the bush
        Breaks in a clearing, through ill-fashioned fields,
She comes to labor, when the first still hush
        Of autumn follows large and recent yields.

Age in her fingers, hunger in her face,
        Her shoulders stooped with weight of work and years,
But rich in tawny coloring of her race,
        She comes a-field to strip the purple ears.

---

112 Published in June 1900 in the *Halifax Herald* (Strong-Boag and Gerson, 227), this text was
reprinted in 1903 as title poem for *Canadian Born* (1903) and again in *Flint and Feather* (1912).
113 Prior to republication in 1903 (*Canadian Born*) and 1912 (*Flint and Feather*), this poem
appeared in September 1896 in *Harper's Weekly* (Strong-Boag and Gerson, 225).

And all her thoughts are with the days gone by,
    Ere might's injustice banished from their lands
Her people, that to-day unheeded lie,
    Like the dead husks that rustle through her hands.

Source texts

Johnson, E. Pauline, *Canadian Born* (Toronto: George N. Morang, 1903).
Johnson, E. Pauline, Tekahionwake, *The White Wampum* (London: John Lane; Toronto: Copp Clark Co; Boston: Lamson, Wolffe & Co., 1895).

References

Adcock, A. St. John, 'The Reader', *The Bookman* (September 1912), 233–53.
Gerson, Carole, '"Rereading Pauline Johnson', *Journal of Canadian Studies* 46.2 (2012), 45–61.
Rose, Marilyn J. 'JOHNSON, EMILY PAULINE', *Dictionary of Canadian Biography* 14 (University of Toronto/Université Laval, 2003), Web.

Ann McNabb (n.d.)

'The Life Story of an Irish Cook' (1906)

After her sister Maria died of typhus fever, Ann McNabb's entire family made the transatlantic journey in what today is termed chain migration, as each one reaching the US then aided others' relocation.

Part of a collection entitled *The Life Stories of Undistinguished Americans*, McNabb's story originally appeared in *The New York Independent* in 1905 in a series by Henry Holt, who also edited the book. Published at a time when US 'nativism' and anti-immigrant discourse abounded, *Life Stories* celebrated diversity and inclusivity. Holt's prefatory note cast the anthology as 'typify[ing] the life of the average worker', while 'mak[ing] each story the genuine experience of a real person'. He declared the narratives' subjects embodied their diverse previous homelands from all over the world (vii). Thus, Holt collected fifteen profiles, including 'A Lithuanian', 'A Polish Sweatshop Girl' and 'An Italian Bootblack'. The introduction, penned by Edwin Slossun, echoed Holt, dubbing the book a 'mosaic picture' of America (6).

Though many chapters were composed by their subjects, McNabb's was one of several oral histories. Slosson assured readers that in those cases 'great pains have been taken' to ensure 'the account is truthful, both as to facts and mode of thought' (7), an assessment Rebecca Harding Davis would affirm in a 1906 book review. Accordingly, while recognising that McNabb's reminiscences were conveyed via her employer, readers can relish a narrative aiming to highlight the perspective of an individual Irish immigrant domestic worker.

'The Life Story of an Irish Cook'

The cook whose story follows, lived for many years in the home of one of America's best known literary women, who has taken down her conversation in this form.

I don't know why anybody wants to hear my history. Nothing ever happened to me worth the tellin' except when my mother died. Now she was an extraordinary person. The neighbors all respected her, an' the minister. "Go ask Mrs. McNabb," he'd say to the women in the neighborhood here when they come wantin' advice.

But about me—I was born nigh to Limavaddy;[114] it's a pretty town close to Londonderry. We lived in a peat[115] cabin, but it had a good thatched roof. Mother put on that roof. It isn't a woman's work, but she—was able for it.

There were sivin childher of us. John an' Matthew they went to Australia. Mother was layin' by for five year to get their passage money. They went into the bush. We heard twice from thim and then no more. Not another word and that is forty year gone now—on account of them not reading and writing. Learning isn't cheap in them old countries as it is here, you see. I suppose they're dead now—John would be ninety now—and in heaven. They were honest men. My mother sent Joseph to Londonderry to larn the weaver's trade. My father he never was a steddy worker. He took to the drink early in life. My mother an' me an' Tilly we worked in the field for Squire Varney. Yes, plowin' an' seedin' and diggin'—any farm work he'd give us. We did men's work, but we didn't get men's pay. No, of course not. In winter we did lace work for a merchant in Londonderry. (Ann still can embroider beautifully.) It was pleasanter nor diggin' after my hands was fit for it. But it took two weeks every year to clean and soften my hands for the needle.

Pay was very small and the twins—that was Maria and Philip—they were too young to work at all. What did we eat? Well, just potatoes. On Sundays, once a month, we'd maybe have a bit of flitch.[116] When the potatoes rotted[117]—that was the hard times! Oh, yes, I mind the famine years. An' the cornmeal that the 'Mericans sent. The folks said they'd rather starve nor eat it. We didn't know how to cook it. Here I eat corn dodgers and fried mush fast enough.

Maria—she was one of the twins—she died the famine year of the typhus and— well, she sickened of the herbs and roots we eat—we had no potatoes.

Mother said when Maria died, "There's a curse on ould green Ireland and we'll get out of it." So we worked an' saved for four year an' then Squire Varney helped a bit an' we sent Tilly to America. She had always more head than me. She came to Philadelphia and got a place for general housework at Mrs. Bent's. Tilly got but two dollars a week, bein' a greenhorn.[118] But she larned hand over hand, and Mrs. Bent kept no other help and laid out to teach her. She larned her to cook and bake and to wash and do up shirts—all American fashion. Then Tilly axed[119] three dollars a

---

114 A market town in Northern Ireland
115 Brown, boggy material, consisting of partly decomposed vegetable matter
116 Cured and salted side of a hog
117 McNabb references an infestation that ruined the potato crops in Ireland between 1845 and 1850.
118 An inexperienced person; a term often applied to recently arrived immigrants
119 Ask/asked

week. Mother always said, "Don't ax a penny more than you're worth. But know your own vally[120] and ax that."

She had no expenses and laid by money enough to bring me out before the year was gone. I sailed from Londonderry. The ship was a sailin' vessel, the "Mary Jane." The passage was $12. You brought your own eating, your tea an' meal, an' most had flitch. There was two big stoves that we cooked on. The steerage was a dirty place and we were eight weeks on the voyage – over time three weeks. The food ran scarce, I tell you, but the captain gave some to us, and them that had plenty was kind to the others. I've heard bad stories of things that went on in the steerage in them old times – smallpox and fevers and starvation and worse. But I saw nothing of them in my ship. The folks were decent and the captain was kind.

When I got here Mrs. Bent let Tilly keep me for two months to teach me – me bein' such a greenhorn. Of course I worked for her. Mr. Bent was foreman then in Spangler's big mills. After two months I got a place. They were nice appearing people enough, but the second day I found out they were Jews. I never had seen a Jew before, so I packed my bag and said to the lady, "I beg your pardon, ma'am, but I can't eat the bread of them as crucified the Saviour." "But," she said, "he was a Jew." So at that I put out. I couldn't hear such talk. Then I got a place for general housework with Mrs. Carr. I got $2 till I learned to cook good, and then $3 and then $4. I was in that house as cook and nurse for twenty-two years. Tilly lived with the Bents till she died, eighteen years. Mr. Bent came to be a partner in the mills and got rich, and they moved into a big house in German-town and kept a lot of help and Tilly was housekeeper. How did we keep our places so long? Well, I think me and Tilly was clean in our work and we was decent, and, of course, we was honest. Nobody living can say that one of the McNabbs ever wronged him of a cent. Mrs. Carr's interests was my interests. I took better care of her things than she did herself, and I loved the childher as if they was my own. She used to tell me my sin was I was stingy. I don't know. The McNabbs are no wasteful folk. I've worn one dress nine year and it looked decent then. Me and Tilly saved till we brought Joseph and Phil over, and they went into Mr. Bent's mills as weaver and spool boy and then they saved, and we all brought out my mother and father. We rented a little house in Kensington for them. There was a parlor in it and kitchen and two bedrooms and bathroom and marble door step, and a bell. That was in '66, and we paid nine dollars a month rent. You'd pay double that now. It took all our savings to furnish it, but Mrs. Bent and Mrs. Carr gave us lots of things to go in. To think of mother having a parlor and marble steps and a bell! They came on the old steamer "Indiana" and got here at night, and we had supper for them and the house all lighted up. Well, you ought to have seen mother's old face! I'll never forget that night if I live to be a hundred. After that mother took in boarders and Joseph and Phil was there. We all put every cent we earned into building associations. So Tilly owned a house when she died and I own this one now. Our ladies told us how to put the money so as to breed

---

120 Value

more, and we never spent a cent we could save. Joseph pushed on and got big wages and started a flour store, and Phil went to night-school and got a place as clerk. He married a teacher in the Kensington public school. She was a showy miss! Silk dress and feathers in her hat!

Father died soon after he come. The drink here wasn't as wholesome for him as it was in Ireland. Poor father! He was a goodhearted man, but he wasn't worth a penny when he died.

Mother lived to be eighty. She was respected by all Kensington. The night she died she said: "I have much to praise God for. I haven't a child that is dependent on the day's work for the day's victuals. Every one of them owns a roof to cover him."

Joseph did well in his flour store. He has a big one on Market Street now and lives in a pretty house out in West Philadelphia. He's one of the wardens in his church out there and his girls gives teas and goes to reading clubs.

But Phil is the one to go ahead! His daughter Ann – she was named for me, but she calls herself Antoinette – is engaged to a young lawyer in New York. He gave her a diamond engagement ring the other day. And his son, young Phil, is in politics and a member of councils. He makes money hand over hand. He has an automobile and a fur coat, and you see his name at big dinners and him making speeches. No saving of pennies or building associations for Phil.

It was Phil that coaxed me to give up work at Mrs. Carr's and to open my house for boarders here in Kensington. His wife didn't like to hear it said I was working in somebody's kitchen. I've done well with the boarders. I know just how to feed them so as to lay by a little sum every year. I heard that young Phil told some of his friends that he had a queer old aunt up in Kensington who played poor, but had a great store of money hoarded away. He shouldn't have told a story like that. But young folks will be young! I like the boy. He is certainly bringing the family into notice in the world. Last Sunday's paper had his picture and one of the young lady he is going to marry in New York. It called him the young millionaire McNabb. But I judge he's not that. He wanted to borrow the money I have laid by in the old bank at Walnut and Seventh the other day and said he'd double it in a week. No such work as that for me! But the boy certainly is a credit to the family!

Source text

McNabb, Ann, 'The Life Story of an Irish Cook', in Hamilton Holt (ed.), *The Life Stories of Undistinguished Americans as Told by Themselves*, With an Introduction by *Edwin E. Slosson* (New York: James Pott & Company, 1906), 143–9.

References

Beck, Hermann, 'Review: The Life Stories of (Undistinguished) Americans as Told by Themselves', *Oral History Review* 19.1/2 (1991), 146–8.

Harding Davis, Rebecca, 'Undistinguished Americans', *The Independent* (26 April 1906), 962.

Lynch-Brennan, Margaret, *Irish Bridget: Irish Immigrant Women in Domestic Service in America, 1840–1930* (Syracuse, NY: Syracuse University Press, 2014).

'The Story of an Irish Cook', *The Independent* (30 March 1905), 715–17.

Henry James (1843–1916)

Figure 5.5 Henry James (1843–1916) *c*.1906, by Alice M. Boughton
(1866–1943). National Portrait Gallery, Smithsonian Institution;
gift of Allan M. Price.

Photographer Alice Boughton revisits her experience creating this image in
Photographing the Famous (New York: Avondale Press, 1928), 94. Admitting Henry James was 'the only sitter who ever terrified me', she struggled
through their formal sitting, then wound up preferring this candid look,
garnered as he was about to leave her studio and paused to appreciate 'a
small painting of a mother and child by Arthur Davies'.

From The American Scene *(1907)*

Henry James, often called 'The Master' due to his influence as writer and
social critic, may be the long nineteenth century's most famous transatlantic literary figure. Born into a New England patrician family, he spent most
of his adult life in Europe.

The *American Scene* chronicles the expatriate's return visit to the US in 1904, after being away for over two decades. James depicts himself as quickly recognising how much his former homeland had changed, making the 'American scene' now before him alternately puzzling and frustrating. Therefore, David Gervais argues, '[T]he more he [James] saw of it, the more he began to feel that it was only able to create its future at the cost of destroying its past' (350). James observes this pattern literally when he tries to revisit sites associated with his own family's past, such as his 1843 birth home in New York's Washington Square – now replaced by one of the city's signature massive buildings. Repeatedly, James describes feeling dislocated by his homeland's apparent rejection of foundational values, embracing, instead, crazed pursuit of economic growth. So, Karen Scherzinger notes, James vacillates between being 'Eurocentric and pompous' and offering up whimsical 'self-parody' of his inability to reclaim native status, since living long abroad has made him alien (168–9).

Ironically, given his own expatriated identity, James identifies one sign of the shift in American values in the explosion of new European immigrants. His visit to the New York City Ghetto, for example, bursts with arrogant racism. His response to the Statue of Liberty presents a stark contrast to the idealised welcome associated with Emma Lazarus's 1883 poem, 'The New Colossus', which appears in our NC section.

From The American Scene

PREFACE

The following pages duly explain themselves, I judge, as to the Author's point of view and his relation to his subject; but I prefix this word on the chance of any suspected or perceived failure of such references. My visit to America had been the first possible to me for nearly a quarter of a century, and I had before my last previous one, brief and distant to memory, spent other years in continuous absence; so that I was to return with much of the freshness of eye, outward and inward, which, with the further contribution of a state of desire, is commonly held a precious agent of perception. I felt no doubt, I confess, of my great advantage on that score; since if I had had time to become almost as "fresh" as an inquiring stranger, I had not on the other hand had enough to cease to be, or at least to feel, as acute as an initiated native. I made no scruple of my conviction that I should understand and should care better and more than the most earnest of visitors, and yet that I should vibrate with more curiosity – on the extent of ground, that is, on which I might aspire to intimate intelligence at all – than the pilgrim with the longest list of questions, the sharpest appetite for explanations and the largest exposure to mistakes.[121]

---

121 On James's perspective in the Preface and throughout the text, see Kevin Piper, who argues that 'James's liminal position in *The American Scene* as a returning exile is both descriptive of the Other and expressive of the self', as the Master 'combines literary self-consciousness with the examination of cultural difference', by using a narrative technique Piper dubs 'the approach' (106).

I felt myself then, all serenely, not exposed to grave mistakes – though there were also doubtless explanations which would find me, and quite as contentedly, impenetrable. I would take my stand on my gathered impressions, since it was all for them, for them only, that I returned; I would in fact go to the stake for them – which is a sign of the value that I both in particular and in general attach to them and that I have endeavoured to preserve for them in this transcription. My cultivated sense of aspects and prospects affected me absolutely as an enrichment of my subject, and I was prepared to abide by the law of that sense – the appearance that it would react promptly in some presences only to remain imperturbably inert in others. There would be a thousand matters – matters already the theme of prodigious reports and statistics – as to which I should have no sense whatever, and as to information about which my record would accordingly stand naked and unashamed. It should unfailingly be proved against me that my opportunity had found me incapable of information, incapable alike of receiving and of imparting it; for then, and then only, would it be clearly enough attested that I *had* cared and understood.

There are features of the human scene, there are properties of the social air, that the newspapers, reports, surveys and blue-books[122] would seem to confess themselves powerless to "handle," and that yet represented to me a greater array of items, a heavier expression of character, than my own pair of scales would ever weigh, keep them as clear for it as I might. I became aware soon enough, on the spot, that these elements of the human subject, the results of these attempted appreciations of life itself, would prove much too numerous even for a capacity all given to them for some ten months; but at least therefore, artistically concerned as I had been all my days with the human subject, with the appreciation of life itself, and with the consequent question of literary representation, I should not find such matters scant or simple. I was not in fact to do so, and they but led me on and on. How far this might have been my several chapters show; and yet even here I fall short. I shall have to take a few others for the rest of my story.

H.J.

'Ellis Island'[123]

In the Bay, the rest of the morning, the dense raw fog that delayed the big boat, allowing sight but [n]ot the immediate ice-masses through which it thumped its way, was not less of the essence. Anything blander, as a medium, would have seemed a mockery of the facts of the terrible little Ellis Island, the first harbour of refuge and stage of patience for the million or so immigrants annually knocking at our official door. Before this door, which opens to them there only with a hundred forms and ceremonies, grindings and grumblings of the key, they stand appealing and wait-ing, marshalled, herded, divided, subdivided, sorted, sifted, searched, fumigated, for longer or shorter periods – the effect of all which prodigious process, an intendedly "scientific" feeding of the mill, is again to give the earnest observer a thousand more things to think of than he can pretend to retail. The impression of Ellis Island, in fine, would be – as I was to find throughout that so many of my impressions would be – a chapter by itself; and with a particular page for recognition of the degree in which

---

122 Victorian-era blue-books were official government-published reports, with 'blue' referencing the colour typically used for their covers.
123 New York harbour through which millions of European immigrants entered the US

the liberal hospitality of the eminent Commissioner of this wonderful service, to whom I had been introduced, helped to make the interest of the whole watched drama poignant and unforgettable. It is a drama that goes on, without a pause, day by day and year by year, this visible act of ingurgitation on the part of our body politic and social, and constituting really an appeal to amazement beyond that of any sword-swallowing or fire-swallowing of the circus. The wonder that one couldn't keep down was the thought that these two or three hours of one's own chance vision of the business were but as a tick or two of the mighty clock, the clock that never, never stops–least of all when it strikes, for a sign of so much winding-up, some louder hour of our national fate than usual. I think indeed that the simplest account of the action of Ellis Island on the spirit of any sensitive citizen who may have happened to "look in" is that he comes back from his visit not at all the same person that he went. He has eaten of the tree of knowledge, and the taste will be for ever in his mouth. He had thought he knew before, thought he had the sense of the degree in which it is his American fate to share the sanctity of his American consciousness, the intimacy of his American patriotism, with the inconceivable alien; but the truth had never come home to him with any such force. In the lurid light projected upon it by those courts of dismay it shakes him–or I like at least to imagine it shakes him–to the depths of his being; I like to think of him, I positively *have* to think of him, as going about ever afterwards with a new look, for those who can see it, in his face, the outward sign of the new chill in his heart. So is stamped, for detection, the questionably privileged person who has had an apparition, seen a ghost in his supposedly safe old house. Let not the unwary, therefore, visit Ellis Island.

The after-sense of that acute experience, however, I myself found, was by no means to be brushed away; I felt it grow and grow, on the contrary, wherever I turned: other impressions might come and go, but this affirmed claim of the alien, however immeasurably alien, to share in one's supreme relation was everywhere the fixed element, the reminder not to be dodged. One's supreme relation, as one had always put it, was one's relation to one's country–a conception made up so largely of one's countrymen and one's countrywomen. Thus it was as if, all the while, with such a fond tradition of what these products predominantly were, the idea of the country itself underwent something of that profane overhauling through which it appears to suffer the indignity of change. Is not our instinct in this matter, in general, essentially the safe one–that of keeping the idea simple and strong and continuous, so that it shall be perfectly sound? To touch it over-much, to pull it about, is to put it in peril of weakening; yet on this free assault upon it, this readjustment of it in *their* monstrous, presumptuous interest, the aliens, in New York, seemed perpetually to insist. The combination there of their quantity and their quality–that loud primary stage of alienism which New York most offers to sight– operates, for the native, as their note of settled possession, something they have nobody to thank for; so that *unsettled* possession is what we, on our side, seem reduced to–the implication of which, in its turn, is that, to recover confidence and regain lost ground, we, not they, must make the surrender and accept the orientation. We must go, in other words, *more* than half-way to meet them; which is all the difference, for us, between possession and dispossession. This sense of dispossession, to be brief about it, haunted me so, I was to feel, in the New York streets and in the packed trajectiles[124] to which one clingingly appeals from the streets, just

---

124 Trajectile: body impelled through air or space (*OED*); a projectile

as one tumbles back into the streets in appalled reaction from *them*, that the art of beguiling or duping it became an art to be cultivated – though the fond alternative vision was never long to be obscured, the imagination, exasperated to envy, of the ideal, in the order in question; of the luxury of some such close and sweet and *whole* national consciousness as that of the Switzer[125] and the Scot.

Source text

James, Henry, *The American Scene* (London: Chapman and Hall, 1907).

References

'The American Scene. By Henry James. (Chapman & Hall)', *The Atheneum* (9 March 1907), 282–3.
Cooper, Frederic Taber, 'New Books Reviewed: "The American Scene"', *North American Review* (17 May 1907), 214.
Gervais, David, 'Deciphering America: "The American Scene"', *Cambridge Quarterly* 18.4 (1989), 349–62.
Piper, Kevin, 'An "interspace worth mention": Henry James's Approach and the Critique of Mastery in *The American Scene*', *Henry James Review* 29.2 (2008), 105–17.
Scharzinger, Karen,'"Lurking Ghosts": Metaphor, *The Ambassadors*, and Henry James's Population of the American Scene', *Henry James Review* 24.2 (2003), 168–79.

Charles Alexander Eastman, MD (Ohiyesa) (1858–1939)

From 'The Transition Period: First Effects of Civilisation' in 'The North American Indian' Address (1911)

Charles Eastman ('Ohiyesa') was a physician, author, and Native rights advocate. The youngest child of a Santee Sioux and a woman of Anglo-Native descent, he faced a lifetime challenge navigating his mixed-race identity.

He completed medical school in Boston and then joined the Bureau of Indian Affairs as resident physician on the Pine Ridge Reservation. There, in late December 1890, while treating victims of the Wounded Knee Massacre, Eastman met his future wife, the New England-bred European-American Elaine Goodale. She had been working in the area as an educator of Native youth. With Elaine as editor-collaborator, Eastman published eleven books, all drawing on his Indigenous identity. He also served as an Indian advocate in Washington, DC, under the Roosevelt and Coolidge administrations.

---

125 Swiss

As a respected lecturer, Eastman represented North American Native peoples at the First Universal Races Congress in London in 1911. The Congress drew more than 2,000 attendees from over fifty countries, assembled to build a network for anti-racist activism. Eastman's speech characterised North American Indigenous life before and after contact with white settlers. In this section of his speech, he emphasised the destructive aspects of North American colonisation. See more in FD and RS.

From 'The Transition Period: First Effects of Civilisation' in 'The North American Indian' Address

The first effects of contact between this primitive race, with its Spartan virtues and non-progressive philosophy, and the strenuous and dominant Anglo-Saxon race were, speaking broadly, destructive and demoralising, leading only after untold misery to an era of reconstruction and progress. These results may be grouped in two classes: those which were natural and inevitable, and those which were the fruits of a deliberate policy.

The conflicts born of a disputed occupancy of the soil were doubtless largely inevitable. It has been plausibly argued that the Indian had no possessory rights in territory he did not use except as a hunting-ground; but no such principle is found in the white man's law, and as a matter of fact his rights were recognised from first to last by treaty and purchase. Unfortunately, the red man did not understand his white brother. He innocently supposed that on this vast continent there was room for both, where each could peaceably develop his peculiar mode of life. It is almost unnecessary to say that he was slow to recognise the superiority of an organised form of society, and unwilling to accept the arts and letters, customs and religion of the invader until brought to see the stern necessity of so doing by starvation, oppression, and suffering in many forms.

It was equally inevitable that the vices of the more sophisticated race should be imitated by the simpler; and being in no degree immune to their effects, the resulting degradation was rapid and apparently hopeless. Trade for furs and other articles of value, initiated by the cupidity of the white man, helped to accomplish the downfall of the red, by substituting a desire for gain for his native uncalculating generosity, but yet more by the unprincipled use of strong drink, which the early traders found to be of invaluable assistance in controlling and defrauding him. In the train of whisky and drunkenness came debauchery and diseases caused by immorality; then the hitherto unknown and frightful small-pox, decimating many tribes and wiping out whole bands; and finally the white plague, tuberculosis, following inevitably upon a sedentary and indoor life in unsanitary dwellings (whose use was suggested or compelled by the white man), together with poor and insufficient food. [. . .]

History makes it plain to us that the European colonists at first shared in the Indians' misconception of their ultimate relation. Vast tracts of land far to the westward of the settlements were set aside from time to time for their perpetual occupancy, only to be again seized upon in a few years as the country developed. Finally, each tribe made its last stand, fighting with wonderful but hopeless courage and temporary success against overwhelming odds, and one by one they were subdued and overthrown, not without the help of such means as the wholesale extermination of game, the use of tribe against tribe, and even the bribery and corruption of chiefs and headmen to induce them to betray their people. The horrors and cruelties of Indian warfare are attributable not only to the desperate situation of the natives and fierce resentment caused by the continual treaty-breaking, but to their possession of knives and modern fire-arms gained in trade.

Upon their complete subjugation followed the "reservation period," in the case of those tribes whose game was destroyed necessarily including the pauperising effect of the issue of regular rations; and in this miserable prison existence, at the mercy of petty officials bent on "graft," the manhood of the Indian suffered its final eclipse, and his beggarly apathy was like that of a wild animal confined in a zoological garden.

We may say now without much fear of contradiction that the reservation policy was a mistake, the fruits of a radical misapprehension of the red man's native capacity. A generation ago it was common to affirm his absolute inability to assimilate the white man's civilisation. There was, of course, no such inability, but merely a lack of motive and opportunity; in other words, it was a simple question of adaptation to environment. Yet this shallow and immoral doctrine has been embodied in such well-known sayings as "There's no good Indian but a dead Indian,"[126] and "You can no more civilise an Indian than you can civilise a rattlesnake"; the one attributed to a famous general, the other to a United States senator. At the opposite extreme, and the one gradually coming into full acceptance by a more enlightened generation, we have General Pratt's unanswerable logic: "To civilise the Indian, get him into civilisation!"[127]

Source text

Eastman, Charles Alexander, MD (Ohiyesa), 'The North American Indian', in Gustav Spiller (ed.), *Papers on Inter-Racial Problems Communicated to the First Universal Races Congress Held at the University of London; July 26–29, 1911* (London: P. S. King; Boston: World's Peace Foundation, 1911), 367–76.

References

Coskan-Johnson, Gale P., 'What writer would not be an Indian for a while? Charles Alexander Eastman, Critical Memory, and Audience', *Studies in American Indian Literatures* 18.2 (2006), 105–31.

Landry, Alysa, 'Theodore Roosevelt: "The Only Good Indians Are the Dead Indians"', *Indian Country Today: Digital Indigenous News*, Web.

Robbins, Sarah Ruffing, 'Reclaiming Voices from Indian Boarding School Narratives', *Learning Legacies: Archive to Action through Women's Cross-Cultural Teaching* (Ann Arbor, MI: University of Michigan Press, 2017).

---

126 This quote apocryphally attributed to US Army General Philip Sheridan (1831–88) reflected a sentiment widespread throughout the US in Eastman's time. For example, upon the death of the Apache chief Geronimo in February 1909, the *Chicago Daily Tribune* trumpeted: 'Geronimo Now a Good Indian'. President Theodore Roosevelt helped popularise the language in 1886, saying, 'I don't go so far as to think that the only good Indians are dead Indians, but I believe nine out of ten are,' adding that 'I shouldn't like to inquire too closely into the case of the tenth'.

127 Richard Henry Pratt's (1840–1924) oppressive boarding school system for Native youth at Carlisle set an approach for assimilationist education that numerous scholars now label 'education for extinction'. Eastman was, to some extent, a product of such programmes, having studied at white-run institutions, including Dartmouth, where he earned his undergraduate degree. Toward the end of his life, however, he would withdraw from white-dominated society, living in a cabin close to his ancestral homelands.

Edith Maude Eaton [Sui Sin Far] (1865–1914)

'Sui Sin Far, the Half Chinese Writer, Tells of Her Career' (1912)

Edith Maude Eaton (pen name Sui Sin Far) was one of the first writers of Asian descent published in North America. She also embodied transatlantic and transnational authorship, as explained in the essay below, where she emphasised both her hybrid identity and her mobility across multiple national borders. Significantly, after years of frustration linked to having her authorial aspirations constrained by family responsibility and economic stress, she mined her mixed-race identity as a source for her writing.

The eldest child of an English merchant and a Chinese mother educated in Britain, Eaton was born in Macclesfield, England. Her family moved to North America in 1872, settling first in Hudson City, New York. In this feature story, Eaton revisited her diverse multinational work experiences. After living in the Caribbean and several US cities (including Boston, San Francisco and Seattle), she returned to Montreal, where she died in 1914.

Eaton's decision to embrace her Chinese heritage, even though her features did not highlight her bi-racial origin, was courageous, considering the rampant Sino-phobia of the time. Chinese Americans were victimised by degrading stereotypes and overt discrimination. The US Chinese Exclusion Act of 1882, restricting Chinese immigration and citizenship, would be in effect until 1954. Her many periodical stories and her best-known work, *Mrs. Spring Fragrance*, resisted this persistently negative context by depicting Chinese and Chinese-American people in positive, complex ways.

Figure 5.6 Sui Sin Far (1865–1914) *c.*1912. From the private collection of Dana Birchall, granddaughter of Winnifred Eaton. Courtesy Canada's Early Women Writers. SFU Library Digital Collections. Simon Fraser University, Burnaby, BC, Canada. 1980–2014.

'Sui Sin Far, the Half Chinese Writer, Tells of Her Career'

As the Globe[128] thinks that my experience in life has been unusual, and that a personal sketch will be interesting to its readers, I will try my best to furnish one. Certainly my life has been quite unlike that of any literary worker of whom I have read. I have never met any to know – save editors.

I have resided in Boston now for about two years.

I came here with the intention of publishing a book and planting a few Eurasian thoughts in Western literature. My collection of Chinese-American stories will be brought out very soon, under the title, "Mrs Spring Fragrance." I have also written another book which will appear next year, if Providence is kind.

In the beginning I opened my eyes in a country place in the county of Cheshire, England. My ancestors on my grandfather's side had been known to the county for some generations back. My ancestors on my grandmother's side were unknown to local history. She was a pretty Irish lass from Dublin when she first won my grandfather's affections.

My father, who was educated in England and studied art in France, was established in business by his father at the age of 22, at the Port of Shanghai, China. There he met my mother, a Chinese young girl, who had been educated in England, and who was in training for a missionary. They were married by the British Consul,[129] and the year following their marriage returned to England.

As I swing the door of my mental gallery I find radiant pictures in the opening, and through all the scenes of that period there walks one figure – the figure of my brother, Edward, a noble little fellow, whose heart and intelligence during the brief years of early childhood led and directed mine. I mention this brother because I have recently lost him through an accident, and his death has affected me more than I can say.

At the age of 4 years I started to go to school. I can remember being very much interested in English history. I remember also that my mother was a fascinating story teller and that I was greatly enamored of a French version of "Little Bo-Peep," which my father tried to teach me.

Arrival in America

When I was 6 years old my father brought us to America. Besides my first brother, who was only 10 months older than myself, I had now three sisters and another brother. We settled in Montreal, Can, and hard times befell, upon which I shall not dwell.

I attended school again and must have been about 8 years old when I conceived the ambition to write a book about the half Chinese. This ambition arose from my sensitiveness to the remarks, criticisms and observations on the half Chinese which continually assailed my ears, also from an impulse, born with me, to describe, to impart to others all that I felt, all that I saw, all that I was. I was not sensitive without reason. Some Eurasians may affect that no slur is cast upon them because of their nationality; but I dislike cant and desire to be sincere. Wealth, of course, ameliorates certain conditions. We children, however, had no wealth.

---

128 *Boston Globe*, the newspaper where this account appeared
129 The 1842 Treaty of Nanjing had ended the First Opium War and given British merchants and their families access to the city of Shanghai. Consuls represented British interests in Shanghai.

I think as well my mind was stimulated by the readings of my teacher, who sought to impress upon her scholars that the true fathers and mothers of the world were those who battled through great trials and hardships to leave to future generations noble and inspiring truths.

I left school at the age of 10, but shortly thereafter attracted the attention of a lovely old lady, Mrs. William Darling of Hochelaga, who induced my mother to send me to her for a few hours each day. This old lady taught me music and French. I remember her telling her husband that I had a marvelous memory and quoting "Our finest hope is finest memory," which greatly encouraged me, as compared with my brother and sister, who had both splendid heads for figures, I ranked very low intellectually. It was Mrs. Darling who first, aside from my mother, interested me in my mother's people, and impressed upon me that I should be proud that I had sprung from such a race. She also inspired me with the belief that the spirit is more than the body, a belief which helped me through many hours of childish despondency, for my sisters were all much heavier and more muscular than I.

When my parents found that family circumstances made it necessary to withdraw me from Mrs. Darling, my old friend's mind seemed to become wrought with me, and she tried to persuade them to permit her to send me to a boarding school. My father, however, was an Englishman, and the idea of having any of his children brought up on charity, hurt his pride.

I, now in my 11th year, entered into two lives, one devoted entirely to family concerns; the other, a withdrawn life of thought and musing. This withdrawn life of thought probably took the place of ordinary education with me. I had six keys to it; one, a great capacity for feeling; another, the key of imagination; third, the key of physical pain; fourth the key of sympathy; fifth, the sense of being differentiated from the ordinary by the fact that I was an Eurasian; sixth, the impulse to create.

Little Lace Girl

The impulse to create was so strong within me that failing all other open avenues of development (I wrote a good deal of secret doggerel[130] verse around this period) I began making Irish crochet lace patterns, which I sold to a clique of ladies to whom I was known as "The Little Lace Girl." I remember that when a Dominion exhibition was held in Montreal a lace pattern which I sent to the art department won first prize—a great surprise to all my people as I was the only little girl competing. My mother was very proud of my work. I remember that when the church asked her to donate something she got me to crochet her a set of my mats as a gift.

At the age of 14 I succumbed to a sickness which affected both head and heart and retarded development both mentally and physically. Which is the chief reason, no doubt, why an ambition conceived in childhood is achieved only as I near the close of half a century. But for all this retardation and the fact that I suffered from recurrent attacks of the terrible fever, I never lost spirit and always maintained my position as the advisory head of the household. We had a large family of children[131] and my father was an artist.

The wiseacres[132] tell us that if we are good we will be big, healthy and contented. I must have been dreadfully wicked. The only thing big about me were my feelings;

---

130 Comic verse composed in irregular rhythm
131 Eaton was then one of fourteen children.
132 Person with an affectation of wisdom or knowledge

the only thing healthy, my color; the only content I experienced was when I peeped into the future and saw all the family grown and settled down and myself, far away from all noise and confusion, with nothing to do but write a book.

To earn my living I now began to sell my father's pictures. I enjoyed this, and no doubt, it was beneficial, as it took me out into the open air and it brought me into contact with a number of interesting persons. To be sure, there was a certain sense of degradation and humiliation in approaching a haughty and contemptuous customer, and also periods of melancholy when disappointed in a sale I had hoped to effect or payment for a picture was not made when promised. But the hours of hope and elation were worth all the dark ones. I remember staring out one morning with two pictures in my hand and coming home in the evening with $20. How happy was everybody!

This avocation I followed for some years. Besides affording me opportunities to study human nature, it also enabled me to gratify my love for landscape beauty—a love which was and is almost a passion.

My 18th birthday saw me in the copying room of the Montreal Star,[133] where for some months I picked and set type. While there I taught myself shorthand.

Became Stenographer

As last I took a position as stenographer[134] in a lawyer's office. I do not think a person of artistic temperament is fitted for mechanical work and it is impossible for such to make a success of it. Stenography, in particular, is torturing to one whose mind must create its own images. Unconsciously I was stultified by the work I had undertaken. But it had its advantages in this respect, that it brought me into contact and communion with men of judgment and mental ability. I know that I always took an interest in my employers and their interests, and, therefore, if I did not merit, at least received their commendation.

I recall that the senior member of the firm, now Judge Archibald of Montreal, occasionally chatted with me about books and writers, read my little stories and verse as they appeared, and usually commented upon them with amused interest. I used to tell him that I was ambitious to write a book. I remember him saying that it would be necessary for me to acquire some experience of life and some knowledge of character before I began the work and I assuring him seriously that I intended to form all my characters upon the model of myself. "They will be very funny people then," he answered with a wise smile.

While in this office I wrote some humorous articles which were accepted by Peck's Sun,[135] Texas Siftings[136] and Detroit Free Press. I am not consciously a humorous person; but now and then unconsciously I write things which seem to strike editors as funny.

One day a clergyman suggested to my mother that she should call upon a young Chinese woman who had recently arrived from China as the bride of one of the local Chinese merchants. With the exception of my mother there was but one other Chinese woman in the city besides the bride. My mother complied with the clergyman's wishes and I accompanied her.

From that time I began to go among my mother's people, and it did me a world of good to discover how akin I was to them.

---

133 *The Montreal Star* was an English-language Canadian newspaper published in Quebec.
134 A stenographer transcribes speech in shorthand.
135 A popular newspaper in Milwaukee, Wisconsin
136 An independent weekly humour magazine in Austin, Texas

Passing by a few years I found myself in Jamaica, W I,[137] working as a reporter on a local paper. It was interesting work until the novelty wore off, when it became absolute drudgery. However, it was a step forward in development. I had reached my 27th year.

Sir Henry Blake was the Governor of the island while I was there, and I found the Legislative Council reporting both instructive and amusing. How noble and high principled seemed each honorable member while on the floor! How small and mean while compelled to writhe under the scorn and denunciation of some opposing brother! I used to look down from the press gallery upon the heads of the honorable members and think a great many things which I refrained from putting into my report.

I got very weary and homesick tramping the hot dusty streets of Kingston; and contracted malarial fever, the only cure for which, in my case, was a trip up North.

I remained in Montreal about a year, during which period I worked, first, as a stenographer for Mr Hugh Graham (now Sir Hugh) of the Star, and then in the same capacity for Mr G.T. Bell of the Grand Trunk Railway.[138] Both of these positions I was compelled to resign because of attacks of inflammatory rheumatism.

At last my physicians declared that I would never gain strength in Montreal, and one afternoon in June what was left of me – 84 pounds – set its face westward. I went to San Francisco, where I had a sister, a bright girl, who was working as a spotter in one of the photograph galleries. I fell in love with the City of the Golden Gate,[139] and wish I had space in which to write more of the place in which all the old ache in my bones fell away from them, never to return again.

As soon as I could I found some work. That is, I located myself in a railway agency, the agent of which promised me $5 a month and as well an opportunity to secure outside work. But despite this agency's fascinating situation at the corner of a shopping highway I made slight progress financially, and had it not been for my nature and my office window might have experienced a season of melancholy. As it was, I looked out of my window, watched a continuously flowing stream of humanity, listened to the passing bands, inhaled the perfume of the curbstone flower sellers' wares, and was very much interested.

To eke out a living I started to canvas Chinatown for subscribers for the San Francisco Bulletin. During my pilgrimages thereto I met a Chinese whom I had known in Montreal. He inquired if I were still writing Chinese stories. Mr. Charles Lummis made the same inquiry. Latent ambition aroused itself. I recommended writing Chinese stories. Youth's Companion[140] accepted one.

But I suffered many disappointments and rejections, and the urgent need for money pressing upon me, I bethought me of Seattle. Perhaps there Fortune would smile a little kinder. This suggestion had come some months before Lyman E. Knapp, ex-Governor of Alaska, who had dropped into my office one day to get some deeds type-written. Observing that I understood legal work, he advised me to try "the old Siwash town," where, he added, he was sure I would do better than in San Francisco.

---

137 West Indies
138 The Grand Trunk Railway system operated in the Canadian provinces of Quebec and Ontario, and in US states of Connecticut, Maine, Michigan, Massachusetts, New Hampshire and Vermont.
139 Nickname for San Francisco
140 A children's magazine published in Boston, Massachusetts

To Seattle I sailed, and the blithe greenness of the shores of Puget Sound seemed to give me the blithest of welcomes. I was in my 29th year, and my sole fortune was $8. Before 5 o'clock of the first day here I had arranged for desk room in a lawyer's office and secured promise of patronage from several attorneys, a loan and mortgage company and a lumber and shingle merchant. I remember that evening I wrote my mother a letter, telling her that I had struck gold, silver, oil, copper, and everything else that luck could strike, in proof of which I grandiloquently shoved into her envelope a part of my remaining wealth.

As always on account of my inaccuracy as a stenographer and my inability to typewrite continuously, my earning capacity was small; but I managed to hold up my head, and worked intermittently and happily at my Chinese stories.

Chinese Mission Teacher

Occasionally I taught in a Chinese mission school, as I do here in Boston, but learned far more from my scholars than ever I could impart to them.

I also formed friendships with women who braced and enlightened me, women to whom the things of the mind and the heart appealed; women who were individuals, not merely the daughters of their parents, the wives of the husbands; women who taught me that nationality was no bar to friendship with those whose friendship was worth while.

Ever and again, during the 14 years in which I lived in Seattle, whenever I had a little money put by, some inward impulse would compel me to use it for a passage home. The same impulse would drive me to work my way across the Continent, writing advertisements for the different lines. Once when I saved up $85 toward a rest in which to write the book of my dreams news from home caused me to banish ambition for a while longer; and I sent my little savings to pay a passage out West for one of my younger sisters. This sister remained with me for seven months, during which time I got her to learn shorthand and typewriting, so that upon her return to Montreal she would be enabled to earn her living. Thus did the ties of relationship belate me; but at the same time strengthen.

A year later, a shock of sudden grief so unfitted me for mechanical work that I determined to emancipate myself from the torture of writing other people's thoughts and words with a heart full of my own, and throwing up my position, worked my way down South as far as the city of Los Angeles. Arrived there, I gave way to my ruling passion – the passion to write all the emotions of my heart away. But it was hard work – artistic expression, if I may so call it. I had been so long accustomed to dictation that when I sat down to compose, although my mind teemed with ideas tumultuously clamoring for release, I hesitated as if I were waiting for a voice behind me to express them. I had to free myself from that spell. My writings might be imperfect, but they had got to bear the impress of thoughts begotten in my own mind and clothed in my own words.

I struggled for many months. The Century Magazine took a story from me; but I remained discontented with my work. I was not discontented with life, however. If there was nothing but bread to eat and water to drink, absorbed in my work I was immune to material things – for a while. You have to come back to them in the end.

Located in Boston

As I have already said, two years ago I came East with the intention of publishing a book of Chinese-American stories. While I was in Montreal my father obtained for me a letter of introduction from a Chinese merchant of that city to his brother in Boston, Mr. Lew Han Son. Through Mr. Lew Han Son I became acquainted with some Americans of the name of Austin who live in Dorchester and who have been my good friends ever since. I am also acquainted with a lady in Charlestown, Mrs Henderson, who is a sister of one of my Western friends. Save, however, some visiting among Chinese friends, I do not mingle much in any kind of society. I am not rich and I have my work to do.

I have contributed to many of the leading magazines.

During the past year I have been engaged in writing my first book, and completed it a couple of months ago. In this undertaking I was encouraged by the managing editor of the Independent.[141] Truth to tell, if I had not received some such encouragement I could not have carried the work to a successful completion, as I am one of those persons who have very little staying power.

To accomplish this work, or to enable me to have the leisure in which to accomplish it, I was obliged to obtain some financial assistance, for one cannot live upon air and water alone, even if one is half-Chinese. Two of my lawyer friends in Montreal kindly contributed toward this end. I hope soon to be in a position to repay them.

My people in Montreal, my mother in particular, my Chinese friends in Boston and also American friends are looking forward to the advent of "Mrs Spring Fragrance" with, I believe, some enthusiasm. I am myself quite excited over the prospect. Would not any one be who had worked as hard as I have – and waited as long as I have – for a book?

Source text

Far, Sui Sin, 'Sui Sin Far, the Half Chinese Writer, Tells of Her Career', *Boston Daily Globe* (5 May 1912), SM6.

References

Chapman, Mary, 'The "Thrill" of Not Belonging: Edith Eaton (Sui Sin Far) and Flexible Citizenship', *Canadian Literature* 212 (2012), 191–5.
Johanningsmeir, Charles, 'Edith Eaton/Sui Sin Far: True "Westerner"?' *American Literary Realism* 51.3 (Spring 2019), 220–45.

Mary Antin (1881–1940)

From Reviews of Mary Antin's The Promised Land (1913)

Mary Antin was born in Polotsk, Vitsyebsk, Russia, a centre of Jewish culture. Because of their Jewish heritage, her family suffered persecution and decided to emigrate. The Antins required two separate transatlantic journeys to transport the family to the US. Israel Antin, the father, embarked

---

141 An American magazine of religion, politics and literature published in the late nineteenth and early twentieth centuries, *The Independent* came out weekly, first in New York, later in Boston.

first, leaving Russia in 1891; Esther Weltman Antin followed with her four children in 1894.

During her family's more prosperous times, Antin had received an education from her brother's private tutors, an experience then unusual for girls. This instruction later enabled Mary to attend school in Boston while her sister, Fetchke (Frieda), worked in a sweatshop. Antin published her first book, *From Plotzk to Boston* (1899), when only eighteen. That text made a transatlantic connection in print, as British author Israel Zangwill (1864–1926), author of *The Melting Pot* (a drama first performed in 1908), wrote an appreciative introduction. A few years later, Antin published serialised memoirs in the US-based *Atlantic Monthly*, and these texts would inform *The Promised Land*.

Antin's contemporaries praised her ability to illuminate the challenges Jewish immigrants faced. For example, a review in the British periodical *Academy and Literature* underscored a particularly terrifying episode where Antin described child kidnappings followed by enforced conversions in Russia and argued that Western readers of *The Promised Land* should help Russian Jews reach a new, safe life. In the US, reviewer George Sampson contended Antin's 'vivid story' served as a 'testimony to the brave spirit of this alien child, once stepchild of the Czar, now a daughter of America' (167).

In the additional reviews of *The Promised Land* below, we see further signs of how British-based periodicals of Antin's day favourably assessed her writing. Through her first-hand perspective on migration and assimilation, she contributed, from across the Atlantic, to the circulation in Britain of a mythologised American Dream.

'Books of the Month: Biography and History: **The Promised Land**'

"An illustration of what the American system of free education and the European immigrant can make of each other." In these words of the authoress there lies the keynote to this brilliant piece of autobiography. Mary Antin, youngest and proudest of America's children, was Mashke, the Russian Jewess, living there within the "Pale of Settlement," and learning in her earliest years that if the Gentile child spat upon her, she, being of her race, must submit. And before you have finished her book you will understand how America takes in that ceaseless stream from the lands of oppression, and moulds them and stamps them with her own image. The book is a notable contrast of the Old World and the New World in their ways of treating the plastic and subtle material which the Jewish race presents.

From '**The Promised Land.** By Mary Antin (Heinemann)'

Miss Antin's memoir suggests comparison with Marguerite Audoux's history of 'Marie Claire.' If not so neatly written or so compact, it is more important in proportion as the stream of life which it presents is broader, more normally human, and in many ways more significant to the student of society. Much has been written about the Jews who live in the Pale of Settlement in Russia. But it has mostly been written from the outside, either by reformers who have dwelt upon the miserable condition of an oppressed people, or by artists who have presented Jewish characters objectively. Here we have a study from within; a realistically minute picture of men and women in humble position living the life of their castes, cooped up in the narrow place of residence allotted them by the Government, paying excessive taxes, compelled to bribe the police and even their Gentile neighbours for the sake of peace, with the last horror of a "pogrom"[142] hanging perpetually over their heads.

Miss Antin was born into this community, and she describes the daily life of her people with that intimacy which is worth so much more than the generalized knowledge of the social student. [...]

[T]here comes a dramatic moment in the narrative when this family, living its "medieval" life in Russia, soaked with the narrow superstitions and ignorance of their restricted community, is translated from Eastern Europe to the Atlantic coast of America. Through the illness of the mother they had fallen into poverty, and the father, unable to make a living in Russia, was driven by his "nervous, restless temperament," which for once inspired him, to emigrate and settle in the city of Boston.

For him it was a veritable "Land of Promise," a place where men were free, where labour had opportunity, where the police were not enemies, where music, light, and protection were given gratis. Above all, it was a place where children were educated; and Miss Antin becomes almost ecstatic in describing the fateful day when her father took her, still in her early teens, to the free school at Boston.

To her Boston was a sort of fairyland. Every one was kind. Teachers took special care of her. She won prizes, and was encouraged to write poems, which editors published. Libraries were open to her; a natural history club accepted her as a member; and from her tenement in the Ghetto she went forth to visit cultured persons in the famous "Back Bay."

On the members of her family the spirit of America left its mark. All that they had brought with them—their traditions, their prejudices, their superstitions—was deeply ingrained in their characters; but they were quickly disorganized by this new, strange influence from without, by the assimilating power of America which in a single generation turns the immigrant into an American citizen. Much as her father and mother gained by the change, they were conscious also of loss—of the loss of something intimately bound up in character.

Miss Antin was young when she went to Boston, and the process of Americanization was simpler with her than with the elder members of her family. But she has not lost her native capacity for quick perception, and the visualizing of the little significant things of life.

Source texts

'Books of the Month: Biography and History: *The Promised Land*. By Mary Antin. Heinemann', *The English Review* 13 (February 1913), 489.

'*The Promised Land*. By Mary Antin (Heinemann.)', *The Athenaeum* 4449 (1 February 1913), 125.

References

'The Alien Immigrant: *The Promised Land*. By Mary Antin. Illustrated. (Wm. Heinemann. 7s. 6d. net.)' *Academy and Literature* 2115 (16 November 1912), 637–8.

---

142 Massacre targeting a particular people; often used to reference assaults on Jews

Butler, Sean, '"Both Joined and Separate": English, Mary Antin, and the Rhetoric of Identification', *MELUS* 27.1 (2002), 53–83.

Sampson, George, 'A Stepchild of the Czar', *The Bookman* 43.255 (December 1912), 166–7.

Sollors, Werner, *Ethnic Modernism* (Cambridge: Cambridge University Press, 2008).

John Muir (1838–1914)

From The Story of My Boyhood and Youth *(1913)*

During the nineteenth century, an estimated 2.7 million emigrants left Scotland for America. One of these was renowned environmentalist John Muir. Muir's memoir begins with descriptions of his pre-emigration home in Dunbar, cast as a place with 'boundless woods full of mysterious good things' (Muir, 54). Striking portraits of the natural world continue throughout his narrative, making the landscape, on both sides of the Atlantic, a central character.

The memoir also explores the effects emigrants from Scotland have on 'Amaraka' (Muir, 55). Muir portrays the 'new wilds' as if they were empty spaces before his family arrived, not as longstanding home to Indigenous communities. Actually, as Donald Worster notes, the Wisconsin region where the Muirs settled was still home to Native American Winnebagoes who, pressured by the US government, had relocated there after selling lands east of the Mississippi. Young Muir occasionally crossed paths with Native people, and his book revisits disagreements between his father and 'a Scotch neighbor, Mr. George Mair', over 'the Indian question' (218). Muir recalls how Mair found it 'pitiful to see how the unfortunate Indians' were 'being robbed of their lands and pushed ruthlessly back into narrower and narrower limits by alien races who were cutting into their means of livelihood' (218). Reflecting then-common prejudices, however, Muir's father countered that 'surely it could never have been the intention of God to allow Indians to rove and hunt over so fertile a country and hold it forever in unproductive wildness, while Scotch and Irish and English farmers could put it to so much better use' (218).

Muir's love for nature led him to his now-well-known role as conservationist. His *Story* adds complex substance to that profile by positioning him as a transatlantic immigrant, significant not only for his later environmentalism, but also for his youthful identity as a white settler being schooled in racist attitudes, as noted in the memoir scene referenced above. For the Sierra Club (which he co-founded), reckoning with that legacy has led to reconsideration of Muir's status (Grad, 'Sierra').

From The Story of My Boyhood and Youth

One night, when David and I were at grandfather's fireside solemnly learning our lessons as usual, my father came in with news, the most wonderful, most glorious, that wild boys ever heard. "Bairns,"[143] he said, "you needna learn your lessons the nicht,[144] for we're gan to America the morn!" No more grammar, but boundless woods full of mysterious good things; trees full of sugar, growing in ground full of gold; hawks, eagles, pigeons, filling the sky; millions of birds' nests, and no game-keepers to stop us in all the wild, happy land. We were utterly, blindly glorious. After father left the room, grandfather gave David and me a gold coin apiece for a keepsake, and looked very serious, for he was about to be deserted in his lonely old age. And when we in fullness of young joy spoke of what we were going to do, of the wonderful birds and their nests that we should find, the sugar and gold, etc., and promised to send him a big box full of that tree sugar packed in gold from the glorious paradise over the sea, poor lonely grandfather, about to be forsaken, looked with downcast eyes on the floor and said in a low, trembling, troubled voice, "Ah, poor laddies, poor laddies, you'll find something else ower the sea forbye gold and sugar, birds' nests and freedom fra lessons and schools. You'll find plenty hard, hard work." And so we did. But nothing he could say could cloud our joy or abate the fire of youthful, hopeful, fearless adventure. Nor could we in the midst of such measureless excitement see or feel the shadows and sorrows of his darkening old age. To my schoolmates, met that night on the street, I shouted the glorious news, "I'm gan to Amaraka the morn!" None could believe it. I said, "Weel, just you see if I am at the skule the morn!"

Next morning we went by rail to Glasgow[145] and thence joyfully sailed away from beloved Scotland, flying to our fortunes on the wings of the winds, care-free as thistle seeds. We could not then know what we were leaving, what we were to encounter in the New World, nor what our gains were likely to be. We were too young and full of hope for fear or regret, but not too young to look forward with eager enthusiasm to the wonderful schoolless bookless American wilderness. Even the natural heart-pain of parting from grandfather and grandmother Gilrye, who loved us so well, and from mother and sisters and brother was quickly quenched in young joy. Father took with him only my sister Sarah (thirteen years of age), myself (eleven), and brother David (nine), leaving my eldest sister, Margaret, and the three youngest of the family, Daniel, Mary, and Anna, with mother, to join us after a farm had been found in the wilderness and a comfortable house made to receive them.

In crossing the Atlantic before the days of steamships, or even the American clippers, the voyages made in old-fashioned sailing-vessels were very long. Ours was six weeks and three days. But because we had no lessons to get, that long voyage had not a dull moment for us boys. Father and sister Sarah, with most of the old folk, stayed below in rough weather, groaning in the miseries of seasickness, many of the passengers wishing they had never ventured in "the auld rockin' creel," as they called our bluff-bowed, wave-beating ship, and, when the weather was moderately calm, singing songs in the evenings, – "The Youthful Sailor Frank and Bold," "Oh, why left I my hame, why did I cross the deep," etc. But no matter how much the old tub tossed about and battered the waves, we were on deck every day, not in the least seasick, watching the sailors at their rope-hauling and climbing work; joining in their songs, learning the names of the ropes and sails, and helping them as far as they would let us; playing games with other boys in calm weather when the deck was dry, and in stormy weather rejoicing in sympathy with the big curly-topped waves.

---

143 Scottish variant of children
144 'The nicht' would convey 'tonight'.
145 Glasgow, large port city on the River Clyde in western Scotland

The captain occasionally called David and me into his cabin and asked us about our schools, handed us books to read, and seemed surprised to find that Scotch boys could read and pronounce English with perfect accent and knew so much Latin and French. In Scotch schools only pure English was taught, although not a word of English was spoken out of school. All through life, however well educated, the Scotch spoke Scotch among their own folk, except at times when unduly excited on the only two subjects on which Scotchmen get much excited, namely religion and politics. So long as the controversy went on with fairly level temper, only gude[146] braid Scots was used, but if one became angry, as was likely to happen, then he immediately began speaking severely correct English, while his antagonist, drawing himself up, would say: "Weel, there's na use pursuing this subject ony further, for I see ye hae gotten to your English."

As we neared the shore of the great new land, with what eager wonder we watched the whales and dolphins and porpoises and seabirds, and made the good-natured sailors teach us their names and tell us stories about them!

There were quite a large number of emigrants aboard, many of them newly married couples, and the advantages of the different parts of the New World they expected to settle in were often discussed. My father started with the intention of going to the backwoods of Upper Canada.[147] Before the end of the voyage, however, he was persuaded that the States offered superior advantages, especially Wisconsin and Michigan, where the land was said to be as good as in Canada and far more easily brought under cultivation; for in Canada the woods were so close and heavy that a man might wear out his life in getting a few acres cleared of trees and stumps. So he changed his mind and concluded to go to one of the Western States.

On our wavering westward way a grain-dealer in Buffalo told father that most of the wheat he handled came from Wisconsin; and this influential information finally determined my father's choice. At Milwaukee a farmer who had come in from the country near Fort Winnebago with a load of wheat agreed to haul us and our formidable load of stuff to a little town called Kingston for thirty dollars. On that hundred-mile journey, just after the spring thaw, the roads over the prairies were heavy and miry, causing no end of lamentation, for we often got stuck in the mud, and the poor farmer sadly declared that never, never again would he be tempted to try to haul such a cruel, heart-breaking, wagon-breaking, horse-killing load, no, not for a hundred dollars. In leaving Scotland, father, like many other home-seekers, burdened himself with far too much luggage, as if all America were still a wilderness in which little or nothing could be bought. One of his big iron-bound boxes must have weighed about four hundred pounds, for it contained an old-fashioned beam-scales with a complete set of cast-iron counterweights, two of them fifty-six pounds each, a twenty-eight, and so on down to a single pound. Also a lot of iron wedges, carpenter's tools, and so forth, and at Buffalo, as if on the very edge of the wilderness, he gladly added to his burden a big cast-iron stove with pots and pans, provisions enough for a long siege, and a scythe and cumbersome cradle for cutting wheat, all of which he succeeded in landing in the primeval Wisconsin woods.

A land-agent at Kingston gave father a note to a farmer by the name of Alexander Gray, who lived on the border of the settled part of the country, knew the section-lines, and would probably help him to find a good place for a farm. So father went away

---

146 Scottish variant of good
147 The region now identified as Ontario

to spy out the land, and in the mean time left us children in Kingston in a rented room. It took us less than an hour to get acquainted with some of the boys in the village; we challenged them to wrestle, run races, climb trees, etc., and in a day or two we felt at home, carefree and happy, notwithstanding our family was so widely divided. When father returned he told us that he had found fine land for a farm in sunny open woods on the side of a lake, and that a team of three yoke of oxen with a big wagon was coming to haul us to Mr. Gray's place.

We enjoyed the strange ten-mile ride through the woods very much, wondering how the great oxen could be so strong and wise and tame as to pull so heavy a load with no other harness than a chain and a crooked piece of wood on their necks, and how they could sway so obediently to right and left past roadside trees and stumps when the driver said *haw* and *gee*. At Mr. Gray's house, father again left us for a few days to build a shanty on the quarter-section he had selected four or five miles to the westward. In the mean while we enjoyed our freedom as usual, wandering in the fields and meadows, looking at the trees and flowers, snakes and birds and squirrels. With the help of the nearest neighbors the little shanty was built in less than a day after the rough bur-oak logs for the walls and the white-oak boards for the floor and roof were got together.

To this charming hut, in the sunny woods, overlooking a flowery glacier meadow and a lake rimmed with white water-lilies, we were hauled by an ox-team across trackless carex[148] swamps and low rolling hills sparsely dotted with round-headed oaks. Just as we arrived at the shanty, before we had time to look at it or the scenery about it, David and I jumped down in a hurry off the load of household goods, for we had discovered a blue jay's nest, and in a minute or so we were up the tree beside it, feasting our eyes on the beautiful green eggs and beautiful birds, – our first memorable discovery. The handsome birds had not seen Scotch boys before and made a desperate screaming as if we were robbers like themselves; though we left the eggs untouched, feeling that we were already beginning to get rich, and wondering how many more nests we should find in the grand sunny woods. Then we ran along the brow of the hill that the shanty stood on, and down to the meadow, searching the trees and grass tufts and bushes, and soon discovered a bluebird's and a woodpecker's nest, and began an acquaintance with the frogs and snakes and turtles in the creeks and springs.

This sudden plash into pure wildness – baptism in Nature's warm heart – how utterly happy it made us! Nature streaming into us, wooingly teaching her wonderful glowing lessons, so unlike the dismal grammar ashes and cinders so long thrashed into us. Here without knowing it we still were at school; every wild lesson a love lesson, not whipped but charmed into us. Oh, that glorious Wisconsin wilderness! Everything new and pure in the very prime of the spring when Nature's pulses were beating highest and mysteriously keeping time with our own![149] Young hearts, young leaves, flowers, animals, the winds and the streams and the sparkling lake, all wildly, gladly rejoicing together!

---

148 A hair-like plant found in the US Great Lakes region
149 Muir's enthusiastic vision here of Nature as teacher foreshadows his eventual conservationist leadership. By 1903, he was so well known in that role that Theodore Roosevelt asked the naturalist to guide a trip to Yosemite that wound up influencing Roosevelt's use of tools like the Monuments and Antiquities Act to safeguard wilderness regions ('How John Muir', 338).

Source text

Muir, John, *The Story of My Boyhood and Youth: With Illustrations from Sketches by the Author* (Boston: Riverside Press, 1913).

References

Grad, Shelby, 'Sierra Club calls out the racism of John Muir', *Los Angeles Times* (22 July 2020), Web.
'How John Muir inspired Roosevelt', *Current Opinion* (1 March 1925), 337–8.
Worster, Donald, *A Passion for Nature: The Life of John Muir* (Oxford: Oxford University Press, 2008).

6

NATIONALISM AND COSMOPOLITANISM

Figure 6.1 *A Union in the Interest of Humanity – Civilization – Freedom and Peace for All Time.* United States Great Britain, *c.*1898. Photograph. Library of Congress Prints and Photographs Division.

The idea of the nation, and more precisely of the nation-state, is a concept borne out of a Romantic understanding of the unproblematic location of collective definition and character. This notion of nationhood as a culturally homogenous, organic whole with a shared history, environment and language was exemplified by the German poet and philosopher Johann Gottfried von Herder's (1744–1803) conception of *Das Volk* ('folk' or 'nation'), which contributed to the collective consciousness (*Der Volksgeist*) of a people.[1] Our anthology begins in the turmoil of the American Revolutionary War and ends in the wake of the First World War, just two of the events over the long nineteenth century which had a profound impact on both the shaping of transatlantic relations and the construction of nationhood in their aftermath. Nationalism and national identity became contested and complicated ideas around the globe, through imperial expansion and resistance, economic exploitation and the displacement of enormous numbers of people as a result. Revolutions against European rule in Latin America in the late eighteenth and early nineteenth centuries, revolutions for national autonomy in Europe itself in the 1840s and the fight for Irish Home Rule in the 1860s and 1870s – these are just three examples of many where the national imaginary was fought over and claimed in ways that resonated across the Atlantic. More peacefully, 1867 saw the founding of Canada as a federal state. Still part of the British imperial family but granted a degree of national autonomy, Canadian federation opened up the possibility of westward expansion, though at the devastating cost of displacing First Nations peoples from their land. We include the poem 'My English Letter', by E. Pauline Johnson (Tekahionwake), as an example of the divided allegiances (Canadian, British, Native) that are often at play during this period. Both internal and external national affiliations collided, putting significant pressure on the idea of the nation itself as a self-evident, coherent 'imagined community'.[2]

To reframe literary analysis in the context of the transatlantic allows us to complicate an understanding of the Atlantic basin as a collection of stable nations of the kind that Herder imagined. It is to conceive of spatial practices as dynamic and unfolding, in which the prefix 'trans-' signifies movement across and against expected or conventional categories, including those of the nation itself. What happens when one nation's attitudes, prejudices, modes of representation are brought into contact with those of a different national tradition? (We see some of the impact of these kinds of collisions in our Travel and Tourism section.) Transatlantic literature, therefore, becomes one means through which we can explore the impact of the Atlantic itself, as a mechanism of exchange and circulation, on the national imaginary. Placing texts within the wider rubric of transatlanticism opens up for reconsideration the assumptions that underlie nationally bounded literary histories, for writing produced within a particular national tradition is inevitably implicated in – or made contagious by – a

---

1 See Alan Patton, '"The Most Natural State": Herder and Nationalism', *History of Political Thought* 31.4 (2010), 657–89.

2 Benedict Anderson, in his highly influential book *Imagined Communities* (London: Verso, 1983), argues that national identity is imagined because 'the members of even the smallest nation will never know most of their fellow-members, meet them, or even hear of them, yet in the minds of each lives the image of their communion' (15). See Dimock for a rebuttal of Anderson's thesis.

network of transnational influences and choices. For Paul Giles, 'in a world of transnational mobility and spatial dislocation, no enclosed community – neither university nor region nor nation – can define itself in a separatist manner'.[3] As the texts in this section illustrate, the relational, contested nature of nationalism is often what is at stake, for even if national formulations are strategically and affectively powerful, they are also simultaneously challenged by modes of encounter that highlight the contingency of that power.

An awareness of the transatlantic as a competitive space – not just economically, but also culturally – helped to inaugurate literature's deployment in the service of national self-assertion. Thomas Paine's *Rights of Man* (the second part of which we excerpt here) argued for a radical break from British rule with the promise of 'a new area to the human race' soon to be established in the embryonic US. Paine's political rhetoric established a comparative perspective against which Old and New Worlds could be measured. Likewise Elizabeth Barrett Browning's powerful anti-slavery poem 'A Curse for a Nation' (1856) triangulates English working conditions, the context of Italian resistance to Austrian rule (Barrett Browning was living in Italy at this time) and the hypocrisy of the US national imaginary in a complex transnational indictment. The transatlantic perspective could also offer more tangible rewards for campaigners against enslavement and its poisonous legacy. We include a report from the *New York Times* of Ida B. Wells's own account of her tour of England to raise awareness and funds in the fight against lynching, in which her national identity is reframed in explicitly extra-national considerations.

LITERARY NATIONALISM

As we note in our Art, Aesthetics and Entertainment section, Sidney Smith's 1820 polemic in *The Edinburgh Review*, scornful of the US's ability ever to match the accomplishments of British literary history, is an exercise in national assertion disguised as literary criticism. The following year, the Scottish poet Thomas Campbell (whom we include in our Migration, Settlement and Resistance section) objected to Smith's nationalist rhetoric, warning that literary battles run the risk of leading to other, more deadly, forms of antagonism: 'our literary feuds with America' generate 'antipathies that prepare the human mind for the guilt of war. The serpent's teeth, though buried in the dirt, produce armed men. The evil of nationally hostile writers lives long after their short reputations.'[4]

On the other side of the Atlantic, US literary nationalism found its voice in the first half of the nineteenth century, most famously in the writings of Ralph Waldo Emerson, Henry David Thoreau and Herman Melville. Thoreau, in his essay 'Walking' (initially a lecture, but posthumously published in the *Atlantic Monthly* in 1862), compared the Atlantic to a 'Lethean stream, in our passage over which we have the opportunity to forget the Old World and its institutions';[5] and Melville, as if in a direct but belated response to Sidney Smith,

---

3 Paul Giles, 'Transnationalism and Classic American Literature', *PMLA* 118.1 (2003), 64.
4 Thomas Campbell, 'Preface', *New Monthly Magazine and Literary Journal* (London: Henry Colburn and Co., 1821), vii, xii.
5 Henry David Thoreau, 'Walking', *Atlantic Monthly* 9.56 (June 1862), 662.

asserted the inevitability of US literary genius through his conviction that 'men, not very much inferior to Shakespeare, are this day being born on the banks of the Ohio'.[6] However, alongside such assertions of US exceptionalism, or at least of US literary competitiveness, can be found a sustained interest in other nations and cultures. For instance, Emerson's advocacy of an ideology of national self-reliance, a view that has long dominated the ways in which he has been read, exists in counterpoint with his detailed, and often sympathetic, response to English society and culture. Our excerpt from his book *English Traits* (1856) explores this oscillation between New and Old World allegiances.

Anglo-American reconciliation and expansion, rather than rupture, was also a strong element of the transatlantic relationship, especially after the end of the American Civil War in 1865. US 'Anglophilia', as Elisa Tamarkin discusses in her important account of the ways in which British culture came to be regarded with sentimental attachment, was matched by a shared British desire to see the growth of an Anglo-Saxon alliance across the Atlantic, stretching its influence and authority into other parts of the globe. The US, from this vantage point, rather than embodying a set of worrying radical republican attitudes, was regarded as the invigorated progenitor of ever increasing numbers of anglicised immigrants, what James Belich has called 'the Rise of the Angloworld'. Even within this broad alliance, though, competitiveness could not be dispelled. So while, for instance, George R. Parkin, a prominent Canadian advocate of British imperialism, noted that '[t]he development of the Anglo-Saxon race [. . .] which has its home in the British Isles, has become, within the last century, the chief factor and central feature of human history',[7] the US clergyman Josiah Strong saw things rather differently. In his best-selling book *Our Country* (1885) he asserted that 'England can hardly hope to maintain her relative importance among Anglo-Saxon peoples where her "pretty island" is the home of only one-twentieth of the race'.[8] Here we read Strong's version of the *translatio studii et imperii* trope, by which locations of power and authority shift across time and space; for Strong the movement is inexorably westward, with the now increasingly insignificant English no longer central to the Anglo-Saxon imperial/racial project. Anna Laetitia Barbauld presents the reader with a similar trajectory in her earlier poem *Eighteen Hundred and Eleven* (1812), an excerpt from which we include here.

These exchanges operate as indicative instances of the kinds of bilateral Anglo-American comparison between the once colonial parent and its rebellious offspring that have tended to define the transatlantic paradigm. While long regarded as the dominant pairing within the Anglophone Atlantic basin, more recent scholarship has sought to expand beyond the US-Great Britain tie to account for the impact of wider hemispheric encounters on the national

---

6 Herman Melville, 'Hawthorne and His Mosses', in Herman Melville, *The Piazza Tales: And Other Prose Pieces, 1839–1860*, Harrison Hayford et al. (eds) (Evanston, IL: Northwestern University Press, 1987), 245.
7 George R. Parkin, 'The Reorganization of the British Empire', *Century* 37 (1888), 187.
8 Josiah Strong, *Our Country: Its Possible Future and the Present Crisis* (New York: American Home Missionary Society, 1885), 166.

imaginary. Our anthology as a whole draws attention to this more diverse geographical terrain (while acknowledging its focus on Anglophone writing, as we explain in the book's Introduction), and many of the excerpts in this section alert the reader to forms of national expression and contestation beyond the Anglo-Saxon binary of Britain and the US. For instance, William Allen, a self-described 'quadroon' from Virginia, writes a celebration of Gabriel Valdés, an Afro-Cuban poet central to a rebellion against Spanish rule, and the institution of slavery, in Cuba in 1844. The collision of different identities and nationalities in this piece is indicative of the complex formations at work in the Atlantic world. Arthur C. Parker's 1918 address, 'The American Indian in the World Crisis', explores the status of Native peoples within the US and Canada in the context of their participation in the First World War.

VARIETIES OF COSMOPOLITANISM

In an 1867 letter to his friend Thomas Sergeant Perry, the young Henry James articulated what he saw as the peculiar problem facing the US writer, who, in the face of established cultural and literary traditions in Europe, struggles to create 'something of our own – something distinctive & homogenous'. James's solution is the cultivation of a cosmopolitan sensibility, selecting between and appropriating different influences:

> We can deal with forms of civilisation not our own, can pick and choose and assimilate and in short (aesthetically &c) claim our property wherever we find it. To have no national stamp has hitherto been a defect & a drawback; but I think it is not unlikely that American writers may yet indicate that a vast intellectual fusion and synthesis of the various National tendencies of the world is the condition of more important achievements than any we have seen.[9]

James presents here a model for US authorship that he would, of course, go on to embody with great success – the carefully attuned cosmopolitan sensibility that can rescue US writing from the provincialism of geographical distance.

Cosmopolitanism – and its personification in the figure of the cosmopolitan – has a long history, with the Greek philosopher Diogenes in the fourth century BCE asserting that he was a citizen of the world, a *kosmopolites*, to distinguish his own expansive sense of community from more local traditions. It has come to be regarded as an ethical stance, in which principles of curiosity, sympathy and conversation are mobilised against a limiting parochialism. The figure of the cosmopolitan remains compelling, if not unproblematic, because of its testing of the parameters of belonging and identity, thereby asking us to consider where the highest value and loyalty reside – with the individual, the group, the nation, or the world – issues which are also central to the kinds of affiliation and commitment explored in our

---

9 Philip Horne (ed.), *Henry James: A Life in Letters* (London: Penguin Books, 1999), 17.

Suffrage and Citizenship section.[10] To what extent is it possible, or even advisable, to relinquish the specifics of the local or the national, in favour of a quasi-transcendent ethical or political position? Kwame Anthony Appiah has proposed the concept of 'partial cosmopolitanism' to negotiate between the imperatives of the local/national and those of the global/universal. An earlier iteration of this question of the place of the cosmopolitan within the national literary project can be seen in Henry Longfellow's novel *Kavanagh* (1849), excerpted below, in which is staged a debate over the relative virtues of US exceptionalism and what one character calls 'universal' values that transcend national particularities. Longfellow's commitment to literary internationalism is shown in his editorship of both one of the earliest anthologies of translated European poetry, *Poets and Poetry of Europe* (1844), and of the 31-volume *Poems of Places* (1876–9), which brought together translations of poetry from around the world.

The mythology of US exceptionalism both drove the expansion of its immigrant population and, in so doing, worked to undermine the presumption of an Anglo-Saxon nation. Emma Lazarus's celebrated 'The New Colossus' (1883), written to assist with the funding of the Statue of Liberty, welcomed the 'huddled masses', yet in turn those arrivals generated quite different responses regarding the composition of the nation. Anzia Yezierzka, in her story 'How I Found America', turned a sceptical eye on the possibilities of immigrant access to the rewards of US acculturation; Theodore Roosevelt, as our excerpt reveals, advocated a chimerical process of robust Americanisation, against which the Europeanised cosmopolitanism of the expatriate US citizen (with perhaps Henry James in mind) displayed effete qualities of the 'over-civilized, over-sensitive, over-refined'; and, in contrast, Randolph Bourne's model of a 'Trans-national America' espoused what we would now call ethnic/racial pluralism, a cosmopolitan society strengthened by its diversity.

References

Anderson, Amanda, *The Powers of Distance: Cosmopolitanism and the Cultivation of Detachment* (Princeton, NJ: Princeton University Press, 2001).

Appiah, Kwame Anthony, *Cosmopolitanism: Ethics in a World of Strangers* (New York: Norton, 2006).

Belich, James, *Replenishing the Earth: The Settler Revolution and the Rise of the Angloworld, 1783–1939* (Oxford: Oxford University Press, 2009).

Brennan, Timothy, *At Home in the World: Cosmopolitanism Now* (Cambridge, MA: Harvard University Press, 1997).

Dimock, Wai Chee, 'Literature for the Planet', *PMLA* 116.1 (2001), 173–88.

Ninkovich, Frank, *Global Dawn: The Cultural Foundation of American Internationalism 1865–1890* (Cambridge, MA: Harvard University Press, 2009).

Tamarkin, Elisa, *Anglophilia: Deference, Devotion, and Antebellum America* (Chicago: University of Chicago Press, 2008).

---

10 For more on the contested theories of cosmopolitanism, see Steven Vertovec and Robin Cohen (eds), *Conceiving Cosmopolitanism: Theory, Context, and Practice* (Oxford: Oxford University Press, 2003).

Phillis Wheatley (1753–84)

'The following Letter and Verses, were written by the famous Phillis Wheatley, the African Poetess, and presented to his Excellency Gen. Washington.' (1776)

One early effort to produce bibliographic resources and analysis of Phillis Wheatley's writings came from Charles Heartman, a German immigrant (to England in 1907 and then to America). Donaldson credits the collector, book-seller and editor with important scholarship for literature studies through a 78-volume book series. One, Heartman's 1915 *Phillis Wheatley*, extended her then-available oeuvre beyond the *Poems* by publishing texts like the lyric below.

Heartman described it as previously 'lost' and identified its original publication in *Pennsylvania Magazine* (19–20). He also printed the grateful letter Washington sent to 'Miss Phillis' in late 1775. Besides documenting Washington's having received Wheatley's missive directly, Heartman provided the General's assessment of the piece as 'elegant' and 'striking proof of [her] poetical talents'. Washington's description of Wheatley as 'favoured by the muses' affirmed their shared engagement in classical learning, while his invitation to visit his headquarters situated them as joined in the battle for nation-making.

Similarly, Heartman's introduction to *Phillis Wheatley* characterised her as, like himself, both a cosmopolitan honouring classical culture and a promoter of American nationhood. He observed that, during her earlier visit to London, 'she was to have been introduced to the king', but for 'her mistress' [poor] health' leading to a rush back to America. Although, Heartman averred, such a meeting might have been 'interesting' to Wheatley, who had 'reaped the highest honors in England', her loyalty was firmly placed with 'the colonies'. Accordingly, Heartman contrasted Wheatley's tone in '"To the Kings Most Excellent Majesty"' with the 'strength and feeling' in her 'poem to George Washington' (19).

Echoing its focus on Washington as hero for the emerging nation, Wheatley's poem confirms her affiliation by turning the rhyming couplets of Pope – long associated with a different national identity – into an anti-colonial statement. Thus, 'Britannia droops the pensive head' while showing 'Cruel blindness to Columbia's [America's] state', suggesting a British stance toward revolutionary righteousness at odds with 'the eyes of [other] nations on the scales', hoping instead that 'Columbia's arm prevails'.

'The following Letter and Verses, were written by the famous Phillis Wheatley, the African Poetess, and presented to his Excellency Gen. Washington.'

SIR,

I have taken the freedom to address your Excellency in the enclosed poem, and entreat your acceptance, though I am not insensible of its inaccuracies. Your being appointed by the Grand Continental Congress to be Generalissimo of the armies of North America, together with the fame of your virtues, excited sensations not easy to suppress. Your generosity, therefore, I presume, will pardon the attempt. Wishing your Excellency all possible success in the great cause you are so generously engaged in. I am,

Your Excellency's most obedient humble servant, Phillis Wheatley.
Providence, Oct. 26, 1775.[11]

His Excellency Gen. Washington.

Celestial choir! enthron'd in realms of light,
Columbia's[12] scenes of glorious toils I write.
While freedom's cause her anxious breast alarms,
She flashes dreadful[13] in refulgent[14] arms.
See mother earth her offspring's fate bemoan,
And nations gaze at scenes before unknown!
See the bright beams of heaven's revolving light
Involved in sorrows and the veil of night!
The goddess comes, she moves divinely fair,
Olive and laurel binds her golden hair:[15]
Wherever shines this native of the skies,
Unnumber'd charms and recent graces rise.
Muse![16] Bow propitious while my pen relates
How pour her armies through a thousand gates,
As when Eolus[17] heaven's fair face deforms,
Enwrapp'd in tempest and a night of storms;
Astonish'd ocean feels the wild uproar,
The refluent[18] surges beat the sounding shore;
Or thick as leaves in Autumn's golden reign,
Such, and so many, moves the warrior's train.
In bright array they seek the work of war,
Where high unfurl'd the ensign[19] waves in air.
Shall I to Washington their praise recite?
Enough thou know'st them in the fields of fight.

---

11 Wheatley's 1775 dating for her letter to Washington, like this poem's original publication date of 1776, marks a significant distance from the 1773 release date of her *Poems on Various Subjects*. After potential Boston-based publishing routes had failed because racist attitudes there prevented publication, *Poems* first appeared in England, not America, with support from Selina Hastings, countess of Huntingdon, to whom Wheatley dedicated that book. Accordingly, several lyrics in that collection locate Wheatley's affiliations with Britain and patrons there just a few years before her Washington text signalled a definitive shift in her loyalties, both political and cultural.
12 Wheatley uses 'Columbia' as a term for America.
13 Awe-inspiring
14 Brightly shining
15 Classical literature often depicted deities as becoming directly involved in human strife. The 'laurel', meanwhile, was an evergreen used to crown victors and poetic excellence.
16 Calling on the muse or muses for inspiration and guidance was a familiar neoclassical poetic technique.
17 God of winds
18 Flowing backwards
19 Flag or banner

Thee, first in place[20] and honours,—we demand
The grace and glory of thy martial band.
Fam'd for thy valour, for thy virtues more,
Hear every tongue thy guardian aid implore!
  One century scarce perform'd its destined round,
When Gallic[21] powers Columbia's fury found;
And so may you, whoever dares disgrace
The land of freedom's heaven-defended race!
Fix'd are the eyes of nations on the scales,
For in their hopes Columbia's arm prevails.
Anon Britannia[22] droops the pensive head,
While round increase the rising hills of dead.
Ah! Cruel blindness to Columbia's state!
Lament thy thirst of boundless power too late.
  Proceed, great chief, with virtue on thy side,
Thy ev'ry action let the goddess guide.
A crown,[23] a mansion, and a throne that shine,
With gold unfading, WASHINGTON! Be thine.

Source text

Wheatley, Phillis, 'The following Letter and Verses, were written by the famous Phillis Wheatley, the African Poetess, and presented to his Excellency Gen. Washington', *The Pennsylvania Magazine; or, American Monthly Museum* 2.4 (April 1776), 193.

References

Donaldson, Gary A., 'The Career of Charles F. Heartman and the Tradition of Collecting Americana', *Papers of the Bibliographical Society of America* 84.4 (December 1990), 377–96.
Heartman, Chas. Fred., *Phillis Wheatley (Phillis Peters): A Critical Attempt and a Bibliography of Her Writings* (New York: Printed for the Author, 1915), 19–23.
Kilgore, John Mac, 'Rites of Dissent: Literatures of Enthusiasm and the American Revolution', *Early American Literature* 48.2 (2013), 367–98.

Thomas Paine (1737–1809)

From Rights of Man. Part the Second *(1792)*

Thomas Paine, one of the foremost American philosophers and political theorists, emigrated from England in 1774 and immediately strove to

---

20 We follow Heartman's edition and the *Pennsylvania Magazine* in using 'place' here, situating Washington as 'first in place'; some versions say 'peace'.
21 French (previously named Gaul and hence Gallic)
22 Great Britain
23 Wheatley, here envisioning a 'crown' for Washington, was not unique then in imagining that he might become a king for America, a role he rejected.

foment the American rebellion against his mother country. Paine is best known for his pamphlet *Common Sense* (1776), which was circulated widely throughout the colonies. Its tremendous influence, along with his subsequent inspirational pamphlet series *The American Crisis* (1776), earned him the moniker 'The Father of the American Revolution'. Paine served in a diplomatic role for the fledgling American government, first as the secretary for Foreign Affairs, then as a de facto ambassador who travelled abroad to secure funding for American military expenses. After the war's conclusion he migrated to Europe and participated in the French Revolution, becoming a favourite of revolutionaries and gaining both honorary citizenship and election to the French National Convention. Later publications including *The Age of Reason* (1794) and *Agrarian Justice* (1797) earned Paine a notoriety for free-thinking and deism; he had accordingly fallen out of favour in the US by the time of his death in 1809.

The *Rights of Man* was written in England and published in two parts – first in March 1791 and thereafter in February 1792. Paine had difficulty securing a publisher for the tract, which faced suppression and opposition by the British government but proved to be popular among revolutionaries, dissenters and the working class, eventually selling one million copies. Intended as a rebuttal to Edmund Burke's *Reflections on the Revolution in France* (1790), Paine's tract argues that human rights originate from nature, not man, and that the purpose of government is merely to protect these inalienable rights from outside intrusion. Any institution superseding these natural, individual rights – whether monarchy or aristocracy – is illegitimate and contrary to human justice. Paine specifically advocated for radical reformations of the English government, including progressive taxation and subsidised education, the elimination of the aristocracy and a written Constitution modelled after the American compact. In response to *Rights of Man* the Crown convicted Paine of seditious libel *in absentia*, but as Paine did not return to England his death sentence was never executed. This excerpt, from the introduction to the second part, posits the US as an example to the rest of the world, arguing that America's constitutional democracy 'promises a new area to the human race'.

From **Rights of Man**

Introduction

What Archimedes[24] said of the mechanical powers, may be applied to Reason and Liberty: *"Had we,"* said he, *"a place to stand upon, we might raise the world."*

The revolution in America presented in politics what was only theory in mechanics. So deeply rooted were all the governments of the old world, and so effectually

---

24 Archimedes (*c.*287–*c.*212 BCE) was a Greek mathematician, physicist, engineer, inventor and astronomer. The full quote is popularised as 'Give me a place to stand and with a lever I will move the whole world'.

had the tyranny and the antiquity of habit established itself over the mind, that no beginning could be made in Asia, Africa, or Europe, to reform the political condition of man. Freedom had been hunted round the globe; reason was considered as rebellion; and the slavery of fear had made men afraid to think.

But such is the irresistible nature of truth, that all it asks, and all it wants, is the liberty of appearing. The sun needs no inscription to distinguish him from darkness; and no sooner did the American governments display themselves to the world, than despotism felt a shock, and man began to contemplate redress.

The independence of America, considered merely as a separation from England, would have been a matter but of little importance, had it not been accompanied by a revolution in the principles and practice of governments. She made a stand, not for herself only, but for the world, and looked beyond the advantages which *she* could receive. Even the Hessian,[25] though hired to fight against her, may live to bless his defeat; and England, condemning the viciousness of its government, rejoice in its miscarriage.

As America was the only spot in the political world, where the principles of universal reformation could begin, so also was it the best in the natural world. An assemblage of circumstances conspired, not only to give birth, but to add gigantic maturity to its principles. The scene which that country presents to the eye of a spectator, has something in it which generates and enlarges great ideas. Nature appears to him in magnitude. The mighty objects he beholds, act upon his mind by enlarging it, and he partakes of the greatness he contemplates. Its first settlers were emigrants from different European nations, and of diversified professions of religion, retiring from the governmental persecutions of the old world, and meeting in the new, not as enemies, but as brothers. The wants which necessarily accompany the cultivation of a wilderness produced among them a state of society, which countries long harassed by the quarrels and intrigues of governments, had neglected to cherish. In such a situation man becomes what he ought. He sees his species, not with the inhuman idea of a natural enemy, but as kindred; and the example shows to the artificial world, that man must go back to nature for information.

From the rapid progress which America makes in every species of improvement, it is rational to conclude, that if the governments of Asia, Africa and Europe, had begun on a principle similar to that of America, or had not been very early corrupted therefrom, that those countries must, by this time, have been in a far superior condition to what they are. Age after age has passed away, for no other purpose than to behold their wretchedness. Could we suppose a spectator who knew nothing of the world, and who was put into it merely to make his observations, he would take a great part of the old world to be new, just struggling with the difficulties and hardships of an infant settlement. He could not suppose that the hordes of miserable poor, with which old countries abound, could be any other than those who had not yet had time to provide for themselves. Little would he think they were the consequence of what in such countries is called government.

If, from the more wretched parts of the old world, we look at those which are in an advanced stage of improvement, we still find the greedy hand of government thrusting itself into every corner and crevice of industry, and grasping the spoil of the multitude. Invention is continually exercised, to furnish new pretences for revenue and taxation. It watches prosperity as its prey, and permits none to escape without a tribute. [. . .]

---

25 German mercenary soldiers who fought on behalf of Britain during the Revolutionary War

If systems of government can be introduced, less expensive, and more productive of general happiness, than those which have existed, all attempts to oppose their progress will in the end be fruitless. Reason, like time, will make its own way, and prejudice will fall in a combat with interest. If universal peace, harmony, civilization, and commerce are ever to be the happy lot of man, it cannot be accomplished but by a revolution in the system of governments. All the monarchical governments are military. War is their trade, plunder and revenue their objects. While such governments continue, peace has not the absolute security of a day. What is the history of all monarchical governments but a disgustful picture of human wretchedness, and the accidental respite of a few years repose? Wearied with war, and tired with human butchery, they sat down to rest and called it peace. This certainly is not the condition that heaven intended for man; and if *this be monarchy*, well might monarchy be reckoned among the sins of the Jews.

The revolutions which formerly took place in the world, had nothing in them that interested the bulk of mankind. They extended only to a change of persons and measures but not of principles, and rose or fell among the common transactions of the moment. What we now behold, may not improperly be called a *"counter revolution."* Conquest and tyranny, at some early period, dispossessed man of his rights, and he is now recovering them. And as the tide of all human affairs has its ebb and flow in directions contrary to each other, so also is it in this. Government founded on a *moral theory, on a system of universal peace, on the indefeasible hereditary rights of man*, is now revolving from west to east by a stronger impulse than the government of the sword revolved from east to west. It interests not particular individuals but nations in its progress, and promises a new area to the human race.

Source text

Paine, Thomas, *The Political Writings of Thomas Paine, Vol. II.* (Charlestown, MA: George Davidson, 1824).

References

Hitchens, Christopher, *Thomas Paine's* Rights of Man (New York: Grove Press, 2006).
Kates, Gary, 'From Liberalism to Radicalism: Tom Paine's *Rights of Man*', *Journal of the History of Ideas* 50.4 (1989), 569–87.
Nelson, Craig, *Thomas Paine: Enlightenment, Revolution, and the Birth of Modern Nations* (New York: Penguin, 2006).

Anna Laetitia Aikin Barbauld (1743–1825)

From Eighteen Hundred and Eleven, A Poem *(1812)*

Qualities British critics initially condemned in Barbauld's darkly satirical *Eighteen Hundred and Eleven* actually contributed to the poem's recovery in the late twentieth century as a critique of imperialism imagining her nation's future as salvageable only through a new transnationalism.

The poem's dismissal of Britain's imperial designs arose from a neoclassically inflected synthesis of Barbauld's longstanding pacifist and Dissenting religious views. By depicting the Napoleonic conflict as debilitating Britain, Birns argues, Barbauld envisioned 'the New World as more important than the Old' via rising cultural prominence of the Americas (549). Similarly, in a proto-feminist move, she proposed that a woman writer like Scottish playwright Joanna Baillie could claim status alongside men of scientific reason she admired, like Benjamin Franklin and transplant-to-America Joseph Priestley.

For over a hundred years, diatribes against Barbauld's poem as antinationalist held sway. Ironically, Lucy Aikin, her niece and editor, enshrined this emphasis in her 1825 *Works* collection, where she dubbed the poem a 'beautiful offspring of her [aunt's] genius', yet cast Barbauld as a Cassandra unjustly vilified (l). Aikin especially excoriated one cowardly 'assassin' as set upon destroying a 'venerable and female author' (li). Aikin's complaint that male critics eviscerated her aunt's literary identity helped marginalise the poem itself, downplaying Barbauld's most passionate engagement with global politics.

More recent calls to recover the text include seeing it as a morally grounded recuperation of Augustan verse's civic vision (Levine) or a striking example of 'historiography of the present' (Sachs). But another important cosmopolitan reading underscores its embrace of cultural imperialism in place of the militaristic brand it critiques (Crocco). As Crocco observes, Barbauld merits credit for avoiding the Orientalist thinking scholars like Edward Said have condemned, since her *translatio imperii* traces a series of transfers of political power from East to West (from Asia to Western Europe to the expanding-westward Americas) while imagining imperial axes like London as no more immune to decay than already disempowered sites in Asia and Classical metropoles. Yet, given her portrayal of pilgrims returning to an Old World Britain, her depiction of an ongoing *translatio studii* across the Atlantic positions that new cultural hegemony as migrating to locales still shaped by the very centre of cultural influence she critiques.

From Eighteen Hundred and Eleven, A Poem

Still the loud death drum, thundering from afar,
O'er the vext nations pours the storm of war:
To the stern call still Britain bends her ear,
Feeds the fierce strife, the alternate hope and fear;
Bravely, though vainly, dares to strive with Fate,
And seeks by turns to prop each sinking state.
Colossal Power with overwhelming force
Bears down each fort of Freedom in its course;
Prostrate[26] she lies beneath the Despot's sway,
While the hushed nations curse him—and obey.[27]

---

26 Lying face-down
27 Barbauld's opening lines evoke the ongoing Napoleonic Wars and their drain on British society.

Bounteous in vain, with frantic man at strife,
Glad Nature pours the means—the joys of life;
In vain with orange blossoms scents the gale,
The hills with olives clothes, with corn the vale;
Man calls to Famine, nor invokes in vain,
Disease and Rapine follow in her train;
The tramp of marching hosts disturbs the plough,
The sword, not sickle, reaps the harvest now,
And where the Soldier gleans the scant supply,
The helpless Peasant but retires to die;
No laws his hut from licensed outrage shield,
And war's least horror is the ensanguined[28] field.

Fruitful in vain, the matron counts with pride
The blooming youths that grace her honoured side;
No son returns to press her widow'd hand,
Her fallen blossoms strew a foreign strand.
Fruitful in vain, she boasts her virgin race,
Whom cultured arts adorn and gentlest grace;
Defrauded of its homage, Beauty mourns,
And the rose withers on its virgin thorns.
Frequent, some stream obscure, some uncouth name
By deeds of blood is lifted into fame;
Oft o'er the daily page some soft-one bends
To learn the fate of husband, brothers, friends,
Or the spread map with anxious eye explores,
Its dotted boundaries and penciled shores,
Asks *where* the spot that wrecked her bliss is found,
And learns its name but to detest the sound.

And thinks't thou, Britain, still to sit at ease,
An island Queen amidst thy subject seas,
While the vext billows, in their distant roar,
But soothe thy slumbers, and but kiss thy shore?
To sport in wars, while danger keeps aloof,
Thy grassy turf unbruised by hostile hoof?
So sing thy flatterers; but, Britain, know,
Thou who hast shared the guilt must share the woe.
Nor distant is the hour; low murmurs spread,
And whispered fears, creating what they dread;
Ruin, as with an earthquake shock, is here,
There, the heart-witherings of unuttered fear,
And that sad death, whence most affection bleeds,
Which sickness, only of the soul, precedes.
Thy baseless[29] wealth dissolves in air away,
Like mists that melt before the morning ray:

---

28 Bloody
29 Unjustifiable

No more on crowded mart or busy street
Friends, meeting friends, with cheerful hurry greet;
Sad, on the ground thy princely merchants bend
Their altered looks, and evil days portend,[30]
And fold their arms, and watch with anxious breast
The tempest blackening in the distant West.

Yes, thou must droop; thy Midas[31] dream is o'er;
The golden tide of Commerce leaves thy shore,
Leaves thee to prove the alternate ills that haunt
Enfeebling Luxury and ghastly Want;
Leaves thee, perhaps, to visit distant lands,
And deal the gifts of Heaven with equal hands.

Yet, O my Country, name beloved, revered,
By every tie that binds the soul endeared,
Whose image to my infant senses came
Mixt with Religion's light and Freedom's holy flame!
If prayers may not avert, if 'tis thy fate
To rank amongst the names that once were great,
Not like the dim cold Crescent[32] shalt thou fade,
Thy debt to Science and the Muse unpaid;
Thine are the laws surrounding states revere,
Thine the full harvest of the mental year,
Thine the bright stars in Glory's sky that shine,
And arts that make it life to live are thine.
If westward streams the light that leaves thy shores,
Still from thy lamp the streaming radiance pours.
Wide spreads thy race from Ganges[33] to the pole,
O'er half the western world thy accents roll:
Nations beyond the Apalachian[34] hills
Thy hand has planted and thy spirit fills:
Soon as their gradual progress shall impart
The finer sense of morals and of art,
Thy stores of knowledge the new states shall know,
And think thy thoughts, and with thy fancy glow;
Thy Lockes, thy Paleys[35] shall instruct their youth,
Thy leading star direct their search for truth;
Beneath the spreading Platan's[36] tent-like shade,

---

30 Serve as an omen
31 As an adjective, like King Midas, able to glean easy financial reward
32 Alluding to the Ottoman Empire, set in contrast in the next line with Britain and its un-fading contributions to science and literature
33 Hallowed (and now polluted) South Asian transboundary river flowing between India and Bangladesh
34 Appalachian: mountain range in eastern North America, running from Georgia to the Canadian–US border
35 John Locke (1632–1704), a British philosopher and medical researcher, and William Paley (1743–1805), a classical scholar and clerical leader.
36 A North American shade tree

Or by Missouri's[37] rushing waters laid,
"Old father Thames"[38] shall be the Poets' theme,
Of Hagley's woods[39] the enamoured virgin dream,
And Milton's[40] tones the raptured ear enthrall,
Mixt with the roar of Niagara's[41] fall;
In Thomson's glass[42] the ingenuous youth shall learn
A fairer face of Nature to discern;
Nor of the Bards that swept the British lyre[43]
Shall fade one laurel, or one note expire.
Then, loved Joanna,[44] to admiring eyes
Thy storied groups in scenic pomp shall rise;
Their high soul'd strains and Shakespear's noble rage
Shall with alternate passion shake the stage.
Some youthful Basil[45] from thy moral lay
With stricter hand his fond desires shall sway;
Some Ethwald,[46] as the fleeting shadows pass,
Start at his likeness in the mystic glass;
The tragic Muse resume her just controul,
With pity and with terror purge the soul,
While wide o'er transatlantic realms thy name
Shall live in light, and gather *all* its fame.

Where wanders Fancy[47] down the lapse of years
Shedding o'er imaged woes untimely tears?
Fond moody Power! as hopes—as fears prevail,
She longs, or dreads, to lift the awful veil,
On visions of delight now loves to dwell,
Now hears the shriek of woe or Freedom's knell:
Perhaps, she says, long ages past away,
And set in western waves our closing day,

---

37 The longest river in North America, running over 2,000 miles from the northern Rocky Mountains to join the Mississippi River
38 A river flowing through southern England and playing a key role in London history and culture
39 Part of the Hagley estate in Worcestershire, England
40 John Milton (1608–74), author of *Paradise Lost* (1667) and an influential intellectual whose *Areopagitica* (1644) condemned censorship
41 Niagara Falls, a monumental natural site between Canada and the US, often linked with the concept of the 'sublime' outlined by Edmund Burke
42 James Thomson (1700–48), Scottish writer much admired by both Barbauld and her brother John Aikin for integrating scientific knowledge and natural philosophy into his poetry, such as *The Seasons* (1730) and his poem honouring Sir Isaac Newton. Barbauld is likely referencing a passage in Thomson's *Autumn* section of *The Seasons* that describes a telescope's power while simultaneously alluding to Milton's invocation of Galileo.
43 'Bards' and 'lyre' honour British poetry, while the next line's 'laurel' alludes to a crown of poetic excellence.
44 Joanna Baillie (1762–1851), prolific Scottish poet and playwright
45 Baillie's play *Basil* (1798) centres on a character of that name who shines as a warrior but cannot achieve a broader brand of leadership.
46 Ethwald, the eponymous character in *Ethwald*, one of Baillie's *Series of Plays: Passions of the Mind* (1802)
47 Often used in Barbauld's era to represent imaginative capability

Night, Gothic night, again may shade the plains
Where Power is seated, and where Science reigns;
England, the seat of arts, be only known
By the gray ruin and the mouldering stone;
That Time may tear the garland from her brow,
And Europe sit in dust, as Asia now.

Yet then the ingenuous youth whom Fancy fires
With pictured glories of illustrious sires,
With duteous zeal their pilgrimage shall take
From the blue mountains, or Ontario's[48] lake,
With fond adoring steps to press the sod
By statesmen, sages, poets, heroes trod;
On Isis'[49] banks to draw inspiring air,
From Runnymede[50] to send the patriot's prayer;
In pensive thought, where Cam's[51] slow waters wind,
To meet those shades that ruled the realms of mind;
In silent halls to sculptured marbles bow,
And hang fresh wreaths round Newton's awful brow.[52]
Oft shall they seek some peasant's homely shed,
Who toils, unconscious of the mighty dead,
To ask where Avon's winding waters stray,
And thence a knot of wild flowers bear away; [...]
With curious search their pilgrim steps shall rove
By many a ruined tower and proud alcove,
Shall listen for those strains that soothed of yore
Thy rock, stern Skiddaw, and thy fall, Lodore;[53]
Feast with Dun Edin's[54] classic brow their sight,
And visit "Melross by the pale moonlight."[55]

But who their mingled feelings shall pursue
When London's faded glories rise to view?
The mighty city, which by every road,
In floods of people poured itself abroad;
Ungirt by walls, irregularly great,
No jealous drawbridge, and no closing gate;
Whose merchants (such the state which commerce brings)
Sent forth their mandates to dependant kings;
Streets, where the turban'd Moslem, bearded Jew,

---

48 A region in Canada
49 An alternative name for the Thames
50 Meadow by the Thames where King John signed the Magna Carta in 1215
51 A river in eastern England that flows through Cambridge
52 References Sir Isaac Newton (1643–1727), English scientist and theologian, with 'awful' in this case connoting 'awe-inspiring'
53 A mountain and a waterfall in England's Lake District
54 Edinburgh
55 Barbauld draws from a poem by Sir Walter Scott (1771–1832), 'The Lay of the Last Minstrel' (1805), set at Melrose Abbey, Scotland.

And woolly Afric, met the brown Hindu;
Where through each vein spontaneous plenty flowed,
Where Wealth enjoyed, and Charity bestowed.
Pensive and thoughtful shall the wanderers greet
Each splendid square, and still, untrodden street;
Or of some crumbling turret, mined by time,
The broken stair with perilous step shall climb,
Thence stretch their view the wide horizon round,
By scattered hamlets trace its antient bound,
And, choked no more with fleets, fair Thames survey
Through reeds and sedge pursue his idle way.

With throbbing bosoms shall the wanderers tread
The hallowed mansions of the silent dead,
Shall enter the long isle and vaulted dome
Where Genius and where Valour find a home;
Awe-struck, midst chill sepulchral marbles breathe,
Where all above is still, as all beneath;
Bend at each antique shrine, and frequent turn
To clasp with fond delight some sculptured urn,
The ponderous mass of Johnson's form to greet,
Or breathe the prayer at Howard's sainted feet.[56]

Perhaps some Briton, in whose musing mind
Those ages live which Time has cast behind,
To every spot shall lead his wondering guests
On whose known site the beam of glory rests: [...]
Or call up sages whose capacious mind
Left in its course a track of light behind;
Point where mute crowds on Davy's lips reposed,
And Nature's coyest secrets were disclosed;
Join with their Franklin, Priestley's injured name,
Whom, then, each continent shall proudly claim.

Oft shall the strangers turn their eager feet
The rich remains of antient art to greet,
The pictured walls with critic eye explore,
And Reynolds be what Raphael was before.[57]
On spoils from every clime their eyes shall gaze,
Egyptian granites and the Etruscan vase;[58]
And when midst fallen London, they survey

---

56 Barbauld envisions her pilgrims visiting statues of Samuel Johnson (1708–84), creator of the groundbreaking *Dictionary of the English Language* (1755), and John Howard (1726–90), a social reformer she admired.

57 Sir Joshua Reynolds (1723–92), British portrait artist, cast here as achieving fame on a par with Italian artist Raphael (1483–1520)

58 Barbauld's classifying items associated with the British Museum ('Egyptian granites and Etruscan vase') as 'spoils' anticipates later critiques of the museum's many thefts of cultural artefacts. She then extends her examples via reference to a sarcophagus assumed to hold Alexander the Great.

The stone where Alexander's ashes lay,
Shall own with humbled pride the lesson just
By Time's slow finger written in the dust.

There walks a Spirit o'er the peopled earth,
Secret his progress is, unknown his birth;
Moody and viewless as the changing wind,
No force arrests his foot, no chains can bind;
Where'er he turns, the human brute awakes,
And, roused to better life, his sordid hut forsakes:
He thinks, he reasons, glows with purer fires,
Feels finer wants, and burns with new desires:
Obedient Nature follows where he leads;
The steaming marsh is changed to fruitful meads;
The beasts retire from man's asserted reign,
And prove his kingdom was not given in vain.
Then from its bed is drawn the ponderous ore,
Then Commerce pours her gifts on every shore,
Then Babel's towers[59] and terraced gardens rise,
And pointed obelisks invade the skies;
The prince commands, in Tyrian purple[60] drest,
And Egypt's virgins weave the linen vest.
Then spans the graceful arch the roaring tide,
And stricter bounds the cultured fields divide.
Then kindles Fancy, then expands the heart,
Then blow the flowers of Genius and of Art;
Saints, Heroes, Sages, who the land adorn,
Seem rather to descend than to be born;
Whilst History, midst the rolls consigned to fame,
With pen of adamant inscribes their name.

The Genius now forsakes the favoured shore,
And hates, capricious, what he loved before;
Then empires fall to dust, then arts decay,
And wasted realms enfeebled despots sway; [...]

Venice the Adriatic weds in vain,
And Death sits brooding o'er Campania's[61] plain;
O'er Baltic shores and through Hercynian groves,[62]
Stirring the soul, the mighty impulse moves;
Art plies his tools, and Commerce spreads her sail,
And wealth is wafted in each shifting gale.

---

59 Genesis 11: 1–9 narrates the Tower of Babel story as an explanation of why people speak different languages in different global locations.
60 Tyrian invokes Tyre, a city in what is now Lebanon; 'Tyrian purple' references an indigo dye favoured by the Greeks and Romans.
61 A region in the southwest of Italy, with Naples its largest city
62 An ancient forest located in Germany

The sons of Odin tread on Persian looms,
And Odin's[63] daughters breathe distilled perfumes;
Loud minstrel Bards, in Gothic halls, rehearse
The Runic rhyme, and "build the lofty verse:"
The Muse, whose liquid notes were wont to swell
To the soft breathings of the Aeolian shell,[64]
Submits, reluctant, to the harsher tone,
And scarce believes the altered voice her own.
And now, where Caesar[65] saw with proud disdain
The wattled hut and skin of azure stain,
Corinthian columns rear their graceful forms,
And light varandas brave the wintry storms,
While British tongues the fading fame prolong
Of Tully's eloquence and Maro's song.[66]
Where once Bonduca[67] whirled the scythed car,
And the fierce matrons raised the shriek of war,
Light forms beneath transparent muslins float,
And tutored voices swell the artful note.
Light-leaved acacias and the shady plane
And spreading cedar grace the woodland reign;
While crystal walls the tenderer plants confine,
The fragrant orange and the nectared pine;
The Syrian grape there hangs her rich festoons,
Nor asks for purer air, or brighter noons:
Science and Art urge on the useful toil,
New mould a climate and create the soil,
Subdue the rigour of the northern Bear,[68]
O'er polar climes shed aromatic air,
On yielding Nature urge their new demands,
And ask not gifts but tribute at her hands.

London exults:—on London Art bestows
Her summer ices and her winter rose;
Gems of the East her mural crown adorn,
And Plenty at her feet pours forth her horn;
While even the exiles her just laws disclaim,
People a continent, and build a name:
August she sits, and with extended hands
Holds forth the book of life to distant lands.

---

63 A Viking/Norse god
64 'Aeolian' as a geographic term alludes to islands in the Tyrrhenian Sea or a region in Asia Minor; in music, a harmonious tonal scale; in mythology and poetry, the Greek god of the winds or the action of wind, as in an Aeolian harp like that in various Romantic-era poems (*OED*).
65 Julius Caesar invaded Britain in 55 and 54 BCE, as recorded in his account of the Gallic Wars.
66 Tully, another name for Marcus Tullius Cicero (106–43 BCE), famous Roman orator and rhetorician; Publius Vergilius Maro (70–19 BCE), generally called Virgil, penned the *Aeneid*, the epic depicting Rome's rise as led by Aeneas, refugee from the Trojan War.
67 Boudica, the British Celtic queen who led a revolt against Roman rule
68 North star

But fairest flowers expand but to decay;
The worm is in thy core, thy glories pass away;
Arts, arms and wealth destroy the fruits they bring;
Commerce, like beauty, knows no second spring.
Crime walks thy streets, Fraud earns her unblest bread,
O'er want and woe thy gorgeous robe is spread,
And angel charities in vain oppose:
With grandeur's growth the mass of misery grows.
For see,—to other climes the Genius soars,
He turns from Europe's desolated shores;
And lo, even now, midst mountains wrapt in storm,
On Andes'[69] heights he shrouds his awful form;
On Chimborazo's summits[70] treads sublime,
Measuring in lofty thought the march of Time;
Sudden he calls:— "'Tis now the hour!" he cries,
Spreads his broad hand, and bids the nations rise.
La Plata[71] hears amidst her torrents' roar;
Potosi[72] hears it, as she digs the ore:
Ardent, the Genius fans the noble strife,
And pours through feeble souls a higher life,
Shouts to the mingled tribes from sea to sea,
And swears—Thy world, Columbus, shall be free.

Source text

Barbauld, Anna Laetitia, *Eighteen Hundred and Eleven, A Poem* (London: J. Johnson and Co., 1812).

References

Aikin, Lucy (ed.), 'Memoir', *The Works of Anna Laetitia Barbauld, with a Memoir by Lucy Aikin*, Vol. 1 (London: Longman, Hurst, 1825), v–lxxii.
Birns, Nicholas, '"Thy World, Columbus!": Barbauld and Global Space, 1803, "1811", 1812, 2003', *European Romantic Review* 16.5 (2005), 545–62.
Crocco, Francesco, 'The Colonial Subtext of Anna Laetitia Barbauld's "Eighteen Hundred Eleven"', *The Wordsworth Circle* 41.2 (Spring 2010), 91–4.
Levine, William, 'The Eighteenth-century Jeremiad and Progress-piece Traditions in Anna Barbauld's "Eighteen Hundred and Eleven"', *Women's Writing* 12.2 (2005), 177–86.
Sachs, Jonathan, 'Future! Decline', *Poetics Today* 37.3 (September 2016), 355–68.

---

69 A vast mountain range along the western coast of South America
70 A mountain in Ecuador
71 A city in Argentina
72 A city in Bolivia

Henry Wadsworth Longfellow (1807–82)

From Kavanagh, A Tale *(1849)*

Henry Wadsworth Longfellow was perhaps the most famous and successful American poet of the mid-nineteenth century. Born in Maine (then a part of Massachusetts) to descendants of the *Mayflower* Pilgrims, he attended Bowdoin College at fifteen and became a professor upon his graduation in 1825. In his twenties and thirties he balanced teaching with travelling in Europe, publishing his first book of poetry in 1839. He mounted a foray into fiction with *Kavanagh,* composed in 1847 and published in 1849. Though the novel made little commercial impact, it had a sizeable influence on his peers, and stands as a fine example of local colour fiction in the romantic mode.

Beyond its somewhat conventional romance plot, the principal subject of *Kavanagh* is the fledgling state of American literature, as evinced by the lengthy discussion in Chapter 20, reproduced below. In the age of colonisation, establishing a national literature was the surest way to gain recognition as an imperial power, and in this venture the US was far behind European powers. Longfellow introduces a gently satirical conversation between two characters with contrasting views about the importance of the national characteristics of literature: Churchill, a writer unable to complete his manuscript, is sceptical of the kind of literary American exceptionalism championed by Hathaway, whose own championing of the native virtues of the poet Honeywell is nevertheless untroubled by Honeywell's indebtedness to British romantic models of authorship. Churchill's appeal to 'universal' qualities that transcend the particularity of the national is nevertheless not immune to the material temptations of an expanding literary marketplace.

From Kavanagh, A Tale

Meanwhile, things had gone on very quietly and monotonously in Mr. Churchill's family. Only one event, and that a mysterious one, had disturbed its serenity. It was the sudden disappearance of Lucy, the pretty orphan girl; and as the booted centipede, who had so much excited Mr. Churchill's curiosity, disappeared at the same time, there was little doubt that they had gone away together. But whither gone, and wherefore, remained a mystery.

Mr. Churchill, also, had had his profile, and those of his wife and children, taken, in a very humble style, by Mr. Bantam, whose advertisement he had noticed on his way to school nearly a year before. His own was considered the best, as a work of art. The face was cut out entirely; the collar of the coat velvet; the shirt-collar very high and white; and the top of his head ornamented with a crest of hair turning up in front, though his own turned down, — which slight deviation from nature was explained and justified by the painter as a license allowable in art.

One evening, as he was sitting down to begin for at least the hundredth time the great Romance,—subject of so many resolves and so much remorse, so often determined upon but never begun,—a loud knock at the street-door, which stood wide open, announced a visitor. Unluckily, the study-door was likewise open; and consequently, being in full view, he found it impossible to refuse himself; nor, in fact, would he have done so, had all the doors been shut and bolted,— the art of refusing one's self being at that time but imperfectly understood in Fairmeadow. Accordingly, the visitor was shown in.

He announced himself as Mr. Hathaway.[73] Passing through the village, he could not deny himself the pleasure of calling on Mr. Churchill, whom he knew by his writings in the periodicals, though not personally. He wished, moreover, to secure the cooperation of one already so favorably known to the literary world, in a new Magazine he was about to establish, in order to raise the character of American literature, which, in his opinion, the existing reviews and magazines had entirely failed to accomplish. A daily increasing want of something better was felt by the public; and the time had come for the establishment of such a periodical as he proposed. After explaining in rather a florid and exuberant manner his plan and prospects, he entered more at large into the subject of American literature, which it was his design to foster and patronize.

"I think, Mr. Churchill," said he, "that we want a national literature commensurate with our mountains and rivers,—commensurate with Niagara,[74] and the Alleghanies,[75] and the Great Lakes!"[76]

"Oh!"

"We want a national epic that shall correspond to the size of the country; that shall be to all other epics what Banvard's Panorama of the Mississippi[77] is to all other paintings,—the largest in the world!"

"Ah!"

"We want a national drama in which scope enough shall be given to our gigantic ideas, and to the unparalleled activity and progress of our people!"

"Of course."

"In a word, we want a national literature altogether shaggy and unshorn, that shall shake the earth, like a herd of buffaloes thundering over the prairies!"

"Precisely," interrupted Mr. Churchill; "but excuse me!—are you not confounding things that have no analogy? Great has a very different meaning when applied to a river, and when applied to a literature. Large and shallow may perhaps be applied to both. Literature is rather an image of the spiritual world, than of the physical, is it not? — of the internal, rather than the external. Mountains, lakes, and rivers are, after all, only its scenery and decorations, not its substance and essence. A man will not necessarily be a great poet because he lives near a great mountain. Nor, being a poet, will he necessarily write better poems than another, because he lives nearer Niagara."

---

73 Hathaway is thought to be based on Cornelius Mathews (1817–89), US editor and journalist, and influential member of the Young America movement that advocated political and cultural national autonomy.
74 A series of large waterfalls on the Niagara River between the US and Canada
75 A large portion of the Appalachian range that runs from Pennsylvania through Virginia
76 The Great Lakes of North America
77 John Banvard (1815–91), whose famous panorama of the Mississippi River valley was twelve feet high and nearly half a mile long

"But, Mr. Churchill, you do not certainly mean to deny the influence of scenery on the mind?"

"No, only to deny that it can create genius. At best, it can only develop it. Switzerland has produced no extraordinary poet; nor, as far as I know, have the Andes, or the Himalaya mountains, or the Mountains of the Moon in Africa."[78]

"But, at all events," urged Mr. Hathaway, "let us have our literature national. If it is not national, it is nothing."

"On the contrary, it may be a great deal. Nationality is a good thing to a certain extent, but universality is better. All that is best in the great poets of all countries is not what is national in them, but what is universal. Their roots are in their native soil; but their branches wave in the unpatriotic air, that speaks the same language unto all men, and their leaves shine with the illimitable light that pervades all lands. Let us throw all the windows open; let us admit the light and air on all sides; that we may look towards the four corners of the heavens, and not always in the same direction."

"But you admit nationality to be a good thing?"

"Yes, if not carried too far; still, I confess, it rather limits one's views of truth. I prefer what is natural. Mere nationality is often ridiculous. Every one smiles when he hears the Icelandic proverb, 'Iceland is the best land the sun shines upon.' Let us be natural, and we shall be national enough. Besides, our literature can be strictly national only so far as our character and modes of thought differ from those of other nations. Now, as we are very like the English,— are, in fact, English under a different sky,— I do not see how our literature can be very different from theirs. Westward from hand to hand we pass the lighted torch, but it was lighted at the old domestic fireside of England."

"Then you think our literature is never to be any thing but an imitation of the English?"

"Not at all. It is not an imitation, but, as some one has said, a continuation."

"It seems to me that you take a very narrow view of the subject."

"On the contrary, a very broad one. No literature is complete until the language in which it is written is dead. We may well be proud of our task and of our position. Let us see if we can build in any way worthy of our forefathers."

"But I insist upon originality."

"Yes; but without spasms and convulsions. Authors must not, like Chinese soldiers, expect to win victories by turning somersets[79] in the air."

"Well, really, the prospect from your point of view is not very brilliant. Pray, what do you think of our national literature?"

"Simply, that a national literature is not the growth of a day. Centuries must contribute their dew and sunshine to it. Our own is growing slowly but surely, striking its roots downward, and its branches upward, as is natural; and I do not wish, for the sake of what some people call originality, to invert it, and try to make it grow with its roots in the air. And as for having it so savage and wild as you want it, I have only to say, that all literature, as well as all art, is the result of culture and intellectual refinement."

---

78 A fabled mountain range and the source of the Nile; currently identified as the Rwenzori Mountains in Uganda

79 Also somersault

"Ah! we do not want art and refinement; we want genius, —untutored, wild, original, free."

"But, if this genius is to find any expression, it must employ art; for art is the external expression of our thoughts. Many have genius, but, wanting art, are for ever dumb. The two must go together to form the great poet, painter, or sculptor."

"In that sense, very well."

"I was about to say also that I thought our literature would finally not be wanting in a kind of universality."

"As the blood of all nations is mingling with our own, so will their thoughts and feelings finally mingle in our literature. We shall draw from the Germans tenderness; from the Spaniards, passion; from the French, vivacity, to mingle more and more with our English solid sense. And this will give us universality, so much to be desired."

"If that is your way of thinking," interrupted the visitor, "you will like the work I am now engaged upon."

"What is it?"

"A great national drama, the scene of which is laid in New Mexico. It is entitled Don Serafin, or the Marquis of the Seven Churches. The principal characters are Don Serafin, an old Spanish hidalgo;[80] his daughter Deseada; and Fra Serapion, the Curate. The play opens with Fra Serapion at breakfast; on the table a game-cock, tied by the leg, sharing his master's meal. Then follows a scene at the cock-pit, where the Marquis stakes the remnant of his fortune—his herds and hacienda—on a favorite cock, and loses."

"But what do you know about cock-fighting?" demanded, rather than asked, the astonished and half-laughing school-master.

"I am not very well informed on that subject, and I was going to ask you if you could not recommend some work."

"The only work I am acquainted with," replied Mr. Churchill, "is the Reverend Mr. Pegge's Essay on Cock-fighting among the Ancients;[81] and I hardly see how you could apply that to the Mexicans."

"Why, they are a kind of ancients, you know. I certainly will hunt up the essay you mention, and see what I can do with it."

"And all I know about the matter itself," continued Mr. Churchill, "is, that Mark Antony was a patron of the pit, and that his cocks were always beaten by Caesar's;[82] and that, when Themistocles[83] the Athenian general was marching against the Persians, he halted his army to see a cock-fight, and made a speech to his soldiery, to the effect, that those animals fought not for the gods of their country, nor for the monuments of their ancestors, nor for glory, nor for freedom, nor for their children, but only for the sake of victory. On his return to Athens, he established cock-fights in that capital. But how this is to help you in Mexico I do not see, unless you introduce Santa Anna,[84] and compare him to Caesar and Themistocles."

---

80 A gentleman
81 A reference to Samuel Pegge's 'A Memoir on Cock-fighting' (1775)
82 Mark Antony (83–30 BCE) and Julius Caesar (100–44 BCE), famous Roman politicians
83 An Athenian politician and general (524–459 BCE) who successfully led the invasion of Persia
84 Antonio López de Santa Anna (1794–1876), a prominent Mexican politician and general

"That is it; I will do so. It will give historic interest to the play. I thank you for the suggestion."

"The subject is certainly very original; but it does not strike me as particularly national."

"Prospective, you see!" said Mr. Hathaway, with a penetrating look.

"Ah, yes; I perceive you fish with a heavy sinker,—down, far down in the future, —among posterity, as it were."

"You have seized the idea. Besides, I obviate your objection, by introducing an American circus company from the United States, which enables me to bring horses on the stage and produce great scenic effect."

"That is a bold design. The critics will be out upon you without fail."

"Never fear that. I know the critics root and branch, —out and out, —have summered them and wintered them, — in fact, am one of them myself. Very good fellows are the critics; are they not?"

"O, yes; only they have such a pleasant way of talking down upon authors."

"If they did not talk down upon them, they would show no superiority; and, of course, that would never do."

"Nor is it to be wondered at, that authors are sometimes a little irritable. I often recall the poet in the Spanish fable, whose manuscripts were devoured by mice, till at length he put some corrosive sublimate into his ink, and was never troubled again."

"Why don't you try it yourself?" said Mr. Hathaway, rather sharply.

"O," answered Mr. Churchill, with a smile of humility, "I and my writings are too insignificant. They may gnaw and welcome. I do not like to have poison about, even for such purposes."

"By the way, Mr. Churchill," said the visitor, adroitly changing the subject, "do you know Honeywell?"

"No, I do not. Who is he?"

"Honeywell the poet, I mean."

"No, I never even heard of him. There are so many poets now-a-days!"

"That is very strange indeed! Why, I consider Honeywell one of the finest writers in the country, —quite in the front rank of American authors. He is a real poet, and no mistake. Nature made him with her shirt-sleeves rolled up."

"What has he published?"

"He has not published any thing yet, except in the newspapers. But, this Autumn, he is going to bring out a volume of poems. I could not help having my joke with him about it. I told him he had better print it on cartridge-paper."

"Why so?"

"Why, to make it go off better; don't you understand?"

"O, yes; now that you explain it. Very good."

"Honeywell is going to write for the Magazine; he is to furnish a poem for every number; and as he succeeds equally well in the plaintive and didactic style of Wordsworth,[85] and the more vehement and impassioned style of Byron,[86] I think we shall do very well."

---

85 William Wordsworth (1770–1850), famous English poet
86 George Gordon Byron (1788–1824), famous English poet

"And what do you mean to call the new Magazine?" inquired Mr. Churchill.

"We think of calling it The Niagara."

"Why, that is the name of our fire-engine! Why not call it The Extinguisher?"

"That is also a good name; but I prefer The Niagara, as more national. And I hope, Mr. Churchill, you will let us count upon you. We should like to have an article from your pen for every number."

"Do you mean to pay your contributors?"

"Not the first year, I am sorry to say. But after that, if the work succeeds, we shall pay handsomely. And, of course, it will succeed, for we mean it shall; and we never say fail. There is no such word in our dictionary. Before the year is out, we mean to print fifty thousand copies; and fifty thousand copies will give us, at least, one hundred and fifty thousand readers; and, with such an audience, any author might be satisfied."

He had touched at length the right strings in Mr. Churchill's bosom; and they vibrated to the touch with pleasant harmonies. Literary vanity! — literary ambition! The editor perceived it; and so cunningly did he play upon these chords, that, before he departed, Mr. Churchill had promised to write for him a series of papers on Obscure Martyrs, — a kind of tragic history of the unrecorded and life-long sufferings of women, which hitherto had found no historian, save now and then a novelist.

Notwithstanding the certainty of success, — notwithstanding the fifty thousand subscribers and the one hundred and fifty thousand readers, — the Magazine never went into operation. Still the dream was enough to occupy Mr. Churchill's thoughts, and to withdraw them entirely from his Romance for many weeks together.

Source text

Longfellow, Henry Wadsworth, *Kavanagh, A Tale* (Boston: Ticknor, Reed, and Fields, 1849).

References

Eckel, Leslie, *Atlantic Citizens: Nineteenth-Century American Writers at Work in the World* (Edinburgh: Edinburgh University Press, 2013).

Irmscher, Christoph and Robert Arbour (eds), *Reconsidering Longfellow* (Madison, WI: Fairleigh Dickinson University Press, 2014).

Figure 6.2 'Closing of the Exhibition: The Amazon Putting on her Bonnet
and Shawl', *Punch* 21 (11 October 1851), 162.
Courtesy Mary Couts Burnett Library, TCU.

'Closing of the Exhibition': Bloomers in the Crystal Palace

The Bloomer costume – a short skirt worn over voluminous trousers – was
a style of reformed dress named after American Amelia Bloomer. The new
fashion caused quite a stir, including in the press, when Bloomer and others
first adopted the ankle-length trousers in the US in 1850. After a number of
American women visiting Britain's Great Exhibition of 1851 appeared there
in Bloomers, the *London Times* and other UK publications weighed in with

critique. In this image originally appearing as a full page within *Punch*, an Exhibition statue of an Amazon, the legendary female warrior, dons more typical gendered attire – a bonnet, shawl and long dress. The Amazon is speaking to Hiram Powers's *Greek Slave* statue, widely considered the high-light of the US exhibit. Shown here as wearing a Bloomer costume, this image of the statue marks the style as distinctly American. *Punch* simultaneously highlights the irony that the Americans' most significant contribution to the Great Exhibition was a statue of an enslaved person, despite the lofty rhetoric of liberty associated with both the United States and, in the case of the Bloomer costume, women's rights. Echoing concern over the propri-ety of women abandoning appropriate attire, the illustration also signals the irony of appropriating slavery onto an aesthetically crafted white female nude body. The original *Punch* cartoon carries this comment in addition to the main caption, thereby suggesting gendered solidarity between the two female figures: 'Amazon (to Greek Slave). "Well, My Dear! I'm very glad it's over. It's very hard work keeping in one attitude for five months together, isn't it?"'.

Sofia Prado Huggins

W. G. Allen (1820–88)

'Placido' (1852)

William Gustavus Allen was a self-described 'quadroon', born in Virginia in 1820 to a white father and free mixed-race mother. His informal schooling culminated with admission to Oneida College, the first in the US to accept African American students, from which he graduated in 1844. Thereafter he moved to Troy, New York, and took up the abolitionist cause with a series of lectures and his newspaper, *National Watchman*. Allen became the target of mob violence for his engagement to the white woman Mary King, which caused the couple to marry in secret and self-exile to England in 1853. There he made a living as an orator and lecturer, earning fame as an eloquent and erudite speaker and considered a credit to his race. He continued to write sympathetic articles on the African diaspora until his death in 1888.

The subject of his essay, 'Placido', is the Afro-Cuban poet Gabriel de la Concepción Valdés, born in 1809 in Havana. After intermittent educa-tion and itinerant career as a labourer Valdés began writing poetry under the pseudonym 'Placido', earning little money though gaining popularity among the Cuban people. His popular cries for liberty also drew the atten-tion of the ruling Spanish authorities; in 1844 Placido was swept up in a targeted action against the 'Ladder Conspiracy', which allegedly sought to foment a slave revolt and abolish slavery in Cuba. Without evidence Placido was subjected to a show trial and sentenced to death, executed via firing squad. He is considered Cuba's foremost Romantic poet, as well as a martyr for his actions.

The following essay was written by Allen as part of the anthology *Autographs for Freedom* (1853), a collection of anti-slavery testimonies by various authors intended to raise money for the abolitionist cause. Its range of reference is indicative of Allen's desire to place Placido within a cosmopolitan culture of letters, even as it celebrates his credentials as a nationalist poet and patriot.

'Placido'

The true wealth and glory of a nation consist not in its gold dust, nor in its commerce, nor in the grandeur of its palaces, nor yet in the magnificence of its cities,—but in the intellectual and moral energy of its people. Egypt is more glorious because of her carrying into Greece the blessings of civilization, than because of her pyramids, however wondrous, her lakes and labyrinths, however stupendous, or her Thebes,[87] though every square marked a palace, or every alley a dome. Who hears of the moneyed men of Athens, of Rome? And who does *not* hear of Socrates,[88] of Plato,[89] of Demosthenes,[90] of Virgil,[91] of Cicero?[92] Are you in converse with him of the "Sea-girt Isle,"[93] and would touch the chord that vibrates most readily in his heart?—then talk to him of Shakespeare,[94] of Milton,[95] of Cowper,[96] of Bacon,[97] of Newton;[98] of Burns,[99] of Scott.[100] To the intelligent son of the "Emerald Isle,"[101] talk of Curran,[102] of Emmett,[103] of O'Connell.[104]

Great men are a nation's vitality. Nations pass away,—great men, never. Great men are not unfrequently buried in dungeons or in obscurity; but they work out great thoughts for all time, nevertheless. Did not Bunyan[105] work out a great thought all-vital and vitalizing, when he lay twelve years in Bedford jail, weaving his tagged lace, and writing his Pilgrim's Progress? The greatest man in all America is now in

---

87 Ancient Egyptian city on the Nile River
88 Socrates (*c*.470–399 BCE), Greek philosopher
89 Plato (c. 429/23–348/7 BCE), Greek philosopher
90 Demosthenes (384–22 BCE), Greek politician and orator
91 Virgil (70–19 BCE), Roman poet
92 Cicero (106–43 BCE) Roman statesman and orator
93 England
94 William Shakespeare (1564–1616), English playwright
95 John Milton (1608–74), English poet
96 William Cowper (1731–1800), English poet and hymn-writer
97 Francis Bacon (1561–1626), English philosopher and statesman
98 Isaac Newton (1643–1727), English mathematician and scientist
99 Robert Burns (1759–96), Scottish poet
100 Walter Scott (1771–1832), Scottish novelist
101 Ireland
102 John Philpot Curran (1750–1817), Irish Protestant politician and orator
103 Robert Emmet (1778–1803), Irish republican and orator
104 Daniel O'Connell (1775–1847), Irish Catholic political leader
105 John Bunyan (1628–88), author of *The Pilgrim's Progress* (1678)

obscurity. It is he who is *"the Lord of his own soul,"*[106] on whose brow wisdom has marked her supremacy, and who, in his sphere, moves

"Stilly as a star, on his eternal way."[107]

A great writer hath said, "Nature is stingy of her great men." I do not believe it. God doeth all his work fitly and well; how, therefore, could he give us great men, not plentifully, but stingily? The truth is, there are great men, and they are plentiful,—plentiful for the times, I mean,—but we do not see them, because we will not come into the sun-light of truth and rectitude where, and where only, dwelleth greatness.

Placido was a great man. He was a great poet besides. He was a patriot, also,—how could he be otherwise? Are not all poets patriots?

"Adios Mundo,"[108] cried he, as with tear-bedimmed eyes he looked up into the blue heavens above him, and upon the green earth beneath him; and upon the portals of the universe read wisdom, majesty, and power. Was there no poetry in this outburst of a full heart, and in this looking upward to heaven? "Adios Mundo," cried he, as now beholding, for the last time, the home of his love,—he bared his bosom to the death-shot of the soldiers.

Great was Placido in life,—he was greater still in death. His was the faith which fastens itself upon the EVERLASTING I AM.

Call you that greatness which Pizarro[109] achieved when, seizing a sword and drawing a line upon the sand from east to west, he himself facing south, he said to his band of pirates:—*"Friends, comrades, on that side are toil, hunger, nakedness, the drenching storm, desertion, and death; on this side, ease and pleasure. There lies Peru with its richness; here Panama with its poverty. Choose, each man what best becomes a brave Castillian. For my part I go to the south;"*—suiting the action to the word? So do I,—but look ye, this is merely the greatness of overwhelming energy and concentrated purpose, not illuminated by a single ray of light from the Divine. See here, how Placido dwarfeth Pizarro when he thus prayeth,

"God of unbounded love, and power eternal!
To Thee I turn in darkness and despair;
Stretch forth Thine arm, and from the brow infernal
Of calumny the veil of justice tear!

O, King of kings!—my father's God!—who only
Art strong to save, by whom is all controlled,—
Who giv'st the sea its waves, the dark and lonely
Abyss of heaven its light, the North its cold,
The air its currents, the warm sun its beams,
Life to the flowers, and motion to the streams:

All things obey Thee; dying or reviving
As thou commandest; all, apart from Thee,
From Thee alone their life and power deriving,
Sink and are lost in vast eternity!

---

106 From *The Last Man* (1826) by Mary Wollstonecraft Shelley: 'Was there indeed anarchy in the sublime universe of Adrian's thoughts, did madness scatter the well-appointed legions, and was he no longer the lord of his own soul?'
107 Paraphrase of lines from Henry Ellison's sonnet, 'Self-greatness': 'He, in his sphere, moves stilly, like a star / Which makes all light about it, 'bove the jar / Of earth's vain cares, on his eternal way.'
108 'Goodbye, world'
109 Francisco Pizarro González (1478–1541), Spanish conquistador of Peru

O, merciful God! I cannot shun Thy presence,
    For through its veil of flesh, Thy piercing eye
Looketh upon my spirit's unsoiled essence,
    As through the pure transparence of the sky;
Let not the oppressor clap his bloody hands,
    As o'er my prostrate innocence he stands.

But if, alas, it seemeth good to Thee
    That I should perish as the guilty dies,
Still, fully in me, Thy will be done, O God!" [110]

Placido had a symmetrically developed character. All great men have this. His intellectual and moral nature blended harmoniously as
"Kindred elements into one." [111]
An ancient philosopher hath said that the passions and the soul are placed in the same body, so that the passions might have ready opportunity to persuade the soul to become subservient to their purpose. A terrible conflict. And yet through it Placido passed triumphantly.

Placido was born a slave on the island of Cuba, on the plantation of Don Terribio De Castro. The year of his birth I am unable to give, but it must have been somewhere between the years 1790 and 1800. He was of African origin. But little is known of his earliest days save that he was of gentle demeanor, and wore an aspect which, though mild, indicated the working of great thoughts within. He was allowed some little advantage of education in his youth, and he evinced great poetic genius. The prayer just quoted was composed by him while he lay in prison, and repeated on his way from his dungeon to his place of execution.

The Heraldo, a leading journal of Havana, thus spoke of him after his arrest:—

"Placido is a celebrated poet,—a man of great genius, but too wild and ambitious. His object was to subdue Cuba, and make himself the chief."

The following lines, also, were found inscribed upon the walls of his dungeon. They were written on the day previous to his execution.

"O Liberty! I wait for thee,
To break this chain, and dungeon bar;
    I hear thy voice calling me,
Deep in the frozen North, afar,
With voice like God's, and vision like a star.

Long cradled in the mountain wind,
Thy mates, the eagle and the storm:
    Arise; and from thy brow unbind
The wreath that gives its starry form,
And smite the strength, that would thy strength deform.
Yet Liberty! thy dawning light,

---

110 From Placido's 'Prayer of Placido' (1844)
111 From Allen's own *The American Prejudice Against Color* (1853). Here he refers to a mob which sought to kill him for attempting to marry a 'white' woman; in this case, he wrote 'the "respectable" and the base were commingled, like Kindred elements into one'.

Obscured by dungeon bars, shall cast
A splendor on the breaking night,
And tyrants, flying thick and fast,
Shall tremble at thy gaze, and stand aghast."

In poetic feeling, patriotic spirit, living faith, and, withal in literary beauty, these lines are not surpassed; and they cannot fail to rank Placido not only with the great-hearted, but with the gifted men of the earth. A tribute to his genius is recorded in the fact, that he was ransomed from slavery by the contributions of slave-holders of Cuba.

Placido was executed on the 7th of July, 1844. On the first fire of the soldiers, no ball entered his heart. He looked up, but with no spirit of revenge, no aspect of defiance,—only sat upon his countenance the desire to pass at once into the region where no death is.

"Pity me," said he, "and fire here,"—putting his hand upon his heart. Two balls then entered his body, and Placido fell.

As Wordsworth[112] said of Toussaint,[113] so may it be said of Placido,—

"Thou hast left behind thee
Powers that will work for thee; air, earth, and skies.
There's not a breathing of the common wind
That will forget thee; thou hast great allies,
Thy friends are exultations, agonies,
And love, and man's unconquerable mind."[114]

The charge against Placido was, that he was at the head of a conspiracy to overthrow slavery in his native island. Blessings on thee, Placido! Nor didst thou fail of thy mission. Did the martyrs, stake-bound, fail of theirs? As the Lord liveth, Cuba shall yet be free.

That Placido was at the head of this conspiracy there is not a doubt; but what his plans in detail were, I know not; the means of acquiring them are not within my reach. Nevertheless, from the treatment throughout of the Cuban authorities towards Placido, we may safely conclude that Placido's plan in detail evinced no lack of ability to originate and execute, nor of that sagacity which should mark a revolutionary leader. Placido hated slavery with a hatred intensified by the remembrance of wrongs which a loving and loved mother had borne. The iron, too, had entered into his own soul; and he had been a daily witness of scenes such as torment itself could scarcely equal, nor the pit itself outdo. Call you this extravagance? You will not,—should you but study a single chapter in the history of Cuban slavery.

Do you honor Kossuth?[115]—then forget not him who is worthy to stand side by side with Hungary's illustrious son.

What may be the destiny of Cuba in the future near at hand, I will not venture to predict. What may be her *ultimate* destiny is written in the fact that,—"God hath

---

112 William Wordsworth (1770–1850), English poet
113 Toussaint L'Ouverture (1743–1803), the leader of the successful Haitian Revolution (1791–1804), which freed previously enslaved Haitian Africans
114 From Wordsworth's 'To Toussaint L'Ouverture' (1802)
115 Lajos Kossuth (1802–94), a Hungarian statesman and revolutionary

no attribute which, in a contest between the oppressed and the oppressor, can take sides with the latter."[116]

This sketch, though hastily written, and eager in detail as it must necessarily be, will show, at least, by the quotations of poetry introduced, that God hath not given to one race alone, all intellectual and moral greatness.

Source text

Allen, W. G., *Autographs for Freedom* (Boston: John P. Jewett and Company, 1853).

References

Fischer, Sybille, *Modernity Disavowed: Haiti and the Cultures of Slavery in the Age of Revolution* (Durham, NC: Duke University Press, 2004).
Stimson, Frederick S., *Cuba's Romantic Poet: The Story of Plácido* (Chapel Hill, NC: University of North Carolina Press, 1964).

Ralph Waldo Emerson (1803–82)

'Result' *from* English Traits *(1856)*

Ralph Waldo Emerson, New England lecturer, poet and essayist, was arguably the foremost public intellectual in the US in the nineteenth century. Following a brief period as a Unitarian minister, he gave up the pulpit to devote himself to a career as a man of letters. Along with Henry David Thoreau, Margaret Fuller, Theodore Parker and others, Emerson was central to the emergence and theorisation of Transcendentalism, a philosophy of self-reliance and spirituality that advocated for the non-conformist individual. By the early 1840s his work was being read and reviewed on both sides of the Atlantic, and he had an important early advocate in Thomas Carlyle, who wrote a 'Preface' to the first British edition of Emerson's *Essays, First Series* (1841). Although regarded as a key figure in the declaration of an independent US literary tradition, Emerson's cosmopolitanism and transatlanticism were also characteristic features from his earliest writings; his reading in major European – and indeed Asian – writers was wide-ranging, establishing a commitment to comparative literary study. If essays like 'Self-Reliance' (1841) and 'The American Scholar' (1837) articulated a vision of

---

116 Paraphrase of Thomas Jefferson's *Notes on the State of Virginia* (1781):

> Indeed I tremble for my country when I reflect that God is just: that his justice cannot sleep for ever: that considering numbers, nature and natural means only, a revolution of the wheel of fortune, an exchange of situation is among possible events: that it may become probable by supernatural interference! The almighty has no attribute which can take side with us in such a contest.

US autonomy, Emerson's engagement with Europe, and Great Britain in particular, found its most extensive formulation in *English Traits*, an account of his second trip to England in 1847–8.

English Traits' first incarnation was as a series of lectures first delivered in 1850, which were then worked up into book form. The chapters cover a range of topics, some describing aspects of English landscape and topography, others focusing on elements of English cultural and political life. Throughout, Emerson's intention is to evaluate both the past greatness of British (read, English) national culture and to judge its viability as a future model. Leslie Eckel has noted that the book demonstrates an acute ambivalence to the very idea of nationality itself; it 'works to undermine its ostensibly national agenda by exposing the "narrowness" and "limited" scope of English nationality, and indeed, of all expressions of patriotic feeling' (105). England may be 'the best of actual nations', but its distance from an 'ideal' incarnation is marked. Both the Old World and the New fail to manifest versions of nationality that, for Emerson, have anything to recommend them. Indeed the category of the 'nation' itself, as a container of identity, may no longer suffice.

'Result', *from* English Traits

England is the best of actual nations. It is no ideal framework, it is an old pile built in different ages, with repairs, additions and makeshifts; but you see the poor best you have got. London is the epitome of our times, and the Rome of to-day. Broad-fronted, broad-bottomed Teutons,[117] they stand in solid phalanx[118] four-square to the points of compass; they constitute the modern world, they have earned their vantage ground and held it through ages of adverse possession. They are well marked and differing from other leading races. England is tender-hearted. Rome was not. England is not so public in its bias; private life is its place of honor. Truth in private life, untruth in public, marks these home-loving men. Their political conduct is not decided by general views, but by internal intrigues and personal and family interest. They cannot readily see beyond England. The history of Rome and Greece, when written by their scholars, degenerates into English party pamphlets. They cannot see beyond England, nor in England can they transcend the interests of the governing classes. "English principles" mean a primary regard to the interests of property. England, Scotland and Ireland combine to check the colonies. England and Scotland combine to check Irish manufactures and trade. England rallies at home to check Scotland. In England, the strong classes check the weaker. In the home population of near thirty millions, there are but one million voters. The Church punishes dissent, punishes education. Down to a late day, marriages performed by

---

117 A synonym for Anglo-Saxon, meaning white descendants of Britons and Germans
118 A 'line or array of battle' (*OED*) drawn into a square facing in all directions

dissenters[119] were illegal. A bitter class-legislation gives power to those who are rich enough to buy a law. The game-laws are a proverb of oppression.[120] Pauperism incrusts and clogs the state, and in hard times becomes hideous. In bad seasons, the porridge was diluted. Multitudes lived miserably by shell-fish and sea-ware. In cities, the children are trained to beg, until they shall be old enough to rob. Men and women were convicted of poisoning scores of children for burial-fees.[121] In Irish districts, men deteriorated in size and shape, the nose sunk, the gums were exposed, with diminished brain and brutal form. During the Australian emigration, multitudes were rejected by the commissioners as being too emaciated for useful colonists. During the Russian war, few of those that offered as recruits were found up to the medical standard, though it had been reduced.[122]

The foreign policy of England, though ambitious and lavish of money, has not often been generous or just. It has a principal regard to the interest of trade, checked however by the aristocratic bias of the ambassador, which usually puts him in sympathy with the continental Courts. It sanctioned the partition of Poland, it betrayed Genoa, Sicily, Parga, Greece, Turkey, Rome and Hungary.

Some public regards they have. They have abolished slavery in the West Indies, and put an end to human sacrifices in the East.[123] At home they have a certain statute hospitality. England keeps open doors, as a trading country must, to all nations. It is one of their fixed ideas, and wrathfully supported by their laws in unbroken sequence for a thousand years. In *Magna Charta*[124] it was ordained that all "merchants shall have safe and secure conduct to go out and come into England, and to stay there, and to pass as well by land as by water, to buy and sell by the ancient allowed customs, without any evil toll, except in time of war, or when they shall be of any nation at war with us." It is a statute and obliged hospitality and peremptorily maintained. But this shop-rule had one magnificent effect. It extends its cold unalterable courtesy to political exiles of every opinion, and is a fact which might give additional light to that portion of the planet seen from the farthest star. But this perfunctory hospitality puts no sweetness into their unaccommodating manners, no check on that puissant[125] nationality which makes their existence incompatible with all that is not English.

What we must say about a nation is a superficial dealing with symptoms. We cannot go deep enough into the biography of the spirit who never throws himself entire into one hero, but delegates his energy in parts or spasms to vicious and defective individuals. But the wealth of the source is seen in the plenitude of English nature. What variety of power and talent; what facility and plenteousness of knighthood, lordship, ladyship, royalty, loyalty; what a proud chivalry is indicated in "Collins's Peerage,"[126] through eight hundred years! What dignity resting on what reality and

---

119 Members of Protestant congregations other than the Anglican Church
120 Laws 'for the preservation or protection of game' (*OED*), which prevented hunting of game on private property, thus privileging landowners and hereditary estates over the hungry
121 Burial insurance covered burial costs or fees
122 The Crimean War (1853–6)
123 Slavery in the British empire was abolished in 1833. 'Human sacrifice' likely refers to *sati* (suttee), or widow burning after a husband's death; Britain often referenced this by no means universal custom as evidence of benefits conferred on India by British control.
124 The Magna Carta Libertatum, a royal charter of rights, was signed by King John in 1215.
125 Powerful
126 Arthur Collins's *The Peerage of England*, first published in 1709 and frequently updated

stoutness! What courage in war, what sinew in labor, what cunning workmen, what inventors and engineers, what seamen and pilots, what clerks and scholars! No one man and no few men can represent them. It is a people of myriad personalities. Their many-headedness is owing to the advantageous position of the middle class, who are always the source of letters and science. Hence the vast plenty of their æsthetic production. As they are many-headed, so they are many-nationed: their colonization annexes archipelagoes and continents, and their speech seems destined to be the universal language of men. I have noted the reserve of power in the English temperament. In the island, they never let out all the length of all the reins, there is no Berserkir rage,[127] no abandonment or ecstasy of will or intellect, like that of the Arabs in the time of Mahomet,[128] or like that which intoxicated France in 1789.[129] But who would see the uncoiling of that tremendous spring, the explosion of their well-husbanded forces, must follow the swarms which pouring now for two hundred years from the British islands, have sailed and rode and traded and planted through all climates, mainly following the belt of empire, the temperate zones, carrying the Saxon seed, with its instinct for liberty and law, for arts and for thought,— acquiring under some skies a more electric energy than the native air allows,— to the conquest of the globe. Their colonial policy, obeying the necessities of a vast empire, has become liberal. Canada and Australia have been contented with substantial independence. They are expiating the wrongs of India by benefits; first, in works for the irrigation of the peninsula, and roads, and telegraphs; and secondly, in the instruction of the people, to qualify them for self-government, when the British power shall be finally called home.

Their mind is in a state of arrested development,— a divine cripple like Vulcan;[130] a blind *savant* like Huber[131] and Sanderson.[132] They do not occupy themselves on matters of general and lasting import, but on a corporeal[133] civilization, on goods that perish in the using. But they read with good intent, and what they learn they incarnate. The English mind turns every abstraction it can receive into a portable utensil, or a working institution. Such is their tenacity and such their practical turn, that they hold all they gain. Hence we say that only the English race can be trusted with freedom,— freedom which is double-edged and dangerous to any but the wise and robust. The English designate the kingdoms emulous[134] of free institutions, as the sentimental nations. Their culture is not an outside varnish, but is thorough and secular in families and the race. They are oppressive with their temperament, and all the more that they are refined. I have sometimes seen them walk with my countrymen when I was forced to allow them every advantage, and their companions seemed bags of bones.

There is cramp limitation in their habit of thought, sleepy routine, and a tortoise's instinct to hold hard to the ground with his claws, lest he should be thrown on his back. There is a drag of inertia which resists reform in every shape; — law-reform,

---

127 'A wild Norse warrior of great strength and ferocious courage, who fought on the battle-field with a frenzied fury known as the "berserker rage"' (*OED*)
128 An alternative name for the founding prophet of Islam, Mohammed
129 Outbreak of the French Revolution
130 The Roman god of fire Vulcan, derived from the Greek god Haephestus, expelled from Olympus after he was born lame
131 François Huber (1750–1830), pioneering Swiss entomologist
132 Nicholas Sanderson (1682–1739), English scientist and mathematician
133 Bodily or material
134 Imitative

army-reform, extension of suffrage, Jewish franchise, Catholic emancipation,— the abolition of slavery, of impressment, penal code and entails.[135] They praise this drag, under the formula that it is the excellence of the British constitution that no law can anticipate the public opinion. These poor tortoises must hold hard, for they feel no wings sprouting at their shoulders. Yet somewhat divine warms at their heart and waits a happier hour. It hides in their sturdy will. "Will," said the old philosophy, "is the measure of power," and personality is the token of this race. *Quid vult valde vult.* What they do they do with a will.[136] You cannot account for their success by their Christianity, commerce, charter, common law, Parliament, or letters, but by the contumacious[137] sharptongued energy of English *naturel*,[138] with a poise impossible to disturb, which makes all these its instruments. They are slow and reticent, and are like a dull good horse which lets every nag pass him, but with whip and spur will run down every racer in the field. They are right in their feeling, though wrong in their speculation.

The feudal system survives in the steep inequality of property and privilege, in the limited franchise, in the social barriers which confine patronage and promotion to a caste, and still more in the submissive ideas pervading these people. The fagging of the schools[139] is repeated in the social classes. An Englishman shows no mercy to those below him in the social scale, as he looks for none from those above him; any forbearance from his superiors surprises him, and they suffer in his good opinion. But the feudal system can be seen with less pain on large historical grounds. It was pleaded in mitigation of the rotten borough,[140] that it worked well, that substantial justice was done. Fox, Burke, Pitt, Erskine, Wilberforce, Sheridan, Romilly, or whatever national man, were by this means sent to Parliament, when their return by large constituencies would have been doubtful.[141] So now we say that the right measures of England are the men it bred; that it has yielded more able men in five hundred years than any other nation; and, though we must not play Providence

---

135 The following dates indicate English reforms: 1829: Catholic emancipation enabling Catholics' election to Parliament; 1832: first reform bill widening the franchise and Parliamentary representation of urban cities; 1833: abolition of slavery in British territories. Only two years after *English Traits* appeared did Jews win the right to sit in Parliament through the 1858 Jews Relief Act.

136 Emerson translates the Latin in his next sentence. The quote is usually traced to Cicero's *Letters to Atticus*.

137 'Stubbornly perverse, insubordinate, rebellious' (*OED*)

138 'Innate character or disposition' (*OED*)

139 A traditional practice in British public schools in which younger boys were expected to act as personal servants to older boys

140 Parliamentary constituencies, often depopulated, still sent a member to Parliament. In effect, these seats were a matter of landowners' patronage and privilege.

141 All those who Emerson mentions were famous MPs: Charles James Fox (1749–1806), who supported American patriots; Edmund Burke (1729–97), who opposed the French Revolution; William Pitt, the Younger (1759–1806), Prime Minister for two terms; Erskine May (1815–86), constitutional theorist and Clerk of the House of Commons; William Wilberforce (1759–1833), who spearheaded the passage of the 1833 abolition of slavery; Richard Brinsley Sheridan (1751–1816), a successful playwright as well as MP; and Samuel Romilly (1757–1818), who worked to mitigate the severity of criminal punishment.

and balance the chances of producing ten great men against the comfort of ten thousand mean men, yet retrospectively, we may strike the balance and prefer one Alfred, one Shakspeare, one Milton, one Sidney, one Raleigh, one Wellington, to a million foolish democrats.[142]

The American system is more democratic, more humane; yet the American people do not yield better or more able men, or more inventions or books or benefits, than the English. Congress is not wiser or better than Parliament. France has abolished its suffocating old *régime*, but is not recently marked by any more wisdom or virtue.

The power of performance has not been exceeded,—the creation of value. The English have given importance to individuals, a principal end and fruit of every society. Every man is allowed and encouraged to be what he is, and is guarded in the indulgence of his whim. "Magna Charta," said Rushworth, "is such a fellow that he will have no sovereign."[143] By this general activity and by this sacredness of individuals, they have in seven hundred years evolved the principles of freedom. It is the land of patriots, martyrs, sages and bards, and if the ocean out of which it emerged should wash it away, it will be remembered as an island famous for immortal laws, for the announcements of original right which make the stone tables of liberty.

Source text

Emerson, Ralph Waldo, *English Traits* (Boston: Phillips, Sampson, and Company, 1856).

References

Belich, James, *Replenishing the Earth: The Settler Revolution and the Rise of the Anglo-world* (Oxford: Oxford University Press, 2009).

Eckel, Leslie, *Atlantic Citizens: Nineteenth-Century American Writers at Work in the World* (Edinburgh: Edinburgh University Press, 2013).

Knobel, Dale T., '"Celtic Exodus": The Famine Irish, Ethnic Stereotypes, and the Cultivation of American Racial Nationalism', in Margaret M. Mulrooney (ed.), *Fleeing the Famine: North America and Irish Refugees 1845–1851* (Westport, CT: Praeger, 2003), 79–96.

Taylor, Andrew, '"Mixture Is a Secret of the English Island": Transatlantic Emerson and the Location of the Intellectual', *Atlantic Studies* 1.2 (2004), 158–77.

---

142 Alfred the Great (849–99), who protected England from invading Danes and promoted education; William Shakespeare (1564–1616), English playwright; John Milton (1608–74), author of *Paradise Lost*; Sir Philip Sidney (1554–86), Elizabethan poet, statesman and soldier; Sir Walter Raleigh (1554–1618), explorer, writer and favourite of Queen Elizabeth I; Arthur Wellesley, Duke of Wellington (1769–1852), commander of the British Army who defeated Napoleon at Waterloo (1815) before becoming a British statesman and prime minister (1828–30).

143 John Rushworth (c.1612–90) documented significant events leading up to the English Civil War (1640–60) and afterward published *Historical Collections*.

Elizabeth Barrett Browning (1806–61)

'A Curse for a Nation' (1856)

Elizabeth Barrett Browning's 'A Curse for a Nation' reverses the convention of the Recording Angel, for here the Angel delegates the task of recording to the woman poet instead. The result is a transatlantic poem in a triple sense. It is written by an Englishwoman who cried out against child labour in mines and factories when she lived in England, who identifies with her adopted homeland in Italy and with Italian resistance to an oppressive Austrian empire, and who, in 'A Curse for a Nation', records and sends an Angel's curse 'over the western sea' to slave-holding America, where the poem appeared in the 1856 issue of the Boston National Anti-slavery Bazaar journal *Liberty Bell*. Within the poem's dramatic scene, the woman poet expresses love for America but is appointed to write out the Angel's curse on the US in general and specifically on its white privilege exercised to exploit and harm the Black bodies of the enslaved (who are invoked in the image of bloodhounds, which were used to hunt fugitive slaves). The primary sin of slavery, according to the Angel, spills over into false national pride and moral blindness in daily life. The woman poet's tears will act as a salve, 'very salt and bitter and good', on America's moral wounds.

This is a more direct attack on slavery in the US than Barrett Browning's 1848 *Liberty Bell* poem 'Runaway Slave at Pilgrim's Point' (see AA). Yet when, according to Stone and Taylor, 'the poem was reprinted as the concluding work in *Poems before Congress* (1860) . . . its new context in a volume bitterly critical of England's non-intervention in the Italian liberation struggle led some English reviewers to interpret it as a curse directed not at America, but at their own country' (279–80).

'A Curse for a Nation'

PROLOGUE.

I heard an angel speak last night,
    And he said, "Write!
Write a nation's curse for me,
And send it over the western sea."

I faltered, taking up the word—
    "Not so, my lord!
If curses must be, choose another
To send thy curse against my brother.

"For I am bound by gratitude,
    In love and blood,

To brothers of mine across the sea,
Who have stretched out kindly hands to me."

"Therefore," the voice said, "shalt thou write
        My curse to-night!
From the summits of love a curse is driven,
As lightning from the tops of heaven."

"Not so!" I answered. "Evermore
        My heart is sore
For my own land's sins! for the little feet
Of children bleeding along the street.

"For parked-up honours, that gainsay
        The right of way!
For almsgiving through a door that is
Not open enough for two friends to kiss.

"For an oligarchic parliament,
        And classes rent.[144]
What curse to another land assign,
When heavy-souled for the sins of mine?"

"Therefore," the voice said, "shalt thou write
        My curse to-night!
Because thou hast strength to see and hate
An ill thing done within thy gate."

"Not so!" I answered once again—
        "To curse, choose men;
For I, a woman, have only known
How the heart melts and the tears run down."

"Therefore," the voice said, "shalt thou write
        My curse to-night!
There are women who weep and curse, I say,
(And no one marvels) night and day.

"And thou shalt take their part to-night—
        Weep and write!
A curse from the depths of womanhood,
Is very salt, and bitter, and good."

So thus I wrote, and mourned indeed,
        What all may read;
And thus, as was enjoined on me,
I send it over the western sea.

---

144 Torn asunder

The Curse.

I.

Because ye have broken your own chain
    With the strain
Of brave men climbing a nation's height,[145]
Yet thence bear down with chain and thong
On the souls of others,—for this wrong
    This is the curse—write!

Because yourselves are standing straight
    In the state
Of Freedom's foremost acolyte,
Yet keep calm footing all the time
On writhing bondslaves,—for this crime
    This is the curse—write!

Because ye prosper in God's name,
    With a claim
To honour in the whole world's sight,
Yet do the fiend's work perfectly
On babes and women—for this lie
    This is the curse—write!

II.

Ye shall watch while kings conspire
Round the people's smouldering fire,
    And, warm for your part,
Shall never dare—O shame!
To utter the thought into flame
    Which burns at your heart.
        This is the curse—write!

Ye shall watch while nations strive
With the bloodhounds—die or survive,—
    Drop faint from their jaws,
Or throttle them backward to death,
And only under your breath
    Shall ye bless the cause.
        This is the curse—write!

Ye shall watch while strong men draw
The nets of feudal law
    To strangle the weak;
Ye shall count the sin for a sin,
But your soul shall be sadder within
    Than the word which ye speak.
        This is the curse—write!

---

145 A reference to the American Revolution

Ye shall watch while rich men dine,
And poor men hunger and pine
    For one crust in seven;
But shall quail from the signs which present
God's judgment as imminent
    To make it all even.
       This is the curse—write!

When good men are praying erect
That Christ may avenge his elect
    And deliver the earth,
The prayer in your ears, said low,
Shall sound like the tramp of a foe
    That's driving you forth.
       This is the curse—write!

When wise men give you their praise,
They shall pause in the heat of the phrase,
    And sicken afar;
When ye boast your own charters kept true,
Ye shall blush!—for the thing which ye do
    Derides what ye are.
       This is the curse—write!

When fools write taunts on your gate,
Your scorn ye shall somewhat abate,
    As ye look o'er the wall;
For your conscience, tradition, and name
Strike back with a deadlier blame
    Than the worst of them all.
       This is the curse—write!

Go! while ill deeds shall be done,
Plant on your flag in the sun
    Beside the ill-doers;
And shrink from clenching the curse
Of the witnessing universe,
    With a curse of yours!
       This is the curse—write!

           Florence, Italy, 1854.

Source text

Browning, Elizabeth Barrett, 'A Curse for a Nation', *The Liberty Bell: By Friends of Freedom* (Boston: National Anti-Slavery Bazaar, 1856), 1–9.

References

Miller, John MacNeill, 'Slavish Poses: Elizabeth Barrett Browning and the Aesthetics of Abolition', *Victorian Poetry* 52.4 (2014), 637–59.

Stone, Marjorie and Beverly Taylor (eds), *Elizabeth Barrett Browning: Selected Poems* (Peterborough, Ont.: Broadview Press, 2009).

Emma Lazarus (1849–87)

'The New Colossus' (1883)

Born in New York City to a wealthy Jewish family, Emma Lazarus was privately educated and began writing poetry in her youth. Her *Poems and Translations* appeared in 1867, followed by *Admetus and Other Poems* in 1871; in all, more than fifty of her poems were published during her lifetime. In response to widescale Russian pogroms during the 1880s Lazarus became an activist and aid-worker for the resettlement of Jewish refugees in the US, a cause she held dearly until her death in 1887.

Lazarus composed 'The New Colossus' in 1883 as a donation to a fundraising campaign for the Statue of Liberty. Although the poem was read during the fundraising exhibit and achieved wide publication in *New York World* and the *New York Times*, it played no part in the statue's opening, and was largely forgotten thereafter. It was not until 1903 that a plaque was affixed to the pedestal bearing the poem. Since the Statue of Liberty stood in New York Harbor directly upon the transatlantic route to Ellis Island, it became an unofficial symbol of welcome for immigrants, and the poem on its pedestal immortalised that message. In years since, the poem has served as an anthem for pro-immigration and pro-refugee American activists, especially the phrase 'Give me your tired, your poor, / Your huddled masses yearning to breathe free', which was quoted recently during protests against President Trump's 2017 Muslim ban.

'The New Colossus'

Not like the brazen giant of Greek fame,[146]
With conquering limbs astride from land to land,
Here at our sea-washed, sunset gates shall stand
A mighty woman, with a torch, whose flame
Is the imprisoned lightning, and her name
Mother of Exiles. From her beacon-hand
Glows world-wide welcome; her mild eyes command
The air-bridged harbor that twin cities frame.

"Keep, ancient lands, your storied pomp!" cries she,
With silent lips. "Give me your tired, your poor,
"Your huddled masses yearning to breathe free;

---

146 The Colossus of Rhodes, a statue of Helios constructed in 280 BCE. By legend it straddled the harbour into that city.

"The wretched refuse of your teeming shore—
"Send these, the homeless, tempest-tost to me—
"I lift my lamp beside the golden door!"

Source text

Lazarus, Emma, 'The New Colossus', in *Catalogue of the Pedestal Fund Art Loan Exhibition at the National Academy of Design* (December 1883), [9].

References

Cavitch, Max, 'Emma Lazarus and the Golem of Liberty', *American Literary History* 18.1 (2006), 1–28.
Lootens, Tricia, *The Political Poetess: Victorian Femininity, Race, and the Legacy of Separate Spheres* (Princeton, NJ: Princeton University Press, 2017).

John A. Macdonald (1815–91)

Letters to and from Sir John A. Macdonald (1884)

An immigrant from Scotland at age five, John Macdonald became a lawyer in Toronto before entering Canadian politics in 1843 as a Conservative alderman from Kingston. He quickly rose in prominence through the colonial government and successively served as Attorney General and premier, then as leader of the Confederation of Canada and the nation's first prime minister beginning in 1867. Though his terms were marked by both progress and scandal, as well as a five-year period in the minority after his resignation, he served a total of nineteen years in office and died in office in 1891. Macdonald is considered one of the founders of the Canadian nation.

What is now Canada was a colony of Great Britain until 1 July 1867 when the Dominion of Canada (including the present and future provinces of Nova Scotia, New Brunswick, Ontario and Quebec) was established through the passage of the British North America Act. Within years several other provinces had been added to the newfound nation, and the completion of the Canadian Pacific Railway in 1885 allowed direct travel from the Atlantic Ocean to its Pacific coast. The latter half of the nineteenth century was a new Age of Empire for many powerful nations (including the United States), which turned their attention overseas in an attempt to open and capture resources and new markets in Africa and Asia. Apparently, this threat was a concern of British colonies in the Caribbean. Indeed, the letters below reveal a significant, if ephemeral, discussion between officials in Canada, Jamaica and Great Britain regarding a political and/or economic alliance. Ultimately Canada never pursued such an arrangement in the Caribbean, and Jamaica did not gain its independence until 6 August 1962. (Barbados did similarly on 30 November 1966.) Still, the epistolary record reveals that Canadians were not immune to these ambitions and had a summer's dalliance in pursuit thereof.

From Sir John Macdonald to Sir Charles Tupper.[147]

Ottawa, June 4th, 1884

My Dear Tupper,
I cabled you that the Hon. M. Solomon[148] of Jamaica would call upon you on the subject of confederation with Canada. It cannot come to anything, but still we should hear what they have to say, as it is a high compliment to Canada to have such a desire to join her political system coming from other Colonies.

Singularly enough, through Sir Francis Hincks,[149] enquiries were made last week from Barbados as to whether we should take them in. Hincks agrees with me that it would not do. You should contrive to let Lord Derby[150] and the Cabinet know all this. It will serve to show them our growing importance.

I suppose you will introduce Mr. Solomon to Tilley and Macpherson. * * *

The crops are looking well, although a severe frost last week has done some damage.

Campbell[151] is looking ill and depressed. Langevin and Chapleau getting on together pretty well.

With kind regards to Lady Tupper,
Yours sincerely,
John A. Macdonald

From Sir Charles Tupper to Sir John Macdonald.

9, Victoria Chambers,
London, S.W.,
8th July, 1884

My Dear Sir John,
I duly received your letter of the 4th ultimo, and have since had a visit from Mr. Solomon and Mr. Ashley, the chairman of the Jamaica Board here. I told that Canada would warmly favour anything to promote the interests of Jamaica, consistent with its own—that I saw many and serious obstacles in the way—all of which would receive careful consideration in case a formal proposal for union as made by Jamaica. I discussed the subject with Lord Derby, who seemed much impressed by the fact that both Jamaica and Barbados were thinking of federation with Canada.

I remain,
Yours faithfully,
Charles Tupper.

---

147 Charles Tupper (1821–1915), a prominent Canadian Father of Confederation and the premier of Nova Scotia between 1864 and 1867
148 Editor's note: The Hon. Michael Solomon, an elected member of the Legislative Council of Jamaica, who visited Canada in 1885 with the object of sounding the statesmen of the Dominion on the question of political union between that Colony and Canada.
149 Francis Hincks (1807–85), a prominent Canadian politician who had previously served as Governor of Barbados
150 Frederick Arthur Stanley (1841–1908), 16th Earl of Derby and Colonial Secretary of the UK from 1885 to 1886
151 Alexander Campbell (1822–92), Canadian politician, Minister of Justice and Attorney General (1881–5)

From Sir John Macdonald to Sir Francis Hincks.

Ottawa,
Private. 18th September, 1884.

My Dear Hincks,
We had yesterday a visit from the Hon. Michael Solomon, one of the legislative Council of Jamaica. He came, as you may suppose, about a political union of the Island with Canada. His visit was informal as he had no authority from his Government to see us, but he was authorized by the Standing Committee of West India proprietors in London to take Canada on his way home and see how the land lies with us. We told him that we had not given the subject much consideration, but were ready to hear what he had to say. All he wants from us now is to say that we should be ready to discuss the subject with a delegation from the Island. I told him that the permission of Her Majesty's Government must first be obtained. That, he said, could be easily procured, as Lord Derby had signified his assent in advance, and that he would take steps to get his Government to ask for the permission on his arrival at Kingston.

We shall probably inform Mr. Solomon that we shall have no objection to discussing the subject of a political union or of a tariff arrangement, either by correspondence or the receipt of a delegation, without in any way expressing our opinion on either. I have seen the articles in the ——,[152] which I presume are from your pen. At all events, I know that you must have considered the subject, and I should like much to get the benefit of your advice.

The commercial union would be valuable, but I dread the political future which a union opens to us—the negro question, defence, etc., etc.

I should like to have it so arranged that you could run up here at some time convenient to us both, and discuss the question in all its bearings, with my colleagues and myself.

Let me know what you can do to help us with your valuable counsel.
Yours very sincerely,
John A. Macdonald.

Sir Francis Hincks, K.C.M.G.,

From Sir John Macdonald to the Hon. Michael Solomon

Ottawa, 25th September, 1884.

Dear Mr. Solomon,
Since we had the pleasure of seeing you here, the subject of your unofficial mission has been discussed in Council. We are of opinion that the question of a political union is one surrounded with difficulties which may however prove not to be insuperable. Our information is exceedingly limited and we are therefore not in a position to express any decided opinion on the subject. If Her Majesty's Government give their consent, the Government of Canada will be quite ready to enter upon the consideration of the two important questions, first of a political union and, failing that, of a commercial arrangement.

The discussion of the subject can be had, either by letter or with a delegation from your Government. Meanwhile, we shall be very much obliged to you if you

---

152 Editorial note in original: Word indecipherable.

will send us such publications relating to Jamaica in the way of Blue Books[153] as are available. We should also like to get copies of your tariff and of you customs and excise laws.

I remain,

Dear Mr. Solomon,

Yours faithfully,

John A. Macdonald.

The Hon. Michael Solomon,
Jamaica.

Source text

Macdonald, John, *Correspondence of Sir John Macdonald* (Garden City, NY: Doubleday, Page & Company, 1921).

Reference

Gwyn, Richard J., *Nation Maker: Sir John A. MacDonald – His Life, Our Times* (Toronto: Random House, 2011).

E. Pauline Johnson (Tekahionwake) (1861–1913)

'My English Letter' (1888)

From birth E. Pauline Johnson straddled two cultures as the daughter of a Mohawk man and an Englishwoman. She grew up on the Six Nations Reserve in Ontario and was educated by her parents at home before enrolling at the Brantford Central Collegiate at 14. Johnson took to writing poetry in 1884 after her father's death, utilising both E. Pauline Johnson and Tekahionwake as authorial names while publishing in various periodicals. (The poem we include below first appeared in the Toronto periodical *Saturday Night*.) As her popularity grew, she began reciting her work on tours of Canada, England and the US, dressing as a Mohawk 'princess' for half of the performance and as an English 'lady' for the other. Her poetry similarly reflected her dual heritage, for she published volumes comprised of both Eng-

Figure 6.3 Copy of a portrait of E. Pauline Johnson (1862–1913), Six Nations poetess. Courtesy Archives of Ontario.

---

153 Yearly periodicals issued by each colonial governor concerning the affairs, records and statistics of their colony

lish poetry and Native folktales, including *The White Wampum* (1895), *Canadian Born* (1903) and *Flint and Feather* (1912). She retired from the stage in 1909 and moved to Vancouver, where she continued writing until her death in 1913.

During this period ties between Canada and the United Kingdom were close; the Dominion had asserted independence only in 1867, though its foreign affairs were controlled by the Imperial Parliament in London. Johnson was a nationalist and strove to promote Canadian pride through her art. She was also well aware of her nation's cultural debt to Britain, from language to literature to landscape, and was herself a child of both traditions.

In the period before transatlantic telegraph and telephone, letters sent by post were the main method of communication, and could take weeks or months between sending and arrival. In 'My English Letter' the speaker waits for a letter from England and yearns for the mother country she loves yet has never visited.

'My English Letter'

When each white moon, her lantern idly swinging,
    Comes out to join the star night-watching band,
Across the grey-green sea, a ship is bringing
    For me a letter, from the Motherland.

Naught would I care to live in quaint old Britain,
    These wilder shores are dearer far to me,
Yet when I read the words that hand has written,
    The parent sod more precious seems to be.

Within that folded note I catch the savour
    Of climes that make the Motherland so fair,
Although I never knew the blessed favour
    That surely lies in breathing English air.

Imagination's brush before me fleeing,
    Paints English pictures, though my longing eyes
Have never known the blessedness of seeing
    The blue that lines the arch of English skies.

And yet my letter brings the scenes I covet,
    Framed in the salt sea winds, aye more in dreams
I almost see the face that bent above it,
    I almost touch that hand, so near it seems.

Near, for the very grey-green sea that dashes
    'Round these Canadian coasts, rolls out once more
To Eastward, and the same Atlantic splashes
    Her wild white spray on England's distant shore.

Near, for the same young moon so idly swinging
   Her threadlike crescent bends the self-same smile
On that old land from whence a ship is bringing
   My message from the transatlantic Isle.

Thus loves my heart that far old country better,
   Because of those dear words that always come,
With love enfolded in each English letter
   That drifts into my sun-kissed Western home.

Source text

Johnson, E. Pauline (Tekahionwake), *The White Wampum* (London: John Lane, 1895).

References

Collett, Anne, 'Red and White: Miss E. Pauline Johnson Tekahionwake and the Other Woman', *Women's Writing* 8.3 (2001), 359–74.
Strong-Boag, Veronica and Carole Gerson, *Paddling Her Own Canoe: The Times and Texts of E. Pauline Johnson (Tekahionwake)* (Toronto: University of Toronto Press, 2000).

Ida B. Wells (1862–1931)

'Miss Wells's Plea for the Negro: She Describes Her Labors in England to Arouse Sentiment Against Lynching' (1894)

Twice in the 1890s, Black activist Ida B. Wells crossed the Atlantic to engage British citizens in her anti-lynching crusade. Her appeal echoed those of previous anti-slavery advocates like Frederick Douglass and Henry 'Box' Brown earlier in the century by using an extra-national strategy to impact a social movement in her home country. Thus, she constructed a cosmopolitan persona and a globally framed moral imperative to resist US white power's destruction of Black bodies.

Complementing the historical precedents that illuminate her British campaign, Kwame Appiah's *The Honor Code* provides an ethical lens for interpreting Wells's transatlantic efforts. Extending his *Cosmopolitanism* (2006), Appiah's 2010 text assembles case studies to define tipping points when a shift in moral value systems finally undermined a social practice not previously considered immoral. For one example – foot-binding in China – Appiah emphasises that changing it required China to embrace a cosmopolitan view, attending to how the practice was judged beyond national borders. Relatedly, he argues, ending the British slave trade necessitated whites' recognition that supporting enslavement violated a code of self-respect tied to an idealised national identity with cosmopolitan implications.

Over a century ahead of Appiah, Wells enacted his argument, pushing British audiences to see anti-lynching work as a necessary extension of anti-slavery's agenda. British allies like Celestine Edwards (1857?–94) and Catherine Impey (1847–1923) bolstered Wells's strategy, described by Silkey as countering American leaders' efforts toward 'preserving the illusion' of lynching as 'honorable' (3). For Silkey, Wells's transatlantic approach capitalised on the US as then 'a nation striving to attract foreign investment and prove itself worthy of becoming an imperial power on par with European nations', and therefore vulnerable to moral mandates revealing lynching to extra-national audiences as un-heroic (3).

'Miss Wells's Plea for the Negro'

Miss Ida B. Wells told a large audience in the Bethel African Methodist Episcopal Church,[154] in Sullivan Street, last night, about her visit to England to arouse public sentiment against the lynching of negroes in the Southern States.

Miss Wells is a slender little woman, with clear-cut features, a very light complexion, and is about the medium height. She speaks readily and has a musical voice.

The meeting was opened by the Rev. Mr. Henderson,[155] pastor of the church, who made a few remarks about lynching, and introduced T. Thomas Fortune,[156] editor of The Age and President of the Afro-American League, who introduced Miss Wells.

"This work of ours is not done, it is but begun," said Miss Wells, "and those who were hereditary bondsmen must strike the blow if they would be free. The negro is not free. The outside world has been deluded into believing he is, but for years the work of Abraham Lincoln has been nullified. The white man's vote in the South is much more dangerous than a white man's vote in the North, because he not only casts his own vote, but the negro's as well."

Miss Wells told how she was lead to make public appeals for her race.

"After trying for two years to get a hearing in the press, after I was banished from my home,"[157] she said, "I met an Englishwoman who had been in the South and

---

154 Bethel, established in 1819 in New York City, moved several times in the nineteenth century while always maintaining its commitment to be led by and to serve African Americans.

155 A prominent religious leader, Rev. J. M. Henderson was pastor of Bethel from 1894–8.

156 Timothy Thomas Fortune (1856–1928) settled in New York in the 1880s. A crusading Black journalist, he edited an influential American newspaper for Black readers and organised the National Afro-American League, which campaigned against lynching and other terrorist violence against African Americans.

157 In 1889, Wells had become part-owner of Memphis's Free Speech and Headlight. In March 1892, three African American Memphis businessmen were lynched as part of an effort by whites, Silkey explains, 'to get rid of Negroes who were acquiring wealth and property' and to thereby frighten other Blacks into accepting social subservience (54). Wells wrote editorials responding to what became known as the 'Lynching at the Curve', and a white mob ransacked the Free Speech offices and threatened the lives of her co-editor and Wells herself.

knew something of the real state of affairs. She asked me if I would go to England and tell the people how the negro was treated in America, and I said I would.[158]

"My reception in Liverpool was a most gracious one, and after holding ten meetings there we started on a tour. Wherever we went we were greeted by large crowds, who listened to my tale of how innocent men were lynched, burned at the stake, and shot down without a trial, and how half-grown boys were allowed to fire bullets into the bodies of dying men. They were horrified to hear these things.

"Newspapers containing the vilest articles about me were sent to England from America to stop my work. At one time I thought I would have to remain in England to defend my own character, but the London Anti-Lynching League[159] decided that my character needed no defense. They also decided that the time was ripe for me to return and make an appeal to the American people, and that is why I am here tonight.

"I may say that never since the days when 'Uncle Tom's Cabin' was first published has the English public and people been stirred as they were by my tales of Southern lynchings.[160]

"I said the hereditary bondsman must strike the blow if he would be free. I do not mean by that he must use dynamite, the bomb, the dagger, or the torch, because the men who have suffered so for the last thirty years do not make Anarchists, strikers, or brigands, but the worm itself will turn at last, and if the colored man can do no less, he can contribute the sinews of war."

Miss Wells made an appeal to the colored people of the North to organize, and urged that a bureau be established to procure authentic news of the outrages perpetrated on negroes in the South, and see that whenever the story of an outrage was sent out by white men in the South the negro's side be told also.

"We do not desire to shield the criminal because he is a black man," she said, "but we want at least to have his guilt established by the court competent to try him before he is executed, and we want the black man's home to be as sacred from invasion as that of any other man in the land."

Source text

'Miss Wells's Plea for the Negro: She Describes Her Labors in England to Arouse Sentiment Against Lynching', *New York Times* (30 July 1894), 8.

References

Appiah, Kwame Anthony, *Cosmopolitanism: Ethics in a World of Strangers* (New York: W. W. Norton, 2006).
—, *The Honor Code: How Moral Revolutions Happen* (New York: W. W. Norton, 2010).
Silkey, Sarah L., *Black Woman Reformer: Ida B. Wells, Lynching, & Transatlantic Activism* (Athens, GA: University of Georgia Press, 2015).

---

158 Silkey reports that Catherine Impey and Isabella Fyvie Mayo, both leaders in the Society for the Recognition of the Brotherhood of Man and of the British periodical *Anti-Caste*, joined together 'on a letter inviting Ida B. Wells to come to England to recount the horrors of lynching before British audiences' (61). The invitation launched Wells's first speaking tour in Britain in 1893. This *NYT* story reports on her second trip in 1894.

159 The enthusiastic responses of British audiences to Wells's speeches helped launch the London Anti-Lynching Committee and other British chapters.

160 In her own 1852 tour of Britain soon after her novel's publication, Harriet Beecher Stowe stoked the popularity of *Uncle Tom's Cabin* there.

Figure 6.4 'The Most Recently Discovered Wild Beast: Irish-American
Dynamite Skunk', *Judy, or the London Serio-comic Journal* 29 (3 August 1881),
50–1. For context, see Kevin Kenny, 'Diaspora and Comparison:
The Global Irish as a Test Case', *Journal of American History* 90.1 (2003),
134–62. Image courtesy Kevin Kenny.

Theodore Roosevelt (1858–1919)

From 'What "Americanism" Means' (1894)

Though in later years Theodore Roosevelt became a soldier, statesman,
Governor and the twenty-sixth President of the United States, during the
1880s and 1890s he was best known as an outdoorsman and author who
epitomised the American West. Born into a powerful New York family,
Roosevelt was a sickly child who found strength in vigorous exercise and
travel. He graduated from Harvard in 1880 and eschewed Columbia Law
School for a series of political appointments in New York City. Thereafter
he took up ranching in Dakota Territory, earning a reputation as a cowboy,
conservationist and deputy sheriff while publishing three books on frontier life. Returning East, Roosevelt successively served in the Civil Service
Commission and as New York City Police Commissioner and Assistant
Secretary of the Navy, emerging as a national figure even before his famous
escapades with the Rough Riders during the Spanish-American War. Roosevelt became Governor of New York in 1898, Vice President in 1900 and
assumed the Presidency after William McKinley was assassinated in 1901.

First published in 1894 in *The Forum* magazine, while Roosevelt was
in the Civil Service Commission, 'What "Americanism" Means' offers a

robust defence of American patriotism. At the time the US had reached the terminus of its westward expansion, and had adopted imperial ambitions, looking beyond its borders to the Caribbean, Pacific and Central America for new markets and colonies. At the same time, the nation saw a swelling wave of immigration from Europe (especially to the large cities of the East Coast) that threatened to shift the ethnic composition and character of the American demographic. Roosevelt attempts to thread the needle between cultural pluralism and xenophobia, arguing that the US must assimilate and 'Americanise' such immigrants with regard to American beliefs and institutions, while simultaneously barring their discrimination and exclusion on grounds of national origin. Such nuanced, practical positions were a hallmark of Roosevelt's later Presidency, as he sought to encourage economic expansion while curtailing the power of Gilded Age trusts.

From 'What "Americanism" Means'

Patriotism was once defined as "the last refuge of a scoundrel;" and somebody has recently remarked that when Dr. Johnson[161] gave this definition he was ignorant of the infinite possibilities contained in the word "reform." Of course both gibes were quite justifiable, in so far as they were aimed at people who use noble names to cloak base purposes. Equally of course the man shows little wisdom and a low sense of duty who fails to see that love of country is one of the elemental virtues, even though scoundrels play upon it for their own selfish ends; and, inasmuch as abuses continually grow up in civic life as in all other kinds of life, the statesman is indeed a weakling who hesitates to reform these abuses because the word "reform" is often on the lips of men who are silly or dishonest.

What is true of patriotism and reform is true also of Americanism. There are plenty of scoundrels always ready to try to belittle reform movements or to bolster up existing iniquities in the name of Americanism; but this does not alter the fact that the man who can do most in this country is and must be the man whose Americanism is most sincere and intense. Outrageous though it is to use a noble idea as the cloak for evil, it is still worse to assail the noble idea itself because it can thus be used. The men who do iniquity in the name of patriotism, of reform, of Americanism, are merely one small division of the class that has always existed and will always exist, – the class of hypocrites and demagogues, the class that is always prompt to steal the watchwords of righteousness and use them in the interests of evil-doing. [. . .]

[. . .] Our nation is that one among all the nations of the earth which holds in its hands the fate of the coming years. We enjoy exceptional advantages, and are menaced by exceptional dangers; and all signs indicate that we shall either fail greatly or succeed greatly. I firmly believe that we shall succeed; but we must not foolishly blink the dangers by which we are threatened, for that is the way to fail. On the

---

161 Samuel Johnson (1709–84), an English writer who published one of the first widespread English dictionaries in 1755. The quote in question was directed at William Pitt, 1st Earl of Chatham, and his supporters.

contrary, we must soberly set to work to find out all we can about the existence and extent of every evil, must acknowledge it to be such, and must then attack it with unyielding resolution. There are many such evils, and each must be fought after a fashion; yet there is one quality which we must bring to the solution of every problem, – that is, an intense and fervid Americanism. We shall never be successful over the dangers that confront us; we shall never achieve true greatness, nor reach the lofty ideal which the founders and preservers of our mighty Federal Republic have set before us, unless we are Americans in heart and soul, in spirit and purpose, keenly alive to the responsibility implied in the very name of American, and proud beyond measure of the glorious privilege of bearing it.

There are two or three sides to the question of Americanism, and two or three senses in which the word "Americanism" can be used to express the antithesis of what is unwholesome and undesirable. In the first place we wish to be broadly American and national, as opposed to being local or sectional. We do not wish, in politics, in literature, or in art, to develop that unwholesome parochial spirit, that over-exaltation of the little community at the expense of the great nation, which produces what has been described as the patriotism of the village, the patriotism of the belfry. Politically, the indulgence of this spirit was the chief cause of the calamities which befell the ancient republics of Greece, the mediaeval republics of Italy, and the petty States of Germany as it was in the last century. It is this spirit of provincial patriotism, this inability to take a view of broad adhesion to the whole nation that has been the chief among the causes that have produced such anarchy in the South American States, and which have resulted in presenting to us not one great Spanish-American federal nation stretching from the Rio Grande to Cape Horn, but a squabbling multitude of revolution-ridden States, not one of which stands even in the second rank as a power.[162] However, politically this question of American nationality has been settled once for all. We are no longer in danger of repeating in our history the shameful and contemptible disasters that have befallen the Spanish possessions on this continent since they threw off the yoke of Spain. Indeed, there is, all through our life, very much less of this parochial spirit than there was formerly. Still there is an occasional outcropping here and there; and it is just as well that we should keep steadily in mind the futility of talking of a Northern literature or a Southern literature, an Eastern or a Western school of art or science. [...] Joel Chandler Harris[163] is emphatically a national writer; so is Mark Twain.[164] They do not write merely for Georgia or Missouri or California any more than for Illinois or Connecticut; they write as Americans and for all people who can read English. It is of very great consequence that we should have a full and ripe literary development in the United States, but it is not of the least consequence whether New York, or Boston, or Chicago, or San Francisco becomes the literary centre of the United States.

There is a second side to this question of a broad Americanism, however. The patriotism of the village or the belfry is bad, but the lack of all patriotism is even worse. There are philosophers who assure us that, in the future, patriotism will be

---

162 The various nations of South America achieved independence from Spain and Portugal between 1810 and 1822.

163 Joel Chandler Harris (1848–1908), US writer often associated with Georgia and the New South

164 Mark Twain (pen name of Samuel Langhorne Clemens, 1835–1910), US author of *The Adventures of Tom Sawyer* (1876) and *Adventures of Huckleberry Finn* (1884/5)

regarded not as a virtue at all, but merely as a mental stage in the journey toward a state of feeling when our patriotism will include the whole human race and all the world. This may be so; but the age of which these philosophers speak is still several aeons distant. In fact, philosophers of this type are so very advanced that they are of no practical service to the present generation. It may be that in ages so remote that we cannot now understand any of the feelings of those who will dwell in them, patriotism will no longer be regarded as a virtue, exactly as it may be that in those remote ages people will look down upon and disregard monogamic marriage; but as things now are and have been for two or three thousand years past, and are likely to be for two or three thousand years to come, the words "home" and "country" mean a great deal. Nor do they show any tendency to lose their significance. At present, treason, like adultery, ranks as one of the worst of all possible crimes.

One may fall very far short of treason and yet be an undesirable citizen in the community. The man who becomes Europeanized, who loses his power of doing good work on this side of the water, and who loses his love for his native land, is not a traitor; but he is a silly and undesirable citizen. He is as emphatically a noxious element in our body politic as is the man who comes here from abroad and remains a foreigner. Nothing will more quickly or more surely disqualify a man from doing good work in the world than the acquirement of that flaccid habit of mind which its possessors style cosmopolitanism.

It is not only necessary to Americanize the immigrants of foreign birth who settle among us, but it is even more necessary for those among us who are by birth and descent already Americans not to throw away our birthright, and, with incredible and contemptible folly, wander back to bow down before the alien gods whom our forefathers forsook. It is hard to believe that there is any necessity to warn Americans that, when they seek to model themselves on the lines of other civilizations, they make themselves the butts of all right-thinking men; and yet the necessity certainly exists to give this warning to many of our citizens who pride themselves on their standing in the world of art and letters, or, perchance, on what they would style their social leadership in the community. It is always better to be an original than an imitation, even when the imitation is of something better than the original; but what shall we say of the fool who is content to be an imitation of something worse? Even if the weaklings who seek to be other than Americans were right in deeming other nations to be better than their own, the fact yet remains that to be a first-class American is fifty-fold better than to be a second-class imitation of a Frenchman or Englishman. As a matter of fact, however, those of our country-men who do believe in American inferiority are always individuals who, however cultivated, have some organic weakness in their moral or mental make-up; and the great mass of our people, who are robustly patriotic, and who have sound, healthy minds, are justified in regarding these feeble renegades with a half-impatient and half-amused scorn.

We believe in waging relentless war on rank-growing evils of all kinds, and it makes no difference to us if they happen to be of purely native growth. We grasp at any good, no matter whence it comes. We do not accept the evil attendant upon another system of government as an adequate excuse for that attendant upon our own; the fact that the courtier is a scamp does not render the dema-gogue any the less a scoundrel. But it remains true that, in spite of all our faults and shortcomings, no other land offers such glorious possibilities to the man able to take advantage of them, as does ours; it remains true that no one of our people can do any work really worth doing unless he does it primarily as an American. It is because certain classes of our people still retain their spirit of colonial dependence on, and exaggerated deference to, European opinion, that they fail to accomplish what they ought to. It is precisely along the lines where we have worked most independently that we have accomplished the greatest results; and it is in those professions where there has been no servility to, but merely a wise profiting by, foreign experience, that we have produced our greatest men. Our soldiers and statesmen and orators; our explorers, our wilderness-winners, and commonwealth-builders; the men who have made our laws and seen that they were executed; and the other men whose energy and ingenuity have created our marvellous material prosperity, – all these have been men who have drawn wisdom from the experience of every age and nation, but who have nevertheless thought, and worked, and conquered, and lived, and died, purely as Americans; and on the whole they have done better work than has been done in any other country during the short period of our national life.

On the other hand, it is in those professions where our people have striven hardest to mold themselves in conventional European forms that they have succeeded least; and this holds true to the present day, the failure being of course most conspicuous where the man takes up his abode in Europe; where he becomes a second-rate European, because he is over-civilized, over-sensitive, over-refined, and has lost the hardihood and manly courage by which alone he can conquer in the keen struggle of our national life. Be it remembered, too, that this same being does not really become a European; he only ceases being an American, and becomes nothing. He throws away a great prize for the sake of a lesser one, and does not even get the lesser one. The painter who goes to Paris, not merely to get two or three years' thorough training in his art, but with the deliberate purpose of taking up his abode there, and with the intention of following in the ruts worn deep by ten thousand earlier travelers, instead of striking off to rise or fall on a new line, thereby forfeits all chance of doing the best work. He must content himself with aiming at that kind of mediocrity which consists in doing fairly well what has already been done better; and he usually never even sees the grandeur and picturesqueness lying open before the eyes of every man who can read the book of America's past and the book of America's present. Thus it is with the undersized man of letters, who flees his country because he, with his delicate, effeminate sensitiveness, finds the conditions of life on this side of the water crude and raw; in other words, because he finds that he cannot play a man's part among men, and so goes where he will be sheltered from the winds that harden stouter souls. This *emigré* may write graceful and pretty verses, essays, novels; but he will never do work to compare with that of his brother, who is strong enough to stand on his own feet, and do his work as an American. Thus it is with the scientist who spends his youth in a German university, and can thenceforth work only in the fields already fifty times furrowed by the German ploughs. Thus it is with that most foolish of parents who sends his children to be educated abroad, not knowing – what every clear-sighted man from Washington[165] and Jay[166] down has known – that the American who is to make his way in America should be brought up among his fellow Americans. It is among the people who like to consider themselves, and, indeed, to a large extent are, the leaders of the so-called social world, especially in some of the northeastern cities, that this

---

165 George Washington (1732–99), first President of the US
166 John Jay (1745–1829), the first Chief Justice of the US Supreme Court

colonial habit of thought, this thoroughly provincial spirit of admiration for things foreign, and inability to stand on one's own feet, becomes most evident and most despicable. We thoroughly believe in every kind of honest and lawful pleasure, so long as the getting it is not made man's chief business; and we believe heartily in the good that can be done by men of leisure who work hard in their leisure, whether at politics or philanthropy, literature or art. But a leisure class whose leisure simply means idleness is a curse to the community, and in so far as its members distinguish themselves chiefly by aping the worst – not the best – traits of similar people across the water, they become both comic and noxious elements of the body politic.

The third sense in which the word "Americanism" may be employed is with reference to the Americanizing of the newcomers to our shores. We must Americanize them in every way, in speech, in political ideas and principles, and in their way of looking at the relations between Church and State. We welcome the German or the Irishman who becomes an American. We have no use for the German or Irishman who remains such. We do not wish German-Americans and Irish-Americans who figure as such in our social and political life; we want only Americans, and, provided they are such, we do not care whether they are of native or of Irish or of German ancestry. We have no room in any healthy American community for a German-American vote or an Irish-American vote, and it is contemptible demagogy to put planks into any party platform with the purpose of catching such a vote. We have no room for any people who do not act and vote simply as Americans, and as nothing else. [. . .]

The mighty tide of immigration to our shores has brought in its train much of good and much of evil; and whether the good or the evil shall predominate depends mainly on whether these newcomers do or do not throw themselves heartily into our national life, cease to be Europeans, and become Americans like the rest of us. More than a third of the people of the Northern States are of foreign birth or parentage. An immense number of them have become completely Americanized, and these stand on exactly the same plane as the descendants of any Puritan, Cavalier, or Knickerbocker among us,[167] and do their full and honorable share of the nation's work. But where immigrants, or the sons of immigrants, do not heartily and in good faith throw in their lot with us, but cling to the speech, the customs, the ways of life, and the habits of thought of the Old World which they have left, they thereby harm both themselves and us. If they remain alien elements, unassimilated, and with interests separate from ours, they are mere obstructions to the current of our national life, and, moreover, can get no good from it themselves. In fact, though we ourselves also suffer from their perversity, it is they who really suffer most. It is an immense benefit to the European immigrant to change him into an American citizen. To bear the name of American is to bear the most honorable titles; and whoever does not so believe has no business to bear the name at all, and, if he comes from Europe, the sooner he goes back there the better. Besides, the man who does not become Americanized nevertheless fails to remain a European, and becomes nothing at all. The immigrant cannot possibly remain what he was, or continue to be a member of the Old-World society. If he tries to retain his old language, in a few generations it becomes a barbarous jargon; if he tries to retain his old customs and ways of life, in a few generations he becomes an uncouth boor. He has cut himself off from the Old World, and cannot retain his connection with it; and if he wishes ever to amount to anything he must throw himself heart and soul, and without reservation, into the new life to which he has come.

---

167 Various religious sects that immigrated to British North America in the seventeenth century

[...] There are certain ideas which he must give up. For instance, he must learn that American life is incompatible with the existence of any form of anarchy, or of any secret society having murder for its aim, whether at home or abroad; and he must learn that we exact full religious toleration and the complete separation of Church and State. Moreover, he must not bring in his Old-World race and national antipathies, but must merge them into love for our common country, and must take pride in the things which we can all take pride in. He must revere only our flag; not only must it come first, but no other flag should even come second. He must learn to celebrate Washington's birthday rather than that of the Queen or Kaiser, and the Fourth of July instead of St. Patrick's Day. Our political and social questions must be settled on their own merits, and not complicated by quarrels between England and Ireland, or France and Germany, with which we have nothing to do: it is an outrage to fight an American political campaign with reference to questions of European politics. Above all, the immigrant must learn to talk and think and *be* United States. [...]

[...] We Americans can only do our allotted task well if we face it steadily and bravely, seeing but not fearing the dangers. Above all we must stand shoulder to shoulder, not asking as to the ancestry or creed of our comrades, but only demanding that they be in very truth Americans, and that we all work together, heart, hand, and head, for the honor and the greatness of our common country.

Source text

Roosevelt, Theodore, 'What "Americanism" Means', *The Forum* 17.2 (April 1894), 196–206.

References

Hansen, Jonathan, 'True Americanism: Progressive Era Intellectuals and the Problem of Liberal Nationalism', in Michael Kazin and Joseph A. McCartin (eds), *Americanism: New Perspectives on the History of an Ideal* (Chapel Hill, NC: University of North Carolina Press, 2006), 73–89.

Oliver, Lawrence J., 'Theodore Roosevelt, Brander Matthews, and the Campaign for Literary Americanism', *American Quarterly* 41.1 (1989), 93–111.

Rudyard Kipling (1865–1936)

'The White Man's Burden' (1899)

Rudyard Kipling was born to British parents in Bombay, where he spent his first six years before immigrating to England for his schooling. He returned to India in 1882 as a journalist for the *Civil and Military Gazette*, and it was there he began to sketch and publish stories influenced by the local colour and characters. Kipling's career ascended with a return to London, and was furthered by a subsequent move to the US, where he lived for a number of years and wrote *The Jungle Book* stories. On the strength of his writing Kipling served as a military correspondent and 'literary advisor' during the Boer War and the First World War, respectively. Though Kipling was popular in his day and was awarded the Nobel Prize for literature in 1907, he leaves a complicated legacy as an emblem of the imperial age.

The late Victorian age was marked by the twin poles of colonialism and empire and the sort of skewed racial thinking that went with it. 'The White Man's Burden' was first published in *The Times* (London) on 4 February 1899 and then in the *New York Tribune*, the *New York Sun* and the *San Francisco Examiner* the following day. It also appeared in the February 1899 issue of the immensely popular New York-based *McClure's Magazine*. Though broadly applied to all colonial situations, Kipling intended the poem to speak to the Philippine-American War, in which the US sought to annex what had been a Spanish colony. Kipling's friend Theodore Roosevelt brought the poem to the attention of the Senate, where stanzas were read aloud in the debate over the Treaty of Paris, which would cede the Philippines to the US. (Senator Henry Cabot Lodge commented that it was rather 'poor poetry', but made 'good sense from the expansion standpoint' [Brantlinger, 172].) As it is, 'The White Man's Burden' has become a rallying cry and rationale for military intervention, with the implication that invasion is a godly sacrifice for the conquerors and to the benefit of those conquered.

'The White Man's Burden'

> Take up the White Man's burden –
>   Send forth the best ye breed –
> Go bind your sons to exile
>   To serve your captives' need;
> To wait in heavy harness,
>   On fluttered folk and wild –
> Your new-caught, sullen peoples,
>   Half-devil and half-child.
>
> Take up the White Man's burden –
>   In patience to abide,
> To veil the threat of terror
>   And check the show of pride;
> By open speech and simple,
>   An hundred times made plain
> To seek another's profit,
>   And work another's gain.
>
> Take up the White Man's burden –
>   The savage wars of peace –
> Fill full the mouth of Famine
>   And bid the sickness cease;
> And when your goal is nearest
>   The end for others sought,
> Watch Sloth and heathen Folly
>   Bring all your hopes to nought.

Take up the White Man's burden –
   No tawdry rule of kings,
But toil of serf and sweeper –
   The tale of common things.
The ports ye shall not enter,
   The roads ye shall not tread,
Go mark them with your living,
   And mark them with your dead.

Take up the White Man's burden –
   And reap his old reward:
The blame of those ye better,
   The hate of those ye guard –
The cry of hosts ye humour
   (Ah, slowly!) toward the light: –
'Why brought he us from bondage,
   Our loved Egyptian night?'

Take up the White Man's burden –
   Ye dare not stoop to less –
Nor call too loud on Freedom
   To cloak your weariness;
By all ye cry or whisper,
   By all ye leave or do,
The silent, sullen peoples
   Shall weigh your Gods and you.

Take up the White Man's burden –
   Have done with childish days –
The lightly proffered laurel,
   The easy, ungrudged praise.
Comes now, to search your manhood
   Through all the thankless years,
Cold, edged with dear-bought wisdom,
   The judgment of your peers!

Source text

Kipling, Rudyard, *The Five Nations* (London: Methuen and Co., 1903).

References

Brantlinger, Patrick, 'Kipling's "The White Man's Burden" and Its Afterlives', *English Literature in Transition, 1880–1920* 50.2 (2007), 172–91.

Jeffries, Laura, 'The White Meme's Burden: Replication and Adaptation in Twenty-First Century White Supremacist Internet Cultures', *Reception* 10.1 (2018), 50–73.

Murphy, Gretchen, *Shadowing the White Man's Burden: U.S. Imperialism and the Problem of the Color Line* (New York: New York University Press, 2010).

The first step towards lightening

The White Man's Burden

is through teaching the virtues of cleanliness.

Pears' Soap

is a potent factor in brightening the dark corners of the earth as civilization advances, while amongst the cultured of all nations it holds the highest place—it is the ideal toilet soap.

Figure 6.5 'The First Step Towards Lightening the White Man's Burden Is Through Teaching the Virtues of Cleanliness. Pears' Soap', *Harper's Weekly* 43 (30 September 1899), 968. Courtesy HathiTrust.

Randolph Bourne (1886–1918)

From 'Trans-national America' (1916)

Randolph Bourne faced physical handicaps his entire life as a result of a botched delivery and spinal tuberculosis at an early age. His mental abilities, however, were unaffected, and he proved a keen public intellectual and enrolled at Columbia University under the tutelage of John Dewey and Charles Beard. By the time he graduated in 1913, he had published a book of magazine essays, and under the Gilder Fellowship travelled Europe for a year before the outbreak of military conflict. Bourne opposed the First World War and especially American involvement in it, writing frequently and fervently on the subject, for which he faced public backlash and editorial censure. He died from the international influenza epidemic after the war, leaving a legacy as a prominent journalist and writer, notably in influential essays such as 'The Handicapped' (1911) and 'Trans-national America' (1916).

'Trans-national America' was published as a three-part essay in the July 1916 issue of the *Atlantic Monthly*, in part as a response to the American notion of the 'melting pot', popularised by Israel Zangwill's play of that phrase first performed in 1908, which described the assimilation of hetero-geneous immigrant cultures into a homogenised US identity. Rather than this model, Bourne espoused what would now be called ethnic/racial plural-ism, in which immigrants retained their native cultures while contributing to a cosmopolitan society made all the greater for its diversity. Written against the rising tide of nationalism and Anglo-Saxon 'race pride', the notion of a 'trans-national' America was as provocative as it was compelling.

From 'Trans-national America'

No reverberatory effect of the great war has caused American public opinion more solicitude than the failure of the 'melting-pot.' The discovery of diverse nationalistic feelings among our great alien population has come to most people as an intense shock. It has brought out the unpleasant inconsistencies of our traditional beliefs We have had to watch hard-hearted old Brahmins[168] virtuously indignant at the spectacle of the immigrant refusing to be melted, while they jeer at patriots like Mary Antin[169] who write about 'our forefathers.' We have had to listen to publicists who express themselves as stunned by the evidence of vigorous nationalistic and cultural movements in this country among Germans, Scandinavians, Bohemians, and Poles, while in the same breath they insist that the mien shall be forcibly assimilated to that Anglo- Saxon tradition which they unquestioningly label 'American.'

As the unpleasant truth has come upon us that assimilation in this country was proceeding on lines very different from those we had marked out for it, we found ourselves inclined to blame those who were thwarting our prophecies. The truth became culpable. We blamed the war, we blamed the Germans. And then we discovered with a moral shock that these movements had been making great headway before the war even began. We found that the tendency, reprehensible and paradoxical as it might be, has been for the national clusters of immigrants, as they became more and more firmly established and more and more prosperous, to cultivate more and more assiduously the literatures and cultural traditions of their homelands. Assimilation, in other words, instead of washing out the memories of Europe, made them more and more intensely real. Just as these clusters became more and more objectively American, did they become more and more German or Scandinavian or Bohemian or Polish.

To face the fact that our aliens are already strong enough to take a share in the direction of their own destiny, and that the strong cultural movements represented by the foreign press, schools, and colonies are a challenge to our facile attempts, is not, however, to admit the failure of Americanization. It is not to fear the failure of democracy. It is rather to urge us to an investigation of what Americanism may rightly mean. It is to ask ourselves whether our ideal has been broad or narrow—whether perhaps the time has not come to assert a higher ideal than the 'melting-pot.' Surely we cannot be certain of our spiritual democracy when, claiming to melt

---

168 A member of the Boston Brahmin, or the unofficial elite class of New England culture, who are primarily Anglo-American and Protestant
169 Mary Antin (1881–1949), a Polish-American immigrant, activist and author of *The Promised Land* (1912), an autobiography detailing her Americanisation

the nations within us to a comprehension of our free and democratic institutions, we fly into panic at the first sign of their own will and tendency. We act as if we wanted Americanization to take place only on our own terms, and not by the consent of the governed. All our elaborate machinery of settlement and school and union, of social and political naturalization, however, will move with friction just in so far as it neglects to take into account this strong and virile insistence that America shall be what the immigrant will have a hand in making it, and not what a ruling class, descendant of those British stocks which were the first permanent immigrants, decide that America shall be made. This is the condition which confronts us, and which demands a clear and general readjustment of our attitude and our ideal. [. . .]

III

The failure of the melting-pot, far from closing the great American democratic experiment, means that it has only just begun. Whatever American nationalism turns out to be, we see already that it will have a color richer and more exciting than our ideal has hitherto encompassed. In a world which has dreamed of internationalism, we find that we have all unawares been building up the first international nation. The voices which have cried for a tight and jealous nationalism of the European pattern are failing. From that ideal, however valiantly and disinterestedly it has been set for us, time and tendency have moved us further and further away. What we have achieved has been rather a cosmopolitan federation of national colonies, of foreign cultures, from whom the sting of devastating competition has been removed. America is already the world-federation in miniature, the continent where for the first time in history has been achieved that miracle of hope, the peaceful living side by side, with character substantially preserved, of the most heterogeneous peoples under the sun. Nowhere else has such contiguity been anything but the breeder of misery. Here, notwithstanding our tragic failures of adjustment, the outlines are already too clear not to give us a new vision and a new orientation of the American mind in the world.

It is for the American of the younger generation to accept this cosmopolitanism, and carry it along with self-conscious and fruitful purpose. In his colleges, he is already getting, with the study of modern history and politics, the modern literatures, economic geography, the privilege of a cosmopolitan outlook such as the people of no other nation of to-day in Europe can possibly secure. If he is still a colonial, he is no longer the colonial of one partial culture, but of many. He is a colonial of the world. Colonialism has grown into cosmopolitanism, and his motherland is no one nation, but all who have anything life-enhancing to offer to the spirit. That vague sympathy which the France of ten years ago was feeling for the world—a sympathy which was drowned in the terrible reality of war—may be the modern American's, and that in a positive and aggressive sense. If the American is parochial, it is in sheer wantonness or cowardice. His provincialism is the measure of his fear of bogies[170] or the defect of his imagination.

Indeed, it is not uncommon for the eager Anglo-Saxon who goes to a vivid American university to-day to find his true friends not among his own race but among the acclimatized German or Austrian, the acclimatized Jew, the acclimatized Scandinavian or Italian. In them he finds the cosmopolitan note. In these youths,

---

170 A ghost or other supernatural being

foreign-born or the children of foreign-born parents, he is likely to find many of his old inbred morbid problems washed away. These friends are oblivious to the repressions of that tight little society in which he so provincially grew up. He has a pleasurable sense of liberation from the stale and familiar attitudes of those whose ingrowing culture has scarcely created anything vital for his America of to-day. He breathes a larger air. In his new enthusiasms for continental literature, for unplumbed Russian depths, for French clarity of thought, for Teuton philosophies of power, he feels himself citizen of a larger world. He may be absurdly superficial, his outward-reaching wonder may ignore all the stiller and homelier virtues of his Anglo-Saxon home, but he has at least found the clue to that international mind which will be essential to all men and women of good-will if they are ever to save this Western world of ours from suicide. His new friends have gone through a similar evolution. America has burned most of the baser metal also from them. Meeting now with this common American background, all of them may yet retain that distinctiveness of their native cultures and their national spiritual slants. They are more valuable and interesting to each other for being different, yet that difference could not be creative were it not for this new cosmopolitan outlook which America has given them and which they all equally possess.

A college where such a spirit is possible even to the smallest degree, has within itself already the seeds of this international intellectual world of the future. It suggests that the contribution of America will be an intellectual internationalism which goes far beyond the mere exchange of scientific ideas and discoveries and the cold recording of facts. It will be an intellectual sympathy which is not satisfied until it has got at the heart of the different cultural expressions, and felt as they feel. It may have immense preferences, but it will make understanding and not indignation its end. Such a sympathy will unite and not divide.

Against the thinly disguised panic which calls itself 'patriotism' and the thinly disguised militarism which calls itself 'preparedness' the cosmopolitan ideal is set. This does not mean that those who hold it are for a policy of drift. They, too, long passionately for an integrated and disciplined America. But they do not want one which is integrated only for domestic economic exploitation of the workers or for predatory economic imperialism among the weaker peoples. They do not want one that is integrated by coercion or militarism, or for the truculent assertion of a medieval code of honor and of doubtful rights. They believe that the most effective integration will be one which coordinates the diverse elements and turns them consciously toward working out together the place of America in the world-situation. They demand for integration a genuine integrity, a wholeness and soundness of enthusiasm and purpose which can only come when no national colony within our America feels that it is being discriminated against or that its cultural case is being prejudged. This strength of cooperation, this feeling that all who are here may have a hand in the destiny of America, will make for a finer spirit of integration than any narrow 'Americanism' or forced chauvinism.

In this effort we may have to accept some form of that dual citizenship which meets with so much articulate horror among us. Dual citizenship we may have to recognize as the rudimentary form of that international citizenship to which, if our words mean anything, we aspire. We have assumed unquestioningly that mere participation in the political life of the United States must cut the new citizen off from all sympathy with his old allegiance. Anything but a bodily transfer of devotion from one sovereignty to another has been viewed as a sort of moral treason against the Republic. We have insisted that the immigrant whom we welcomed escaping from the very exclusive nationalism of his European home shall forthwith adopt a nationalism just as exclusive, just as narrow, and even less legitimate because it is founded on no warm traditions of his own. Yet a nation like France is said to permit a formal and legal dual citizenship even at the present time. Though a citizen of hers may pretend to cast off his allegiance in favor of some other sovereignty, he is still subject to her laws when he returns. Once a citizen, always a citizen, no matter how many new citizenships he may embrace. And such a dual citizenship seems to us sound and right. For it recognizes that, although the Frenchman may accept the formal institutional framework of his new country and indeed become intensely loyal to it, yet his Frenchness he will never lose. What makes up the fabric of his soul will always be of this Frenchness, so that unless he becomes utterly degenerate he will always to some degree dwell still in his native environment.

Indeed, does not the cultivated American who goes to Europe practice a dual citizenship, which, if not formal, is no less real? The American who lives abroad may be the least expatriate of men. If he falls in love with French ways and French thinking and French democracy and seeks to saturate himself with the new spirit, he is guilty of at least a dual spiritual citizenship. He may be still American, yet he feels himself through sympathy also a Frenchman. And he finds that this expansion involves no shameful conflict within him, no surrender of his native attitude. He has rather for the first time caught a glimpse of the cosmopolitan spirit. And after wandering about through many races and civilizations he may return to America to find them all here living vividly and crudely, seeking the same adjustment that he made. He sees the new peoples here with a new vision. They are no longer masses of aliens, waiting to be 'assimilated,' waiting to be melted down into the indistinguishable dough of Anglo-Saxonism. They are rather threads of living and potent cultures, blindly striving to weave themselves into a novel international nation, the first the world has seen. In an Austria-Hungary or a Prussia the stronger of these cultures would be moving almost instinctively to subjugate the weaker. But in America those wills-to-power are turned in a different direction into learning how to live together.

Along with dual citizenship we shall have to accept, I think, that free and mobile passage of the immigrant between America and his native land again which now arouses so much prejudice among us. We shall have to accept the immigrant's return for the same reason that we consider justified our own flitting about the earth. To stigmatize the alien who works in America for a few years and returns to his own land, only perhaps to seek American fortune again, is to think in narrow nationalistic terms. It is to ignore the cosmopolitan significance of this migration. It is to ignore the fact that the returning immigrant is often a missionary to an inferior civilization.

This migratory habit has been especially common with the unskilled laborers who have been pouring into the United States in the last dozen years from every country in southeastern Europe. Many of them return to spend their earnings in their own country or to serve their country in war. But they return with an entirely new critical outlook, and a sense of the superiority of American organization to the primitive living around them. This continued passage to and fro has already raised the material standard of living in many regions of these backward countries. For these regions are thus endowed with exactly what they need, the capital for the exploitation of their natural resources, and the spirit of enterprise. America is thus educating these laggard peoples from the very bottom of society up, awaking vast masses to a new-born hope for the future. In the migratory Greek, therefore, we have not the parasitic alien, the doubtful American asset, but a symbol of that cosmopolitan interchange which is coming, in spite of all war and national exclusiveness.

Only America, by reason of the unique liberty of opportunity and traditional isolation for which she seems to stand, can lead in this cosmopolitan enterprise. Only the American—and in this category I include the migratory alien who has lived with us and caught the pioneer spirit and a sense of new social vistas—has the chance to become that citizen of the world. America is coming to be, not a nationality but a trans-nationality, a weaving back and forth, with the other lands, of many threads of all sizes and colors. Any movement which attempts to thwart this weaving, or to dye the fabric any one color, or disentangle the threads of the strands, is false to this cosmopolitan vision. I do not mean that we shall necessarily glut ourselves with the raw product of humanity. It would be folly to absorb the nations faster than we could weave them. We have no duty either to admit or reject. It is purely a question of expediency. What concerns us is the fact that the strands are here. We must have a policy and an ideal for an actual situation. Our question is, What shall we do with our America? How are we likely to get the more creative America—by confining our imaginations to the ideal of the melting-pot, or broadening them to some such cosmopolitan conception as I have been vaguely sketching?

The war has shown America to be unable, though isolated geographically and politically from a European world-situation, to remain aloof and irresponsible. She is a wandering star in a sky dominated by two colossal constellations of states. Can she not work out some position of her own, some life of being in, yet not quite of, this seething and embroiled European world? This is her only hope and promise. A trans-nationality of all the nations, it is spiritually impossible for her to pass into the orbit of any one. It will be folly to hurry herself into a premature and sentimental nationalism, or to emulate Europe and play fast and loose with the forces that drag into war. No Americanization will fulfill this vision which does not recognize the uniqueness of this trans-nationalism of ours. The Anglo-Saxon attempt to fuse will only create enmity and distrust. The crusade against 'hyphenates' will only inflame the partial patriotism of trans-nationals, and cause them to assert their European traditions in strident and unwholesome ways. But the attempt to weave a wholly novel international nation out of our chaotic America will liberate and harmonize the creative power of all these peoples and give them the new spiritual citizenship, as so many individuals have already been given, of a world.

Is it a wild hope that the undertow of opposition to metaphysics in international relations, opposition to militarism, is less a cowardly provincialism than a groping for this higher cosmopolitan ideal? One can understand the irritated restlessness with which our proud pro-British colonists contemplate a heroic conflict across the seas in which they have no part. It was inevitable that our necessary inaction should evolve in their minds into the bogey of national shame and dishonor. But let us be careful about accepting their sensitiveness as final arbiter. Let us look at our reluctance rather as the first crude beginnings of assertion on the part of certain strands in our nationality that they have a right to a voice in the construction of the American ideal. Let us face realistically the America we have around us. Let us work with the forces that are at work. Let us make something of this trans-national spirit instead of outlawing it. Already we are living this cosmopolitan America. What we need is everywhere a vivid consciousness of the new ideal. Deliberate headway must be made against the survivals of the melting pot ideal for the promise of American life.

Source text

Bourne, Randolph, 'Trans-national America', *Atlantic Monthly* 118 (July 1916), 86–97.

References

Clayon, Bruce, *Forgotten Prophet: The Life of Randolph Bourne* (Columbia, MO: University of Missouri Press, 1998).
Nichols, Christopher McKnight, 'Rethinking Randolph Bourne's Trans-National America: How World War I Created an Isolationist Antiwar Pluralism', *Journal of the Gilded Age and Progressive Era* 8.2 (April 2009), 217–57.

Arthur C. Parker (1881–1955)

From 'The American Indian in the World Crisis' (1918)

Arthur C. Parker grew up on the Cattaraugus Reservation of the Seneca Nation in Western New York, though he was not born a tribal member since the matrilineal descent of the Seneca did not extend to his white mother. At twelve he was given honorary membership as well as the name *Gawaso Wanneh* ('Big Snowsnake'). His family moved to White Plains, New York, thereafter and Parker attended public schools and eventually Dickinson Seminary, though he was not ordained. His adult career was spent as an archaeologist at various positions in New York, largely conducting research on the Iroquois and the history of other Native American tribes. Related to his heritage and interest, he co-founded the Society of American Indians (1911) and the National Congress of American Indians (1944), and served as the editor of the *American Indian Magazine* (1915–20), where he often wrote editorials on issues important to Indigenous peoples.

Native Americans had historically not been considered US citizens. The Dawes Act of 1887 allowed Native Americans to claim individual land holdings and thereby gain citizenship, but many still remained marginalised and were considered foreigners or savages who could not be incorporated into the larger body of American society. Yet, at the outset of the First World War, Native Americans were declared eligible for the draft, and over 6,000 were conscripted with more than 5,000 others enlisting voluntarily. Native Americans supported the war in non-combat roles as well, with many Native women serving as nurses through the Red Cross and civilians purchasing millions of dollars of war bonds. In so doing Native Americans asserted their allegiance as extending beyond their own tribal nations to include affiliation with the US. Native American veterans were granted US citizenship in 1919, a status extended to all Native Americans in 1924, in part due to displays of patriotism during the Great War.

Parker delivered the following address before the Albany Institute, one of the nation's oldest museums of history and art, on 5 February 1918. It was reprinted in *American Indian Magazine* shortly thereafter.

Figure 6.6 *American Indian Magazine*, cover for Spring 1918 issue. Courtesy University of Kansas Library.

From 'The American Indian in the World Crisis'

There are several sorts of patriotism and as many kinds of patriots. There is the patriot who shouts at a passing parade, or perhaps leads the parade carrying the flag, and who the next day audits the profits his store has made because of the holiday crowd. Then there is the patriot who, in the primitive sense, loves his native land and believes it the greatest in the universe; loves it because it contains his possessions and because he derives his livelihood there. There is another sort of patriot who, holding himself as merely an individual unit in his country, and more largely an individual of human society, has within himself the consciousness of his individual responsibility to society, and who recognizes that his real safety and profit comes from the safety and prosperity of all mankind, not merely himself. Thus, we have with us the shouting patriot, the emotional patriot, who for the sake of the good opinion of his fellows waves the flag; we have the selfish patriot who measures patriotism by his individual comfort and freedom; we have the world-patriot who pledges his life and fortune that his fellow countrymen and his brothers in the world fellowship may enjoy life, liberty and pursuit of happiness.

The Indian a World Patriot

The American Indian today stands before the world today as a "world patriot." He has pledged all his possessions, the lives of 10,000 his keenest and most physically sound men, and with them all his ideals of universal justice,—to the service of the United States of America and to the cause of world-wide democracy.

The most conservative of estimates place the value of Indian possessions in the United States of America at one billion dollars. There are three hundred thousand

Indians in the country today. Once they numbered more than a million and once they owned a continent with all its undeveloped resources. Yet, notwithstanding, these shrunken figures, an Indian of the Kaw tribe, a United States Senator from Kansas named Charles Curtis,[171] arose in the United States Senate and introduced a bill by which all the funds of the Indian tribes within the United States held in the Federal treasury were pledged to the financial support of the Government. Specifically this Indian in behalf of his kindred by blood pledged $100,000,000 to the Liberty Loan.[172] If every white man had pledged an equal individual amount the first Liberty Loan would have totalled fifty billion dollars. If dollars pledged indicate any measure of patriotism the measure of the red man of America is full and running over.

Indian patriotism is no new thing. Once any Indian tribe fully understood the moral justice of any patriotic cause they entered it fully and freely. There were Indians in the regiments of Washington, there were Indians in the first battles of the Revolutionary war, at Lexington and at Bunker Hill,[173] in the campaigns in the Hudson valley and about New York. In every battle of the nation since that time there have been Indian patriots willing to lay down their lives for the triumph of a nation conceived as this nation was conceived. It was only when Indians were encroached upon and confused as to the policy of the country that they took up arms against it,—the only effective way by which they could protest. Though they have suffered much injustice, though every treaty forced upon the Indians has been broken by the Nation, though their lands have been taken from them, their women and children massacred by our military units, though they have been repressed and segregated, yet in this world struggle, this gigantic war for human freedom, for the establishment of government of men by the consent and cooperation of the governed, the American Indian is loyal to the United States and to the cause of the Allies. There is absolutely no doubt of this. They are in America and with America to the finish. [...]

Indians in Europe

When the war burst over Europe there were perhaps forty American Indians in Germany and Austria, some as opera singers and others with American wild west shows. Among them were a dozen or more Onondaga Indians from New York State. The war destroyed all their business hopes and the shows were stranded. With great difficulty these Onondagas made their way from Vienna and Posen to Holland. They were frequently mobbed, stoned and in other ways abused, the populace thinking them Russians or Serbians. At length a good Yankee consul sent them home, and what a good place America did seem to these war stranded red skins. A few years ago one of the Seneca Chiefs toured Germany. Before he went he told me that he hoped to see the Kaiser and preach the Indian religion to him. He came back disappointed in not being able to talk to the Kaiser, but more than this he came back to his family with a tale that Germany was a country of warriors getting ready to fight somebody. A month ago I had a letter from the reservation

---

171 Charles Curtis (1860–1936) later served as Vice President from 1929 to 1933, thereby becoming the highest-ranking Native American to serve in the US Executive Branch.

172 A series of four bonds sold by the American government during 1917 and 1918 in support of the Allied cause

173 The battles of Lexington and Bunker Hill (1775), both in Massachusetts, two of the earliest military engagements of the Revolutionary War

telling that Jesse Cornplanter,[174] son of this chief, has enlisted in the United States Army and was going over to Germany with another sort of message for the Kaiser. Young Cornplanter will find himself in good company and with a couple of million men ready to carry a pretty potent message over the top to take to Berlin. Be sure of this that before the war is over, feet that once wore moccasins will tread the streets of Potsdam, and that the American red man,—call him by what other name you may,—will help civilize an autocracy gone mad with the lust for power.

The Indians did not wait for the draft. Long before we entered the struggle Indians had gone over the border and enlisted with the Canadian forces. Indeed on some of the Canadian reservations the Dominion Government had encouraged the formation of Indian companies and battalions. Thus when the first blood was shed the Canadian Indians were ready and went their way to the transports eager for the fray "over there." Hundreds more joined such regiments as they could, some of the best equipped enlisting in the famous Princess Pat regiment.[175] Many Indian boys from the United States joined that regiment and won immortal honors in its heroic work in the front line. Among these are Lieutenant Longlance the Cherokee who was about to enter West Point[176] when a real chance for service came. Then there was Ernest Kick the Oneida who lost his life at Vimey Ridge,[177] and Harold Griffis whose father was a Kiowa. Griffis' real name is Tahan, meaning Fighting-man. Thrice he was wounded, the last time being one of eight survivors of his company. Had his companion not pulled a Hun's bayonet from his leg and shot the Hun, Harold might never have lived to re-enlist in the engineers' troops back of the lines. To the Canadians, Indians are Canadians,—brothers in the big fight. Just so they are here in the United States, where more than 5,000 Indians have enlisted voluntarily. They are in all branches of the service. [...]

The Indian in The Fight for Democracy

The rational world is demanding democracy for all nations, respect for the rights of the smaller groups, the sanctity of treaties and open diplomacy. The Indians of America have suffered long the woes of these things ignored. Patiently they have submitted to the inevitable and obeyed the laws of the land. They have sought as their light gave them vision to win back their heritage by labor and thrift. They are entering the body politic to become a force for weal or woe in it. For the time being they are forgetting themselves, and with the manhood of America challenged by an infamous autocracy they have responded,—they fight.

Some day the thousands from abroad will return to ask for the freedom, the citizenship and the right of self government for which they fought and shed their blood on the other side. If America today will think, and care and give the few simple things for which the Indians of America have memorialized the President and

---

174 Jesse Cornplanter (Hayonhwonhish) (1889–1957), US actor, author, decorated First World War veteran

175 Princess Patricia's Canadian Light Infantry, the first Canadian regiment formed at the outset of the First World War

176 The United States Military Academy at West Point, New York

177 The Battle of Vimy Ridge, fought between Canadian-British and German forces from 9 to 12 April 1917 in Nord-Pas-de-Calais, France; often touted as a key moment in the development of shared Canadian identity, Vimy has been glorified in that nation's celebrations and memorials. Parker's citation of Vimy here also recognises that Native communities' views on national affiliations are not directly aligned with white boundaries such as between the US and Canada.

Congress there will be some recompense. If not the three hundred thousand red men will struggle on with aching hearts and with the feeling that they have been denied the justice that so great a nation should give and freely give. In that measure by which you who hear this message ignore the red man's call you will have contributed to the continuation of his present difficulties.

But whatever you do or any one else does, the Indian, you may be sure will render every possible service, to America, his country, and will struggle on not only for his own regeneration but for the even greater ennoblement of this Republic.

Source text

Parker, Arthur C., 'The American Indian in the World Crisis', *American Indian Magazine* 6.1 (1918), 15–24.

References

Bruchac, Joseph, 'Being Iroquois: Arthur C. Parker', *Voices: The Journal of New York Folklore* 41.1 (Spring 2015), 38–9.
Porter, Joy, *To Be Indian: The Life of Seneca-Iroquois Arthur Caswell Parker* (Norman, OK: Oklahoma University Press, 2001).
Smithers, Gregory D., 'The Soul of Unity: The Quarterly Journal of the Society of American Indians, 1913–1915', *American Indian Quarterly* 37.3 (Spring 2013), 263–89

Anzia Yezierska (1880–1970)

From 'How I Found America' (1920)

Anzia Yezierska was one of the millions of Europeans who immigrated to the US in the last decades of the nineteenth century, arriving in New York City around 1890 from the village of Plinsk, Poland. Her Orthodox Jewish family was strongly patriarchal; her father was a Talmudic scholar who expected his wife and daughters to support him through labour outside the home, an experience she would later fictionalise throughout her career. This paternal demand led young Anzia to work in factories and sweatshops throughout her youth, until finally enrolling at Columbia Teacher's College under John Dewey, with whom she had a romantic relationship. She began writing at thirty-two, first with a number of stories collected in *Hungry Hearts* (1920), then in novels such as *Salome of the Tenements* (1923) and *Bread Givers* (1925). At various junctures she expanded her scope with stints of screenwriting in Hollywood and for the WPA Writers' Project, but returned to write about her lived experience of immigrant life in Manhattan. Though her writing was once considered crude and mawkish alongside other immigrant fiction, feminist and ethnic studies scholars have recovered Yezierska as a pioneer of modernism cast in a vernacular idiom.

'How I Found America' touches on the common themes of Yezierska's writing: immigration and Americanisation. Though nominally equal under the law, immigrants faced discrimination, exploitation and abiding poverty. Nonetheless, for many, compared to life in their home nations, they had religious freedom and opportunity for education and advancement, as well as a path to citizenship. The tension between these visions served as the basis for much of Yezierska's fiction, blending consternation and aspiration.

From 'How I Found America' (1920)

[..]

Between buildings that loomed like mountains, we struggled with our bundles, spreading around us the smell of the steerage. Up Broadway, under the bridge, and through the swarming streets of the ghetto, we followed Gedalyeh Mindel.

I looked about the narrow streets of squeezed-in stores and houses, ragged clothes, dirty bedding oozing out of the windows, ash-cans and garbage-cans cluttering the side-walks. A vague sadness pressed down my heart—the first doubt of America.

"Where are the green fields and open spaces in America?" cried my heart. "Where is the golden country of my dreams?"

A loneliness for the fragrant silence of the woods that lay beyond our mud hut welled up in my heart, a longing for the soft, responsive earth of our village streets. All about me was the hardness of brick and stone, the stinking smells of crowded poverty.

"Here's your house with separate rooms like in a palace." Gedalyeh Mindel flung open the door of a dingy, airless flat.

"Oi weh!" my mother cried in dismay. "Where's the sunshine in America?"

She went to the window and looked out at the blank wall of the next house. "Gottuniu! Like in a grave so dark ..."

"It ain't so dark, it's only a little shady." Gedalyeh Mindel lighted the gas. "Look only"—he pointed with pride to the dim gaslight. "No candles, no kerosene lamps in America, you turn on a screw and put to it a match and you got it light like with sunshine."

Again the shadow fell over me, again the doubt of America!

In America were rooms without sunlight, rooms to sleep in, to eat in, to cook in, but without sunshine. And Gedalyeh Mindel was happy. Could I be satisfied with just a place to sleep and eat in, and a door to shut people out—to take the place of sunlight? Or would I always need the sunlight to be happy?

And where was there a place in America for me to play? I looked out into the alley below and saw pale-faced children scrambling in the gutter. "Where is America?" cried my heart.

My eyes were shutting themselves with sleep. Blindly, I felt for the buttons on my dress, and buttoning I sank back in sleep again—the deadweight sleep of utter exhaustion.

"Heart of mine!" my mother's voice moaned above me. "Father is already gone an hour. You know how they'll squeeze from you a nickel for every minute you're late. Quick only!"

I seized my bread and herring and tumbled down the stairs and out into the street. I ate running, blindly pressing through the hurrying throngs of workers—my haste and fear choking each mouthful.

I felt a strangling in my throat as I neared the sweatshop prison; all my nerves screwed together into iron hardness to endure the day's torture.

For an instant I hesitated as I faced the grated window of the old dilapidated building—dirt and decay cried out from every crumbling brick.

In the maw of the shop, raging around me the roar and the clatter, the clatter and the roar, the merciless grind of the pounding machines. Half maddened, half deadened, I struggled to think, to feel, to remember—what am I—who am I—why was I here?

I struggled in vain—bewildered and lost in a whirlpool of noise.

"America—America—where was America?" it cried in my heart.

The factory whistle—the slowing-down of the machines—the shout of release hailing the noon hour.

I woke as from a tense nightmare—a weary waking to pain.

In the dark chaos of my brain reason began to dawn. In my stifled heart feelings began to pulse. The wound of my wasted life began to throb and ache. My childhood choked with drudgery—must my youth too die—unlived?

The odor of herring and garlic—the ravenous munching of food—laughter and loud, vulgar jokes. Was it only I who was so wretched? I looked at those around me. Were they happy or only insensible to their slavery? How could they laugh and joke? Why were they not torn with rebellion against this galling grind—the crushing, deadening movements of the body, where only hands live and hearts and brains must die?

A touch on my shoulder. I looked up. It was Yetta Solomon from the machine next to mine.

"Here's your tea."

I stared at her, half hearing.

"Ain't you going to eat nothing?"

"Oi weh! Yetta! I can't stand it!" The cry broke from me. "I didn't come to America to turn into a machine. I came to America to make from myself a person. Does America want only my hands—only the strength of my body—not my heart—not my feelings—my thoughts?"

"Our heads ain't smart enough," said Yetta, practically. "We ain't been to school like the American-born."

"What for did I come to America but to go to school—to learn—to think—to make something beautiful from my life ..."

"Sh-sh! Sh-sh! The boss—the boss!" came the warning whisper.

A sudden hush fell over the shop as the boss entered. He raised his hand. Breathless silence.

The hard, red face with pig's eyes held us under its sickening spell. Again I saw the Cossack and heard him thunder the ukaz.[178]

Prepared for disaster, the girls paled as they cast at each other sidelong, frightened glances.

---

178 An imperial decree issued by a Russian tsar or religious leader. This particular order, issued by the tsar and delivered by a Cossack, had threatened a fine of a thousand rubles if the Hebrew religion was taught in the Jewish home.

"Hands," he addressed us, fingering the gold watch-chain that spread across his fat belly, "it's slack in the other trades and I can get plenty girls begging themselves to work for half what you're getting—only I ain't a skinner.[179] I always give my hands a show to earn their bread. From now on, I'll give you fifty cents a dozen shirts instead of seventy-five, but I'll give you night-work, so you needn't lose nothing." And he was gone.

The stillness of death filled the shop. Each one felt the heart of the other bleed with her own helplessness.

A sudden sound broke the silence. A woman sobbed chokingly. It was Balah Rifkin, a widow with three children.

"Oi weh!" She tore at her scrawny neck. "The blood-sucker—the thief! How will I give them to eat—my babies—my babies—my hungry little lambs!"

"Why do we let him choke us?"

"Twenty-five cents less on a dozen—how will we be able to live?"

"He tears the last skin from our bones!"

"Why didn't nobody speak up to him?"

"Tell him he couldn't crush us down to worse than we had in Russia?"

"Can we help ourselves? Our life lies in his hands."

Something in me forced me forward. Rage at the bitter greed tore me. Our desperate helplessness drove me to strength.

"I'll go to the boss!" I cried, my nerves quivering with fierce excitement. "I'll tell him Balah Rifkin has three hungry mouths to feed."

Pale, hungry faces thrust themselves toward me, thin, knotted hands reached out, starved bodies pressed close about me.

"Long years on you!" cried Balah Rifkin, drying her eyes with a corner of her shawl.

"Tell him about my old father and me, his only bread-giver," came from Bessie Sopolsky, a gaunt-faced girl with a hacking cough.

"And I got no father or mother and four of them younger than me hanging on my neck." Jennie Feist's beautiful young face was already scarred with the gray worries of age.

America, as the oppressed of all lands have dreamed America to be, and America as it is, flashed before me—a banner of fire! Behind me I felt masses pressing—thousands of immigrants—thousands upon thousands crushed by injustice, lifted me as on wings.

I entered the boss's office without a shadow of fear. I was not I—the wrongs of my people burned through me till I felt the very flesh of my body a living flame of rebellion.

I faced the boss.

"We can't stand it!" I cried. "Even as it is we're hungry. Fifty cents a dozen would starve us. Can you, a Jew, tear the bread from another Jew's mouth?"

"You, fresh mouth, you! Who are you to learn me my business?"

"Weren't you yourself once a machine slave—your life in the hands of your boss?"

"You—loaferin[180]—money for nothing you want! The minute they begin to talk English they get flies in their nose ... A black year on you—trouble-maker! I'll have no smart heads in my shop! Such freshness! Out you get ... out from my shop!"

---

179 Slang for a mule driver – in this sense, one who works his wards too hard
180 Yiddish slang for loafer or a lazy person

Stunned and hopeless, the wings of my courage broken, I groped my way back to them—back to the eager, waiting faces—back to the crushed hearts aching with mine.

As I opened the door they read our defeat in my face.

"Girls!" I held out my hands. "He's fired me."

My voice died in the silence. Not a girl stirred. Their heads only bent closer over their machines.

"Here, you! Get yourself out of here!" The boss thundered at me. "Bessie Sopolsky and you, Balah Rifkin, take out her machine into the hall . . . I want no big-mouthed Americanerins[181] in my shop."

Bessie Sopolsky and Balah Rifkin, their eyes black with tragedy, carried out my machine.

Not a hand was held out to me, not a face met mine. I felt them shrink from me as I passed them on my way out.

In the street I found I was crying. The new hope that had flowed in me so strong bled out of my veins. A moment before, our togetherness had made me believe us so strong—and now I saw each alone—crushed—broken. What were they all but crawling worms, servile grubbers for bread?

I wept not so much because the girls had deserted me, but because I saw for the first time how mean, how vile, were the creatures with whom I had to work. How the fear for bread had dehumanized their last shred of humanity! I felt I had not been working among human beings, but in a jungle of savages who had to eat one another alive in order to survive.

And then, in the very bitterness of my resentment, the hardness broke in me. I saw the girls through their own eyes as if I were inside of them. What else could they have done? Was not an immediate crust of bread for Balah Rifkin's children more urgent than truth—more vital than honor?

Could it be that they ever had dreamed of America as I had dreamed? Had their faith in America wholly died in them? Could my faith be killed as theirs had been?

Gasping from running, Yetta Solomon flung her arms around me.

"You golden heart! I sneaked myself out from the shop—only to tell you I'll come to see you to-night. I'd give the blood from under my nails for you—only I got to run back—I got to hold my job—my mother—"

I hardly saw or heard her—my senses stunned with my defeat. I walked on in a blind daze—feeling that any moment I would drop in the middle of the street from sheer exhaustion.

Every hope I had clung to—every human stay—every reality was torn from under me. I sank in bottomless blackness. I had only one wish left—to die.

Was it then only a dream—a mirage of the hungry-hearted people in the desert lands of oppression—this age-old faith in America—the beloved, the prayed-for "golden country"?

Had the starved villagers of Sukovoly lifted above their sorrows a mere rainbow vision that led them—where—where? To the stifling submission of the sweatshop or the desperation of the streets!

"O God! What is there beyond this hell?" my soul cried in me. "Why can't I make a quick end to myself?"

A thousand voices within me and about me answered:

---

181 Yiddish slang for American

"My faith is dead, but in my blood their faith still clamors and aches for fulfillment—*dead generations whose faith though beaten back still presses on—a resistless, deathless force!*"

"In this America that crushes and kills me, their spirit drives me on—to struggle—to suffer—but never to submit."

In my desperate darkness their lost lives loomed—a living flame of light. Again I saw the mob of dusty villagers crowding around my father as he read the letter from America—their eager faces thrust out—their eyes blazing with the same hope, the same age-old faith that drove me on—

A sudden crash against my back. Dizzy with pain I fell—then all was darkness and quiet.

I opened my eyes. A white-clad figure bent over me. Had I died? Was I in the heaven of the new world—in America?

My eyes closed again. A misty happiness filled my being.

"Learning flows free like milk and honey," it dreamed itself in me.

I was in my heaven—in the schools of America—in open, sunny fields—a child with other children. Our lesson-books were singing birds and whispering trees—chanting brooks and beckoning skies. We breathed in learning and wisdom as naturally as flowers breathe in sunlight.

After our lessons were over, we all joined hands skipping about like a picture of dancing fairies I had once seen in a shop-window.

I was so full of the joy of togetherness—the great wonder of the new world; it pressed on my heart like sorrow. Slowly, I stole away from the other children into silent solitude, wrestling and praying to give out what surged in me into some form of beauty. And out of my struggle to shape my thoughts beautifully, a great song filled the world.

"Soon she's all right to come back to the shop—yes, nurse?" The voice of Yetta Solomon broke into my dreaming.

Wearily I opened my eyes. I saw I was still on earth.

Yetta's broad, generous face smiled anxiously at me. "Lucky yet the car that run you over didn't break your hands or your feet. So long you got yet good hands you'll soon be back by the machine."

"Machine?" I shuddered. "I can't go back to the shop again. I got so used to sunlight and quiet in the hospital I'll not be able to stand the hell again."

"Shah!—Shah!" soothed Yetta. "Why don't you learn yourself to take life like it is? What's got to be, got to be. In Russia, you could hope to run away from your troubles to America. But from America where can you go?"

"Yes," I sighed. "In the blackest days of Russia, there was always the hope from America. In Russia we had only a mud hut; not enough to eat and always the fear from the Cossack, but still we managed to look up to the sky, to dream, to think of the new world where we'll have a chance to be people, not slaves."

"What's the use to think so much? It only eats up the flesh from your bones. Better rest ..."

"How can I rest when my choked-in thoughts tear me to pieces? I need school more than a starving man needs bread."

Yetta's eyes brooded over me. Suddenly a light broke. "I got an idea. There's a new school for greenhorns[182] where they learn them anything they want ..."

---

182 Someone new or inexperienced; term often applied to immigrants

"What—where?" I raised myself quickly, hot with eagerness. "How do you know from it—tell me only—quick—since when—"

"The girl next door by my house—she used to work by cigars—and now she learns there."

"What does she learn?"

"Don't get yourself so excited. Your eyes are jumping out from your head."

I fell back weakly: "Oi weh! Tell me!" I begged.

"All I know is that she likes what she learns better than rolling cigars. And it's called 'School for Immigrant Girls.'"

"Your time is up. Another visitor is waiting to come in," said the nurse.

As Yetta walked out, my mother, with the shawl over her head, rushed in and fell on my bed kissing me.

"Oi weh! Oi weh! Half my life is out from me from fright. How did all happen?"

"Don't worry yourself so. I'm nearly well already and will go back to work soon."

"Talk not work. Get only a little flesh on your bones. They say they send from the hospital people to the country. Maybe they'll send you."

"But how will you live without my wages?"

"Davy is already peddling with papers and Bessie is selling lolly-pops after school in the park. Yesterday she brought home already twenty-eight cents."

For all her efforts to be cheerful, I looked at her pinched face and wondered if she had eaten that day.

Released from the hospital, I started home. As I neared Allen Street,[183] the terror of the dark rooms swept over me. "No—no—I can't yet go back to the darkness and the stinking smells," I said to myself. "So long they're getting along without my wages, let them think I went to the country and let me try out that school for immigrants that Yetta told me about."

So I went to the Immigrant School.

A tall, gracious woman received me, not an employee, but a benefactress.

The love that had rushed from my heart toward the Statue in the Bay,[184] rushed out to Mrs. Olney. She seemed to me the living spirit of America. All that I had ever dreamed America to be shone to me out of the kindness of her brown eyes. She would save me from the sordidness that was crushing me I felt the moment I looked at her. Sympathy and understanding seemed to breathe from her serene presence.

I longed to open my heart to her, but I was so excited I didn't know where to begin.

"I'm crazy to learn!" I gasped breathlessly, and then the very pressure of the things I had to say choked me.

An encouraging smile warmed the fine features.

"What trade would you like to learn—sewing-machine operating?"

"Sewing-machine operating?" I cried. "Oi weh!" I shuddered. "Only the thought 'machine' kills me. Even when I only look on clothes, it weeps in me when I think how the seams from everything people wear is sweated in the shop."

"Well, then"—putting a kind hand on my shoulder—"how would you like to learn to cook? There's a great need for trained servants and you'd get good wages and a pleasant home."

"Me—a servant?" I flung back her hand. "Did I come to America to make from myself a cook?"

---

183 A street on the Lower East Side of Manhattan
184 The Statue of Liberty

Mrs. Olney stood abashed a moment. "Well, my dear," she said deliberately, "what would you like to take up?"

"I got ideas how to make America better, only I don't know how to say it out. Ain't there a place I can learn?"

A startled woman stared at me. For a moment not a word came. Then she proceeded with the same kind smile. "It's nice of you to want to help America, but I think the best way would be for you to learn a trade. That's what this school is for, to help girls find themselves, and the best way to do is to learn something useful."

"Ain't thoughts useful? Does America want only the work from my body, my hands? Ain't it thoughts that turn over the world?"

"Ah! But we don't want to turn over the world." Her voice cooled.

"But there's got to be a change in America!" I cried. "Us immigrants want to be people—not 'hands'—not slaves of the belly! And it's the chance to think out thoughts that makes people."

"My child, thought requires leisure. The time will come for that. First you must learn to earn a good living."

"Did I come to America for a living?"

"What did you come for?"

"I came to give out all the fine things that was choked in me in Russia. I came to help America make the new world .... They said, in America I could open up my heart and fly free in the air—to sing—to dance—to live—to love .... Here I got all those grand things in me, and America won't let me give nothing."

"Perhaps you made a mistake in coming to this country. Your own land might appreciate you more." A quick glance took me in from head to foot. "I'm afraid that you have come to the wrong place. We only teach trades here."

She turned to her papers and spoke over her shoulder. "I think you will have to go elsewhere if you want to set the world on fire." [...]

Source text

Yezierska, Anzia, *Hungry Hearts* (New York: Grosset & Dunlap, 1920).

References

Campos, Rebecca E., 'Charity Institutions as Networks of Power: How Anzia Yezierska's Characters Resist Philanthropic Surveillance', *Journal of English Studies* 15.15 (2017), 31–52.

Hefner, Brooks E., '"Slipping back into the vernacular": Anzia Yezierska's Vernacular Modernism', *MELUS: Multi-Ethnic Literature of the U.S.* 36.3 (2011), 187–211.

7

RELIGION AND SECULARISM

Figure 7.1 'The American River Ganges', *Harper's Weekly* 15 (30 September 1871), 916. A related essay, 'The Priests and the Children', appears on p. 915. There, Eugene Lawrence claimed the 'Romish Church' was a threat to 'our free schools, and perhaps our free institutions', since priests and Catholic-run schools were undermining public education and American children. Courtesy HathiTrust.

The US author Elizabeth Stuart Phelps first rose to transatlantic prominence when barely twenty years old by publishing *The Gates Ajar* (1868), a novel with a religious message on the afterlife. Even so mixed a review as appeared in *Hours at Home* credited her text as compellingly 'giv[ing] the author's views of Heaven' ('Literature', 386). Phelps's embrace of an explicit religious focus would continue across a long authorial career. In 1893, for instance, when invited to revisit *The Gates Ajar* and its sequels (*Beyond the Gates* [1883] and *The Gates Between* [1887]), she recollected a publisher's joke to her that '"Heaven is your hobby"' ('Immortality', 567). Phelps's initial narrative had tapped into US readers' intense grief over the loss of loved ones in the Civil War but had resonated more broadly through Anglo-Protestant religious sentimentalism. Thus, revisiting her writing process in an 1896 reflection for London's *Review of Reviews*, she recalled how the novel's content moved her like 'a tear or a sigh or a prayer' to provide spiritual comfort by depicting a Heavenly afterlife ('What Led', 440).

Phelps was hardly alone among transatlantic women novelists in embracing religious themes. Charlotte Brontë's eponymous heroine Jane Eyre finds refuge with her cousin St John Rivers's family after fleeing Thornfield and considers joining him in a missionary career. As Hosanna Krienke has observed, two well-known novels by Unitarian (and minister's wife) Elizabeth Gaskell – *Mary Barton* (1848) and *Ruth* (1853) – address questions about sin, repentance and the after-life. Relatedly, this section's excerpt from *Lois the Witch* (1859) exemplifies Gaskell's sustained engagement with religious topics.

Yet to pigeonhole such women authors as 'religious writers' ignores their self-aware navigation of secular, business dimensions of their authorship, not to mention their engagement with politics. Addressing religious themes hardly precluded authors like Phelps or Gaskell from writing on secular issues of social justice from a pragmatic, realist stance.[1] Similarly, as a daughter, wife and sibling of ministers, Harriet Beecher Stowe made her first trip to Britain mainly to garner money through the popularity of *Uncle Tom's Cabin* – though she made time to meet with many religious groups there.

SPIRITUALITY WITHIN WORLDLY SPACES

If the most religiously inclined writings and daily experiences of nineteenth-century transatlantic culture included secular dimensions, a flip side is equally evident. Take, for instance, the oceanic business of seafaring, or more specifically whaling. Richard J. Callahan demonstrates that whaling was deeply infused with religious influences, including constant prayers for sailors by those at home (as reflected in the Anglican *Book of Common Prayer*), and outreach efforts by organisations like the American Seamen's Friend Society ('Religious Spaces'). Indeed, whalers were a frequent target of religious organisations seeking to reform – or at least ameliorate – the bad behaviour of mariners who faced

---

1 See Elizabeth Starr on 'Gaskell's social-problem novels' and contributions to 'authorship as a legitimate part of the often aggressive, contentious world of public streets and factories' (385). Despite readers' persistent association of Phelps with heavenly concerns, she also published incisive examinations of worldly social problems such as 'The Tenth of January' (1868), *The Silent Partner* (1871) and *Doctor Zay* (1886).

a thousand sinful temptations when finally returning to land.[2] Stereotypes (and real cases) of seamen's post-cruise rowdiness led to such interventions as a Port of London 'floating chapel' aiming 'to induce sailors to attend public worship' rather than heading to a port town's bar.[3]

Transatlantic literature tied to seafaring spotlights how shipboard sites – while themselves traversing fluid oceanic space – blended secular and religious concerns. In that context, see scenes from John Marrant's narrative in this section, such as his account of the Lord's saving him from drowning when cast overboard during a storm. Meanwhile, a fluid blending of religious and worldly concerns is echoed, Bryan Sinche argues, in Lydia Sigourney's *Poems for the Sea*. Sinche interprets Sigourney's collection as connecting the sentimentalised spiritual stance for which the poet is sometimes satirised with a realistic portrayal of seamen as facing so many hardships in their commercial duties that would-be reformers should temper expectations for saving sailors' souls.

RELIGION *AND* SECULARISM

As indicated above, nineteenth-century religion and secularism exercised interconnected influences on transatlantic life, for both individuals and social groups. Accordingly, our use of 'and' between the two terms (rather than 'versus') resists a commonplace binary view, offering in its place an emphasis on interactivity operating through multiple transatlantic pathways.

Admittedly, individual authors sometimes self-positioned on either side of an imagined divide to attack failings associated with the opposite end. Charles Bradlaugh's principled critique of religion, excerpted here, offers one example. But many writings linked to this theme explored interrelationships between religion and secularism, as Woods Hutchinson did in *The Gospel According to Darwin* (1898), also excerpted here.

Joseph Priestley's 'Preface' to *The Present State of Europe Compared with the Ancient Prophesies*, another entry, explicates his reasons for leaving Britain for America and defends himself against his opponents on both religious and secular grounds. He bemoans the 'rioting and violence' directed against affiliates of the Dissenting religious tradition (vi), himself among them (vii).[4] At the same time, Priestley draws on Enlightenment-associated appeals to Reason to justify his emigration, such as his perception that the new nation where his friend Benjamin Franklin would welcome him was more genuinely dedicated to the political principle of '*civil and religious liberty*' (xi, emphasis in original).

---

2 'Thoughtlessness of Sailors', *Chambers Edinburgh Journal* (5 June 1841), 156.

3 One account reported that 'Ministers of different denominations' officiated at services that were 'well attended by thousands of sailors', many of whom declared that the Chapel convinced them 'to join themselves with the Christian societies', moving from 'utter carelessness' to 'seriously thoughtful' religious practice (208). See 'Port of London and Bethel Union Society', *Wesleyan-Methodist Magazine* 11 (March 1832).

4 Dissenters rejected elements of the official national Anglican religion, not all religion. Unlike in the US, where separation of Church and State was enshrined in the Constitution's first amendment, in Britain the Anglican Church was the nation's official religion, with the King or Queen designated as 'Defender of the Faith'. Though Protestants had freedom to worship as of 1688, they were denied equal access to universities and serving in Parliament until well into the nineteenth century.

RELIGION-GUIDED REFORM AS SECULARISED ENTERPRISE

The nineteenth century's many transatlantic reform campaigns consistently evoked religious principles as rationale and guide to action. As documented within 'Abolition and Aftermath' earlier, anti-slavery leaders cast their appeals in moral terms. Thus writers like William Craft forcefully condemned pro-slavery advocates in the US for religious hypocrisy, as seen in our entry from his memoir. If the opening text in this section, Phillis Wheatley's 'On Being Brought from Africa to America', seems to affirm the arguments Craft sought to refute, careful readers will note the sense of cultural loss also recorded in her lyric, which thereby questions, if indirectly, the Christian 'civilising' practices the poem also praises.

However important religious features were to transatlantic reform campaigns like those for abolition and temperance, or against prostitution, these same movements required prolonged and purposeful engagement with secular institutions. Along those lines, Candace Ward highlights astute political manoeuvring by the founders of *The Jamaica Watchman* even as they fought pro-slavery forces on spiritual and moral grounds.[5] Similarly, in literature, Anthony Trollope's Barsetshire novels (including *Barchester Towers* [1857]) show religious institutions caught up in secular relations and institutional power politics, as does Margaret Oliphant's Chronicles of Carlingford series.

Several texts in this section exemplify transatlantic literature linked to missionary enterprises and their complicated connection with extra-religious agendas. 'Irish Jim', a story appearing in *Youth's Companion* in 1857, enshrines the efforts by Protestant US-based 'home missions' to acculturate Catholic immigrant children. Ethnic stereotypes in the story depict Jim's Irish mother as unfit, anticipating nativist anti-immigrant rhetoric today; Jim is welcomed into American-ness mainly through embracing Protestantism. On a parallel front, Helen Barrett Montgomery's *Western Women in Foreign Lands* celebrates women like British missionary Charlotte Tucker, whose biography here was echoed by many magazine profiles honouring 'civilising' religious teachers abroad. Notably, such texts simultaneously furthered imperial political agendas. Thus, speaking at an international congress on race soon after Montgomery's compendium on missionary successes lauded movement supporters, Charles Eastman (Ohiyesa) lamented the complicity of missionaries in colonising lands and Native people as far back as early conquest days in the Americas.

---

5 See '"An Engine of Immense Power": *The Jamaica Watchman* and Crossings in Nineteenth-Century Print Culture', *Victorian Periodicals Review* 51.3 (Fall 2018), 483–503. Ward tracks the *Watchman*'s progress from its 1829 launch through politicised conflicts with pro-slavery 'planto-cratic interests' who had their own publications (483). Founders Edward Jordon and Robert Osborn, she demonstrates, resisted the planter class on moral grounds but also via rhetorical prowess shaped by political skill. For a broader survey showing how religious reform movements were bound up with political radicalism, thereby 'undercutting the opposition between religious and secular political orientations that has been the focus of so much scholarship', see Abigail Green, 'Humanitarianism in Nineteenth-Century Context: Religious, Gendered, National', *Historical Journal* 57.4 (2014), 1157–75.

Whose Religious and Secular Experiences Count?

Voices from multiple perspectives – including satirical ones – circulated portraits of religion in action to transatlantic audiences. An entry from Frances Trollope's *Domestic Manners of the Americans* (1832) and a Washington Irving sketch, 1819's 'The Country Church', illustrate how the secular site of print publication provided a venue for playful yet thought-provoking commentary on religion's shortcomings. Trollope's and Irving's texts make for a generative pairing – one a British author's deft skewering of US evangelical revivals, the other an American writer's gentle but incisive look at class differences in an English country church. Our excerpt from Anna Jameson's thoughts on Indigenous people's 'Religious Opinions' is more complex – in tone, standpoint and individual diction choices – reflecting both her own seemingly self-assured analysis and signs of her assessments' limitations.

Anglophone Protestants dominated the transatlantic print marketplace for texts about nineteenth-century religion, but they did not hold complete sway. Multiple entries here affirm the nineteenth century's diversity of authors and religious traditions, as seen in texts by Muslim author Abon Becr Sadika and two poets: Latter-Day Saints author Eliza Snow and Jewish writer Grace Aguilar. In their writings, as well as in Cecil Frances Alexander's popular hymn 'All Things Bright and Beautiful', we note that, however much nineteenth-century religion could merit critique of its practices, its positive social force in the lives of individuals and groups cannot be ignored. As Michael Rectenwald reminds us, historically sensitive study should avoid perceiving secularisation as a 'progressive and teleological' process, moving in a clean, inexorable line of cultural change (2). Rather, he urges, we should see secularism as more complicated than 'the mere absence of religion', while acknowledging the persistent energy of religiosity (3).

Two authors in this section can foster such analysis. Pairing E. Pauline Johnson's 'Brier: Good Friday' and 'The Happy Hunting Grounds' honours her lifelong affirmation of spiritual traditions from both her white settlers' and her First Nations' heritages. An excerpt from Anglo-Irish author Frances Power Cobbe, in line with our section's emphasis on interactions between religion and secularism, chronicles another transatlantic synthesis-seeking in her record of reconciling her initial religious training with studies of Deism, supported by careful study of American thinker Theodore Parker.

References

Callahan, Richard J., Jr, 'The Religious Spaces of American Whaling', in John Corrigan (ed.), *Religion, Space, and the Atlantic World* (Columbia, SC: University of South Carolina Press, 2017), 133–51.

Krienke, Hosanna, 'The "After-Life" of Illness: Reading Against the Deathbed in Gaskell's *Ruth* and Nineteenth-Century Convalescent Devotionals', *Victorian Literature and Culture* 45 (2017), 35–53.

'Literature of the Day: The Gates Ajar', *Hours at Home: A Popular Monthly of Instruction and Recreation* 8.4 (February 1869), 385–8.

Phelps, Elizabeth Stuart, 'Immortality and Agnosticism: "The Gates Ajar" – Twenty-Five Years After', *North American Review* 156.438 (May 1893), 567–76.

Rectenwald, Michael, *Nineteenth-Century British Secularism: Science, Religion, and Literature* (New York: Palgrave Macmillan, 2016).

Sinche, Bryan, 'Lydia Sigourney's Sailors and the Limits of Sentiment', *Legacy* 29.1 (2012), 62–85.

Starr, Elizabeth, '"A Great Engine for Good": The Industry of Fiction in Elizabeth Gaskell's "Mary Barton" and "North and South"', *Studies in the Novel* 34.4 (Winter 2002), 385–402.

Werner, Winter Jade, *Missionary Cosmopolitanism in Nineteenth-Century British Literature* (Columbus, OH: Ohio State University Press, 2020).

'What Led to "The Gates Ajar"', *Review of Reviews* (May 1896), 440.

Phillis Wheatley (1753–84)

'On being brought from AFRICA to AMERICA' (1773)

Phillis Wheatley's being the first published African American poet in an emerging national culture marks a key moment in literary history. But her role addressing religious issues associated with transatlantic enslavement is also noteworthy.

She was purchased in Boston in 1761 and ironically renamed for the ship that had brought her from Africa: *Phillis*. The Wheatley family used their kind treatment of her to navigate the moral conflict between their religion and ownership of a human. John and Susanna Wheatley had two adolescent children (Mary and Nathaniel). Mary shared her literacy with Phillis. In 1770, Phillis's poem memorialising the British Reverend George Whitefield became a sensation on both sides of the Atlantic. By 1772, Susanna Wheatley was seeking to publish a collection of Phillis's poems – a goal achieved only through the help of English supporters willing to believe an enslaved young girl capable of authorship.

One recurring theme in Wheatley's *Poems* addresses a question which Jeffrey Bilbro has explained was then tormenting British evangelicals such as William Cowper and John Newton: how to reconcile God's sovereign goodness with the plight of enslaved people. Wheatley's poem below offers one answer. However evil enslavement may be, God may enable some good to arise for enslaved individuals: gaining Christianity. Embedded within this assertion of hope for individual Blacks' salvation, some readers also see Wheatley's critique of the racial hierarchy then enabling so many professed Christians to justify slavery's stain on their religion. Further, as Keith Byerman argues, if we take her subtitle's signalling of 'religious and moral' subjects as one focus of her writing, we can see how 'she uses her faith as an alternative source of sustenance, identity, and authority in a society that refused to acknowledge her fundamental humanity' ('Talking Back').

Figure 7.2 Phillis Wheatley. Courtesy American Antiquarian Society.

'On being brought from AFRICA to AMERICA'

'Twas mercy brought me from my *Pagan* land,
Taught my benighted soul to understand
That there's a God, that there's a *Saviour* too:
Once I redemption neither sought nor knew.
Some view our sable race with scornful eye,
"Their colour is a diabolic die."[6]
Remember, *Christians*, *Negros*, black as *Cain*,
May be refin'd, and join th' angelic train.

Source text

Wheatley, Phillis, *Poems on various subjects, religious and moral* (London: A. Bell, 1773).

References

Bilbro, Jeffrey, 'Who Are Lost and How They're Found: Redemption and Theodicy in Wheatley, Newton, and Cowper', *Early American Literature* 47.3 (2012), 561–89.

---

6 Byerman urges a careful reading of this line, which he sees as using 'word play with "diabolic" and "die"' to ironically appropriate 'the voice of her antagonists' for critique of 'racism in her time' ('Talking Back', Web).

Byerman, Keith, 'Talking Back: Phillis Wheatley, Race, and Religion', *Religions* 10.6 (2019), Web.

John Marrant (1755–91)

From A Narrative of the Lord's Wonderful Dealings with John Marrant: A Black *(1785)*

Born a free Black in New York City, John Marrant had an itinerant childhood, migrating with his mother to Florida, Georgia and South Carolina. At 13 he converted to Christianity upon hearing the preaching of famous Methodist minister George Whitefield, after which Marrant travelled the wilderness, winding up in a Cherokee village where he was condemned to death for trespassing. In a miraculous stroke of fortune, Marrant converted the Cherokee chief and his daughter to Christianity and remained in their community for two years thereafter. Though official records do not corroborate his claim, Marrant was avowedly impressed into the British Navy for nearly seven years, serving as a sailor and musician and participating in several battles during the Revolutionary War. Marrant eventually settled in London and worked as a clerk before becoming ordained as a Methodist minister and gaining appointment to pastoral positions in Nova Scotia, then Boston, where he ministered to Native American and Black Christians.

His autobiographical *Narrative*, excerpted here, chronicles his picaresque journey to London, where the volume was published. Though a unique figure as a free Black transatlantic traveller, Marrant skirts many of these details to emphasise his religious conversion and devotion, praising God's mercy and providence. Thus the text functions as both a conversion and captivity narrative, even though Marrant never was enslaved. His *Narrative* sold well both in the US and UK, going through seventeen editions, some unauthorised. The following excerpt begins with his late-1770s impressment aboard a British ship and concludes with his 1785 journey from London to Nova Scotia.

From *A Narrative of the Lord's Wonderful Dealings with John Marrant*

In those troublesome times, I was pressed on board the Scorpion[7] sloop of war, as their musician, as they were told all I could play on music.—I continued in his majesty's service six years and eleven months; and with shame confess, that a lamentable stupor crept over all my spiritual vivacity, life and vigor; I got cold and dead.

---

7 The HMS *Scorpion*, a sloop in Britain's Navy of Virginia

My gracious God, my dear Father in his dear Son, roused me every now and then by dangers and deliverances.—I was at the siege of Charles-Town,[8] and passed through many dangers. When the town was taken, my old royal benefactor and convert, the king of the Cherokee Indians,[9] riding into the town with general Clinton,[10] saw me, and knew me: He alighted off his horse,[11] and came to me; said he was glad to see me; that his daughter was very happy, and sometimes longed to get out of the body.

Some time after this I was cruising about in the American seas, and cannot help mentioning a singular deliverance I had from the most imminent danger, and the use the Lord made of it to me. We were overtaken by a violent storm; I was washed overboard, and thrown on again; dashed into the sea a second time, and tossed upon deck again. I now fastened a rope round my middle, as a security against being thrown into the sea again; but, alas! forgot to fasten it to any part of the ship; being carried away the third time by the fury of the waves, when in the sea, I found the rope both useless and an incumbrance. I was in the sea the third time about eight minutes, and the sharks came round me in great numbers; one of an enormous size, that could easily have taken me into his mouth at once, passed and rubbed against my side. I then cried more earnestly to the Lord than I had done for some time; and he who heard Jonah's prayer, did not shut out mine, for I was thrown aboard again; these were the means the Lord used to revive me, and I began now to set out afresh.[12]

I was in the engagement with the Dutch off the Dogger Bank,[13] on board the Princess Amelia, of 84 guns.[14] We had a great number killed and wounded; the deck was running with blood; six men were killed, and three wounded, stationed at the same gun with me; my head and face were covered with the blood and brains of the slain: I was wounded, but did not fall, till a quarter of an hour before the engagement ended, and was happy during the whole of it. After being in the hospital three months and 16 days, I was sent to the West-Indies on board a ship of war, and, after cruising in those seas, we returned home as a convoy. Being taken ill of my old wounds, I was put into the hospital at Plymouth, and had not been there long, when the physician gave it as his opinion, that I should not be capable of serving the king again; I was therefore discharged, and came to London, where I lived with a respectable and pious merchant three years,[15] who was unwilling to part with me. During this time I saw my call to the ministry fuller and clearer; had a feeling concern for the salvation of my country-men: I carried them constantly in the arms of prayer and faith to the throne of grace, and had continual sorrow in my heart for my brethren, for my kinsmen, according to the flesh.—I wrote a letter to my brother, who returned me an answer, in which he prayed some ministers would come and preach to them, and desired me to shew it

---

8 A major battle fought between 29 March and 12 May 1780, the result being a decisive British victory and the subsequent occupation of Charleston

9 Many Cherokee fought on the side of the British.

10 General Henry Clinton (1730–95), British Commander-in-Chief in North America

11 [Author's note] Though it is unusual for Indians to have a horse, yet the king accompanied the general on the present successful occasion riding on horse-back.—If the king wished to serve me, there was no opportunity; the town being taken on Friday afternoon, Saturday an express arrived from the commander in chief at New-York, for a large detachment, or the town would fall into the hands of the Americans, which hurried us away on Sunday morning.

12 An extended allusion to the Bible's book of Jonah

13 The Battle of Dogger Bank (5 August 1781), fought in the North Sea

14 [Author's note] This action was on the 5th of August, 1781.

15 [Author's note] About three years; it might be a few weeks over or under.

to the minister whom I attended. I used to exercise my gifts on a Monday evening in prayer and exhortation, and was approved of, and ordained at Bath. Her Ladyship[16] having seen the letter from my brother in Nova-Scotia,[17] thought Providence called me there: To which place I am now bound, and expect to sail in few days.

I have now only to intreat the earnest prayers of all my kind Christian friends, that I may be carried safe there; kept humble, made faithful, and successful; that strangers may hear of and run to Christ; that Indian tribes may stretch out their hands to God; that the black nations may be made white in the blood of the Lamb; that vast multitudes of hard tongue, and of a strange speech, may learn the language of Canaan, and sing the song of Moses, and of the Lamb; and, anticipating the glorious prospect, may we all with fervent hearts, and willing tongues, sing hallelujah; the kingdoms of the world are become the kingdoms of our God, and of his Christ. Amen and Amen

London
Prescot-Street, No. 60,
July 18, 1785.

Figure 7.3 Frontispiece, *A Narrative of the Life of John Marrant, of New-York, in North America* (Halifax, England: J. Nicholson & Co., 1815). Courtesy HathiTrust; digitised by University of Michigan.

---

16 Selina Hastings, Countess of Huntingdon (1707–91), a major booster of Methodism and benefactor of mission work in North America
17 A Loyalist member of the African-American church in Birchtown, established by Huntingdon after the close of the Revolutionary War

Source text

Marrant, John, *A Narrative of the Lord's Wonderful Dealings with John Marrant, A Black* (London: Gilbert and Plummer, 1785).

References

Brooks, Joanna, *American Lazarus: Religion and the Rise of African-American and Native American Literatures* (Oxford: Oxford University Press, 2003).
Bynum, Tara, 'A Silent Book, Some Kisses, and John Marrant's Narrative', *Criticism* 57.1 (2015), 71–90.
May, Cedrick, 'John Marrant and the Narrative Construction of an Early Black Methodist Evangelical', *African American Review* 38.4 (2004), 553–70.

Joseph Priestley (1733–1804)

From 'Preface' to The Present State . . .; A Sermon (1794)

When he died at age 70 in rural Pennsylvania, Joseph Priestley closed out a remarkable transatlantic career. A productive author in multiple genres, Priestley has been credited as the first scientist to capitalise on experimental chemistry's potential, including identifying the properties of oxygen and the process of photosynthesis. He was equally admired as a leading theologian among British Dissenters.

'Dissenters' in Priestley's day actually referenced many groups sharing identities outside the official Church of England yet embodying among themselves numerous doctrinal differences and affiliations. Dissenters ranged from 'separatists, such as Baptists, Quakers and Independents (or Congregationalists), who rejected the concept of a national church' and sought toleration to worship in their own way, to 'most Presbyterians, who could not accept the terms of conformity, but who considered themselves the heirs of a reformed Elizabethan Church and who hoped in vain for . . . a more accommodating Church of England' (Rivers and Wykes, 4). Priestley's Dissenting leadership incorporated his religious writing as well as innovative teaching at Warrington (1761–7), where he developed curricula embraced at other dissenting academies, which served students ineligible for Anglican institutions. Some non-Dissenters came to view him as a threat to their authority.

While several early biographies focused on either his science or his theology, Priestley's own work cultivated connections between the two, stressing links between his rational study of the natural world and his scriptural knowledge. He affirms this stance in the meditation below, defending himself against criticism – which he casts as religious persecution and identifies as leading him to abandon his homeland for America.

From 'Preface' to The Present State . . .; A Sermon

This discourse, and those on the *Evidences of Divine Revelation,* which will be published about the same time, being the last of my labours in this country, I hope my friends, and the public, will indulge me while I give the reasons of their being the last, in consequence of my having at length, after much hesitation, and now with reluctance, come to a resolution to leave this kingdom.

After the riots in Birmingham,[18] it was the expectation, and evidently the wish, of many persons, that I should immediately fly to France, or America. But I had not consciousness of guilt to induce me to fly my country.[19] On the contrary, I came directly to London, and instantly, by means of my friend Mr. Russell, signified to the king's ministers, that I *was* there, and ready, if they thought proper, to be interrogated on the subject of the riot. But no notice was taken of the message. [. . .]

Whatever good or evil I have been capable of is now chiefly done; and I trust that the same consciousness of integrity, which has supported me hitherto, will carry me through any thing that may yet be reserved for me. Seeing, however, no great prospect of doing much good, or having much enjoyment, here, I am now preparing to follow my sons;[20] hoping to be of some use to them in their present unsettled state, and that Providence may yet, advancing in years as I am, find me some sphere of usefulness along with them.

As to the great odium that I have incurred, the charge of *sedition* or my being an enemy to the constitution or peace of my country, is a mere pretence for it; though it has been so much urged, that it is now generally believed, and all attempts to undeceive the public with respect to it avail nothing at all. The whole course of my studies, from early life, shews how little *politics* of any kind have been my object. Indeed to have written so much as I have in *theology* and to have done so much in *experimental philosophy* and at the same time to have had my mind occupied, as it is supposed to have been, with factious politics, I must have had faculties more than human. Let any person only cast his eye over the long list of my publications, and he will see that they relate almost wholly to theology, philosophy, or general literature. [. . .]

I never preached a political sermon in my life, unless such as, I believe, all Dissenters[21] usually preach on the fifth of November,[22] in favour of *civil and religious liberty,* may be laid to be political. And on these occasions, I am confident, that I never advanced any sentiment but such as, till of late years, would have tended to recommend rather than render me obnoxious, to those who direct the administration of this country. And the doctrines which I adopted when young and which,

---

18 The Birmingham (or Priestley) Riots, from 14 to 17 July 1791, targeted Priestley and other Dissenters. Homes, chapels and businesses of Dissenters were burned; English officials responded very slowly and, seemingly, reluctantly.

19 The source text here includes a long note from Priestley describing his dramatic escape from Birmingham.

20 Priestley's sons had already emigrated to America.

21 A catch-all term for those who refused to belong to and/or recognise the primacy of authority of the Church of England

22 The fifth of November, or Guy Fawkes Night, commemorates the Gunpowder Plot of 1605, wherein a number of Catholic conspirators plotted to assassinate King James I, a Protestant. Thereafter the celebration of the King's deliverance became a rally for anti-Catholic sentiment, including the burning of effigies of the Pope.

were even popular then (except with the clergy who were at that time generally disaffected to the family on the throne) I cannot abandon, merely because the times are so changed, that they are now become unpopular, and the expression and communication of them hazardous.

Farther, though I by no means disapprove of societies for political information, such as are now every where discountenanced, and generally suppressed, I never was a member of any of them; nor, indeed, did I ever attend any public meeting, if I could decently avoid it, owing to habits acquired in studious and retired life. [...]

If then, my real crime has not been *sedition*, or *treason*, what has it been? For every *effect* must have some adequate *cause*, and therefore the odium that I have incurred must have been owing to something in my declared sentiments, or conduct, that has exposed me to it. In my own opinion, it cannot have been any thing but my open hostility to the doctrines of the established church, and more especially to all civil establishments of religion whatever. This has brought upon me the implacable resentment of the great body of the clergy; and they have found other methods of opposing me besides *argument*, and that use of the *press* which is equally open to us all. They have also found an able ally and champion in Mr. Burke,[23] who (without any provocation except that of answering his book on the French Revolution) has taken several opportunities of inveighing against me, in a place where he knows I cannot reply to him, and from which he also knows that his accusation will reach every corner of the country, and consequently thousands of persons, who will never read any writings of mine.[24] They have had another, and still more essential vehicle of their abuse in what are called the treasury newspapers and other popular publications. [...]

Many times, by the encouragement of persons from whom better things might have been expected, I have been burned in effigy along with Mr. Paine;[25] and numberless insulting and threatening letters have been sent to me from all parts of the kingdom. It is not possible for any man to have conducted himself more peaceably than I have done all the time that I have lived at Clapton, yet it has not exempted me not only from the worst suspicions, but very gross insults. A very friendly and innocent club, which I found in the place, has been considered as *Jacobine*[26] chiefly on my account; and at one time there was cause of apprehension that I should have been brought into danger for lending one of Mr. Paine's books. But with some difficulty the neighbourhood was satisfied that I was innocent. [...]

A farther proof of the excessive bigotry of this country is that, though the clergy of Birmingham, resenting what I advanced in the first part of my *Appeal*,[27] replied to it, and pledged themselves to go through with the enquiry along with me, till the whole truth should be investigated, they have made no reply to the

---

23 Edmund Burke (1729–97), Irish-Anglo statesman and politician who promoted a close relationship between church and state
24 Note in original: Mr. Burke having said in the House of Commons, that "I was made a citizen of France on account of my declared hostility to the conditions of this country," I, in the public papers, denied the charge. [. . .]
25 Thomas Paine (1737–1809), whose writings helped stoke the American Revolution (see elsewhere in the anthology, Paine, 'From *Common Sense*' and 'From *The Rights of Man*')
26 A movement during the French Revolution; more broadly, used to make revolutionary and radical politics, which could include violence
27 *An Appeal to the Public on the Subject of the Riots in Birmingham* (Birmingham: J. Thompson, 1791)

Second Part of my Appeal,[28] in which I brought specific charges against themselves, and other persons by name, proving them to have been the promoters and abettors of the riot;[29] and yet they have as much respect shewn to them as ever, and the country at large pays no attention to it. Had the clergy been the injured persons, and Dissenters the rioters, unable to answer the charges brought against them, so great would have been the general indignation at their conduct, that I am persuaded it would not have been possible for them to continue in the country.

I could, if I were so disposed, give my readers many more instances of the bigotry of the clergy of the church of England with respect to me, which could not fail to excite, in generous minds, equal indignation and contempt; but I forbear. Had I, however, foreseen what I am now witness to, I certainly should not have made any attempt to replace my library or apparatus, and I soon repented of having done it. But this being done, I was willing to make some use of both before another interruption of my pursuits; I began to philosophize, and make experiments, rather late in life, being near forty, for want of the necessary means of doing any thing in this way; and my pursuits have been much interrupted by removals (never indeed chosen by myself, but rendered necessary by circumstances) and my time being now short, I hoped to have had no occasion for more than one, and that a final, remove. But the circumstances above mentioned have induced me though with great and sincere regret, to undertake another, and to a greater distance than any that I have hitherto made.

I profess not to be unmoved by the aspect of things exhibited in this Discourse. But notwithstanding this, I should willingly have awaited my fate in my native country, whatever it had been, if I had not had sons in America, and if I did not think that a field of public usefulness, which is evidently closing upon me here, might open to more advantage there. [. . .]

I cannot refrain from repeating again, that I leave my native country with real regret, never expecting to find any where else society so suited to my disposition and habits, such friends as I have here (whose attachment has been more than a balance to all the abuse I have met with some others). [. . .] I sincerely wish my countrymen all happiness; and when the time for reflection (which my absence may accelerate) shall come, my countrymen, I am confident, will do me more justice. They will be convinced that every suspicion they have been led to entertain to my disadvantage has been ill founded, and that I have even some claims to their gratitude and esteem. In this case, I shall look with satisfaction to the time when, if my life be prolonged, I may visit my friends in this country; and perhaps I may, notwithstanding my removal for the present, find a grave (as I believe is naturally the wish of every man) in the land that gave me birth.

Source text

Priestley, Joseph, *The Present State of Europe Compared with the Ancient Prophecies: A Sermon, Preached at the Gravel Pit Meeting in Hackney, February 28, 1794, Being the Day Appointed for the General Fast: with a Preface, Containing the Reasons for the Author's Leaving England* (London: J. Johnson, 1794).

---

28 *An Appeal to the Public on the Subject of the Riots in Birmingham, Part II* (London: J. Johnson, 1792)
29 The Birmingham Riots, referenced above

References

Priestley, Joseph, *Memoirs of Dr. Joseph Priestley, To the Year 1795, Written by Himself, with a Continuation, to the Time of His Decease, by His Son, Joseph Priestley* (London: J. Johnson, 1806).

Rivers, Isabel and David L. Wykes (eds), *Joseph Priestley, Scientist, Philosopher, Theologian* (Oxford: Oxford University Press, 2008).

Washington Irving (1783–1859)

'The Country Church' (1819)

One of the foremost American writers of the nineteenth century, Washington Irving was also a diplomat, biographer and historian who earned the moniker 'first American man of letters'. Irving's writing career began in 1802 when he served as a commentator for the New York *Morning Chronicle*. In 1807 Irving created a literary magazine using the pseudonym Diedrich Knickerbocker, which he would employ intermittently for the rest of his career. In 1815 he departed the United States for England and remained in Europe for the next seventeen years. When he returned in 1832, he had become a literary celebrity, though sometimes criticised for being more European than American.

'The Country Church' is part of Irving's *The Sketch Book* of *Geoffrey Crayon, Gent.*, published serially in 1819 and 1820. Irving feared piracy and arranged for publication on both sides of the Atlantic, hoping to retain the bulk of royalties. Reviews were positive in both locales, as Irving gained renown in Europe as the rare American author of quality. For Americans, the 'Country Church' sketch is full of curiosities, including the 'well-fed' vicar and 'the family of a nobleman of high rank'. Thus the narrator is a surrogate for the American audience, presumably astounded to behold such mixes of antiquity and haughtiness, dignified humility and vulgar excess as seen here.

'The Country Church'

> A gentleman!
> What, o'the woolpack? or the sugar chest?
> Or lists of velvet? which is't, pound, or yard,
> You vend your gentry by?
>
> Beggar's Bush

THERE are few places more favorable to the study of character than an English country church. I was once passing a few weeks at the seat of a friend, who resided in the vicinity of one, the appearance of which particularly struck my fancy. It was one of those rich morsels of quaint antiquity which give such a peculiar charm to English landscape. It stood in the midst of a county filled with ancient families, and contained, within its cold and silent aisles, the congregated dust of many noble generations. The interior walls were encrusted with monuments of every age and style. The light streamed through windows dimmed with armorial bearings, richly emblazoned in stained glass. In various parts of the church were tombs of knights, and high-born dames, of gorgeous workmanship, with their effigies in colored marble. On every side the eye was struck with some instance of aspiring mortality; some haughty memorial which human pride had erected over its kindred dust, in this temple of the most humble of all religions.

The congregation was composed of the neighbouring people of rank, who sat in pews, sumptuously lined and cushioned, furnished with richly-gilded prayer books, and decorated with their arms upon the pew doors; of the villagers and peasantry, who filled the back seats, and a small gallery beside the organ; and of the poor of the parish, who were ranged on benches in the aisles.

The service was performed by a snuffling well-fed vicar, who had a snug dwelling near the church. He was a privileged guest at all the tables of the neighbourhood, and had been the keenest fox-hunter in the country; until age and good living had disabled him from doing any thing more than ride to see the hounds throw off, and make one at the hunting dinner.

Under the ministry of such a pastor, I found it impossible to get into the train of thought suitable to the time and place: so, having, like many other feeble Christians, compromised with my conscience, by laying the sin of my own delinquency at another person's threshold, I occupied myself by making observations on my neighbours.

I was as yet a stranger in England, and curious to notice the manners of its fashionable classes. I found, as usual, that there was the least pretension where there was the most acknowledged title to respect. I was particularly struck, for instance, with the family of a nobleman of high rank, consisting of several sons and daughters. Nothing could be more simple and unassuming than their appearance. They generally came to church in the plainest equipage, and often on foot. The young ladies would stop and converse in the kindest manner with the peasantry, caress the children, and listen to the stories of the humble cottagers. Their countenances were open and beautifully fair, with an expression of high refinement, but, at the same time, a frank cheerfulness, and an engaging affability. Their brothers were tall, and elegantly formed. They were dressed fashionably, but simply; with strict neatness and propriety, but without any mannerism or foppishness. Their whole demeanor was easy and natural, with that lofty grace, and noble frankness, which bespeak freeborn souls that have never been checked in their growth by feelings of inferiority. There is a healthful hardiness about real dignity, that never dreads contact and communion with others, however humble. It is only spurious pride that is morbid and sensitive, and shrinks from every touch. I was pleased to see the manner in which they would converse with the peasantry about those rural concerns and field-sports, in which the gentlemen of this country so much delight. In these conversations there was neither haughtiness on the one part, nor servility on the other; and you were only reminded of the difference of rank by the habitual respect of the peasant.

In contrast to these was the family of a wealthy citizen, who had amassed a vast fortune; and, having purchased the estate and mansion of a ruined nobleman in the neighbourhood, was endeavoring to assume all the style and dignity of an hereditary lord of the soil. The family always came to church en prince.[30] They were rolled majestically along in a carriage emblazoned with arms. The crest glittered in silver radiance from every part of the harness where a crest could possibly be placed. A fat coachman, in a three-cornered hat, richly laced, and a flaxen wig, curling close round his rosy face, was seated on the box, with a sleek Danish dog beside him. Two footmen, in gorgeous liveries, with huge bouquets, and gold-headed canes, lolled behind. The carriage rose and sunk on its long springs with peculiar stateliness of motion. The very horses champed their bits, arched their necks, and glanced their eyes more proudly than common horses; either because they had caught a little of the family feeling, or were reined up more tightly than ordinary.

I could not but admire the style with which this splendid pageant was brought up to the gate of the church-yard. There was a vast effect produced at the turning of an angle of the wall; — a great smacking of the whip, straining and scrambling of horses, glistening of harness, and flashing of wheels through gravel. This was the moment of triumph and vainglory to the coachman. The horses were urged and checked until they were fretted into a foam. They threw out their feet in a prancing trot, dashing about pebbles at every step. The crowd of villagers sauntering quietly to church, opened precipitately to the right and left, gaping in vacant admiration. On reaching the gate, the horses were pulled up with a suddenness that produced an immediate stop, and almost threw them on their haunches.

There was an extraordinary hurry of the footman to alight, pull down the steps, and prepare every thing for the descent on earth of this august family. The old citizen first emerged his round red face from out the door, looking about him with the pompous air of a man accustomed to rule on 'Change, and shake the Stock Market with a nod. His consort, a fine, fleshy, comfortable dame, followed him. There seemed, I must confess, but little pride in her composition. She was the picture of broad, honest, vulgar enjoyment. The world went well with her; and she liked the world. She had fine clothes, a fine house, a fine carriage, fine children, every thing was fine about her: it was nothing but driving about, and visiting and feasting. Life was to her a perpetual revel; it was one long Lord Mayor's day.[31]

Two daughters succeeded to this goodly couple. They certainly were handsome; but had a supercilious air, that chilled admiration, and disposed the spectator to be critical. They were ultra-fashionable in dress; and, though no one could deny the richness of their decorations, yet their appropriateness might be questioned amidst the simplicity of a country church. They descended loftily from the carriage, and moved up the line of peasantry with a step that seemed dainty of the soil it trod on. They cast an excursive glance around, that passed coldly over the burly faces of the peasantry, until they met the eyes of the nobleman's family, when their countenances immediately brightened into smiles, and they made the most profound and elegant courtesies, which were returned in a manner that showed they were but slight acquaintances.

I must not forget the two sons of this aspiring citizen, who came to church in a dashing curricle,[32] with outriders. They were arrayed in the extremity of the mode, with all that pedantry of dress which marks the man of questionable pretensions to style.

---

30 In a princely manner; lavishly, luxuriously
31 A pageant day in England where the mayor of London is presented to the Royal Judiciary, traditionally by being conveyed to Westminster in a gilded and elaborately decorated equipage
32 A light, open, two-wheeled carriage pulled by two horses side by side

They kept entirely by themselves, eyeing every one askance that came near them, as if measuring his claims to respectability; yet they were without conversation, except the exchange of an occasional cant phrase. They even moved artificially; for their bodies, in compliance with the caprice of the day, had been disciplined into the absence of all ease and freedom. Art had done every thing to accomplish them as men of fashion, but nature had denied them the nameless grace. They were vulgarly shaped, like men formed for the common purposes of life, and had that air of supercilious assumption which is never seen in the true gentleman.

I have been rather minute in drawing the pictures of these two families, because I considered them specimens of what is often to be met with in this country—the unpretending great, and the arrogant little. I have no respect for titled rank, unless it be accompanied with true nobility of soul; but I have remarked in all countries where artificial distinctions exist, that the very highest classes are always the most courteous and unassuming. Those who are well assured of their own standing are least apt to trespass on that of others; whereas nothing is so offensive as the aspirings of vulgarity, which thinks to elevate itself by humiliating its neighbour.

As I have brought these families into contrast, I must notice their behavior in church. That of the nobleman's family was quiet, serious, and attentive. Not that they appeared to have any fervor of devotion, but rather a respect for sacred things, and sacred places, inseparable from good breeding. The others, on the contrary, were in a perpetual flutter and whisper; they betrayed a continual consciousness of finery, and a sorry ambition of being the wonders of a rural congregation.

The old gentleman was the only one really attentive to the service. He took the whole burden of family devotion upon himself, standing bolt upright, and uttering the responses with a loud voice that might be heard all over the church. It was evident that he was one of those thorough church and king men, who connect the idea of devotion and loyalty; who consider the Deity, somehow or other, of the government party, and religion "a very excellent sort of thing, that ought to be countenanced and kept up."

When he joined so loudly in the service, it seemed more by way of example to the lower orders, to show them that, though so great and wealthy, he was not above being religious; as I have seen a turtle-fed[33] Alderman swallow publicly a basin of charity soup, smacking his lips at every mouthful, and pronouncing it "excellent food for the poor."

When the service was at an end, I was curious to witness the several exits of my groups. The young noblemen and their sisters, as the day was fine, preferred strolling home across the fields, chatting with the country people as they went. The others departed as they came, in grand parade. Again were the equipages wheeled up to the gate. There was again the smacking of whips, the clattering of hoofs, and the glittering of harness. The horses started off almost at a bound; the villagers again hurried to right and left; the wheels threw up a cloud of dust; and the aspiring family was rapt out of sight in a whirlwind.

Source text

Irving, Washington, *The Sketch Book of Geoffrey Crayon, Gent., Vol. I* (London: John Murray, 1820).

---

33 As turtle was a delicacy, the alderman is painted as deigning to eat 'charity soup' as a gesture of solidarity with common people.

References

Delogu, Christopher Jon, '"How Did I Get Here?": An Untimely Meditation on *The Sketchbook of Geoffrey Crayon, Gent.* by Washington Irving', *Revue de la Société d'études anglo-américaines des XVIIe et XVIIIe siècles* (2001), 219–28.
Hanssen, Jessica Allen, 'Transnational Narrativity and Pastoralism in *The Sketch Book of Geoffrey Crayon, Gent by Washington Irving*', *Transnational Literature* 9.1 (November 2016), Web.

Figure 7.4 'Children in the Churchyard', Washington Irving, *Sketch Book of Geoffrey Crayon, Gent. Artist's Edition* (New York: G. P. Putnam, 1864), 195. Illustration by Alfred F. Bellows. Courtesy HathiTrust.

Frances Trollope (1779–1863)

'Chapter VIII', Domestic Manners of the Americans (1832)

In 1827, 'Fanny' Trollope moved herself and three of her children from England to a small community in the backwoods of Tennessee. When the supposedly utopian community did not live up to its ideals, Trollope relocated her family to Cincinnati, Ohio. After a series of failed business ventures, Trollope travelled the East Coast for a year and returned to England in 1831.

Her *Domestic Manners of the Americans*, published in March 1832, presents a critical view of US society, commenting on everything from clothing to manners, architecture to food. In this excerpt, Trollope writes about revivals and religion in Cincinnati.

Nineteenth-century America saw a boom in revivals, particularly in Ohio, eventually leading to the Second Great Awakening and a substantial increase in membership of Baptist and Methodist congregations long after the First Great Awakening, almost one hundred years earlier, centred in Britain and British colonies. Here, Trollope describes a revival she attended and prayer meetings she learned of second-hand. The scenes are charged with emotion, sometimes comical, and book-ended by her own analysis. Trollope finds women to be engaging in questionable behaviours highlighting differences between British Anglicanism and American Baptist and Methodist customs and their respective reflections of the larger society.

'Chapter VIII', Domestic Manners of the Americans

Absence of public and private Amusement—Churches and Chapels—Influence of the Clergy—A Revival

I never saw any people who appeared to live so much without amusement as the Cincinnatians. Billiards are forbidden by law, so are cards. To sell a pack of cards in Ohio subjects the seller to a penalty of fifty dollars. They have no public balls, excepting, I think, six during the Christmas holidays. They have no concerts. They have no dinner parties.

They have a theatre, which is, in fact, the only public amusement of this triste little town; but they seem to care little about it, and either from economy or distaste, it is very poorly attended. Ladies are rarely seen there, and by far the larger proportion of females deem it an offence against religion[34] to witness the representation of a play. It is in the churches and chapels of the town that the ladies are to be seen in full costume; and I am tempted to believe that a stranger from the continent of Europe would be inclined, on first reconnoitering the city, to suppose that the places of worship were the theatres and cafés of the place. No evening in the week but brings throngs of the young and beautiful to the chapels and meeting-houses, all dressed with care, and sometimes with great pretension; it is there that all display is made, and all fashionable distinction sought. The proportion of gentlemen attending these evening meetings is very small, but often, as might be expected, a sprinkling of smart young clerks makes this sedulous display of ribands and ringlets intelligible and natural. Were it not for the churches, indeed, I think there might be a general bonfire of best bonnets, for I never could discover any other use for them.

The ladies are too actively employed in the interior of their houses to permit much parading in full dress for morning visits. There are no public gardens or lounging shops

---

34 Revivalists of the Second Great Awakening largely adhered to 'postmillennialism', which advocated for a purification of society in preparation for the return of Christ.

of fashionable resort, and were it not for public worship, and private tea-drinkings, all the ladies in Cincinnati would be in danger of becoming perfect recluses.

The influence which the ministers of all the innumerable religious sects through America have on the females of their respective congregations, approaches very nearly to what we read of in Spain, or in other strictly Roman Catholic countries.[35] There are many causes for this peculiar influence. Where equality of rank is affectedly acknowledged by the rich, and clamorously claimed by the poor, distinction and pre-eminence are allowed to the clergy only. This gives them high importance in the eyes of the ladies. I think, also, that it is from the clergy only that the women of America receive that sort of attention which is so dearly valued by every female heart throughout the world.[36] With the priests of America the women hold that degree of influential importance which, in the countries of Europe, is allowed them throughout all orders and ranks of society, except, perhaps, the very lowest; and in return for this they seem to give their hearts and souls into their keeping. I never saw, or read, of any country where religion had so strong a hold upon the women, or a slighter hold upon the men.

I mean not to assert that I met with no men of sincerely religious feelings, or with no women of no religious feelings at all; but I feel perfectly secure of being correct as to the great majority in the statement I have made.

We had not been many months in Cincinnati when our curiosity was excited by hearing the "revival" talked of by every one we met throughout the town.[37] "The revival will be very full"—"We shall be constantly engaged during the revival"— were the phrases we constantly heard repeated, and for a long time without in the least comprehending what was meant; but at length I learnt that the un-national church of America[38] required to be roused, at regular intervals, to greater energy and exertion. At these seasons the most enthusiastic of the clergy travel the country, and enter the cities and towns by scores, or by hundreds, as the accommodation of the place may admit, and for a week or fortnight, or, if the population be large, for a month; they preach all day, and often for a considerable portion of the night, in the various churches and chapels of the place. This is called a Revival.

I took considerable pains to obtain information on this subject; but in detailing what I learnt I fear that it is probable I shall be accused of exaggeration; all I can do is cautiously to avoid deserving it. The subject is highly interesting, and it would be a fault of no trifling nature to treat it with levity.

These itinerant clergymen are of all persuasions, I believe, except the Episcopalian, Catholic, Unitarian, and Quaker. I heard of Presbyterians of all varieties; of Baptists of I know not how many divisions; and of Methodists of more denominations that I can remember; whose innumerable shades of varying belief it would require much time to explain and more to comprehend. They enter all the cities, towns, and villages of the Union in succession; I could not learn with sufficient certainty to repeat, what the interval generally is between their visits. These itinerants are, for the most part, lodged in the houses of their respective followers, and every

---

35 Spain and its state apparatuses were officially, formally Catholic. In the seventeenth century, Spanish monarchs began appointing priests to important dioceses, effectively ranking clergy.

36 See Ann Douglas's *The Feminization of American Culture* (New York: Knopf, 1977).

37 Ohio and northern Kentucky experienced a series of 'Great Revivals' in the early nineteenth century. Trollope also refers here to the Second Great Awakening.

38 In Britain, the Church of England is explicitly tied to the national state; in contrast, because of the dictates of the separation of church and state, the US has no national religious structures.

evening that is not spent in the churches and meeting-houses, is devoted to what would be called parties by others, but which they designate as prayer-meetings. Here they eat, drink, pray, sing, hear confessions, and make converts. To these meetings I never got invited, and therefore I have nothing but hearsay evidence to offer, but my information comes from an eye witness, and one on whom I believe I may depend. If one half of what I heard may be believed, these social prayer-meetings are by no means the most curious, or the least important part of the business.

It is impossible not to smile at the close resemblance to be traced between the feelings of a first-rate Presbyterian or Methodist lady, fortunate enough to have secured a favourite Itinerant for her meeting, and those of a first-rate London Blue,[39] equally blest in the presence of a fashionable poet. There is a strong family likeness among us all the world over.

The best rooms, the best dresses, the choicest refreshments solemnize the meetings. While the party is assembling, the load-star of the hour is occupied in whispering conversations with the guests as they arrive. They are called brothers and sisters, and the greetings are very affectionate. When the room is full, the company, of whom a vast majority is always women, are invited, entreated, and coaxed to confess before their brothers and sisters all their thoughts, faults, and follies.

These confessions are strange scenes; the more they confess, the more invariably are they encouraged and caressed. When this is over, they all kneel, and the itinerant prays extempore. They then eat and drink; and then they sing hymns, pray, exhort, sing, and pray again, till the excitement reaches a very high pitch indeed. These scenes are going on at some house or other every evening during the revival, nay, at many at the same time, for the churches and meeting-houses cannot give occupation to half the Itinerants, though they are all open throughout the day, and till a late hour in the night, and the officiating ministers succeed each other in the occupation of them.

It was at the principal of the Presbyterian churches that I was twice witness to scenes that made me shudder; in describing one, I describe both, and every one; the same thing is constantly repeated.

It was in the middle of summer, but the service we were recommended to attend did not begin till it was dark. The church was well lighted, and crowded almost to suffocation. On entering, we found three priests standing side by side, in a sort of tribune, placed where the altar usually is, handsomely fitted up with crimson curtains, and elevated about as high as our pulpits. We took our places in a pew close to the rail which surrounded it.

The priest who stood in the middle was praying; the prayer was extravagantly vehement, and offensively familiar in expression; when this ended, a hymn was sung, and then another priest took the centre place, and preached. The sermon had considerable eloquence, but of a frightful kind. The preacher described, with ghastly minuteness, the last feeble fainting moments of human life, and then the gradual progress of decay after death, which he followed through every process up to the last loathsome stage of decomposition. Suddenly changing his tone, which had been that of sober accurate description, into the shrill voice of horror, he bent forward his head, as if to gaze on some object beneath the pulpit. And as Rebecca made known to Ivanhoe what she saw through the window,[40] so the preacher made

---

39 Blue-stocking: an (overly) intellectual woman. The term sometimes critiqued a (supposed) lack of feminine grace and a disrespect for men's 'natural' intellectual superiority.

40 In Sir Walter Scott's *Ivanhoe* (1820), one of the historical novels stoking his popularity in America, Rebecca relays details of a battle to Ivanhoe.

known to us what he saw in the pit that seemed to open before him. The device was certainly a happy one for giving effect to his description of hell. No image that fire, flame, brimstone, molten lead, or red-hot pincers could supply, with flesh, nerves, and sinews quivering under them, was omitted. The perspiration ran in streams from the face of the preacher; his eyes rolled, his lips were covered with foam, and every feature had the deep expression of horror it would have borne, had he in truth been gazing at the scene he described. The acting was excellent. At length he gave a languishing look to his supporters on each side, as if to express his feeble state, and then sat down, and wiped the drops of agony from his brow.

The other two priests arose, and began to sing a hymn. It was some seconds before the congregation could join as usual; every up-turned face looked pale and horror-struck. When the singing ended, another took the centre place, and began in a sort of coaxing affectionate tone, to ask the congregation if what their dear brother had spoken had reached their hearts? Whether they would avoid the hell he had made them see? "Come, then!" he continued, stretching out his arms toward them, "come to us and tell us so, and we will make you see Jesus, the dear gentle Jesus who shall save you from it. But you must come to him! You must not be ashamed to come to him! This night you shall tell him that you are not ashamed of him; we will make way for you; we will clear the bench for anxious sinners to sit upon. Come, then! come to the anxious bench, and we will show you Jesus! Come! Come! Come!"

Again a hymn was sung, and while it continued, one of the three was employed in clearing one or two long benches that went across the rail, sending the people back to the lower part of the church. The singing ceased, and again the people were invited, and exhorted not to be ashamed of Jesus, but to put themselves upon "the anxious benches," and lay their heads on his bosom. "Once more we will sing," he concluded, "that we may give you time." And again they sung a hymn.

And now in every part of the church a movement was perceptible, slight at first, but by degrees becoming more decided. Young girls arose, and sat down, and rose again; and then the pews opened, and several came tottering out, their hands clasped, their heads hanging on their bosoms, and every limb trembling, and still the hymn went on; but as the poor creatures approached the rail their sobs and groans became audible. They seated themselves on the "anxious benches;" the hymn ceased, and two of the three priests walked down from the tribune, and going, one to the right, and the other to the left, began whispering to the poor tremblers seated there. These whispers were inaudible to us, but the sobs and groans increased to a frightful excess. Young creatures, with features pale and distorted, fell on their knees on the pavement, and soon sunk forward on their faces; the most violent cries and shrieks followed, while from time to time a voice was heard in convulsive accents, exclaiming, "Oh Lord!" "Oh Lord Jesus!" "Help me, Jesus!" and the like.

Meanwhile the two priests continued to walk among them; they repeatedly mounted on the benches, and trumpet-mouthed proclaimed to the whole congregation, "the tidings of salvation," and then from every corner of the building arose in reply, short sharp cries of "Amen!" "Glory!" "Amen!" while the prostrate penitents continued to receive whispered comfortings, and from time to time a mystic caress. More than once I saw a young neck encircled by a reverend arm. Violent hysterics and convulsions seized many of them, and when the tumult was at the highest, the priest who remained above again gave out a hymn, as if to drown it.

It was a frightful sight to behold innocent young creatures, in the gay morning of existence, thus seized upon, horror-struck, and rendered feeble and enervated for ever. One young girl, apparently not more than fourteen, was supported in the arms of another some years older; her face was pale as death; her eyes wide open, and perfectly devoid of meaning; her chin and bosom wet with slaver;[41] she had every appearance of idiotism.[42] I saw a priest approach her; he took her delicate hands, "Jesus is with her! Bless the Lord!" he said, and passed on.

Did the men of America value their women as men ought to value their wives and daughters, would such scenes be permitted among them?

It is hardly necessary to say, that all who obeyed the call to place themselves on the "anxious benches" were women, and by far the greater number, very young women. The congregation was, in general, extremely well dressed, and the smartest and most fashionable ladies of the town were there; during the whole revival, the churches and meeting-houses were every day crowded with well-dressed people.

It is thus the ladies of Cincinnati amuse themselves; to attend the theatre is forbidden; to play cards is unlawful; but they work hard in their families, and must have some relaxation. For myself, I confess that I think the coarsest comedy ever written would be a less detestable exhibition for the eyes of youth and innocence than such a scene.

Source text

Trollope, Frances Milton, *Domestic Manners of the Americans, Vol. I* (London: Whitaker, Treacher, & Co., 1832).

References

Devine, Christine (ed.), *Nineteenth-century British Travelers in the New World* (Farnham: Ashgate, 2013).
Martineau, Harriet, *Society in America* (London: Saunders and Otley, 1837).
Neville-Sington, Pamela, *Fanny Trollope: The Life and Adventures of a Clever Woman* (London: Viking, 1997).

Abon Becr Sadika (c.1750–?) and Richard Robert Madden (1798–1886)

From Madden's 'Letter XXXI: The Scherife of Timbuctoo' (1835)

Few accounts of West Indian slavery written from the point of view of an enslaved person have come down to us – far fewer than texts by North American Black authors. Those we can access today – like Mary Prince's memoir and Abon Becr Sadika's – typically reach us as the proverbial Black letter in a white envelope (a mediated text whose publication was controlled by white editors). In Sadika's case, one intermediary is Irish Catholic writer Richard

---

41 Saliva falling from the mouth
42 Extreme mental deficiency

Robert Madden. A talented physician, enthusiastic traveller and zealous abolitionist, Madden arrived in Jamaica in October 1833, having been appointed as a Special Magistrate to help facilitate the island's transition to post-Emancipation after Parliament's abolishment of slavery throughout the British empire. His two-volume account of his experiences in this challenging role appeared in 1835, published, as his introduction noted, 'in the form of Letters' (I, vii) to various allies in the anti-slavery cause back in England.

Abon Becr Sadika's autobiographical narrative is uniquely valuable in presenting the experiences of a Black African Muslim who managed to maintain his religious identity. Having studied with prominent scholars before being caught up in the Ashanti revolution, around 1805 Abu Becr Sadika found himself on a British ship bound for Jamaica. Renamed Edward Donlan, Sidika was working for store owner Alexander Anderson when Madden arrived in the Indies. Also unusual for an African author of this era, Sadika apparently (with Madden's help) returned to his original home and family.

Sadika's account envisions a white Christian audience. He spotlights similarities between his Muslim religion and Christianity, while pointing to contradictions between enslaving others and professing to be godly. Meanwhile, Madden's self-deprecating depiction of his own efforts to secure Sadika's release from a labour contract (the status then required of former Caribbean enslaved people as a transition to actual freedom) illustrates how slavery continued its force in the Indies after legislation supposedly ended it.

From Madden's[43] 'Letter XXXI: The Scherife [Abon Becr Sadika[44]] of Timbuctoo'

TO J. BUCKINGHAM, ESQ.

Kingston, Sept. 29, 1834

My Dear Sir,

Having made up my mind in the case of the negro Edward Donlan, to purchase the unexpired period of his apprenticeship,[45] (which is the jargon now in use, to

---

43 At least one other somewhat longer version of Sadika's memoir reached transatlantic audiences: a dictation to George Renouard published by the Royal Geographical Society. Renouard (foreign secretary of the society) describes this second version as 'written after his [Sadika's/Siddik's] arrival' in Britain, 'in the presence of a friend with whom he was spending a few days in the neighbourhood of London' and dubs it 'no doubt the same in substance as that complied from his oral communication by Dr. Madden while in Jamaica'. Renouard also characterises his version as 'agree[ing], almost word for word, with another account of his life, drawn up while he was on his voyage from New York, at the request of Captain Oldrey'. Observing that all three narratives were originally 'written in the Arabic language', Renouard signals yet another mediating layer between Black composition and white readership: translation (102). Notably, nonetheless, Renouard presents his edited version as aiming 'to allow Abú Bekr to speak for himself' (102).

44 Alternative spellings of this author's name include Abu Bakr al-Siddiq.

45 Though the British Act of Emancipation freed all children younger than six years, and technically designated all other enslaved people as free, those older than six were required to serve apprenticeships for periods ranging from four to six years – or until a manumission payment as set by one of the special magistrates like Madden was made.

express the act of redeeming a man from slavery,) I made an application to his master, to request he would nominate a local magistrate, to act with the special justice of some adjoining parish, for the purpose of proceeding to a valuation of his apprentice. Whatever that valuation might be, I hoped to indemnify myself by a public subscription for so large an outlay.

I was given to understand, by Mr. Anderson, that the man was invaluable to him—that he kept his books (in Arabic characters)—and that the accounts of the whole of his vast business were kept by him—in short, that no sum of money which could be awarded to him could compensate for the loss of the man's services. [...]

I now waited on Mr. Anderson, and I frankly stated to him what my wishes and intentions were. [...]

This gentleman, I should think, is upwards of sixty; his hair is white as snow: but a hale, fresh-coloured, happy-looking, kind-hearted person, whose patriarchal mien, and genuine old-English-gentlemanism[46] (if I may coin with impunity) of air and manner, give even a stranger a favourable impression of one to whom Nature has been so kind, and Time itself more indulgent than usual.

There are some men whom, perhaps, you see for the first time in your life, and why or wherefore you know not, but you feel your spirit in communion with theirs from the first moment of your intercourse. Anderson was one of these men. A great many words did not pass between us: I expressed the wish I felt to obtain the man's release: he said, I need say no more on the subject. The man was valuable to him; his services were worth more to him than those of negroes for whom he had paid £300; but the man had been a good servant to him—a faithful and a good negro–and he would take no money for him—he would give him his liberty!!! I pressed him to name any reasonable sum for his release, but he positively refused to receive one farthing[47] in the way of indemnity for the loss of the man's services.

The following day was appointed to execute the act of manumission, at the public office of the special magistrate. [...]

The time appointed for carrying the release into effect having become known, a great number of the respectable inhabitants of Kingston attended: the office was, indeed, crowded at an early hour with persons of all complexions, who had come to witness the ceremony. Mr. Anderson and his negro, Edward Donlan, being in attendance, the manumission papers were prepared; but before they were signed, the nature of the circumstances which had led to the effort that had been made to obtain the man's freedom, and the manner in which that boon had been granted by his master, were dwelt on at some length; and the merits of the fidelity of the one, and the generosity of the other were feebly perhaps described, however forcibly they might be felt. Indeed, the merits of the latter could not be overrated. It might be very easy for a stranger to recommend Mr. Anderson to be generous when nothing is to be given and very agreeable to be philanthropic when the exercise of our humanity is indulged at no expense. But with Mr. Anderson it was very different, for no sums of money that a bench of magistrates could honestly award, could adequately compensate him for the loss of this man's services. But, nevertheless, he performed this most generous act of manumission as it became a good man to perform a gracious action—freely and without hesitation or condition. Though I do say it, who perhaps should not say it, the scene was one of no ordinary interest.

---

46 Invoking a race-based affiliation with Anderson's 'old-English-gentlemanism', Madden also honours the merchant's generosity in agreeing to Sadika's manumission.
47 A piece of British money

Beside the bench stood a negro of exalted rank in his own country, in the act of obtaining his liberty, after many a long year of slavery, and near him his venerable master, "prepared to give unto his servant that which was just and equal, knowing that he also had a Master in heaven."[48] There were tears of joy on some of the black features before me, and there were smiles of satisfaction even on white faces in that assemblage. It is said that the gods are pleased to behold the successful exertions of a good man struggling with adversity; but if we are justified in estimating what is pleasing to that intelligence by the extent of the advantages conferred on man by human beneficence, perhaps the sight of a good master, voluntarily making a faithful bondsman free and laying down authority which it may not be in his nature to abuse, but yet which he knows it is not safe for mortal man to be intrusted with, is one of the exhibitions of humanity in which its affinity with a higher nature appears at a distance less remote than in almost any other situation in which we can conceive it. And on such an occasion one might address the chief actor in that scene in the words of sacred commendation, in speaking of the redemption of the slave,—"It shall not seem hard unto thee when thou sendest him away from thee, for he hath been worth a double hired servant to thee in serving thee six years, and the Lord thy God shall bless thee in all that thou doest."

I did not allow the public to be unmindful of the concluding part of the injunction, "When thou sendest him out free, thou shalt not let him go away empty;" for the following notice was presented to the public attention, and in a few days I had the satisfaction of putting twenty pounds in the hands of the liberated negro of Timbuctoo.

"Kingston, Sept. 9, 1834.

"To the humane attention of the inhabitants of Kingston, the case is earnestly recommended of Abon Becr Sadiki, lately the apprentice of Mr. Anderson; a man of noble rank in his own country, who for many years has been in servitude in this island, and has demeaned himself in such a manner as to have obtained a reputation for good conduct, and even for attainments as a scholar, which few of his countrymen have ever gained, or at least preserved in slavery. The benevolent assistance of this community is now solicited to enable him to turn to his own advantage the unexpired period of his apprenticeship. The history of his life, which accompanies this paper, is written in his own language, and couched in terms at once credible to his acquirements as a scholar, and his character as a man of discretion and integrity. How he could have attained so competent a knowledge of his native language at so early an age as that which he had been taken his country, and have kept up his knowledge of it in the unfavourable circumstances in which he was placed in a foreign land, it is difficult to conceive; and it is only for the considerate to appreciate the extent of so much perseverance, and the encouragement that should be the reward of so much patient merit."

"The History of Abon Becr Sadika,[49] known in Jamaica by the name of Edward Donlan

---

48 Madden here quotes Anderson to underscore an admirable religious motivation promoting the freeing of Donlan/Sidika.

49 Costanzo notes the particular value of Sidika's narrative as one originally written in Arabic (117).

"My name is Abon Becr Sadika, born in Timbuctoo,[50] and brought up in Geneh.[51] I acquired the knowledge of the Alcoran[52] in the country of Gounah, in which country there are many teachers for young people: they are not of one country, but come from different parts, and are brought here to dwell for their instruction. The names of the different masters in the country called Gounah are Aboudoulaki, a son of Ali Aga; Mohamet Wadiwahoo; Mohamet Ali Mustaphi; Ibrahim, son of Yussuf, a native; and Ibrahim, son of Abou Hassan, from Footatoroo. The whole of these masters are in our school, and under the direction of a head master, the son of Ali Aga Mahomed Tuffosere. My father's name is Kara-Mousa, *Scheriff*, (the interpretation of which is, 'of a noble family.') The names of my father's brothers are Aderiza, Abdriman, Mahomet, and Abon Becr. Their father, my grandfather, lived in the country of Timbuctoo and Geneh: some say he was the son of Ibrahim, the founder of my race in the country of Geneh.

"And it came to pass, after the death of my grandfather, jealousy arose among the sons and the rest of the family, which scattered them into the different parts of Soudan. Aderiza went to the country of Marsina, where he dwelt a little time: after that he went over the river and dwelt in Geneh: he married a daughter of Maroulhaide Abon Becr, for his wife. Abdriman went to the country of Cong, and married the daughter of Samer Ali, the lord of that country, where dwelt his wife. Mahomet went to the country of Gounah. Abon Becr remained in the country of Timbuctoo along with the rest of the family who were not yet married. My father was always travelling to the country of Cassina and Bournoo, where he married and returned with my mother to Timbuctoo. After two years elapsed, my father then thought upon his brothers, whom he repented having parted with, which grieved him exceedingly, and he desired his servants to prepare themselves to go along with him to see how and where they were.[53] The servants obeyed, and, accordingly, went with him to Geneh, from there to Cong, and from there to Gounah, where they stopped; and the servants there gathered a quantity of gold for their master; for there is a great deal of gold in that country, from the wilderness down to the river-side, also from the rocks. They are obliged to break the stones to dust, and put them into a vessel of water, when all the gold will sink down separate, the dust will float, and the gold will remain in the vessel; and then they purify the same, and make it ready for use. The money they make use of is a shell called Jagago: they are in the habit of bartering goods for goods, according to prices. In this said country (Gounah) my father gathered a large quantity of gold and silver, some of which he sent his father-in-law: he also sent horses, mules, and rich silks, from Egypt, as presents for Ali Aga Mahomad Tassere, my grandfather, in the country of Bournoo and Cassina. My father afterwards took the bad fever, which was the cause of his death in Gounah, where he was buried. At this time I was a child, and knew nothing then; but some of my old relations told me all about the life of my departed father. My uncles, after the death of my father, returned to their different countries, and only left my uncle, named Mahomet, at Gounah, where he dwelt.

---

50 Also spelled 'Timbuktu'; ancient city in Mali, north of the Niger River

51 The modern name for Geneh is Jenné.

52 Alcoran references the sacred book of Islam, also known as the 'Qur'an' and sometimes spelled Koran. Gounah is sometimes called Bouna, but Abu Bakr uses an Arabic naming.

53 A notable difference in word choice appears in Renouard's *Royal Geographical* version here, where the text reads 'that he remembered his brethren, repented on account of them and wept bitterly. He then ordered his *slaves* to make ready for their departure with him' (103, emphasis added).

"And it came to happen, about five years after the death of my father, I got the consent of my teacher to go to the country of Gounah, to see the grave of my father. Whereupon he said to me, that, with the blessing of God, he would accompany me. He then prepared proper provision for our journey, and took along with us many of his eldest scholars to bear us company. We departed, and, after long fatigue, we arrived at Cong; from there we went to Gounah, and stopped there for about two years, as we considered the place a home, having much property therein. After a lapse of two years, my master took it into his mind to travel to Agi. In the mean time he made inquiries of different people who had travelled in that country; and some of them told him that Mohamed Cassina and Adama Anina, his brothers, were then going to that country. He then asked his informant where those people were to be found: they told him that they were already gone, except Adama, who was now pre-paring to go. My master then set out, and left us with my uncle Mohamad in Gounah, until he returned. In the mean time, we heard that Abdengara, king of Buntuco, having slain Iffoa, the king of Bandara, in battle, also wanted to kill Cudjoe, the captain of an adjoining district. Abdengara sent to inform Cudjoe that, if he would pay him such a quantity of gold as he required for a ransom, he would be content. Cudjoe then sent much gold to him, which he refused. He said to the messenger, "Return to thy master, and tell him, that, if he do not send two hundred pieces of gold, I will not be satisfied, and my sword shall take off his head." When this messenger returned to his lord, and related the message he received, Cudjoe took away the ransom and kept it, and sent a message to the king of Gounah relating the transaction. When Abdengara came to hear of Cudjoe sending to inform the king of Gounah of his doings, he became wrath, and ordered all his army to battle against Cudjoe. And when the king of Gou-nah heard that Abdengara had come in with his army to fight him, he then called all his men to meet the enemy in the country of Bolo, where they commenced fighting from the middle of the day until night. After that they went to their different camps: seven days after that they gathered up again, and commenced the war in the town Anacco, where they fought exceedingly, and there were many lives lost on both sides; but Abdengara's army, being stronger than the king of Gounah's, took possession of the town. Some of Gounah's people were obliged to fly to Cong, and on that very day they made me a captive.[54] As soon as I was made prisoner, they stripped me, and tied me with a cord, and gave me a heavy load to carry, and led me into the country of Buntocoo,— from thence to the town of Cumasy, where the king of Shantee reigned, whose name is Ashai,—and from thence to Assicuma,—and from thence to Agimaca, which is the country of the Fantees:[55] from thence to the town of Dago, by the sea-side (all the way on foot, and well loaded;) there they sold me to the Christians in that town—there one of the ship's captains purchased me, and delivered me over to one of his sailors: the boat immediately pushed off, and I was carried on board the ship. We were three months at sea before we arrived in Jamaica, which was the beginning of bondage. —I have none to thank but those that brought me here. But, praise be to God, who has every thing in his power to do as he thinks good, and no man can remove whatever burden he chooses to put on us. As he said, 'Nothing shall fall on us except what he shall ordain; he is our Lord, and let all that believe in him put their

---

54 The Renouard version here reads: 'On that day was I made a slave' (106).
55 People from the southern coast of Ghana between Accra and Sekindi-Takoradi

trust in him.'[56] My parents' religion is of the Mussulman:[57] they are all circumcised, and their devotions are five times a day; they fast in the month Ramadan; they give tribute according to the law; they are married to four wives, but the fifth is an abomination to them. They fight for their religion, and they travel to Hedjaz[58] (those who are capable.) They don't eat any meat except what they themselves kill. They do not drink wine nor spirits, as it is held an abomination so to do. They do not associate with any that worship idols, or profane the Lord's name, or do dishonor to their parents, or commit murder, or bear false witness, or who are covetous, proud, or boastful; for such faults are an abomination unto my religion. They are particularly careful in the education of their children, and in their behaviour, but I am lost to all these advantages: since my bondage I am become corrupt; and I now conclude by begging the Almighty God to lead me into the path that is proper for me, for he alone knows the secrets of my heart and what I am in need of.

"Abon Becr Sadika.

"Kingston, Jamaica, Sept. 20, 1834."

The above was written in Arabic. The man speaks English well and correctly for a negro, but does not read or write it. I caused him to read the original, and translate it word by word; and, from the little knowledge I have of the spoken language, I can safely present you with this version of it as a literal translation. There are other letters of his, and some of his brethren, which I will send you in my next. The letter of the latter, addressed to me by some native Africans, who have obtained their liberty in this city, is written in English by one of them, and is an epistle which, I think, you will read with much interest.

I am, my dear Sir,
Yours, very truly,
R. R. M.

Source text

Madden, R. R., *A Twelvemonth's Residence in the West Indies, During the Transition from Slavery to Apprenticeship; With Incidental Notices of the State of Society, Prospects, and Natural Resources of Jamaica and Other Islands*, Vol. 2 (Philadelphia: Carey, Lea and Blanchard, 1835).

References

Costanzo, Angelo, 'The Narrative of Archibald Monteith, a Jamaican Slave', *Callaloo* 13.1 (January 1990), 115–30.

---

56 The Renouard version is more expansive: 'but praise be to God, under whose power are all things, He doth whatsoever he willeth! No one can turn aside that which He hath ordained, nor can any one withhold that which He hath given! As God Almighty himself hath said: – Nothing can befall us unless it be written for us (in his book)! He is our master: in God, therefore, let all the faithful put their trust!' (106).

57 Muslim; the Renouard/Royal Geographical reads: 'The faith of our families is the faith of Islám' (106).

58 A region of western Saudi Arabia where Mecca is located

D'Costa, Jean and Barbara Lalla (eds), 'Richard Robert Madden, *A Twelvemonth Residence in the West Indies*', *Voices in Exile: Jamaican Texts of the 18th and 19th Centuries* (Tuscaloosa, AL: University of Alabama Press, 1989), 67–75.

Es Siddík, Abú Bekr, 'Routes in North Africa. Communicated by the Rev. G. C. Renouard', *Journal of the Royal Geographical Society of London* 6 (1836), 100–13.

Anna Brownell Jameson (1794–1860)

From 'Religious Opinions', Winter Studies and Summer Rambles in Canada *(1838)*

Born in Dublin, Anna Jameson immigrated with her family to England at an early age, eventually settling in London. A precocious child and headstrong student, she became governess to a series of prominent families. A formative tour of the Continent in 1821 generated her first travel book, *The Diary of an Ennuyée*. In 1825 she wed Robert Sympson Jameson, who shared her love of literature and encouraged her writing, though their marriage soon became unhappy. Meanwhile, she published several well-received books on female subjects, including *The Loves of the Poets* (1829), *Memoir of Celebrated Female Sovereigns* (1831) and *The Beauties of the Court of King Charles the Second* (1833). After travels in North America she separated from her husband and returned to England, where she turned her attention to Christian art.

When her husband was appointed Attorney General of Upper Canada in 1833, he sent for her; out of duty, she came. *Winter Studies and Summer Rambles in Canada* is the travelogue of her subsequent eight-month journey to and from Toronto. Composed as a journal, the book chronicles her trip through lower Canada (then a backwater British colony), including several tales from Native peoples based on conversations with Henry Rowe Schoolcraft. Jameson blends her account of both seasons from her title with astute political analysis and keen observation of the natural landscape. Published in London in 1838, the book achieved both popular and critical success.

From 'Religious Opinions', Winter Studies and Summer Rambles in Canada

It is a mistake to suppose that these Indians are idolaters; heathens and pagans you may call them if you will; but the belief in one Great Spirit, who created all things, and is paramount to all things, and the belief in the distinction between body and soul, and the immortality of the latter—these two sublime principles pervade their wildest superstitions; but though none doubt of a future state, they have no distinct or universal tenets with regard to the condition of the soul after death. Each individual seems to have his own thoughts on the subject, and some doubtless never think about it at all. In general, however, their idea of a paradise (the land of spirits) is some far off country towards the south-west, abounding in sunshine, and placid lakes, and rivers full of fish, and forests full of game, whither they are transported by the Great Spirit, and where those who are separated on earth meet again in happiness, and part no more.

Not only man, but everything animate, is spirit, and destined to immortality. According to the Indians, (and Sir Humphry Davy,[59]) nothing dies, nothing is destroyed; what we look upon as death and destruction is only transition and change. The ancients, it is said—for I cannot speak from my own knowledge – without telescopes or logarithms, divined the grandest principles of astronomy, and calculated the revolutions of the planets; and so these Indians, who never heard of philosophy or chemistry, have contrived to hit upon some of the profoundest truths in physics and metaphysics; but they seem content, like Jaques, "to praise God, and make no boast of it."

In some things, it is true, they are as far as possible from orthodox. Their idea of a hell seems altogether vague and negative. It consists in a temporary rejection from the land of good spirits, in a separation from lost relatives and friends, in being doomed to wander up and down desolately, having no fixed abode, weary, restless, and melancholy. To how many is the Indian hell already realised on this earth? Physical pain, or any pain which calls for the exercise of courage, and which it is manliness to meet and endure, does not apparently enter into their notions of punishment. They believe in evil spirits, but the idea of the Evil Spirit, a permitted agency of evil and mischief, who divides with the Great Spirit the empire of the universe – who contradicts or renders nugatory His will, and takes especially in hand the province of tormenting sinners – of the devil, in short, they certainly had not an idea, till it was introduced by Europeans.[60] Those Indians whose politeness will not allow them to contradict this article of the white man's faith, still insist that the place of eternal torment was never intended for the Red-skins, the especial favourites of the Great Spirit, but for white men only.

Formerly it was customary with Chippewas to bury many articles with the dead, such as would be useful on their journey to the land of spirits.

Henry[61] describes in a touching manner the interment of a young girl, with an axe, snow-shoes, a small kettle, several pairs of moccasins, her own ornaments, and strings of beads; and, because it was a female—destined, it seems, to toil and carry burthens in the other world as well as this—the carrying-belt and the paddle. The last act before the burial, performed by the poor mother, crying over the dead body of the child, was that of taking from it a lock of hair for a memorial. "While she did this," says Henry, "I endeavoured to console her by offering the usual arguments, that the child was happy in being released from the miseries of this life, and that she should forbear to grieve, because it would be restored to her in another world, happy and everlasting. She answered, that she knew it well, and that by the lock of hair she should know her daughter in the other world, for she would take it with her – alluding to the time when this relic, with the carrying-belt and axe, would be placed in her own grave." [. . .]

---

59 (1778–1829), a prominent British chemist and inventor
60 Note in original: History of the Moravian Missions. Mr. Schoolcraft.
61 Alexander Henry 'The Elder', a British-Canadian fur trader, lived with the Ojibwa from 1763 1764 and published *Travels and Adventures in Canada and the Indian Territories between the Years 1760 and 1776* (New York: T. Riley, 1809) (see 150–1).

This custom of burying property with the dead was formerly carried to excess from the piety and generosity of surviving friends, until a chief, greatly respected and admired among them for his bravery and talents, took an ingenious method of giving his people a lesson. He was seized with a fit of illness, and after a few days expired, or seemed to expire. But after lying in this death-trance for some hours, he came to life again, and recovering his voice and senses, he informed his friends that he had been half-way to the land of spirits; that he found the road thither crowded with the souls of the dead, all so heavily laden with the guns, kettles, axes, blankets, and other articles buried with them, that their journey was retarded, and they complained grievously of the burthens which the love of their friends had laid on them. "I will tell you," said Gitchee Gauzinee,[62] for that was his name, "our fathers have been wrong; they have buried too many things with the dead. It is too burthensome to them, and they have complained to me bitterly. There are many who, by reason of the heavy loads they bear, have not yet reached the land of spirits. Clothing will be very acceptable to the dead, also his moccasins to travel in, and his pipe to refresh him on the way; but let his other possessions be divided among his relatives and friends."[63]

This sensible hint was taken in good part. The custom of kindling a fire on the grave, to light the departed spirit on its road to the land of the dead, is very general, and will remind you of the oriental customs. [. . .]

The Indians have a very fanciful mythology, which would make exquisite machinery for poetry. It is quite distinct from the polytheism of the Greeks. The Greek mythology personified all nature, and materialised all abstractions: the Indians spiritualise all nature. They do not indeed place dryads and fauns in their woods, nor naiads in their streams; but every tree has a spirit; every rock, every river, every star that glistens, every wind that breathes, has a spirit; everything they cannot comprehend is a spirit: this is the ready solution of every mystery, or rather makes everything around them a mystery as great as the blending of soul and body in humanity. A watch, a compass, a gun, have each their spirit. The thunder is an angry spirit; the aurora borealis, dancing and rejoicing spirits; the milky way is the path of spirits. Birds, perhaps from their aerial movements, they consider as in some way particularly connected with the invisible world of spirits. Not only all animals have souls, but it is the settled belief of the Chippewa Indians that their souls will fare the better in another world, in the precise ratio that their lives and enjoyments are curtailed in this: hence, they have no remorse in hunting; but when they have killed a bear or rattle-snake, they solemnly beg his pardon, and excuse themselves on the plea of necessity.

Besides this general spiritualisation of the whole universe, which to an Indian is all spirit in diversity of forms (how delighted Bishop Berkeley[64] would have been with them!), they have certain mythologic existences. Manabozho is a being very analogous to the Seeva of the Hindoo mythology. The four cardinal points are spirits, the west being the oldest and the father of the others, by a beautiful girl, who, one day while bathing, suffered the west wind to blow upon her. Weeng is the spirit of sleep, with numerous little subordinate spirits, his emissaries, whose employment is to close the eyes of mortals, and by tapping on their foreheads knock them to

---

62 A great and legendary (perhaps mythical) Ojibwa warrior
63 Mr Schoolcraft (author's note)
64 George Berkeley, an Irish philosopher, argued in favour of immaterialism.

sleep. Then they have Weendigos – great giants and cannibals, like the Ascaparts and Morgantes of the old romances; and little tiny spirits or fairies, which haunt the woods and cataracts. The Nibanàba, half human half fish, dwell in the waters of Lake Superior. Ghosts are plentiful, and so are transformations, as you have seen. The racoon was once a shell lying on the lake shore, and vivified by the sun-beams: the Indian name of the raccoon, aisebun, is literally, he was a shell. The brains of a wicked adulteress, whose skull was beaten to pieces against the rocks, as it tumbled down a cataract, became the white fish.[65]

As to the belief in sorcery, spells, talismans, incantations, all which go by the general name of medicine, it is unbounded. Henry mentions, that among the goods which some traders took up the country to exchange for furs, they had a large collection of the little rude prints, published for children, at a halfpenny a piece – I recollect such when I was a child. They sold these at a high price, for medicines (i.e. talismans,) and found them a very profitable and popular article of commerce. One of these, a little print of a sailor kissing his sweetheart, was an esteemed medicine among the young, and eagerly purchased for a love-spell. A soldier presenting his gun, or brandishing his sabre, was a medicine to promote warlike courage – and so on.

The medicines and manitos[66] of the Indians will remind you of the fetishes of the negroes.

With regard to the belief in omens and incantations, I should like to see it ascertained how far we civilized Christians, with all our schools, our pastors, and our masters, are in advance of these (so-called) savages?[67]

Source text

Jameson, Anna, *Winter Studies and Summer Rambles in Canada*, Vol. III (London: Saunders and Otley, 1838).

References

Buss, Helen M., 'Anna Jameson's *Winter Studies and Summer Rambles in Canada* as Epistolary Dijournal', in Marlene Kadar (ed.), *Essays on Life Writing: From Genre to Critical Practice* (Toronto: University of Toronto Press, 1992), 42–60.

---

65 [Author's note] I have heard the particulars of this wild story of the origin of the white-fish, but cannot remember them. I think the woman was put to death by her sons. Most of the above particulars I learned from oral communication, and from some of the papers published by Mr. Schoolcraft. This gentleman and others instituted a society at Detroit (1832) called the *Algic Society*, for 'evangelising the north-western tribes, inquiring into their history and superstitions, and promoting education, agriculture, industry, peace, and temperance among them.'

66 An Algonquin word for spirit, deity or supernatural being

67 [Author's note] 'One of the most distinguished men of the age, who has left a reputation which will be as lasting as it is great, was, when a boy, in constant fear of a very able but unmerciful schoolmaster, and in the state of mind which that constant fear produced, he fixed upon a great spider for his fetish, (or manito,) and used every day to pray to it that he might not be flogged.'—*The Doctor*, vol. v.

When a child, I was myself taken to a witch (or medicine woman) to be cured of an accidental burn, by charms and incantations. I was then about six years old, and have a very distinct recollection of the whole scene, which left a strong and frightful impression on my childish fancy.

Gerry, Thomas M. F., '"I Am Translated": Anna Jameson's Sketches and Winter Studies and Summer Rambles in Canada', *Journal of Canadian Studies/Revue d'études canadiennes* 25.4 (Winter 1990–1), 34–49.

Johnston, Judith, *Anna Jameson: Victorian, Feminist, Woman of Letters* (Aldershot: Scolar Press, 1997).

Grace Aguilar (1816–47)

'The Wanderers' (1845)

The child of Portuguese Jewish refugees who settled in London, Grace Aguilar was a precocious product of both cultures, home-educated in religion, history and perhaps Hebrew by her parents. Her family was sickly during this period, and Aguilar herself contracted measles at age nineteen. From predilection and for financial support, she began to write, publishing an initial book of poems in 1839. During her twenties Aguilar composed prolifically: a translation of *Israel Defended*, a tract on *The Spirit of Judaism*, and a history titled the *Women of Israel,* as well as domestic fiction well received in England. Her most prominent work was poetry, however, much of it published by American Rabbi and editor Isaac Leeser in his magazine, *The Occident and American Jewish Advocate*. Diagnosed with spinal paralysis in 1847, she died at only thirty-one in Frankfurt, Germany, while visiting her brother.

Given her background, her *oeuvre* unsurprisingly conveys strong Jewish themes. 'The Wanderers', for example, published in 1838, is a poetic explication of the story of Hagar, Abraham's handmaiden and mother of his firstborn child, Ishmael. Hagar was sent with her fourteen-year-old son into the Desert of Beersheba, where, in Aguilar's words, exhaustion and 'the heavy scorching air' gave little hope of survival. But, hearing their despair, the poem continues, God's 'still small voice' uplifts them, leading Hagar to 'a well of water' and promising that her son will 'a nation make'.

In its emotional drama, as well as its affirmation of God's pledge to the Jewish people, 'The Wanderers' clearly affiliated with the aims of its initial publication site, Isaac Leeser's Philadelphia situated but globally oriented magazine. By 'follow[ing] our contemporaries in the old world . . . and mak[ing] use of their labours' (that is of European-based writers like Aguilar), Leeser had explained in the periodical's first issue in 1843, he aimed to produce a publication 'devoted to the advancement of the religious interests of the whole Jewish people' ('Introductory Remarks', 3).

'The Wanderers'

Genesis, xxi. 14–20.

WITH sadden'd heart and tearful eye the mother went her way,
The Patriarch's mandate had gone forth, and Hagar must not stay.

Oh! who can tell the emotions deep that pressed on Abra'am's heart—
As thus, obedient to his God, from Ismael called to part!

But God had spoken, and he knew His word was changeless truth,
He could not doubt His blessing would protect the friendless youth;
He bade him go, nor would he heed the anguish of his soul;
He turned aside,—a father's wo in silence to control.

Now hand in hand they wend their way, o'er hills and vale and wild;
The mother's heart was full of grief, but smiled in glee her child:
Fearless and free, he felt restraint would never gall him now—
And hail'd with joy the fresh'ning breeze that fann'd his fair young brow.

His mother's heart was desolate, and tears swell'd in her eye;
Scarce to his artless words of love her quiv'ring lips reply.
She only saw the *future* as a lone and dreary wild:
The *present* stood before the lad in joyance undefil'd.

She knew, alas! his boyish strength too soon would droop and fade;
And who was, in that lonely scene, to give them food and aid?
With trembling gaze she oft would mark the flushing of his cheek,
And list in terror, lest he should 'gin falteringly to speak!

Fatigue she felt not for herself, nor heeded cure nor pain—
But nearer, nearer to her breast her boy at times she'd strain;
Beersheba's wilderness they see before them dark and wide;
Oh, who across its scorching sands their wandering steps will guide?

The flush departed from the cheek which she so oft has kiss'd;
To his glad tones of childish glee no longer may she list;
A pallor as of death is spread o'er those sweet features now—
She sees him droop before the blast that fann'd his aching brow.

"Oh, mother, lay me down," he cried, "I know not what I feel,
But something cold and rushing seems thro' all my limbs to steal—
Oh kiss me, mother dear, and then ah, lay me down to sleep—
Nay, do not look upon me thus—kiss me and do not weep!"

Scarce could her feeble arms support her child, and lay him where
Some clustering shrubs might shield him from the heavy scorching air;
His drooping eyelids closed; his breath came painfully and slow—
She bent her head on his a while in wild yet speechless wo.

Then from his side she hurried, as impelled she knew not why,
Save that she could not linger there—she could not see him die—
She lifted up her voice and wept—and o'er the lonely wild
"Let me not see his death!" was borne, "my Ismael, my child!"

And silence came upon her then, her stricken soul to calm;
And suddenly and strange there fell a soft and soothing balm—

And then a voice came stealing, on the still and fragrant air—
A still small voice that would be heard, tho' solitude was there.

"What aileth thee, oh Hagar?" thus it spoke: "fear not, for God hath heard
The lad's voice where he is,—and thou, trust in thy Maker's word!
Awake! arise! lift up the lad and hold him in thine hand—
I will of him a nation make, before Me, he shall stand."

It ceased, that voice; and silence now, as strangely soft and still,
The boundless desert once again with eloquence would fill—
And strength returned to Hagar's frame, for God hath oped her eyes—
And lo! amid the arid sands a well of water lies!

Quick to her boy, with beating heart, the anxious mother flies,
And to his lips, and hands, and brow, the cooling draught applies—
He wakes! he breathes! the flush of life is mantling on his cheek—
He smiles! he speaks ! oh those quick tears his mother's joy shall speak!

She held him to her throbbing breast, she gazed upon his face—
The beaming features, one by one, in silent love to trace.
She bade him kneel to bless the Hand that saved him in the wild—
But oh! few words her lips could speak, save these—"My child, my child!"

Source text

Aguliar, Grace, 'The Wanderers', *The Occident and American Jewish Advocate* 3.7 (October 1845), 330–2.

References

Harris, Daniel, 'Hagar in Christian Britain: Grace Aguilar's "The Wanderers"', *Victorian Literature and Culture* 27 (1999), 143–69.
[Leeser, Isaac], 'Introductory Remarks', *The Occident and the American Jewish Advocate* 1.1 (April 1843), 1–6.
Scheinberg, Cynthia. '"Measure to Yourself a Prophet's Place": Biblical Heroines, Jewish Difference and Women's Poetry', in Isobel Armstrong and Virginia Blain (eds), *Women's Poetry, Late Romantic to Late Victorian: Gender and Genre, 1830–1900* (New York: Palgrave, 1999), 263–91.

Cecil F. H. Alexander (1818–95)

'All Things Bright and Beautiful' (1848)

Child poet Cecil Frances Alexander emerged as a young adult hymn writer for the Church of Ireland in her twenties. In 1850 she married William Alexander, a poet himself, and later the Bishop of Derry, launching what would become a long and fruitful marriage. In all, she composed over

400 hymns in her lifetime, including collections such as *Verses for Holy Seasons*, *The Lord of the Forest and His Vassals* and *Hymns for Little Children*, the last being especially popular (with 69 editions). Proceeds from her writing went to charitable causes such as the Derry Institution for the Deaf and Dumb and the Derry Home for Fallen Women. Anglican hymnals still reprint her hymns, and a stained glass window memorialises her in the north vestibule of St Columb's Cathedral.

'All Things Bright and Beautiful' appeared under the title 'Maker of Heaven and Earth' in the 1848 *Hymns for Little Children*, which sold between 250,000 and 275,000 copies in the United States. With simple rhyme and rhythm the song enshrines Anglican doctrine with vivid imagery. The third stanza ('The rich man in his castle, / The poor man at his gate, / God made them high and lowly, / And ordered their estate') underscores Alexander's support of the English class system and is rarely included in today's versions.

'All Things Bright and Beautiful'

MAKER OF HEAVEN AND EARTH

ALL things bright and beautiful,
　　All creatures great and small,
All things wise and wonderful,
　　The LORD GOD made them all.

Each little flower that opens,
　　Each little bird that sings,
He made their glowing colours,
　　He made their tiny wings.

The rich man in his castle,
　　The poor man at his gate,
GOD made them, high or lowly,
　　And ordered their estate.

The purple-headed mountain.
　　The river running by,
The sunset and the morning,
　　That brightens up the sky,

The cold wind in the winter,
　　The pleasant summer sun,
The ripe fruits in the garden,
　　He made them every one.

The tall trees in the greenwood,
　　The meadows where we play,

The rushes by the water,
　　We gather every day;—

He gave us eyes to see them,
　　And lips that we might tell,
How great is GOD Almighty,
　　Who has made all things well.

Source text

[Alexander, Cecil Frances], *Hymns for Little Children: First American Edition* (Philadelphia: Herman Hooker, 1850).

References

Wallace, Valerie, *Mrs. Alexander: A Life of the Hymn-Writer, Cecil Frances Alexander, 1818–1895* (Dublin: Lilliput Press, 1995).

Eliza R. Snow (1804–87)

'Queen Victoria' (1856)

A prolific poet, Eliza R. Snow lived at the centre of nineteenth-century Mormondom as a transnational enterprise. Members of the Church of Jesus Christ Latter-day Saints revered her as Matriarch of the Church. Also claiming renown as the sister of a church president, Lorenzo Snow, she enacted gendered leadership by serving as longtime President of the LDS's Relief Society.

With composition dates ranging from the 1820s to the 1880s, Snow's poems tracked her trajectory from an unmarried-by-choice, piously intellectual Baptist authoress writing for frontier Ohio periodicals to becoming an activist in the LDS community. In the latter role, Snow envisioned her lyrics as drawing readers to God. She had been slower to convert than her mother and sister, both of whom were baptised by Joseph Smith soon after the 1830 publication of the *Book of Mormon*. Though impressed by other converts' testimonies, Snow held back, along with her brother Lorenzo (who became one of the LDS's twelve apostles). By 1835, however, she was ready to be baptised; she would join the travels of Latter-day Saints to Missouri, Illinois and Utah, becoming one of Smith's wives and, after his 1844 death, a 'plural wife' of Brigham Young.

The poem below records a pivotal 1840–1 period in Lorenzo's service to the Church, when he travelled to Britain to seek transatlantic converts during a period when such practices as plural marriage (cast in secular legal terms as polygamy) often brought negative scrutiny. Snow composed her 'Queen Victoria' poem as a celebration of the monarch's gracious welcoming of Lorenzo and, implicitly, the LDS community. For that community's members, in fact, Eliza Snow herself was a sovereign, regularly referenced as a prophetess and Zion's poetess.

'Queen Victoria'

The following lines were suggested by the circumstance of the presentation of the Book of Mormon to Her Majesty Queen Victoria and His Royal Highness Prince Albert, by Elder L. Snow,[68] through the politeness of Sir Henry Wheatley, in 1842.[69]

Of all the monarchs of the earth
    That wear the robes of royalty,
She has inherited by birth
    The broadest wreath of majesty.

From her wide territorial wing
    The sun does not withdraw its light,
While earth's diurnal motions bring
    To other nations day and night.

All earthly thrones are tott'ring things,
    Where lights and shadows intervene;
And regal honor often brings
    The scaffold or the guillotine.

But still *her* sceptre is approv'd—
    All nations deck the wreath she wears;
Yet, like the youth whom Jesus lov'd,
    One thing is lacking even there.

But lo! A prize possessing more
    Of worth than gems with honor rife—
A herald of salvation bore
    To her the words of endless life.

---

68 Snow reports in her *Biography* of Lorenzo that he looked back on this journey as signalling 'the providence of God' in guiding his work 'as an ambassador' carrying His 'message to the nations of the earth' (48). Stopping in Liverpool and then Manchester and Birmingham after a rough Atlantic passage, Lorenzo addressed converts and sought new ones before reaching London, where he was named head of the Church there and, in turn, ordained several new ministers. One of Eliza's 1841 poems, 'To Elder Lorenzo Snow, London, England', urged him to complete his service abroad and return home to his 'warm friends' in America (*Biography*, 56–7). Yet, she recognised the importance of his work abroad.

69 Snow includes a reference to the poem's origin in the *Biography*, where she salutes Victoria's acceptance, along with Prince Albert's, of the 'two neatly bound copies of the *Book of Mormon*, which had been donated by President Brigham Young, and left in the care of Elder Snow for that purpose' (*Biography*, 63). We thank our colleague Larisa Schumann, an LDS-affiliated scholar, for assistance with the headnote and footnotes for this entry.

That *gift*, however fools deride,
  Is worthy of her royal care:
She'd better lay her crown aside
  Than spurn the light reflected there.

O would she now her influence lend—
  The influence of royalty,
Messiah's kingdom to extend,
  And Zion's "*nursing mother*" be;

She, with the glory of her name
  Inscrib'd on Zion's lofty spire,
Would win a wreath of endless fame,
  To last when other wreaths expire.

Though over millions call'd to reign—
  Herself a powerful nation's boast,
'Twould be her everlasting gain
  To serve the King, the Lord of Hosts.

For there are crowns and thrones on high,
  And kingdoms *there* to be conferr'd;
There honors wait that never die,
  There fame's immortal trump is heard.

Truth speaks—it is Jehovah's word:
  Let kings and queens and princes hear:
In distant isles the sound is heard—
  Ye heavens, rejoice; O earth, give ear.

The time, the time is now at hand
  To give a glorious period birth—
The Son of God will take command,
  And rule the nations of the earth.

Source text

Snow, Eliza R., *Poems, Religious, Historical, and Political* (Liverpool: F. D. Richards; London: Latter-Day Saints' Book, 1856).

References

Beecher, Maureen Ursenbach and Lavina Fielding Anderson (eds), *Sisters in Spirit: Mormon Women in Historical and Cultural Perspective* (Urbana, IL: University of Illinois Press, 1987).

Derr, Jill Mulvay and Karen Lynn Davidson, 'A Wary Heart Becomes "Fixed Unalterably": Eliza R. Snow's Conversation to Mormonism', *Journal of Mormon History* 30.2 (Fall 2004), 98–128.

Smith, Eliza R. Snow, *Biography and Family Record of Lorenzo Snow, One of the Twelve Apostles of the Church of Jesus Christ of Latter-Day Saints, Written and Compiled by His Sister* (Salt Lake City, UT: Deseret News Company, 1884).

Youth's Companion (1827–1929)

'Irish Jim' (1857)

Youth's Companion, a Protestant periodical aimed at acculturating Anglo-American children, was launched in Boston in 1827 by Asa Rand and Nathaniel Willis, publishing monthly until 1929. Daniel Sharp Ford eventually took over as editor-publisher, a role held until his death in 1899. Under Ford's leadership, the periodical cultivated a more literary and transatlantic bent by commissioning internationally known authors (including Rudyard Kipling and Thomas Hardy) while continuing to publish unsigned didactic pieces.

This brief story called upon prejudice associated with what, from the mid-1850s to the 1890s, was the largest and most regularly vilified immigrant group coming to America: the Irish. Attacked on the basis of ethnic identity, Irish newcomers were doubly marginalised for being Catholic, a concern repeatedly raised by that era's nativists when lobbying against immigration. Print and visual texts – including in popular periodicals like *Harper's Weekly* and (later) *WASP* – reinforced opposition to the ongoing Irish influx. Stereotypes attacking Irish Americans included unrefined language (cast as exaggerated brogue), negative social behaviours (especially drunkenness), lack of self-restraint (such as in domestic violence) and, in extreme versions, an equivalency with brute animalism (sometimes using blackface figures with simian features). Suggesting that individual Irish might be transformed into acceptable Americans via Protestant-sponsored education, this *Youth's Companion* story also transferred the role of maternal teacher from Catholic failure in Jim's Irish home to a safe Methodist school space affirming nativist dominion.

'Irish Jim'

A friend has written me an account of a boy named Jim M'C, who belongs to the Methodist Mission School in Bedford-street, Philadelphia. If you would like to know about him, read on:

About a year ago Jim went into the school, in no very nice plight. His clothes were ragged, his face and hands dirty, and his hair matted. He was tipsy withal, for though scarcely thirteen summers old, he had been taught to love the drink that fills the drunkard's bowl. Alas, poor Jim!

But the singing of the scholars had a charm for him which he could not resist. There was music in his soul, and the songs he heard at school waked it into life, and there was melody in poor Jim's heart.—Again and again he went there. He was idle, and owing to his habit of doing as he pleased, he found it hard to submit to rule; but by degrees he grew quiet, left off drinking, and went also to the day school.

Jim's mother is a Catholic. It was from her he learned to drink. She tried to keep him from the Sunday school, but, having had his own way of things evil so long, he would have it in this one good act of his life. So Jim is still a scholar in the Sunday school.

Not long since the lady who teaches Jim's day school met his mother. 'How do you do, mem?' said she to the teacher, 'and how to you git along wid Jim?'

'Pretty well,' replied the teacher; 'he gives us a little trouble at times, but, on the whole, we manage him quite easily.'

Jim's mother, on hearing this, looked sternly into the teacher's face, and said: 'Och! But Jim is a bad boy. An' I wish ye'd be after bating him well, for wasn't it last night that he locked me up in the cellar? Och! But he's a bad boy, he is.'

'I'll talk to him,' answered the teacher. Then wishing the angry mother good morning, she walked to her school-room.

At a fitting time the teacher called Jim to her side and said, 'Jim, why did you fasten your mother down the cellar last night?'

Jim smiled and replied: 'Why, you see, ma'am, I was singing one of the hymns we learn at school, and mother wanted me to stop. She said it was wrong to sing it. But I wanted to sing, so I just put her down the cellar, locked the door, and sung my hymn, and after I was done I let her up!'

I don't know what the teacher said to Jim, but I think there is hope in his case. It was right for him to sing. It was wrong for his mother to forbid him. But it was also wrong for him to lock his mother up in the cellar. Wicked as his mother may be, she is still his mother, and he should treat her with kindness. No doubt Jim meant right. There is good seed in Jim's heart, which, I hope, will spring up in due time. When it does Jim will sing louder than ever; but he will be too meek then to lock his mother down in the cellar.

Let all good children pray that Irish Jim may soon become a true Christian, and that, instead of putting his mother down stairs, he may lead her to the cross of Jesus, where they will sing sweet songs of praise together. Pray for Irish Jim, my children! – S.S. Adv.

Source text

'Irish Jim', *The Youth's Companion* 31.33 (13 August 1857), 130.

References

Bryne, James P., 'The Genesis of Whiteface in Nineteenth-Century American Popular Culture', *MELUS* 29.3–4 (Fall–Winter, 2004), 133–49.

Moran, Edward, 'The Youth's Companion', *St. James Press Encyclopedia of Popular Culture Online* (Detroit, MI: Gale, 2013), Web.

Elizabeth Gaskell (1810–65)

From 'Part the Third', Lois the Witch (1859)

Englishwoman Elizabeth Gaskell won immediate success with *Mary Barton* (1848), which addressed cross-class communication and worker–employer relations and ended transatlantically when Mary Barton and her husband migrated to Canada to start a new life. Charles Dickens recruited the newly prominent Gaskell for *Household Words*, which he edited, and then *All the Year Round*, in which Gaskell's dramatic depiction of the Salem witch trials appeared between 8 and 22 October 1859. It was immediately reprinted in *Harper's Weekly* in the US between 22 October and 12 November with unauthorised cuts (e.g. the protagonist's continued loyalty to crown and church in England – see Hughes). During an 1857 holiday in Rome, Gaskell joined an American circle including Charles Eliot Norton and expatriate US sculptor William Wetmore Story (1819–95); earlier she had met Harriet Beecher Stowe (Uglow, 353, 417–18; Pettit, 599). A Unitarian who thus applied reason to religion, Gaskell relied for her tale's historical details on US Unitarian minister Charles Upham's *Lectures on Witchcraft, Comprising a History of the Delusion in Salem in 1692* (1831), sometimes copying verbatim (Uglow, 475; Hughes). *Lois the Witch* portrays the dangers of hysteria and superstition and leads to a shocking ending; along the way it offers comparisons of religious beliefs in England and America in the seventeenth and nineteenth centuries and a sympathetic representation of the suffering endured by Native Americans. The excerpt below occurs after the newly orphaned Lois Barclay leaves England to live with her uncle's family in Salem, Massachusetts, and the first accusation of witchcraft has been proclaimed.

From 'Part the Third', Lois the Witch

Lois sat spinning with Faith.[70] Both were silent, pondering over the stories that were abroad. Lois spoke first.

"Oh, Faith! this country is worse than ever England was, even in the days of Master Matthew Hopkinson, the witch-finder.[71] I grow frightened of every one, I think. I even get afeared sometimes of Nattee!"

Faith coloured a little. Then she asked,

"Why? What should make you distrust the Indian woman?"

"Oh! I am ashamed of my fear as soon as it arises in my mind. But, you know, her look and colour were strange to me when I first came; and she is not a christened woman; and they tell stories of Indian wizards; and I know not what the mixtures are which she is sometimes stirring over the fire, nor the meaning of the strange chants she sings to herself. And once I met her in the dusk, just close by Pastor Tappau's house, in company with Hota, his servant; it was just before we heard of the sore disturbance in his house, and I have wondered if she had aught to do with it."

Faith sat very still, as if thinking. At last she said,

---

70 Cousin to Lois, along with Prudence and the mentally unstable Manasseh; their mother is Grace Hickson

71 Matthew Hopkins (n.d.–1647) was a notorious English witchfinder who tried twenty-six purported witches in Essex and sparked similar trials across the nation (*ODNB*).

"If Nattee has powers beyond what you and I have, she will not use them for evil; at least not evil to those whom she loves."

"That comforts me but little," said Lois. "If she has powers beyond what she ought to have, I dread her, though I have done her no evil; nay, though I could almost say she bore me a kindly feeling. But such powers are only given by the Evil One; and the proof thereof is, that, as you imply, Nattee would use them on those who offend her."

"And why should she not?" asked Faith, lifting her eyes, and flashing heavy fire out of them, at the question.

"Because," said Lois, not seeing Faith's glance, "we are told to pray for them that despitefully use us, and to do good to them that persecute us.[72] But poor Nattee is not a christened woman. I would that Mr. Nolan would baptize her: it would, maybe, take her out of the power of Satan's temptations."

"Are you never tempted?" asked Faith half-scornfully; "and yet I doubt not you were well baptised!"

"True," said Lois sadly; "I often do very wrong; but, perhaps, I might have done worse, if the holy form had not been observed."

They were again silent for a time.

"Lois," said Faith, "I did not mean any offence. But do you never feel as if you would give up all that future life, of which the parsons talk, and which seems so vague and so distant, for a few years of real, vivid blessedness, to begin tomorrow – this hour – this minute? Oh! I could think of happiness for which I would willingly give up all those misty chances of heaven –"

"Faith, Faith!" cried Lois in terror, holding her hand before her cousin's mouth, and looking around in fright. "Hush! you know not who may be listening; you are putting yourself in his power."

But Faith pushed her hand away, and said, "Lois, I believe in him no more than I believe in heaven. Both may exist; but they are so far away that I defy them. Why all this ado about Mr. Tappau's house—promise me never to tell living creature, and I will tell you a secret."

"No!" said Lois, terrified. "I dread all secrets. I will hear none. I will do all that I can for you, Cousin Faith, in any way; but just at this time I strive to keep my life and thoughts within the strictest bounds of godly simplicity, and I dread pledging myself to aught that is hidden and secret."

"As you will, cowardly girl, full of terrors, which, if you had listened to me, might have been lessened, if not entirely done away with." And Faith would not utter another word, though Lois tried meekly to entice her into conversation on some other subject. [. . .]

At length a day was appointed when, after solemn fasting and prayer, Mr. Tappau invited the neighbouring ministers and all godly people to assemble at his house, and unite with him in devoting a day to solemn religious services, and to supplication for the deliverance of his children, and those similarly afflicted, from the power of the Evil One. All Salem poured out towards the house of the minister. There was a look of excitement on all their faces; eagerness and horror was [sic] depicted on many, while stern resolution, amounting to determined cruelty, if the occasion arose, was seen on others.

---

72 Luke 6: 27–8

In the midst of the prayer, Hester Tappau, the younger girl, fell into convulsions; fit after fit came on, and her screams mingled with the shrieks and cries of the assembled congregation. In the first pause, when the child was partially recovered, when the people stood around, exhausted and breathless, her father, the Pastor Tappau, lifted his right hand, and adjured[73] her, in the name of the Trinity, to say who tormented her. There was a dead silence; not a creature stirred of all those hundreds. Hester turned wearily and uneasily, and moaned out the name of Hota, her father's Indian servant. Hota was present, apparently as much interested as any one; indeed, she had been busying herself much in bringing remedies to the suffering child. But now she stood aghast, transfixed, while her name was caught up and shouted out in tones of reprobation[74] and hatred by all the crowd around her. Another moment, and they would have fallen upon the trembling creature and torn her limb from limb—pale, dusky, shivering Hota, half guilty-looking from her very bewilderment. But Pastor Tappau, that gaunt, grey man, lifting himself to his utmost height, signed to them to go back, to keep still while he addressed them; and then he told them that instant vengeance was not just, deliberate punishment; that there would be need of conviction, perchance of confession—he hoped for some redress for his suffering children from her revelations, if she were brought to confession. They must leave the culprit in his hands, and in those of his brother ministers, that they might wrestle with Satan before delivering her up to the civil power. He spoke well; for he spoke from the heart of a father seeing his children exposed to dreadful and mysterious suffering, and firmly believing that he now held the clue in his hand which should ultimately release them and their fellow-sufferers. And the congregation moaned themselves into unsatisfied submission, and listened to his long, passionate prayer, which he uplifted even while the hapless Hota stood there, guarded and bound by two men, who glared at her like bloodhounds ready to slip, even while the prayer ended in the words of the merciful Saviour. Lois sickened and shuddered at the whole scene; and this was no intellectual shuddering at the folly and superstition of the people, but tender moral shuddering at the sight of guilt which she believed in, and at the evidence of men's hatred and abhorrence, which, when shown even to the guilty, troubled and distressed her merciful heart. She followed her aunt and cousins out into the open air, with downcast eyes and pale face. Grace Hickson was going home with a feeling of triumphant relief at the detection of the guilty one. Faith alone seemed uneasy and disturbed beyond her wont, for Manasseh received the whole transaction as the fulfilment of a prophecy, and Prudence was excited by the whole scene into a state of discordant[75] high spirits. [. . .]

That evening the news spread through Salem, that Hota had confessed her sin, had acknowledged that she was a witch.[76] Nattee was the first to hear the intelligence. She broke into the room where the girls were sitting with Grace Hickson, solemnly doing nothing, because of the great prayer-meeting in the morning, and

---

73 To bind under oath (*OED*)
74 Rejection of a person or thing (*OED*)
75 Conflicting (*OED*)
76 The first victim of the Salem witch trials was Tituba, an enslaved Indigenous woman. Hota's story mirrors Tituba's, although Tituba was ultimately let go.

cried out, "Mercy, mercy, mistress, everybody! take care of poor Indian Nattee, who never do wrong, but for mistress and the family! Hota one bad wicked witch; she say so herself; oh, me! oh, me!" and stooping over Faith, she said something in a low, miserable tone of voice, of which Lois only heard the word "torture." But Faith heard all, and turning very pale, half accompanied, half led Nattee back to her kitchen. [...]

Hota had confessed all – had owned to signing a certain little red book[77] which Satan had presented to her, had been present at impious sacraments,[78] had ridden through the air to Newbury Falls,[79] and, in fact, had assented to all the questions which the elders and magistrates, carefully reading over the confessions of the witches who had formerly been tried in England, in order that they might not omit a single inquiry, had asked of her. More she had owned to, but things of inferior importance, and partaking more of the nature of earthly tricks than of spiritual power. She had spoken of carefully adjusted strings, by which all the crockery in Pastor Tappau's house could be pulled down or disturbed; but of such intelligible malpractices the gossips of Salem took little heed. One of them said that such an action showed Satan's prompting; but they all preferred to listen to the grander guilt of the blasphemous[80] sacraments and supernatural rides. The narrator ended with saying that she was to be hung the next morning, in spite of her confession, even although her life had been promised to her if she acknowledged her sin; for it was well to make an example of the first-discovered witch, and it was also well that she was an Indian, a heathen, whose life would be no great loss to the community. Grace Hickson on this spoke out. It was well that witches should perish off the face of the earth, Indian [or] English, heathen or, worse, a baptized Christian who had betrayed the Lord, even as Judas[81] did, and had gone over to Satan. For her part, she wished that the first-discovered witch had been a member of a godly English household, that it might be seen of all men that religious folk were willing to cut off the right hand, and pluck out the right eye, if tainted with this devilish sin. She spoke sternly and well. The last comer said that her words might be brought to proof, for it had been whispered that Hota had named others, and some among the most religious families of Salem, whom she had seen among the unholy communicants[82] at the sacrament of the Evil One. And Grace replied that she would answer for it, all godly folk would stand the proof, and quench all natural affection rather than that such a sin should grow and spread among them. She herself had a weak bodily dread of witnessing the violent death even of an animal; but she would not let that deter her from standing among those who cast the accursed creature out from among them on the morrow morning.

---

77 Witches were believed to have signed the devil's book, often in blood.
78 Solemn ceremonies or religious acts (*OED*); it was assumed witches had their own perverted sacraments.
79 Newbury, MA, north of Salem, has waterfalls on the Parker River.
80 Irreverent of God or anything sacred (*OED*)
81 Judas: the disciple who betrayed Jesus; see Matt. 26, Mark 14 or Luke 22
82 Those in communion with a particular church (*OED*); the term continues the theme of perverted sacraments.

Source text

Gaskell, Elizabeth, 'Lois the Witch', *All the Year Round* 1 (22 October 1859), 609–24.

References

Foster, Louisa Jayne, 'The Monstrous Transatlantic Witchcraft Narrative: Elizabeth Gaskell's Lois the Witch', in Robin Peel and Daniel Maudlin (eds), *Transatlantic Traffic and (Mis)translations* (Durham, NH: University of New Hampshire Press, 2013), 68–80.

Hughes, Linda K. (ed.), *Novellas and Shorter Fiction: Cousin Phillis and other Tales from* All the Year Round *and the* Cornhill Magazine *1859–64*. Vol. 4, *Works of Elizabeth Gaskell*, Joanne Shattock (gen. ed.) (London: Pickering & Chatto, 2006).

Pettit, Clare. 'Time Lag and Elizabeth Gaskell's Transatlantic Imagination', *Victorian Studies* 54.4 (2012), 599–623.

Uglow, Jenny, *Elizabeth Gaskell: A Habit of Stories* (London: Faber & Faber, 1999).

William Craft (1824–1900) and Ellen Craft (1826–91)

From Running a Thousand Miles for Freedom *(1860)*

Nineteenth-century religious leaders were divided as to whether slavery, as an institution or as an individual's practice, could be compatible with Biblical teachings. One strategy for reconciling righteousness with the enslavement of African people and their descendants involved the assertion, expressed earlier in this section by Phillis Wheatley, that being enslaved provided access to religious salvation. In contrast, some religious leaders pointed to a fundamental moral conflict between a Christian identity and the enslavement of humans. For example, in 1846, the Rev. Isaac Nelson, leader of a Presbyterian Church in Belfast, Ireland, tried (though unsuccessfully) to persuade his colleagues to deny American enslavers' participation in an Evangelical Alliance meeting.

Arguments seeking either to reconcile Christianity with slavery or to demonstrate such a stance as unconscionable played out in periodicals on both sides of the Atlantic. For instance, an 1860 article in *The Liberator*, on the 'Attitude of the "Religious" Press Towards Slavery and Anti-Slavery', juxtaposed a pro-slavery piece appearing in *The Congregationalist* with what *The Liberator* writer argued: that true Christian civilisation would not arrive in the American South until all slaves were freed.

That same year, in London, William and Ellen Craft published their memoir of a daring escape from enslavement and their transatlantic passage to freedom. Within their opening pages, the Crafts entered this ongoing debate by condemning slaveholding as un-Christian.

From **Running a Thousand Miles for Freedom**

PART I.

"God gave us only over beast, fish, fowl,
Dominion absolute; that right we hold
By his donation. But man over man
He made not lord; such title to himself
Reserving, human left from human free."
Milton.[83]

MY wife and myself were born in different towns in the State of Georgia, which is one of the principal slave States. It is true, our condition as slaves was not by any means the worst; but the mere idea that we were held as chattels, and deprived of all legal rights—the thought that we had to give up our hard earnings to a tyrant, to enable him to live in idleness and luxury—the thought that we could not call the bones and sinews that God gave us our own: but above all, the fact that another man had the power to tear from our cradle the new-born babe and sell it in the shambles like a brute, and then scourge us if we dared to lift a finger to save it from such a fate, haunted us for years.

But in December, 1848, a plan suggested itself that proved quite successful, and in eight days after it was first thought of we were free from the horrible trammels of slavery, rejoicing and praising God in the glorious sunshine of liberty. [...]

I have known worthless white people to sell their own free children into slavery; and, as there are good-for-nothing white as well as coloured persons everywhere, no one, perhaps, will wonder at such inhuman transactions: particularly in the Southern States of America, where I believe there is a greater want of humanity and high principle amongst the whites, than among any other civilized people in the world.

I know that those who are not familiar with the working of "the peculiar institution," can scarcely imagine any one so totally devoid of all natural affection as to sell his own offspring into returnless bondage. But Shakespeare, that great observer of human nature, says:—

> "With caution judge of probabilities.
> Things deemed unlikely, e'en impossible,
> Experience often shows us to be true."

WILLIAM CRAFT.

ELLEN CRAFT.

Figure 7.5 William and Ellen Craft, from William Still, *The Underground Railroad. A Record of Facts, Authentic Narratives, Letters, &c.* (Philadelphia: Porter & Coates, 1872), inter-page 368–9. Courtesy HathiTrust.

---

83 *Paradise Lost*, Book 12. In quoting from such a high-culture religious source, the Crafts lend ethos to their memoir and the arguments therein.

My wife's new mistress was decidedly more humane than the majority of her class. My wife has always given her credit for not exposing her to many of the worst features of slavery. For instance, it is a common practice in the slave States for ladies, when angry with their maids, to send them to the calybuce[84] sugar-house, or to some other place established for the purpose of punishing slaves, and have them severely flogged; and I am sorry it is a fact, that the villains to whom those defenceless creatures are sent, not only flog them as they are ordered, but frequently compel them to submit to the greatest indignity. Oh! if there is any one thing under the wide canopy of heaven, horrible enough to stir a man's soul, and to make his very blood boil, it is the thought of his dear wife, his unprotected sister, or his young and virtuous daughters, struggling to save themselves from falling a prey to such demons!

It always appears strange to me that any one who was not born a slaveholder, and steeped to the very core in the demoralizing atmosphere of the Southern States, can in any way palliate slavery. It is still more surprising to see virtuous ladies looking with patience upon, and remaining indifferent to, the existence of a system that exposes nearly two millions of their own sex in the manner I have mentioned, and that too in a professedly free and Christian country. There is, however, great consolation in knowing that God is just, and will not let the oppressor of the weak, and the spoiler of the virtuous, escape unpunished here and hereafter.

I believe a similar retribution to that which destroyed Sodom[85] is hanging over the slaveholders. My sincere prayer is that they may not provoke God, by persisting in a reckless course of wickedness, to pour out his consuming wrath upon them.

I must now return to our history.

My old master had the reputation of being a very humane and Christian man, but he thought nothing of selling my poor old father, and dear aged mother, at separate times, to different persons, to be dragged off never to behold each other again, till summoned to appear before the great tribunal of heaven. But, oh! what a happy meeting it will be on that great day for those faithful souls. I say a happy meeting, because I never saw persons more devoted to the service of God than they. But how will the case stand with those reckless traffickers in human flesh and blood, who plunged the poisonous dagger of separation into those loving hearts which God had for so many years closely joined together—nay, sealed as it were with his own hands for the eternal courts of heaven? It is not for me to say what will become of those heartless tyrants. I must leave them in the hands of an all-wise and just God, who will, in his own good time, and in his own way, avenge the wrongs of his oppressed people.

My old master also sold a dear brother and a sister, in the same manner as he did my father and mother. The reason he assigned for disposing of my parents, as well as of several other aged slaves, was, that "they were getting old, and would soon become valueless in the market, and therefore he intended to sell off all the old stock, and buy in a young lot." A most disgraceful conclusion for a man to come to, who made such great professions of religion!

This shameful conduct gave me a thorough hatred, not for true Christianity, but for slave-holding piety.

---

84 Prison or place of punishment
85 A prominent city in the Bible, destroyed for being sinful

Source text

Craft, William and Ellen, *Running a Thousand Miles for Freedom; or, the Escape of William and Ellen Craft from Slavery* (London: William Tweedie, 1860).

References

C. K. W., 'Attitude of the "Religious" Press Towards Slavery and Anti-Slavery', *The Liberator* 30.7 (17 February 1860), 28.
'Pro-Slavery Fanaticism', *The Independent* 6.293 (13 July 1854), 1.
Ritchie, Daniel, 'Abolitionism and Evangelicalism: Isaac Nelson, the Evangelical Alliance, and Transatlantic Debate over Christian Fellowship with Slaveholders', *Historical Journal* 57.2 (2014), 421–46.

Charles Bradlaugh (1833–91)

From 'Humanity's Gain from Unbelief' (1889)

When Charles Bradlaugh voiced doubts about the Anglican faith as a teenager, he was suspended from the church and evicted from his family home. He found open arms in the local atheist community and emerged as a 'freethinker' in his adult life, advocating for birth control, unionism and universal suffrage. Though he followed his father into work as a solicitor's clerk, he became aligned with secular causes and took positions as editor of the *National Reformer* (a secularist newspaper), president of the London Secular Society and co-founder of the National Secular Society. He was also on the vanguard of the transatlantic secularism movement, travelling to the United States for a vibrant lecture tour in three consecutive winters (1873–5). In 1880 Bradlaugh was elected to Parliament but refused to take the Oath of Allegiance, for which he was eventually arrested and imprisoned.

Published only two years before his death, 'Humanity's Gain From Unbelief' displays many features of Bradlaugh's characteristic iconoclasm. Bradlaugh explores the chequered history of the church, arguing that humanity's progress has been made in spite of, not because of, Christianity. In this way the essay couples with the larger transatlantic secularism movement, which sought to frame agnosticism and atheism as a positive force rather than springing from apostasy or heathenism. As a result of the book's tremendous reception, Bradlaugh engaged in a debate with Rev. Marsden Gibson, in Newcastle, described by one bystander in as 'a matter of Bradlaugh launching cannon-balls while his opponent spun cobwebs' (Bonner Bradlaugh, 407). The following selection was prepared at the request of Allen Thorndike Rice and published in *North American Review* in March 1889.

From 'Humanity's Gain from Unbelief'

As an unbeliever, I ask leave to plead that humanity has been a real gainer from scepticism, and that the gradual and growing rejection of Christianity—like the rejection of the faiths which preceded it—has in fact added, and will add, to man's happiness and well-being. I maintain that in physics science is the outcome of scepticism, and that general progress is impossible without scepticism on matters of religion. I mean by religion every form of belief which accepts or asserts the supernatural. [...] Each religion is slowly, but certainly, modified in its dogma and practice by the gradual development of the peoples amongst whom it is professed. Each discovery destroys in whole or part some theretofore-cherished belief. No religion is suddenly rejected by any people; it is, rather, gradually outgrown. None see a religion die; dead religions are like dead languages and obsolete customs; the decay is long and—like the glacier-march—is only perceptible to the careful watcher by comparisons extending over long periods. A superseded religion may often be traced in the festivals, ceremonies, and dogmas of the religion which has replaced it. Traces of obsolete religions may often be found in popular customs, in old-wives' stories, and in children's tales. [...]

Take one clear gain to humanity consequent on unbelief, i.e., in the abolition of slavery in some countries, in the abolition of the slave trade in most civilized countries, and in the tendency to its total abolition. I am unaware of any religion in the world which in the past forbade slavery. The professors of Christianity for ages supported it; the Old Testament repeatedly sanctioned it by special laws; the New Testament has no repealing declaration. Though we are at the close of the nineteenth century of the Christian era, it is only during the past three-quarters of a century that the battle for freedom has been gradually won. It is scarcely a quarter of a century since the famous emancipation amendment was carried to the United States Constitution. And it is impossible for any well-informed Christian to deny that the abolition movement in North America was most steadily and bitterly opposed by the religious bodies in the various States. Henry Wilson, in his "Rise and Fall of the Slave-Power in America",[86] Samuel J. May, in his "Recollections of the Anti-Slavery Conflict",[87] and J. Greenleaf Whittier,[88] in his poems, alike are witnesses that the Bible and pulpit, the Church and its great influence, were used against abolition and in favor of the slaveowner. I know that Christians in the present day often declare that Christianity had a large share in bringing about the abolition of slavery, and this because men professing Christianity were Abolitionists. I plead that these so-called Christian Abolitionists were men and women whose humanity—recognizing freedom for all—was, in this, in direct conflict with Christianity. It is not yet fifty years since the European Christian powers jointly agreed to abolish the slave trade. What of the effect of Christianity on these powers in the centuries which had preceded? [...] For some 1,800 years almost all Christians kept slaves, bought slaves, sold slaves, bred slaves, stole slaves. Pious Bristol and godly

---

86 (1812–75), a Massachusetts Senator and the 18th Vice President of the US under Ulysses S. Grant; his book was published in three volumes between 1872 and 1877.
87 (1797–1871), a prominent American reformer; his book was published in 1869.
88 (1807–92), an American poet famous for his anti-slavery writing

Liverpool[89] less than 100 years ago, openly grew rich on the traffic. Daring the ninth century Greek Christians sold slaves to the Saracens. In the eleventh century prostitutes were publicly sold in Rome as slaves, and the profit went to the church.

It is said that William Wilberforce[90] was a Christian, but, at any rate, his Christianity was strongly diluted with unbelief. As an Abolitionist, he did not believe Leviticus c. 25, v. 44–46;[91] he must have rejected Exodus c. 21, v. 2–6;[92] he could not have accepted the many permissions and injunctions by the Bible Deity to his chosen people to capture and hold slaves. In the House of Commons on 18th of February, 1796, Wilberforce reminded that Christian assembly that infidel and anarchic France had given liberty to the Africans, whilst Christian and monarchic England was "obstinately continuing a system of cruelty and injustice." Wilberforce, whilst advocating the abolition of slavery, found the whole influence of the English court, and the great weight of the Episcopal bench against him. George III, a most Christian king, regarded abolition theories with abhorrence, and the Christian House of Lords was utterly opposed to granting freedom to the slave. When Christian missionaries, some sixty-two years ago, preached to Demerara[93] negroes under the rule of Christian England, they were treated by Christian judges, holding commission from Christian England, as criminals for so preaching. A Christian commissioned officer, member of the Established Church of England, signed the auction notices for the sale of slaves as late as the year 1824. [. . .]

Take the further gain to humanity consequent on the unbelief, or rather disbelief, in witchcraft and wizardry. Apart from the brutality by Christians towards those suspected of witchcraft, the hindrance to scientific initiative or experiment was incalculably great so long as belief in magic obtained. The inventions of the past two centuries, and especially those of the nineteenth century, might have benefitted mankind much earlier and much more largely, but for the foolish belief in witchcraft and the shocking ferocity exhibited against those suspected of necromancy. After quoting a large number of cases of trial and punishment for witchcraft from official records in Scotland, J. M. Robertson[94] says: "The people seem to have passed from cruelty to cruelty, precisely as they became more and more devoted to their church, till, after many generations, the slow spread of human science began to counteract the ravages of superstition, the clergy resisting reason and humanity to the last." [. . .]

Is it not also fair to urge the gain to humanity which has been apparent in the wiser treatment of the insane consequent on the unbelief in the Christian doctrine that these unfortunates were examples either of demoniacal possession or of special visitation of Deity? For centuries, under Christianity, mental disease was most ignorantly treated. Exorcism, shackles, and the whip were the penalties, rather than

---

89 Large economic hubs in England
90 (1759–1833), perhaps the most prominent English abolitionist, who brought about the Slave Trade Act 1807 and the Slavery Abolition Act 1833; see one of his speeches in the 'Abolition and Aftermath' section of this anthology.
91 These verses of Leviticus envision passing the ownership of bonded peoples to the next and future generations 'for ever', excepting 'your brethren the children of Israel'.
92 These lines from Exodus describe some situations where even Hebrew bondmen might have their children remain enslaved after their terms of service have expired.
93 A Dutch colony now part of present-day Guyana
94 (1856–1933), a British journalist and member of Parliament who held that the historical Jesus Christ was a myth

the curatives, for mental maladies. From the heretical departure of Pinel,[95] at the close of the last century to the position of Maudsley[96] to-day, every step illustrates the march of unbelief. Take the gain to humanity in the unbelief, not yet complete, but now largely preponderant, in the dogma that sickness, pestilence, and famine were manifestations of divine anger, the results of which could neither be avoided nor prevented. The Christian churches have done little or nothing to dispel this superstition. The official and authorised prayers of the principal denominations even to-day reaffirm it. Modern study of the laws of health, experiments in sanitary improvements, more careful applications of medical knowledge, have proved more efficacious in preventing or diminishing plagues and pestilence than have the inter-vention of the priest or the practice of prayer. Those in England who hold the old faith that prayer will suffice to cure disease are to-day termed "peculiar people," and are occasionally indicted for manslaughter, when their sick children die, because the parents have trusted to God instead of appealing to the resources of science.[97]

It is certainly a clear gain to astronomical science that the Church which tried to compel Galileo to unsay the truth, has been overborne by the growing unbelief of the age, even though our little children are yet taught that Joshua made the sun and moon stand still,[98] and that for Hezekiah the sun-dial reversed its record.[99] [...]

As in astronomy, so in geology, the gain of knowledge to humanity has been almost solely in measure of the rejection of the Christian theory, a century since it was almost universally held, that the world was created six thousànd years ago, or at any rate, that by the sin of the first man, Adam, death commenced about that period. Ethnology and anthropology have only been possible in so far as, adopting the regretful words of Sir W. Jones,[100] "intelligent and virtuous persons are inclined to doubt the authenticity of the accounts delivered by Moses concerning the primi-tive world."

Surely it is clear gain to humanity that unbelief has sprung up against the divine right of kings, that men no longer believe that the monarch is "God's anointed," or that "the powers that be are ordained of God." In the struggles for political freedom, the weight of the Church was mostly thrown on the side of the tyrant. The homilies of the Church of England declare that "even the wicked rulers have their power and authority from God," and that "such subjects as are disobedient or rebellious against their princes, disobey God and procure their own damnation." It can scarcely be necessary to argue to the citizens of the United States of America that the origin of their liberties was in the rejection of this faith in the divine right of George III. [...]

At the last Southwell Diocesan Church-of-England Conference at Derby, the Bishop of the Diocese presiding, the Rev. J. G. Richardson said of the Old Testa-ment that "it was no longer honest, or even safe to deny that this noble literature, rich in all the elements of moral or spiritual grandeur, given—so the Church had

---

95 Philippe Pinel (1745–1826), a French physician who some call 'the father of modern psychiatry'
96 Henry Maudsley (1835–1918), a British psychiatrist and proponent of degeneration theory, agnostic and a critic of religion
97 Cf. the Church of Christ, Scientist (Christian Science), which was founded in 1879 and grew quickly across North America and Europe
98 Cf. Joshua 10: 12–13
99 Cf. Isaiah 38: 7–8
100 William Jones: (1746–94), prominent English linguist who proposed a relation between Indo-European languages

always taught, and would always teach—under the inspiration of Almighty God, was sometimes mistaken in its science, was sometimes inaccurate in its history, and sometimes only relative and accommodatory in its morality. It resumed theories of the physical world which science had abandoned and could never resume; it contained passages of narrative which devout and temperate men pronounced discredited both by external and internal evidence; it praised, or justified, or approved, or condoned, or tolerated conduct which the teaching of Christ and the conscience of the Christian alike condemned." Or— as I should urge—the gain to humanity by unbelief is that "the teaching of Christ" has been modified, enlarged, widened, and humanized, and that "the conscience of the Christian" is, in quantity and quality, made fitter for the ever-increasing additions of knowledge of these later and more heretical days.

Source text

Bradlaugh, Charles, 'Humanity's Gain from Unbelief', *North American Review* 148.388 (March 1889), 294–306.

References

Alexander, Nathan G., 'Atheism and Polygenesis in the Nineteenth Century: Charles Bradlaugh's Racial Anthropology', *Modern Intellectual History* 16.3 (2019), 835–61.
Bonner Bradlaugh, Hypatia, *Charles Bradlaugh: A Record of His Life and Work By His Daughter* (London: T. Fisher Unwin, 1908).
Has Humanity Gained from Unbelief? Two Nights' Debate Between Rev. Marsden Gibson, M. A., and Charles Bradlaugh (London: Freethought Publishing Company, 1889).

E. Pauline Johnson (Tekahionwake) (1861–1913)

'Brier: Good Friday' (1893) and 'The Happy Hunting Grounds' (1889)

E. Pauline Johnson embodied transatlantic hybridity through mixed-race identity. Her mother emigrated from England at an early age, and her father, from a leading Mohawk family, became influential in Canadian politics. Johnson compellingly displayed her hybrid self by dividing recitations of her poetry into two parts, wearing Native dress when presenting poems honouring her First Nations heritage, juxtaposed with a Victorian outfit for her more English-aligned verses. Her efforts to synthesise both dimensions of her background extended beyond such performances, as shown in writings addressing her spirituality.

Soon after her 1913 death, salutes to Johnson appeared on both sides of the Atlantic. Charles Mair's 'Appreciation' in *Moccasin Maker* demonstrated how, even for critics inclined to praise, Johnson's artistic engagement with spiritual thought was tempting to bifurcate. Mair characterised her religious standpoint thus: 'Though of the Christian faith, there is yet an almost pagan yearning manifest in her work, which she undoubtedly drew from her Indian ancestry' (19).

Johnson acknowledged the complexity of her religious thought in a 1906 essay published in the *London Daily Express* and later repurposed for *The Moccasin Maker*. 'A Pagan in St. Paul's' describes her visit to the cathedral. Meditatively, she celebrates this stately place, filled with music from a boys' choir and a 'deep-throated organ', 'where the paleface worships the Great Spirit' ('Pagan,' *Moccasin*, 160). Yet, even in that moment, she is drawn imaginatively back to scenes of Iroquois dancing, 'the soft swish, swish of moccasined feet', in another kind of musical worship of the Great Spirit, which she claims is equally spiritual (161). In bringing together the two poems below from earlier periodical publications, Johnson's 1895 *The White Wampum* collection had already similarly honoured both traditions important to her personal spirituality.

'Brier: Good Friday'[101]

> BECAUSE, dear Christ, your tender, wounded arm
>   Bends back the brier that edges life's long way.
> That no hurt comes to heart, to soul no harm,
>   I do not feel the thorns so much to-day.
>
> Because I never knew your care to tire,
>   Your hand to weary guiding me aright,
> Because you walk before and crush the brier,
>   It does not pierce my feet so much to-night.
>
> Because so often you have hearkened to
>   My selfish prayers, I ask but one thing now,
> That these harsh hands of mine add not unto
>   The crown of thorns upon your bleeding brow.

'The Happy Hunting Grounds'[102]

> INTO the rose gold westland, its yellow prairies roll,
> World of the bison's freedom, home of the Indian's soul.
> Roll out, O seas! in sunlight bathed,
> Your plains wind-tossed, and grass enswathed.

---

101 In their detailed bibliography of Johnson's writings, Veronica Strong-Boag and Carole Gerson note that this poem was originally published in April 1893 in *Saturday Night*. *Paddling Her Own Canoe: The Times and Texts of E. Pauline Johnson (Tekahionwake)* (Toronto: University of Toronto Press, 2000), 224.
102 Originally published in January 1889 in *Saturday Night* (Strong-Boag and Gerson, 221).

Farther than vision ranges, farther than eagles fly,
Stretches the land of beauty, arches the perfect sky,
Hemm'd through the purple mists afar
By peaks that gleam like star on star.

Fringing the prairie billows, fretting horizon's line,
Darkly green are slumb'ring wildernesses of pine,
Sleeping until the zephyrs throng
To kiss their silence into song.

Whispers freighted with odour swinging into the air,
Russet needles as censers[103] swing to an altar, where
The angels' songs are less divine
Than duo sung twixt breeze and pine.

Laughing into the forest, dimples a mountain stream,
Pure as the airs above it, soft as a summer dream,
O! Lethean[104] spring thou'rt only found
Within this ideal hunting ground.

Surely the great Hereafter cannot be more than this,
Surely we'll see that country after Time's farewell kiss.
Who would his lovely faith condole?
Who envies not the Red-skin's soul,

Sailing into the cloud land, sailing into the sun,
Into the crimson portals ajar when life is done?
O! dear dead race, my spirit too
Would fain sail westward unto you.

Source text

Johnson, E. Pauline (Tekahiohwake), *The White Wampum* (London: J. Lane; Toronto: Copp Clark, 1895).

References

Johnson, E. Pauline, *The Moccasin Maker. With an Introduction by Sir Gilbert Parker and an Appreciation by Charles Mair* (Toronto: William Briggs, 1913).
Jones, Manina and Neal Ferris, 'Flint, Feather, and Other Material Selves: Negotiating the Performance Poetics of E. Pauline Johnson', *American Indian Quarterly* 41.2 (Spring 2017), 125–57.
MacKay, Isabel Ecclestone, 'Pauline Johnson: A Reminiscence' *Canadian Magazine* 41 (July 1913), 273–8.

---

103 A container in which incense is burned, typically during a religious ceremony
104 Lethe is the Greek spirit of forgetfulness and oblivion.

Frances Power Cobbe (1822–1904)

From 'Religion' in Life of Frances Power Cobbe (1894)

In October 1894, Boston's *The Literary World* published a review of Frances Power Cobbe's memoir, praising it as 'full of cheerfulness, and equally marked by religious earnestness and philanthropic fervor'. Situating Cobbe's narrative transnationally, this review began by asserting the author's renown 'all over the civilized world as a writer of books on ethics and religion' and closed with a prediction of her text's 'large circulation in America', since she already had 'many American friends'. If, as the article suggested, her accomplishments deserved admiration because she had grown up during an era when women's educational opportunities were limited, her cultivation of intellect was simultaneously enabled by birth into an Anglo-Irish 'family . . . of good rank' ('Frances', 326). Meanwhile, the reviewer also identified Cobbe's impressive knowledge and spiritual commitment as having American roots in the study of Unitarian minister Theodore Parker's writings, as Cobbe herself acknowledges in the excerpt from her memoir below.

Sally Mitchell outlines many veiled elements in Cobbe's *Life*, attributing those gaps to 1890s life-writing conventions. Some silences, Mitchell observes, involve various 'family secrets', including potentially scandalous details about her brothers' lives (133). Mitchell finds 'Cobbe's extreme reticence about her beloved friend Mary Lloyd' (139), with whom the social activist and early 'New Woman' 'shared a house' in marriage-like domesticity (132), the most notable, if also the most understandable gap.

Yet, Mitchell also highlights a letter Cobbe wrote to the American Sarah Wister, declaring the autobiography aimed for openness, including in the treatment of religion: 'I have tried to write not merely a book of sketches & *souvenirs* but a real *Life*, seen *from inside* – though it cost me something to make the effort[,] I have told my real story – of my old religious struggles & of the various joys & sorrows of a very varied life' (133, emphases in original).

From 'Religion', Life of Frances Power Cobbe

I had read a good number of books by Deists. [. . .]

But the epoch-making book for me was Theodore Parker's "Discourse of Religion."[105] Reading a notice of it in the "Athenaeum,"[106] soon after its publication (somewhere about the year 1845), I sent for it, and words fail to tell the satisfaction

---

105 (1810–60), an American theologian, pastor, scholar and social reformer active in the anti-slavery movement; his *A Discourse of Matters Pertaining to Religion* divided Christianity into the 'transient' (scriptural dogma) and the 'permanent' (moral truths).
106 Literary magazine published in London from 1828 to 1921

and encouragement it gave me. One must have been isolated and care-laden as I to estimate the value of such a book. I had come, as I have narrated above, to the main conclusions of Parker, namely, the absolute goodness of God and the non-veracity of popular Christianity, three years before; so that it has been a mistake into which some of my friends have fallen when they have described me as converted from orthodoxy by Parker. But his book threw a flood of light on my difficult way. It was, in the first place, infinitely satisfactory to find the ideas which I had hammered out painfully and often imperfectly, at last welded together, set forth in lucid order, supported by apparently adequate erudition and heart-warmed by fervent piety.[107] But, in the second place, the Discourse helped me most importantly by teaching me to regard Divine Inspiration no longer as a miraculous and therefore incredible thing; but as normal, and in accordance with the natural relations of the infinite and finite spirit; a Divine inflowing of mental Light precisely analogous to that moral influence which divines call Grace. As every devout and obedient soul may expect to share in Divine Grace, so the devout and obedient souls of all the ages have shared (as Parker taught) in Divine Inspiration. And, as the reception of grace, even in large measure, does not render us impeccable, so neither does the reception of Inspiration make us *Infallible*. It is at this point that Deism stops and Theism begins: namely, when our faith transcends all that can be gleaned from the testimony of the bodily senses and accepts as supremely trustworthy of the direct Divine teaching, the "original revelation" of God's holiness and love in the depths of the soul. Theodore Parker adopted the alternative synonym to mark the vital difference in the philosophy which underlies the two creeds; a theoretic difference leading to most important practical consequences in the whole temper and spirit of Theism as distinct from Deism. I saw all this clearly ere long, and ranged myself thenceforth as a THEIST; a name now familiar to everybody, but which, when my family came to know I took it, led them to tell me with some contempt that it was "a word in a Dictionary, not a Religion."

A few months after I had absorbed Parker's Discourse, the great sorrow of my life befell me. My mother, whose health had been feeble ever since I could remember her, and who was now seventy years of age, passed away from a world which has surely held few spirits so pure and sweet. She died with her weeping husband and sons beside her bed and with her head resting on my breast. Almost her last words were to tell me I had been "the pride and joy" of her life. The agony I suffered when I realized that she was gone I shall not try to tell. She was the one being in the world whom I truly loved through all the passionate years of youth and early womanhood; the only one who really loved me. Never one word of anger or bitterness had passed from her lips to me, nor (thank God!) from mine to her in the twenty-four years in which she blessed my life; and for the latter part of that time her physical weakness had drawn a thousand tender cares of mine around her. No relationship in all the world, I think, can ever be so perfect as that of mother and daughter under such circumstances, when the strength of youth becomes the support of age, and the sweet dependence of childhood is reversed.

---

107 A memoir review ('Seventy-One Years') in the *Chicago Daily Tribune* cites the mutual regard between Cobbe and Parker ('the spiritual guide of her life') and points to his welcoming her to numerous conversations during his last days, in Italy, and her later editing of twelve volumes of his writing.

But it was all over I was alone; no more motherly love and tenderness were ever again to reach my thirsting heart. But this was not, as I recall it, the worst pang in that dreadful agony. I had (as I said above) ceased to believe in a future life, and therefore I had no choice but to think that that most beautiful soul which was worth all the kingdoms of earth had actually ceased to be. She was a "Memory;" nothing more.

I was not then or at any time one of those fortunate people who can suddenly cast aside the conclusions which they have reached by careful intellectual processes, and leap to opposite opinions at the call of sentiment. I played no tricks with my convictions, but strove as best I could to endure the awful strain, and to recognize the Divine Justice and Goodness through the darkness of death. I need not and cannot say more on the subject.

Happily for me, there were many duties waiting for me, and I could recognize even then that, though pleasure seemed gone forever, yet it was a relief to feel I had still *duties*. "Something to do for others" was an assuagement of misery. My father claimed first and much attention, and the position I now held of the female head of the family and household gave me a good deal of employment. To this I added teaching in my village school a mile from our house two or three times a week, and looking after all the sick and hungry in the two villages of Donabate and Balisk.[108] Those were the years of Famine and Fever in Ireland, and there was abundant call for all our energies to combat them. [. . .]

I had, though with pain, kept my heresies secret during my mother's declining years and till my father had somewhat recovered from his sorrow. I had continued to attend family prayers and church services, with the exception of the Communion, and had only vaguely allowed it to be understood that I was not in harmony with them all. When my poor father learned the full extent of my "infidelity," it was a terrible blow to him, for which I have, in later years, sincerely pitied him. He could not trust himself to speak to me, but though I was in his house he wrote to tell me I had better go away. My second brother, a barrister, had a year before given up his house in Queen Anne Street under a terrible affliction, and had gone, brokenhearted, to live on a farm which he hired in the wilds of Donegal.[109] There I went as my father desired and remained for nearly a year; not knowing whether I should ever be permitted to return home and rather expecting to be disinherited. He wrote to me two or three times and said that if my doubts only extended in certain directions he could bear with them, "but if I rejected Christ and disbelieved the Bible, a man was called upon to keep the plague of such opinions from his house." Then he required me to answer him on those points categorically. Of course I did so plainly, and told him I did not believe that Christ was God; and I did not (in his sense) believe in the inspiration or authority of the Bible. After this ensued a very long silence, in which I remained entirely ignorant of my destiny and braced myself to think of earning my future livelihood. I was absolutely lonely; my brother, though always very kind to me, had not the least sympathy with my heresies, and thought my father's conduct (as I do) quite natural; and I had not a friend or relative from whom I could look for any sort of comfort. [. . .]

As I had no duties in Donegal, and seldom saw our few neighbors, I occupied myself, often for seven or eight or even nine hours a day, in writing an "Essay

---

108 Villages in Ireland
109 Northernmost county in Ireland

on True Religion." I possess this MS. still, and have been lately examining it. Of course, as a first literary effort, it has many faults, and my limited opportunities for reference render parts of it very incomplete; but it is not a bad piece of work. [. . .]

Reading Parker's "Discourse," as I did very naturally in my solitude once again, it occurred to me to write to him and ask him to tell me on what ground he based the faith which I perceived he held, in a life after death? It had seemed to me that the guarantee of Revelation having proved worthless, there remained no sufficient reason for hope to counter-weigh the obvious difficulty of conceiving of a survival of the soul. Parker answered me in a most kind letter, accompanied by his "Sermon of the Immortal Life." Of course I studied this with utmost care and sympathy, and by slow, very slow degrees, as I came more to take in the full scope of the Theistic, as distinguished from the Deistic, view I saw my way to a renewal of the Hope of the Human Race which, twenty years later, I set forth as best I could in the little book of that name. I learned to trust the intuition of Immortality which is "written in the heart of man by a Hand which writes no false-hoods." I deemed also that I could see (as Parker says) the evidence of a "summer yet to be in the buds which lie folded through our northern winter;" the presence in human nature of many efflorescences[110] – and they the fairest of all – quite unaccountable and unmeaning on the hypothesis that the end of man is in the grave. In later years I think, as the gloom of the evil and cruelty of the world has shrouded more the almost cloudless skies of my youth, I have most fervently held by the doctrine of Immortality because it is to me the indispensable corollary of that of the goodness of God. I am not afraid to repeat the words, which so deeply shocked, when they were first published, my old friend, F. W. Newman:[111] "If Man be not immortal, God is not just."

Recovering this faith, as I may say, rationally and not by any gust of emotion, I had the inexpressible happiness of thinking henceforth of my mother as still existing in God's universe, and (as well I knew) loving me wherever she might be, and under whatever loftier condition of being. To meet her again "spirit to spirit, ghost to ghost," has been to me for forty years the sweetest thought connected with death. Ere long, now, it must be realized.

After nine or ten months of this, by no means harsh, exile, my father summoned me to return home. I resumed my place as his daughter in doing all I could for his comfort, and as the head of his house; merely thenceforth abstaining from attendance either at Church or at family prayer. I had several favorite nooks and huts near and far in the woods, which I made into little Oratories for myself, and to one or other of them I resorted almost every evening at dusk; making it a habit – not broken for many years afterwards, to repeat a certain versified Litany of Thanksgiving which I had written and read to my mother. On Sundays, when the rest of the family went to the village church, I had the old garden for a beautiful cathedral. Having let myself in with my own key and locked the doors, I knew I had the lovely six acres within the high walls, free for hours

110 Blossoming
111 Francis William Newman (1805–97), religious scholar and social reformer; brother of his more famous sibling, Catholic theologian John Henry Newman

from all observation or intrusion. How much difference it makes in life to have at command such peace and solitude it is hard to estimate. I look back to some of the summer forenoons spent alone in that garden as to the flowering time of my seventy years. God grant that the afterglow of such hours may remain with me to the last, and that "at eventide it may be light!" [...]

My inner life was made happy by my simple faith in God's infinite and perfect love; and I never had any doubt whether I had erred in abandoning the creed of my youth. On the contrary, as the whole tendency of modern science and criticism showed itself stronger and stronger against the old orthodoxy, my hopes were unduly raised of a not distant New Reformation which I might even live to see. These sanguine hopes have faded. As Dean Stanley[112] seems to have felt, there was, somewhere between the years '74 and '78, a turn in the tide of men's thoughts (due, I think, to the paramount influence and insolence which physical science then assumed), which has postponed any decisive "broad" movement for years beyond my possible span of life. But though nothing appears quite so bright to my old eyes as all things did to me in youth, though familiarity with human wickedness and misery, and still more with the horrors of scientific cruelty to animals, have strained my faith in God's justice sometimes even to agony, —I know that no form of religious creed could have helped me any more than my own or as much as it has done to bear the brunt of such trial; and I remain to the present unshaken both in respect to the denials and the affirmations of Theism. There are great difficulties, soul-torturing difficulties besetting it; but the same or worse beset every other form of faith in God; and infinitely more, and to my mind insurmountable ones, beset Atheism.

For fifty years Theism has been my staff of life. I must soon try how it will support me down the last few steps of my earthly way. I believe it will do so well.

Source text

Cobbe, Frances Power, *Life of Frances Power Cobbe, by Herself*, Vol. 1 (Boston: Houghton, Mifflin, 1894).

References

'Frances Power Cobbe', *The Literary World; a Monthly Review of Current Literature* 25.20 (6 October 1894), 326.

Mitchell, Sally, 'Frances Power Cobbe's *Life* and the Rules for Women's Autobiography', *English Literature in Transition, 1880–1920* 50.2 (2 November 2007), 131–57.

'Seventy-One Years: "Life of Frances Power Cobbe" Nearly Reviews the Century', *Chicago Daily Tribune* (6 October 1894), 10.

---

112 Formally known as Arthur Penrhyn Stanley, Dean Stanley (1815–81) was an English churchman and academic.

Figure 7.6 Darwin as depicted in a caricature from 'Punch's Fancy Portraits. – No. 54: Charles Robert Darwin, L.L.D., F.R.S.', *Punch* 81 (22 October 1881), 190. Courtesy Mary Couts Burnett Library, TCU.

Punch added text below the caption:

> In his *Descent of Man* he brought his own Species down as low as possible – i.e. to 'A Hairy Quadruped furnished with a Tail and Pointed Ears, and probably *Arboreal* in its Habits' – which is a reason for the very general interest in a 'Family Tree.' He has lately been turning his attention to the 'Politic Worm.'

For analysis of the image see Anna Henchman, 'Charles Darwin's Final Book on Earthworms, 1881', *Branch*, Web. Honouring the impact of earthworms on the environment, Darwin (in Henchman's view) challenged the dominance of anthropocentric ideas in his final book, *The Formation of Vegetable Mould through the Action of Worms* (1881). The cartoon's depiction of a worm in the form of a question mark could indicate that the visual artist (perhaps Linley Sambourne?) was resisting the *Worms* book's argument. Yet, setting this image in dialogue with Woods Hutchinson's appreciation of Darwin's commitment to scientific inquiry encourages another interpretation: questions raised by science may promote critical thinking about humans' relationships with the environment.

Woods Hutchinson (1862–1930)

From 'The Fifth Gospel', The Gospel According to Darwin *(1898)*

Born in Yorkshire in 1862, Woods Hutchinson immigrated to the United States at an early age and settled in Iowa. After receiving his medical degree from the University of Michigan, he embarked upon a long career as a professor of anatomy (University of Iowa), comparative pathology (University of Buffalo) and clinical medicine (New York Polyclinic). Along the way he served as editor of multiple medical journals and published volumes on health-related issues such as exercise, consumption and preventable diseases.

Of his written works *The Gospel According to Darwin* was his first and most famous, and the only book not directly related to his medical profession. Drawing upon the most prominent intellectual movement of in the nineteenth century, Hutchinson promoted Charles Darwin as a new evangelist who had brought a revisionist testament to humanity. For Hutchinson, Darwin's doctrine made atheism tenable by providing an alternative explanation for a host of religious dogma: notably good and evil, and the origin of people and the natural world.

From The Gospel According to Darwin

THE FIFTH GOSPEL

EVERY revelation granted to man is at the outset denounced as atheistic and sacrilegious. The flash that follows the "Let there be light" sadly changes the faces of the gods, whether they be the Dagons[113] born of man s fingers, or the Dogmas of his fancy, as they stand in their twilight shrines, thick with the smoke of incense or hazy with the "dim religious light" of mystic contemplation. Not only this, but the dazzling glare pains to the blinding-point the eye of faith, until the familiar features, nay, even the majestic outlines of the Divine Form seem utterly lost, and it is little wonder that the shuddering cry goes up, "Great Pan[114] is dead !"

The instant impulse, almost too strong to be resisted, is to turn the back upon the light which has wrought this havoc, declare it a bale-fire,[115] an *ignis fatuus*,[116] a lying illumination, and thus save both eyes and theology. There is plenty of darkness left to construct another shrine. And this is the course usually taken, in point of fact; but is it wisest, not to say bravest, or manliest? Whoever follows it, proves himself to have been worshipping, *not* the Deity, but his own pet conception of Him; Light cannot alter Being, only its appearance. And yet "Thou that destroyest the law and the prophets" is the denunciation hurled at every new light-bringer.

A courageous few, however, turn and unshrinkingly face the dazzling ray of golden sunlight, which has shot unbidden across the purple twilight of the sanctuary, proudly

---

113 A reference to Dagon, an ancient god of the Philistines
114 Greek god of shepherds and their flocks
115 Large fire used as a signal
116 *Ignis fatuus*: will-o'-the-wisp

secure that whatever is true cannot be altered, whatever is untrue is unworthy of their homage. As ever the bravest course is the happiest, and although the shrine is seen shattered and empty, while the rich vestments, brain-woven and fancy-dyed, with which, with unconscious irony, divinity has been "adorned," lie folded upon the floor like the grave-clothes at the feet of Lazarus,[117] yet the roof is found to have been but a veil of twilight and shadows, and heaven above is revealed.

And as their glad eyes gaze up into the sapphire, star-sprinkled vault, they are again aware of a Presence of far lovelier, though vaguer outline, and though more remote, of a grandeur never before conceived.

This is peculiarly true of that great burst of eternal truth which broke upon the world chiefly through the work and genius of Charles Darwin.[118] Its dawning was heralded by a shudder and a shriek from every pew and pulpit, and "Darwinism" became a synonym for blasphemy. Its truth was vehemently denied, its logic mercilessly ridiculed, its "debasing tendencies" furiously denounced. It was to be given no quarter, for if tolerated for a moment it would utterly destroy every vestige, not only of religion, but of the religious spirit, and yet I venture to herald it to-day as the long-missing "Fifth Evangel,"[119] "The Gospel according to Darwin." Instead of destroying the religious spirit, it reanimates it, and places it upon stronger foundations than ever before.

This may seem an extravagant and extraordinary statement, but it can be shown to be far from unfounded. In the first place, it restores the grand unity of the universe, and proves the fundamental harmony of its conflicting forces. There is no hanging in the balance between the forces of good and evil, no perilous and often doubtful conflict between a beneficent World Spirit and a malevolent one: no such thing as abstract or essential "evil": nothing but a magnificent scheme of glorious progress through conflict. Storm and darkness, hunger and cold, war and wanderings, nay, even pestilence and famine, are seen to be spurs to progress, mothers of invention, and the stern nurses of all the virtues. Never has the doctrine of the Old Gospel that "all things work together for good to them that love the Good" received such tremendous endorsement. Instead of gazing upon a world of blind, remorseless chance, or inevitable fate, so full of cruelty, injustice, and needless suffering, as to absolutely require the conception or invention of "another world," to even partially remedy its inequalities, the Darwinist sees all things and all forces moving steadily forward in one grand and gloriously beneficent scheme of advancement. Nature's only and unvarying war-cry is "Excelsior!"[120]

The old Evangelists did at times catch glimpses of this truth from the mountain-peaks of their loftiest spiritual raptures, but it was soon lost sight of, in the mist of the valley and fog of the fen, into which the churches were plunged in that palsied time which heralded the death of the great Roman Empire.

None of them, however, even dreamed of a light which should reveal a harmony and an order in that far more bitter, more hopeless and perplexing conflict which is incessantly present in the soul of man itself. Even to Paul's magnificent intellect, the only possible result is that one of the conflicting forces *must* and inevitably will utterly destroy the other. "The carnal mind is enmity against God, and is not subject to the law of God, neither indeed can it be.... To be carnally minded is death."[121] In

---

117 Lazarus of Bethany was raised from the dead four days after death according to the Gospel of John.
118 See, in 'Travel and Tourism', part of Darwin's account of the journal that played a central role in his theories.
119 An addition to the Four Evangelists, Matthew, Mark, Luke and John, and their Gospels
120 In Latin, 'ever upward' or 'still higher'
121 Paraphrase of Romans 8: 6–10; Paul the Apostle probably wrote his Epistle to this specific congregation while in Corinth in about AD 57.

the mild radiance of the Fifth Gospel even this struggle, like every other, is seen to surely and inevitably result in progress, to which both forces are absolutely necessary. The "enmity" between them is merely that between the steam-chest and the driving-wheel in the great engine, or, more accurately, between the panting young giant in the cylinder and the piston-rod, each fiercely asserting itself against the other, and between them driving the great wheel. Browning[122] has caught the same ray of dawn when he cries:

> "As the bird wings and sings
> Let us cry, "All good things
> Are ours, nor soul helps flesh more, now, than flesh helps soul."

Our passions and appetites are seen to be the great driving forces of our nature, and even the term "animal," as applied to them, carries with it no stigma of degradation; on the contrary, it suggests much that is brave, faithful, and self-denying. By far the longest, and not by any means the least noble part of our pedigree lies outside of the human family.

One of Darwin s greatest services was the proving that our moral impulses are derived, not from education nor external revelation, nor from the cold calculations and experimental deductions of "refined selfishness," according to either Bentham[123] or Spencer,[124] but from the warm and beautiful family affections, those ties of blood, whose golden links are alike binding upon the dove upon its nest, the deer in its covert, the lioness in her lair, and the mother by the hearthstone. The courage, the patience, the cheerfulness, the affections, that are in us are just as essentially "carnal" as are the "lusts of the flesh" and the "pride of life," and what is more, are more numerous and more powerful. Our deepest and strongest instincts in the long run are found to be on the side of right.

The most exquisite result of this perception is a delicious sense of harmony and sympathy with nature and all that she contains. The world is no longer either "vile" or "unfriendly" in either its human or its physical aspects. "The Prince of the Power of it"[125] has disappeared; all men of all races, become brethren upon the common ground of the great, noble, primitive instincts, and even the beasts of the field and the fowls of the air are glowing with that "touch of nature" which "makes the whole world kin." The only thing in it that we could profitably alter is our own conceited, babyish selves.

Another proof of the inspiration of the Fifth Gospel is the calm and rational view which it enables us to take of death. To remove the fear of this has been a leading aim of all former revelations, but it is to be doubted whether they have not the rather intensified it, as they all unite in characterizing it as the King of Terrors, the bitterest of evils, and the great enemy of the race.

The new light pierces these grisly, ghostly draperies, woven of fear and darkness, and shows behind them a gentle, painless, grandly-beneficent process of nature, by which the old is tenderly and reverently laid away to dissolve and reappear in the new.

Bracken dies and enriches the mold so that the anemone, violet, and the primrose may lift their dainty heads and scatter their perfume through copse and glen. Here is the Resurrection of the Body. Nothing is lost, but much is gained by the change.

The Mexican aloe lives a century, scatters its myriad seeds, then peacefully fades and dies, but its seeds take root upon its very grave, and give birth to other winged seeds, and so on through thousands of centuries. The vital spark has never

---

122 Robert Browning (1812–89), English poet; the lines below are from the 12th stanza of his 'Rabbi Ben Ezra'.
123 Jeremy Bentham (1748–1832), a pioneer of utilitarianism
124 Herbert Spencer (1820–1903), an English philosopher and theorist of evolution
125 A reference to Satan, 'The Prince of the Power of the Air' (Ephesians 2: 2)

once gone out, but burns with a brighter, richer, intenser glow in each succeeding generation. The primitive aloe is still alive and in a fuller, richer sense than ever before. This is Life Eternal, and what is better, Life Improving. Is not this a nobler, higher, more unselfish conception than that of an indefinite prolongation of our own petty, personal existence? This is an immortality worth having, for it provides for progress.

We are immortal physically, in the course of nature, and mentally and morally in our influence, so far as this is for good. All that is true, all that is good, in us and in our influence, will survive to all the ages; all that is false and base will be ruthlessly crushed and destroyed, ground into powder by the mills of the gods. It is not a question of whether we, as a whole, will be "saved" or "lost" but *of how much* of us. [. . .]

One of the strongest claims to recognition of the Fifth Gospel is the light which it throws upon that problem, "The Origin and Relations of Evil." By its rays evil is seen, and can even be demonstrated to be mainly one of the necessary accompaniments of the development of Good into Better. If movement is to occur, it must be possible in all directions, and the power of advancing inevitably carries with it the possibility of retreat. The possibility of growth must include that of decay. Evil is the shadow thrown by the sunlight of the good. Good is positive and absolute, evil negative and relative. Almost every evil, viewed broadly and attentively, is seen to be at bottom mainly a relative or temporary absence of good, and in many cases, repulsive as it may be at first sight, to be ultimately beneficent in its nature.

More than this, much of what we term evil is a necessary part of the scheme of progress. To use a mechanical illustration, not only is falling an indispensable corollary of, or antithesis to, rising, but also an essential factor in forward motion. That incarnate poetry of motion, the flight of the lordly eagle, consists of a quick, short dash, with a few score strokes of his powerful wings to a dizzy height, followed by a circling, swooping, triumphant descent on motionless, outstretched pinions, a veritable riding upon the wings of the wind, covering half a country side in its sweep. Here progress is attained, not so much by the rise, as by the long, sweeping descent which follows it, and *both* movements are alike indispensable.

To soar aloft merely to brave the eye of the sun-god, or to excite the admiration and reverence of the rest of the feathered tribes, as the classic myth of the kingly bird supposes, would be simply a fruitless and foolish waste of energy; and yet in the spiritual realm, many a pinnacle of saintliness, many a state of ecstasy, has been attained from highly similar motives, and proved equally barren of results. Much of what we term absolute good would be sterile unless mixed with apparent evil. The whole process of human locomotion, not only physical but mental, is literally a series of interrupted falls. Our only chance of advancing is to fall in the right direction and keep at it. Our only struggle should be, not to avoid falling, but to fall forward.

Of all the innumerable forms of evil probably none is so obtrusively self-evident, or so universally denounced and deplored by philosophers of every system, priests of every creed, and observers of every age, as pain. On its presence and frequency alone have been founded most of the doubts and denials of the goodness of God, or the benevolence of the universe. It is generally accepted as almost pure evil, and by its mere presence, a standing reflection upon the intelligence and competence of the Great Architect. The sight, or even thought, of suffering is abhorrent to us, and we are sure that "Providence" ought not to "permit" it in any form. But is not this, after all, a somewhat short-sighted and childish way of regarding the question?

Pain is indeed hard to bear, and harder to look upon, but is there no harvest which its sharp sickle reaps? Of a surety there is, and a golden one, which can be gathered by no other means. [...]

And here is where the Fifth Gospel gently but decidedly parts company with the Fourth. Although it goes even further in the direction of proving the necessity and even the beneficence of pain, it stops far short of exalting suffering into a virtue, or regarding it as the dominant and commonest element in the lot of mankind. The essential benefit of pain lies in the avoidance of its cause, and the reward is to be reaped from the thorny barrens of discomfort by determined effort and incessant struggle and not by tame and pulpy submission. It has no sympathy whatever with the morbid delusion that suffering is *per se* purifying and exalting, and the mere endurance of it a grace; still less that the submission to it is the one principal duty of man. It declines to regard this sun-kissed, grass-carpeted, flower-gemmed world of ours as a "vale of tears" or "wilderness of woe," and instead of holding that the more disagreeable anything is, the more likely it is to be "good for us," it would deem the fact of any object or action being repugnant to our natural tastes and instincts as at least good presumptive evidence of its injuriousness.

It furnishes a scientific and rational basis for Pestalozzi's[126] dictum that "we do not desire certain things because we believe them to be good, but we hold them to be good because we instinctively desire them." It unhesitatingly declares enjoyment (harmony with environment) to be the normal condition of organized being, suffering the abnormal—comfort the rule, pain the exception; in short, our appetites, impulses, and instincts are the exquisite fruits of the experience of myriads of ancestral generations. If anything about us be divine, they emphatically are, and may be, freely, boldly, joyfully followed—instead of sternly repressed and distorted.

That strange distortion of the teachings of the Master known as orthodox Christianity, too often alas a mixture of one-fourth Christ, one-fourth Paul, and one-half pure superstition, regards our passions and appetites as our chiefest enemies, necessary evils, only valuable for the discipline gained in fighting them, permits their indulgence only under protest and with an air of apology, and would like to crush them out entirely were it not for the trifling drawback that life itself would be destroyed in the process. And even this consideration has been, alas, no bar to its zeal, especially in the case of other persons. From this belief more than from any other have sprung those dark and disgraceful shadows of monasticism, self-torture, and persecution, which have always dogged and too often utterly dimmed its shining course.

Nature's revenge for this contemptuous treatment of her heralds and prophets is swift and signal, and the carrying out of this belief must logically, and always has, resulted in either asceticism or hypocritical licentiousness, and generally in both.

From the standpoint of the Darwinist, our passions are our best friends and trustiest servants, and our instincts and appetites our safest guides. The one may be humored too far, and the other followed too blindly; but in the long run they will be found to have done us at least ten times as much good as harm. Like Solomon's "virtuous woman," they will "do us good and not evil all the days of our life."[127] This once recognized, the pleasure which comes from their legitimate gratification becomes something to be freely and frankly enjoyed as a mark of nature's approval, instead of a thing to be ashamed of, acknowledged with apologies, and indulged in with grave misgivings.

---

126 Johann Heinrich Pestalozzi (1746–1827), Swiss educational reformer
127 Proverbs 31: 10–12; Solomon was a Biblical King known for his wisdom.

In short, joy becomes as integral a part of the Fifth Gospel as grief is of the Fourth.

The grand old Greek "joy of living" comes back in broader, manlier, more enduring form, and is of itself a sufficient reason for existing. Once more the mellow glow of the golden sunlight becomes the smile of the great heart of the universe. The mist-wreath upon the blue mountain, the silver flash of the rushing river amid the rich green of the reeds, the gorgeous, crimson pageantry of the hosts of heaven in the western sky, and the amethyst light in the eye of woman, are but reflections of His beauty; the warbling of birds, the song of the wind in the pine-forests, and the murmuring of pebbly brooks, are the echoes of the music of the spheres; and the joyous response which all these stir up in us is part of the grand sympathy of the universe, the love between those of one blood and one lineage. Nor does "Lebenslust"[128] stop here: far from it. Deeper, but even sweeter and more lasting than any of these is the stern joy of battle, the warm throb which answers the touch of the frost-king, the breath of the storm-wind, the dash of the salt spray over the bulwarks, the plunge of the frantic steed. Best of all, the glorious ecstasy of taking our lives between our teeth, and looking danger and death in the face, of daring everything in defence of our loved ones, the fierce music of the clash of swords, and the rattle of musketry, the sweet "smell of the battle afar off."[129] Life is a brave, red-blooded, warm-hearted, joyous thing, which needs no sickly phantasmic "after world" to render it worth the living.

Source text

Hutchinson, Woods, *The Gospel According to Darwin* (Chicago: Open Court Publishing Company, 1898).

References

Livingstone, David, *Dealing with Darwin: Place, Politics, and Rhetoric in Religious Engagements with Evolution* (Baltimore, MD: Johns Hopkins University Press, 2014).
Pleins, J. David, *The Evolving God: Charles Darwin on the Naturalness of Religion* (London: Bloomsbury, 2013).

Helen Barrett Montgomery (1861–1934); Charlotte Tucker (1821–93)

'Charlotte Tucker: A Lady of England', Western Women in Eastern Lands (1910)

In the long nineteenth century, foreign mission work represented one of the most accessible opportunities for (mainly white) middle-class women

---

128 German for 'love of life'
129 Job 39: 25

to claim major, visible leadership in an ambitious social enterprise. By the time Helen Montgomery wrote her influential history, the movement had produced numerous role models, partly through Protestant periodicals like *Woman's Work for Woman*, which circulated profiles designed to promote a sense of shared transnational commitment – and donations.

Montgomery presented narratives about women mission workers from both the US and the UK. For one of these, the American Montgomery borrowed the 'Lady of England' subtitle for her chapter on Charlotte Tucker from a biography Agnes Giberne had published in London in 1895. This designation, long used as a pseudonym by Tucker herself, was already firmly linked to the British missionary among transatlantic audiences. Thus one review of Giberne's text for Boston's *The Literary World* needed only the acronym 'A.L.O.E.' as title (dubbing them 'mystic but familiar initials'). Tucker's own publications included many didactic texts for children and adults before she journeyed in 1875 to India, where, in her fifties, she re-cast herself as a missionary heroine, while acquiring an exotic new setting for storytelling. Montgomery's profile reinforced that characterisation, simultaneously reaffirming the women's foreign mission enterprise as a vital gendered movement. Today, we can add a critical lens examining how mission work like Tucker's played a complicit part in empire-building.

'Charlotte Tucker: A Lady of England'

How shall one in a few brief paragraphs capture the fragrance and beauty of a personality like that of Charlotte Tucker? The leisurely biography in which Miss Giberne has lovingly pictured "A Lady of England" seems all too short.[130] Can one carry into an abstract the elusive charm? If the failure shall drive any to consult the biography from which these random notes are drawn, I shall rejoice at a good turn done.

Early life

Charlotte Tucker, one of a splendid family of ten sons and daughters, was born in 1821 to an English gentleman, Mr. Henry St. George Tucker, and his wife, Jane Boswell. Her father had been a director of the East India Company and a government officer in Bengal; and her five brothers were all in the Indian service. Her early life is full of quiet simplicity and charm. The family were united in the tenderest affection. There were parties, games, charades, and all sorts of merry pastimes, as well as the serious concerns of a household earnestly religious. Charlotte was from the first a person of marked individuality. Her eager imagination revelled in the plays of Shakespeare which her father delighted to read aloud. As a child she began to

---

130 Reviews of Giberne's biography appeared on both sides of the Atlantic, with responses seeming to differ mainly on the basis of the assessor's stance toward women's writings in general rather than whether the periodical was British or American. Accordingly, for example, R. Brimley Johnson, writing for Britain's *The Academy*, skewered Tucker as 'always religious and affectionate', but 'not domestic' and (evidently a problem then) 'personally ambitious' (502). Despite some praise of Tucker for becoming a missionary relatively late in life, Johnson wove in asides demeaning her 'entirely didactic' writings, suggesting, 'It is probable that had she preached less her readers would have profited more' (502). See 'A Lady of England: The Life and Letters of Charlotte Maria Tucker', in *The Academy* (7 December 1895), 502.

compose plays which the other children acted out. She had a fund of story and of gay humor that made any place where she was charming and full of life.

Writings

When not quite thirty years old, Charlotte Tucker sent one of the numerous stories written for the pleasure of little nieces and nephews to a publisher. The quaint, unworldly little letter which accompanied the manuscript had no name given and no address. "She asked," she said, "for no earthly remuneration."

One can imagine with what eagerness she saw, some months later, her "Claremont Tales" actually in print. From that time to the end of her long life there was no year in which she did not publish one book; and several years in which her facile pen was credited with a half dozen or more. "Wings and Stings," "The Giant Killer," "History of a Needle," "Old Friends with New Faces," "The Young Pilgrim," "Fairy Know-a-bit," are some of the hundred or more titles of her published works.

Many of her books were wholesome and fanciful tales for children, with a decidedly didactic strain running through them, and the steadfast purpose to advance Christ's kingdom. Very early she developed a highly figurative and parabolic style, which did not add to the vogue of her books among practical Anglo-Saxons, but actually prepared her for the greater work of her life, in writings that appealed to the Oriental mind.

Becomes a missionary

For the twenty-five years after she began to write the current of her life flowed on in its accustomed channels, and then, when she was fifty-four years old, came a great, an astonishing break. These years of middle life had seen the changes and sorrows that so often had come. A dear brother, Robert, a judge in Futteypore,[131] had been killed during the terrible days of the Indian mutiny, and she had the care of his children; her idolized younger sister had married, a beloved niece and godchild had died suddenly, she had tenderly cared for her father and mother and an older sister until they too were taken from her. At last, with three-fourths of her life journey behind her, she was free from all the dear home ties and duties, able to let a controlling desire of her heart speak. She offered herself as a missionary to India, to go out paying her own expenses as a zenana worker.[132]

Personality

Let us get a clear picture of her when this step was taken. "She had soft gray hair drawn smoothly away from a fine brow, her clear gray eyes full of intelligence, and the frank sweet smile playing over her features made hers a very attractive face." Her tall figure was slight and spare. The years had not saddened her, but only made more gentle her strong and impetuous nature. To nieces and nephews she was the beloved "Aunt Char" who read Shakespeare to them while her busy knitting needles flashed back and forth, who studied Dante with them, reading the sonorous Italian with such joy, who danced with them those evenings at home, gavottes[133] with springy grace they remembered for years afterward. "No one could play games like

---

131 Futteypore is about seven miles from the Ganges.
132 Zenana workers were female missionaries who visited Indian women in their own homes to convert them to Christianity. 'Zenana' refers to women's quarters where Indian women were confined under the purdah system. Since men were forbidden to enter, this work provided a special opportunity for mission women.
133 French dance form developed during the sixteenth century but still popular in the nineteenth

Aunt Char; she seemed younger than the youngest of us," they said. They remembered too the lively little songs she sang, accompanying herself on the guitar. One of them wrote years afterward:

"I think things were only a trouble to her when she had to do them for herself. Nothing was a trouble if it helped another. Work for the Master whom she loved was her life's motive ... She was, I think, the most unselfish character I ever knew. She lived for others; whether in the great work of her life, the use of her pen, the proceeds of which went to fill in her charity purse, or in the simple act of leaving her quiet room, on a dull, rainy day, to play a bright country dance or a Scotch reel,[134] and set the little ones dancing to vent their superfluous spirits."

Motives

Imagine the consternation when this beloved sister and adorable aunt, this popular author and woman of affairs, announced her intention to leave home and friends as a foreign missionary. "Preposterous, fantastic, romantic," said the startled friends and relatives. It was no sudden fancy of Charlotte Tucker's part, but a settled purpose quietly taken after looking the whole ground over. India had terrible, crying needs; there were pitifully few who were willing to go. God had left her free of responsibility and ties holding her back. She had means of her own so that no missionary funds need be risked on what might prove an unwise venture.

In her letter to that sister Laura with whom she had shared every single thought since babyhood she said, "Do not grudge me, dear one, to the work for which my soul yearns ... I only fear I am presumptuous in coming forward, but it seems as if my dear Lord were calling me to it, and my heart says, 'Here am I; send me.'" The dear sister did not try to dissuade her though the pain of parting was like death to them both. So it came about in 1875 there sailed away to Bombay an eager, gray-haired woman, still young in heart, to begin eighteen years of blessed ministry among a strange people in a strange land.

First experiences

She feared that it might be difficult for her to acquire a language at her age, but applied herself with such intensity that at the end of a year she passed her examination in Hindustani.[135] She did not even wait to speak correctly before attempting conversation; but practised her first word learned on the first one she met. An amusing instance of this is given in her biography. On her way up from Bombay she attended a wedding at a mission station. Though a stranger, she threw herself into the preparations, helped trim the chapel, and was left for a half-hour to entertain a very grand lady, a Begum,[136] who came to see the festivities. "I made gallant attempts to keep up a conversation with my dreadfully bad Hindustani, I dashed at it, tried to explain ... answered questions regarding my family, etc. The Begum laughed and I laughed, for I knew my Hindustani was very bad; but I did not remember always to use the respectful, 'Ap' to the princess [honorary mode of address]." Evidently the princess liked this vivacious white-haired lady, so unaffected and unconscious of self, so merry and entertaining; for she walked with her to the wedding in the church, and stayed during the service. And then this undaunted missionary managed to say

---

134 Type of Scottish country dance
135 Hindustani: group of Indic dialects spoken in northwestern India, principally Hindi and Urdu
136 Begum: Muslim woman of high rank in India or Pakistan

in her poor, stammering Hindustani, "The Lord Jesus Christ is here; He gives blessing," to which the princess nodded assent.

Orientalizing[137]

She came into the station at Amritsar[138] like a fresh breeze. She sat on the floor
with the native Christians at the first church service. She was eager to see all, to
hear all, to learn all. "I want to Orientalize my mind," was her frequent word. But all
the missionaries, marvelling at the way she seemed to understand the people and
sympathize with them, said, "She was born Oriental, her thoughts seemed naturally
to clothe themselves in those figures of speech in which the children of the East are
wont to express themselves." She would have been glad to adopt native dress if the
other missionaries would have been permitted; and seemed perfectly comfortable
in positions that are very trying to most Europeans. She rode, for example, in a
native conveyance called the ekka, a springless platform on wooden wheels. On this
bedding was placed, and there she sat, gracefully unconcerned, with her feet tucked
under her, native fashion.

Her work: zenanas

Her missionary service falls into three divisions.

Without sparing herself, she gave hours of every day to patient visitation of
the zenanas. During the last years of her life her diary shows that she had access
to one hundred and seventy homes. Her methods were individual and original. A
picture, a mechanical toy, an allegorical design, served to introduce the topic nearest her heart, the Gospel of Christ. Her love of little children was a passion, and
often opened to her jealously guarded doors. "I found myself stroking little brown
cheeks," she writes in her journal. This tenderness overflowed to animals. One of
her letters while in England had told of meeting a mole one day and stooping to
stroke its smooth head, – "it was not in the least afraid."

In her zenana visitation she seems to have undertaken little systematic instruction, but to have poured out her loving heart in all the gracious, gentle, beautiful
ministries she knew so well how to give.

Her influence among the native Christians was very great. She loved them and
they knew it, and she fell so easily into their modes of thought, was so generously
unselfish in relieving distress, that she became to them a holy woman, a saint.

There was an indescribable lighting up of her features when she sang or played
the harmonium. Indian Christians sometimes walked a long distance to see this
unconscious illumination of her whole face as she sang of Jesus. When she was an
old woman, some one expressed surprise that she could sing. "Oh, I sing every day,"
she said; "if I should stop a day, my throat might find out how old I am."

---

137 In Montgomery's time, 'Oriental' and 'Orientalizing' would have been generally acceptable
wording in Anglophone texts, whereas scholarship in our day has led writers to avoid such usage.
See Edward W. Said's *Orientalism* (1978; rpt. New York: Vintage, 1979), where he explicates his
title as a term for Western colonial 'othering' and subordination of Middle Eastern and Asian cultures. See also this *OED* definition: 'representation of the Orient (esp. the Middle East) in Western
academic writing, art, or literature; *spec.* this representation perceived as stereotyped or exoticizing
and therefore embodying a colonialistic attitude'.
138 City in northwestern India, later infamous for the 1919 massacre of unarmed Indians by British
forces

Her work: teaching

The second division of her work was teaching. When, within a year of her settling at Amritsar, a new station was opened at Batala, she felt called to go. Her missionary friends, in view of the isolation and greater hardships, and of her social gifts and graces, urged her to stay where she could devote more time to literary work, have more comforts, and meet the Europeans she was so well fitted to influence. But the inward call was clear, and Charlotte Tucker went to Batala to make her home in the old palace which had been bought for the boys' school.

"From this time forth," writes one of the teachers, "for years to come, Miss Tucker was a mainstay of the Boys' Boarding School, teaching the older boys English and history, taking a motherly interest in all their pursuits, writing for them Batala school songs, inviting them in the evening to little entertainments enlivened by parlor games, visiting the sick, comforting the homesick new boy; mothering the young convert; besides carrying on without fail her regular visits to the town and villages, and her literary work in India and England."

Her work: writings

Third came the literary work already alluded to, the writing of books for Indian readers. In this she had a genius. Her fables and allegories, her meditations on the parables of Jesus, went straight to the native heart. They were translated into many languages, and sold in the most inexpensive form by the thousands. Indeed, these tiny books may well prove to be her most important contribution; for their good work seems just begun; the demand for them is continually increasing. The titles of some of them are: "Two Pilgrims to Kashi," "The Prophet and the Leper," "The Wonderful Medicine," "Eight Pearls of Blessing," "Story of the Pink Chaddar," "Turban with a Border of Gold," "The Intercessor," "Widows and the Bible," "The Bag of Treasure." One or more of these were written in the month of vacation that she allowed herself each year of her eighteen years of continuous service.

Influence

Her personal influence among the missionaries might well be enumerated as her fourth form of service. She became "Auntie" to them all.[139] No wedding festivities were complete without her inimitable fun and frolic. Her extreme simplicity of life was a challenge to those younger and stronger. She allowed herself only the bare necessities of life, and gave away all the rest of her income in such secret and unostentatious ways that only the recipient will ever know.

Her exquisite humility of spirit smoothed away any irritation that her impetuous, impulsive manner might have caused. "She is beloved and honored by rich and poor, young and old. She is our sunshine. Her bright fancies, her quick perceptions, her wise suggestions, are invaluable to all of us in the mission. Life has seemed to me a different thing since God brought her to us," wrote Mrs. Elmslie.[140] The real

---

139 In this guise, an extended 1896 sketch of Tucker for *The Missionary Herald*, a major publication of the American Board of Commissioners for Foreign Missions, includes these quotes from Tucker emphasising her close association with American missionaries: 'I am particularly delighted with the American missionaries I have seen,' and 'It seems to me as if both England and America had sent their cream to India' (174).

140 The quote likely comes from Margaret Duncan Elmslie (1852–82), wife and co-missionary with William J. Elmslie (1832–72), a Presbyterian doctor from Aberdeen, Scotland, who served in India under the sponsorship of the Church Missionary Society (CMS).

inspiration, after all, was not in what she did or said, but in what she was. When she read the life of Bishop Gobal, she said: "A humbling book; I feel like a barnyard chicken looking up at in eagle, and chirping, 'I'm a bird, too.'"

Speaking to another missionary, she said: "We are only the housemaids. We open the door, but they come in, and go themselves up to the king."

Conference notes

In one of her letters to her sister is a delicious description of a "conference" where feeling had run high over some question of policy when she was in the chair:

"The question was brought up again by a strong lady on one side, and then a paper was read by a strong lady on the other, and I proposed that the vote should be taken again, which resulted in a majority of four, I being one of the four. A lady in the minority called out, 'It does not matter what is voted, we will all do just the same as before,' which was more true than polite. Then there was another lady who got up, time after time, to make the most impracticable propositions; and she got snubbed and sat down and cried. Oh, dear, it does not do to be so thin-skinned! So you see, dear, all did not go *quite* smoothly when I sat in the chair, with the bonnet on my head which you wore at dear Fred's wedding."

"It was clear that M. did not admire my way of presiding. I had been voted the thanks of the meeting, but her honesty made me feel more than ever that I had not been efficient. It is a good thing to know the truth.["]

"Is not this a funny glimpse of life? ... I doubt myself that there is much use in conferences, except that it is nice that some dear workers should meet and know each other. We had many choice ones."

The dear, sweet-souled old body, and the dear, naughty but very human missionary ladies!

After more than eighteen years of faithful labor, God called his old servant home; so frail and worn, so brave and trusting, still pouring out her remnant of strength ungrudgingly, but oh, so weary and so glad to go!

In the model Christian village, Clarkabad, that has risen to memorialize Clark of the Punjab,[141] where cleanliness and thrift, happy children and happy mothers, schools and churches, take the place of filth and misery, there has been placed a pure white stone in memory of A Lady of England who became A Lady of India.

Note.—Miss Tucker went out under the Indian Female Normal Society;[142] and when in 1880 that agency divided, she followed the part which became the Church of England Zenana Missionary Society. The other section, under undenominational auspices, became known as the Zenana Bible and Medical Mission. [Montgomery's note]

---

141 Robert Clark: (1825–1900), from Lincolnshire, England, one of the first CMS missionaries to serve in the Punjab
142 The Indian Female Normal School and Instruction Society (IFNS) was one of the earliest missionary societies capitalising on the zenana as the target of special feminine mission. The society also provided women teachers for girls' schools.

Source text

Montgomery, Helen Barnett, *Western Women in Eastern Lands: An Outline Study of Fifty Years of Woman's Work in Foreign Missions* (New York: Macmillan, 1910).

References

'A.L.O.E', *The Literary World; a Monthly Review of Current Literature* 26.24 (30 November 1895), 418.

Brackney, William H., 'The Legacy of Helen B. Montgomery and Lucy W. Peabody', *International Bulletin of Missionary Research* 15.4 (October 1991), 174–8.

'For Young People. A.L.O.E', *Missionary Herald* 92.4 (April 1896), 173–6.

Mobley, Kendal P., *Helen Barrett Montgomery: The Global Mission of Domestic Feminism* (Waco, TX: Baylor University Press, 2009).

Charles Alexander Eastman, MD (Ohiyesa) (1858–1939)

From 'Religion' and 'The Transition Period: The Christian Missionary' in 'The North American Indian' Address (1911)

A major rhetorical strategy supporting white settler colonialism in the Americas entailed depicting indigenous people as morally unworthy and uncivilised savages, incapable of self-governance. For Native people resisting colonialism's power, one path involved overt warfare; another – increasingly the only available one after Removals and massacres like Wounded Knee – was to demonstrate Indians' ability to assimilate into white culture. If Charles Eastman and other Native leaders of his generation can be critiqued today as 'red apple' figures (Indian in appearance but having whitened themselves through affiliation), his determined efforts to serve as a spokesman affirming the worth of indigenous cultures should also be recognised. His 1911 speech to the Universal Races Conference (URC) in London provided a notable opportunity to make this case to an international audience of more than two thousand people, including influential political figures and intellectuals from Britain and America, as well as representatives of other colonised peoples from across the world.

Kyle Mays argues that American race leaders like W. E. B. DuBois and Eastman viewed the event as a platform for claiming 'full citizenship' rights in an era when both Blacks and Native peoples were facing constraints limiting them to only a 'partial citizenship' role, nationally and beyond (244). But Mays also underscores the conference's broader ethical focus and, indeed, pre- and post-event press coverage of the URC situated the Congress's goals in moral terms. Eastman's presentation accordingly included details turning the tables on rhetoric deprecating indigenous nations as savage. His section on 'Religion' emphasised the enlightened spiritual stance of Native thought and traditions; then, he juxtaposed that portrayal with an incisive critique of Christian missionaries' negative impact on indigenous communities.

From 'Religion' and 'The Transition Period: The Christian Missionary' in 'The North American Indian' Address

Religion.—The religion of the American Indian has been generally misunderstood, and that by reason of his own reticence as much as the intolerance and prejudice of the outsider. He was trained from infancy to hold the "Great Mystery" sacred and unspeakable. That spirit which pervades the universe in its every phase and form was not to be trifled with by him in express terms. The Indian cultivated his mind and soul so as to feel, hear and see God in Nature. He distinguished clearly between intellect and spirit, and while conceding to man superior intelligence, as evidenced by the gift of articulate speech, he perceived in the unerring instinct of the dumb creation something mysterious and divine.

He had absolute faith in the immortality of the spirit, believing that the "Great Mystery" had breathed something of himself into every human frame. The highest type of prayer was offered fasting and alone in a solitary place, if possible upon a mountain-top, and was a true communion of spirits, far above all earthly or selfish desire. There was also a secondary form of prayer for bodily welfare or the satisfaction of material needs, in which the Indian appealed to his father the Sun, the great-grandfather Rock, or the spirits of animals as intermediaries. The rites of this worship were purely symbolic. He believed in the intercession of the souls of the departed, and there were totems or emblematic devices to which a certain sacredness was attached, as talismans, not as idols.

His religious teachers were the women, and, above all, the mothers, who cultivated the spiritual nature of the child before its birth, by thinking pure and high thoughts in nature's solitudes, and continued it later by the continual suggestion of a listening attitude—one of openness to the Unseen Powers. In a word, this simple religion of his was an attitude of mind rather than a dogma, and consisted in the all but universal sentiments of humility, reverence, and devotion. [. . .]

The Transition Period: [The Christian Missionary.—] The Christian missionary, especially the "Black Robe," pressed close upon the heels of the trader, and though urged by the best of motives nevertheless made grave mistakes. Misunderstanding and denouncing the Indian's own religion as "devil-worship," he often succeeded only in overthrowing the native philosophy without substituting anything better, and many of the early converts were such in name only, being recruited from among the loafers and sycophants of the tribes, while the stronger characters held proudly aloof.

Source text

Eastman, Charles Alexander, MD (Ohiyesa), 'The North American Indian', in Gustav Spiller (ed.), *Papers on Inter-racial Problems, Communicated to the First Universal Races Conference, held at the University of London, July 26–29, 1911* (London: P. S. King & Son; Boston: World's Peace Foundation, 1911), 367–76.

References

Mays, Kyle T., 'Transnational Progressivism: African Americans, Native Americans, and the Universal Races Congress of 1911', *Studies in American Indian Literatures* 25.2 (Summer 2013), 241–61.
'Positive Suggestions for Promoting Inter-Racial Friendliness', *Century Path* (12 March 1911), 2–3.
'Universal Races Congress', *New York Observer and Chronicle* (6 July 1911), 33.

Troß der Trauer wieder brachte er dahin mich, daß ich lachte;
Einen Armstuhl endlich rollte ich zu Thür und Vogel her.
In den sammt'nen Kiffen liegend, in die Hand die Wange schmiegend,
Sann ich, hin und her mich wiegend, was des Wortes Deutung wär'—
Was der grimme, finst're Vogel aus dem nächt'gen Schattenheer
    Wollt' mit seinem „Nimmermehr."

Diefes faß ich still ermeffend, doch des Vogels nicht vergeffend,
Deffen Feueraugen jetzo mir das Herz beklemmten fehr;
Und mit schmerzlichen Gefühlen ließ mein Haupt ich lange wühlen

Figure 7.7 Poe, Edgar Allan and Carl Theodor Eben, *Der Rabe: Ein Gedicht Von Edgar Allan Poe. Metrically translated from English by Carl Theodor Eben. Illustrations by David Scattergood* (Philadelphia: Barclay & Company, 1869), 7. Courtesy HathiTrust.

Carl Theodor Eben (1836–1909), one of numerous translators of Poe's 'The Raven' for multiple transatlantic communities, emigrated to the US in the 1850s. Charles Baudelaire's more renowned French renderings helped establish Poe's place as a serious artist with transnational reach, but Eben's *Der Rabe* reminds us that some translations of English-language literature addressed US immigrant audiences.

David Scattergood's illustrations for this text, meanwhile, anticipated a wide array of visually stunning responses to the poem, including Gustav Dore's 1884 *Raven* artist's edition. Such images demonstrate that Poe's psychologically focused writings evoked complex nineteenth-century links connecting mesmerism, spiritualism and séance-inflected communications with the dead, whereby social practices operated in liminal spaces between the sciences and the spirit world.

8

SCIENCE AND TECHNOLOGY

Figure 8.1 'The Coiling of the Atlantic Telegraph Cable on Board H.M.S. Agamemnon', *Illustrated London News* 31 (1 August 1857), 108. Courtesy TCU Center for Instructional Services.

A famous transatlantic exchange of science and technology predates the long nineteenth century: Tisquantum (or Squanto), one of the last surviving Patuxets and an English speaker from earlier captivity and residence in England, taught the applied science of agriculture to the Puritan colonists at Plymouth, enabling them to survive (Mann; see also Cajete). The Native technology of snowshoes, also previously unknown to English colonists, later helped them endure the severe winters of the 1690s (Wickman, 66, 82).

Though important work by indigenous scientists and inventors and people of colour continued, relatively few travelled or were published transatlantically in the long nineteenth century, when the very term 'scientist' was coined.[1] Throughout this era, the synergy of science and technology was fundamental, whether derived from the principle of Francis Bacon (1561–1626) that science should help improve the human condition or from patrons like Britain's Prince Albert (1819–61), who helped integrate natural sciences into the curriculum at Cambridge University as Chancellor and promoted industrial manufactures through his initiative of the Great Exhibition (1851), the first world's fair (Resetarits, 6; Rauch, 1510). Both in theoretical and technological contributions, the nineteenth century generated key developments, as well as the problems that accompanied them, familiar today. Steam engines were vital to transatlantic travel as well as industry but were propelled by fossil fuels (usually coal) on such a wide scale that they instigated the Anthropocene. (See on the anthology's affiliated website, for example, the 1860 account in *Scientific American*, 'The Arrival of the Great Eastern', the 'mammoth' steamship designed by engineer Isambard Brunel (1806–59), which required huge amounts of coal on board.) New nineteenth-century technologies also fostered what Anthony E. Kaye terms the Atlantic World's 'second' stage of slavery as 'the collective process of technological innovation', exemplified in tools like the saw gin (633), enabled increased cultivation of US land for cotton, while 'biological innovations' in seeds for both sugar and cotton (634) additionally increased commitments to a slave economy in both the US South and the Caribbean.[2]

FORMS OF CONNECTIVITY

The development of the telegraph, represented by our selections involving Samuel Morse and the transatlantic cable, helped create a connected world of information predating the internet. The earliest prototype of the computer itself, moreover, was designed by Englishman Charles Babbage, whose innovations were reported in the US as early as 1822, as our selection from the journal *Minerva* indicates. His colleague Ada Lovelace, née

---

1 William Whewell (1794–1866), Master of Trinity College, Cambridge and tutor to poet Alfred Tennyson in the early 1830s, coined the term 'scientist' in reviewing Mary Somerville's *On the Connection of the Physical Sciences* (1834) in the *Quarterly Review*; he also coined the influential terms 'Uniformitarian' and 'Catastrophic' for alternative models of geological change (*ODNB*).

2 Anthony E. Kaye, 'The Secondary Slavery: Modernity in the Nineteenth-Century South and the Atlantic World', *Journal of Southern History* 75.3 (August 2009), 627–50.

Byron (the daughter of the famed Romantic poet), wrote the earliest computer program, a feat memorialised in the transatlantic allied development of the military computer programming language Ada in the 1970s, when a UK team member obtained permission from a Lovelace descendant to use the name.[3]

Successive new technologies were swiftly applied to business and industry, which generated wealth beyond what the earlier transatlantic slave trade had enabled. Yet, as our section on Business, Industry and Labour reports, in the absence of labour laws or worker protections, new technologies intensified the divisions between affluence and poverty among transatlantic populations, especially in an era with few laws regulating the workplace or minimum wages. Such disparities also inspired numerous literary works, from Charles Kingsley's novel *Alton Locke* (1850) to Rebecca Harding Davis's 1861 short story 'Life in the Iron Mills', with its epigraph drawn from Alfred Tennyson's *In Memoriam*. Other technical breakthroughs in gun manufacture made warfare and murder on increasingly wide scales possible. (See, for example, 'The Gun of the Century', first published in *All the Year Round*, on this anthology's affiliated website.)[4] Expanding weapons trade also served the oppressions of British imperialism or the US surge westward across Native land (albeit many settlers relied on guns to hunt for subsistence). Guns and westward settlement alike also created the ecological disaster of the buffalo's near extermination and quickened the displacement of Native Americans for whom the buffalo was an essential part of the culture, providing food and clothing. And of course improvements in the machine gun made possible the wholesale slaughter of trench warfare in the First World War, which drew in both Britain and America.

The theoretical contributions of science were a more benign development of the long nineteenth century. Scientific concepts were widely disseminated in both popular and scientific print culture, especially periodicals (Cantor et al., xvii–xviii; Resetarits, 6), so that science itself became part of the era's literature. Some theories nonetheless troubled received assumptions in religion and secular cultures, or posited processes that could not be directly observed, increasing the distance between public and specialist knowledges that is familiar today. For example, the 1860 review we feature of Charles Darwin's 1859 *On the Origin of Species* by leading US scientist Asa Gray was favourable to Darwin yet simultaneously registered some of the threats to settled religious belief posed by his theory of evolution through natural selection. Nor, for that matter, could any scientist directly observe in one lifetime the evolutionary change posited by Darwin in 1859. Darwin was unable to specify the mechanism of evolution, which enabled some scientists to doubt his model of slow change. Yet once scientists in the early twentieth century rediscovered the 1865 article by Gregor Mendel (1822–84) on genetics, this former conundrum

---

3 William A. Whitaker, 'Ada – The Project: The DoD High Order Language Working Group', *ACM SIGPLAN Notices* 28.3 (March 1993), 318–20.
4 See also Lindsay Schakenbach Regele, 'Industrial Manifest Destiny: American Firearms Manufacturing and Antebellum Expansion', *Business History Review* 92 (Spring 2018), 57–83.

was resolved, supported by the isolation of DNA by Swiss scientist Friedrich Miescher (1844–95) in 1869, and the foundation for contemporary genetics had been laid.

The era also saw the formulation by transnational scientists of the first and second laws of thermodynamics, namely the conservation of energy and entropy. Both had direct implications for industry and the survival of the human species (and solar system), but they relied on abstruse mathematics not directly accessible to the public. The mathematical work of Scot James Clerk Maxwell (1831–79) on force and electromagnetic theory would be important to Albert Einstein (1879–1955), who introduced his 'special theory of relativity' in 1905 (Rauch, 1516–17). Both thermodynamics and relativity further eroded human ability to observe scientific processes directly as well as assumptions of empirical certitude. We represent one response to thermodynamics by an article in *Friends' Review*, an American Quaker journal that also suggests the latitude with which many religious believers could respond to cutting-edge nineteenth- and early twentieth-century science.

Medicine inherently relies on both scientific research and technological innovation to treat disease. Though microscopes were in common use and cells along with bacteria had been observed since the seventeenth century, transmission of disease was imperfectly understood until fairly late in the nineteenth century. Famously, British physician John Snow (1813–58) traced a London cholera outbreak to a single water pump in 1854, but further investigations were needed before the outlines of germ theory were generally adopted. In the mid-1860s, a new medical technology advocated by surgeon Joseph Lister (1827–1912) discovered the use of carbolic acid to sterilise surgical instruments and treat wounds, thereby further helping prevent contagion and deaths from germs. A global pandemic occurred only in 1918 with the outbreak of the 'Spanish flu', but repeated outbreaks of epidemics, especially of cholera, were sufficiently mystifying and terrifying to cause disruptions and promote competing theories for responding productively (as in our own era). We represent the fears and successive waves of cholera through transatlantic medical journal reports from 1851 and 1871, along with illustrations that register the terror these outbreaks inspired.

Medical education was crucial to the implementation of new treatments and expanded patient access to care. Medicine became fully professionalised in the nineteenth century around the Atlantic basin (Shortt, 51–68), but this immediately raised the question of who would, and would not, be admitted. Women on both sides of the Atlantic faced repeated obstacles, in part because the needful anatomical studies were considered too indelicate for women. Elizabeth Blackwell's and Sophia Jex-Blake's excerpted life histories below register women's struggles and the transatlantic travel they often undertook to achieve their career goals. Though African physician Lucas Santomee Peter practised medicine in the New York colony as early as 1667 (Sullivan, 182), qualified Black students also faced rampant discrimination, likewise necessitating education abroad for some, especially prior to the first Black medical school that opened at Howard University in 1868 (Sullivan, 182–3).

Indeed, throughout the long nineteenth century an abiding question was what and who counted in science and technology – even as spurious sciences of 'race' and eugenics gained recognition in some quarters of the scientific community.

Women such as English textbook author Mary Somerville and US astronomer Maria Mitchell gained recognition, but Native, Black and white women's expertise in botany, adapted to everything from treating disease to cookery, remained outside the charmed circle of professional recognition and payment, though we are able to include Fanny Calderon de la Barca's account of Native women's role in the Mexican production of the liquor pulque. Agriculture was another crucial applied science, which we represent through a British journal article recounting the innovations of Booker T. Washington at several institutions, culminating at Tuskeegee. Navigation, too, was a critical applied science for transatlanticism, and it could entail unexpected convergences between First Nations navigators in Canada, known as *voyageurs*, and British imperialism in the anthology's excerpt by Mohawk author Louis Jackson, one of several Indigenes Jace Weaver aligns with the 'Red Atlantic'. This too is supplemented by a further excerpt from Jackson on our affiliated website reflecting his challenges in managing labourers onsite in Egypt.

All facets of nineteenth-century science and technology entailed transatlantic travel, whether as part of scientific research (as with Darwin's visit to South America on board the *Beagle*), lectures, training, joint ventures such as the laying of the transatlantic cable, or dissemination through print. We have striven to be as inclusive in representing the manifold forms of science and technology and their practitioners in this historical era. Yet we acknowledge inevitable gaps and absences and invite readers of this anthology to pursue inquiry into additional historical figures, inventions and emergent fields (such as ecology, foreglimpsed in our John Muir selection) to help form a more complete understanding of transatlantic science and technology.

References

Cajete, Gregory, *Native Science: Natural Laws of Interdependence* (Santa Fe, NM: Clear Light Publishers, 2000).

Cantor, Geoffrey et al., 'Introduction', in Louise Henson et al. (eds), *Culture and Science in the Nineteenth-century Media* (2004; rpt. London: Routledge, 2016), xvii–xxv.

Mann, Charles C., 'Squanto and the Pilgrims: Native Intelligence', *Smithsonian* 36.9 (December 2005), 94–108.

Rauch, Alan, 'Science', in Dino Felluga (ed.) with Pamela Gilbert and Linda K. Hughes (associate eds), *Encyclopedia of Victorian Literature*, 4 vols (Oxford: Wiley Blackwell, 2015), 4.1505–19.

Resetarits, C. R. (ed.), *An Anthology of Nineteenth-Century American Science Writing* (London: Anthem, 2012).

Shortt, S. E. D., 'Physicians, Science, and Status: Issues in the Professionalization of Anglo-American Medicine in the Nineteenth Century', *Medical History* 27 (1983), 51–68.

Sullivan, Louis W., 'The Education of Black Health Professionals', *Phylon* 38.2 (1977), 181–93.

Weaver, Jace, *The Red Atlantic: American Indigenes and the Making of the Modern World, 1000–1927* (Chapel Hill, NC: University of North Carolina Press, 2014).

Wickman, Thomas, '"Winters Embittered with Hardships": Severe Cold, Wabanaki Power, and English Adjustments, 1690–1710', *William and Mary Quarterly* 72.1 (January 2015), 57–98.

Benjamin Franklin (1706–90)

'Letter from Dr. Franklin to Mr. M. Collinson' (1776)

First-generation American Benjamin Franklin has an important place in the history of science as well as in US history and literature. In addition to inventing the Franklin stove, which burned more efficiently while using less wood, he became a towering figure in science after publishing his experiments in electricity. He established that, contrary to earlier hypotheses, there were not two kinds of electricity but only one, with positive and negative poles, and that its discharge did not involve loss of matter (an early demonstration of the conservation of matter). His experiments were inspired when he learned from botanist and Royal Society member Peter Collinson (1694–1768) about recent experiments in Germany conducted with a Leyden jar (which acted as a capacitor). Franklin and Collinson, who was also a merchant in the cloth trade, became acquainted through Collinson's American business transactions. Collinson also befriended John Bartram (1697–1777), considered to be the father of American botany.

'Letter from Dr. Franklin to Mr. M. Collinson'

To the Editor of the London Magazine,
Sir,

In your January magazine you favoured the public with some valuable memoirs of the late worthy Mr. Peter Collinson. Among his particular friends stands the name of Dr. Benjamin Franklin, to whom he communicated many valuable particulars. Their minds were congenial, and ever intent on promoting the public good.—The following letter is one proof thereof, and therefore deserves a place in your valuable repository.
Y.[5]
To MICHAEL COLLINSON, Esq;[6]

Dear Sir,
UNDERSTANDING that an account of our dear departed friend Mr. Peter Collinson is intended to be given to the public, I cannot omit expressing my approbation of the design. The character of good men are exemplary, and often stimulate the well disposed to an imitation, beneficial to mankind, and honourable to themselves. And as you may be unacquainted with the following instances of his zeal and usefulness in promoting knowledge, which fell within my observation, I take the liberty of informing

---

5 Unidentified
6 The eldest son (1727–95) of Peter Collinson, Michael was also a botanist

you, that in 1730, a Subscription Library[7] being set on foot at Philadelphia, he encouraged the design by making several very valuable presents to it, and procuring others from his friends: and as the Library Company had a considerable sum arising annually to be laid out in books, and needed a judicious friend in London to transact the business for them, he voluntarily and chearfully undertook that service, and executed it for more than thirty years successively; assisting in the choice of books, and taking the whole care of collecting and shipping them, without ever charging or accepting any consideration for his trouble. The success of this library (greatly owing to his kind countenance and good advice) encouraged the erecting others in different places on the same plan; and it is supposed there are now upwards of thirty subsisting in the several colonies, which have contributed greatly to the spreading of useful knowledge in that part of the world; the books he recommended being all of that kind, and the catalogue of this first library being much respected and followed by those libraries that succeeded.

During the same time he transmitted to the directors of the library the earliest accounts of every new European Improvement in agriculture and the arts, and every philosophical discovery: among which, in 1745, he sent over an account of the new German experiments in electricity, together with a glass tube, and some directions for using it, so as to repeat those experiments. This was the first notice I had of that curious subject, which I afterwards prosecuted with some diligence, being encouraged by the friendly reception he gave to the letters I wrote to him upon it. Please to accept this small testimony of mine to his memory, for which I shall ever have the utmost respect; and believe me, with sincere esteem, Dear Sir,

Your most humble servant,
R. Franklin.

Source text

Franklin, Benjamin, 'Letter from Dr. Franklin to Mr. M. Collinson', *London Magazine, or, Gentleman's Monthly Intelligencer* 45 (April 1776), 189–90.

Charles Babbage (1791–1871)

'Application of Machinery to the Calculating and Printing of Mathematical Tables' (1822)

This brief report on a pamphlet by Charles Babbage addressed to the President of the Royal Society of London demonstrates both the pervasive practice of transatlantic reprinting and the immediate transatlantic circulation of news about Babbage's calculating engine. The weekly American newspaper *The Minerva*, published in New York, placed the article in its 'Scientific Notices from Foreign Journals' column but did not identify its British source. Babbage published his twelve-page pamphlet in London

---

7 Available only to dues-paying members; not a free library

in July; within two months the news of it appeared in *The Minerva*. The article underscores the accuracy and speed of computation by machine rather than humans and identifies the mathematical principle on which Babbage's invention was based. Babbage secured funding to build a full-scale 'difference engine' but did not complete it. He went on to design an 'analytical engine', generally viewed as the nineteenth-century prototype of the modern computer today.

'Application of Machinery to the Calculating and Printing of Mathematical Tables'

A very eminent mathematician, Charles Babbage, Esq. F. R. S. London and Edinburgh, &c. in a letter addressed to Sir Humphry Davy, President of the Royal Society of London, has announced to the world that he has invented various machines by which some of the more complicated processes of arithmetical calculation may be performed with certainty and despatch; so that if the sanguine expectations of the ingenious inventor shall be completely realized, the mathematician may in many cases be relieved from the dull drudgery of arithmetical computation, and tables of almost every kind may be constructed with a facility and accuracy hitherto unknown, by a process purely mechanical.[8] Mathematicians are well aware that tables of every kind may now be constructed by the aid of one of the finest inventions of modern analysis, the theory of finite differences.[9] It is in this way that Mr. Babbage proposes to apply his machines to the purpose of calculation. He states that his first engine is capable of computing any table by the aid of differences, whether they are positive or negative, or of both kinds: and that with perfect confidence he would venture to construct an engine that should compute numbers depending on ten or twelve successive orders of differences. It is a remarkable property of the machine, that the greater the number of differences, the more it will outstrip the most rapid calculator.[10] This machine, by the application of certain parts, may be employed in extracting the roots of equations, and the degree of approximation will depend on its magnitude.

Mr. Babbage has sketches of two other machines, one by which the product of any number by any other number may be found; and another, by which all prime numbers from 0 to ten millions may be determined. He has also a fourth machine, whose plans are in a more advanced state, by which tables having no order of differences constant, may be constructed. This last is immediately applicable to the construction of logarithmic and astronomical tables of every kind; and in order to avoid the errors which might be produced in copying and printing the numbers in the common way, the ingenious inventor states, that he has contrived means by which the machines shall take, from several boxes containing type, the numbers which they calculate, and place them side by side; thus becoming at once a substitute for the computer and the compositor.

---

8 F. R. S.: Fellow of the Royal Society; Sir Humphry Davy (1778–1829), chemist and inventor
9 Finite difference: 'any of the differences between the successive values of a function when its independent variable takes on the values of an arithmetical progression' (*OED*)
10 Refers to a human as opposed to machine calculator

In order to demonstrate the practicability of executing these views, Mr. Babbage has actually constructed a machine which will produce any tables where second differences are constant, and has exhibited it to some friends, who have witnessed its performance. In the computation of a series of numbers from the formula $x2$ add x add 41, they were at first produced rather slower than they could be taken down by a person that undertook to write the numbers as they appeared, but as soon as four figures were required, the machine was at least equal in speed to the writer.

Source text

'Application of Machinery to the Calculating and Printing of Mathematical Tables', *The Minerva* 1.23 (14 September 1822), 183.

References

Hyman, Anthony, *Charles Babbage: Pioneer of the Computer* (Princeton, NJ: Princeton University Press, 1982).
ODNB

Frances Calderón de la Barca (1804–82)

From Life in Mexico, During a Residence of Two Years in That Country *(1843)*

Frances Erskine Inglis Calderón de la Barca was a transatlantic writer. Born in Edinburgh, Scotland, Fanny moved to Boston, Massachusetts with her mother and sisters to start a school. While in Boston, Calderón de la Barca was rumoured to have helped circulate a pamphlet that disparaged a prominent Bostonian family. Consequently, the school closed and the family moved to Long Island, New York, where Frances Erskine made the acquaintance of William Prescott, a writer and historian, who was acquainted with Angel Calderón de la Barca, the first Spanish minister to Mexico.

Frances Erskine married Angel Calderón, and they moved to Mexico. Frances Calderón de la Barca wrote *Life in Mexico* in which she recounts her experiences not as a traveller but as a migratory resident. Of note are the author's transatlantic life and publication history since *Life in Mexico* was published both in Boston (Little Brown, 1843) and in London (Chapman and Hall, 1843).

Life in Mexico, a series of letters dated from 27 October 1839 to 28 April 1842, offers insight into one woman's experiences with the impacts of colonialism in Mexico. We excerpt from the tenth letter, which recounts the writer's impressions of indigenous agricultural advancements and pulque production. An iconic indigenous drink, pulque is made from the fermented sap of the maguey plant, and Calderón de la Barca describes indigenous cultivation and fermentation methods that endured in spite of colonial efforts to stop them. Although she does not claim to be an agricultural historian, Calderón de la Barca offers her transatlantic insight into agricultural practices indigenous to Mexico.

From Life in Mexico

Making of Pulque–Organos and Nopal–

26th [February 1840].—We went yesterday with Mr. M— , his wife and daughter and a padre to visit the archbishop's palace at Tacubaya, a pretty village about four miles from Mexico, and a favourite ride of ours in the morning. The country round Mexico, if not always beautiful, has the merit of being original, and on the road to Tacubaya, which goes by Chapultepec, you pass large tracts of country, almost entirely uncultivated, though so near the city, or covered by the mighty maguey plant, the American agave, which will flourish on the most arid soil, and, like a fountain in a desert place, furnishes the poorest Indian with the beverage most grateful to his palate. It seems to be to them what the reindeer is to the Esquimaux, fitted by nature to supply all his wants.[11] The maguey and its produce, *pulque*, were known to the Indians in the most ancient times, and the primitive Aztecs may have become as intoxicated on their favourite *octli*, as they called it, as the modern Mexicans do on their beloved pulque.

It is not often that we see the superb flower with its colossal stem, for the plant that is in blossom is a useless beauty. The moment the experienced Indian becomes aware that his maguey is about to flower, he cuts out the heart, covers it over with the side leaves of the plant, and all the juice which should have gone to the great stem of the flower, runs into the empty basin thus formed, into which the Indian, thrice a day, and during several months in succession, inserts his *acojote* or gourd, a kind of siphon, and applying his mouth to the other end, draws off the liquor by suction; a curious-looking process.[12] First it is called honey-water, and is sweet and scentless; but easily ferments when transferred to the skins or earthen vases where it is kept. To assist in its fermentation, however, a little old pulque, *Madre pulque*, as it is called, which has fermented for many days, is added to it, and in twenty-four hours after it leaves the plant, you may imbibe it in all its perfection. It is said to be the most wholesome drink in the world, and remarkably agreeable when one has overcome the first shock occasioned by its rancid odour. At all events, the maguey is a source of unfailing profit, the consumption of pulque being enormous, so that many of the richest families in the capital owe their fortune entirely to the produce of their magueys. When the owners do not make the pulque themselves, they frequently sell their plants to the Indians; and a maguey, which costs a real[13] when first planted, will, when ready to be cut, sell for twelve or eighteen dollars; a tolerable profit, considering that it grows in almost any soil, requires little manure, and, unlike the vine, no very special or periodical care. They are planted in rows like hedges,

---

11 A term considered controversial; Inuit is preferred in Greenland and Canada.
12 Refers to Indigenous ritual drinking practices
13 A unit of currency

and though the individual plant is handsome, the general effect is monotonous. Of the fibres is made an excellent strong thread called *pita*, of which pita they make a strong brownish paper, and might make cloth if they pleased. There is, however, little improvement made by the Mexicans upon the ingenuity of their Indian ancestors, in respect to the maguey. Upon paper made of its fibres, the ancient Mexicans painted their hieroglyphical figures. The strong and pointed thorns which terminate the gigantic leaves, they used as nails and pins; and amongst the abuses, not the uses of these, the ancient sanguinary priests were in the habit of piercing their breasts and tearing their arms with them, in acts of expiation. Besides, there is a very strong brandy distilled from pulque, which has the advantage of producing intoxication in an infinitely shorter period.

Together with the maguey, grows another immense production of nature, the *organos*, which resembles the barrels or pipes of an organ, and being covered with prickles, the plants growing close together, and about six feet high, makes the strongest natural fence imaginable, besides being covered with beautiful flowers. There is also another species of cactus, the nopal, which bears the tuna,[14] a most refreshing fruit, but not ripe at this season. The plant looks like a series of flat green pin-cushions fastened together, and stuck full of diminutive needles.

But though the environs of Mexico are flat, though there are few trees, little cultivation, and uninhabited haciendas, and ruined churches in all directions, still, with its beautiful climate and ever-smiling sky, the profusion of roses and sweet-peas in the deserted gardens, the occasional clumps of fine trees, particularly the graceful Arbold de Peru (*shinum molle*, the Peruvian pepper-tree), its bending branches loaded with bunches of coral-coloured berries, the old orchards with their blossoming fruit-trees, the conviction that everything necessary for the use of man can be produced with scarcely any labour, all contributes to render the landscape one which it is impossible to pass through with indifference.

A magnificent ash-tree (the Mexican *fresno*), the pride of Tacubaya;[15] which throws out its luxuriant branches, covering a large space of ground, was pointed out to us as having a tradition attached to it. It had nearly withered away, when the Ylustrisimo Señor Fonti,[16] the last of the Spanish archbishops, gave it his solemn benediction, and prayed that its vigour might be restored. Heaven heard his prayer; new buds instantly shot forth, and the tree has since continued to thrive luxuriantly. [...]

Source text:

Calderón de la Barca, Frances, *Life in Mexico, During a Residence of Two Years in That Country* (London: Chapman and Hall, 1843).

References

Caballero, Soledad and Jennifer Hayward, '"An Occasional Trait of Scotch Shrewdness": Narrating Nationalism in Frances Calderón de la Barca's *Life in Mexico*', in Joselyn M. Almeida (ed.), *Romanticism and the Anglo-Hispanic Imaginary* (Leiden: Editions Rodopi, 2010), 290–319.

---

14 Spanish for prickly pear, the fruit produced by the nopal, a prickly pear cactus
15 An area in present-day Mexico City
16 Pedro José de Fonte y Hernández Miravete (1777–1839), Archbishop of Mexico from 1815 to 1837

Méndez Rodenas, Adriana, *Transatlantic Travels in Nineteenth-Century Latin America: European Women Pilgrims* (Lewisburg, PA: Bucknell University Press, 2014).

Harriet Martineau (1802–76)

'Miss Martineau on Mesmerism' (1844)

Martineau's transatlantic identity is presented in more detail under the headnote for her work appearing in the anthology's 'Abolition and Aftermath' section. Here, Martineau's transatlantic publication history is broadened to include a letter she wrote regarding her personal experiences with Mesmerism, a form of hypnotism first popularised by the German doctor Franz Anton Mesmer (1734–1815). In 1839, Martineau fell acutely ill in Italy with gynaecological complications, likely a prolapsed uterus and ovarian cyst (Frawley, 18). After Thomas Greenhow, her brother-in-law and physician, and other friends and acquaintances encouraged her to try Mesmerism as a possible remedy, Martineau believed she had been healed a few months later.

Mesmerism was a controversial treatment, and in 1844 Martineau wrote a series of seven letters for the *Athenaeum*, a well-regarded nineteenth-century weekly paper, to affirm her positive experiences with her course of therapy. Shortly after Martineau published her letters, Greenhow published 'A Medical Report of the Case of Miss H------- M-------', a telling and personal pamphlet about Martineau's gynaecological health; he did so to discredit her acknowledgment of the role Mesmerism played in her recovery (Frawley, 20–1). Unsurprisingly, Martineau was embarrassed by Greenhow's actions.

In the letter that follows, reprinted in the US periodical the *Anglo American*, Martineau mentions that her letters about Mesmerism were first published in the *Athenaeum*. She argues that her treatment plan, like other forms of healing with more spiritual connections, deserves to be recognised.

'Miss Martineau on Mesmerism'

LETTER VII. Tynemouth, November 28, 1844.

Many persons suppose that when the truth, use and beauty of Mesmerism are established, all is settled; that no further ground remains for a rejection of it. My own late experience, and my observation of what is passing abroad, convince me that this is a mistake. I know that there are many who admit the truth and function of Mesmerism, who yet discountenance it. I know that the repudiation of it is far more extensive than the denial. It gives me pain to hear this fact made the occasion of contemptuous remark, as it is too often by such as know Mesmerism to be true. The repudiation I speak of proceeds from minds of a high order; and their superstition (if superstition it be) should be encountered with better weapons than the arrogant compassion which I have heard expressed.

I own I have less sympathy with those who throw down their facts before the world, and then despise all who will not be in haste to take them up, than with some I know of, who would seriously rather suffer to any extent, than have recourse to relief which they believe unauthorized; who would rather that a mystery remain sacred than have it divulged for their own benefit: who tell me to my face that they would rather see me sent back to my couch of pain than witness any tampering with the hidden things of Providence. There is a sublime rectitude of sentiment here, which commands and wins one's reverence and sympathy; and if the facts of the history and condition of Mesmerism would bear out the sentiment, no one would more cordially respond to it than I—no one would have been more scrupulous about procuring recovery by such means—no one would have recoiled with more fear and disgust from the work of making known what I have experienced and learned. But I am persuaded that a knowledge of existing facts clears up the duty of the case, so as to prove that the sentiment must, while preserving all its veneration and tenderness, take a new direction, for the honour of God and the safety of man.

Granting to all who wish, that the powers and practice of Mesmerism (for which a better name is sadly wanted) are as old as man and society; that from age to age there have been endowments and functions sacred from popular use, and therefore committed by providential authority to the hands of a sacred class; that the existence of mysteries ever has been, and probably must ever be, essential to the spiritual welfare of man; that there should ever be a powerful sentiment of sanctity investing the subject of the ulterior powers of immortal beings in their mortal state; that it is extremely awful to witness, and much more to elicit, hidden faculties, and to penetrate by their agency into regions of knowledge otherwise unattainable;—admitting all these things, still the facts of the present condition of Mesmerism in this country, and on two continents, leave to those who know them, no doubt of the folly and sin of turning away from the study of the subject. It is no matter of choice whether the subject shall remain sacred—a deposit of mystery in the hands of the church—as it was in the Middle Ages, and as the Pope and many Protestants would have it still. The Pope has issued an edict against the study and practice of Mesmerism in his dominions; and there are some members of the Church of England who would have the same suppression attempted by means of ecclesiastical and civil law at home. But for this it is too late: the knowledge and practice are all abroad in society; and they are no more to be reclaimed than the waters, when out in floods, can be gathered back into reservoirs. The only effect of such prohibitions would be to deter from the study of Mesmerism, the very class who should assume its administration, and to drive disease, compassion and curiosity into holes and corners to practice as a sin what is now done openly and guiltlessly, however recklessly, through an ignorance for which the educated are responsible. The time is past for facts of natural philosophy to be held at discretion by priesthoods; for any facts which concern all human beings to be a deposit in the hands of any social class. Instead of re-enacting the scenes of old—setting up temples with secret chambers, oracles, and miraculous ministrations—instead of reviving the factitious sin and cruel penalties of witch craft, (all forms assumed by mesmeric powers and faculties in different times), instead of exhibiting false mysteries in an age of investigation, it is clearly our business to strip false mysteries of their falseness, in order to secure due reverence to the true, of which there will ever be no lack. Mystery can never fail while man is finite: his highest faculties of faith will, through all time and all eternity, find ample exercise in waiting on truths above his ken: there will ever be in advance of the human soul, a region "dark through excess of light;" while all labour spent on surrounding clear facts with artificial mystery is just so much profane effort spent in drawing minds away from the genuine objects of faith. And look at the consequences! Because philosophers will not study the facts of that mental *rapport* which takes place in Mesmerism, whereby the mind of the ignorant often gives out in echo the knowledge of the informed, we have claims of inspiration springing up right and left. Because medical men will not study the facts of the mesmeric trance, nor ascertain the extremest of its singularities, we have tales of Estaticas, and of sane men going into the Tyrol and elsewhere to contemplate, as a sign from heaven, what their physicians ought to be able to report of at home as natural phenomena easily producible in certain states of disease.[17] Because physiologists and mental philosophers will not attend to facts from whose vastness they pusillanimously shrink, the infinitely delicate mechanism and organization of brain, nerves and mind are thrown as a toy into the hands of children and other ignorant persons, and of the base. What, again, can follow from this but the desecration, in the eyes of the many, of things which ought to command their reverence? What becomes of really divine inspiration when the commonest people find they can elicit marvels of prevision and insight? What becomes of the veneration for religious contemplation when Estaticas are found to be at the command of very unhallowed—wholly unauthorized hands? What becomes of the respect in which the medical profession ought to be held, when the friends of the sick and suffering, with their feelings all alive, see the doctors' skill and science overborne and set aside by means at the command of an ignorant neighbor—means which are all ease and pleasantness? How can the profession hold its dominion over minds, however backed by law and the opinion of the educated, when the vulgar see and know that limbs are removed without pain, in opposition to the will of the doctors, and in spite of their denial of the facts? What avails the decision of a whole College of Surgeons that such a thing could not be, when a whole town full of people know that it was? Which must succumb, the learned body or the fact? Thus are objects of reverence desecrated, not sanctified, by attempted restriction of truth, or of research into it. Thus are human passions and human destinies committed to reckless hands, for sport or abuse. No wonder if somnambules are made into fortune-tellers—no wonder if they are made into prophets of fear, malice and revenge, by reflecting in their somnambulism the fear, malice and revenge of their questioners;—no wonder if they are made even ministers of death, by being led from sick bed to sick bed in the dim and dreary alleys of our towns, to declare which of the sick will recover, and which will die! Does anyone suppose that powers so popular, and now so diffused, can be interdicted by law—such oracles silenced by the reserve of the squeamish,—such appeals to human passions hushed, in an age of universal communication, by the choice of a class or two, to be themselves, dumb? No: this is not the way. It is terribly late to be setting about choosing a way, but something must be done; and that something is clearly for those whose studies and art relate to the human frame to take up, earnestly and avowedly, the investigation of this weighty matter; to take its practice into their own hands, in virtue of the irresistible claim of qualification. When they become the wisest and the most skilful in the administration of Mesmerism, others, even the most reckless vulgar, will no more think of interfering than they now do of using the lancet, or operating on the eye. Here, as elsewhere, knowledge is power. The greater knowledge will ever insure the superior power. At present, the

---

17 References to controversial states of ecstasy, primarily experienced by female clergy

knowledge of Mesmerism, superficial and scanty as it is, is out of the professional pale. When it is excelled by that which issues from within the professional pale, the remedial and authoritative power will reside where it ought; and not till then. These are the chief considerations which have caused me to put forth these letters in this place;—an act which may seem rash to all who are unaware of the extent of the popular knowledge and practice of Mesmerism. The *Athenaeum* is not likely to reach the ignorant classes of our towns; and if it did, the cases I have related would be less striking to them than numbers they have learned by the means of the itinerant Mesmerists. The *Athenaeum* does reach large numbers of educated and professional men; and I trust some of them may possibly be aroused to consideration of the part it behoves them to take.

As for the frequent objection brought against inquiry into Mesmerism, that there should be no countenance of an influence which gives human beings such power over one another, I really think a moment's reflection, and a very slight knowledge of Mesmerism would supply both the answers which the objection requires. First, it is too late, as I have said above; the power is abroad, and ought to be guided and controlled. Next, this is but one addition to the powers we have over one another already; and a far more slow and difficult one than many which are safely enough possessed. Every apothecary's shop is full of deadly drugs—every workshop is full of deadly weapons—wherever we go, there are plenty of people who could knock us down, rob, and murder us; wherever we live there are plenty of people who could defame and ruin us. Why do they not?[18] Because moral considerations deter them. Then bring the same moral considerations to bear on the subject of Mesmerism. If the fear is of laying victims prostrate in trance, and exercising spells over them, the answer is, that this is done with infinitely greater ease and certainty by drugs than it can ever be by Mesmerism; by drugs which are to be had in every street. And as sensible people do not let narcotic drugs lie about in their houses, within reach of the ignorant and mischievous, so would they see that Mesmerism was not practiced without witnesses and proper superintendence. It is a mistake, too, to suppose that Mesmerism can be used at will to strike down victims, helpless and unconscious, as laudanum does, except in cases of excessive susceptibility from disease; cases which are, of course, under proper ward. The concurrence of two parties is needful in the first place, which is not the case in the administration of narcotics: and then the practice is very uncertain in its results on most single occasions; and again, in the majority of instances, it appears that the intellectual and moral powers are more, and not less vigorous than in the ordinary state. As far as I have any means of judging, the highest faculties are seen in their utmost perfection during the mesmeric sleep; the innocent are stronger in their rectitude than ever, rebuking levity, reproving falsehood and flattery, and indignantly refusing to tell secrets, or say or do anything they ought not; while the more faulty then confess their sins, and grieve over and ask pardon for their offences. The volitions of the Mesmerist may actuate the movements of the patient's limbs, and suggest the material of his ideas; but they seem unable to touch his *morale*. In this state the *morale* appears supreme, as it is rarely found in the ordinary condition. If this view is mistaken, if it is founded on too small a collection of facts, let it be brought to the test and corrected. Let the truth be ascertained and established; for it cannot be extinguished, and it is too important to be neglected.

---

18 Apothecaries served in the capacity of chemists or pharmacists.

And now one word of respectful and sympathizing accost unto those reverent and humble spirits who painfully question men's right to exercise faculties whose scope is a new region of insight and foresight. They ask whether to use these faculties be not to encroach upon holy ground, to trespass on the precincts of the future and higher life. May I inquire of these in reply, what they conceive to be the divinely appointed boundary of our knowledge and our powers? Can they establish, or indicate, any other boundary than the limit of the knowledge and powers themselves? Has not the attempt to do so, failed from age to age? Is it not the most remarkable feature of the progress of time, that, in handing over the future into the past, he transmutes its material incessantly, and without pause, converting what truth was mysterious, fearful, impious to glance at, into that which is safe, beautiful and beneficent to contemplate and use,—a clearly consecrated gift from the Father of all to the children who seek the light of his countenance? Where is his pleasure to be ascertained but in the ascertainment of what he gives and permits, in the proof and verification of what powers he has bestowed on us, and what knowledge he has placed within our reach? While regarding with shame all pride of intellect, and with fear the presumption of ignorance, I deeply feel that the truest humility is evinced by those who most simply accept and use the talents placed in their hands; and that the most childlike dependence upon their Creator appears in those who fearlessly apply the knowledge he discloses to the furtherance of that great consecrated object, the welfare of the family of man.

Harriet Martineau.

Source text

Martineau, Harriet, 'Miss Martineau on Mesmerism', *The Anglo American, a Journal of Literature, News, Politics, the Drama, Fine Arts, Etc.* 4.18 (22 February 1845), 416–17.

References

Frawley, Maria (ed.), Harriet Martineau, *Life in the Sickroom* (1844) (Peterborough: Broadview Press, 2003).

Martineau, Harriet, 'Mesmerism Forty Years Ago', *Hall's Journal of Health* 34.10 (October 1887), 225–9.

Charles Darwin (1809–82)

From Voyage of the Beagle *(1845)*

Charles Darwin needs little biographical introduction given his contributions to the field of biology. His *Origin of Species* (1859) continues to generate controversy. In his *Voyage of the Beagle* (published as the *Journal of Researches* in 1839 and as a second edition in 1845), he records his personal observations as scientific. He weaves his travel writing and field notes alongside other findings from scientists (Richard Owen and Andrew Smith) as a way of illuminating his scientific ethos.

In the following excerpt from chapter 5, Darwin documents his findings of fossils in the River Plate region of South America. He connects his research to his own experiences and other studies of large animals in South Africa and finds that previously held understandings about the dietary requirements of larger animals may not be correct due to the types of vegetation that grow in the Global South.

A transatlantic/transnational figure, Darwin's findings are complicated by Britain's global imperial pursuits. Britain had failed at a series of attempted invasions in the Rio de la Plata region (1806–7). A scientific representative of the empire, Darwin is positioned as a European traveller engaging with the natural world, lands, people, and animals for the first time. Darwin is not finding new people, territories, species and ways of life; they existed long before his arrival in South America. His observations often result in his 'othering' of non-European individuals he encounters (Almeida, 171).

From Voyage of the Beagle

The Beagle arrived here on the 24th of August, and a week afterwards sailed for the Plata.[19] With Captain FitzRoy's[20] consent I was left behind, to travel by land to Buenos Ayres. I will here add some observations, which were made during this visit and on a previous occasion, when the Beagle was employed in surveying the harbour.

The plain, at the distance of a few miles from the coast, belongs to the great Pampean[21] formation, which consists in part of a reddish clay, and in part of a highly calcareous marly rock. Nearer the coast there are some plains formed from the wreck of the upper plain, and from mud, gravel, and sand thrown up by the sea during the slow elevation of the land, of which elevation we have evidence in upraised beds of recent shells, and in rounded pebbles of pumice scattered over the country. At Punta Alta[22] we have a section of one of these later-formed little plains, which is highly interesting from the number and extraordinary character of the remains of gigantic land-animals embedded in it. These have been fully described by Professor Owen,[23] in the Zoology of the voyage of the Beagle, and are deposited in the College of Surgeons. I will here give only a brief outline of their nature.

First, parts of three heads and other bones of the Megatherium, the huge dimensions of which are expressed by its name.[24] Secondly, the Megalonyx, a great allied animal. Thirdly, the Scelidotherium, also an allied animal, of which I obtained a nearly perfect skeleton. It must have been as large as a rhinoceros: in the structure of its head it comes according to Mr. Owen, nearest to the Cape Ant-eater, but in some other respects it approaches to the armadilloes. Fourthly, the Mylodon Darwinii, a

---

19 The Rio de la Plata, an estuary formed by the Paraná and Uruguay Rivers
20 Robert FitzRoy (1805–65), captain of the *Beagle*
21 The flat, fertile plains of the Pampa region in Argentina
22 Punta Alta, a city southeast of Bahía Blanca
23 Richard Owen (1804–92), English biologist and palaeontologist
24 Darwin mentions several extinct ground sloths in this paragraph.

closely related genus of little inferior size. Fifthly, another gigantic edental quadruped. Sixthly, a large animal, with an osseous coat in compartments, very like that of an armadillo. Seventhly, an extinct kind of horse, to which I shall have again to refer. Eighthly, a tooth of a Pachydermatous animal, probably the same with the Macrauchenia, a huge beast with a long neck like a camel, which I shall also refer to again. Lastly, the Toxodon,[25] perhaps one of the strangest animals ever discovered: in size it equalled an elephant or megatherium, but the structure of its teeth, as Mr. Owen states, proves indisputably that it was intimately related to the Gnawers, the order which, at the present day, includes most of the smallest quadrupeds: in many details it is allied to the Pachydermata: judging from the position of its eyes, ears, and nostrils, it was probably aquatic, like the Dugong and Manatee, to which it is also allied. How wonderfully are the different Orders, at the present time so well separated, blended together in different points of the structure of the Toxodon!

The remains of these nine great quadrupeds, and many detached bones, were found embedded on the beach, within the space of about 200 yards square. It is a remarkable circumstance that so many different species should be found together; and it proves how numerous in kind the ancient inhabitants of this country must have been. At the distance of about thirty miles from Punta Alta, in a cliff of red earth, I found several fragments of bones, some of large size. Among them were the teeth of a gnawer, equalling in size and closely resembling those of the Capybara, whose habits have been described; and therefore, probably, an aquatic animal. There was also part of the head of a Ctenomys;[26] the species being different from the Tucutuco, but with a close general resemblance. The red earth, like that of the Pampas, in which these remains were embedded, contains, according to Professor Ehrenberg,[27] eight fresh-water and one salt-water infusorial animalcule; therefore, probably, it was an estuary deposit.

The remains at Punta Alta were embedded in stratified gravel and reddish mud, just such as the sea might now wash up on a shallow bank. They were associated with twenty-three species of shells, of which thirteen are recent and four others very closely related to recent forms. [...] From the bones of the Scelidotherium, including even the knee-cap, being intombed in their proper relative positions, and from the osseous armour of the great armadillo-like animal being so well preserved, together with the bones of one of its legs, we may feel assured that these remains were fresh and united by their ligaments, when deposited in the gravel together with the shells. Hence we have good evidence that the above enumerated gigantic quadrupeds, more different from those of the present day than the oldest of the tertiary quadrupeds of Europe, lived whilst the sea was peopled with most of its present inhabitants; and we have confirmed that remarkable law so often insisted on by Mr. Lyell,[28] namely, that the "longevity of the species in the mammalia is upon the whole inferior to that of the testacea."[29]

The great size of the bones of the Megatheroid animals, including the Megatherium, Megalonyx, Scelidotherium, and Mylodon, is truly wonderful. The habits of life of these animals were a complete puzzle to naturalists, until Professor Owen lately solved the problem with remarkable ingenuity. The teeth indicate, by their simple structure, that

---

25 An extinct South American mammal with curved teeth
26 Species of rodents indigenous to South America
27 Christian Gottfried Ehrenberg (1795–1876), German naturalist and zoologist
28 Charles Lyell (1797–1875), Scottish geologist and close friend of Darwin
29 A quotation from Lyell's *Principles of Geology* (1830–3)

these Megatheroid animals lived on vegetable food, and probably on the leaves and small twigs of trees; their ponderous forms and great strong curved claws seem so little adapted for locomotion, that some eminent naturalists have actually believed, that, like the sloths, to which they are intimately related, they subsisted by climbing back downwards on trees, and feeding on the leaves. It was a bold, not to say preposterous, idea to conceive even antediluvian trees, with branches strong enough to bear animals as large as elephants. Professor Owen, with far more probability, believes that, instead of climbing on the trees, they pulled the branches down to them, and tore up the smaller ones by the roots, and so fed on the leaves. The colossal breadth and weight of their hinder quarters, which can hardly be imagined without having been seen, become on this view, of obvious service, instead of being an incumbrance: their apparent clumsiness disappears. With their great tails and their huge heels firmly fixed like a tripod on the ground, they could freely exert the full force of their most powerful arms and great claws. Strongly rooted, indeed, must that tree have been, which could have resisted such force! The Mylodon, moreover, was furnished with a long extensile tongue like that of the giraffe, which, by one of those beautiful provisions of nature, thus reaches with the aid of its long neck its leafy food. I may remark, that in Abyssinia[30] the elephant, according to Bruce, when it cannot reach with its proboscis the branches, deeply scores with its tusks the trunk of the tree, up and down and all round, till it is sufficiently weakened to be broken down.

The beds including the above fossil remains, stand only from fifteen to twenty feet above the level of high-water; and hence the elevation of the land has been small (without there has been an intercalated period of subsidence, of which we have no evidence) since the great quadrupeds wandered over the surrounding plains; and the external features of the country must then have been very nearly the same as now. What, it may naturally be asked, was the character of the vegetation at that period; was the country as wretchedly sterile as it now is? As so many of the co-embedded shells are the same with those now living in the bay, I was at first inclined to think that the former vegetation was probably similar to the existing one; but this would have been an erroneous inference for some of these same shells live on the luxuriant coast of Brazil; and generally, the character of the inhabitants of the sea are useless as guides to judge of those on the land. Nevertheless, from the following considerations, I do not believe that the simple fact of many gigantic quadrupeds having lived on the plains round Bahia Blanca, is any sure guide that they formerly were clothed with a luxuriant vegetation: I have no doubt that the sterile country a little southward, near the Rio Negro, with its scattered thorny trees, would support many and large quadrupeds.

That large animals require a luxuriant vegetation, has been a general assumption which has passed from one work to another; but I do not hesitate to say that it is completely false, and that it has vitiated the reasoning of geologists on some points of great interest in the ancient history of the world. The prejudice has probably been derived from India, and the Indian islands, where troops of elephants, noble forests, and impenetrable jungles, are associated together in every one's mind. If, however, we refer to any work of travels through the southern parts of Africa, we shall find allusions in almost every page either to the desert character of the country, or to the numbers of large animals inhabiting it. The same thing is rendered evident by the many engravings which have been published of various parts of the

---

30 Abyssinia, the northern part of present-day Ethiopia

interior. When the Beagle was at Cape Town, I made an excursion of some days' length into the country, which at least was sufficient to render that which I had read more fully intelligible. [...]

The belief that where large quadrupeds exist, the vegetation must necessarily be luxuriant, is the more remarkable, because the converse is far from true. Mr. Burchell[31] observed to me that when entering Brazil, nothing struck him more forcibly than the splendour of the South American vegetation contrasted with that of South Africa, together with the absence of all large quadrupeds. In his Travels, he has suggested that the comparison of the respective weights (if there were sufficient data) of an equal number of the largest herbivorous quadrupeds of each country would be extremely curious. If we take on the one side, the elephant, hippopotamus, giraffe, bos caffer, elan, certainly three, and probably five species of rhinoceros; and on the American side, two tapirs, the guanaco, three deer, the vicuna, peccari, capybara (after which we must choose from the monkeys to complete the number), and then place these two groups alongside each other, it is not easy to conceive ranks more disproportionate in size. After the above facts, we are compelled to conclude, against anterior probability, that among the mammalia there exists no close relation between the *bulk* of the species, and the *quantity* of the vegetation, in the countries which they inhabit. [...]

We know that the extreme regions of North America, many degrees beyond the limit where the ground at the depth of a few feet remains perpetually congealed, are covered by forests of large and tall trees. In a like manner, in Siberia, we have woods of birch, fir, aspen, and larch, growing in a latitude (64°), where the mean temperature of the air falls below the freezing point, and where the earth is so completely frozen, that the carcass of an animal embedded in it is perfectly preserved. With these facts we must grant, as far as *quantity alone* of vegetation is concerned, that the great quadrupeds of the later tertiary epochs might, in most parts of Northern Europe and Asia, have lived on the spots where their remains are now found. I do not here speak of the kind of vegetation necessary for their support; because, as there is evidence of physical changes, and as the animals have become extinct, so may we suppose that the species of plants have likewise been changed.

These remarks, I may be permitted to add, directly bear on the case of the Siberian animals preserved in ice. The firm conviction of the necessity of a vegetation possessing a character of tropical luxuriance, to support such large animals, and the impossibility of reconciling this with the proximity of perpetual congelation, was one chief cause of the several theories of sudden revolutions of climate, and of overwhelming catastrophes, which were invented to account for their entombment. I am far from supposing that the climate has not changed since the period when those animals lived, which now lie buried in the ice. At present I only wish to show, that as far as *quantity* of food *alone* is concerned, the ancient rhinoceroses might have roamed over the *steppes* of central Siberia (the northern parts probably being under water) even in their present condition, as well as the living rhinoceroses and elephants over the *Karros* of Southern Africa.[32]

---

31 William John Burchell (1781–1863), English explorer and naturalist
32 Karros, or Karoo, a semi-arid region in South Africa

Source text

Darwin, Charles, *Journal of the Researches into the Natural History and Geology of the Countries Visited During the Voyage of the H.M.S. Beagle Round the World, Under the Command of Capt. FitzRoy, R.A.* (London: John Murray, 1845), 81–9.

References

Almeida, Joselyn M., *Reimagining the Transatlantic, 1780–1890* (Farnham: Ashgate, 2011).
Schmitt, Cannon, *Darwin and Memory of the Human: Evolution, Savages, and South America* (Cambridge: Cambridge University Press, 2009).

Transatlantic Responses to Nineteenth-Century Cholera Epidemics

Figure 8.2 'At the Gates: Our safety depends upon official vigilance', *Harper's Weekly* 29 (5 September 1885), 592. Courtesy National Library of Medicine [US].

Two scientific articles about cholera epidemics in the British *Lancet* (founded 1823) and US *Scientific American* (founded 1845) demonstrate the rapid transatlantic exchange of nineteenth-century medical research as part of what Christopher Hamlin terms 'the rise of global biomedical science' (Hamlin, 4). Successive waves of cholera began to move from Asia westward in 1817 (Hamlin, 4; Gilbert, 3), leading many to compare cholera to the medieval 'Great Plague' (Gilbert, 2). The fear that cholera inspired remained late into the century (Hamlin, 1), as two of this section's illustrations, 'Back!' (*Punch* magazine, 1892) and 'At the Gates' (*Harper's Weekly*, 1885), confirm. Fears increased because medical experts were so long uncertain of cholera's cause or how it spread. Scientists debated two major theories: miasmic contamination (in twenty-first-century terms, 'community spread') by bad air exacerbated by poor weather conditions, which necessitated quarantine; and poor sanitation, which required reform to maintain clean water and cleanliness (Gilbert, 93–4; Bezio, 64). A death-dealing disease combined with the medical establishment's partial knowledge of how to stop or treat it became a powerful precedent for the global COVID-19 pandemic which began in 2019.

Like later pandemics, nineteenth-century cholera interacted with social conditions. Steam ships and international trade further spread the disease, but quarantines were stoutly resisted by merchants on economic grounds (Gilbert, 2). And transatlantic epidemics negatively impacted race and class (Hamlin, 12; Gilbert, 3; Graham, 63–6). The disease also challenged dominant transatlantic groups because it challenged faith in 'progress' and modernity (Hamlin, 4). Fears and anxiety eased after 1883–4, when Robert Koch isolated this water-borne microbe, proving the sanitationists right after all (Hamlin, 8). But the epidemic left its imprint on the transatlantic history of medicine.

J. Watson (dates unknown)

From 'Cholera in Jamaica. An Account of the First Outbreak of the Disease in That Island' (1851)

The ancient but decayed town of Port Royal consists of perhaps the filthiest collection of hovels, occupied by the filthiest inmates, which the whole civilized world can show. It is built on a peninsula of sand, which is only about two or three feet above the sea level. Any rain that falls soon percolates through the sand; the sea-breezes blow constantly by day, and in general the place is looked upon as salubrious for Jamaica, in spite of its filth. Indeed it is frequently resorted to by invalids from other quarters, for the sake of its fresh sea-breezes. By the last census, the population was between 900 and 1000. The past summer was unusually rainy, and the tides, in the latter part of September and beginning of October, were uncommonly high, two coincident circumstances, which rendered the ground floor of houses damp. It is the practice of the great majority of the natives to sleep on those floors, with nothing more than a mat under them, and commonly in the same rags which they wear during the day. The doors and windows are shut, and from six to twelve persons are thus pent up in a space less than is comprised in the dimensions of a common sitting-room. The temperature in the shade, during the day, has averaged 88° Fahr., and a few degrees lower at night, and the barometer was observed to range lower than usual. The natives, who are of all shades of colour from black to white, but mostly black or dark brown, live chiefly on fish salt or fresh, and large quantities of the crude vegetables of the country, such as yams and plantains. Drunkenness is not particularly their besetting sin.

Everything being thus admirably disposed to encourage the full development of any pestilence, I[33] was, on the 7th of October, requested to see a woman, about fifty years of age; she complained of having been purged the preceding night, and was, when first seen, cold, and had cramps of the extremities. She was also passing upwards and downwards the rice-water-looking fluid characteristic of Asiatic cholera. She died the same day. At this time, no one entertained any suspicion that such a pestilence was hovering over the island. In consideration of the mischief which would be caused by the announcement that cholera had appeared, if it should turn out to be unfounded, the coroner, who was furnished with a written statement of the case, consented to dispense with an inquest.

On the night of the 7th and on the 8th two other persons became affected with similar symptoms, in the same neighbourhood, and died rapidly. After making two post-mortem examinations, I reported formally to the authorities that malignant Asiatic cholera existed in the town. At first the report was received with incredulity, and poo-poo'd; but the danger of the reported calamity was too terrible to permit it to be disregarded. The custos of the parish (I believe this official corresponds with our lord lieutenant of a county) and some medical gentlemen were deputed from Kingston to investigate here, when only the three cases above mentioned had occurred.

I am not quite certain whether they were at once convinced when I detailed the histories of those cases. However, the disease very quickly spread abroad through this town in such a way as to be unmistakable. In less than a month it destroyed upwards of 250 of the inhabitants, or one-fourth of the entire population.

About a week or less after cholera appeared in Port Royal, a few stray cases were reported in Kingston, a large city of 50,000 inhabitants, situated at the head of the harbor. Somewhat later, it was found in Spanish Town, which is the capital, and which is about twelve miles from Kingston inland; and simultaneously the low-lying villages on the plain, and near the margins of this extensive harbor, were most severely attacked. Cholera gradually advanced into the central parts of the island, and is reported to have reached the towns on the north side.

In Kingstown and Spanish Town, which I think might successfully dispute with Port Royal its acknowledged pre-eminence in filth, fœtor,[34] and all unwholesome abominations, and which are so far worse because they are much larger there, in both towns, the mortality has been terrible, but it is yet of unascertained magnitude, and unchecked.

There was of course very soon a general panic. Some said the disease was imported by the medium of contagion; there consequently appeared in many places

---

33 John Watson was already working as Surgeon to the Naval Hospital, Port Royal, Jamaica, when he published this account of the Jamaican cholera outbreak in January 1851. By early 1853 Watson had been promoted to the post of Deputy Medical Inspector in the naval lists.
34 An offensive smell (*OED*)

great unwillingness to attend to the sick, and even difficulty in procuring people to inter the dead. The latter were reported, in many instances, to have been cast away in by-places to get rid of their bodies, and they were only discovered by the John Crows, or carrion crows of the island. Husbands refused to put their hands on the dead bodies of their wives to lift them into coffins, and even mothers deserted their children when the latter took the disease. Such were the mature fruits of teaching the people to believe cholera to be contagious. In Port Royal, where we preach, I believe, a truer and certainly a more comforting belief, the poor people showed no unwillingness to help one another in deep distress.

I do not propose now to attempt a medical history of this epidemic. The symptoms in the persons attacked here were similar to those which I witnessed in Lisbon in 1833, and which are reported to exist in cholera patients in all parts of the world. The treatment has embraced the usual remedies, and they have in most instances been equally ineffectual here as elsewhere after the disease fairly developed itself. My present object is to throw as much light on the statistics of cholera in Jamaica, on this its first visit to the colony, as my opportunities of observation and my abilities will permit me to do.

For many months past, American steamers have been in the custom of touching here and at Kingston on their voyage between New York and Chagres,[35] for the purpose of coaling, receiving and discharging passengers, &c. Their passengers and crews landed, of course, at both places.

About a week before cholera appeared in Port Royal, two young men arrived from Chagres at this place. They reported that their father died of cholera at Chagres shortly before they left. Those two were the only individuals, so far as I can learn, who, about that time, became resident here after returning from Chagres, where cholera was said to exist, and they were suspected to have introduced the disease. They both laboured under common intermittent fever on their debarkation, for which I attended them, and they were soon restored to perfect health, after taking some doses of quinine. No case of cholera has up to this time occurred in their house, nor in the two adjoining houses, right and left of theirs. No ship is known to have arrived in this port with a case of cholera on board, or which has had any one ill of that disease during the voyage from Chagres, or elsewhere, to Port Royal.

The disease exhausted itself here in less than a month from the date of its first appearance. Nine medical officers were assiduously employed for that space of time, day and night, attending to the sick in the fœtid hovels of the town, and in the hospital, not one of whom was seized. There is here a small respectable community, belonging to the church, the navy, and army, who, with their families, are placed in circumstances favourable to health. Not one of them has yet taken cholera, nor any member of their families, although they formed part of a community which was losing one-fourth its number.

In Spanishtown and Kingstown, the well fed and proper housed portion of the inhabitants have not experienced the same immunity, as many of them have died. It may be observed, however, that persons of a similar class here are generally in the prime and vigour of life, as they are necessarily occupied in the performance of duties which could not be discharged at the advanced age to which many of the respectable civilians in the island have attained. Moreover, the persons alluded to here are mostly unmarried, and have therefore less of the class of young children and other predisposed individuals among them.

---

35 The former chief Atlantic port on the isthmus of Panama

On the first outbreak of cholera, the Naval Hospital contained about thirty patients, most of whom were far advanced in convalescence from intermittent fever, which they had contracted in the *Bermuda* schooner, at Grey Town, Nicaragua. One of them died of cholera.

Five days after cholera showed itself, the *Indefatigable* frigate arrived, also from Grey Town. Her crew was sickly, from a similar fever to that with which the *Bermuda*'s people were affected, and it was contracted at the same place. Her men, however, were very weak on their arrival; whereas the crew of the *Bermuda*, as has been just stated, was nearly restored to health.

We are quite accustomed, in this hospital, to the type of fever which generally prevails in ships returning from Nicaragua: it is, when the patients reach this place, usually intermittent, manageable, and curable by proper nourishment, quietude, and medicine. [...]

To recapitulate: *Bermuda*'s people, being nearly restored to health, before cholera appears, lose only one man in hospital by cholera.

Indefatigable comes in when the disease is raging with the utmost virulence in the place, and suffers very severely.

Persian arrives when cholera has ceased, or nearly on shore, and although her patients are exposed to every imaginable source of contagion, they totally escape contamination, and have convalesced as favourably as such patients usually do.

I cannot reconcile those very remarkable and interesting facts with the opinion which a great number of people entertain, that contagion has been the principal agent in the spread of cholera in Jamaica. On the contrary, I think they prove, that if it acted at all, it played only a secondary part, and that some totally different influence mainly directed the march of the present fatal epidemic.

Certain learned Pundits tell us that the contagion of cholera is so virulent as to attach itself in some miraculous way to two lads, who, however, are not themselves attacked; that these two individuals carry their invisible charge through a sea voyage, and then contaminate the whole population of Jamaica. Will they be pleased to explain how it happened, that, if this contagion be so virulent, fifty highly predisposed men were thrust into hospital wards which were still reeking with the emanations from the bodies of cholera patients, and not one of them took cholera!

While the above-mentioned melancholy scenes were being enacted in the town, and in the hospital, the soldiers in the garrison, white and black troops, who with their wives and children amounted to about three hundred individuals, became subject to the disease, and lost in a few days, I think about eighty out of their number. They were marched to Stoney-hill barracks, which at the time was very deficient in sleeping accommodation, and in every way less comfortable than the quarters they left. The march (through a swampy country) of twelve miles or thereabout, was performed under a heavy incessant rain. The change under these adverse circumstances was so beneficial, that the pestilence was checked among them.

Port Royal, Jamaica, Nov. 26, 1850.

'The Fear of Cholera' (1871)

It is said that a merchant, during one of the former visitations of cholera to this country, having become so unduly alarmed as to flee incontinently into the country, closing his place of business during his absence, a wag[36] placed upon the door of the absentee the following notice:

> "Not cholera sick, nor cholera dead;
> But through the fear of cholera fled.
> Will soon return, when cholera's over;
> If from his fright he should recover."

The unreasonable and excessive fear of some people is well ridiculed in the lines above quoted, but such foolish terror differs very widely from the proper caution which should mark the action of public authorities upon the approach of this scourge. Such caution will receive the praise of all intelligent men, for although the nature of the disease is still problematical, and although there are yet wide differences as to its treatment when acquired, there is unanimity of opinion as to the causes which tend to aggravate and increase the disease, the removal of which surely lessens its mortality.

This country has had a scarce defined fear, that the cholera would reach us ere long, and that the ravages it has made in the east would be transferred to our shores. In England the fear of the disease has assumed definite form, and the municipal officers of most of its cities have taken decided action upon the removal of nuisances and the enforcement of cleanliness. In London, the dustmen[37] have been ordered to remove rubbish and refuse twice each week from every house, and daily to clean out every public dust bin, and cart away its contents. Owners or occupiers of houses allowing stagnant water to remain in water closets,[38] etc., are fined ten dollars for each offence, and penalties are imposed upon all who pursue offensive trades after notice to discontinue them. It is also made penal to tolerate common nuisances in houses, or to admit into them live hogs, goats, geese, etc., which has been practiced by some of the lower classes. Butchers who sell stale meat, or dealers in fish or fruit who sell damaged or stale articles, are fined one hundred dollars, and the damaged articles are seized and destroyed.

The commissioners instruct and encourage the people in the free use of disinfectants, and warn them against uncleanly habits. Inspectors are constantly on the lookout for violators of health ordinances, and owners and occupants are exhorted to be more than usually vigilant in the care of their buildings.

This does not look like senseless fright. It is evident the health officers of London apprehend the advent of cholera before long, and are anxious to limit its horrors by every means in their power. The season is too far advanced to admit of much danger from cholera in this country during the present autumn and ensuing winter; but unless its progress shall have been stayed, the next summer will be likely to bring it to our shores. Should this occur, it is to be hoped all our cities, New York city in particular, will be better prepared for its reception than it has been during the recent hot weather, when a walk by either of the two great markets was equal in effect upon sensitive stomachs to a full dose of ipecacuanha,[39] and a trip through some of the tenant house districts was enough to make the stoutest stomach rebel.

---

36 A habitual joker (*OED*)
37 Trash collectors
38 Flush toilets
39 A South American small shrubby plant possessing purgative properties (*OED*)

Source texts

Watson, J., 'Cholera in Jamaica. An Account of the First Outbreak of the Disease in That Island', *Lancet* (11 January 1851), 40–1.

'The Fear of Cholera', *Scientific American* 25.14 (30 September 1871), 215.

References

Bezio, Kelly, 'The Nineteenth-Century Quarantine Narrative', *Literature and Medicine* 31.1 (Spring 2013), 63–90.

Gilbert, Pamela, *Cholera and Nation: Doctoring the Social Body in Victorian England* (Albany, NY: State University of New York Press, 2008).

Graham, Aaron, 'Politics, Persuasion and Public Health in Jamaica, 1800–1850', *History* 104 (2019), 63–82.

Hamlin, Christopher, *Cholera: The Biography* (Oxford: Oxford University Press, 2009).

Figure 8.3 '"Back!"', *Punch* 103 (10 September 1892), 115. Courtesy Mary Couts Burnett Library, TCU.

The Advent of a Transatlantic Communications Network: The Atlantic Cable

From George Wilson (1818–59) 'The Atlantic Wedding-Ring' (1858) and 'Ocean Telegraphy' (1866)

The first signal transmitted across the Atlantic Cable on 5 August 1858 was a defining event to contemporaries, a triumph quickly succeeded by dismay when the initial cable laid across the Atlantic failed due to inadequate gutta percha insulation and wiring. Efforts immediately began to lay a second cable that would permanently establish speedy transatlantic communications, which was accomplished in 1866. This technological landmark anticipated today's electronically connected world and further speeded the travel of news and ideas across the Atlantic.

Acclaimed as Britain's first technology professor, George Wilson, a chemist from Edinburgh, Scotland, was appointed Professor of Technology at the University of Edinburgh and founding director of the Industrial Museum of Scotland in 1855. These appointments charged him with developing a new academic discipline and curating a new museum. Although technology was a new field in Britain, for Wilson 'it was the capacity for technology which gave our species mastery over the environment' (182). Wilson approached technology not as 'an object – in the sense of being a commodity, a piece of technology – but rather a dynamic network in which objects are produced and maintained by the flow of the material and non-material' (Swinney, 180). He illuminated his thoughts by writing about this nineteenth-century technology marvel in poetic form, presenting the scientific advancement of wired communication across an ocean as a symbol of transatlantic unity. However, the unity he imagined was a raced one, denoting a wedding of Anglo-Saxons only.

The new transatlantic communications network, as well as works like Wilson's, inspired a popular genre of transatlantic telegraphic literature consisting of 'innumerable odes and hymns, of which it must be said that, whatever their merit is as poetry, their spirit at least was noble, celebrating the event chiefly as promoting the brotherhood of the human family' (Field, 203).

An excerpt from Wilson's 'Atlantic Wedding-Ring' appears below, followed by the periodical article 'Ocean Telegraphy'.

From 'The Atlantic Wedding-Ring'

IT is customary, in referring to the Atlantic and other submarine Telegraphs, to mention only the submerged cable, as if that constituted the entire telegraph. In reality, however, the cable forms but one-half of the requisite electric circuit, the other and equally essential half being furnished by the ocean. Thus, excluding from consideration the small portions of land occupied above water-mark on either side of the Atlantic, by the station houses nearest the brink of the sea, the cable, some two thousand miles long, conveys the electric current from shore to shore in one direction, and the sea conveys it in the other. Such a double channel must be provided in all telegraphs, and the half supplied by the earth or sea, although it costs nothing, is as important as the insulated metallic half which is so costly to produce, and so difficult to preserve in working order. The Atlantic Telegraph, accordingly, when considered as a link of union between the old and new worlds, cannot be compared to the ordinary wedding-ring, a circle consisting entirely of metal. Its symbol is one of those finger-rings at present out of fashion, where a part only of the circle is gold, the remaining portion consisting of a jewel held between the ends of the golden crescent, and completing the circle. If we suppose the stone in such a ring to be that which jewellers term the "Aqua Marine," we shall have a perfect symbol of a submarine Telegraph.

Since the lines which follow were written, an unexpected derangement of the Atlantic Cable has stopped the working of the telegraph. But even if the worst apprehensions are realised, and no future signal pass along it, it must for ever be sacred in the eyes of the historian and poet. The wedding of the Old and the New World is an accomplished fact, and the thread like wire which conveyed across the Atlantic the Angelic song, as the first greeting from the fatherland, has, in one sense, done its work. Nor is there any reason to doubt that the wise, and brave, and patient men who have so nobly carried out this great enterprise, will before long reap the full reward, as they have already gathered the first-fruits of their labours.

"THE way is far across the sea,
My Daughter,' England said:—
"Thy Land and mine each other love,
'Tis time that they should wed."—
"The way is far across the sea,"
America replied:—
"Thou hast the Bridegroom, Fatherland,
And I the willing Bride."

"Doth any one forbid the bans?
Will any one declare,
Why these should not be wedded,
This long betrothed pair?"

Then rose the nations of the world,
And shouted as one man:—
"Wed, Anglo-Saxons, if ye will?
Wed rather if ye can."

"Who talks of weddings? We forbid
The bans:—The Atlantic gales
That shatter ships, and slaughter men,
And turn to shrouds their sails.
Ho! cease thy vauntings, Bridegroom bold,
And stay thy longings, Bride,
The Wedding-Ring shall never pass
Across the stormy tide."

[…]

Then rose a voice, sweet, soft, and clear;—
The Earth spake to the Sea:—
"I will give half the wedding-ring,
If half is given by thee. My half shall be this costly chain
Of copper and dusky steel,
Woven together, and darkly clad
To last through woe and weal.
It bendeth like a crescent moon:
If thou wilt place between
Its crescent horns, like jewel-stone,
Thy waters, emerald green;—
Then we together shall complete
The wondrous wedding-ring,
Round which the Silent Lightnings
Their voiceless flight shall Wing."

"Thou art a Queen, O Ancient Earth!
And I a King of old;
The Brides of Venice wedded me
With many a ring of gold.
But better far than golden ring,
I'll prize thy darksome chain;
The beryl of my purest depth
Shall help to wed the twain."

"O! promise not too much thou Earth!"
Exclaimed the scornful wind;
"Thy wedding-gift is strong indeed
If I no flaw can find:
And trust thou not too much the Sea,
He is my Vassal-slave:—
His wrathful hands to mar thy gift,
Shall start from every wave."

[…]

Before an eyelid rose and fell,
Ere scarce the words were given,
It could engirdle Earth and Sea
With its lightning-pace of Heaven.

On England's shores through many a day
And night they forged the chain,
A thousand, thousand miles in length
To stretch across the main.
Within the stately battle-ships,
Through many an hour of toil,
Like two great sleeping serpents,

They wound it coil on coil.
One ship was from the Bridegroom-land,
And one was from the Bride,
And so they sailed together
Across the Atlantic Tide.
They steered across the exulting Sea,
Straight for the middle-deep,
That Bridal-land and Bridegroom-land
Their settled tryst might keep.
And there about midsummer-time,
Like lovers who have broken
A ring in twain, and each one-half
Keeps as a troth-plight token
Till they can join the halves again,
They welded fast the link
That wove the kindred coils in one,
And watched the welding sink
Beneath the Sun, the Stars, the Sea,
Till it could sink no more;
And then its prow each good ship turned
Home to its native shore.
One sailed to East, and one to West:
Between, they unwound the chain,
Down deepest ocean-valley
Along the deep sea-plain.
From ship to ship along the line,
Where death and silence dwell,
The voiceless listening went and came,
And signalled "All is well."
Onward by night, onward by day!
They saw arise and set the sun;
They counted all the anxious hours,
And thought their work was done.

[. . .]

The sailed by night, they sailed by day!—
The long betrothed lands
From bridegroom passed to bride the ring
And joined their willing hands.
Loud when the ships had reached each shore,
The cannon spake in thunder;
"Whom God hath joined," they seemed to say,
"Let no man put asunder."
And then around the wondrous ring
The blessed greeting ran,
"Glory to God! On Earth be Peace,
Goodwill to every man."

[. . .]

'Ocean Telegraphy'

Beyond doubt, the event of the present century, and one which will mark an epoch in the world's history, is the discovery of the magnetic telegraph, an account of which, and its inventor, or, more properly speaking, discoverer, we gave in our last number. Dr. Morse,[40] however, in his most sanguine moments, could scarcely have dreamed that the child of his brain and genius would have produced so stupendous a result as the laying of cables by which two continents are brought into instant communication, and bound together by a multitude of ties. Of the importance of this result for the world's good, we may gather an idea from the words of the great American Statesman, Mr. Seaward,[41] who, in congratulating Mr. Cyrus Field on the success of the scheme, said: "If the Atlantic Cable had not failed in 1858, European States (and for the most part they had Southern proclivities) would not have been led, in 1861, into the great error (and this error is, assuredly, now a proven fact) of supposing that civil war in America could either perpetuate African slavery or divide the Republic."

Last week we endeavored to give our readers a notion of the vast extent to which the telegraph wires had been applied. The story, however, of submarine telegraph is even of more absorbing interest.

The first successful submarine telegraph was laid between England and France, a distance of twenty-four miles, in 1850, since which time a number of lines have been laid and satisfactorily worked. No one then dreamed of an Atlantic Cable, and in the development of electrical science then existing, such a dream would have proved wholly illusory. Experiments, however, soon demonstrated the fact that, under certain conditions, currents of electricity could be sent through submerged wires for any distance, and also showed how certain scientific difficulties attending their transmission could be obviated or removed. These facts established, the way for an ocean telegraph was fairly open, and all required were the genius to plan, and the energy and capital to execute. These were happily found, and through the efforts of Mr. Field, who had devoted a large share of attention to the subject, a company was formed in 1854 for the purpose of connecting the Old and New World with an ocean telegraph. In 1858 the cable was stretched across the Atlantic from Ireland to Newfoundland; messages were transmitted, and for a few days everything promised success, when, from some unknown cause, the wires ceased to convey signals, and the project proved a failure. But the possibility and feasibility of the scheme were now demonstrated. Only its details required attention, and it was confidently believed that science and skill could overcome the difficulties in the way of success, and that the actual working of such a line was only a question of time.

That these difficulties were surmounted we have seen by the successful laying of the cable in 1866, which promises commercially to prove to the enterprising share-holders in the company who have found the capital a very Eldorado far exceeding even that of the New River, the shares of which are now of fabulous value.

This success, however, it must be remembered, was gained by the experience earned by more than one failure. To mention the last, in 1865, the cable, after having been paid out 1,040 miles, broke asunder, and became silent at the depth of 2,400

---

40 Samuel Morse (1791–1872), American inventor of the telegraph and Morse code
41 Presumably Frederick W. Seward (1830–1915), son of William Seward (1801–72), respectively the Assistant Secretary and Secretary of State at the time; and Cyrus Field (1819–92), financier who conceived and promoted the venture of the transatlantic cable

fathoms, and for a time the public mind, and capitalists lost all faith in an ultimate success; but – another proof of the power of mind over matter – it came at last, and monarch and president spoke their wondering congratulations to each other through it.

That success, however, astounding as it was, has been since surpassed by a feat, combined of science, perseverance, and capital, that has no peer in the world's history.

Success in laying the cable of the present year giving encouragement to the noble workers, they resolved to snatch it once more out of the very jaws of failure; in other words, to recover the lost cable of 1865, and so, almost at one and the same time to have a double line of communication. That they have done so is now patent to all, and by so doing they have achieved one of those marvelous and matchless feats whose importance it is difficult to estimate, and whose antecedent difficulties it is almost impossible to realize.

The enormous advantages of such a triumph can scarcely be overrated. It shows more than the possibility of merely laying a cable across the floor of the ocean. It shows that if a cable should become damaged, it may be brought again to the surface, and the faulty part rectified. So perfect are the present appliances of electricity that the *locality* of a "fault" is now readily discovered. It is now clearly shown that the breaking of an electric line – even in mid-ocean – is not necessarily a fatal blow to the undertaking. After a year's immersion a severed cable is recovered, spliced, and completed. To go out into the Atlantic and fish for a line as thick as one's thumb, at the depth where the peak of Teneriffe[42] might plant its base, and yet fail to send its summit above the waters, would seem about as hopeless an instance of deep-sea fishing as the mind of man could imagine. [...]

It was no wonder that the public did not believe in the possibility of such an achievement, but now that the thing *has* been done, and we see *how* it has been done, it may always be said that the difficulty has not been overestimated. It has been overcome by men who thought the achievement not impossible, but exceedingly difficult. They could measure the difficulty and adapt their means. They cannot even be called lucky, as having met with fine weather, or happened to hit on the right spot, for they had rather more than their share of gales, and dead calms, and fogs, and drifting currents, accidental failures, drawing of splices, miles of rope lost, twisting of grapnel flukes, breaking of strands, and noiseless slipping of the cable out of hold, no one knew how. The means were in proportion to the end, and were only just sufficient. Here was the largest ship ever built (the Great Eastern),[43] and it was aided by two ships, one of them the Terrible, which once ranked high in the navy. [...]

It was necessary, at last, to sacrifice eighty miles of the cable, and to try a less depth, which, however, proved not much less. Who, indeed, can say that the task was found a bit less difficult than had been supposed when he attempts to realize this struggle with known and unknown difficulties? Think of the sunless skies, the midnight darkness, the loss of bearings, the separations, and the general absence of certain information or safe conjecture in which these ships were dredging for a cable hoped to be still in existence *three miles below* their keels. It was midnight when it made its appearance, as if from another world, and was secured. With this messenger from the deep a communication was immediately opened with fellow-laborers

---

42 The largest of the Canary Islands
43 Designed by engineer Isambard Brunel (1806–59) and built in 1858

sitting on the cliffs of Valentia two thousand miles off, and with all the inhabitants of the civilized world.

Who, after this, dare say there is such a word as *impossible?*

The scene on board the Great Eastern on Sunday morning, September the 2nd, will be for ever memorable; its description reads like the pages of a romance. The Atlantic Cable of 1865 having been at length fished up, the excitement on board was indescribable, but for a time it was doubtful whether it retained its original powers. In the electrician's room awaiting the arrival of the "end," for the purpose of test, were Mr. Gooch, Mr. Cyrus Field, Captain Hamilton, Mr. Canning, Mr. Clifford, Professor Thomson, Mr. Deane, and others.[44] At last Mr. Willoughby Smith, the chief electrician, made his appearance at the door with the end of the cable in his hand, and the connections having been made, he sat down opposite the instrument. A breathless silence prevailed. Not a word was spoken, all eyes being directed upon the operator, whose expression of countenance indicated the deep anxiety he felt in making the test. At the expiration of some ten minutes he relieved their suspense by stating that as far as he had then gone he believed the tests to be perfect; but another minute had scarcely elapsed when he took off his hat and gave a cheer, which, as can be easily understood, was hastily taken up in the room, and having been heard outside, it was echoed from stem to stern of the ship with a heartiness which everyone can appreciate. [...]

How it was received at Heart's Content, the point of junction between the two continents, a view of which we give to our readers, the following, from an eye-witness, may best describe: "The harbor," he says, "of the Heart's Content presented a scene on the evening of Friday, the 27th of July, which will not easily be effaced from the memory of those who witnessed the final triumph of the Atlantic Telegraph Expedition of 1866. Securely anchored in its waters lay the Great Eastern, surrounded by her faithful convoy, while boats of all sizes and kinds flocked about her, laden with the inhabitants, who rushed on board to see the leviathan ship and all her wonders. While this crowd of visitors were on board there was a silent gathering on shore, awaiting the landing of the cable from the Medway by the boats of the Terrible, to which that honor was assigned. [...] The Terrible's crew, accompanied by the leading cable-men, jumped into the water, and there was a hearty and animated struggle between them to see who should first bring the cable on shore." [...]

A salute then was given in honor of Her Majesty of twenty-one guns each from the Great Eastern, Terrible, Niger, and Lily, announcing the landing of the cable, and the cheers which were given on shore were answered by those from the ships, over and over again. Early in the morning, before the Great Eastern entered the harbor, Mr. Gooch had received a reply to the message from the Queen to the President of the United States.

---

44 Daniel Gooch (1816–89), engineer and company head of the newly formed Anglo-American Telegraph Company, who superintended the laying of the original and replacement cables and was knighted in 1866 for his achievement; Captain A. T. Hamilton (dates unknown), Director, Atlantic Telegraph Company; Samuel Canning (1823–1908), Chief Engineer, Telegraph Construction and Maintenance Company, also knighted in 1866 for the achievement of recovering the 1865 cable; Henry Clifford (1821–1905), electrician and Telegraph engineer; William Thomson (1824–1907), mathematician and physicist, holder of the Glasgow Chair of natural philosophy, member of the Telegraph's Consulting Scientific Committee, inventor of instruments for measuring submarine current, who upon being knighted for his role in the 1865 and 1866 cables became better known as Lord Kelvin; and John C. Deane (1816–87), secretary of the Anglo-American Telegraph Company.

Source texts

Wilson, George, 'The Atlantic Wedding Ring', *Blackwood's Edinburgh Magazine* 84 (October 1858), 458-61.
'Ocean Telegraphy', *The London Reader: of literature, science, art and general information* (13 October 1866), 641-2.

References

ANB
Field, Henry, *History of the Atlantic Telegraph* (New York: Charles Scribner, 1869).
Flint, Kate, 'Transatlantic Currents', *American Literary History* 21.2 (Summer 2009), 324–34.
ODNB
Russell, William H., *The Atlantic Cable* (London: Day & Son, Ltd., 1866).
Swinney, George, 'George Wilson's Map of Technology: Giving Shape to the "industrial arts" in Mid-nineteenth-century Edinburgh', *Journal of Scottish Historical Studies* 36.2 (2016), 165–90.

Asa Gray (1810–88)

From 'Review of Darwin's Theory on the Origin of Species by means of Natural Selection' (1860)

A path-breaking American scientist, Gray is considered the founder of American botany. Born in New York, his transatlantic reach included corresponding with and visiting European botanists as well as exchanging plant specimens with them. Gray's most significant correspondence emerged from his support of Charles Darwin's theory of evolution. In 1838, Gray and Darwin reportedly met in England at Kew Gardens. In 1855, the two scientists initiated an epistolary scientific discussion about North American flora and biogeography and continued to correspond until Darwin's death in 1882.

Because of his prominence in American botanical studies, Gray's endorsement of Darwin's theory led most other American naturalists to accept Darwinian evolution as well. Still, Gray's support of Darwin met with religious challenges, given his assertion that 'natural theological' persuasions were compatible with Darwinian natural selection. Gray's review compares Darwin's theory, whereby new species arise due to natural selection, with the theory of species advocated by Louis Agassiz (1807–73), the Harvard Professor of Zoology who resisted the concept of new species through natural (versus supernatural) means (Jordan). Doubly transatlantic in consequence, the review also underscores the rapidity with which new scientific findings circulated transatlantically by 1860.

From 'Review of Darwin's Theory on the **Origin of Species**'

This book is already exciting much attention. Two American editions are announced, through which it will become familiar to many of our readers, before these pages are issued. An abstract of the argument [...] is unnecessary. [...] For the volume itself is an abstract, a prodromus[45] of a detailed work upon which the author has been laboring for twenty years, and which "will take two or three more years to complete." [...] The volume itself [...] is just condensed enough for its purpose. It will be far more widely read, and perhaps will make deeper impression than the elaborate work might have done. [...]

The ordinary and generally received view assumes the independent, specific creation of each kind of plant and animal in a primitive stock, which reproduces its like from generation to generation, and so continues the species. [...] [T]he primordial differences between species and species at their beginning have not been effaced, nor largely obscured, by blending through variation. Consequently, whenever two reputed species are found to blend in nature through a series of intermediate forms, community of origin is inferred, and all the forms, however diverse, are held to belong to one species. Moreover, since bisexuality[46] is the rule in nature (which is practically carried out, in the long run, far more generally than has been suspected), and the heritable qualities of two distinct individuals are mingled in the offspring, it is supposed that the general sterility of hybrid progeny, interposes an effectual barrier against the blending of the original species by crossing.

From this generally accepted view the well-known theory of Agassiz and the recent one of Darwin diverge in exactly opposite directions.

That of Agassiz differs fundamentally from the ordinary view only in this, that it discards the idea of a common descent as the real bond of union among the individuals of a species, and also the idea of a local origin—supposing, instead, that each species originated simultaneously, generally speaking over the whole geographical area it now occupies or has occupied, and in perhaps as many individuals as it numbered at any subsequent period.

Mr. Darwin, on the other hand, holds the orthodox view of the descent of all the individuals of a species not only from a local birth-place, but from a single ancestor or pair; and that each species has extended and established itself, through natural agencies, wherever it could; so that the actual geographical distribution of any species is by no means a primordial arrangement, but a natural result. He goes farther, and this volume is a protracted argument intended to prove that the species we recognize have not been independently created, as such, but have descended, like varieties, from other species. Varieties, on this view, are incipient or possible species: species are varieties of a larger growth and a wider and earlier divergence from the parent stock: the difference is one of degree, not of kind.

The ordinary view—rendering unto Caesar the things that are Caesar's—looks to natural agencies for the actual distribution and perpetuation of species, to a supernatural for their origin.

The theory of Agassiz regards the origin of species and their present distribution over the world as equally primordial, equally supernatural; that of Darwin, as equally derivative, equally natural.

---

45 A book which is introductory or preliminary to another, usually larger, work (*OED*)
46 As used here, the state of having two sexes

The theory of Agassiz, referring as it does the phenomena both of origin and distribution directly to the Divine will [...] may be said to be theistic to excess. The contrasted theory is not open to this objection. Studying the facts and phenomena in reference to proximate causes, and endeavoring to trace back the series of cause and effect as far as possible, Darwin's aim and processes are strictly scientific, and his endeavor, whether successful or futile, must be regarded as a legitimate attempt to extend the domain of natural or physical science. [...] Mr. Darwin thinks that, acting upon an inherent predisposition to vary, [physical influences] have sufficed even to modify the species themselves and produce the present diversity. Mr. Agassiz believes that they have not even affected the geographical range and the actual association of species, still less their forms; but that every adaptation of species to climate and of species to species is as aboriginal, and therefore as inexplicable, as are the organic forms themselves. [...]

We have contrasted these two extremely divergent theories, in their broad statements. It must not be inferred that they have no points nor ultimate results in common.

In the first place they practically agree in upsetting, each in its own way, the generally received definition of species, and in sweeping away the ground of their objective existence in Nature. The orthodox conception of a species is that of lineal descent: all the descendants of a common parent, and no other, constitute a species; they have a certain identity because of their descent, by which they are supposed to be recognizable. [...] But if species were created in numberless individuals over broad spaces of territory, these individuals are connected only in idea, and species differ from varieties on the one hand and from genera, tribes, &c. on the other only in degree; and no obvious natural reason remains for fixing upon this or that degree as specific. [...] Species upon this view are enduring, but subjective and ideal. Any three or more of the human races, for example, are species or not species, according to the bent of the naturalist's mind. Darwin's theory brings us the other way to the same result. In his view, not only all the individuals of a species are descendants of a common parent but of all the related species also. Affinity, relationship, all the terms which naturalists use figuratively to express an underived, unexplained resemblance among species, have a literal meaning upon Darwin's system, which they little suspected, namely, that of inheritance. Varieties are the latest offshoots of the genealogical tree in "an unlineal" order; species, those of an earlier date, but of no definite distinction; genera, more ancient species, and so on. The human races, upon this view likewise may or may not be species according to the notions of each naturalist as to what differences are specific; but, if not species already, those races that last long enough are sure to become so. It is only a question of time. [...]

It may also be noted that there is a significant correspondence between the rival theories as to the main facts employed. Apparently every capital fact in the one view is a capital fact in the other. [...]

The one naturalist, perhaps too largely assuming the scientifically unexplained to be inexplicable, views the phenomena only in their supposed relation to the Divine mind. The other, naturally expecting many of these phenomena to be resolvable under investigation, views them in their relations to one another, and endeavors to explain them as far as he can (and perhaps farther) through natural causes.

But does the one really exclude the other? Does the investigation of physical causes stand opposed to the theological view and the study of the harmonies between mind and Nature? [...] Even if the doctrine of the origin of species through natural selection should prevail in our day, we shall not despair; being confident that the genius of an Agassiz will be found equal to the work of constructing, upon the mental and material foundations combined, a theory of nature as theistic and as scientific, as that which he has so eloquently expounded.

Source text

G[ray]., A[sa]., 'Review of Darwin's Theory on the Origin of Species by means of Natural Selection', *American Journal of Science and Arts*, 2nd series, 29 (May 1860), 153–84.

References

ANB

Dupree, A. Hunter, *Asa Gray: American Botanist, Friend of Darwin* (Baltimore, MD: Johns Hopkins University Press, 1959).

Jordan, David Starr, 'Louis Agassiz', Britannica.com. Web.

Maria Mitchell (1818–89)

Figure 8.4 Bust of Mary Somerville sculpted by Lawrence Macdonald (1884), Vassar College; gift of Frances Power Cobbe. Photograph by Colton Johnson, courtesy of Colton Johnson

'Mrs. Somerville', From Life, Letters, and Journals (1896)

Maria Mitchell (1818–89) in the US and Mary Somerville (1780–1872) in Britain both enjoyed distinguished careers in science despite little formal education; each influenced university education in their respective countries. Somerville College, Oxford, is named for the latter, but only Mitchell made an original contribution to science. Trained by her father in precise, systematic astronomical observations, Mitchell observed a previously unrecorded comet on 1 October 1847 and was awarded a gold medal by the king of Denmark. As a computer (arithmetical calculator) for the *American Ephemeris and Nautical Almanac*, she was the sole US woman to earn an income in science in the 1850s. She was invited to join the faculty of Vassar College, a women's college, in 1865 and continued her astronomical observations and astronomy professorship until ill health forced her resignation in 1888.

When Mitchell met Mary Somerville in 1858, Somerville had achieved renown as a widely read science expositor. Somerville's first book, *The Mechanism of the Heavens*, was published in 1831 and became a required Cambridge University textbook for advanced mechanics. *On the Connection of the Physical Sciences* (1834) and *Physical Geography* (1848), which was the first English language textbook on this subject, followed, earning her a civil list pension. As had Mitchell before her, Somerville went on to earn a gold medal – two, in fact, in 1869, one from the Royal Geographical Society and the other from the Geographical Society of Florence.

Besides Mitchell's reminiscence of meeting Somerville, another artistic production linking the two was the gift to Vassar of a bust of Somerville sculpted in 1844 by Lawrence Macdonald (1799–1878). The gift came from British feminist activist and theologian Frances Power Cobbe (1822–1904) after Mitchell described Vassar College to her. The bust can be seen in the Maria Mitchell Observatory at Vassar College today, testimony not only to two transatlantic women of science but also to transatlantic feminist networks supporting higher education for women.

From Life, Letters, and Journals

"I had no hope, when I went to Europe,[47] of knowing Mrs. Somerville. American men of science did not know her, and there had been unpleasant passages between the savants of Europe and those of the United States which made my friends a little reluctant about giving me letters.

"Professor Henry[48] offered to send me letters, and said that among them should be one to Mrs. Somerville; but when his package came, no such letter appeared, and I did not like to press the matter, – indeed, after I had been in England I was not

---

47 Mitchell's chapters V–VIII detail her 'First European Tour', 1857–8
48 Joseph Henry (1797–1878), physicist and first secretary of the Smithsonian Institution from 1846 until his death

surprised at any amount of reluctance. They rarely asked to know my friends, and yet, if they were made known to them, they did their utmost.

"So I went to Europe with no letter to Mrs. Somerville, and no letter to the Herschels.[49]

"I was very soon domesticated with the Airys,[50] and really felt my importance when I came to sleep in one of the round rooms of the Royal Observatory. I dared give no hint to the Airys that I wanted to know the Herschels, although they were intimate friends. 'What was I that I should love them, save for feeling of the pain?' But one fine day a letter came to Mrs. Airy from Lady Herschel, and she asked, 'Would not Miss Mitchell like to visit us?' Of course Miss Mitchell jumped at the chance! Mrs. Airy replied, and probably hinted that Miss Mitchell 'could be induced,' etc.

"If the Airys were old friends of Mrs. Somerville, the Herschels were older. The Airys were just and kind to me; the Herschels were lavish, and they offered me a letter to Mrs. Somerville.

"So, provided with this open sesame to Mrs. Somerville's heart, I called at her residence in Florence, in the spring of 1858.[51]

"I sent in the letter and a card, and waited in the large Florentine parlor. In the open fireplace blazed a wood fire very suggestive of American comfort – very deceitful in the suggestion, for there is little of home comfort in Italy.

"After some little delay I heard a footstep come shuffling along the outer room, and an exceedingly tall and very old man entered the room, in the singular head-dress of a red bandanna turban, approached me, and introduced himself as Dr. Somerville, the husband.

"He was very proud of his wife, and very desirous of talking about her, a weakness quite pardonable in the judgment of one who is desirous to know. He began at once on the subject. Mrs. Somerville, he said, took great interest in the Americans, for she claimed connection with the family of George Washington.

"Washington's half-brother, Lawrence, married Anne Fairfax, who was one of the Scotch family.[52] When Lieutenant Fairfax was ordered to America, Washington wrote to him as a family relative, and asked him to make him a visit. Lieutenant Fairfax applied to his commanding officer for permission to accept, and it was refused. They never met, and much to the regret of the Fairfax family the letter of Washington was lost. The Fairfaxes of Virginia are of the same family, and occasionally some member of the American branch returns to see his Scotch cousins.

"While Dr. Somerville was eagerly talking of these things, Mrs. Somerville came tripping into the room, speaking at once with the vivacity of a young person. She was seventy-seven years old, but appeared twenty years younger. She was not handsome, but her face was pleasing; the forehead low and broad; the eyes blue; the

---

49 Sir John Frederick William Herschel (1792–1871), astronomer and mathematician, and his wife Lady Margaret (1810–84); John Herschel was elevated to a baronetcy at the coronation of Queen Victoria in 1838 for his groundbreaking discoveries about nebulae.
50 Not yet knighted for his distinguished scientific achievements and service to the crown when Mitchell met him, George Biddle Airy (1801–92) and his wife Richarda (1804–75) resided at Greenwich, where Airy served as astronomer royal from 1835 to 1881 and oversaw the Royal Observatory. Airy had known Herschel since the 1820s.
51 In 1838 Somerville and her husband William (1771–1860), a former army doctor, moved to Italy in the interests of William's health.
52 The details are confirmed by the Mount Vernon digital library in the US: 'Fairfax Family: George Washington's Mount Vernon', Web.

features so regular, that in the marble bust by Chantrey,[53] which I had seen, I had considered her handsome.

"Neither bust nor picture, however, gives a correct idea of her, except in the outline of the head and shoulders.

"She spoke with a strong Scotch accent, and was slightly affected with deafness, an infirmity so common in England and Scotland.

"While Mrs. Somerville talked, the old gentleman, seated by the fire, busied himself in toasting a slice of bread on a fork, which he kept at a slow-toasting distance from the coals. An English lady was present, learned in art, who, with a volubility worthy of an American, rushed into every little opening of Mrs. Somerville's more measured sentences with her remarks upon recent discoveries in *her* specialty. Whenever this occurred, the old man grew fidgety, moved the slice of bread backwards and forwards as if the fire were at fault, and when, at length, the English lady had fairly conquered the ground, and was started on a long sentence, he could bear the eclipse of his idol no longer, but, coming to the sofa where we sat, he testily said, 'Mrs. Somerville would rather talk on science than on art.'

"Mrs. Somerville's conversation was marked by great simplicity; it was rather of the familiar and chatty order, with no tendency to the essay style. She touched upon the recent discoveries in chemistry or the discovery of gold in California, of the nebulae, more and more of which she thought might be resolved, and yet that there might exist nebulous matters, such as compose the tails of comets, of the satellites, of the planets, the last of which she thought had other uses than as subordinates. She spoke with disapprobation of Dr. Whewell's attempt to prove that our planet was the only one inhabited by reasoning beings; she believed that a higher order of beings than ourselves might people them.[54]

"On subsequent visits there were many questions from Mrs. Somerville in regard to the progress of science in America. She regretted, she said, that she knew so little of what was done in our country.

"From Lieutenant Maury, alone, she received scientific papers.[55] She spoke of the late Dr. (Nathaniel) Bowditch with great interest, and said she had corresponded with one of his sons.[56] She asked after Professor Peirce, whom she considered a great mathematician, and of the Bonds, of Cambridge.[57] She was much interested in their photography of the stars, and said it had never been done in Europe. At that time photography was but just applied to the stars. I had carried to the Royal Astronomical Society the first successful photograph of a star. It was that of Mizar and Alcor,[58] in the Great Bear. (Since that time all these things have improved.)

---

53 Francis Legatt Chantrey (1781–1841) sculpted the bust in 1840.
54 William Whewell (1794–1866), historian and philosopher of science, was Master of Trinity College, Cambridge from 1841 until his death. He invented the term 'scientist' in an 1834 review of a book by Somerville. His *Of the Plurality of Worlds* (1853) rejected the possibility of extraterrestrial life.
55 Matthew Fontaine Maury (1806–73), US naval officer and oceanographer
56 Nathaniel Bowditch (1773–1838), a US astronomer and mathematician internationally known for his work on celestial mechanics
57 Benjamin Peirce (1809–80), US mathematician, astronomer and Harvard professor; astronomer father and son William Cranch Bond (1789–1859), director of the Harvard College Observatory, and George Phillips Bond (1825–65), who collaboratively discovered Saturn's satellite Hyperion and Ring C
58 Stars in the constellation also known as the Big Dipper

"The last time I saw Mrs. Somerville, she took me into her garden to show me her rose-bushes, in which she took great pride. Mrs. Somerville was not a mathematician only, she spoke Italian fluently, and was in early life a good musician.

"I could but admire Mrs. Somerville as a woman. The ascent of the steep and rugged path of science had not unfitted her for the drawing-room circle; the hours of devotion to close study have not been incompatible with the duties of wife and mother; the mind that has turned to rigid demonstration has not thereby lost its faith in those truths which figures will not prove. 'I have no doubt,' said she, in speaking of the heavenly bodies, 'that in another state of existence we shall know more about these things.'

"Mrs. Somerville, at the age of seventy-seven, was interested in every new improvement, hopeful, cheery, and happy. Her society was sought by the most cultivated people in the world. [She died at ninety-two.]"[59]

Source text

Mitchell, Maria, *Life, Letters, and Journals*, ed. Phebe Mitchell Kendall (Boston: Lee and Shepard Publishers, 1896).

References

ANB
Bergland, Renée, *Maria Mitchell and the Sexing of Science: An Astronomer Among the American Romantics* (Boston: Beacon Press, 2008).
ODNB

'Professor Morse' (1872)

A transatlantic painter and inventor, Samuel F. B. Morse (1791–1872), along with Leonard D. Gale (1800–83), a professor of chemistry, and Alfred Vail (1807–59), a student at what is now New York University, is credited as co-developing Morse Code and single-wire telegraphy. Morse attended Yale University and had aspirations of becoming a great artist. As detailed in the obituary below, Morse's contributions to telecommunications reached beyond national boundaries, time, land and sea.

'Professor Morse'

Samuel Finley Breese Morse has passed away from amongst us; he died on Tuesday evening, the 2nd of April, at the ripe age of eighty-one. Prof. Morse's name will be for ever so closely associated with the development of the electric telegraph, that we feel it our duty to give some notice, though it be a brief one of his life. He was the son of

---

59 The bracketed sentence was a later addition, presumably Mitchell's given the date of Somerville's death.

the Rev. Jedediah Morse, well known as a geographer, and was born in Charlestown, Massachusetts, on the 27th of April, 1791. Samuel Morse was educated at Yale College, but, having determined to become a painter he came to England in 1811, formed a friendship with Leslie, whose portrait he painted, and in 1813 he exhibited at the Royal Academy a colossal picture of 'The Dying Hercules.'[60] He returned to America and endeavoured to establish himself as a portrait painter, but without much success, until in 1822 he settled in New York, and painted for the corporation a full-length portrait of Lafayette, who was then on a visit to the United States. We find Mr. Morse again in England in 1829, remaining here until 1832, when he returned to his own country. His companion on this voyage was Prof. Jackson, the eminent American chemist and geologist, who was then returning from Paris, where the question of the time occupied in the passage of the electric current through a good conducting wire was occupying the attention of scientific men. From Dr. Jackson Mr. Morse appears to have first learnt that the passage of the electric fluid was absolutely instantaneous, and it occurred to him that it might be used for conveying intelligence from one place to another. The friends of Prof. Morse claim for him, that during the voyage he had written out the general plan of his telegraphic arrangement. In 1835 he certainly placed in the New York University a model of his "Recording Electric Telegraph," and in 1837 he filed his caveat at the Patent Office in Washington. It was not, however, until 1840 that the patent was perfected, and then Prof. Morse set about getting his telegraph used. Four years, however, passed away before he succeeded, the first electric telegraph completed in the United States being the line between Washington and Baltimore, which began to work in 1844. Since that time the recording electric telegraph of Morse has been adopted over the whole country, and at the time of his death there were not less than twenty thousand miles of electric wires, stretching over the States between the Atlantic and Pacific Oceans.

Mr. Morse's first telegraph was a chemical one, the electric current being used to decompose the acetate or carbonate of lead, or turmeric paper moistened with a solution of sulphate of soda. He, however, gave up this arrangement, and adopted the electro-magnetic system instead. This was, however, in his hands, a rather ponderous affair, his electro-magnet weighing 158 pounds, and the instrument was not sufficiently delicate for long distances. Experience enabled Mr. Morse to simplify his arrangements, and his "Simple Morse Circuit" was thought to be so complete, that in 1857 the French Administration of Telegraphs adopted the Morse instrument before all others. The "Morse Code," the "Morse's Transmitting Plate," his "Embosser," and Morse's telegraph worked by induction currents, are sufficient to show how completely the American artist has connected his name with the system of employing electricity to pass as the messenger from man to man, over earth and under the sea.

Source text

'Professor Morse', *The Atheneaum* 2321 (20 April 1872), 500.

References

ADNB
Staiti, Paul, *Samuel F. B. Morse* (Cambridge: Cambridge University Press, 1989).

---

60 Charles Robert Leslie (1794–1859), an English painter

Antoinette Brown Blackwell (1825–1921)

'Sex and Evolution', From The Sexes Throughout Nature (1875)

In *The Sexes Throughout Nature* (1875), American Antoinette Brown Blackwell presented the earliest feminist critique of Charles Darwin. Darwin had positioned women as inferior to men in *The Descent of Man* (1871); similarly, Herbert Spencer contended in *The Principles of Biology* (1864–7) that women's physiological development was compromised by their necessary diversion of bodily resources to their reproductive systems. Blackwell's opening chapter in her book, 'Sex and Evolution', explicitly charges Darwin and Spencer with male bias; their standpoints as men rather than any verifiable scientific evidence, she claims, underlay their prejudicial assertions about women.

Blackwell was not a scientist but a feminist intellectual and activist who had directly encountered male bias and exclusion at Oberlin College, where she matriculated in 1846 and became the friend of activist Lucy Stone (1818–93). After earning a degree in literature Brown studied theology for three years but was denied a degree and even regular enrollment in courses required for those planning to enter the ministry. She triumphed nonetheless, first being hired as a Congregationalist minister in Butler, New York and then becoming the first female ordained minister in the US (1853). Later still Oberlin conferred honorary Ministry and Doctorate of Divinity degrees on her in the early twentieth century.

Blackwell turned to writing after doubts about religious orthodoxy led her to resign her pulpit. She then met and married activist reformer Samuel Blackwell in 1853 and gave birth to seven children, five of whom—all daughters—survived. Blackwell was also an ardent abolitionist and suffragist and supporter of temperance. She lived long enough to cast her first vote in a presidential election in 1920.

'Sex and Evolution'

The Statement.

It is the central theory of the present volume that the sexes in each species of beings compared upon the same plane, from the lowest to the highest, are always true equivalents – equals but not identicals in development and in relative amounts of all normal force. This is an hypothesis which must be decided upon the simple basis of fact.

If the special class of feminine instincts and tendencies is a fair offset in every grade of life to corresponding masculine traits, this is a subject for direct scientific investigation. It is a question of pure quantity; of comparing unlike but strictly measureable terms. In time it can be experimentally decided, and settled by rigidly mathematical tests. We do not weigh lead and sunbeams in the same balance; yet the *savants*[61] can estimate their equivalent forces on some other basis than avoirdu-pois.[62] So if the average female animal is the natural equivalent of the average male of its own type in the whole aggregate of their differentiated qualities, science, by turning concentrated attention to this problem, and applying the adequate tests, can yet demonstrate this fact beyond controversy.

Or if the male is everywhere the established superior, then science in time can undoubtedly affirm that truth upon a basis of such careful and exact calculation that every opponent must learn to acquiesce.

But the question is still very far from reaching the point of accurate solution. It is decided on both sides by inferences drawn from yet untested data.

Nor is it in any way dependent upon the hypothesis of Evolution or upon any phase of that hypothesis. The leopard and the leopardess either are or are not mathematical equivalents when fairly estimated as to all their powers and capacities, physical and psychical. No question as to their origin or their mode of growth can affect that equation.

But each writer can best treat of any subject from his own standpoint, and hence, in the present paper, the equivalence of the sexes is considered in the light of certain theories of development.

Mr. Spencer and Mr. Darwin, the accredited exponents of Evolution, are both constructive reasoners.[63] Each, with a special line of investigation, is intent upon the unfolding of related facts and conclusions; and every fresh topic is destined to be examined as to its bearing upon the central points of *the system*.

Any positive thinker is compelled to see everything in the light of his own convictions. The more active and dominant one's opinions, the more liable they must be to modify his rendering of related facts – roping them inadvertently into the undue service of his theories. Add to this the immense concentrated work which both these famous investigators have undertaken for years past, and one may readily understand that on certain points to which they have not given special attention, these great men may be equally liable with lesser ones to form mistaken judgments. When, therefore, Mr. Spencer argues that women are inferior to men because their development must be earlier arrested by reproductive function, and Mr. Darwin claims that males have evolved muscle and brains much superior to females, and entailed their pre-eminent qualities chiefly on their male descendants, these conclusions need not be accepted without question, even by their own school of evolutionists.

Men see clearly and think sharply when their sympathies are keenly enlisted, but not otherwise. But neither of these high authorities evinces the least vital inter-est in the dogma of male superiority. Smaller men, who are not pre-eminent over the majority of their own sex, might glory in the relative inferiority of the other. But here there seems to be but small temptation to narrow-mindedness. They accept the theory as a foregone conclusion. Of course they are bound to regard it philosophically when it is thrust upon their attention, and to ground it, like every other fact, upon a common scientific basis. But they both content themselves by pushing forward a few stones of strength, wedging them hastily into their places as underpinning, and leaving them there without being welded together by the cement

---

61 Extremely learned or scholarly persons (*OED*)
62 Standard measure of weight
63 British social theorist Herbert Spencer (1820–1903) and scientist Charles Darwin (1809–82); Spencer coined the phrase 'the survival of the fittest'.

of long and intent thinking. It is the more annoying therefore, that we should be called on to accept their conclusions on this point, because of their great authority in closely related departments to which they have given almost exclusive attention.

When "Social Statics" was written, Mr. Spencer had some belief in the equivalence of the sexes.[64] Reverting to First Principles, he became so intent on evolving a *system*, that *woman's place in nature* fell out of perspective in his thoughts.[65] The subject must have seemed of too little importance to require long and laborious investigation. The four weighty volumes of Biology and Psychology all indicate that his attention was absorbed elsewhere; but in a line often running so marvellously near to that of the relation of the sexes, as affected by evolution, that he very narrowly missed giving it his fullest recognition.[66]

In a subsequent paper on the "Psychology of the Sexes," Mr. Spencer does give us a strong, clearly-lined statement of his position; but the further exposition of it is brief and, for him, only feebly sustained.[67] Now, as Mr. Spencer never yet woke up to any topic around which he was not able to recognize a thousand side considerations, all tending to special modifications of the main conclusion, it is apparent that he has not yet aroused his energies to an adequate consideration of this question. It is analogically certain that, otherwise, he never would have attempted to crowd the discussion into half-a-dozen brief pages.

Mr. Darwin, also, eminently a student of organic structures, and of the causes which have produced them, with their past and present characters, has failed to hold definitely before his mind the principle that the difference of sex, whatever it may consist in, must itself be subject to *natural selection* and to evolution. Nothing but the exacting task before him of settling the Origin of all Species and the Descent of Man, through all the ages, could have prevented his recognition of ever-widening organic differences evolved in two distinct lines.[68] With great wealth of detail, he has illustrated his theory of how the male has probably acquired additional masculine characters; but he seems never to have thought of looking to see whether or not the females had developed equivalent feminine characters.

The older physiologists not only studied nature from the male standpoint – as, indeed, they must chiefly, being generally men – but they interpreted facts by the accepted theory that the male is the representative type of the species – the female a modification preordained in the interest of reproduction, and in that interest only or chiefly. To them, physiology was an adjunct of the special creation theory. They believed that Sovereign Power and Wisdom had created one vessel to honor, and the other to dishonor. Evolutionists depart widely from this time-honored basis. But how are we to understand the want of balance in their interpretation of natural methods? It is difficult to perceive what self-adjusting forces, in the organic world, have developed men everywhere the superiors of women, males characteristically the superiors of females.

Other things equal, children of the same parents must begin embryo life on the same plane. As many successive stages of growth have arisen between primordial forms and women, as between these and men. Mr. Spencer reasons, that the cost

---

64 *Social Statics* was published in 1851.
65 An allusion to Spencer's *First Principles* (1862)
66 *The Principles of Psychology* (1855); revised and enlarged as *The Principles of Psychology* (1870, 1872); *The Principles of Biology* (volume 1, 1864; volume 2, 1867)
67 See Spencer, 'The Psychology of the Sexes', *Popular Science Monthly* 4 (November 1873), 30–8.
68 Darwin's *Origin of Species* (1859) and *The Descent of Man* (1871)

of reproduction being greater for the female than the male, female development is earlier arrested in proportion. Hence woman can never equal men, physically or mentally.

Mr. Darwin's theory of Sexual Selection supposes that a male superiority has been evolved in the male line, and entailed chiefly to the male descendants. The females, sometimes, inherit characters originally acquired by the males; but this form of evolution is carried forward principally from father to son, from variety to variety, and from species to species, beginning with the lowest unisexual beings and continuing upwards to man. With a few inconsiderable exceptions, the more active progressive male bears off the palm, among all higher animals in size, and among all animals high and low, in development of muscles, in ornamentation, in general brightness and beauty, in strength of feeling, and in vigor of intellect. Weighed, measured, or calculated, the masculine force always predominates.

Possibly the cause to which Mr. Spencer assigns the *earlier arrest of feminine development* may be alleged as the sufficient reason for Mr. Darwin's *male evolution*. At any rate, Mr. Spencer scientifically *subtracts from the female*, and Mr. Darwin as scientifically *adds to the male*. The inequality between them is steadily increasing along the whole length of all the internodes;[69] and it seems to grow both upwards and downwards, as plants do, from all the nodes. Unless it meet with a check in some unknown law, the causes which originally superinduced the inequality between the sexes must continue to increase it to a degree which it is startling to contemplate!

These philosophers both believe that inheritance is limited in a large degree to the same sex, and both believe in mathematical progression. Where, then, is male superiority to end? Are all the races, because of it, threatened with decadence and death somewhere in the remote future? Or must the time arrive when inferior males will be systematically chosen, and the superior ones thus eliminated from existence? But would this be Evolution? Moreover, if we must fall back upon certain natural checks which will be able in the future to prevent too great an inequality between the sexes, it cannot be preposterous to suppose that in the past and in the present similar natural checks always have been, and still are, in active operation. These, from the beginning, may have been able, progressively, to maintain a due balance, an approximate equilibrium and equivalence of forces, between the males and females of each species, as it has been successively evolved. To point out the nature of these functional checks, to show that they have produced many various structural modifications in different species, corresponding in each with varying habits and development, but all tending to maintain a virtual equivalence of the sexes, is the aim of the present paper.

The facts of Evolution may have been misinterpreted, by giving undue prominence to such as have been evolved in the male line; and by overlooking equally essential modifications which have arisen in the diverging female line. It is claimed that average males and females, in every species, always have been approximately equals, both physically and mentally. It is claimed that the extra size, the greater beauty of color, and wealth of appendages, and the greater physical strength and activity in males, have been in each species mathematically offset in the females by corresponding advantages – such as more highly differentiated structural

---

69 Structures located between two nodes or joints (*OED*)

development; greater rapidity of organic processes; larger relative endurance, dependent upon a more facile adjustment of functions among themselves, thus insuring a more prompt recuperation after every severe tax on the energies. It is claimed that the stronger passional force in the male finds its equivalent in the deeper parental and conjugal affection of the female; and that, in man, the more aggressive and constructive intellect of the male, is balanced by a higher intellectual insight, combined with a greater facility in coping with details and reducing them to harmonious adjustment, in the female. It is also claimed that in morals – development still modified by the correlative influences of sex – unlike practical virtues and vices and varied moral perceptions, must still be regarded as scientific equivalents.

All characters, being equally transmitted to descendants of both sexes, may remain undeveloped in either, or may be developed subject to sexual modifications; and yet, as a whole, the males and females of the same species, from mollusk up to man, may continue their related evolution, as true equivalents in all modes of force, physical and psychical. If this hypothesis can be shown to have a sufficient basis in nature, then Mr. Spencer and Mr. Darwin are both wrong in the conclusion that, in the processes of Evolution, man has become the superior of woman.

I do not underrate the charge of presumption which must attach to any woman who will attempt to controvert the great masters of science and of scientific inference. But there is no alternative! Only a woman can approach the subject from a feminine standpoint; and there are none but beginners among us in this class of investigations. However great the disadvantages under which we are placed, these will never be lessened by waiting. And are there any who will read this paper, and yet feel that it deals with a class of topics improper for a woman to investigate, and still more unfitting for her to discuss before the public? Not among men of science, surely; but in the appeal to a popular audience, one may expect to meet some remnant of this sentiment. Then, in the graver phases of relations which may involve modesty, I can but appeal to the old motto of chivalry – *Honi soit qui mal y pense*.[70] Psychology and physiology are inseparable. Who can escape from the first requisite of knowledge – "know thyself?"

Source text

Blackwell, Antoinette Brown, *The Sexes Throughout Nature* (New York: G. P. Putnam's Sons, 1875).

References

ANB
Cazden, Elizabeth, *Antoinette Brown Blackwell: A Biography* (Old Westbury, NY: Feminist Press, 1983).
Deutscher, Penelope, 'The Descent of Man and the Evolution of Woman', *Hypatia* 19.2 (2004), 35–55.

---

70 The maxim 'may he be shamed who thinks badly of it'

P. E. C.

'Facts and Theories' (1876)

The Quaker doctrine of 'continuous revelation' (Hamm, 132), which held that the inner light of revelation begun in Christ's time continued into the present, meant that transatlantic Quakers not only contributed to science but often approached scientific discoveries as continuing revelations of God manifested in nature. The article below from *Friends' Review* registers the transatlantic debate between nineteenth-century geologists and physicists about the earth's age. Evolutionists emphasised gradual, continuous change through uplift and erosion established by geologists ('uniformitarianism'), which required a hugely ancient earth to account for contemporary geological formations. Within this framework, evolution was also ancient.

The new nineteenth-century science of thermodynamics suggested a younger earth. Germans Rudolph Clausius (1822–88), Hermann von Helmholtz (1821–94) and others had formulated the first and second law of thermodynamics. The first, the conservation of energy, was a reassuring principle that nothing was lost, only transformed into another energy state. The second, known originally as the 'dissipation theory' (Neswald, 15) and today as entropy, posited heat death, the gradual loss of heat or energy within a system. This implied as a corollary the eventual death of the sun and hence earth itself, and also had implications for steam-driven technologies, which needed constant restoking from coal, a finite resource. Because the earth was hot at its formation and had to lose heat before life could arise, physicists argued for more recent development of life forms. Besides referencing this debate, 'Facts and Theories' demonstrates that among transatlantic believers, science and religion did not necessarily form binaries (see Woods Hutchinson, *The Gospel According to Darwin* [1898], RS). The article additionally underscores the importance of travel to nineteenth-century scientists, since 'Darwin's Bulldog' Thomas Henry Huxley (1825–95), the Englishman so named for his fierce defence of Darwin, presented lectures on evolution in New York in mid-September 1876 (Jensen, 191–2).

FACTS AND THEORIES

An interesting discussion is now going on between the geologists and the physicists, as to the possible age of our globe. The testimony of the rocks is thought to indicate a series of changes which would require hundreds of millions of years for their accomplishment, while it is claimed, on the other hand, that the laws of thermodynamics and the indications of astronomy will not admit of a greater period than fifteen million years.

The discussion is important, not only from the zeal and ability of the men who are engaged in it, but also on account of the evidence it gives of the limitations of science. In these fertile days of invention and discovery, our curiosity, our fondness for novelty, and our admiration of talent or genius, incline us to accept all the teachings of sanguine investigators as authoritative. We may, therefore, often overlook the important distinction between facts, which are God's truths, and theories or interpretations, which are fallible, like their inventors.

Every new fact should be gladly welcomed, come from what source it may. The gatherers of facts, men like Tyndall[71] and Darwin and Huxley, are doing better service than they know, to religious as well as to physical culture, by their earnest and honest study of the inscriptions in the book of nature. It is true that the service would be still greater, if their understandings were opened to perceive and proclaim the greatest of all facts, that the Word which speaks from the rocks and from the stars is the All-Creative Word, "and the Word was made flesh, and dwelt among us (and we beheld His glory, the glory of the only begotten of the Father), full of grace and truth."[72] If it is too much to expect that men who are devoted to special lines of physical study, should also hold themselves open to spiritual influences, it is not too much to ask that those who deny our right to judge of facts which we can only imperfectly comprehend, should not attempt to judge of matters which are beyond their own comprehension.

Prof. Huxley's recent lectures furnish pertinent illustrations of the views here expressed. His presentation of some of the most important facts which have been elicited by modern research, is admirable; his display of caution in confessing the incompleteness of his evidence is commendable; his inference that the facts which he has collected point to some kind of evolution, as an important method in the plans of Divine wisdom, is reasonable; his utter repudiation of the doctrine that the universe was made or is governed by chance, is in entire accordance with the views of the ablest scientists of our day; his acknowledgment of his own unfitness for Biblical exegesis, is praiseworthy. But the tacit sarcasm of his occasional thrusts at real or supposed opponents, is two-edged, and may be readily turned against himself. Take, for example, the following extract from his first New York Lecture:—

"If we are to listen to them we must believe that what seem so clearly defined as days of creation—as if very great pains had been taken that there should be no mistake—that these are not days at all, but periods that we may make just as long as convenience requires. We are also to understand that it is consistent with that phraseology to believe that plants and animals may have been evolved by natural processes, lasting for millions of years, out of similar rudiments. A person who is not a Hebrew scholar can only stand by and admire the marvellous flexibility of a language which admits of such diverse interpretations." [Applause and laughter.][73]

It is easy to excite "applause and laughter" in a sympathizing audience, but it is not always easy to justify them after seasons of cool reflection. Is it any disparagement to science, that its observations not only admit, but even seem to require, "such diverse interpretations" as the geological and the astronomical limitations of time, or that physical estimates of solar heat should range between a few thousands and a few millions of degrees? Are the varying standards of scientific orthodoxy,

---

71 British physicist John Tyndall (1820–93) translated the papers on thermodynamics by Clausius and Helmholtz in 1851 and 1854 respectively, making them available to the Anglophone world.
72 John 1: 14
73 The New York *Times* and *Tribune* printed Huxley's lectures given on the nights of 18, 20 and 22 September (Jensen, 191).

which claim homage to Agassiz as the infallible pontiff to day,[74] and to Darwin to morrow, any evidence that there is no such thing as scientific truth? If a record is so flexible as to be always abreast, or in advance of the most advanced research, is not its adaptability to all possible progress an evidence of supernatural origin?

Many of us can remember the various phases of geological speculation, from the one which regarded fossils as "sports"[75] of nature, to the one which finds in them indications of a blind, unknowing, and yet wondrously skilful law of evolution. In like manner we have seen changes, though far less marked, in some details of Biblical interpretation. The world moves, and it is quite as important that our religious insight should expand with the growth of our religious experience, as that our scientific insight should expand with the growth of our scientific experience.

The truths of revelation, whether they are thrilled through the inmost recesses of our souls for our personal guidance, or written in the sacred volume "that the man of God may be perfect, thoroughly furnished unto all good works,"[76] or displayed in the heights and depths of heaven and earth for the instruction and elevation and sanctification of our intellects, are all as eternal as their Author. Past ages have never fully comprehended them, but He who stands at the door and knocks has always sufficiently enlightened those who have opened their hearts to Him. We have no reason to believe that we are wiser in our own generation than our fathers were in theirs, or that we can arrive at such partial apprehension of truth as we need, except through the help of Him who is "the Way, the Truth, and the Life."[77] But as He is unchangeable, and as all truth is His truth, it becomes us to keep our minds childlike and teachable, striving to avoid the arrogance of prejudice and one-sidedness, accepting and welcoming all the facts of faith and science, and praying that their interpretation may be blessed to the glory of Him who is over all.

P. E. C.

Source text

P. E. C., 'Facts and Theories', *Friends' Review: A Religious, Literary and Miscellaneous Journal* 30.10 (21 October 1876), 145– 6.

References

Hamm, Thomas D., *The Quakers in America* (New York: Columbia University Press, 2003).

Jensen, J. V., 'Thomas Henry Huxley's Lecture Tour of the United States, 1876', *Notes and Records of the Royal Society of London* 42.2 (July 1988), 181–95.

Meisel, Martin, 'On the Age of the Universe', *Britain, Representation, and Nineteenth-Century History*, Web.

Neswald, Elizabeth, 'Saving the World in the Age of Entropy: John Tyndall and the Second Law of Thermodynamics', in Bernard Lightman and Michael S. Reidy (eds), *The Age of Scientific Naturalism: Tyndall and His Contemporaries* (Pittsburgh, PA: Pittsburgh University Press, 2016), 15–31.

---

74 Louis Agassiz (1807–73), Harvard biologist who opposed Darwin's theory of the origin of species; see Asa Gray's review of *On the Origin of Species* in this section.

75 A 'freak' or 'curiosity' of nature (*OED*)

76 2 Timothy 3: 17

77 John 14: 6

Walt Whitman (1819–92)

'ORIGINS – Darwinism — (Then Furthermore.)', Two Rivulets (1876)

In Horace Traubel's record of conversations late in Whitman's life, Traubel recorded, 'W. spoke tenderly of Darwin. Darwin is one of his loves that will last' (Traubel, 3: 166). Whitman may have initially absorbed evolutionary ideas from Jean-Baptiste Lamarck (1744–1829), but once Darwin had published *On the Origin of Species* (1859) Whitman assigned Darwin a central place in his thought and writings. Acting as both 'Poet' and 'Priest' (terms he uses in his essay), Whitman seeks to merge science and metaphysics. Whitman also referenced his commitment to an overarching fusion of spirit, body, science, poetry and democracy in a conversation dated 31 July 1888 by Traubel:

> I quoted something Huxley said about evolution—that he did not hold it as a dogma but as a working hypothesis. W. exclaimed: "It is beautiful—beautiful—such a confession as that: the most glorious and satisfying spiritual statement of the nineteenth century. Can the churches, the priests, the dogmatists, produce anything to match it? How can we ever forget Darwin? Was ever a great man a more simple man than Darwin? Was ever a beautiful character a more simple character than Darwin? He was one of the *acme* men—he was at the top. I could hope for no better fate for my book than that it should grow strong in so beneficent an atmosphere—breathe the breath of its life" (Traubel, 2: 65)

The title *Two Rivulets* refers to Whitman's poetry and prose and signals Whitman's innovative printing style in this slender volume: his verse appears in the top halves of pages, his prose below, the two separated by a wavy line suggestive of a river.

'ORIGINS – Darwinism'

Running through prehistoric ages—coming down from them into the day-break of our records, founding theology, suffusing literature, and so brought onward—(a sort of verteber[78] and marrow to all the antique races and lands, Egypt, India, Greece, Rome, the Chinese, the Jews, &c., and giving cast and complexion to their art, poems, and their politics as well as ecclesiasticism, all of which we more or less inherit,) appear those venerable claims to origin from God himself, or from Gods and Goddesses—ancestry from divine beings of vaster beauty, size and power than ours ... But in current and latest times, the theory of human origin that seems to

---

78 American term (now obsolete) for vertebra

have most made its mark, (curiously reversing the antique) is, that we have come on, originated, developt, from monkeys, baboons ... a theory more significant perhaps in its indirections, or what it necessitates, than it is even in itself.

(Of the foregoing speculations twain, far apart as they seem, and angrily as their conflicting advocates to-day oppose each other, are not both theories to be possibly reconciled, and even blended? Can we, indeed, spare either of them? Better still, out of them, is not a Third Theory, the real one, or suggesting the real one, to arise?)

Of this old theory, Evolution, as broach'd anew, trebled, with indeed all-devouring claims, by Darwin, it has so much in it, and is so needed as a counterpoise to yet widely prevailing and unspeakably tenacious, enfeebling superstitions—is fused, by the new man, into such grand, modest, truly scientific accompaniments—that the world of erudition, both moral and physical, cannot but be eventually better'd and broaden'd from its speculations—from the advent of Darwinism. Nevertheless, the problem of origins, human and other, is not the least whit nearer its solution. In due time the Evolution theory will have to abate its vehemence, cannot be allow'd to dominate every thing else, and will have to take its place as a segment of the circle, the cluster—as but one of many theories, many thoughts, of profoundest value—and re-adjusting and differentiating much, yet leaving the divine secrets just as inexplicable and unreachable as before—may-be more so.

Then furthermore—What is finally to be done by Priest or Poet—and by Priest or Poet only—amid all the stupendous and dazzling novelties of our Century, with the advent of America, and of Science and Democracy—remains just as indispensable, after all the work of the grand astronomers, chemists, linguists, historians, and explorers, of the last hundred years—and the wondrous German and other metaphysicians of that time—and will continue to remain, needed, America and here, just the same as in the World of Europe or Asia, of a hundred, or a thousand, or several thousand years ago. I think indeed more needed, to furnish statements from the present points, the added arriere,[79] and the unspeakably immenser vistas of to-day ... Only the Priests and Poets of the modern, at least as exalted as any in the past, fully absorbing and appreciating the results of the past, in the commonalty of all Humanity, all Time, (the main results already, for there is perhaps nothing more, or at any rate not much, strictly new, only more important modern combinations, and new relative adjustments,) must indeed recast the old metal, the already achiev'd material, into and through new moulds, current forms ... Meantime, the highest and subtlest and broadest truths of modern Science wait for their true assignment and last vivid flashes of light—as Democracy waits for its—through first-class Metaphysicians and Speculative Philosophs[80]—laying the basements and foundations for those new, more expanded, more harmonious, more melodious, freer American Poems.

Source text

Whitman, Walt, *Two Rivulets* (Camden, NJ: Author's edition, 1876).

References

Traubel, Horace. *With Walt Whitman in Camden*, volume 2 (New York: D. Appleton & Co., 1908).

---

79 Behind the times, backward
80 Philosophers, a term especially associated with the rationalists preceding the French Revolution

Traubel, Horace. *With Walt Whitman in Camden*, volume 3 (New York: Mitchell Kennerley, 1914).

Wong, Hertha D. '"This Old Theory Broach'd Anew": Darwinism and Whitman's Poetic Program', *Walt Whitman Quarterly Review* 5.4 (1988), 27–39.

Walt Whitman (1819–92)

Section 31, 'Song of Myself', Leaves of Grass (1855; rpt. 1881)

Section 31 of 'Song of Myself' registers the impact on Whitman's poetry of new findings by British scientist Charles Lyell (1797–1875), whose *Principles of Geology* (1830–3) posited uniform geological processes acting on the formation and erosion of the earth's surface over millennia. His poem's relation to geology is especially evident in Whitman's references to gneiss (a metamorphic rock), coal (a carbon mineral formed principally from former plant life beneath the earth's surface), 'plutonic rocks' (also formed beneath the earth's surface) and the extinct mastodon's fossil remains ('powder'd bones'). The general sense in Section 31 of a universe of organic and non-organic forms in constant process also harmonised with Darwin's subsequent theory of evolution (cf. Whitman's 'Darwinism'). The source text of Whitman's section, an 1881 London imprint, also registers Whitman's British readership. Though Whitman remained a controversial figure in North America and Great Britain to the end of his life due to his bold experimentalism and sexual candour, as early as 1868 William Michael Rossetti (1829–1919), brother to Christina (1830–94), published a circumspectly edited volume of Whitman's poetry. By 1881 Whitman's copyright edition could be published in London without editorial precautions.

Section 31, 'Song of Myself'

> I believe a leaf of grass is no less than the journey-work of the stars,
> And the pismire[81] is equally perfect, and a grain of sand, and the
> egg of the wren,
> And the tree-toad is a chef-d'oeuvre[82] for the highest,
> And the running blackberry would adorn the parlors of heaven,
> And the narrowest hinge in my hand puts to scorn all machinery,
> And the cow crunching with depress'd head surpasses any statue,
> And a mouse is miracle enough to stagger sextillions of infidels.
>
> I find I incorporate gneiss, coal, long-threaded moss, fruits, grains,
>   esculent[83] roots,
> And am stucco'd with quadrupeds and birds all over,

---

81 Ant (*OED*)
82 Masterpiece (*OED*)
83 Edible (*OED*)

And have distanced what is behind me for good reasons,
But call any thing back again when I desire it.

In vain the speeding or shyness,
In vain the plutonic[84] rocks send their old heat against my approach,
In vain the mastodon retreats beneath its own powder'd bones,
In vain objects stand leagues off and assume manifold shapes,
In vain the ocean settling in hollows and the great monsters lying
    low,
In vain the buzzard houses herself with the sky,
In vain the snake slides through the creepers and logs,
In vain the elk takes to the inner passes of the woods,
In vain the razor-bill'd auk[85] sails far north to Labrador,
I follow quickly, I ascend to the nest in the fissure of the cliff.

Source text

Whitman, Walt, *Leaves of Grass* (London: David Bogue, 1881).

Reference

Blodgett, Harold, *Walt Whitman in England* (Ithaca, NY: Cornell University Press, 1934).

Louis Jackson (1843–?)

From Our Caughnawagas in Egypt *(1885)*

Figure 8.5 'Louis Jackson, Captain of the Contingent', frontispiece,
Our Caughnawagas in Egypt (Montreal: Wm. Drysdale & Co., 1885).
Courtesy Toronto Public Library.

---

84 Rocks formed by the action of heat at great depths in the earth's crust (*OED*)
85 A sea bird specific to North America

The science of navigation was essential to transatlantic oceanic travel and British imperialism. Louis Jackson's *Our Caughnawagas in Egypt* reveals Canadian Mohawks' participation in both transatlantic travel and an imperial expedition in 1884–5. First Nations author Louis Jackson was an Iroquois Mohawk born in Kahnawake (Caughnawaga in Jackson's narrative) across the St Lawrence river from Montreal. At the age of forty-one he led a contingent of fifty-six Mohawk voyageurs, or boatmen, as their captain (Benn, 205) on an expedition up the Nile to relieve Khartoum in Sudan.

Egypt controlled the Sudan until the 1880s, when Britain invaded Egypt, ostensibly to eradicate its notorious slave trade, and subsequently governed Egypt as a protectorate until 1956. British and its allied Egyptian and Sudanese forces were themselves attacked in the early 1880s by followers of El Mahdi, the son of a Nile boat builder who claimed descent from Muhammad and fought to reinstate Islamic law as practised in Muhammad's time. Backed by troops committed to that religious aim, the Mahdi conquered extensive Sudanese territory, prompting Prime Minister William Gladstone to send Major-General Charles Gordon (1833–85), a hero from British wars in China (1862–4), to stabilise Khartoum, evacuate if necessary, and provide intelligence. Instead of working toward a safe exit, Gordon attacked but could not defeat the Mahdi; instead the Mahdi surrounded and lay siege to Khartoum (Benn, 38–43).

To save this famous military icon the British organised an expedition from upper Egypt to Khartoum to relieve Gordon and the city. This required navigation by imperial forces up the Nile, a matter requiring great skill and support. The British commander expressly ordered the commissioning of Canadian indigenous voyageurs to achieve this feat. Louis Jackson, an experienced foreman, led his Kahnawake boatmen as they travelled some 12,000 miles aboard a steamship across the Atlantic to Egypt, then upriver. He and his contingent successfully established transport channels, then returned to Canada via Great Britain. (Their success was not matched by the larger mission; the Mahdi's troops overran Khartoum and beheaded Gordon before the British could arrive.) The frontispiece accompanying Jackson's narrative was an etching of Jackson that underscored both his authorship and his Mohawk ethnicity.

The rhetoric and underlying cultural politics of Jackson's narrative and the preface by Anglo-Canadian Thomas Storrow Brown (1833–88), sometime hardware merchant and journalist, illuminate the global mobility and cosmopolitanism often occluded from historical accounts of indigenes and the complex negotiations of First Nations people with Anglo-Canadian and British colonisers – as well as their encounter with other colonised people of colour.

(See Louis Jackson's excerpted commentary on his efforts to manage labour practices in Egypt from this same work, at teachingtransatlanticism.tcu.edu.)

From Our Caughnawagas in Egypt

PREFACE.

The Indians of Caughnawaga are an offshoot from the Mohawks, one of the divisions of the Six Nations, formerly in pseudo occupation[86] of western New York, and known to the French by the general name of Iroquois. Long before the cession of this Province to Great Britain, they were settled at the head of the rapids of the St. Lawrence opposite Lachine, on a tract of land ten miles square, or 64,000 acres held in common, but lately separated into lots to be divided among the people as individual property.

Contrary to what has been the too common fate of aborigines brought into close contact with foreigners, the Caughnawagas, with some mixture of white blood, have maintained throughout, their Indian customs, manners and language, with the manhood of their ancestors, in an alertness, strength and power of endurance wherever these qualities have been required: in the boating or rafting on our larger rivers and the hardships of *Voyageurs* in the North-West.

As a high tribute to this known excellence, the call for Canadian *Voyageurs* to assist in the boat navigation of the Nile was accompanied by a special requirement that there should be a contingent of fifty Caughnawagas. They responded quickly to the call, performed the task committed to them in a manner most satisfactory as described in these pages, and returned to their homes at the end of six months, after a voyage of more than 12,000 miles, sound and resolute as when they started, with the loss of but two men.

There is something unique in the idea of the aborigines of the New World being sent for to teach the Egyptians how to pass the Cataracts of the Nile, which has been navigated in some way by them for thousands of years, that should make this little book attractive to all readers, especially as it is written by one born and bred in Caughnawaga, who, with the quick eye of an Indian, has noticed many things unnoticed by ordinary tourists and travellers.

It is written in a most excellent spirit that might wisely be imitated by other travellers. The writer finds no faults, blames nobody, and always content, is generous in his acknowledgments for every act of kindness and proper consideration shown to him and his party, by Her Majesty's Officers of all ranks in command of the expedition. It was written off-hand and goes forth to the public as it came from the pen of the writer, to be judged in its style and the matter contained, by no standard but its own.

Montreal, April, 1885.

OUR CAUGHNAWAGAS IN EGYPT.

When it was made known by Lord Melgund[87] in the early part of September, 1884, that it was the express desire of General Lord Wolseley[88] to have Caughnawaga

---

86 As Benn observes, this term 'reflected a Euro-American view that did not interpret native land use or title as possessing the same status as that of white settlers and powers' (245 n.2).
87 In 1884 Gilbert Elliot, Viscount Melgund, later fourth Earl of Minto (1845–1914), was serving as military secretary to Lord Lansdowne (1845–1927), Governor-General of Canada 1883–1900.
88 Garnet Joseph Wolesley, Viscount Wolesley (1833–1913), commanded the Khartoum expeditionary force.

Indians form part of the Canadian Contingent, the required number was soon obtained, in spite of discouraging talk and groundless fears. [...]

Now came the tug of war, the shooting of all the cataracts. Coming up we used all eddies, now we had to avoid them, coming up also if unable to proceed we could draw back and try another channel, now, everything depended on quick judgment and prompt action, the more so as keel boats are not considered fit for rapid work.[89] I ordered my captains to follow at such distances as to give them time to avoid following should the leading boat err in the choice of channel. After shooting the Dal cataract, all safe I asked my captains how the boats behaved. All agreed that they were slow in answering their helm and required close watching. Travelling between the cataracts against a strong headwind was slow work and we longed for the next one to get along faster. Shooting the Dal, there had been much dodging of rocks and islands, which gave some excitement. In Akaska cataract we discovered a smooth, straight channel in the middle of the river and not very long.

This shooting of the rapids was a surprise to the Egyptian soldiers, a number of whom were stationed at every cataract. The natives came rushing out of their huts with their children, goats and dogs and stood on the beach to see the North American Indian boatmen. I had more leisure now to look round. I have not seen the place yet where I would care to settle down.

The next cataract is Tangur, which I considered the most dangerous of all for shooting. The river is wide and there are many islands and rocks, the rocks are high, and there are many channels to choose from, and as I had noticed coming up, many of these channels are too crooked for shooting especially with a keel boat, all of which makes this rapid, a dangerous one to shoot. The rocks hide each other and if you clear the first one you find yourself close on the other. A narrow escape I had on the east side of Tangur island. The boat following me had taken a sheer and was obliged to take another channel, which having a swifter current than the one I had taken, brought this boat up with me below the rock so close as nearly to cause a disaster.

Colonel Alleyne[90] ordered lunch near the place, where the steamer Gizeh was wrecked. We could see her high and dry on the rock, where she had laid some time as I was told. After lunch we started for Ambigol cataract. On our way we met several large nuggars[91] with their peculiar sails, going at good speed. These nuggars never track but go up with a strong breeze. We shot Ambigol cataract between three and four o'clock and met five whalers at the foot of it. Colonel Alleyne ordered me to go ashore to speak to them. They were manned by Royal Engineers with foreman Graham and his voyageurs. We started again downwards and made Semnah cataract after sunset shortly before dark. Shooting Semnah gate, finished our day's work and we camped. We had made this day 61 miles.

---

89 A laudatory notice of Jackson's narrative in the *Saturday Review* pointed to the challenge of this navigation: 'The gallant Canghnawaga [*sic*] Captain . . . seems to have been convinced by what he saw that preliminary surveys were not of much use, as in bad places the river was totally different one day from what it had been a few days before' (143).
90 Brevet Lieutenant-Colonel James Alleyne (n.d.) of the Royal Artillery
91 A type of large, broad-beamed boat to carry cargo (*OED*)

Dal cataract	5 miles.
From the foot of Dal to the head of Akaska	9 "
Akaska cataract	1 "
From the foot of Akaska to Tangur	14 "
Tangur cataract	3 "
From the foot of Tangur to Ambigol	9 "
Ambigol cataract	1 "
From the foot of Ambigol to Semneh	17 "
Semneh cataract	2 "
	61 "

This day's experience decided my opinion about the boats. Many of my men had been portaging on the Ottawa for different lumber firms and all agreed with me, that whilst the Nile river boats would have been of no use on the Ottawa, they could not be improved upon for the Nile service on account of the nature of the river. For the ascents of the river as well as the cataracts, the sailing qualities of the boats were all important, and when towed by line the keel would give a chance to shoot out into the current to get round rocks, where a flat bottom would have followed the line broadside and fetched up against the rock. In shooting the cataracts the boats did not answer the helm as quickly as would flat bottoms, but this drawback was not sufficient to condemn the keel.

Next day, Thursday, November 6th, we ran some more swift water to Sarras, nine miles below foot of Semnah. We met there thirty whalers with troops and stores ready to ascend. Colonel Denison[92] asked me to give him one man to act as pilot, so I gave him Mathias Hill,[93] an Iroquois. Colonel Denison went up with this fleet.

Most of the Canadian voyageurs asked me how I found the Rapids. I told them that I had no trouble, considering it unadvisable to give a minute description, as I had already discovered how the fast falling water daily changed the appearance of the river, and what was a good place for me to go up, would be bad now, whilst a bad place might be better. I was well aware that these voyageurs would have more trouble than I had. They had not only larger loads but soldier crews, whilst I had my Caughnawaga boys with whom I had worked from youth up and who promptly caught at a sign from me, while the soldiers had to be talked to, and, although having the best of will, could not always comprehend the situation.

After thirty whalers had started, I was informed by Lord Avonmore[94] of the order to camp. Next day the 7th November, another fleet of twenty-eight boats started, for which Lord Avonmore asked me a pilot. I gave him John Bruce[95] of St. Regis. [...]

We sailed from Alexandria on February 6th, 1885, well pleased with what we had seen in the land of the Pharos and proud to have shown the world that the dwellers on the banks of the Nile, after navigating it for centuries, could still learn something of the craft from the Iroquois Indians of North America and the Canadian voyageurs of many races.

I cannot conclude without expressing my satisfaction at the handsome treatment accorded us by the British Government, and should our services be of assistance in

---

92 Brevet Lieutenant-Colonial Frederick G. Denison (n.d.), Governor General's Bodyguard and Commander of the Canadian voyageurs

93 A river pilot, Hill had been born in Kahnawake and was forty-eight at the time of the expedition; he had earlier served in the US Army during the Civil War (Benn, 205).

94 William Charles Yelverton (1825–83), fourth Viscount Avonmore

95 Bruce was evidently another experienced river pilot; he was also fluent in English and translated for the Mohawks (Benn, 200).

the proposed Fall campaign in Egypt, they will be freely given. We were allowed just double the amount of clothing stipulated in the contract, the overcoats being given to us at Malta on our way home.

Source text

Jackson, Louis, *Our Caughnawagas in Egypt: A narrative of what was seen and accomplished by the Contingent of North American Indian Voyageurs who led the British Boat Expedition for the Relief of Khartoum up the Cataracts of the Nile* (Montreal: W. Drysdale & Co., 1885).

References

Benn, Carl, *Mohawks on the Nile: Natives Among the Canadian Voyageurs in Egypt 1884–1885* (Toronto: Natural Heritage Books, 2009).
Dictionary of Canadian Biography
Flint, Kate, *The Transatlantic Indian, 1776–1930* (Princeton, NJ: Princeton University Press, 2009).
ODNB
'Voyageurs on the Nile', *Saturday Review* (1 August 1885), 142–3.
Weaver, Jace, *The Red Atlantic: American Indigenes and the Making of the Modern World, 1000–1927* (Chapel Hill, NC: University of North Carolina Press, 2014).

Elizabeth Blackwell (1821–1910)

From Pioneer Work in Opening the Medical Profession to Women: Autobiographical Sketches (1895)

The transatlantic physician Elizabeth Blackwell (1821–1910) was Britain's first woman licensed to practise medicine. The daughter of an abolitionist sugar refiner in Bristol and his wife, Blackwell emigrated with her family at age eleven, first to New York then Cincinnati. After her father died suddenly in 1838, she began teaching to help support the family and save money for medical school, principally inspired in this goal by a woman who died of uterine cancer because she was too modest to be examined by a male doctor early on. The excerpt below narrates Blackwell's admission to the Geneva Medical School in New York state after repeated denials elsewhere.

After graduating first in her class in 1849, Blackwell travelled to Paris for further training, where she lost the sight of one eye from purulent ophthalmia after treating an infant with the disease. Thus ended her plan to become a surgeon. She returned to New York and founded in 1853 what became a women's hospital run by women. Visiting London in 1858, she entered her name into the General Medical Council's Register, thus becoming the first British woman physician and influencing in the process Elizabeth Garrett (1836–1917), who became the second. She continued her career back in New York and later helped organise women nurses for Union troops in the Civil War. In 1869 she returned to England, where she lived the rest of her life with the Irish orphan she had adopted in 1856. There, in addition to joining women's reform campaigns, she served as consulting physician at Elizabeth Garrett Anderson's hospital for women and a lecturer on midwifery at the London Medical School for Women. After her death she was buried neither in the US nor England but at Kilmun in western Scotland, a favourite holiday retreat.

From Pioneer Work in Opening the Medical Profession to Women

In the summer of 1847, with my carefully hoarded earnings, I resolved to seek an entrance into a medical school. Philadelphia was then considered the chief seat of medical learning in America, so to Philadelphia I went; taking passage in a sailing vessel from Charleston for the sake of economy.

In Philadelphia I boarded in the family of Dr. William Elder. He and his admirable wife soon became warm and steadfast friends. Dr. Elder (author of the life of Dr. Kane, the Arctic voyager) was a remarkable man, of brilliant talent and genial nature.[96] He took a generous interest in my plans, helping by his advice and encouragement through the months of effort and refusals which were now encountered.

Applications were cautiously but persistently made to the four medical colleges of Philadelphia for admission as a regular student. The interviews with their various professors were by turns hopeful and disappointing. Whilst pursuing these inquiries I commenced my anatomical studies in the private school of Dr. Allen.[97] This gentleman by his thoughtful arrangements enabled me to overcome the natural repulsion to these studies generally felt at the outset. With a tact and delicacy for which I have always felt grateful, he gave me as my first lesson in practical anatomy a demonstration of the human wrist. The beauty of the tendons and exquisite arrangements of this part of the body struck my artistic sense, and appealed to the sentiment of reverence with which this anatomical branch of study was ever afterwards invested in my mind.

During the following months, whilst making applications to the different medical colleges of Philadelphia for admission as a regular student, I enlisted the services of my friends in the search for an Alma Mater. The interviews with the various professors, though disappointing, were often amusing.

Extracts from the Journal of 1847

May 27. – Called on Dr. Jackson (one of the oldest professors in Philadelphia), a small, bright-faced, grey-haired man, who looked up from his newspaper and saluted me with, 'Well, what is it? What do you want?'[98] I told him I wanted to

---

96 The 1858 biography of physician and explorer Dr Elisha Kane (1820–57) by Dr William Elder (1806–85), physician turned writer

97 Jonathan Moses Allen (1815–67), later a professor at Pennsylvania Medical College, was author of *The Practical Anatomist; or, the Student's Guide in the Dissecting-Room* (1856).

98 Drs Samuel Jackson, William Darrach and William Ashmead (see below) were all practising physicians affiliated with medical training in Philadelphia, but few details are available.

study medicine. He began to laugh, and asked me why. Then I detailed my plans. He became interested; said he would not give me an answer then; that there were great difficulties, but he did not know that they were insurmountable; he would let me know on Monday. I came home with a lighter heart, though I can hardly say I hope. On Monday Dr. Jackson said he had done his best for me, but the professors were all opposed to my entrance. Dr. Horner advised me to try the Filbert Street and Franklin schools. A professor of Jefferson College thought it would be impossible to study there, and advised the New England schools.

June 2. – Felt gloomy as thunder, trudging round to Dr. Darrach. He is the most non-committal man I ever saw. I harangued him, and he sat full five minutes without a word. I asked at last if he could give me any encouragement. 'The subject is a novel one, madam, I have nothing to say either for or against it; you have awakened trains of thought upon which my mind is taking action, but I cannot express my opinion to you either one way or another.' 'Your opinion, I fear, is unfavourable.' 'I did not say so. I beg you, madam, distinctly to understand that I express no opinion one way or another; the way in which my mind acts in this matter I do not feel at liberty to unfold.' 'Shall I call on the other professors of your college?' 'I cannot take the responsibility of advising you to pursue such a course.' 'Can you not grant me admittance to your lectures, as you do not feel unfavourable to my scheme?' 'I have said no such thing; whether favourable or unfavourable, I have not expressed any opinion; and I beg leave to state clearly that the operation of my mind in regard to this matter I do not feel at liberty to unfold.' I got up in despair, leaving his mind to take action on the subject at his leisure.

Dr. Warrington[99] told me that he had seen his friend Dr. Ashmead, who had told him that Paris was such a horrible place that I must give up my wish for a medical education – indeed, his communication would be so unfavourable that he would rather not meet me in person. I told the Doctor that if the path of duty led me to hell I would go there; and I did not think that by being with devils I should become a devil myself – at which the good Doctor stared.

Nevertheless, I shrink extremely from the idea of giving up the attempt in America and going to France, although the suggestion is often urged on me.

The fear of successful rivalry which at that time often existed in the medical mind was expressed by the dean of one of the smaller schools, who frankly replied to the application, 'You cannot expect us to furnish you with a stick to break our heads with;' so revolutionary seemed the attempt of a woman to leave a subordinate position and seek to obtain a complete medical education. A similarly mistaken notion of the rapid practical success which would attend a lady doctor was shown later by one of the professors of my medical college, who was desirous of entering into partnership with me on condition of sharing profits over 5,000 dollars on my first year's practice.

During these fruitless efforts my kindly Quaker adviser, whose private lectures I attended, said to me: 'Elizabeth, it is of no use trying. Thee cannot gain admission to these schools. Thee must go to Paris and don masculine attire to gain the necessary knowledge.' Curiously enough, this suggestion of disguise made by good Dr. Warrington was also given me by Doctor Pankhurst, the Professor of Surgery in the largest college in Philadelphia. He thoroughly approved of a woman's gaining complete medical knowledge; told me that although my public entrance into the

---

99 Joseph Warrington, Jr (1808–88), a Philadelphia obstetrician; both Warrington and Elder were Quakers (Sahli, 337 n.6).

classes was out of the question, yet if I would assume masculine attire and enter the college he could entirely rely on two or three of his students to whom he should communicate my disguise, who would watch the class and give me timely notice to withdraw should my disguise be suspected.

But neither the advice to go to Paris nor the suggestion of disguise tempted me for a moment. It was to my mind a moral crusade on which I had entered, a course of justice and common sense, and it must be pursued in the light of day, and with public sanction, in order to accomplish its end.

The following letter to Mrs. Willard of Troy, the well-known educationalist,[100] describes the difficulties through which the young student had to walk warily:

Philadelphia: May 24.

I cannot refrain from expressing my obligations to you for directing me to the excellent Dr. Warrington. He has allowed me to visit his patients, attend his lectures, and make use of his library, and has spoken to more than one medical friend concerning my wishes; but with deep regret I am obliged to say that all the information hitherto obtained serves to show me the impossibility of accomplishing my purpose in America. I find myself rigidly excluded from the regular college routine, and there is no thorough course of lectures that can supply its place. The general sentiment of the physicians is strongly opposed to a woman's intruding herself into the profession; consequently it would be perhaps impossible to obtain private instruction, but if that were possible, the enormous expense would render it impracticable, and where the feelings of the profession are strongly enlisted against such a scheme, the museums, libraries, hospitals, and all similar aids would be closed against me. In view of these and numerous other difficulties Dr. Warrington is discouraged, and joins with his medical brethren in advising me to give up the scheme. But a strong idea, long cherished till it has taken deep root in the soul and become an all-absorbing duty, cannot thus be laid aside. I must accomplish my end. I consider it the noblest and most useful path that I can tread, and if one country rejects me I will go to another.

Through Dr. Warrington and other sources I am informed that my plan can be carried out in Paris, though the free Government lectures, delivered by the faculty, are confined to men, and a diploma is strictly denied to a woman, even when (as in one instance, as it is said) she has gone through the course in male attire; yet every year thorough courses of lectures are delivered by able physicians on every branch of medical knowledge, to which I should be admitted without hesitation and treated with becoming respect. The true place for study, then, seems open to me; but here, again, some friendly physicians raise stronger objections than ever. 'You, a young unmarried lady,' they say, 'go to Paris, that city of fearful immorality, where every feeling will be outraged and insult attend you at every step; where vice is the natural atmosphere, and no young man can breathe it without being contaminated! Impossible, you are lost if you go!'

Now, dear madam, I appeal to you, who have had the opportunity of studying the French in their native land, is not this a false view, a greatly exaggerated fear? Is it not perfectly true everywhere that a woman who respects herself will be respected by others; that where the life is directed by a strong, pure motive to a noble object,

100 Emma Hart Willard (1787–1870), founder of the Troy Female Seminary, which opened in Troy, NY in 1837

in a quiet, dignified, but determined manner, the better feelings of mankind are enlisted, and the woman excites esteem and respectful sympathy? To my mind this is perfectly clear, and I trust that your more experienced judgment will confirm my opinion. Probably, then, if all the information which I am still collecting agree with what I have already received, I may sail for France in the course of the summer, that I may familiarise myself with a rapid French delivery before the commencement of the winter lectures.

I have tried to look every difficulty steadily in the face. I find none which seem to me unconquerable, and with the blessing of Providence I trust to accomplish my design.

After a short, refreshing trip with my family to the seaside, the search was again renewed in Philadelphia. But applications made for admission to the medical schools both of Philadelphia and of New York were met with similarly unsuccessful results.

I therefore obtained a complete list of all the smaller schools of the Northern States, 'country schools,' as they were called. I examined their prospectuses, and quite at a venture sent in applications for admission to twelve of the most promising institutions, where full courses of instruction were given under able professors. The result was awaited with much anxiety, as the time for the commencement of the winter sessions was rapidly approaching. No answer came for some time. At last, to my immense relief (though not surprise, for failure never seemed possible), I received the following letter from the medical department of a small university town in the western part of the State of New York:–

Geneva: October 20, 1847.

To Elizabeth Blackwell, Philadelphia.

I am instructed by the faculty of the medical department of Geneva University to acknowledge receipt of yours of 3rd inst. A quorum of the faculty assembled last evening for the first time during the session, and it was thought important to submit your proposal to the class (of students), who have had a meeting this day, and acted entirely on their own behalf, without any interference on the part of the faculty. I send you the result of their deliberations, and need only add that there are no fears but that you can, by judicious management, not only 'disarm criticism,' but elevate yourself without detracting in the least from the dignity of the profession.

Wishing you success in your undertaking, which some may deem bold in the present state of society, I subscribe myself,
Yours respectfully,
CHARLES A. LEE,
Dean of the Faculty.
15 Geneva Hotel.

This letter enclosed the following unique and manly letter, which I had afterwards copied on parchment, and esteem one of my most valued possessions:–

At a meeting of the entire medical class of Geneva Medical College, held this day, October 20, 1847, the following resolutions were unanimously adopted:–

1. *Resolved* – That one of the radical principles of a Republican Government is the universal education of both sexes; that to every branch of scientific education the door should be open equally to all; that the application of Elizabeth Blackwell to become a member of our class meets our entire approbation; and in extending our

unanimous invitation we pledge ourselves that no conduct of ours shall cause her to regret her attendance at this institution.

2. *Resolved* – That a copy of these proceedings be signed by the chairman and transmitted to Elizabeth Blackwell.

T. J. STRATTON, *Chairman.*

With an immense sigh of relief and aspiration of profound gratitude to Providence I instantly accepted the invitation, and prepared for the journey to Western New York State.

Source text

Blackwell, Elizabeth, *Pioneer Work in Opening the Medical Profession to Women: Autobiographical Sketches* (London: Longmans, Green, and Co., 1895).

References

ANB

ODNB

Sahli, Nancy, 'A Stick to Break Our Heads With: Elizabeth Blackwell and Philadelphia Medicine', *Pennsylvania History: A Journal of Mid-Atlantic Studies* 44.4 (October 1977), 335–47.

H. C. Foxcroft (1865–1950)

From 'A Negro On Efficiency' (1906)

Helen Charlotte Foxcroft was an English historian and literary editor. The daughter of Victorian gentry, she was an avid researcher and focused her studies on George Savile, first marquess of Halifax (1633–95), a Restoration-era statesman (*ODNB*). Foxcroft's interests did not lie solely in British history. She also wrote about Booker Taliaferro Washington (1856–1915), a leading American in higher education, politics and race relations, though her words included racist terminology and ideology.

Booker T. Washington, the son of Jane, was enslaved for the first nine years of his life; he details his upbringing in his autobiography *Up from Slavery* (1900). Washington attended an elementary school for Black students in West Virginia, simultaneously working in coal mines. Washington later attended the Hampton Normal and Agricultural Institute in Hampton, Virginia. After graduating in 1875, Washington returned to West Virginia to teach and was placed in charge of the night school at the Hampton Institute. His success there led to his nomination to found a training college for Blacks at Tuskegee, Alabama. Alabama education commissioners wanted a white principal; Washington's reputation convinced them otherwise.

A transatlantic figure, Washington went to Europe where he toured, lectured and learned about agricultural practices. Washington's publications include *The Future of the American Negro* (1899), *Up from Slavery* (1900), *Character Building* (1902), *Working with the Hands* (1904), *Tuskegee & Its People* (1905) and *The Negro in the South* with W. E. B. Du Bois (1907).

From 'A Negro On Efficiency'

EFFICIENCY is a word of the moment. Enveloped in a halo of vague political sanctity, it exhales a mystic virtue—undefined, undefinable. Its devotees fall back on the figure of Circumlocution; it is Something Lord Rosebery[101] preaches—and the War Office[102] has not practised. It is Something lacked by the Englishman of to-day—enjoyed by his rivals; and should therefore be provided, in bulk, by a vote of the House of Commons.[103] To the Black Race, meanwhile, no one ascribes the attribute; and it is thus remarkable that one of the most efficient among living Americans is a man of colour. On his writings we found the following essay.

Born a slave about 1858, "near a cross-roads post office," Mr. Booker Washington would seem to be a mulatto. On this he lays no stress. He welcomes that complete identification with the coloured race imposed by American custom upon all "touched with the tar brush;" and claims to derive from his mother, a negress, whatever energies he possesses. The fact, however, that he is not a pure black cannot be ignored by anyone interested in the problem of potential negro capacity.

A slave during his first six years, he testifies to the patriarchal relations often prevalent on the plantations, and admits that Abolition found the slave on a higher plane than the savage. Yet he denounces the system in the interests not only of morality, but of efficiency. "The whole machinery of slavery," he says, "... cause[d] labour ... to be looked on as a badge of degradation." Indifferent to the interests of the estate, the slaves were too ignorant for any but the rudest methods; and even in the wealthiest houses reigned a coarse and slovenly plenty.

Once free, he worked in furnaces and mines, and somehow learned to read; for in common with his race, he was fired with a passion for instruction. This zeal, of course, was not always "according to knowledge." Freedom from manual toil seemed to most the end to be desired; and book-learning a royal road towards that blissful consummation. The boy could not escape the contagion of these opinions. He longed, however, to improve the lot of his mother; and vaguely questioned the theory which completely identified education with progress *in the use of language*.

A simple experience left on him its mark for life. The wife of the mine-owner – a New Englander, wealthy and cultivated – "a high respect for manual labour ... well done, and ... was not ashamed to use her hands." To the coloured boys she seemed a stern mistress; but Booker so hated the coal-mine that he braved her terrors. A kindly reception reassured him; her requirements, if rigid, were simple. Truthfulness and promptitude—cleanliness, order, and method—in a word, thorough-

---

101 Archibald Philip Primrose (1847–1929), fifth Earl of Rosebery and Prime Minister, March 1894 to June 1895
102 The department of the British government that was the result of fusing formerly independent bodies responsible for various parts of Army administration into one governing body
103 The lower body of the British Parliament

ness, proved essential. "Excuses and explanations," she warned him, "could never . . . take . . . the place of results."

Charming is his account of the struggles which, under her watchful superintendence, transformed the neglected garden into a paradise of order; and of the sudden realization—that he had created this. "My whole nature began to change. I felt a self-respect . . . a satisfaction" hitherto unknown. Never again could physical toil appear a degradation; never again could he fear the lady he still reveres as "one of" his "greatest teachers."

He now planned to pursue his education at the Hampton Normal [Training] and Agricultural Institute[104] in Virginia, where the course was partly industrial. Encouraged by his mistress, and supplied with a scanty purse by sympathetic negro neighbours, he started at the age of fourteen. Now walking, then begging or earning a lift, at times sleeping under platforms, he completed the 500 miles, and reached Hampton with about 2s. in his pocket. His unkempt appearance might have disqualified him had not the headmistress desired him to *sweep out the room*; which done, she quietly observed, "I guess you'll do." He earned his board by acting as porter; a generous Northerner paid his fees; in the vacations (*more Americano*) he served in a shop.

Of his literary studies he says little; but lays stress on his initiation into the "value of the Bible," in its spiritual and literary aspects. He had also lessons in elocution. Longing "to do something to make the world better," he coveted the power of "speak[ing] about that thing;" and obtained from a teacher private instruction in breathing, articulation, and emphasis.

The industries practised at Hampton were of a simple description. The pupils helped in the house, cultivated the farm, kept tools and buildings in repair. Meanwhile the whole life was a revelation to the ex-slave, who had never slept in sheets, and to whom household regularity and "the use [and moral value] of the bath-tub" were new and surprising experiences.

All other influences he, however, subordinates to that of the Principal—"a type," as he tells us, "of that Christ-like body of Northern men and women who went into the negro schools at the close of the war."—"Daily . . . contact with General Armstrong[105]. . . alone," he declares, "would have been a liberal education." From General Armstrong he imbibed the strong and practical religious energy which inspired his subsequent labours; and learned, as he touchingly explains, that those are happiest who do most for others.

Leaving Hampton at the age of eighteen, he went as waiter to an hotel. Ignorant of the art, he was degraded to the rank of dish-washer, but determining to recover his position, was soon reinstated. Which thing we fancy is a parable.

After an interlude of teaching he resumed his studies at a negro institute in Washington. The pupils dressed fashionably, and boasted of mental attainments. In character, however, they compared to him unfavourably with the Hampton product. If they knew more Latin and Greek, they knew "less about life and its conditions as they would meet it at their homes." Penniless girls taken from the poorest classes were thrown on the world with expensive tastes and accomplishments not

---

104 Present-day Hampton Institute opened in 1868 as the 'Hampton Normal and Agricultural Institute', aiming to teach young African American youth trades and industrial skills that they could use to become self-sufficient and create better foundations for their people overall.

105 Samuel Chapman Armstrong (1839–93) commanded Black troops in the Civil War and founded the Hampton Institute.

in demand; with results which may be guessed. Again, a system which supplied from charitable sources board and lodging in semi-luxurious surroundings seemed to him a mistake. At Hampton each student was responsible for his modest expenses, the effort to supply which proved of high value as a means of character building. Men so trained were the readier to seek "the country districts of the South, where there was little of comfort," and there "take up work for our people."

His talents suggested a political career, which he declined in favour of "other service . . . of more permanent value" to his race. At the age of twenty he returned to Hampton, and was employed to found a subsidiary night-school for impecunious[106] but aspiring blacks. These worked *ten* hours a day in the school saw-mills and laundries; and gave two hours per evening to book-work, their surplus earnings accumulating for subsequent day-school expenses. "I never," says Mr. Washington," taught pupils who gave me such genuine satisfaction." In May, 1881, however, General Armstrong selected him to organize a proposed training college for negroes at Tuskegee, Alabama, and he thus, at the age of twenty-two, entered on his life work. To an apparently modest sphere he brought lofty aspirations, an experience already extensive, a trained intelligence with some technical skill, and almost inexhaustible energy.

His aim was to make his humble school a substantial contributor to the welfare of the coloured race. Some have reproached him with the fact that the ideals he has set before it are simply the white man's ideals. Mr. Washington, we admit, has not evolved a civilisation. But races whose native organisation has been rudely obliterated cannot possibly develop on the line of their original traditions; and the American negro, if he is to retain American citizenship, must adopt American standards. The actual situation he gauged with shrewd discrimination. Penniless and illiterate when emancipated, the race, in fifteen years, had made considerable progress in wealth and education; while Congressmen and even Governors had risen from its ranks. But the general outlook was far from satisfactory, for all parties concerned had tried "to begin at the top." Potential capacity apart, the negroes, when freed, were generally without training, moral, mental, or technical. A few, educated as artisans, constituted the efficient element. The remainder had never even worked; they had only been worked. They had never thought; others had thought for them. Under stringent discipline, self-control had been unknown. And it was these untutored barbarians whom the North had tried to force into electoral and official equality. The results were disastrous. Statesmen who could not read, and whose morals were as weak as their education, provoked the cruel reaction embodied in the "Ku Klux Klan;" while political agitation distracted the rank and file "from more fundamental matters." Elsewhere he saw the same premature ambition. Scorning the humbler avocations, incompetent men and women crowded into the professions. [. . .]

In Alabama, meanwhile, with eighty per cent. of agriculturists, the outlook was little better. Everything seemed sacrificed to cotton-growing without, and senseless extravagance within. Antiquated methods and unsound finance intensified the inherent evils of a one-crop system; while cabins almost bare of the commonest utensils displayed costly clocks and harmoniums which the family could not use. Amid such surroundings he found "educated" men and women; persons, that is, who had committed to memory certain rules of arithmetic and grammar, valued in inverse ratio to their bearing on the facts around them. "Art and elegant accomplishments" failed to

---

106 Having few or no financial resources

refine. Adepts in "compound interest" never asked why their father lost money on every bale of cotton. Girls who could read the map could not lay a table. No room was bright with the beautiful flowers which abound; and among people destined to a country life he found text-books solely concerned with the phenomena of cities. Unselfish educational labour had, in fact, been wasted in preparing people for any circumstance but their own. He himself resolved to civilise rather than to "cram," and to turn the mental energies of his disciples towards a reform of their actual surroundings. Especially he dreaded "educat[ing] them out of sympathy with agricultural life, so that they would be attracted ... to the cities." By transforming the agricultural, no less than the moral, intellectual, and religious ideals of his people; by proving the reconcilability of the yeoman's career with the mental interests and the reasonable aspirations of man, even ambitious youths might be kept, he felt, on the land.

But his heart almost sank on comparing his aims with his means. He had neither buildings nor plant; and the State grant, about £800[107] a year, had been strictly appropriated to salaries.

From a dilapidated shanty in the town, he removed the school to a dilapidated shanty in the country. Here he proposed to cultivate land; and thus minimize household expenses, while vindicating the dignity of physical toil, and the value of modern methods. This his pupils resented. To a dislike of manual labour they added a belief ("by no means," hints Mr. Washington, "confined to my race") that books alone are the orthodox vehicle of instruction. Some aspired to a professional, many to a city career; all supposed that their country breeding had exhausted the mysteries of farming. Mr. Washington, however, "took off his own coat" in earnest; nor could a poor soil, scanty apparatus, and slovenly workers daunt his ready courage. Agriculture, he contended, is the art which makes poor soil rich; implements slowly accumulated; and Mr. Washington, with genial decision, kept the entire school waiting till careless students had returned theirs spades under cover. To the girls he explained that a dish is either well washed, or it is not; and that anyone who takes pay for work ill done receives money on false pretences. Such practical examples he found more potent than reams of abstract morality.

His system was the Hampton method, emphasized on its industrial side. The night-school specially appealed to him; as trying, more especially, the "grit" of students, with corresponding benefit to their characters. The night students, he maintains, "take up their studies with a degree of enthusiasm ... that is not equaled in the day classes;" and there is, he declares, "something in the [constant] handling of a tool that has a ... relation to close, accurate thinking."

And what are the results? After twenty years' work the school owns 2,300 acres, of which 700 are under cultivation on the most modern principles; and the extensive experiments carried on are keenly appreciated by the neighbours of both races. Thirty-six buildings, duly fitted with elaborate plant, which have been built, designed, and equipped by the staff and the students, attest the efficiency of the technical instruction. The students number 1,100, and include recruits from Africa, Cuba, Porto Rico, Jamaica, &c. About 6,000 have benefited, and of these one half are regarded as specially successful. Large yeoman farmers, thriving merchants, ministers, teachers, physicians, nurses, besides artisans, and those engaged in domestic avocations, are numbered in the list. "After diligent investigation," Mr. Washington has not found a dozen old pupils idle—or as many in prison. Moreover, "[these] men

---

107 Roughly $5,500 in 1868

and women ... by their own example, or by direct effort"—often, be it noted, at the cost of much self-denial—"are showing the masses of our race how to improve their material, educational ... moral, and religious" status; exhibiting, meanwhile, "a degree of common-sense and self-control which is causing better relations ... between the races ... Whole communities are fast being revolutionised through the instrumentality of these men and women." Sixteen industrial schools of some size inherit the Tuskegee tradition, while a civilising influence is exerted over natives in British, German, and Belgian Africa, through Tuskegee men despatched, by request, to diffuse improved methods of cotton cultivation.

Once a year, moreover, a Negro Farmers' Conference is held at Tuskegee, not to mention educational and business congresses. Political agitation is barred; for Mr. Washington argues that the negro's admission to his full political rights will automatically follow his ascent in the scale of civilisation. Whining or complaint is equally deprecated; the discussion is confined to matters "which the race ha[s] under itscontrol." The practice of thrift, honesty, and self-discipline; the adoption of improved methods, financial and agricultural; the advancement of education, and the introduction of agriculture and household economy into the curriculum of the country school, are urged upon all present. The farmer is reminded that frugality, energy, and intelligence can raise him to the status of a proprietor; the tenant is encouraged to a higher standard of demand in respect of household accommodation, and all are adjured to further, in every possible way, amicable relations between the races. A widespread propaganda, meanwhile, is carried on among the women of the race, and Tuskegee controls an elementary school on the lines dear to Mr. Washington. Moreover, Mr. Washington has so inoculated his subordinates with his own principles that he can extend his influence by prolonged lecturing tours, through which money is obtained for the many needs of the establishment, and the negro population, in all parts of the States, is successfully stimulated to fresh efforts after a higher efficiency. For Mr. Washington is not merely, as we might expect, an efficient speaker; he is also a consummate orator, whose power over audiences of either race has been compared by an American publicist to the influence of Gladstone.[108] In method, however, they must differ entirely; since even the most impassioned admirers of the "old man eloquent" would hardly define him as giving "an idea for every word." Master, moreover, of a written style, which, if hardly polished, is at least easy and forcible, he appeals to both races through the medium of the Press; witness his autobiography; his account of Tuskegee; his "open letter" on lynching,[109] addressed to the State Legislature; and those frank strictures on the morality of negro preachers, which, after bringing upon him a storm of obloquy, initiated a much-needed reform.

Source text

Foxcroft, H. C., 'A Negro on Efficiency', *Fortnightly Review* 86 (1906), 461–7.

---

108 William Gladstone (1809–98), British Prime Minister on four occasions between 1868 and 1894

109 Foxcroft may be referencing Washington's letter to a Birmingham, Alabama, newspaper, which appeared in 1904 under the title 'Booker T. Washington Expresses Opinion on Recent Burnings at the Stake', or, more likely, a reprint, such as 'A Protest Against the Burning and Lynching of Negroes', a brief pamphlet subsequently published with its first page referencing the original newspaper article as having 'also [been] sent out by the Associated Press to the newspapers of the country' (1).

References

ANB

'Washington', in Henry Louis Gates and Evelyn Brooks Higgonbothom (eds), *Harlem Renaissance Lives from the African American National Biography* (Oxford: Oxford University Press, 2009), 510–15.

Washington, Booker T., 'Expresses Opinion on Recent Burnings at the Stake', *Birmingham Age-Herald* (29 February 1904), 2.

Washington, Booker T., 'A Protest Against the Burning and Lynching of Negroes', Daniel Murray Pamphlet Collection, Library of Congress (Alabama: s.n.?, 1904).

Washington, Booker T., *Up From Slavery* (New York: Double Day, 1900).

John Muir (1838–1914)

From The Story of My Boyhood and Youth *(1913)*

This excerpt complements the selection from John Muir's memoir *The Story of My Boyhood and Youth* in MSR. A transatlantic environmentalist and writer, Muir pursued his passion and enthusiasm for nature and wildlife in Britain and America. Muir's environmentalism is not unproblematic; he characteristically envisioned 'pristine wilderness' as one emptied of the Native Americans who occupied it and privileged white settlers for whose use and enjoyment land was to be preserved (DeLuca and Demo, 541–5).

Born in Scotland, Muir developed a fascination with field-based learning as he lived near the North Sea and spent time as a child exploring the area near Dunbar. His playtime consisted of learning about birds and marine life, and these cherished memories also inspired his fascination with American natural history. When he learned of his father's decision to move to the United States, Muir and David, his brother, were ecstatic because of what they perceived as the limitless possibilities in spending time outdoors engaging with American forestry and wildlife.

The Story of My Boyhood and Youth underscores the importance of appreciating and caring for one's environment. Muir supplements his recollections with references to John James Audubon (1785–1851), the famed transatlantic ornithologist and painter, and Alexander Wilson (1766–1813), a prominent transatlantic ornithologist and poet.

From The Story of My Boyhood and Youth

'A Boyhood in Scotland'

WHEN I was a boy in Scotland I was fond of everything that was wild, and all my life I've been growing fonder and fonder of wild places and wild creatures. Fortunately around my native town of Dunbar, by the stormy North Sea, there was no lack of wildness, though most of the land lay in smooth cultivation. With red-blooded playmates, wild as myself, I loved to wander in the fields to hear the birds sing, and along the seashore to gaze and wonder at the shells and seaweeds, eels and crabs in the pools among the rocks when the tide was low; and best of all to watch the waves in awful storms thundering on the black headlands and craggy ruins of the old Dunbar Castle when the sea and the sky, the waves and the clouds, were mingled together as one. We never thought of playing truant, but after I was five or six years old I ran away to the seashore or the fields almost every Saturday, and every day in the school vacations except Sundays, though solemnly warned that I must play at home in the garden and back yard, lest I should learn to think bad thoughts and say bad words. All in vain. In spite of the sure sore punishments that followed like shadows, the natural inherited wildness in our blood ran true on its glorious course as invincible and unstoppable as stars.

My earliest recollections of the country were gained on short walks with my grandfather when I was perhaps not over three years old. On one of these walks grandfather took me to Lord Lauderdale's gardens, where I saw figs growing against a sunny wall and tasted some of them, and got as many apples to eat as I wished. On another memorable walk in a hay-field, when we sat down to rest on one of the haycocks I heard a sharp, prickly, stinging cry, and, jumping up eagerly, called grandfather's attention to it. He said he heard only the wind, but I insisted on digging into the hay and turning it over until we discovered the source of the strange exciting sound, — a mother field mouse with half a dozen naked young hanging to her teats. This to me was a wonderful discovery. No hunter could have been more excited on discovering a bear and her cubs in a wilderness den.

I was sent to school before I had completed my third year. The first schoolday was doubtless full of wonders, but I am not able to recall any of them. I remember the servant washing my face and getting soap in my eyes, and mother hanging a little green bag with my first book in it around my neck so I would not lose it, and its blowing back in the sea-wind like a flag. [. . .]

Nature saw to it that besides school lessons and church lessons some of her own lessons should be learned, perhaps with a view to the time when we should be called to wander in wildness to our heart's content. Oh, the blessed enchantment of those Saturday runaways in the prime of the spring! How our young wondering eyes reveled in the sunny, breezy glory of the hills and the sky, every particle of us thrilling and tingling with the bees and glad birds and glad streams! Kings may be blessed; we were glorious, we were free, — school cares and scoldings, heart thrashings and flesh thrashings alike, were forgotten in the fullness of Nature's glad wildness. These were my first excursions, — the beginnings of lifelong wanderings.

'A New World'

OUR grammar-school reader, called, I think, "Maccoulough's Course of Reading," contained a few natural-history sketches that excited me very much and left a deep impression, especially a fine description of the fish hawk and the bald eagle by the Scotch ornithologist Wilson, who had the good fortune to wander for years in the

American woods while the country was yet mostly wild. I read his description over and over again, till I got the vivid picture he drew by heart, — the long-winged hawk circling over the heaving waves, every motion watched by the eagle perched on the top of a crag or dead tree; the fish hawk poising for a moment to take aim at a fish and plunging under the water; the eagle with kindling eye spreading his wings ready for instant flight in case the attack should prove successful; the hawk emerging with a struggling fish in his talons, and proud flight; the eagle launching himself in pursuit; the wonderful wing-work in the sky, the fish hawk, though encumbered with his prey, circling higher, higher, striving hard to keep above the robber eagle; the eagle at length soaring above him, compelling him with a cry of despair to drop his hard-won prey; then the eagle steadying himself for a moment to take aim, descending swift as a lightning-bolt, and seizing the falling fish before it reached the sea.

Not less exciting and memorable was Audubon's wonderful story of the passenger pigeon, a beautiful bird flying in vast flocks that darkened the sky like clouds, countless millions assembling to rest and sleep and rear their young in certain forests, miles in length and breadth, fifty or a hundred nests on a single tree; the overloaded branches bending low and often breaking; the farmers gathering from far and near, beating down countless thousands of the young and old birds from their nests and roosts with long poles at night, and in the morning driving their bands of hogs, some of them brought from farms a hundred miles distant, to fatten on the dead and wounded covering the ground.

In another of our reading-lessons some of the American forests were described. The most interesting of the trees to us boys was the sugar maple, and soon after we had learned this sweet story we heard everybody talking about the discovery of gold in the same wonder-filled country. [. . .]

Source text

Muir, John, *The Story of My Boyhood and Youth: With Illustrations from Sketches by the Author* (Boston: Riverside Press, 1913).

References

ANB
DeLuca, Kevin and Anne Demo, 'Imagining Nature and Erasing Class and Race: Carleton Watkins, John Muir, and the Construction of Wilderness', *Environmental History* 6.4 (2001), 54–60.
'How John Muir inspired Roosevelt', *Current Opinion* 78 (1 March 1925), 337–8.
ODNB
Worster, Donald, *A Passion for Nature: The Life of John Muir* (Oxford: Oxford University Press, 2008).

Margaret Todd (1859–1918)

From **The Life of Sophia Jex-Blake** *(1918)*

Like Elizabeth Blackwell's *Pioneer Work in Opening the Medical Profession to Women* (1895), *The Life of Sophia Jex-Blake* (1918) by Margaret Todd, physician, novelist and intimate companion of Jex-Blake for twenty-five years, recounts the challenges faced by women seeking rigorous medical training to become practising physicians. Like Blackwell's, the story of physician and feminist campaigner Jex-Blake is also explicitly transatlantic, as the excerpts from Todd's account of Jex-Blake's sojourn in the US (1865–8) demonstrate.

Sophia Jex-Blake (1840–1912) attended private boarding schools, then Queen's College, London once she decided to become a teacher. In 1865 Jex-Blake travelled to the US to observe American educational institutions, publishing *A Visit to Some American Schools and Colleges* in 1867. More important for her subsequent career, in Boston she met Dr Lucy Ellen Sewall (1837–90), resident physician of the New England Hospital for Women and Children. While serving as clerk and nursing assistant in Sewall's hospital during a second US trip, Jex-Blake observed that many women avoided medical attention from male doctors due to concerns about modesty. This realisation fired Jex-Blake's determination to become a physician herself and serve women. She acquired all the training she could under Sewall, then sought admission to Harvard Medical School, which rejected her on grounds of sex.

Forced by her father's death to return to England in 1868, Jex-Blake had to fight again in London and Edinburgh for training and certification as a medical doctor. Because of her private income, she could sustain her campaign for women's medical school admission over several years. After earning her MD degree in 1877, she went on to found a medical school for women in Edinburgh in 1886, where she had opened her practice.

One of her students was Margaret Todd. By 1888 Todd moved in with Jex-Blake, remaining her companion until Jex-Blake's death. In 1892, still a medical student, Todd published the novel *Mona Maclean, Medical Student* under the pseudonym Graham Travers, which reflected the approaches to training at Jex-Blake's medical school (Swenson, 131). Todd practiced medicine only five years after earning her degree in 1894, retiring to move with Jex-Blake to Sussex once the latter's health declined. After Jex-Blake's death, Todd undertook a biography of Jex-Blake that drew largely from Jex-Blake's own diaries and letters. Not long after publishing the biography in 1918, Todd committed suicide (Swenson, 129).

From The Life of Sophia Jex-Blake

Dr. Lucy Sewall was at this time a young woman of 28, a worthy descendant of "a long line of truly noble ancestry."[110] She held the appointment of Resident Physician to the New England Hospital for Women and Children (an institution which had been founded in great measure through the exertions of her father, the Hon. Samuel Sewall), but there was nothing about her to suggest that she had adopted what was at that time an unusual line of life for a woman. Singularly girlish in appearance,

---

110 After graduating from the New England Female Medical College in Boston in 1862, Sewall had herself completed transatlantic training with physicians and hospitals in England and France. Her father was a lawyer, politician and abolitionist activist, and her mother came from a prominent Quaker family.

she was and remained throughout life so gentle and womanly that, until one knew her well, her reserves of strength were a source of repeated surprise. "So simple and humble and kindly," writes S. J.-B.[111] at this time, – "said she '*could* not succeed in learning to think enough before she spoke about a case.'"

No wonder S. J.-B. was attracted. A warm friendship sprang up between the two young women, a friendship by means of which S. J.-B. was introduced primarily to the world of Medicine, and, secondarily, to the wide question of Feminism. She had been living, of course, in a feminist world at home, and a very choice world of its kind; but here the movement had become more explicit, its aims were clearly defined and partially realized. It had, no doubt, lost a certain amount of charm in the process, but that is the fate of all movements the world over. They too have to be worked out "in the commonplace clay with which the world provides us."[112] [. . .]

> "Sat for a couple of hours in Dr. Sewall's dispensary this morning. Some 36 cases heard and helped more or less. Some coming with bright faces, – 'So much better, Doctor,' – some in pain enough, poor souls. Dr. Sewall with such a kindly ready sympathy, and such clear firm treatment for them all. Certainly the right woman in the right place, except in as far as she herself gets to look sadly fagged and tired sometimes."[113] [. . .]

[. . .] "You don't know," she writes to her Mother, "what an immense thing it is for us to have got free admission to the Woman's Hospital life here, – we are always doing something jolly together with the students and doctors, – all women, by the way.

> Dr. Sewall is resident Physician, and is always asking us to spend jolly evenings there, – or to join them in going to theatres, etc. Yesterday we made an expedition in the evening to a famous place for ice-cream, 8 of us there were – 4 M.D.s (one of whom is a splendid surgeon, – the first female surgeon I have heard of) two students and we two. After the ices we went back to the Hospital, and played a most ridiculous game of cards called 'Muggins', keeping us in roars of laughter half the time. Then Dr. Tyng[114] (the surgeon) sang, and, among other things gave us a specimen of the 'Shaker' singing – with its very peculiar religious dance, – have you heard about the Shakers?[115] I hope to see them and then I will tell you.
>
> But can't you understand how refreshing it is to slip into the bright life of all these working people – working hard all day, and then so ready for fun when work's over? It reminds me of the full colour and life of the old London times when all we working women were together." [. . .]

[. . .]

[. . .] Already in October one had heard of S. J.-B. "helping the doctor through oceans of figures in hospital reports," and one can well believe that she was an efficient member of the little community. The very day after she took up her residence

---

111 Margaret Todd's abbreviation throughout for Sophia Jex-Blake
112 What follows is an excerpt from S. J.-B.'s diary in the same chapter of Todd's biography.
113 In the following paragraphs Todd first quotes a letter from S. B.-J. to her mother, then a two-paragraph excerpt in the letter from S. J.-B.'s diary commenting on the sociability practised among US women physicians.
114 Anita E. Tyng (1837–1913), gynaecological surgeon
115 The Shakers were a radical Protestant communal sect whose distinctive worship practices gave rise to their name.

in the hospital precincts the "student" who did the dispensing was summoned away, and as – of course! – there was a run of arduous cases at the same time, S. J.-B. cheerfully volunteered to do the dispensing, – "and was very thankfully accepted" to fill the gap! Within a week she writes to her Mother:

"It's very amusing, dear, to learn to write and make up prescriptions so easily, – I shall be up to the doctors in future you see! I have just been making one up for myself under the doctor's directions, to my great amusement, – ... Besides being apothecary, I'm general secretary, – write all the business letters (which the doctor hates) and post up the hospital records of cases, etc. ; and besides this I requested to be and got appointed what I call 'chaplain' with discretionary powers. The only people who visit in the hospital (besides friends at visiting hours) are the Lady Managers, each of whom has a month on duty, and besides that Mr. Barnard comes and holds a short service and preaches every Sunday afternoon. So I thought that the patients would like some reading, etc., sometimes, and Dr. Sewall gave me leave to do all I liked ... You can't think how pleased they were all of them, and how heartily they asked me to come again, which I shall do pretty often." [...]

"Nov. 27th. We get up at 6.30 a.m., – breakfast at 7, then go round the wards with the doctors, then I make up the hospital medicines and see what drugs need to be ordered into the dispensary. The Dispensary opens at 9, or two days in the week at 10, and on Mondays and Thursdays (Dr. Sewall's days) I am there all the morning, making up prescriptions as fast as she writes them (two of us generally have our hands full, but sometimes I am alone), and very often we have not got through our work when the dinner-bell rings at 1 p.m. Dr. Sewall always has an enormous number of patients – from 60 to 70, and if I go down into the Dispensary waiting-room I get seized on so eagerly – 'Is Dr. Sewall here herself?' as she is occasionally obliged to be absent part of the time.

I think anyone who passed a couple of mornings in this dispensary would go away pretty well convinced of the enormous advantage of women doctors; and one sees daily how the poor women feel it by the crowds that come on the four days in the week when the lady physicians are in charge, and the handful that comes on the two days when a man presides ... They say that they have cases again and again of long-standing diseases which the women have borne rather than go to a man with their troubles, – and I don't wonder at it." [...]

[September 1866][116]
Excellent work was done at that Women's Hospital in Boston, as a number of our English women doctors have had reason to testify: sickness was relieved, and – what is quite as much to the point – competent and able doctors were turned out year by year. But of course the scholastic side of the work was on a very different level. Even for those days, the practical scientific education, and, above all, the sheer supply of material, were inadequate in the extreme. Then as now, of course, it was true that "la carrière ouverte aux talents,"[117] and when women doctors were so rare there was little doubt that a competent woman would make her way. Certainly it was not the hallmark of a good University degree that helped her, for good Universities existed

116 In between the prior events recorded in S. J.-B.'s 27 November 1865 diary and September 1866, she had journeyed back to England. In this excerpt, S. J.-B., has rejoined Sewall at the hospital.
117 'The course is open to men of talent', quotation attributed to Napoleon Bonaparte

for the male sex only. Graduation in America to this day may mean a great deal or it may mean just nothing at all. It was not the fault of the woman doctor of that period if her "degree" was one that failed to inspire the enthusiasm of those that understood.

Now S. J.-B.'s entry on any new sphere in life could seldom be fitly described as the addition of a little more of the same stuff. For better or worse, she was apt to come somewhat as the yeast comes to the dough, and yet that metaphor, too, falls short, for the medium reacted upon her as intensely perhaps as she acted on the medium. In the present case she had drifted into medical work all uncritical and full of admiration; but a visit to England brought her back as an outsider with her critical faculty fully awake. She saw that the need of adequate Graduation – urgent though it might be – was as nothing compared to the need of adequate Education. It *was* hard to make bricks without straw. In America women doctors had proved, against heavy odds, that women doctors were wanted. Why not give them a fair field? One heard on every side of the splendid advantages laid, so to speak, at the feet of men students at Harvard.

Why should not women be admitted to Harvard?

Why not ask?

In April, 1867, the following correspondence was published in *The Boston Daily Advertiser.*

"March 11th. 1867.

GENTLEMEN,

Finding it impossible to obtain elsewhere in New England a thoroughly competent medical education, we hereby request permission to enter the Harvard Medical School on the same terms and under the same conditions as other students, there being, as we understand, no university statute to the contrary.

On applying for tickets for the course, we were informed by the Dean of the Medical Faculty that he and his coadjutors were unable to grant them to us in consequence of some previous action taken by the corporation, to whom now therefore we make request to remove any such existing disability. In full faith in the words recently spoken with reference to the University of Harvard, – 'American colleges are not cloisters for the education of a few persons, but seats of learning whose hospitable doors should be always open to every seeker after knowledge' – we place our petition in your hands and subscribe ourselves,

Your obedient servants,
SOPHIA JEX-BLAKE
SUSAN DIMOCK[118]

To the President and Fellows of the University of Harvard."

"Harvard University. April 8th. 1867.

MY DEAR MADAM,

After consultation with the faculty of the Medical College, the corporation direct me to inform you and Miss Dimock that there is no provision for the education of women in any department of this university.

Neither the corporation nor the faculty wish to express any opinion as to the right or expediency of the medical education of women, but simply

---

118 Miss Susan Dimock was a student of great promise who afterwards completed her education at Zurich. She was lost at sea in the wreck of the steamer *Schiller* in May 1875. [Todd's note]

to state the fact that in our school no provision for that purpose has been made, or is at present contemplated.

Very respectfully yours,
THOMAS HILL.[119]

Miss S. Jex-Blake."

A few days later the following paragraph appeared in *The Advocate*:

"*The Beginning of the End.* A correspondence between the President and two lady applicants for admission to the Medical School was published some days since in the 'Boston Advertiser.' We understand that the friends of female education have no notion of resting satisfied with their first rebuff; and that prominent Alumni of Boston are already taking measures for the prolonged agitation of the question."

A month later S. J.-B. had obtained introductions to each of the professors in the Medical Faculty at Harvard, and to each member of the staff of the Massachusetts General Hospital and of the Eye and Ear Infirmary: as well as to many people of standing connected with these various institutions: and she now proceeded to canvass them systematically. In addition to a number of influential friends, she was ably supported by Miss Dimock.

On the whole their reception was encouraging. The individual letters, indeed, are so favourable, that the hopes of the inexperienced young applicants must have run high. The following from Dr. Oliver Wendell Holmes[120] is typical of some half dozen at least:

"I should not only be willing, but I should be much pleased, to lecture to any number of ladies for whom we can find accommodation in the anatomical lecture room, always provided that any special subject which seemed not adapted for an audience of both sexes should be delivered to the male students alone."

Dr. Brown Séquard[121] is even more emphatic in a letter to Dr. Holmes:

"MY DEAR PROFESSOR,
Miss Blake, who will hand you this note, wishes me to say that I am strongly in favour of the admission of persons of her sex at the Medical College. As such is my decided opinion, I write very willingly.

Very faithfully yours,
C. E. BROWN-SEQUARD"

The corporation of Harvard, however, exerted its power to veto any such inclinations on the part of individual professors.

---

119 Thomas Hill (1818–91), president of Harvard University from 1862–8
120 Oliver Wendell Holmes (1809–94), a physician and professor of anatomy at Harvard, is also known today for his writings, including *The Autocrat at the Breakfast Table* and poems such as 'The Chambered Nautilus'.
121 Dr Charles-Édouard Brown-Séquard (1817–94), physician and physiological researcher, taught at Harvard University 1864–8.

S. J.-B. quotes the above and a number of similar letters in the diary, and adds the comment:

      "All which ends in . . . smoke!"

Source text

Todd, Margaret, *The Life of Sophia Jex-Blake* (London: Macmillan, 1918).

References

ANB
ODNB
Swenson, Kristine, *Medical Women and Victorian Fiction* (Columbia, MO: University of Missouri Press, 2005).

9

SUFFRAGE AND CITIZENSHIP

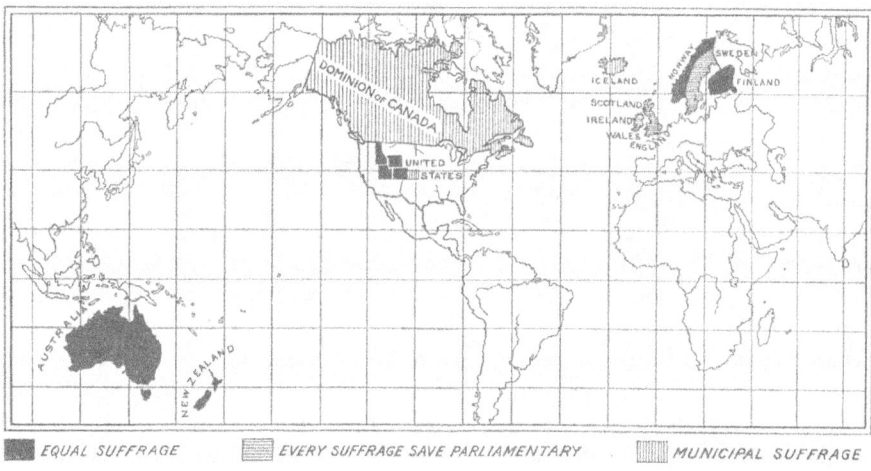

EQUAL SUFFRAGE   EVERY SUFFRAGE SAVE PARLIAMENTARY   MUNICIPAL SUFFRAGE

Figure 9.1 'Votes for Women: An Object-Lesson by Bertha Damaris Knobe:
Woman-Suffrage Map of the World, Showing the Forms of Enfranchisement
Granted in Various Countries', *Harper's Weekly* 52 (25 April 1908), 20.
Library of Congress Public Domain Archive.

Today the question of citizenship, of who counts as a citizen and has the right
to elect democratic representatives, continues to be vexed around the Atlantic basin in the face of global instability and debates over immigration and
national identity. These matters, however, were also salient features of politics and polemics on both sides of the Atlantic in the long nineteenth century.

Debates over citizenship actually began earlier still and, according to Dominique Leydet, revolved around two competing concepts of citizenship in the classical world: the republican model of citizenship advanced by Aristotle, and liberal approaches to citizenship maintained within the Roman empire.[1]

Republican citizenship requires a capacity for self-rule and active participation in governmental institutions, so that legal citizens are disposed both to rule and be ruled. The very term 'citizen', an Anglo-Norman hence intrinsically transatlantic word, derives from a root designating a resident of a city. The republican model was especially suited to Athenian democracy, which was predicated on direct rule of the city by citizens. Athenian citizenship was defined very narrowly, however, for it explicitly excluded women, the enslaved and foreigners. Among those holding the legal status of citizens, citizenship was an active practice among equals who rotated in holding political office.

The Roman model, in contrast, separated citizenship from political office but radically extended the boundaries of legal citizenship, since the Roman empire extended citizen rights to the peoples whose territories it conquered. Only the privileged few (again excluding women) held office, but citizenship within the empire was inclusive and multi-racial.

TRANSATLANTIC CITIZENSHIP

As new ideas about democracy and representative government emerged in the Atlantic world against the backdrop of the American and French Revolutions, these contrasting classical models of citizenship continued to inform debates over citizenship and suffrage throughout the long nineteenth century. These debates in turn entered transatlantic print culture as both prominent and marginalised writers registered in books and periodicals their contrasting arguments about who was capable of self-rule and governance, and who should be welcomed as citizens and given democratic rule's highest privilege: the right to vote and determine political leadership.

Until 4 July 1776, all English-speaking colonial residents in the Caribbean territories and North America, as well as in the British Isles, were subjects of British rule and the unwritten British constitution that guaranteed (to those who were free) rights such as trial by jury. But only a very few held suffrage rights. No women, children, Indigenes or enslaved persons could vote, while the vast majority of middle- and lower-class white men were also excluded from the vote as only property owners whose land was valued at forty shillings or more in potential rents held suffrage rights. Thus somewhat less than three per cent of free men could vote in Parliamentary elections. In the pre-Revolution colonies of America, many local governments were run on the ancient republican model of self-rule and highly participatory governance, yet colonial governors were mostly selected by the Crown in England.

After the American Revolution and into the twentieth century, the transatlantic history of suffrage and citizenship was gradual movement toward widening the franchise and definitions of who counted as citizens – counterpointed by firm opposition among many (not all) of those already holding power. A central

---

1 Dominique Leydet, 'Citizenship', in Edward N. Zalta (ed.), *The Stanford Encyclopedia of Philosophy* (Fall 2017 edition), Web.

reference point in reforms promoting liberal citizenship and the extension of suffrage rights was the document with which this section begins: the collaboratively written Declaration of Independence attributed to Thomas Jefferson that declared, in keeping with universalist Enlightenment principles, that all 'men' were inherently equal with the right to pursue 'happiness' in whatever way seemed most fitting to individuals.

The American Revolution initially attracted sporadic European interest since this involved only Britain and a distant colony across the rough waters of the Atlantic. The French Revolution, in contrast, was more immediately cataclysmic since an entire ancient order of monarchy and privileged nobles was overthrown. In Britain, famously, Edmund Burke (1729–97) immediately wrote in opposition to the British-born emigrant to America Thomas Paine (1737–1809), whose *Common Sense* (1776) had bolstered the American cause of independence and who immediately endorsed the French Revolution. Burke's *Reflections on the Revolution in France* (1790) repudiated Paine's support of revolutions based on human rights. Instead, he urged a strictly republican model of a state governed by an elite under a constitutional monarch that changed only gradually as 'organic' developments emerged from longstanding institutions and principles. Still, the inspiring preamble to the American *Declaration of Independence* steadily expanded in influence and inspired efforts within and without its own borders toward reforms that ensured full citizenship and democratic rights for ever more inclusive populations.

In practice the new nation followed a far less robust programme of equality and liberty and, from the beginning, legalised a number of oppressions and exclusions based on race and gender. One clause of the Declaration itself justified revolution because George III had not sufficiently protected white colonists against 'the merciless Indian savages', and in the face of European-American desire to expand westward, Native Americans were repeatedly objects of conquest and displacement. Concurrently, though, at the very outset of US history Abigail Adams wrote to her husband John to 'Remember the Ladies' as members of the Constitutional Congress gathered to enact a 'New Code of Laws' that formed the newly born nation's governing principles. US women would not achieve suffrage rights until 1920, our concluding date in this anthology.[2] And even then Native and Chinese American women were excluded from this citizenship right, as were their counterparts in Canada. The very personhood of enslaved Blacks was denied in the notorious compromise of the 1787 Constitution of the US, which counted an enslaved human only as 3/5 of a person. As for the first peoples under both British and US rule, majority white governments repeatedly made treaties in support of Indigenes' sovereign status and as repeatedly violated them when it suited governmental interests (see also Joseph Brant's speech in 'Migration and Settlement').

SUFFRAGE AND OTHER REVOLUTIONS

The obverse side of this history and the print culture it inspired was born of activist efforts in Britain, the US, Canada and the Caribbean by those who resisted exclusion and oppression and repeatedly pressed for full legal status

---

2 Letter from Abigail Adams to John Adams, 31 March 1776, in Margaret A. Hogan and C. James Taylor (eds), *My Dearest Friend: Letters of Abigail and John Adams* (Cambridge, MA: Harvard University Press, 2007), 110.

as citizens – efforts that met with some decided advances but remain as yet incomplete today. The push toward liberal citizenship and citizens' rights to participate in governance opens below with the 1804 Haitian declaration of independence from French rule by Jean-Jacques Dessalines, a French document quickly translated into English. Haiti, as an independent country governed by Blacks, stood as a symbol of possible transformation elsewhere to transatlantic peoples of colour. And for that very reason the Haitian Revolution and its leaders were a source of anxiety for proponents of exclusive white rule. Hence Haiti (or Hayti, as it was often spelled) would figure as an antagonist to the prominent man of letters Thomas Carlyle in 1849, who insisted that formerly enslaved Blacks lacked capacity for self-rule. But more than eighty years after Dessalines's declaration, John Jacob Thomas hailed that revolution as a beacon of Black empowerment and self-rule in *Froudacity* (1889), a systematic critique of a more recent polemic against Caribbean Blacks by another prominent Englishman of letters, James Anthony Froude.

Another hotbed of revolutionary activity in the long nineteenth century (and into the twentieth) was Ireland, a predominantly white nation nestled close to Britain but nonetheless another colonised land. Here the Anglo-Irish Ascendancy, a network of Protestant landlords, clergy and office-holders, governed the mainly Catholic, Gaelic-speaking people of Ireland and excluded them from any central role as citizens. Jonah Barrington cited the American Revolution as a motivating precedent for the 1798 Irish uprising, which sought to overthrow British rule but was brutally suppressed, leading to the 1801 Act of Union that annexed Ireland to Britain to form the United Kingdom. Barrington's protests would be reprised later in the century by Fenian and related movements, and some of the notorious dynamiters in London in the 1880s and beyond were planned by Irish exiles in North America who travelled transatlantically to join Irish-based resistance.[3]

Almost three decades before US President Abraham Lincoln issued his Emancipation Proclamation in 1862 that declared US enslavement null and void, British writer Harriet Martineau measured US enslavement against that country's Declaration of Independence and decried the blatant hypocrisy in *Society in America* (1837), published transatlantically. Autobiographer, journalist and abolitionist Frederick Douglass also looked back to 4 July 1776 in his Independence Day oration of 1852, 'What to the American Slave is your 4th of July?', as he addressed the Ladies' Anti-Slavery Society in Rochester, New York. Douglass's critique of US governmental hypocrisy was given added ethos since he could speak both as one who had been enslaved and one who held citizenship rights in the present. And his repeated formal address to his hearers as 'Fellow Citizens' throughout his speech rhetorically enacted the difference made by the full conferral of citizenship rights upon the free. Eventually legal enslavement was eradicated throughout the Atlantic world. But as many of the selections in the Abolition section of this anthology make clear, it was long before Black US, Canadian and Caribbean citizens secured full access to active political participation.

Another critique of US society lodged by Harriet Martineau in 1837 was that, contrary to the US Declaration and Constitution, women were subjected to taxation without representation and had no means, as non-voting residents

---

3 Niall Whelehan, *The Dynamiters: Irish Nationalism and Political Violence in the Wider World, 1867–1900* (Cambridge: Cambridge University Press, 2012), 83ff.

of the US, of giving their consent to be governed. US Abolitionist writers Maria Weston Chapman (1837) and Elizabeth Cady Stanton (1848) similarly resisted patriarchal governance, whether by Protestant clergymen in Chapman's case or exclusively male Congressional representation in Stanton's address. Part and parcel of full citizenship was the franchise, and subsequent decades witnessed ever more transatlantic women demanding the vote. The full-blown transatlantic female suffragist movement is represented in our anthology by British militant suffragist Emmeline Pankhurst, whose Hartford, Connecticut address in 1913 reprised the democratic principle of the necessary consent of the governed and justified British suffragists' turn to violent protest to register their refusal of consent, inspiring some US suffragists in turn. That same year saw the US nurse Ellen La Motte travel to London as a foreign correspondent to report on suffragist militancy to the *Baltimore Sun*, only to be knocked down as police set upon the suffragists, culminating in La Motte's futile if humorous attempt to testify against police brutality in court.

White feminists, unlike Black suffragists like Sojourner Truth who were also abolitionist activists, did not always take care to extend rhetorical and protest efforts toward gaining suffrage for Black citizens. Indeed, Elizabeth Cady Stanton objected to formerly enslaved Blacks who had had no access to education being granted the franchise before white middle-class women. Black writer and philosopher Anna Julia Cooper, a US citizen who would later earn a PhD from the Sorbonne, advocated for women's equal access to the education needed for empowerment as citizens in 1892; but unlike Stanton she explicitly proclaimed the need to ensure higher education for Black women. A US activist for civil rights for Blacks and women alike, Frances Ellen Watkins Harper deliberately fashioned her poetry, speeches and fiction as interventions, whether declaiming her poetry in public or printing her work. She demonstrated the global impetus of reformist action in her poem 'Maceo' near the century's end, celebrating the eponymous Afro-Cuban general who had helped lead the Free Cuba movement.

Another woman poet, Pauline Johnson, linked support for women's rights to First Nation rights within the British Commonwealth. The daughter of a Mohawk chief and an Anglo-American mother, Johnson also performed her verse under the name Tekahionwake, and in 'The Lodge of the Lawmakers' (1896) she contrasted the Iroquois nation's long tradition of participatory, inclusive governance councils open to men and women with the inferior model offered up by the British Parliament that persisted in denying rights to women despite public protests. This section concludes with US Indigenous writer Gertrude Simmons Bonnin, who issued the demand for full citizenship rights for Native Americans in an explicitly international transatlantic context of peace and social justice movements across gender, ethnicity and national borders following the 1918 Armistice that concluded the First World War.

References

Bonner, Christopher James, *Remaking the Republic: Black Politics and the Creation of American Citizenship* (Philadelphia, PA: University of Pennsylvania Press, 2020).

Hall, Catherine, *Civilising Subjects: Metropole and Colony in the English Imagination 1830–1867* (Chicago: University of Chicago Press, 2002).

Krauthamer, Barbara, *Black Slaves, Indian Masters: Slavery, Emancipation, and Citizenship in the Native American South* (Chapel Hill, NC: University of North Carolina Press, 2015).

McFadden, Margaret, *Golden Cables of Sympathy: The Transatlantic Sources of Nineteenth-Century Feminism* (Lexington, KY: University Press of Kentucky, 1999).

Smith, Donald B. and Nellie Oosterom, 'Worlds Apart', *Canada's History* 97.5 (October–November 2017), 30–7.

Thomas Jefferson (1743–1826) et al.

From The Declaration of Independence *(1776)*

In the summer of 1776 delegates from thirteen British colonies in North America met in Philadelphia to draft an official declaration of independence from Great Britain. On 11 June a 'Committee of Five' delegates (John Adams, Benjamin Franklin, Robert Livingston, Roger Sherman and Thomas Jefferson) was appointed to draft a document in support of this aim. What was produced resulted from a collaborative process of deliberation, amendment and revision, yet since the first draft was written in Jefferson's hand, authorship has traditionally been attributed to him.

Beyond recording a litany of grievances the colonies had with the Crown of England, the document makes several radical assertions regarding human nature and government. First, it declares the right of a given people to form their own government. Second, it holds that 'all men are created equal' and that those 'men' have 'unalienable Rights' including 'Life, Liberty and the pursuit of Happiness' that have been bestowed by the Creator. Finally, it argues that any government proving deficient or abusive may be abolished and reformed via the will of the people. While the subjects of these were originally limited to free white men of property, the principle has since been extended to people around the world. Widely distributed domestically and abroad, the American *Declaration of Independence* became the basis for subsequent declarations by rebels and revolutionaries, notably the *Haitian Declaration of Independence* and Seneca Falls *Declaration of Rights and Sentiments*. The preamble to the Declaration is reprinted below, from the London periodical *The Gentleman's Magazine and Historical Chronicle*, indicative of the degree to which the text circulated on both sides of the Atlantic.

From The Declaration of Independence

IN CONGRESS, JULY 4, 1776
The unanimous Declaration of the thirteen United States of America

When in the Course of human events it becomes necessary for one people to dissolve the political bands which have connected them with another and to assume among the powers of the earth, the separate and equal station to which the Laws of Nature and of Nature's God entitle them, a decent respect to the opinions of mankind requires that they should declare the causes which impel them to the separation.

We hold these truths to be self-evident, that all men are created equal, that they are endowed by their Creator with certain unalienable Rights, that among these are Life, Liberty and the pursuit of Happiness. — That to secure these rights, Governments are instituted among Men, deriving their just powers from the consent of the governed, — That whenever any Form of Government becomes destructive of these ends, it is the Right of the People to alter or to abolish it, and to institute new Government, laying its foundation on such principles and organizing its powers in such form, as to them shall seem most likely to effect their Safety and Happiness. Prudence, indeed, will dictate that Governments long established should not be changed for light and transient causes; and accordingly all experience hath shewn that mankind are more disposed to suffer, while evils are sufferable than to right themselves by abolishing the forms to which they are accustomed. But when a long train of abuses and usurpations, pursuing invariably the same Object evinces a design to reduce them under absolute Despotism, it is their right, it is their duty, to throw off such Government, and to provide new Guards for their future security. — Such has been the patient sufferance of these Colonies; and such is now the necessity which constrains them to alter their former Systems of Government. The history of the present King of Great Britain is a history of repeated injuries and usurpations, all having in direct object the establishment of an absolute Tyranny over these States. To prove this, let Facts be submitted to a candid world.

Source text

[Jefferson, Thomas], 'The Declaration of Independence', *The Gentleman's Magazine and Historical Chronicle* 66 (1776), 361–2.

References

Armitage, David, *The Declaration of Independence: A Global History* (Cambridge, MA: Harvard University Press, 2007).

Deroin, Jeanne and Pauline Roland, 'Letter to the Convention of the Women of America, 15 June 1851', in Elizabeth Cady Stanton, Susan B. Anthony and Matilda Joslyn Gage (eds), *History of Woman Suffrage, Vol. 1, 1848–1861* (New York: Fowler & Wells, 1881), 234–7.

Jean-Jacques Dessalines (1758–1806)

From The Haitian Declaration of Independence *(1804)*

In 1804, as the Declaration excerpted below affirms, a conflict of over a decade culminated in a new Caribbean nation (St Domingue, today's Haiti) forged through 'an alliance of African-born, black creole, and mixed-race insurgents' (Perry, 45). A conflict with huge casualties, the result was historic, including the expulsion of the French, the creation of the first independent nation in Latin America and the launch of the first Black-led sovereign republic. Beyond its seismic transatlantic impact on Haiti and France, the Declaration struck awe and fear into slaveholders and their supporters in the English-speaking transatlantic, where the term 'declaration' first began to circulate in many reprinted translations of the document versus the French terms *proclamation* or *acte*, more in tune with the original (Armitage and Gaffield, 11). Although twenty-first-century Haiti is now in the throes of environmental, political and social crises, the impact of this earlier nineteenth-century history on transatlantic culture cannot be overstated.

Proclaimed on 1 January 1804, the 'Acte d'indépendance', a three-part document, departed from the model offered by American and French predecessors. The first section, labelled 'Armée Indigène' in the original French, presented an oath in which Jean-Jacques Dessalines's generals affirm the break with France and swear to die rather than live under her domination. The second section entails a formal statement addressed to all the people and signed by Dessalines himself, presenting a rationale for why freedom from France is necessary. The final section enshrines yet another oath by Haitian generals, affirming Dessalines as ruler for life. We excerpt from all three sections below.

Since Jean-Jacques Dessalines had limited ability for composing in formal French of the day, many scholars attribute at least part of the text as 'scripted by [Louis Félix] Boisrond-Tonnerre', as well as bearing his signature as secretary (Armitage and Gaffield, 13). But the document can also be viewed as a combination of dictation and multiple collaborations, with Dessalines speaking in its 'conceptual voice', at the least (Jenson, 76).

Patricia Killian prepared the translation below, in collaboration with anthology co-editor Sarah Ruffing Robbins, taking an approach of using language that would be accessible to today's student readers.

From The Haitian Declaration of Independence

Liberty or Death
Army of the People

Today, the first of January, 1804,[4] the Commander in Chief of the Armed Forces of Saint Domingue, Dessalines, met with [our] Generals, the Leaders of the Armed Forces, to discuss the independence of Haiti.[5] The Generals were summoned in

---

4 An earlier formal declaration, issued on 29 November 1803, by Dessalines, along with Henri Christophe and Augustin Clerv[e]aux, had already proclaimed the 'independence of Saint. Domingue under the authority of the "Black People and Men of Colour of St. Domingo"' (Armitage and Gaffield, 'Introduction', 5). Recent scholarship has questioned the relationship between the earlier document and the tripartite one excerpted here: 'Why is January 1 celebrated as Independence Day and not November 29? What was the motivation in the writing and distribution of the January 1 document in place of the November 29 document?' (Armitage and Gaffield, 6).

5 Armitage and Gaffield emphasise that the early stages of the Haitian Revolution, under Toussaint Louverture's leadership, had a different character than under Dessalines: 'While Louverture had struggled for greater colonial autonomy, the revolution had not been about political independence. The French army's arrival [in 1802] changed this', they say, leading to outright revolution ('Introduction', 4).

order to take steps which are intended to ensure the happiness of the people. Dessalines explained his true goal for the country.

He made known to the Generals his true intention and his deepest concern, which was to assure the indigenous peoples[6] of Haiti that they would have a stable government forever. He imparted this idea in a speech which communicates to Foreign Powers his determination to make the country independent and to allow the people to enjoy a freedom consecrated by their own blood.

After having gathered the views of those present, the Commander in Chief has asked that each one of the Generals in attendance take an oath to renounce France forever, to die rather than to live under her domination, and to fight for freedom until their last breath.

The Generals, instilled with these sacred principles, after having given their unanimous support to the clearly communicated proposal of independence, have all sworn to posterity, to the entire universe, to renounce all ties with France, and to die rather than live under her domination.

Declared in Gonaïves,[7] this 1st of January 1804 and the first day of the independence of Haiti.[8]

[Part 2: Formal Declaration Statement]

The Commander in Chief[9]
To the people of Haiti
Citizens,

It is not enough to have thrown out of your country the barbarians who have bloodied it for two centuries; it is not enough to have put an end to the continually reemerging factions which were each in turn, playing with the illusion of liberty that France was setting before your eyes; we must, through a final act of national authority, put in place forever the empire of freedom in the country of our birth. We must snatch away from the inhumane government which has been for a long time keeping our spirits in the most humiliating stupor, any hope whatsoever of enslaving us once again. We must finally live free or die. [...]

And you, invaluable men, fearless Generals, who, paying no heed to your own troubles, have brought liberty back to life by sacrificing all your blood for freedom, know that you have done nothing unless you give to all nations, a frightening yet just example of the vengeance that a people, proud to have won back their freedom and protective of its conservation; will do all that is needed to maintain it. Let us frighten all those who would dare to seize it again from us: let us begin with the French. May

---

6 In using the term 'indigène', the Declaration would seem both to claim a common birthplace for all Haiti's peoples and to assert that these same people were the island's original inhabitants – neither of which was true. Indigenous people of the Caribbean preceded the arrival of enslaved Africans. Yet, as Amanda Perry points out, 'As of 1791, more than half the total population of colonial Saint-Domingue had been born in Africa'. Promoting a solidarity grounded in imagined shared indigeneity, the Declaration 'not only reimagines these Africans as "natives"; it addresses all the subjects of the new state as indigenous, the Indigenous Citizens led by Dessalines as the Chief of the Indigenous Army' (45).
7 Identified at the close of the second document as the army's headquarters
8 This statement is followed by a list of signatures, including the generals' various titles and ranks, beginning with Dessalines himself, seconded by Henri Christophe and Alexandre Pétion, along with several others, then finalised by Boisrond-Tonnerre as secretary.
9 Note Dessalines's assertion of authority here.

they tremble in reaching our coasts, if not from the memory of the cruelties which they carried out there, at least from the terrifying resolution that we are going to make: that we promise to put to death any native-born Frenchman who would soil with his unholy step, the land of liberty.

We have dared to be liberated, let us dare to be free by ourselves and for ourselves. Let us imitate the child who is growing up: his own weight is breaking the boundary which becomes useless and keeps him from moving ahead. Which people fought for us? Which people would like to reap the fruits of our labor? And what could be more of a dishonorable absurdity than to win in order to be enslaved. Enslaved! . . . let us leave to the French this name; they have won,[10] but now, in doing so, they have ceased to be free.

Let us follow other paths; let us imitate these peoples who, considering the importance of the future and learning to leave to the past the example of cowardice, have preferred to be destroyed rather than stricken from the list of free peoples.

Nevertheless, let us hold back from preaching, which could destroy our work. Let us allow our neighbours to breathe in peace; let them live peacefully under the laws which they made for themselves. Let us not go about like revolutionaries, setting ourselves up on a pedestal as the sole law-makers of the Antilles.[11] Let us not, in our glory, trouble the rest of the islands which are our neighbours. Contrary to our own experience, their islands have not been drenched in the blood of their innocent inhabitants. They have no vengeance to carry out against the authority that protects them. They have no reason to take revenge on the leadership that protects them.

These neighboring islands are fortunate never to have known the scourges that destroyed us. All they can do is express wishes for our prosperity.

For our neighbours, we wish peace, but we curse the French name and express our eternal hatred of France: that is our cry.

People of Haiti! It was my fortunate destiny to be the sentry who had to ensure the well-being of the revered quality for which you are sacrificing. I have watched over and fought, sometimes alone, and if I was lucky enough to put back into your hands the sacred gift which you entrusted to me, know that it is now up to you to conserve it. In fighting for your freedom, I worked for my own happiness. Before strengthening this liberty through laws that ensure your individual freedom, your Leaders, whom I have brought together here, as well as myself, we owe you this last proof of our devotion.

Generals, and you, Leaders, brought together close to me for the happiness of our country, the day has come, this day which must make our glory and our independence live on forever.

If among us, there is one whose support is only half-hearted, may he pull back, trembling in fear, from taking the oath which must unite us.

Let us swear to the entire universe, to posterity, and to ourselves, to give up all ties to France forever, and to die rather than live under her domination. Let us promise to fight until our last breath, for the independence of our country.

And you, people who have been ill-fated for too long, witness the oath that we are taking. Remember that it is your courage and your faithfulness on which I counted when I threw myself into the work of freedom in order to fight the despotism and the tyranny that you had been struggling against for 14 years; remember that I have sacrificed everything to fly to your defense: parents, children, and

---

10 The tone for 'won' is delivered ironically, or even sarcastically, here.
11 Islands of the West Indies in the Caribbean

fortune. Now the only wealth I possess is your liberty. Remember also that my name has become terrifying to all people who support slavery, and that despots and tyrants only say my name while cursing the day I was born. If ever you were to refuse or receive half-heartedly the laws that the spirit who watches over your destiny assigns to me to manage for your well-being, then you would deserve the fate of ungrateful peoples.

But put aside that horrible thought; you the people will be the support of the liberty you cherish, and the support of your Commander in Chief.

From the hands of your Commander, therefore, take the oath to live freely and independently, and to prefer death to anything that would put you again under the yoke. Swear finally, to pursue forever the traitors and the enemies of your independence.

Declared at the Headquarters of Gonaïves on January 1st, 1804, the first year of Independence,
Signed,   J.J. Dessalines

Figure 9.2 'Jean-Jacques Dessalines; Governor-General of Haiti, 1804; Jacques I, Emperor of Haiti, 1804–6'. Schomburg Center for Research in Black Culture, Jean Blackwell Hutson Research and Reference Division, New York Public Library. *The New York Public Library Digital Collections.* 1910.

Figure 9.3 'Toussaint Louverture, about 1802'. Schomburg Center for Research in Black Culture, Jean Blackwell Hutson Research and Reference Division, New York Public Library. *The New York Public Library Digital Collections.* 1910.

Jean-Jacques Dessalines and Touissant Louverture – both formerly enslaved heroes of the initial Haitian Revolution – emerged from the extended conflict to face distinct yet similar fates. Louverture (1743–1803), who consolidated his leadership of the entire island in the years after the 1791 initial rebellion, accepted an offer to meet with a French general in 1802, was arrested and deported to France, and died imprisoned there in 1803. After Louverture's capture, Dessalines assumed the office of Governor-General, as outlined in the Acte d'indépendance, though he was assassinated in 1806.

In the Name of the Haitian People

We the Generals and Commanders of the Armed Forces of Haiti are filled with gratitude for the blessings we have received from the Commander in Chief, Jean-Jacques Dessalines, defender of the liberty which our people now enjoy.

In the name of liberty, in the name of independence, in the name of the people he has made happy, we proclaim him to be Haitian Governor General for life; we swear to obey without question the laws coming from his authority, the only one that we will recognise; we give him the right to make peace, to make war, and to name his successor.[12]

Declared at the Headquarters of Gonaïves, on this day, the first of January 1804, the first day of our independence. [...][13]

At Port-au-Prince

From the Printing Press of the Government[14]

Source text

Haitian Declaration of Independence. 1 January 1804. The National Archives, KEW. Records of the Colonial Office and predecessors: Jamaica, Original Correspondence. CO 137/111/1.

---

12 In *Haitian Connections*, Julia Gaffield notes an important context for this claim: 'There was no legal document conceding France's defeat and the granting to Haiti of its independence and sovereignty, as had been the case with the Treaty of Paris in 1783, through which the British Empire had acknowledged the independence of the United States of America' (7). Further, with war ongoing between France and Britain, foreign governments had to navigate complex transnational relations involving Haiti – one factor which may have contributed to what Gaffield dubs an inaccurate '"isolation thesis"', viewing Haiti as cut off from the world after independence (2). She provides extensive evidence of transnational interactions, alongside Haitians' continued assertions of sovereignty, like Dessalines's given here and tempered by his calls to his countrymen to avoid calling for revolutions elsewhere.

13 Like the first of the three documents, this one closes with affirming signatures from a group of generals. For Jenson, different dignitaries being listed as signing the first and third documents suggests that, despite repetition of the January 1 inscribed date, all three texts may not have been generated on the same day.

14 Printing by a Press designated as official to the new government helped enable wide circulation of the 'Acte' text, which was translated and reprinted throughout the Atlantic world.

References

Armitage, David and Julia Gaffield, 'Introduction: The Haitian Declaration of Independence in an Atlantic Context', in Julia Gaffield (ed.), *The Haitian Declaration of Independence: Creation, Context, and Legacy* (Charlottesville, VA: University of Virginia Press, 2016), 1–22.

Gaffield, Julia, *Haitian Connections in the Atlantic World: Recognition after Revolution* (Chapel Hill, NC: University of North Carolina Press, 2015).

Girard, Philippe R., 'Jean-Jacques Dessalines and the Atlantic System: A Reappraisal', *William and Mary Quarterly* 69.3 (July 2012), 549–82.

Jenson, Deborah, 'Dessalines's American Proclamations of the Haitian Independence', *Journal of Haitian Studies* 15.1–2 (2009), 72–102.

Perry, Amanda T., 'Becoming Indigenous in Haiti, from Dessalines to *La Révue Indigène*', *Small Axe* 21.2 (July 2017), 45–61.

Jonah Barrington (1756?–1834)

From Rise and Fall of the Irish Nation *(1833)*

Contra the rising tide of revolution in the US, France and Latin America, Ireland established closer ties with England in the late eighteenth century as a result of the Union Act. In response Jonah Barrington, an Irishman and fierce opponent of Unionisation, laboured to expose the secret records, letters and papers precipitating the National Convention, the 1798 Rebellion and the Act of Union. His *Historic Memoirs of Ireland* was published in two volumes, with the first arriving in 1809. Publication of the second volume was delayed, perhaps in exchange for his safe exile in France, until 1835. His writing was notorious for relaying salacious and racy material (often of dubious veracity) about prominent Irishmen of the period.

The following excerpt is from 'Prefatory Observations' and Chapter One of Barrington's 1833 *Rise and Fall of the Irish Nation*, which was first published in London and later France and the US. The volume's subtitle is 'A full account of the bribery and corruption by which the union was carried; the family histories of the members who voted away the Irish parliament; with an extraordinary Black list of the Titles, places, and pensions which they received for their corrupt votes'. In the excerpt Barrington reflects on the pernicious changes to Ireland in the three decades since Union and laments how the Irish were unable to follow the model of the US in gaining liberty from Great Britain.

From Rise and Fall of the Irish Nation

More than thirty summers have now passed by, since that disastrous measure, called a "legislative Union" extinguished at one blow, the pride, the prosperity, and the Independence of the Irish Nation.[15]

---

15 In 1800 the Parliaments of Great Britain and Ireland passed parallel acts which created the United Kingdom. In Ireland the act was controversial, as its passage was secured on the second vote through extensive bribery of dozens of Irish MPs.

A measure which, under the false colours of guarding for ever against a disunion of the Empire, has taken the longest, and surest stride, to lead it to dismemberment.

A measure which, instead of "*consolidating the strength and resources of the Empire*," as treacherously expressed from the Throne of the Viceroy,[16] has, through its morbid operation, paralysed the resources of Ireland; whilst England is exhausting her own strength, squandering her own treasures, and clipping her own constitution, to uphold a measure, effected by corruption, and maintained by oppression.

A measure which, pretending to tranquillize, has in fact excited more hostile, and I fear, interminable disgust, than had ever before existed between the two nations, and has banished from both, that mutual and invigorating attachment, which was daily augmenting, under the continuance of the federative connexion.

The protecting body of the country gentlemen have evacuated Ireland, and in their stead, we now find official clerks, griping agents, haughty functionaries and proud Clergy — the resident Aristocracy of Ireland, if not quite extinguished, is hourly diminishing; and it is a political truism, that the coexistence of an oligarchy, without a cabinet — a resident executive, and an absent legislation—tenants without landlords, and magistrates without legal knowledge — must be, from its nature, a form of constitution at once incongruous, inefficient, and dangerous. The present is a state which cannot exist; it is a struggle, that cannot continue — there is "a tide" in the affairs of Empires, as well as of individuals; every fever has a crisis: Ireland is in one now — I am not fanatic, I am the partisan only of tranquillity, in the country where I drew my first breath.

The people of England, and also of some continental kingdoms, are fully aware of the distracted state of Ireland, but are at a loss to account for it; it is now however in proof, that thirty-three years of Union have been thirty-three years of beggary and disturbance, and this result, I may fairly say, I always foresaw. [. . .]

In fact the world has now become not only enlightened, but illuminated, by the progress of political information; and it is as clear as day that there are but two ways, through which eight millions of Irish population can ever be governed with security: either through the re-enjoyment of her own constitution, and voluntary affection to her rulers, or by physical force of arms, and the temporary right of conquest — the former even now requires only the will of England, and the word reconciliation; but both ancient and modern examples fully prove, that the whole physical force and power of Great Britain might find itself dangerously deceived in trying to establish by the sword, a system so repugnant to the very nature of the English people. [. . .]

It was about this period, when the short-sighted policy of the British Government had by its own arbitrary proceedings planted the seeds of that political philosophy, afterwards so fatal to the most powerful monarchies of Europe, that Ireland began to feel herself affected by the struggles of America: — the spirit of independence had crossed the Atlantic, and the Irish people, awakened from a trance, beheld with anxiety the contest, in which they now began to feel an interest. They regarded with admiration the exertions of a colony combating for the first principles of civil liberty, and giving to the world an instructive lesson of fortitude and perseverance.

---

16 Lord Charles Cornwallis (1738–1805) served as the Lord Lieutenant or Viceroy of Ireland from 1798 to 1801. Only Protestant English noblemen could be appointed to the position.

Spread over a vast expanse of region, America, without wealth — without resources — without population — without fortresses — without allies — had every thing to contend with, and every thing to conquer: — but freedom was her call and as if she had been designed by Providence for an example to the universe of what even powerless states can achieve by enthusiasm and *unanimity*, her strength increased with her deprivations, and the firmness of one great and good man converted the feebleness of a colony into the power of an Empire. The defeats of Washington[17] augmented his armies — his wants and necessities called forth his intellect — while his wisdom, firmness, and moderation, produced him powerful friends, and secured him ultimate victory. — The strength of Great Britain at length yielded to the vigor of his mind, and the unflinching fortitude of his people; and Lord Cornwallis (the chosen instrument for oppressing heroic nations), by his defeat, and his captivity, established the independence of America. The arrogance of England bowed its proud head to the shrine of liberty and her favorite general led back the relics of his conquered army, to commemorate in the mother country the impotence of her power, and emancipation of her colonies.

While these great events were gradually proceeding towards their final completion, Ireland became every day a more anxious spectator of the arduous conflict — every incident in America began to communicate a sympathetic impulse to the Irish people: — the moment was critical: — the nation became enlightened — a patriotic ardor took possession of her whole frame, and, before she had well considered the object of her solicitude, the spark of constitutional liberty had found its way into her bosom.

The disposition of Ireland to avail herself of the circumstances of those times, so favourable to the attainment of her rights, now openly avowed itself. — Her determination to claim her constitution from the British Government became unequivocal, and she began to assume the attitude and language of a nation "*entitled to independence*."[18] — The sound of arms and the voice of freedom echoed from every quarter of the island — distinctions were forgotten, or disregarded — every rank, every religion, alike caught the general feeling, — but firmness and *discretion* characterized her proceedings: — she gradually arose from torpor and obscurity — her native spirit drew aside the curtain, that had so long concealed her from the world; and exhibited an armed and animated people, claiming their natural rights, and demanding their constitutional liberty.

Source text

Barrington, Jonah, *Rise and Fall of the Irish Nation* (Paris: G. G. Bennis, 1833).

References

Barrington, Jonah, *Historic Memoirs of Ireland* (London: Henry Colburn, 1835).

---

17 General George Washington; in 1776–7 Washington's army suffered defeats by the British at White Plains, Fort Washington, Brandywine and Germantown.
18 Religious minorities formed the Society of the United Irishmen in 1791 which, influenced by the American and French Revolutions, sought to overthrow British Rule. Under principles of liberty and equality the rebels pushed for independence, only for the Irish Rebellion of 1798 to be crushed by British forces.

Maria Weston Chapman (1806–85)

'The Times That Try Men's Souls' (1837)

Abolitionist and reformer Maria Weston Chapman was born in Weymouth, Massachusetts, but educated in England. In 1828 she returned to the US to serve as principal of Ebenezer Bailey's Young Ladies High School. Two years later she married businessman Henry Chapman and the couple had four children. The Chapmans were active in reform movements, especially abolition, and Maria was a prominent member of the Boston Female Anti-Slavery Society, the Massachusetts Anti-Slavery Society, the New England Anti-Slavery Society and the American Anti-Slavery Society. Maria published the pamphlet *Right and Wrong in Massachusetts* in 1839, and served as editor of the anti-slavery annual *The Liberty Bell* from 1839 to 1858 and the *Non-Resistant*, the publication of William Lloyd Garrison's New England Non-Resistance Society, from 1839 to 1842, as well as ancillary editor of Garrison's *The Liberator*. The following satirical poem reprinted in *The Liberator* was Chapman's response to orthodox clergymen who had issued a pastoral letter in 1837 that sharply criticised female abolitionists as a danger to female character (Goodwin, Web).

Henry Chapman died from tuberculosis in 1842, and Maria relocated to Europe from 1848 to 1855 to provide her daughters with an educational experience similar to her own. While abroad, she remained devoted to anti-slavery efforts and successfully sought financial contributions for the cause from prominent members of French and British society. She continued her efforts after returning to the US, but following the Emancipation Proclamation of 1863, Chapman resigned from nearly all of her anti-slavery work. Chapman died of heart disease on 12 July 1885 in Weymouth, Massachusetts.

'The Times That Try Men's Souls'[19]

> Confusion has seized us, and all things go wrong,
>   The women have leaped from "their spheres,"
> And, instead of fixed stars, shoot as comets along,
>   And are setting the world by the ears!
> In courses erratic they're wheeling through space,
> In brainless confusion and meaningless chase.
>
> In vain do our knowing ones try to compute
>   Their return to the orbits designed;
> They're glanced at a moment, then onward they shoot,
>   And are 'neither to hold nor to bind;'
> So freely they move in their chosen ellipse,
> The "Lords of Creation" do fear an eclipse.

---

19 In *The Liberator*, the poem had the subtitle of 'Language of the Revolution'

They've taken a notion to speak for themselves,
 And are wielding the tongue and the pen;
They've mounted the rostrum;[20] the termagant[21] elves,
 And—oh horrid!—are talking to men!
With faces unblanched in our presence they come,
To harangue us, they say, in behalf of the dumb.

They insist on their right to petition and pray,
 That St. Paul, in Corinthians, has given them rules
For appearing in public;[22] despite what those say
 Whom we've trained to instruct them in schools;[23]
But vain such instruction, if women may scan
And quote texts of Scripture to favor their plan.

Our grandmothers' learning consisted, of yore
 In spreading their generous boards;
In twisting the distaff,[24] or mopping the floor,
 And *obeying the will of their lords.*
Now, misses may reason, and think, and debate,
Till unquestioned submission is quite out of date.

Our clergy have preached on the sin and the shame
 Of woman, when out of "her sphere,"
And labored *divinely* to ruin her fame,
 And shorten this horrid career;
But for spiritual guidance no longer they look
To Fulsom, or Winslow, or learned PARSON Cook.

Our wise men have tried to exorcise in vain
 The turbulent spirits abroad;
As well might we deal with the fetterless main,
 Or conquer ethereal essence with sword;
Like the devils of Milton,[25] they rise from each blow,
With spirit unbroken, insulting the foe.

Our patriot fathers, of eloquent fame,
 Waged war against tangible forms;
Aye, *their* foes were men—and if ours were the same,
 We might speedily quiet their storms.
But, ah! their descendants enjoy not such bliss—
The assumptions of Britain were nothing to this.

---

20 'Any platform, stage, or similar structure adapted for public speaking' (*OED*)
21 'Violent, unruly; overbearing; bad-tempered' (*OED*)
22 In *The Liberator*, an asterisked note here identified 1 Cor. 11: 5 as the relevant biblical passage, which censures women praying or prophesying with uncovered heads as if they were men
23 *The Liberator* original version specified 'orthodox schools'.
24 'A cleft staff about 3 feet long, on which, in the ancient mode of spinning, wool or flax was wound' (*OED*)
25 Reference to *Paradise Lost* (1667) by John Milton (1608–74)

Could we but array all our force in the field,
    We'd teach these usurpers of power
That their bodily safety demands they should yield,
    And in the presence of manhood should cower;
But, alas! for our tethered and impotent state,
Chained by notions of knighthood—we can but debate.

Oh! shade of the prophet Mahomet, arise!
    Place woman again in "her sphere,"
And teach that her soul was not born for the skies,
    But to flutter a brief moment here.
This doctrine of Jesus, as preached up by Paul,[26]
If embraced in its spirit, will ruin us all.
                    —*Lords of Creation.*

Source text

Chapman, Maria Weston, 'The Times That Try Men's Souls', in Elizabeth Cady Stanton, Susan B. Anthony and Matilda Joslyn Gage (eds), *History of Woman Suffrage Vol. 1, 1848–1861* (New York: Fowler & Wells, 1881), 82–3.

References

ANB
Britannica
Chapman, Maria Weston, 'The Times That Try Men's Souls', *The Liberator* 9.10 (8 March 1839), 40.
Goodwin, Joan, 'Maria Weston Chapman and the Weston Sisters', *Dictionary of Unitarian and Universalist Biography* (Web).
OED
Stone, Marjorie, 'Frederick Douglass, Maria Weston Chapman, and Harriet Martineau: Atlantic Abolitionist Networks and Transatlanticism's Binaries', in Linda K. Hughes and Sarah R. Robbins (eds), *Teaching Transatlanticism: Resources for Teaching Nineteenth-Century Anglo-American Print Culture* (Edinburgh: Edinburgh University Press, 2015), 107–23.

Harriet Martineau (1802–76)

From Society in America *(1837)*

Harriet Martineau was a British author and activist often cited as the first female sociologist. Martineau began her career by publishing anonymously for the *Monthly Repository*, but after her family's textile business failed, she used her writing to support her family. Although Martineau originally

---

26 Another footnote in *The Liberator* cited Gal. 3: 28.

published religious articles, she found fame by the age of thirty after publishing *Illustrations on Political Economy* (1832–4), a serialised work that sold more copies in the period than the work of Charles Dickens. After achieving financial security, Martineau travelled to the United States in September 1834 and spent two years touring the country and documenting her observations for what would become her most celebrated work of social criticism, *Society in America*. This was published in three volumes in London in 1837, just five years after Frances Trollope's *Domestic Manners of the Americans*. *Society in America* is Martineau's most comprehensive social criticism as her lengthy stay in the United States allowed her to see several regions, including New Orleans in the south and Chicago in the west. Martineau's popularity enabled her to move in prominent American social circles and to witness the political proceedings of the American government in Washington, DC, which she documents in her narrative. While Martineau states in her introduction that she intends to relate her experiences to determine whether America upholds the ideals expressed in its Constitution and asserts that she has no desire to teach or judge Americans, she forcefully expresses her transatlantic perspective on the status of women and the treatment of African Americans in the US. She went on to spend the remainder of her life working for the advancement of women and the anti-slavery campaign.

From Society in America

'Citizenship of People of Colour'

Before I entered New England, while I was ascending the Mississippi, I was told by a Boston gentleman that the people of colour in the New England States were perfectly well-treated; that the children were educated in schools provided for them; and that their fathers freely exercised the franchise. This gentleman certainly believed he was telling me the truth. That he, a busy citizen of Boston, should know no better, is now as striking an exemplification of the state of the case to me as a correct representation of the facts would have been. There are two causes for his mistake. He was not aware that the schools for the coloured children in New England are, unless they escape by their insignificance, shut up, or pulled down, or the school-house wheeled away upon rollers over the frontier of a pious State, which will not endure that its coloured citizens should be educated. He was not aware of a gentleman of colour, and his family, being locked out of their own hired pew[27] in a church, because their white brethren will not worship by their side. But I will not proceed with an enumeration of injuries, too familiar to Americans to excite any feeling but that of weariness; and too disgusting to all others to be endured. The other cause of this gentleman's mistake was, that he did not, from long custom, feel some things to be injuries, which he would call anything but good treatment, if he had to bear them himself. Would he think it good treatment to be forbidden

---

27 It was commonplace for families to rent pews as a means of financial support for the church; the pew's location also signified a family's social status in the community.

to eat with fellow-citizens; to be assigned to a particular gallery in his church; to be excluded from college, from municipal office, from professions, from scientific and literary associations? If he felt himself excluded from every department of society, but its humiliations and its drudgery, would he declare himself to be "perfectly well-treated in Boston?" Not a word more of statement is needed.

A Connecticut judge lately declared on the bench that he believed people of colour were not considered citizens in the laws. He was proved to be wrong. He was actually ignorant of the wording of the acts by which people of colour are termed citizens. Of course, no judge could have forgotten this who had seen them treated as citizens: nor could one of the most eminent statesmen and lawyers in the country have told me that it is still a doubt, in the minds of some high authorities, whether people of colour are citizens. He is as mistaken as the judge. There has been no such doubt since the Connecticut judge was corrected and enlightened. The error of the statesman arose from the same cause; he had never seen the coloured people treated as citizens. "In fact," said he, "these people hold an anomalous situation. They are protected as citizens when the public service requires their security; but not otherwise treated as such." Any comment would weaken this intrepid statement.

The common argument, about the inferiority of the coloured race, bears no relation whatever to this question. They are citizens. They stand, as such, in the law, and in the acknowledgment of every one who knows the law. They are citizens, yet their houses and schools are pulled down, and they can obtain no remedy at law. They are thrust out of offices, and excluded from the most honourable employments, and stripped of all the best benefits of society by fellow-citizens who, once a year,[28] solemnly lay their hands on their hearts, and declare that all men are born free and equal, and that rulers derive their just powers from the consent of the governed.

This system of injury is not wearing out. Lafayette, on his last visit to the United States, expressed his astonishment at the increase of the prejudice against colour.[29] He remembered, he said, how the black soldiers used to mess[30] with the whites in the revolutionary war. The leaders of that war are gone where principles are all,—where prejudices are nothing. If their ghosts could arise, in majestic array, before the American nation, on their great anniversary, and hold up before them the mirror of their constitution, in the light of its first principles, where would the people hide themselves from the blasting radiance? They would call upon their holy soil to swallow them up, as unworthy to tread upon it. But not all. It should ever be remembered that America is the country of the best friends the coloured race has ever had. The more truth there is in the assertions of the oppressors of the blacks, the more heroism there is in their friends. The greater the excuse for the pharisees[31] of the community, the more divine is the equity of the redeemers of the coloured race. If it be granted that the coloured race are naturally inferior, naturally depraved, disgusting, cursed,—it must be granted that it is a heavenly charity which descends among them to give such solace as it can to their incomprehensible

---

28 Reference to the Fourth of July (or Independence Day) holiday in the United States
29 Marie Joseph Paul Yves Roche Gilbert du Motier, Marquis de Lafayette (1757–1834), fought beside Americans in the American Revolutionary War upon his first trip to the US and returned in 1784 at the invitation of George Washington.
30 'To serve up (food); to divide and measure out (ingredients and portions)' (OED).
31 'A person of the spirit or character commonly attributed to the Pharisees in the New Testament; a legalist or formalist; a self-righteous person, a hypocrite' (OED).

existence. As long as the excuses of the one party go to enhance the merit of the other, the society is not to be despaired of, even with this poisonous anomaly at its heart.

Happily, however, the coloured race is not cursed by God, as it is by some factions of his children. The less clear-sighted of them are pardonable for so believing. Circumstances, for which no living man is answerable, have generated an erroneous conviction in the feeble mind of man, which sees not beyond the actual and immediate. No remedy could ever have been applied, unless stronger minds than ordinary had been brought into the case. But it so happens, wherever there is an anomaly, giant minds rise up to overthrow it: minds gigantic, not in understanding, but in faith. Wherever they arise, they are the salt of their earth, and its corruption is retrieved. So it is now in America. While the mass of common men and women are despising, and disliking, and fearing, and keeping down the coloured race, blinking the fact that they are citizens, the few of Nature's aristocracy are putting forth a strong hand to lift up this degraded race out of oppression, and their country from the reproach of it. If they were but one or two, trembling and toiling in solitary energy, the world afar would be confident of their success. But they number hundreds and thousands; and if ever they feel a passing doubt of their progress, it is only because they are pressed upon by the meaner multitude. Over the sea, no one doubts of their victory. It is as certain as that the risen sun will reach the meridian. Already are there overflowing colleges, where no distinction of colour is allowed;—overflowing, *because* no distinction of colour is allowed. Already have people of colour crossed the thresholds of many whites, as guests, not as drudges or beggars. Already are they admitted to worship, and to exercise charity, among the whites.

The world has heard and seen enough of the reproach incurred by America, on account of her coloured population. It is now time to look for the fairer side. The crescent streak is brightening towards the full, to wane no more. Already is the world beyond the sea beginning to think of America, less as the country of the double-faced pretender to the name of Liberty, than as the home of the single-hearted, clear-eyed Presence which, under the name of Abolitionism, is majestically passing through the land which is soon to be her throne.

From 'Political Non-Existence of Women'
One of the fundamental principles announced in the Declaration of Independence is, that governments derive their just powers from the consent of the governed. How can the political condition of women be reconciled with this?

Governments in the United States have power to tax women who hold property; to divorce them from their husbands; to fine, imprison, and execute them for certain offences. Whence do these governments derive their powers? They are not "just," as they are not derived from the consent of the women thus governed.

Governments in the United States have power to enslave certain women; and also to punish other women for inhuman treatment of such slaves. Neither of these powers are "just;" not being derived from the consent of the governed.

Governments decree to women in some States half their husbands' property; in others one-third. In some, a woman, on her marriage, is made to yield all her property to her husband; in others, to retain a portion, or the whole, in her own hands. Whence do governments derive the unjust power of thus disposing of property without the consent of the governed?

The democratic principle condemns all this as wrong; and requires the equal political representation of all rational beings. Children, idiots, and criminals, during the season of sequestration, are the only fair exceptions.

The case is so plain that I might close it here; but it is interesting to inquire how so obvious a decision has been so evaded as to leave to women no political rights whatever. The question has been asked, from time to time, in more countries than one, how obedience to the laws can be required of women, when no woman has, either actually or virtually, given any assent to any law. No plausible answer has, as far as I can discover, been offered; for the good reason, that no plausible answer can be devised. The most principled democratic writers on government have on this subject sunk into fallacies, as disgraceful as any advocate of despotism has adduced. In fact, they have thus sunk from being, for the moment, advocates of despotism. Jefferson in America, and James Mill at home,[32] subside, for the occasion, to the level of the author of the Emperor of Russia's Catechism for the young Poles.[33]

Jefferson says, "Were our State a pure democracy, in which all the inhabitants should meet together to transact all their business, there would yet be excluded from their deliberations,

"1. Infants, until arrived at years of discretion;
"2. Women, who, to prevent depravation of morals, and ambiguity of issue, could not mix promiscuously in the public meetings of men;
"3. Slaves, from whom the unfortunate state of things with us takes away the rights of will and of property."

If the slave disqualification, here assigned, were shifted up under the head of Women, their case would be nearer the truth than as it now stands. Woman's lack of will and of property, is more like the true cause of her exclusion from the representation, than that which is actually set down against her. As if there could be no means of conducting public affairs but by promiscuous meetings! As if there would be more danger in promiscuous meetings for political business than in such meetings for worship, for oratory, for music, for dramatic entertainments,— for any of the thousand transactions of civilized life! The plea is not worth another word.

Mill says, with regard to representation, in his Essay on Government, "One thing is pretty clear; that all those individuals, whose interests are involved in those of other individuals, may be struck off without inconvenience ... In this light, women may be regarded, the interest of almost all of whom is involved, either in that of their fathers or in that of their husbands."[34]

The true democratic principle is, that no person's interests can be, or can be ascertained to be, identical with those of any other person. This allows the exclusion of none but incapables.

The word "almost," in Mr. Mill's second sentence, rescues women from the exclusion he proposes. As long as there are women who have neither husbands nor fathers, his proposition remains an absurdity.

---

32 Martineau quotes an 1816 letter from Thomas Jefferson (1743–1826) to Samuel Kercheval (1767–1845) and connects Jefferson's political views with those of James Mill (1773–1836), a British philosopher as well as father to John Stuart Mill (1806–73) who published political essays.
33 After Poland fell under Russian domination, Polish cadets revolted against the Russian government in the 'Cadet Revolution of 1830', but the Russian army of Tsar Nicholas I (1796–1855; r. 1825–55) annihilated them.
34 James Mill's 'Essay on Government' was written in 1820 for the *Encyclopaedia Britannica*.

The interests of women who have fathers and husbands can never be identical with theirs, while there is a necessity for laws to protect women against their husbands and fathers. This statement is not worth another word.

Some who desire that there should be an equality of property between men and women, oppose representation, on the ground that political duties would be incompatible with the other duties which women have to discharge. The reply to this is, that women are the best judges here. God has given time and power for the discharge of all duties; and, if he had not, it would be for women to decide which they would take, and which they would leave. But their guardians follow the ancient fashion of deciding what is best for their wards. The Emperor of Russia discovers when a coat of arms and title do not agree with a subject prince. The King of France early perceives that the air of Paris does not agree with a free-thinking foreigner. The English Tories feel the hardship that it would be to impose the franchise on every artizan, busy as he is in getting his bread. The Georgian planter perceives the hardship that freedom would be to his slaves. And the best friends of half the human race peremptorily decide for them as to their rights, their duties, their feelings, their powers. In all these cases, the persons thus cared for feel that the abstract decision rests with themselves; that, though they may be compelled to submit, they need not acquiesce.

It is pleaded that half of the human race does acquiesce in the decision of the other half, as to their rights and duties. [...]

But this acquiescence is only partial; and, to give any semblance of strength to the plea, the acquiescence must be complete. I, for one, do not acquiesce. I declare that whatever obedience I yield to the laws of the society in which I live is a matter between, not the community and myself; but my judgment and my will. Any punishment inflicted on me for the breach of the laws, I should regard as so much gratuitous injury; for to those laws I have never, actually or virtually, assented. I know that there are women in England who agree with me in this—I know that there are women in America who agree with me in this. The plea of acquiescence is invalidated by us.

It is pleaded that, by enjoying the protection of some laws, women give their assent to all. This needs but a brief answer. Any protection thus conferred is, under woman's circumstances, a boon[35] bestowed at the pleasure of those in whose power she is. A boon of any sort is no compensation for the privation of something else; nor can the enjoyment of it bind to the performance of anything to which it bears no relation. Because I, by favour, may procure the imprisonment of the thief who robs my house, am I, unrepresented, therefore bound not to smuggle French ribbons? The obligation not to smuggle has a widely different derivation.

I cannot enter upon the commonest order of pleas of all;—those which relate to the virtual influence of woman; her swaying the judgment and will of man through the heart; and so forth. One might as well try to dissect the morning mist. I knew a gentleman in America who told me how much rather he had be a woman than the man he is;—a professional man, a father, a citizen. He would give up all this for a woman's influence. I thought he was mated too soon. He should have married a lady, also of any acquaintance, who would not at all object to being a slave, if ever the blacks should have the upper hand; "it is so right that the one race should be subservient to the other!" Or rather,—I thought it a pity that the one could not be a woman, and the other a slave; so that an injured individual of each class might

---

35 'A favour, a gift, a thing freely or graciously bestowed' (OED)

be exalted into their places, to fulfil and enjoy the duties and privileges which they despise, and, in despising, disgrace. [. . .]

That woman has power to represent her own interests, no one can deny till she has been tried. The modes need not be discussed here: they must vary with circumstances. The fearful and absurd images which are perpetually called up to perplex the question,—images of women on wool-sacks[36] in England, and under canopies[37] in America, have nothing to do with the matter. The principle being once established, the methods will follow, easily, naturally, and under a remarkable trans-mutation of the ludicrous into the sublime. The kings of Europe would have laughed mightily, two centuries ago, at the idea of a commoner, without robes, crown, or sceptre, stepping into the throne of a strong nation. Yet who dared to laugh when Washington's super-royal[38] voice greeted the New World from the presidential chair, and the old world stood still to catch the echo?

The principle of the equal rights of both halves of the human race is all we have to do with here. It is the true democratic principle which can never be seriously controverted,[39] and only for a short time evaded. Governments can derive their just powers only from the consent of the governed.

Source text

Martineau, Harriet, *Society in America*, Vol. 1 (New York: Saunders and Otley, 1837).

References

Hunter, Shelagh, *Harriet Martineau: The Poetics of Moralism* (Aldershot: Scolar, 1995).
Logan, Deborah A., *Harriet Martineau, Victorian Imperialism, and the Civilizing Mission* (Burlington: Ashgate, 2010).
—, *The Hour and the Woman: Harriet Martineau's 'Somewhat Remarkable' Life* (DeKalb, IL: Northern Illinois University Press, 2002).

Elizabeth Cady Stanton (1815–1902)

From 'Address on Woman's Rights' (1848)

Elizabeth Cady Stanton recoiled from sexism early in life, having been denied admission to Union College and going so far as to remove from her nuptial vows the commandment to 'obey' her husband, Henry Brewster Stanton. Her initial foray into activism came as an abolitionist, when she attended the 1840 World Anti-Slavery Convention in London and met Lucretia Mott. She was

---

36 'A seat made of a bag of wool for the use of judges when summoned to attend the House of Lords; [. . .] also, the usual seat of the Lord Chancellor in the House of Lords, made of a large square bag of wool without back or arms and covered with cloth. Often *allusively* with reference to the position of the Lord Chancellor as the highest judicial officer' (*OED*)
37 An architectural canopy was added over the bench of the Chief Justice of the Supreme Court during the renovations of 1830.
38 'Above royal rank; higher than or beyond royal' (*OED*)
39 Disputed or argued about

also involved in the temperance movement (along with Susan B. Anthony). Yet she campaigned against extending civil rights to emancipated Blacks on grounds of the injustice when white women were denied voting rights.

Her longstanding activism in support of women's rights and suffrage underlay her authorship of the Seneca Falls Declaration of Sentiments (1848), modelled on the US *Declaration of Independence*, which listed grievances against 'the repeated injuries and usurpation on the part of man toward woman'. Following the convention she began to deliver her 'first speech', excerpted below, initially in Waterloo, New York (Gordon, 94).

Stanton inspired women's rights activists (and later suffragettes) both domestic and abroad, like Frenchwomen Jeanne Deroin and Pauline Roland, who composed an 1851 'Letter to the Convention of the Women of America' extolling their 'courageous declaration'. Though she would not live to see it, women gained suffrage with the ratification of the Nineteenth Amendment in 1920, albeit with limited access at the polls along the lines of race and class.

From 'Address on Woman's Rights'

Ladies and gentlemen, when invited some weeks ago to address you I proposed to a gentleman of this village to review our report of the Seneca Falls convention and give his objections to our Declaration, resolutions and proceedings to serve me as a text on which to found an address for this evening—the gentleman did so, but his review was so laconic that there was the same difficulty in replying to it as we found in replying to a recent sermon preached at Seneca Falls—there was nothing of it.

Should that gentleman be present this evening and feel disposed to give any of his objections to our movement, we will be most happy to answer him.

I should feel exceedingly diffident to appear before you wholly unused as I am to public speaking, were I not nerved by a sense of right and duty—did I not feel that the time had fully come for the question of woman's wrongs to be laid before the public— did I not believe that woman herself must do this work—for woman alone can understand the height and the depth, the length and the breadth of her own degradation and woe. Man cannot speak for us—because he has been educated to believe that we differ from him so materially, that he cannot judge of our thoughts, feelings and opinions by his own. Moral beings can only judge of others by themselves—the moment they give a different nature to any of their own kind they utterly fail. The drunkard was hopelessly lost until it was discovered that he was governed by the same laws of mind as the sober man. Then with what magic power, by kindness and love, was he raised from the slough of despond and placed rejoicing on high land. Let a man once settle the question that woman does not think and feel like himself and he may as well undertake to judge of the amount of intellect and sensation of any of the animal creation as of woman's nature. He can know but little with certainty, and that but by observation.

Among the many important questions which have been brought before the public, there is none that more vitally affects the whole human family than that which is technically termed Woman's rights. Every allusion to the degraded and inferior position occupied by woman all over the world, has ever been met by scorn and abuse. From the man of highest mental cultivation, to the most degraded wretch who staggers in the streets do we hear ridicule and coarse jests, freely bestowed upon those who dare assert that woman stands by the side of man—his equal, placed here by her God to enjoy with him the beautiful earth, which is her home as it is his—having the same sense of right and wrong and looking to the same Being for guidance and support. So long has man exercised a tyranny over her injurious to himself and benumbing to *her* faculties, that but few can nerve themselves against the storm, and so long has the chain been about her that however galling it may be she knows not there is a remedy.

The present social, civil and religious condition of women is a subject too vast to be brought within the limits of one short lecture. Suffice it to say for the present, that wherever we turn the history of woman is sad and drear and dark, without any alleviating circumstances, nothing from which we can draw consolation. As the nations of the earth emerge from a state of barbarism, the sphere of woman gradually becomes wider but not even under what is thought to be the full blaze of the sun of civilization is it what God designed it to be. In every country and clime does man assume the responsibility of marking out the path for her to tread,—in every country does he regard her as a being inferior to himself and one whom he is to guide and controul. From the Arabian Kerek whose wife is obliged to steal from her Husband to supply the necessities of life,—from the Mahometan who forbids pigs dogs women and other impure animals to enter a mosque, and does not allow a fool, madman or women to proclaim the hour of prayer,—from the German who complacently smokes his meerschaum while his wife, yoked with the ox draws the plough through its furrow,—from the delectable gentleman who thinks an inferior style of conversation adapted to women—to the legislator who considers her incapable of saying what laws shall govern her, is this same feeling manifested. In all eastern countries she is a mere slave bought and sold at pleasure. There are many differences in habits, manners, and customs, among the heathen nations of the old world, but there is little change for the better in woman's lot—she is either the drudge of man to perform all the hard labour of the field and the menial duties of the hut, tent, or house, or she is the idol of his lust the mere creature of his ever varying whims and will. Truly has she herself said in her best estate,

> I am a slave, a favoured slave
> At best to share his pleasure and seem very blest,
> When weary of these fleeting charms and me,
> There yawns the sack and yonder rolls the sea,
> What! am I then a toy for dotards play
> To wear but till the gilding frets away?[40]

In christian countries, boasting a more advanced state of civilization and refinement, woman still holds a position infinitely inferior to man. In France the Salic law[41] tells much although it is said that woman there has ever had great influence in all political revolutions. In England she seems to have advanced a little— There she has a right to the throne, and is allowed to hold some other offices and some women have a right to vote too— But in the United States of America woman has no right either to hold office, nor to the elective franchise, we stand at this moment, unrepresented in this government—our rights and interests wholly overlooked.

---

40 On the title page of Child's *History of the Condition of Women*, from Lord Byron, 'The Corsair,' the first two lines are found in canto 2, pt. 14, and the last four in canto 3, pt. 8. Neither author copied Byron's lines precisely. The 'sack' alludes to purging the harem by tossing an unwanted woman into the Bosphorus in a sack (Gordon, 117 n.4).

41 'By the Salic law, females were excluded from the line of succession to the throne of France' (Gordon, 117 n.4).

Let us now glance at some of the popular objections to this whole question. There is a class of men who believe in the natural inborn, inbred superiority both in body and mind and their full complete Heaven descended right to lord it over the fish of the sea, the fowl of the air, the beast of the field[42] and last tho' not least the immortal being called woman. I would recommend this class to the attentive perusal of their Bibles— to historical research, to foreign travel—to a closer observation of the manifestations of mind about them and to an humble comparison of themselves with such women as Catharine of Russia, Elizabeth of England distinguished for their statesmanlike qualities, Harriet Martineau and Madame de Stael for their literary attainments, or Caroline Herschel and Mary Summerville for their scientific researches, or for physical equality to that whole nation of famous women the Amazons.[43] We seldom find this class of objectors among liberally educated persons, who have had the advantage of observing their race in different countries, climes, and under different phases, but barbarians tho' they be in entertaining such an opinion—they must be met and fairly vanquished.

Source text

Gordon, Ann D. (ed.), 'Address by ECS on Woman's Rights', *Selected Papers of Elizabeth Cady Stanton and Susan B. Anthony*, Vol. I (New Brunswick, NJ: Rutgers University Press, 1998), 95–8.

References

McMillen, Sally G., *Seneca Falls and the Origins of the Women's Rights Movement* (New York: Oxford University Press, 2008).
Wellman, Judith, *The Road to Seneca Falls: Elizabeth Cady Stanton and the First Woman's Rights Convention.* (Chicago: University of Illinois Press, 2004).

Thomas Carlyle (1795–1881)

From 'Occasional Discourse on the Negro Question' (1849)

Born in Scotland, Thomas Carlyle (1795–1881) gained early fame and a transatlantic audience with *Sartor Resartus* (1833; rpt. 1840), *The French Revolution* (1837), *On Heroes and Hero-Worship* (1841) and *Past and*

---

42 Genesis 1: 28

43 'This standard list of capable women can be found in both [Lydia Maria] Child[, *History of the Condition of Women, in Various Ages and Nations*, 1835] and [Sarah] Grimké[, *Letters on the Equality of the Sexes*, 1838]. Monarchs in Russia and England, Catherine II or Catherine the Great (1729–96) ruled from 1762 to her death, and Elizabeth I (1533–1603) ruled from 1558 to 1603. In the field of letters, Harriet Martineau (1802–1876), a British writer and ardent abolitionist, visited the United States from 1834 to 1836 and, under the influence of the Grimké sisters, became an advocate of woman's rights. Germaine de Stael (1766–1817), a French writer and leader of an intellectual and political salon, went into exile during Napoleon's reign. British astronomers, Caroline Lucretia Herschel (1750–1848) and Mary Fairfax Somerville (1780–1872) (see also ST) were honoured for their discoveries by the Royal Astronomical Society. For evidence of women's physical potential, the most popular example was the Amazons, a tribe of warrior women in antiquity who fought the Greeks' (Gordon, 117–18 n.8).

Present (1843), all concerned in part with social reform. Carlyle's admiration for strong rulers and increasingly reactionary impulses later produced one of the most repugnant essays by a major transatlantic writer, his 'Occasional Discourse on the Negro Question' in the December 1849 issue of *Fraser's Magazine*. John Stuart Mill was sufficiently disturbed to issue a refutation of Carlyle in the magazine's following number. As a reminder of the barriers faced by persons of colour and the platform allotted to racist writing by celebrity writers, the essay nonetheless serves transatlantic studies today.

The immediate spur to Carlyle's essay was the collapsing sugar markets in post-abolition Jamaica exacerbated by labour shortages. As Douglas Hall explains, 'the ex-slaves had carved out small-holdings in the mountain areas, and on the remaining estates wage-rates had been pushed down after 1846 and the labour supply was unreliable' (173). Witnesses testifying in London before the 1848 Select Committee on Sugar and Coffee Planting as well as Benjamin Hawes, Under-Secretary of State for the Colonies, complained of Black persons' refusal to work, attributing it to laziness – a stance encouraged by white Caribbean plantation owners. This immediate historical context, Carlyle's staunch Calvinism (which inspired his fervent belief in the value of work) and Carlyle's close friendship with Henry Taylor in the Colonial Office (Catherine Hall, 348, 351) propelled his 'discourse'.

From 'Occasional Discourse on the Negro Question'

My Philanthropic Friends,—It is my painful duty to address some words to you, this evening, on the Rights of Negroes. Taking, as we hope we do, an extensive survey of social affairs, which we find all in a state of the frightfullest embroilment, and as it were, of inextricable final bankruptcy, just at present; and being desirous to adjust ourselves in that huge upbreak, and unutterable welter of tumbling ruins, and to see well that our grand proposed Association of Associations, the UNIVERSAL ABOLITION-OF-PAIN ASSOCIATION, which is meant to be the consummate golden flower and summary of modern Philanthropisms all in one, do *not* issue as a universal 'Sluggard-and-Scoundrel Protection Society,'—we have judged that, before constituting ourselves, it would be very proper to commune earnestly with one another, and discourse together on the leading elements of our great Problem, which surely is one of the greatest. With this view the Council[44] has decided, both that the Negro Question, as lying at the bottom, was to be the first handled, and if possible the first settled; and then also, what was of much more questionable wisdom, that—that, in short, I was to be Speaker on the occasion. An honorable duty; yet, as I said, a painful one!—Well, you shall hear what I have to say on the matter; and you will not in the least like it.

West-Indian affairs, as we all know, and some of us know to our cost, are in a rather troublous condition this good while. In regard to West Indian affairs,

---

44 A fictional council within Carlyle's fictive 'Association' based on the British Anti-Slavery Society

however, Lord John Russell[45] is able to comfort us with one fact, indisputable where so many are dubious, that the Negroes are all very happy and doing well. A fact very comfortable indeed. West Indian Whites, it is admitted, are far enough from happy; West Indian Colonies not unlike sinking wholly into ruin: at home too, the British Whites are rather badly off; several millions of them hanging on the verge of continual famine; and in single towns, many thousands of them very sore put to it, at this time, not to live 'well,' or as a man should, in any sense temporal or spiritual, but to live at all:—these, again, are uncomfortable facts; and they are extremely extensive and important ones. But, thank Heaven, our interesting Black population,—equaling almost in number of heads one of the Ridings of Yorkshire,[46] and in *worth* (in quantity of intellect, faculty, docility, energy, and available human valour and value) perhaps one of the streets of Seven Dials,[47]—are all doing remarkably well. 'Sweet blighted lilies,'—as the American epitaph on the Nigger child has it,—sweet blighted lilies, they are holding up their heads again![48] How pleasant, in the universal bankruptcy abroad, and dim dreary stagnancy at home, as if for England too there remained nothing but to suppress Chartist riots,[49] banish united Irishmen,[50] vote the supplies, and *wait* with arms crossed till black Anarchy and Social Death devoured us also, as it has done the others; how pleasant to have always this fact to fall back upon: Our beautiful Black darlings are at last happy; with little labour except to the teeth, *which* surely, in those excellent horse-jaws of theirs, will not fail!

Exeter Hall,[51] my philanthropic friends, has had its way in this matter. The Twenty Millions,[52] a mere trifle despatched with a single dash of the pen, are paid; and far over the sea, we have a few black persons rendered extremely 'free' indeed. Sitting yonder with their beautiful muzzles up to the ears in pumpkins, imbibing sweet pulps and juices; the grinder and incisor teeth ready for every new work, and the pumpkins cheap as grass in those rich climates: while the sugar-crops rot round them uncut, because labour cannot be hired, so cheap are the pumpkins;—and at home, we are but required to rasp from the breakfast loaves of our own English labourers some slight 'differential sugar-duties,' and lend a poor half-million or a few poor millions now and then, to keep that beautiful state of matters going on.[53] A state of matters

---

45 Lord John Russell (1792–1878): Whig Prime Minister of Great Britain 1846–52 and 1865–6
46 Yorkshire county in north-central England, then divided into three Ridings: North, East and West
47 An area of London long associated with urban poverty, memorably described by Charles Dickens in Chapter Five of *Sketches by Boz* (1836)
48 Alludes to the gravestone inscription for a Black infant reported by Harriet Martineau in *Society in America*, vol. 2, Section III, chp. 1 ('Intercourse)', 222
49 A movement among activist workers of the late 1830s and 1840s seeking a charter of democratic rights, including universal male suffrage and private ballots. Large-scale demonstrations, occasionally involving property damage, had stoked middle-class and government anxieties and repressive government action.
50 Amid the Irish famine of 1845–9 resulting from failed crops, many starving Irish migrated both to Britain and the US, stirring anxieties about how to stop them in both countries.
51 Exeter Hall (1831–1907) was the center of the anti-slavery campaign and played a vital role in ameliorative efforts to better society.
52 The amount paid by the government, not to the formerly enslaved but to former British enslavers, to compensate for their losses following the 1833 act abolishing slavery in Britain and British territories
53 The Sugar Duties Act of 1846 stipulated that the protection of colonial sugar against foreign competition – which assured greater profitability to West Indian planters – would be gradually phased out. But protectionism did not cease until 1854, so that sugar was more expensive for workers in 1849. Meantime anxieties about long-term viability of the sugar industry increased.

lovely to contemplate, in these emancipated epochs of the human mind; which has earned us not only the praises of Exeter Hall, and loud long-eared halleluiahs of laudatory psalmody[54] from the Friends of Freedom everywhere, but lasting favour (it is hoped) from the Heavenly Powers themselves;—which may at least justly appeal to the Heavenly Powers, and ask them, If ever in terrestrial procedure they saw the match of it? Certainly, in the past history of the human species it has no parallel; nor, one hopes, will it have in the future. [...]

Our own white or sallow Ireland, sluttishly[55] starving from age to age on its act-of-parliament 'freedom,' was hitherto the flower of mismanagement among the nations: but what will this be to a Negro Ireland, with pumpkins themselves fallen scarce like potatoes! Imagination cannot fathom such an object; the belly of Chaos never held the like. The human mind, in its wide wanderings, has not dreamt yet of such a 'freedom' as that will be. Towards that, if Exeter Hall and science of supply and demand are to continue our guides in the matter, we are daily travelling, and even struggling, with loans of half-a-million and such-like, to accelerate ourselves. [...]

And first, with regard to the West Indies, it may be laid down as a principle, which no eloquence in Exeter Hall, or Westminster Hall,[56] or elsewhere, can invalidate or hide, except for a short time only, That no Black man who will not work according to what ability the gods have given him for working, has the smallest right to eat pumpkin, or to any fraction of land that will grow pumpkin, however plentiful such land may be; but has an indisputable and perpetual *right* to be compelled, by the real proprietors of said land, to do competent work for his living. This is the everlasting duty of all men, black or white, who are born into this world. To do competent work, to labour honestly according to the ability given them; for that and for no other purpose was each one of us sent into this world; and woe is to every man who, by friend or by foe, is prevented from fulfilling this the end of his being. [...] If it be his own indolence that prevents and prohibits him, then his own indolence is the enemy he must be delivered from: and the first 'right' he has,—poor indolent blockhead, black or white, is, That every *unprohibited* man, whatsoever wiser, more industrious person may be passing that way, shall endeavour to 'emancipate' him from his indolence, and by some wise means, as I said, compel him to do the work he is fit for. This is the eternal law of nature for a man, my beneficent Exeter Hall friends; this, that he shall be permitted, encouraged, and if need be compelled to do what work the Maker of him has intended by the making of him for this world! Not that he should eat pumpkin with never such felicity in the West India Islands is, or can be, the blessedness of our black friend; but that he should do useful work there, according as the gifts have been bestowed on him for that. And his own happiness, and that of others round him, will alone be possible by his and their getting into such a relation that this can be permitted him, and in case of need that this can be compelled him. I beg you to understand this; for you seem to have a little forgotten it, and there lie a thousand inferences in it, not quite useless for Exeter Hall, at present. The idle black man in the West Indies had not long since the right, and will again under better form, if it please Heaven, have the right (actually the first 'right of man' for an indolent person) to be *compelled* to work as he was fit, and to *do* the Maker's

---

54 Hymn-singing
55 'Untidily, dirtily' (*OED*)
56 Parliament building

will who had constructed him with such and such prefigurements of capability. And I incessantly pray Heaven, all men, the whitest alike and the blackest, the richest and the poorest, in other regions of the world, had attained precisely the same right, the divine right of being compelled (if 'permitted' will not answer) to do what work they are appointed for, and not to go idle another minute, in a life so short! Alas, we had then a perfect world; and the Millennium, and true 'Organization of Labour,' and reign of complete blessedness, for all workers and men, had then arrived,—which, in these, our own poor districts of the Planet, as we all lament to know, it is very far from having yet done. [...]

And now observe, my friends, it was not Black Quashee[57] or those he represents that made those West India Islands what they are, or can by any hypothesis be considered to have the right of growing pumpkins there. For countless ages, since they first mounted oozy, on the back of earthquakes, from their dark bed in the Ocean deeps, and reeking saluted the tropical Sun, and ever onwards till the European white man first saw them some three short centuries ago, those Islands had produced mere jungle, savagery, poison-reptiles and swamp-malaria: till the white European first saw them, they were as if not yet created,—their noble elements of cinnamon, sugar, coffee, pepper black and grey, lying all asleep, waiting the white Enchanter who should say to them, Awake! Till the end of human history, and the sounding of the Trump of Doom, they might have lain so, had Quashee and the like of him been the only artists in the game. Swamps, fever-jungles, man-eating Caribs, rattle-snakes, and reeking waste and putrefaction, this had been the produce of them under the incompetent Caribal[58] (what we call Cannibal) possessors till that time; and Quashee knows, himself, whether ever he could have introduced an improvement. Him, had he by a miraculous chance been wafted thither, the Caribals would have eaten, rolling him as a fat morsel under their tongue; for him, till the sounding of the Trump of Doom, the rattle-snakes and savageries would have held on their way. It was not he, then; it was another than he! Never by art of his could one pumpkin have grown there to solace any human throat; nothing but savagery and reeking putrefaction could have grown there. [...]

Source text

Carlyle, Thomas, 'Occasional Discourse on the Negro Question', *Fraser's Magazine* 40 (December 1849), 670–9.

References

Dickerson, Vanessa D., *Dark Victorians* (Urbana, IL: University of Illinois Press, 2008).
Hall, Catherine, *Civilising Subjects: Colony and Metropole in the English Imagination, 1830–1867* (Chicago: University of Chicago Press, 2002).
Hall, Douglas, *Five of the Leewards, 1834–1870: The Major Problems of the Post-Emancipation Period in Antigua, Barbuda, Mont/serrat, Nevis, and St. Kitts* (Kingston: Caribbean Universities Press, 1971).
Martineau, Harriet, *Society in America*, 2 vols (New York: Saunders and Otley, 1837).

---

57 A 'generic name for: a black person, esp. one considered as credulous or insignificant' (*OED*)
58 Carlyle accurately notes the historical association by Europeans of 'Carib' with 'cannibal'.

Frederick Douglass (1818–95)

From 'What to the American Slave is your 4th of July?' (1852)

Perhaps the most prominent African American of the nineteenth century, Frederick Douglass was born into slavery on a plantation on the Chesapeake shore of Maryland. During his early years he was raised by his grandmother and prohibited from gaining literacy by his owners, yet secretly learned to read from neighbourhood white children and odd books. In 1833 Douglass was sent to a 'slave-breaker', a measure of punishment which backfired when the tormented Douglass rebelled and refused to be further beaten. He escaped slavery in 1838 and with his wife settled in New Bedford, Massachusetts, where he became a licensed preacher in the African Methodist Episcopal Zion Church. In subsequent years he grew to become a famous orator and abolitionist, speaking regularly for various anti-slavery causes. In 1845 he embarked upon a two-year tour of Ireland and England and offered dozens of lectures. Upon his return Douglass started an abolitionist newspaper, the *North Star*, which split from William Lloyd Garrison and his *National Anti-Slavery Standard*. He was an early and fervent supporter of women's rights, school desegregation and military enlistment for free Blacks during the Civil War. Along with his advocacy and oratory Douglass's later years were spent in a series of political positions: a New York presidential elector; United States Marshal for the District of Columbia; consul-general to Haiti and Santo Domingo. After the death of his first wife he married a white woman in 1884, to some controversy, dying of a heart attack in 1895.

On 5 July 1852 Douglass was invited to give a speech to the Ladies' Anti-Slavery Society in Rochester, New York. Though the address was intended to commemorate Independence Day and he referred to his audience as 'friends' and 'fellow citizens', Douglass drew a clear distinction between whites and Blacks, freely utilising the pronoun 'you' rather than 'we' and excoriating the hypocrisy of the United States. Excerpts from the address, which include references to Britain, appear below.

From 'What to the American Slave is your 4th of July?'

Mr. President, Friends and Fellow Citizens:

He who could address this audience without a quailing sensation, has stronger nerves than I have. I do not remember ever to have appeared as a speaker before any assembly more shrinkingly, nor with greater distrust of my ability, than I do this day [...] Should I seem at ease, my appearance would much misrepresent me. The little experience I have had in addressing public meetings, in country schoolhouses, avails me nothing on the present occasion. [...]

The fact is, ladies and gentlemen, the distance between this platform and the slave plantation, from which I escaped, is considerable — and the difficulties to be overcome in getting from the latter to the former, are by no means slight. That I am here to-day is, to me, a matter of astonishment as well as of gratitude. You will not, therefore, be surprised, if in what I have to say I evince no elaborate preparation, nor grace my speech with any high sounding exordium.[59] With little experience and with less learning, I have been able to throw my thoughts hastily and imperfectly together; and trusting to your patient and generous indulgence, I will proceed to lay them before you.

This, for the purpose of this celebration, is the 4th of July. It is the birthday of your National Independence, and of your political freedom. This, to you, is what the Passover was to the emancipated people of God. It carries your minds back to the day, and to the act of your great deliverance; and to the signs, and to the wonders, associated with that act, and that day. This celebration also marks the beginning of another year of your national life; and reminds you that the Republic of America is now 76 years old. I am glad, fellow-citizens, that your nation is so young. Seventy-six years, though a good old age for a man, is but a mere speck in the life of a nation. Three score years and ten is the allotted time for individual men; but nations number their years by thousands. According to this fact, you are, even now, only in the beginning of your national career, still lingering in the period of childhood. I repeat, I am glad this is so. There is hope in the thought, and hope is much needed, under the dark clouds which lower above the horizon. The eye of the reformer is met with angry flashes, portending disastrous times; but his heart may well beat lighter at the thought that America is young, and that she is still in the impressible stage of her existence. May he not hope that high lessons of wisdom, of justice and of truth, will yet give direction to her destiny? [...]

Fellow-citizens, I shall not presume to dwell at length on the associations that cluster about this day. The simple story of it is that, 76 years ago, the people of this country were British subjects. The style and title of your "sovereign people" (in which you now glory) was not then born. You were under the British Crown. Your fathers esteemed the English Government as the home government; and England as the fatherland. This home government, you know, although a considerable distance from your home, did, in the exercise of its parental prerogatives, impose upon its colonial children, such restraints, burdens and limitations, as, in its mature judgment, it deemed wise, right and proper.

But, your fathers, who had not adopted the fashionable idea of this day, of the infallibility of government, and the absolute character of its acts, presumed to differ from the home government in respect to the wisdom and the justice of some of those burdens and restraints. They went so far in their excitement as to pronounce the measures of government unjust, unreasonable, and oppressive, and altogether such as ought not to be quietly submitted to. I scarcely need say, fellow-citizens, that my opinion of those measures fully accords with that of your fathers. Such a declaration of agreement on my part would not be worth much to anybody. It would, certainly, prove nothing, as to what part I might have taken, had I lived during the great controversy of 1776. To say *now* that America was right, and England wrong, is exceedingly easy. Everybody can say it; the dastard, not less than the noble brave, can flippantly discant[60] on the tyranny of England towards the American Colonies. It is fashionable to do so; but there was a time when to pronounce against England,

---

59 A beginning or introduction, especially to a discourse or composition
60 A discourse or comment on a theme

and in favor of the cause of the colonies, tried men's souls. They who did so were accounted in their day, plotters of mischief, agitators and rebels, dangerous men. To side with the right, against the wrong, with the weak against the strong, and with the oppressed against the oppressor! here lies the merit, and the one which, of all others, seems unfashionable in our day. [. . .]

The greatest and best of British statesmen admitted its justice, and the loftiest eloquence of the British Senate came to its support. But, with that blindness which seems to be the unvarying characteristic of tyrants, since Pharaoh and his hosts were drowned in the Red Sea, the British Government persisted in the exactions complained of. [. . .]

On the 2d of July, 1776, the old Continental Congress, to the dismay of the lovers of ease, and the worshipers of property, clothed that dreadful idea with all the authority of national sanction. They did so in the form of a resolution . . . "Resolved, That these united colonies are, and of right, ought to be free and Independent States; that they are absolved from all allegiance to the British Crown; and that all political connection between them and the State of Great Britain is, and ought to be, dissolved."[61]

Citizens, your fathers made good that resolution. They succeeded; and to-day you reap the fruits of their success. The freedom gained is yours; and you, therefore, may properly celebrate this anniversary. The 4th of July is the first great fact in your nation's history — the very ring-bolt in the chain of your yet undeveloped destiny. [. . .]

Fellow Citizens, I am not wanting in respect for the fathers of this republic. The signers of the Declaration of Independence were brave men. They were great men too — great enough to give fame to a great age. It does not often happen to a nation to raise, at one time, such a number of truly great men. The point from which I am compelled to view them is not, certainly, the most favorable; and yet I cannot contemplate their great deeds with less than admiration. They were statesmen, patriots and heroes, and for the good they did, and the principles they contended for, I will unite with you to honor their memory. [. . .]

They were peace men; but they preferred revolution to peaceful submission to bondage. They were quiet men; but they did not shrink from agitating against oppression. They showed forbearance; but that they knew its limits. They believed in order; but not in the order of tyranny. With them, nothing was "*settled*" that was not right. With them, justice, liberty and humanity were "*final*;" not slavery and oppression. You may well cherish the memory of such men. They were great in their day and generation. Their solid manhood stands out the more as we contrast it with these degenerate times. [. . .]

Your fathers have lived, died, and have done their work, and have done much of it well. You live and must die, and you must do your work. You have no right to enjoy a child's share in the labor of your fathers, unless your children are to be blest by your labors. [. . .] Washington could not die till he had broken the chains of his slaves.[62] Yet his monument is built up by the price of human blood,[63] and the traders

---

61 The text of Lee's Resolutions, introduced in the Continental Congress by Richard Henry Lee (Virginia). Historical records indicate it was introduced on 7 June 1776 and approved on 2 July.
62 In his will George Washington mandated the release of his 123 enslaved people after the deaths of himself and his wife – the only slave-holding Founding Father who did so.
63 Construction of the Washington Monument began in 1848. While it cannot be conclusively proven, enslaved labour was likely utilised in the initial phase of construction.

in the bodies and souls of men shout — "We have Washington to *our father*." — Alas! that it should be so; yet so it is.

> "The evil that men do, lives after them,
> The good is oft' interred with their bones."[64]

Fellow-citizens, pardon me, allow me to ask, why am I called upon to speak here to-day? What have I, or those I represent, to do with your national independence? Are the great principles of political freedom and of natural justice, embodied in that Declaration of Independence, extended to us? and am I, therefore, called upon to bring our humble offering to the national altar, and to confess the benefits and express devout gratitude for the blessings resulting from your independence to us?

Would to God, both for your sakes and ours, that an affirmative answer could be truthfully returned to these questions! Then would my task be light, and my burden easy and delightful. For *who* is there so cold, that a nation's sympathy could not warm him? Who so obdurate and dead to the claims of gratitude, that would not thankfully acknowledge such priceless benefits? Who so stolid and selfish, that would not give his voice to swell the hallelujahs of a nation's jubilee, when the chains of servitude had been torn from his limbs? I am not that man. In a case like that, the dumb might eloquently speak, and the "lame man leap as an hart."[65]

But, such is not the state of the case. I say it with a sad sense of the disparity between us. I am not included within the pale of this glorious anniversary! Your high independence only reveals the immeasurable distance between us. The blessings in which you, this day, rejoice, are not enjoyed in common. — The rich inheritance of justice, liberty, prosperity and independence, bequeathed by your fathers, is shared by you, not by me. The sunlight that brought life and healing to you, has brought stripes and death to me. This Fourth July is *yours*, not *mine*. *You* may rejoice, *I* must mourn. To drag a man in fetters into the grand illuminated temple of liberty, and call upon him to join you in joyous anthems, were inhuman mockery and sacrilegious irony. Do you mean, citizens, to mock me, by asking me to speak to-day? If so, there is a parallel to your conduct. And let me warn you that it is dangerous to copy the example of a nation whose crimes, lowering up to heaven, were thrown down by the breath of the Almighty, burying that nation in irrecoverable ruin! I can to-day take up the plaintive lament of a peeled and woe-smitten people! [. . .]

Fellow-citizens; above your national, tumultuous joy, I hear the mournful wail of millions! whose chains, heavy and grievous yesterday, are, to-day, rendered more intolerable by the jubilee shouts that reach them. If I do forget, if I do not faithfully remember those bleeding children of sorrow this day, "may my right hand forget her cunning, and may my tongue cleave to the roof of my mouth!"[66] To forget them, to pass lightly over their wrongs, and to chime in with the popular theme, would be treason most scandalous and shocking, and would make me a reproach before God and the world. My subject, then fellow-citizens, is AMERICAN SLAVERY. I shall see, this day, and its popular characteristics, from the slave's point of view. Standing, there, identified with the American bondman, making his wrongs mine, I do not hesitate to declare, with all my soul, that the character and conduct of this nation never looked blacker to me than on this 4th of July! Whether we turn to the declarations of the

---

64 William Shakespeare, *Julius Caesar* III.ii.80–1
65 Isaiah 35: 6
66 Psalms 137: 5–6

past, or to the professions of the present, the conduct of the nation seems equally hideous and revolting. America is false to the past, false to the present, and solemnly binds herself to be false to the future. Standing with God and the crushed and bleeding slave on this occasion, I will, in the name of humanity which is outraged, in the name of liberty which is fettered, in the name of the constitution and the Bible, which are disregarded and trampled upon, dare to call in question and to denounce, with all the emphasis I can command, everything that serves to perpetuate slavery — the great sin and shame of America! [. . .]

One is struck with the difference between the attitude of the American church towards the anti-slavery movement, and that occupied by the churches in England towards a similar movement in that country. There, the church, true to its mission of ameliorating, elevating, and improving the condition of mankind, came forward promptly, bound up the wounds of the West Indian slave, and restored him to his liberty.[67] There, the question of emancipation was a high religious question. It was demanded, in the name of humanity, and according to the law of the living God. The Sharps, the Clarksons, the Wilberforces, the Buxtons, and Burchells and the Knibbs,[68] were alike famous for their piety, and for their philanthropy. The anti-slavery movement *there* was not an anti-church movement, for the reason that the church took its full share in prosecuting that movement: and the anti-slavery movement in this country will cease to be an anti-church movement, when the church of this country shall assume a favorable, instead of a hostile position towards that movement.

Americans! your republican politics, not less than your republican religion, are flagrantly inconsistent. You boast of your love of liberty, your superior civilization, and your pure Christianity, while the whole political power of the nation (as embodied in the two great political parties), is solemnly pledged to support and perpetuate the enslavement of three millions of your countrymen. You hurl your anathemas at the crowned headed tyrants of Russia and Austria, and pride yourselves on your Democratic institutions, while you yourselves consent to be the mere *tools* and *body-guards* of the tyrants of Virginia and Carolina. [. . .] You discourse eloquently on the dignity of labor; yet, you sustain a system which, in its very essence, casts a stigma upon labor. You can bare your bosom to the storm of British artillery to throw off a threepenny tax on tea;[69] and yet wring the last hard-earned farthing from the grasp of the black laborers of your country. You profess to believe "that, of one blood, God made all nations of men to dwell on the face of all the earth,"[70] and hath commanded all men, everywhere to love one another; yet you notoriously hate, (and glory in your hatred), all men whose skins are not colored like your own. You declare, before the world, and are understood by the world to declare, that you *"hold these truths to be self evident, that all men are created equal; and are endowed by their Creator with certain inalienable rights; and that, among these are, life, liberty, and the pursuit of happiness;"*[71] and yet, you hold securely, in a bondage which, according to your own Thomas Jefferson, *"is worse*

---

67 Enslavement was abolished across the British Empire (with the exception of the Territories in the Possession of the East India Company) in 1833.

68 Prominent British abolitionists: Granville Sharp (1735–1813), Thomas Clarkson (1760–1846), William Wilberforce (1759–1833), Thomas Fowell Buxton (1786–1845), Thomas Burchell (1799–1846) and William Knibb (1803–45)

69 In response to the Tea Act of 1773, which levied a three-penny tax on imports to British colonies in North America, the colonists dumped boxes of tea into Boston Harbour, known as the Boston Tea Party.

70 Acts 17: 26

71 Text from the Declaration of Independence

than ages of that which your fathers rose in rebellion to oppose,"[72] *a seventh part* of the inhabitants of your country. [. . .]

Allow me to say, in conclusion, notwithstanding the dark picture I have this day presented of the state of the nation, I do not despair of this country. There are forces in operation, which must inevitably work the downfall of slavery. *"The arm of the Lord is not shortened,"*[73] and the doom of slavery is certain. I, therefore, leave off where I began, with *hope*. While drawing encouragement from the Declaration of Independence, the great principles it contains, and the genius of American Institutions, my spirit is also cheered by the obvious tendencies of the age. Nations do not now stand in the same relation to each other that they did ages ago. No nation can now shut itself up from the surrounding world, and trot round in the same old path of its fathers without interference. The time *was* when such could be done. Long established customs of hurtful character could formerly fence themselves in, and do their evil work with social impunity. Knowledge was then confined and enjoyed by the privileged few, and the multitude walked on in mental darkness. But a change has now come over the affairs of mankind. Walled cities and empires have become unfashionable. The arm of commerce has borne away the gates of the strong city. Intelligence is penetrating the darkest corners of the globe. It makes its pathway over and under the sea, as well as on the earth. Wind, steam, and lightning are its chartered agents. Oceans no longer divide, but link nations together. From Boston to London is now a holiday excursion. Space is comparatively annihilated. Thoughts expressed on one side of the Atlantic, are distinctly heard on the other. The far off and almost fabulous Pacific rolls in grandeur at our feet. The Celestial Empire,[74] the mystery of ages, is being solved. The fiat of the Almighty, *"Let there be Light,"*[75] has not yet spent its force. No abuse, no outrage whether in taste, sport or avarice, can now hide itself from the all-pervading light. The iron shoe, and crippled foot of China must be seen, in contrast with nature. *Africa must rise and put on her yet unwoven garment. "Ethiopia shall stretch out her hand unto God."*[76] In the fervent aspirations of William Lloyd Garrison, I say, and let every heart join in saying it:

> *God speed the year of jubilee*
> *The wide world o'er!*
> *When from their galling chains set free,*
> *Th' oppress'd shall vilely bend the knee [. . .]*[77]

Source text

Douglass, Frederick, *Oration, Delivered in Corinthian Hall, Rochester, by Frederick Douglass, July 5th, 1852* (Rochester: Lee, Mann, and Co. 1852).

References

Colaiaco, James A., *Frederick Douglass and the Fourth of July* (New York: St. Martins, 2007).
Levine, Robert S., *The Lives of Frederick Douglass* (Cambridge, MA: Harvard University Press, 2016).

72 From Jefferson's 26 June 1786 letter to Jean Nicholas Démeunier, French author and politician
73 Isaiah 59: 1
74 China
75 Genesis 1: 3
76 Psalms 68: 31
77 From William Lloyd Garrison's poem 'Triumph of Freedom' (1845)

John Jacob (J.J.) Thomas (1841–89)

From Froudacity: West Indian Fables (1889)

Of African descent, Trinidadian linguist John Jacob Thomas was born in San Fernando, Trinidad, only a few years after slavery was abolished in the British West Indies. He attended one of the first Trinidadian primary schools and entered the Model School – an institution for training teachers – in 1859. During his first teaching appointment he taught himself patois and published *The Theory and Practise of Creole Grammar* (1869). After civil service positions were opened to competitive examination, he earned a series of clerkships in Port of Spain, gaining recognition in that community. By then Thomas had become a prominent intellectual respected for his work in the Trinidadian literary milieu. Thomas advocated tirelessly for increased educational and intellectual development, serving as a secretary of *The Trinidad Monthly*, the colony's inaugural literary journal, and founding its first literary society, *The Trinidad Athenaeum*.

Froudacity: West Indian Fables was composed in 1889 as a response to the controversial work published in 1888 by James Anthony Froude, a British historian who had earlier written a biography of Carlyle (1882). Froude's polemic, *The English in the West Indies; or, The Bow of Ulysses*, contended that the Caribbean had been the seat of English pride and power during the seventeenth and eighteenth centuries, and that its decline across the nineteenth was due to the increased power and presence of freed Blacks. In particular Froude scoffed at Caribbean self-government, arguing that the majority Black population was unfit for autonomy and would go the way of Haiti in repressing whites. As F. S. J. Ledgister comments in reference to Carlyle's 'Occasional Discourse on the Negro Question' (see this section's excerpt), 'Froude is Carlyle in the West Indies' (Ledgister, 118).

Thomas immediately countered Froude's claims with articles in the *St George's Chronicle and Grenada Gazette* that became *Froudacity*, published in London. Thomas systematically deconstructs and denounces Froude for a host of faults: casual racism, inaccuracies, sweeping generalisations and overall lack of knowledge of the Caribbean. Thomas has sometimes been critiqued for working within a Western rather than Pan-African framework, but he defined Creole culture as encompassing both African and East Indian descendants (Ledgister, 126–9). *Froudacity* was well received but failed to gain momentum when Thomas died the same year.

From Froudacity: West Indian Fables

PREFACE

Last year had well advanced towards its middle—in fact it was already April, 1888—before Mr. Froude's book of travels in the West Indies[78] became known and generally accessible to readers in those Colonies.

---

78 *The English in the West Indies; or, The Bow of Ulysses*, a polemic published by James Anthony Froude in 1888

My perusal of it in Grenada about the period above mentioned disclosed, thinly draped with rhetorical flowers, the dark outlines of a scheme to thwart political aspiration in the Antilles. That project is sought to be realized by deterring the home authorities from granting an elective local legislature, however restricted in character, to any of the Colonies not yet enjoying such an advantage. An argument based on the composition of the inhabitants of those Colonies is confidently relied upon to confirm the inexorable mood of Downing Street.[79]

Over-large and ever-increasing,—so runs the argument,—the African element in the population of the West Indies is, from its past history and its actual tendencies, a standing menace to the continuance of civilization and religion. An immediate catastrophe, social, political, and moral, would most assuredly be brought about by the granting of full elective rights to dependencies thus inhabited. Enlightened statesmanship should at once perceive the immense benefit that would ultimately result from such refusal of the franchise. The cardinal recommendation of that refusal is that it would avert definitively the political domination of the Blacks, which must inevitably be the outcome of any concession of the modicum of right so earnestly desired. The exclusion of the Negro vote being inexpedient, if not impossible, the exercise of electoral powers by the Blacks must lead to their returning candidates of their own race to the local legislatures, and that, too, in numbers preponderating according to the majority of the Negro electors. The Negro legislators thus supreme in the councils of the Colonies would straightway proceed to pass vindictive and retaliatory laws against their white fellow-colonists. For it is only fifty years since the White man and the Black man stood in the reciprocal relations of master and slave. Whilst those relations subsisted, the white masters inflicted, and the black slaves had to endure, the hideous atrocities that are inseparable from the system of slavery. Since Emancipation,[80] the enormous strides made in self-advancement by the ex-slaves have only had the effect of provoking a resentful uneasiness in the bosoms of the ex-masters. The former bondsmen, on their side, and like their brethren of Hayti, are eaten up with implacable, blood-thirsty rancour against their former lords and owners. The annals of Hayti form quite a cabinet of political and social object-lessons which, in the eyes of British statesmen, should be invaluable in showing the true method of dealing with Ethiopic subjects of the Crown.[81] The Negro race in Hayti, in order to obtain and to guard what it calls its freedom, has outraged every humane instinct and falsified every benevolent hope. The slave-owners there had not been a whit more cruel than slave-owners in the other islands. But, in spite of this, how ferocious, how sanguinary, how relentless against them has the vengeance of the Blacks been in their hour of mastery! A century has passed away since then, and, notwithstanding that, the hatred of Whites still rankles in their souls, and is cherished and yielded to as a national creed and guide of conduct. Colonial administrators of the mighty British Empire, the lesson which History has taught and yet continues to teach you in Hayti as to the best mode of dealing with your Ethiopic colonists lies patent, blood-stained and terrible before you, and should be taken definitively to heart. But if you are willing that Civilization and Religion—in short, all the highest developments of individual and social life—should at once be swept away by a desolating vandalism of African birth; if you do not recoil from the blood-guiltiness that would stain your consciences through the massacre of our fellow-countrymen in the West Indies, on account of

---

79 The seat of British municipal government in London
80 The Slavery Abolition Act of 1833 abolished slavery throughout the British Empire, including the West Indies.
81 That is those descended from Africa

their race, complexion and enlightenment; finally, if you desire those modern Hesperides[82] to revert into primeval jungle, horrent[83] lairs wherein the Blacks, who, but a short while before, had been ostensibly civilized, shall be revellers, as high-priests and devotees, in orgies of devil-worship, cannibalism, and obeah[84]—dare to give the franchise to those West Indian Colonies, and then rue the consequences of your infatuation! [...]

Alas, if the foregoing summary of the ghastly imaginings of Mr. Froude were true, in what a fool's paradise had the wisest and best amongst us been living, moving, and having our being! Up to the date of the suggestion by him as above of the alleged facts and possibilities of West Indian life, we had believed (even granting the correctness of his gloomy account of the past and present positions of the two races) that to no well-thinking West Indian White, whose ancestors may have, innocently or culpably, participated in the gains as well as the guilt of slavery, would the remembrance of its palmy days be otherwise than one of regret. We Negroes, on the other hand, after a lapse of time extending over nearly two generations, could be indebted only to precarious tradition or scarcely accessible documents for any knowledge we might chance upon of the sufferings endured in these Islands of the West by those of our race who have gone before us. Death, with undiscriminating hand, had gathered in the human harvest of masters and slaves alike, according to or out of the normal laws of nature; while Time had been letting down on the stage of our existence drop-scene after drop-scene of years, to the number of something like fifty, which had been curtaining off the tragic incidents of the past from the peaceful activities of the present. Being thus circumstanced, thought we, what rational elements of mutual hatred should *now* continue to exist in the bosoms of the two races?

With regard to the perpetual reference to Hayti, because of our oneness with its inhabitants in origin and complexion, as a criterion for the exact forecast of our future conduct under given circumstances, this appeared to us, looking at actual facts, perversity gone wild in the manufacture of analogies. The founders of the Black Republic, we had all along understood, were not in any sense whatever equipped, as Mr. Froude assures us they were, when starting on their self-governing career, with the civil and intellectual advantages that had been transplanted from Europe. On the contrary, we had been taught to regard them as most unfortunate in the circumstances under which they so gloriously conquered their merited freedom. We saw them free, but perfectly illiterate barbarians, impotent to use the intellectual resources of which their valour had made them possessors, in the shape of books on the spirit and technical details of a highly developed national existence. We had learnt also, until this new interpreter of history had contradicted the accepted record, that the continued failure of Hayti to realize the dreams of Toussaint[85] was due to the fatal want of confidence subsisting between the fairer and darker sections of the inhabitants, which had its sinister and disastrous origin in the action of the Mulattoes in attempting to secure freedom for themselves, in conjunction with the Whites, at the sacrifice of their darker-hued kinsmen. Finally, it had been explained to us that the remembrance of this abnormal treason had been underlying and perniciously influencing the whole course of Haytian national history. All

---

82 In Greek mythology, nymphs of the sunset and evening
83 'Shuddering; feeling or expressing horror' (*OED*)
84 Sorcery or witchcraft
85 François-Dominique Toussaint Louverture (1743–1803), the most prominent leader of the Haitian Revolution

this established knowledge we are called upon to throw overboard, and accept the baseless assertions of this conjuror-up of inconceivable fables! He calls upon us to believe that, in spite of being free, educated, progressive, and at peace with all men, we West Indian Blacks, were we ever to become constitutionally dominant in our native islands, would emulate in savagery our Haytian fellow-Blacks who, at the time of retaliating upon their actual masters, were tortured slaves, bleeding and rendered desperate under the oppressors' lash—and all this simply and merely because of the sameness of our ancestry and the colour of our skin! One would have thought that Liberia[86] would have been a fitter standard of comparison in respect of a coloured population starting a national life, really and truly equipped with the requisites and essentials of civilized existence. But such a reference would have been fatal to Mr. Froude's object: the annals of Liberia being a persistent refutation of the old pro-slavery prophecies which our author so feelingly rehearses.

Let us revert, however, to Grenada and the newly-published "Bow of Ulysses," which had come into my hands in April, 1888.

It seemed to me, on reading that book, and deducing therefrom the foregoing essential summary, that a critic would have little more to do, in order to effectually exorcise this negrophobic political hobgoblin, than to appeal to impartial history, as well as to common sense, in its application to human nature in general, and to the actual facts of West Indian life in particular.

History, as against the hard and fast White-master and Black-slave theory so recklessly invented and confidently built upon by Mr. Froude, would show incontestably—(a) that for upwards of two hundred years before the Negro Emancipation, in 1838, there had never existed in one of those then British Colonies, which had been originally discovered and settled for Spain by the great Columbus or by his successors, the *Conquistadores*, any prohibition whatsoever, on the ground of race or colour, against the owning of slaves by any free person possessing the necessary means, and desirous of doing so; (b) that, as a consequence of this non-restriction, and from causes notoriously historical, numbers of blacks, half-breeds, and other non-Europeans, besides such of them as had become possessed of their "property" by inheritance, availed themselves of this virtual license, and in course of time constituted a very considerable proportion of the slave-holding section of those communities; (c) that these dusky plantation-owners enjoyed and used in every possible sense the identical rights and privileges which were enjoyed and used by their pure-blooded Caucasian brother-slaveowners. The above statements are attested by written documents, oral tradition, and, better still perhaps, by the living presence in those islands of numerous lineal representatives of those once opulent and flourishing non-European planter-families.

Common sense, here stepping in, must, from the above data, deduce some such conclusions as the following. First that, on the hypothesis that the slaves who were freed in 1838—full fifty years ago—were all on an average fifteen years old, those vengeful ex-slaves of to-day will be all men of sixty-five years of age; and, allowing for the delay in getting the franchise, somewhat further advanced towards the human life-term of threescore and ten years. Again, in order to organize and carry out any scheme of legislative and social retaliation of the kind set forth in the "Bow of Ulysses," there must be (which unquestionably there is not) a considerable, well-educated, and very influential number surviving of those who had actually been

---

86 Founded by freed and free-born American Blacks in 1847, the African nation of Liberia served as a model for the modern Black republic.

in bondage. Moreover, the vengeance of these people (also assuming the foregoing nonexistent condition) would have, in case of opportunity, to wreak itself far more largely and vigorously upon members of their own race than upon Whites, seeing that the increase of the Blacks, as correctly represented in the "Bow of Ulysses," is just as rapid as the diminution of the White population. And therefore, Mr. Froude's "Danger-to-the-Whites" cry in support of his anti-reform manifesto would not appear, after all, to be quite so justifiable as he possibly thinks.

Feeling keenly that something in the shape of the foregoing programme might be successfully worked up for a public defence of the maligned people, I disregarded the bodily and mental obstacles that have beset and clouded my career during the last twelve years, and cheerfully undertook the task, stimulated thereto by what I thought weighty considerations. I saw that no representative of Her Majesty's Ethiopic West Indian subjects cared to come forward to perform this work in the more permanent shape that I felt to be not only desirable but essential for our self-vindication. I also realized the fact that the "Bow of Ulysses" was not likely to have the same ephemeral existence and effect as the newspaper and other periodical discussions of its contents, which had poured from the press in Great Britain, the United States, and very notably, of course, in all the English Colonies of the Western Hemisphere. In the West Indian papers the best writers of our race had written masterly refutations, but it was clear how difficult the task would be in future to procure and refer to them whenever occasion should require. Such productions, however, fully satisfied those qualified men of our people, because they were legitimately convinced (even as I myself am convinced) that the political destinies of the people of colour could not run one tittle of risk from anything that it pleased Mr. Froude to write or say on the subject. But, meditating further on the question, the reflection forced itself upon me that, beyond the mere political personages in the circle more directly addressed by Mr. Froude's volume, there were individuals whose influence or possible sympathy we could not afford to disregard, or to esteem lightly. So I deemed it right and a patriotic duty to attempt the enterprise myself, in obedience to the above stated motives.

At this point I must pause to express on behalf of the entire coloured population of the West Indies our most heartfelt acknowledgments to Mr. C. Salmon for the luminous and effective vindication of us, in his volume on "West Indian Confederation," against Mr. Froude's libels.[87] The service thus rendered by Mr. Salmon possesses a double significance and value in my estimation. In the first place, as being the work of a European of high position, quite independent of us (who testifies concerning Negroes, not through having gazed at them from balconies, decks of steamers, or the seats of moving carriages, but from actual and long personal intercourse with them, which the internal evidence of his book plainly proves to have been as sympathetic as it was familiar), and, secondly, as the work of an individual entirely outside of our race, it has been gratefully accepted by myself as an incentive to self-help, on the same more formal and permanent lines, in a matter so important to the status which we can justly claim as a progressive, law-abiding, and self-respecting section of Her Majest's liege subjects.

It behoves me now to say a few words respecting this book as a mere literary production.

---

87 *The Caribbean Confederation* (1888), a volume by the British author Charles Spencer Salmon (1832–96) that proposes a confederation of the fifteen British West Indian colonies

Alexander Pope, who, next to Shakespeare and perhaps Butler, was the most copious contributor to the current stock of English maxims, says:

"True ease in writing comes from Art, not Chance,
As those move easiest who have learnt to dance."[88]

A whole dozen years of bodily sickness and mental tribulation have not been conducive to that regularity of practice in composition which alone can ensure the "true ease" spoken of by the poet; and therefore is it that my style leaves so much to be desired, and exhibits, perhaps, still more to be pardoned. Happily, a quarrel such as ours with the author of "The English in the West Indies" cannot be finally or even approximately settled on the score of superior literary competency, whether of aggressor or defender. I feel free to ignore whatever verdict might be grounded on a consideration so purely artificial. There ought to be enough, if not in these pages, at any rate in whatever else I have heretofore published, that should prove me not so hopelessly stupid and wanting in self-respect, as would be implied by my undertaking a contest in artistic phrase-weaving with one who, even among the foremost of his literary countrymen, is confessedly a master in that craft. The judges to whom I do submit our case are those Englishmen and others whose conscience blends with their judgment, and who determine such questions as this on their essential rightness which has claim to the first and decisive consideration. For much that is irregular in the arrangement and sequence of the subject-matter, some blame fairly attaches to our assailant. The erratic manner in which he launches his injurious statements against the hapless Blacks, even in the course of passages which no more led up to them than to any other section of mankind, is a very notable feature of his anti-Negro production. As he frequently repeats, very often with cynical aggravations, his charges and sinister prophecies against the sable objects[89] of his aversion, I could see no other course open to me than to take him up on the points whereto I demurred, exactly how, when, and where I found them.

My purpose could not be attained up without direct mention of, or reference to, certain public employés in the Colonies whose official conduct has often been the subject of criticism in the public press of the West Indies. Though fully aware that such criticism has on many occasions been much more severe than my own strictures, yet, it being possible that some special responsibility may attach to what I here reproduce in a more permanent shape, I most cheerfully accept, in the interests of public justice, any consequence which may result.

A remark or two concerning the publication of this rejoinder. It has been hinted to me that the issue of it has been too long delayed to secure for it any attention in England, owing to the fact that the West Indies are but little known, and of less interest, to the generality of English readers. Whilst admitting, as in duty bound, the possible correctness of this forecast, and regretting the oft-recurring hindrances which occasioned such frequent and, sometimes, long suspension of my labour; and noting, too, the additional delay caused through my unacquaintance with English publishing usages, I must, notwithstanding, plead guilty to a lurking hope that some small fraction of Mr. Froude's readers will yet be found, whose interest in the West Indies will be temporarily revived on behalf of this essay, owing to its direct bearing on Mr. Froude and his statements relative to these Islands, contained in his recent book of travels in them. This I am led to hope will be more particularly the case when it is borne in mind that

88 Alexander Pope (1688–1744), *An Essay on Criticism* (1711), Part 2, lines 362–3
89 That is Black persons

the rejoinder has been attempted by a member of that very same race which he has, with such eloquent recklessness of all moral considerations, held up to public contempt and disfavour. In short, I can scarcely permit myself to believe it possible that concern regarding a popular author, on his being questioned by an adverse critic of however restricted powers, can be so utterly dead within a twelvemonth as to be incapable of rekindling. Mr. Froude's "Oceana,"[90] which had been published long before its author voyaged to the West Indies, in order to treat the Queen's subjects there in the same more than questionable fashion as that in which he had treated those of the Southern Hemisphere, had what was in the main a formal rejoinder to its misrepresentations published only three months ago in this city. I venture to believe that no serious work in defence of an important cause or community can lose much, if anything, of its intrinsic value through some delay in its issue; especially when written in the vindication of Truth, whose eternal principles are beyond and above the influence of time and its changes.

At any rate, this attempt to answer some of Mr. Froude's main allegations against the people of the West Indies cannot fail to be of grave importance and lively interest to the inhabitants of those Colonies. In this opinion I am happy in being able to record the full concurrence of a numerous and influential body of my fellow-West Indians, men of various races, but united in detestation of falsehood and injustice.

J. J. T.

LONDON, *June*, 1889.

Source text

Thomas, J. J., *Froudacity: West Indian Fables by James Anthony Froude* (London: T. Fisher Unwin, 1889).

References

Froude, James Anthony, *The English in the West Indies; Or, the Bow of Ulysses* (London: Longmans, Green, and Co., 1888).
Ledgister, F. S. J., 'Racist Rantings, Travelers' Tales, and a Creole Counterblast: Thomas Carlyle, John Stuart Mill, J. A. Froude, and J. J. Thomas on British Rule in the West Indies', in Paul E. Kerry and Marylu Hill (eds), *Thomas Carlyle Resartus: Reappraising Carlyle's Contribution to the Philosophy of History, Political Theory, and Cultural Criticism* (Madison, WI: Fairleigh Dickinson University Press, 2010), 106–32.

Anna Julia Cooper (1858?–1964)

From 'The Higher Education of Women', A Voice from the South (1892)

Anna Julia Haywood Cooper was born in Raleigh, North Carolina, to an enslaved mother. At age nine, she became a student-teacher at St Augustine

---

90 *Oceana, or, England and Her Colonies* (1886), published after Froude spent six months travelling in South Africa, Australasia and America, but not the West Indies

School in Raleigh, where she graduated in 1877 and married fellow student-teacher, Reverend George C. Cooper, who died two years later. Cooper entered Oberlin College in 1881, graduating with her bachelor's degree in 1884 and received an honorary master's degree in 1887. After teaching at Wilberforce University in Ohio, she became principal of the M Street Colored High School in Washington, DC, the nation's most prestigious preparatory school for African Americans, but was dismissed in 1906 for resisting a new emphasis on vocational training and asserting the necessity of keeping college preparatory classes. Cooper next taught at Lincoln Institute in Jefferson City, Missouri, for four years before returning to M Street as a teacher until her retirement in 1930. During this time, she worked toward her doctoral degree, often studying abroad in Europe during her summer breaks, and in 1925 she earned her doctorate in modern languages from the Sorbonne in Paris.

Cooper was a prominent figure in the Black women's club movement and a member of the National Association of Educators and the National Association for the Advancement of Colored People. She lectured on feminist, racial and educational topics and spoke at the London Pan-African Conference in 1900. *A Voice from the South* was Cooper's first book; she continued to publish articles and essays throughout her life. Cooper died at her home in Washington on 27 February 1964.

From 'The Higher Education of Women'

In soul-culture woman at last dares to contend with men, and we may cite Grant Allen[91] (who certainly cannot be suspected of advocating the unsexing of woman) as an example of the broadening effect of this contest on the ideas at least of the men of the day. He says in his *Plain Words on the Woman Question*, recently published:

"The position of woman was not [in the past] a position which could bear the test of nineteenth-century scrutiny. Their education was inadequate, their social status was humiliating, their political power was nil, their practical and personal grievances were innumerable; above all, their relations to the family—to their husbands, their children, their friends, their property—was simply insupportable."

And again: "As a body we 'Advanced men' are, I think, prepared to reconsider, and to reconsider fundamentally, without prejudice or misconception, the entire question of the relation between the sexes. We are ready to make any modifications in those relations which will satisfy the woman's just aspiration for personal independence, for intellectual and moral development, for physical culture, for political activity, and for a voice in the arrangement of her own affairs, both domestic and national."

Now this is magnanimous enough, surely; and quite a step from eighteenth century preaching, is it not? The higher education of Woman has certainly developed the men;—let us see what it has done for the women.

---

91 Charles Grant Allen (1848–99) was a science writer and novelist who upheld the theory of evolution in the second half of the nineteenth century.

Matthew Arnold[92] during his last visit to America in '82 or '83, lectured before a certain co-educational college in the West. After the lecture he remarked, with some surprise, to a lady professor, that the young women in his audience, he noticed, paid as close attention as the men, ["]*all the way through*." This led, of course, to a spirited discussion of the higher education for women, during which he said to his enthusiastic interlocutor, eyeing her philosophically through his English eyeglass: "But—eh—don't you think it—eh—spoils their *chawnces*, you know!"

Now, as to the result to women, this is the most serious argument ever used against the higher education. If it interferes with marriage, classical training has a grave objection to weigh and answer.

For I agree with Mr. Allen at least on this one point, that there must be marrying and giving in marriage even till the end of time.

I grant you that intellectual development, with the self-reliance and capacity for earning a livelihood which it gives, renders woman less dependent on the marriage relation for physical support (which, by the way, does not always accompany it). Neither is she compelled to look to sexual love as the one sensation capable of giving tone and relish, movement and vim to the life she leads. Her horison is extended. Her sympathies are broadened and deepened and multiplied. She is in closer touch with nature. Not a bud that opens, not a dew drop, not a ray of light, not a cloud-burst or a thunderbolt, but adds to the expansiveness and zest of her soul. And if the sun of an absorbing passion be gone down, still 'tis night that brings the stars. She has remaining the mellow, less obtrusive, but none the less enchanting and inspiring light of friendship, and into its charmed circle she may gather the best the world has known. She can commune with Socrates about the *daimon*[93] he knew and to which she too can bear witness; she can revel in the majesty of Dante, the sweetness of Virgil, the simplicity of Homer, the strength of Milton. She can listen to the pulsing heart throbs of passionate Sappho's encaged soul, as she beats her bruised wings against her prison bars and struggles to flutter out into Heaven's æther,[94] and the fires of her own soul cry back as she listens. "Yes; Sappho, I know it all; I know it all." Here, at last, can be communion without suspicion; friendship without misunderstanding; love without jealousy.

We must admit then that Byron's[95] picture, whether a thing of beauty or not, has faded from the canvas of to-day.

> "Man's love," he wrote, "is of man's life a thing apart,
> 'Tis woman's whole existence.
> Man may range the court, camp, church, the vessel and the mart,
> Sword, gown, gain, glory offer in exchange.
> Pride, fame, ambition, to fill up his heart—
> And few there are whom these cannot estrange.
> Men have all these resources, we *but one*—
> *To love again and be again undone*."[96]

---

92 Matthew Arnold (1822–88) was a prominent English poet and cultural critic who worked as an inspector of schools in nineteenth-century Britain.
93 One's genius (*OED*)
94 The clear sky; the upper regions of space beyond the clouds; the medium supposed to fill the upper regions of space, as the air fills the lower regions (*OED*)
95 George Gordon, Lord Byron (1788–1824) was a British poet and leading figure in the Romantic Movement.
96 Lord Byron, George Gordon, *Don Juan*, Canto 1, stanza 194

This may have been true when written. *It is not true to-day.* The old, subjective, stagnant, indolent and wretched life for woman has gone. She has as many resources as men, as many activities beckon her on. As large possibilities swell and inspire her heart.

Now, then, does it destroy or diminish her capacity for loving?

Her standards have undoubtedly gone up. The necessity of speculating in 'chawnces' has probably shifted. The question is not now with the woman "How shall I so cramp, stunt, simplify and nullify myself as to make me elegible to the honor of being swallowed up into some little man?" but the problem, I trow, now rests with the man as to how he can so develop his God-given powers as to reach the ideal of a generation of women who demand the noblest, grandest and best achievements of which he is capable; and this surely is the only fair and natural adjustment of the chances. Nature never meant that the ideals and standards of the world should be dwarfing and minimizing ones, and the men should thank us for requiring of them the richest fruits which they can grow. If it makes them work, all the better for them. [...]

The high ground of generalities is alluring but my pen is devoted to a special cause: and with a view to further enlightenment on the achievements of the century for THE HIGHER EDUCATION OF COLORED Women, I wrote a few days ago to the colleges which admit women and asked how many colored women had completed the B. A. course in each during its entire history. These are the figures returned: Fisk leads the way with twelve; Oberlin next with five; Wilberforce, four; Ann Arbor and Wellesley three each, Livingstone two, Atlanta one, Howard, as yet, none.

I then asked the principal of the Washington High School how many out of a large number of female graduates from his school had chosen to go forward and take a collegiate course. He replied that but one had ever done so, and she was then in Cornell.[97]

Others ask questions too, sometimes, and I was asked a few years ago by a white friend, "How is it that the men of your race seem to outstrip the women in mental attainment?" "Oh," I said, "so far as it is true, the men, I suppose, from the life they lead, gain more by contact; and so far as it is only apparent, I think the women are more quiet. They don't feel called to mount a barrel and harangue by the hour every time they imagine they have produced an idea."

But I am sure there is another reason which I did not at that time see fit to give. The atmosphere, the standards, the requirements of our little world do not afford any special stimulus to female development.

It seems hardly a gracious thing to say, but it strikes me as true, that while our men seem thoroughly abreast of the times on almost every other subject, when they strike the woman question they drop back into sixteenth century logic. They leave nothing to be desired generally in regard to gallantry and chivalry, but they actually do not seem sometimes to have outgrown that old contemporary of chivalry—the idea that women may stand on pedestals or live in doll houses, (if they happen to have them) but they must not furrow their brows with thought or attempt to help men tug at the great questions of the world. I fear the majority of colored men do not yet think it worth while that women aspire to higher education. Not many will subscribe to the "advanced" ideas of Grant Allen already quoted. The three R's, a little music and a good deal of dancing, a first rate dress-maker and a

---

97 [Author's note] Graduated from Scientific Course, June, 1890, the first colored woman to graduate from Cornell.

bottle of magnolia balm, are quite enough generally to render charming any woman possessed of tact and the capacity for worshipping masculinity.

Source text

Cooper, Anna Julia, *A Voice from the South by a Black Woman of the South* (Xenia, OH: Aldine Printing House, 1892).

References

ANB
Hack, Daniel, *Reaping Something New: African American Transformations of Victorian Literature* (Princeton, NJ: Princeton University Press, 2017), 148–50.
Hubbard, LaRese, 'Anna Julia Cooper and Africana Womanism: Some Early Conceptual Contributions', *Black Women, Gender and Families* 4.2 (Fall 2010), 31–53.
OED

Frances E. W. Harper (1825–1911)

'Maceo' (1900)

Frances Ellen Watkins Harper, the daughter of free Blacks, was born in Baltimore, Maryland. Though she attended the free Blacks' school run by her uncle only until age thirteen, she became a major African American poet of the nineteenth century as well as a groundbreaking novelist who dealt with Reconstruction, passing and miscegenation. She was also an activist for abolition and women's rights and her performances of her poems, much like spoken word poet-activists in the twenty-first century, brought further attention to her causes while also helping turn her collected poems into a best-seller. She additionally co-founded the National Association of Colored Women in the 1890s for which she acted as Vice President until her death.

Antonio Maceo y Grajales (1845–96) was a prominent Afro-Cuban military leader of Afro-Cuban troops fighting against Spanish colonial rule of Cuba. Known as 'the Bronze Titan', he conceptually linked the enslavement of Africans and their descendants to the domination of Cuba by Spain and more generally European colonialism (Callahan 49, 52). Just as he exemplified a form of pan-African understanding (see also Celestine Edwards, 'Introduction', AA), so Harper's tribute to him demonstrates the transnational scope of Harper's commitments to freedom and social justice. Monique-Adelle Callahan asserts that the full context for the poem, first published in the 1900 reprinting of Harper's *Poems*, is the retreat from Reconstruction and a policy of white supremacy in the US South. If Maceo figures only in the first three stanzas (Callahan, 53; Gruesser, 27), Callahan adds that the invocation of Christ's martyrdom in the poem's later stanzas aligns Christ and Maceo, so that 'the Bronze Titan' becomes a type of Christ in his deliberate self-sacrifice to free others (Callahan, 53–6).

'Maceo'

Maceo dead! A thrill of sorrow
    Through our hearts in sadness ran
When we felt in one sad hour
    That the world had lost a man.

He had clasped unto his bosom
    The sad fortunes of his land—
Held the cause for which he perished
    With a firm, unfaltering hand.

On his lips the name of freedom
    Fainted with his latest breath.
Cuba Libre[98] was his watchword
    Passing through the gates of death.

With the light of God around us,
    Why this agony and strife?
With the cross of Christ before us,
    Why this fearful waste of life?

Must the pathway unto freedom
    Ever mark a crimson line,
And the eyes of wayward mortals
    Always close to light divine?

Must the hearts of fearless valor
    Fail 'mid crime and cruel wrong,
When the world has read of heroes
    Brave and earnest, true and strong?

Men to stay the floods of sorrow
    Sweeping round each war-crushed heart;
Men to say to strife and carnage—
    From our world henceforth depart.

God of peace and God of nations,
    Haste! Oh, haste the glorious day
When the reign of our Redeemer
    O'er the world shall have its sway.

When the swords now blood encrusted,
    Spears that reap the battle field,
Shall be changed to higher service,
    Helping earth rich harvests yield.

Where the widow weeps in anguish,
    And the orphan bows his head,
Grant that peace and joy and gladness
    May like holy angels tread.

---

98 Free Cuba. Callahan translates an 1879 statement by Maceo to contextualise the dying words
that Harper ascribes to him: 'The opportune moment has arrived that we will make the whole world
know that the Cuban knows how to die for the redemption of his country' (Callahan, 49).

Pity, oh, our God the sorrow
    Of thy world from thee astray,
Lead us from the paths of madness
    Unto Christ the living way.

Year by year the world grows weary
    'Neath its weight of sin and strife,
Though the hands once pierced and bleeding
    Offer more abundant life.

May the choral songs of angels
    Heard upon Judea's plain
Sound throughout the earth the tidings
    Of that old and sweet refrain.

Till our world, so sad and weary,
    Finds the balmy rest of peace—
Peace to silence all her discords—
    Peace till war and crime shall cease.

Peace to fall like gentle showers,
    Or on parchéd flowers dew,
Till our hearts proclaim with gladness:
    Lo, He maketh all things new.

Source text

Harper, Frances E. W., *Poems* (Philadelphia: Ferguson, 1900).

References

ANB
Callahan, Monique-Adelle, *Between the Lines: Literary Transnationalism and African American Poetics* (Oxford: Oxford University Press, 2011).
Gruesser, John Cullen, *The Empire Abroad and the Empire at Home: African American Literature and the Era of Expansion* (Athens, GA: University of Georgia Press, 2012).
Lootens, Tricia, *The Political Poetess: Victorian Femininity, Race, and the Legacy of Separate Spheres* (Princeton, NJ: Princeton University Press, 2017).

E. Pauline Johnson (Tekahionwake) (1861–1913)

'The Lodge of the Law-Makers' (1906)

From birth E. Pauline Johnson straddled two cultures as the daughter of a highly educated Mohawk father and English mother. She grew up on the Six Nations Reserve in Ontario and was educated by her parents at home before enrolling at the Brantford Collegiate Institute at 14. Johnson began writing poetry in 1884 after her father's death, utilising both E. Pauline Johnson and Tekahionwake as pen names while publishing in various periodicals. As her popularity grew, she began reciting her work on tours of Canada, England and the US, dressing as a Mohawk 'princess' for half of the poetry and an English 'lady' for the other. Her poetry similarly reflected her dual heritage, as she published volumes comprised of both English poetry and Native folk-tales, including *The White Wampum* (1895), *Canadian Born* (1903) and *Flint and Feather* (1912). She retired from the stage in 1909 and moved to Vancouver, where she continued writing until her death in 1913.

Her poetry often expresses a desire for peace and reconciliation between Native peoples and the British/Canadians, and she is recognised as one of the foremothers of Canadian literature. Her writings also support Canadian independence and women's rights. She has at times been criticised for performing Native identity for white audiences for profit, though she needed the income and faced both discrimination and poverty. Certainly, as a First Nations writer, she promoted Native institutions and culture and resisted white supremacy.

'The Lodge of the Law-Makers' juxtaposes the 'Parliaments of the White Man and the Red'. The piece, composed while Johnson was touring England, ridicules the supposed democracy and enlightenment of the British, whose Parliament features regular elections but supports primogeniture and bars women from representation or power. As Johnson observes, the supposedly uncivilised and backwards Iroquois nation has held legislative assemblies and accepted women's guidance for centuries.

'The Lodge of the Law-Makers'

Contrasts between the Parliaments of the White Man and the Red.

The Paleface is a man of many moods; what he approves to-day he will disapprove to-morrow.

He is never content to let his mighty men rule for more than four or five years, after which time he wearies of their council fires, their law-giving, and their treaties with other tribes; he wants new chiefs, warriors, and braves, and he secures them by the voice and vote of the nation.

We of the ancient Iroquois[99] race can but little understand this strange mode of government. We and our fathers, and their fathers before them, have always been pleased with our own Parliament,[100] which has never varied through the generations—save when death leaves one seat empty, and another chief in the line of lineage steps forward to fill the vacancy.

But to more fully learn the wisdom of the white man's superior civilization, I followed the wide crowded trail that leads to his council-house. I knew I would find it on the banks of a river,[101] for any trails, even in my own country, whether they are beaten by man, horse, or buffalo, lead always to the edge of a stream.

---

99 A powerful tribe of Native Americans and First Nations situated in North America
100 The Iroquois Confederacy, an assembly of the five nations of Iroquois (Mohawk, Oneida, Cayuga, Onondaga and Seneca)
101 Here, the Thames

As I neared the place I knew it for the abode of the wise men of this nation, for the voice of power and diplomacy, and tactics and skillful intrigue, thundered out from the white man's strange timepiece set in the carven square tower that rises majestic and inviolate as the tallest pine in the undiscovered wilderness of the West; and as the mountain tornado thrashes through the topmost branches, waking them to murmuring voices that dominate all other sounds of the forest, so do the tongues of these mighty men beneath the tower proclaim their dominion over all the wilderness of mankind in these island kingdoms of the East.

Old men and young were debating with great spirit. Their speech was not so pleasant, or so diplomatic, or so fraught with symbols, as is the speech of our Indian rulers; the law-making for the nation is not pleasant councilling; therefore, we say, use the speech that may breed dissension as one would use the stone war-club. We hide and wrap the stone in vari-coloured beads and brilliantly stained moose-hair; it is then more acceptable to the eye and the touch, but the weapon and the force are there nevertheless. The white man's speech shows the grim baldness of the stone alone—no adornment, no coloring to render it less aggressive, but his tongue is arrow-headed, fleet, and direct, and where he aims is the spot he strikes.

Do the white law-makers in this great council-house on the Thames river know that there exists within my own Indian race the oldest constitutional government of America—a free Commonwealth older than any in Europe, save that of this ancient England and the land of the crags and cañons which they call Switzerland?[102]

Hiawatha's Work

And this Commonwealth, which dominated the vast continent of North America even after the white traders set their feet on our territory, was devised and framed through the brain of the young Onondaga diplomat, Hiawatha,[103] who, conceiving an idea for a universal peace, called together the representative chiefs of all the hostile tribes. It mattered not that war and bloodshed had existed for many decades between the tribes that these envoys represented, the words of Hiawatha were as oil.

The council fires burned ceaselessly, the council pipes were filled and smoked endlessly, until the fifty chiefs in conclave all ratified the policy under discussion. And thus was framed the constitution of a government that was to live through the ages, that does exist in absolute authority to-day, where the chiefs who are the final descendants of those fifty noble families still meet, and direct the affairs of their people with no less wisdom and judgment than is displayed by these Palefaces here beneath the square tower by the Thames.[104]

Our fifty titles[105] are not necessarily borne by the eldest sons of the noble families,[106] for he may be greatly lacking in the qualities that make a statesman. Is not his second, or maybe his youngest brother, of as noble birth as he? Why not then, put

---

102 The Iroquois Confederacy was established sometime between 1570 and 1600.
103 Also known as Ayenwatha or Aiionwatha, one of the founders of the Iroquois Confederacy. Various accounts list him as an Onondaga or Mohawk, or adopted from the former to the latter at some point.
104 Either Victoria Tower or Elizabeth Tower, square-shaped towers that house the British Parliament
105 The Grand Council of the Confederacy is comprised of fifty Sachems, called Hoyaneh, passed down on a hereditary basis.
106 At this time the British House of Lords was comprised of hereditary peers, usually based on primogeniture.

him in high places, to let him use the brain and mind that, perhaps, his elder brother lacks? This is the Iroquois policy, and we practice it; but the white man knows little of the intricate workings of our inflexible league, for we are a silent people. Will the white man who considers us a savage, unenlightened race wonder if I told him the fate of the "Senate"[107] lies in the hands of the women of our tribes?

The Daughters

I have heard that the daughters of this vast city cry out for a voice in the Parliament of this land.[108] There is no need for an Iroquois woman to clamor for recognition in our councils; she has had it for upwards of four centuries.[109] The highest title known to us is that of "chief matron." It is borne by the oldest woman of each of the noble families.

From her cradle-board she is taught to judge men and their intellectual qualities, their aptness for public life, and their integrity, so that when he who bears the title leaves his seat in council to join the league-makers in the happy hunting grounds she can use her wisdom and her learning in nominating his fittest successor. She must bestow the title upon one of his kinsmen, one of the blood royal, so that the heritage is unbroken, so, perhaps, she passes by the inadequate eldest son and nominates the capable younger one. Thus is the council given the best of the brain and blood of the nation.

The old and powerful chiefs-in-council never attempt to question her decision; her appointment is final, and at the "condoling council," when he is installed, and his title conferred as he first takes his seat, the chief matron may, if she desires, enter the council-house and publicly make an address to the chiefs, braves, and warriors assembled, and she is listened to not only with attention, but with respect.

There are fifty matrons possessing this right in the Iroquois Confederacy. I have not yet heard of fifty white women even among those of noble birth who may speak and be listened to in the lodge of the law-makers here.

Source text

Johnson, E. Pauline. 'The Lodge of the Law-Makers: Contrasts between the Parliaments of the White Man and the Red', *Daily Express*, 14 August 1906, 4.

References

Dictionary of Canadian Biography, Web.
Monture, Rick, *We Share Our Matters: Two Centuries of Writing and Resistance at Six Nations of the Grand River* (Winnipeg: University of Manitoba Press, 2014).
Strong-Boag, Veronica and Carole Gerson, *Paddling Her Own Canoe: The Times and Texts of E. Pauline Johnson (Tekahionwake)* (Toronto: University of Toronto Press, 2000).

---

107 The Upper House of Legislature in Canada is the Senate
108 The Parliament (Qualification of Women) Act of 1918 allowed British women over 21 to serve as a Member of Parliament.
109 The Iroquois are a matrilineal tribe, with clan mothers who nominate the chief and may remove leaders from power.

Ellen Newbold La Motte (1873–1961)

**From 'Caught in Suffragette Riot, Ellen N. La Motte, of Baltimore,
Is Knocked Down and Then—Well, She Writes About It' (1913)**

Figure 9.4 Miss La Motte in Court, in 'Caught in Suffragette Riot',
The Baltimore Sun (7 September 1913), 19.

US nurse and activist Ellen Newbold La Motte grew up in Louisville, Kentucky and Wilmington, Delaware; completed nursing training at the Johns Hopkins Hospital Training School for Nurses in Baltimore, Maryland, in 1902; and became a tuberculosis nurse soon after. In 1909 she joined the Baltimore Health Department and became the first woman there to work as an executive, supervising fifteen nurses.

She was additionally an outspoken suffragist, marching in suffrage parades, lecturing and serving on the editorial board of the suffrage journal the *New Voter*. In June 1913 she took a leave of absence from the Baltimore health department and became special correspondent (July–September 1913) covering militant suffragism in London for the *Baltimore Sun*.

She next moved to Paris and later served as a First World War I nurse, publishing *The Backwash of War*, a highly sceptical series of fictional sketches, in 1916; this was censored by the US government in 1918 due to its grim portrayal of war's effects. She continued as an activist and writer, if curbing her activism after moving back to Washington, DC, around 1931. La Motte's lively *Sun* report, like Pankhurst's Connecticut address in this section, further confirms suffragist transatlantic alliances.

From 'Caught in Suffragette Riot'

It was nearly 3 o'clock on a Monday afternoon, July 28, and the London Pavilion[110] was crowded for the weekly meeting of the women's Social and Political Union. Mary Richardson[111] and I entered together and found seats at the back somewhere on the aisle, which she said were good because we could get out again quickly.

"After this is over," she said, "meet me at the Cottage Tea Room, Piccadilly, and we'll have tea."

"But why meet you?" I inquired innocently. "Didn't we come together? Aren't we sitting together? Why aren't we going out together?"

"When this meeting is over," went on Mary Richardson, ignoring the question, "if either one of us is left, let us go to the Cottage Tea Room, Piccadilly, and either wait for the other a reasonable time. Now don't ask any more questions. The whole place is full of plain-clothes men and there is going to be a lot of trouble."

Everyone in the audience seemed to be aware that there was trouble brewing, and to be expecting it. On the Monday before Mrs. Pankhurst[112] had been arrested in the Pavilion before the meeting began, and the Monday before that Annie Kenney[113] had been arrested as she was leaving the Pavilion after the meeting, and on this Monday both of them were due to speak—with what results no one could tell. That is, they were both due to speak if they could pass unrecognized through the lines of police waiting for them outside. And if by chance they managed to pass the lines and enter the building, the police would be all the more furious and all the more determined to arrest them afterward. A fight, either way.

TENSITY[114]—THAT'S IT

We in America who are used to perfectly peaceful suffrage meetings, where the sole emotion engendered is apt to be a slight feeling of boredom over the shop-worn, if sound, arguments, can have little idea of the intense, exciting atmosphere of these W. P. S. U. meetings.

Everyone is on edge with nervous apprehension; every unusual sound or unusual pause causes a springing up from the seats, or a rush to the place of disturbance. The arrival of the leaders is a signal for the most enthusiastic demonstration. Always at Mrs. Pankhurst's appearance, and in a lesser degree at Annie Kenney's, the audience rises to its feet, many leaping on the seats, and there follows a storm of cheers, handclaps and waving handkerchiefs, which lasts for many minutes. We have not in the whole of America a leader capable of calling forth such demonstrations of love, loyalty and admiration. But then we have no leaders, and no members of the rank and file either, whose sincerity and belief has been put through the awful tests that these women have suffered.[115]

---

110 The Women's Social and Political Union (WPSU) met weekly at the London Pavilion near Piccadilly Circus.

111 Mary Raleigh Richardson (1882/3–1961) was a militant suffragist arrested nine times (*ODNB*). She sheltered with LaMotte in Paris in October 1913 to avoid arrest back home (Crawford, 597).

112 See also the headnote to Pankhurst's *Verbatim Report of Mrs. Pankhurst's Speech* in this section.

113 Annie Kenney (1879–1953), working-class suffragist, is credited with helping launch suffragist militancy when she and Christabel Pankhurst interrupted a Liberal political meeting in Manchester on 13 October 1905 (*ODNB*).

114 'a state of tension' (*OED*)

115 Both women had been arrested and waged debilitating hunger strikes.

But both Annie Kenney and Mrs. Pankhurst arrived on the platform in safety. Mrs. Pankhurst was wheeled on in an invalid's chair, and although unable to rise from it, in a voice trembling with weakness and emotion she made a short speech. She was out of prison only four days after a hunger strike and she was at liberty under the protection of her license. Therefore it was Annie Kenney whom the police would arrest—if they could—after the meeting.

And then little Annie Kenney spoke—a vivacious, brave, stirring appeal, the burden of which was "No surrender." She herself was like a vivid flame, contained in a body so frail and wasted by starvation that one suffered to look at her.

THE TRAP

Then we all watched to see her leave the stage. She could only reach the street through the main entrance, and as she left the platform and passed down the passageway at the side of the theatre, suffragettes from all over the house sprang up to go with her. Those who were on the aisle seats got there first.

Only the narrow strip of sidewalk outside the Pavilion had to be crossed. Two taxis were waiting at the curb—one belonging to the Women's Social and Political Union, the other to the police of Scotland Yard. One meant safety, the other arrest. The doors of both stood open, the engines of both were whirring, each ready to dash off with its passenger when the struggle should be decided.

She had worn a disguise when she entered the pavilion—a long, dark cloak and a dark hat, which came well down over her face. In it she had slipped past police on entering and they were determined that she should not do so again. However, they were unable to recognize her, but knew that she was one among the outpouring crowd, concealed somewhere in the midst of the tight, close marching mass of people moving slowly out of the pavilion doors, and they determined to find her in their own way.

THE ASSAULT

A certain number of the crowd were allowed to pass by in safety and then suddenly from both sides of the lane of uniformed men through which it was moving a furious assault was made.

The police rushed into the hemmed-in crowd with terrible violence, using both fists and clubs.

Both men and women were savagely struck in the face, knocked down, kicked and trampled on.

In a second there was a terrible fight raging all up and down the sidewalk and out into the roadway—a fight between furious, armed police on one side and on the other a mass of women, together with a few men who tried to assist them. And this took place in Piccadilly Circus, in the greatest capital of Europe, in a nation that calls itself the most highly civilized in the world. Moreover, the police who instigated this brutal assault were acting under the orders of Reginald McKenna, Home Secretary of England.[116]

When the smoke of battle had cleared away and I had got rid of the marks of some of it from my person I went to the Cottage Tea Room to wait for Mary Richardson. As she did not come within the reasonable time allotted I concluded that she had been arrested, which I afterward found to have been the case.

---

116 Reginald McKenna (1863–1943), Liberal politician and MP

THE COURT

There are many police courts in London, and as I did not know to which one she would be brought up for trial I went to Lincoln's Inn House the next morning and asked for the prisoner's secretary. [. . .]

The prisoner's secretary was rather glad to see me. [. . .] [and] glad to have some one to whom she could consign Mary Richardson's satchel. [. . .]

As I made my way through the crowd [in the courtroom] a woman came toward me with great cordiality.

"I see you're one of us!" she exclaimed.

I explained my commission with much pride. Then she went on to ask if I had been at the fight the day before.

I certainly had.

She went on to further explanation. A man, she said, an employe [sic] of the Colonial Office, has been badly injured by a constable the day before on leaving the pavilion. He had not provoked the attack. He had succeeded in getting the constable's number and wished to bring a charge against him, but it was necessary to have witnesses to corroborate his statements. Had I by any chance seen anything of it—could I possibly be a witness in the case?

I had seen one man mercilessly attacked and beaten, but unfortunately it was not the one she had reference to. A glance about the crowded waiting room, however, soon showed me the young fellow whom I had seen so badly hurt; he had a great gash over one eye, which had been partly closed by the blow, and his coat and shirt were covered with dried blood. I pointed him out to my new-found friend.

HE GOT HER BLOW

"I shall be glad to witness for that young man," I explained. "Happened to walk out of the pavilion right behind him and he got the blow that otherwise would have fallen on me."

Whereupon, with the easy camaraderie born of the police court, I offered my services to the young man. He was a painter and imprisonment meant a serious thing for him, since many were dependent upon him for support. With him was a man who had known him for some years—the cartoonist of the Suffragette[117]—who had come to testify as to his character, to prove that he was a hard-working, honest man and not some hooligan that the police had chanced to run in.

We talked over the matter carefully together since it had been my fortune to witness the very blow which had laid Ryan's head open.

"It's not that I mind going to prison," he began somewhat apologetically. "Not today in England, when all the best and finest among us are being sent there—but it's my sister—she's a widow, and has a lot of children—and I help look after them." [. . .]

DENMAN,[118] THE BEAK

"Who's the magistrate?" we asked one of our neighbors.

"Who's the Beak? Denman—looks like a Beak doesn't he?" was the scornful reply.

The Beak—it seemed much more suitable—was a thin, shriveled old man, who looked as if his last idea had been taken aboard during the Victorian epoch, about the date of the Prince Consort's death.[119]

---

117 *The Suffragette* (1912–15), a weekly newspaper, was the official publication of the WPSU.
118 The eldest son of George Denman (1819–96), judge and politician, G. L. Denman was named a Metropolitan Police magistrate in 1890 (*ODNB*).
119 Prince Albert of Saxe-Coburg and Gotha, Prince Consort to Queen Victoria, died in December 1861 at age forty-two.

These English magistrates are appointed for life, so have nothing to fear as to removal from office—a freedom which gives them considerable latitude in the administration of justice.

Moreover, since there is no necessity for keeping an ear to the ground, there is no necessity for intellectual or moral progress in any direction.

What one is most struck with in England is the rockiness, the solidity and impregnability of these British institutions.

One glance at the Beak's face, and we could have prophesied the outcome of each case that was tried before him. [. . .]

Ryan's case was called, in which we had been such a close and unwilling witness the day before. The usual charge was made—assaulting an officer, with the further charge of having behaved in most refractory and unruly manner when taken into custody. The constable testified that the prisoner had thrown himself down on the floor of the station house and had to be carried into his cell. Two officers testified to this latter piece of resistance. Then Ryan was put on the stand. He made but a poor showing, being rather frightened and evidently suffering from the blow over his eye. He could not tell accurately at what place the blow was given him—whether on leaving the Pavilion or when on his way to the station house. He was unshaken, however, in his statement that it was not he but the officer who had struck the first blow, and he freely admitted having struck back in self-defense. He also admitted having thrown himself to the floor of the police station when in custody, but explained that that was because the officers had screwed his arms so tightly behind his back.

The policeman who made the charge accused Ryan of having injured him—given him a blow on the forehead and a cut lip. There was no sign whatever of the cut lip; as for the injury to the forehead, it was a small red mark, looking very much like a birthmark, and was without swelling or contusion of any kind. Ryan, on the contrary, stood before them with a half-closed eye, with a cut on his forehead two inches long and blood all over his clothes.

MISS LA MOTTE TESTIFIES

Then my turn came to go into the witness box. The Bible was offered me to swear by, but it had been a tool in the hands of too many barefaced liars, so I said that I would dispense with this farce in this most Christian country and would affirm instead. I was allowed to make my statement without interruption.

I had been to the Pavilion meeting the afternoon before and happened by chance to walk out directly behind the prisoner, who seemed a comfortable, tall, broad-shouldered person to march behind. I walked out slowly in a dense crowd, between two lines of police. As I reached the curb, where more police were standing, I saw one of them suddenly strike out and give Ryan a tremendous blow in the face, followed by another and another in instant succession. This attack was entirely unprovoked and uncalled for in any way. Then, and not till then, did Ryan strike back, trying in a vain effort to defend himself, but as far as I could see his efforts had fallen short. He did not seem to be able to reach his opponent nor to land one blow upon him. I also saw the policeman strike the blow which laid the prisoner's head open. I had seen the blood fly.

"Ha! This is a new version!" exclaimed Muskett,[120] spring to his feet. "Perhaps you can identify the constable whom you say did all this?"

---

120 Muskett (otherwise unidentified) was the prosecuting attorney mentioned earlier in the article.

"Quite easily," I replied.

Half a dozen policemen were lined along the wall behind me. I pointed one out.

"That one—with the small birthmark on his forehead."

"Birthmark!" exclaimed Muskett, indignantly. "Birthmark, indeed! An injury given to this man by Ryan!"

"It will bear watching then, for it certainly doesn't look like a flat mark. Pretty slight and insignificant anyway, compared with those that Ryan got," I ventured. [. . .]

"And now may I ask, put in the magistrate, "just what happened after you saw the prisoner get his head cut?"

"At that point," I replied, regretfully, "I was unable to witness anything further. A man knocked me down—from behind. Which seems to be a good British custom."

Witness was excused!

THE SUMMING UP

In a few minutes the magistrate summed up the case and delivered sentence. [. . .]

"The testimony of the last witness, which seems to be at variance with what has gone before, we will not consider. Therefore, we find the prisoner guilty of the charge of assaulting and injuring an officer in the discharge of his duty, and will accordingly sentence the prisoner to 21 days' imprisonment, without option of a fine."

––––––

Somewhere at the back of the court room I saw a couple of the law-abiding suffragists who had come up to London two days before. I recognized them as law-abiding from the colors in their hats.[121] They were watching the administration of the law with awe and respect—admiration, too, perhaps—who knows?

For myself, I called to mind a banner that had been stood up on the plinth of the Nelson column at Trafalgar Square, during the riot two days before. It was a huge green banner, bearing upon it the words:

"LAWS—THEREFORE—REBELS."

Source text

La Motte, Ellen N. 'Caught in Suffragette Riot, Ellen N. La Motte, of Baltimore, Is Knocked Down and Then—Well, She Writes About It', *The Baltimore Sun*, 7 September 1913, 3.

References

ANB

Crawford, Elizabeth, *The Women's Suffrage Movement: A Reference Guide 1866–1928* (London: UCL Press, 1999).

ODNB

––––––

121 Presumably members of the National Union of Women's Suffrage Societies, a non-militant rival to the WPSU, whose colours were green, white and red in contrast to the WPSU's green, white and purple

Emmeline Pankhurst (1858–1928)

From **Verbatim Report of Mrs. Pankhurst's Speech, Delivered Nov. 13, 1913 at Parsons' Theatre, Hartford, Conn.** *(1913)*

Figure 9.5 Emmeline Pankhurst. Gerritsen Collection of Women's History, Howey 6234. Courtesy Kenneth Spencer Research Library, University of Kansas.

Emmeline (née Goulden) Pankhurst was a British suffragette leader and founder of the Women's Social and Political Union (WSPU). The eldest of ten children, Pankhurst was raised in a politically active family; reading the daily newspaper to her father at breakfast roused her own political interests. At the age of fourteen, her mother allowed her to attend a suffrage meeting to hear Lydia Becker (1827–90), editor of the *Woman's Suffrage Journal*. Pankhurst's continued involvement with the women's suffrage movement led to her introduction to Dr Richard Marsden Pankhurst (1835/6–98), a lawyer and fellow advocate for women's rights. The two married in December 1879 and had five children. In 1915 Pankhurst adopted four girls as part of a proposed WSPU effort to alleviate the 'war babies' problem, though she later relinquished custody of three girls due to financial strain.

Pankhurst was a member of several political groups and in 1894 was elected as an Independent Labour Party (ILP) candidate for the Chorlton board of guardians. In this role she introduced many improvements to workhouse conditions for women and girls. However, after the ILP built a hall in honour of her late husband but refused to allow women to participate in the branch headquarters at the hall, she resigned from the ILP and formed the WSPU on 10 October 1903. Dedicated to the women's suffrage movement, the WSPU became known for its militant tactics, including property destruction, heckling politicians and hunger strikes. Pankhurst, a gifted speaker, earned money to support herself and the WSPU through her speaking engagements in the UK, US and Canada. She was imprisoned several times, but she maintained that the only way for women to get the vote was to use the same methods that men used when unfairly governed. Emmeline Pankhurst died on 14 June 1928, less than a month before the second Representation of the People Act, the bill which granted women over the age of twenty-one the right to vote on equal terms with men, became law on 2 July.

From Verbatim Report of Mrs. Pankhurst's Speech

I do not come here as an advocate, because whatever position the suffrage movement may occupy in the United States of America, in England it has passed beyond the realm of advocacy and it has entered into the sphere of practical politics. It has become the subject of revolution and civil war, and so tonight I am not here to advocate woman suffrage. American suffragists can do that very well for themselves. I am here as a soldier who has temporarily left the field of battle in order to explain – it seems strange it should have to be explained – what civil war is like when civil war is waged by women. I am not only here as a soldier temporarily absent from the field at battle; I am here – and that, I think, is the strangest part of my coming – I am here as a person who, according to the law courts of my country, it has been decided, is of no value to the community at all; and I am adjudged because of my life to be a dangerous person, under sentence of penal servitude in a convict prison. [. . .][122]

It is not at all difficult if revolutionaries come to you from Russia, if they come to you from China, or from any other part of the world, if they are men, to make you understand revolution in five minutes, every man and every woman to understand revolutionary methods when they are adopted by men. [. . .] But since I am a woman it is necessary in the twentieth century to explain why women have adopted revolutionary methods in order to win the rights of citizenship. [. . .]

[W]e women, in trying to make our case clear, always have to make as part of our argument, and urge upon men in our audience the fact – a very simple fact – that women are human beings. [. . .]

Suppose the men of Hartford had a grievance, and they laid that grievance before their legislature, and the legislature obstinately refused to listen to them,

---

122 On 24 February 1913 Pankhurst was arrested for violating the Malicious Injuries to Property Act 1861 and sentenced to three years in prison. She was released under the Exploiting Prisoners Act after serving less than six weeks, but she was still under sentence when she travelled to the US.

or to remove their grievance, what would be the proper and the constitutional and the practical way of getting their grievance removed? Well, it is perfectly obvious at the next general election [...] the men of Hartford in sufficient numbers would turn out that legislature and elect a new one. [...] But let the men of Hartford imagine that they were not in the position of being voters at all, that they were governed without their consent being obtained, that the legislature turned an absolutely deaf ear to their demands, what would the men of Hartford do then? They couldn't vote the legislature out. They would have to choose; they would have to make a choice of two evils: they would either have to submit indefinitely to an unjust state of affairs, or they would have to rise up and adopt some of the antiquated means by which men in the past got their grievances remedied. We know what happened when your forefathers decided that they must have representation for taxation, many, many years ago. When they felt they couldn't wait any longer, when they laid all the arguments before an obstinate British government that they could think of, and when their arguments were absolutely disregarded, when every other means had failed, they began by the tea party at Boston, and they went on until they had won the independence of the United States of America. [...]

[I]t is about eight years since the word militant was first used to describe what we were doing. [...] It was not militant at all, except that it provoked militancy on the part of those who were opposed to it. When women asked questions in political meetings and failed to get answers, they were not doing anything militant. [...] [I]n Great Britain it is a custom, a time-honored one, to ask questions of candidates for parliament and ask questions of members of the government. No man was ever put out of a public meeting for asking a question until Votes for Women came onto the political horizon. The first people who were put out of a political meeting for asking questions, were women; they were brutally ill-used; they found themselves in jail before 24 hours had expired.[123] [...] However, we were called militant for doing that, and we were quite willing to accept the name. [...] We were determined to press this question of the enfranchisement of women to the point where we were no longer to be ignored by the politicians. [...]

You have two babies very hungry and wanting to be fed. One baby is a patient baby, and waits indefinitely until its mother is ready to feed it. The other baby is an impatient baby and cries lustily, screams and kicks and makes everybody unpleasant until it is fed. Well, we know perfectly well which baby is attended to first. That is the whole history of politics. [...] You have to make more noise than anybody else, you have to make yourself more obtrusive than anybody else, you have to fill all the papers more than anybody else, in fact you have to be there all the time and see that they do not snow you under.

[W]hen you have warfare things happen; people suffer; the non-combatants suffer as well as the combatants. And so it happens in civil war. When your forefathers threw the tea into Boston Harbor, a good many women had to go without their tea. It has always seemed to me an extraordinary thing that you did not follow it up by throwing the whiskey overboard; you sacrificed the women; and there is a good deal of warfare for which men take a great deal of glorification which has involved

---

123 WSPU members Christabel Pankhurst and Annie Kenney were arrested for interrupting a Liberal Party meeting in Manchester on 13 October 1905 by repeatedly asking, 'Will the Liberal Government, if returned, give votes to women?'

more practical sacrifice on women than it has on any man. It always has been so. The grievances of those who have got power, the influence of those who have got power commands a great deal of attention; but the wrongs and the grievances of those people who have no power at all are apt to be absolutely ignored. That is the history of humanity right from the beginning. Well, in our civil war people have suffered, but you cannot make omelettes without breaking eggs; you cannot have civil war without damage to something. The great thing is to see that no more damage is done than is absolutely necessary, that you do just as much as will arouse enough feeling to bring about peace, to bring about an honorable peace for the combatants; and that is what we have been doing. [...] [W]e entirely prevented stockbrokers in London from telegraphing to stockbrokers in Glasgow, and vice versa: for one whole day telegraphic and telephonic communication was entirely stopped.[124] I am not going to tell you how it was done. I am not going to tell you how the women got to the mains and cut the wires; but it was done. It was done, and it was proved to the authorities that weak women, suffrage women, as we are supposed to be, had enough ingenuity to create a situation of that kind.

Now, I ask you, if women can do that, is there any limit to what we can do except the limit we put upon ourselves? If you are dealing with an industrial revolution, if you get the men and women of one class rising up against the men and women of another class, you can locate the difficulty; if there is a great industrial strike, you know exactly where the violence is, and every man knows exactly how the warfare is going to be waged; but in our war against the government you can't locate it. [...] We wear no mark; we belong to every class; we permeate every class of the community from the highest to the lowest; and so you see in the woman's civil war the dear men of my country are discovering it is absolutely impossible to deal with it: you cannot locate it, and you cannot stop it. "Put them in prison," they said; "that will stop it. [...] But it didn't happen so at all: instead of the women giving it up, more women did it, and more and more and more women did it until there were three hundred women at a time, who had not broken a single law, only "made a nuisance of themselves" as the politicians say.

Well then they felt they must do something else, and they began to legislate. I want to tell men in this meeting that the British government, which is not remarkable for having very mild laws to administer, has passed more stringent laws to deal with this agitation than it ever found necessary during all the history of political agitation in my country. They were able to deal with the revolutionaries of the Chartists' time; they were able to deal with the trades union agitation; they were able to deal with the revolutionaries later on when the Reform Acts of 1867 and 1884 were passed: but the ordinary law has not sufficed to curb insurgent women. [...] They had to dip back into the middle ages to find a means of repressing the women in revolt. [...] They have said to us, government rests upon force, the women haven't force, so they must submit. Well, we are showing them that government does not rest upon force at all: it rests upon consent. As long as women consent to be unjustly governed, they can be: but directly women say: "We with-hold our consent, we will not be governed any longer so long as that government is unjust," not by the forces of civil war can you govern the very weakest woman. You can kill that woman, but she escapes you then; you cannot govern her. [...] [N]o power on earth can govern a human being, however feeble,

---

124 On 8 February 1913, suffragists in Glasgow and London blew up fuse boxes and used scissors to cut aerial telegraph and telephone wires ('More Suffragist Violence').

who with-holds his or her consent. [...] When they put us in prison at first, simply for taking petitions, we submitted; we allowed them to dress us in prison clothes; we allowed them to put us in solitary confinement; we allowed them to treat us as ordinary criminals, and put us amongst the most degraded of those criminals; [...] we learned of some of the appalling evils of our so-called civilization that we could not have learned in any other way. [...] It was valuable experience, and we were glad to get it. [...] I have seen men smile when they heard the words "hunger strike," and yet I think there are very few men today who would be prepared to adopt a "hunger strike" for any cause. It is only people who feel an intolerable sense of oppression who would adopt a means of that kind. [...] It means you refuse food until you are at death's door, and then the authorities have to choose between letting you die, and letting you go; and then they let the women go.

Now, that went on so long that the government felt they had lost their power, and that they were unable to cope with the situation. Then it was that, to the shame of the British government, they set the example to authorities all over the world of feeding sane, resisting human beings by force. There may be doctors in this meeting: if so, they know it is one thing to [...] feed by force an insane person; [...] but it is quite another thing to feed a sane, resisting human being who resists with every nerve and with every fibre of her body the indignity and the outrage of forcible feeding. Now, that was done in England, and the government thought they had crushed us. But they found that it did not quell the agitation, that more and more women came in and even passed that terrible ordeal. [...] They were obliged to let them go.

Then came the legislation [...] the Cat and Mouse Act.[125] [The home secretary] said: "Give me the power to let these women go when they are at death's door, and leave them at liberty under license until they have recovered their health again and then bring them back [...]."[126] [I]t was passed to repress the agitation, to make the women yield – because that is what it has really come to, ladies and gentlemen. It has come to a battle between the women and the government as to who shall yield first, whether they will yield and give us the vote, or whether we will give up our agitation. Well, they little know what women are. Women are very slow to rouse, but once they are aroused, once they are determined, nothing on earth and nothing in heaven will make women give way; it is impossible. And so this Cat and Mouse Act which is being used against women today has failed. [...] [T]here are women lying at death's door, recovering enough strength to undergo operations, who have had both systems applied to them, and have not given in and won't give in, and who will be prepared, as soon as they get up from their sick-beds, to go on as before. There are women who are being carried from their sick-beds on stretchers into meetings. They are too weak to speak, but they go amongst their fellow-workers just to show that their spirits are unquenched, and that their spirit is alive, and they mean to go on as long as life lasts.

Now, I want to say to you who think women cannot succeed, we have brought the government of England to this position, that it has to face this alternative: either women are to be killed or women are to have the vote. I ask American men in this meeting, what would you say if in your State you were faced with that alternative,

---

125 The Exploiting the Prisoners (Temporary Discharge for Ill-Health) Act, commonly known as the Cat and Mouse Act, was passed in April 1913.
126 Reginald McKenna (1863–1943), member of the Liberal Party, served as Home Secretary from 1911 to 1915.

that you must either kill them or give them their citizenship [. . .]? Well, there is only one answer to that alternative, there is only one way out [. . .] you must give those women the vote. Now that is the outcome of our civil war.

You won your freedom in America when you had the revolution, by bloodshed, by sacrificing human life. You won the civil war by the sacrifice of human life when you decided to emancipate the negro. You have left it to women in your land, the men of all civilized countries have left it to women, to work out their own salvation. That is the way in which we women of England are doing. Human life for us is sacred, but we say if any life is to be sacrificed it shall be ours; we won't do it ourselves, but we will put the enemy in the position where they will have to choose between giving us freedom or giving us death. [. . .]

So here am I. I come in the intervals of prison appearance: I come after having been four times imprisoned under the Cat and Mouse Act, probably going back to be rearrested as soon as I set my foot on British soil.[127] I come to ask you to help to win this fight. If we win it, this hardest of all fights, then, to be sure, in the future it is going to be made easier for women all over the world to win their fight when their time comes.

Source text

Pankhurst, Emmeline, *Verbatim Report of Mrs. Pankhurst's Speech, Delivered Nov. 13, 1913 at Parsons' Theatre, Hartford, Conn.* (Hartford, CT: Connecticut Woman Suffrage Association, 1913).

References

'More Suffragist Violence', *The Times*, 11 February 1913, 6.

Gertrude Simmons Bonnin (Zitkala-Ša[128]) (1876–1938)

'Editorial Comment' (1919)

Zitkala-Ša was born on the Yankton Sioux Reservation, where she lived until the age of eight. In 1884 she was recruited by missionaries to the White's Indiana Manual Labor Institute, a Quaker school where she spent three miserable years, somewhat mitigated by learning to read, write and play the violin. Throughout her childhood she alternated time between the

---

127 Pankhurst was re-arrested upon arrival back in England, but went to Paris after being released due to a hunger strike.

128 In her 1900 series for *Atlantic Monthly*, the author's name was listed as 'Zitkala-Sa', using an umlaut symbol over the 'S', a marking matched by her grave's headstone. Many scholars who focus on her career, including Tadeusz Lewandowski (whom we cite below) use Š as the accent mark, as we do here and elsewhere. Some recent printings of the name include additional accent marks, perhaps to signal which syllables are stressed orally, as in 'Zitkála-Šá'.

Reservation and various white educational institutions – including Earlham College, and the New England Conservatory of Music – before taking a position as a music teacher at the Carlisle Indian Industrial School in 1889. It was during her tenure there that she began freelance journalism, composing articles for the *Atlantic Monthly*, *Harper's Monthly* and the *North American Review*. She also began to work on larger projects in both writing and music: *Old Indian Legends* (1901), a collection of Native American stories, and *Sun Dance Opera*, the first opera co-authored by a Native American, which premiered in 1913. During her second period of publishing she authored a number of influential political texts, including *American Indian Stories* (1921) and *Oklahoma's Poor Indians* (1924), which chronicled the exploitation of Native American tribes by oil corporations.

Beyond her authorship Zitkala-Ša was engaged in political activism, criticising the Bureau of Indian Affairs and advocating for a sovereign Native American identity. With her husband Raymond Bonnin, she helped found the National Council of American Indians (NCAI) and served in leadership from its 1926 inception to her death in 1938. She also worked for feminist causes, in 1921 joining the General Federation of Women's Clubs, through which she created the Indian Welfare Committee. The piece below originally appeared in *American Indian Magazine*, for which Zitkala-Ša served as editor and contributor in 1918 and 1919 in the shadow of the Great War. In light of Native Americans' contributions to the war effort, and writing as Gertrude Simmons Bonnin, she argued that the time for Indian citizenship had come.

'Editorial Comment'

THE eyes of the world are upon the Peace Conference[129] sitting at Paris.

Under the sun a new epoch is being staged!

Little peoples are to be granted the right of self- determination!

Small nations and remnants of nations are to sit beside their great allies at the Peace Table; and their just claims are to be duly incorporated in the terms of a righteous peace.

Paris, for the moment, has become the center of the world's thought. Divers human petitions daily ascend to its Peace Table through foreign emissaries, people's representatives and the interest's lobbyists. From all parts of the earth, claims for adjustments equitable and otherwise are cabled and wirelessed. What patience and wisdom is needed now to render final decisions upon these highly involved and delicate enigmas reeking with inhumanities! The task may be difficult and the exposures of wrongs innumerable, still we believe,——yes, we know, the world is to be made better as a result of these stirring times.

Immortal justice is the vortex around which swing the whirl of human events!

We are seeking to know, justice, not as a fable but as a living, active, practical force in all that concerns our welfare!

---

129 The Versailles Peace Conference was held in Paris from January to June 1919. Diplomats from the victorious nations of the Great War redrew new national boundaries of defeated European powers, creating a number of new nations.

Actions of the wise leaders assembled in Paris may be guided ostensibly by temporary man-made laws and aims, dividing human interests into domestic and international affairs, but even so those leaders cannot forget the eternal fact that humanity is essentially one undivided, closely intertwined, fabric through which spiritual truth will shine with increasing brightness until it is fully understood and its requirements fulfilled. The universal cry for freedom from injustice is the voice of a multitude united by afflictions. To appease this human cry the application of democratic principles must be flexible enough to be universal.

Belgium is leading a historic procession of little peoples seeking freedom!

From the very folds of the great allied nations are many classes of men and women clamoring for a hearing. Their fathers, sons, brothers and husbands fought and died for democracy. Each is eager to receive the reward for which supreme sacrifice was made. Surely will the blood-soaked fields of No-Man's Land unceasingly cry out until the high principles for which blood spilled itself, are established in the governments of men.

Thus in this vast procession to Paris, we recognize and read their flying banners.

Labor organizations are seeking representation at the Peace Conference. Women of the world, mothers of the human race, are pressing forward for recognition.[130] The Japanese are taking up the-perplexing problem of race discrimination.[131]

The Black man of America is offering his urgent petition for representation at the Conference; and already President Wilson has taken some action in his behalf by sending to Paris, Dr. Moton,[132] of Tuskegee Institute accompanied by Dr. DuBois.[133]

A large New York assembly of American men and women wirelessed, it is reported, to President Wilson while he was in mid-ocean, enroute to Paris, requesting his aid in behalf of self-government for the Irish people.

The Red man asks for a very simple thing,—citizenship in the land that was once his own—America. Who shall represent his cause at the World's Peace Conference? The American Indian, too, made the supreme sacrifice for liberty's sake. He loves democratic ideals. What shall world democracy mean to his race?

There never was a time more opportune than now for America to enfranchise the Red man!

Source text

Bonnin, Gertrude, 'Editorial Comment', *American Indian Magazine* 6.4 (Winter 1919), 161–2.

References

Krouse, Susan Applegate, *North American Indians in the Great War* (Lincoln, NE: University of Nebraska Press, 2007).
Lewandowski, Tadeusz, *Red Bird, Red Power: The Life and Legacy of Zitkala-Ša* (Norman, OK: University of Oklahoma Press, 2016).

---

130 A small contingent of feminist activists travelled to Paris to lobby the delegates for equal rights, but their appeals were not recognised.
131 The Japanese delegation proposed a 'racial equality clause' to the Covenant of the League of Nations; since it did not win unanimous approval, the measure did not pass.
132 Robert Russa Moton (1867–1940), a prominent African-American author and the principal of Tuskegee Institute from 1915–35
133 W. E. B. Du Bois (1868–1963), a prominent author, activist and intellectual, and the first African American to earn a doctorate at Harvard

10

TRAVEL AND TOURISM

Figure 10.1 Thos. Hunter, Lith., Thompson Westcott, and H. J. Schwarzmann. *Cook's World's Ticket Office: Centennial International Exhibition, 1876*. Philadelphia, PA: Thos. Hunter, Lith., 1876. Courtesy of the Free Library of Philadelphia, Print and Picture Collection.

The appropriateness of travel narratives as an important genre for thinking about the geometries of circulation, exchange and transformation that structure our understanding of the Atlantic space is perhaps self-evident. From at least the sixteenth century onwards, accounts of the Americas by European travellers created a set of powerful images of a 'New World' ripe for exploration and exploitation, as well as a narrative problem of how to find a suitable correlative in writing for an experience of often radical otherness – perhaps the core issue for every narrative of travel. In the opposite direction, from the end of the eighteenth century the flow of travellers across the Atlantic increased, as an elite and commercial class of American citizen experienced European cultural and business opportunities. Travel narratives encode forms of spatial and temporal disruption, for to travel is to be in motion, to observe the world from a series of shifting, dynamic viewpoints that, consciously or otherwise, have the effect of structuring knowledge through comparative perspectives. As our chapter also illustrates, travel narratives can be expansive and compendious, often concerning themselves with areas beyond the merely 'touristic' or 'autobiographical': they can take in questions of history, politics, anthropology and linguistics, as well as offering interventions in travel theory and writing itself. Travel writing can create an awareness of the situatedness of knowledge, the intrinsic relation between the location of the knower (which may be unfamiliar, foreign) and that which is observed. The effects of this are, potentially, liberating, offering a way of contesting, and maybe escaping, the ideological and, in some cases, political/legal repressions of home. Edward Said's understanding of the figure of the 'exile' is useful for us in this regard, viewed as an identity self-consciously aware of her or his contingent, situated status, one in which 'homes are provisional. Border and barriers, which enclose us within the safety of familiar territory, can also become prisons, and are often defended beyond reason or necessity. Exiles cross borders, break barriers of thought and experience.'[1] Alternatively, as this chapter also demonstrates, the comparative lens through which unfamiliar space is evaluated can lead to a retrenchment of national identity or characteristics, or a nostalgia for them. And Said's model of exilic identity is one that pays scant attention to those whose travel is determined by ongoing economic or political displacement.

FORMS OF TRAVEL

The growth of what we might regard as privileged, non-economic travel occurred in the context of much broader structures of transatlantic movement during the nineteenth century. Before the abolition by Great Britain of the Atlantic trade in enslaved peoples in 1807, transatlantic travel for millions of Africans during the Middle Passage was a coercive and brutal experience, as we highlight in our MSR thematic chapter. Fugitive enslaved Americans would travel to Britain and Europe in the first half of the century, evading capture in the US and working to inspire transatlantic abolitionist movements abroad. Political upheavals in Europe saw increased migration of people to North American and British cities, and the Irish famine in the 1840s led to emigration in large numbers to both destinations. William O'Reilly has calculated that the nineteenth century mapped a transition from primarily enforced to voluntary movement in the Atlantic world, and that before 1850, only 10 per cent of migrants to the Americas were free, with most enslaved or indentured.[2] The Atlantic was a space of continuous

---

1 Edward Said, 'Reflections on Exile', in *Reflections on Exile and Other Essays* (Cambridge, MA: Harvard University Press, 2000), 185.
2 William O'Reilly, 'Movements in the Atlantic World, 1450–1850', in Nicholas Canny and Philip Morgan (eds), *The Oxford Handbook of the Atlantic World 1450–1850* (Oxford: Oxford University Press, 2011), 307, 318. See also Lisa Lowe, *The Intimacies of Four Continents* (Durham, NC: Duke University Press, 2015).

mobility, with the global economy more interconnected than ever before and reasons for travel ranging from enslavement, commerce, education, asylum and, increasingly, tourism.

Technological advances brought about massive transformations in the speed, cost and viability of transatlantic travel across the long nineteenth century. In 1815 Washington Irving spent almost six weeks at sea before arriving in Liverpool. By 1853 Harriet Beecher Stowe was able to make the same journey in ten days on a steamship. The first non-stop transatlantic flight was seen in 1919, inaugurating what would become the preferred means of transatlantic travel in the twentieth century and beyond. As travel became easier, so expanded the opportunities for writing to respond to unfamiliar geographies and cultures, and the rapidity with which that writing could be published and distributed. Travel writing during the period was a capacious, eclectic genre, deployed in the service of multiple ambitions, both personal and public. Our selection illustrates this diversity, travelling itself from models of ethnographic and scientific exploration (Charles Darwin) to a modernist poet's return to a lost European landscape (Ezra Pound), and everything in between. William Stowe has observed that it was a 'form of narrative that served as a meeting place for various narrative voices, literary styles, levels of speech and kinds of subjects, combining disparate modes of discourse without necessarily generating any tension among them or forging them into a "higher unity"'.[3] Nevertheless within this heterogeneity could also be found the conventions of expected sites of touristic pilgrimage, inaugurated within US literature perhaps most famously by Washington Irving's *Sketchbook* (1819–20), an excerpt from which we include elsewhere in this anthology (see RS). But as Irving's narrative achieves so cleverly, and as several of the examples from this chapter illustrate, the faithful reporting of cultural or geographical highlights on both sides of the Atlantic was only part of the motivation behind accounts of travel, as these texts often deployed the experience of foreign encounter to perform ideological work. To observe, and to observe comparatively (either implicitly or explicitly), is to take a position that resonates with cultural and political assumptions or resistances.

We include excepts from two important travel narratives in the first half of the nineteenth century that introduced the still-young United States to a British readership eager to read about the rebellious child of empire and its republican project. Frances Trollope's *Domestic Manners* (1832) and Charles Dickens's *American Notes* (1842) recount in detail, and with some admiration, the diversity and expanse of the US; but both, ultimately, succumb to judging the nation a failure in its social and political structures. Travel here institutes a form of comparativism that works to re-enforce hierarchies of national value, rather than to undermine or unsettle them. The often tense political relationship between Great Britain and the US during the nineteenth century, exacerbated by war between the two nations in 1812–14 and by the global economic impact of the Civil War between 1861 and 1865, resonated within transatlantic literary culture generally and within travel writing more specifically, as the characteristics and qualities of each were placed in dialogue and juxtaposition. For both

---

3 William W. Stowe, 'Conventions and Voices in Margaret Fuller's Travel Writing', *American Literature* 63 (June 1991), 243.

Trollope and Dickens, the encounter with North America worked to re-inscribe certain ideas of home that the comparison with abroad helped to solidify.

TOURISM AND ANTI-TOURISM

The confluence of travel with an enlarged, cheaper print culture created the possibility of a traveller being able to demonstrate her or his acquisition of cultural capital, something that could then be possessed, in turn, by the text's reader. Part of the attraction of Europe for the New World traveller was the encounter with the artefacts and edifices of 'Culture', the appreciation of which would provide evidence of a 'civilised' mind. As William Stowe has explored, the nineteenth century witnessed the explosion of cheap travellers' guidebooks to accompany the growth in international tourism. Thomas Cook's first overseas travellers (to Europe in 1855) may likely have consulted the appropriate *Handbook for Travellers* published by John Murray in London, beginning in 1836, and Karl Baedeker's German guidebooks were translated into English by the 1860s. These books, Stowe notes, became as sacred texts articulating a 'liturgy' of travel, 'handbooks of devotion' that offered a stable point of view, promised information and orientation, and minimised the dangers of alienation: 'Like a ritual celebrant, the traveller returns with a boon: with knowledge, memories of exalting, ennobling experience, and a magically transformed sensitivity to history and to art.'[4] Some literary texts, such as Nathanael Hawthorne's novel *The Marble Faun* (1860) and George Eliot's novel *Romola* (1863), were explicitly marketed as a hybrid mixture of fiction and guidebook (with the German publisher Tauchnitz producing editions of both books with blank spaces onto which tourists could paste postcards or images, or write up impressions). Other authors were more sceptical of the commercialisation of travel, with Henry James, for one, lamenting in 1882 the democratisation of the cultural scene. In an essay on Venice he writes that 'The Venice of to-day is a vast museum where the little wicket that admits you is perpetually turning and creaking, and you march through the institution with a herd of fellow-gazers'. Instead of joining the crowd, James's tourist 'likes to be alone; to be original; to have (to himself, at least) the air of making discoveries'.[5]

The 'anti-tourism' of such a stance, a self-conscious resistance to being one of the crowd, to participating in the expected rituals of the leisure traveller, is marked most strongly in our excerpt from Mark Twain's *The Innocents Abroad* (1869), a satirical account of its narrator's travels through Europe and to the Holy Land in the company of his fellow American tourists.[6] Twain's persona refuses to be impressed by the seductions of Old World culture or to participate in the affect of awe that it is expected to induce. Built into this account of overseas travel is a determined resistance to the authorised narratives of sensibility

---

4 William W. Stowe, *Going Abroad: European Travel in Nineteenth-Century American Culture* (Princeton, NJ: Princeton University Press, 1994), 44. See also Jan Palmowski, 'Travels with Baedeker: The Guidebook and the Middle Classes in Victorian and Edwardian Britain', in Rudy Koshar (ed.), *Histories of Leisure* (London: Berg, 2002), 105–31.
5 Henry James, *Portraits of Places* (London: Macmillan, 1883), 5–6.
6 For more on anti-tourism as a motif of travel writing, see James Buzard, *The Beaten Track: European Tourism, Literature, and the Ways to 'Culture', 1800–1918* (Oxford: Oxford University Press, 1993), ch. 2.

and comparative judgement that the business of tourism was well on the way to encoding. Margaret Fuller's journalism as a foreign correspondent for the *New York Tribune* newspaper is similarly concerned to theorise the forms that tourism takes, and our excerpt from a letter of 1848 highlights the ways in which her taxonomy of American tourists in Rome allows Fuller to open up her localised observations to reflect on the moral health of the US. 'Abroad' as a category is the platform on which 'home' can be more properly evaluated. Over sixty years later, the modernist writer Djuna Barnes, in a newspaper article from 1913 that we include in this chapter, would complicate the distinction between home and abroad still further by pointing to the kinds of internal travel that can be undertaken within an increasingly cosmopolitan US itself.

Our excerpts from books by William Wells Brown and Nancy Gardner Prince are indicative of the multiple uses to which travel narrative can be put. In *The American Fugitive in Europe* (1855) Brown explicitly inhabits the role of an educated tourist, writing knowledgably about the sites of Europe and claiming for himself what Brigitte Bailey has described as 'the privileged gaze of the cultural traveller'.[7] Yet, as our excerpt illustrates, Brown shows a sophisticated awareness of how the sites and edifices of cultural capital are implicated in the projects of imperialism and enslavement, under which he himself has suffered. Travel writing here becomes a vehicle through which a transatlantic understanding of the legacies of oppression can be articulated. Likewise Prince's *Narrative of the Life and Travels* (1850), which recounts her travels to imperial Russia and then to Jamaica, operates both as spiritual autobiography and as travel narrative, establishing both a keen observational eye and a larger perspective in which racial and class differences can be explored.

As Susan Basnett has noted, 'the travel text as ethnography or social commentary transcends gender boundaries',[8] and with the expansion of literacy and print culture across the nineteenth century, and with increasing numbers of women travellers over the same period, women gained access to the kinds of cultural authority that the genre had always afforded men. In addition to the women already mentioned, this chapter includes work by Anna Brownwell Jameson, Fanny Calderón de la Barca and Edith Wharton, each of whom narrate a response to unfamiliar cultural and racial scenes from a complex intersection of perspectives: a white British traveller encountering a First Nation family in the case of Jameson; a Scottish woman representative, through marriage, of Spanish imperial power in Mexico in the case of de la Barca; and a wealthy US white woman, guest of the French governing forces in Morocco, in the case of Wharton. Each of these narratives embodies both a desire to understand cultural difference and yet, at the same time, risks re-inscribing hierarchies of privilege that acts of travel can enforce.

The chapter's final text, Langston Hughes's 1921 poem 'The Negro Speaks of Rivers', brings our anthology full circle: like Phillis Wheatley's lyric that

---

7 Brigitte Bailey, 'Urban Reform, Transatlantic Movements and US Writers: 1837–1861', in Leslie Elizabeth Eckel and Clare Frances Elliott (eds), *The Edinburgh Companion to Atlantic Literary Studies* (Edinburgh: Edinburgh University Press, 2016), 206.

8 Susan Basnett, 'Travel Writing and Gender', in Peter Hulme and Tim Youngs (eds), *The Cambridge Companion to Travel Writing* (Cambridge: Cambridge University Press, 2002), 225.

begins our 'Abolition and Aftermath' section, Hughes shows how Black voices have always been central to the ways in which the transatlantic has been imagined and experienced. Travelling across space and time, the poem speaks both of the wider, global contexts of Black identity and the ongoing oppression of Black citizens within the US of our contemporary moment.

References

Castillo, Susan and David Seed (eds), *American Travel Writing and Empire* (Liverpool: Liverpool University Press, 2009).

Pratt, Mary Louise, *Imperial Eyes: Travel Writing and Transculturation* (London: Routledge, 1992).

Renella, Mark and Whitney Walton, 'Planned Serendipity: American Travelers and the Transatlantic Voyage in the Nineteenth and Twentieth Centuries', *Journal of Social History* 38.2 (2004), 365–83.

Thompson, Carl, *Travel Writing* (London: Routledge, 2011).

Urry, John, *The Tourist Gaze: Leisure and Travel in Contemporary Societies* (London: Sage, 1990).

Frances Trollope (1779–1863)

From Domestic Manners of the Americans *(1832)*

Domestic Manners of the Americans, the English writer Frances Trollope's first book, appeared the year after she returned from a four-year visit to the US (1827–31), during which she observed and described many aspects of that country's society, politics and culture, living for a time in a utopian community in Tennessee before establishing an emporium selling European goods in Cincinnati. As Clare Cotugno has noted, the book charts Trollope's disappointment and growing dislike of US culture, most trivially (and famously) focused around her disgust at New World manners, more importantly underwritten by her rejection of US principles of expanded democracy (242–3). The book's publication three days before the passage of the first Reform Bill in the British parliament in 1832, an Act which significantly broadened the franchise, was, for Trollope, the political first step on a retrograde path that the US, to her mind, had fully embraced.

In this excerpt from Chapter Two of *Domestic Manners*, Trollope writes about her first experience of New Orleans, and her trip to Frances Wright's utopian community, the Nashoba Commune, in Tennessee. She is fascinated by the winter vegetation, warm climate and the transatlantic Francophone-Anglophone cultural mingling. Her view of slavery is an uneasy mixture of critique and romanticisation. Trollope was a confirmed opponent of slavery before her US trip, yet while she would attack the hypocrisy of slave-owners 'with one hand hoisting the cap of liberty, and with the other flogging their slaves' (180), she also noted that 'much kind attention' (198) was given to the health of the enslaved.

Trollope's time in America illuminates what Tamara Wagner has suggested was 'her development as an author, and her resultant contribution to genre formation provides a revealing case study of the divergent ways in which transatlantic emigration worked as a theme and plot structure in nineteenth-century literature' (Wagner, 251). Trollope's travels would also inform her works of fiction: *Jonathan Jefferson Whitlaw* (1836), *The Refugee in America* (1842), *The Barnabys in America; or Adventures of the Widow Wedded* (1843) and *The Old World and the New* (1849).

From Domestic Manners of the Americans

New-Orleans—Society—Creoles and Quadroons—Voyage up the Mississippi.
On first touching the soil of a new land, [...] it is impossible not to feel considerable excitement and deep interest in almost every object that meets us. New Orleans presents very little that can gratify the eye of taste, but nevertheless there is much of novelty and interest for a newly-arrived European. The large proportion of blacks seen in the streets, all labour being performed by them; the grace and beauty of the elegant Quadroons,[9] the occasional groups of wild and savage looking Indians, the unwonted aspect of the vegetation, the huge and turbid river, [...] all help to afford that species of amusement which proceeds from looking at what we never saw before.

The town has much the appearance of a French Ville de Province,[10] and is, in fact, an old French colony taken from Spain by France.[11] The names of the streets are French, and the language about equally French and English. The market is handsome and well supplied, all produce being conveyed by the river. We were much pleased by the chant with which the Negro boatmen regulate and beguile their labour on the river; it consists but of very few notes, but they are sweetly harmonious, and the Negro voice is almost always rich and powerful.

By far the most agreeable hours I passed at New Orleans were those in which I explored with my children the forest near the town. It was our first walk in "the eternal forests of the western world," and we felt rather sublime and poetical. The trees, generally speaking, are much too close to be either large or well grown; and, moreover, their growth is often stunted by a parasitical plant, for which I could learn no other name than "Spanish moss;" it hangs gracefully from the boughs, converting the outline of all the trees it hangs upon into that of weeping willows. The chief beauty of the forest in this region is from the luxuriant undergrowth of palmetos,[12] which is decidedly the loveliest coloured and most graceful plant I know. The pawpaw,[13] too, is a splendid shrub, and in great abundance. We here, for the first time, saw the wild vine, which we afterwards found growing so profusely in every part of

---

9 A term in slave societies to designate a person with one quarter African and three-quarters European ancestry
10 A provincial French town
11 New Orleans, founded as a French colony in 1718, was ceded to Spain in 1763, reverting back to French rule for just one year (1802–3), before the US bought it, and Louisiana, in 1803.
12 Palm trees native to the American South
13 A shrub that can grow to a small fruit-bearing tree

America, as naturally to suggest the idea that the natives ought to add wine to the numerous productions of their plenty-teeming soil. [...]

Notwithstanding it was mid-winter when we were at New Orleans, the heat was much more than agreeable, and the attacks of the mosquitos incessant, and most tormenting; yet I suspect that for a short time we would rather have endured it, than not have seen oranges, green peas, and red pepper, growing in the open air at Christmas. In one of our rambles we ventured to enter a garden, whose bright orange hedge attracted our attention; here we saw green peas fit for the table, and a fine crop of red pepper ripening in the sun. A young Negress was employed on the steps of the house; that she was a slave made her an object of interest to us. She was the first slave we had ever spoken to, and I believe we all felt that we could hardly address her with sufficient gentleness. She little dreamed, poor girl, what deep sympathy she excited; she answered us civilly and gaily, and seemed amused at our fancying there was something unusual in red pepper pods; she gave us several of them, and I felt fearful lest a hard mistress might blame her for it. How very childish does ignorance make us! and how very ignorant we are upon almost every subject, where hear-say evidence is all we can get!

I left England with feelings so strongly opposed to slavery, that it was not without pain I witnessed its effects around me. At the sight of every Negro man, woman, and child that passed, my fancy wove some little romance of misery, as belonging to each of them; since I have known more on the subject, and become better acquainted with their real situation in America, I have often smiled at recalling what I then felt.

The first symptom of American equality that I perceived, was my being introduced in form to a milliner;[14] it was not at a boarding-house, under the indistinct outline of "Miss C*****," nor in the street through the veil of a fashionable toilette, but in the very penetralia of her temple, standing behind her counter, giving laws to riband and to wire, and ushering caps and bonnets into existence. She was an English woman, and I was told that she possessed great intellectual endowments, and much information; I really believe this was true. Her manner was easy and graceful, with a good deal of French tournure;[15] and the gentleness with which her fine eyes and sweet voice directed the movements of a young female slave, was really touching: the way, too, in which she blended her French talk of modes with her customers, and her English talk of metaphysics with her friends, had a pretty air of indifference in it, that gave her a superiority with both.

I found with her the daughter of a judge, eminent, it was said, both for legal and literary ability; and I heard from many quarters, after I had left New Orleans, that the society of this lady was highly valued by all persons of talent. Yet were I, traveller-like, to stop here, and set it down as a national peculiarity, or republican custom, that milliners took the lead in the best society, I should greatly falsify facts. I do not remember the same thing happening to me again, and this is one instance, among a thousand, of the impression every circumstance makes on entering a new country, and of the propensity, so irresistible, to class all things, however accidental, as national and peculiar. On the other hand, however, it is certain that if similar anomalies are unfrequent in America, they are nearly impossible elsewhere. [...]

---

14 Maker of women's hats
15 Affect or air

Our stay in New Orleans was not long enough to permit our entering into society, but I was told that it contained two distinct sets of people, both celebrated, in their way, for their social meetings and elegant entertainments. The first of these is composed of Creole families,[16] who are chiefly planters and merchants, with their wives and daughters; these meet together, eat together, and are very grand and aristocratic; each of their balls is a little Almack's,[17] and every portly dame of the set is as exclusive in her principles as a lady patroness. The other set consists of the excluded but amiable Quadroons, and such of the gentlemen of the former class as can by any means escape from the high places, where pure Creole blood swells the veins at the bare mention of any being tainted in the remotest degree with the Negro stain.

Of all the prejudices I have ever witnessed, this appears to me the most violent, and the most inveterate. Quadroon girls, the acknowledged daughters of wealthy American or Creole fathers, educated with all of style and accomplishments which money can procure at New Orleans, and with all the decorum that care and affection can give; exquisitely beautiful, graceful, gentle, and amiable, these are not admitted, nay, are not on any terms admissable, into the society of the Creole families of Louisiana. They cannot marry; that is to say, no ceremony can render a union with them legal or binding; yet such is the powerful effect of their very peculiar grace, beauty, and sweetness of manner, that unfortunately they perpetually become the objects of choice and affection. If the Creole ladies have privilege to exercise the awful power of repulsion, the gentle Quadroon has the sweet but dangerous vengeance of possessing that of attraction. The unions formed with this unfortunate race are said to be often lasting and happy, as far as any unions can be so to which a certain degree of disgrace is attached.

There is a French and an English theatre in the town; but we were too fresh from Europe to care much for either; or, indeed, for any other of the town delights of this city, and we soon became eager to commence our voyage up the Mississippi.

Miss Wright,[18] then less known (though the author of more than one clever volume) than she has since become, was the companion of our voyage from Europe; and it was my purpose to have passed some months with her and her sister at the estate she had purchased in Tennessee. This lady, since become so celebrated as the advocate of opinions that make millions shudder, and some half-score admire, was at the time of my leaving England with her, dedicated to a pursuit widely different from her subsequent occupations. Instead of becoming a public orator in every town throughout America, she was about, as she said, to seclude herself for life in the deepest forests of the western world, that her fortune, her time, and her talents might be exclusively devoted to aid the cause of the suffering Africans. Her first object was to shew that nature had made no difference between blacks and whites, excepting in complexion; and this she expected to prove by giving an education perfectly equal to a class of black and white children. Could this fact be once fully established, she conceived that the Negro cause would stand on firmer ground than it had yet done, and the degraded rank which they have ever held amongst

---

16 People descended from colonial French or colonial Spanish settlers
17 A reference to social clubs and rooms in London, with a small set of aristocratic women controlling admission
18 Frances Wright (1795–1852), a Scottish-born American reformer, who advocated for social change in the US. She established the Nashoba Community (1825–8) in Tennessee to educate formerly enslaved peoples.

civilized nations would be proved to be a gross injustice. This question of the mental equality, or inequality, between us and the Negro race, is one of great interest, and has certainly never yet been fairly tried; and I expected for my children and myself both pleasure and information from visiting her establishment, and watching the success of her experiment. [...]

On the 1st of January, 1828, we embarked on board the Belvidere [...]. We found the room destined for the use of the ladies dismal enough, as its only windows were below the stern gallery; but both this and the gentlemen's cabin were handsomely fitted up, and the former well carpeted; but oh! that carpet! I will not, I may not describe its condition; indeed it requires the pen of a Swift[19] to do it justice. Let no one who wishes to receive agreeable impressions of American manners, commence their travels in a Mississippi steam boat; for myself, it is with all sincerity I declare, that I would infinitely prefer sharing the apartment of a party of well-conditioned pigs to the being confined to its cabin.

I hardly know any annoyance so deeply repugnant to English feelings, as the incessant, remorseless spitting of Americans. I feel that I owe my readers an apology for the repeated use of this, and several other odious words; but I cannot avoid them, without suffering the fidelity of description to escape me. It is possible that in this phrase "Americans," I may be too general. The United States form a continent of almost distinct nations, and I must now, and always, be understood to speak only of that portion of them which I have seen. In conversing with Americans I have constantly found that if I alluded to any thing which they thought I considered as uncouth, they would assure me it was local, and not national; the accidental peculiarity of a very small part, and by no means a specimen of the whole. "That is because you know so little of America," is a phrase I have listened to a thousand times, and in nearly as many different places. *It may be so*—and having made this concession, I protest against the charge of injustice in relating what I have seen.

Source text

Trollope, Frances, *Domestic Manners of the Americans*, Vol. 1 (London: Whittaker, Treacher, & Co., 1832).

References

Cotugno, Clare, '"Stay Away from Paris!" Frances Trollope Rewrites America', *Victorian Periodicals Review* 38.2 (2005), 240–57.

Heineman, Helen, 'Frances Trollope in the New World: *Domestic Manners of the Americans*', *American Quarterly* 21 (1969), 544–59.

Neville-Singon, Pamela A., *Fanny Trollope: The Life and Adventures of a Clever Woman* (London: Viking, 1997).

Wagner, Tamara S., '"Did you ever hear of such a thing as settlements?": Settling Outstanding Accounts in Frances Trollope's American novels', *Women's Writing* 18.2 (2011), 233–55.

---

19 Jonathan Swift (1667–1745), Anglo-Irish satirist, poet, Dean of St. Patrick's Cathedral, Dublin, and author of *Gulliver's Travels* (1726)

Anna Brownell Jameson (1794–1860)

From Winter Studies and Summer Rambles *(1838)*

This brief excerpt demonstrates a receptive response to cultural differ-ence by a white woman British traveller encountering a First Nation family. Prior to arriving in Canada (see the Jameson headnote in RS), Jameson had resided almost two years in Germany, having met Ottilie von Goethe (1796–1872), daughter-in-law of Johann Wolfgang von Goethe (1749–1832), in 1833 and entered into Goethe's social network despite challenging cultural differences. Hence Jameson was practised in negotiating cultural differences and embraced opportunities to learn more about other cultures.

Winter Studies and Summer Rambles, a transnational as well as trans-atlantic book, was largely formed from letters she was writing to Goethe and their mutual German friend Sibylle Mertens-Schaaffhausen (1797–1857), first as Jameson read widely and critically commented upon con-temporary German writers (her 'Winter Studies'). With summer's arrival she seized the opportunity to travel and meet Native North Americans, assisted by a new friendship network. She first met William McMurray (1810–94), a Church of England clergyman and Canadian agent to First Peoples, and his wife Charlotte (1806–71), the daughter of Ojibwe mother Oshaguscodawaqua ('Susan', d. 1843, the daughter of Ojibwe chieftain Waubojeeg, *c.*1747–93) and Irish-Canadian fur trader John Johnston. Charlotte was sister to Jane Johnston Schoolcraft (1800–42), married to the US Indian agent Henry Rowe Schoolcraft (1793–1864). After Jameson visited the Schoolcrafts, Jane Schoolcraft then accompanied Jameson to visit Schoolcraft's mother. There is some question as to whether Jameson creatively embellished her account of adoption by the Ojibwe (also nar-rated in *Winter Studies and Summer Rambles* [Birkwood, 39]), and with-out question Jameson writes from the perspective of white governmental and cultural dominance. But as an alternative model for white response to First Peoples, Jameson's writing forms a marked contrast to William F. Cody's much later Wild West show (see 'Buffalo Bill', AAE).

From Winter Studies and Summer Rambles

One of the gratifications I had anticipated in coming hither [Sault Ste. Marie on the Canadian side]—my strongest inducement perhaps—was an introduction to the mother of my two friends, of whom her children so delighted to speak, and of whom I had heard much from other sources. A woman of pure Indian blood, of a race celebrated in these regions as warriors and chiefs from generation to genera-tion, who had never resided within the pale of what we call civilised life, whose habits and manners were those of a genuine Indian squaw, and whose talents and domestic virtues commanded the highest respect, was, as you may suppose, an object of the deepest interest to me. [...]

The old lady herself is rather large in person, with the strongest marked Indian features, a countenance open, benevolent, and intelligent, and a manner perfectly easy—simple, yet with something of motherly dignity, becoming the head of her large family. She received me most affectionately, and we entered into conversation—Mrs. Schoolcraft, who looked all animation and happiness, acting as interpreter. Mrs. Johnston speaks no English, but can understand it a little, and the Canadian French still better; but in her own language she is eloquent, and her voice, like that of her people, low and musical; many kind words were exchanged, and when I said anything that pleased her, she laughed softly like a child. I was not well and much fevered, and I remember she took me in her arms, laid me down on a couch, and began to rub my feet, soothing and caressing me. She called me Nindannis, daughter, and I called her Neengai, mother, (though how different from my own fair mother, I thought, as I looked up gratefully in her dark Indian face!). [...]

[There follows a dialogue on 'Savagery' with George Johnston.]

"It is a constant and favourite subject of reproach against the Indians—this barbarism of their desultory warfare; but I should think more women and children have perished in *one* of your civilised sieges, and that in late times, than during the whole war between the Chippewas and Sioux, and *that* has lasted a century."[20]

I was silent, for there is a sensible proverb about taking care of our own glass windows: and I wonder if any of the recorded atrocities of Indian warfare or Indian vengeance, or all of them together, ever exceeded Massena's retreat from Portugal,—and the French call themselves civilised.[21] A war-party of Indians, perhaps two or three hundred, (and that is a very large number,) dance their war-dance, go out and burn a village, and bring back twenty or thirty scalps. *They* are savages and heathens. We Europeans fight a battle, leave fifty thousand dead or dying by inches on the field, and a hundred thousand to mourn them, desolate; but *we* are civilised and Christians. Then only look into the motives and causes of our bloodiest European wars as revealed in the private history of courts:—the miserable, puerile, degrading intrigues which set man against man—so horridly disproportioned to the horrid result! and then see the Indian take up his war-hatchet in vengeance for some personal injury, or from motives that rouse all the natural feelings of the natural man within him! Really I do not see that an Indian warrior, flourishing his tomahawk, and smeared with his enemy's blood, is so very much a greater savage than the pipe-clayed, padded, embroidered personage, who, without cause or motive, has sold himself to slay or be slain: one scalps his enemy, the other rips him open with a sabre; one smashes his brains with a tomahawk, and the other blows him to atoms with a cannon-ball: and to me, femininely speaking, there is not a needle's point difference between the one and the other. If war be unchristian and barbarous, then war as a *science* is more absurd, unnatural, unchristian, than war as a *passion*.

Source text

Jameson, Anna Brownell, *Winter Studies and Summer Rambles in Canada*, Vol. 3 (London: Saunders and Otley, 1838).

---

20 Jameson here quotes George Johnston (1796–1861), younger brother of Jane Schoolcraft. 'Chippewa' is an older English name for the Ojibwe.

21 Jameson cites an episode from the Peninsular Wars, when Napoleon's trusted Marshal André Méssina, Prince D'Essling (1758–1817) invaded Portugal with 60,000 troops but, unable to dislodge the forces of the Duke of Wellington (1769–1852), perforce retreated in 1811 with great losses.

References

ANB

Armour, David A., 'JOHNSTON, JOHN', *Dictionary of Canadian Biography*, vol. 6 (University of Toronto/Université Laval, 2003), Web.

Birkwood, Susan, 'True or False: Anna Jameson on the Position of Women in European and in Anishinaubae Society', *Nineteenth-Century Feminisms* 2 (2000), 32–47.

Johnston, Judith, *Anna Jameson: Victorian, Feminist, Woman of Letters* (Aldershot: Ashgate, 1997).

Thomas, Clara, *Love and Work Enough: The Life of Anna Jameson* (Toronto: University of Toronto Press, 1967).

Charles Dickens (1812–70)

From American Notes for General Circulation *(1842)*

American Notes is Charles Dickens's humorous yet sobering travel account of his first visit to the US (January–June 1842). He came to America an abolitionist and was eager to witness American democracy first-hand. He would soon become disillusioned by the treatment of enslaved individuals and was taken aback by American directness. He found little time for privacy as large crowds followed him in many places. However, he made transatlantic literary connections by meeting Washington Irving, Henry Wadsworth Longfellow and Edgar Allan Poe.

Dickens's unfavourable outlook on America was deeply rooted in his experience with American printing houses' pirating of his books; he arrived in the US intending to make a transatlantic case for implementing international copyright. As he would learn, the American press eventually attacked him for these attempts since he wished to gain additional profits from a people who had welcomed him so warmly.

In the excerpt from Chapter Four that follows, Dickens laments the poor quality of American railway transportation and the racially segregated train cars for passengers. He describes visiting Boston and Lowell, and is broadly supportive of the treatment American factory labourers received, chiefly young women and adolescent girls. He suggests that British mill workers might live more respectably if the British class system would permit workers to have access to reading materials and dreams of what 'might be', instead of living with the inability to transcend their current social status, something that would be a key theme in his novel *Hard Times* (1854). Through his support of reform movements, 'Dickens's tour participated in some Anglo-American networks (suffrage and anti-slavery reform) while attempting to regulate another (the literary marketplace)' (Claybaugh, 440). His overall disappointment with the US would find fictional form in the novel published immediately after *American Notes*, *Martin Chuzzlewit* (1842).

From **American Notes for General Circulation**

'An American Railroad. Lowell and its Factory System'

Before leaving Boston, I devoted one day to an excursion to Lowell.[22] I assign a separate chapter to this visit; not because I am about to describe it at any great length, but because I remember it as a thing by itself, and am desirous that my readers should do the same.

I made acquaintance with an American railroad, on this occasion, for the first time. As these works are pretty much alike all through the States, their general characteristics are easily described.

There are no first and second class carriages as with us; but there is a gentleman's car and a ladies' car: the main distinction between which is that in the first, everybody smokes; and in the second, nobody does. As a black man never travels with a white one, there is also a negro car; which is a great blundering clumsy chest, such as Gulliver put to sea in, from the kingdom of Brobdingnag.[23] There is a great deal of jolting, a great deal of noise, a great deal of wall, not much window, a locomotive engine, a shriek, and a bell.

The cars are like shabby omnibusses, but larger: holding thirty, forty, fifty, people. The seats, instead of stretching from end to end, are placed crosswise. Each seat holds two persons. There is a long row of them on each side of the caravan, a narrow passage up the middle, and a door at both ends. In the centre of the carriage there is usually a stove, fed with charcoal or anthracite coal; which is for the most part red-hot. It is insufferably close; and you see the hot air fluttering between yourself and any other object you may happen to look at, like the ghost of smoke.

In the ladies' car, there are a great many gentlemen who have ladies with them. There are also a great many ladies who have nobody with them: for any lady may travel alone, from one end of the United States to the other, and be certain of the most courteous and considerate treatment everywhere. The conductor or check-taker, or guard, or whatever he may be, wears no uniform. He walks up and down the car, and in and out of it, as his fancy dictates; leans against the door with his hands in his pockets and stares at you, if you chance to be a stranger; or enters into conversation with the passengers about him. A great many newspapers are pulled out, and a few of them are read. [...]

If a lady take a fancy to any male passenger's seat, the gentleman who accompanies her gives him notice of the fact, and he immediately vacates it with great politeness. Politics are much discussed, so are banks, so is cotton. Quiet people avoid the question of the Presidency, for there will be a new election in three years and a half, and party feeling runs very high: the great constitutional feature of this institution being, that directly the acrimony of the last election is over, the acrimony of the next one begins; which is an unspeakable comfort to all strong politicians and true lovers of their country: that is to say, to ninety-nine men and boys out of every ninety-nine and a quarter.

Except when a branch road joins the main one, there is seldom more than one track of rails; so that the road is very narrow, and the view, where there is a deep cutting, by no means extensive. When there is not, the character of the scenery

---

22 Lowell, a city in northeast Massachusetts, was founded in 1820 as a centre for textile manufacturing, becoming the largest producer of woven cotton in the US by the 1850s.

23 References to racially segregated train cars and Jonathan Swift's *Gulliver's Travels* (1726)

is always the same. Mile after mile of stunted trees: some hewn down by the axe, some blown down by the wind, some half fallen and resting on their neighbours, many mere logs half hidden in the swamp, others mouldered away to spongy chips. [...] Now you emerge for a few brief minutes on an open country, glittering with some bright lake or pool, broad as many an English river, but so small here that it scarcely has a name; now catch hasty glimpses of a distant town, with its clean white houses and their cool piazzas, its prim New England church and schoolhouse; when whir-r-r-r! almost before you have seen them, comes the same dark screen: the stunted trees, the stumps, the logs, the stagnant water—all so like the last that you seem to have been transported back again by magic. [...]

I was met at the station at Lowell by a gentleman intimately connected with the management of the factories there; and gladly putting myself under his guidance, drove off at once to that quarter of the town in which the works, the object of my visit, were situated. Although only just of age—for if my recollection serve me, it has been a manufacturing town barely one-and-twenty years—Lowell is a large, populous, thriving place. Those indications of its youth which first attract the eye, give it a quaintness and oddity of character which, to a visitor from the old country, is amusing enough. It was a very dirty winter's day, and nothing in the whole town looked old to me, except the mud, which in some parts was almost knee-deep, and might have been deposited there, on the subsiding of the waters after the Deluge. In one place, there was a new wooden church, which, having no steeple, and being yet unpainted, looked like an enormous packing-case without any direction upon it. In another there was a large hotel, whose walls and colonnades were so crisp, and thin, and slight, that it had exactly the appearance of being built with cards. I was careful not to draw my breath as we passed, and trembled when I saw a workman come out upon the roof, lest with one thoughtless stamp of his foot he should crush the structure beneath him, and bring it rattling down. The very river that moves the machinery in the mills (for they are all worked by water power), seems to acquire a new character from the fresh buildings of bright red brick and painted wood among which it takes its course; and to be as light-headed, thoughtless, and brisk a young river, in its murmurings and tumblings, as one would desire to see. One would swear that every "Bakery," "Grocery," and "Bookbindery," and other kind of store, took its shutters down for the first time, and started in business yesterday. The golden pestles and mortars fixed as signs upon the sun-blind frames outside the Druggist's, appear to have been just turned out of the United States' Mint; and when I saw a baby of some week or ten days old in a woman's arms at a street corner, I found myself unconsciously wondering where it came from: never supposing for an instant that it could have been born in such a young town as that.

There are several factories in Lowell, each of which belongs to what we should term a Company of Proprietors, but what they call in America a Corporation. I went over several of these; such as a woollen factory, a carpet factory, and a cotton factory: examined them in every part; and saw them in their ordinary working aspect, with no preparation of any kind, or departure from their ordinary every-day proceedings. I may add that I am well acquainted with our manufacturing towns in England, and have visited many mills in Manchester and elsewhere in the same manner.

I happened to arrive at the first factory just as the dinner hour was over, and the girls were returning to their work; indeed the stairs of the mill were thronged with them as I ascended. They were all well dressed, but not to my thinking above their condition; for I like to see the humbler classes of society careful of their dress and appearance, and even, if they please, decorated with such little trinkets as come within the compass of their means.[...]

These girls, as I have said, were all well dressed: and that phrase necessarily includes extreme cleanliness. They had serviceable bonnets, good warm cloaks, and shawls; and were not above clogs and pattens.[24] Moreover, there were places in the mill in which they could deposit these things without injury; and there were conveniences for washing. They were healthy in appearance, many of them remarkably so, and had the manners and deportment of young women: not of degraded brutes of burden. If I had seen in one of those mills (but I did not, though I looked for something of this kind with a sharp eye), the most lisping, mincing, affected, and ridiculous young creature that my imagination could suggest, I should have thought of the careless, moping, slatternly, degraded, dull reverse (I *have* seen that), and should have been still well pleased to look upon her.

The rooms in which they worked, were as well ordered as themselves. In the windows of some, there were green plants, which were trained to shade the glass; in all, there was as much fresh air, cleanliness, and comfort, as the nature of the occupation would possibly admit of. Out of so large a number of females, many of whom were only then just verging upon womanhood, it may be reasonably supposed that some were delicate and fragile in appearance: no doubt there were. But I solemnly declare, that from all the crowd I saw in the different factories that day, I cannot recal or separate one young face that gave me a painful impression; not one young girl whom, assuming it to be a matter of necessity that she should gain her daily bread by the labour of her hands, I would have removed from those works if I had had the power.

They reside in various boarding-houses near at hand. The owners of the mills are particularly careful to allow no persons to enter upon the possession of these houses, whose characters have not undergone the most searching and thorough inquiry. Any complaint that is made against them, by the boarders, or by any one else, is fully investigated; and if good ground of complaint be shown to exist against them, they are removed, and their occupation is handed over to some more deserving person. There are a few children employed in these factories, but not many. The laws of the State forbid their working more than nine months in the year, and require that they be educated during the other three. For this purpose there are schools in Lowell; and there are churches and chapels of various persuasions, in which the young women may observe that form of Worship in which they have been educated. [...]

I am now going to state three facts, which will startle a large class of readers on this side of the Atlantic, very much.

Firstly, there is a joint-stock piano in a great many of the boarding-houses. Secondly, nearly all these young ladies subscribe to circulating libraries. Thirdly, they have got up among themselves a periodical called THE LOWELL OFFERING, "A repository of original articles, written exclusively by females actively employed in the mills,"—which is duly printed, published, and sold; and whereof I brought away from Lowell four hundred good solid pages, which I have read from beginning to end.[25]

---

24 Protective outdoor shoes
25 *The Lowell Offering* was a monthly periodical that ran from 1840 to 1845.

The large class of readers, startled by these facts, will exclaim, with one voice, "How very preposterous!" On my deferentially inquiring why, they will answer, "These things are above their station." In reply to that objection, I would beg to ask what their station is.

It is their station to work. And they *do* work. They labour in these mills, upon an average, twelve hours a day, which is unquestionably work, and pretty tight work too. Perhaps it is above their station to indulge in such amusements, on any terms. Are we quite sure that we in England have not formed our ideas of the "station" of working people, from accustoming ourselves to the contemplation of that class as they are, and not as they might be? I think that if we examine our own feelings, we shall find that the pianos, and the circulating libraries, and even the Lowell Offering, startle us by their novelty, and not by their bearing upon any abstract question of right or wrong.

For myself, I know no station in which, the occupation of to-day cheerfully done and the occupation of to-morrow cheerfully looked to, any one of these pursuits is not most humanizing and laudable. I know no station which is rendered more endurable to the person in it, or more safe to the person out of it, by having igno-rance for its associate. I know no station which has a right to monopolize the means of mutual instruction, improvement, and rational entertainment; or which has ever continued to be a station very long, after seeking to do so.

Of the merits of the Lowell Offering as a literary production, I will only observe, putting entirely out of sight the fact of the articles having been written by these girls after the arduous labours of the day, that it will compare advantageously with a great many English Annuals. It is pleasant to find that many of its Tales are of the Mills and of those who work in them; that they inculcate habits of self-denial and contentment, and teach good doctrines of enlarged benevolence. A strong feeling for the beauties of nature, as displayed in the solitudes the writers have left at home, breathes through its pages like wholesome village air; and though a circulating library is a favourable school for the study of such topics, it has very scant allusion to fine clothes, fine marriages, fine houses, or fine life. Some persons might object to the papers being signed occasionally with rather fine names, but this is an American fashion. One of the provinces of the state legislature of Massachusetts is to alter ugly names into pretty ones, as the children improve upon the tastes of their par-ents. These changes costing little or nothing, scores of Mary Annes are solemnly converted into Bevelinas every session. [. . .]

In this brief account of Lowell, and inadequate expression of the gratification it yielded me, and cannot fail to afford to any foreigner to whom the condition of such people at home is a subject of interest and anxious speculation, I have carefully abstained from drawing a comparison between these factories and those of our own land. Many of the circumstances whose strong influence has been at work for years in our manufacturing towns have not arisen here; and there is no manufacturing population in Lowell, so to speak: for these girls (often the daugh-ters of small farmers) come from other States, remain a few years in the mills, and then go home for good.

The contrast would be a strong one, for it would be between the Good and Evil, the living light and deepest shadow. I abstain from it, because I deem it just to do so. But I only the more earnestly adjure all those whose eyes may rest on these pages, to pause and reflect upon the difference between this town and those great haunts of desperate misery: to call to mind, if they can in the midst of party strife and squabble, the efforts that must be made to purge them of their suffering and danger: and last, and foremost, to remember how the precious Time is rushing by.

Source text

Dickens, Charles, *American Notes for General Circulation*, Vol. 1 (London: Chapman & Hall, 1842).

References

Claybaugh, Amanda, 'Toward a New Transatlanticism: Dickens in the United States', *Victorian Studies* 48 (Spring 2006), 439–60.
Ingham, Patricia, Introduction, *American Notes for General Circulation* (London: Penguin, 2000), xi–xxxi.
Meckier, Jerome, *Innocent Abroad: Charles Dickens's American Engagements* (Lexington, KY: University Press of Kentucky, 1990).

Frances Calderón de la Barca (1804–82)

From Life in Mexico During a Residence of Two Years in That Country *(1843)*

For important biographical details about Fanny Calderón de la Barca and the transatlantic publication history of *Life in Mexico*, see ST. The following excerpt underscores Calderón de la Barca's experience as a Scottish-born woman living in Mexico and negotiating the customs and conventions of that society. She was invited to a ball in Puebla, Mexico, an event where she was expected to make an appearance given her position as a diplomat's wife.

Calderón de la Barca's understanding of the importance of regional variations and local customs comes to the forefront when she feels that her Scottish heritage is mocked by Mexican society at the ball for Puebla's elites. Despite being advised against donning a traditional costume of a Mexican woman, for the sake of social propriety, she observes that among the attendees was an individual who attempted to dress as a Scottish Highlander. This reflection on the mimicry of dress highlights the complex set of performances where markers of cultural identity are adopted or refused according to rules that often remain a mystery to the reporting narrator. Calderón de la Barca occupies a number of different identities, not just of nationality but also of class, gender and ethnicity. She is a curious traveller and a representative, through marriage, of the Spanish court. Each of these colliding selves is refracted through her concentration in this passage on the resonances of dress.

From Life in Mexico During a Residence of Two Years in That Country

'Letter the Ninth'

Yesterday (Sunday) a great day here for visiting after mass is over. We had a concourse of Spaniards, all of whom seemed anxious to know whether or not I intended to wear a Poblana dress[26] at the fancy ball, and seemed wonderfully interested about it. Two young ladies or women of Puebla, introduced by Señor — came to proffer their services in giving me all the necessary particulars, and dressed the hair of Josefa, a little Mexican girl, to show me how it should be arranged; mentioned several things still wanting, and told me that every one was much pleased at the idea of my going in a Poblana dress. I was rather surprised that *every one* should trouble themselves about it. About twelve o'clock the president, in full uniform, attended by his aides-de-camp, paid me a visit, and sat about half an hour, very amiable, as usual. Shortly after came more visits, and just as we had supposed they were all concluded, and we were going to dinner, we were told that the secretary of state, the ministers of war and of the interior, and others, were in the drawing-room. And what do you think was the purport of their visit? To adjure me by all that was most alarming, to discard the idea of making my appearance in a Poblana dress! They assured us that Poblanas generally were *femmes de rien*, that they wore no stockings, and that the wife of the Spanish minister should by no means assume, even for one evening, such a costume. I brought in my dresses, showed their length and their propriety, but in vain; and, in fact, as to their being in the right, there could be no doubt, and nothing but a kind motive could have induced them to take this trouble; so I yielded with a good grace, and thanked the cabinet council for their timely warning, though fearing, that in this land of procrastination, it would be difficult to procure another dress for the fancy ball; for you must know, that our luggage is still toiling its weary way, on the backs of mules, from Vera Cruz to the capital. They had scarcely gone, when Señor — brought a message from several of the principal ladies here, whom we do not even know, and who had requested, that as a stranger, I should be informed of the reasons which rendered the Poblana dress objectionable in this country, especially on any public occasion like this ball. I was really thankful for my escape.

Just as I was dressing for dinner, a note was brought, marked *reservada* (private) the contents of which appeared to me more odd than pleasant. I have since heard, however, that the writer, Don José Arnaiz, is an old man, and a sort of privileged character, who interferes in everything, whether it concerns him or not. I translate it for your benefit.

"The dress of a Poblana is that of a woman of no character. The lady of the Spanish minister is a *lady* in every sense of the word. However much she may have compromised herself, she ought neither to go as a Poblana, nor in any other character but her own. So says to the Señor de C—n, José Arnaiz, who esteems him as much as possible." [. . .]

10th.— The fancy-ball took place last evening in the theatre [. . .]. Having discarded the costume of the light-headed Poblamanas, I adopted that of a virtuous Roman Contadina,[27] simple enough to be run up in one day; a white skirt, red bodice with blue ribbons, and lace veil put on square behind; *à propos* to which head-dress, it is very common amongst the Indians to wear a piece of stuff folded square, and laid flat upon the head, in this Italian fashion; and as it is not fastened, I cannot imagine how they trot along, without letting it fall.

[. . .] The ball, given for the benefit of the poor, was under the patronage of the ladies C—a, G—a, Guer—a, and others, but such was the original dirtiness and bad condition of the theatre, that to make it decent, they had expended nearly all the

---

26 A traditional Mexican dress, often regarded as risqué and provocative
27 An Italian peasant woman

proceeds. As it was, and considering the various drawbacks, the arrangements were very good. Handsome lustres had superseded the lanterns with their tallow candles, the boxes were hung with bright silk draperies, and a canopy of the same drawn up in the form of a tent, covered the whole ball-room. The orchestra also was tolerably good. The boxes were filled with ladies, presenting an endless succession of China crape shawls of every color and variety, and a monotony of diamond ear-rings; while in the theatre itself, if ever a ball might be termed a fancy-ball, this was that ball. Of Swiss peasants, Scotch peasants, and all manner of peasants, there were a goodly assortment; as also of Turks, Highlanders, and men in plain clothes. But being public, it was not, of course, select, and amongst many well-dressed people, there were hundreds who, assuming no particular character, had exerted their imagination to appear merely fanciful, and had succeeded. One, for example, would have a scarlet satin petticoat, and over it a pink satin robe, with scarlet ribbons to match. Another, a short blue satin dress, beneath which appeared a handsome purple satin petticoat; the whole trimmed with yellow bows. They looked like the signs of the zodiac. All had diamonds and pearls; old and young, and middle-aged; including little children, of whom there were many.

The lady patronesses were very elegant. The Señora de Gu—a, wore a head-dress in the form of a net, entirely composed of large pearls and diamonds; in itself a fortune. The Señora de C—a, as Madame de la Vallière,[28] in black velvet and dia-monds, looking pretty as usual, but the cold of the house obliged her to muffle up in furs and böas, and so to hide her dress. The Señora de G—a, as Mary, Queen of Scots,[29] in black velvet and pearls, with a splendid diamond necklace, was extremely handsome; she wore a cap, introduced by the Albini, in the character of the Scottish Queen, but which, though pretty in itself, is a complete deviation from the beautiful simplicity of the real Queen-Mary cap. She certainly looked as if she had arrived at her prime without knowing Fotheringay.[30]

Various ladies were introduced to me who are only waiting to receive our cards of *faire part* before they call. Amongst the girls, the best dresses that I observed were the Señoritas de F—d, the one handsome, with the figure and face of a Span-ish peasant; the other much more graceful and intelligent-looking, though with less actual beauty. However, so many of the most fashionable people were in their boxes, that I am told this is not a good occasion on which to judge of the beauty or style of toilet of the Mexican women; besides which, these fancy balls being uncom-mon, they would probably look better in their usual costume. Upon the whole, I saw few striking beauties, little grace, and very little good dancing. There was too much velvet and satin, and the dresses were too much loaded. The diamonds, though superb, were frequently ill-set. The dresses, compared with the actual fash-ion, were absurdly short, and the feet, naturally small, were squeezed into shoes still smaller, which is destructive to grace, whether in walking or dancing. [...]

There was a young gentleman pointed out to me as being in the costume of a Highlander! How I wished that Sir William Cumming, Macleod of Macleod, or some veritable Highland chieftain could suddenly have appeared to annihilate him, and show the people here what the dress really is! There were various unfortunate children, bundled up in long satin or velvet dresses, covered with blonde and jewels, and with artificial flowers in their hair.

---

28 Louise de La Vallière (1644–1710), mistress of Louis XIV of France
29 Mary I (1542–87), queen of Scotland, 1542–67
30 Fotheringay Castle in England, where Mary, Queen of Scots, was imprisoned and executed in 1587

The room was excessively cold, nor was the ancient odor of the theatre entirely obliterated; nor indeed do I think that all the perfumes of Arabia would overpower it. Having walked about, and admired all the varieties of fancy costumes, I being nearly frozen, went to the Countess C—a's box on the pit tier, and enveloped myself in a cloak. They pointed out the most distinguished persons in the boxes, amongst others the family of the E—s, who seem very handsome, with brilliant colors and fine teeth. We remained until three in the morning, and declined all offers of refreshment, though, after all, a cup of hot chocolate would not have been amiss. There was supper somewhere, but I believe attended only by gentlemen. I had the satisfaction in passing out to see numerous ladies on their partners' arms, and all bedizened as they were with finery, stop under the lamps, and light their cigars, — cool and pretty.

Source text

Calderón de la Barca, Frances, *Life in Mexico During a Residence of Two Years in That Country*, Vol. 1 (Boston: Charles C. Little and James Brown, 1843).

References

Caballero, Soledad and Jennifer Hayward, '"An occasional trait of Scotch shrewdness": Narrating Nationalism in Frances Calderón de la Barca's Life in Mexico', in Joselyn M. Almeida (ed.), *Romanticism and the Anglo-Hispanic Imaginary* (Leiden: Editions Rodopi, 2010), 290–319.
Lindsay, Claire, 'Postcolonial Anxieties: Fetishizing Frances Calderón de la Barca', *Women: A Cultural Review* 17.2 (2006), 171–87.
Méndez Rodenas, Adrianam, *Transatlantic Travels in Nineteenth-Century Latin America: European Women Pilgrims* (Lewisburg, PA: Bucknell University Press, 2014).

Charles Darwin (1809–82)

From Voyage of the Beagle *(1845)*

In this excerpt from Chapter Eleven of *Voyage of the Beagle*, Charles Darwin provides observations about his encounters in Tierra del Fuego, an archipelago near the southernmost part of South America. In transatlantic terms, he speaks to the rapid increase in the horse population since the arrival of sixteenth-century Europeans, and he provides a comparison of the climate and geographic formations with others present in Europe – contextualising so as to place the South American experience in a perspective accessible to European readers. Of particular note is how Darwin comments on meeting a group of individuals from Patagonia, referring to them as 'half civilised' and 'proportionally demoralised', indicative of the sometimes uncomfortable relationship between scientific documentation and moral framing in his account. While ostensibly writing a narrative of ethnographic analysis, Darwin is unable to abandon taxonomies of hierarchy grounded in assumptions of racial privilege. (See ST for biographical details about Darwin that describe his service as a scientific representative of imperial endeavours.)

Clearly, Darwin is curious about the evolutionary states of people, places and animals in Latin America, and, as Marisa Palacios Knox has suggested, 'only the vital possibilities of educational and evolutionary "improvement" . . . enable Darwin to understand the paradox of primitive and modern' (Palacios Knox, 6). In this excerpt, Darwin positions people within proto-evolutionary contexts, and, perhaps through his scientific-evolutionary approach, Darwin reveals British attempts at establishing an informal empire since he presents himself as a scientist who is 'master of all he surveys' (Pratt, 201; see also Reeder).

Darwin's account of his trip was first published in 1839 as the third volume of the captain of the *Beagle*, Robert FitzRoy's, account of the voyage. We reprint from the second edition of 1845, in which Darwin was able to take into account his developing ideas about evolution.

Figure 10.2 *H.M.S. Beagle*. Frontispiece to Charles Darwin, M.A., F.R.S., *Journal of Researches into the Natural History and Geology of the Countries Visited During the Voyage Round the World of H.M.S. 'Beagle'* (New York: D. Appleton and Company, 1890).

From Voyage of the Beagle

In the end of May, 1834, we entered for a second time the eastern mouth of the Strait of Magellan.[31] The country on both sides of this part of the Strait consists of nearly level plains, like those of Patagonia.[32] Cape Negro, a little within the second Narrows, may be considered as the point where the land begins to assume the marked features of Tierra del Fuego. On the east coast, south of the Strait, broken park-like scenery in a like manner connects these two countries, which are opposed to each other in almost every feature. It is truly surprising to find in a space of twenty miles such a change in the landscape. If we take a rather greater distance, as between Port Famine and Gregory Bay, that is about sixty miles, the difference is still more wonderful. At the former place, we have rounded mountains concealed by impervious forests, which are drenched with the rain, brought by an endless succession of gales; while at Cape Gregory, there is a clear and bright blue sky over the dry and sterile plains. The atmospheric currents, although rapid, turbulent, and unconfined by any apparent limits, yet seem to follow, like a river in its bed, a regularly determined course.

During our previous visit (in January), we had an interview at Cape Gregory with the famous so-called gigantic Patagonians,[33] who gave us a cordial reception. Their height appears greater than it really is, from their large guanaco mantles,[34] their long flowing hair, and general figure: on an average, their height is about six feet, with some men taller and only a few shorter; and the women are also tall; altogether they are certainly the tallest race which we anywhere saw. In features they strikingly resemble the more northern Indians [...], but they have a wilder and more formidable appearance: their faces were much painted with red and black, and one man was ringed and dotted with white like a Fuegian.[35] Capt. Fitz Roy offered to take any three of them on board, and all seemed determined to be of the three. It was long before we could clear the boat; at last we got on board with our three giants, who dined with the Captain, and behaved quite like gentlemen, helping themselves with knives, forks, and spoons: nothing was so much relished as sugar. This tribe has had so much communication with sealers and whalers that most of the men can speak a little English and Spanish; and they are half civilised, and proportionally demoralised.

The next morning a large party went on shore, to barter for skins and ostrich-feathers; fire-arms being refused, tobacco was in greatest request, far more so than axes or tools. The whole population of the toldos,[36] men, women, and children, were arranged on a bank. It was an amusing scene, and it was impossible not to like the so-called giants, they were so thoroughly good-humoured and unsuspecting: they asked us to come again. They seem to like to have Europeans to live with them; and old Maria, an important woman in the tribe, once begged Mr. Low to leave any one of his sailors with them. They spend the greater part of the year here; but in summer they hunt along the foot of the Cordillera:[37] sometimes they travel as far as the Rio Negro 750 miles to the north. They are well stocked with horses, each man

---

31 A sea-route in southern Chile that separates mainland South America from the Tierra del Fuego
32 Region of South America shared by Chile and Argentina
33 Since the sixteenth century, travellers' accounts of a giant race of humans living in Patagonia had circulated.
34 A type of covering made from the hair of an animal similar to a llama
35 Indigenous populations from the Tierra del Fuego region
36 A tent, hut or simple dwelling of the native Indians of South America (*OED*)
37 A mountain range

having, according to Mr. Low, six or seven, and all the women, and even children, their one own horse. In the time of Sarmiento (1580),[38] these Indians had bows and arrows, now long since disused; they then also possessed some horses. This is a very curious fact, showing the extraordinarily rapid multiplication of horses in South America. The horse was first landed at Buenos Ayres in 1537, and the colony being then for a time deserted, the horse ran wild; in 1580, only forty-three years afterwards, we hear of them at the Strait of Magellan! Mr. Low informs me, that a neighbouring tribe of foot-Indians is now changing into horse-Indians: the tribe at Gregory Bay giving them their worn-out horses, and sending in winter a few of their best skilled men to hunt for them.

June 1st.—We anchored in the fine bay of Port Famine. It was now the beginning of winter, and I never saw a more cheerless prospect; the dusky woods, piebald with snow, could be only seen indistinctly, through a drizzling hazy atmosphere. We were, however, lucky in getting two fine days. On one of these, Mount Sarmiento, a distant mountain 6800 feet high, presented a very noble spectacle. I was frequently surprised in the scenery of Tierra del Fuego, at the little apparent elevation of mountains really lofty. I suspect it is owing to a cause which would not at first be imagined, namely, that the whole mass, from the summit to the water's edge, is generally in full view. I remember having seen a mountain, first from the Beagle Channel, where the whole sweep from the summit to the base was full in view, and then from Ponsonby Sound across several successive ridges; and it was curious to observe in the latter case, as each fresh ridge afforded fresh means of judging of the distance, how the mountain rose in height.

Before reaching Port Famine, two men were seen running along the shore and hailing the ship. A boat was sent for them. They turned out to be two sailors who had run away from a sealing-vessel, and had joined the Patagonians. These Indians had treated them with their usual disinterested hospitality. They had parted company through accident, and were then proceeding to Port Famine in hopes of finding some ship. I dare say they were worthless vagabonds, but I never saw more miserable looking ones. They had been living for some days on mussel-shells and berries, and their tattered clothes had been burnt by sleeping so near their fires. They had been exposed night and day, without any shelter, to the late incessant gales, with rain, sleet, and snow, and yet they were in good health.

During our stay at Port Famine, the Fuegians twice came and plagued us. As there were many instruments, clothes, and men on shore, it was thought necessary to frighten them away. The first time a few great guns were fired, when they were far distant. It was most ludicrous to watch through a glass the Indians, as often as the shot struck the water, take up stones, and, as a bold defiance, throw them towards the ship, though about a mile and a half distant! A boat was sent with orders to fire a few musket-shots wide of them. The Fuegians hid themselves behind the trees, and for every discharge of the muskets they fired their arrows; all, however, fell short of the boat, and the officer as he pointed at them laughed. This made the Fuegians frantic with passion, and they shook their mantles in vain rage. At last, seeing the balls cut and strike the trees, they ran away, and we were left in peace and quietness. During the former voyage the Fuegians were here very troublesome, and to frighten them a rocket was fired at night over their wigwams; it answered effectually, and one of the officers told me that the clamour first raised, and the

---

38 Pedro Sarmiento de Gamboa (1532–92), Spanish explorer who wrote *The History of the Incas* in 1572

barking of the dogs, was quite ludicrous in contrast with the profound silence which in a minute or two afterwards prevailed. The next morning not a single Fuegian was in the neighbourhood.

When the Beagle was here in the month of February, I started one morning at four o'clock to ascend Mount Tarn, which is 2600 feet high, and is the most elevated point in this immediate district. We went in a boat to the foot of the mountain (but unluckily not to the best part), and then began our ascent. The forest commences at the line of high-water mark, and during the first two hours I gave over all hopes of reaching the summit. So thick was the wood, that it was necessary to have constant recourse to the compass; for every landmark, though in a mountainous country, was completely shut out. In the deep ravines, the death-like scene of desolation exceeded all description; outside it was blowing a gale, but in these hollows, not even a breath of wind stirred the leaves of the tallest trees. So gloomy, cold, and wet was every part, that not even the fungi, mosses, or ferns could flourish. In the valleys it was scarcely possible to crawl along, they were so completely barricaded by great mouldering trunks, which had fallen down in every direction. When passing over these natural bridges, one's course was often arrested by sinking knee deep into the rotten wood; at other times, when attempting to lean against a firm tree, one was startled by finding a mass of decayed matter ready to fall at the slightest touch. We at last found ourselves among the stunted trees, and then soon reached the bare ridge, which conducted us to the summit. Here was a view characteristic of Tierra del Fuego; irregular chains of hills, mottled with patches of snow, deep yellowish-green valleys, and arms of the sea intersecting the land in many directions. The strong wind was piercingly cold, and the atmosphere rather hazy, so that we did not stay long on the top of the mountain. Our descent was not quite so laborious as our ascent, for the weight of the body forced a passage, and all the slips and falls were in the right direction. [...]

Recapitulation.—I will recapitulate the principal facts with regard to the climate, ice-action, and organic productions of the southern hemisphere, transposing the places in imagination to Europe, with which we are so much better acquainted. Then, near Lisbon, the commonest sea-shells, namely, three species of Oliva, a Voluta, and a Terebra, would have a tropical character. In the southern provinces of France, magnificent forests, intwined by arborescent grasses and with the trees loaded with parasitical plants, would hide the face of the land. The puma and the jaguar would haunt the Pyrenees. In the latitude of Mont Blanc, but on an island as far westward as Central North America, tree-ferns and parasitical Orchideae would thrive amidst the thick woods. Even as far north as central Denmark, humming-birds would be seen fluttering about delicate flowers, and parrots feeding amidst the evergreen woods; and in the sea there, we should have a Voluta, and all the shells of large size and vigorous growth. Nevertheless, on some islands only 360 miles northward of our new Cape Horn in Denmark, a carcass buried in the soil (or if washed into a shallow sea, and covered up with mud) would be preserved perpetually frozen. If some bold navigator attempted to penetrate northward of these islands, he would run a thousand dangers amidst gigantic icebergs, on some of which he would see great blocks of rock borne far away from their original site. Another island of large size in the latitude of southern Scotland, but twice as far to the west, would be "almost wholly covered with everlasting snow," and would have each bay terminated by ice-cliffs, whence great masses would be yearly detached: this island would boast only of a little moss, grass, and burnet, and a titlark would be its only land inhabitant. From our new Cape Horn in Denmark, a chain of mountains, scarcely half the height of the

Alps, would run in a straight line due southward; and on its western flank every deep creek of the sea, or fiord, would end in "bold and astonishing glaciers." These lonely channels would frequently reverberate with the falls of ice, and so often would great waves rush along their coasts; numerous icebergs, some as tall as cathedrals, and occasionally loaded with "no inconsiderable blocks of rock," would be stranded on the outlying islets; at intervals violent earthquakes would shoot prodigious masses of ice into the waters below. Lastly, some missionaries attempting to penetrate a long arm of the sea, would behold the not lofty surrounding mountains, sending down their many grand icy streams to the sea-coast, and their progress in the boats would be checked by the innumerable floating icebergs, some small and some great; and this would have occurred on our twenty-second of June, and where the Lake of Geneva is now spread out!

Source text

Darwin, Charles, *Journal of the Researches into the Natural History and Geology of the Countries Visited During the Voyage of the H.M.S. Beagle Round the World, Under the Command of Capt. FitzRoy, R.A.* (London: John Murray, 1845).

References

Knox, Marisa Palacios, 'Imagining Informal Empire: Nineteenth-century British Literature and Latin America', *Literature Compass* (2019), 1–13.
Pratt, Mary Louise, *Imperial Eyes: Travel Writing and Transculturation* (New York and London: Routledge, 1992).
Reeder, Jessie, *The Forms of Informal Empire: Britain, Latin America, and Nineteenth-Century Literature* (Baltimore, MD: Johns Hopkins University Press, 2020).
Schmitt, Cannon, 'Darwin's Savage Mnemonics', *Representations* 88.1 (2004), 55–80.

Margaret Fuller (1810–50)

From 'New and Old World Democracy' (1848)

Margaret Fuller was a pioneering editor, journalist, author and early advocate of feminism in the US. A voracious reader of European writing, including that of the French novelist George Sand and, especially, the German dramatist and novelist Goethe, Fuller's most significant personal and intellectual relationship in the United States was with the transcendentalist philosopher Ralph Waldo Emerson, with whom she began an often difficult friendship in 1836. She edited the Transcendentalist journal *The Dial* from 1840 to 1842, and published her book *Woman in the Nineteenth Century*, a key document in the fight against proscriptive social and gendered roles, in 1845. Fuller was hired by Horace Greeley, editor of the highly influential New York *Tribune* newspaper as, first, a literary critic and then, between 1846 and 1850, its foreign correspondent in

Italy, France and England. In Rome in 1848 she witnessed, and reported on, the Italian revolution, one of a series of upheavals that spread across Europe that year. At this time, Italy was not a unified nation, but a series of often-warring states and kingdoms, with the Austrian Empire an important ruling presence. Rome was governed by the Papal States, and Fuller's dispatches to the *Tribune* report on the rising clamour against the Vatican in favour of a republican government. The piece excerpted here focuses on Fuller's analysis of the types of American traveller, and challenges the political and cultural complacency of her fellow US citizens, who are unwilling to recognise the moral evils of slavery and seemingly blind to the failures of democracy. Fuller drowned, along with her husband and son, in a shipwreck off the coast of New York on 19 July 1850, as she returned to the United States from Europe. Her body was never recovered.

From 'New and Old World Democracy'

The American in Europe, if a thinking mind, can only become more American. In some respects it is a great pleasure to be here. Although we have an independent political existence, our position toward Europe, as to Literature and the Arts, is still that of a colony, and one feels the same joy here that is experienced by the colonist in returning to the parent home. What was but picture to us becomes reality; remote allusions and derivations trouble no more: we see the pattern of the stuff, and understand the whole tapestry. There is a gradual clearing up on many points, and many baseless notions and crude fancies are dropped. Even the post-haste passage of the business American through the great cities, escorted by cheating couriers and ignorant *valets de place*,[39] unable to hold intercourse with the natives of the country, and passing all his leisure hours with his countrymen, who know no more than himself, clears his mind of some mistakes—lifts some mists from his horizon.

There are three species: first, the servile American—a being utterly shallow, thoughtless, worthless. He comes abroad to spend his money and indulge his tastes. His object in Europe is to have fashionable clothes, good foreign cookery, to know some titled persons, and furnish himself with coffee-house gossip, which he wins importance at home by retailing among those less traveled, and as uninformed as himself.

I look with unspeakable contempt on this class—a class which has all the thoughtlessness and partiality of the exclusive classes in Europe, without any of their refinement, or the chivalric feeling which still sparkles among them here and there. However, though these willing serfs in a free age do some little hurt, and cause some annoyance at present, they cannot last: our country is fated to a grand, independent existence, and as its laws develop, these parasites of a bygone period must wither and drop away.

Then there is the conceited American, instinctively bristling and proud of—he knows not what—He does not see, not he, that the history of Humanity for many centuries is likely to have produced results it requires some training, some devotion,

---

39 Tour guides for travellers

to appreciate and profit by. With his great clumsy hands only fitted to work on a steam-engine, he seizes the old Cremona violin,[40] makes it shriek with anguish in his grasp, and then declares he thought it was all humbug before he came, and now he knows it; that there is not really any music in these old things; that the frogs in one of our swamps make much finer, for *they* are young and alive. To him the etiquettes of courts and camps, the ritual of the Church, seem simply silly—and no wonder, profoundly ignorant as he is of their origin and meaning. Just so the legends which are the subjects of pictures, the profound myths which are represented in the antique marbles, amaze and revolt him; as, indeed, such things need to be judged of by another standard than that of the Connecticut Blue-Laws.[41] He criticises severely pictures, feeling quite sure that his natural senses are better means of judgment than the rules of connoisseurs—not feeling that to see such objects mental vision as well as fleshly eyes are needed, and that something is aimed at in Art beyond the imitation of the commonest forms of Nature.

This is Jonathan[42] in the sprawling state, the booby truant, not yet aspiring enough to be a good school-boy. Yet in his folly there is meaning; add thought and culture to his independence, and he will be a man of might: he is not a creature without hope, like the thick-skinned dandy of the class first specified.

The Artistes form a class by themselves. Yet among them, though seeking special aims by special means may also be found the lineaments of these two classes, as well as of the third, of which I am now to speak.

3d. The thinking American—a man who, recognizing the immense advantage of being born to a new world and on a virgin soil, yet does not wish one seed from the Past to be lost. He is anxious to gather and carry back with him all that will bear a new climate and new culture. Some will dwindle; others will attain a bloom and stature unknown before. He wishes to gather them clean, free from noxious insects. He wishes to give them a fair trial in his new world. And that he may know the conditions under which he may best place them in that new world, he does not neglect to study their history in this. [...]

Eighteen hundred years of this Christian culture in these European Kingdoms, a great theme never lost sight of, a mighty idea, an adorable history to which the hearts of men invariably cling, yet are genuine results rare as grains of gold in the river's sandy bed! Where is the genuine Democracy to which the rights of all men are holy? where the child-like wisdom learning all through life more and more of the will of God? where the aversion to falsehood in all its myriad disguises of cant, vanity, covetousness, so clear to be read in all the history of Jesus of Nazareth? Modern Europe is the sequel to that history, and see this hollow England, with its monstrous wealth and cruel poverty, its conventional life and low, practical aims; see this poor France, so full of talent, so adroit, yet so shallow and glossy still, which could not escape from a false position with all its baptism of blood; see that lost Poland and this Italy bound down by treacherous hands in all the force of genius; see Russia with

---

40 Cremona, Italy, has been a centre for classical violin-making since the sixteenth century.
41 The Blue Laws of Connecticut were invented in 1781 as a hoax by Samuel Peters, an Anglican clergyman, who had been forced to leave America for London in 1774, shortly before the outbreak of the Revolutionary War, because of his hostility to the cause of American independence. The laws themselves – forty-five in total – were excessively harsh, bordering on ridiculous, in order to discredit America's ability to govern itself.
42 'Jonathan', from 'Brother Jonathan', is a stock figure applied to, at first, rebellious colonists during the American Revolution and, later, to (especially) Yankee and New England Americans.

its brutal Czar and innumerable slaves; see Austria and its royalty that represents nothing, and its people who, as people, are and have nothing! If we consider the amount of truth that has really been spoken out in the world, and the love that has beat in private hearts—how Genius has decked each spring-time with such splendid flowers, conveying each one enough of instruction in its life of harmonious energy, and how continually, unquenchably the spark of faith has striven to burst into flame and light up the Universe—the public failure seems amazing, seems monstrous.

Still Europe toils and struggles with her idea, and, at this moment, all things bode and declare a new outbreak of the fire, to destroy old palaces of crime! May it fertilize also many vineyards!—Here at this moment a successor of St. Peter,[43] after the lapse of near two thousand years, is called "Utopian" by a part of this Europe, because he strives to get some food to the mouths of the *leaner* of his flock. A wonderful state of things, and which leaves as the best argument against despair that men do not, *cannot* despair amid such dark experiences—and thou, my country! will thou not be more true? does no greater success await thee? All things have so conspired to teach, to aid! A new world, a new chance, with oceans to wall in the new thought against interference from the old!—Treasures of all kinds, gold, silver, corn, marble, to provide for every physical need! A noble, constant, starlike soul, an Italian,[44] led the way to its shores, and, in the first days, the strong, the pure, those too brave, too sincere for the life of the Old World hastened to people them. A generous struggle then shook off what was foreign and gave the nation a glorious start for a worthy goal. Men rocked the cradle of its hopes, great, firm, disinterested men who saw, who wrote, as the basis of all that was to be done, a statement of the rights, the inborn rights of men, which, if fully interpreted and acted upon, leaves nothing to be desired.

Yet, oh Eagle, whose early flight showed this clear sight of the Sun, how often dost thou near the ground, how show the vulture in these later days! Thou wert to be the advance-guard of Humanity, the herald of all Progress; how often hast thou betrayed this high commission! Fain would the tongue in clear triumphant accents draw example from thy story, to encourage the hearts of those who almost faint and die beneath the old oppressions. But we must stammer and blush when we speak of many things. I take pride here that I may really say the Liberty of the Press works well, and that checks and balances naturally evolve from it which suffice to its government. I may say that the minds of our people are alert, and that Talent has a free chance to rise. It is much. But dare I say that political ambition is not as darkly sullied as in other countries? Dare I say that men of most influence in political life are those who represent most virtue or even intellectual power? Is it easy to find names in that career of which I can speak with enthusiasm? Must I not confess in my country to a boundless lust of gain? Must I not confess to the weakest vanity, which bristles and blusters at each foolish taunt of the foreign press; and must I not admit that the men who make these undignified rejoinders seek and find popularity so? Must I not confess that there is as yet no antidote cordially adopted that will defend even that great, rich country against the evils that have grown out of the commercial system in the old world? Can I say our social laws are generally better,

---

43 Fuller refers here to Pope Pius IX, pope from 1846 to 1878, whose early years as pontiff had seen an embrace of liberal and reformist policies within the Papal States (territories in Italy under the direct control of the Pope). Fuller's later opinion of Pius would considerably darken, as his reformist credentials faded.

44 A reference to Christopher Columbus

or show a nobler insight into the wants of man and woman? I do, indeed, say what I believe, that voluntary association for improvement in these particulars will be the grand means for my nation to grow and give a nobler harmony to the coming age. But it is only of a small minority that I can say they as yet seriously take to heart these things; that they earnestly meditate on what is wanted for their country,—for mankind,—for our cause is, indeed, the cause of all mankind at present. Could we succeed, really succeed, combine a deep religious love with practical development, the achievements of Genius with the happiness of the multitude, we might believe Man had now reached a commanding point in his ascent, and would stumble and faint no more. Then there is this horrible cancer of Slavery, and this wicked War, that has grown out of it.[45] How dare I speak of these things here? I listen to the same arguments against the emancipation of Italy, that are used against the emancipation of our blacks; the same arguments in favor of the spoliation of Poland as for the conquest of Mexico. I find the cause of tyranny and wrong everywhere the same—and lo! my Country the darkest offender, because with the least excuse, foresworn to the high calling with which she was called,—no champion of the rights of men, but a robber and a jailer; the scourge hid behind her banner; her eyes fixed, not on the stars, but on the possessions of other men.

Source text

Fuller, Margaret, 'Things and Thoughts in Europe. No. XVIII', *New-York Daily Tribune* 1 January 1848, 1.

References

Bailey, Brigitte, *American Travel Literature, Gendered Aesthetics and the Italian Tour, 1824–62* (Edinburgh: Edinburgh University Press, 2018).
Reynolds, Larry J., *European Revolutions and the American Literary Renaissance* (New Haven, CT: Yale University Press, 1989).

Nancy Gardner Prince (1799–?)

From A Narrative of the Life and Travels of Mrs. Nancy Prince (1850)

Nancy Gardner Prince was a free-born African American, a member of the Anti-Slavery Society in Boston, a missionary, reformer, businesswoman, and, following her marriage to Nero Prince, a traveller to Russia. Her *Narrative of the Life and Travels*, first published in 1850 before going through two further editions, is the first work by an African American woman to combine spiritual autobiography and travel narrative. Born

---

45 Fuller refers here to the Mexican War (1846–8), which she regarded as being motivated by the desire to expand slavery further into western and southern territories.

into poverty, Prince supported her family from an early age, hiring herself out as a domestic servant. She moved to St Petersburg in 1824, to
join her husband, who was employed as a footman in the court of the
Russian emperor Alexander I. Prince left Russia in 1833, widowed, to
return to Boston, becoming active in abolitionist and missionary circles,
before moving to Jamaica in 1840 to establish a manual labour school for
orphaned children. As Cheryl Fish notes, Prince's 'evangelical New England voice registers outrage from the scenes of empire and emancipation
in Russia and then Jamaica' (25). The extract from the *Narrative* reprinted
here describes Prince's arrival in the Russian court and her observations
of its habits, traditions and practices. Hers is a documenting eye, keen to
explain the exotic to her readers. The comparative perspective she implicitly establishes between Russia and the United States is generated through
a keen sense of her own social and economic freedoms in St Petersburg, as
well as the preferable conditions of Russia's servant class.

From A Narrative of the Life and Travels of Mrs. Nancy Prince

September 1st, 1823, Mr. Prince arrived from Russia; February 15th, I was married;
April 14th, embarked in brig Romulus, arrived at Elsinore[46] May 24th, left the same
day for Copenhagen, where we remained twelve days. We visited the King's Palace, and several other extensive and beautiful buildings. We attended a number of
entertainments among the Danes and English, who were religiously observed; their
manners and customs are similar; they are very attentive to strangers; the Sabbath
is strictly observed; the principal religion is the Lutheran and Calvinistic, but persuasions are tolerated. The languages of that people are Dutch, French, English, &c. The
Danes are very modest and kind, but, like all other nations, they well know how to
take the advantage. I left there the 7th of June, and arrived at Cronstradt[47] on the
19th; left there the 21st for St. Petersburg, and in a few hours were happy to find
ourselves at our place of destination, through the blessing of God, in good health,
and soon made welcome from all quarters. We took lodgings with a Mrs. Robinson,
a native of our country, who was Patience Mott, of Providence, who left there in
the year 1813, in the family of Alexander Gabriel, the man who was taken for Mr.
Prince.[48] There I spent six weeks very pleasantly, visiting and receiving friends, after
the manner of the country. We then commenced housekeeping. While there I
attended two of their parties; there were various amusements in which I did not
participate, which caused them much disappointment. I told them my religion did
not allow of dancing or dice playing, which formed part of the amusements. As they
were very strict in their religion, they indulged me in the same privilege. By the help
of God I was ever enabled to maintain my stand.

---

46 A city in eastern Denmark
47 Kronstadt, a major Russian trading and military centre in the nineteenth century, is located on
Kotlin Island, west of St Petersburg.
48 Patience Mott first travelled to St Petersburg in 1811 with Prudy Jenkins, the wife of Claude
Gabriel, a Haiti-born merchant sailor who settled in Russia, at the request of Tsar Alexander I, to
become his servant (Clauson, 73–5).

Mr. Prince was born in Marlborough, and lived in families in this city. In 1810 he went to Gloucester,[49] and sailed with captain Theodore Stanwood, for Russia; he returned with him, and remained in his family, and at this time visited my mother's family. He again sailed with him in 1812, for the last time. Captain Stanwood took with him his son Theodore, for the purpose of attending school in the city of St. Petersburg. Mr. Prince went to serve Princess Purtossozof, one of the noble ladies of Court. It is well known that the color of one's skin does not prohibit from any place or station that he or she may be capable of occupying.

The Palace, where the Emperor resides, is called the Court, the seat of government. This magnificent building is adorned with all the ornaments that possibly can be explained; there are hundreds of people that inhabit it, besides the soldiers that guard. There are several of these splendid edifices in the city and vicinity. The one that I was presented in, was in a village, three miles from the city. After leaving the carriage, we entered the first ward; the usual salutation by the guards was performed. As we passed through the beautiful hall, a door was opened by two colored men, in official dress, and there stood the Emperor Alexander[50] on his throne, in royal apparel. The throne is circular, elevated two steps from the floor, and covered with scarlet velvet, tasseled with gold. As I entered, the Emperor stepped forward with great politeness and condescension, and welcomed and asked me several questions; he then accompanied us to the Empress Elizabeth;[51] she stood in her dignity, and received me in the same manner. They presented me with a watch, and fifty dollars in gold.

The number of colored men that filled this station was twenty; when one dies, the number is immediately made up. Mr. Prince filled the place of one that had died. They serve in turns, four at a time, except on some great occasions, when all are employed. Provision is made for the families within or without the Palace. Those without go to Court at 8 o'clock in the morning; after breakfasting, they take their station in the halls, for the purpose of opening the doors, at signal given, when the Emperor and Empress pass. [...]

The present Emperor and Empress[52] are courteous and affable. The Empress would often send for the ladies of the court at 8 o'clock in the evening to sup with her, when they arrive at court they form a procession and she takes the lead. On entering the hall, the band strikes up; there are two long tables on each side, and in the midst circular tables for the Imperial family. The tables are spread apparently with every variety of eatable and deserts, but every thing is artificial, presenting a novel appearance. When the company are seated, the Emperor and Empress walk around the tables and shake hands with each individual as they pass. The prisoners of war who are nobles, are seated by themselves with their faces veiled. There is a tender or waiter to each person, with two plates, one with soup and the other with something else. After a variety of courses, in one hour they are dismissed by the band. They then retire to another part of the palace to attend a ball or theatrical amusements. At the Empress's command they are dismissed. She carries power and

---

49 Before travelling to Russia, Nero Prince was the deputy grandmaster of the Prince Hall Grand Lodge of freemasons, which in the nineteenth century had a predominantly African American membership. Marlborough and Gloucester are both cities in Massachusetts.
50 Czar Alexander I (1777–1825), Emperor of Russia from 1801 to 1825
51 Elizabeth Alexeievna (1779–1826), Empress of Russia from 1801 to 1825
52 Nicholas I (1796–1855), Emperor of Russia from 1825 to 1855, and Alexandra Feodorovna (1798–1860), Empress of Russia from 1825 to 1855

dignity in her countenance well adapted to her station. And after her late amusements at night she would be out at an early hour in the morning visiting the abodes of the distressed, dressed in as common apparel as any one here, either walking or riding in a common sleigh. At her return she would call for her children, take them in her arms and talk to them. "She riseth while it is yet night and giveth meat to her household and a portion to her maidens, she stretcheth out her hands to the poor, yea, she reacheth out her hands to the needy; she is not afraid of the snow for all her household are clothed in scarlet."[53] Then she would go to the cabinet of his Majesty; there she would write and advise with him. [...]

There is another spacious building called the Market, half a mile square, where all kinds of articles may be bought. Between the Market and the church there is a block of buildings where silver articles of all kinds are to be purchased. These stores present a very superb appearance and are visited by every foreigner that comes into the place. Besides these buildings, Main Street is lined with elegant buildings with projecting windows, to the extent of twelve miles. Nearly at the termination of the street there is a spacious building of stone which encloses the Taberisey Garden, so called from its having every kind of tree, shrub, flower and fruit, of the known world, which flourish alike in winter as in summer. There is an extensive Frozen Market which forms a square as large as Boston Common. This space of ground is covered with counters, on which may be purchased every variety of eatable, such as frozen fish, fowl, and meats of every description, besides every other article of commerce which will bear the extreme cold of a St. Petersburg winter. This city was founded by Peter the Great, and built upon a bog which was occupied by a few fishermen's huts, and belonged to the Finns. It is situated at the extremity of the Gulf of Finland, and is built partly on the main land and partly on several small islands. The foundation of the city is extremely marshy, which subjects it to frequent inundations. For this reason there are canals which are cut through the streets, very beautifully laid out, faced with granite, railed with iron chains nubbed with brass, with bridges to cross from one street to the other. The city houses are built of stone and brick, and twice the thickness of American houses. [...] The village houses are built of logs corked with oakum, where the peasants reside. This class of people till the land, most of them are slaves and are very degraded. The rich own the poor, but they are not suffered to separate families or sell them off the soil. All are subject to the Emperor, and no nobleman can leave without his permission. The mode of travelling is principally by stages which are built something like our omnibuses, with settees upon the top railed and guarded by soldiers, for the purpose of protecting the travellers from the attacks of wild beasts. The common language is a mixture of Sclavonian[54] and Polish. The nobility make use of the modern Greek, French, and English. I learned the languages in six months, so as to be able to attend to my business, and also made some proficiency in the French. My time was taken up in domestic affairs; I took two children to board the third week after commencing housekeeping, and increased their numbers. The baby linen making and children's garments were in great demand. I started a business in these articles and took a journeywoman and apprentices. The present Empress is a very active one, and inquired of me respecting my business and gave me much encouragement by purchasing of me garments for herself and children, handsomely wrought in French and English styles, and many of the nobility also followed her example.

---

53 Prince conflates Proverbs 31: 15 and 31: 20–1.
54 An archaic English form for Slavonia

Source text

Prince, Nancy Gardner, *A Narrative of the Life and Travels of Mrs. Nancy Prince* (Boston: The Author, 1850).

References

Clauson, J. Earl, *These Plantations* (Providence, RI: Roger Williams Press, 1937).
Fish, Cheryl J., *Black and White Women's Travel Narratives: Antebellum Explorations* (Gainesville, FL: University Press of Florida, 2004).
Peterson, Carla L., *Doers of the Word: African-American Women Speakers and Writers in the North (1830–1880)* (New York: Oxford University Press, 1995).

William Wells Brown (c.1814–84)

From **The American Fugitive in Europe. Sketches of Places and People Abroad** *(1855)*

Figure 10.3 William Wells Brown, in Julia Griffiths (ed.), *Autographs for Freedom* (Auburn: Alden, Beardsley & Co., 1854). Schomburg Center for Research in Black Culture, Manuscripts, Archives and Rare Books Division, New York Public Library. 'Wm. Wells Brown', *The New York Public Library Digital Collections.*

William Wells Brown, as he would name himself, was born enslaved in Lexington, Kentucky. After twenty years of indentured service, Brown escaped to freedom in 1834, taking the name of a Quaker benefactor who had helped him, and settled in Buffalo, New York, a key station on the Underground Railroad. That year he met Frederick Douglass for the first time and became a travelling lecturer for the Western New York Anti-Slavery Society. In 1847 he moved to Boston, which would become his permanent home, and published his *Narrative of William Wells Brown, A Fugitive Slave*. Brown's travels to Europe were instigated by his nomination as a delegate to the International Peace Congress in Paris in 1849, where he gave a speech on abolitionism. With the passing of the Fugitive Slave Law in 1850, his stay in Europe, where he also visited and lectured in Ireland, England and Scotland, was prolonged. Brown's novel *Clotel* was first published in London in 1853.

The American Fugitive was a reworking and expansion of an earlier collection of travel sketches, *Three Years in Europe: or Places I Have Seen and People I Have Met* (London, 1852). The book presents Brown's experience of, and exposure to, a variety of cultural scenes and encounters. In the first of the two passages excerpted here, his engagement with the cultural edifices of Paris is described for the reader. It is indicative of Brown's desire to present himself not just as a tourist (though this is an important identity he wishes to assume), but someone who is also fully engaged with the histories of imperialism and oppression that lie behind the markers of French sophistication. The second passage draws attention to a wider Black presence in Europe – this time in London – through the figure of Joseph Jenkins, whose picaresque adaptability points to a Black reclaiming of Franklinian industry.

From The American Fugitive in Europe. Sketches of Places and People Abroad

CHAPTER VII.

"The moon on the east oriel shone
Through slender shafts of shapely stone,
By foliaged tracery combined.
Thou wouldst have thought some fairy's hand
'Twixt poplars straight the osier wand
In many a freakish knot had twined:
Then framed a spell, when the work was done,
And changed the willow wreaths to stone."

SIR WALTER SCOTT.[55]

---

55 From 'Canto Second' of *The Lay of the Last Minstrel* (1805) by Walter Scott. Scott's home, Melrose Abbey, is described here.

HERE I am, within ten leagues of Paris, spending the time pleasantly in viewing the palace and grounds of the great chateau of Louis XIV.[56] Fifty-seven years ago, a mob, composed of men, women and boys, from Paris, stood in front of this palace, and demanded that the king should go with them to the capital. I have walked over the same ground where the one hundred thousand stood on that interesting occasion. I have been upon the same balcony, and stood by the window from which Marie Antoinette looked out upon the mob that were seeking her life.[57]

Anxious to see as much of the palace as I could, and having an offer of the company of my young friend, Henry G. Chapman,[58] to go through the palace with me, I set out early this morning, and was soon in the halls that had often been trod by royal feet. We passed through the private as well as the public apartments; through the secret door by which Marie Antoinette had escaped from the mob of 1792; and viewed the room in which her faithful guards were killed, while attempting to save their royal mistress. I took my seat in one of the little parlor carriages that had been used in days of yore for the royal children, while my friend H. G. Chapman drew me across the room. The superb apartments are not now in use. Silence is written upon these walls, although upon them are suspended the portraits of men of whom the world has heard.

Paintings representing Napoleon in nearly all his battles are here seen; and, wherever you see the emperor, there you will also find Murat, with his white plume waving above.[59] Callot's painting of the battle of Marengo,[60] Hue's of the retaking of Genoa,[61] and Bouchat's of the 18th Brumaire,[62] are of the highest order; while David has transmitted his fame to posterity by his splendid painting of the coronation of Napoleon and Josephine in Notre Dame.[63] When I looked upon the many beautiful paintings of the last-named artist that adorn the halls of Versailles, I did not wonder that his fame should have saved his life when once condemned and sentenced to death during the reign of terror. The guillotine was robbed of its intended victim; but the world gained a great painter.[64] As Boswell transmitted his own name to posterity with his life of Johnson,[65] so has David left his with the magnificent paintings that are now suspended upon the walls of the palaces of the Louvre, the Tuileries, St. Cloud, Versailles, and even the little Elysee.

After strolling from room to room, we found ourselves in the Salle du Sacre, Diane, Salon de Mars, de Mercure, and D'Apollon. I gazed with my eyes turned to

---

56 The Palace of Versailles, the construction of which was started during the reign of Louis XIV, King of France, 1643–1715
57 On 5 October 1789 thousands of Parisians marched the twelve miles to Versailles, to protest initially against the high price of bread. Events turned violent, and the King, Louis XVI, agreed to the crowd's demands to return to Paris, along with his wife, Marie-Antoinette, and children.
58 Henry Grafton Chapman Jr. (1833–83), son of Maria Weston Chapman, a leading Garrisonian abolitionist
59 Napoleon Bonaparte (1769–1821), Emperor of France, 1804–14, and again in 1815; Joachim Murat (1767–1815), Marshal of France during Napoleon's reign, and King of Naples (1808–15)
60 Antoine-François Callet's 'Allegory of the Battle of Marengo, 14 June 1800' (1800–15)
61 Jean-François Hue's 'Entrance of the French Army into Gênes, 24 June 1800' (1810)
62 François Bouchot's 'Coup of 18 Brumaire' (1840)
63 Jacque-Louis David's 'The Coronation of Napoleon' (1805–7)
64 With the execution of his friend Robespierre in 1794, an act which effectively ended the Reign of Terror (a period of the French Revolution dominated by massacres and public executions), David was also at risk of a similar fate. Although arrested and imprisoned in both 1794 and 1795, he avoided the guillotine.
65 James Boswell (1740–95), the friend and biographer of Samuel Johnson (1709–84)

the ceiling till I was dizzy. The Salon de la Guerre is covered with the most beautiful representations that the mind of man could conceive, or the hand accomplish. Louis XIV. is here in all his glory. No Marie Antoinette will ever do the honors in these halls again.

After spending a whole day in the palace, and several mornings in the gardens, I finally bade adieu to the bronze statue of Louis XIV. that stands in front of the palace, and left Versailles, probably forever.

I am now on the point of quitting the French metropolis. I have occupied the last two days in visiting places of note in the city. I could not resist the inclination to pay a second visit to the Louvre. Another hour was spent in strolling through the Italian Hall, and viewing the master workmanship of Raphael, the prince of painters. Time flies, even in such a place as the Louvre, with all its attractions; and, before I had seen half that I wished, a ponderous clock near by reminded me of an engagement, and I reluctantly tore myself from the splendors of the place.[66]

During the rest of the day I visited the Jardin des Plantes,[67] and spent an hour and a half pleasantly in walking among plants, flowers, and, in fact, everything that could be found in any garden in France. From this place we paid our respects to the Bourse,[68] or Exchange, one of the most superb buildings in the city. The ground floor and sides of the Bourse are of fine marble, and the names of the chief cities in the world are inscribed on the medallions which are under the upper cornice. The interior of the edifice has a most splendid appearance as you enter it.

The cemetery of Père la Chaise[69] was too much talked of by many of our party at the hotel for me to pass it by; so I took it, after the Bourse. Here lie many of the great marshals of France, the resting-place of each marked by the monument that stands over it, except one, which is marked only by a weeping willow and a plain stone at its head. This is the grave of Marshal Ney.[70] I should not have known that it was his, but some unknown hand had written, with black paint, "Bravest of the Brave," on the unlettered stone that stands at the head of the man who followed Napoleon through nearly all his battles, and who was shot, after the occupation of Paris by the allied army. Peace to his ashes! During my ramble through this noted place, I saw several who were hanging fresh wreaths of "everlasting flowers" on the tombs of the departed.

A ride in an omnibus down the Boulevards, and away up the Champs Elysees, brought me to the Arc de Triomphe; and, after ascending a flight of one hundred and sixty-one steps, I was overlooking the city of statuary. This stupendous monument was commenced by Napoleon in 1806; and in 1811 it had only reached the cornice of the base, where it stopped, and it was left for Louis Philippe to finish. The first stone of this monument was laid on the 15th of August, 1806, the birth-day of the man whose battles it was intended to commemorate. A model of the arch was erected for Napoleon to pass through as he was entering the city with Maria Louisa, after their marriage. The inscriptions on the monument are many, and the different scenes here represented are all of the most exquisite workmanship. The genius of

---

66 The Louvre Museum, housed in the Louvre Palace, opened as a museum and gallery in 1793. By the time of Brown's visit to Paris in 1849 it had expanded rapidly to become a major cultural repository.
67 The largest botanical garden in Paris, first opening to the public in 1640
68 Headquarters of the Paris Stock Exchange, built between 1808 and 1826
69 The largest cemetery in Paris, first opened in 1804
70 Michel Ney (1769–1815), military commander with a distinguished record in the French Revolution and Napoleonic Wars

War is summoning the obedient nations to battle. Victory is here crowning Napoleon after his great success in 1810. Fame stands here recording the exploits of the warrior, while conquered cities lie beneath the whole. But it would take more time than I have at command to give anything like a description of this magnificent piece of architecture.

That which seems to take most with Peace Friends is the portion representing an old man taming a bull for agricultural labor; while a young warrior is sheathing his sword, a mother and children sitting at his feet, and Minerva, crowned with laurels, stands shedding her protecting influence over them. The erection of this regal monument is wonderful, to hand down to posterity the triumphs of the man whom we first hear of as a student in the military school at Brienne; whom in 1784 we see in the Ecole Militaire, founded by Louis XV. in 1751; whom again we find at No. 5 Quai de Court, near Rue de Mail; and in 1794 as a lodger at No. 19 Rue de la Michandère. From this he goes to the Hotel Mirabeau, Rue du Dauphin, where he resided when he defeated his enemies on the 13th Vendemaire. The Hotel de la Colonade, Rue Nouve des Capuchins, is his next residence, and where he was married to Josephine. From this hotel he removed to his wife's dwelling in the Rue Chanteriene, No. 52. In 1796 the young general started for Italy, where his conquests paved the way for the ever-memorable 18th Brumaire, that made him Dictator of France. Napoleon was too great now to be satisfied with private dwellings, and we next trace him to the Elysee, St. Cloud, Versailles, the Tuileries, Fontainebleau, and, finally, came his decline, which I need not relate to you.

After visiting the Gobelins,[71] passing through its many rooms, seeing here and there a half-finished piece of tapestry, and meeting a number of the members of the late Peace Congress,[72] who, like myself, had remained behind to see more of the beauties of the French capital than could be seen during the Convention week, I accepted an invitation to dine with a German gentleman at the Palais Royal, and was soon revelling amid the luxuries of the table. I was glad that I had gone to the Palais Royal, for here I had the honor of an introduction to M. Beranger, the poet; and, although I had to converse with him through an interpreter, I enjoyed his company very much. "The people's poet," as he is called, is apparently about seventy years of age, bald on the top of the bead, and rather corpulent, but of active look, and in the enjoyment of good health. Few writers in France have done better service to the cause of political and religious freedom than Pierre Jean de Beranger.[73] He is the dauntless friend and advocate of the downtrodden poor and oppressed, and has often incurred the displeasure of the government by the arrows that he has thrown into their camp. He felt what he wrote; it came straight from his heart, and went directly to the hearts of the people. He expressed himself strongly opposed to slavery, and said, "I don't see how the Americans can reconcile slavery with their professed love of freedom." Dinner out of the way, a walk through the different apartments, and a stroll over the court, and I bade adieu to the Palais Royal, satisfied that I should partake of many worse dinners than I had helped to devour that day.

---

71 A historic tapestry factory and gallery in Paris

72 Brown was chosen by the American Peace Society as a delegate to an International Peace Congress held in Paris in August 1849, where he spoke on the abolition of slavery.

73 Pierre-Jean de Béranger (1780–1857), popular and prolific songwriter and poet, whose writings advocated social justice and were often highly critical of government policy. His poem 'Les nègres et le marionettes' (c.1821) addresses the slave trade.

Few nations are more courteous than the French. Here, the stranger, let him come from what country he may, and be ever so unacquainted with the people and language, is sure of a civil reply to any question that he may ask. With the exception of the egregious blunder I have mentioned of the cabman driving me to the Elysee, I was not laughed at once while in France. [. . .]

Chapter XXVIII

"Look here, upon this picture, and on this."

HAMLET.[74]

No one accustomed to pass through Cheapside[75] could fail to have noticed a good-looking man, neither black nor white, engaged in distributing bills to the thousands who throng that part of the city of London. While strolling through Cheapside, one morning, I saw, for the fiftieth time, Joseph Jenkins, the subject of this chapter, handing out his bills to all who would take them as he thrust them into their hands. I confess that I was not a little amused, and stood for some moments watching and admiring his energy in distributing his papers. A few days after, I saw the same individual in Chelsea, sweeping a crossing; here, too, he was equally as energetic as when I met him in the city. Some days later, while going through Kensington, I heard rather a sweet, musical voice singing a familiar psalm, and on looking round was not a little surprised to find that it was the Cheapside bill-distributor and Chelsea crossing-sweeper. He was now singing hymns, and selling religious tracts. I am fond of patronizing genius, and therefore took one of his tracts and paid him for a dozen.

During the following week, I saw, while going up the city road, that Shakspeare's tragedy of Othello was to be performed at the Eagle Saloon[76] that night, and that the character of the Moor was to be taken by "Selim, an African prince." Having no engagement that evening, I resolved at once to attend, to witness the performance of the "African Roscius,"[77] as he was termed on the bills. It was the same interest that had induced me to go to the Italian opera to see Madames Sontag and Grisi in Norma,[78] and to visit Drury Lane to see Macready take leave of the stage.[79] My expectations were screwed up to the highest point. The excitement caused by the publication of "Uncle Tom's Cabin"[80] had prepared the public for anything in the African line, and I felt that the prince would be sure of a good audience; and in this I was not disappointed, for, as I took my seat in one of the boxes near the stage, I saw that the house was crammed with an orderly company. The curtain was already up when I entered, and Iago and Roderigo were on the stage. After a while Othello came in, and was greeted with thunders of applause, which he very gracefully acknowledged. Just black enough to take his part with out coloring his face, and being tall, with a good figure and an easy carriage, a fine, full and musical voice, he

---

74 *Hamlet* III.iv.54
75 A street in the City of London, historically the financial centre of London
76 A theatre in Hoxton, east London, built in 1830
77 A reference to Quintus Roscius (126–62 BCE), a Roman actor born into slavery
78 Henriette Songat (1806–54), a celebrated German soprano who performed at the Covent Garden Theatre, London, in 1849, and Giulia Grisi (1811–69), an Italian opera singer who also regularly appeared in London
79 William Charles Macready (1793–1873) was a celebrated English actor, who took leave of the stage in a performance of *Macbeth* at Drury Lane, London, in February 1851.
80 Harriet Beecher Stowe's novel *Uncle Tom's Cabin*, published in 1852

was well adapted to the character of Othello. I immediately recognized in the countenance of the Moor a face that I had seen before, but could not at the moment tell where. Who could this "prince" be, thought I. He was too black for Douglass, not black enough for Ward, not tall enough for Garnet, too calm for Delany, figure, though fine, not genteel enough for Remond.[81] However, I was soon satisfied as to who the star was. Reader, would you think it? it was no less a person than Mr. Jenkins, the bill-distributor from Cheapside, and crossing-sweeper from Chelsea! For my own part, I was overwhelmed with amazement, and it was some time before I could realize the fact. He soon showed that he possessed great dramatic power and skill; and his description to the senate of how he won the affections of the gentle Desdemona stamped him at once as an actor of merit. "What a pity," said a lady near me to a gentleman that was by her side, "that a prince of the royal blood of Africa should have to go upon the stage for a living! It is indeed a shame!" When he came to the scene,

> "O, cursed, cursed slave!—whip me, ye devils,
> From the possession of this heavenly sight!
> Blow me about in winds, roast me in sulphur!
> Wash me in steep-down gulfs of liquid fire!
> O, Desdemona Desdemona! dead?
> Dead? O! O! O!"[82]

the effect was indeed grand. When the curtain fell, the prince was called upon the stage, where he was received with deafening shouts of approbation, and a number of bouquets thrown at his feet, which he picked up, bowed, and retired. I went into Cheapside the next morning, at an early hour, to see if the prince had given up his old trade for what I supposed to be a more lucrative one; but I found the hero of the previous night at his post, and giving out his bills as energetically as when I had last soon him. Having to go to the provinces for some months, I lost sight of Mr. Jenkins, and on my return to town did not trouble myself to look him up. More than a year after I had witnessed the representation of Othello at the Eagle, I was walking, one pleasant Sabbath evening, through one of the small streets in the borough, when I found myself in front of a little chapel, where a number of persons were going in. As I was passing on slowly, an elderly man said to me, "I suppose you have come to hear your colored brother preach." "No," I answered; "I was not aware that one was to be here." "Yes," said he; "and a clever man he is, too." As the old man offered to find me a seat, I concluded to go in and hear this son of Africa. The room, which was not large, was already full. I had to wait but a short time before the reverend gentleman made his appearance. He was nearly black, and dressed in a black suit, with high shirt-collar, and an intellectual-looking cravat, that nearly hid his chin. A pair of spectacles covered his eyes. The preacher commenced by reading a portion of Scripture; and then announced that they would sing the twenty-eighth hymn in "the arrangement." O, that voice! I felt sure that I had heard that musical

---

81 Brown here references a number of important Black abolitionist figures: Frederick Douglass (1818–95), Samuel Ringgold Ward (1817–c.66), Henry Highland Garnet (1815–82), Martin Delany (1812–85) and Charles Lenox Remond (1810–73).
82 *Othello* V.ii.290–5

voice before; but where, I could not tell. I was not aware that any of my countrymen were in London; but felt that, whoever he was, he was no discredit to the race; for he was a most eloquent and accomplished orator. His sermon was against the sale and use of intoxicating drinks, and the bad habits of the working classes, of whom his audience was composed.

Although the subject was intensely interesting, I was impatient for it to come to a close, for I wanted to speak to the preacher. But, the evening being warm, and the room heated, the reverend gentleman, on wiping the perspiration from his face (which, by the way, ran very freely), took off his spectacles on one occasion, so that I immediately recognized him, and saved me from going up to the pulpit at the end of the service. Yes; it was the bill-distributor of Cheapside, the crossing-sweeper of Chelsea, the tract-seller and psalm-singer of Kensington, and the Othello of the Eagle Saloon. I could scarcely keep from laughing right out when I discovered this to be the man that I had seen in so many characters. As I was about leaving my seat at the close of the services, the old man who showed me into the chapel asked me if I would not like to be introduced to the minister, and I immediately replied that I would. We proceeded up the aisle, and met the clergyman as he was descending. On seeing me, he did not wait for a formal introduction, but put out his hand and said, "I have seen you so often, sir, that I seem to know you." "Yes," I replied; "we have met several times, and under different circumstances." Without saying more, he invited me to walk with him towards his home, which was in the direction of my own residence. We proceeded; and, during the walk, Mr. Jenkins gave me some little account of his early history. "You think me rather an odd fish, I presume," said he. "Yes," I replied. "You are not the only one who thinks so," continued he. "Although I am not as black as some of my countrymen, I am a native of Africa. Surrounded by some beautiful mountain scenery, and situated between Darfour and Abyssinia, two thousand miles in the interior of Africa, is a small valley going by the name of Tegla. To that valley I stretch forth my affections, giving it the endearing appellation of my native home and fatherland. It was there that I was born, it was there that I received the fond looks of a loving mother, and it was there that I set my feet, for the first time, upon a world full of cares, trials, difficulties and dangers. My father being a farmer, I used to be sent out to take care of his goats. This service I did when I was between seven and eight years of age. As I was the eldest of the boys, my pride was raised in no small degree when I beheld my father preparing a farm for me. This event filled my mind with the grand anticipation of leaving the care of the goats to my brother, who was then beginning to work a little. While my father was making those preparations, I had the constant charge of the goats; and, being accompanied by two other boys, who resided near my father's house, we wandered many miles from home, by which means we acquired a knowledge of the different districts of our country.

"It was while in those rambles with my companions that I became the victim of the slave-trader. We were tied with cords, and taken to Tegla, and thence to Kordofan, which is under the jurisdiction of the Pacha of Egypt. From Kordofan I was brought down to Dongola and Korti, in Nubia,[83] and from thence down the Nile to Cairo; and, after being sold nine times, I became the property of an English gentleman, who brought me to this country and put me into school. But he died before I finished my education, and his family feeling no interest in me, I had to seek

---

83 Dongola and Korti are both towns in Sudan, but at the time of Brown's narrative were part of Egypt.

a living as best I could. I have been employed for some years in distributing hand-bills for a barber in Cheapside in the morning, go to Chelsea and sweep a crossing in the afternoon, and sing psalms and sell religious tracts in the evening. Sometimes I have an engagement to perform at some of the small theatres, as I had when you saw me at the Eagle. I preach for this little congregation over here, and charge them nothing; for I want that the poor should have the Gospel without money and without price. I have now given up distributing bills; I have settled my son in that office. My eldest daughter was married about three months ago; and I have presented her husband with the Chelsea crossing, as my daughter's wedding portion." "Can he make a living at it?" I eagerly inquired. "O, yes! that crossing at Chelsea is worth thirty shillings a week, if it is well swept," said he. "But what do you do for a living for yourself?" I asked. "I am the leader of a band," he continued; "and we play for balls and parties, and three times a week at the Holborn Casino."

By this time we had reached a point where we had to part; and I left Joseph Jenkins, impressed with the idea that he was the greatest genius that I had met in Europe.

Source text

Brown, William Wells, *The American Fugitive in Europe: Sketches of Places and People Abroad* (Boston: John P. Jewett and Company, 1855).

References:

Buzinde, Christine and Iyunolu Osagie, "William Wells Brown: Fugitive Subjectivity, Travel Writing, and the Gaze", *Cultural Studies* 25.3 (2011), 405–25.
Edwards, Justin D., *Exotic Journeys: Exploring the Erotics of U.S. Travel Literature, 1840–1930* (Hanover, NH: University Press of New England, 2001).
Greenspan, Ezra, *William Wells Brown: An African American Life* (New York: W. W. Norton & Company, 2014).

Kahkewāquonāby (Peter Jones) (1802–56)

From Life and Journals of Kah-ke-wa-quo-nā-by: (Rev. Peter Jones,) Wesleyan Missionary *(1860)*

Kahkewāquonāby (Peter Jones) was born in present-day Hamilton, Ontario. His father, born in New York and of Welsh descent, moved to Canada for work. Kahkewāquonāby's mother was Tuhbenahneequay, the daughter of Wahbanosay, a chief of the Mississauga Ojibway; she raised him in the culture and religion of the Ojibwas until he was fourteen, after which he lived with his father and converted to Methodism. He married Eliza Field, whom he met on his first English tour in 1832.

Kahkewāquonāby served as a Methodist preacher who supported First Nations communities. Because of his bilingualism, he was instrumental in the church's project to convert Native peoples in Upper Canada, translating

Biblical texts and hymns into Ojibwe and Mohawk as well as preaching. Kahkewāquonāby was also a successful fund-raiser for the Methodist church in Canada, and travelled to the US and the UK to give speeches and sermons. He drew crowds in their thousands, and would often appear in Native dress; emphasising his exotic appeal in this way is something that he would later regret.

In the following excerpt from Chapter Eleven of the *Life and Journals of Kah-ke-wa-quo-nā-by*, the author provides an account of the first of his three tours to Britain (1832). He discusses his meeting with King William IV at Windsor and notes British interest in his faith and ministry.

From Life and Journals of Kah-ke-wa-quo-nā-by:
(Rev. Peter Jones,) Wesleyan Missionary

Wednesday 4th.—At 1 called at the Colonial Secretary's Office to enquire whether the articles sent by the Indian women, had been presented to Her Majesty the Queen.[84] I was informed that they had been presented some time last summer. I informed the gentleman whom I saw at the Office, that I was going to-morrow to see the King and Queen at Windsor.

Thursday 5th.—I took an early breakfast and set off at 8 o'clock in the morning by a Windsor coach, and arrived there about noon. On getting out of the coach, I saw a gentleman with an Indian and a boy going straight to the Royal Palace. I at once thought that this party were going to be introduced to the King and Queen at the same time I was. I went to the Inn and put on my Indian dress as soon as I could, but to my great disappointment I found I had forgotten my medal, so I had to go without it. On arriving at the Palace, I enquired for Mr. Hudson, the person whom I was recommended to enquire for. He came out and I shewed him the note from Mrs. Vansittart; he replied and said it was all right, and then informed me that a Chief and his son were here, and asked me if I knew them? I said I did not. He then said that they were now going round to see the different apartments, and asked me if I would like to go with them? to which I was glad to consent. I met with the Indian Chief and his party in the room where the King's gold plate is deposited. I shook hands with him, and we tried to talk to each other in our own language, but we could not understand one another, so we were obliged to speak to each other in the English, which, he spoke very well. This Chief and his son were from Nova Scotia, and were of the Micmack Tribe,[85] and belonged to the Roman Catholic religion. Went through the castle and saw all the state rooms, which I had seen before, and we were highly pleased with what we saw. I was struck with the manner in which the kitchen was fitted up. A long table is heated with steam, which keeps all the provisions hot till they go on the King's table. We then went to the King's hot houses and gardens, and the fountain, which were all in the best style. Two or three of the Lords in waiting, or those who surround the throne, were with us all the time, and seemed desirous to shew us that which might be interesting to us.

---

84 Adelaide of Saxe-Meiningen (1792–1849), Queen consort of William IV
85 The Mi'kmaq or Mi'gmaq, a First Nations people indigenous to Canada's Atlantic provinces

At 2 o'clock word came to us that their Majesty's would soon be ready to receive us very graciously. We then went to the waiting room, and in a few minutes we were conducted to the drawing room, where the King and Queen received us very graciously. The gentleman who was with the Micmack Chief, was introduced first to the King, and then introduced his friend the Micmack. I was introduced by one of the Lords. Their Majesties bowed their heads when we bowed to them. They were standing when we entered the room, and stood the whole time while we remained with them. The King asked whether we were of one party, and one of the Lords answered that we were not. He then enquired if we could talk English, and when he was informed that we could, he asked us what nation we belonged to; I told him that I belonged to the Chippeway nation, residing in Upper Canada. He then asked how many of us there were in the nation. I told him about 40 or 50,000. He asked me how old I was. I replied thirty-one. When I was baptized? I told him about nine or ten years ago. What my name was? I replied, Kahkewaquonaby, in the Indian— Peter Jones in the English. Similar questions were put to the Nova Scotia Indian. On being introduced to the King, one of the Lords in waiting informed the King that I wished to present to him a copy of the Chippeway Translation of the Gospel of St. John,[86] which he received out of my hand and opened it, and said "Very good." Some one asked who was the translator. The Queen then replied, "It is his own." The King asked the Micmack if he was a Catholic; to which he replied "Yes." The King then pointing to me, said to him, "He is not." I told the Queen that the Indian women in Canada had sent by me a few articles of Indian work, to be presented to Her Majesty, which I had sent to Lord Goderich. She replied that she had received them, and was happy to accept them, and hoped the Indian women would do well in their undertaking. The King and those around him talked for some time about our dress. The King remarked that my dress was the real Chippeway costume. The Nova Scotia Indian's son, the King said, was a complete model of the American Indians; and that he should have known him to belong to that country, if he had seen him any where in the street. After being with them about half an hour, the King made a signal that the interview was over, so we bowed to them, and retired with the Lords into a lower room, where we sat down to take a lunch.

We had roasted chickens, beef, potatoes, tarts, wines, &c., and ate out of silver dishes. I ate very heartily of the roasted chickens and potatoes. The gentleman at the head of the table, filled his glass full of champagne, and proposed the King's health. All rose up and drank the King's health. After eating a little while, the same gentleman said, "The Queen" upon which all rose up and drank the Queen's health. I understand one of the gentleman to say, "The King's squaw."[87] Before we rose up from the table, a message was sent to us that Lady— and the family would like to see the Indian Chiefs after lunch. Another word came to inform us that the King had ordered two medals to be struck and presented to the two Chiefs as soon as possible. After dinner we went into a long beautiful hall, where we met the ladies and the children belonging to the Royal family, amongst whom was Prince George.[88] Some of the children shook hands with us. After this we were shown the King's private apartments, which were the most beautiful I ever saw—all glittered with

---

86 *The Gospel According to St. John. Translated into the Chippeway Tongue by John Jones, and Revised and Corrected by Peter Jones, Indian Teachers* (London: British and Foreign Bible Society, 1831)
87 An offensive term today
88 George FitzClarence, 1st Earl of Munster (1794–1842), eldest illegitimate son of William IV

gold tapestry. We were also taken to see the horses belonging to the Royal family, and they were the most handsome creatures I ever saw.

I forgot to mention in its proper place, that while we were present with their Majesty's, one of the Lords in waiting, asked me in their presence if I was a Wesleyan Methodist. I replied I was, and that they (the Methodists) were the first who came and preached to us. I moreover replied to the gentleman who asked me the question, that the doctrines taught by the Methodists were the same as those of the Church of England, only differing a little in the mode of government. He said there was no difference. Mr. Hudson told me that when the Queen received those articles sent by the Indian women, she had ordered him to send a reply to their address, but not knowing my address, he did not know where to send it, and consequently it had been omitted till the present time. He would now be most happy to forward the same to me. So I gave him my address in London, where he might send the Queen's talk and also the Medal. The Nova Scotia Chief, I was informed, came over to England to purchase farming implements, which business he and his people were going to follow. Left the Palace about 4, P. M.; called and took tea with Mr. Ford, who afterwards drove me in his gig to the Bath road, where I met with a coach and rode to London, highly gratified with my visit to our great father the King, and our great mother the Queen. The King and Queen were dressed very plain, and were very open, and seemed not at all to be proud. They both looked very healthy and in good spirits. Long may they live to be a blessing to their nation and people! May God direct them in the good and right path of righteousness! God bless the King and Queen!

Source text

Kahkewãquonãby (Peter Jones), *Life and Journals of Kah-ke-wa-quo-nã-by: (Rev. Peter Jones,) Wesleyan Missionary* (Toronto: Anson Green, 1860).

References

Smith, Donald B., *Sacred Feathers: The Reverend Peter Jones (Kahkewaquonaby) and the Mississauga Indians*, 2nd edn (Toronto: University of Toronto Press, 2013).
Weaver, Jace, 'Native American Authors and Their Communities', *Wicazo Sa Review* 12.1 (Spring 1997), 47–87.

Samuel Langhorne Clemens (Mark Twain) 1835–1910

From The Innocents Abroad, or The New Pilgrims' Progress (1869)

Perhaps best known for *The Adventures of Tom Sawyer* (1876) and *The Adventures of Huckleberry Finn* (1884), Twain offers an ethnographic and slyly humorous account of American travellers undertaking a chartered voyage to Europe and the Holy Land in *The Innocents Abroad*. The book was Twain's most commercially successful publication and remains a highly popular travel guide.

The 'Mark Twain' that narrates this book is a self-consciously imaginative creation. His narrator is unapologetically sceptical of the reverence directed at all things European; the historical moment of the voyage, the period after the Civil War, was one in which a more confident national consciousness felt less beholden to Europhile allegiances. Twain's ideal observer is one who is unencumbered by previous tourist accounts of culture, able instead (as he writes in the Preface to *The Innocents Abroad*) to 'see Europe and the East if he looked at them with his own eyes instead of those who traveled in countries before him' (v). In a lecture called 'The American Vandal', delivered after his return to the US, he would celebrate 'the roving, independent, free-and-easy character of that class of travelling Americans who are not elaborately educated, cultured and refined, and gilded and filigreed with the ineffable graces of the first society' (27).

The excerpt from Chapter 23 exhibits these qualities of a determined American refusal to be impressed by the seductions of Venetian high culture. Twain employs a strategy of familiarisation, making the exotic or unique appear commonplace, so that the hierarchies of value between Old and New Worlds collapse into each other. One distinction that is drawn comes as a result of the narrator's encounter with a Black tour guide, whose enslaved parents had moved to Italy from South Carolina. His linguistic fluency and sophisticated knowledge of European art impresses Twain, noting a cultivation beyond the expertise of the Americans that the guide encounters. The meeting between the two men enables Twain to reflect on the relative status of race relations in Italy and the US.

From The Innocents Abroad, or The New Pilgrims' Progress

The Venetian gondola is as free and graceful, in its gliding movement, as a serpent. It is twenty or thirty feet long, and is narrow and deep, like a canoe; its sharp bow and stern sweep upward from the water like the horns of a crescent with the abruptness of the curve slightly modified.

The bow is ornamented with a steel comb with a battle-ax attachment which threatens to cut passing boats in two occasionally, but never does. The gondola is painted black because in the zenith of Venetian magnificence the gondolas became too gorgeous altogether, and the Senate decreed that all such display must cease, and a solemn, unembellished black be substituted. [...] Reverence for the hallowed Past and its traditions keeps the dismal fashion in force now that the compulsion exists no longer. So let it remain. It is the color of mourning. Venice mourns. The stern of the boat is decked over and the gondolier stands there. He uses a single oar—a long blade, of course, for he stands nearly erect. [...] I am afraid I study the gondolier's marvelous skill more than I do the sculptured palaces we glide among. He cuts a corner so closely, now and then, or misses another gondola by such an imperceptible hair-breadth that I feel myself "scrooching," as the children say, just as one does when a buggy wheel grazes his elbow. But he makes all his calculations with the nicest precision, and goes darting in and out among a Broadway confusion of busy craft with the easy confidence of the educated hackman. He never makes a mistake. [...]

We sit in the cushioned carriage-body of a cabin, with the curtains drawn, and smoke, or read, or look out upon the passing boats, the houses, the bridges, the people, and enjoy ourselves much more than we could in a buggy jolting over our cobble-stone pavements at home. This is the gentlest, pleasantest locomotion we have ever known. [...]

We see the ladies go out shopping, in the most natural way, and flit from street to street and from store to store, just in the good old fashion, except that they leave the gondola, instead of a private carriage, waiting at the curbstone a couple of hours for them,—waiting while they make the nice young clerks pull down tons and tons of silks and velvets and moire antiques;[89] [...] And they always have their purchases sent home just in the good old way. Human nature is very much the same all over the world; and it is so like my dear native home to see a Venetian lady go into a store and buy ten cents' worth of blue ribbon and have it sent home in a scow.[90] Ah, it is these little touches of nature that move one to tears in these far-off foreign lands. [...]

We have been pretty much every where in our gondola. We have bought beads and photographs in the stores, and wax matches in the Great Square of St. Mark.[91] The last remark suggests a digression. Every body goes to this vast square in the evening. The military bands play in the centre of it and countless couples of ladies and gentlemen promenade up and down on either side, and platoons of them are constantly drifting away toward the old Cathedral, and by the venerable column with the Winged Lion of St. Mark on its top,[92] and out to where the boats lie moored; and other platoons are as constantly arriving from the gondolas and joining the great throng. Between the promenaders and the side-walks are seated hundreds and hundreds of people at small tables, smoking and taking *granita*, (a first cousin to ice-cream;) on the side-walks are more employing themselves in the same way. [...] Very many of the young women are exceedingly pretty and dress with rare good taste. We are gradually and laboriously learning the ill-manners of staring them unflinchingly in the face—not because such conduct is agreeable to us, but because it is the custom of the country and they say the girls like it. We wish to learn all the curious, outlandish ways of all the different countries, so that we can "show off" and astonish people when we get home. We wish to excite the envy of our untraveled friends with our strange foreign fashions which we can't shake off. All our passengers are paying strict attention to this thing, with the end in view which I have mentioned. The gentle reader will never, never know what a consummate ass he can become, until he goes abroad. I speak now, of course, in the supposition that the gentle reader has not been abroad, and therefore is not already a consummate ass. If the case be otherwise, I beg his pardon and extend to him the cordial hand of fellowship and call him brother. I shall always delight to meet an ass after my own heart when I shall have finished my travels.

---

89 A textile (often silk) with a wavy appearance
90 A flat-bottomed barge
91 Piazza San Marco, the main public square in Venice
92 St Mark's Campanile

On this subject let me remark that there are Americans abroad in Italy who have actually forgotten their mother tongue in three months—forgot it in France. They can not even write their address in English in a hotel register. I append these evidences, which I copied *verbatim* from the register of a hotel in a certain Italian city:

"John P. Whitcomb, *Etats Unis*.

"Wm. L. Ainsworth, *travailleur* (he meant traveler, I suppose,) *Etats Unis*.

"George P. Morton *et fils, d'Amerique*.

"Lloyd B. Williams, *et trois amis, ville de Boston, Amerique*.

"J. Ellsworth Baker, *tout de suite de France, place de naissance Amerique, destination la Grand Bretagne*."

I love this sort of people. A lady passenger of ours tells of a fellow-citizen of hers who spent eight weeks in Paris and then returned home and addressed his dearest old bosom friend Herbert as Mr. "Er-bare!" He apologized, though, and said, "'Pon my soul it is aggravating, but I cahn't help it—I have got so used to speaking nothing but French, my dear Erbare—damme there it goes again!— got so used to French pronunciation that I cahn't get rid of it—it is positively annoying, I assure you." This entertaining idiot, whose name was Gordon, allowed himself to be hailed three times in the street before he paid any attention, and then begged a thousand pardons and said he had grown so accustomed to hearing himself addressed as "M'sieu Gor-r-dong," with a roll to the r, that he had forgotten the legitimate sound of his name! He wore a rose in his button-hole; he gave the French salutation—two flips of the hand in front of the face; he called Paris *Pairree* in ordinary English conversation; [...] he cultivated a moustache and imperial,[93] and did what else he could to suggest to the beholder his pet fancy that he resembled Louis Napoleon—and in a spirit of thankfulness which is entirely unaccountable, considering the slim foundation there was for it, he praised his Maker that he was *as* he was, and went on enjoying his little life just the same as if he really *had* been deliberately designed and erected by the great Architect of the Universe.

Think of our Whitcombs, and our Ainsworths and our Williamses writing themselves down in dilapidated French in foreign hotel registers! We laugh at Englishmen, when we are at home, for sticking so sturdily to their national ways and customs, but we look back upon it from abroad very forgivingly. It is not pleasant to see an American thrusting his nationality forward *obtrusively* in a foreign land, but Oh, it is pitiable to see him making of himself a thing that is neither male nor female, neither fish, flesh, nor fowl—a poor, miserable, hermaphrodite Frenchman! [...]

We have seen famous pictures until our eyes are weary with looking at them and refuse to find interest in them any longer. And what wonder, when there are twelve hundred pictures by Palma the Younger[94] in Venice and fifteen hundred by Tintoretto?[95] And behold there are Titians[96] and the works of other artists in proportion. We have seen Titian's celebrated Cain and Abel, his David and Goliath, his Abraham's Sacrifice. We have seen Tintoretto's monster picture,[97] which is seventy-four feet long and I do not know how many feet high, and thought it a very commodious picture. We have seen pictures of martyrs enough, and saints enough, to regenerate the world. I ought not to confess it, but still, since one has no opportunity in America to acquire a critical

---

93 A small beard growing beneath the lower lip
94 Giacomo Palma il Giovane (*c.*1540–1628), Venetian painter
95 (1518–94), Venetian painter
96 Tiziano Vecelli, or Titian (*c.*1488–1576), Venetian painter, whose works 'Cain and Abel' (1544), 'David and Goliath' (1544) and 'The Sacrifice of Isaac' (1542) are referenced here
97 A reference to Tintoretto's painting 'Il Paradiso', completed in 1594

judgment in art, and since I could not hope to become educated in it in Europe in a few short weeks, I may therefore as well acknowledge with such apologies as may be due, that to me it seemed that when I had seen one of these martyrs I had seen them all. [. . .]

It seems to me that whenever I glory to think that for once I have discovered an ancient painting that is beautiful and worthy of all praise, the pleasure it gives me is an infallible proof that it is *not* a beautiful picture and not in any wise worthy of commendation. This very thing has occurred more times than I can mention, in Venice. In every single instance the guide has crushed out my swelling enthusiasm with the remark:

"It is nothing—it is of the *Renaissance*."

I did not know what in the mischief the Renaissance was, and so always I had to simply say,

"Ah! so it is—I had not observed it before."

I could not bear to be ignorant before a cultivated negro, the offspring of a South Carolina slave. But it occurred too often for even my self-complacency, did that exasperating "It is nothing—it is of the *Renaissance*." I said at last:

"*Who* is this Renaissance? Where did he come from? Who gave him permission to cram the Republic with his execrable daubs?"

We learned, then, that Renaissance was not a man; that *renaissance* was a term used to signify what was at best but an imperfect rejuvenation of art. The guide said that after Titian's time and the time of the other great names we had grown so familiar with, high art declined; then it partially rose again—an inferior sort of painters sprang up, and these shabby pictures were the work of their hands. Then I said, in my heat, that I "wished to goodness high art had declined five hundred years sooner." The Renaissance pictures suit me very well, though sooth to say its school were too much given to painting real men and did not indulge enough in martyrs.

The guide I have spoken of is the only one we have had yet who knew any thing. He was born in South Carolina, of slave parents. They came to Venice while he was an infant. He has grown up here. He is well educated. He reads, writes, and speaks English, Italian, Spanish, and French, with perfect facility; is a worshipper of art and thoroughly conversant with it; knows the history of Venice by heart and never tires of talking of her illustrious career. He dresses better than any of us, I think, and is daintily polite. Negroes are deemed as good as white people, in Venice, and so this man feels no desire to go back to his native land. His judgment is correct.

Source text

Twain, Mark, *The Innocents Abroad, or The New Pilgrims' Progress* (Hartford, CT: American Publishing Company, 1869).

References

Kaplan, Paul H. D., 'Contraband Guides: Twain and His Contemporaries on the Black Presence in Venice', *Massachusetts Review* 44.1–2 (2003), 182–202.

Morris, Roy, Jr, *American Vandal: Mark Twain Abroad* (Cambridge, MA: Harvard University Press, 2015).

Twain, Mark, 'The American Vandal Abroad', *Mark Twain Speaking*, ed. Paul Fatout (Iowa City, IA: University of Iowa Press, 1976), 27–36.

Figure 10.4 'The Ladies' Cabin', *Harper's New Monthly Magazine* 41 (July 1870), 194. Courtesy HathiTrust.

Figure 10.5 'Horrors of the Emigrant Ship – Scene in the Hold of the "James Foster, Jr."', *Harper's Weekly* 13 (27 March 1869), 204. Courtesy HathiTrust.

Jack London (1876–1916)

From **The People of the Abyss** *(1903)*

Jack London was a prolific US journalist, novelist, short-story writer and political activist, who, at the time of his early death, had acquired an international reputation and significant wealth, for his writing career coincided with the development and expansion of US periodical culture. A life-long socialist, his belief in the inevitable ascendancy of the working-class informs several of his works, including *The Iron Heel* (1908), *War of the Classes* (1905) and *The People of the Abyss*. His work as a journalist saw him report on the Russo-Japanese War in 1904 for the *San Francisco Examiner*. Prior to this, in 1902 London lived in the East End of London for several weeks, experiencing the conditions of workhouse living and the hardships of extreme poverty. There were a number of earlier models of extended reportage on urban life, on both sides of the Atlantic, of which London was very aware – most famously Friedrich Engels's *The Condition of the Working Class in England* (1845) and Jacob Riis's *How the Other Half Lives* (1890), an exposé of New York slum living. George Orwell's later books, *Down and Out in Paris and London* (1933) and *The Road to Wigan Pier* (1937), are influenced by London's strategy of immersive journalism.

Our excerpt, the opening chapter, demonstrates London's awareness of how the visible and oral markers of class – clothes, speech – once acquired generate new forms of social interaction and (potential) political solidarity. London's desire to experience the conditions of East End life are also explicitly set apart from the more conventional aspirations of US tourism.

From **The People of the Abyss**

CHAPTER I—THE DESCENT
Christ look upon us in this city.
And keep our sympathy and pity
  Fresh, and our faces heavenward;
  Lest we grow hard.

           THOMAS ASHE.[98]

"But you can't do it, you know," friends said, to whom I applied for assistance in the matter of sinking myself down into the East End of London. "You had better see the police for a guide," they added, on second thought, painfully endeavoring to adjust themselves to the psychological processes of a madman who had come to them with better credentials than brains.

---

98 From Thomas Ashe (1836–89), 'London Lyrics', ll.1–4

"But I don't want to see the police," I protested. "What I wish to do, is to go down into the East End and see things for myself. I wish to know how those people are living there, and why they are living there, and what they are living for. In short, I am going to live there myself."

"You don't want to *live* down there!" everybody said, with disapprobation writ large upon their faces. "Why, it is said there are places where a man's life isn't worth tu'pence."

"The very places I wish to see," I broke in.

"But you can't, you know," was the unfailing rejoinder.

"Which is not what I came to see you about," I answered brusquely, somewhat nettled by their incomprehension. "I am a stranger here, and I want you to tell me what you know of the East End, in order that I may have something to start on."

"But we know nothing of the East End. It is over there, somewhere." And they waved their hands vaguely in the direction where the sun on rare occasions may be seen to rise.

"Then I shall go to Cook's,"[99] I announced.

"Oh yes," they said, with relief. "Cook's will be sure to know."

But O Cook, O Thomas Cook & Son, pathfinders and trail-clearers, living sign-posts to all the world and bestowers of first aid to bewildered travellers—unhesitatingly and instantly, with ease and celerity, could you send me to Darkest Africa or Innermost Thibet, but to the East End of London, barely a stone's throw distant from Ludgate Circus, you know not the way!

"You can't do it, you know," said the human emporium of routes and fares at Cook's Cheapside branch. "It is so—hem—so unusual."

"Consult the police," he concluded authoritatively, when I had persisted. "We are not accustomed to taking travellers to the East End; we receive no call to take them there, and we know nothing whatsoever about the place at all."

"Never mind that," I interposed, to save myself from being swept out of the office by his flood of negations. "Here's something you can do for me. I wish you to understand in advance what I intend doing, so that in case of trouble you may be able to identify me."

"Ah, I see; should you be murdered, we would be in position to identify the corpse."

He said it so cheerfully and cold-bloodedly that on the instant I saw my stark and mutilated cadaver stretched upon a slab where cool waters trickle ceaselessly, and him I saw bending over and sadly and patiently identifying it as the body of the insane American who *would* see the East End.

"No, no," I answered; "merely to identify me in case I get into a scrape with the 'bobbies.'" This last I said with a thrill; truly, I was gripping hold of the vernacular.

"That," he said, "is a matter for the consideration of the Chief Office."

"It is so unprecedented, you know," he added apologetically.

The man at the Chief Office hemmed and hawed. "We make it a rule," he explained, "to give no information concerning our clients."

"But in this case," I urged, "it is the client who requests you to give the information concerning himself."

Again he hemmed and hawed.

---

99 Thomas Cook & Son, originally founded in 1841, was a travel agency that organised tours within Great Britain and internationally. By the time of London's visit to its Cheapside office in London, it also had branches throughout Europe, Australasia and North America.

"Of course," I hastily anticipated, "I know it is unprecedented, but—"

"As I was about to remark," he went on steadily, "it is unprecedented, and I don't think we can do anything for you."

However, I departed with the address of a detective who lived in the East End, and took my way to the American consul-general. And here, at last, I found a man with whom I could 'do business.' There was no hemming and hawing, no lifted brows, open incredulity, or blank amazement. In one minute I explained myself and my project, which he accepted as a matter of course. In the second minute he asked my age, height, and weight, and looked me over. And in the third minute, as we shook hands at parting, he said: "All right, Jack. I'll remember you and keep track."

I breathed a sigh of relief. Having burnt my ships behind me, I was now free to plunge into that human wilderness of which nobody seemed to know anything. But at once I encountered a new difficulty in the shape of my cabby, a gray-whiskered and eminently decorous personage, who had imperturbably driven me for several hours about the 'City.'

"Drive me down to the East End," I ordered, taking my seat.

"Where, sir?" he demanded with frank surprise.

"To the East End, anywhere. Go on."

The hansom pursued an aimless way for several minutes, then came to a puzzled stop. The aperture above my head was uncovered, and the cabman peered down perplexedly at me.

"I say," he said, "wot plyce yer wanter go?"

"East End," I repeated. "Nowhere in particular. Just drive me around, anywhere."

"But wot's the haddress, sir?"

"See here!" I thundered. "Drive me down to the East End, and at once!"

It was evident that he did not understand, but he withdrew his head, and grumblingly started his horse.

Nowhere in the streets of London may one escape the sight of abject poverty, while five minutes' walk from almost any point will bring one to a slum; but the region my hansom was now penetrating was one unending slum. The streets were filled with a new and different race of people, short of stature, and of wretched or beer-sodden appearance. We rolled along through miles of bricks and squalor, and from each cross street and alley flashed long vistas of bricks and misery. Here and there lurched a drunken man or woman, and the air was obscene with sounds of jangling and squabbling. At a market, tottery old men and women were searching in the garbage thrown in the mud for rotten potatoes, beans, and vegetables, while little children clustered like flies around a festering mass of fruit, thrusting their arms to the shoulders into the liquid corruption, and drawing forth morsels but partially decayed, which they devoured on the spot.

Not a hansom did I meet with in all my drive, while mine was like an apparition from another and better world, the way the children ran after it and alongside. And as far as I could see were the solid walls of brick, the slimy pavements, and the screaming streets; and for the first time in my life the fear of the crowd smote me. It was like the fear of the sea; and the miserable multitudes, street upon street, seemed so many waves of a vast and malodorous sea, lapping about me and threatening to well up and over me.

"Stepney, sir; Stepney Station," the cabby called down.

I looked about. It was really a railroad station, and he had driven desperately to it as the one familiar spot he had ever heard of in all that wilderness.

"Well?" I said.

He spluttered unintelligibly, shook his head, and looked very miserable. "I'm a strynger 'ere," he managed to articulate. "An' if yer don't want Stepney Station, I'm blessed if I know wotcher do want."

"I'll tell you what I want," I said. "You drive along and keep your eye out for a shop where old clothes are sold. Now, when you see such a shop, drive right on till you turn the corner, then stop and let me out."

I could see that he was growing dubious of his fare, but not long afterwards he pulled up to the curb and informed me that an old-clothes shop was to be found a bit of the way back.

"Won'tcher py me?" he pleaded. "There's seven an' six owin' me."

"Yes," I laughed, "and it would be the last I'd see of you."

"Lord lumme, but it'll be the last I see of you if yer don't py me," he retorted.

But a crowd of ragged onlookers had already gathered around the cab, and I laughed again and walked back to the old clothes shop.

Here the chief difficulty was in making the shopman understand that I really and truly wanted old clothes. But after fruitless attempts to press upon me new and impossible coats and trousers, he began to bring to light heaps of old ones, looking mysterious the while and hinting darkly. This he did with the palpable intention of letting me know that he had 'piped my lay,' in order to bulldose me, through fear of exposure, into paying heavily for my purchases. A man in trouble, or a high-class criminal from across the water, was what he took my measure for—in either case, a person anxious to avoid the police.

But I disputed with him over the outrageous difference between prices and values, till I quite disabused him of the notion, and he settled down to drive a hard bargain with a hard customer. In the end I selected a pair of stout though well-worn trousers, a frayed jacket with one remaining button, a pair of brogans[100] which had plainly seen service where coal was shovelled, a thin leather belt, and a very dirty cloth cap. My underclothing and socks, however, were new and warm, but of the sort that any American waif, down in his luck, could acquire in the ordinary course of events.

"I must sy yer a sharp 'un," he said, with counterfeit admiration, as I handed over the ten shillings finally agreed upon for the outfit. "Blimey, if you ain't ben up an' down Petticut Lane[101] afore now. Yer trouseys is wuth five bob to hany man, an' a docker 'ud give two an' six for the shoes, to sy nothin' of the coat an' cap an' new stoker's singlet an' hother things."

"How much will you give me for them?" I demanded suddenly. "I paid you ten bob for the lot, and I'll sell them back to you, right now, for eight! Come, it's a go!"

But he grinned and shook his head, and though I had made a good bargain, I was unpleasantly aware that he had made a better one.

I found the cabby and a policeman with their heads together, but the latter, after looking me over sharply, and particularly scrutinizing the bundle under my arm, turned away and left the cabby to wax mutinous by himself. And not a step would he budge till I paid him the seven shillings and sixpence owing him. Where-upon he was willing to drive me to the ends of the earth, apologizing profusely for his insistence, and explaining that one ran across queer customers in London Town.

---

100 Ankle-high boots
101 Petticoat Lane Market, a clothing and fashion market in East London

But he drove me only to Highbury Vale, in North London, where my luggage was waiting for me. Here, next day, I took off my shoes (not without regret for their lightness and comfort), and my soft, grey travelling suit, and, in fact, all my clothing; and proceeded to array myself in the clothes of the other and unimaginable men, who must have been indeed unfortunate to have had to part with such rags for the pitiable sums obtainable from a dealer.

Inside my stoker's singlet, in the armpit, I sewed a gold sovereign (an emergency sum certainly of modest proportions); and inside my stoker's singlet I put myself. And then I sat down and moralised upon the fair years and fat, which had made my skin soft and brought the nerves close to the surface; for the singlet was rough and raspy as a hair shirt, and I am confident that the most rigorous of ascetics suffer no more than I did in the ensuing twenty-four hours.

The remainder of my costume was fairly easy to put on, though the brogans, or brogues, were quite a problem. As stiff and hard as if made of wood, it was only after a prolonged pounding of the uppers with my fists that I was able to get my feet into them at all. Then, with a few shillings, a knife, a handkerchief, and some brown papers and flake tobacco stowed away in my pockets, I thumped down the stairs and said good-bye to my foreboding friends. As I paused out of the door, the 'help,' a comely, middle-aged woman, could not conquer a grin that twisted her lips and separated them till the throat, out of involuntary sympathy, made the uncouth animal noises we are wont to designate as 'laughter.'

No sooner was I out on the streets than I was impressed by the difference in status effected by my clothes. All servility vanished from the demeanor of the common people with whom I came in contact. Presto! in the twinkling of an eye, so to say, I had become one of them. My frayed and out-at-elbows jacket was the badge and advertisement of my class, which was their class. It made me of like kind, and in place of the fawning and too respectful attention I had hitherto received, I now shared with them a comradeship. The man in corduroy and dirty neckerchief no longer addressed me as 'sir' or 'governor.' It was 'mate' now—and a fine and hearty word, with a tingle to it, and a warmth and gladness, which the other term does not possess. Governor! It smacks of mastery, and power, and high authority—the tribute of the man who is under to the man on top, delivered in the hope that he will let up a bit and ease his weight. Which is another way of saying that it is an appeal for alms.

This brings me to a delight I experienced in my rags and tatters which is denied the average American abroad. The European traveller from the States, who is not a Croesus, speedily finds himself reduced to a chronic state of self-conscious sordidness by the hordes of cringing robbers who clutter his steps from dawn till dark, and deplete his pocket-book in a way that puts compound interest to the blush.

In my rags and tatters I escaped the pestilence of tipping, and encountered men on a basis of equality. Nay, before the day was out I turned the tables, and said, most gratefully, "Thank you, sir," to a gentleman whose horse I held, and who dropped a penny into my eager palm.

Other changes I discovered were wrought in my condition by my new garb. In crossing crowded thoroughfares I found I had to be, if anything, more lively in avoiding vehicles, and it was strikingly impressed upon me that my life had cheapened in direct ratio with my clothes. When before I inquired the way of a policeman, I was usually asked, "Bus or 'ansom, sir?" But now the query became, "Walk or ride?" Also, at the railway stations, a third-class ticket was now shoved out to me as a matter of course.

But there was compensation for it all. For the first time I met the English lower classes face to face, and knew them for what they were. When loungers and work-men, at street corners and in public-houses, talked with me, they talked as one man to another, and they talked as natural men should talk, without the least idea of getting anything out of me for what they talked or the way they talked.

And when at last I made into the East End, I was gratified to find that the fear of the crowd no longer haunted me. I had become a part of it. The vast and malodor-ous sea had welled up and over me, or I had slipped gently into it, and there was nothing fearsome about it—with the one exception of the stoker's singlet.

Source text

London, Jack, *The People of the Abyss* (New York: Macmillan, 1903).

References

McLaughlin, Joseph, *Writing the Urban Jungle: Reading Empire in London from Doyle to Eliot* (Charlottesville, VA: University Press of Virginia, 2000).
Peluso, Robert, 'Gazing at Royalty: Jack London's "The People of the Abyss" and the Emergence of American Imperialism', in Leonard Cassuto and Jeanne Campbell Rees-man (eds), *Rereading Jack London* (Stanford, CA: Stanford University Press), 55–74.

Djuna Barnes (1892–1982)

'Why Go Abroad—See Europe in Brooklyn!' (1913)

Djuna Barnes was a US novelist and journalist, most famous for her 1936 novel, *Nightwood*, now regarded as an important work of modernist fic-tion. She began her writing career in 1913 as a freelance illustrator and journalist for the *Brooklyn Daily Eagle*, a popular newspaper first appear-ing in New York since 1841. Her reputation as a journalist grew, and her work was published in several other newspapers, including *McCall's*, *The World* and the *New York Press*, often accompanied by her own drawings. Much of her journalism is subjective, based on observation or experience. In the 1920s Barnes lived in Paris, interviewing expatriate writers and art-ists for US publications, as well as becoming part of a Parisian lesbian life that she would go on to satirise gently in her 1928 work *Ladies Almanack*.

The example of Barnes's journalism that we include here is indicative of her mode of reportage – mobile, anecdotal, observational, mildly ironic. It is one of a number of expressions of urban America's cosmopolitan credentials: for instance, Henry James's *The American Scene* (1907) had worried about the visibility of European immigrants to New York, and in 1927 Ford Madox Ford would state clearly his belief in that city's cosmopolitan exceptionalism in *New York Is Not America*. Barnes's report from a bustling Brooklyn looks with affection at the national diversity on display in America's marketplace.

'Why Go Abroad—See Europe in Brooklyn!'

Wallabout Market Has the Real Flavor of Continental Towns.

Atmosphere of Foreign Lands Pervades Squares Where Produce Is Bartered.

Three thousand miles away, on a foreign shore, pictured to us in the graphic language of men who went and saw, and, seeing, wrote; painted for us by dreamers who unite conception with oil; dwelt on by us as something yet to realize, of its sorrow, of its charm, of its serenity; of its splendor of color, united with splendor of line; of the splendor of little things and the splendor of great – this is the land of our hearts. We are going to it when we have saved enough; some day when the teapot bank can hold no more, or some day when our uncles decide to rent a seat in ether, when we are grown. This is the land that is swarming with incidents and is profligate with gasps. We are even now in the throes of the mental shiver of expectancy.

And yet we have opportunity, we stay-at-homes, to go down to it and see it for ourselves. How many of us have discovered it? Just how many know that Europe is in Brooklyn?

Wallabout![102] Wallabout! Wallabout! Why in the world haven't you sensed it? Here you can see the colored quilt that covers a spavined horse, the tambourine that receives the proceeds of a soul in that soul's metal; music which brings forth a dime or an onion from the listeners in the shops.

Why, oh, why, my feet, have you not dodged the pungent, omnipotent pepper, the crescendo of screaming peanuts roasting, the howl of the hucksters and the background of tired, silent horses ruminating in the sunset?

Over this presides the genius of Time, represented by the clock in the market square, in the tower house where sits the market clerk over his ledger counting up the quarters he has collected from the farmer for standing rent in the aisles of the square. As its hands come around toward 5 you know that the few who are widest awake are due. Between the clock and the restaurant abutting, with tall glasses of spaghetti and crushed brown figs, hangs a low, swinging, lax line of clothes beating a flapping tatoo upon the blue of an awakening sky. Giuseppi grew up to its tune. The clock and the stores and the streets and the very city itself he has learned to sense by smell, as he handles his bananas. Giuseppi soaked in it, no longer knows that his very coat tails spell Florida; that his floating tie and his rakish, bagging shirt all are weaved with the flax of fruit.

Life is changing, but Wallabout goes on, stark calm in the gray of a winter dawn. Night is pierced by an upward thrust chimney which smokes in great lazy gasps; low boats purr in the harbour and the wet canvas flaps upon a wet deck and there is the spray and the rime and the tumult of the sea, and then the dusk lifts and the houses become buildings and the windows and doors take form and the cobbles come into existence as slowly stealing in from the forty roads of produce, the horses come. Carts piled to the point of satisfaction with cabbages and turnips and beets, and upon the seats, their heads upon their breasts, the Long Island farmers sleep as they bring our dinner in.

From the hold of the dusky boats that murmured in the dawn come the imports, the grapes, the nuts, the figs, up from sheltering decks, hauled and cursed over by men in open shirts and dirt colored trousers. So comes our dessert.

And then we must sing of the "mulligan,"[103] that brews in the pot of our little Italy, that pot of soup that simmers upon the hob in some humble home; that

---

102 In the early twentieth-century Wallabout Market on the Brooklyn waterfront was the second largest food market in the world. It remained in operation until 1941.

103 A term for an Irishman, and mulligan stew is an Irish dish made from scraps of meat, vegetables and potatoes.

lyrical street-gathered mulligan, gleaned by women in monstrously tucked skirts and enveloping shawls, caught at with furtive eyes, for even though it is not forbidden, the getting makes it sweet.

By twelve the market must be clear of carts; and rubbish men and women make room for the street cleaners, who gather up anything that may have been overlooked. The square has to be cleaned for the night renting, when the 6 o'clock loads come in. The commission merchant has got through handling the beets and the cauliflower and the beans and the celery. He has put his price on the load as it stands, and he has already by 12, disposed of it all to the merchants of the market. He folds his hands and loiters about waiting for the next line, and the marketeers handle the goods and smell of the fruits and count up their profit and their loss and never seem to know that they have been done out of so many cents to the pound by a few yards, for these Long Island farmers stand within a block of their markets and yet they wait for the commission merchant to buy first.

Every bit of broken box is reduced to kindling and run off with by bare-legged boys with their soap box carts, every hoop and every nail and every scrap of paper is likewise collected and the busy mother stands behind and goads with little hissing foreign curses and menacing circles of the arm.

Life, bustle, color, Europe, barter, gain, loss, Wallabout, Wallabout, Wallabout, somebody, anybody, something is here to be learned. No trip to the foreign land is needed, if it's atmosphere you want. No need is there to stifle in the body of a ship for six or seven days, if it's accent you want. No need to count the money in the teapot if it's movement and music that you seek. The organ grinder with his tambourine-beating wife, wedges between the crowds and receives in the soul's metal, a dime or an onion.

Source text

Barnes, Djuna, 'Why Go Abroad? – See Europe in Brooklyn!', *Brooklyn Daily Eagle* 7 December 1913, Part 2, 3.

References

Edwards, Justin D., '"Why Go Abroad?": Djuna Barnes and the Urban Travel Narrative', *Journal of Urban History* 29.1 (2002), 6–24.
Parsons, Deborah L., *Djuna Barnes* (Tavistock: Northcote House Publishers, 2003).

Ezra Pound (1885–1972)

'Provincia Deserta' (1915)

Ezra Pound was a central figure in the emergence and development of literary modernism in the early decades of the twentieth century. A prolific poet, translator and editor, he left the US for Europe in 1908, settling in London, where he was embedded in its high literary culture. Forming friendships with T. S. Eliot, H. D., William Carlos Williams and Marianne Moore, among others, Pound was at the vanguard of an international literary movement dedicated to transforming poetry's form and content at the start of the new century. His transnational credentials were marked from the first, with early poetic work translating Chinese, Japanese and Provencal languages. In the summer of 1912, Pound went on a walking tour of southern France, visiting the locations mentioned in 'Provincia Deserta'. During the period he was greatly influenced by the writing of the French troubadour poets of the Middle Ages, positing their songs of chivalry and courtly love as superior to the 'effete' decadence of Pound's contemporary modernity. The poem cites several examples of troubadour writers, and is, in effect, an attempt to capture the traces of this earlier poetic culture in the French landscape. In this, Pound adopts an *'ubi sunt'* motif (meaning, literally, 'where are . . . [they]?'), as the poem performs a pilgrimage that can never be sure of its ability to reconnect with a past long gone.

The poem first appeared in the influential monthly magazine *Poetry*, a Chicago-based publication with a mission to promote new writing. Pound later published it in the collection *Lustra* (London, 1916). His expansive geographical and temporal reach, displayed here, is most obviously marked in his *Cantos*, a series of 116 poems written between 1915 and 1962, in which troubadour culture would again be celebrated.

'Provincia Deserta'

At Rochecoart,[104]
Where the hills part
     in three ways,
And three valleys, full of winding roads,
Fork out to south and north,
There is a place of trees . . . gray with lichen.
I have walked there
     thinking of old days.
At Chalais[105]
     is a pleached arbor;
Old pensioners and old protected women
Have the right there—
     it is charity.
I have crept over old rafters,
     peering down
Over the Dronne,[106]
     over a stream full of lilies.
Eastward the road lies,
     Aubeterre[107] is eastward,
With a garrulous old man at the inn.
I know the roads in that place:

---

104 Rochechouart, a town in west-central France
105 A commune (the French equivalent of a municipal township) in southwestern France
106 A 125-mile long river flowing through southwestern France
107 Aubeterre-sur-Dronne, a commune in southwestern France

Mareuil[108] to the north-east,
        La Tour,
There are three keeps near Mareuil,
And an old woman,
        glad to hear Arnaut,[109]
Glad to lend one dry clothing.

I have walked
        into Perigord,[110]
I have seen the torch-flames, high-leaping,
Painting the front of that church,
And, under the dark, whirling laughter.
I have looked back over the stream
        and seen the high building,
Seen the long minarets, the white shafts.
I have gone in Ribeyrac[111]
        and in Sarlat,[112]
I have climbed rickety stairs, heard talk of Croy,
Walked over En Bertran's[113] old layout,
Have seen Narbonne, and Cahors and Chalus,[114]
Have seen Excideuil,[115] carefully fashioned.

I have said:
        "Here such a one walked.
"Here Coeur-de-Lion was slain.[116]
        "Here was good singing.
"Here one man hastened his step.
        "Here one lay panting."
I have looked south from Hautefort,[117]
        thinking of Montaignac,[118] southward.
I have lain in Rocafixada,[119]
        level with sunset,
Have seen the copper come down
        tinging the mountains,

---

108 Mareuil en Périgord, a commune in southwestern France
109 Arnaut de Mareuil, a twelfth-century troubadour poet, reimagined by Pound in his poem 'Marvoil'
110 Périgord, a region of France, whose major town is Périguex, and whose twelfth-century cathedral Pound goes on to describe
111 Ribérac, a commune in southwestern France, and the birthplace of the troubadour Arnaut Daniel
112 Sarlat-la-Canéda, a commune in southwestern France
113 Bertrand de Born was one of the most important troubadour poets of the twelfth century.
114 Narbonne, a commune in southern France; Cahors, a commune in southwestern France; Chalus, a commune in western France
115 A commune in southwestern France and the birthplace of the troubadour Giraut de Borneil
116 Richard I (1157–99), King of England from 1189 until his death at the Château de Chalus-Chabrol
117 A commune in southwestern France
118 Montignac, a commune in southwestern France
119 Roquefixade, a commune in southwestern France

I have seen the fields, pale, clear as an emerald,
Sharp peaks, high spurs, distant castles.
I have said: "The old roads have lain here.
"Men have gone by such and such valleys,
"Where the great halls are closer together."
I have seen Foix on its rocks, seen Toulouse, and Arles[120] greatly
     altered,
I have seen the ruined "Dorata."[121]
        I have said:
"Riquier! Guido."[122]
           I have thought of the second Troy,
Some little prized place in Auvergnat:[123]
Two men tossing a coin, one keeping a castle,
One set on the highway to sing.
       He sang a woman.
Auvergne rose to the song;
       The Dauphin backed him.
"The castle to Austors!"
       "Pieire kept the singing—
"A fair man and a pleasant."
       He won the lady,
Stole her away for himself, kept her against armed force:
So ends that story.[124]
That age is gone;
Pieire de Maensac is gone.
I have walked over these roads;
I have thought of them living.

Source text

Pound, Ezra, 'Provincia Deserta', *Poetry: A Magazine of Verse* 5.6 (March 1915), 251–4.

References

Grieve, Thomas F., *Ezra Pound's Early Poetry and Poetics* (Columbia, MO: University of Missouri Press, 1997).
McDougal, Stuart Y., *Ezra Pound and the Troubadour Tradition* (Princeton, NJ: Princeton University Press, 1972).

---

120 Foix, a commune in southwestern France, its castle is built on a rocky hill; Toulouse, the capital city of the region of Occitanie; Arles-Espénan, a commune in southwestern France
121 A reference to the church of Notre-Dame de la Daurade, in Toulouse
122 Girault Riquier was one of the last of the thirteenth-century troubadour poets. Guido Cavalcanti (*c.*1255–1300) was an Italian troubadour poet; he would be a continuing focus for Pound's work.
123 Auvergne, a region of south-central France in which Auvergnat, a unique dialect to the region, is spoken
124 Pound describes how two brothers from Auvergnat, Peire and Austors de Maensac, both troubadours, agreed that one of them (Austors) would claim the family inheritance, the other (Peire) would possess poetic artistry.

Sieburth, Richard (ed.), *A Walking Tour in Southern France: Ezra Pound Among the Troubadours* (New York: New Directions, 1992).

Edith Wharton (1862–1937)

From In Morocco *(1920)*

The US writer Edith Wharton's reputation was made through her acute ability to describe the nuances of social interaction, often among the elite of the transatlantic travelling world. Her work is concerned to dramatise the ways in which sometimes hidden social codes exert forms of control and authority on characters (often women) who find themselves trying to negotiate them. Her most famous novels, *The House of Mirth* (1905) and *The Age of Innocence* (1920), are celebrated examples of this kind of forensic fictionalised anthropology. Wharton would cross the Atlantic sixty times, and became a devotee of French and Italian culture in particular, as shown in her travel narratives *Italian Backgrounds* (1905) and *A Motor-Flight Through France* (1908). With the outbreak of the First World War, and while living in Paris, she became an outspoken supporter of the French war effort and organised relief efforts for Belgian refugees. In the summer of 1917 Wharton took a trip to French Morocco, France's colony in North Africa, convincing her publisher, Scribner's, to publish a book of her travels. The resulting book, *In Morocco*, is a curious hybrid combining travel narrative, social observation, and pro-colonial propaganda. (Wharton's host was Hubert Lyautey, the resident-general of French Morocco.)

The passage excerpted here describes Wharton's encounter with a harem in the ancient city of Fez, access to which was a rare privilege for a foreign traveller. Her interest in, and concern for, the status of women who are effectively imprisoned in a form of sterile luxury echoes her more familiar preoccupations around Anglo-American female agency and its obstruction.

From In Morocco

"In Fez"

What thoughts, what speculations, one wonders, go on under the narrow veiled brows of the little creatures destined to the high honour of marriage or concubinage in Moroccan palaces?

Some are brought down from mountains and cedar forests, from the free life of the tents where the nomad women go unveiled. Others come from harems in the turreted cities beyond the Atlas,[125] where blue palm-groves beat all night against the stars and date-caravans journey across the desert from Timbuctoo.[126] Some, born

---

125 Mountains stretching across northwestern Africa
126 An ancient city in Mali, governed by the French from 1893 to 1960

and bred in an airy palace among pomegranate gardens and white terraces, pass thence to one of the feudal fortresses near the snows, where for half the year the great chiefs of the south live in their clan, among fighting men and falconers and packs of *sloughis*.[127] And still others grow up in a stifling Mellah,[128] trip unveiled on its blue terraces overlooking the gardens of the great, and, seen one day at sunset by a fat vizier or his pale young master, are acquired for a handsome sum and transferred to the painted sepulchre of the harem.

Worst of all must be the fate of those who go from tents and cedar forests, or from some sea-blown garden above Rabat,[129] into one of the houses of Old Fez.[130] They are well-nigh impenetrable, these palaces of Elbali:[131] the Fazi dignitaries do not welcome the visits of strange women. On the rare occasions when they are received, a member of the family (one of the sons, or a brother-in-law who has "studied in Algeria") usually acts as interpreter; and perhaps it is as well that no one from the outer world should come to remind these listless creatures that somewhere the gulls dance on the Atlantic and the wind murmurs through olive-yards and clatters the metallic fronds of palm-groves.

We had been invited, one day, to visit the harem of one of the chief dignitaries of the Makhzen[132] at Fez, and these thoughts came to me as I sat among the

Figure 10.6 'Women Watching a Procession from a Roof'. In Edith Wharton, *In Morocco* (New York: Charles Scribner's Sons, 1920), facing 194–5.

---

127 North African breed of dog
128 Walled Jewish-quarters, often found in Moroccan cities
129 The capital city of Morocco
130 The capital of modern Morocco until 1912
131 Fes el Bali, the oldest walled area of Fez
132 Dar el-Makhzen, a Sultan's palace in Fez

pale women in their mouldering prison. The descent through the steep tunnelled streets gave one the sense of being lowered into the shaft of a mine. At each step the strip of sky grew narrower, and was more often obscured by the low vaulted passages into which we plunged. The noises of the Bazaar had died out, and only the sound of fountains behind garden walls and the clatter of our mules' hoofs on the stones went with us. Then fountains and gardens ceased also, the towering masonry closed in, and we entered an almost subterranean labyrinth which sun and air never reach. At length our mules turned into a *cul-de-sac* blocked by a high building. On the right was another building, one of those blind mysterious house-fronts of Fez that seem like a fragment of its ancient fortifications. Clients and servants lounged on the stone benches built into the wall; it was evidently the house of an important person. A charming youth with intelligent eyes waited on the threshold to receive us: he was one of the sons of the house, the one who had "studied in Algeria" and knew how to talk to visitors. We followed him into a small arcaded *patio* hemmed in by the high walls of the house. On the right was the usual long room with archways giving on the court. Our host, a patriarchal personage, draped in fat as in a toga, came toward us, a mountain of majestic muslins, his eyes sparkling in a swarthy silver-bearded face. He seated us on divans and lowered his voluminous person to a heap of cushions on the step leading into the court; and the son who had studied in Algeria instructed a negress to prepare the tea.

Across the *patio* was another arcade closely hung with unbleached cotton. From behind it came the sound of chatter, and now and then a bare brown child in a scant shirt would escape, and be hurriedly pulled back with soft explosions of laughter, while a black woman came out to readjust the curtains.

There were three of these negresses, splendid bronze creatures, wearing white djellabahs over bright-coloured caftans, striped scarves knotted about their large hips, and gauze turbans on their crinkled hair. Their wrists clinked with heavy silver bracelets, and big circular earrings danced in their purple earlobes. A languor lay on all the other inmates of the household, on the servants and hangers-on squatting in the shade under the arcade, on our monumental host and his smiling son; but the three negresses, vibrating with activity, rushed continually from the curtained chamber to the kitchen, and from the kitchen to the master's reception-room, bearing on their pinky-blue palms trays of Britannia metal[133] with tall glasses and fresh bunches of mint, shouting orders to dozing menials, and calling to each other from opposite ends of the court; and finally the stoutest of the three, disappearing from view, reappeared suddenly on a pale green balcony overhead, where, profiled against a square of blue sky, she leaned over in a Veronese attitude[134] and screamed down to the others like an excited parrot.

In spite of their febrile activity and tropical bird-shrieks, we waited in vain for tea; and after a while our host suggested to his son that I might like to visit the ladies of the household. As I had expected, the young man led me across the *patio*, lifted the cotton hanging and introduced me into an apartment exactly like the one we had just left. Divans covered with striped mattress-ticking stood against the white walls, and on them sat seven or eight passive-looking women over whom a number of pale children scrambled.

---

133 Silvery pewter alloy used for household goods and cutlery
134 After the Italian painter Veronese (1528–88), whose work often depicted figures in contorted poses

The eldest of the group, and evidently the mistress of the house, was an Algerian lady, probably of about fifty, with a sad and delicately-modelled face; the others were daughters, daughters-in-law and concubines. The latter word evokes to occidental ears images of sensual seduction which the Moroccan harem seldom realizes. All the ladies of this dignified official household wore the same look of somewhat melancholy respectability. In their stuffy curtained apartment they were like cellar-grown flowers, pale, heavy, fuller but frailer than the garden sort. Their dresses, rich but sober, the veils and diadems put on in honour of my visit, had a dignified dowdiness in odd contrast to the frivolity of the Imperial harem. But what chiefly struck me was the apathy of the younger women. I asked them if they had a garden, and they shook their heads wistfully, saying that there were no gardens in Old Fez. The roof was therefore their only escape: a roof overlooking acres and acres of other roofs, and closed in by the naked fortified mountains which stand about Fez like prison-walls.

After a brief exchange of compliments silence fell. Conversing through interpreters is a benumbing process, and there are few points of contact between the open-air occidental mind and beings imprisoned in a conception of sexual and domestic life based on slave-service and incessant espionage. These languid women on their muslin cushions toil not, neither do they spin. The Moroccan lady knows little of cooking, needlework or any household arts. When her child is ill she can only hang it with amulets and wail over it; the great lady of the Fazi palace is as ignorant of hygiene as the peasant-woman of the *bled*.[135] And all these colourless eventless lives depend on the favour of one fat tyrannical man, bloated with good living and authority, himself almost as inert and sedentary as his women, and accustomed to impose his whims and ceremonies on them ever since he ran about the same *patio* as a little short-smocked boy.

The redeeming point in this stagnant domesticity is the tenderness of the parents for their children, and western writers have laid so much stress on this that one would suppose children could be loved only by inert and ignorant parents. It is in fact charming to see the heavy eyes of the Moroccan father light up when a brown grass-hopper baby jumps on his knee, and the unfeigned tenderness with which the childless women of the harem caress the babies of their happier rivals. But the sentimentalist moved by this display of family feeling would do well to consider the lives of these much-petted children. Ignorance, unhealthiness and a precocious sexual initiation prevail in all classes. Education consists in learning by heart endless passages of the Koran, and amusement in assisting at spectacles that would be unintelligible to western children, but that the pleasantries of the harem make perfectly comprehensible to Moroccan infancy. At eight or nine the little girls are married, at twelve the son of the house is "given his first negress"; and thereafter, in the rich and leisured class, both sexes live till old age in an atmosphere of sensuality without seduction.

The young son of the house led me back across the court, where the negresses were still shrieking and scurrying, and passing to and fro like a stage-procession with the vain paraphernalia of a tea that never came. Our host still smiled from his cushions, resigned to Oriental delays. To distract the impatient westerners, a servant unhooked from the wall the cage of a gently-cooing dove. It was brought to us, still cooing, and looked at me with the same resigned and vacant eyes as the

---

135 Arabic for field, countryside

ladies I had just left. As it was being restored to its hook the slaves lolling about the entrance scattered respectfully at the approach of a handsome man of about thirty, with delicate features and a black beard. Crossing the court, he stooped to kiss the shoulder of our host, who introduced him as his eldest son, the husband of one or two of the little pale wives with whom I had been exchanging platitudes.

From the increasing agitation of the negresses it became evident that the ceremony of tea-making had been postponed till his arrival. A metal tray bearing a Britannia samovar and tea-pot was placed on the tiles of the court, and squatting beside it the newcomer gravely proceeded to infuse the mint. Suddenly the cotton hangings fluttered again, and a tiny child in the scantest of smocks rushed out and scampered across the court. Our venerable host, stretching out rapturous arms, caught the fugitive to his bosom, where the little boy lay like a squirrel, watching us with great sidelong eyes. He was the last-born of the patriarch, and the youngest brother of the majestic bearded gentleman engaged in tea-making. While he was still in his father's arms two more sons appeared: charming almond-eyed schoolboys returning from their Koran-class, escorted by their slaves. All the sons greeted each other affectionately, and caressed with almost feminine tenderness the dancing baby so lately added to their ranks; and finally, to crown this scene of domestic intimacy, the three negresses, their gigantic effort at last accomplished, passed about glasses of steaming mint and trays of gazelles' horns and white sugar-cakes.

Source text

Wharton, Edith, *In Morocco* (New York: Charles Scribner's Sons, 1920).

References

Ammons, Elizabeth, *Edith Wharton's Argument with America* (Athens, GA: University of Georgia Press, 1980).
Edwards, Justin D., *Exotic Journeys: Exploring the Erotics of U.S. Travel Literature, 1840–1930* (Hanover, NH: University Press of New England, 2001).
Hunter, Robert F., 'Manufacturing Exotica: Edith Wharton and Tourism in French Morocco, 1917–20', *Middle Eastern Studies* 46.1 (2010), 59–77.

Langston Hughes (1902–67)

'The Negro Speaks of Rivers' (1921)

In 1920, the year designated as a closing point for this anthology, a youthful Langston Hughes composed a fitting bookend to our opening text, an equally brief yet significant lyric by another Black author, Phillis Wheatley. Read together, these poems signal the centrality of Black voices to transatlantic literature of the long nineteenth century.

For Hughes, years ahead of Harlem Renaissance fame, 'The Negro Speaks of Rivers' emerged in a sudden surge of words movingly recalled in his 1940 autobiography, *The Big Sea*. On his way, after high-school graduation, to visit a father he 'did not like', a man divorced from Langston's mother and 'interested only in making money' (*Big Sea*, 55), Hughes rode a train from Cleveland, Ohio, to Mexico. Musing, he struggled to reconcile his positive vision of 'Negroes from the Southern ghettos – facing tremendous odds, working and laughing and trying to get somewhere in the world' – with his father's 'dislike of his own people'. Crossing the Mississippi River, he 'began to think what that river [. . .] had meant to Negroes in the past – how to be sold down that river was the worst fate that could overtake a slave' (65). Recalling stories of Lincoln travelling those waters, he 'began to think about other rivers in our past', and then came to the line: '"I've known rivers"', which he wrote 'on the back of an envelope' (66).

Born of cross-Americas train travel linked across time to affirming far-away sites, 'Rivers' foreshadowed numerous aspects of Hughes's just-then-unfolding authorial career. Travel writer (on Spain, Cuba and more), translator (of Caribbean poets) and student of South African politics (see Graham, *Cultural Entanglements*), he would inspire allusive, border-crossing adaptations of his works. Thus, as Shane Graham observed in connection with the poem's 100th anniversary, already here Hughes expressed an 'expansive global vision' (6) promoting 'international circulation', that merits 'reading him less exclusively as an American writer and emphasizing the transnational nature of his work and legacy' ('Assessing', 7).

With its initial June 1921 publication in *The Crisis*, a monthly co-edited by Jessie Fauset and W. E. B. Du Bois, Hughes's free-verse meditation affiliated with an endeavour both artistic and political, one Du Bois would later describe as 'interpreting to the world the hindrances and aspirations of American Negroes' (qtd in Dzanouni et al., 2). As such, like Phillis Wheatley's poem to Dartmouth opening this anthology, Hughes's text underscores the continued power of Black voices speaking on social issues of global relevance.

'The Negro Speaks of Rivers'

I've known rivers:[136]
I've known rivers ancient as the world and older than the flow
      of human blood in human veins.

My soul has grown deep like the rivers.

---

136 In one example of how Hughes's text and cross-cultural connections have fostered translingual intertextuality, N. Michelle Murray traces how a short story by Donato Ndongo builds a web of 'Rivers' allusions toward 'a literary geography that moves beyond the Middle Passage and slavery to examine the linkages currently connecting Africa, the Americas, and Europe' (40) ('The African Dreams of Migration: Donato Ndongo's "El sueño," Langston Hughes, and the Poetics of the Black Diaspora', *Symposium: A Quarterly Journal in Modern Literatures* 72.1 (2018), 39–52).

I bathed in the Euphrates when dawns were young.
I built my hut near the Congo and it lulled me to sleep.
I looked upon the Nile and raised the pyramids above it.[137]
I heard the singing of the Mississippi when Abe Lincoln went
        down to New Orleans,[138] and I've seen its muddy bosom turn
        all golden in the sunset.

I've known rivers;[139]
Ancient, dusky rivers.

My soul has grown deep like the rivers.

Source text

Hughes, Langston, 'The Negro Speaks of Rivers', *The Crisis* 22 (June 1921), 71.

References

Dzanouni, Lamia, Helene Le Dantec-Lowry and Claire Parfait, 'From One *Crisis* to the Other: History and Literature in *The Crisis* from 1910 to the Early 1920s', *European Journal of American Studies* 11.1 (2016), 1–24.

Graham, Shane, 'Assessing the Legacy of "The Negro Speaks of Rivers" on its Centennial', *Langston Hughes Review* 27.1 (2021), 1–11.

Graham, Shane, *Cultural Entanglements: Langston Hughes and the Rise of African and Caribbean Literature* (Charlottesville, VA: University of Virginia Press, 2020).

Hughes, Langston, *Autobiography: The Big Sea*, in Joseph McLaren (ed.), *The Collected Works of Langston Hughes*, Vol. 13 (Columbia, MO: University of Missouri Press, 2002).

Rampersad, Arnold, *The Life of Langston Hughes Vol 1: I, Too, Sing America, 1902–1941*, 2nd edn (Oxford: Oxford University Press, 2002).

---

137 Graham suggests Hughes's 'favored technique of listing place-names (in this case the Euphrates, the Congo, the Nile, and the Mississippi)' generates 'kinship and solidarity across national and colonial borders' ('Assessing', 5); Graham connects this approach with Ira Dworkin's proposal that, as early as this poem, Hughes tapped into issues of 'colonial subjugation' like those in 'the Belgian-occupied Congo and the Egyptian Revolution against British rule in 1919' ('Assessing', 5), thus refuting readings that cast the poem as ahistorically romantic, only.

138 An apocryphal journey by Lincoln travelling North to South, here invoked by Hughes as an implicit nod to the later-president's role as Emancipator of enslaved Blacks

139 Graham's reading in 'Assessing' affiliates with others' that link its first-person 'I' voice with a diasporic 'universe of identities and practices [. . .] under the umbrella of Blackness', rather than a monolithic, essentialising speaker (5). This interpretation also aligns with Graham's study of Hughes's *Cultural Entanglements* as seeking 'a negotiated, concentrically organized, borderless black collectivity – a transnational entanglement that resembles Paul Gilroy's model of the black Atlantic' (62).

AUTHOR LISTINGS

Section Abbreviations:

Abolition and Aftermath: AA; Art, Aesthetics and Entertainment: AAE; Business, Industry and Labour: BIL; Family and Domesticity: FD; Migration, Settlement and Resistance: MSR; Nationalism and Cosmopolitanism: NC; Religion and Secularism: RS; Science and Technology: ST; Suffrage and Citizenship: SC; Travel and Tourism: TT

Barlow, Joel
    From *The Columbiad* (1807) [AAE]
Barnes, Djuna
    'Why Go Abroad—See Europe in Brooklyn!' (1913) [TT]
Barrington, Jonah
    From *Rise and Fall of the Irish Nation* (1833) [SC]
Blackwell, Antoinette Brown
    'Sex and Evolution', From *The Sexes Throughout Nature* (1875) [ST]
Blackwell, Elizabeth
    From *Pioneer Work in Opening the Medical Profession to Women: Autobiographical Sketches* (1895) [ST]
Bonnin, Gertrude Simmons (Zitkala-Ša)
    'Editorial Comment' (1919) [SC]
Boswell, James
    'An Account of the Chief of the Mohock Indians, who lately visited England' (1776) [MSR]
Bourne, Randolph
    From 'Trans-national America' (1916) [NC]
Bradlaugh, Charles
    From 'Humanity's Gain from Unbelief' (1889) [RS]
Brant, Joseph (Thayendenegeh)
    'Speech of Captain Brant to Lord George Germain' (1776) [MSR]
Brown, William Wells
    London Anti-slavery Speech of September (1849) [AA]
    From *The American Fugitive in Europe. Sketches of Places and People Abroad* (1855) [TT]
Browning, Elizabeth Barrett
    'The Runaway Slave at Pilgrim's Point' (1848) [AA]
    'A Curse for a Nation' (1856) [NC]
Bryant, William Cullen
    'Sonnet – To an American Painter Departing for Europe' (1829) [AAE]
Burnett, Frances Hodgson
    From *Little Lord Fauntleroy* (1885–6) [FD]
Calderón de la Barca, Frances
    From *Life in Mexico, During a Residence of Two Years in That Country* (1843) [ST]
    From *Life in Mexico, During a Residence of Two Years in That Country* (1843) [TT]
Campbell, Thomas
    'The Emigrant' (1823) [MSR]
Carlyle, Thomas
    From 'Occasional Discourse on the Negro Question' (1849) [SC]
[Cary], Mary Ann Shadd
    From *A Plea For Emigration; Or, Notes Of Canada West* (1852) [MSR]
    'A Voice of Thanks': Letter to William Lloyd Garrison, Esq.' (1861) [AA]
Chapman, Maria Weston
    'The Times That Try Men's Souls' (1837) [SC]

EU representative:
Easy Access System Europe
Mustamäe tee 50, 10621 Tallinn, Estonia
Gpsr.requests@easproject.com